16
31

SOCIOLOGY

SOCIOLOGY

John E. Farley

Southern Illinois University at Edwardsville

Prentice Hall, Englewood Cliffs, New Jersey 07632

Library of Congress Cataloging-in-Publication Data

Farley, John E.
    Sociology.

    Includes bibliographical references.
        1. Sociology.   I. Title.
HM51.F33   1990   301   89-25525
ISBN 0-13-816000-7

Acquisitions editor: Nancy Roberts
Development editor: Robert Weiss
Editorial/production supervision: Susan E. Rowan
Interior and cover design: Lorraine Mullaney
Manufacturing buyer: Ed O'Dougherty
Photo research: Teri Stratford
Photo editor: Lorinda Morris-Nantz
Cover photo: Maurice Prendergast, "Untitled"/
    Art Resource, New York

© 1990 by Prentice-Hall, Inc.
A Division of Simon & Schuster
Englewood Cliffs, New Jersey 07632

Printed in the United States of America

10   9   8   7   6   5   4   3   2   1

ISBN 0-13-816000-7

Prentice-Hall International (UK) Limited, *London*
Prentice-Hall of Australia Pty. Limited, *Sydney*
Prentice-Hall Canada Inc., *Toronto*
Prentice-Hall Hispanoamericana, S.A., *Mexico*
Prentice-Hall of India Private Limited, *New Delhi*
Prentice-Hall of Japan, Inc., *Tokyo*
Simon & Schuster Asia Pte. Ltd., *Singapore*
Editora Prentice-Hall do Brasil, Ltda., *Rio de Janeiro*

To my teachers: Henry Silverman, for teaching me the meaning of good writing; Arthur Vener, for enabling me to discover and develop my interest in the social sciences; Bernard Finifter, for introducing me to the process of social research; and Charles Tilly, for acting as a source of guidance and motivation without which I could never have completed my first major research and writing project.

Brief Contents

Contents

PART 1
INTRODUCTION   1

PART 2
SOCIETY AND HUMAN INTERACTION   55

PART 3

Stratification:
Structured Social Inequality   235

PART 4
SOCIAL INSTITUTIONS

333

PART 5
SOCIAL CHANGE
487

Polls Apart Boxes

Personal Journey Into Sociology Boxes

Special Topics Boxes

Photo Acknowledgments

Part 1 clockwise from top left: Shopper / Stock, Boston. Lawrence Migdale / Photo Researchers. United Nations Photo. Luis Villota / The Stock Market.

Chapter 1 2 Betty Press / Monkmeyer Press. 5 (left) no credit, (right) Arlene Collins / Monkmeyer Press. 9 Ken Levinson / Monkmeyer Press. 13 Historical Pictures Service. 14 (left to right) New York Public Library, New York Public Library, Historical Pictures Service, New York Public Library. 15 Historical Pictures Service. 16 Historical Pictures Service. 17 (left) Courtesy University of Chicago Archives, (right) Harvard University News Office. 19 Paolo Koch / Photo Researchers.

Chapter 2 22 Anthro-Photo. 27 Ken Karp. 29 UPI / Bettmann Newsphotos. 31 (left) Ed Bock / The Stock Market, (right) Laima Drushis. 37 Mark Mangold / Bureau of the Census. 40 Professor Philip G. Zimbardo, Stanford Univ. 48 Marmel Studios / The Stock Market. 49 Larry Mulvehill / Photo Researchers.

Part 2 54 clockwise fr top left: Audrey Gottlieb / Monkmeyer Press. Bill Wassman / The Stock Market. Cary Wolinsky / Stock, Boston. Harvey Lloyd / The Stock Market, Rhoda Sidney.

Chapter 3 61 Rami Haidar / Gamma-Liaison. 68 (left) UPI / Bettmann Newsphotos, (right) UPI / Bettman Newsphotos. 70 Jan Halaska / Photo Researchers. 73 P-H Photo Archives. 74 J-L Atlan / Sygma. 78 George Goodwin / Monkmeyer Press.

Chapter 4 82 George Riley / Stock, Boston. 87 David Austen / Stock, Boston. 88 (left) Laima Drushis, (right) Shirley Zeiberg. 96 David Austen / Stock, Boston. 98 Historical Picture Service. 100 (no credit). 102 Torin Boyd / Gamma-Liaison. 103 Eugene Gordon. 107 Laima Druskis.

Chapter 5 116 Edgeworth Productions / The Stock Market. 119 Harlow Primate Laboratory, University of Wisconsin. 121 Ed Bock / Stock Market. 124 Brown Brothers. 126 (top) Mimi Forsyth / Monkmeyer Press, (bottom) Wayne Behling / Upsilanti Press. 127 Harvard Graduate School of Education. 134 Hazel Hankin / Stock, Boston. 140 Roy Morsch / The Stock Market. 141 U.S. Marine Corps photo.

Chapter 6 146 Ellis Herwig / Stock, Boston. 149 Library of Congress. 152 (left) Historical Pictures Service, Inc., (right) Cary Molinsky / Stock, Boston. 154 Carl Wolinsky / Stock, Boston. 159 Owen Franken / Stock, Boston. 161 Renate Hiller / Monkmeyer Press. 170 Bettye Lane / Photo Researchers, Inc. 171 National Archives. 172 Riche Browne / Stock, Boston.

Chapter 7 176 Gabe Palmer / The Stock Market. 179 (left) Joseph Nettis / Photo Researchers, (right) Murray & Assoc. / The Stock Market. 185 (top) Campus Verlag Frankfurt, (bottom) Wide World Photos. 187 Courtesy Ford Archives, Henry Ford Museum, Dearborn, Michigan. 190 (top) Sygma, (bottom) Sygma. 193 (left) Sue Klemmons Stock, Boston, (right) Gabe Palmer / The Stock Market. 194 Joseph Nettis / Photo Researchers.

Chapter 8 204 Owen Franken / Stock, Boston. 206 Library of Congress. 208 P-H Photo Archives. 209 Laimiete Druskis. 210 Arlene Collins / Monkmeyer Press. 211 Michael Mella / Sygma. 223 Ken Hawkins / Sygma. 224 (left) Ellis Herwig / Stock, Boston, (right) Bill Anderson / Monkmeyer Press. 230 (top) Owen Franken / Stock, Boston., (bottom) R. P. Kingston / Stock, Boston.

Part 3 234 clockwise from top left: Joseph Nettis / Photo Researchers. Laima Druskis. Tromson Monroe Public Relations. Laima Druskis.

Chapter 9 236 Peter Menzel / Stock, Boston. 239 Owen Franken / Stock, Boston. 243 courtesy New York Stock Exchange. 244 Owen Franken / Stock, Boston. 246 Anna Kaufman Moon. 250 Cary Wolinsky / Stock, Boston. 251 Owen Franken / Stock, Boston. 253 Thomas Ives / The Stock Market. 254 P-H Photo Archives. 261 (left to right) Gabe Palmer / The Stock Market, Peter Vadnai / The Stock Market, Bill Gallery / Stock, Boston.

Chapter 10 270 Markel / Gamma-Liaison. 273 P-H Photo Archives. 274 (top) D. Hudson / Sygma., (bottom) UPI / Bettmann Newsphotos. 276 Robert J. Capece / Monkmeyer Press. 281 S. M. Wakefield. 285 Brown Brothers / Sterling, PA. 286 Michael A. Keller / The Stock Market. 289 Arthur Grace / Sygma. 290 Courtesy U.S. Army.

Chapter 11 300 Bob Daemmrich / Stock, Boston. 302 (top row, left to right) UN Photo / Ray Witlin., Laima Druskis., United Nations. (bottom row, left to right) United Nations., Peter Buckley., Harvey Lloyd / The Stock Market. 306 Library of Congress / Russell Lee. 309 (left) Peter Buckley (right) Robert Frerck / The Stock Market. 310 Library of Congress. 319 Woolaroc Museum, Bartlesville, Oklahoma. 321 C. Albers, National Archives. 324 Owen Franken / Stock, Boston.

Part 4 332 clockwise from top left: Diane M. Lowe / Stock, Boston. Andree Abecassis / The Stock Market. United Nations Photo. Blaine Harrington / The Stock Market. Shirley Zeiberg.

Chapter 12 334 Historical Pictures Service. 338 (left) Victor Englebert / Photo Researchers. (right) United Nations. 339 Historical Pictures Service. 342 TASS from Sovfoto. 348 Mimi Forsyth / Monkmeyer Press. 349 Library of Congress. 351 Laura Sikes / Sygma. 353 A. Nogues / Sygma. 354 J. Pavlovsky / Sygma. 359 UPI / Bettmann Newsphotos.

Chapter 13 364 Richard Steedman / The Stock Market. 367 (top) Donald Dietz / Stock, Boston., (bottom) Harvey Lloyd / The Stock Market. 368 Charles Gupton / Stock, Boston. 369 Laima Druskis. 373 Kenneth P. Davis. 376 Bob Daemmrich / Stock, Boston. 377 Winnie Denker / The Stock Market. 382 Robert V. Eckert Jr. / Stock, Boston.

Chapter 14 394 Spencer Grant / Monkmeyer Press. 397 Historical Picture Service. 402 Tom Marotta. 403 UPI / Bettmann Newsphotos. 406 Jeffry W. Myers / Stock, Boston. 410 Mimi Forsyth / Monkmeyer Press. 415 J. Pinderhughes / The Stock Market. 418 Springmann / The Stock Market. 419 Mike Kagan / Monkmeyer Press. 420 Ray Ellis / Photo Researchers.

Chapter 15 424 Tim Thompson / The Stock Market. 432 (top left) Luis Villota / The Stock Market., (top right) Bill Wassman / The Stock Market., (bottom left) Michele Burgess / The Stock Market., (bottom right) Ray Shaw / The Stock Market. 438 UPI / Bettmann Newsphotos. 439 J. Langevin / Sygma. 442 (top) Stanley Tretich / Sygma., (bottom) Owen Franken / Stock, Boston. 444 Ira Wyman / Sygma. 445 A. Nogues / Sygma. 447 Ken Hawkins / Sygma.

Chapter 16 454 Bob Daemmrich / Stock, Boston. 457 Michel Heron / Monkmeyer Press. 458 Laima Druskis. 461 John Running / Stock, Boston. 463 Novosti / Gamma-Liaison. 464 David Madison. 468 Gabe Palmer / The Stock Market. 471 Nick Sapieha / Stock, Boston. 476 UPI / Bettmann Newsphotos. 478 P-H Photo Archives.

Part 5 486 Cary Wolinsky / Stock, Boston. Barbara Alper / Stock, Boston. no credit. Laima Druskis. Simon Nathan / The Stock Market.

Chapter 17 488 Luis Villota / The Stock Market. 496 (left) The Bettmann Archive, (right) Lionel Delevingne / Stock, Boston. 498 Diane M. Lowe / Stock, Boston. 500 United Nations. 502 M. Reichental / The Stock Market. 512 Library of Congress. 515 Gabe Palmer / The Stock Market. 516 Art Stein / Photo Researchers. 517 Anthony Edgeworth / The Stock Market. 520 Nathan Benn / Stock, Boston.

Chapter 18 524 Donald Dietz / Stock, Boston. 529 (left) The Bettmann Archive, (right) The Bettmann Archive. 531 New York Library Collection. 533 Luis Villota / The Stock Market. 534 The University of Chicago Library. 538 W. Campbell / Sygma. 543 Martin Rogers / Stock, Boston. 547 Billy E. Barnes / Stock, Boston. 549 Blair Seitz / Photo Researchers.

Chapter 19 554 Susan Steinkamp / Picture Group, Washington DC. 557 Neal Peters. 561 Moyer / Gamma-Liaison. 562 UPI / Bettmann Newsphotos. 563 Robin Loznak / Gamma Liaison. 565 AP/Wide World Photos. 573 Raymond Depardon / Gamma Liaison. 578 Heiner / Gamma-Liaison. 582 D. Hudson / Sygma.

Chapter 20 586 Ira Kirschenbaum / Stock, Boston. 590 UPI / Bettmann Newsphotos. 591 Marcello Bertinetti / Photo Researchers. 593 Charles Gupton / The Stock Market. 594 The Bettmann Archive. 595 The Bettmann Archive. 600 P-H Photo Archives. 605 Paul Conklin / Monkmeyer Press.

Preface

An introductory sociology text attempts to do many things. On one level, it must impart basic information on a variety of subjects to the students. At the same time, it must develop students' ability to think critically and to analyze everyday events through the sociological perspective. Ideally, students who complete the introductory course should be able to transcend the common-sense approach to social phenomena that most of them bring to the class.

My textbook has been written with both objectives in mind. To increase students' store of sociological knowledge, I have included the most up-to-date information, accompanied by current and recent citations. In my conversations with faculty members who teach the introductory course, I have found that their most frequent complaint about introductory texts is their tendency to jump from topic to topic in a disconnected manner as they try to mention every concept that any instructor might want included. The result is that such texts fail to explain most topics adequately and to show how one topic or issue relates to another. In this text, I have deliberately introduced slightly fewer concepts than most competing books, although all major topical areas are covered. By adopting this approach, I have been able to discuss the concepts I cover in greater depth than most introductory texts. I also show how theories, issues, and debates in different specialities of sociology relate to one another. I believe that this will help students to see relationships among ideas that are often missed in the attempt to cover every possible concept in an encyclopedic manner.

To assist students in developing critical-thinking skills, I have organized my text around the three basic sociological perspectives: the functionalist, conflict, and symbolic-interactionist perspectives. Rather than introducing these concepts briefly in the opening chapter and referring to them intermittently in later chapters, I have devoted an entire chapter to explaining them, including the strengths and weaknesses of each and the ways students can use all three to achieve a more complete understanding of social phenomena. This analysis is carried through all remaining chapters, as the key concepts in each chapter are analyzed from these different perspectives. I genuinely believe that each perspective helps us to understand an important piece of social reality. Thus, throughout the book each perspective is discussed with respect to those sociological issues and debates to which it is relevant. Special attention is paid to synthesizing these different approaches. A major focus of this discussion is current efforts by several leading sociologists to integrate macro- and microsociological theories. The goal is to teach students to see the perspectives not as competing arguments, but as approaches that can each contribute to the student's understanding of social phenomena. Ultimately, this will help students to develop their own perspectives.

Organization

I have divided my book into five parts. The first introduces sociology as a discipline. Chapter 1 begins with a brief discussion of the key theories and theorists of sociology and discusses the social conditions that gave rise to sociology and that continue to make it relevant. The book then moves on in Chapter 2 to research methodology, with special focus on the scientific method. Two end-of-book appendixes are also linked to Part I. The first discusses careers in sociology and offers many real-life examples of former students who have entered careers within and outside of the profession. The second provides an overview of certain quantitative concepts, including standard deviation and correlation coefficients.

Part II focuses on society and interaction. It begins with a chapter devoted exclusively to the key perspectives, a chapter unique to this text. Chapter 4 combines culture and social structure. These two topics are treated together because they are so closely interrelated that they cannot be separated realistically into two chapters. This approach provides students with a better-integrated view of the basis of social organization. After discussing socialization in Chapter 5, I move immediately to sex and gender, unlike most texts, which treat sex and gender in a later chapter. The reasoning here is that because people are *taught* to be male or female, the gender chapter incorporates and illustrates the major topics introduced in socialization. The remaining chapters in Part II deal with groups and organizations, deviance, and social control.

Part III deals with the crucial concept of stratification. There are two stratification chapters: economic and prestige, and political. This division reflects the standard analysis of Weber. I then conclude with the race and ethnicity chapter, which includes such current issues as race versus class and affirmative action. Part IV, social institutions, focuses on the basic human institutions: economic and political systems, marriage and the family, education, religion, and health care. We then conclude with Part V, which examines change and social behavior on a mass scale.

Features

My book contains a number of special features, including boxes, photo essays, and pedagogical aids, designed to assist students in developing a sociological perspective. The major ones are listed below.

Photo Essays   Each part opens with a photo essay that ties together the main concepts introduced in the chapters. This will provide students with a well-integrated overview of each part.

Personal Journey into Sociology   Major figures in sociology, including Harry Edwards, Joan McCord, William Domhoff, and Charles Tilly, have written boxes especially for this text explaining both the nature and the personal meaning of their work.

Polls Apart   Special interactive boxes based on research data help students analyze their responses to surveys and research questions on the basis of popular opinion. Exercises are useful for critical thinking and understanding the relevance of sociological research.

Pedagogy   This book contains a number of valuable pedagogical aids, including a variety of boxes on special topics, end-of-chapter glossaries, chapter summaries, further readings, and real-life opening vignettes. It is clearly written and carefully edited, always with the introductory student as the intended audience. Although it is highly readable, it is also comprehensive and thorough.

Bibliographic Style   This text uses the name-date referencing style, which has come to predominate in sociology and many other disciplines. Each reference is identified at the relevant point within the text with an author's surname, a date, and, in some cases, the page numbers on which the specifically relevant material appears. To look up the information on any reference, go to the alphabetic list of references at the end of the book and find the author's name and the item published in that year. That entry will give the full bibliographic information on the publication cited. If more than one item by a particular author in a given year is cited, the date in the first citation is followed by the letter *a*, the date in the second citation by *b*, and so forth. Initials are used in the text to distinguish two authors with the same last name who published items in the same year.

The Development Story

Prentice Hall invested a great deal of time and resources into devloping this textbook. Central to this development was soliciting the feedback of specialists within the discipline. Early in this process a focus group was assembled to review the overall organization and approach of the manuscript. As specific chapters were submitted, they were carefully reviewed by a full-time development editor at Prentice Hall and by a number of outside experts and classroom teachers. After the first draft was completed, a number of college and university faculty were invited to Englewood Cliffs, where the manuscript was reviewed chapter by chapter. All of this feedback has been assessed and, where appropriate, incorporated into the manuscript. In addition, several chapters have been class-tested; students and faculty rated them very highly against the competition. As a result of all this input, I am confident that faculty and students will find this text to be a highly effective tool for teaching and learning.

Supplements

Accompanying this book is a first-rate supplements package. In fact, Prentice Hall offers the most comprehensive supplements package currently available in the sociology market. The key supplements are listed below.

Annotated Instructor's Edition Our Annotated Instructor's Edition (AIE), one of the few on the market, consists of two parts: the Instructor's Manual (IM) and margin notes and comments. The IM, which is bound to the front of the AIE, was prepared by Professor Lee Frank of the Community College of Allegheny County. It contains a chapter outline, discussion questions, additional lectures, and ideas for classroom activities and interactive software. The text itself contains notes and critical-thinking questions in the margins written by the author.

Critical-Thinking Booklet We have prepared a special booklet, available upon adoption, to assist students in developing the critical-thinking skills that most instructors see as a major objective of an introductory sociology course.

Transparencies Each instructor who adopts this text will receive a special package of full-color transparencies, plus an instructor's guide that ties them into the text.

Video Package Video series available upon adoption.

Complete Testing Package Hard-copy tests, computer testing, and telephone test preparation service will be available to adopters. Computer tests are available for Mac, Apple, and IBM systems.

Sociology on a Disk Software for IBM or Apple II series computers, this interactive software has activities that allow students to apply textbook theory to real life situations.

Study Guide Guide for students that includes chapter outlines, key concepts, and self-tests.

Study Guide for Non-Native Speakers Written in English by ESL specialists for people whose native language is not English.

Acknowledgments

This book reflects the efforts of a large number of people. Many reviewers offered their time and suggestions, and many people at Prentice Hall contributed to the success of this project. I especially wish to thank Bill Webber for initiating the project; Nancy Roberts for overseeing the entire process; Robert Weiss for carefully editing the manuscript and serving as an indispensable resource person; Susan Rowan for guiding the manuscript through the production process; Terri Peterson and Roland Hernandez for directing the marketing campaign; Joe Sengotta and Wendy Helft for advertising and copywriting; Kim Byrne for putting together the excellent supplements package; and Ray Mullaney and Susan Willig for their many contributions. I would also like to acknowledge the following people for participating in our reviewers' conference: Glenn Currier of El Centro College, Lee Frank of the Community College of Allegheny County, Peter Morrill of Bronx Community College, and Michael Woodard of the University of Missouri. I want to thank Ann Pasarella for her various contributions to this text. I am grateful to my colleagues at the Department of Sociology and Social Work at Southern Illinois University at Edwardsville, and to graduate students Don Conway-Long, Ming Yan, John Egel, and Julie Dare, who provided key assistance at several important points during the writing of the book. I would also like to thank the following reviewers:

Frank Hearn, SUNY-Cortland
Joseph Behar, Dowling College
Dean A. Boldon, Maryville College
Arnold S. Brown, Northern Arizona University
Paul S. Gray, Boston College
Charles L. Harper, Creighton University
James R. Hudson, Pennsylvania State University-Harrisburg
Craig Jenkins, Ohio State University
David Karp, Boston College
Wade Clark Roof, University of Massachusetts
Susan D. Rose, Dickinson College
Walter L. Wallace, Princeton
Jon Darling, University of Pittsburgh
Glenn Currier, El Centro College

Norman K. Denzin, University of Illinois
Joseph M. Garza, Georgia State University
Harry H.L. Kitano, University of California at Los Angeles
Rhoda Lois Blumberg, Rutgers University
Anthony Orum, University of Illinois-Chicago
Jeanne Ballantine, Wright State University
Peter B. Morrill, Bronx Community College
Lee Frank, Community College of Allegheny County
D. James Dingman, Jackson Community College
Carl R. Redden, University of Central Arkansas
Novella Perrin, Central Missouri State University
Michael D. Woodard, University of Missouri
William H. McBroom, University of Montana
Jonathan C. Gibralter, Morrisville College

I would like to thank the following people for making major research contributions to various sections of the text: Larry Koch, Ball State University; Marlene Lehtinen, University of Utah; Christine M. Von Der Haar, Baruch College; Steven Vago, St. Louis University; and Thomas D. Hall, DePauw University.

Finally, I would like to thank my wife Margi and my daughters Kelly and Megan, who provided both emotional support and assistance with a variety of tasks, as well as making the sacrifices that inevitably result when a member of the family decides to write a book.

John E. Farley

About the Author

John E. Farley is Professor of Sociology at Southern Illinois University at Edwardsville, where he regularly teaches the introductory course, among others. He conducted his undergraduate studies at Michigan State University, where he received a B.A. in political science. He continued his studies at the University of Michigan, where he received an M.A. and a Ph. D. in sociology, as well as the master of urban planning degree. He has taught at Southern Illinois University at Edwardsville since 1977. He is the author of two other Prentice Hall books, Majority-Minority Relations *(second edition, 1988) and* American Social Problems: An Institutional Analysis *(1987). He is an active researcher in urban sociology and race and ethnic relations, and his articles have appeared in the* American Journal of Sociology, *the* American Journal of Economics and Sociology, Urban Affairs Quarterly, *and a number of other journals. He also regularly presents the results of his research at professional meetings, and has addressed such meetings in Canada and Sweden as well as in the United States. He has provided expert testimony in a number of federal court cases pertaining to racial discrimination and segregation in housing, and he serves as a member of the editorial board of* Urban Affairs Quarterly. *He enjoys spending time with his children Kelly and Megan, and is an avid skier, fisherman, and camper. Now that this book is finished, he also looks forward to getting caught up on various projects on the older house that he and his wife Margi are renovating.*

PART 1

INTRODUCTION

A s I think back to my own first course in sociology, the most important thing I learned was a new way of thinking about my world, which enabled me to see and understand things that I had been unable to see and understand before. In large part, it was nothing more than learning to ask questions that I otherwise would never have thought of. By asking the right questions, I could often understand why people thought and acted as they did, even when in the past the same thoughts and behaviors had seemed impossible to understand.

Based on this experience, it seems to me that the most important thing that most of you can learn from an introductory sociology course is a new—and to me, very exciting—way of thinking, analyzing, and asking questions about the world in which you live. That is what Part 1, consisting of Chapters 1 and 2, is all about. In Chapter 1, sociology is presented as a new way of understanding human thought and behavior. You will see examples of questions you probably could not answer without using sociology. Two key aspects of the sociological way of understanding human thought and behavior are addressed in Chapter 1. First, you will see how sociology uses the methods of scientific inquiry. Second, you will see that sociology enables us to see the influence on our lives of human collectivities, ranging from small informal groups up to entire societies.

In Chapter 2, we shall explore the scientific method of inquiry used by sociologists in greater detail. This method involves asking questions, then collecting information in a systematic way in order to answer those questions. Once the information has been collected, its meaning must be interpreted, which usually leads to new questions. Thus, the scientific method is an ongoing cycle of building theory and conducting research. Sociology has developed a number of methods specifically designed for the study of human society, human thought, and human behavior. Chapter 2 will familiarize you with these methods.

CHAPTER 1

Sociology: The Discipline

When I made the decision to enter graduate study in sociology, many of my friends and relatives asked me "What is sociology?" I am sure that many of you have the same question. The question could be answered in a number of ways because there is tremendous diversity both in the topics that sociologists study and in the ways that they approach these topics. Sociology is a broad field with many different theories, methodologies, and areas of interest. Sociologists constantly debate and challenge one another, and no consensus regarding sociological "truth" is likely to emerge any time in the future. A beginning student who asks, "How do sociologists feel?" about a particular issue will not find an easy answer.

espite the limitations we have just mentioned, we can develop an acceptable definition of **sociology:**. *Sociology is a systematic approach to thinking about, studying, and understanding society, human social behavior, and social groups.* It is different from other approaches to understanding human behavior, and it offers insights and findings that other approaches cannot. This sociology course will help you to develop new tools for understanding how and why people behave as they do.

What Is Sociology?

Sociology and Common Sense

Common sense is one way of understanding the world. Almost everyone understands the importance of common sense. Common sense could be defined as the ability to see and act upon that which is obvious. We can all think of examples where people's lack of common sense got them into serious trouble. One such incident occurred some years ago in the Minneapolis area. A series of tornadoes struck one evening, but thanks to adequate warning, there were no deaths and only one serious injury—a broken leg suffered by a man who fell off the roof of his garage while taking pictures of one of the tornadoes. Common sense tells most of us that we should not stand on the roof during a tornado, and we do not have to think very long to reach such a conclusion. Clearly, everyone needs such common sense.

Like everything else, though, common sense is good for some things and not for others. Try using common sense to answer the following true/false quiz:

1. Making contraceptives available to teenagers through school clinics will push them to be more sexually active because they won't have to worry about pregnancy.
2. People who live in the southern part of the United States drink less alcohol than people who live in the North.
3. The welfare laws of the United States work in such a way that most poor people become chronically dependent upon welfare.

4. Soldiers about to be "rotated" home on leave are more relaxed than those who have just begun a tour of duty.
5. The higher the percentage of people in a population who drink, the higher the percentage of alcoholics there will be in that population.
6. Two people are paid different amounts to do a silly, boring task and then tell someone else they enjoyed it. Later on, the person who is paid *less* will typically say the task was more enjoyable than the person who was paid more.
7. The civil rights laws of the 1960s considerably narrowed the gap between black and white family income in the United States.
8. Juvenile delinquents generally commit the same kinds of crime as adult criminals.
9. Overcrowding in American cities is an important reason for the much higher urban crime rates in the last 2 decades compared to earlier decades.
10. The incidence of homosexuality in the United States today is no greater relative to the population than it was 40 or 50 years ago.

Common sense probably suggested an answer to many of these questions. But was it the right answer? Turn ahead now to the box entitled "Answers to the Common-Sense Quiz" and find out.

How did you do? If you are like most students, you got several answers wrong. In fact, based on similar quizzes I've given in my own introductory classes, I am sure that some of you got half or more of them wrong. The point? Common sense is great for some things (like telling you to stay off the roof during tornadoes), but in many other situations it is totally inadequate, and we must use other means of understanding the world. Sociology is one such way.

Characteristics of Sociology

Basically, sociology has three key characteristics. First, sociology is regarded as a **science** by most sociologists. Science is one of several possible ways of understanding reality. It is a general approach to asking and answering questions based on observation, generalization, and interpretation. Second, sociology is a *social science:* It uses the methods of science in order to study *human social behavior.* Third, sociology is for the most part concerned with human social behavior on a *relatively large scale*. In other words, sociologists are more likely to be interested in predicting how the majority of people will respond to a particular social situation than in predicting the response of a given individual to that situation. Similarly, sociology is concerned with the influence on people's behavior of the *groups* and *societies* to which they belong. Let us explore each of these ideas a bit further.

Sociology as a Science

Science as a Way of Thinking

Science is one of several possible ways of understanding reality. As we have already seen, common sense is another way of understanding reality, and faith and tradition are yet others. Each of these is useful for understanding certain kinds of things. However, as the previous common-sense example illustrated, each also has its limitations. Science, because it is based on *observation,* is useful for testing things that can be seen

Both the natural and the social sciences are based on the scientific method.

or measured. It is not the only approach useful for this, but in modern industrial societies, it has become the dominant approach. Science is of limited value, however, in addressing issues that cannot be directly observed, such as the existence of heaven and hell. Science, then, is based on repeated *observation* or *measurement*. This systematic observation is called **research.** Through this kind of observation, scientists look for patterns and regularities, a process called *generalization*. They try to find patterns that occur so regularly that they can predict that a given set of conditions will be accompanied by the same result, even in similar situations that they have not directly observed. When scientists find such regularities, they seek to *explain* them through a **theory.** In other words, they try to say *why* a pattern they have observed so regularly takes place. Essentially, science deals with cause and effect: Scientists observe what usually happens under a given set of conditions (research) and try to explain why it happened (theory). If this explanation is correct, the scientist has produced a theory that should be able to *predict* what will usually happen in the future under similar conditions. Science, then, is a way of understanding reality that consists of a cycle of observation, generalization, explanation, and prediction. These predictions are then tested by a new round of observation, and the cycle is repeated. Ideally, each round of the cycle generates new knowledge. This cycle is known as the *scientific method*.

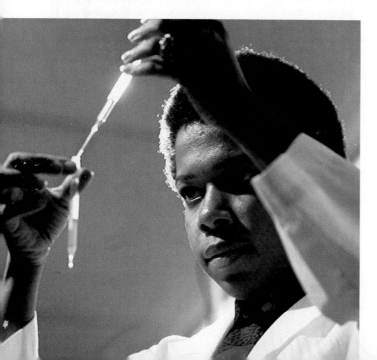

Answers to the Common-Sense Quiz

1. False   The limited number of studies of the effects of distributing contraceptives in high-school clinics have all shown that this practice either had no effect on, or slightly *reduced,* the amount of teenage sexual activity. The apparent reason: Students in schools with clinics became more informed about the consequences of their sexual behavior and felt more in control of their sexual behavior, and thus were more willing to say no (Moore and Caldwell, 1977).

2. True   Among those who do drink, there is little regional difference in the amount of alcohol consumed. However, average per-person alcohol consumption in the South is lower because a larger proportion of the southern population does not drink at all. The apparent reason for this is that more people in the South belong to religions that forbid or discourage drinking (see Gallup, 1984; U.S. Bureau of the Census, 1988a).

3. False   Actually, recent research has shown that the majority of all poor people at any given time are poor only for a limited period, and their poverty is due to some personal or family crisis such as divorce or unemployment. Most people use welfare to get through such crises; only a minority of recipients become dependent on welfare for an extended period (Duncan et al., 1984).

4. False   Soldiers about to return home experience great stress, whereas those who have just settled into a tour of duty accept and adjust to their situation (Stouffer et al., 1949).

5. False   Some populations, such as Italians and Jews, have very high incidences of drinking (nearly all adults drink), but their rates of alcoholism are well below the average. Other groups, such as some fundamentalist Protestants in the United States, contain relatively few drinkers, but those who do drink exhibit very high alcoholism rates, in part because they do their drinking on the sly. Among some of these groups, the alcoholism rate is well above that of Italians and Jews (Clinard, 1974, pp. 466–471, 479–484).

6. True   Experiments have shown that this is exactly how people behave. Apparently, those who were paid well to lie and say they enjoyed the task could rationalize and say they lied for the money. Those who were paid poorly could not do this and apparently responded by convincing themselves that the task hadn't been so bad after all (Festinger and Carlsmith, 1959).

7. False   The ratio of black-to-white family income has consistently been around 55 to 60 percent ever since the major civil rights laws were passed in the 1960s. The processes of discrimination that produce or perpetuate such inequalities are apparently more subtle than those addressed by the laws (Farley, 1988).

8. False   By and large, young people and adults commit different types of crimes. Adult criminals are more likely to commit serious assaults and major thefts and are responsible for the great majority of homicides. Juvenile delinquents are likely to commit smaller thefts, vandalism, joy riding as well as *status offenses*—things that are legal for adults to do but illegal for juveniles (for example, drinking) (Barlow, 1987; Federal Bureau of Investigation, 1989).

9. False   The crime rates of American cities *have* been higher over the past few decades than in the past. This trend, however, cannot be blamed on overcrowding, because by any measure (for example, people per square mile of the city or people per room in housing units), American cities have been getting progressively *less* crowded since 1960 or earlier and are much less crowded now than they were in the past (Palen, 1987, p. 169).

10. True   Ever since the famous Kinsey Reports on sexual behavior were published in the late 1940s and early 1950s, survey data have found that the proportion of people with a predominant homosexual preference has remained steady at around 3 or 4 percent for males and 2 or 3 percent for females. The proportion with some homosexual experience is considerably larger, but it, too, has remained constant.

The Scientific Method

Organized Skepticism The basic approach discussed above—a cycle of inquiry consisting of observation, generalization, explanation, and prediction—is shared by all sciences, both the **natural sciences,** such as physics, chemistry, astronomy, and biology, and the **social sciences,** such as psychology and anthropology, which study human behavior. Certain principles apply in all sciences (Merton, 1973), the most important of which is **organized skepticism.** This principle states that science accepts nothing on the basis of faith or common sense; anything accepted by science must ultimately be demonstrated by *observation*. In other words, if you want a scientist to accept something as true, you had better be prepared to prove it. Scientific issues are often marked by competing theories, each of which claims to be the *true* explanation. For scientists to accept a theory, they must be able to observe enough patterns consistent with the theory to convince their colleagues that the theory is correct. In other words, the things that a theory predicts must consistently be shown through research to be true. If this happens, the scientific community will accept the theory as correct; if it does not, the theory will not be accepted and might even be rejected.

Sharing of Findings and Methods Another important principle in science is *sharing*. This norm specifies that scientists have an obligation to share the knowledge they produce with other scientists, even when such findings are not consistent with their theories. They are expected to be honest and complete in doing this. Reporting only those findings that support the theory while keeping others secret violates scientific ethics. Moreover, scientists have an obligation to describe fully how they conducted the research that produced their findings. This obligation is important for two reasons. First, other scientists cannot determine whether a finding is trustworthy if they do not know how the observations were done and how the finding was arrived at. The principle of *organized skepticism* would discourage scientists from accepting such a finding. Second, sharing of methods used permits *replication*. Other scientists should be able to reproduce the findings by performing the same or similar obser-

vations. If other scientists cannot reproduce the findings, the validity of these findings will almost certainly be suspect.

Sociology as a Social Science

Can Human Behavior Be Studied Scientifically?

As noted above, sociology is one of the social sciences, which are concerned with the study of human thought and behavior and human social institutions. All of the social sciences share the common assumption that human social behavior can be studied scientifically, although there are great debates concerning how best to accomplish this. Social scientists believe that certain patterns and regularities in human behavior enable them to predict and explain human behavior to a substantial extent. Is this assumption true? Can human behavior be studied scientifically?

Many people would argue that it cannot. Because each person is an individual, capable of making free choices about an almost infinite number of things, how can we view human behavior as regular and predictable? The best answer is that every one of you experiences the regularities and predictable elements of human behavior every day. Every time you drive a car, you rely on the predictability of the other people on the road. You assume that they will go in the right direction, stop at stop signs, wait for lights to turn green, and so on. In most cases, they do. Only on the infrequent occasions when people behave *unpredictably* are accidents likely to occur. The behavior of people in other situations is similarly predictable. Imagine yourself in class; at religious services; at a football game. In each of these situations, your behavior and that of the other people present is for the most part predictable. Even less structured situations such as parties and nightclubs have fairly regular patterns of behavior. In each case, if you have had a reasonable amount of experience, you have a pretty good idea of how you are "supposed to" behave, and you will usually act accordingly.

Survey Questions: What Do They Tell Us?

Please write down your answers to the following questions:

1. Some people feel that the 1975 Public Affairs Act should be repealed. Do you agree or disagree with this idea?
2. Congress has been considering the Agricultural Trade Act of 1984. Do you favor or oppose the passage of this act?
3. Congress has also been considering the Monetary Control Bill of 1990. Do you favor or oppose the passage of this act?

If these bills don't sound familiar to you, don't be discouraged. The fact is that each of these bills is a fictitious one. However, in the Greater Cincinnati Survey, 22 percent of the sample of people expressed an opinion on Question 1, 35 percent on Question 2, and 38 percent on Question 3, despite the fact that no such legislation existed. The point of this survey is the unwillingness of many people questioned by pollsters to concede "I don't know."

How likely are people to express an opinion about a fictitious topic? Researchers find that people can be more readily tempted into giving opinions on a fictitious topic when it seems familiar (agriculture) than when it doesn't (Public Affairs Act), probably because they confuse the fictitious issue with something on which they really *do* have an opinion. Indeed, the more knowledgeable a person is about a particular area, the less likely that he or she will give a decided opinion on an imaginary topic.

Why are respondents reluctant to answer they "don't know"? Apparently, they feel pressured to answer the questions because of the way in which they are asked and the manner in which the interviewer handles the "don't know" responses. What can the researcher do to encourage frank answers? Give people a chance to plead ignorance, and don't keep probing for more information. The media may be disappointed if one-fourth of the people surveyed have no opinion on a burning issue of the day, but at least pollsters can feel that they have honestly reported the situation.

QUESTIONS: Polls are a key source of information in sociological research. Do the results of the Cincinnati survey affect your opinion of the accuracy of polls? Why or why not? How should sociologists use polls in their work?

Limitations of the Social Sciences

Beyond such obvious cases of predictable behavior, however, social scientists have developed an impressive record of predicting behavior based on careful and systematic (scientific) measurement. In a large population of newly married couples, for example, a social scientist could predict with reasonable accuracy what kinds of couples are at the highest risk of divorce. A social scientist would predict — on the basis of findings of past research — that those couples with lower income and education levels, those who marry at a younger age, those in which the wife has a high income relative to her husband, and those with partners from sharply different social backgrounds have a higher risk of divorce than couples with the opposite characteristics. Not every couple with "high-risk" characteristics will get a divorce, but a social scientist could predict that a large group of couples with these characteristics will experience a higher divorce rate than a similar-sized group of couples without them. On this large scale, divorce is predictable, even if the error rate does increase when you try to predict whether a *particular* couple will get a divorce.

An Analogy: Meteorology An analogy can be seen in the natural science of *meteorology,* the study of weather. Over a large area (such as a state), meteorologists can make fairly accurate predictions that, for example, thunderstorms will occur and will affect about one-third of the area. However, they are far less accurate at predicting exactly what will happen at one spot. They know that thunderstorms will occur and will affect a certain proportion of a large area, but they cannot pinpoint exactly where the storms will occur. This does not mean that meteorology is not scientific or that weather is totally unpredictable. Rather, it means that the large pattern is easier to predict than the isolated experience of one location. The same is true of the social sciences: The overall behavior patterns in groups of people are frequently predictable; the exact behavior of a given individual is less so. In individual situations, predictions of behavior become much more *probabilistic:* Given what we know about an individual, we can state a rough level of probability that the individual will think or behave in a particular way, but we cannot predict the exact behavior with complete certainty, just as the meteorologist cannot predict the weather in a particular location with precise certainty.

Complications in the Study of Human Behavior

Although human behavior does display considerable regularity and predictability, certain elements of complexity are present in the social sciences that are not present in the natural sciences. These complexities make human behavior somewhat more difficult to study than natural processes, and they help to explain why the predictions of social scientists are frequently less precise than those of natural scientists. These complexities also offer some explanation for the fact

Although individual behavior is often unpredictable, sociologists can predict the behaviors of groups of people with a high degree of accuracy.

that social scientists disagree sharply about what are the best methods for studying human behavior, even when they do agree that it can be systematically studied.

Reactivity One problem in the social sciences is **reactivity;** that is, the tendency of people to behave differently when they are being studied than they normally would. In most social-science research, the people being studied know they are being studied, interact with the person studying them, or both. In surveys, most experiments, and some participant observation (three common methods of social research described in Chapter 2), the people being studied know that they are the subjects of some kind of research project. Consequently, they might try to please the researcher, make themselves look good, cover up their faults, or act defensively. Thus, what the researcher observes is not normal everyday behavior, but, in part, a reaction to the research process. Even if the subjects don't know they are being studied, their interactions with the researcher can shape the way they behave. Natural scientists generally don't have to worry about these difficulties. For example, under specified temperature and atmospheric conditions, two chemicals will react with one another the same way whether anyone is watching or not. The same is *not* true of two people. Thus, one of the great challenges of social-science research is to measure correctly what the researcher intends to measure — not the reaction of the person being studied to the research, and not the social scientist's sometimes incorrect interpretation of the meaning of that person's behavior.

Change Over Time and Place Another complicating factor in the social sciences is that relationships can change significantly over time, and even from one place to another. This problem can be illustrated by the relationship between race and voter turnout. At one time, it was almost universally true that white voters turned out at a higher rate than black voters in the United States. In the 1980s, however, as black majorities emerged in many local electorates and black candidates became influential on the local, state, and national levels, black voter turnout surpassed white turnout in many areas. Thus, the finding that whites were more likely to vote than blacks, once true, is no longer valid.

This complication exists to a much lesser extent, if at all, in the natural sciences. Fifty years ago, protons had a positive electrical charge and electrons had a negative charge, and they still do today and still will 50 years from now. Moreover, this will hold true whether one is in Detroit, New York, St. Louis, or San Francisco, whereas the pattern of blacks turning out to vote at a higher rate than whites will not. This adds another complication to the study of human behavior, and it underlines two important points about the social sciences:

1. Research must be kept up to date; patterns demonstrated to be true in the past do not always hold true in the present. Only current research can indicate whether they do.
2. Research findings generated in one locality might not hold for another locality. Thus, large-scale national research is preferable to local studies for many purposes, and caution should always be used in generalizing social- science findings to or from a particular local area.

The "Newness" of Sociology   Two additional facts are worth mentioning in comparing the social sciences to the natural sciences. First, the social sciences are relatively young disciplines. The term *sociology* was not coined until around 150 years ago, and all the people regarded as influential in the discipline were born within the past 200 years. In contrast, most of the natural sciences have been in existence much longer — in some cases for thousands of years — and hence have had more time to build up a body of knowledge.

Studying Ourselves   The second point is that approaching the social sciences in a detached manner is more difficult because we are, in effect, studying ourselves. Social scientists often have strong personal feelings about the material they are studying. As has been illustrated by Thomas Kuhn (1962), natural scientists can also have strong feelings about the subject matter they are studying and even set out to "prove a point." However, this is probably more typical of the social sciences, where the scientist, as a human being, is often very close emotionally to what he or she is studying. As Kuhn points out, this does not in any way invalidate science (either natural or social), but it in-

creases the need for social scientists to adhere to the principle of organized skepticism.

By now, I suspect that some of you agree that human behavior can be studied scientifically, and some do not. Even sociologists disagree on the *extent* to which sociology constitutes a science (Denzin, 1987; Collins, 1987), and some have argued that the difficulties of observing and interpreting human behavior make sociology less a science than one of the liberal arts (Denzin, 1989). In large measure, this is because sociologists have increasingly recognized that their observations are not simply descriptions of human behavior as it "really happens," but rather descriptions of the sociologist's *understanding* of the behavior that he or she has observed. Thus, two sociologists observing the same behavior can and do sometimes "see" different things (Denzin, 1989, p. 67). Beyond the difficulties of observation, many social scientists are uncomfortable with, and do not accept, the idea that human behavior is governed by some set of laws such that, if only we could discover all of them and measure people's social and psychological characteristics with perfect accuracy, we could totally predict human behavior.

Even so, the majority of sociologists do subscribe to the view that much human behavior *can* be observed and understood through the methods of science, even though certain difficulties make the social world harder to study than the natural or physical world (Collins, 1975). Similarly, although no set of "laws" exists that totally determines human behavior, there *are* patterns and regularities to human behavior that make it largely, if far from totally, predictable.

The Sociological Imagination

One source of discomfort to nonsociologists is that sociology often tells us things that we believe are not true. For this very reason, however, sociology can be a source of very useful insights. Sociologist C. Wright Mills (1959) refers to such insights as the **sociological imagination.** By using the sociological imagination, we gain understandings that we could not achieve through other modes of reasoning. The sociological imagination helps us to understand how the social situation shapes our private realities — often in ways over which we have limited control. In many societies, but especially in the United States, people usually think in terms of *individuals* and what *individuals* do. From this viewpoint, when something good happens to you, it is because of what you have accomplished or what some other person—a parent, sibling, friend, or lover—has done for you. Similarly, when something bad happens, it is because of your own failing, or perhaps because some other individual has treated you unfairly.

Divorce and the Sociological Imagination   Consider the case of divorce, mentioned earlier in this chapter. If you are ever divorced, you will likely ask yourself "Where did I go wrong?" or perhaps "Why did my spouse treat me that way?" Undoubtedly, thinking about such questions will give you some useful insights. At the same time, though, there is another part of understanding why you got a divorce that such questions can't answer. The fact is that divorce has become much more common in the United States than it was in the past, for a variety of reasons that have nothing to do with how you or your spouse treat each other. These causes of divorce, which are explored in greater detail in Chapter 13, include changes in the economic meaning of the family, longer life expectancy, changes in the roles of men and women, changed views of marriage, and changes in the law. Today, you are getting married in a different social situation from that of your parents or grandparents, and a much higher percentage of marriages end in divorce as a result of those changes. Thus, your divorce results only in part from your behavior or your spouse's behavior; in the past, similar behavior would not have resulted in divorce. Rather, part of the reason for your divorce has to do with social changes that have increased *everyone's* risk of divorce.

Using the sociological imagination is helpful for understanding a wide variety of events that occur in your life. The sociological imagination, for example, can be used to understand such diverse events as obtaining a college degree, losing a job, and getting sick. This can be tremendously useful to both individuals and the larger society. From the individual viewpoint, it gives us a better understanding of why things happen to us, and why others behave as they do. From a societal viewpoint, it can be a very useful tool for alleviating problems that arise from human behavior or human social arrangements.

Finally, if you are still skeptical about the usefulness of sociology, consider this: Like it or not, you live in a world where "scientific" claims about human behavior are made all the time. This is done in advertising, in politics, even in sports and entertainment. Some such claims are based on sound social research, but many are not and are merely intended to persuade (or in some cases entertain) you. The ability to distinguish valid social science from hucksterism and propaganda is a useful tool in the media age.

Sociology and the Other Social Sciences

Sociology shares some important things with the other social sciences: the use of the scientific method, the assumption that human behavior has patterns and regularities, and the belief that behavior can be studied and largely understood through systematic observation, generalization, and interpretation. Sociology also differs in certain ways from the other social sciences, which include psychology, social anthropology, economics, and political science. (Some people also include history, whereas others classify it as a humanity.) Several applied professions, including social work and urban planning, rely heavily on knowledge generated by the social sciences. In colleges and universities, programs in these professions are sometimes located under schools or divisions of social science, and sometimes in separate professional schools.

The various social sciences differ in the aspects of human behavior that they study, the level (individual versus group or society) at which they study human behavior, and, to a considerable extent, the methods by which they study human behavior. Although they are regarded as distinct academic disciplines, they overlap considerably. Many areas of human behavior are studied by more than one of the social sciences, sometimes with very similar methods of research. Keeping this in mind, we shall briefly describe sociology, then discuss each of the other social sciences and how it relates to sociology.

Sociology

Sociology is concerned with virtually all aspects of human social behavior. In this sense, it is less specialized than some of the other social sciences, particularly political science and economics. The second feature that distinguishes sociology from the other social sciences is its scale: Its emphasis is on *societies* and groups within society rather than on individuals. Among the things that sociologists consider in any society they study are the major forms of organization and ways of doing things that become accepted in that society, which sociologists call *institutions*. Sociologists are interested in how these institutions address basic needs in society and how they relate to the interests, needs, and desires of the various groups of people within societies (ethnic groups, gender groups, religious groups, social classes). Sociologists also study such *social groups* to see how they develop, how they relate to one another, and how they divide (and sometimes struggle over) the society's scarce resources. In addition, they study the beliefs, values, and rules about behavior that emerge in a society, as well as how and why these things differ among the various social groups within the society. Finally, sociologists examine the ways in which both societies and social groups train and indoctrinate new members, as well as the ways in which some social groups recruit new members. As you can see, the subject matter of sociology is nearly limitless. About the only limit is that sociology generally addresses these issues at least partly on a collective level — that of the society or social group — rather than entirely at the individual level.

Psychology

Psychology, perhaps the oldest of the social sciences, is like sociology in that it is interested in a very broad range of human thought and behavior. The main difference is that psychology studies human behavior primarily on the *individual* level. By doing this, psychologists seek to understand and predict (and sometimes alter) the thoughts and behavior of individuals. Insofar as it considers the physiological influences on human thought and behavior, psychology overlaps with one of the natural sciences, biology. It also has one important area of overlap with sociology, known

as **social psychology.** Social psychology concerns the interaction between the individual and society, with a particular emphasis on the influences of society and social groups on the thought and behavior of the individual. Because of its interests in both the individual and society, social psychology is an important subdiscipline within both sociology and psychology, and social psychology courses are commonly taught in both sociology and psychology departments.

Economics

Economics involves the study of human behavior as it relates to the production, exchange, distribution, and consumption of wealth and income. Economic behaviors include buying and selling, barter, employment, wages, and spending patterns of individuals, businesses, and governments. Economics is highly quantitative, with a heavy emphasis (at least in Western capitalist countries) on how markets set prices and wage rates. Attempts are made at the national and world levels to predict and explain price changes, employment levels, and trade balances. Like psychology, economics has an important area of overlap with sociology, sometimes called *economic sociology* or the *sociology of economics*. This area is concerned with societal and group processes as they relate to income, wealth, consumption of goods and services, unemployment, and other economic issues. It is also concerned with the social impact of different economic systems, such as capitalism and socialism.

Political Science

As the name suggests, political science is concerned with human behavior as it relates to government and politics. Like sociology, it tends to operate on a group or societal level, but its focus is more narrow. Among the areas of interest to political scientists are the development of political institutions, such as systems of government and political parties, and how the public relates to these institutions through such means as voting, political-party participation, running for office, writing letters, and participating in protest marches. The latter set of concerns is the focus of an area of overlap with sociology called *political sociology*. Political science also considers the conditions under which political institutions break down or change radically, as in the case of revolutions and civil wars.

Social Anthropology

Social anthropology is the study of human *culture:* attitudes, beliefs, and rules of behavior that become generalized in society. Clearly, this interest overlaps significantly with sociology, but there is a difference in emphasis. Anthropology places a somewhat greater emphasis on *describing* the cultures of various societies: Its primary objective is to understand these cultures. Sociology, in contrast, tends to relate these cultures to a larger context, including the institutions, the distribution of resources, and the interactions among social groups within the societies. Social anthropology also relies more heavily than sociology on direct observation—for example, observing the culture of a society or social group by living in it for an extended period of time. Some anthropologists, known as *physical anthropologists,* use the techniques of archaeology to understand cultures of the past and the historical and prehistorical roots of today's cultures; other anthropologists study the process of evolution, and their work overlaps heavily with that of biologists.

The Evolution of Sociology

The Nineteenth Century

As was noted earlier, the term *sociology* was coined only about 150 years ago. That period—the nineteenth century—witnessed some of the most profound social change in all of human history, particularly in Europe. For the first time, cities were becoming the dominant influence in what had always been rural societies. After thousands of years of relative stability, the world's population had entered a period of rapid growth that has continued to the present (what we now call the *population explosion*). Tradition and religion were being displaced by science and economic rationalism as ways of understanding reality and as forces shaping people's lives. Perhaps most dramatic of all was the effect of the Industrial Revolution on the lives of ordinary people.

The social and economic problems created by the Industrial Revolution provided the incentive for the development of sociology as a discipline.

As the urban industrial economic order replaced the rural agricultural order, thousands flocked to the cities of Europe and, later, North America. In the cities, the migrants often endured horrible working conditions, child labor, low wages, and filthy, overcrowded neighborhoods that could not begin to accommodate them. Of course, urbanization made conditions such as these more visible, and some of the great minds of the era turned their attention to trying to understand why society was changing in the ways it was. Much of their concern was focused on new social problems, such as overcrowding, poverty, crime, depersonalization, and suicide, that seemed to be outgrowths of industrialization, urbanization, and related changes.

Early Sociologists

The Frenchman August Comte (1798–1857) first used the term "sociology." He set the stage for future developments within the discipline when he argued that societies contained both forces for stability and cooperation, which he called *social statics,* and forces for conflict and change, which he called *social dynamics.* Even today, one of the greatest debates in sociology—and one we will consider throughout this book—concerns the relative influences upon societies of forces for change versus forces for stability.

Although Comte named the discipline and to a large extent set the agenda for its debates, the most lasting early influence on sociology came from three other great social thinkers: the Germans Karl Marx and Max Weber and the Frenchman Emile Durkheim.

Karl Marx The earliest of the three, Karl Marx (1818–1883), was an economist and a political philosopher as much as a sociologist. His influence upon world politics has probably not been exceeded by any other individual. Although Marx did not consider himself a sociologist, his theories have been as influential in sociology as in philosophy or any of the other social sciences. Marx was deeply angered by the brutal treatment of workers and their families during the Industrial Revolution. He sought to understand the causes of this situation in order to change it. Thus, as Comte had done previously, Marx combined the role of social scientist and social activist; in fact, he saw the two as inseparable. Emphasizing what Comte called social dynamics, Marx saw virtually all societies as being shaped by a struggle between those who owned the **means of production** (whatever you need to own in order to produce something that can be sold) and those who did not. He then developed theories about the dynamics of this struggle in the emerging industrial capitalist societies of his time. In such societies, the owners of the means of production were those who possessed industrial capital—the **bourgeoisie.** The rest of the society, whom he called the **proletariat,** worked for this group in exchange for wages and salaries that Marx saw as being less than the value that the workers added to the goods they produced. Marx saw these two groups as having fundamentally opposing interests, as well as very unequal power. He developed theories about the ways that the bourgeoisie acted to keep its great wealth and about how the proletariat could force a fair distribution of that wealth. Marx then applied those theories to assume a position of leadership on the proletarian side of that struggle.

Max Weber Like Marx, Max Weber (1864–1920) was highly interested in the changes brought about by the Industrial Revolution. Like Marx, too, he was aware of the forces for *alienation* that were being unleashed by these changes. However, Weber focused on potential benefits in these changes that Marx recognized but did not emphasize because of his concerns with the problems of the new industrial order. Weber saw a great potential for increased productivity and, as a result, an increased standard of living in what he called *rationalization*—the replacement of tradition and favoritism with a model of choice based on who and what works best in achieving a given objective. Weber saw this process of rationalization as the cornerstone of modern economic and political systems. Yet, at the same time, he recognized that such systems could only flourish within a cultural and social

Four prominent early European sociologists (left to right): August Comte, Karl Marx, Max Weber, and Emile Durkheim. Comte was the first person to use the term "sociology."

context favorable to their development. In particular, he developed an important theory about the role of the Protestant Reformation in bringing about a social climate favorable to the emergence of capitalism. Thus, whereas Marx saw society as largely a product of economic forces (especially economic struggle), Weber saw economic systems as being heavily influenced by the society and culture in which they developed. Because Marx and Weber offered opposite views on several important social issues, Weber has sometimes been described as carrying on a debate with the ghost of Karl Marx. Another important difference between Marx and Weber is that, whereas Marx felt that social scientists should base their work on their values, Weber felt that they should attempt to be value-neutral. Even so, Weber realized that total value neutrality in the social sciences is an impossible ideal. He recognized that values influence the choice of topics to study, and he also saw the usefulness of personal experiences and viewpoints for developing insights about human social behavior. Like other aspects of the disagreements between Marx and Weber, debate about the role of values in sociology continues to this very day.

Emile Durkheim   Emile Durkheim (1858–1917), the third great social thinker of this era, was less interested in economic change than either Marx or Weber. Perhaps Durkheim's greatest accomplishment was to do what Comte had said could be done—apply the scientific method to the study of human behavior. In his analysis of the social factors that contributed to suicide, Durkheim was the first to carry out a study involving the large-scale collection of data to test a social theory. Durkheim, however, was important not only as the first social researcher but also as a theorist par excellence. In contrast to Marx, Durkheim focused on the forces that hold society together and bond its members in common interest. A particular interest of Durkheim's was how these forces change as a society evolves from a traditional, rural, agrarian society into a complex, interdependent, urban society. Thus, as with both Marx and Weber, important elements of Durkheim's work concentrate on the effects of modernization on society, which was one of the prime intellectual questions of his era.

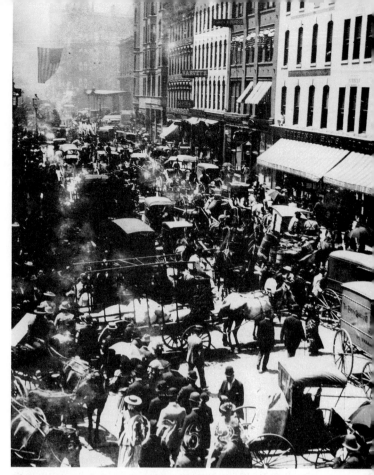

Chicago around the turn of the century. Many U.S. sociologists used this city as a "social laboratory" for urban reforms.

The Development of Sociology in the United States

The conditions that brought sociology into being in Europe developed somewhat later in the United States. As a result, the development of sociology in the United States also lagged somewhat behind European sociology. The vast American frontier acted as a safety valve in the early industrial era by giving people a choice between moving to the cities and heading west. By the mid-nineteenth century, however, the Industrial Revolution and urban growth were well under way. In fact, the Civil War was in part a struggle between the agricultural interests of the rural South and the industrial interests of the urban North. American intellectuals, like their European counterparts, focused on the consequences of these trends: By the turn of the century, sociology had begun to find its way into the curriculum of American colleges and universities.

The discipline ultimately flourished in this country to a greater extent than almost anywhere else.

The Chicago School

The first department of sociology in the United States was established at the University of Chicago in 1893 and dominated American sociology for more than half a century thereafter. The American Sociological Association (ASA) was founded in 1905. (It was originally called the American Sociology Society, but the name was changed because of jokes about the initials.)

From the establishment of the discipline until around World War II, American sociology for the most part adopted an activist, reformist orientation. Urban problems such as crime, overcrowding, drug abuse, and poverty were a central focus of the Chicago School of sociologists. The tone for this reformist orientation was set by the earliest major American sociologist, Lester Ward (1841–1913). Ward saw sociology as a tool for understanding and trying to solve these problems. At the University of Chicago, early American sociologists such as Robert E. Park (1864–1944), Ernest W. Burgess (1886–1966), and Louis Wirth (1897–1952) continued this philosophy by studying such problems as juvenile delinquency and, in some cases, by setting up institutes to apply sociology to alleviating them. The burgeoning city of Chicago served as a natural laboratory for these sociologists by providing opportunities both to study urban problems and to try out solutions that were suggested by their research. (For an excellent overview of the work of the early Chicago School sociologists, see Faris, 1979.)

Symbolic-Interactionism

By the 1920s, another branch of sociology was also blossoming at the University of Chicago. Rooted in social psychology, it asked questions about how individuals learn, fit into, interact with, and alter the *roles* that exist within the social system. This school of thought, known as *symbolic-interactionism,* has remained a dominant influence in social psychology (or at least the sociological branch thereof) ever since. The early leader of this school of thought was University of Chicago sociologist George Herbert Mead (1863–1931). Interestingly, Mead hated to write and therefore never wrote a book. However, his graduate students, recognizing the brilliance and importance of his work, published a book, *Mind, Self, and Society* (Mead, 1934), based on their notes from his lectures. Much of Mead's thinking constituted an elaboration of ideas that had been developed around the turn of the century by Charles Horton Cooley of the University of Michigan.

1940–1960: A Turn from Activism

By the 1940s and 1950s, sociology had become established in most major American universities. During this time, it also underwent two important changes: It began to make greater use of numbers and statistics, and it became dominated by the view that it should be "value-neutral" rather than activist. In part, these changes reflected the desire of sociologists to gain acceptance of their field as a legitimate science in an era when the prevailing view was that science should be value-free. In part, too, they reflected the economic recovery sparked by World War II that produced an era of prosperity, relative social stability, and economic growth. In the 1950s, social problems were further from the public mind than they had been in earlier decades, and sociology turned its attention away from them. This illustrates an important point: *To a large extent, the concerns and values of sociology reflect the concerns and values of the society within which*

Robert E. Park, a prominent sociologist associated with the University of Chicago.

George Herbert Mead was the leader of the Chicago school of sociology.

Talcott Parsons was the most prominent U.S. sociologist of the 1950s.

it operates. In the 1950s, public interest centered on growth, science, and technology, not on social problems—and sociology generally followed this trend.

The most influential American sociologist of this time was undoubtedly Talcott Parsons (1902–1979). Parsons viewed society as a stable, though complex, system of interdependent parts, each of which performed a function important to the system. He was influenced by several of the early European sociologists, particularly Durkheim, and his work in turn influenced that of other important American sociologists, such as Robert Merton. Parsons's approach was challenged by C. Wright Mills (1916–1962), one of the few major sociologists of this era who retained an activist bent. Mills, influenced by the intellectual tradition of Karl Marx, argued that the decision-making process within the U.S. government occurred largely behind the scenes and was dominated by a narrowly defined interest group composed of corporate, political, and military officials whom he called the *power elite.* Although Mills's influence on American sociology was limited throughout most of his life, today he is regarded as one of the more influential American sociologists, and his theories about the power elite set the stage for a good deal of important research on the American power structure.

The 1960s: Return to Activism

Sociology's retreat from social activism did not last. By the mid-1960s, the nation's attention had again turned to social problems, as exemplified by the civil rights movement and the "war on poverty." The conflicts generated by these social changes were intensified by the sometimes violent disputes over the Vietnam War. Suddenly, it was not science and prosperity but burning cities, disrupted campuses, a "sexual revolution," and an explosive increase in the use of illegal drugs that held the attention of the public and of sociologists. Many sociologists and their students (some of whom are today's sociologists) were very much caught up in the conflict, and activism and reformism again became important forces within the profession. As had happened in the past, the sudden emergence of social change and upheaval brought a surge of interest in sociology, and in the late 1960s and early 1970s sociology became one of the most popular majors on campus.

The 1970s and 1980s: A New Diversity

Since that time, conflict and upheaval in American society have declined (although this trend might again be shifting), and enrollment in sociology courses has declined to its pre-1960s levels on many campuses. However, the effect of the 1960s and early 1970s on sociology has been lasting. American sociology in the 1970s and 1980s has been very diverse: Some sociologists have followed the activist tradition of Comte, Marx, Ward, and Mills, while others have followed the "value-free science" tradition of Weber, Durkheim, and Parsons. Still others have chosen the interactionist tradition of Cooley, Mead, and, more recently, Herbert Blumer. No single theoretical perspective has dominated sociology over the past 2 decades, nor has any one sociologist or small group of sociologists influenced the field to the extent that Marx, Durkheim, Weber, Mead, and Parsons did in the past. Although some experts see this trend as a sign of incoherence in the field, more people see it as healthy. No single approach does have all the answers, and the challenges that the different approaches offer to one another help to bring out the best in sociologists of every theoretical orientation. Indeed, the failure of the sociologists of the 1950s to predict the upheavals of the 1960s is a good illustration of what happens when one view comes to dominate the field excessively: It goes unchallenged, not only when it is right, but also when it is wrong, as nearly every theoretical orientation is *part* of the time.

Sociology: What Use Today?

A question that every sociologist confronts sooner or later is "What can you use this stuff for?" Some sociologists answer this question with a general response, along the lines of "Knowledge is power." The idea is that, whether or not sociology is applied to some specific problem or issue, it is useful for everyone to know something about the forces that shape human behavior. I firmly believe this, and for me it is reason enough to expose every college student to sociology, or at least to one of the social sciences. However, in an era when jobs are scarce and incomes often rise more slowly than the cost of living, I also think some concern about the practical usefulness of any discipline is warranted.

Fortunately, sociology is not simply a theoretical science. The fact is that sociological knowledge and research techniques are relevant to an almost infinite variety of practical concerns. Government, business, labor, education, and even religion use sociology as a tool to get useful information for solving problems they face. Consider the following examples.

Faced with a declining patient clientele, the administrators of a university hospital want to purchase physician practices in order to attract admissions. However, they do not know which locations are good places to purchase these practices in terms of attracting the maximum number of patients. The solution: Hire a team of sociologists to obtain and analyze data on population, physician supply, physician productivity, and the frequency of visits to the doctor, for the purpose of identifying various locations as medically overserved or underserved.

A university campus is beset with racial problems. A racist joke is told on the campus radio station, antiblack leaflets are passed under dormitory doors, many black students at the school are dropping out, and both black and white students refuse to interact with each other. A sociologist points out that neither racial group really sees things from the perspective of the other. Whites assume that the passage of civil rights laws means that opportunities for blacks are equal when, in fact, blacks still must overcome disproportionate poverty, poor education, inadequate medical care, and high rates of unemployment. Blacks assume that whites are genuinely aware of all these things and simply don't care. The solution: A required course on race relations for all students to correct the misperceptions that each group has about the other. In this example, teaching students some of the sociology of race relations could go a long way toward easing the tensions.

A county government is seeking federal funds for housing. One requirement for such assistance is that the county address the housing needs of its disabled population. The county officials have no idea how many disabled people live in their county, much less what their housing needs are. The solution: Hire a sociologist to review various sources of data and develop an estimate of the number of disabled people in the county, as well as to review the findings of social research on the appropriateness of various types of housing arrangements for people with various types of disabilities.

As these examples illustrate, sociology is a problem-solving tool. In fact, the examples are not made up: they are all real-life situations with which I am personally familiar. The range of problems and questions that sociologists have been called upon to

Among the issues that sociologists have been asked to study is declining attendance at Sunday Mass by U.S. Catholics.

help with in recent years is tremendous. It includes the absence of blacks and Hispanics from the upper management of baseball, declining Sunday Mass attendance in the U.S. Catholic Church, problems of absenteeism and low productivity in automobile plants, income differences in student achievement in American schools, the question of what name a product should be marketed under to maximize sales, and yes, even what combination of topics covered will produce the best sales in an introductory sociology textbook! Sociologists have participated in commissions advising the federal government on a number of issues, including urban riots, the effects of pornography, the causes of violence in American society, the consequences (or lack thereof) of smoking marijuana, and the possible results of deregulating certain industries. Some businesses, government agencies, and other organizations employ sociologists permanently on their staffs, and others hire them on a short-term basis to address specific problems.

As important as sociology is as a problem-solving tool, however, its greatest usefulness arises from use of the *sociological imagination,* discussed earlier in this chapter. Sociology enables us to gain a new perspective on the forces that define our situation, thereby enabling us to see that our society sometimes acts in ways that severely limit human opportunity. It allows us to step back and look at ourselves. In so doing, it makes us aware of the presence and extent of such conditions as poverty, unemployment, crime, family conflict, racism, and sexism—conditions that, at one time or another, affect nearly all of us. It allows us to act as constructive social critics of our (or any) society, by enabling us to seek and discover, for example, the forces that throw people out of work or lead them to behave violently.

Although such discovery can be painful—we sometimes learn things about ourselves and our society that frighten or disappoint us—we cannot improve things unless we understand what is wrong. Precisely because such insight is often threatening or disappointing, people, particularly those with wealth and power, often prefer to avoid it. In Hitler's Germany, for example, university sociology departments were disbanded, and sociology has been severely restricted in a number of undemocratic countries in our own time. Even in the United States, the wealthy and powerful have often questioned the value of sociology, or at best valued it only for its practical applications. When it is allowed the freedom to do so, sociology can serve as a voice of dissent, asking important questions that otherwise would go unasked. In the long run, this is every bit as beneficial—perhaps even more so—than the more obvious and practical "social engineering" applications discussed in the preceding section. The point is that, in different ways, sociology is useful both to individuals or organizations confronted with specific problems, and to all of us in the larger society, by helping us to see and understand problems that we might otherwise remain unaware of.

Most of you, of course, will not become professional sociologists, even if you choose to major in sociology at the undergraduate level. However, the use of the knowledge and tools of sociology to address practical problems and issues is not limited to sociologists. As the appendix at the end of this book illustrates, sociology majors are entering a range of careers and making use of their skills and knowledge at all degree levels from B.A. through Ph.D.

Summary

Sociology operates on the basic principle that human behavior has important elements of regularity and predictability. It uses scientific methods of observation and generalization to describe, explain, and predict human behavior. Sociology is useful because there are distinct limits to what common sense can tell us about human behavior: Some things that "make sense" turn out, on careful observation of behavior, to be wrong. Sociology is one of the social sciences, and it is distinguished from the others by the broad range of behavior with which it is concerned and by its emphasis on understanding human behavior on the group or societal level. It emerged in the nineteenth century out of a desire to understand the rapid social changes associated with urbanization and the Industrial Revolution. However, as society has changed, the concerns and emphases of sociology have changed with it. Sociology can be applied to a wide range of problems and issues of concern to government, business, education, labor, and religion. Employment opportunities for people trained in sociology exist in all of these areas, although an undergraduate degree does not prepare a student for any specific "sociologist" job. Nonetheless, most people who earn a bachelor's degree in sociology get a job in a field related to their training, where they frequently outperform co-workers with professional degrees.

Glossary

sociology The systematic study of society, human social behavior, and social groups.

science An approach to understanding the world based on systematic observation and generalization, which is used to generate theories to explain what is observed and to predict future results under similar conditions.

research The process of systematic observation used in all sciences.

theory A set of interrelated statements about reality, usually involving one or more cause-and-effect relationships.

natural sciences Those sciences that are concerned with the natural or physical world, including chemistry, biology, physics, astronomy, geology, oceanography, and meteorology.

social sciences Those sciences that are concerned with the study of human behavior, including sociology, anthropology, psychology, economics, political science, and, by some definitions, history.

organized skepticism A norm or principle specifying that scientists will be required to support their claims about reality through observed evidence.

reactivity The tendency of people being studied by social scientists to react to the researcher or to the fact that they are being studied.

sociological imagination A series of insights or perspectives toward society that is achieved through the study of sociology.

social psychology An important subspecialty of both sociology and psychology that is concerned with the interaction of the individual with larger societal forces.

means of production Those goods or resources, including land in an agricultural society and capital in an industrial society, that a person must own to produce things of value.

bourgeoisie In a capitalist economy, those who own capital, who constitute the dominant group or ruling class.

proletariat In a capitalist economy, the class who work for wages or salaries and who are employed by the owners of capital.

Further Reading

BART, PAULINE, AND LINDA FRANKEL. 1986. *The Student Sociologist's Handbook*, 4th ed. New York: Random House. Discusses major theoretical perspectives in sociology and offers students information on how to search the sociological literature to gather information for writing papers on sociological topics.

BERGER, PETER. 1963. *Invitation to Sociology: A Humanistic Per-*

spective. New York: Doubleday Anchor. A classic and highly readable introduction to the sociological perspective. An excellent starting point for learning what it means to think sociologically.

COLLINS, RANDALL, AND MICHAEL MAKOWSKY. 1988. *The Discovery of Society,* 4th ed. New York: Random House. Discusses, in a highly readable way, the conditions that gave rise to sociology as an academic discipline in nineteenth-century Europe; it also relates the history of the discipline's intellectual development.

Encyclopedia of Sociology. 1986. Guilford, CT: Dushkin Publishing Group. A comprehensive sourcebook on concepts and theories in sociology, as well as on major sociologists. Contains short entries providing overviews of a very wide range of sociological topics.

MILLS, C. WRIGHT. 1959. *The Sociological Imagination.* New York: Oxford University Press. Another classic work, also aimed at helping you understand the meaning of the sociological perspective. Shows how things that we think of as personal troubles are often the results of larger societal processes.

CHAPTER 2

How Sociology Is Done

You wake up late. Your first class has already started, but you are still sleepy. After all, that was quite a party on the new coed floor of your dorm last night — somebody brought some super grass to share, and it seemed as though half the dorm was there. Then you remember — you didn't set the alarm because you weren't going to class today. Nixon just invaded Cambodia, and today is the first day of the student strike called in protest. You look out your window and see dozens of students picketing every classroom building. Over on the main quad, more than 1,000 students have already gathered for the big rally that starts at 10:00. You had better get dressed; you told several of your friends that you'd meet them downstairs in time to walk to the rally. It's obvious from the number of pickets and people already at the rally that you won't have to worry about getting in trouble for missing class; hardly anyone will be there, and besides, a couple of your professors are really into the peace movement and probably won't hold class anyway. Your parents, of course, are another matter. They'll probably see all this on television and call tonight to see if you are going to class. Should you tell them the truth? As you dress, you turn on the radio and hear the awful news: four students were killed by National Guardsmen yesterday at Kent State University in Ohio. Now you realize how far things have gone. This isn't just protest anymore. This is war.

    The scene described above is almost certainly a lot different from your experience of college. Yet it is a good description of the experiences of thousands of students in nearly every large university in the United States during the first week of May 1970. (The experience was quite different at some other types of college, however.) Do you ever wonder why things seem to have been so different then from the way they are now? Was it just the Vietnam War, or were there other reasons? Can such a question be answered? If so, how?

These are precisely the kinds of questions that sociologists try to answer. They try to explain how and why society changes over time, and how and why one society differs from another. They try, too, to explain why different groups of people respond differently to similar situations. Some people in 1970, for example, were just as outraged by the student demonstrations as others were by the shootings at Kent State. Some people, in fact, thought that the students "had it coming." In asking such questions, sociologists make the important assumption that *they can be answered:* People think and behave as they do for identifiable reasons. Thus, if we can measure the right things, we can answer such questions as why one generation of college students is relatively uninterested in politics while another generation seems to center its entire lifestyle around politics. (In Chapter 19, on social movements, we will see in some detail how sociologists have answered this question.)

Social Theory and Research

The opening vignette illustrates the point, noted briefly in Chapter 1, that sociology is largely concerned with *cause and effect.* Sometimes it seeks to *explain,* as, for example: Why did students protest and use drugs so much more in the late 1960s and early 1970s than during other periods? Sometimes, too, it seeks to *predict:* Under what conditions might students once again become strongly interested in political issues? Of course, there are times when sociology merely seeks to *describe:* To what extent do students currently use drugs, and how and to what extent do they participate politically? Most of the time, though, description is a step toward either explanation or prediction, both of which involve the notion of cause and effect.

Cause and Effect

By **cause and effect,** social scientists mean that the presence of one condition (the *cause*) makes the occurrence of some other condition (the *effect*) more likely than it would otherwise have been. This is a somewhat broader definition than the popular notion of cause and effect. To social scientists, the cause does not *always* have to be followed by the effect, but the effect does occur more often when the cause is present than when it is absent. Consider the example of unemployment and divorce. Social research has indicated that unemployment is a cause of divorce. By this, I mean that when one of the breadwinners in a family becomes unemployed, the family is more likely to experience a divorce than it would have been had that unemployment not occurred. It does *not* mean that a divorce will *always* follow the loss of a job, nor does it mean that the absence of unemployment guarantees that a couple will not get divorced. It simply means that, all other things being equal, divorce is more likely in the presence of unemployment than in its absence.

Theory and Research

Values and Theories As explained in Chapter 1, a *theory* can be defined as a set of interrelated statements about reality, usually involving one or more cause-effect relationships. Ideally, these statements can be tested through *research*—the process of systematic observation introduced in Chapter 1. This is what distinguishes theories from other kinds of arguments: Theories are made up of verifiable statements about reality that, with the right information, can be tested (Lenski, 1988).

In contrast to theories are **values.** Values are personal judgments or preferences about what is considered good or bad, or about what is liked or disliked. Unlike theories, values can never be proved or disproved because they reflect personal preferences or judgments. Such judgments, of course, are largely products of culture, and people from different cultures have different values. Still, no culture's values are "right" or "wrong," "true" or "false."

Consider the following statement: "Poverty causes conflict in society." This is a statement about reality that — given the right information — could be shown to be either true or false. Thus, this statement could stand as a part of a theory. In contrast, consider the following statement: "Conflict in society is undesirable." This statement is a *value judgment*. It cannot be proved true or false because it is simply a matter of what people consider good or bad. Some people regard conflict as bad per se because it often leads to anger, violence, and hatred. Others consider at least some conflict to be good because it can help to change society for the better. Which group of people is "right"? That question cannot be answered. The two groups simply have different desires and priorities. In other words, they have different *values*.

Distinguishing Theories from Values Why this discussion of theories and values? These concepts are important because our thinking about society and human behavior is bound to be influenced by both values and factual questions. This is true for sociologists as well as for "ordinary people." Therefore, you must be able to look at an argument and distinguish what part of the argument involves testable theories and what part involves values, which cannot be tested. This principle is illustrated by the example above. When we speak about social conflict, we are likely to ask and debate questions about what causes it. These are factual questions concerning cause and effect, which is exactly what theories address. Questions of this type can be answered by research. However, when we speak about social conflict, we are also likely to debate whether it is good or bad, and the answer, at least in part, involves values. Science, through theory and research, might be able to identify some consequences of conflict (for example, how likely it is to bring about a certain kind of change), but it *cannot* prove that conflict and its consequences are either good or bad. Judgments of this type are a matter of values and cannot be answered scientifically, even though scientists, like everyone else, have their values.

You will often encounter arguments such as the following: "Conflict is bad because it usually leads to violence, and it rarely changes anything anyway." This argument is a mix of values and theories, and to evaluate it you have to be able to determine which is which. The part asserting that "conflict is bad" is a value judgment because it reflects a personal preference. In fact, even if the rest of the statement were true, you could still reasonably disagree with the "conflict is bad" part. (Perhaps conflict also challenges people and leads them to work harder and be more creative, so it could be seen as good for that reason.) However, the parts of the statement concerning the effects of conflict on violence and social change concern factual reality. Those parts of the statement could be thought of as a rudimentary social theory, and, given the right information, could be proved either true or false. Thus, when you encounter statements or arguments about society, you should ask yourself the following questions:

1. What parts of the statement or argument reflect people's values and therefore are a matter of personal attitude or preference that cannot be judged true or false through observation?
2. What parts of the statement concern reality and therefore could be demonstrated to be true or false if you could get the right information?

Values and the Social Sciences The above discussion holds true whether you are studying the works of social scientists, reading a newspaper, watching a television program, or having a discussion with your friends. Although social scientists place a primary emphasis on theory and research — that is, on addressing factual questions about the realities of human behavior — they, too, are human, and their work is often influenced by their values. Inevitably, the topics that social (or, for that matter, natural) scientists choose to study will be influenced by their values. In addition, scientists are not value-free concerning their theories. Science today is a very competitive business, and every scientist wants to gain recognition (and grant money and publications) by developing a theory that works better than anyone else's. Consequently, scientists sometimes try to interpret their results to fit their theories. Finally, because social scientists study human beings, they frequently bring strong values to their research that can influence their interpretations of their findings. Both social scientists and natural scientists often have a strong interest in applying their research for some useful purpose, and they frequently make policy recommendations. These recommendations can be influenced by both their research findings and their values. All of this is fine, as long as the principle of *sharing* discussed in Chapter 1 is followed. The scientific community can thus debate the interpretations, the policy recommendations, and even the appropriateness of the topic for study. Such debate strengthens rather than weakens science, and for this reason few people today argue that science can or should be totally value-free.

The Relationship between Theory and Research

Recall from Chapter 1 that science consists of a cycle that includes observation (research), generalization, explanation, and prediction. This leads to a new round of the cycle, which may begin with new research to test the predictions generated from the previous round. This cycle is illustrated in Figure 2.1. This diagram illustrates the reciprocal relationship between research and theory. Research findings are most meaningful when considered in the context of a theory, which *explains* the findings by proposing cause-effect relationships that can account for them. Similarly, theory is of little use unless it can be shown by research to be correct.

Explanation versus Prediction Consider the top half of Figure 2.1, which shows research being used to *generate* theory. Here a research finding is obtained, assumed, or found to generalize, and a theory is then developed to *explain* it. Jiobu (1988) used this method of reasoning to develop a theory to explain the relatively high income of Japanese Americans. Compared to most other racial minority groups in the United States — even compared to much of the white major-

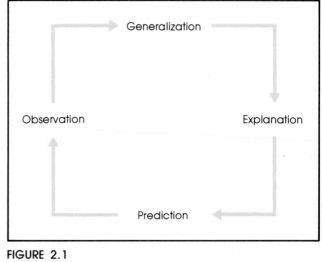

FIGURE 2.1
The Cycles of Scientific Inquiry

ity group — Japanese Americans on the average have high levels of income and education. How did the Japanese succeed where others could not? Jiobu developed a theory that their success was based in part on their ability to gain control of certain segments of the California vegetable industry — including tomatoes, asparagus, and spinach — that required high levels of labor but little land to produce, and had wide market demand that extended far beyond the Japanese-American market.

Now, consider the bottom half of the figure. Here, research is being used to *test* theory. The theory predicts a particular result, and the scientist does the research to see if the predicted result can be obtained. Again, the ethnic-group success example can be used to illustrate this procedure. Jiobu's theory predicts that *any* ethnic group that gains control of an industry that produces a product for which there is a wide market should experience success to a greater extent than other ethnic groups. An obvious way to test this theory is to examine the economic history of a wide variety of ethnic groups. If we were to do such a study and find that, consistently, ethnic groups that at some point in history gained control of such an industry today have higher incomes than comparable groups that did not gain control of such an industry, we would

have an important piece of evidence in support of
Jiobu's theory. If, however, we found no difference in
the average incomes of ethnic groups that did and did
not gain control of such an industry at some time in the
past, we would probably conclude that Jiobu's theory
was wrong.

As shown in Figure 2.1, the relationship between
theory and research works two ways. Sometimes, as in
the top half of the figure, scientists do research in order
to develop theories, or develop theories in order to
explain a research finding. In this case, the scientists
are engaging in a process of *explanation,* or *theory
generation.* Other times, as in the bottom half of the
figure, scientists do research in order to test a theory.
In this case, the scientists are engaging in a process of
prediction, or *theory testing.*

Research and Theory Testing When social scientists use research for theory testing, they usually make
use of a **hypothesis,** a single testable statement about
reality that is developed for the purpose of testing a
piece of a theory. A hypothesis always takes the form
of a statement, not a question. It usually involves some
kind of cause-effect relationship between two or more
variables. (Some examples of hypotheses, as well as
related examples that are not hypotheses, are shown
in the box entitled "Which Ones Are Hypotheses?")
The reason a hypothesis is used is that a theory is

usually too large and complex to test at one time.
Hence, scientists test one part of the theory at a time
and develop a hypothesis. A hypothesis, then, may be
thought of as an educated guess, based on a theory, of
what finding a research project will obtain. When
research is done for the purpose of theory testing, the
scientist develops a hypothesis from a theory, then
conducts research to see whether the actual evidence
obtained is consistent with the hypothesis.

*An important part of every social-research project is to
become familiar with past research and relevant theories.*

A CASE STUDY: DURKHEIM ON SUICIDE   This process can be illustrated by the first sociological study conducted according to the scientific model, Emile Durkheim's *Suicide* (1964; [orig. 1897]). Durkheim sought to explain why some people commit suicide while others don't. He developed the theory that suicide was often the result of isolation or a lack of social integration. This theory suggests several hypotheses. If we can identify groups of people who are more individualistic and less integrated into some type of group life, we would expect such people to have a higher rate of suicide. Durkheim identified three such groups of people: Protestants, men, and unmarried people. Protestant religions emphasize an individual relationship with God rather than the community orientation stressed by Catholics and Jews. Men are expected to be "strong" and do things on their own, whereas the traditional female role emphasizes family and community relationships. Unmarried people may be alone much of the time and often do not have the kinds of relationships that married people have with their spouse and (usually) children.

Thus, Durkheim developed three hypotheses: Suicide rates would be higher among Protestants than among Catholics and Jews, higher among men than among women, and higher among unmarried than among married people. He then tested the hypotheses by examining data archives on suicide cases and computing suicide rates for different categories of the population in several European countries. As he expected, he found higher suicide rates among Protestants, men, and unmarried people than among Catholics and Jews, women, and unmarried people. These findings supported his hypotheses. Moreover, they offered an important piece of evidence in support of his larger theory.

Usually no single study suffices to accept or reject a theory. At best, it will support or refute a few hypotheses that are derived from, or consistent with, a theory. Still, each confirmed hypothesis adds support to a theory (as in the case of Durkheim's theory about the causes of suicide), and if enough hypotheses relating to a theory are confirmed on a consistent basis, the theory will come to be widely supported. In the case of Durkheim's theory, the notion of isolation and disconnection from others as a cause of suicide has become widely accepted among sociologists. This is because (1) Durkheim and others have confirmed a number of hypotheses, all of which are consistent with the theory; and (2) many of the hypothesized relationships have held up consistently over time and in a number of different societies. Although Durkheim conducted his research in a number of European nations during the nineteenth century, similar patterns can be found in the United States today. American males today, for example, remain much more likely than American females to commit suicide. Also, church members in the United States have lower suicide rates than do nonmembers, and married people are less likely to commit suicide than are divorced people (Breault, 1986, 1988).

Research and Theory Generation Researchers who are interested in topics about which there is no well-developed theory are likely to engage in research for the purpose of *theory generation*. The main purpose of such research is to develop some theory to explain some pattern of behavior. Rather than use a hypothesis to predict the research result, the researcher conducts research as a way of *generating* or developing hypotheses that can then be used to build a theory.

FASCISM: A CASE STUDY An example of this can be seen in the research of Theodor Adorno, Else Frenkel-Brunswick, and others (1950) concerning *fascism*. Adorno, who fled Germany to escape the Nazis, was interested in why people would support a movement like Nazism. Because Nazism and fascism were very recent developments at the time, no sizable body of theory on these subjects existed. Thus, researchers either had to develop their own theory or adopt theories about related topics that might be relevant to fascism. They reasoned that some clues to the thinking of people who supported fascism might be found in the speeches and writings of Nazi leaders. Thus, they analyzed these speeches and writings for common themes. Assuming that personality need might be relevant to support for the Nazis, they particularly looked for themes that appeared regularly even though they were not directly related to fascism's political message. They found a number of such themes, including superstition, stereotyped thinking, simplistic good/bad categorization, aggression against nonconformers, and cynicism. These same themes appeared repeatedly in the speeches and writings of Nazis, fascists, Ku Klux Klan members, and other right-wing extremists. This led researchers to hypothesize that a personality test could be developed to predict intolerance of the type practiced by such extremists. They developed such a test and found that people with the personality traits measured by the test were indeed more prejudiced against racial and religious minority groups. The purpose of their initial analysis of the speeches and writings of extremists, however, was simply to generate the hypothesis, not to test it.

Steps in a Social Research Project

In any social science research project, a certain sequence of steps must be followed. These steps vary somewhat depending upon whether the objective of the research is to generate hypotheses or to test hypotheses. These steps are outlined in a general form in Figure 2.2 and are discussed in greater detail in the following pages.

Why did so many Germans accept Hitler and the Nazis? Theodor Adorno conducted research to determine why people support authoritarian personalities.

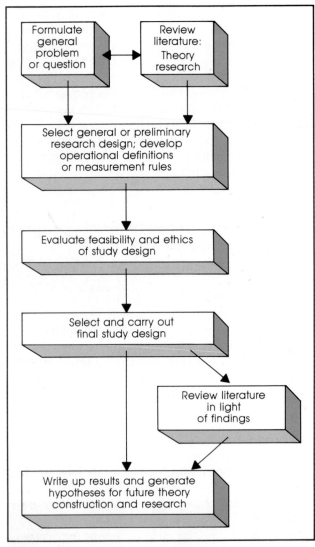

FIGURE 2.2a
Steps in Hypothesis-Generation Research Projects

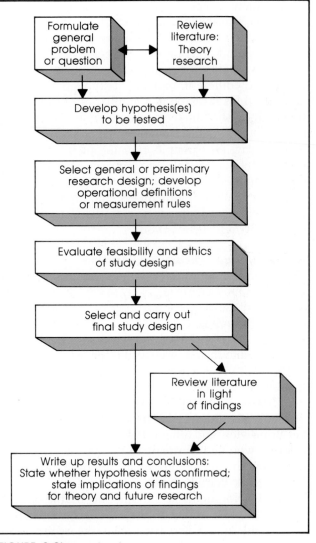

FIGURE 2.2b
Steps in Hypothesis-Testing Research Projects

Defining the Research Problem

Regardless of whether a social scientist is interested in theory testing or theory generation, the first (and perhaps most important) step in any research project is to define clearly the problem the researcher wishes to study. Thus, scientists usually begin by stating a ques-

tion that the research is intended to answer. In our first example, Durkheim (who engaged in theory testing) asked whether sex, religion, and marital status influenced the likelihood of suicide. In our second example (involving theory generation), the researchers asked whether any identifiable personality pattern might predispose people toward fascism. Although

How does childhood play affect adult behavior? Which factors affect the amount of education a person receives, and how does education in turn affect a person's chances of success? To answer questions such as these, sociologists conduct research both to generate and test theories.

the question may be more narrowly defined in the theory-testing mode of research, a clear identification of the question to be answered is important in both types of research. By identifying the research problem or question in this manner, the researcher is able to limit his or her inquiries to those things that are relevant to answering the question. In other words, the research problem gives definition or focus to the entire research project. Although a good, clear definition of the problem does not guarantee a successful research project, the absence of a clear definition often results in a bad one.

In order to define a problem to be researched, the researcher must be thoroughly familiar with theory and past research concerning the chosen topic. A good research question will usually accomplish one of two things. If the mode of research is theory testing, the question will identify some hypothesis to be tested, which will help to confirm or disconfirm some part of a theory. If the purpose is to generate theory,

the objective will be to look for some pattern or regularity that might serve as the basis for a theory or hypothesis. Neither objective can be accomplished, however, without a thorough knowledge of what is already known, what is plausible but unconfirmed, what is already disproved, and what is uncharted territory.

Variables

As previously stated, social scientists are interested in cause and effect. To measure cause and effect they use *variables*. A **variable** is any concept that can take on different values or that has two or more categories. In other words, the concept can *vary* among the different values or categories. Temperature is a variable, as are age and income. All of them vary from time to time in the same people and places, as well as between people or places. These variables can be expressed as numbers—75 degrees, $50,000, or 18 years old. Other variables cannot be expressed as numbers. Religion and ethnicity are examples of this type of variable. Religion, for example, can be classified as Protestant, Catholic, Jewish, Muslim, or "all other." However, none of these categories is "more" or "greater" than another in the sense that $50,000 is more than $25,000. They are simply different categories. Beginning students sometimes confuse categories of variables with the variables themselves. Protestant, Catholic, Jewish, Muslim, and "all other" are *not* variables. They are simply *categories* of the same variable, religion.

Independent variables Social science research typically involves cause-effect relationships among variables. Similarly, most hypotheses concern such relationships. Some variables in the social sciences represent causes, others represent effects. In a hypothesis or a research project, a variable that the researcher thinks is a *cause* is called an **independent variable** (or sometimes, a *predictor variable*). In a study involving a relationship between two variables, then, the independent variable is the variable that the researcher thinks influences the other variable or precedes it in time.

Dependent Variables A variable that a researcher thinks is the effect is called the **dependent variable.** This variable is thought to follow the independent variable in time or to be influenced by the independent variable. It is called the dependent variable because, if the researcher is right, its value in part *depends on* the value of the independent variable. If education is the independent variable and income is the dependent variable, for example, then a person's income depends, in part, on the amount of education that he or she has. In this example, education represents the cause and income the effect. For more examples — and to see how well you can identify independent and dependent variables — see the box entitled "Identifying Independent and Dependent Variables."

Measurement

Operational Definitions Once the variables to be included in a study have been decided upon, the researcher must decide how to *measure* them. The precise means by which the variables will be measured depends on the type of study being done. Measurement is the process of determining the value of a variable. This is accomplished by using an **operational definition,** a precise statement of the meaning of a variable or of the categories of a variable for the purpose of measurement. An operational definition of income could be "the adjusted gross income that the survey respondent claims to have reported on his or her income tax form for the most recent tax year." In observational research, the racial categories white, black, Asian, Hispanic, and other might be defined according to the observer's judgment: A person is white if the observer in the study judges him or her to be white, and so forth.

There is no "right" or "wrong" way to define a variable operationally. Take, for example, the operational definition of a Jewish person. If a researcher were interested in the effects of religious identity, anyone who considers himself or herself to be Jewish might be defined as Jewish. If the researcher were interested in the effects of religious participation, a Jewish person might be operationally defined as someone who has attended temple on the Sabbath at least once within the past month. Neither operational definition is "right" or "wrong"; they just capture different aspects of what it means to be Jewish.

Although any variable can be operationally defined in several ways, all operational definitions *must* be clear and unambiguous. We would not, for example, want to define as Jewish "anyone who believes in the Jewish faith." That definition is too ambiguous because it does not tell us how to decide who believes in the Jewish faith and who doesn't.

Validity and Reliability However we measure our variables, two conditions must be met for successful measurement: validity and reliability. Reliability is the easier of the two to assess. **Reliability** refers to consistency in measurement. When a given variable is measured several times, do we get the same result? If we ask the same person his or her race several times and get different answers each time, we clearly have a reliability problem. Similarly, if we have five questions in a survey intended to measure social class, and every question produces different results in the same individuals, the reliability of our instrument is poor: Questions that are supposed to be measuring the same thing are in fact measuring different things.

Even if we have good reliability, we may have a problem of poor validity. **Validity** refers to measuring correctly the concept we intend to measure. Consider an example. You are using a yardstick to measure the width of a desk. You see that the width of the desk is exactly two times the length of the yardstick. You can measure the desk 20 times, and you will get the same result each time. However, you didn't notice that your "yardstick" is really a meter stick. Your measurement is therefore *not valid*. The desk is wider than you thought, because it is really 2 meters wide, not 2 yards wide.

As a practical matter, validity is much harder to assess than reliability. Social scientists look for clues that support the validity of their measures, but in some instances they can never be sure. This is particularly true when they are attempting to measure some abstract concept, such as intelligence, happiness, or power. Sociologists refer to such concepts as **constructs** because, to some extent, their precise meaning must be constructed by the researcher. They are too abstract to measure directly. Take the case of intelligence tests. Are they valid measures of intelligence? Well, just what is intelligence? We could define it as the ability to learn. That is a reasonable definition, but there is no way to measure this ability directly. It is a truism among educators that some people don't work up to their ability. Yet, all we can measure directly is what people know or can do at some point in time — and in one way or other, that is what all intelligence tests measure.

We cannot directly judge the validity of intelligence tests because we have no way to measure intelligence precisely and directly. We can get some hints about the validity of such tests, though. If a new intelligence test produced similar results to several existing tests of intelligence, we would have more faith in its validity than if it did not. Similarly, we would have more faith in the test if those who score high on it get better grades in school than those who score low. Even in these cases, however, questions of validity would remain. Perhaps all the tests are measuring social class, not intelligence, and children from higher social classes do better in school. If this were the case, our test could give similar results to other tests and predict school grades, but still not be measuring intelligence.

Identifying Cause-Effect Relationships

Consider a situation in which a scientist is trying to find out whether a cause-effect relationship exists between two variables. Let us call the independent variable the *presumed cause* and the dependent variable the *presumed effect*. How does the scientist decide whether or not such a cause-effect relationship exists? In other words, how do we determine whether the independent variable causes the dependent variable? Basically, the scientist must ask three questions. The first is: "Is there *correlation* between the two variables?" The second is: "Is the *time order* correct?" If

Here are the answers to the quiz on identifying independent and dependent variables that appeared on the preceding page.

1. The independent variable is religion (whether one is Protestant or Catholic), and the dependent variable is voting preference. Because people are usually born into a religious affiliation and develop their political preferences later, religion would be the independent variable because it normally comes first in time.

2. Because the question clearly specified crime as the result, the incidence or amount of crime is the dependent variable; poverty or lack thereof is the independent variable.

3. Presumably, what the students are debating is whether studying raises one's GRE score. Therefore, the independent variable is whether one studies (or how much one studies), whereas the dependent variable is the score on the GRE.

the answers to these questions are both "yes," the scientist then asks: "Are there any *alternative explanations* for the observed correlation?" Let us consider each question in more detail.

Correlation The term **correlation** means that when the independent variable changes, the dependent variable also has a tendency to change. Consider again the first two examples from the box on independent and dependent variables. In the first example, the hypothesis was that Catholics are more likely to vote Democratic than Protestants. Suppose you conducted an exit poll at a presidential election and found that a higher percentage of Catholics than Protestants reported voting for the Democratic candidate. Such a finding would be an example of correlation: There was a difference in the voting patterns of Catholics and Protestants. Similarly, in the second example, if climatological records revealed that northern locations did have colder average temperatures than southern ones, you would again have evidence of correlation: Location does correlate with temperature. Conversely, if you found no difference between the voting patterns of Catholics and Protestants or no difference in average temperatures between northern and southern locations, you would have an absence of correla-

tion. In such situations you would usually conclude that there is no cause-effect relationship between the variables. Some reports of scientific studies use the terms *covariation* or *statistical relationship*. These terms mean the same thing as correlation.

Positive and Negative Correlation Correlation can be *positive* (direct) or *negative* (inverse). Consider the example in the box concerning the relationship between studying and GRE scores. In this example, the hypothesis assumes that the more you study, the higher your score. If research showed this to be true, there would be a *positive* relationship between the amount of studying and the score. In other words, as one variable increases, the other also increases. In contrast, a researcher investigating the example of poverty and crime might find that as people's incomes rise, the likelihood of their committing certain crimes decreases. In this case, where one variable (income) increases, the other (crime rate) decreases. This is what is meant by a *negative* relationship.

Correlation alone is never enough to prove a cause-effect relationship between the independent variable and the dependent variable. Consider the following example. The more hospital beds a city has, the more deaths it will have each year. If you compare all

Sorting Out Cause-Effect Relationships: Single-Parent Homes and Teenage Pregnancy

How sociologists sort out cause-effect relationships using control variables can be illustrated by the findings of a recent study of the effect of parental absence resulting from separation or divorce (the independent variable) on teenage pregnancy (the dependent variable) (McLanahan and Bumpass, 1988). We know that teenage girls from single-parent homes are more likely than other girls to become pregnant. But is it because they are from *single-parent families,* or is it because of other aspects of their *social background?* People from low-income families, for example, have above-average divorce and separation rates, and therefore their children frequently grow up in single-parent families. At the same time, growing up poor may by itself put a person at a high risk of teenage pregnancy. Thus, to determine whether growing up in a one-parent family "causes" a higher rate of teenage pregnancy, we must introduce one or more *control variables.* (We shall slightly simplify the McLanahan and Bumpass study by combining their social background and education variables into one control variable.)

The diagrams below illustrate two possibilities. In Example 1, the relationship is spurious: There is a relationship between growing up in a single-parent home and teenage pregnancy *only* because people of certain social backgrounds are more likely to grow up in single-parent homes *and* to become pregnant as teenagers. This spurious relationship is represented by a dotted line, while the true cause-effect relationships are represented by solid arrows. In this example, there is no relationship between growing up in a single-parent home and teenage pregnancy *among people whose social background is otherwise similar.*

In Example 2, there *is* a real cause-effect relationship between growing up in a single-parent home and teenage pregnancy. In this example, the relationship between growing up in a single-parent home and teen pregnancy remains present even among people with similar backgrounds. Introducing a control variable does not eliminate the covariation between the independent variable (single-parent home) and the dependent variable (teenage pregnancy). Thus, there is a solid arrow between single-parent home and teenage pregnancy. The arrow between social background and teenage pregnancy has a question mark because in this case a cause-effect relationship might or might not exist.

What did the study actually find? It found that even among people with similar backgrounds, those who grew up in single-parent families were more likely to become pregnant as teenagers. In the population as a whole, white teenagers who grew up in one-parent families were 111 percent more likely than other white teenagers to give birth as teens. Among those whose social background and education were similar, those from one-parent homes were 58 percent more likely to give birth. Among black teenagers, the difference was 50 percent in the whole population and 36 percent for those with similar education and background. Thus, for both races, the control variables of education and background explained away only part of the relationship between growing up in a one-parent home and having a baby as a teenager. In this case, Example 2 was the correct choice.

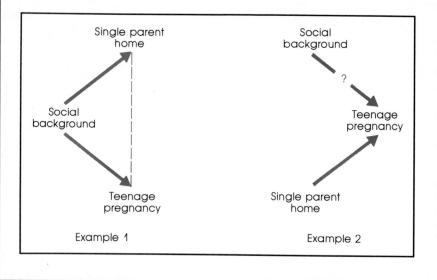

Example 1

Example 2

American cities, you will find that this correlation is true. However, it does *not* mean that having more hospital beds will cause more people to die. Rather, larger cities have more hospital beds because they have more people, and for the same reason, they also have more deaths. This is why we must answer the other two questions: Is the time order between the variables correct, and are there any alternative explanations for the correlation between the two variables?

Time Order   If correlation between two variables is established, the next step in trying to determine whether the independent variable causes the dependent variable is to determine whether the variables occurred in the correct time order. This step is very simple: *The cause must happen before the effect.* Something taking place today cannot cause something that happened yesterday. As was previously pointed out, religious affiliation generally is acquired before political preference. Hence, it is reasonable to argue that religious affiliation could cause or influence political preference; it is not plausible to argue the contrary. Sometimes in social research it is very clear which variable came first, but in other cases the social scientist must make a judgment. In general, when correlation exists between two variables, the researcher must determine the time order of the two variables. If evidence indicates that the presumed cause came before the presumed effect, the scientist can move on to address the question of alternative explanations. If there is no such plausible evidence, the scientist will probably conclude that the independent variable is *not* causing or influencing the dependent variable.

Eliminating Alternative Explanations   Once a social scientist has established correlation and correct time order between two variables, the remaining task is to ask whether anything else — some third variable or combination of variables — could be causing the correlation without the independent variable actually causing or influencing the dependent variable. Consider again the example of religion and voting preference. As the example has been stated, we have correlation (the exit poll showed that Catholics were more

likely to vote Democratic than Protestants), and we have correct time order (religious affiliation is usually acquired before political preference.) We still cannot conclude that being Catholic by itself has any effect on voting, however. We must consider *alternative explanations* for the relationship we have observed. Consider, for example, the possibility that Catholics as a group have lower incomes than Protestants. If this were true, it could be income, not religion, that is influencing voting preference. In general, people of lower incomes *are* more likely to vote Democratic, and people of higher incomes *are* more likely to vote Republican. If Catholics did have lower average incomes than Protestants, they would then be more likely to vote Democratic, even if religion by itself had no effect on voting.

How would we know whether religion made any difference in voting if Protestants had higher incomes than Catholics? We would have to compare Catholics and Protestants *with the same income*. If, among Catholics and Protestants with the same income, the Catholics were still more likely to vote Democratic, we would be more likely to conclude that religion has a cause-effect relationship with voting. If, however, Catholics and Protestants of the same income were equally likely to vote Democratic, we would conclude that religion has no effect on income and that the original correlation was *spurious;* that is, it was a product of a third variable. In other words, an alternative explanation — income differences between Catholics and Protestants — accounted for the relationship.

Control Variables   In the example above, income was introduced as a **control variable.** A control variable is a third variable that is introduced to determine whether the relationship between the independent variable and the dependent variable can be accounted for by an alternative explanation. In this example, we wanted to know whether the correlation between religion and voting preference represented a true cause-effect relationship or whether it was merely a product of income differences between Catholics and Protestants. We answered this question by introducing income as a *control variable.* In the box ''Sorting Out

Cause-Effect Relationships,'' you can see how a control variable was used in a real sociological study.

Interpretation and Dissemination

The final stage in a research project is to interpret and disseminate the findings. This process involves writing up the results and making them available to others. Professional sociologists do this by publishing books, reports, and journal articles, and by presenting research papers at professional meetings. You might do it by submitting a paper to your instructor. In addition to describing the results, this process involves interpreting them: *Why* did the researcher get the results she or he obtained? Sometimes, particularly when the purpose of the research was to test a hypothesis, all of the appropriate control variables were included, and the hypothesis was confirmed, the meaning of the findings seems quite clear. If the hypothesis was not supported by the data, of course, the question becomes "Why not?" In other cases, the objective is to generate hypotheses, and this, by its very nature, requires interpretation of the findings. Interpretation takes the researcher full circle, because once again he or she must use theory and past research to make a judgment about what interpretations are plausible. Once an interpretation has been offered, an addition has been made to existing theory. A new cycle of theory and research can now begin, as the same researcher or other researchers develop and test hypotheses arising from the interpretation.

For a real-life example of how sociologists conduct this process of theory and research, see "Personal Journey into Sociology: Joan McCord."

Key Research Methods in Sociology

The principles discussed thus far in this chapter are applicable to all of the social sciences, and often to the natural sciences as well. Now we shall narrow our focus somewhat to consider the particular research methods that are used in sociology. Once a sociologist has selected a research problem and reviewed the sociological literature to identify theories and past research that relate to the topic, the next task is to design and carry out the research. Sociologists use four major approaches to research: *experiments, surveys, field observation,* and *analysis of existing data.*

Experiments

An **experiment** is research that is carried out in a situation, such as a laboratory or classroom, that is under the control of the researcher. In an experiment, the researcher changes or manipulates the independent variable, tries to keep everything else constant,

An experiment on infant behavior. Scientists often conduct experiments in order to test hypotheses.

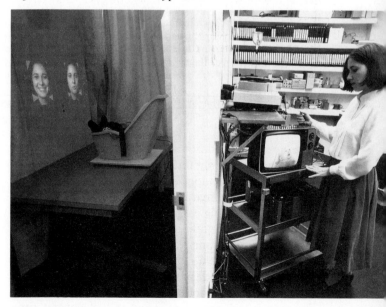

Changing Times

The year 1956 was a beginning, of sorts, for me. That was the year H. L. A. Hart was teaching a seminar on Causation and the Law. One day, several of us spent hours arguing that it was impossible to know more than that events were or were not "conjoined." Hart suddenly reached for a heavy glass ashtray and slid it across the table against the stomach of Henry Aiken, a Humean. "I caused that!" he announced. Hart's shove issued the challenge that drove my interest in longitudinal research.

How can we learn that one thing causes another? Despite the appeal of radical skepticism, it was impossible to reject the idea that at least sometimes, people cause things to happen. And, as Hart's gesture indicated, detection of causal relations cannot be entirely dependent on perceiving constancy of conjunction. Hart had not previously shoved anything across the conference table—much less an ashtray. Yet it seemed clear that Hart had been the cause of his colleague's pain. We had seen Hart touching the ashtray; the touching had preceded the ashtray's movement; and we could follow the trail as the ashtray crossed the table en route to Aiken's stomach.

Joan McCord, *Temple University*

Temporal priority seemed to be central to the causal relationship.

Also in 1956, I became a Research Assistant at Palfrey House, the study center for Child Psychology at Harvard. My first assignment introduced me to the Human Relations Area Files then being created. I was asked to code for the child-rearing section of these cross-cultural resources. Fascinating anecdotes. We were supposed to classify societies on the basis of reports for which, often, only one or two cases had been described. I could not overcome my doubts about generalizing from what might well be

atypical families or erroneous reports. We were to rate cultures on such things as maternal warmth, use of physical punishment, and permissiveness of aggression. After classifying a culture on a particular dimension, we recorded our confidence in the rating as representing a picture of the society. My constant rating of "doubtful" led to a reassignment! I became Eleanor Maccoby's research assistant.

Data for the classic Sears, Maccoby, and Levin study had been collected by asking parents to describe their children and to respond to questions about their own child-rearing techniques. The source of information both for the child's behavior and for the home environment had been the mother. Alternative explanations for the relationships were equally plausible. Although mothers might be accurately reporting their own and their children's behavior, for example, their reports might merely reflect justifications of their behavior. Alternatively, the reports of both sets of data could be reflections of different biases about idealized parent-child relationships. At least partly to overcome these problems, we were coding children's behavior from an independent source:

and measures the dependent variable before and after the change in the independent variable. Suppose, for example, that a researcher wanted to find out if seeing a movie advocating tolerance would reduce people's levels of racial prejudice. The researcher could give a group of people a questionnaire measuring prejudice, show them the movie, then give them the scale again to see if their attitudes had changed. If they had, there would be evidence both of correlation between seeing the movie and prejudice score and of correct time order.

Experimental and Control Groups

To be really confident of their results, however, researchers must use not one, but two, groups of people in their experiments. One group, called the **experimental group,** goes through an experience like that described above. They are given a "before" measure of the dependent variable (called the *pretest*), the independent variable is changed or manipulated (as in the showing of the movie), and the dependent variable is measured again (the *posttest*). The other group, the

the children's "doll play." Doll play had been developed as a technique for understanding how children perceived the world. The children in the Sears, Maccoby, and Levin study had told stories using dolls to represent their families. The measure assumed that a child identified with a doll assigned the same sex as the child. We were measuring conscience by counting punishing events for which the cause was unknown.

A few months earlier, Gordon Allport had asked William and me to reevaluate The Cambridge-Somerville Youth Study, a program designed to prevent delinquency. The Cambridge-Somerville Youth Study had included random assignment of high-risk children to treatment and control groups. Almost a decade earlier, Edwin Powers and Helen Witmer had evaluated the program and concluded that no beneficial effect had been demonstrated. Hoping to understand the development of conscience, we extended our work beyond comparing the randomly assigned treated and control groups.

On December 10, 1956, I put the finishing touches on our book, *Origins of Crime*. Then I went to the hospital to deliver the first of our two sons.

Although 1956 marks an important beginning for me, my interest in studying society began, of course, much earlier. As a child, I had to cope with understanding why people threw snowballs with rocks inside—calling "Jew, Jew"—as I walked home from first grade. We moved from Scarsdale to New York City to Tucson, Arizona. I was perpetually an "outsider."

My high school boy friend and I were married as Stanford undergraduates and went to Harvard together. I taught elementary school while my husband earned his Ph.D. Just as my turn came to complete graduate school, my husband was invited to become Assistant Dean of Humanities and Sciences at Stanford.

Upon our return from a year in France in 1961 I resumed studies aiming toward a Ph.D. in Philosophy. At about that time, our marriage broke down. I struggled to keep food on the table. Without a Ph.D., I could not get the positions for which my experience and training had qualified me; yet employers were unwilling to hire me in assistant positions because, they said, "You will be bored." Finally in 1965, the National Institute of Mental Health funded my return to graduate school. I earned a Ph.D.

in Sociology, from Stanford, in 1968.

During these years the boys from the Cambridge-Somerville Youth Study had become middle-aged. During the 1950s, I had directed coding of the records describing family interactions. These records included detailed information about how fathers, mothers, and siblings interacted. The lure of discovering delayed benefits of treatment—which I fully expected—in combination with the possibility of a more adequate study of the influence of child rearing on adult behavior drove me and a small cadre of assistants to retrace the group although 30 years had passed without contact. In the process of tracing, we learned much about mobility and case retrieval (for we found 98 percent of the men). We also learned that self-reports of benefits from treatment were untrustworthy. Despite their descriptions of how the treatment had been beneficial, men in the treatment group actually turned out worse than those in the matched control group. The early records have proved their value in showing that child-rearing differences predict many features of adult behavior. I am still working with the mountains of data produced from this retracing.

control group, goes through the pretest and posttest, but there is no manipulation of the independent variable. In the example above, the *control group* would be given the "before" and "after" prejudice questionnaire but would *not* be shown the movie. Why is this necessary? Without the control group, the scientist would have no way of knowing whether people's attitudes changed because of seeing the movie or for some other reason. It could be, for example, that their attitudes changed because answering the questionnaire made them think in ways that changed their minds.

Using the control group eliminates this alternative explanation because that group also took the questionnaire twice. If the experimental group (the group that saw the movie) changed more than the control group, it was clearly influenced by something more than just taking the test—most likely by the movie.

Of course, other possibilities exist. Perhaps the people in the experimental group were more easily persuaded than the people in the control group and thus were more likely to change their minds. Fortunately, there is also a way of dealing with problems like

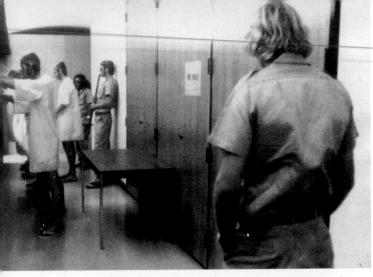

In a classic social-science experiment, Philip Zimbardo divided a group of students into prisoners and guards. So thoroughly did the students internalize these new roles that the experiment had to be stopped well ahead of the original deadline.

this, which involve preexisting differences between the people in the two groups. It is important in experiments that people in the experimental group be as similar to people in the control group as possible in all respects. The safest way to assure this is to have large experimental and control groups (100 or more) and to assign people *randomly* between the two groups. This will assure that the groups are similar in all respects. If this cannot be done, the next best thing is to see that people in the two groups are similar with respect to any social characteristics that the researcher considers important, such as age, sex, race, and educational level.

Reactivity in Experimental Research

The experimental research design described here, sometimes called the "classic experimental design," is outlined in Table 2.1. This design eliminates possible effects of preexisting differences between the groups, of taking the pretest and posttest, and of passage of time between the pretest and posttest. Thus, it narrows considerably the number of explanations for any differences between the two groups in the degree to which the dependent variable changes between the pretest and the posttest. When such differences are found in this experimental design, there is strong reason to suppose that the cause of the change is the independent variable — though this cannot be proved

conclusively in most cases. Why not? Because there is still the potential problem of *reactivity,* discussed in Chapter 1. It is possible, for example, that nobody's attitudes really changed, but that subjects wanted to please the researcher, and that those who saw the movie advocating tolerance were tipped off to what the researcher "wanted." Hence, they could have reported greater tolerance on the posttest, not because they had really changed their minds, but rather because they thought that was what the researcher wanted them to do. This behavior is an example of what is known as the **Hawthorne effect,** described in the accompanying box. Researchers usually cannot be completely sure when their results are being influenced by the Hawthorne effect or by other types of reactivity. By being alert to the possibility, however, they can often detect it and interpret their findings accordingly.

Field Experiments

Although true experiments are conducted in situations where the researcher can control all the elements, the experimental technique is sometimes taken into situations not fully under the control of researchers, in an approach called *field experiments.*

Natural Experiments Two common types of field experiments are natural experiments and social experiments. *Natural experiments* use pretests and post-

TABLE 2.1
The Classic Experimental Design.

STEP	EXPERIMENTAL GROUP	CONTROL GROUP
1. Random assignment of subjects between groups	Yes	Yes
2. Pretest (measurement of dependent variable)	Yes	Yes
3. Change or manipulation of independent variable	Yes	No
4. Posttest (measurement of dependent variable)	Yes	Yes

I n the 1930s social psychologist Elton Mayo was hired by the Western Electric Company to study productivity at its Hawthorne plant. Mayo tested the effects on productivity of various changes in working conditions, such as lighting, supervision, and wage incentives. At first, it appeared that various changes had increased productivity among the workers. However, researchers then noticed something curious: opposite changes (such as increased or decreased lighting) both increased productivity. In fact, *any* change in working conditions seemed to lead to increased productivity. Moreover, when a change that had been made was later reversed, productivity increased again! Why? It seems that the workers were so happy that somebody was showing some interest in them that they increased their productivity in order to please the researchers who were the source of that interest. In other words, the fact that research was being done, not the specific changes in work conditions, was responsible for the increased productivity. It is to Mayo's credit that he tried enough different changes in working conditions to notice that all of them produced a change in productivity. Suppose he had made only one change — say, increased lighting.

Then he might have falsely concluded that plants with more lighting would be more productive than plants with less lighting. There are two important points here for all social researchers. First, the possibility that subjects are reacting to the fact that they are being studied must always be taken into consideration. Second, there is a better chance (though not always a certainty) of detecting such reactivity in experimental research if various manipulations of the independent variable are tried out and if control groups are used. (For more information on Mayo's discovery, see Roethlisberger and Dickson, 1939.)

tests with naturally occurring events to assess the effects of such events on some dependent variable. My own Ph.D. dissertation can serve as an example of a natural experiment. I was interested in the effect of different types of housing on children's day-to-day activities. I was permitted to use data from a survey conducted at the University of Toronto (Michelson, 1977), which had asked questions of both children and their parents about their daily activities before and after they moved into either single-family houses or high-rise apartments. By so doing, I was able to compare the activities of children both before (pretest) and after (posttest) they moved into one type of housing or the other. In this example, the naturally occurring event of the family's move substituted for the manipulation of the independent variable that would have taken place in a true experiment.

Social Experiments In *social experiments,* some type of social policy is tried out in a real-life setting, and a pretest, posttest, and control group are used to assess its effects. An example of this can be seen in the federal government's Housing Allowance Experiment of the mid-1970s (U.S. Department of Housing and Urban Development, 1979). In this study, low-income families in the experimental group were given housing allowances — money to be used for the purpose of helping them pay for their housing. In pretests and posttests, the amount of money spent on housing by the experimental and control groups was measured to see if the people in the experimental group used their housing allowances to increase what they spent on housing and thereby increase the quality of their housing. For the most part, the experiment found that they did not. Instead, by paying for their housing with the housing allowance, they freed up personal funds to cover other expenses.

Survey Research

Actually, both of the housing examples above (like most field experiments) did not strictly use the experimental method of research. Rather, they combined that method with *survey research,* which is the most widely used type of research design in sociology. **Survey research** is any research in which a population or a sample of a population is asked a set of questions that are worked out in advance by the researcher. In survey research, the variables are constructed from people's responses to the survey questions. Researchers attempt to measure all of the independent and control variables that might be relevant to whatever dependent variable they are interested in.

Kinds of Surveys

Survey research is conducted in three common ways: the questionnaire, the telephone interview, and the personal interview.

Questionnaire In the *questionnaire,* the people answering the survey read the questions and mark or write their answers on the survey form or an answer sheet. Questionnaires are simple and inexpensive to administer. However, the researcher might not always know when people have a problem understanding questions. Also, depending on how the survey is administered, the response rate can be low. Mail-out/mail-back questionnaires have notoriously low response rates, often well under 50 percent and sometimes as low as 10 percent. The response rate can be improved if the survey is handed out to a group and people fill it out on the spot. As we shall see later, however, both of these methods present problems in terms of obtaining a sample that is representative of the population of interest to the researcher.

Telephone Interview A second way of doing survey research is the *telephone interview,* in which people are asked questions over the telephone. This practice produces a better response rate. It is especially good if quick results are needed because answers can be entered immediately into a computer by the interviewer and then quickly analyzed. However, telephone-survey results can be biased because some people do not own telephones and others have unlisted numbers. In some cases, the latter problem can be avoided by using random-dialing computer programs. Because of such programs and because of the ease of getting quick

results at low cost, use of telephone surveys increased dramatically in the 1980s (Babbie, 1989).

During the 1930s and 1940s (when more households lacked telephones than today), telephone polls occasionally made incorrect predictions of election outcomes because Democrats, with lower average incomes, were less likely to have telephones. Thus, they were missed by the pollsters, and the polls predicted Republican victories in elections that were won by the Democrats. A classic case is the famous *Literary Digest* presidential poll of 1936. Although it was not a telephone poll, it got into trouble by drawing much of its sample from telephone directories. Because the poll greatly overrepresented Republicans, it predicted that Alf Landon would defeat Franklin D. Roosevelt by about 15 percentage points. Roosevelt subsequently won in a landslide, carrying every state but two.

Personal Interview The third way of doing survey research is the *personal interview*. Unless results are needed very quickly, the personal interview is usually the most thorough and reliable method of survey research. If done properly, most of the intended sample can be reached, interviewers can recognize ambiguous questions, and visual aids can be used. The main drawback of this method of research is its expense. Each interview can take an hour, and another hour or more may be spent traveling. The researcher must pay trained interviewers for this work. Someone else must then code the results and enter them into the computer for analysis. Thus, one of the biggest factors researchers must take into consideration when they decide what kind of survey research to do is what they can afford.

Multivariate Analysis

A great advantage of survey research is its ability to measure and analyze the effects of large numbers of variables at once. The ability to conduct such *multivariate analysis* has been greatly enhanced by computer technology. Multivariate analysis can accomplish two important things. First, a researcher can hold a large number of control variables constant and sort out the effect of one independent variable. Thus, in one of the examples used earlier, a researcher could assess the effect of religion on voting behavior while

Consider the following questions that might be used in survey research. Do some of these questions bias the results by leading the respondent to answer in a particular way? Are some of the questions here better survey questions than others?

1. Indicate below your opinion about the current level of spending by the federal government on social services:

   a. Much too high
   b. Too high
   c. About right
   d. Too low

2. Do you agree that the death penalty should be abolished?

3. Should the United States give military aid in order to stop the spread of communism in Central America?

4. Should the United States provide military aid for the purpose of intervening in the internal affairs of Nicaragua and overthrowing that country's sovereign government?

5. Would you favor or oppose a law that would forbid the distribution of contraceptives at any clinic located on school property in this state?

Now turn the page to see what's wrong or right with these questions.

---

holding constant not only income but other variables such as sex, race, educational level, and membership in a labor union. To put it differently, computerized multivariate analysis could compare Catholics and Protestants who are identical on all of these other variables to determine whether Catholics are still more likely to vote for Democrats.

Multivariate analysis can also assess the relative influence of a number of independent variables all at once. Suppose, for example, that we were *not* merely interested in the effect of religion on voting behavior, but were trying to learn as much as possible about voting behavior, using any independent variable that might be relevant. With multivariate analysis, we could look at the effects of religion, age, sex, race, educational level, income, and union membership on voting all at once. Through multivariate analysis, we could find out which of these independent variables influences voting the most, which the least, and how influential each variable is relative to each of the others. We would also get information on the direction of the effect of each variable. Moreover, with modern high-speed computers, any of this information could be obtained from a data archive in a matter of seconds or minutes.

Multivariate analysis of survey data is a very pow-erful tool for sorting out alternative explanations for correlation. Still, it must be used with caution for several reasons. First, a researcher conducting a multivariate analysis must specify which variables are to be treated as independent, control, and dependent variables. This must be done in a manner consistent with the time order in which the variables occurred. If the researcher specifies as an independent variable a variable that actually is an effect, not a cause, he or she will still get results back from the computer, but they will be wrong. Second, the question must be worded so that it accurately measures what it is intended to measure. Third, the survey must be conducted either on the population of interest to the researcher or on a proper sample of that population. In the following sections, we shall consider question wording and sampling a bit further.

Survey Questions

Two general types of question are commonly used in survey research: fixed-response and open-ended. *Fixed-response* questions are like multiple-choice exam questions: The respondent (the person answering the survey) is asked a question and then chooses

1. This question will tend to produce an excessive number of "too high" responses because respondents are given two choices on the "too high" side—"too high" and "much too high"—but only one choice on the "too low" side. On fixed-response items, there should always be an equal number of choices on both sides of the issues. Politicians and advocacy groups often deliberately violate this principle in order to make their surveys come out in favor of their views.

2. This question leads respondents in the direction of agreeing by starting out "Do you agree" without mentioning disagreement. More neutral wording would be "Should the death penalty be abolished?" or "Do you agree or disagree with the view that the death penalty should be abolished."

3. and 4. These items, on another controversial topic, show opposite biases. Both of them contain loaded phrases. Item 3 contains the phrase "stop the spread of communism." This has the effect of defining the insurgency in Central America as "communist aggression," a definition not everyone agrees with. Moreover, by specifically calling to mind people's emotions about communism, the question will likely evoke a "yes" response. Question 4 contains phrases that produce the opposite effect. By using the phrase "internal affairs," it suggests we have no business being involved. The phrase "sovereign government" establishes the legitimacy of the Nicaraguan government, a notion not all Americans accept. Thus, this wording will lead people in the direction of responding "no." A wording preferable to either of the above would be, "Should the United States provide military aid to the forces opposing the government of Nicaragua?"

5. This is probably the most neutral of the questions listed. It uses both "favor" and "oppose," thus avoiding the tendency to lead people either way. It is also relatively free of any words or phrases that would evoke an emotional response in one direction or the other.

---

one of several possible answers listed on the questionnaire or by the interviewer. Advantages of this approach are that the results are easy to process and the respondent picks the category that his or her answer will be placed in, rather than having that done by the researcher. The disadvantage, of course, is that none of the categories may represent the respondent's true feelings about the question. The other kind of question is the *open-ended* question. This type of question has no fixed choices; rather, the respondent states or writes an answer to the question in his or her own words. This offers the advantage of enabling respondents to say what they really think without limiting them to a preconceived set of categories. However, in order to analyze large numbers of such responses, researchers must usually code each response according to its meaning, so that similar responses from different people can be grouped together. This process involves a great deal of work, and there is always the risk that the coder will interpret the response differently than the respondent intended. Thus, open-ended and fixed-response questions both have their advantages and disadvantages.

How to Phrase Survey Questions Regardless of the types of questions they use, researchers must be careful not to word their questions in a way that will bias their results. As is illustrated in the box on loaded questions, such elements as the particular words used in the question, leading phrases, and the number of response choices offered on each side of the issue can all affect questionnaire results. Sometimes, though, the bias in question wording is not as obvious as it is in the examples given in the box. Some sociologists argue that *any* wording of a question contains some bias, because different question wordings call to mind different aspects of an issue. In addition, the nature of such biases may vary from one survey respondent to another, because the same word often calls to mind different meanings, or evokes different emotions, for different people (Denzin, 1989, pp. 148–150).

The problems associated with the wording of questions are especially critical when people are confused and uncertain in the first place. Research has shown, for example, that question wording has an especially strong effect in research on attitudes toward abortion (Cohut, 1982). Despite strong opinions at the extremes on this issue, most Americans are not firmly committed to one side or the other and have somewhat ambiguous feelings about abortion (Farley, 1987, p. 218). Thus, different question wordings get different results. Another example can be seen in polls rating the president. Different pollsters have different ideas about which characteristics people value in a president. For this reason, they word their poll questions somewhat differently and thus obtain somewhat different ratings of the same president. For these reasons, you should always pay attention to the wording of the questions when considering the results of survey research, and the researcher should always make this information available to the reader.

Sampling

Although some surveys include everyone in the population the researcher is interested in, most surveys are based on *samples*. A **sample** is a subset of a population that is used to represent the entire population. If a sample is properly drawn, it can produce a result that is almost as trustworthy as if the entire population had been surveyed—and at a tremendously lower cost. A poorly drawn sample can render a research project useless. In order to be trustworthy, a sample must have two key characteristics. First, and most important, it must be *representative* of the population. Second, it must be *large* enough to give reliable results.

Representative Samples In order for a sample to be representative of a population, everyone in the population must have the same chance of getting in the sample. This assures that no one segment of the population, such as males, Lutherans, college students, or poor people, will be overrepresented or underrepre-

sented in the sample. Were this the case, such a group would influence the results of the sample more or less than its numbers in the population warrant. The basic way to obtain a representative sample is by a random draw from everyone in the population in question. In a very large population, such as the United States, this may be done in a complicated process involving several steps. However, such procedures follow two important principles that are the same as in a simple random sample. First, everyone in the population of interest to the researcher must have the same chance of getting in the sample. Second, individuals to be included are drawn on a random basis.

Probably you have heard of, or even participated in, certain types of surveys that violate these principles. "Person on the street" interviews violate it, because who is on a given street at a given time is far from random. If the survey is conducted downtown at lunch time, for example, clerical workers will probably be overrepresented relative to their numbers in a city's population. Also violating this principle are "phone-in" surveys conducted by television stations in which people call one number if they agree and another if they disagree with a certain proposition, and the mail-in surveys that are sometimes included in magazines. In both cases, the respondent has to initiate the response to the survey—a process that is hardly random. People who choose to respond are almost certainly different in important ways from those who do not. Moreover, there is no way to tell who saw the television show or read the magazine where the survey appeared, and thus no way to tell which population the sample was drawn from. That is why people who conduct such surveys often note that they are "not scientific." They most certainly are not, and their results cannot be assumed to generalize to any population.

Sample Size Surveys where the sample *is* representative can very accurately represent the responses that would have been obtained by surveying the entire population, if one additional condition is met. The sample must be of adequate size for the population in question. Adequate size does not vary in direct proportion to the population. Even for a very small local population, a sample size of a few hundred will usually be needed to get reliable results. At the same time, a representative national sample of 2,000 or 3,000 people is adequate for a population as large as that of the United States.

Social researchers have developed elaborate methods to measure the reliability of survey results based on the size of their samples. An estimate, such as the proportion of people who favor capital punishment, can be placed in a *confidence interval*. In other words, based on a given sample size, a researcher can be 95 percent certain that the true percentage favoring capital punishment is within, say, 2 percentage points of the figure obtained in the survey. When researchers obtain a statistical relationship between an independent and a dependent variable in their sample, they can use a measure called *statistical significance* to judge the likelihood that the relationship exists in the population the sample represents. If the result comes out to be statistically significant, the researchers can be confident that the result did not occur by chance and that it holds for the population they are interested in. In general, the stronger the correlation and the larger the sample, the more likely that any given relationship between two variables will be statistically significant.

Field Observation

Field observation is a method of research in which human behavior is observed by researchers as it occurs in ordinary, "real-life" situations. It is the only method of research that permits social scientists to see directly how people actually behave in ordinary situations not under the control of the researcher. In experiments, the behavior is ordinarily observed in artificial settings such as classrooms or laboratories, so the researcher cannot assume that people will behave the same way in real-life situations. In survey research, researchers must depend upon what respondents tell them. We know that when it comes to behavior, people do not always know how they would behave in some situations, so the answers they give survey takers are not always accurate. Even accounts of what people have actually done in the past frequently contain considerable inaccuracies. Field observation gets around

these problems by observing carefully and systematically how people actually behave in ordinary situations.

Field Observation and Theory Generation

Field observation is especially useful for theory generation. Often, if a researcher does not have a clear theory or a body of past research findings to work with, field observation can disclose patterns that can be used to generate hypotheses. Field observation is similar in some ways to the ordinary observations of the behavior of others that we all make. The difference is that field observations are more systematic. Field observers take care to make prompt and detailed notes about their observations and to distinguish *observations* ("the woman was smiling") from *interpretations* ("the woman was happy").

Although field observation has the important advantage over other research methods in that the social scientist sees real behavior in uncontrived situations, this method also has some limitations. Most important is that the observer is never sure whether or not the behavior observed is representative of anyone beyond the people actually observed. In field observations there is no way to draw a random sample of the population. The observer must, rather, observe the behavior of those with whom he or she comes into contact in the situation in which the observation is being done.

Participant Observation

The two main types of field observation are *participant observation* and *unobtrusive observation*. In **participant observation,** the researcher participates in some way in the behavior being observed. This can be accomplished by attending a meeting, participating in a group activity, or perhaps living for a time with the people being studied. A critical question here is whether the researcher should reveal his or her identity. There are arguments both for and against doing this. The main argument against it is that when people realize that they are being studied, they behave differently. Those in favor of revealing their identity argue that people may alter their behavior even more if they suspect they are secretly being studied. There is also an ethical argument in support of researchers' revealing their identities: Some social scientists feel that people have a right to know when they are being studied and a right not to be studied if they don't want to be. Others, however, argue that when people are in a public place, social scientists have the same right to observe them that anyone else has.

In most cases, participant observation is less quantitative and more qualitative than other methods of research. Whereas surveys and experiments produce numbers that can be used to test hypotheses and clarify relationships between variables, participant observation is often more subjective in nature. It offers less-precise numbers, but it allows far greater depth of knowledge. No matter what group of people a sociologist is trying to study, there are some things that he or she will not find out simply by asking questions as an "outsider." Every group of people has its informal norms and "inside information." It is not likely that the answers given to a survey taker will reveal much about this aspect of group life. To get this information, a sociologist must literally become a part of the group and often must remain so for some time. Participant observers have moved into neighborhoods, or even lived with families, for periods ranging from 1 year to 4 or 5 years.

Many social scientists feel that no other method can gain the degree of insight that is possible through ongoing, intimate contact. Many of sociology's most important studies have been based on participant observation, and they have often produced results that have contradicted conventional wisdom—even sometimes the conventional wisdom of sociologists. Sociologists William F. Whyte (1981 [originally published in 1943]) and Herbert Gans (1962) conducted long-term participant observation studies in Boston's low-income Italian neighborhoods. They found that the neighborhoods, which were generally regarded as disorganized, vice-ridden slums, were actually stable, well-organized neighborhoods where the residents worked hard and took care of one another. The residents had low incomes and were uninvolved in the city's political life, but these neighborhoods were nothing like the dens of social pathology that they were widely believed to be. Some of the things Whyte learned were surprising even to him. In his words: "As I sat and listened, I learned the answers to questions that I would not even have had the sense to ask."

Participant Observation and Reactivity Participant observation, like experiments and surveys, faces the problem that its results can be influenced by reactivity. If, for example, a social scientist attends a meeting, his or her attendance might influence the behavior of others there. Even if the observer tries to avoid getting involved in the debate, *that* behavior might attract notice. Although this problem cannot be entirely avoided in participant observation, there are things the social scientist can do to lessen it. One, as mentioned, is to remain as uninvolved as possible. Another strategy is to try to act like most of the people being observed. There is, however, one method of field observation that avoids problems of reactivity entirely—*unobtrusive observation*.

Unobtrusive Observation

Unobtrusive observation can be defined as field observation in which the researcher does not in any way become involved in the behavior being observed. One type of unobtrusive observation is observing human behavior from a position out of sight—through a window, across the street, and so forth. Another type is observation of *physical traces*—evidence that people leave behind them. A sociologist might, for example, get an idea of how safe people feel in a neighborhood by examining the proportion of cars that are locked. Frequently, such methods lead to the development of *unobtrusive measures,* which are quantifiable measures such as the percentage of males and females entering a grocery store at a certain time of day, that result from unobtrusive observation.

The great advantage of unobtrusive observation over all the methods of research discussed thus far is that, if done properly, it avoids problems of reactivity. The disadvantage is that it tends to be somewhat lacking in depth. One can obtain only so much information without any direct interaction with other people. Still, unobtrusive observation is an important social research tool, particularly in urban sociology, where researchers are interested in the characteristics of people living in and using different kinds of city neighborhoods.

Use of Existing Data Sources

A final type of research that is of great importance in sociology is the use of existing data sources. Very often a social scientist need not collect original data to study an issue or a problem because the necessary data have already been collected by someone else and are available. There are three main sources of existing data: various public and private data archives, the U.S. Census and related sources, and published or broadcast media suitable for content analysis. Let us consider each further.

Data Archives

As you are probably aware, thousands of surveys have been taken in recent decades by college- and university-based researchers, private organizations and corporations, and various government agencies. Most of these surveys have resulted in computerized data archives, many of which are available to researchers. Many college professors conducting research are willing to share their data with others whose research interests are slightly different from their own. In fact, some do this on a regular basis through organizations like the Inter-University Consortium for Social and Political Research (ICPSR), a national organization in which most major universities participate. Professional organizations often conduct surveys of participants in their professions and sometimes make such data available to researchers with related interests. Many government agencies conduct surveys and other forms of research and then sell computer archives of the data at cost. The U.S. government also has a registration system that records births, deaths, marriages, and divorces as they occur, which is an important source for researchers interested in these topics.

The U.S. Census

A second major source of data, available to anyone with access to a good library, is the U.S. Census. The Census, conducted every 10 years, includes compre-

The National Archives building in Washington, D. C.

hensive data on a wide range of population and housing characteristics for areas as small as a city block and as big as the entire country. A glance through any major sociological journal will reveal that the Census is one of the most important sources of data for sociological research. In addition to population and housing, regular censuses are also conducted on manufacturing, wholesale trade, retail trade, service industries, agriculture, mineral industries, and government. The results of all of these censuses can be looked up at any major library or purchased on computer tape from the Census Bureau or any number of universities and private firms.

The population Census is only conducted every 10 years, however, and there is a need for more current data. This need is met by the Census Bureau's *Current Population Survey*. This survey, conducted on an ongoing basis, provides annual updates on such things as population size, age structure, racial composition, income, education, and employment and unemployment. If you need up-to-date data on any of these issues, the *Current Population Survey* is the place to look.

Content Analysis

A slightly different approach to using existing data sources is *content analysis*. We have already seen one example of this—Adorno's research on the speeches and writings of Nazis and similar extremists. **Content analysis** involves some type of systematic examination of the content of books, articles, speeches, movies, television programs, or other similar communications. Such analysis can look for regular patterns, as Adorno's research did, or it can examine the handling of some area of subject matter. One might, for example, compare the number and types of roles filled by male and female characters in a set of television programs. Is there any difference, for example, in the proportion of males and females who are portrayed as people in a position to make important decisions? Such portrayals can tell a good deal about how the writers of the television programs felt about the roles of men and women in society. They also say a lot about what television is teaching youngsters about men and women in society.

The U.S. Census is a major source of sociological data.

Expressing Social Research Results as Numbers

Measures of Central Tendency

The results of social research methods ranging from experiments to surveys to unobtrusive observation to analysis of census data are commonly expressed as numbers. Such a system allows a more precise measurement than simply saying "some," "many," or "most." One common numerical concept used in social research is **central tendency**—what we commonly think of as an average. Measures of central tendency tell us where the middle or typical people fall on some distribution of scores, ages, incomes, or other numerical variables. The three common measures of central tendency are the *mean, median,* and *mode.*

Mean The **mean** is the statistic you probably learned to compute in elementary or high school when you were taught to "take an average." To compute the mean, you add up all of the scores (or ages, incomes, or whatever) and divide by the number of people. Consider the following example, based on the scores of a small class on a 10-point sociology quiz:

Compute the mean score for this quiz. To the nearest hundredth, you should have obtained a mean score of 6.77. If you didn't, did you remember to add in 9, 6, and 5 twice, and 8 three times? You need to do this because those are the numbers of people who got those scores. You then divide the total of scores, which is 88, by the total number of people, which is 13.

SCORE	NUMBER OF PEOPLE
10	1
9	2
8	3
7	1
6	2
5	2
4	1
3	1
2	0
1	0

Although the mean will often give a good picture of where the typical person falls in a distribution, sometimes it will not. The reason is that the mean is affected by extreme high or low values in the distribution. To see an example of this, look at the box "Five Old Prospectors." When you are working with distributions involving variables, such as income, where a few individuals fall far above (or below) most of the rest, it is often preferable to use another measure of central tendency, the median.

Median The **median** is whatever number falls exactly in the middle of the distribution. It is the score (or age, income, or whatever is being measured) of the middle person, such that half of the people score higher and half lower. Look again at the distribution of test scores above. What is the median score?

If you said 7, you are right: Six people got scores above 7; six people got scores below 7. As noted, the median is usually preferable for distributions like income that are heavily affected by extreme values.

I magine an old western mining town with a population of six people. In this town live five old prospectors, none of whom, unfortunately, has found any gold this year. Each of them therefore has an

Note: This example, as well as other parts of the discussion of measures of central tendency and dispersion, is based on materials developed by graduate assistants for the introductory sociology course at The University of Michigan during the mid-1970s.

income of $0. Also in this town lives one old mine owner who had an income of $1,200,000 last year. What is the mean income in the town?

The *mean* income in this town is $200,000. This is the total income of everyone in the town, $1,200,000, divided by the number of people in the town, six. Obviously, this is not representative of typical income in the town: Most of the people in this town had an income of zero. Although this is an extreme example, it illustrates an important point: The mean is

disproportionately affected by even a small number of scores or numbers that fall far above or below what is typical of the population being studied. Thus, for any variable—such as income—where a few people score far higher (or lower) than the majority, the mean can be a misleading statistic. For such distributions, it is preferable to use the median, discussed in the text. In this example, the median income is $0, which is much more representative of the "typical" miner than $200,000.

Mode   The third common measure of central tendency is the **mode.** The mode is whatever score the most people obtain. In the distribution above, the mode is 8, because three people had that score—more than any other. It is possible to have two, or even three or more, modes—if there are two or more scores that tie for the most people. Because the mode occasionally falls well away from the center of the distribution, it is probably the least-used of the three measures of central tendency in sociology.

Although measures of central tendency are widely used in the social sciences, it is also important to consider whether most people score near the average or whether scores are very spread out. This issue is addressed further in the appendix "Statistics in Sociology," found at the end of this text.

Reading Tables

In reports of sociological research, results are often presented in *tables,* like Table 2.2. Thus, being able to read tables is an essential skill for anyone who wishes to make sense of sociological research. It is also a skill of some broader usefulness, because many other kinds of information also appear in tables. In fact, in many

sociological research reports, most of the actual research findings appear in the tables rather than in the text. As one of my professors in graduate school put it, "If you don't have time to read both the tables and the verbiage, skip the verbiage and read the tables." Using Table 2.2 as an example, we shall go through the things you need to know as you read tables.

The Table Title   The title of the table should give you a clear description of the information that appears in the table. It should tell you specifically what the two variables in the table are. In this example, one variable is race, and the other is the number of people who agree with the statement that "Political officials don't care much about people like me." Here, because the item is fairly short, the full statement is included in the title. In some cases, though, the title may contain an asterisk or a superscript referring you to a footnote containing the question wording. Of course, in other cases, the variables may be simpler to describe, as in a table showing race by sex for a population.

Headers   Every table will also contain headers that describe the variables or categories of variables that appear in the table. In this case, the headers reveal that the race variable has three categories—"White,"

TABLE 2.2
Number and Percentage Agreeing that "Political officials don't care much about people like me," by race, 1976.

| | RACE | | | |
	White	Black	Other	Total
Agree	1049 (52.1%)	140 (68.2%)	26 (58.4%)	1214 (53.7%)
Disagree	964 (47.9%)	65 (31.8%)	19 (41.6%)	1047 (46.3%)
Total	2012	205	45	2261

SOURCE: University of Michigan, Institute for Social Research, 1976 Election Survey. Data obtained by author through Inter-University Consortium for Social and Political Research.

"Black," and "Other"—and that the responses to the statement were classified as "Agree" or "Disagree."

Unit of Analysis The title or the headers should indicate the *unit of analysis* of the table; that is, what the numbers represent. In this case, the title tells you that the numbers in the table represent the number of people and the percentage of people who agree with the statement. Thus, for example, the results show that 1,049 of the white people surveyed agreed with the statement (upper left number in the table). In other tables, the unit of analysis might be cities. In such a case, each number would tell you how many cities fell into a particular category of the table. Other possible units of analysis are countries, organizations, companies, and, perhaps, thousands of people. The title or headers should always contain this information as well as whether you are being given *raw frequencies* —the number of people, places, and so forth—or *percentages*. Some tables, like Table 2.2, give you both. Some tables, rather than classifying people, places, or groups of people, show some statistical measures of correlation. Tables of this type are discussed in the chapter appendix.

Marginals Many tables, like Table 2.2, have a column at the right and a row at the bottom labeled "Total." This row and column, called the *marginals,* give you important information about the breakdown of each variable. In Table 2.2, for example, the marginal column at the right tells you that, of the total of 2,261 people who answered the item, 1,214, or 53.7 percent, agreed with the statement, and 1,047, or 46.3 percent, disagreed. From the marginal row at the bottom, you can see that of the same 2,261, 2,012 were white, 205 were black, and 45 were of some

other racial group. A little further computation based on these numbers would tell you that of the 2,261, 89 percent were white, 9 percent were black, and 2 percent were of other racial groups.

Table Cells The data for people with each possible combination of the variables are shown in the *cells* of the table. Again, look at the upper left number in Table 2.2, 1,049. This cell represents the number of people in the sample who were white *and* agreed with the statement. The number in the cell to the right, 140, represents the number who were black and agreed, and the number in the cell below, 964, represents the number who were white and disagreed. To determine the meaning of the number in any cell, read down from the column header and across from the row header. These headers will identify the particular combination of categories represented by any given cell. In this particular table, each cell also contains a percentage, which we shall explore next.

Percentages As noted above, some tables will give you percentages. If this is the case, you need to know how to interpret them. For example, the upper left cell gives a percentage, 52.1 percent. To interpret the percentages properly, you must know which way they total. In this case, they total down: 52.1 percent plus 47.9 percent = 100 percent. Whether they total down or across is arbitrary, but an important rule is at work here. Ordinarily, *the dependent variable will be broken down into percentages within each category of the independent variable.* Thus, you must know—from the text or from your own knowledge of which variable would come first in time—which variable in the table is the independent variable and which is the dependent variable. In this case, the independent variable is clearly race, because people are born with this characteristic and attain political views later. Thus, we look at each category of the independent variable — white, black, and other — and within each category we convert the dependent variable (agreement or disagreement with the statement) to percentages. Thus, we see that among whites, 52.1 percent agreed with the statement, and 47.9 percent disagreed; among blacks, 68.2 percent agreed, and 31.8 percent disagreed; and so forth.

Why are tables read this way? Because this system best illustrates how the independent variable correlates with the dependent variable. In this case, for example, we can immediately see that the percentage of blacks agreeing was about 16 points higher than the percentage of whites. Thus, we can see clearly that blacks are more likely than whites to feel that political officials don't care about them.

Sometimes you will encounter tables that only show raw frequencies and not percentages. If this happens, you can always convert the table to percentages yourself. Just remember the principle stated above: Within each category of the independent variable, convert the dependent variable to percentages.

Source of Data Finally, any table should tell you the source of the data (occasionally you will be told this in the text). In the case of Table 2.2, the data came from the 1976 Election Survey, a nationwide survey conducted by the University of Michigan's Institute for Social Research, which I obtained through the ICPSR.

Summary

In this chapter, we have elaborated upon the scientific method and explored the relationship between theory and research. Research generates theory, as theorists seek to explain research findings. These theories then stimulate new research by predicting what such research may be expected to find. When researchers operate in the mode of prediction and theory testing, they often use hypotheses. Hypotheses are specific statements about reality, derived from theories as a way of testing parts of those theories. A hypothesis usually contains one or more independent variables (presumed causes) and a dependent variable (presumed effect). Scientists test for such cause-effect relationships by looking for correlation between independent and dependent variables, by checking the time order (cause must precede effect), and by eliminating alternative explanations, often through the use of control variables.

In sociology, the major methods of research are experiments, survey research, field observation, and use of existing data sources. Which of these methods a sociologist will use depends in part on that sociologist's purpose in research (for example, theory testing versus theory generation), and in part on the sociologist's judgment concerning the strengths and weaknesses of each method.

Results derived from any method of research are commonly expressed as numbers. Comparison of different groups or populations often involves use of measures of central tendency, such as the mean, median, and mode. Such results frequently are presented in tables; being able to read tables correctly is an essential skill for anyone trying to make sense of sociological research.

Glossary

cause and effect A relationship in which some condition (the effect) is more likely to occur when some other condition (the cause) is present than it otherwise would be.

values Personal preferences, likes and dislikes, or judgments about what is good and desirable or bad and undesirable.

hypothesis A testable statement about reality, usually derived from a theory and developed for purposes of testing some part of that theory.

variable Any concept that can take on different values or be classified into different categories in different cases.

independent variable A variable that is presumed by the

researcher to be the cause of some other variable, called the dependent variable.

dependent variable A variable that is presumed by the researcher to be the effect of some other variable, called the independent variable.

operational definition A precise statement of the meaning of a variable or of the categories of a variable for the purposes of measurement.

reliability The ability of a measurement process to produce consistent results when the same variable is measured several times.

validity The ability of a measurement process to measure correctly that which it is intended to measure.

constructs Abstract concepts that cannot be measured directly; examples are intelligence, happiness, and power.

correlation A relationship between two variables in which a change in one is accompanied by a change in the other.

control variable A variable that is introduced into an experiment to determine whether correlation between an independent and a dependent variable is the product of some other influence operating on both of them.

experiment A research method in which the researcher manipulates the independent variable while keeping everything else constant in order to measure the effect on the dependent variable.

experimental group In experimental research, the group that experiences some manipulation or change of the independent variable.

control group In experimental research, the group that experiences no manipulation of the independent variable; it is used for purposes of comparison to the experimental group.

Hawthorne effect A source of error in social research, in which the people being studied attempt to please the researcher or otherwise respond to the attention they receive from the researcher rather than to the condition that the researcher is attempting to study.

survey research Any research in which a population is asked a set of questions by a researcher, who then analyzes the responses.

sample A subset of a population that is studied for the purpose of drawing conclusions about the larger population.

field observation A research method in which the researcher observes human behavior as it occurs in natural, "real-life" situations.

participant observation A form of field observation in which the researcher participates in some way in the behavior that is being studied.

unobtrusive observation A type of field observation in which the researcher does not interact with the people being studied, participate in the behavior being studied, or reveal his or her identity as a researcher.

content analysis A research method based on the systematic examination of the content of some message or communication.

central tendency A measure of where the center of a distribution lies, or where the middle, average, or typical person falls in some distribution of scores or characteristics.

mean The arithmetic average of a set of numbers or scores, obtained by dividing the sum of the scores by the number of scores.

median The middle score or number in a distribution of scores or numbers.

mode The most frequently occurring number or score in a distribution of numbers or scores.

Further Reading

BABBIE, EARL. 1989. *The Practice of Social Research,* 5th ed. Belmont, CA: Wadsworth. A detailed and well-written text covering all major social science research methods, including the advantages and disadvantages of using any particular method.

DENZIN, NORMAN. 1989. *The Research Act,* 3rd ed. Englewood Cliffs, NJ: Prentice Hall. An introduction to research methods that explores both the possibilities and limitations of social science research. Considerable attention is devoted to the meaning of "science" and the extent to which the positivist scientific model is appropriate for sociology.

MONETTE, DUANE R., THOMAS SULLIVAN, AND CORNELL R. DEJONG. 1986. *Applied Social Research.* New York: Holt, Rinehart, and Winston. An introduction to social research methods, with emphasis on the application of such research to the human services, including counseling, criminal justice, social work, day care, community psychology, teaching, and nursing.

REYNOLDS, PAUL D. 1982. *Ethics and Social Science Research.* Englewood Cliffs, NJ: Prentice Hall. An introductory discussion of ethical issues that arise in social research and of ways of handling these issues.

PART 2

SOCIETY AND HUMAN INTERACTION

I n Part 2, we shall examine human societies and the interactions that take place between individuals within societies, and between individuals and the societies in which they live. We begin this process in Chapter 3 by examining three sociological perspectives on society and interaction. Throughout the book, we will see how sociologists use insights arising from these perspectives to aid in our understanding of virtually every aspect of society and human interaction.

We begin this process in Chapter 4 by examining culture (beliefs, knowledge, attitudes, and ways of life that are shared within a society) and social structure (the arrangement of social positions in a society. Culture and social structure are perhaps the two most central concepts in sociology, and they are intricately interrelated. Culture is a product of social structure, but at the same time it can act either to perpetuate or to change that social structure. In order to participate in society, everyone must learn about his or her culture and social structure. This process, called socialization, is discussed in Chapter 5. How we experience this socialization process is in very large part a product of whether we are born male or female — one of the very few social distinctions that exists in some form in all societies. The different and unequal roles of men and women, the reasons these roles persist, the means by which they are learned, and changes in these roles are the topics of Chapter 6.

In Chapter 7, we shall examine social structure at levels below that of entire societies — groups and organizations. We will see how the dynamics of interaction within groups can lead people to make decisions and take actions that they would never do on their own.

Finally, in Chapter 8, we shall examine how societies and cultures interact with individuals in ways that lead those individuals to conform to the will of the larger collectivity. At the same time, we shall examine why some people don't conform. We shall discover that there are sometimes important things that such nonconformity does for society, as well as the more familiar ways that it may threaten or change society.

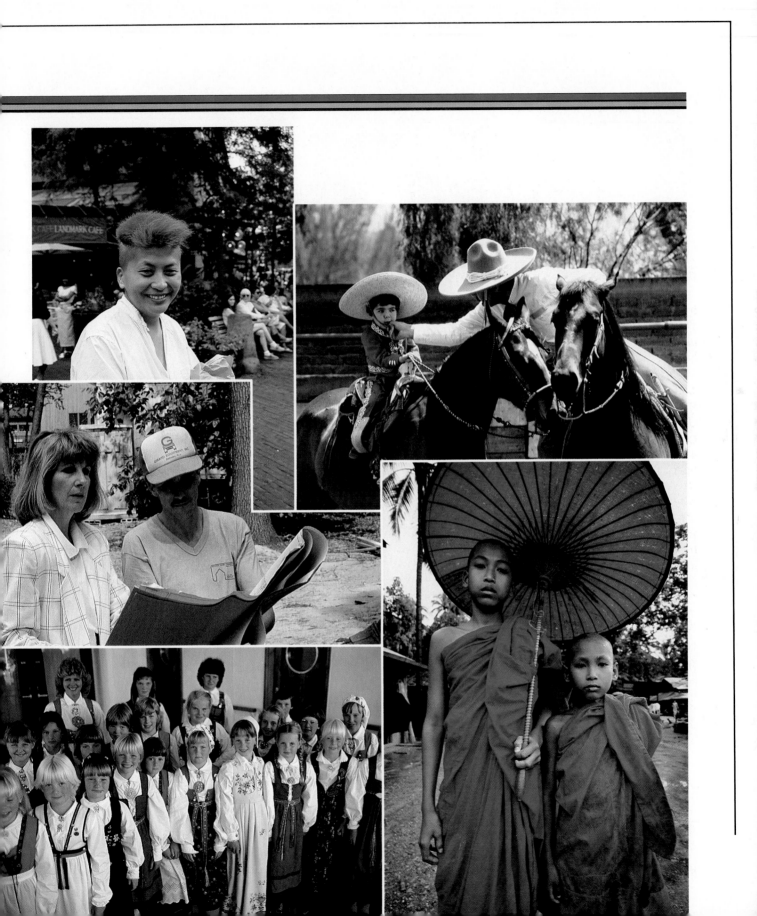

CHAPTER 3

Perspectives on Society and Interaction

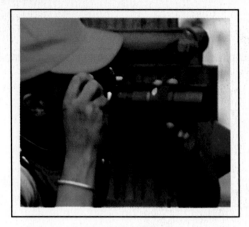

Consider the following three quotations, all written by sociologists:

In the contemporary historical situation, under capitalism, our species-being (our basic human nature) is deprived. Under capitalism, our work has become alienated. . . . Our otherwise productive activity is now directed against us; it has become independent of us and no longer belongs to us as producers (Quinney, 1979, p. 211).

In general, the system of stratification creates a discontent among those who are lowly placed, and is hence a source of cleavage, but it is also the principal means for placing people in different positions and motivating them to fulfill their roles. The organization of workers into trade-unions or a labor party, for example, . . . integrates the workers into the body politic by giving them a legitimate means of obtaining their wants (Lipset, 1959, p. 24).

Established patterns of group life exist and persist only through the continued use of the same schemes of interpretation. . . . Let the interpretations that sustain them be undermined or disrupted by changed definitions from others, and the patterns can quickly collapse (Blumer, 1966, p. 538).

learly, these three quotations reflect very different views about the essence of society and human behavior. The third quote differs from the first two in that it sees society as the product of the thoughts and actions of individuals. Change those thoughts and actions, it argues, and society can quickly change. The other two look at things the opposite way: They see society as a force acting upon the individual. However, they see the nature of the force quite differently. According to the first quote, society makes us slaves by turning the products of our work against us. According to the second quote, society integrates us into a system and gives us a way of getting what we want.

Perspectives in Sociology

Each of the three sociologists quoted above was operating from one of the three main *perspectives* that have been influential in sociology. A **perspective** can be defined as an overall approach or viewpoint toward a subject, including (1) a set of *questions* to be asked about the subject, (2) a general *theory* or theoretical approach to explaining the nature of the subject, and often (3) a set of *values* relating to the subject.

Sociologists propose dozens of important theories and ask thousands of questions, but to a large extent these theories and questions can be linked to one or more of the three major perspectives in the field. These perspectives are the *functionalist perspective* (represented by the Lipset quote above), the *conflict perspective* (represented by the Quinney quote), and the *symbolic-interactionist perspective* (represented by the Blumer quote). Each of these perspectives offers a distinct theory concerning the key social forces that shape human behavior and society. In other words, they offer different explanations for why people behave as they do. For this reason, each of them asks and attempts to answer somewhat different kinds of questions. A sociologist's preference for one or the other of these perspectives may also reflect his or her values to some extent. Here I am referring to

two kinds of values: views about what society should be like, and preferences concerning the kinds of questions the sociologist asks.

Macrosociology I: The Functionalist Perspective

Two of the three perspectives we shall be considering, the functionalist perspective and the conflict perspective, fall under the category of **macrosociology**. In other words, they are mainly concerned with explaining large-scale social patterns. Often the unit of analysis is an entire society, and these perspectives may compare different societies or the same society in different historical periods. The third perspective, the symbolic-interactionist perspective, is *microsociological,* which is to say that it is largely concerned with the subfield of sociology known as *social psychology,* introduced in Chapter 1. In other words, it is more concerned with processes that operate at the individual level and with the interaction between individuals and the larger society. We shall turn our attention first to the functionalist perspective.

The Functionalist Perspective Defined

The **functionalist perspective** is known by a number of different names, including *order perspective* and *structural-functionalism,* all of which refer to the same general theoretical viewpoint. The basic social theory underlying this perspective is sometimes referred to as *systems theory.* The early sociologist who probably had the greatest influence over the development of this theory was Emile Durkheim. Among the most influential modern functionalist theorists have been the American sociologists Talcott Parsons and Robert Merton. These individuals are examined in the box entitled "Functionalist Theory."

The functionalist perspective is primarily concerned with why a society assumes a particular form. This perspective assumes that *any society takes its par-*

Functionalist Theory

EMILE DURKHEIM (1858–1917)

Much of functionalist thinking about the importance of interdependency as a force for cohesion in society can be traced to the writings of Emile Durkheim. In his first major work, *De la Division du Travail Social* (*The Division of Labor in Society*) (Durkheim, 1947 [1893]), he argued that in preindustrial societies, tradition, unquestioned belief, and forced conformity are the main forces holding society together. He referred to this as *mechanical solidarity.* In modern societies, these forces are replaced by interdependency. Durkheim called this new pattern *organic solidarity* because he saw the interdependency in society as being similar to the interdependency of the organs of a living being.

Durkheim's recognition of the importance of consensus can be seen in another major concept he developed, *anomie* or the state of normlessness (Durkheim, 1964 [1897]). By this Durkheim meant that in certain situations norms—rules of behavior—break down and become inoperative. This may occur during periods of rapid social change or intense conflict, and when it does, people are more likely to engage in behavior that is destructive to them or their society (as Durkheim (1964 [orig. 1897]) illustrated in his pioneering study of suicide).

TALCOTT PARSONS (1902–1979)

Functionalist theory became especially influential in the United States, where its leading proponent was Talcott Parsons. One of Parsons's major contributions to sociology was the notion that each piece of the social structure represents some underlying function. According to his theory of *structural-functionalism,* there are four particularly crucial functions, necessary in any society, that in turn are met by particular *systems of action* within society (Parsons, 1966, 1971): *integration,* holding the society together and forming a basis for cooperation, which is attained through the social system; *pattern maintenance,* the development and maintenance of common values, which is attained through the cultural system; *goal attainment,* a motivational force that creates the incentive to work and cooperate, which is attained through the personality system; and *adaptation* to the environment, which is attained through the behavioral organism, which Parsons took to include the economic system.

ROBERT MERTON (1910–)

Although Robert Merton studied under Parsons and is generally identified with the functionalist perspective, certain elements of his thinking have been influenced by the conflict perspective as well. Unlike Durkheim and Parsons, who attempted to develop grand theories to explain the basic nature of society, Merton has often sought to develop *middle-range theories* that seek to describe and explain a narrower range of behaviors with a greater degree of precision. Merton (1967) has argued that such theories better lend themselves to testing through research than do larger-scale theories.

In keeping with his notion of middle-range theories, Merton has written on a number of specialty areas within sociology, including the sociology of science and race and ethnic relations and especially deviant behavior (Merton, 1938, 1968).

ticular form because that form works well for the society given its particular situation. Societies exist under a wide range of environmental situations. Some, for example, exist in harsh Arctic, desert, or mountain climates, whereas others exist in temperate climates and fertile environments. Levels of technology also vary widely. Some societies have highly advanced industrial technologies, whereas others engage in subsistence farming. Societies also differ in terms of their interactions with other societies. Some have hostile neighbors; others have friendly neighbors. All of these elements make up the total environment within which a society must exist, and each combination of these elements forces a society to adapt in a particular set of ways. Thus, what works for one society cannot be expected to work for another.

In any society, however, the functionalist theoretical perspective makes one basic argument. Whatever the characteristics of the society, *those characteristics developed because they met the needs of that society* in its particular situation. Having now provided a general statement describing the functionalist perspective, let us look at several of its key principles in greater detail. These principles include *interdependency, functions of social structure and culture, consensus and cooperation,* and *equilibrium.*

Key Principles of the Functionalist Perspective

Interdependency   One of the most important principles of functionalist theory is that *society is made up of interdependent parts.* This means that every part of society is dependent to some extent on other parts of society, so that what happens at one place in society has important effects elsewhere. Early social thinkers in this tradition often likened the operation of society to that of a living organism. August Comte, Herbert Spencer, and Emile Durkheim all used this analogy. Think of your own body. Your entire body depends upon your heart, brain, lungs, stomach, and liver for its survival. Each of these organs provides a vital function. A malfunction in any one of them can affect the health of your entire body. These early sociologists saw society as operating in much the same way.

If this was true a century ago when Comte and Spencer were developing their social theories, it is even more true today. Society has become more complex and more interdependent, not less so. Just think for a moment of all the people upon whom your participation in your introductory sociology course depends. Obviously, the class requires a faculty member to teach it and students to take it. However, it also depends on many other people and organizations. Someone has to provide the electricity to light the room, and in order for that electricity to be provided, someone had to build a dam or mine some coal, oil, or uranium and get that fuel to the power plant. Someone also had to decide when the class would be held and in what room, communicate that information to you, and enroll you in that class. Someone (in this case, me) had to write the book, with the assistance of many other people: printers, editors, proofreaders, salespeople, and bookstore employees. Thus, a class that seems to involve just you, your fellow students, and your professor is in fact the product of the efforts of hundreds of people. Consider also that a failure on the part of any element of this complicated system could affect your participation in this class. Your name could be left off the instructor's class list; the book could arrive late or in insufficient numbers at the bookstore; there could be a power failure; the class could be announced in the same room as another class.

Functions of Social Structure and Culture   Closely related to interdependency is the idea that each part of the social system exists because it serves some **function**. This notion is applied by functionalists to both social structure and culture. *Social structure* refers to the organization of society, including its institutions, its social positions, and its distribution of resources. *Culture* refers to a set of beliefs, language, rules, values, and knowledge held in common by the members of a society. (These concepts are discussed in more detail in Chapter 4.) According to the functionalist perspective, each of the various elements of social structure performs a function for society. In other words, it meets some need in the society or somehow contributes to the effective operation of the society. Here again, the analogy to a living organism is apparent: Just as each organ has its function to perform, so does each part of society.

Much the same is true of culture. If a society has a rule or belief, the theory argues, that rule or belief likely exists because it is in some way useful for the society. Consider, for example, the *postpartum sex taboo,* a common rule in many preindustrial societies. This rule specifies that a woman may not have sex for some set period after the birth of a child. The length of time covered by the postpartum taboo has ranged from a few weeks to several years. Although few people realized it, this rule was very useful. When the mother is breast-feeding her baby and her own diet is barely adequate, becoming pregnant could so deplete the nutrients in her breast milk that her baby could become seriously malnourished. Thus, in such societies, the health of babies — and consequently, the perpetuation of the society itself — depended on the mother's not becoming pregnant again too soon after giving birth. The postpartum sex taboo prevented this. Therefore, whatever religious or mystical beliefs may have served as the basis for this rule, it turns out that the rule performed an important function for society.

MANIFEST AND LATENT FUNCTIONS   Societal functions that are obvious and openly stated are referred to as **manifest functions.** A manifest function

Lebanon is a graphic example of what happens when consensus on basic social values breaks down.

of education, for example, is to teach children about such subjects as reading, writing, and arithmetic. Sometimes, however, functions are not obvious or openly acknowledged. These are called **latent functions**. A latent function of education is baby-sitting: School relieves parents of the responsibility of taking care of their children. Thus, the parents are free to pursue other efforts or simply to take a break from child care. Latent functions are often unintentional: The school system was not set up for the purpose of baby-sitting, but it does serve that purpose. Although latent functions are less obvious than manifest functions, they can be just as important to society. For this reason, sociologists operating out of the functionalist perspective have devoted much effort to identifying the latent functions of social structure and culture.

Consensus and Cooperation Another key principle in functionalist theory is that societies have a tendency toward *consensus;* that is, to have certain basic values that nearly everyone in the society agrees upon. Americans, for example, nearly all agree that they believe in freedom and democracy. They may not agree on exactly what they mean by either freedom or democracy, and they also may disagree on the extent to which the United States has attained these ideals. However, as ideals or principles that a society ought to strive for, the overwhelming majority of Americans express support for freedom and democracy.

According to functionalists, societies tend toward consensus in order to achieve *cooperation*. As we have already seen, the interdependency in society requires that people cooperate. If people in even one part of such an interdependent system fail to cooperate with people elsewhere in the system, the effects will be felt throughout the entire system. People are more likely to cooperate when they share similar values and goals. According to Durkheim (1947 [orig. 1893]; 1957 [orig. 1898]), they are especially likely to cooperate when they feel that they share things in common with one another; he referred to such unity as *solidarity*.

What happens when a society lacks consensus? According to functionalists, inability to cooperate will paralyze the society, and people will devote more and more effort to fighting one another rather than getting anything done. Perhaps the clearest example in today's world is that of Lebanon, a society that lacks consensus about any key values. Sunni Muslims, Shi'ite Muslims, Christians, and several other religious groups all have sharply different and opposing beliefs. A number of international powers have chosen to fight their conflicts on Lebanese soil, and in the process they have recruited various interest groups through a combination of bargaining and intimidation. As a result, many Lebanese are loyal, not to Lebanon, but to Syria, Iran, Israel, or one of several Palestinian factions. So extreme is the lack of consensus in Lebanon that the Lebanese government does not even attempt to govern much of the country. At least some of the various interest groups are always in a state of military conflict with others, and people traveling within the capital city of Beirut must pass by a host of military checkpoints armed by different factions. Most of the city's economic activity has been destroyed, as many hotels, stores, and factories have been destroyed by bombs and rockets. Foreign business-people and diplomats risk being kidnapped by one of the factions. Lebanon is admittedly an extreme case, whose situation has been worsened greatly by the fact that it has become a battleground for Israel, Syria, the Palestineans, Iran, and even Western powers such as France and the United States. However, it does illustrate a point: A society that lacks consensus will have a very hard time surviving as a society.

Equilibrium A final principle of functionalist theorists is that of *equilibrium*. This view holds that, once a society has achieved the form that is best adapted to its situation, it has reached a state of balance or equilibrium, and it will remain in that condition until it is forced to change by some new condition. New technology, a change in climate, or contact with an outside society are all conditions to which a society might have to adapt. When such conditions occur, *social change* will take place: society will change just enough to adapt to the new situation. However, once that adaptation has been made, the society has attained a new state of balance with its environment, and it will not change again until some new situation requires further adaptation. The picture that emerges from the functionalist perspective, then, is that of a basically stable, well-functioning system that changes only when it has to, and then only enough to adapt to changes in its situation. In short, the natural tendency of society is to be stable, because society is a smoothly operating, interdependent system.

Functions and Dysfunctions

An important refinement of the functionalist perspective has been made by Robert Merton (1968). Merton has argued that even social arrangements that are useful to society can have **dysfunctions** or consequences that are harmful to society. No matter how useful something is, it can still have negative side effects. In general, functionalist theory argues that when the functions outweigh the dysfunctions, a social arrangement will likely continue to exist because, on balance, it is useful to society. However, because situations change, a condition that is functional today can become dysfunctional in the future. Thus, when studying any element of social structure or culture, sociologists typically raise questions about its possible functions and dysfunctions.

Macrosociology II: The Conflict Perspective

Although the **conflict perspective** can trace its intellectual roots to ancient Chinese, Greek, and Arabian philosophers, modern conflict theory is largely an outgrowth of the theories of Karl Marx. There are many kinds of conflict theories today, a number of which disagree in important ways with Marx's analysis. Nonetheless, the basic Marxian notion of different groups in society having conflicting self-interests remains influential in most modern conflict theories. Modern conflict theory has been refined by the German theorist Ralf Dahrendorf (1959) and by American sociologists C. Wright Mills (1956) and Randall Collins (1979, 1975).

The Conflict Perspective Defined

Like the functionalist perspective, the conflict perspective is a macrosociological perspective that addresses the question, "Why does society take the form that it does?" However, conflict theory gives a very different answer to this question. Its answer is that *different groups in society have conflicting self-interests, and the nature of the society is determined by the outcome of the conflict among these groups.* To conflict theorists, the most important force shaping society is conflicting self-interests among different groups within society. The conflict perspective is examined in the "Conflict Theory" box.

Conflicting Self-Interests Why, according to conflict theorists, do different groups in society have conflicting self-interests? The reason is that every society experiences competition over **scarce resources**. A scarce resource is anything that does not exist in sufficient amounts for everyone to have all that he or she wants. The most important scarce resources in society, which produce the greatest competition, are money (and the things it can buy) and power. Whenever a resource is scarce, one person's gain is potentially another's loss. If you have more money or power, the result may very well be that I have less, because there is only so much to go around. It is this feature that produces conflict: Groups struggle with one another to increase their share of money and power, often by reducing the money and power of others. In this struggle, the interests of those who have a good deal of money and power conflict with the interests of those who do not. The self-interest of those who have money and power is to keep things as they are so that they can continue to enjoy an advantaged position.

Conflict Theory

KARL MARX (1818–1883)

K arl Marx has probably had more influence over conflict theory than any other sociologist. Marx's theories concerning ownership of the means of production and concerning the bourgeoisie and the proletariat were discussed in Chapter 1. He argued that in industrial societies, the bourgeoisie uses its power to assure that all elements of the social structure and ideology support its continued ownership of the means of production. The proletariat, in contrast, has an interest in change.

Much of Marx's social thinking can be found in *Capital* (1967), originally published in three volumes between 1867 and 1894.

RALF DAHRENDORF (1929–)

The German sociologist Ralf Dahrendorf is credited with making important modifications in conflict theory to make it more applicable to twentieth-century industrial societies. One way his theories differ from those of Marx is that he gives *power* a more central role than Marx did. Marx saw power as purely an outgrowth of owning the means of production, whereas Dahrendorf has identified other bases of power, including legal authority. Thus, conflicts of interest exist between those who have power and those who lack it, just as they exist between those who own wealth and those who do not. Like Marx, Dahrendorf does not believe that people are always aware of what their self-interests are. When a group of people share a common social position (such as being employed in similar types of work around the country by the same employer), they have common self-interests. When they are unaware of these self-interests, they have what Dahrendorf (1959) calls *latent interests*. At some point, however, they may become aware of their common self-interests and try to advance them. At this stage, they have developed and articulated *manifest interests*.

This step represents an intermediate step between the existence of conflicting interests (always present in society) and the actual emergence of social conflict (only sometimes present).

C. WRIGHT MILLS (1916–1962)

Probably the most influential conflict theorist in American sociology has been C. Wright Mills. Like Dahrendorf, Mills sought to apply conflict theory to modern industrial capitalism. He felt that one consequence of the massive scale of corporations and governments in modern society is to make the elite less visible and more removed from the people. As a result, the elite have greater power, and the masses feel powerless and, therefore, increasingly cynical and apathetic about politics (Mills, 1956a, 1956b).

Mills (1956b) believed that in the United States major political decisions are made by a *power elite* consisting of top corporate executives, high military commanders, and the executive branch of the federal government. Mills's ideas set the stage for an important tradition of research in sociology, described in Chapter 10, and there are some who say that they offer a good explanation of such events as the Vietnam War, Watergate, and the Iran-Contra scandal.

Mills also spoke and wrote often of "the sociological imagination"; in fact, he published a book with that title in 1961. By this term, Mills meant that we should seek to distinguish *personal troubles*— problems affecting particular individuals as a result of something they did or didn't do—from *social problems*— conditions affecting many people, which, although they may think of them in personal terms, are in reality a product of larger societal processes or conditions.

This group will attempt to preserve the **status quo**— the existing set of arrangements. The self-interest of those who lack money and power is just the opposite. They want to create *change* so that they can get a bigger share of wealth and power.

This point of view differs significantly from the functionalist perspective. Whereas the functionalist perspective sees the various elements of society as being interdependent, conflict theorists believe that the various human elements of society are in conflict with one another because one group's gain is potentially another group's loss.

Bias in Social Structure and Culture As noted above, the distribution of scarce resources such as money and power is usually unequal. Those who have money often have power, and vice versa. There are many debates among conflict theorists about the precise relationship between money and power, but there is one key point on which most conflict theorists agree: Those who have disproportionate amounts of money and power can use their power to maintain their privileged position. In other words, they have the power to shape society to their own advantage. The result of this is that a society tends to take on characteristics that work to the further advantage of the dominant groups within that society.

Here, too, there is an important parallel to functionalist theory. As we saw, functionalists argue that societies assume the characteristics they do because those characteristics are functional—useful to the society. Conflict theorists agree up to a point—but they ask the question, "Functional for *whom?*" In other words, they believe that social arrangements exist because they are useful—but *not* to the whole society. Rather, they are useful to the *dominant group* in society—whatever advantaged group has the power to shape society according to its own interests. This power can be exercised in a variety of ways. The wealthy are frequently in positions to influence public opinion. Dominant groups in many societies try (often successfully) to gain control of the media, which is why freedom of the press is repressed in much of the world. Even where it is not, those with money have a better chance than others of being able to communicate through the media. The wealthy may be overrepresented in governments or may even control them directly. Other key institutions such as education and religion are often disproportionately influenced by dominant groups, or if not, they may be unwilling to challenge such groups. Finally, there is always the possibility of a dominant group using force to shape a society to its own interests.

Conflicting Values and Ideologies Because different groups in society have conflicting self-interests, it is virtually certain, according to conflict theory, that they will have different views about social issues. In short, their values and *ideologies*—systems of beliefs about reality—will be based in large part on what serves their self-interests. Those in the dominant group use their considerable power to promote belief in the values and ideologies that support the existing order (Marx, 1964; Manheim, 1936 [orig. 1929]). When they succeed, as they often do, subordinate groups accept the dominant group's ideology and believe things that are not in their own interest to believe, a condition Marx called *false consciousness*. (This concept will be explored further in Chapter 4.) Sooner or later, however, subordinate groups come to see that their interests conflict with those of the dominant group, and when this happens, they develop their own values and beliefs, which naturally conflict with those advocated by the dominant group. Thus, the inherent tendency of society is toward conflict, not consensus. Conflict comes from within society because different groups have conflicting self-interests and thus try to shape society and its values in different and conflicting ways.

CONFLICT VERSUS VIOLENCE It is very important to stress here that *conflict does not mean the same thing as violence.* Certainly conflict can be violent, as in the case of riots and revolutions. However, nonviolent conflict is more common. Conflict occurs in legislatures, as opposing interest groups seek to pass laws and policies from which they can benefit. It occurs in the courts, as different groups pursue legal strategies to get the law interpreted in their interests. Collective bargaining and civil rights panels are other mechanisms for dealing with conflict. All of these processes reflect the **institutionalization** of conflict. They reflect the fact that society has recognized that conflict will occur and has developed ways of dealing with it. You can argue, as many conflict theorists do, that dominant groups develop institutions for dealing with conflict that favor their own interests. Even so, the fact remains that conflict does often occur in peaceful, institutional settings. It also sometimes occurs peacefully outside such institutional settings, as in the case of mass demonstrations and nonviolent civil disobedience. In general, when institutional means of resolving conflict exist, *and* when disadvantaged groups perceive that such institutional settings offer a fair opportunity for resolving conflict, these groups will use them. If such means do not exist, however, or if disadvantaged groups believe that these means favor the advantaged groups, conflict will occur outside institutional settings (Coser, 1956). In this situation, violence becomes more likely.

THE ROLES OF CONFLICT Conflict theorists see conflict not only as natural and normal, but also as useful to society. Conflict, they argue, brings social change, which makes two things possible. First, it offers disadvantaged groups an opportunity to improve their position in society through a more equitable distribution of scarce resources. Second, it offers society an opportunity to function better, because conflict creates the possibility of eliminating social arrangements that are harmful to the society as a whole but serve the interests of the dominant group.

Consider environmental pollution as an example of this principle. At one time, there was very little regulation of industrial activities that pollute the air or water or of dumping of hazardous wastes. Because it was cheaper to discharge hazardous materials into the environment than to dispose of them properly, some industries did so. These industries invoked the potential evils of government regulation as an ideological justification for their behavior. During the 1960s and 1970s, however, Americans became more aware of the threat to their health and quality of life presented by such pollution, and a strong environmental movement developed. This development generated political conflict between environmentalists and industrial polluters. As a direct result of this conflict, the government passed laws and established means of regulation to control pollution. By the mid-1980s, the environment was cleaner and healthier in many areas than it had been 15 or 20 years earlier. (For evidence of reductions in air pollution, see Council on Environmental Quality, 1984, pp. 16–38). Thus, conflict benefited society in the form of a cleaner and healthier environment.

Conflict and Social Change The example above illustrates a case where conflict resulted in social change. One place where the functionalist and conflict perspectives disagree most strongly is on the source of social change. Functionalists see social change as coming largely from outside society. They see it as a response to some new technology, some change in the environment, or some interaction with another society. Conflict theorists, however, see change as coming from within society. Different

groups have opposing interests and thus engage in conflict; that conflict produces change. Therefore, to conflict theorists, it was not simply the presence of air pollution that brought about regulations to control it. Rather, change arose from people's reaction to the fact that they were threatened by pollution. They developed a social movement, engaged in conflict with those who had a self-interest in continuing to pollute, and helped to bring about a new policy and a cleaner environment.

Conflict of Interest versus Value Conflict

One issue that has not been resolved by conflict theorists is the relative importance of *conflicting interests* and *conflicting values* as causes of conflict in society. One view is that of Marx, who is generally regarded as an *economic determinist*. Marx believed that the question of who owns the *means of production* (whatever one must own in order to be able to produce and sell things of value) determines virtually all other characteristics of society. Values in society, for example, represent someone's self-interests. According to Marx, if people correctly understand their self-interests, their values will reflect this understanding. Therefore, to understand conflict, you must examine the economic self-interests that underlie the values.

Other conflict theorists believe that values and beliefs can operate independently of self-interest. Karl Mannheim (1936 [orig. 1929]), for example, argued that academic intellectuals could look at conflicts among interest groups and draw objective conclusions that would be detached from any particular group's interests. This would enable them to seek *utopias* that would operate in the best interest of the most people. On a more modern note, you could argue that values, and not economic interest, play a key role in some controversies, such as conflicts between religious conservatives and the advocates of sexual freedom.

It is probably fair to say that values often do reflect underlying self-interests, so that many value conflicts are products of conflicting self-interests, as Marx argued. However, cultural belief systems linked, for example, to religion and ethnicity can also generate considerable conflict. Thus, it is likely that both conflicting values and conflicting self-interests can operate as sources of conflict in society.

Macrosociological Perspectives: Is Synthesis Possible?

The differences between the functionalist and conflict schools have led sociologists to ask an important question: Are the two theories incompatible, or are societies sufficiently complex so that both theories could be right at the same time?

This question has not been answered to the satisfaction of all sociologists, and debate continues concerning the compatibility or incompatibility of the two perspectives. However, I believe — and I think most sociologists believe — that although they disagree on key points, the functionalist and conflict perspectives are not totally incompatible. In the first place, certain social arrangements might be useful to society in some ways and useful to the dominant group in others. Society might also contain forces both for consensus and conflict; under different conditions, one or the other can predominate. Let us examine each of these ideas a bit further.

Can Social Structure Be Simultaneously Biased and Functional?

Can social structure serve the interests of the dominant group and society as a whole at the same time? Let us illustrate this question with an example. Functionalist and conflict sociologists have been debating the causes of social inequality for decades. In short, functionalists have argued that inequality exists because it creates incentives that make society more productive, whereas conflict theorists have argued that inequality exists because it benefits the rich and powerful. They argue that the level of inequality in the United States cannot be explained by a need for productivity, partly because much of the inequality is inherited and thus cannot operate as an incentive. To this, the functionalists reply, "Show me a society without inequality. Inequality exists in all societies

that produce a surplus because it serves a useful purpose in those societies." I shall explore this debate much further in Chapter 9 and have no intention of trying to resolve it here. However, I would like to point out that *both* theories could be partly correct. Perhaps inequality does produce incentives that societies need, and perhaps that is why it exists in essentially every society, as functionalists point out. It may also be true, however, that *more* social inequality exists in the United States than is needed to create incentives for productivity, and the reason for this could be the use of power by the wealthy to keep and expand their wealth. Assuming that each theory is partly right, the key sociological question becomes: What is the relative importance of the two causes of social inequality? That is a challenging research question. Suppose for a moment that each reason — society's productivity needs and the desire of the powerful to maintain their wealth — offers part of the answer. If this were the case — and it is very possible that it is (see Lenski, 1966) — we would have to consider both the functionalist and conflict theories in order to ask the right research questions and to understand the causes of social inequality in the United States. (For some elaboration of this idea, see the "Eclectic Macrosociology" box.)

Simultaneous Forces for Conflict and Cooperation

As was noted in Chapter 1, Talcott Parsons and his structural-functionalist theories heavily dominated American sociology from the end of World War II into the early 1960s. Since that time, however, conflict theories have become much more influential in American sociology, and since the late 1960s, Marx has been taken far more seriously as a sociological theorist than he was in the 1950s. Today, no single theoretical paradigm dominates American sociology the way functionalism did in the 1950s. Why? Although there are undoubtedly many reasons, one likely reason is that society changed.

In the United States in the 1950s, the economy was growing, we had recently been victorious in two wars that had enjoyed popular support, and, to all outward appearances, we enjoyed consensus on basic values. By 1970, things had changed dramatically.

Eclectic Macrosociology

MAX WEBER (1864–1920)

No sociologist has had a greater influence over the field than the social theorist Max Weber (pronounced vā.ber). Weber's thinking drew on a variety of ideas, some associated with conflict theory, some with what we now call the functionalist perspective, and some with neither. Thus, he cannot be clearly linked to any particular perspective.

Like other sociologists of his time, Weber was greatly interested in the process of modernization associated with urbanization and the Industrial Revolution. A key element of modernization, according to Weber (1962), is rationalization—a process whereby decisions are made on the basis of what is effective in helping people attain their goals rather than on the basis of tradition. This notion is similar to functionalist theory in the sense that it focuses on what *works*. However, Weber was aware of conflicts and competing interests in society, and rationalization included the notion of what is effective for one group in its competition or conflict with another, a concept that borrows heavily from the conflict perspective.

GERHARD LENSKI (1924–)

The American sociologist Gerhard Lenski (1966) has drawn upon the functionalist and conflict theories to explain social inequality. He agrees with the functionalists—but only up to a point—that inequality creates incentives and rewards people in accordance with their skills. However, he also argues that much inequality exists beyond what can be accounted for on this basis, and that the power arising from wealth allows the advantaged to hang on to their wealth long after their advantage serves any use to society. Lenski also notes that the degree of inequality in any society is linked to its system of production. As societies advance from the hunting-and-gathering stage to agriculture (and, usually, some form of feudalism), the degree of social inequality increases dramatically. Once society industrializes, however, this trend is reversed. Although modern industrial societies have considerable inequality, they have less than preindustrial societies. The reasons for this include the complexity of the division of labor and the presence of a large skilled and educated segment that pushes society in the direction of democratization.

LEWIS COSER (1913–)

The American sociologist Lewis Coser has been interested in group dynamics, although he defines a group as everything from a small gathering to an entire social system. Much of his work has focused on ways that conflict—both within groups and between groups—can improve the functioning of those groups (Coser, 1956). Thus, it could be said that Coser has conducted a functional analysis of conflict. He argues that conflict within groups can benefit the group as long as it does not challenge the group's purpose for existence. He sees the normal state as a combination of consensus on core values and conflict over specifics. Conflict offers groups ways to adapt to changing needs and can also increase long-run group cohesion by offering a way to address dissatisfactions. Conflict in general is more likely to produce breakdown in small, close-knit groups, and adaptation in large, diverse ones. Conflict over many unrelated issues is also less disruptive than sustained conflict over one issue. Conflict between groups (external conflict) can perform the functions of defining group boundaries and of promoting cohesion within groups.

The country was bitterly divided over the war in Vietnam, and the civil rights movement had brought dramatic changes in race relations (legally, at least). Hundreds of cities had experienced racial violence. John and Robert Kennedy and Martin Luther King had been assassinated, demonstrators had been beaten outside the 1968 Democratic Convention in Chicago, and students had been shot by National Guardsmen on college campuses. Old rules no longer seemed to operate, as young people smoked marijuana, preached "free love," and dressed and wore their hair in ways that shocked many in the older generation. In short, conflict seemed to have become the rule overnight.

These photos contrast the supposedly "calm" 1950s with the "violent" 1960s. Although there is some truth to these descriptions, the 1950s did experience many underlying conflicts, and the forces of consensus held the nation together during the tumultuous 1960s.

Sociologists responded to these developments by rethinking their theories. Those theories that emphasized change and conflict became far more popular than they had been a decade earlier. From the hindsight of another 2 decades, though, many sociologists have come to believe that forces for conflict and change both exist in American society, and that the different conditions of the 1950s and 1960s brought different forces to the surface. From this viewpoint, society always had a need to cooperate, but it also always had certain conditions that divided it.

In the 1950s, consensus was easy to attain. Most people's lives were getting better (the economy was growing dramatically), and the world seemed simple (communism was an enemy feared by much of the world). Hence, the forces for cooperation predominated, and conflict, though present, was low-key. Still, certain underlying conflicts simmered. Black Americans remained disadvantaged, even if the promise of civil rights seemed to offer a better future. Women were becoming more educated, yet they were still expected to remain in the home if they could afford to do so, a situation that was to bring about great conflict and change in the future.

By the late 1960s, though, things had changed. We were in a war we did not understand and seemed unable to win. Many African Americans, their hopes buoyed by the prosperity of the 1950s and the idealism of the early 1960s, realized that their economic situation was not getting better. The antiwar and Black

Power movements ended the appearance of consensus, and the conflict spread to other areas as well —as it usually does during periods of social change and upheaval. In particular, American women began to change and equalize gender roles in American society. None of this meant that the forces of cooperation were no longer operative. Despite the deep divisions, society did not collapse, the economy continued to produce, and many of the old rules that had been rejected were eventually replaced by new ones— different, indeed, but still rules. Thus, just as the forces for conflict were present but subdued in the 1950s, the forces of cooperation remained present but were less evident in the 1960s.

From the mid-1970s through the 1980s, there was a more even balance between the forces of conflict and cooperation in American society than in either the 1950s or the 1960s. Social conflict, as represented in such events as riots and mass demonstrations, was less common during this period, but it did occasionally occur, as in the case of racial violence in Miami in 1980 and 1989. A conservative who extolled traditional societal values was twice elected president by big majorities—but massive opposition forced him to abandon certain policies, such as aid to the Nicaraguan contras. The excesses of the "free love" mentality of the 1960s had been soundly rejected by the end of the 1980s, but even AIDS could not bring about a return to the restrictive sexual values of the 1950s. Not surprisingly, U.S. sociology became theoretically balanced during this time. Functionalists reasserted the validity of their viewpoint, and a view that came to be known as *neofunctionalism* gained significant support among sociologists (Alexander, 1985, 1988). At the same time, however, a Section on

Marxist Sociology was formed within the American Sociological Association, and its sessions were among the best attended at the annual meetings.

The point of this discussion is that, rather than simply saying that society tends toward cooperation and stability or toward conflict and change, it is important to recognize that both kinds of forces are present. The functionalist theory is useful for understanding one kind; the conflict theory for understanding the other. The true challenge to sociology is to identify social conditions that bring one force or the other to the fore. That is why many of sociology's most important theorists have recognized that forces for integration and forces for conflict are both present in society and have tried to understand the conditions under which each force predominates. In fact, this tradition of balanced use of the two approaches can be traced at least to Max Weber, though Weber also created new theories that are not easily classified under either perspective. The views and contributions of Weber and two contemporary theorists—Gerhard Lenski and Louis Coser—are further explored in the box entitled "Eclectic Macrosociology."

Macrosociological Perspectives: A Final Note

As we finish our discussion of macrosociological perspectives, we have seen important areas of consistency and overlap between functionalist and conflict thinking. We have seen, too, that social arrangements can be useful to society in some ways, but—at the same time—useful to special interests and perhaps even dysfunctional to society in other ways. Forces for conflict and forces for cooperation are both present in society, and each may dominate under different conditions. Moreover, as Coser notes, even conflict can in some ways be useful for the larger society. Finally, society is in part shaped by relationships of exchange that involve elements of both cooperation and domination. All of these things suggest that the most useful macrosociology may be one that incorporates ideas from both theoretical perspectives.

Even so, the debate goes on between functionalist and conflict sociologists. This is not just a debate about theories; it is also a debate about values. Functionalism, because it notes society's tendencies toward stability and balance, appeals to conservatives and cautious liberals. It stresses the advantages of the status quo, which appeals to those who oppose major change. Its emphasis on conformity has a similar appeal, warning of the dangers of a divided society and opposing suggestions to do things in any radically different way.

Similarly, conflict theory appeals to radicals and strong liberals who favor fundamental changes in social institutions. It stresses society's inequalities, which liberals and radicals see as society's unfairnesses. It is favorable to new ideas and to social change, which appeals to those who think society needs to change.

Although political views may well influence sociologists' preferences for one perspective or the other, it is important to distinguish such views, which represent *values,* from what the two perspectives say about social reality, which is a matter of *theory.* One can never prove that a conservative, moderate, liberal, or radical political view is "right" or "wrong," because that is a matter of values. However, sociology has gone a long way toward understanding the forces that shape society, and the evidence here suggests that both the functionalist and the conflict perspectives have important insights to offer in this regard. Thus, it would be highly incorrect to say that these perspectives are "just a matter of opinion."

Microsociology: The Symbolic-Interactionist Perspective

Almost from the time sociology emerged as an academic discipline, some people within the field felt that, to understand even large-scale patterns of human behavior, it was not enough to study only the characteristics of society. Rather, these social theorists argued that you must study the *processes by which human interaction occurs.* These processes of interaction involve social psychology or **microsociology**, in that they often include interactions *between individuals and the larger society.* Societies do present situations, send messages, and give rules to individuals, but it is on the individual level that these situations, messages, and rules are interpreted. Moreover, how these situations, messages, and rules are interpreted is a key factor in determining how people behave. These realizations have given rise to the third major perspective in sociology, the **symbolic-interactionist perspective**. Because of its concern with the interaction between the individual and the larger society, it is also sometimes called the *microinteractionist perspective* (Collins, 1985), or simply the *interactionist perspective*.

The Interactionist Perspective Defined

If the interactionist perspective could be summarized in one general statement, that statement might begin with the notion that the *interpretation* of reality can often be an important factor in *determining* the ultimate reality. As previously noted, society continually presents individuals with situations, messages, and rules. Taken together, these elements, and the *meaning* given to them by the individual, define the individual's experience of social reality. Sometimes the meaning of these situations, messages, and rules is clear, and to the extent that this is the case, the individual's social reality is obvious to him or her. Usually, however, the meaning of the situations, messages, and rules is not completely clear to the individual, and the individual must *interpret* them as best he or she can (Blumer, 1962). This interpretation occurs, of course, in the context of past messages the individual has received from society. Nonetheless, it *is* interpretation, and individuals with different sets of past experiences frequently interpret the same message or situation differently. Hence, the individual's understanding of social reality depends in part on the content of the messages and situations he or she encounters and in part on how he or she interprets those messages and situations. How the individual understands reality, of course, will have an important effect on how he or she will behave, which can further alter the situation. For these reasons, *the interactionist perspective focuses first on how messages are sent and received and on how social situations are encountered by individuals, then upon how people interpret the meanings of these messages and situations, and finally on how these processes shape human behavior and society.*

Interpreting Situations and Messages

As noted above, one key concern of the interactionist perspective is how people interpret the messages they receive and the situations they encounter. Interactionists believe these issues are important because people's interpretations of reality are an important factor in determining how they will behave. Consider an example. You are waiting at the bus stop, and the person next to you says, "Hello. Isn't this a nice day?" Your behavior in response to this message will depend on your interpretation of the message, which in turn will be a product of past messages and experiences. If, for example, your experience has been that people at the bus stop like to chat to pass the time while waiting for the bus, you will probably respond in a friendly way and carry on a conversation with the person until the bus arrives. If, however, your experience has been different, you will probably respond differently. Suppose your experience has been that people at the bus stop usually don't talk to one another, but keep to themselves. On the few occasions when people did try to strike up a conversation with you, it turns out they were trying to sell you something, begging for money, or seeking to convert you to their religious beliefs. In this case, you would interpret the situation differently, assume the person wanted something from you, and would likely try to avoid further interaction.

Our reactions to people's behavior in different social settings depends on our interpretation of those behaviors.

The Social Construction of Reality

What is significant about the above example is that *the real intentions of the person speaking to you were not important.* Even the person's behavior does not give us the entire explanation of why you experienced the reality of the situation as you did. Rather, it was your understanding of the meaning of the person's behavior, including your interpretation of his or her intentions, that determined the reality that you experienced (Charon, 1985, p. 36). Sociologists refer to this process as the **social construction of reality** (Berger and Luckmann, 1966). By this, they mean that the reality that you experience is not simply determined by what goes on in an objective sense; rather, it is determined by your understanding of the meaning of what happens. Thus, depending on that understanding, the reality you experienced could have been either "This person is friendly" or "This person is trying to hit me up for something."

There are two additional important points concerning this process. First, the meaning you attribute to the person's behavior is largely a product of your past experiences in similar social situations. Thus, *there is a clear social influence on your interpretation of situations you encounter.* This point is made forcefully by a short book titled *One Hundred Dollar Misunderstanding* (Gover, 1981), about a sheltered college freshman who comes into contact with a prostitute. He does not know that she is a prostitute, and she does not know that he is anything besides a "customer." As a result, every behavior by each of them is misunderstood by the other. Second, how you interpret the meaning of the situation you encounter will influence how you respond to it. This principle was recognized as early as the 1920s by W. I. Thomas, in a statement today known as the **Thomas theorem**: "If men define situations as real, they are real in their consequences" (Thomas, 1966). In other words, whatever the objective reality, people behave on the basis of their *understanding* of reality, and that behavior in turn shapes subsequent realities, including objective realities of human behavior. As Collins (1985a, p. 199) put it, "If the definition of reality can be shifted, the behavior it elicits will switch, sometimes drastically." Consider, for example, likely changes in the freshman's behavior toward his new friend once he realizes that she is a prostitute.

Ethnomethodology Symbolic-interactionist theory, then, argues that your interpretations of reality are in part socially determined, and that these interpretations in turn partly determine how you will behave. To put this a bit more broadly, human behavior is in part a product of the structure of society and in part a product of how individuals interpret that social structure. Attempting to understand the forces that influence how individuals interpret the situations and messages they encounter has developed into a major subfield within the interactionist perspective known as **ethnomethodology**. It was given this name by Harold Garfinkel, who has written extensively about it (see Garfinkel, 1967; and Handel, 1982). Ethnomethodology has been applied to a variety of topics in sociology. It has been suggested, for example, that one factor influencing people's scores on intelligence tests is their interpretation of the meaning and importance of the test and what it will be used for (Ogbu, 1978).

The Looking-Glass Self Another important concept that has long been used by symbolic-interactionists is the **looking-glass self**. This concept was developed by the early symbolic-interactionist theorist Charles Horton Cooley, who is discussed further in the box entitled "Symbolic-Interactionist Theory." The basic notion of the looking-glass self could be summed up as, "We see ourselves as others see us." In other words, we come to develop a self-image on the basis of the messages we get from others, as we understand them. If your teachers and fellow students give you the message, in various ways, that you are "smart," you will come to think of yourself as an intelligent person. If others tell you that you are attractive, you will likely think of yourself as attractive. Conversely, if people repeatedly laugh at you and tease you about being clumsy, you will probably come to decide that you are clumsy. Over the years, you gradually develop a complex set of ideas about what kind of person you are, and to a large extent, these ideas are based on the messages you get from others. In Cooley's terms, you use other people as a mirror into which you look to see what you are like.

Symbolic-Interactionist Theory

CHARLES HORTON COOLEY (1864–1929)

Much of what later came to be known as the symbolic-interactionist perspective is based on the ideas of Charles Horton Cooley. Cooley is best known for his theories concerning self-image and the looking-glass self, which are discussed in this chapter. Cooley also proposed that the formation of self-image occurs mainly through communication with a fairly limited number of individuals, called *significant others,* with whom a person interacts on a regular basis. In childhood, parents, peers, teachers, relatives, neighbors, and religious leaders are most likely to be the significant others. In later life, co-workers, supervisors, spouses or lovers, and children are the most important significant others.

GEORGE HERBERT MEAD (1863–1931)

George Herbert Mead's thinking was similar in many ways to that of Cooley, but he added two important elements to Cooley's theories. First, he clarified the means by which the communication processes of interest to Cooley occurred. Mead (1934) pointed out that one of the features that distinguishes human beings from animals is their ability to use *symbols.* A symbol can be defined as anything that stands for or represents something else. This includes words, gestures, signs, and images. Most human communication uses symbols, and it is through symbols that the processes of interest to symbolic-interactionists occur. Symbols are used to communicate the expectations associated with roles, and, in response, they are used to present the image to others that an individual is attempting to fulfill the expectations of those roles. Finally, symbols are used by others to let the individual know how well or poorly he or she is doing in meeting those role expectations.

Mead's other important addition to Cooley's thinking was the concept of the *generalized other.*

HERBERT BLUMER (1900–1987)

Herbert Blumer was one of Mead's many students in his famous social psychology course, which formed the basis of *Mind, Self, and Society* (Mead, 1934). Blumer went on to become the most influential symbolic-interactionist theorist of recent years, although he also made important contributions to macrosociological analysis, particularly in the area of race relations (for example, Blumer, 1965).

It was Blumer who first used the term *symbolic-interactionism* in a 1937 article. According to Blumer (1969), symbolic-interactionism is based on three key premises. The first is that human beings behave toward things on the basis of the meaning that those things have for them. The second is that the meanings of things for each individual are derived from social interaction with other people. This premise challenged two dominant views in the social sciences: the belief that the meaning of things is a matter of objective reality and the conviction that the meaning of things a person observes is a product of the person's psychological makeup. Blumer's third key premise is that meanings are shaped through an interpretive process used by the individual in dealing with the things he or she encounters. Thus, the actions of others are interpreted, and this interpretation is part of what defines meaning. Moreover, because of this process of interpretation, meanings of things can change as the interpretation changes.

Of course, the message we get from others about ourselves is partly a product of the intended content of the message and partly a product of how we *perceive* the message. To Cooley, an important part of the looking-glass self was how we understand the messages we get from others. In Cooley's terms, we *imagine* what others think of us on the basis of our understanding of the messages we get from them. Thus, if we misunderstand the messages of others, we may form our self-image on the basis of a different message than what was intended. For this reason, processes of communication — the sending and receiving of messages about our personal characteristics — play a key role in the formation of self-image.

The kind of self-image this process produces, moreover, will influence many aspects of your life. Self-esteem, clearly part of this process, has been shown to be linked to success in business life and in personal life, and the lack of it has been linked to substance abuse, unemployment, suicide, and a host of other personal and social problems.

The Self-Fulfilling Prophecy A concept closely related to the looking-glass self, but applicable to an even broader range of human behavior, is the **self-fulfilling prophecy**. The self-fulfilling prophecy is a situation in which people *expect* something to happen, and because they expect it to happen, they behave in such a way that they cause it to happen. Sociologists have discovered numerous examples of self-fulfilling prophecies. The best known concerns teacher expectations and student achievement (Rosenthal and Jacobson, 1968; Brophy, 1983). Generally speaking, students will outperform others of equal ability when teachers have higher expectations of them. (For a more detailed discussion, see Chapter 14.) Similarly, countries sometimes engage in military buildups because they expect to be attacked, which their potential enemies interpret as an aggressive move that requires a response. A cycle of this type between two polarized alliances in Europe was one of the causes of World War I (Farrar, 1978). Another example concerns the often poor relations between inner-city black and Hispanic youths and the police. The police view the

youths as troublemakers who must be shown the "force of the law." The youths see the police as brutal and often racist, and they frequently respond with behavior to show them that "Nobody's going to push us around." In other words, both the police and the youth "act tough" toward each other because each expects trouble from the other. These responses virtually assure conflict between the two groups (Kuykendall, 1970).

Social Roles

An important concept in symbolic-interactionist sociology is the notion of **social roles**; that is, sets of behavioral expectations attached to positions within the social system. Human interaction is defined by the relationships among various roles, such as student, teacher, parent, and school-bus driver. In the course of a day, everyone fills a variety of social roles, each carrying a set of behavioral expectations that are *situation-specific*. The exact content of these roles depends on the nature of the particular social system. Moreover, knowledge of how to behave in roles is learned through contact with others and through the messages we receive from others about (1) what expectations are attached to a particular role and (2) how well we are meeting the expectations associated with the roles we fill. The latter process, of course, is part of what Cooley meant by the looking-glass self.

However, a major concern of symbolic-interactionists has also been with the questions: How do people learn the content of roles, and how do people learn the relationships among various roles in the social system? In both cases, the general answer is that people learn these things through the messages they receive from other people. These learning processes, in turn, have a key impact on how people actually behave: People usually attempt to behave in a way that will fill the expectations of their roles as they understand them. As discussed in the box entitled "Symbolic-Interactionist Theory," the contributions of George Herbert Mead have been particularly important in this area. Symbolic-interactionists have been particularly interested in the childhood socialization process, because the learning of social roles is such a critical part of that process.

Charles Horton Cooley developed the concept of the looking-glass self.

Sending Messages: The Presentation of Self

Just as the symbolic-interactionist perspective is concerned with how people get and interpret social messages, it is also concerned with how messages are sent. In particular, people want to convince others that they are succeeding in meeting the expectations of the roles they are attempting to fill. Thus, just as people respond to the expectations and messages they get from others, they also attempt to send messages regarding their own behavior and characteristics. To any given individual, the importance of different roles will vary. In addition, people exercise some choice in the roles they fill. Most of us, for example, must fill the role of "employee" in some way or other. However, the particular job we hold — and thus the particular characteristics of our employment role — varies widely. Moreover, it is something over which people have some choice. In part, people manage the self-image that they project to others by choosing what roles to fill and emphasize in their lives (see Backman and Secord, 1968). They also manage their self-image by presenting to other people the image that they feel is appropriate to the particular role that they are in at any particular time. The early Chicago School sociologist Robert Park (1927) put it this way: "One thing that distinguishes man from the lower animals is the fact that he has a conception of himself, and once he has defined his role, he tries to live up to it. He not only acts, but he dresses the part, assumes quite spontaneously all the manners and attitudes he conceives as proper to it." Sociologists refer to this process as the *presentation of self,* or *impression management.*

The Dramaturgical Perspective The analogy of human behavior to acting is made most explicitly by a particular interactionist theory known as the **dramaturgical perspective**. This theory, generally identified with Erving Goffman (1959, 1967, 1971), argues that in each role we fill, we try to convince people that we are filling it in a particular way, generally the way to which we think they will respond positively. Thus, the self-image a person attempts to project at work will be different, for example, from the self-impression he or she would likely try to project on a weekend "singles" ski excursion. In Goffman's terms, people give differ-

What image did Oliver North try to project during the Iran-contra hearings? Was this a "performance," as Goffman would use the word?

ent performances on different occasions. These performances, however, are always shaped by what people think others expect and will respond to positively. Thus, it is only through messages from others that we develop our ideas of what is a proper image to project at work or on a ski trip.

FRONT-STAGE AND BACK-STAGE BEHAVIOR An important distinction in the dramaturgical approach is that of "front-stage" and "back-stage" behavior (Goffman, 1959). "Front-stage" behavior — the performances aimed at impression management — takes place in settings where others can see us. However, there are also private settings in which we "let our guard down" and behave in ways that we would not want others to see. Goffman called this "back-stage" behavior. Collins (1985, p. 157) illustrated the distinction this way:

[Front stage] is the storefront where the salesperson hustles the customer, [back stage] the backroom where the employees divide up their sales territories, establish their sales line, and let their hair down after the manipulation they have gone through. In another sphere, there is an analogous distinction between the cleaned-up living room and a carefully laid table where the ritual of a dinner party is to reaffirm status membership with one's guests, and the backstage of bathroom, kitchen, and bedroom before and afterwards, where emotional as well as physical garbage is disposed of.

A fascinating aspect of the process of impression management is that we generally assist one another with our performances (Goffman, 1959). Most of us are sufficiently insecure about our own performances that we do not make others aware of the flaws in theirs. Imagine, for example, that your professor or a classmate enters your classroom with his zipper open or her blouse unbuttoned. There may be a bit of snickering, but most people will try to spare the person involved embarrassment by pretending nothing is wrong. In fact, some people will experience discomfort or embarrassment over the situation, even though it is someone else whose performance is flawed. This embarrassment or discomfort will probably increase if anyone says anything about it in front of the class. Many people will think, "That could just as easily be me." Therefore, people usually engage in what Goffman called "studied nonobservance": They go out of their way to ignore flaws in others' performances. To create or even acknowledge awareness of flaws in performances is to "create a scene": It leads to embarrassment, not only for the person whose performance is flawed, but for others as well.

The dramaturgical perspective has sometimes been criticized for attempting to reduce human behavior to a continuous process of impression management. To do this would clearly be an oversimplification, for two reasons. First, as macrosociology tells us, a person's position in the larger social structure clearly is an important force in shaping behavior. By position in the social structure, I am referring to the functions a person's roles must fill (as stressed by the functionalist perspective) and the resources attached to those roles (as stressed by the conflict perspective). Second, whatever self-image we try to project to others, we are likely to influence our own self-image in the attempt. In other words, if we "act" to impress others, we will often come to believe our own act. This will be particu-

larly true if *others* respond positively to the act. In other words, the messages from others are once again affecting our own self-images.

Micro- and Macrosociology: Is Synthesis Possible?

Simultaneous Effects of Function, Conflict, and Interaction

As we saw earlier, there has been considerable effort among sociologists to combine the insights of the functionalist and conflict perspectives in order to understand social situations more fully. Is it similarly possible to combine the microsociological interactionist perspective with the two macrosociological perspectives? Increasingly, sociologists like George Homans and Randall Collins (see box) have been attempting to do exactly this. It is my view that most social situations can be more fully understood by using all three perspectives (or theories that combine them) than by using just one or two. I shall briefly outline the reasons why I think this is so, discuss some examples of theories combining the perspectives, and then give a concrete example of a common social situation that is best understood by using all three perspectives.

Although most sociologists operate primarily as either macrosociologists or microsociologists, I believe that there is one sense in which few would dispute the usefulness of both types of approach. To put it simply, the different approaches may be useful for understanding different aspects of the social situation. Any social arrangement may exist in part because it is useful to the society—as argued by the functionalist perspective. At the same time, it may also exist partly because it meets the needs of some particular interest group within the society—as argued by the conflict perspective. It may, in fact, even be harmful to other interest groups or, in some way, to the larger society. Despite these larger societal influences, though, the exact form of the social arrangement is likely to be shaped by the understandings of reality held by those participating in it, and by their consequent behavior —which is what the symbolic-interactionist view argues. These understandings are partly a product of

Micro-Macro Links

GEORGE C. HOMANS (1910–)

T he American sociologist George Homans (1961) has been one of the leading advocates in sociology of *exchange theory,* discussed in the text. He argues that in any human exchange, the objective is to maximize profit, which he defines broadly as reward minus cost. Because people bring unequal resources into such exchanges, they often expect and receive unequal profits.

Homans (1950) has also devoted a good deal of effort to studying group dynamics. He believes that human interaction within groups is shaped by an *external system* and an *internal system.* The external system refers to the interactions of the group with its larger environment, including other groups: an environment to which the group must adapt if it is to survive. The internal system refers to the interactions of individuals and coalitions within the group, which define group sentiment and lead to the development of a group culture. These processes involve elements of both cooperation and conflict.

RANDALL COLLINS (1941–)

Randall Collins has been one of the most prolific writers among sociological theorists in the 1970s and 1980s. His early work centered around the conflict perspective, addressing a wide range of issues relating to that perspective. In *Conflict Sociology* (1975), he discusses ways in which the propositions arising from conflict theory (and other sociological theories as well) can be scientifically tested, and he assesses the contribution of the conflict perspective to the understanding of several areas of social life. He has applied the conflict perspective to religion (1975), marriage (1985b), gender inequality (1971a), and education (1971b).

Recently, however, Collins has sought to combine insights from the conflict perspective with those from microsociology. Like other sociologists in recent years, he stresses the idea that individual actions shape social structures. His interaction ritual chain theory, discussed in the text, is one example of this thrust. He has also devoted some effort to understanding the intellectual roots of the three main sociological perspectives, noting, among other things, that several philosophical viewpoints that were prominent in the early days of sociology have influenced all three perspectives (Collins, 1985a). Thus, from the very start, the three sociological traditions have had at least something in common.

---

the objective reality of the larger social structure, but they are also partly a product of people's response to that reality (Handel, 1979, pp. 863–867).

Attempts at Synthesis Sociology has witnessed many recent attempts to establish links between micro and macro social influences. One example is Giddens's (1979, 1985) *structuration theory.* Giddens takes both functionalism and conflict theory to task for viewing social structure as an unchanging force that shapes the individual. Although he acknowledges that structure does influence the individual, he also argues that individuals are to some extent aware of these influences, and through their awareness and action they also influence the social structure. Similarly, Randall Collins has integrated important notions from the symbolic-interactionist perspective into his recent work (Collins, 1981; 1988). He sees *interaction ritual chains* as a means by which processes of interaction can lead to changes in social structure. By interaction rituals, Collins (1985, p. 171) means exchanges of performances in the dramaturgical sense defined by Goffman. As people move from one interaction to another, they go through a series of such rituals (the interaction ritual chain), and each ritual negotiates a relationship, the nature of which is determined by the *cultural capital* (knowledge, ways of thinking, ideas, lifestyles) of the people involved. At the same time, these cultural resources are exchanged. Depending on the nature of such exchanges, social inequality may be either perpetuated or broken down.

Study of the mechanisms by which social inequality is maintained or broken down is an important area in which both micro and macro perspectives are utilized in sociology today. Conflict theorists, for example, argue that social inequality largely reflects unequal access to education and to the kinds of cultural capital of interest to Collins. They contend that the educational system systematically makes it difficult or impossible for people of lower socioeconomic status to gain educational credentials, knowledge, or cultural capital. When sociologists ask *how* the educational system may perpetuate such inequalities, however, they usually focus on microsociological processes, such as the effect of teacher expectations on student achievement. Thus, the *outcome* may be structured inequality, as argued by conflict theory, but to understand the *process* that leads to that outcome, we must use interactionist theory.

Exchange Theory

One important theory that represents a linkage between macro- and microsociology is **exchange theory** (Homans, 1961, 1984; Blau, 1964; for examples of recent work in this tradition, see Yamagishi, Gilmore, and Cook, 1988; Clark, 1987; Mortensen, 1987). Exchange theory, like conflict theory, begins with the assumption that people seek to advance their self-interests. These interests sometimes conflict and sometimes coincide with those of other people. According to this theory, people enter into relationships with one another when each participant has something to offer that the other desires. Thus, each person has something to give and something to gain. Exchange theory has been applied to a wide range of relationships, from pure business relationships such as that between buyer and seller to intimate personal relationships such as that between husband and wife. In the latter case, for example, consider the personal needs of two individuals who get married. One partner may primarily have a need for companionship, whereas the other seeks status through the marriage relationship. According to Blau, people assess their needs and pick their partners accordingly, and, as long as these needs stay the same and each partner meets the other's need, the relationship is likely to remain stable. Of course, should either partner's needs change, or should one partner stop meeting the other's needs, the marriage could be in trouble.

Exchange relationships also can operate between groups and individuals. Consider the case of an individual joining a club. The club gains increased membership, dues money, and possibly someone new to work on its projects. The individual gains the personal interaction the club provides, as well as whatever activities and programs it offers members. However, if the relationship does not prove to be mutually beneficial, it will likely end.

Exchanges and Power Ideally, social exchanges are equal. Each partner in the exchange gets a fair "return" for what he or she puts in. Many business and personal relationships in our society are governed by a norm of *reciprocity* — the view that a fair exchange is one in which there is a more-or-less even trade. Similarly, studies of attractiveness show that, in the majority of cases, partners in love relationships rate fairly similarly to one another on attractiveness (Berscheid et al., 1971; Walster and Walster, 1969; Penrod, 1986, pp. 189–190). Thus, attractiveness operates as a resource for which partners in courtship make an "even" trade. Sometimes, however, people accept a lower level of attractiveness in their mate in order to get more of something else, such as money or prestige.

Exchange theorists also note that many exchange relationships are characterized by *unequal power,* in which one partner sometimes brings greater resources to the exchange than the other, as in the case of the relationship between employer and employee. When this happens, the more powerful partner usually expects and gets more. Those who lack resources —the poor, the sick, the unattractive—may have little choice but to enter relationships of unequal exchange. This concept also explains one reason why women have traditionally been more concerned about appearance than men: In a sexist society, they have had fewer alternative resources like wealth and power to offer to a potential mate (Melville, 1983). Thus, although exchange theory resembles functionalism in the sense that each partner often benefits from the exchange, it resembles conflict theory in the sense that one partner can benefit much more than the other. Although it resembles the macro theories in some regards, its focus is on the actions of individuals

A yard sale, like most social realities, can be analyzed from the functionalist, conflict, and interactionist perspectives.

(Alexander, 1988, p. 87), which arise largely from their perceptions about what they have to gain or lose in a relationship.

Although exchange theory has been influential in both macrosociology and social psychology and acts as something of a bridge between the two, it has its critics. The strongest criticism is that it reduces all human interactions to calculated, rational exchanges. The critics argue that in reality people enter into social relationships for all kinds of reasons — some rational, some based heavily on emotion. A more balanced view, then, might be that people enter into relationships with one another partly for reasons of exchange and partly for other reasons.

Finally, even if each sociologist were to study a social arrangement from only one perspective, sociology would still build a cumulative body of knowledge about the social arrangement through the work of different sociologists analyzing it from different theoretical perspectives. Through the cycle of theory and research discussed in Chapter 2, claims arising from each perspective are put to the test: some are supported by research findings; others are not. Let us now consider an everyday example where the three perspectives combined can give us insights that go beyond those of any perspective by itself.

Using All Three Perspectives: An Example

Every Saturday morning from late spring through early fall, hundreds of thousands, perhaps even millions, of Americans participate in an event that takes place in big cities and small towns; in rural areas and suburbs; in all 50 states. I am speaking of the yard sale or garage sale. This is an ordinary event, not the stuff of which headline news or path-breaking sociological studies are made. Nonetheless, it is important to millions of Americans. Moreover, I would argue that it is precisely for the ordinary, everyday event like the yard sale that sociology is useful for giving us special insights. Hence, I choose the yard sale, not only as an event about which sociology offers interesting insights, but also as one that illustrates the usefulness of each of the three perspectives for letting us see a part of the social reality that is occurring.

Consider how a yard sale might be analyzed from the functionalist perspective. A yard sale performs the important function of allowing things that would otherwise go to waste to be used and, for the seller, to be turn d into a little extra cash. These are the functions of a yard sale that readily come to mind — in other words, its *manifest functions*. Consider, though, some *latent functions* of yard sales. For one, they offer people an enjoyable outing, an opportunity to get out of the house. In addition, they may perform the important social function of enabling people to see one another on a regular basis.

Yard sales can also be analyzed from a conflict perspective. In fact, I first became aware of this when I saw an article about yard sales in an "underground newsletter" published by a group of politically radical students on the campus where I teach. The article touted yard sales as "striking a blow at capitalism through people's recycling." In a sense, it was right. Those who attend yard sales can be seen as an interest group; specifically, people with limited incomes who have a particular interest in getting things inexpensively rather than purchasing "flashy and new" merchandise. Surely this interest runs contrary to that of another set of interest groups: the manufacturers, advertisers, and department stores, whose interests lie in persuading people to buy the "newest and best," even if something older and less flashy would work equally well. Thus, shopping at yard sales could be seen as being in the interest of those with limited incomes, and there is evidence suggesting that this is happening. In the past decade or 2, as people's purchasing power has failed to grow as much as it did in the past, the popularity of yard sales has soared. Some evidence does indicate that the established business interests have come to see yard sales as a threat. In my town, for example, several city council members have called for a crackdown on the posting of signs advertising yard sales, proclaiming them to be an unsightly nuisance. (Interestingly, no similar argument had been made by the city council a few months earlier when the town was flooded with political campaign signs!)

Finally, yard sales can be analyzed from a symbolic-interactionist perspective. They are often characterized by considerable bargaining between buyer and seller, and the course of this bargaining is certainly shaped by the perceptions the buyer and seller have of each other. If the seller is perceived as "wanting too much," the entire interaction can come to a quick end. Evidence of "wanting too much" can include not only prices that are too high, but also an unwillingness to bargain. As symbolic-interactionists point out, it is the person's perception of the meaning of the other's behavior that is critical. In other words, the reality that each of us experiences is socially constructed. It may be that the seller is having his or her first yard sale and doesn't know what prices to charge or that one is supposed to bargain. That doesn't really matter to the buyer, though, because it is the buyer's *perception* that determines his or her behavior. If the buyer misinterprets the seller's lack of experience as greed, the buyer experiences the seller as "wanting too much" rather than not knowing you're supposed to bargain. With this understanding of reality, the buyer will likely end the interaction.

Of course, the seller's behavior is also influenced by the process of interaction. A novice seller may realize, after a few such interactions, that something is wrong. If the disgruntled buyers give the seller the right set of messages, the seller may learn from them that buyers expect the prices to be lower and to be subject to bargaining. Once the seller lowers his or her prices and begins to bargain, the entire interaction may be different. In short, the communication that occurs between buyer and seller, as well as how each interprets the other's messages, has a crucial impact on the outcomes of the yard sale. To put it in Blumer's terminology, behavior has been influenced by the meanings of the yard sale situation to the participants, which in turn is largely a product of their communication with one another.

We have seen, then, that each perspective — functionalist, conflict, and interactionist — has added something to our understanding of the yard sale. Each has helped us to understand a somewhat different part of its reality. In this particular case, none of the three perspectives is in any sense "wrong," even though proponents of the three perspectives can and do debate their relative usefulness for understanding reality. Rather, as noted, each helps us understand a slightly different aspect of what is taking place. Most important, our understanding of the social meaning and significance of the yard sale is greater when we use all three perspectives than when we use any one, because each offers us part of the "big picture."

The Three Perspectives and This Book

I have provided an extensive introduction to the three sociological perspectives in this chapter because I believe that they give greater meaning to the more specific theorizing and research that will be discussed in the remainder of this book. The rest of the book will concern a number of major topics that make up the key subject matter of sociology. Each of these topics has a number of specific theories and lines of research pertaining to it. Many of these theories and lines of research, though specific to the topic of interest, arise in large part from one of the three perspectives introduced here. Some go further and attempt to combine insights from two or all three of the perspectives and to apply them to a particular topic. I believe that your understanding of sociology will be enhanced if you see how a theory about, for example, race relations, may relate to theories about aging, or drug use, or formal organizations. The best way to do this is to try throughout the book to link specific theories to the larger sociological perspectives from which they arise. Thus, in virtually every chapter in this book, that linkage will be made. As you read this text, I hope you will see that at least one of the major perspectives, and often all three, can be used to gain important insights about every major topic discussed in the rest of this book.

Summary

In this chapter, we have examined the three theoretical perspectives that have had the greatest influence in sociology. Two of them, the functionalist and conflict perspectives, are macrosociological, focusing mainly on large-scale societal processes. The functionalist perspective holds that social arrangements exist because they meet needs in society, and it stresses interdependency, the functions of social structure and culture, consensus, cooperation, and equilibrium. The conflict perspective holds that society is made up of competing interest groups with unequal power and that social structure exists because it meets the needs of interest groups, usually those with power. It stresses conflicting interests, the relationship of culture and social structure to group interests, and the inevitability of conflict and change.

In part, these perspectives reflect competing values that cannot be judged scientifically. In larger part, though, they reflect different theories about human behavior and society, which are subject to scientific evaluation. Although the two macrosociological perspectives disagree on some key points, many sociologists believe that the two schools are not incompatible. Social structure, for example, may meet society's needs in some ways and the needs of dominant groups in other ways. Similarly, it is reasonable to argue that forces for both stability and change are always present in society, but that under different social conditions, different forces predominate.

The microsociological symbolic-interactionist perspective gives greater attention to processes involving individuals. It holds that people's understanding of reality is determined by the messages they get from others and by how they interpret these messages. This, in turn, is an important influence over how people behave. Among key concepts stressed by interactionists are social roles, the looking-glass self, the self-fulfilling prophecy, and the social construction of reality.

Attempts have been made to build links between micro- and macrosociology. As illustrated by the example of the yard sale, each perspective — the functionalist, conflict, and interactionist — can add to our understanding of a social situation. In large part, this is true because each addresses a different piece of the reality of that situation.

Glossary

perspective A general approach to a subject, including a set of questions to be addressed, a theoretical framework, and, often, a set of values.

macrosociology Those areas of sociology that are concerned with large-scale patterns operating at the level of the group or society.

functionalist perspective A macrosociological perspective stressing the basic notion that society is made up of interdependent parts that function together to produce consensus and stability.

function A consequence of a social arrangement that is in some way useful for the social system.

manifest function A function of a social arrangement that is evident and, often, intended.

latent function A function of a social arrangement that is not evident and is often unintended.

dysfunction A consequence of a social arrangement that is in some way damaging or problematic to the social system.

conflict perspective A macrosociological perspective based on the key premise that society is made up of groups that compete, usually with unequal power, for scarce resources; conflict and change are seen as the natural order of things.

scarce resources Material goods, statuses, and other things that people want, but that do not exist in sufficient quantities to satisfy everybody's needs or desires.

status quo The existing set of arrangements within a society.

institutionalization A process whereby a condition or social arrangement becomes accepted as a normal and necessary part of a society.

microsociology An area of sociology that is concerned with the interaction of the individual with larger societal influences.

symbolic-interactionist perspective A major microsociological perspective stressing the importance of messages from others and from society, how people understand and interpret these messages, and how this process affects people's behaviors.

social construction of reality A process in which people's experience of reality is largely determined by the meanings they attach to that reality.

Thomas theorem A sociological principle that states that situations defined by people as real are real in their consequences.

ethnomethodology A theory arising from the symbolic-interactionist perspective that argues that human behavior is a product of how people understand the situations they encounter.

looking-glass self A self-image based on an individual's understanding of messages from others about what kind of person that individual is.

self-fulfilling prophecy A process in which people's belief that a certain event will occur leads them to behave in such a way that they cause the event to happen.

social role A set of behavioral expectations that are attached to a social position or status.

dramaturgical perspective A theory arising from the symbolic-interactionist perspective that holds that human behavior is often an attempt to present a particular self-image to others.

exchange theory A theory holding that people enter a relationship because each participant expects to gain something from it.

Further Reading

ABRAHAMSON, MARK. 1978. *Functionalism*. Englewood Cliffs, NJ: Prentice Hall. An introduction to the functionalist perspective, including assessments of its contributions to our understanding of society and its limitations.

CHARON, JOEL. 1985. *Symbolic Interactionism: An Introduction, An Interpretation, An Integration*. Englewood Cliffs, NJ: Prentice Hall. A highly readable introduction to the symbolic-interactionist perspective. It also includes a useful discussion of what is meant by a perspective.

COLLINS, RANDALL. 1985. *Three Sociological Traditions*. New York: Oxford University Press. An excellent discussion of major sociological theoreticians, which locates each major theorist in terms of the three major perspectives, explores the intellectual origins of each perspective, and examines the possibilities of combining ideas arising from each perspective for a better understanding of human society.

COLLINS, RANDALL. 1975. *Conflict Sociology: Toward an Explanatory Science*. New York: Academic Press. A bit more technical than the work described above, this book offers a thorough assessment of the contribution of the conflict perspective to our understanding of human society. It also includes some valuable insights about the nature of scientific inquiry in sociology.

GIDDENS, ANTHONY. 1986. *Sociology: A Brief but Critical Introduction*. New York: Harcourt, Brace, Jovanovich. An examination of the role sociology has to play in society—and of some major theoretical viewpoints in sociology—by a theorist who has taken a leading role in attempts to combine insights from microsociology and macrosociology.

MERTON, ROBERT. 1968. *Social Theory and Social Structure*, 2nd ed. New York: Free Press. Discusses Merton's midlevel variety of functionalist theory, applied to a wide variety of issues of interest to sociologists.

CHAPTER 4

Culture and Social Structure

In the United States, women were once considered attractive only if they wore a corset—a rigid, tight-fitting garment that made their waist appear narrower and their bust larger. In ancient China, the definition of a beautiful woman included tiny, dainty feet; thus, from childhood Chinese women tightly bound their feet to keep them from growing. In the modern world, practices such as foot binding and the wearing of corsets have disappeared, but virtually every country still has standards of attractiveness for women.

Standards of attractiveness are one part of what sociologists call culture: They are a set of ideas that are shared within a society. As the above examples illustrate, culture is widely shared within a society, yet it also changes over time. If we think of standards of attractiveness only as a part of culture, however, we miss an important part of their significance. Standards of attractiveness also tell us something about the positions of men and women in society. The wearing of corsets and the practice of foot binding, for example, were both physically painful. Foot binding often led to serious physical deformity. It is highly significant that women in many societies had to endure painful and sometimes harmful practices to make themselves attractive to men, while men had to do no such thing to make themselves attractive to women. Thus, the wearing of corsets and the binding of feet reflect the subordinate social position of women in traditional American and Chinese societies. Such positions are a part of social structure, the system of social positions and rewards (or lack thereof) that are attached to these positions.

Just as culture changes, so does social structure. The elimination of corsets and foot binding suggests that the position of women has improved in these societies. However, women continue to be judged more than men on the basis of physical attractiveness; for example, a number of women in America today make themselves physically and emotionally ill trying to become or stay thin. Thus, the change has been far from complete.

I n this chapter, we shall explore culture and social structure in greater detail. To understand these concepts, we must first understand the concept of **society.** A society can be defined as a relatively self-contained and organized group of people interacting under some common political authority within a specific geographic area. Societies exist over an extended period of time, outliving the individual people of whom they are composed. A society can refer to a nation-state with millions of people, such as the United States, the Soviet Union, China, Nigeria, France, and Chile. It can also refer to tribal groups with a population of only a few hundred. If a group has some type of governmental system, if its members interact with one another while limiting contact with outsiders, if it exists within some reasonably well-defined territory and persists over time, that group fits the definition of a society.

Society, Culture, and Social Structure

Every society, large or small, has a culture and a social structure. **Culture** refers to the shared knowledge, beliefs, values, and rules about behavior that exist within a society. **Social structure** refers to the organization of society — its social positions and the ongoing relationships among these social positions; the different resources allocated to these social positions; and the social groups that make up the society (Smelser, 1988). Although culture and social structure are distinct, they are not separate. Each influences and is influenced by the other. This linkage is a major focus of this chapter.

What Is Culture?

Social scientists use the term *culture* in a somewhat different way than it is commonly used. In popular use, we often talk of people as being "cultured" or

"uncultured." "Cultured" people are well read, knowledgeable, and enjoy literature, art, and classical music. In the social-scientific sense, however, there are no "uncultured" people. Rather, the term refers to those things that are *shared* within a group or society: shared truths (that is, knowledge and beliefs), shared values, shared rules about behavior, and material objects that are shared in the sense that they are widely used or recognized. Sociologists generally recognize two kinds of culture: nonmaterial and material. **Nonmaterial culture** consists of abstract creations: knowledge, beliefs, values, and rules concerning behavior. **Material culture** consists of physical objects that are the product of a group or society: buildings, works of art, clothing, literary and musical works, and inventions. The two, of course, are linked together: A society whose nonmaterial culture is based on scientific knowledge may, for example, produce a material culture including moon rockets and computers. In contrast, a society whose nonmaterial culture consists primarily of religious beliefs and traditions may produce elaborate temples and religious writings or music.

One final important point is that no society is without culture. For reasons explored in greater detail later in this chapter, every society requires *some* degree of common understanding of reality and common rules for behavior in order to function. Without this, people could not cooperate or even interact in a meaningful way, and nobody would know how to behave.

Shared Truths: Knowledge and Beliefs

The first item mentioned in our definition of nonmaterial culture is shared truths; that is, shared knowledge and beliefs. This item is mentioned first because knowledge and belief are at the core of the definition of culture. More than anything else, culture is a matter of what people in a society know or believe to be true (Goodenough, 1957). The concepts of *knowledge* and *beliefs* are very similar to each other in the sense that both refer to shared understanding of *truth*. Both concern what people believe to be true, and both are subject to testing, if the right information is available. However, in terms of understanding cultures, it does not really matter whether the knowledge and beliefs ever get tested, or even whether they are true in an objective sense. What matters is that people within a society *agree* on a certain reality, a certain set of knowledge and beliefs. If "everybody knows" that something is true, then it might as well be true, because people will behave as though it were.

When sociologists and anthropologists study cultures, they are interested in such social agreements about truth and reality. These social agreements are what shape people's behavior, and they are what determine how people understand their world. In Europe for many centuries, "everybody knew" that the earth was flat. Hence, everyone behaved as though it were, and for many years nobody was so foolish as to attempt to travel around the earth. The first people who suggested that the earth might be round were treated the way you would be treated today if you said the earth was flat. Today, in modern industrial societies, "everybody knows" that the earth is round. Thus, shared knowledge and beliefs, and not reality, determine human behavior. Each society has its culture, and each culture is composed of a distinct set of knowledge and beliefs. Cultures can and do change over time, and what people "know" at one time will not necessarily be the same as what people in the same society will "know" at some other time.

Language One particularly important area of knowledge carried by culture is **language.** Language can be defined as the set of symbols by which the people who share a common culture communicate. Language makes possible a type of communication among human beings that is unknown to animals, because of its use of **symbols**—in this case, words, which are used to represent concepts and ideas. Language also serves the function, through written records or oral traditions, of passing information from generation to generation. In this book, for example, use of the English language permits you to learn about the ideas of great social thinkers like Marx, Durkheim, and Weber, even though they have been dead for many years. Although language's main functions are to make communication possible and to preserve ideas across the

generations, it also has important symbolic functions. Speaking the same language is an important symbol of cultural unity. For this reason, conquered or subordinate minority groups often cling vigorously to their language as a means of preserving their culture, and dominant groups try with equal vigor to get the minorities to speak their languages.

LANGUAGE AS A CULTURAL SYMBOL: AN EXAMPLE An example of the cultural symbolism attached to language can be seen in the recent history of Canada (Porter, 1972). Canada has two major cultural groups, English and French. About two-thirds of the country's population is English-speaking; about one-third is French-speaking. The French-speaking group is concentrated almost entirely in one province, Quebec. In recognition of the desire of both groups to preserve their cultural heritage, Canada has proclaimed itself to be officially bilingual. Both English and French are official languages of Canada, and all activities of the national government are carried on in both languages. In spite of this, it is hard to describe Canada as a truly bilingual country. Although most Quebecois can speak English, the province has declared French to be its only official language. In the remainder of Canada, the overwhelming majority of the population speaks English, and nobody but the federal government makes any serious attempt to be bilingual. In fact, official attempts at bilingualism are usually treated with scorn. In Ontario Province, for example, some stop signs have the French ARRET printed below the English STOP. More often than not, the ARRET is covered with spray paint.

A similar conflict has developed recently in the United States with the growth of the Hispanic population. Like the French-Canadians, many Hispanic Americans have sought to preserve their native culture by speaking Spanish. Just as the English-speaking majority in Canada opposes bilingualism, the English-speaking majority in the United States has reacted strongly to the growing use of Spanish. Several cities and states, for example, have passed legislation specifying English as their only official language.

THE LINGUISTIC RELATIVITY DEBATE Clearly, language can operate as an important symbol of a culture. Equally clearly, it can tell us a good deal about what is important in a culture. Eskimos have 20 different words to describe different types of snow; the Sami of Lapland have 80. This reflects the fact that snow is important in the Eskimo and Sami experiences and that differences in snow that would be unimportant to most people are noticeable to them. Americans have a large number of words to describe different types of automobiles. Although cultures where cars are not so common have only one word, it is important for Americans—the most auto-oriented society in the world—to distinguish among different types of cars. Thus, we speak of convertibles, station wagons, compacts, subcompacts, sport models, sedans, coupes, fastbacks, four-by-fours, T-tops, and clunkers.

We know, then, that the language spoken in a society reflects that society's culture to a large extent. However, does it also *influence* aspects of that culture? A group of specialists known as **linguistic-relativity** theorists (Sapir, 1921; Whorf, 1956) believe that it does. They argue that different languages categorize things differently, thus forcing people to create different categories in their own thinking. Different societies, for example, define colors differently. Where we see a spectrum of red, orange, yellow, green, blue, and purple, other societies in the world see only two or three colors. Some, for example, lump together what Americans consider the "warm" colors in one category and the "cool" colors in another category. To cite another example, we already noted that Laplanders have 80 different words for snow. In contrast, some warm-weather cultures have only one word to cover snow, ice, frost, and cold. Finally, tenses vary. Some languages contain tenses that English lacks, and others lack tenses that we have, such as the past and future tenses. Sapir and Whorf argued that these differences inevitably affect how people think, and, thus, what they can know and believe. How, for example, can a people conceptualize the future if their language has no tense for it?

In the sense of language strictly determining knowledge, the linguistic-relativity hypothesis is difficult to accept. Linguistic relativists undermine their own argument to a certain extent when they explain the meaning of different Eskimo words for snow, or of tenses in one language that do not exist in another language. Hence, language probably does not *determine* the content or organization of our knowledge and beliefs. However, language almost certainly does *influence* our knowledge and beliefs. For example, the English language often uses "black" and "dark" to represent evil and hopelessness. This usage undoubtedly has subtle influences on people's thinking about race. In fact, experiments with schoolchildren have indicated strongly that this is the case (Williams and Stabler, 1973). Thus, although a determinist notion that language defines what we *can* know and think is clearly an overstatement, there is good evidence that language can influence how we *do* think and know.

Shared Values

In addition to the shared realities represented by common knowledge and beliefs, cultures also carry common values. This is not to say that people within a society agree on everything—merely that there are certain common values in their culture that most or all people agree on. In another society with a different culture, the commonly held values will be different.

Ideology

The system of knowledge, beliefs, and values that is shared in a society is often referred to by sociologists as an **ideology,** that is, a set of ideas. In fact, the term *ideology* is very similar in meaning to the term *culture*, except that culture also includes rules concerning behavior. The term ideology has one additional use, however. In the tradition of Marx (1967) and Mannheim (1936 [orig. 1929]), ideology is often taken to mean a set of knowledge, values, and beliefs that gives legitimacy to the social structure. Such ideology is promoted by those in influential positions in the society, but it may be widely accepted throughout the society. Although this notion is associated with conflict sociologists, the basic idea that the culture supports the social structure is something that sociologists of both the functionalist and the conflict perspectives generally acknowledge. This is one reason that functionalist theorists stress the need for consensus: They believe that society works best when people's values and beliefs are consistent with the organization of their society. In any stable society, what people believe to be true will generally support their social arrangements. If this is not the case, the society will experience pressure for change. Attempts may be made by the elite of the society to impose a new ideology, or the people in the society will attempt to change the social structure to match their ideology. Very often, both things happen.

Social Norms

Besides shared realities and shared values, culture also involves shared expectations about behavior. These expectations about behavior are called social **norms.** Sociologists commonly recognize three types of social norms. The most informal are **folkways** — informal, minor norms that usually carry only minor and informal *sanctions,* or punishments, when they are violated. Being over- or underdressed for an occasion is an example of a behavior that violates folkways. Another type of informal norm, called **mores** (pronounced morăys), may or may not be written into law, but violations are usually taken seriously. This is so because mores are more likely than folkways to be viewed as essential to society. Reverence in church and respect for the flag are examples of mores. The flag is a symbol of the society and what it stands for; to challenge it is to challenge the very rightness of the

society. Because mores are often seen as being critical to the maintenance of society, violations often evoke an emotional response. The sanctions for violating mores include ostracism, angry words, and sometimes physical violence. Finally, there are **laws:** formal, codified norms of which everyone is expected to be aware. Violations of laws carry specific sanctions, such as fines or imprisonment, that are usually stated as part of the law. Laws are usually consistent with mores. The concepts of folkways, mores, and laws, as well as the relationship among them, will be discussed in greater detail in Chapter 8.

As is the case with values and beliefs, each culture contains some social norms that are held in common by most or all of the people in the society. Moreover, the norms that are held in common in one culture are different from those in another culture. This can lead to misunderstandings when people with different cultures come into contact with one another, as in international travel. It has been frequently observed, for example, that when North Americans interact with South Americans, different norms are at work concerning the proper distance between two people speaking to each other. South Americans stand closer together when speaking than do North Americans. This leads to an interesting dynamic when a North American and a South American get into a conversation. The South American will keep approaching, and the North American will keep backing away because the South American is "too close." Thus, the two may move across the room or around in circles as the South American keeps trying to get closer and the North American farther away.

I had a similar experience while attending an international research conference in Sweden. At lunch one day, some Americans commented on the "rudeness" of people in Sweden. I was surprised at this statement because I had found everyone I had spoken to or done business with to be pleasant and polite. That evening, however, when a group of us attending the conference went out to a crowded nightclub, I realized the source of my fellow Americans' feelings. Almost immediately upon entering the nightclub, I was bumped by another person, who made no attempt to excuse himself. My reaction was, "That was rude." In fact, had the same act occurred in the United States, it easily could have caused a fight. A

Misunderstandings and even conflicts can arise when people from different cultures are not aware of differences in values.

few minutes later, it happened again, and I soon noticed that it was not uncommon for people gently to push aside a person in their way without saying anything. Significantly, I also noticed that nobody (except the foreign visitors) seemed bothered by it.

As the week went on, I noticed that in any crowded situation gentle bumping and pushing without comment was common and accepted behavior among the Swedes. Not once did I see anyone get angry over it. From the American viewpoint, one could explain this behavior in two ways. One way was to conclude that "Swedes are rude." The other way was to conclude that "Swedes are exceptionally patient" because they never became upset over being bumped. Either conclusion, however, would reflect a misunderstanding of Swedish culture, as a result of looking at it only from the viewpoint of American culture. The correct explanation simply was that Swedes and Americans have different social norms about behavior in crowded places. In the United States, you are expected to avoid bumping people and to excuse yourself when you do. In Sweden, gentle bumping in crowded situations is acceptable and does not require excusing yourself. Imagine for a moment a Swede in the United States unfamiliar with American norms. If that Swede bumped someone and got yelled at, he or she would undoubtedly conclude that "Americans are impatient and belligerent." Any time people interpret the actions of people of another culture in terms of their own cultural norms, such misunderstandings can occur.

What Is Social Structure?

Recall our discussion of corsets and foot binding at the start of this chapter. This discussion showed us that culture and social structure are closely related to each other. By way of review, the concept of social structure refers to the organization of society, including its social positions, the relationships among those positions, and the different resources attached to those positions. Social structure also includes the groups of people who make up society and the relationships that exist among those groups (Smelser, 1988). We shall begin our discussion of social structure by discussing social positions.

A person's educational level, such as college graduate, is an achieved status. The characteristics of the family into which you are born, including your family name, are ascribed statuses.

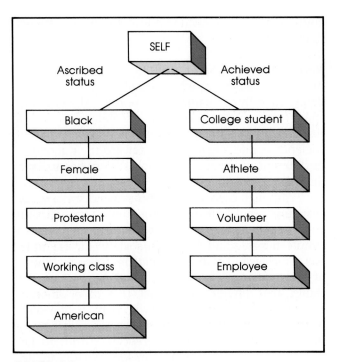

FIGURE 4.1
Achieved and Ascribed Statuses.
This diagram depicts the statuses occupied by a black female college undergraduate who works part time, does volunteer work, and belongs to the track team. How many of these statuses do you share?

Statuses

Society can be thought of as being made up of a set of social positions. Sociologists refer to such a position as a **status.** Imagine that you are a single, black, 20-year-old female who is working part time, attending college, and majoring in physics. You are occupying a number of social positions, or statuses. You are a young single female, an employee, a black person, and a college student majoring in physics. Each of these social positions is defined, in part, by its relationship to other positions in society, which are occupied by other people. Moreover, each of these social positions, or statuses, is occupied by a number of other people besides yourself. There are other black women, other physics majors, other part-time employees. You share a common status with these people, and you are very

likely to share with them some common experiences and behaviors.

Achieved versus Ascribed Status Continuing with the same example, some of your statuses were ones that you were born into. You were, for example, born black and female. Statuses that people are born into are called **ascribed statuses** (Linton, 1936). Besides race and sex, other ascribed statuses include characteristics of the family into which you were born, including your parents' family name, their economic level, their religion, and their national ancestry. In addition to ascribed statuses are statuses that result from something you did. You decided to go to college, to major in physics, to work part time. Statuses that people get at least partially as a result of something that they do are called **achieved statuses** (Linton, 1936). Among the most important achieved statuses are occupations, educational levels, and incomes. Your religion could also be an achieved status, if you changed at some time from the religion you were born into. Achieved statuses need not be things that are seen by society as positive. You might, for example, become a school dropout, a runaway, or a prison inmate. These, too, are achieved statuses, because they result, at least in part, from things that people do.

Obviously, some statuses are more central and important in people's lives than others. For most people, one status stands above all others in terms of its influence over the person's life. Such a status is called a **master status.** For adults, the master status is most likely to be occupation, or possibly a position in the family such as parent, husband, or wife. For children, it may be the status of student or simply that of male or female.

Roles

Each social status, in turn, is attached to one or more *social roles.* As was pointed out in Chapter 3, a social role is a set of expectations for behavior that is attached to a status. Thus, a status is a social position, and a role is a set of behaviors that are expected of anyone who fills the position. As Linton (1936) put it, we *occupy* statuses, but we *play* roles. Each role in society is related to other social roles, through relationships of interdependency and cooperation (as noted by functionalist theory) and through relationships of competition, domination, and subordination (as noted by conflict theory). These roles, of course, are played by people — but the roles and the relationships between them persist independently of which people are playing the roles. Different people may play the same role somewhat differently, but there are certain things that anyone playing a given role (such as that of a physics major) must accomplish and certain other roles with which that person must interact in socially defined ways.

Role Conflict and Role Strain   Each person must play a number of different roles, and sometimes these roles carry conflicting expectations. Returning to our example, you might experience conflicting expectations between your roles of college student, part-time worker, and single woman. These conflicting expectations are called **role conflict.** Sometimes even the same role contains conflicting expectations. This condition is called **role strain.** Thus, you are told that the expectations of you as a college student include academic achievement and enjoying what is supposed to be one of the most "fun" times of your life. Obviously, too much of one can get in the way of the other.

One reason for role strain is that any given role often calls for interaction with a variety of other statuses. Thus, what appears to be one role may in some aspects really be several roles. Consider, for example, the status of retail sales employee. At first, this status seems to give you a clear role to play: sell things to the customers in the manner expected by your supervisor. However, this role actually involves interacting with several different statuses: supervisor, fellow employee, customer. To some extent, each of these interactions defines a *different* role because it carries different expectations. What pleases the boss might not please your fellow employees, and what pleases the customer might not please either your boss or your co-workers. Yet, to some extent, you must please all of them in order to succeed in your job. Thus, the status of retail sales employee in one sense carries several roles: that of subordinate (with respect to your supervisor), that of co-worker (with respect to your fellow employees), and that of seller (with respect to your customers). Merton (1968, pp. 41–45) refers to these combined roles attached to one status as the **role set** of that status.

Roles and Social Structure   In large part, the organization of society, or what we call social structure, is determined by the nature of these roles, the relationships between them, and the distribution of scarce resources among the people who play them. Different societies define, organize, and reward their activities in different ways, and thus each society has its own distinct social structure.

Although each society has its own distinct social structure, almost all social structures contain certain common elements. Any society more complex than a simple hunting and gathering society, for example, has some system of *division of labor* and some system of *stratification.* These differences mean, among other things, that different roles exist, they carry different expectations, and the people who play them are rewarded in different ways. Moreover, the social structure is arranged into some set of social *institutions.* Let us address each of these areas in somewhat more detail.

Division of Labor

One reason for the existence of diverse roles in any social structure is that any society more complicated than a simple hunting and gathering society requires a **division of labor,** or specialization. In other words, there are a variety of jobs to be done, and it is more efficient for each person to do one job than it is to try to teach everyone to do all of the jobs. The larger and more complex the society, the more essential and complex the division of labor becomes. Each job can be thought of as a social role in that it has a particular set of expectations that must be met if the job is to be done properly. Moreover, in large, interdependent societies, each of these jobs or roles relates in some way to a number of other jobs or roles. Thus, the social structure becomes, in part, *a system of roles that divides labor into specialized tasks, all of which are interdependent.* How labor is divided will vary, even among societies (and organizations within the same society) that are otherwise similar. In other words, the content of work roles and the relationships between them will not always be the same. There is no set formula for the division of labor.

One factor that has a major influence on the division of labor is the level of development of a society. As societies develop economically, their division of labor becomes more complex. Thus, modern industrial societies have far more complex divisions of labor than do preindustrial societies. This issue, along with a number of other ways that level of development influences society, is discussed in detail in Chapter 12. However, even at a given level of economic development, there is no one formula for the division of labor. Exactly how that division is accomplished is a key question to be answered whenever a sociologist tries to describe or understand a social structure.

Stratification

Besides carrying different expectations, different roles carry different rewards. As we shall see in much greater detail in Chapter 9, different occupations carry different levels of prestige and different economic rewards. Ascribed statuses also vary widely in prestige and in economic rewards. This system of inequality is called social **stratification,** and it is an important part of virtually every social structure. Social stratification is related in part to a society's division of labor. Some jobs that require detailed technical training are more difficult to learn than others. In part, such jobs are rewarded because they are harder to fill with qualified people, and some incentive is required to encourage people to get the necessary training (Davis and Moore, 1945). However, stratification exists for reasons independent of the division of labor. Even in modern societies, a good deal of economic inequality is inherited and is thus a product of the ascribed status of the family that a person was born into (Tumin, 1955).

Relationships between Roles and Statuses

Because of social stratification, relationships of inequality exist between different roles and statuses in the social structure. Because of division of labor, relationships of cooperation and interdependency also exist among different roles and statuses. These rela-

tionships largely define social structure. Imagine again that you are a single, black, female college student, 20 years old, majoring in physics, and employed part time. We can see that you fit into both a stratification system and a system for the division of labor. You are in relationships of social inequality, or stratification, on the basis of both your ascribed statuses and your achieved statuses. Because of your ascribed statuses of race and sex, your society has placed you in a subordinate position relative to others with different ascribed statuses (whites and males). In other words, your opportunities may be restricted, or people may react to you in some negative way, because of your race and sex. The roles linked to your achieved statuses also in part define your position in the stratification system. You are in a subordinate, or lower, position relative to your professors and your supervisors. However, you are in an advantaged position relative to your peers who did not go to college, because going to college gives you a certain degree of prestige and a better chance of finding a well-paying job.

Besides fitting into a stratification system, you fit into a system of division of labor. In your part-time job, you fulfill a set of expectations (role) that relates in some way to the work roles of others and performs some function within the larger system of division of labor. In the role of student, you are undergoing preparation for some new, and possibly more central, role within that system of division of labor.

In short, social structure is composed of systems of stratification and division of labor, each of which is an interrelated system of roles and statuses. Each person living in a society occupies a number of statuses and plays a number of roles within both of those systems, which define the social structure of that society.

Institutions

Another key element of social structure is that of social **institutions.** Institutions can be defined as forms of organization that perform basic functions in a society, are strongly supported by that society's culture, and are generally accepted as essential elements of the social structure. Like the larger social structure, institutions are made up of relationships among statuses and roles that involve both division of labor and stratification. However, each institution consists of a particular set of such interrelated statuses and roles as well

TABLE 4.1
American Institutions and Their Key Functions.

INSTITUTION	KEY FUNCTIONS
Family (Monogamous)	Replacement of generation
	Socialization of young/cultural transmission
	Status transmission
	Shelter; care for young and elderly
	Emotional support
Capitalist economic system	Economic production
	Provision of goods and services
	Means to distribute scarce resources
	Means to determine what is produced
Government	Provision of needed public services
	Representation of interest groups
	Protection from foreign powers
	Symbols of national unity
	Social control
Legal system	Protection of members of society from illegal actions by other members of society
	Orderly settlement of disputes
	Source of legitimacy for government
	Social control
Education	Socialization of young/cultural transmission
	Passage of knowledge between generations
	Creation of new knowledge through research (universities)
	Allocation of individuals to careers
	Personal development/enhancement of awareness
Health-care system	Treatment of illness
	Extension of life
	Development of new medical technology
Judeo-Christian religion	Provision of societal belief system
	Socialization of young/cultural transmission
	Social control
	Personal support

as specific systems of division of labor and stratification and is tied to a particular function or set of functions. Table 4.1 illustrates some of the key institutions in the social structure of the United States and identifies the functions those institutions perform.

As the definition indicates, a society's institutions are strongly supported by its culture. As a result, people learn to regard these institutions as essential and frequently take them for granted. Specific individuals who play roles within institutions may be criticized, but it is less common for the institution itself to be questioned. Americans might, for example, deplore the behavior of abusive parents, but their disapproval would be directed at the people involved and not at the traditional American family. Suppose for a moment that you heard the following argument:

> The American family is by its nature a brutal, authoritarian institution that encourages abuse by making parents all-powerful authority figures over children. Therefore, abuse is not a problem of bad individuals, but is inherent in the family. If you want to stop abuse, stop blaming the people who abuse their children and put the blame where it belongs: on an authoritarian, antiquated structure that by its very nature encourages abuse. As long as parents have authority over their children, abuse will result in a sizable number of cases.

Most of you would not accept this argument, and some of you would be angry at the person who made it. Although a well-reasoned counterargument could be developed against this argument, many of you would not respond this way but, instead, would reject the argument out of hand. Why? Because, beyond whatever logical flaws it may have, this argument attacks a cherished institution that is close — important — to all of us. In other words, the importance of the family (and other key American institutions) is strongly supported by our social norms and is something that we don't have to think about because we take it for granted.

Institutions are so strongly supported by social values and norms that when a practice or social arrangement becomes widely accepted in society, sociologists say that it has become *institutionalized*. Some sociologists even include the values and norms supporting an institution as part of the definition of an institution. At the very least, for a form of organization to qualify as an institution, it must be central to the culture of the society in which it exists.

Compatibilities between Culture and Social Structure

As we have already noted, social structure and culture are closely linked, and the normal condition is for a society's culture to be compatible with, and support-ive of, its social structure. There are, however, at least occasional periods when culture and social structure are not compatible, and these are the times when social change is most likely to occur. Significantly, sociologists of both the functionalist perspective and the conflict perspective have developed explanations of the conditions that produce compatibility and in-compatibility between culture and social structure. Not surprisingly, these explanations are often at odds, or at least emphasize very different processes.

The Functionalist Perspective and Culture

Adaptation of Culture and Social Structure to the Environment As we saw in Chapter 3, functionalists see society as basically a stable, interdependent sys-tem that has adopted a particular form because that form works well. To maintain this stability requires a consensus in support of the society's basic social ar-rangements. Culture performs this function. It pro-motes cooperation by creating solidarity and provides specific support for the social structure, which oper-ates in such a manner as to meet the basic needs of the society. This basic paradigm of an interdependent and harmonious social structure and culture has been rec-ognized by sociological functionalists dating at least to Emile Durkheim. It is functionalists in the tradition of social anthropology, however, who have best ad-dressed the closely related question of cultural and structural variation. If social structure and culture exist because they are basically functional, then why is there so much variation in social structure and culture among different societies? In brief, their answer is that different societies have developed different structures

and cultures as adaptations to the different environ-ments in which they exist. Social structure and cul-ture, then, are seen as being in harmony with each other, and both of them are adapted to the environ-ment of the social system (Buckley, 1967).

A CASE STUDY: MAGIC   Much of the early insight on this issue is attributable to social anthropologist Branislaw Malinowski, who conducted extended field observation in the Trobriand Islands in the South Pa-cific during the early twentieth century (Malinowski, 1967, 1948, 1926, 1922). Malinowski noted that ar-rangements among the people he studied existed not because they were merely functional but because they were *functional given the presence of a particular envi-ronment.* An example of this can be seen in the Tro-briand Islanders' use of magic. Although they used magic extensively, they seemed to use it primarily when they were entering situations they perceived as dangerous. For example, they used magic when fish-ing on the treacherous open seas, but not when fishing in protected lagoons. Thus, Malinowski concluded that the function of magic was to alleviate fears and make fishing on the open seas seem less threatening.

Malinowski focused primarily on the individual, *psychological function* of magic in relieving anxiety in the context of a dangerous environment. However, because magic also enhanced the Trobriand Islanders' willingness to fish in the bountiful open seas, it also performed the clear function *on the societal level* of helping the Trobriand Islanders to deal with their en-vironment. The idea that culture (in this case, belief in magic) can be useful to a *society* in helping it adapt to its environment is generally associated with the theor-ist A. R. Radcliffe-Brown, who had been trained in the theories of Emile Durkheim. Radcliffe-Brown (1952, 1950, 1935), like Durkheim, saw society as being much like a biological organism, made up of many interrelated parts and having evolved in a way so as to adapt to its environment. To Radcliffe-Brown, then, the important aspect of magic was not its contribution to the individual (alleviate anxiety), but its contribu-tion to the larger society (facilitate fishing on the open seas). Implicit in the work of both Malinowski and Radcliffe-Brown, as well as in that of theorists such as Walter Buckley (1967), is the idea that what is func-tional for a society depends on that society's environ-ment, so that the social structure and culture that develop in any society will be in sizable part a product of that society's environment.

Aspects of the Environment What do we mean by a society's environment? The concept includes the full range of realities to which the society must adapt. There is the *physical environment,* which includes climate, terrain, plant and animal life, and presence or absence of bodies of water. There is the *social environment,* which includes any other societies with which a society must interact. Finally, there is the *technological environment,* which is defined by the level of technology available to a society. All of these represent realities to which a society must adapt, and they interactively define the conditions to which a society must respond. It is obvious that a society in a cold, wet climate will have different needs for shelter and clothing and different ways of obtaining or producing food than one in a desert. However, it is also true that for either the desert or the cold-climate society, reality will be quite different if it is a modern society with electric heating and cooling devices than it would be if it were a primitive one with no technological means of indoor temperature control. Hence, it is the *combination* of the physical, social, and technological environments that defines the total environment to which a society must adapt. Functionalists see social structure and culture as reflecting adaptation to this total environment, and believe that this accounts for variation in culture and social structure from place to place and over time.

Cultural and Structural Variation

Do Cultural or Structural Universals Exist? One question that sociologists and anthropologists have asked for many years is whether cultural or structural *universals* exist. The answer to this question probably depends on how specific something has to be in order to count as a cultural pattern or a structural arrangement. Consider the example of attempts to modify weather, cited by Murdock (1945) as a cultural universal. Are Indian rain dances really a common cultural element with modern cloud-seeding techniques? Although each is intended to induce rain, the assumptions and world-view behind the two are almost diametrically opposed. The Indian rain dances were based on tradition, religion, and mysticism: If one pleased the spirits, one could induce rain. Modern cloud seeding, in contrast, is based on rationalism, science, and technology.

When we speak of cultural universals, then, it makes sense to speak of broad patterns found in all societies. A list of these is shown in Table 4.2. Beyond these broad patterns, however, there are few, if any, specific cultural or structural universals. Weather is important, so people try to change it. But when we get down to *how* they try to change it, we find tremendous variation.

UNIVERSAL SOCIAL TASKS As was already noted in our discussion of social structure, there are certain issues that must be addressed in every society. We have already discussed the most critical ones: division of labor and stratification. In addition, there are other key tasks that every society must accomplish. Thus, every culture must carry some knowledge about these tasks, and every social structure must provide a means for accomplishing them (Aberle et al., 1950). Among these tasks are the following:

> *Dealing with the physical environment*: Getting food and shelter, adapting to the physical terrain, protecting oneself from weather, disease, and natural hazards.
>
> *Governing reproduction and relations between the sexes*: Establishing some rules assuring that the society will reproduce itself and establishing some ground rules for sexual behavior.
>
> *Role assignment*: Deciding who will fill what roles within society's system of division of labor and how the stratification system will reward those who fill various roles.
>
> *Communication*: Enabling people to communicate with one another through language and other symbols.
>
> *Government*: Having some system through which rules are established, disputes resolved, and common goals set up.
>
> *Norms concerning violence*: A set of rules specifying conditions under which violence is and is not acceptable.
>
> *Socialization*: Some way of teaching children and anyone else entering the society how to function and survive within its culture.

Although these issues must be addressed by all societies, the means by which they are addressed are almost limitlessly diverse. Thus, it can be said that cultural universals exist in two broad senses. First, there are regular practices or norms that occur in virtually all societies, although in different forms. Many

TABLE 4.2
Cultural Universals Identified by George Peter Murdock.

Age grading	Etiquette	Inheritance rules	Personal names
Athletic sports	Faith healing	Joking	Population policy
Bodily adornment	Family	Kin groups	Postnatal care
Calendar	Feasting	Kinship nomenclature	Pregnancy usages
Cleanliness training	Fire making	Language	Property rights
Community organization	Folklore	Law	Propitiation of supernatural beings
Cooking	Food taboos	Luck superstitions	Puberty customs
Cooperative labor	Funeral rites	Magic	Religious ritual
Cosmology	Games	Marriage	Residence rules
Courtship	Gestures	Mealtimes	Sexual restrictions
Dancing	Gift giving	Medicine	Soul concepts
Decorative art	Government	Modesty about body functions	Status differentiation
Divination	Greetings	Mourning	Surgery
Division of labor	Hair styles	Music	Tool making
Dream interpretation	Hospitality	Mythology	Trade
Education	Housing	Numerals	Visiting
Eschatology	Hygiene	Obstetrics	Weaning
Ethics	Incest taboos	Penal sanctions	Weather control
Ethnobotany			

SOURCE: George Peter Murdock, 1945, "The Common Denominator of Culture," pp. 123–142 in Ralph Linton, ed., *The Science of Man in the World Crisis* (New York: Columbia University Press).

of the items on Murdock's list fall into this category. Even the incest taboo, sometimes cited as the "only true cultural universal," is an example of this: There is no regularity among societies about what is considered incest and what is not. Second, there are issues that must be addressed by all societies, although in practice each society addresses them in different ways. Thus, cultural variation is much more the pattern than cultural or structural universals. Various aspects of cultural and structural variation, such as religion, sex roles, and marriage and family systems, will be discussed in greater detail in later chapters.

However much culture varies from one society to another, it is true that within any given culture various aspects of the culture tend to be fairly consistent with one another. This tendency is called *cultural integration*. An example can be seen in the consistencies between religious beliefs and the family system in Judeo-Christian societies. Christians and Jews believe that the law of God calls for monogamous marriage, as reflected in the commandments "Thou shalt not commit adultery" and "Thou shalt not covet thy neighbor's wife." Family norms are likewise supportive of religion, as in the saying "The family that prays together stays together." And, indeed, this particular

saying appears to be largely true: divorce rates are significantly lower among devoutly religious people than among the nonreligious.

Ethnocentrism versus Cultural Relativism Recall the example of the Americans in Sweden who misinterpreted the behavior of people in crowded situations as rude. This example illustrates a pattern known as **ethnocentrism,** in which people, consciously or unconsciously, view their own culture as normal and natural and judge other cultures accordingly. Throughout history, people of various cultural backgrounds have labeled those of different backgrounds as "savage," "barbaric," "hedonistic," and "primitive" because these people's behaviors differed from their own.

Ethnocentrism exists in all societies, for several reasons. First, we take much of our behavior for granted, not really thinking about why we do certain things and don't do other things. To most Americans, eating pork or beefsteak is appetizing, but the thought of eating worms or grasshoppers is repulsive. In other cultures, though, these same things are viewed very differently. Worms and grasshoppers are eaten in many societies, and in some societies few things could be more repulsive than eating the meat of a pig or a cow. In many Middle Eastern societies, eating pork is strictly forbidden; it is against the rules of the stricter segments of both Judaism and Islam. In India, cows are considered sacred, and people would be horrified at the thought of killing one, much less eating it.

FUNCTIONS OF ETHNOCENTRISM   A second reason for the universality of ethnocentrism is that it performs a function: In a society where people have a common culture, ethnocentrism in relation to other societies helps to promote *solidarity* (Sumner, 1906). To a certain extent, any society can promote internal unity and cooperation by comparing itself favorably to those outside. Significantly, the ever-present tendency toward ethnocentrism becomes most pronounced during wartime, as each country in the conflict emphasizes its righteousness and civility as contrasted with its evil and barbaric enemy. From a conflict perspective, ethnocentrism is also useful for justifying or rationalizing one group's exploitation of another. After all, "they're just helpless primitives whom we're actually civilizing" in the process of making them slaves or taking their land. With this type of

thinking, even the most brutal exploitation can be made to seem acceptable.

DYSFUNCTIONS OF ETHNOCENTRISM   Despite the fact that it is functional in certain ways, most sociologists see ethnocentrism as generally dysfunctional, and they try to discourage it. For one thing, it can be a major source of conflict and inequality in any society with a significant degree of cultural diversity—which, in today's world, means most societies. Second, it is a major cause of international conflict because societies that view one another ethnocentrically create international conflicts through self-fulfilling prophecies. Third, as previously noted, it is often used as an excuse for one group to treat another in a brutal and exploitative manner. Finally, ethnocentrism creates misunderstanding of social reality. In fact, one of the greatest challenges of social-science research is to avoid ethnocentrism when studying human behavior.

Cultural Relativism   In contrast to ethnocentrism, social scientists try to look at human behavior and culture from a viewpoint of **cultural relativism.** Cultural relativism recognizes that cultures are different but does not view difference as deficiency. Rather, it realizes that different societies develop different cultures and different social structures in response to the different environmental conditions they face. Thus, even if our ways seem natural and are best for us, they are not natural but a social product, and they certainly may not be best for someone else. Cultural relativism also means trying to understand the behavior of people in other cultures according to what it means to them and not what it would mean to someone in *our* culture. Even for social scientists trained in detached observation, this is not easy to do.

It should be stressed that cultural relativism does not always mean value neutrality. Occasionally, cultures become despotic, as in the case of Nazi Germany. Sociologists do not carry cultural relativism to the point of accepting such cultures, but they do try to understand the social forces that produce them.

The Conflict Perspective and Culture

Recall from Chapter 3 that, to the conflict theorist, a society's social structure is arranged so that whatever group holds power in that society controls a dispro-

One reason that ethnocentrism exists is because people consider their cultural values to be "normal" and different values to be "bad." Do these grubs look appetizing to you? Why or why not?

portionate share of scarce resources. To the conflict theorist, the function of culture is to justify such social arrangements — to get people in society to accept the notion that those who have a disproportionate share of scarce resources *should* have that large share. This view is expressed most clearly in the theories of Karl Marx (1964).

Marx on Social Structure and Culture Marx believed strongly that any society's culture is an outgrowth of its social structure. In other words, the basic social and economic arrangements in a society largely determine what people in that society will know and believe. All societies, Marx argued, have an *economic structure* and an *ideational superstructure*. By **economic structure,** Marx was referring to those elements of social structure that relate to production, wealth, and income. It includes the economic stratification system — the distribution of income and particularly wealth — but it also is defined by the society's production system (industrial versus agricultural, for example). By **ideational superstructure,** Marx was referring to those aspects of culture that we have called ideology. Marx used the term superstructure because he saw ideology and culture as arising from the social structure, not having a life of their own. The true structure of a society is defined by its distribution of wealth; culture is simply a product of that economic structure.

SOCIAL STRUCTURE The relationship between social structure (or in Marxian terms, *economic structure*) and culture (or *ideational superstructure*) is depicted in Figure 4.2. The blocks at the top and bottom of the figure represent the social or economic structure. As the figure shows, this structure is composed of a *ruling class* and a *subordinate class*. The ruling class is the group that owns the means of production, and the subordinate class is everyone else. In general, people in the subordinate class work for people in the ruling class. Thus, as shown on the left side of Figure 4.2, the subordinate class provides labor for the ruling class. Those in the ruling class are able to sell the products of that labor for more than the cost of the labor, and this profit — or *surplus value of labor,* as Marx called it — enables the ruling class to enjoy a much higher standard of living than everyone else. Marx saw this as exploitation because the actual work is done by the

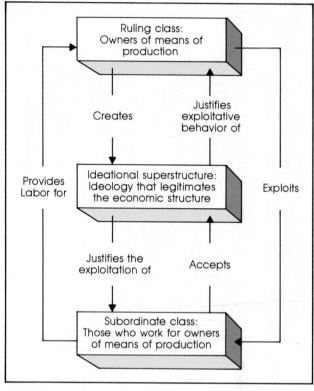

FIGURE 4.2
The Relationship between Economic Structure and Ideational Superstructure (ideology) in Marxian Theory.
SOURCE: Adapted from Dushkin Publishing Group, *The Study of Society,* p. 34. Copyright 1974, Dushkin Publishing Group, Guilford, CT. Used by permission.

subordinate class, who suffer a low standard of living while the ruling class monopolizes the products of their labor. Thus, as shown at the right side of the figure, the ruling class exploits the subordinate class.

IDEOLOGY Of course, because the social structure is fundamentally one of inequality and exploitation, the ruling class always faces the risk of an uprising by the subordinate class. The function of ideology, or ideational superstructure, is to prevent this. A culture's ideology thus explains why the ruling class should enjoy disproportionate wealth. In Figure 4.2, culture or ideology is represented by the middle oval. Note the arrows between the top two ovals. The ruling class creates the ideology, and the ideology justifies its exploitative relationship with the subordinate class.

According to Marxian theory, ideology serves the interests of the ruling classes. How did the "divine right of kings" perform this function?

How ideology justifies such exploitative relationships will depend, of course, on the broader characteristics of the society. Traditional, preindustrial societies might justify the social structure on the grounds that it is the will of God. Thus, the royalty and nobility of preindustrial Europe — the owners of wealth in feudal society — were protected by an ideology known as the *divine right of kings,* which held that kings received their authority from God. In a modern industrial society, the concentration of wealth in the hands of a few might be justified on the grounds of productivity and incentive: Placing any limit upon the wealth that people can earn might take away their incentive to come up with innovations that improve productivity. If this sounds more persuasive to you than God's willing that the king should rule, that is not surprising. You live, after all, in a modern society that values rationality, productivity, and innovation. However, Marx and those who follow his theories would hold that this

argument is merely a cultural mechanism designed to uphold the great wealth of the economic ruling class, and that society could be just as productive without such a concentration of wealth. The relationship between stratification and productivity is explored further in Chapter 9 on economic stratification.

False Consciousness As the bottom half of Figure 4.2 illustrates, not only does the ruling class create and promote an ideology that justifies its exploitative behavior, but the subordinate class accepts this ideology. Marx referred to this acceptance as *false consciousness.* In medieval society, for example, what was critical was that people *believed* in the divine right of kings. Such a belief served the interest of the king, but it went directly against the interests of the serfs and peasants, who labored for long hours day after day, only to see the wealth that they produced taken away by a lord, noble, or king. **False consciousness,** then, can be defined as acceptance by a group of people — usually a subordinate group — of a belief or value that works against that group's self-interests.

False consciousness is a critical concept in conflict theories about culture and social structure because it is the key means by which the ruling class prevents protest or revolution. *Why do subordinate groups so often accept ideologies that go against their own interests?* According to Marx, the answer lies in the power of the ruling class over key institutions and sources of information.

FALSE CONSCIOUSNESS AND SOCIAL STRUCTURE Consider again the example of medieval European society. In that time and place, the key social institution was the Church. Kings were crowned in cathedrals, and bishops were consecrated in the presence of the king. Bishops, like kings and nobles, were often major landowners. Thus, the Church and the royalty shared a common position in the ruling class, and because religion was the source of truth in such traditional societies, the ruling class could promote its interests through the Church. Thus, the divine right theory was not seriously questioned until the beginnings of urbanization and industrialization created a new and powerful capitalist class whose interests often conflicted with those of the rural landowners.

In modern societies, false consciousness can be promoted through other means. Conflict theorists

POLLS APART

What's in the American Dream?

A s discussed in this chapter, most Americans share certain core beliefs, including the right to use your abilities to create a better life for yourself and those around you. This concept, often referred to as the "American Dream," is a crucial part of American ideology.

Take a few minutes to consider the following questions. Do you believe in the "American Dream"? If so, what does this dream mean to you? How would you define *success*? How important is money to this definition?

If you answered "Yes" to the first question, you are not alone. In fact, the majority of Americans (86 percent according to one survey) believe in an American Dream, and two out of three people believe that this dream has some personal meaning for them. What does this dream consist of? Over two-thirds of those questioned defined the dream in terms of education for themselves and their children, freedom of personal choice, and ownership of their homes. Most respondents believed that they

had a good chance of realizing their dreams.

Perhaps surprisingly, advancing from worker to company president, or just plain "wealth," was not a part of most people's dream. This result does not indicate that Americans reject material success. Rather, it demonstrates that Americans are practical, even in their dreams. Most Americans want to live in relative comfort, and they agree that to do so would require more money than they are currently making. Exactly how much more depends on their present income, as is indicated in the following table.

CURRENT INCOME	DREAM FIGURE
Under $15,000	$50,000
$15,000–$25,000	$60,000
Over $50,000	$100,000

Thus, most Americans do dream of having more money, but the amounts they dream about are limited by their current financial status.

If Americans define their dream in this manner, how do they define success? Although there is no single definition, polls indicate that success includes satisfying personal relationships, financial security, and outstanding job performance.

How important is money to this definition? Although money is again a consideration, it is not the major

consideration, at least according to a 1986 survey of high-school seniors. Here is how they ranked the five components they considered most important in selecting a career.

COMPONENT	PERCENT WHO SELECTED
1. Interesting	87%
2. Uses skills and abilities	72%
3. Good chance for advancement	67%
4. Predictable, secure future	64%
5. Chance to earn a good deal of money	58%

These values, of course, can vary from group to group. In a different poll, for example, senior personnel executives in large corporations defined an "exceptional manager" as a person whose income (in thousands of dollars) is twice his or her age.

How did your responses compare to those listed in the polls? What conclusions can you draw concerning the American Dream? Think for a moment of your friends and acquaintances who are currently working or attending school. How would they define success? Do you feel that the American Dream will remain a part of American culture for future generations?

SOURCE: *The American Dream*, A National Survey by the *Wall Street Journal*, 1987, as reported in Dennis A. Gilbert, 1988, *Compendium of American Public Opinion* (New York: Facts on File); Lee Tony, 1987, "Are You Exceptional" *National Business Employment Weekly*, March 8, pp. 13-14; Jerald G. Bachman, 1987, "An Eye on the Future," *Psychology Today* 21 (July), pp. 6-8.

point out, for example, that the media are owned and controlled by large corporations, who are the wealthiest class in contemporary capitalist societies (Mo-

lotch, 1979). This does not mean that the media will speak with a unified voice, or even that they will not criticize the wealthy. However, conflict theorists do

Working-class rejection of George McGovern's proposal for an inheritance tax can be seen as an example of false consciousness.

argue that there is a definite limit to how far the media will go in advocating fundamental change in the economic system, and that the media encourage people to take certain economic arrangements for granted. Often, too, the media focus heavily on entertainment rather than information, giving people largely what they want but also giving them little real information. According to some conflict theorists, this policy distracts the public from social issues that might lead to conflict that could threaten the ruling class (Gouldner, 1976, especially pp. 167–178).

FALSE CONSCIOUSNESS: A CASE STUDY The concept of false consciousness can be illustrated by the 1972 presidential election, during which the Democratic candidate, Senator George McGovern, proposed a major revision of the nation's inheritance laws. The McGovern plan would have taxed away any money inherited by one individual in excess of $500,000. This proposal became so controversial that McGovern was forced to withdraw it, and many observers feel that it contributed to the candidate's landslide defeat by Richard Nixon.

As might be expected, McGovern's proposal aroused tremendous hostility among the wealthy. Significantly, however, although less than 1 percent of the population would have been affected by the plan, some of the major opposition came from the working class (Clelland and Robertson, 1974, pp. 204-205). Why did so many people who would never be in a position to pass along this sum of money react this way? Apparently, most Americans still believed

strongly in the "American Dream"—the belief that they *might* someday possess that kind of wealth. (For a more detailed discussion of the American Dream, see the "Polls Apart" box in this chapter.) To support McGovern's proposal would be to deny this possibility, which they were unwilling to do.

Working-class opposition to the McGovern plan can be interpreted as an act of false consciousness because, in terms of objective interests, these people would have benefited from the proposal. Higher taxes for the wealthy could have meant lower taxes or expanded government programs (for example, college scholarships) for working people, as well as reduced deficits, which would have lowered the inflation rate. Because they were unable to distinguish their interests from those of a wealthy minority, working-class voters lost an opportunity to change government policy to their benefit.

Incompatibilities between Culture and Social Structure

Both the functionalist and conflict perspectives agree that under certain circumstances culture and social structure become at odds with each other. We shall examine this issue from the viewpoints of the two schools.

Culture against Structure: The Functionalist Perspective

How Social Equilibrium Gets Unbalanced Functionalist theory holds that a society's social structure and culture will help it to adapt to its physical, social, and technological environment. This would seem to suggest that society could be very stable once it reached a state of equilibrium with that environment. However, the environment is always changing. The society comes into contact with societies it did not have to deal with before, which represents a change in the social environment. New technologies are invented, which represents a change in the technological environment. Even the physical environment can change and force a society to adapt. In 1986, for example, the Chernobyl nuclear disaster contaminated the reindeer herd of northern Sweden and Norway with radiation, which forced many people who had been herding reindeer for centuries to change their lifestyle, as is discussed in Chapter 20. Although this is a particularly dramatic change in the physical environment, there are many more gradual changes that require societies to adapt. Changes in climate, environmental damage, depletion of natural resources or discovery of new ones, changes in the mix of animal life, and even changes in lake or ocean levels can all require substantial adaptation by human societies. Thus, they can all be important sources of social and cultural change.

Cultural Lag When a society must change in response to its environment, the social structure and the culture often do not change at the same rate. The social structure, for example, can often adapt quickly to new technology. However, the culture is usually slower to change, because people resist giving up important values and beliefs. This creates a condition sociologists call **cultural lag.** When this situation exists, a value, norm, or belief that once was functional persists even though it is no longer functional or has become dysfunctional. Cultural lag occurs any time a society's culture fails to keep up with changes in its social structure, or when one part of the culture changes and another part does not (Ogburn, 1966 [orig. 1922]). Numerous examples of cultural lag can be found in American society.

You can see an example of cultural lag every time that you eat. Americans, after they cut their meat, put down the knife and switch the fork from the left hand to the right. Only then do they put the food in their mouths. This differs from the European practice of simply raising the food to the mouth with the fork in the left hand after cutting the meat. Why did Americans change this practice? Some experts conjecture that the change originated on the frontier, where people needed to keep a hand free in case they had to grab a weapon to fight off an attacker. Today, the frontier is gone, and putting down the knife and switching the fork to the other hand has no practical use. We continue to do it anyway, however, and to eat in the European style is considered to be "bad manners" here.

Cultural Diffusion Another condition that can produce incompatibilities between culture and social structure is **cultural diffusion,** a condition that occurs when aspects of the culture of one society are gradually adopted by other societies. Examples of cultural diffusion abound. One is the worldwide popularity of American and British rock music, which is often sung in English regardless of the local language. Another can be seen in the ease with which Americans today will identify certain forms of behavior as *macho,* a concept that originated not in the United States but in Latin America.

Like cultural lag, cultural diffusion can produce situations where the culture and social structure are incompatible. The culture of one society may not work very well with the social structure of another. In this case, the process happens in the opposite way from cultural lag: the culture changes in some way that may make it incompatible with the social structure. In the 1960s, for example, many young Americans were influenced by mystical Asian religious thought. Trancedental meditation, Zen Buddhism, and other forms of Eastern mysticism stressing inner peace and self-knowledge attracted a sizable interest among the disaffected youth of the period. To other Americans, however—including many parents—a mode of thinking that emphasized introspection and inner peace seemed out of place in an economic system that required achievement motivation and a certain amount of interest in material wealth. Some even saw the spread of these new ideas as a threat to the productivity of the American economy. Thus, it was not at all clear that the cultural diffusion of Eastern religious philosophies into the American youth culture was compatible with the American economic system.

POSSIBLE OUTCOMES When either cultural lag or cultural diffusion produces a situation where the culture and social structure are incompatible, several things can happen. The culture or the structure can change in ways that make the two more compatible. Sometimes a *subculture* will develop. In the case of cultural lag, some people will continue to hang on to the old culture, while others adopt new ways of thinking that are more consistent with the new structural realities. In the case of cultural diffusion, some people are usually quicker than others to borrow ideas from other cultures. In both of these cases, society becomes

The international popularity of U.S. rock stars is an example of cultural diffusion. What elements of Japanese culture have spread to Western countries?

more culturally diverse as different belief systems and different sets of norms emerge among different groups of people in society. This can bring conflict if the groups confront one another, but it can also be an important source of social adaptation.

Subcultures in Mass Society A **subculture** can be defined as a set of cultural characteristics shared among a group within a society that (1) are distinct in some ways from the larger culture within which the group exists, but (2) also have some features in common with the larger culture. Usually, a group that forms a subculture has some sense of identity, some recognition that people in the group share something among themselves that others in the larger society do not. A subculture can develop any time a group of people share some situation or experience that is different from that of others in their society. Some of the groups of people that commonly form subcultures are age groups, racial and ethnic groups, religious groups, people in a particular geographic area, and people with a common occupation, recreational interest, or

economic situation. Each of these examples involves some common situation or experience among people in the group that is not shared with the larger society. It is important to stress that the preface "sub" does not imply that subcultures are inferior to, or less fully developed than, cultures. Rather, it is used to convey the notion that subcultures exist within some larger cultural context.

CASE STUDIES: CHICANO YOUTH AND "COMPUTER JOCKS" In some cases, the values, norms, and beliefs of a subculture are in conflict with those of the larger culture, whereas in other cases, they are largely irrelevant to those of the larger culture. An example of conflict can be seen in the many young Chicanos (Mexican-Americans) who choose to speak Spanish as a way of preserving their own culture and asserting independence from the larger English-speaking culture. As a result, the Chicano youth subculture is to a certain extent in conflict with the larger culture over the issue of language. An example of a subculture whose norms are largely irrelevant to the larger culture can be seen in what are commonly called "computer jocks." Like Chicano youth, this group speaks a language different from that of most Americans, full of terms like "bits and bytes, RAM, infinite loops, DOS, uploads and downloads, and interfacing." However, this group uses such language not as a challenge to the supremacy of English or as an attempt to assert independence from the English-speaking culture, but because of its special interest in the details of computers that ordinary English doesn't describe very well. "Computer jocks" are not really in conflict with the larger culture. They are simply, at least at times, totally absorbed in their own subculture.

Although both groups share knowledge, beliefs, values, and norms that are different from those of the larger culture, neither Chicano youth nor "computer jocks" are totally independent of the larger American culture. Both groups, for example, are for the most part capable of speaking ordinary English when the situation calls for it. They also—at least some of the time—dress very much the same as others, watch the same television programs and movies, and eat at the same restaurant chains. Thus, although they are in some ways distinct from the larger American culture, both Chicano youth and "computer jocks" also "fit in" in a number of ways. This is what makes both of them subcultures rather than totally independent cultures.

A subculture's norms may conflict with those of the larger society, or they may simply be irrelevant to the larger society, as in the case of recreational subcultures. Although such recreational subcultures do not conflict with the larger culture, they do have distinct norms that are well understood by those familiar with the subculture but largely unknown to people outside it. For an example, see the box entitled "Drift Fishing: The Norms of a Subculture."

Jargon in Subcultures   We have already seen examples of language and symbol variation among subcultures in our discussion of Chicano youth and "computer jocks." When a subculture develops its own distinct terminology, this terminology is often referred to as *jargon*. Jargon has both manifest and latent functions. Its manifest function can be seen in the example of the computer jocks. There are areas of particular interest to people sharing the subculture, such as technical computer procedures, that ordinary lan-

guage is not sufficiently detailed to describe easily. The professions — including sociology — also have extensive jargon, for much the same reason. Sociology, chemistry, law, medicine, and other professions involve detailed and specialized subject matter that requires precise terminology.

Besides this manifest function of describing specialized concepts, jargon has the important latent function of setting boundaries concerning who is "in" and who is "out of" a particular subculture. This process of *boundary maintenance* is important to the group identity of those who share a subculture. Thus, part of becoming accepted among the community of professional sociologists is the ability to use the jargon. Similarly, computer jocks and other recreational subcultures use knowledge of the jargon to distinguish novices and outsiders from "insiders."

Functions of Subcultures   We have already identified one of the functions of subcultures: permitting specialized activity. As we saw earlier in this chapter, the division of labor is essential in any society and becomes more so as society becomes larger and more complex. Because subcultures (particularly occupational subcultures) carry the knowledge necessary to perform specialized tasks, they are essential to the division of labor.

IDENTITY IN MASS SOCIETY   Subcultures also provide a source of identity in mass society, thus preventing feelings of isolation and **anomie** (see Chapter 3). In modern mass societies, where people read the same newspapers and watch the same television programs, and where your account number, student number, and social security number are often more important than your name, anomie easily occurs. People want to distinguish themselves from the crowd in order to feel that "I am somebody" (Reissman, 1961). Subcultures permit this by enabling people with a common interest, situation, or set of experiences to stand out from the crowd. They provide effective norms for the small group when the norms of the larger society seem meaningless.

CULTURAL ADAPTATION AND CHANGE   Another important function of subcultures is to serve as a *source of adaptation* in society. Recall our previous discussion of cultural lag and cultural diffusion. Often a subculture is the mechanism through which cultural diffu-

Ethnic groups often form subcultures to keep certain cultural elements alive.

Drift Fishing: The Norms of a Subculture

Some years ago, on a fishing trip, I received a good lesson in the extent to which recreational groups such as fishing people develop their own subcultures. At the lake where I was fishing, a method of fishing known as "drift fishing" is commonly used. Basically, drift fishing consists of fishing off the windward side of a boat that is allowed to drift with the wind. The boat will turn at a 90 degree angle to the wind direction and move sideways in the direction the wind is blowing, and the people fish facing into the wind. The motion extends the line away from the boat, and the moving bait is more attractive to the fish than a still bait. This fishing method also has the advantage that if the fish are concentrated in a small area, a number of boats can take their turns drifting over the "hot spot," and everyone gets a chance to catch fish as he or she passes over. This method is shown in the diagram below.

On this particular day, with about half a dozen boatloads of people fishing this way and catching lots of fish over a small spot, another boatload of fishermen suddenly arrived. To everyone's surprise, they used their motor to position themselves motionless over the spot where the fish were biting—thus blocking everyone else's access to the spot. In addition, they caught very few fish, because their bait wasn't moving enough. Everyone else was angry, but nothing was said; people just left in search of another spot.

That night in the lodge, however, plenty was said. The offending boat was the main topic of conversation, as several boatloads of people from the place I was staying had been fishing that spot. After a number of comments were made about the rudeness and selfishness of the people, the owner of our resort said, "Did you know those people are staying here? You know, what

happened on the lake isn't really their fault. They come here every year, but they just sit in their cabin in the evening and never come to the lodge. They never talk to anyone while they're here. They just don't know they're not supposed to fish that way."

Later, when I thought about this, I realized I had gotten a free lesson in sociology. The people in the lodge belonged to the local fishing subculture and knew the rules so well that they took them for granted and assumed everyone else did, too. Hence, they (perhaps a bit ethnocentrically) defined the behavior of the other group as selfish and inconsiderate. But because the other group of people never talked to anyone familiar with the fishing subculture, they were not part of it and had no way of knowing its norms. They probably would have been very surprised to find out that anyone was mad at them.

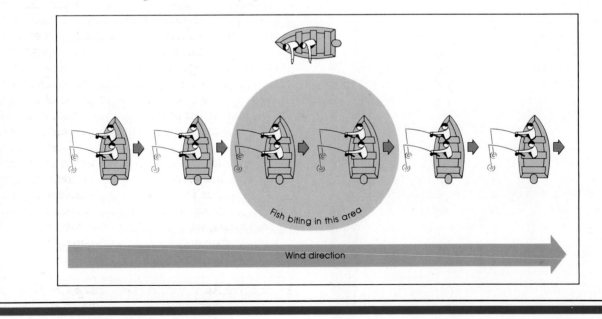

Fish biting in this area

Wind direction

sion occurs. In such cases, some group of people in the society — often the young, the well-educated, or those at the forefront of developing new technologies — adopts a new set of values and beliefs that are better adjusted to the new realities. This group thus develops a subculture in response to the new conditions. Eventually, a process of cultural diffusion occurs within the society, and the values of this subculture spread to the larger society.

A process very much like this has taken place in the United States with respect to the roles of men and women. In today's highly technological and automated society, the notion of determining social roles by sex, which may once have had some basis in differences in physical strength, no longer makes much sense. The idea of more equal roles for men and women was first adopted by young, urban, well-educated people, particularly women (Yankelovich, 1981, 1974). Because the idea of different roles for men and women has been with us for centuries, there was considerable resistance to this new idea. Gradually, though, the notion that women belong in the work place and can perform most jobs spread to the mainstream (Roper Organization, 1980; Yankelovich, 1981). Thus, what had been an adaptation to a new social and technological environment by a particular subculture gradually became accepted in mainstream American culture through a process of cultural diffusion.

Dysfunctions of Subcultures   Although subcultures perform important functions in society, they can also be dysfunctional. The most important potential dysfunction, from the point of view of the functionalist perspective, is that they can erode society's consensus. If a culture contains subcultures whose attitudes are too different from one another, or who are excessively at odds with the larger culture, cooperation can be inhibited. Each group may think of itself first and the concerns of the larger society only later. Hence, functionalists generally seek to place bounds on cultural diversity, opposing policies that encourage it, such as bilingual education (Glazer, 1981; Thernstrom, 1980), and criticizing social programs that emphasize group rights rather than individual rights or the needs of the larger society (Bolce and Gray, 1979; Glazer, 1976).

Culture against Structure: The Conflict Perspective

The Emergence of Class Consciousness   Unlike functionalists, conflict theorists see incompatibility between culture and social structure as something more fundamental than adaptation to the society's environment. They see such incompatibilities as inherent in the nature of the society itself. As we saw, conflict theorists hold that social structure is shaped in the interests of the dominant group in the society and survives because of the false consciousness of other groups. Eventually, however, the people in the society may come to attain **class consciousness;** that is, they will recognize that their true interests do not lie in maintaining the social structure as it was created by the dominant group. In other words, they have now adopted beliefs, values, and norms that support their objective self-interests. This, of course, places their culture at odds with the social structure, and, as a group, the subordinate class is in conflict with the dominant group. To conflict theorists, this conflict offers the possibility of social change.

Class Consciousness and Symbolic Interaction   The process by which people's consciousness is altered involves communication within disadvantaged or oppressed groups, which leads people in those groups to redefine the meaning of their situation. Until rather recently, a shortcoming of conflict theories was their failure to focus sufficiently on the process by which such changes of consciousness occur. Several contemporary theorists who began as conflict theorists have set out to combine the insights of the symbolic-interactionist perspective with those of conflict theory in order to understand this process (Giddens, 1985, 1978; Collins, 1985, 1981). These theorists point out that individual interpretations of meaning collectively define how groups view their situation. They argue that in order for us to understand such changes as shifts from false consciousness to class consciousness, we must understand the processes of communication and interpretation through which individual views of reality are changed.

Subculture As a Weapon in Group Conflict   Because class consciousness develops in groups that share a common interest among themselves (and an interest opposed to that of the dominant group), it is clear that subcultures play an important role in social change. Conflict theorists emphasize the idea that subcultures develop among groups that share a common self-interest. To the conflict theorist, the most important function of subcultures is to enable groups to act on behalf of a common self-interest. Consider again the example of Chicano youth as a group sharing a subculture. From a functionalist perspective, this subculture would give Chicano youth a sense of identity in a mass society. However, from a conflict perspective, the subculture does more than that. It forms a basis for them to act upon the common self-interests they share as Chicanos and as young people. Thus, speaking Spanish is more than a source of identity in mass society; it becomes a political statement that Chicanos are not willing to accept Anglo culture. *Chicanismo*—consciousness of Chicano culture— serves as an organizing base for issues of interest to Mexican-Americans ranging from immigration legislation to unionization of agricultural workers to improvement of inner-city schools. To conflict theorists, this is the most important function of subcultures.

Cross-Cutting and Overlapping Cleavages Although diversity of culture can lead to conflict in some cases, it can also help to keep conflict under control. For example, Chicano youth who opposed the Vietnam War provided an example of what sociologists call **overlapping cleavages.** Both young people and Chicanos were at disproportionate risk of dying in Vietnam and thus shared a common interest in opposing the war. Often, however, the different groups to which people belong have different self-interests. Consider the example of a Catholic couple, both public-school teachers, who send their children to a Catholic school. As public-school teachers, they belong to a group with an occupational subculture. Part of that subculture is a set of values holding that the public schools should be the first priority for educational spending by government. Of course, this set of values is motivated in part by self-interest, as conflict theory would predict. As Catholics with children in a Catholic school, however, the parents belong to another group with a different subculture. This group believes in government support to private schools, pointing

out that private schools save the public money by reducing the number of children that the public schools must educate, even though the parents of private-school students pay the same taxes. This view, too, is motivated at least in part by self-interest. But now consider the position of our couple. Their interest as public-school teachers leads them one way, and their interest as the parents of Catholic-school students leads them the opposite way. The likely result is that their views will not fall strongly in either direction; they will be moderated by their two opposite self-interests and subcultural affiliations. This is an example of what is called **cross-cutting cleavages:** religion and occupation cut different ways. In mass societies, cross-cutting cleavages are often the rule, and they are an important force for keeping conflicts among interest groups and subcultures to a manageable level (Lipset, 1959).

Countercultures Sometimes, particularly when cleavages are overlapping rather than cross-cutting, subcultures become so opposed to the larger culture that sociologists call them **countercultures** (Roszak, 1969; Yinger, 1982). A counterculture exists when a subculture adopts values and beliefs that are predominantly in opposition to those of the larger society. Examples of countercultures are religious cults such as the Hare Krishnas, the Children of God, and the Rajneesh movement of the early 1980s; extremist political groups such as the Ku Klux Klan and the Aryan Nations on the right and the Weather Underground on the left; and groups espousing radically different lifestyles such as the Hell's Angels. Some groups combine lifestyle with politics, such as the hippies of the 1960s or, at the opposite end of the political spectrum, the skinheads of the late 1980s. Such groups often challenge authority and sometimes engage in direct conflict with its representatives.

At times, countercultures become widespread and influential in society, as in the 1960s when diverse groups of young people, seemed to challenge nearly every social norm. Although these groups were popularly referred to as "the counterculture," it is not clear whether it was really one counterculture or many. Certainly there were some common threads that united these diverse groups—opposition to the Vietnam war, enjoyment of rock music, and new ideas

The Hare Krishnas are an example of a counterculture. What others can you think of?

concerning such topics as sexuality, the roles of minorities and women, and the recreational use of drugs. However, the diversity in this so-called counterculture was so great that it is hard to describe it as one counterculture. It is very doubtful whether middle-class college students, Black Panthers, and societal "dropouts" who used psychedelic drugs really had much in common besides challenging authority. Each of these groups had very different lifestyles, experiences, and concerns. Some, for example, were out to change society (and not always in the same ways), whereas others were simply seeking to withdraw from it (Kenniston, 1971).

It should be mentioned that some social scientists question the entire notion of countercultures. They argue that even countercultures reflect a mix of rejection and acceptance of the larger culture. Extreme rightist groups such as the Ku Klux Klan, Posse Comitatus, and the Aryan Nations may engage in violence against the police and fellow citizens, but they also carry the American flag and call themselves "true patriots." In the 1960s and early 1970s, the youth counterculture was said to be rejecting materialism and questioning technology, but you'd hardly know it

by looking at the stereos and amplifiers they used to play rock music (Slater, 1970). From this perspective, these elements of acceptance and rejection of the dominant culture make it very hard to draw the line between a subculture and a counterculture. Regardless of terminology, however, the development of subcultures that at least partly oppose the larger culture is an important source of social change. We shall see an example of that in our discussion of American culture, with which we now conclude this chapter.

American Culture

Core American Values and Beliefs

What are the beliefs and values associated with American culture, and how do they differ from those of other cultures? A number of sociologists have addressed this question and have achieved a fairly broad consensus on some of the core values and beliefs that are shared by the majority of Americans. The most important work in this area has been that of Robin Williams (1970), although a number of other sociologists have made important contributions concerning particular values. Table 4.3 lists some of the most basic American values.

Ideal versus Real Culture

The core values contained in Table 4.3 raise certain questions and issues. Clearly, some of these values conflict with others. For example, our humanitarian belief in helping the "deserving poor" is not always compatible with our emphasis on self-sufficiency and our disdain for "welfare." To resolve this tension, our society continually distinguishes between those we consider to be victims of misfortune and those we feel are responsible for their situation, however unfortunate it might be.

In examining this list you might also have concluded that our actions, both as individuals and as a nation, frequently do not reflect these values. Although we claim to believe in equal opportunity, we have erected numerous obstacles, such as racism, sex-

TABLE 4.3
Core American Values and Beliefs.

Freedom	Belief in personal rights, as expressed in the Bill of Rights of the U.S. Constitution, and the need to extend and defend these rights around the world.
Democracy	The belief that people should be free to choose their own government and that government decisions should be a product of the public will.
Individualism and individual responsibility	The belief that success and failure are individual, and not governmental or societal, responsibilities. People should support themselves and their family and not rely on "welfare."
Religion and morality	A concern with issues of right and wrong, which permeates most political issues. Might reflect the fact that Americans are more religious than most industrialized peoples.
Science and technology	The belief in solving problems through the application of scientific knowledge.
Equality of opportunity	The belief that all people should have the chance to succeed according to their own abilities, rather than because of special privileges.
Competition	Strong belief in outperforming others, as expressed by current rhetoric concerning the "failure" of U.S. schools and businesses to compete with foreign nations.
Work ethic	A major emphasis on achievement through hard work. Tied to the idea that success is measured in terms of material wealth.
Humanitarianism	Belief in assisting the "deserving poor" as well as the victims of serious diseases and natural disasters (floods, famines, earthquakes).
Practicality	Americans value those things they consider "useful." Business and the natural sciences are seen as more valuable than the humanities and social sciences.
Nationalism	Americans are highly patriotic and frequently label as "un-American" ideas that violate the public ethos.
Romantic love	Marriage is associated with romance and love. Differs from preindustrial societies, where marriage was often seen as an economic arrangement.
Sexual restriction	Despite changes in attitudes toward sexuality, Americans maintain more restrictive attitudes toward sex than most Western (and many non-Western) nations.

SOURCES: Williams, 1970; Kluegel and Smith, 1986; Jones et al., 1986; Myrdal, 1944; Henslin, 1975; Ford and Beach, 1981.

ism, and poverty, that prevent entire sections of the population from competing on equal terms (Myrdal, 1944). We consider ourselves a "freedom-loving" people, but we often prevent other people from expressing unpopular views, and our government has supported, and in some cases helped to install, authoritarian regimes throughout the world. These examples illustrate the gap between **ideal culture,** the norms and beliefs that a people accept *in principle,* and **real culture,** those norms and principles that are actually practiced (Myrdal, 1944; Mann, 1970). Look again at Table 4.3. What other discrepancies between real and ideal culture can you think of?

As was previously suggested, there is evidence of some change in American core values over the past 3 decades. Some sociologists see the 1960s and 1970s as a time in which some key American values underwent rather fundamental change. We shall conclude our discussion of American culture by looking at some of these changes.

Recent Changes in American Values and Beliefs

Seeds of Cultural Change: The 1960s and Early 1970s In large part, the social and political activism of the 1960s and early 1970s developed out of opposition in a large segment of the population to the Vietnam War and racism within U.S. society. This activism was most pronounced among young, well-educated children of the middle class (particularly college students) and minority-group members (Bensman and Vidich, 1984, Chap. 16). These two groups, of course, had somewhat different concerns, but they did share a sense of rebellion against the system, and they were targets of efforts by the government to restore order and repress dissent. Thus, both middle-class college youth and minority group activists increasingly thought in terms of "us versus them," creating a situation in which it was easy to challenge a wide variety of cultural norms, values, and beliefs.

Before long, issues of conflict in American society had expanded from war and racism to include the roles of men and women; norms about sexuality, drug use, and the importance of work; the role of authority; and such cultural elements as music, style of dress, and hair length. There was a surge of political activism,

BLOOM COUNTY   by Berke Breathed

This cartoon highlights a key American value — competition.

both in the traditional electoral arena (as young people campaigned for Eugene McCarthy, Robert Kennedy, and George McGovern) and in less traditional forms such as teach-ins, marches, sit-ins, boycotts, and, occasionally, riots.

As time passed, some of the activities and values of the so-called counterculture quickly faded. By the late 1970s, for example, young people were back to their historic pattern of low voting rates and limited political participation. The continuing influence of conservatism in American society was demonstrated by the election of Ronald Reagan to the presidency in 1980 and 1984, although political scientists debate the relative importance of personality versus issues in his victories. Nonetheless, there is compelling evidence that the youth and minority subcultures (or, if you prefer, countercultures) of the 1960s and 1970s did make a lasting difference in American culture. Four areas in which this is evident are:

1. The roles of men and women
2. The rights of racial and ethnic groups
3. Human sexuality
4. Self-fulfillment

Research by Yankelovich (1974) indicates that the new values in these areas spread from college and minority youth into the larger group of noncollege white youth by the early 1970s. Yankelovich (1981) later found that these new values next spread through the adult population, to the point that they had become the dominant values of the nonelderly adult population by the beginning of the 1980s. This represents a classic case of *cultural diffusion*.

Rights of Racial and Ethnic Groups   When Robin Williams published the third edition of his *American Society* in 1970, it still listed *group superiority* as one of the 15 core American values. Although this idea has not disappeared from American thought, it would be hard to list it as a core value in today's America. Survey instruments of all types indicate that most Americans reject notions of one group being superior to another and in principle support racial integration and oppose deliberate acts of segregation and discrimination. Contrast these responses to 1968, when only 60 percent agreed that "white children and black children should attend the same schools." In contrast, in the most recent survey, 89 percent agreed (Skolnick, 1969; National Opinion Research Center, 1983). This does not mean we have eliminated racial inequality or have developed the attitudes necessary to accomplish that goal (see Chapter 11). It does, however, indicate a fundamental shift in attitudes and beliefs.

Sex Roles   A similar shift has occurred in American beliefs about the roles of men and women. Most Americans today, for example, reject the notion that the

PERSONAL JOURNEY INTO SOCIOLOGY

The Sociology of Sport

From my earliest days as a graduate student in the Department of Sociology at Cornell University, I have considered myself a "scholar-activist." Over the ensuing years, my career in sociology has coalesced into virtually a seamless tapestry of academic and activist pursuits and projects.

It now seems clear, in retrospect, that two principal influences propelled me along my established path of professional development. First, there were my experiences growing up Black, poor, and athletically inclined in East St. Louis, Illinois, at the dawn of both the Civil Rights Movement and the age of televised, racially integrated sports. This convergence of history and biography had an enduring impact upon my perceptions of myself and what I eventually came to define as priority challenges confronting me as a Black citizen of this nation.

Second, and perhaps even more important, I was profoundly influenced by "significant others." Initially, these were Black men and women of high status and accomplishment who lived and worked in my community and who took the time and had the patience to become involved with me as informal mentors and counselors. Later the "significant others" in my life came to be comprised mostly of people with whom I had no personal contact at all, but who, through striving to fulfill the promise and potential of their own lives and careers, achieved levels of excellence that gave direction to my own aspirations and goals. Through their works, writings, and public involvements, E. Franklin Frazier, W. E. B. DuBois, Paul

Harry Edwards

Athletic sports are among the cultural universals identified by George Peter Murdock that are listed in Table 4.2. Because all cultures practice some sort of athletic activity, sociologists study sports to gain insights into the values, behaviors, and social structure of a people. Perhaps no individual is as closely identified with this area of study as Harry Edwards. Professor Edwards first achieved prominence when he helped organize a boycott by Black-American athletes of the 1968 Olympic games in Mexico City. More recently, he was hired by several professional sports teams as a consultant on racial problems within the sports world. He also teaches at the University of California at Berkeley.

Robeson, C. Wright Mills, Malcolm X, Richard Wright, Martin Luther King, Jr., Bill Russell, Maya Angelou, and James Baldwin, along with other writers, academicians, political activists, and athletes, became my role models during what, for me, were my intellectually and politically formative years as an undergraduate sociology major and scholarship

student-athlete at San Jose State University in California.

It was against this background that I developed my interest in relationships between sport and society in general, and between race and sport in particular. Following completion of my master's degree and a good deal of research into the role, status, and circumstances of Black people in American sport, I organized a movement among Black athletes aimed at both dramatizing and provoking rectification of widespread, deeply rooted social inequities in American domestic and international sports. In domestic sport, this effort culminated in what was popularly termed "The Revolt of the Black Athlete." This "revolt" was manifested in a series of incidents occurring on over 100 traditionally White college campuses across the nation, where Black athletes and their student supporters, threatening boycotts or disruptions of athletic events, made demands upon athletic directors and campus administrations for more equitable treatment and opportunities for Blacks involved in their sports programs.

At the international level, the movement produced "The Olympic Project for Human Rights," which proposed a Black American boycott of the 1968 Mexico City Olympic Games. The "OPHR" was also the motivating force behind the demonstration atop the Olympic Podium by Tommie Smith and John Carlos during victory ceremonies for medalists in the 200 meter dash.

Following the 1968 Olympics, I returned to Cornell University to complete a Ph.D. in sociology. I subsequently joined the faculty of the

Department of Sociology at the University of California at Berkeley, where I have continued my academic and activist involvements, the results of which, I believe, have been of both practical and sociological significance.

One important product of my work is what I term "the first principle of the sociology of sport": *Sport inevitably recapitulates the character, dynamics and structure of human and institutional relationships within and between societies and the ideological sentiments and values that rationalize those relationships.* Nowhere is the validity of this principle more evident than in my ongoing work on relationships between race, sport, and society.

In sum, a society with long-standing, ongoing traditions of discrimination and inequality that are rationalized by ideologies that associate certain deficiencies or behaviors with particular social groups inevitably exhibits powerful strains of inequity in its sports institution. In the case of the United States, then, institutional racism within professional and college sports is inextricably intertwined with the broader Black experience in America.

Owing largely to (1) a long-standing, widely held, and *racist* presumption of innate, race-linked Black athletic superiority and intellectual deficiency, (2) media propaganda about sports as a broadly accessible route to Black social and economic mobility, and (3) a lack of comparably visible, high-prestige Black role models beyond the sports arena, Black families are four times more likely than White families to push their children toward sports-career aspirations, often to the neglect

and detriment of other critically important areas of personal and cultural development. Indeed, the single-minded pursuit of sports fame and fortune is today approaching an institutionalized *triple tragedy* in Black society: the tragedy of thousands and thousands of Black youths in obsessive pursuit of sports goals that the overwhelming majority of them will never attain; the tragedy of the personal and cultural underdevelopment that afflicts so many successful and unsuccessful Black sports aspirants; and the tragedy of cultural and institutional underdevelopment in Black society overall, partially as a consequence of the *talent drain* toward sports and away from other critically vital areas of occupational and career emphasis, such as medicine, law, economics, politics, education, and the technical fields.

Only *5 percent* of high-school athletes go on to compete in their sports at the collegiate level — including those who participate in junior college — which is to say that over 95 percent of all athletes must face the realities of life after sports at the conclusion of their last high-school athletic competition. Of those Black athletes who do attend 4-year institutions on athletic scholarship or grants-in-aid, 65 to 75 percent *never* graduate from the schools they represent in sports. Of the 25 to 35 percent who do graduate, an unconscionable proportion graduate in what are often less-marketable academic majors riddled with "keep 'em eligible," less-competitive "jock courses" of dubious educational and occupational value.

Of the Black athletes who participate in collegiate football, bas-

ketball, or baseball, less than 2 percent ever make a professional roster. Among these chosen few, 60 percent are out of professional sports within 3 to 4 years and, more often than not, financially destitute or in debt or simply on the street without either the credentials or the skills to succeed in our society.

Even in sports in which Blacks predominate as athletes, they are routinely passed over as candidates for top coaching and sports-administration jobs, often despite having the combination of academic preparation in physical education and substantial practical experience at the *assistant* level in major athletic programs. There are only two Black athletic directors, three Black head football coaches, and fewer than 30 Black head basketball coaches at major Division I, NCAA colleges and universities. There are no Black head baseball coaches at such institutions.

In the professional ranks the record concerning Black access to top positions is even more dismal. Although 63 percent of the players in the National Football League are Black, there has never been a Black head coach in the NFL, and only 6 percent of the assistant coaches are Black. Today, major league baseball has only one Black field manager, and it has never had a Black general manager, though 16 percent of the players are Black. In the National Basketball Association, where 75 percent of the players are Black, only four Blacks are working in front-office, decision-making positions throughout the entire league. And although professional basketball did count six Black head coaches on its rosters at the end of the 1987–88 basketball season, these six Black head coaches had a total of 22 NBA championships and 57 years of NBA playing experience among them. Of the White head coaches in the league, 12 never played in the NBA at all, and of those who did play, only 3 had playing careers of any note or consequence. In short, it appears that Black coaching candidates must be demonstrably superior to their White counterparts in professional basketball experience to gain access to head coaching jobs in the NBA.

American sport, like American society overall, practices a virtual "plantation system" of relations wherein Whites hold a near-monopoly on high-prestige, high-authority occupational positions, while Blacks, when they have access at all, are consigned in disproportionately high numbers to the most vulnerable, most exploitable, most expendable, least powerful production roles—in the case of sport, that of athlete.

There are today ongoing efforts by a broad array of media, academic, civil rights, and sports interests to publicize and rectify the tragedies of Black sports involvement. These efforts have met with only fair success. The challenges are many and complex. Aside from the problems of racism and discrimination are difficulties perpetuated by Black people themselves. Black families and Black athletes must assume greater responsibility for remedying the situation. Through a blind belief in the ability of sports to serve as a socioeconomic mobility vehicle, Black families have unwittingly contributed to the tragedies of Black sports involvement. Too many of us have set up our children for personal and cultural underdevelopment, academic victimization, and athletic exploitation by our encouragement of the primacy of sports achievement over all else. We have then bartered away the services of the more competitive among our children to the highest bidders among collegiate athletic recruiters in exchange for what are typically hollow promises of ethical educational opportunities or, even worse, promises of sports fame, fortune, and Fat City forever.

Black families have the responsibility to inform themselves about the realities of Black sports involvement—its advantages and liabilities, its triumphs and tragedies. As a culture and as a people, we simply can no longer permit many among our most competitive and gifted youths to sacrifice a wealth of human potential on the altar of athletic aspiration, to put playbooks ahead of textbooks. This does not mean that Blacks should abandon sports, but that we *must* learn to deal with the realities of sport more intelligently and constructively. Black parents must insist upon the establishment and pursuit of high academic standards and personal development goals by their children, *high goals and standards that will be principally established and enforced not on the campus, but in the home.*

And, finally, it must be stated unequivocally that Black athletes themselves must shoulder a substantial portion of the responsibility for improving Black circumstances and outcomes in American sports. Black athletes must insist upon intellectual discipline no less than athletic discipline among themselves, and upon educational integrity in athletic programs rather than, as is all too often the case, merely seeking the easiest route to maintaining athletic eligibility. If Black athletes fail to take a conscious, active, and informed role in changing the course and character of Black sports involvement, nothing done by any other party to this tragic situation is likely to be effective.

Currently, along with my full-time position on the Berkeley faculty, I am staff consultant with the San Francisco Forty-Niners of the National Football League and the Golden State Warriors of the National Basketball Association. I have also been appointed Special Assistant to the Commissioner of Major League Baseball. My role in all of these positions is, among other responsibilities, to generate progress in resolving problems of race-based inequities. This is an old and continuing struggle that has changed only in the character of the immediate battles.

In the 1930s, Paul Robeson, Joe Louis, and Jesse Owens led the fight for Black *legitimacy* as athletes. In the late 1940s and into the 1950s, Jackie Robinson, Althea Gibson, Larry Doby, Roy Campanella, and others struggled to secure Black *access* to the mainstream of American sports. From the late 1950s through the 1960s and into the 1970s, Jim Brown, Bill Russell, Curt Flood, Tommie Smith and John Carlos, Muhammad Ali, Arthur Ashe, Kareem Abdul-Jabbar, Michael Warren, and Lucius Allen fought to secure *dignity and respect* for Blacks in sports. Even as all of these battles continue, today we have embarked upon yet another phase of the struggle—the battle for minority access to power and decision-making authority in executive-level roles in American sport.

woman's place is in the home, and in principle they support equal pay for equal work. In fact, work outside the home for pay, not the housewife role, has become the norm for most American women. Some, though not all, historically male professions have witnessed a major surge in the number of women seeking and gaining entry. By the early 1980s, for example, over one-quarter of medical-school students and one-third of law-school students were female (Simmons and Broyler, 1983). As in the case of race relations, attitudes have in many ways outstripped reality when it comes to attaining real social equality for men and women. The important point though, is that today the norms support the idea of equal opportunity for women; as recently as 3 decades ago, they did not.

Human Sexuality   Although the "free love" mentality of the 1960s was on the way out even before the AIDS epidemic, the "sexual revolution" has left a lasting legacy. Today, marriage is no longer a prerequisite for having sex. The majority of Americans today do not object to a sexual relationship between two unmarried people who love and care about each other. As recently as 1969, a Gallup poll showed that two-thirds of Americans viewed premarital sex as "wrong"; just 5 years later, 80 percent of men and 70 percent of women believed that premarital sex was permissible under at least some conditions (Hunt, 1974). The practice of unmarried men and women living together, which once brought social ostracism, is commonplace today. Another major change is the much greater acceptance of divorce and remarriage. Thus, even if American sex norms remain restrictive compared to those in other industrialized countries, they are less restrictive than they were just a few years ago.

Self-Fulfillment   What some people regard as the most fundamental of all the value changes is a greatly increased emphasis upon *self-fulfillment* (Yankelovich, 1981). Self-fulfillment represents a different form of individualism than has traditionally characterized American culture. The self-fulfillment norm emphasizes attaining your potential, but not in the economic sense of maximizing wealth. Rather, you attain your potential to know yourself, to attain a higher consciousness, to perfect a skill, or to experience the world. Thus, work becomes important not as an end in itself but as a means to self-fulfillment. The goal becomes to have a fulfilling job or a job that provides income to support activities (such as travel, sports participation, or creative activities) that bring self-fulfillment.

Based on survey research, Yankelovich (1981) estimates that about 80 percent of the U.S. population had been affected by this new norm by the beginning of the 1980s; about one in six considered it the dominant force in their lives. As you might expect, different social observers view this and other new norms differently. Many functionalists have argued that the search for self-fulfillment has caused parents to be irresponsible toward their children; husbands and wives to be irresponsible toward each other; workers to be irresponsible toward their jobs (Packard, 1983; Etzioni, 1982; see also Bell, 1976). In all these cases, they argue that people place fulfilling experiences ahead of meeting responsibilities, so key social functions go unfulfilled.

Conflict theorists, in contrast, argue that the decline of racism and sexism in part reflects the fact that these discriminations are seen as barriers to people's self-fulfillment. They also argue that a deemphasis on the maximization of wealth could lessen the greed that leads people to exploit one another. Finally, they note that, to an extent, the search for self-fulfillment represents an effort to extend to everyone the opportunities that once were reserved for a small, privileged group.

Summary

In this chapter, we have seen that every society has a culture and a social structure that are closely linked to each other. Culture consists of common knowledge, beliefs, values, and norms, whereas social structure consists of a set of social arrangements. These arrangements consist of interlinked social positions organized into a set of institutions. Each social position, or status, carries behavioral expectations known as roles. Social positions also carry unequal rewards, which are a part of society's system of stratification by which scarce resources are distributed unequally.

Both functionalists and conflict theorists agree, for different reasons, that culture and social structure are usually in harmony with each other, but sometimes at odds. The functionalist perspective sees social structure and culture as meeting basic needs, the specifics of which depend largely on the society's outside environment. For this reason harmony between the culture and the social structure is important. To conflict theorists the social structure is seen as providing disproportionate wealth and reward to the dominant group, or ruling class. Culture serves the function of justifying this privileged position. Its success in doing so is illustrated by false consciousness: the tendency of disadvantaged groups to accept the dominant group's ideology, even though it is against their self-interests to do so.

According to functionalists, culture and structure can become imbalanced with each other through the combination of structural change and cultural lag. Cultural diffusion resulting from contact with another society can bring a similar result. When this happens, either the culture or the structure must change to restore the balance, but must not change so much that key functions can no longer be performed. Conflict theorists, in contrast, see opportunities for society to change and improve when culture and social structure become incompatible. Often this occurs when subordinate groups attain class consciousness: They become aware of their true interests and reject the dominant group's ideology.

Both the functionalist and conflict perspectives recognize the importance of subcultures, which arise among groups in society with some shared experience that is different from that of others in the society. Through cultural diffusion, the values of subcultures can spread into the larger society; thus, subcultures are important sources of cultural change. This has been the case in the United States, as certain values that began with youth and minority subcultures have spread into the larger culture. Still, a number of enduring features distinguish American culture from the cultures even of other industrial, democratic societies.

Glossary

society A relatively self-contained and organized group of people who interact under some shared political authority within some reasonably well-defined geographic area.

culture A set of knowledge, beliefs, attitudes, and rules for behavior that are held commonly within a society.

social structure The organization of society, including institutions, social positions, the relationships among social positions, the groups that make up the society, and the distribution of scarce resources within the society.

nonmaterial culture Abstract creations, such as knowledge and values, that are produced by a society.

material culture Physical objects that are the product of a group or society.

language A set of symbols through which the people in a society communicate with one another.

symbol Anything, including words, signs, and gestures, that is used to represent something else.

linguistic relativity A theory holding that language not only reflects but also helps to shape people's perceptions of reality.

ideology A system of beliefs about reality that often serves to justify a society's social arrangements.

norms Socially defined rules and expectations concerning behavior.

folkways Relatively minor informal norms that carry only informal sanctions, such as mild joking or ridicule, when they are violated.

mores Informal but serious norms, violations of which result in strong sanctions.

laws Officially stated social norms that carry formal, specific, and publicized sanctions when violated, and which are enforced through formal agencies of social control.

status Any position within a social system.

ascribed status Any status that a person receives through birth, including race, sex, and family of origin.

achieved status Any status that a person has attained at least in part as a result of something the person has done.

master status A status that has a dominant influence in shaping a person's life and identity.

role conflict Conflicting or opposing expectations attached to roles.

role strain A condition in which one role contains conflicting expectations.

role set A set of related roles attached to one social position or status.

division of labor A characteristic of most societies in which different individuals or groups specialize in different tasks.

stratification A pattern whereby scarce resources, such as wealth, income, and power, are distributed unequally among the members of a society.

institution A form of organization, with supporting sets of norms, that performs basic functions in a society, is strongly supported by that society's culture, and is generally accepted as an essential element of the society's social structure.

ethnocentrism A pattern whereby people view their own culture as normal, natural, and superior, and judge other cultures accordingly.

cultural relativism A view that recognizes cultures other than one's own as different, but not odd or inferior; other cultures are not judged by the standards of one's own.

economic structure In Marxian terminology, those aspects of social structure that relate to production, wealth, and income.

ideational superstructure A Marxian name for ideology; so named because Marx considered ideology an outgrowth of the economic structure.

false consciousness A condition in which people, usually in groups that are relatively powerless, accept beliefs that work against their self-interests.

cultural lag A pattern whereby some aspect of culture that was once functional persists after social or technological change has eliminated its usefulness.

cultural diffusion A process whereby a belief, value, norm, symbol, or practice spreads from one culture into another, or from a subculture into the larger culture.

subculture A set of knowledge, beliefs, attitudes, symbols, and norms held by a group sharing some common experience or situation within a larger society.

anomie A situation in which social norms either do not exist or have become ineffective.

class consciousness A situation in which a group of people with a common self-interest correctly perceive that interest and develop beliefs, values, and norms consistent with advancing that interest.

overlapping cleavages Divisions or issues of conflict in society that divide people along generally similar lines on different issues.

cross-cutting cleavages Situations in which divisions or issues of conflict divide a society in different ways on different issues.

counterculture A subculture that has developed beliefs, values, symbols, and norms that stand in opposition to those of the larger culture.

ideal culture The norms and beliefs that people in a society accept in principle.

real culture The norms and principles that people in a society actually practice.

Further Reading

BELLAH, ROBERT N., RICHARD MADSEN, WILLIAM M. SULLIVAN, ANN SWIDLER, AND STEVEN M. TIPTON. 1986. *Habits of the Heart: Individualism and Commitment in American Life.* New York: Harper and Row. An analysis of American cultural values and beliefs, with emphasis upon the strain between individualism and achievement on the one hand and commitment to community on the other.

COAKLEY, JAY. 1986. *Sport in Society: Issues and Controversies,* 3rd ed. St. Louis: Mosby. An introduction to the sociology of sport, showing how the social structure of sports reflects the social structure of the larger society. Expands upon issues addressed in Harry Edwards's *Personal Journeys into Sociology* vignette in this chapter.

HARRIS, MARVIN. 1986. *Good to Eat: Riddles of Food and Culture.* New York: Simon and Schuster. This book provides first-hand evidence of how the need to adapt to different environments produces different beliefs and practices in different cultures. It does so in a highly entertaining way, by examining the origins of different eating habits in different cultures.

JONES, ELISE F., ET AL. 1986. *Teenage Pregnancy in Industrialized Countries.* New Haven, CT: Yale University Press. By studying the reasons for the very different levels of teenage pregnancy in five industrialized countries, this book tells us a great deal about how the cultures and social structures of these countries differ, despite their similar levels of industrialization. Also illustrates the intricate relationships between culture and social structure by showing how cultural values influence the levels of teenage pregnancy, which in turn shape (but also reflect) the stratification systems of the various countries.

KLUEGEL, JAMES R., AND ELIOT R. SMITH. 1986. *Beliefs About Inequality: Americans' Views of What Is and What Ought To Be.* New York: Aldine de Gruyter. Another powerful illustration of the interrelationship between culture and social structure. Kluegel and Smith examine American ideas about what is "fair" and perceptions concerning the fairness of American society. They show how these values and beliefs both reflect and shape the American social and economic structure.

YANKELOVICH, DANIEL. 1981. *New Rules: Searching for Self-Fulfillment in a World Turned Upside Down.* New York: Random House. An extensive analysis, based on public opinion polling data, of long-term changes in American culture that resulted from the social upheavals of the 1960s and early 1970s.

CHAPTER 5

Socialization

Human history is replete with legends of lost or deserted children who were raised by wolves, monkeys, or other animals. Legend has it, for example, that Rome was founded by Romulus and Remus, who had been raised in the wild by a wolf. More recently, Walter Cronkite reported that a child in Africa had been raised by monkeys. Legend and reality are quite different, however. No such case has ever been authenticated. Cronkite, for example, was obliged to report the next night that news reporters had been unable to verify the story about the child raised by monkeys.

There are known cases of children raised in isolation who are sometimes called "feral children" (wolf children) because, like the Romulus and Remus of legend, they were raised essentially without human contact. However, unlike Romulus and Remus, such children usually are unable to participate in human society in a normal way.

Two well-known and authenticated cases of isolated children are "Anna" and "Genie." "Anna" was locked in an attic in a Pennsylvania farmhouse for 6 years, her existence denied because she had been born out of wedlock. She had received some physical care but no social interaction. When discovered, tied to a chair, she was unable to walk, talk, or feed herself (Davis, 1940, 1948). She was taken to the University of Chicago, where efforts were made to socialize her with other socially isolated children. In 1 year, a staff member there required medical treatment more than a dozen times as a result of being bitten by Anna (Bettelheim, 1959). Although Anna learned to walk, say some words, and wash her hands and brush her teeth, she never learned to speak in sentences. By the time she died at the age of 11, 4 years after being taken to the university, she was functioning only on the level of a 2- or 3-year old.

A more recent case is that of "Genie" (Pines, 1981; Curtiss, 1977). She had been kept harnessed to a potty seat until the age of

13 *in a small room in a California house, hidden away to avoid the wrath of her father, who hated children. She was fed only milk and baby food, and never spoken to by anyone. Occasionally, in fits of rage, her father beat her, usually when she tried to speak or made noise. She was discovered after her mother fled with her following a fight with her father, and she was placed in a children's hospital. At that time, Genie could not stand straight, chew, or see beyond 10 feet. She blew her nose into the air and urinated and masturbated in the presence of others. Like Anna, she was later able to learn a few words and phrases, but not to ask questions or speak sentences. She did, however, use gestures well, and was able to learn sign language. She was inquisitive, and after 7 years in the hospital, increased her IQ score from 38 to 74. When her mother eventually removed her from the hospital, she still had not come close to normality in many aspects of her behavior and development.*

The cases described in the opening vignette show that, while a newborn baby has the *capacity* to become a member of human society, this capacity can be realized only through interaction with other human beings. In the first few years of life, a baby is completely dependent upon other human beings for survival. In the first few months, he or she literally can survive for only a matter of hours without assistance from other people. In addition to assistance with physical needs, a newborn baby requires consistent social interaction with other human beings. This need is so great that if a baby is deprived of it for an extended period, he or she may never be capable of becoming "normal." As illustrated by "Anna" and "Genie," the total absence of interaction with other human beings produces personalities that cannot participate in human society or even display what would be regarded as normal behavior. Even a partial absence of interaction can be quite harmful: Babies whose parents do not isolate them but who do largely ignore them over an extended time typically show poor intellectual development and high rates of personality difficulties, as do institutionalized children who have sometimes been deprived of interaction because their harried caretakers simply don't have time to provide it (Spitz, 1945; Goldfarb, 1945). Such children typically experience ongoing developmental and emotional problems, even if they receive all the necessary *physical* care. Spitz (1945) referred to this pattern as "hospitalism." Even after placement in foster homes where they do experience normal human interaction, children frequently do not fully recover from the effects of their earlier deprivation.

Becoming "Human" through Socialization

These effects of social isolation dramatically illustrate the human need for **socialization.** Socialization is the process whereby people learn, through interaction with others, that which they must know in order to survive and function within their society. Through this process, people learn their *roles* and the roles of others in their society, and they develop a **self-image.**

Similar effects have also been obtained in animal studies. The best-known example is a series of studies of monkeys by Harry Harlow and his colleagues (Harlow, 1958; Harlow and Harlow, 1970, 1962; Harlow and Zimmerman, 1959). Two key findings of these studies illustrate the importance of interaction for normal development.

First, monkeys raised in isolation from other monkeys did not develop normal behavior. Rather, they were withdrawn, responded to other monkeys with fear or aggression, and did not engage in sex. If the females were artificially impregnated, they usually neglected or abused their offspring. Among the behaviors observed were sitting on the baby monkeys, holding them upside down, and attacking them. Significantly, the effects of such isolation became harder to reverse the longer the monkeys were kept in isolation.

Second, consistent patterns were observed when monkeys in isolation were given a choice between a cloth "dummy mother" and a wire "dummy mother." Even when the wire "mother" had a feeding bottle and the cloth "mother" did not, the monkeys preferred the soft cloth "mother."

Learning about Norms and Social Roles

Studies like the ones discussed above show that primates, including human beings, have an innate need for interaction with others of their kind. Thus, we have seen that babies are dependent on others for (1) the meeting of basic physical needs, without which they cannot survive; and (2) the meeting of the need for interaction, without which their learning capacity is lost and normal behavior is impossible. Two key functions of the socialization process, then, are to provide needed care and needed interaction. The third key function of socialization is to teach people the basic information they need in order to survive in their society. Everyone must learn the social roles that exist in his or her society and how to play them. Furthermore, everyone must learn the norms of his or her society. (Roles and norms are discussed in Chapter 4.) As social animals, people must know how to participate in the society into which they are born.

Theories of Socialization and Development

Social scientists have developed a number of theories about how this process of learning norms and roles takes place. Although these theories disagree on some key points, many of the differences arise from the fact that different theories emphasize different aspects of the socialization and development processes. Among the most important and influential theories of socialization and development are *interactionist theories*, *Freudian theories*, and *cognitive-developmental* theories.

Nature versus Nurture

In psychology and, to a lesser extent, sociology, there has been considerable debate about the relative importance of nature versus nurture in shaping human behavior. The term *nature* refers to natural or biological influences over human behavior. Those who argue

Harlow's experiments with baby monkeys demonstrated the devastating effects of social isolation during the early stages of life.

on behalf of nature as the more significant force shaping human behavior believe that human behavior is in substantial part a product of:

> The individual's genetic or hormonal makeup (Pines, 1982).
>
> Natural instincts or drives that act as influences on the behavior of all human beings (Freud, 1970 [orig. 1920]; 1962 [orig. 1930]; Lorenz, 1966; E. Wilson, 1978).
>
> Physiological processes of development that place limits on the range of thought and behavior of which a person is capable at any given age (Piaget, 1952, 1926; Piaget and Inhelder, 1969).

Although these theories do not all argue that human behavior is *entirely* a product of nature, they do argue that nature has extensive influence over human behavior.

The term *nurture* refers to the influence of *social forces* in shaping human behavior. Those who emphasize nurture as the major influence over human behavior argue that behavior is a product of interactions with other people (emphasized by symbolic-interactionists such as Mead, 1934, and Cooley, 1964) and the situations in which people find themselves, including their share of scarce resources and the relationship of their situations to larger societal needs.

In no area of human behavior has this debate been more intense than in childhood socialization. All schools agree that what happens in childhood has important influences throughout a person's life, because it is in childhood that people first develop their patterns of thought and behavior. Although sociologists generally give greater attention to nurture than to nature, the theories we will be considering do disagree about the relative importance of nature versus nurture. We shall consider first interactionist theories of socialization, which weigh in heavily on the side of nurture.

Interactionist Theories of Socialization

Of all the substantive areas of sociology, socialization is the one in which theories arising from the symbolic-interactionist perspective have had their greatest influence. As we saw in Chapter 3, interactionists see human behavior as the result of how people understand their situations, which in turn is the result of messages they get from others and how they interpret those messages. Because a child is born without *any* understanding of his or her situation, it is clear that these processes are especially important in childhood socialization. Thus, interactionist theories of socialization focus on the ways that messages from others do the following things:

Provide the child with an understanding of his or her situation

Teach the child about the roles that he or she will be expected to play

Teach the child the norms that govern his or her behavior and the ways that some of these norms differ from role to role

Provide the child with messages concerning how well the child is doing at playing his or her roles. These messages, in turn, lead to the development of the child's self-image.

One of the first sociologists to examine the socialization process from the interactionist perspective was George Herbert Mead, whose ideas were introduced briefly in Chapter 3. They continue to rank among the most influential theories about socialization.

Mead on Socialization   As we saw in our examples of feral children, normal human development is impossible without human interaction. Mead believed, in fact, that human behavior is almost totally a product of interaction with others. As he put it:

The self, as that which can be an object to itself, is essentially a social structure, and it arises in social experience . . . it is impossible to conceive of a self arising outside of social experience. (Mead, 1934, p. 13)

Thus, to Mead, social, not biological, forces are the primary source of human behavior. To a large extent, he accepted the notion that a newborn baby is *tabula rasa,* or a "blank slate," without predispositions to develop any particular type of personality. The personality that develops is thus a product of that person's interactions with others. Mead referred to the spontaneous, unsocialized, unpredictable self as the *I.* In the process of socialization, others interact with the individual, developing in him or her the attitudes, behaviors, and beliefs needed to fit into society. Mead referred to the socialized self that emerges from this process, reflecting the attitudes of others, as the *me* (Mead, 1934, pp. 175–178). Although the *me* becomes predominant with socialization, the *I* still exists, and is the source of the spontaneous and seemingly unpredictable side of a person's behavior (Mead, 1934, pp. 174, 177–178). As Ames (1973, pp. 51–52) explains:

The "me" is the result of dealing with other people. It is an internalization of the community, with its institutions, whereas the "I" remains more isolated, more untamed, though cautioned and controlled by the "me." . . . [T]here is always an unstable equilibrium between society, representing what has been achieved or bungled in the past, and the exploring, reforming, revolutionary "I." This sets the problem and promise of education confronting parents, teachers, and statesmen.

THE PLAY STAGE   Social interactions begin in early childhood—a period Mead referred to as the **play stage**—with contacts with **significant others.** These are particular individuals with whom a child interacts on a regular basis early in life, including parents, teachers, and schoolmates. In the play stage, which begins with the acquisition of language, typically around the age of 1 year, children learn several important things through interaction with significant others. First, they learn that they exist as a separate object — the **self.** As Charon (1985, p. 68) puts it:

> The self is pointed out and labeled by the significant others. "Hi, Andrew!" (Here, Andrew stands for this object, *me, myself*). . . . As others point us out to ourselves, we see ourselves. We become social objects to ourselves.

Children also learn at this stage that others, too, have separate identities, separate selves. They learn that different people behave differently, and that different people also *expect* children to behave in different ways. This leads to the third key role of significant others at this point: they teach children social norms. Children learn norms both through concrete messages given by significant others ("Do this, but don't do that") and by using significant others as **role models.** In other words, children learn what is appropriate behavior in part by observing the behavior of significant others and then trying out that behavior themselves.

Why does Mead call this the "play stage"? Essentially, the reason is that the child at this stage is capable only of play and cannot yet engage in the organized activity necessary, for example, to participate in a game such as baseball. To put it a bit differently, at the play stage children are interacting with particular *individuals* (Mommy, Daddy, Kelly, Christopher) and not *roles* (mother, father, big sister, outfielder). They do not yet really understand that, to a large extent, how they are expected to behave toward people is determined by those people's roles. Rather, they just know that different people act differently and expect them to act differently.

THE GAME STAGE   As they get older and interact with a wider range of significant others, children move beyond thinking merely in terms of particular individuals. They begin, in effect, to learn the concept of social roles. They learn that certain positions are occupied by a variety of people, such as mothers, fathers, salespeople, and teachers. They also learn that people in similar social positions frequently behave alike, and that they, in turn, are expected to behave in particular ways toward people with particular social positions. To a large extent, this is true regardless of who fills

A child has reached the game stage when he or she can interact with roles rather than merely with individuals.

these social positions. When a child has learned this, he or she has moved beyond interacting with *particular individuals* and has begun to interact with roles. In Mead's terms, the child has gone from interacting with significant others to a new and higher stage of interacting with the **generalized other.** At this stage, the child has generalized from the behavior and expectations of particular individuals to those of anyone playing various roles that relate to whatever role the child is playing at the time. He or she has, in effect, learned to respond to the expectations of his or her society.

When the child has learned to do this, he or she has reached the **game stage.** The ability to play roles and to interact with other roles makes organized activity, such as games, possible. Take, for example, the game of baseball. Each position in the game, such as shortstop or outfielder, has a set of expectations — a role — attached to it. If you play shortstop, you must know that you are expected not only to stop the ball if it is hit to you, but also what base you should throw to. Anybody playing shortstop needs to know this; the expectations are the same regardless of who plays the position. The same is true of any other organized activity.

What is important, of course, is that a person attains this game stage through repeated messages from others. It is also through communication with others that the specific expectations of each role, such as shortstop, are learned. Thus, through social interaction, the child learns to play different roles attached to positions that he or she occupies at various times, and to respond appropriately to the behavior of others playing various roles.

Socialization and the Looking-Glass Self

In addition to teaching us to play our own social roles and to respond appropriately to the roles of others, the socialization process helps us to develop a self-image — a sense of what kind of person we are. This self-image relates closely to the various roles that we play. We normally come to think of ourselves as being very good at playing some roles and not so good at playing others. This self-image is developed through the process of the *looking-glass self* (Cooley, 1964 [orig. 1902]), which was introduced in Chapter 3. As children try out playing new roles, they try to imagine how they appear to others, and they pay attention to others in order to get messages about how well they are doing in these roles.

Children, then, try to imagine what other people think about how they are doing in their various roles and look for explicit and implicit messages from others to find out. Once they get such messages, they develop ideas about what kind of person they are based on their interpretation of these messages. This process, in turn, affects how they think of themselves. Two elements are critical to this process: the *content* of the messages a child gets from others, and the child's *interpretation* of these messages.

Self-Esteem and Significant Others

As we have indicated, a child will normally come to think of himself or herself as being good at playing some roles and not as good at playing others. In most cases, this process leads to the gradual development of a balanced self-image. Sometimes, though, children are intentionally or unintentionally given messages that are harmful to their overall self-image. Excessive criti-

cism, for example, can lead a child to think of himself or herself as not very good at anything, which produces low *self-esteem*. Self-esteem refers to your judgment of yourself: Do you look upon yourself positively or negatively? This can refer to your *overall* judgment of yourself — called *global self-esteem* — or to your judgment of your performance in a particular role.

Overly busy parents who consistently fail to take time to do things with their children and to respond to their children's concerns can unintentionally give their children messages harmful to their self-esteem. To a young child, "I'm too busy" can easily sound like "I don't want anything to do with you" or "You're a pest." A child who comes to think of himself or herself in these terms might never develop good self-esteem. Young children develop images of themselves that, to a substantial degree, will influence how they think of themselves throughout life. Thus, poor global self-esteem at this stage can be a source of lifelong difficulties. This does not mean that children need to be told they are good at everything. Few people are, and a balanced self-image is much healthier than one that cannot accept any shortcomings. However, it is important for children to:

Get sufficient attention and emotional support from their parents to know that they are loved and wanted

Be given credit and praise when they do things well

Be reassured that it is not necessary to be good at everything

Freudian Theories of Socialization

Id versus Superego

Whereas symbolic-interactionists such as Mead and Cooley see human behavior and personality as almost totally the product of social interaction, their contemporary Sigmund Freud (1856–1939) saw behavior and personality as being the product of the interaction between nature and nurture. Unlike Mead and Cooley, Freud believed that human beings are born with certain innate *natural drives,* or behavioral needs. Freudian theory views the socialization process as a struggle between these natural drives and society's expectations. Freud referred to these natural drives as the **id.** The most important of these drives, according to Freud (1962 [orig. 1930]), are a tendency toward aggression and the drive to obtain sexual pleasure, although more broadly there is a drive to obtain physical or sensual pleasure of any type.

Is Violence a Natural Human Tendency?

Sigmund Freud believed that aggression, if not violence, was a basic natural drive present in all human beings. Ethologists—people who study animal behavior—have in some cases taken this notion a step further, arguing that violent or aggressive behavior is present not only in humans but in all animal species. These ideas have been most thoroughly developed by the ethologist Konrad Lorenz (1966). Lorenz argues that virtually all animals fight their own species, but that they rarely kill them, for two main reasons. Animals such as wolves and ravens, which possess the ability to kill their own kind quickly with a single blow, peck, or bite, do not do so because they have inhibitions against such behavior (Lorenz, 1966, p. 240). Most animals, however, are not physically capable of killing their own species quickly. Significantly, these animals have no inhibition against killing their own species and will in fact do so if one corners another in such a way that escape is impossible. However, this does not usually happen, because the fact that

they cannot *quickly* kill one another usually enables the defeated participant in a fight to flee and escape. These animals have no inhibition against killing their own kind because they do not need it—the ability to escape serves the same purpose.

Lorenz argues that human beings fall naturally into the second category—without weapons or special training, few people can kill another person with a single blow. Thus, the weaker or defeated participant in a fight has time either to escape or to appeal to the compassion of the attacker. Lorenz argues that the invention of weapons turned human violence deadly and transformed humans into one of the very few animals with a high rate of killing its own species. Weapons enable us to kill quickly, and because we do not have the ability to kill quickly without them, we never evolved the inhibitions that keep a raven or wolf from killing its own.

There is little doubt that Lorenz is right when he says that weapons make human violence lethal. Most experts agree, for example, that the high

rate of gun ownership in the United States leads to more lethal assaults and is one of the reasons that the U.S. homicide rate is one of the highest in the world (Farley, 1987, p. 155; see also Newton and Zimring, 1969; R. Farley, 1980). Even so, there is reason to question whether violence is really a human instinct. In many human societies, violence and aggression between human beings are rare, and the killing of one human by another is unheard of. Margaret Mead (1935) cites the Arapesh of New Guinea as an example. Other examples are Africa's Pygmies, the Lepchas of Sikkim, and the Shoshone Indians of the western United States. If violence and aggression are really instinctual in human beings, it is very hard to explain why they do not occur in certain societies. Moreover, in even the most violent societies, most people are peaceful most of the time. Thus, although people clearly have the *capacity* for violence, it remains debatable whether they have an innate *tendency* toward violence.

Freud argued that these tendencies are present even in infancy and early childhood. The sexual drive appears in subtle forms, such as a need for oral sensual stimulation in the first year of life, play with the sexual organs by ages 3 or 4, and unrecognized sexual desires for the opposite-sex parent a year or 2 later. The tendency toward aggression is more evident, in the form of tantrums, hitting, kicking, biting, and so forth. (For a further exploration of the question of whether human beings are innately aggressive and violent, see the box "Is Violence a Natural Human Tendency?")

Both in childhood and throughout life, people are required to control the natural drives—the id—

because these drives result in behaviors that are not acceptable to society. You can neither obtain sexual pleasure from every source from which you desire it nor act out every violent or aggressive impulse that you feel. Opposing the id, then, are the values or norms of society that limit our pleasure-seeking and aggressive tendencies. Freud referred to these as the **superego** —the *conscience* that arises from messages we get from others concerning what is and is not acceptable behavior. The id—a product of our natural drives— says "I *want* to do that," while the superego—a product of the expectations of others—says "You *can't* do that." In effect, everyone experiences an *inner conflict* between his or her natural drives and the expectations and rules imposed by society.

Ego: The Resolution of the Conflict Depending on the strictness of the home in which they were raised and, to a lesser degree, the restrictiveness of significant others outside the home, all people develop a somewhat different balance between the id and the superego. According to Freud, this balance is managed by the **ego,** the ultimate personality that a person develops. The superego will be the dominant influence in people raised in extremely restrictive environments, and the id will play a larger role in the personality of those raised with a greater degree of freedom. To a large extent, then, the degree of restrictiveness experienced in childhood will determine the individual's ultimate personality throughout life.

In general, Freud felt that society placed more restrictions on people's natural drives than is necessary or desirable. He believed that too much repression of the id by the superego early in life leads to

---

Sigmund Freud defined the socialization process in terms of internal drives and cultural restraints rather than social interaction.

pent-up drives that will surface later in dangerous and unhealthy ways. If we deny our sexuality, for example, the sex drive does not go away. Rather, it remains and becomes increasingly frustrated. Similarly, unreleased aggression can build up until it explodes in a way that is much more dangerous than regular, but less explosive, releases of aggression. Less commonly, excessive permissiveness has been said to lead to an underdeveloped conscience that in turn produces a personality called a **sociopath** — a person with no sense of right and wrong and no sense of guilt or remorse for anything he or she does.

Thus, although it is impossible to say exactly how much of human behavior is a product of natural tendencies or drives, it is fair to say that the manner in which conflicts between individual drives or desires and the expectations of society are resolved in childhood will have significant effects on behavior in later life. At the same time, most sociologists argue that the situations people encounter in later life are important social forces in their own right, and they reject the notion that *all* behavior in adulthood is a product of childhood experiences. Recent research supports the notion that both sociological *and* biological influences are at work in shaping human behavior (Udry, 1988; Udry and Billy, 1987).

According to Freud, the drive for physical and sexual pleasure takes different forms at different stages of life, which he called *psychosexual stages.* Freud believed that an unresolved — or inappropriately resolved — conflict between the id and the superego at any of these stages could lead to *fixation* at that stage, or even *regression* to an earlier stage.

Erikson's Eight Stages of Life Freud's notion that people face different conflicts at different stages in life laid the groundwork for important theoretical advances by Erik Erikson. Erikson argued in *Childhood and Society* (1950) that although people do experience different dilemmas at different stages of life, these dilemmas relate more to social expectations and self-identity than to the need to control the drives for sex or aggression. In contrast to Freud's psychosexual stages, Erikson argued that people go through a series of *psychosocial* stages, each of which contains opposing positive and negative components. At each stage, people face a dilemma or crisis as they confront issues and, in effect, make choices between the two components. As Mead and Cooley suggested, the choices that are made are largely a product of the social environment and messages that children receive from significant others. In the first several stages, children who receive encouragement and positive messages about themselves tend to achieve healthy modes of adaptation; children who are ignored or who get excessively negative messages tend to adapt poorly. As with Freud's psychosexual stages, some people fail to resolve the dilemmas they face at any given stage, which can be a major source of problems later in life. Like Freud, Erikson believed that in some instances, adult problems may be resolved by addressing and seeking to resolve issues and dilemmas left over from earlier stages. However, Erikson accorded a greater role to nurture, and a lesser one to nature, in defining the dilemmas to be resolved at various stages of life.

Although both Freud's psychosexual stages and Erikson's psychosocial stages serve as a useful framework outlining some of the major dilemmas that must be addressed in socialization, both have their limitations. They are not precise descriptions of the process of development, and discrete stages have not, for the most part, been scientifically validated. To the extent that such stages do occur in a sequence, they overlap considerably. In addition, there is always the possibility that an unresolved issue from one stage can be addressed successfully later in life. Finally, with respect to Freud, there is considerable question about the role that natural drives play in human development and the extent to which pleasure-seeking behavior in early childhood is properly described as sexual.

Theories of Cognitive Development

Cognitive-developmental theories resemble the theories of Freud and Erikson in two important ways. First, they rely on the idea that people move through a series of stages as they develop and experience the socialization process. Second, they include a place for the forces of nature as well as those of nurture. However, they also differ in two important ways. First, rather than dilemmas or choices, cognitive-developmental theories focus on **cognitive processes:** learning, reasoning, and the actions by which knowledge is obtained and processed. Second, they relate the role

of nature to physiological development in that they acknowledge that the development of the body and brain places an upper limit on the child's capacity to learn, reason, and process knowledge at any given age.

However, although the limits on human potential may be physiologically defined, the actual level and process of learning and reasoning in any individual is mostly a function of social influences. For most of us, learning and modes of reasoning and information processing are very much influenced by the social environment. To see how this occurs, let us begin with the cognitive theories of the Swiss psychologist Jean Piaget.

Piaget: Stages of Cognitive Development Central to Piaget's theory of development was the concept of a *schema*—a behavior sequence involving recognition of a stimulus (sight, sound, object, person, or message) in the environment and a motor (behavioral) response to that stimulus based on our understanding of its meaning. As new information becomes available, it is assimilated into existing schemas, and these schemas may be modified to accommodate new information that does not fit the existing schemas. Thus, cognitive reasoning becomes a process of assimilation and accommodation of new information into existing schemas, which become increasingly complex as new information becomes available. According to Piaget (1926), this process of cognitive reasoning develops through the following four stages:

1. *Sensorimotor stage (until age 2).* This stage involves the development of a physical understanding of the environment by touching, seeing, hearing, and moving around. At this stage, schemas involve purely physical objects and properties. Children learn *object permanence*—if you show a child something and then hide it, the child will learn that it is still there and look for it.

2. *Preoperational stage (ages 2–7).* Children learn to represent schemas in their minds. They engage in symbolic play, using one object as a symbol to represent another. They may, for example, pretend that a block is a car and move it around the way a car would move. At this stage, children also develop *language*—not merely saying words, but putting them together in sentences that express increasingly complex ideas. This clearly demonstrates that they are using mental, not purely physical, schemas. They still, however, look at things from their own viewpoint, not that of

Not until a child reaches the stage of concrete operations can he or she understand that equal amounts of a liquid can appear unequal in different containers.

someone else, and they have trouble with any task that requires them to look at themselves or their environment from someone else's viewpoint. A boy at this stage, for example, may report having two brothers, Henry and Paul. If asked how many brothers Henry has, however, the child will mention only Paul—not himself (Foss, 1973).

3. *Stage of concrete operations (ages 7–11)*. At this stage, children gain several new capabilities. Although they still think mainly in terms of concrete, readily visible objects rather than abstract concepts, they are able to think in terms of cause and effect. They can draw conclusions about the likely physical consequences of an action without always having to try it out. They also learn that quantities can remain constant even if they take different shapes and forms. They understand, for example, that if a given amount of milk is poured from a tall thin glass into a short wide one, or from a large glass into two small ones, it is still the same amount of milk. Finally, as stressed earlier in our discussion of George Herbert Mead, children at this stage can respond to the roles of others, consider things from the viewpoint of others, and play different roles themselves. Thus it is now possible for them to play games.

4. *Stage of formal operations (ages 12 and up)*. When they reach this stage, children can reason not only in terms of the physical world, but also in terms of abstract concepts, such as love, happiness, wealth, intelligence, and remorse. They can think in terms of future consequences and evaluate the probable outcomes of several alternative courses of action. They can also evaluate their own thoughts and self-image. Finally, they can begin to think about major philosophical issues, such as why pain and suffering exist.

Limits on Cognitive Development As was indicated earlier, cognitive theorists believe that the *capacity* to attain these stages is defined by physiological development, but that the actual extent to which people attain them, and the ages at which they attain them, are socially determined. The ability to do these

things is learned from others, and if a child is not exposed to others engaging in the type of reasoning that normally occurs at a given stage, the child may have difficulty developing that reasoning ability on his or her own. Both the larger culture in which a child grows up and the child's immediate social environment influence this process. If a culture places little value on abstract reasoning—for example, a culture in which reality is determined by tradition and not by scientific discovery—a child is much less likely to develop abstract reasoning skills. At the more immediate level, if a child's parents do not think in terms of abstract concepts, and this skill is not emphasized in school, the child has little or no way of learning it. For this reason, a sizable part of the population—even in countries like the United States where scientific knowledge is valued—never reaches the cognitive stage of formal operations. The four stages of cognitive reasoning do appear to occur in sequence, but how far people get through that sequence seems to vary.

Piaget on Moral Reasoning Cognitive reasoning enables people to make moral judgments—that is, to distinguish between right and wrong. Piaget (1932) offered the important insight that how children (and adults) distinguish right from wrong is greatly in-

Jean Piaget with children. According the Piaget, the process of cognitive reasoning develops through four basic stages: sensorimotor, preoperational, concrete operations, and formal operations.

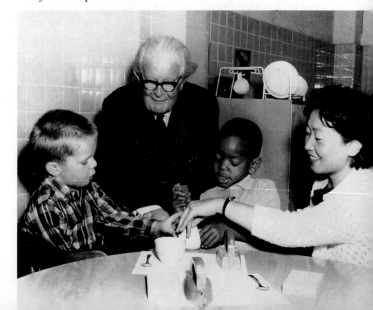

fluenced by their process of cognitive reasoning. A child at the preoperational stage, for example, cannot and will not make judgments about right and wrong in the same way as a child at the stage of formal operations.

THE MORALITY OF CONSTRAINT According to Piaget, children at young ages act on the basis of reward and punishment: They avoid behaviors that bring punishment and repeat ones that are rewarded. They see rules as existing for their own sake (not some larger social purpose), and they do not realize that rules are subject to change. Because it is the punishment or consequence that makes something bad, the rightness or wrongness of an act is judged purely on the basis of its consequences, not its intent. In one experiment, for example, Piaget (1932) found that children thought it was worse to break 15 cups left behind a door where they could not be seen than to break one cup climbing to get some jam that had been placed out of reach. In other words, the *consequences* were greater in the first case. Significantly, the younger children typically paid little attention to the fact that in the second case the child's *intentions* had been worse — to get at something his mother had intended him not to have. Piaget referred to this stage of moral behavior as the *morality of constraint*.

THE MORALITY OF COOPERATION Piaget argued that, given the appropriate social environment, children will move from the morality of constraint to a *morality of cooperation*. As Piaget's theory suggests, young children will often admit doing the right thing only because it brings a cookie or prevents a punishment. Among older children, *intention* becomes a more important factor in determining right and wrong. In Piaget's experiments, for example, older children were more likely to say that the child climbing up to get the jam had behaved worse, because he was doing something he knew his mother didn't want him to do.

Most sociologists agree that for the majority of people moral behavior is more than a matter of reward and punishment. Most crimes — particularly, but not only, minor ones like petty theft — are not solved, and the offenders are never punished. Even so, most people most of the time do not steal. According to Piaget, the reason they don't is that they realize that stealing is wrong. If everyone stole, nobody would be secure in his or her property, and the world would be a miserable place. Thus, the recognition that stealing prevents cooperation and hurts everyone's quality of life keeps most people from stealing. This is what is meant by the morality of cooperation.

Unfortunately, many people never fully develop the morality of cooperation. Even among some adults, consequence and punishment are the main factors influencing moral behavior. At the same time, some very young children have been shown to understand intention and take it into consideration (Shultz et al., 1980). Morality of constraint always appears to precede morality of cooperation, but the age at which morality of cooperation develops, if it develops at all, is quite variable. Thus, moral reasoning, like other aspects of cognitive development, is heavily influenced by social interaction. This is clearly shown in the work of Lawrence Kohlberg, who has elaborated on Piaget's theories of moral reasoning.

Kohlberg's Stages of Moral Development

Lawrence Kohlberg (1974, 1969) expanded on Piaget's ideas by conducting research in which people were presented with moral dilemmas and asked what they would do and why they would do it. In one such dilemma, a man's wife was dying, and the druggist

Lawrence Kohlberg claimed that human behavior could be classified according to stages of moral development.

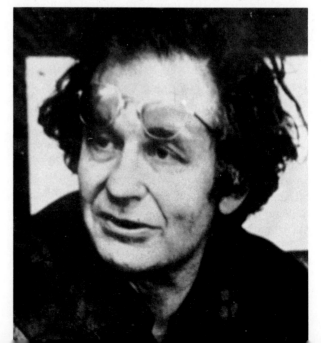

who had invented the only medicine that could save her was charging ten times what the medicine cost to produce — far more than the man could afford. As a result, the man stole the drug. Subjects in Kohlberg's experiments were then asked questions such as whether or not the man was right to steal the drug, and why. It was the "why" part that was of greatest interest to Kohlberg. He found that, based on the *reasons* they gave for their responses to his moral dilemmas, his subjects could be classified into three general levels of moral reasoning, each of which could be subdivided into two more specific stages of moral reasoning. Kohlberg argues that these six stages generally occur in a set sequence: One must pass through Stage 1 before going on to Stage 2, and so forth. However, many people never develop beyond Stage 3 or 4, and some do not even get that far.

THE PRECONVENTIONAL LEVEL Subjects at the preconventional level, consisting of Stages 1 and 2, are self-centered. They view the world in terms of their own interests, needs, and desires, without giving much consideration to the views of others. In Stage 1, *punishment avoidance,* people are concerned with avoiding that which brings punishments or bad consequences. It is very much like Piaget's morality of constraint. In the sample story, a Stage 1 subject might say "Steal the drug if you can get away with it; don't if it looks like you'll get caught." At Stage 2, *need satisfaction,* moral reasoning is a little more developed but remains very self-centered. At this stage, behavior is acceptable if it satisfies your wants or desires. A Stage 2 subject might say the man should steal the drug because his wife needs it, without addressing the druggist's behavior at all.

THE CONVENTIONAL LEVEL At the *conventional level,* which Kohlberg believes characterizes most adult behavior in industrialized countries, behavior is considered right if it is approved by others. Thus, a Stage 3 subject might say stealing is acceptable behavior because the druggist is a bad man, or not acceptable because stealing "isn't nice." A bit more developed is Stage 4, *law and order.* At this stage of moral reasoning, right and wrong are defined on the basis of rules and laws. By and large, such rules and laws are not thought of as changeable, and to violate any of them is nearly always seen as wrong. This group would

be more likely than others to say that stealing the drug is wrong because stealing is against the law. It appears that Stage 4 is the most prevalent in the adult U.S. population (Colby et al., 1983).

THE POSTCONVENTIONAL LEVEL People at the *postconventional level* of morality realize that laws and the approval of others do not simply happen; rather, they often have some basis in people's needs and the general welfare. The stages in this level are harder to define because relatively few people — only about one in five Americans — reach this level (Kohlberg, 1975; see also Colby et al., 1983; Kohlberg, 1986, 1984). In Stage 5, people are governed by *social contracts* — agreements, implicit or explicit, that they enter into for their mutual benefit. People have an obligation, out of fairness, to live up to their end of the bargain. Stage 5 people recognize that laws exist for a reason and that there are bad laws that — even if one obeys them — can and should be changed. In Stage 6, *universal ethical principles,* people live by principles based on human rights that transcend government and laws. Stage 6 people believe that sometimes these ethical or moral principles obligate them to violate laws that work against basic human rights. Dr. Martin Luther King, Jr., is often cited as an example of a person with Stage 6 moral reasoning (Penrod, 1986, p. 74).

Like most of the other theories we have considered, Kohlberg's theory sees social interaction as highly important. Although the sequence always begins with Stage 1 and develops in order, when and how far it develops depends on the messages and examples a child gets from others. In general, urban and well-educated children attain higher levels in Kohlberg's classification system than rural and poorly educated children. Overall, people in modern industrial societies outscore those in rural and less economically developed ones.

Kohlberg's work has been criticized as containing both social class and sex biases. In fact, a general problem with all developmental theories is that the stages may vary among different groups and societies (Danneter, 1984). Middle-class people score higher on Kohlberg's scale than those of lower socioeconomic status, a difference that no doubt reflects both real differences in reasoning and social-class differences in self-expression. Men also score higher than women. This may reflect Kohlberg's system of classification. Men tend to emphasize "justice," which is closely linked to Kohlberg's Stages 5 and 6. Women, however, emphasize "caring," which also reflects a concern with the welfare of others, but is not as highly rated by Kohlberg's coding system (Gilligan, 1982). Thus, both people's actual mode of moral reasoning and the way they express or conceptualize their reasoning are socially influenced.

Moral Reasoning and Moral Behavior

Does moral reasoning affect human behavior? In other words, do people who display different levels of moral reasoning respond differently when confronted with a real-life moral dilemma? Evidence that they do is supplied by a study of student participation in the Free Speech Movement (FSM) at the University of California at Berkeley in 1964, the first of the major student demonstrations of the 1960s.

The Free Speech Movement began when the university announced that it would no longer permit students and student organizations to set up tables in a specified area of the campus. By the time the university capitulated and permitted the tables, its administration building, Sproul Hall, had been taken over by student demonstrators, and a police car had been surrounded by a crowd of several thousand students and abandoned by the officers.

Haan, Smith, and Block (1968) interviewed a large sample of students on the campus, administering moral-reasoning tests developed by Kohlberg and asking the students what they thought of the FSM. In this college population, virtually everyone had reached at least Stage 2, and the sample included people from Stages 2 through 6. Students who supported or participated in the protest were more likely to have achieved certain stages of moral reasoning than other students. Although the majority of students at every stage expressed support of the movement, the percentage who did so was much higher among those at Stages 2, 5, and 6 than among those at Stages 3 or 4. It is not surprising that those at Stage 3 (be nice) or Stage 4 (follow rules) would be less likely to participate.

Of particular interest were the reasons for support or participation given by those at various stages of moral reasoning. The Stage 2 people participated out of self-centered motivation, as Kohlberg's theory predicts: "No university administrator is going to tell *me* what I can and can't do." Protestors in Stage 3 or 4 who supported the movement emphasized bad university administrators who violated the university's own rules or those of the United States Constitution concerning free speech. The Stage 5 and 6 students emphasized the basic human right to free speech. Thus, the probability of supporting the FSM and the reasoning of those who did support it were greatly influenced by where students fell in Kohlberg's six-stage model.

These findings suggest that although moral reasoning is related to behavior, it is more closely related to the process by which people decide *how* to behave when confronted with a moral dilemma such as fellow students requesting their support for the FSM. In fact, a review of the literature on moral development and behavior by Blasi (1980) indicates that the relationship between moral development, as defined by Kohlberg, and moral behavior is far from consistent. Although the majority of studies have found such a link, others have not (see also Kutnick, 1986). Certainly, other factors, such as peer pressures and the particular characteristics of a situation, also have important effects on behavior. However, even if people at different stages of moral development do not always *behave* differently, they do appear to *reason* differently—in real life as well as the laboratory.

Overview of Theories of Socialization

As is evident from the material above, theorists such as Mead, Freud, Erikson, Piaget, and Kohlberg emphasized different aspects of the socialization process, and had different ideas about the roles of nature and nurture and their relative importance in the socialization process. The ideas of these theorists are summarized in Table 5.1. Although they do offer us very different views of the socialization process, these theories cannot be classified as "right" or "wrong." In an important sense, they are all at least partially "right," in that they emphasize different aspects of socialization and development, and seek to under-

TABLE 5.1
Summary of Key Theorists on Socialization and Development

THEORIST	MEAD	FREUD	ERIKSON	PIAGET	KOHLBERG
Socialization viewed as process of:	Learning roles & self-concept through interaction with others.	Struggle between natural drives & societal expectations.	Series of dilemmas to be resolved, relating to social expectations & self-identity.	Development of increasingly sophisticated interpretations of physical & social environment.	Development of increasingly sophisticated moral reasoning, through cognitive development and interaction with others.
Views on nature (natural/biological influences) versus nurture (social influences)	Emphasized nurture; little if any consideration of nature.	Socialization seen as struggle between nature & nurture.	Emphasized nurture, in context of natural development.	Emphasized natural development of reasoning ability, which allows understanding of social environment.	Reasoning seen as joint outcome of natural development and social interaction.

Stages of socialization and development, with typical age range	1. Play Stage:* interaction with specific persons, "I" predominates
	2. Game Stage: interaction with roles, "me" predominates.
		1. Oral (0–1)
		2. Anal (1–3)
		3. Phallic (3–4)
		4. Oedipal (4–6)
		5. Latency (6–11)
		6. Genital (11 & up)
		[See Table 5.1 for further detail.]
			1. Trust vs. mistrust (0–1)
			2. Autonomy vs. doubt, shame (1–2)
			3. Initiative vs. guilt (3–5)
			4. Industry vs. inferiority (6–11)
			5. Identity vs. role confusion (12–18)
			6. Intimacy vs. isolation (young adult)
			7. Generativity vs. self-absorption (middle adult)
			8. Integrity vs. despair (old age)
				1. Sensorimotor (0–2)
				2. Preoperational (2–7)
				3. Concrete operations (7–11)
				4. Formal operations (12 & up)
					Preconventional Level*
					  Stage 1: punishment avoidance
					  Stage 2: need satisfaction
					Conventional Level
					  Stage 3: nice person
					  Stage 4: law and order
					Postconventional Level
					  Stage 5: social contracts
					  Stage 6: universal ethical principles

* Stages are not strongly linked to age; they depend on social interaction.

stand different processes that contribute to the overall course of socialization and development.

Agents of Socialization

All the theories that we have discussed agree that significant others play a prominent role in the socialization process. What we have not yet addressed is the fact that *social institutions* also play an important role.

In fact, both people and institutions can act as **agents of socialization.** Agents of socialization influence the development of people's attitudes, beliefs, self-images, and behavior. In a sense, it could be said that they carry out the process of socialization, interacting with the individual in a way that permits him or her to become a participating member of human society. Agents of socialization may or may not have the primary purpose of carrying out the socialization process, but they always have that effect.

Who They Are

The most important agents of socialization are the family (particularly parents), the school, religion, peers, and the media. Some of these—the family, religion, the school—are institutions whose manifest function is, at least in part, to be agents of socialization. They exist at least partly to provide children with knowledge, values, or—most often—both. These are not the only influential agents of socialization, however. Peers and the mass media also play an important role. Neither peers nor the media exist for the *purpose* of socialization; that is, socialization is not their manifest function. However, they do have the *effect* of shaping knowledge, beliefs, and attitudes—in some cases, just as much as the family, religion, or school. Thus, socialization can be described as an important latent function of peers and the media.

The Family　In the early years, the family is the most important agent of socialization. This is especially true of parents, but it is also true to a lesser extent of older siblings who are present. More than anyone else, the parents define the attitudes and beliefs of a young child. To a large extent, truth to preschool children is what their parents tell them. Parents remain important as agents of socialization throughout childhood and adolescence, although as children age, parents increasingly share their role with other agents of socialization.

The effects of socialization in the family are often lifelong. The family's religion usually becomes the child's, and the child's political attitudes, world view, and lifestyle are substantially influenced by those of the family. Children who experience undesirable behaviors or attitudes in the home are more likely than other children to repeat them in adulthood. Child and spouse abuse, alcoholism and drug abuse, and racial prejudice are all passed on through the family.

Even within the same family, however, not all children are treated the same way. Boys and girls usually undergo a different socialization experience, as we shall see in a later chapter. First-born and only children receive greater attention and often grow up to be greater achievers. A child who is highly active from infancy on is usually treated differently than one who is less active. The child's size and health status also

influence parental behavior. Thus, although certain common patterns appear in every family, even brothers or sisters in the same family do not have exactly the same socialization experience.

The School　As we shall see in Chapter 14, the school is an institution with a profound effect not only on children's knowledge, but also on their self-image, their understanding of reality, and their mode of reasoning. The school also plays an important role in teaching students the beliefs and values of their society. The role of the school in the socialization process has become more important in modern industrial societies, as the amount of specialized technical and scientific knowledge has expanded beyond what parents could possibly teach in the home. Some of the teaching of both knowledge and values that used to occur in the home today takes place in the school. Even more recently, as the two-career family and single-parent family have become more commonplace, school influences children at an early age in the form of day care.

Religion　The influence of religion as an agent of socialization varies widely. Although most Americans identify with some organized religion, only about half attend religious services at some time during the typical week. Of those who do, however, many bring their children to religion classes, and some children attend religious rather than public schools. Among people who are religious, religion is a powerful agent of socialization because it specifies what is right and what is wrong. Moreover, in religious families, religion and the family frequently (though not always) give similar messages. Religion is an important influence on the values and beliefs of the parents, who join with it to pass those values on to their children.

Peers　Peers begin to be an influence at a very young age, as children form friendships with other children. However, it is in the junior-high- and high-school years that peer influence is the greatest, as young people seek to establish their independence by turning to influences other than the home and the school. Although peer subcultures are often at odds with those of the parents and the school, peers in another sense demand a tremendous amount of conformity. Often,

BLOOM COUNTY   by Berke Breathed

The mass media have become increasingly important agents of socialization in modern societies.

little deviation from the peer-group norm in dress, speech, attitude, and behavior is tolerated. The price the peer group exacts for nonconformity is high: ridicule or ostracism precisely at a time when a young person must gain acceptance from a group outside the family in order to establish independence from it. Because of this need and because of the strong pressure for conformity, the influence of the peer group on attitudes and behaviors is, for a time during adolescence, very high—perhaps greater than that of any other agent of socialization. This effect is greatest in the areas of dress, speech, entertainment preferences, and leisure activity. Often it can extend to attitudes and behaviors in the areas of sexuality and drug and alcohol use. However, it is somewhat weaker (though often still significant) in such areas as religious and political beliefs.

The Media   In recent decades, the media have become very influential as agents of socialization. This is especially true of television. The average American child spends well over 3 hours per day watching television—in many cases, more time than he or she spends talking with parents or siblings. The spread of cable television and VCRs has probably enhanced the influence of the media by encouraging people to watch more television.

THE MEDIA AND BEHAVIOR   Although there is

great debate over precisely how television influences attitudes and behavior, there is no doubt that television has become an important means by which young people come to understand their world. As children grow into adolescence, rock music and motion pictures also play some role in the socialization process. Again, there is considerable debate as to which is cause and which is effect, but definite parallels exist between the ideas expressed in the lyrics of rock music and the attitudes and values of youth. In the 1960s and early 1970s, for example, a rebellious and idealistic youth culture was accompanied—and perhaps reinforced—by rebellious and idealistic music, featuring such songs as "The Times They Are a-Changin'," "Blowing in the Wind," "Revolution," and "Volunteers of America."

One area of particular concern has been media portrayals of sexuality and violence. Most Americans have seen thousands of people killed in television dramas, and there is some evidence that this desensitizes people to violence and, at least in the short term, increases aggressive behavior (National Institutes of Mental Health, 1982). Whether or to what degree this increases the overall level of violence in American society remains unclear. American children, like children in many other societies where television is widespread, also view a great deal of actual or implied sexual activity. However, in contrast to most European countries, in the United States television provides little information concerning how to avoid the undesired consequences of sexual activity, such as unwanted pregnancy or sexually transmitted diseases (Jones et al., 1986). Again in contrast to practice in most European countries, the advertising of condoms was forbidden on American television until 1987, and even now the great majority of stations refuse to accept such advertising. This gives American youngsters a mixed message — sex is glamorized but its consequences are not discussed frankly.

ONE-WAY COMMUNICATION   A significant difference between the media and all other agents of socialization is that the media usually communicate one way. Unlike all other agents of socialization, the people we experience through television, movies, radio, and music videos are *not* personal acquaintances, and we cannot really exchange ideas with them. All of the communication is in one direction — from the media to the viewer or listener.

What They Do

How do agents of socialization shape the thinking and behavior of those being socialized? Social scientists have focused on three main processes: *selective exposure and modeling, reward and punishment,* and *nurturance and identification.* Let us consider each.

Selective Exposure   One of the ways that agents of socialization influence attitudes and behaviors is through selective exposure. Children are exposed to those behaviors and attitudes considered desirable and sheltered from those regarded as undesirable. Parents do this by the ways they speak and behave in front of their children and by the reading material and television shows to which they expose their children. Parents try to maximize exposure to "good influences" and protect their children from "bad influences."

It is not only the parents who do this. Peer cultures, for example, expose children to certain modes of dress, speech, and behavior, and not to others. The school attempts — through the content of classroom materials, for example — to expose children to sets of ideas and role models that are supportive of core cultural values. In the United States, such values include individual rights, hard work, and private ownership. Even the media, in the content of their entertainment, largely reinforce such values, although there may be other areas — most notably sex and violence — where

their content differs from what children experience in the home.

Modeling   We know that children do repeat behavior to which they are repeatedly and systematically exposed, through a process called **modeling** (Bandura, 1977). Modeling begins with attention to the behavior of significant others and with retention of the images of such behavior in a person's memory. The next stage is imitation, or reproduction, of that behavior. Eventually, however, this goes beyond mere imitation: The behavior is repeated until it becomes a matter of habit, and it is repeated in situations beyond that in which it was originally observed (Bandura, 1977). Moreover, the child comes to develop attitudes and beliefs that are supportive of the behavior. Obviously, you cannot imitate behaviors to which you are not exposed, which is what makes selective exposure such a powerful tool of socialization. Of course, what agents of socialization *say* and what they *do* are not always the same, and when there is a discrepancy between the two, what they do seems to have a greater effect than what they say (Bryan and Walbek, 1970a, 1970b; Rushton, 1975). If, for example, a parent preaches patience but shows a child impatience, the child will likely learn impatience to a greater extent than patience.

Reward and Punishment   When children imitate and repeat behaviors they learned from significant others, these significant others respond with approval. Approval can be verbal or nonverbal, sometimes taking the form of a concrete reward, such as a cookie or a trip to the beach. Such rewards reinforce the modeling of the significant others' behavior (Sears et al., 1957). Thus, the processes of reward and punishment (Skinner, 1938, 1968) reinforce what is already being learned through selective exposure and modeling. Both behavior and the expression of attitudes can be rewarded or punished by agents of socialization. Because merely expressing an attitude increases the probability that we will come to believe that attitude (see Festinger and Carlsmith, 1959), the process of reward and punishment acts to shape not only behavior, but attitudes and beliefs as well (Insko and Melson, 1969).

Reward and punishment are not always as obvious as giving or denying a child a cookie. Peer groups, for example, have a variety of ways to reward conformity and punish nonconformity. A friendly slap on the back or an invitation to join a group activity may be a reward for an approved action or viewpoint. Conversely, peer groups can be very harsh in their punishment of nonconformity, through ridicule, collective expressions of anger, or — worst of all — ostracism. In fact, with the exception of the mass media, which can only communicate one way, all agents of socialization use some form of reward and punishment to shape attitudes and behavior.

Nurturance and Identification Both of the processes discussed above — selective exposure and modeling, and reward and punishment — are more effective if the child *identifies* with the person who is acting as an agent of socialization. By **identification,** we mean positive feelings toward that individual that lead the child to want to be like that person. These feelings are built in large part by the agent of socialization's nurturant behavior toward the child. These agents love and care about the child, and, in the case of parents, are the child's main source of support. When they help the child, he or she has an obligation to cooperate. All of this leads the child to love, admire, and want to please these agents.

Of all the means that peer groups use to punish nonconformity, ostracism is probably the most extreme.

Conflicting Messages

Agents of socialization do not always give a person the same message. The kind of person your parents want you to be is not always the same kind of person your teachers, your clergy, or your peers want you to be. The media, too, present you with images of the ideal person, which may vary widely depending on what you read or watch. Handling these conflicting messages and expectations is a very important part of the socialization process. How do you respond when your parents want you to go to a family gathering, your athletic coach wants you to work out, your teacher expects you to do homework, and your friends want you to party with them, *all at the same time?* More fundamentally, how do you respond when different agents of socialization want you to be a different kind of person? What happens when you have to decide whether you want to be fun-loving and carefree or serious and achievement-oriented? These choices present both opportunities and difficulties.

Conflicting Agents and Stress Clearly, these conflicting pressures from significant others can be a real source of stress in life. For many, they are the first experience with the condition of role conflict introduced in Chapter 4. In some cases, it is simply impossible to do what all of the agents of socialization are demanding. When this happens, there are two possible responses. One is to try to do part of what each agent of socialization wants: go to the family event this week, party with your friends next week, work out at some other available time, and stay up late to finish your homework. If the demands are too many, you can wind up exhausted or burned out, but most people seem to manage without reaching these extremes.

One strategy people use is to cite the demands of one agent of socialization as the reason for not complying with those of another: "My parents say I can't go with you because we have to go to my family reunion," or "If I don't go to this dance when all my friends are going, people will think there's something wrong with me!" The alternative is to block out or withdraw from some agents of socialization. To please one's parents, you may stop seeing your friends and classmates socially. Or, to please your friends, you may skip your homework or even drop out of school. To use this mode of adaptation with the most important agents of socialization, such as family, school, and peers, is more risky. Often it results in a poorly developed personality.

Conflicts among Agents   The values that different agents of socialization emphasize vary enough in some cases to create conflict, not only within the individual being socialized, but also among the agents of socialization. What happens, for example, when two important agents of socialization — such as the family and the school — want to expose someone selectively to different and conflicting ideas? As shown in the box "School and Library Book Controversies," such conflicts can be explosive.

Just as the content of the messages we get from various agents of socialization differs, so does the process of interaction by which the messages are given. Parents, teachers, and clergy teach from a position of authority, whereas peers do so from a position of equality. Peer interaction is the first interaction that occurs on an equal basis. To be integrated successfully into peer cultures, children must discover how to learn from equals as well as from authority figures.

Another example can be seen in the way the school interacts with the individual. As noted earlier, parents normally interact with their children from an orientation of unconditional love. Children are important because of *who they are,* and, at home, a child is a special person in the family. At school, however, a child is one of the crowd, subject to standard rules and expectations. Moreover, children in school are rewarded because of *what they do* — nothing is automatic. This is a sharp transition for many children that requires some adjustment.

Conflicting Agents and Choice   Although the conflicting messages of different agents of socialization can be a source of considerable stress, they also make choices possible in life. Indeed, they are largely what teaches us how to make choices. Think about it: Would you really want to live in a society where your parents, your school, your friends, and the mass media all gave you exactly the same messages? Would freedom have any meaning in such a society?

The different messages of different agents of socialization also help us to develop beliefs, values, and skills in different areas of life. Political, religious, and goal-related attitudes are largely learned in the home, and aspects of lifestyle relating to entertainment and leisure, and skills related to cooperation, intimacy, and interpersonal relations, are more likely to be learned from peers (Davies and Kandel, 1981; Youniss, 1980). Work habits and how to participate in organizations are largely learned in school (Jackson, 1968; Bowles and Gintis, 1976).

Conflicting Agents and Social Change   In addition to offering choices at the individual level, the different messages of different agents of socialization perform an important function at the societal level: They are an important source of social change. As was noted in Chapter 4, several fundamental changes in the values of Americans concerning sex roles, discrimination, and self-fulfillment occurred in the 1960s and 1970s. Much of the change in attitudes began among middle-class youth and minority groups, and then spread through the larger society (Yankelovich, 1974, 1981). On college campuses, and in some high schools, a strong peer subculture developed that espoused the new values. In effect, one agent of socialization — the peer group — was teaching a very different set of values from those that other agents were teaching. Gradually, major elements in the media also began to convey this message, as can be seen in much of the era's popular music and in movies such as *The Graduate, M*A*S*H,* and *Easy Rider.* Many parents tried to protect their children from these "bad influences." Thus, there was a stronger conflict than usual among different agents of socialization, leading some to talk about a "generation gap." Yet, the messages coming from peer groups and from parts of the media offered young people new choices, and their acceptance of some (though by no means all) of these alternatives led to several important changes in American culture.

Another major source of social change during the 1960s was young minority-group members. For many African Americans, religion operated as an agent of socialization that favored a new response to their minority status. While some black ministers had been taught not to "make trouble," a new generation of-

School and Library Book Controversies: Agents of Socialization in Conflict

Q *uestion:* What do *Huckleberry Finn; Our Bodies, Ourselves; The Grapes of Wrath; Black Boy; The Canterbury Tales;* and a host of history, science, and family-life textbooks have in common?
Answer: Somewhere in the United States, somebody has tried to ban them, either from the classroom or from library shelves.

Controversies have erupted over school or library books in hundreds of communities throughout the United States in the past few decades. In a few cases, the conflict has even become violent. During the 1974–75 school year, some coal miners in West Virginia were so angry about the books being used in their children's schools that they went on strike and shut down the mines for an extended time. Children were withdrawn from school, and a number of school buildings were vandalized. This case was unusual only for the severity of the conflict. In fact, not only rural areas but big cities and "sophisticated" college towns as well have experienced attempts to ban certain books from the school curriculum or the library. A national survey of high-school librarians in 1982 showed that about one-third had experienced some attempt to get books out of the library; such efforts were most common in the Northeast. About half of the attempts to remove books from school libraries were successful (*The New York Times*, 1982).

The 12 most frequently censored books as of 1988 were the following (Mitgang, 1988):

Go Ask Alice, by parents of an anonymous teenage girl
Catcher in the Rye, by J. D. Salinger
Our Bodies, Ourselves, by Boston Women's Health Collective
Forever, by Judy Blume
Of Mice and Men, by John Steinbeck
My Darling, My Hamburger, by Paul Zindel
The Grapes of Wrath, by John Steinbeck
Huckleberry Finn, by MTwain
The Learning Tree, by Gordon Parks
1984, by George Orwell
Black Boy, by Richard Wright
The Canterbury Tales, by Geoffrey Chaucer

Why do school and library books generate such intense and widespread controversy? The answer lies in disagreement among different agents of socialization concerning what children should be exposed to. Some of the disagreement is between teachers and parents. Often teachers want to expose children to the ideas contained in great literary works, while parents regard the ideas, language, or behavior depicted in the books as setting a bad example.

Some critics, for example, object to *Huckleberry Finn* because it contains language that is considered racist. Their opponents argue that the book presents a certain historical context, and in fact makes an important statement against racism. What is more important — the risk that children may imitate the language, or the possibility that they will benefit from the message? Even more controversial are books like *Our Bodies, Ourselves,* where some parents and teachers cannot agree on the desirability of the message itself. Many people want children to be exposed only to material consistent with their own viewpoint, which is impossible in a community with divergent views.

The fight is not just between parents and teachers. Even parents do not agree on what they want their children exposed to because their values differ. What some parents regard as a "bad influence," others regard as a "broadened perspective." Thus, school boards have been placed in a position whereby they will anger teachers and some parents if they do ban a book and other parents if they do not. The mere fact that such controversies are so common and can become so intense is powerful evidence of the extent to which agents of socialization engage in selective exposure.

---

fered a new message of resistance. To many, this message made a lot more sense than merely tolerating discrimination, and thus religion became an important force in the growth of the civil rights movement (Morris, 1984). Thus, once again, the different messages of different agents of socialization became an important source of social change.

Both of these examples show that conflicting messages from different agents of socialization create choices that can lead to major social changes. Thus, part of the way society adapts to new realities is through young people's choices among the different messages of different agents of socialization. The examples illustrate a second point. What often appears to be a failure of socialization to bring the desired outcome is not that at all. Rather, it may reflect the success of another agent of socialization. Many parents in the 1950s—black and white—did not teach their children to participate in such activities as street demonstrations and sit-ins. When their children later did such things, they often asked "What went wrong?" In fact, it would be an oversimplification to say that the young people who did such things were going against what they had been taught. Rather, they were making a choice among the different things that different agents of socialization had taught them. Thus, the white, middle-class student protester could be seen as conforming to the expectations of the peer group and parts of the media, and the young, black civil rights activist could similarly be seen as conforming to the expectations of religious leaders and the peer group.

Adult Socialization

Thus far, we have spoken of the socialization process primarily with reference to how it works in childhood and adolescence. It is in childhood that we encounter the most new roles and new situations, and thus it is in childhood that the socialization process is experienced most intensely. For this reason, childhood socialization is sometimes referred to as *primary socialization*. Socialization, however, does not end when you become an adult. Although many attitudes, beliefs, and behavior patterns have become fairly well established by this time, the process of socialization continues throughout life. Every time we enter a new situation or learn to play a new role, we go through a socialization process.

One example of adult socialization can be seen in the parenting process. While parents are socializing their children concerning how to take care of themselves and participate in society, their children are also socializing *them*. The adults are, in effect, learning the role of parent. In part, parents learn this role from

their children, as they find out what "works" and what doesn't in the rearing of their children.

Life-Cycle Roles

The adult life cycle presents us with numerous new situations that require the learning of new roles. In each of these, a socialization process occurs. Among these situations are leaving home to live on your own, entering college, beginning a career, changing jobs, getting married or cohabiting, becoming a parent, getting divorced or "breaking up," adjusting when your children grow up and leave home, retiring, and losing parents or a spouse through death. Not everyone experiences all of these things, and others experience some of them more than once. Thus, these changes should not be thought of as a clearly defined cycle through which everyone passes. In fact, the life cycle has become less uniform today than it was in the past. Even so, every adult experiences *some* of these changes, and every change requires a socialization process. For purposes of illustration, we shall examine the socialization processes that occur when you get a new job or start a family. Other situations requiring socialization are discussed in later chapters.

Getting a Job A good deal of socialization occurs when you begin your career. You must learn what it really means to be a teacher, a salesperson, a police officer, a lawyer, or an accountant. If the job was preceded by a period of training, you must learn what part of the training applies and what part doesn't. For many people starting out, it is distressing to hear "Forget everything you learned in————." (Fill in the blank with "education school," "police academy," "law school," "sales training," or whatever.) To survive in any career or profession, you must learn the norms of that career or profession and how to play the role in an acceptable way. To do so requires learning and accepting the profession's definition of that career as opposed to the public's. The meaning of a "good cop" from the viewpoint of other police officers may be different from the public's meaning of that term or from the meaning learned in the police academy. Similarly, a teacher who meets only the expectations of his or her students, and not those of other teachers, is not likely to feel accepted as a teacher and may doubt his or her success in that role.

This leads to a second point: Every place of employment has its own subculture, which must be learned by any new employee who wants to succeed. To be effective, even new supervisors must learn this subculture. To complicate matters further, there may be more than one subculture to which the new employee must accommodate. He or she must please not only co-workers, but also supervisors, whose norms may be quite different. For some, there are also customers, clients, voters, patients, or students to keep happy. In a very real way, all of these different groups act as agents of socialization, and their messages concerning the work role are usually different.

Marriage and Family Changes   No matter how much two people may be "in love," getting married or even cohabiting requires major adjustments that in turn require a good deal of socialization. Different ideas concerning such things as money, orderliness of the house, division of housework, and even food preferences can be major sources of conflict unless both parties can learn to compromise or find a mutually satisfactory way of doing things. Those who have lived on their own experience a loss of freedom. Those who have not run the risk of dependency. Women, in particular, who have lived with their parents for all their lives until getting married risk becoming dependent on their husbands the same way they were dependent

upon their parents. Having to deal with these issues comes as a shock to too many Americans, who place great emphasis on the concept of romantic love. Clearly the most important agent of socialization at this stage is the partner. However, to adjust successfully to this new reality, most young people must also interact with peers who are facing the same issues. Parents (and now in-laws) continue to act as agents of socialization at this stage and can be either helpful or a source of additional problems.

BECOMING A PARENT   When people become parents, time management can become a critical issue, particularly if both parents are employed full time. Conflicts between spouses or with parents over child rearing can require additional adjustment. As noted, children are important agents of socialization concerning how to be a parent. Typically, parents and peers also play a major role in this socialization process, as do the media, with their abundant material on parenting techniques.

An increasing number of American women now enter the role of parent before marriage, in which case they must both raise and support the child by themselves. Teenagers who become parents, for whom this may be the first adult role to which they must become socialized, must learn this difficult role under highly adverse conditions.

RETURN TO SINGLEHOOD   Another new role that large numbers of Americans now face is returning to singlehood after a divorce or the end of a "live-in" relationship. About half of all marriages in the United States now end in divorce, so this is an adjustment that a large number of people must make. This adjustment is the subject of Professor Diane Vaughan's *Personal Journey into Sociology*. As Professor Vaughan illustrates, an important part of this socialization process is the development of a new (uncoupled) self-image or identity.

Resocialization in Total Institutions

A less ordinary type of adult socialization, which some experience and others do not, is resocialization in

Marriage requires a great deal of adjustment, which occurs through a socializaton process.

Total institutions carry out the process of resocialization.

total institutions. The term **total institution,** developed by Goffman (1961), refers to any group or organization that has almost total, continuous control over the individual and that attempts to erase the effects of the individual's previous socialization and instill a new set of values, habits, and beliefs. This process is referred to as **resocialization.** There are many examples of total institutions. One is the military, which takes people who generally believe that killing is wrong and seeks to convert them into fighting machines who will kill and risk their lives on orders, without asking questions. Mental hospitals, which use their total control over their patients to replace the attitudes, beliefs, and behavior patterns defined as "mental illness" with "normal" ones, are another example. So are prisons, which seek to eliminate criminal habits and tendencies and convert offenders into law-abiding citizens. Other examples are religious cults, "deprogramming" aimed at weaning people away from religious cults, prisoner-of-war camps, many boarding schools, orphanages, some residential substance-abuse programs, reform schools, some nursing homes, and the environments created by kidnappers.

The Korean War: A Case Study How do total institutions accomplish this? It is often said that they *brainwash* people. Thus, American prisoners of war on occasion defected to the North Koreans and North Vietnamese; Patty Hearst joined her kidnappers in robbing a bank; peace-loving people have turned into fierce fighters after being drafted and put through boot camp. Actually, though, what goes on in total institu-tions—"brainwashing," if you will—bears some striking similarities to ordinary socialization processes. Consider, for example, studies of the "brainwashing" of American prisoners of war during the Korean War. It is said that the Chinese prisoner-of-war camps were especially effective at this. How did they do it?

Studies of Americans who returned from Chinese P.O.W. camps revealed several important findings (Schein, 1957, 1961; Bauer, 1957). First of all, reward and punishment were used. Those who behaved and expressed ideas consistent with the desires of their captors were given somewhat greater freedom, whereas those who rebelled were placed in solitary confinement and, in some cases, were physically punished. Second, selective exposure was used. Some P.O.W.'s were allowed to spend as many hours as they wanted reading in libraries, as good a way as any to pass what was essentially a very boring time. These libraries, of course, were stocked only with materials sympathetic to the Chinese and North Korean viewpoints. Contacts with their own culture were forbidden to the prisoners. Mail, for example, was not allowed to go through. The one exception was "bad mail"—unpaid bills, repossession notices, "Dear John" letters. The effect of this program, of course, was to foster a positive image of the Chinese and North Koreans while isolating P.O.W.'s from all but the unpleasant aspects of their own background.

Most effective of all, perhaps, was the Chinese policy of "lenience" (Schein, 1961, pp. 286–289). This was intended to create an atmosphere of nurturance, a sense of obligation. Most American P.O.W.'s had originally been captured in North Korea and were later taken to Chinese P.O.W. camps. Because they had been captured in the immediate war zone, conditions in Korea were harsh. Long forced marches were the rule, and they were fatal to many P.O.W.'s. Scarce food and clothing went to Chinese and North Korean soldiers before it went to prisoners. In the Chinese prison camps behind the lines, however, conditions were somewhat better. Food and shelter were generally adequate, and forced marches were unnecessary. The Chinese military used this to considerable advantage. "Look how much better we treat you," they said. "We care about you and wouldn't treat you the way

PERSONAL JOURNEY INTO SOCIOLOGY

Uncoupling

I was married for 20 years. As I reflected on the relationship after our separation, the marriage seemed to have been coming slowly apart for the last 10. Certainly we had our good times, but I could retrospectively pick out turning points—moments when the relationship changed, times when the distance between us increased. These turning points did not hinge around arguments or the typical emotional catastrophes that beset any relationship. Instead, they appeared to be related to changes in each of our social worlds. For example, I started college because I realized I was never going to have the steady companionship of my partner and needed something of my own to do. This step, innocently taken, changed me—and us. As our marriage aged, we reacted to our difficulties by altering our relation to the world around us. Those changes, in turn, affected the relationship, changing us as individuals and our relationship to each other.

What's more, when I thought about our relationship in terms of our maneuverings in the social world, it seemed as if our marriage had eroded slowly and steadily over time in a regular, orderly way. Although we personally experienced the ending of the relationship as chaotic and disruptive, its ending took on a kind of social rhythm. That an experience could be orderly and disorderly at the

Diane Vaughan is Associate Professor of Sociology, Boston College. Her research interests are the sociology of organizations, deviance and social control, and transitions.

She is the author of *Controlling Unlawful Organizational Behavior: Social Structure and Corporate Misconduct* (University of Chicago Press, 1983) and *Uncoupling: Turning Points in Intimate Relationships* (Oxford University Press, 1986).

same time was counterintuitive. Perhaps this orderliness was because ours was a long marriage, and thus its ending extended over a long period, giving the appearance of an orderly dissolution. Perhaps it was a natural reflection of my occupation then: a graduate student in sociology, being trained to look for order.

During the same period, I came across an article describing marriage as a process in which two individuals renegotiate who they are with respect to each other and the world around them. They restructure their lives around each other. They create common friends, belongings, memories, and a common future. They redefine themselves as a couple, in their own eyes and in the eyes of others, who respond to the coupled identity they are creating. They are invited out as a twosome, mail comes addressed to both, the IRS taxes them jointly. Single friends may hesitate to call, while the two people are readily incorporated into the social world of those who also are coupled. The coupled identity they create is constantly reaffirmed, not only by the words and deeds of others, but also by the way others come to take the relationship for granted. This continual public confirmation gives them a stable location in the social world and validates their identity.

These ideas immediately captured my interest, for what appeared to have happened as my own relationship deteriorated was a reversal of this process: We slowly and over time began redefining ourselves as separate people. Rather than an abrupt ending, ours appeared to have been a gradual transition.

you were treated in Korea." Implicit, and sometimes explicit, was the threat that the prisoners could always be sent back to the far harsher conditions of Korea. This, of course, accomplished two things. First, many P.O.W.'s became grateful for being treated better in China than in Korea and wanted to cooperate for that reason alone. Second, the fear of being sent back to Korea was enough to get most of the rest to cooperate, even if they didn't really want to.

We see, then, that the prisoner-of-war camp used some of the same techniques that are used in ordinary socialization processes—selective exposure

Long before we physically separated, we had been separating socially—developing separate friends, experiences, and futures. We reacted to our changing relationship in ways that altered the definitions that we held of ourselves and that others held of us.

In order to answer the questions raised by my own experience, I began interviewing people about how their relationships ended. I wanted to learn about the relationships of people who had lived together as well as those who were married. Thus, my interest was not divorce, but uncoupling—how people living together in a sexually intimate relationship (gay and straight couples as well as the married) make transitions out of their relationships. I began collecting biographies of individual relationships. In interviews, I asked people to tell me about their relationships, beginning with the moment they first sensed something was wrong. I tape recorded their narratives, interjecting questions.

As a result of my inquiry, I discovered that uncoupling occurs in a uniform way—a describable pattern that is the same regardless of sexual preference or marital status. In a reversal of coupling, the partners redefine themselves, both in their own eyes and in the eyes of others, as separate entities once again. Getting out of a relationship entails a redefinition of self at several levels: in the private thoughts of the individual, between partners, and in the larger social context in which the relationship exists. Uncoupling is complete when the partners have defined themselves and are defined by others as separate and independent of each other—when being partners is no longer a major source of identity.

Typically, uncoupling happens like this: One person, the initiator, becomes discontented with the relationship. This person begins lobbying for change and, unable to achieve it, unintentionally begins responding to his or her personal problems in a way that begins to divide the couple. The initiator begins socially and psychologically leaving the relationship. At some point, what began unintentionally becomes intentional: The initiator, though deeply affected by the possibility of the loss, wants out.

By the time the partner realizes something is seriously wrong, the initiator has already gone in many ways. The initiator has mourned the relationship, thought about living apart, begun creating a separate lifestyle and, in many cases, experimented with it. The partner, in contrast, has done none of these things. In fact, it is often at the moment of separation that the partner first realizes the relationship is in trouble. At this point, the initiator has been in transition for some time, and the partner's efforts to save the relationship are likely to fail. The rejected partner then begins the transition that the initiator began long before: acknowledging the problems, lobbying for change, mourning the relationship, developing separate friends, seeking alternatives to the relationship, and gradually preparing for a life alone.

When relationships come apart, both people make the same transition, but it starts and ends at different times for each. Consequently, understanding the impact of uncoupling hinges upon whether one is the initiator or partner in a relationship. Initiators have the advantage of time—time to think about and, in many instances, prepare for a life without the partner. When separation occurs, the partner is thrust into an unwanted new life for which he or she is socially and psychologically unprepared. Admittedly, identifying who is the initiator and who is being left behind is not so easy in some cases. Over the course of a long relationship, these roles may be passed back and forth, with one person assuming the role of initiator at one time and the other acting to end the relationship at another. How these roles get passed back and forth is, in fact, one of the more intriguing aspects of the uncoupling process.

and modeling, reward and punishment, and nurturance and identification. The same is true of other total institutions. Boarding schools, for example, seek to isolate children from bad influences (selective exposure) and use reward and punishment and a message that "We care about you more than the people out there who are trying to use you" to shape behavior, and—over the longer run—attitudes and beliefs.

Ordinary Socialization versus Total Institutions

There are, however, four very important differences between resocialization in total institutions and ordinary socialization. First, the total institution seeks to eliminate the effects of previous socialization, whereas ordinary agents of socialization do not usually do this. Second, the total institution seeks to resocialize the individual strictly in accordance with its objectives. In short, the goal is to make a "good soldier," "sane person," "communist sympathizer," or "cooperative inmate" out of the person. Thus, the objectives of the total institution, as opposed to the wishes or self-interests of the individual, are the entire purpose behind the process. Third, the total institution has complete, round-the-clock control of the individual and therefore does not have to compete with other agents of socialization. Finally, some total institutions, including the P.O.W. camps in the Korean War, use fatigue and physical brutality as additional ways of wearing people down. Endless questions and indoctrination and sleep deprivation are common. Eventually, the individual becomes so worn down that he or she has no energy left to resist the forced socialization, at least outwardly. Despite these very important differences, it remains true that there are important parallels between resocialization in total institutions and ordinary socialization.

Functionalist and Conflict Perspectives on Socialization

We shall conclude our discussion of the socialization process by briefly considering some opposing ideas from the functionalist and conflict perspectives about the meaning of socialization.

The Functionalist Perspective

From the viewpoint of the individual, we have already considered the functionalist view of socialization. We noted that the socialization process meets the individual's needs for social interaction and that the process teaches that individual what he or she needs to know in order to participate in the society. The functionalist perspective, however, is most concerned with the ways in which socialization contributes to the perpetuation and strengthening of the *society*.

On this level, the socialization process plays several important roles. It provides knowledge about survival and adaptation to the environment that must be passed from generation to generation in order for the society to survive. Closely related to the preservation of knowledge is the preservation of *culture*. If, as functionalists believe, American values and beliefs are basically well adapted to America's social, physical, and technological environment, then there must be a way to pass along those values and beliefs from generation to generation. Socialization is the means by which this occurs.

The socialization process also promotes *consensus* and *solidarity* by teaching core values upon which people in a society generally agree. Because functionalists see such consensus and solidarity as the basis for human cooperation, there must be a way to assure that one generation's consensus is passed along to the next. Again, the socialization process is the means by which this occurs.

Functionalists also realize that society must adapt to changes in its physical, social, and technological environments. Here again, the socialization process offers one way by which this can occur. Because different agents of socialization offer different messages, the individual has the opportunity to choose the message that promotes change. In this regard, the youthful peer group as an agent of socialization plays an especially important role.

The Conflict Perspective

Functionalists see the socialization process as a means of preserving and strengthening society; conflict theorists see it largely as a weapon in group conflict. They argue that the socialization process very often serves the interests of the dominant group in a society. It does this in two ways: by supporting practices and ideologies that serve dominant-group interests, and by *social channeling*.

Support of Dominant-Group Interests Obedience, compliance, and hierarchy are, to varying degrees, important themes in the socialization practices of most societies. Parents, teachers, and clergy generally teach children to accept rules and societal values. Conflict theorists see this process as preserving values, beliefs, and practices that serve the interests of the dominant group. To the conflict theorist, the socialization process teaches young people *not* to ask "Why do we have to do these things?", "Do things have to be the way they are?", or "Would a different kind of society be better?" Rather, the dominant theme that most parents, schools, and religions teach is that "Ours is a wonderful society and a great country: Learn its values and be grateful you were born here."

Significantly, this message is not just taught in the United States. It is, in fact, taught in nearly every society. And, conflict theorists argue, its effect in every society is to get people to concentrate on what is good about their societies and ignore what is bad. This, of course, inhibits social change and works to the advantage of whatever group is already most advantaged in the society.

Social Change Sometimes, though, rebellions occur in virtually every society. Why does this happen? According to conflict theorists, it happens because different groups in the society have self-interests that conflict with those of the dominant group. When these groups attain a group consciousness or class consciousness, they develop subcultures that promote ideologies that oppose the dominant ideology. Thus, they can become agents of socialization in opposition to those of the dominant group.

We have already seen examples of this: A youthful peer culture or a black church can offer a message different from that of other agents of socialization. The conflict perspective makes two points concerning this process that we have not yet considered. First, these different messages come out of subcultures that developed in response to the self-interests of a group that opposes the dominant group's wishes or interests. Second, the social change that occurs often enhances the interests of subordinate groups in society (like racial minorities or young people). Thus, agents of socialization that arise in opposition to the dominant pattern of socialization offer a means by which society can attain a fairer and more equal power structure.

Social Channeling According to conflict theorists, the second key way that the socialization process serves the interests of dominant groups is through **social channeling.** This concept states that children born into any social group will be prepared for roles in life that fit that group's position in the larger society. Thus, for example, women are prepared either for housework or for the lower-paying jobs that they have traditionally held. Minority-group members experience a socialization process that assures that their education will be limited and poor, thus preparing them for a life of intermittent employment and low-paying jobs. Finally, lower- and working-class children, regardless of race and sex, are taught values that prepare them for taking orders and fitting into jobs where they have little autonomy or opportunity for upward advancement. In contrast, middle- and upper-class males (who are also disproportionately white) are taught to work and think independently (though within a hierarchy), to plan for the highest-paying jobs, and to assume that they will go to college and, increasingly, to graduate or professional schools.

Summary

This chapter explained that social interaction is necessary for normal human development and that such interaction plays a central role in all theories about socialization. Besides meeting the need for interaction, socialization also teaches people the things they need to know in order to survive and develop in their physical and social environments. Particularly critical is the learning of social roles and norms.

Social scientists disagree about the roles of nature and nurture in human development. Interactionists see nurture — social interaction — as the dominant force, with personality being determined by the messages you get from others and your interpretation of those messages. As children develop, they learn the concept of roles, and they shift from interacting with individuals to playing roles and interacting with other roles. Freudian theory, in contrast, sees the expectations of others as being in fundamental conflict with basic drives such as aggression and sexuality. They believe that the ways in which these conflicts are resolved (or left unresolved) in childhood has a major impact on adult personality.

The cognitive-developmental approach, which focuses on reasoning processes, sees the child's physiological development as a limiting factor. Actual development of reasoning capacity is largely determined though social interaction. People pass through a series of stages, which occur in a particular order determined largely by the development of the person's reasoning capabilities. How far a person proceeds and when, though, are mostly determined by social interaction. Closely related are theories concerning moral reasoning, such as those of Kohlberg. These theories see moral reasoning as progressing through a similar series of stages linked to reasoning ability. However, the ability to relate to the roles of others is necessary in order to move to higher stages. This, as well as a good part of the individual's reasoning ability, is gained through interaction with others.

The socialization process is carried out by agents of socialization, which include the family, the school, religion, peer groups, and the media. Although the family is probably the most influential of these agents, different agents predominate at different stages of life. To a greater or lesser extent, all of them shape behavior through processes of selective exposure and modeling, reward and punishment, and nurturance and identification. Most agents of socialization also deliver messages to the individual that play a critical role in defining his or her self-image.

Socialization is a lifelong process, even though it occurs most intensively during the childhood period of primary socialization. In adulthood, people undergo a new socialization process each time they enter a new role, such as leaving their parents' home, starting college, getting a job, getting married or divorced, having children, retiring, or experiencing the death of a spouse. In extraordinary circumstances, they may experience resocialization in a total institution, which uses its complete control over the individual to erase old values and beliefs and instill new ones.

The functionalist and conflict theories offer different explanations of the meaning and purpose of the socialization process. To functionalists, the process helps people learn to participate in society, perpetuates social knowledge and culture, and supports consensus and solidarity. To conflict theorists, it tends to serve the interests of the dominant group by bringing about false consciousness and social channeling. Both perspectives, though, recognize that conflicting messages from different agents of socialization can act as an important source of social change. It is this social change that allows society to adapt to new conditions. Social change also offers a source of opportunity for disadvantaged groups to improve their position in society.

Glossary

socialization The process whereby new members of a society are taught to participate in that society, learn their roles, and develop a self-image.

self-image The totality of the type of person that one perceives oneself to be.

play stage According to George Herbert Mead, a stage of socialization in which the child acquires language, recognizes the self as a separate entity, and learns norms from significant others.

significant others Specific individuals with whom a person interacts and who are important in that person's life.

self A distinct identity attached to a person; an awareness of that person's existence as a separate entity.

role model A significant other from whom a child learns to play a role.

generalized other Classes of people with whom a person interacts on the basis of generalized roles rather than individual characteristics.

game stage According to George Herbert Mead, a stage of socialization at which organized activity becomes possible.

id In Freudian theory, that part of the human personality that is a product of natural drives such as hunger, aggression, and sexual desire.

superego In Freudian psychology, that part of the personality that internalizes the norms and expectations of society and of significant others.

ego In Freudian theory, that part of the personality that mediates between the id and the superego.

sociopath A personality type characterized by a poorly developed sense of right and wrong and the absence of guilt for harm caused to others.

cognitive-development theories Theories of socialization that emphasize the development of reasoning ability.

cognitive processes Mental processes involved in reasoning and learning.

agents of socialization People and institutions that carry out the process of socialization; they act as important influences on the individual's attitudes, beliefs, self-image, and behavior.

modeling A process whereby the behavior of a significant other is observed and imitated.

identification A process whereby an individual develops strong positive feelings toward a person acting as an agent of socialization.

total institution An organization or group that has complete control over an individual and that usually engages in a process of resocialization.

resocialization A process occurring in total institutions designed to undo the effects of previous socialization and teach an individual new and different beliefs, attitudes, and behavior patterns.

social channeling A process whereby socialization prepares an individual for a particular role in life.

Further Reading

BECKER, HOWARD, ET AL. 1961. *Boys in White*. Chicago: University of Chicago Press. In an examination of the socialization process in medical education, Becker presents a fine example of how learning any new role involves a socialization process — including unlearning of old ways of thinking and behaving.

CURTISS, SUSAN. 1977. *Genie: A Psycholinguistic Study of a Modern-Day "Wild Child."* New York: Academic Press. The story of a girl who was kept locked in a room for 12 years, as told by a social scientist who worked for several years trying to socialize her.

ELKIN, FREDERICK, AND GERALD HANDEL. 1984. *The Child and Society,* 4th ed. New York: Random House. A brief but thorough and well-written overview of childhood socialization, which draws upon both sociological and social-psychological perspectives. Examines how race, sex, social class, place of residence, and other social characteristics relate to the socialization process.

GILLIGAN, CAROL. 1982. *In a Different Voice: Psychological Theory and Women's Development*. Cambridge, MA: Harvard University Press. A feminist analysis of the socialization process that considers differences in the ways males and females experience that process, as well as the consequences for men and women of those differences.

ROSE, PETER I. (ed.) 1979. *Socialization and the Life Cycle*. New York: St. Martin's Press. A collection of articles, both recent and classic, that explore the socialization process as it occurs throughout life.

CHAPTER 6

Sex, Gender, and Society

Two people walk into a telephone company's personnel office. They both have the same amount of education, and neither has any specialized training in telephone work. Despite the lack of training, both of them say, "I'll work hard and I'm willing to learn." The company has some openings, so both are hired. Two months later, both people are hard at work. But their work situation is not the same. One of them repairs equipment; the other is an operator. The one repairing equipment receives a salary that is 50 percent higher than that of the operator, with an opportunity for promotion to supervisory work in a few years. The other person has been offered no such opportunity. Why did two people with identical qualifications end up in such different situations? For one reason, and one reason only: The person who became a repairman was male, and the person who became an operator was female.

This is not a hypothetical example. It is based on a 1972 case brought by the Equal Employment Opportunity Commission (EEOC) against the American Telephone and Telegraph Company (AT&T) (Equal Employment Opportunity Commission, 1972; Hacker, 1979). The EEOC found that AT&T was systematically steering male applicants with no training toward jobs as linemen and repairmen, while women with no training were steered toward jobs as operators. The linemen and repairmen were higher paid and had greater opportunity for advancement. There was no basis for such a pattern in job applicants' qualifications, because neither the male nor the female applicants had any prior training. The EEOC ordered a stop to the practice. Although this particular instance of sex discrimination was corrected, the larger pattern it represents remains in U.S. society. Equally educated men and women continue to be steered to different and unequal jobs, and, more broadly, to different and unequal life statuses. This steering begins with the childhood socialization process and continues throughout life.

As we saw in Chapter 5, boys and girls experience the socialization process differently and are prepared for different roles in life. In this chapter, we shall explore how and why society defines the roles of men and women as being different and unequal, and we shall consider in greater detail the socialization processes that prepare men and women for these different roles. At the same time, we shall see that society's expectations concerning the roles of men and women have in some ways changed dramatically over the past 30 years. Indeed, this is one of the more profound social changes of our age. Nonetheless, we shall also see that a good deal has not changed, and that we cannot yet say that equality of the sexes has been attained in the United States or in most other industrialized countries.

What Are Sex and Gender Roles?

To begin our discussion, we should define several important terms. The chapter title mentions *sex* and *gender,* but precisely what is the difference between the two? Basically, sex is biologically defined, whereas gender is socially defined. Thus, **sex** refers to the biological fact that a person is either a man or a woman. **Gender** refers to socially learned traits associated with, and expected of, men or women (Giele, 1988, p. 294). Therefore, to be *male* or *female* is a matter of sex, but to be *masculine* or *feminine* is a matter of gender. Gender, in short, refers to socially learned behaviors and attitudes, such as mannerisms, styles of dress, and activity preferences.

Sex and Gender Roles

A concept closely related to sex and gender is that of **sex roles** or **gender roles.** Sex or gender roles can be defined as roles society expects people to play on account of their sex. One example of sex roles can be seen in the world of work (Spence, Deaux, and Helmreich, 1985). Society expects women to fill certain occupations and men to fill others. Thus, male nurses and female firefighters are still the exception to the rule. Men wishing to be nurses and women wishing to be firefighters will discover that their wishes go against the expectations of many people, and that they can become the objects of ridicule or hostility.

Gender roles also exist with respect to interpersonal behavior (it is still more common for men to ask women for dates than vice versa), the family (the wife and mother is still expected to take primary responsibility for matters pertaining to the home, even if she is employed), and recreational activities (how many women are on your college football team, and how many men do you know who sew because they enjoy it?). In fact, men and women are expected to fill different roles in virtually every area of life. Even if these roles are less rigidly defined than in the past, they are still around.

Sociologists do not agree on whether the appropriate term is *sex roles* or *gender roles.* Some prefer "sex roles" because society determines the roles a person is expected to play on the basis of his or her biological sex. Others prefer "gender roles" because the roles, like gender, are themselves socially defined. Because of this disagreement, we shall, following Giele (1988), use the terms *sex roles* and *gender roles* interchangeably.

Sexism

Sex roles are not only different, they are often unequal. Structured inequality between men and women, and the norms and beliefs that support such inequality, are called **sexism.** Sexism takes a variety of forms. One form is *ideological sexism,* the belief that one sex is inferior to another. Ideological sexism is often used to justify *sexual discrimination,* unequal treatment on the basis of sex. Some men believe incorrectly that women are "too emotional" for certain jobs that require high levels of responsibility—an example of ideological sexism. They then use that belief as an excuse or justification for sexual discrimination—refusal to hire or promote women into jobs with high levels of responsibility. Today, however, the most important form of sexism is probably **institutional sexism.** This term refers to systematic practices and patterns within social institutions that lead to inequality between men and women. One such pattern, which will be discussed later in this chapter, is the relatively low pay of occupations in which most workers are women — even compared to predominantly male occupations with similar educational requirements and levels of responsibility.

Traditional American Sex Roles

Different and unequal sex roles have long been a part of Western culture. In the United States and most other Western societies, social positions involving leadership, power, decision making, and interacting with the larger world have traditionally gone to men. Positions centering around dependency, family concerns, child care, and self-adornment have traditionally gone to women.

The Male Role These unequal sex roles mean that men and women are expected to behave differently in a number of situations (Broverman et al., 1972; Deaux and Lewis, 1984, 1983). Men are expected to be leaders, to take control, to make decisions, and to be active, worldly, unemotional, and aggressive. Through his actions, a man is said to determine his own status. At the same time, men are not expected to talk about (or even necessarily understand) their inner feelings. They are permitted to be blunt, loud, and a bit sloppy. In their relationships with women, men are expected to take the initiative, and sexual gratification is often a higher priority than interpersonal intimacy.

The Female Role Women, in contrast, are expected to be dependent, emotional, and unable to exercise leadership, think quantitatively, or make decisions. As a result, their status in life is often seen as a product not of their own actions but of the actions of the man to whom they are married. Women are also expected to be neater and more considerate than men, to have a better understanding of their own feelings and those of others, to have a higher standard of morality, and to be more appreciative of art, religion, and literature. In relationships, intimacy is more important than sexual

gratification, and women who take the initiative have traditionally been regarded as "pushy."

Although basic differences in sex roles are deeply embedded in our culture, some changes have occurred. In early American history, for example, property ownership and the right to vote were reserved for males. Even in the area of child rearing — where the day-to-day work was done by women — ultimate authority lay with males. Today, women in theory enjoy the same rights of voting and property ownership as men, although in reality both politics and material wealth remain disproportionately controlled by males. Authority over child rearing is regarded as a joint matter between fathers and mothers.

The Housewife Role The familiar role of housewife — the dominant role of middle-class American women in the early and mid-twentieth century — is a fairly recent invention (Degler, 1980, pp. 5–9). In early American history, both women and men engaged in the production of goods to be sold. In that time, most goods were produced in, and sold from, the home, and the majority of people worked at home (often on their farms). Thus, both sexes played a major role in economic production, and the notion of the woman as being *only* the caretaker of children and

Farm and Fireside *by Currier and Ives, 1878. The husband and wife are both helping to produce something that can be sold. Note also who has responsibility for the children.*

keeper of the home was unheard of. Women were in a subordinate and dependent social role, to be sure, because property rights, political power, and household authority were all in the hands of men. Even so, women were not isolated from economic production as they later were.

The housewife role, it turns out, was primarily a product of the Industrial Revolution. After about 1850, the increasing role of manufacturing in the economy meant that more and more work was done outside the home. This occurred, of course, in a social and cultural context in which power and economic control had always been in the hands of men. Because employment outside the home preserved their economic control, it was men who left the home to work.

It must be added, however, that many women viewed the housewife role as an advance. No longer were they expected to be *both* the primary keeper of the home and children *and* make an important contribution to the economic support of the family. Moreover, the housewife role afforded a certain protection from the dangers and physical stresses of industrial employment. Significantly, the housewife role was largely the realm of white middle-class women. Black women, immigrant women, and working-class women did not have the ''luxury'' of leaving the paid labor force (Jones, 1985; Glenn, 1980; Seifer, 1973).

The housewife role fit in well with the Victorian morality that reigned throughout much of the Industrial Revolution. Women were seen as fragile and delicate creatures who were inherently more moral than men. They were to be protected from the risks of the ''harsh world,'' and they had a special role in teaching morality to children and upholding the family unit.

Women, Men, and Work   The housewife role was supported by powerful norms, which stated that, because the family was the wife's primary responsibility, no woman should be employed after marriage except out of economic necessity. Some women, of course, chose a career rather than marriage, but it was not usually acceptable to choose *both* career and marriage, and getting married and raising children was clearly presented as the *ideal* female role. This system contained restraints for men as well as women: It was even less acceptable for a man *not* to work and support his family than it was for a married woman to have a

career. In fact, men have been expected to make major sacrifices of time and comfort in order to advance in their careers and provide for their families. Also, the main role of men has been to provide *economic* support, while emotional support has been the domain of women.

In spite of all this, considerable numbers of American women did work outside the home. Many worked out of economic necessity, and at least a few chose to disregard the norms and have both a marriage and a career. When women did enter the world of work, they found that their experience was different from that of men in several ways.

OCCUPATIONAL SEGREGATION   First, they worked at different jobs. Nearly half of all working women have been concentrated in just three occupations: secretary, nurse, and teacher. It is notable that these occupations involve substantial elements of care taking, service, and nurturance, just as does the traditional housewife role. Men, in contrast, have worked in a much greater range of jobs, including management, manufacturing, physical labor, and the top professions such as law and medicine. This pattern, which sociologists refer to as *occupational segregation,* will be examined in greater detail later in this chapter.

PROMOTIONS   Moreover, once in the work force, men have enjoyed a better chance of getting promoted, whereas women have usually remained in the same occupational position for life (De Prete and Soule, 1988). A secretary rarely becomes a manager, a nurse almost never becomes a doctor, and until recently, a female teacher rarely became a principal.

PAY   Women who work have never received as much money for their work as men have. Full-time working women receive only about 65 cents for every dollar paid to full-time working men, up from about 60 cents in 1970 (see Figure 6.1). The causes of this income inequality will be explored later in this chapter.

Cultural Variation in Sex Roles

Sex Roles: A Cultural Universal?   Now that we have seen some of the main characteristics of sex roles as they have existed in the United States, we must ask whether these patterns occur throughout the world.

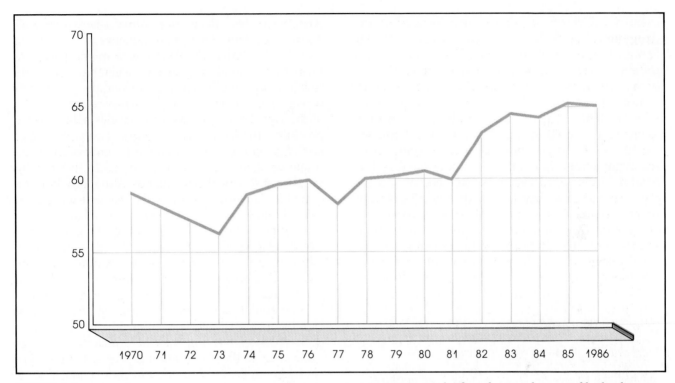

FIGURE 6.1
Median Women's Income as a Percentage of Median Men's Income: Year-Round, Full-Time Workers, 1970–1986
SOURCE: Computed from U.S. Bureau of the Census, 1987a, p. 20.

This is a difficult question to answer, but it appears that in some regards our system is almost universal, whereas in other regards it differs from those of other societies. The United States is typical in the sense that it *has* sex roles. In a classic study, Murdock (1935) found that the overwhelming majority of societies do divide at least some tasks by sex. However, the *content* of those sex roles—that is, precisely what men and women are expected to do and to be—varies widely. Murdock found only a few tasks that are nearly always done by men or by women. In over 80 percent of the societies he studied, hunting, fishing, and trapping were predominantly or exclusively the jobs of males, whereas cooking, carrying water, grinding grain, and gathering roots and seeds were primarily female chores. However, most tasks were done by males in

some societies, by females in others, and by both sexes in yet others. Examples of such tasks are various farming activities, constructing shelter, starting and maintaining care of fires, carrying objects, and preparing drinks and medicine.

The housewife role, so engrained in American society, is far from universal, even among modern industrial societies. In the Soviet Union and several Western European nations, both men and women are expected to contribute to the financial support of the household through employment. In many Asian countries, the norm is for women to be employed. In Japan, Thailand, and the Philippines, the majority of adult women are employed outside the home, and in China, virtually all women are. Similarly, patterns of occupational segregation vary considerably. In the Soviet Union, for example, over two-thirds of all medical doctors are women. As we shall see shortly, however, all of the aforementioned societies have sexual inequality, despite the absence of the housewife role.

Androgynous Societies There are at least a few societies where the roles of men and women differ little, if at all. Social scientists refer to such societies as **androgynous societies.** Margaret Mead's (1935) famous studies of three societies in New Guinea present two such examples. In one of them, the Arapesh, both men and women play what in America would be considered a feminine role. Both are gentle, strongly child-oriented, and giving. In the second, the Mundugumor, both men and women play a role we would consider masculine. They are loud and aggressive, fight a great deal, and are very uninterested in children. In the third society she studied, the Tchambuli, sex roles exist, but they are the opposite of what we are familiar with. Economic production is the role of women, whereas men concern themselves with self-adornment and trying to gain favors and approval from women. In fact, this society could be defined as *female-dominant.*

The photo at left shows the traditional and painful practice of foot-binding in China, while the photo at right illustrates the new roles of women in modern China. Although this change has been especially rapid in China, modernization has brought about new roles for women in many societies.

Are Societies Becoming More Androgynous?

There is evidence that many societies are becoming more androgynous than they were in the past. We mentioned a number of societies where the housewife role has declined significantly. In fact, the proportion of women in the paid labor force has risen across much of the world over the past few decades. China today proclaims the legal equality of men and women, yet just two generations ago women were virtually the property of men and were expected to live for the purpose of serving their husbands. Although China is a dramatic case that undoubtedly changed more than most countries because of the revolution that occurred there after World War II, its direction of change parallels that of much of the world. In most countries, including the United States, modernization eventually has been accompanied by the large-scale entry of women into the paid labor force (see Figure 6.2), and by increased legal recognition of the rights of women. Dozens of countries today, both capitalist and socialist, have laws forbidding sex discrimination in at least some areas of life. As recently as a century ago, such laws were unheard of in many of these countries.

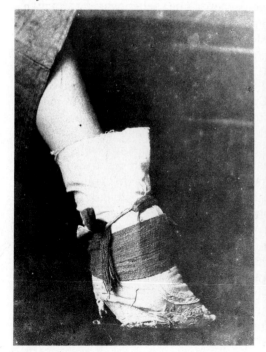

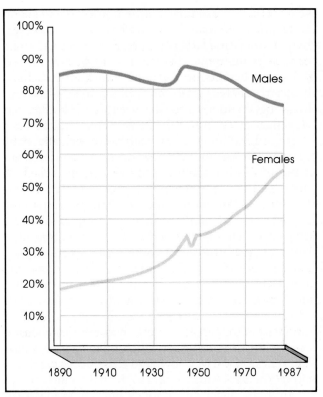

FIGURE 6.2
Labor Force Participation Rates of Men and Women in the United States, 1890–1984
Note that, although rates for men still substantially exceed those for women, the gap has closed significantly. What implications does this hold for the U.S. economy in the twenty-first century?
SOURCE: Adapted from Francine D. Blau and Marianne A. Ferber, *The Economics of Women, Men, and Work,* 1986 (Englewood Cliffs, NJ: Prentice Hall), p. 70; and *Statistical Abstracts of the United States,* 1988, Table 608.

Male Dominance: A Cross-Cultural View Nevertheless, the vast majority of the world's societies have historically been *male-dominant* and remain so. Although many societies are becoming more androgynous, they have yet to eliminate either distinct sex roles or gender inequality. In the Soviet Union, for example, where most doctors are women, that profession enjoys neither the prestige nor the high pay that it does in the United States. In Soviet society, the true centers of power—the government and the Commu-

nist Party—are both male domains. Like the United States, the Soviet Union has never been headed by a woman; in fact, women are almost totally absent from important government posts and from the Communist Party leadership. To only a slightly lesser extent, the same is true of China. The Scandinavian countries have long been regarded as leaders in the effort to bring about equality between the sexes, yet significant inequalities exist there, too. Their parliaments are three-quarters male, and Swedish women earn about 80 percent of what Swedish men earn (Reimer, 1986), better than the situation of American women, but still not equality.

In virtually all societies studied by Murdock (1935) and others, political structures are controlled more by males than by females. This remains so even though women such as Indira Gandhi, Margaret Thatcher, and Golda Meier have become prominent world leaders. The significance of these findings is that, in most societies, *power* is predominantly in the hands of males. In most societies, too, economic activities performed away from the home are largely a male domain, whereas the home and family are more the domain of women. Until the past few decades, whenever women did engage in economic production, it was usually in the home. Even today, when women are active in the labor force in many societies, they nearly always earn less on the average than men. Taking all of these things into consideration, it is hard to avoid the conclusion that male dominance, though not universal, is much more the rule than the exception among the world's societies.

Sex-Role Socialization: An Interactionist Analysis

Sex or gender roles, like all social roles, are learned through *socialization.* There are probably some behavioral differences between the sexes that reflect biological influences. Males may, for example, have a slight natural tendency to be more aggressive than females (Frieze et al., 1978; Gove, 1985). This tendency is almost a cultural universal (Whiting and Edwards, 1976), and even newborn males tend to be slightly more active than females. Part of the reason may be hormonal (Maccoby and Jacklin, 1974). However, some women are far more aggressive than some men; there are wide variations among societies in the levels of aggressiveness of both men and women; and male-female differences in aggression are highly situation-specific (Maccoby, 1980). When the norms of the situation support it, women can be as aggressive as men.

There may also be a slight biological basis for the development of different skills in men and women (Rossi, 1985), perhaps because girls usually develop earlier than boys, and this development is associated with dominance of the left hemisphere of the brain (Waber, 1977; 1979). However, male-female differences in literary, mathematical, and scientific aptitude are not consistent across cultures (Tobias, 1978), nor are they present in all schools, even in the United States. Moreover, these differences have declined in the past 20 years in the United States (Rosenthal and Rubin, 1982), suggesting that they are mainly social, not biological, in origin. If there is any biological basis for sexual differences in reasoning ability, it is certainly small compared to social influences. Although the evidence conflicts concerning moral development, there is no evidence of innate differences between males and females in such areas as conformity, dependency, social orientation, and overall achievement. Thus, nurture, not nature, is the prime determinant of sex-linked behavior. (For a comprehensive analysis of the basis for this conclusion, see Fausto-Sterling, 1985.) From infancy through adulthood, male and female human beings are treated differently and given different messages. The result is that small, natural differences in behavioral predisposition become greatly exaggerated, and men and women come to think of themselves in different ways and to play different roles in life. In effect, "man" and "woman" become distinct social roles. This process is known as **sex-role socialization.** In this part of the chapter, we shall examine how four key agents of socialization teach sex roles: the family, the school, the media, and the peer group.

Teaching Sex Roles in the Home

From infancy, boys and girls are treated differently to prepare them for different roles in life. In the first 2 years of life, for example, mothers smile at and talk to baby girls more than they do to baby boys. However, both mothers and fathers frequently touch and handle baby boys more than baby girls, and they do so less delicately. Parents are also quicker to attend to a fussy baby girl, whereas a baby boy is likely to be allowed to fuss longer without receiving attention (Hoyenga and Hoyenga, 1979, pp. 207–209). Some experts have suggested that the reason for this behavior is that baby boys are fussier and respond less to attention, but actual research findings on this point are mixed at best (Sayers, 1980, pp. 48–49; see also Maccoby and Jacklin, 1974). A more important reason that parents give a fussy baby girl more attention appears to be that they *expect* girls to respond better to attention than boys. What are the effects of this difference? Among other things, even at this early age, boys are encouraged to be more independent than girls, and girls are encouraged to relate interpersonally more than boys.

Different treatment of boys and girls occurs in a number of other areas in early childhood. Obviously, boys and girls are dressed differently. There are also differences in the way boys' and girls' rooms are decorated (Rheingold and Cook, 1975), in the kinds of toys children are given, the kinds of household jobs they are expected to help with, and the kinds of interests they are encouraged to pursue (Maccoby and Jacklin, 1974). In general, girls are rewarded for what they *are*

Through what they do "for fun," children are taught the roles of men and women in their society at an early age.

(charming, attractive), whereas boys are rewarded for what they *do* (Hartley, 1970). Especially in father-dominated families, boys are given greater freedom than girls, with the result that they experience greater control over their situation (Hagan, Simpson, and Gillis, 1987). This socialization does not take long to produce its results. By the age of 5, boys and girls *prefer* different toys and can identify different occupations as being "men's jobs" and "women's jobs" (Garrett et al., 1977; Masters and Wilkinson, 1976). They can identify stereotypical male and female traits even earlier—sometimes as young as 3 (Reis and Wright, 1982).

Teaching Sex Roles in the School

Sex-role socialization continues when children reach school. The tendency to prefer different kinds of toys —which symbolize different roles in life—continues. One study, for example, showed that in kindergarten, girls are encouraged to play with dolls, and boys are encouraged to play with wheeled toys and building blocks (Best, 1983). Girls' toys thus come to represent a domestic, child-oriented role, whereas boys' toys represent going out into the world and doing and building. Children also see different images of males and females in their school books and materials. Studies of school books and materials indicate the following patterns:

> The main characters in stories are more likely to be male than female (Women on Words and Images, 1974).
>
> Male characters display creativity, bravery, achievement, and similar themes, whereas female characters display emotion, fear, and dependency (Key, 1975; Women on Words and Images, 1974; Kolbe and LaVoie, 1980).
>
> Good things that happen to male characters result from their own efforts, whereas good things that happen to female characters result either from luck or from someone else's efforts (Penrod, 1985, p. 88).
>
> Even math books contain sexual stereotypes in their illustrations and word problems (Federbush, 1974).
>
> The late 1970s and early 1980s witnessed an increase in the number of female characters and a decline in stereotyping. However, parity in male and female lead characters had not been attained, nor had stereotyping been eliminated (Hoffman, 1982; Kolbe and LaVoie, 1980).

Children get a similar message from what they

TABLE 6.1
Percentage of Bachelor's Degrees Awarded to Women by Discipline, 1966 and 1981 (Selected Fields)

DISCIPLINE	1966 (%)	1981 (%)
Agriculture	2.7	30.8
Architecture	4.0	18.3
Biological sciences	28.2	44.1
Business	8.5	36.7
Computer and information science	13.0[a]	32.5
Education	75.3	75.0
Engineering	0.4	10.3
English and English literature	66.2	66.5
Foreign languages	70.7	75.6
Health	76.9	83.5
Home economics	97.5	95.0
Mathematics	33.3	42.8
Physical sciences	13.6	24.6
Psychology	41.0	65.0
Social sciences	35.0	44.2
Economics	9.8	30.5
History	34.6	37.9
Sociology	59.6	69.6

[a] Data are for 1969, the earliest year available.

Note that women are most highly represented in home economics and health, which reflect the traditional female role, and are most underrepresented in such "technical" areas as engineering and architecture.

SOURCE: U.S. Department of Health, Education and Welfare, Office of Education, "Earned Degrees Conferred: 1965–66"; U.S. Department of Education, National Center for Education Statistics, "Earned Degrees Conferred, 1980–81."

see first-hand in their schools. Although the teaching profession has historically been a largely female occupation, the proportion of women in the profession falls as the importance and status of the job increase. As you move from kindergarten through grade school, junior high school, high school, and on to college, there are progressively fewer female teachers and more male teachers. At every level of education, the proportion of women among principals and administrators is lower than it is among teachers (see, for example, Baker, 1980). The message children get from this is clear: The most important and highest-status jobs are for men.

Subject Channeling Another process that takes place in schools is *subject channeling*. Boys are expected to excel in math, science, and logic; girls are expected to excel in reading, art, and music. These expectations occur in the home and in school. Parents frequently believe that learning math and science is more important for boys than for girls (Parsons et al., 1982) and thus do more to encourage boys to learn these subjects. In the school, teachers and counselors have similar beliefs. Thus, they encourage boys to take more math and science than girls, and they expect higher achievement from boys than from girls in these subjects (Curran, 1980; Coakley, 1972).

Teaching Sex Roles on Television

Most children in the United States today spend more time watching television than they spend either in school or talking to their parents. What kinds of messages do they get from television about the roles of men and women? Whether we consider television entertainment or television advertising, the evidence is that they get highly stereotyped messages.

Television entertainment, for example, gives messages that reinforce the segregation of men and women into separate occupations. Between 1950 and 1980, 95 percent of doctors on television were men, and 99 percent of nurses were women (Kalisch and Kalisch, 1984). In general, television roles that involve leadership and decision making are played by men, whereas women's roles are likely to be either home-centered or, if at work, involve following more than leading. There has undoubtedly been some change in these stereotypes over the past decades. Women have appeared on television in recent years as tough cops, savvy lawyers, and private investigators. However, two important points must be made here. First, such portrayals remain the exception to the rule. Second, there is some evidence that although women are now sometimes portrayed in these roles, they are portrayed as playing such roles differently than men play them (Roman, 1986). Female police officers, for example, may be portrayed as either more caring than male officers or more devious and conniving; male officers are shown as more aggressive and quicker to use force.

Although sex stereotyping may have become more subtle in television entertainment, it is hardly subtle in television advertising. Very attractive and often thinly clad females are used to sell everything from cars to shaving products to electronic gadgets.

Sometimes the message is more about sex than about the product. When a woman is the lead in a commercial, the message is much more likely to be based on attractiveness than when a man is the lead (Downs and Harrison, 1985). In contrast, the voice of authority on most commercials is male (Klemesrud, 1981). Significantly, male voice-overs are most common when the actors on the commercial are attractive women (Downs and Harrison, 1985). The hidden message is that women are pretty and men are knowledgeable and authoritative. Besides attractiveness, women are also portrayed as engaging in rather mindless behaviors, usually in the home. They frequently become excited about a small improvement in a detergent or floor cleaner or about the softness of facial tissues or toilet paper.

Under these circumstances, it is hardly surprising that social scientists have found that children who watch more television are more stereotyped in their own thinking than children who watch less (Frueh and McGhee, 1975; Beuf, 1974; see also Tan, 1979). Moreover, those who are exposed to stereotypical television become more stereotyped in their own thinking, whereas those who see counterstereotypical television become less stereotyped (Johnson et al., 1980; Johnson and Davidson, 1981; McArthur and Eisen, 1976; Miller and Reeves, 1976; Geis et al., 1984). Taking all this into consideration, there is no doubt that television has been and remains an important means by which sex roles are taught.

How Peers Teach Sex Roles

Some of the strongest pressures for sex-role conformity come from peers. The peer group enforces the principle that boys and girls are supposed to enjoy different activities and play different roles. The reward for conforming to such norms is approval and inclusion; the costs of violating them include rejection, ridicule, and social isolation. In general, peer pressures for sex-role conformity are stronger among boys than among girls (Hartley, 1974). It is worse for a boy to be labeled a "sissy" than for a girl to be labeled a "tomboy." The "tomboy," after all, is only seeking to move from what society has defined as an inferior role into one that society views more favorably; the "sissy" is doing the reverse. In fact, boys are sometimes so negative toward the traditional female role that even girls look down upon it as a result. Best (1983), for example, has noted cases in which girls became reluctant to be seen playing with dolls by the third grade. Why? Because boys made fun of them. The message here, of course, is that the traditional female role of domesticity is inferior and is therefore to be avoided.

Pressures for conformity to ''boys' play'' and ''girls' play'' start young; they have even been found among preschoolers as young as 3 (Lamb et al., 1980). However, these pressures increase as children move through their education, and by the third or fourth grade they are reinforced by a strong system of sex segregation in play: Boys play with boys and girls play with girls. Within each group, strong pressures exist for ''sex-appropriate'' behavior. Peer pressures for boys to be masculine and for girls to be attractive appear to be strongest in adolescence (Coleman, 1961; Bernard, 1981, p. 137).

How Sex Roles Are Learned

We have seen that the family, the school, the media, and the peer group all send children messages about the different roles of men and women. We shall now explore further the process by which these sex roles are learned, and we will see evidence that if the socialization process were different, girls and boys would not be channeled toward different roles in life in the ways that they are now.

The Looking-Glass Self and Sex-Role Socialization

Recall from Chapters 3 and 5 Charles Horton Cooley's (1909) concept of the *looking-glass self*. Consider this concept in the light of the kind of messages that boys and girls get from infancy on.

According to Cooley, our self-image is a product of the messages we receive from others and the ways we understand and interpret those messages. When the messages are like those outlined here—all of which are typical messages given to boys and girls—it is hardly surprising that boys and girls come to see

MESSAGES TO GIRLS	MESSAGES TO BOYS
''You are delicate.''	''You are hardy.''
''You need our help.''	''You can take care of yourself.''
''You understand people.''	''You don't understand people.''
''You are pretty.''	''You can accomplish things.''
''Your dolls are stupid.''	''The things you build are important.''
''You are good in art and reading.''	''You are bad in art and reading.''
''You are bad at math and science.''	''You are good at math and science.''
''You are polite and well behaved.''	''Boys will be boys.''

themselves differently. As a result of these different self-images, they do in fact become different kinds of people. Thus, for example, boys *become* better than girls at math and science. Although there is no difference in their ability test scores in the early grades, boys do score higher than girls by seventh or eighth grade, with the difference increasing until high-school graduation (see Benbow and Stanley, 1980; Curran, 1980; Fairweather, 1976).

However, a variety of evidence suggests that when boys and girls are exposed to similar expectations and messages, such differences either do not develop or can be largely reversed (Newcombe et al., 1983; Coser, 1986; Tobias, 1978). There are at least three conditions under which this is the case. First, such differences do not develop in societies that do not channel girls away from jobs involving math, science, and reasoning, even if other types of sexual inequality exist. The Soviet Union has been cited as one example of such a society (Tobias, 1978). Second, such differences do not develop in some schools even in the United States, quite possibly because these schools make efforts *not* to channel boys and girls toward separate occupations. Finally, girls who, for whatever reason, resist the message and develop a sufficiently strong interest in math and science to take advanced courses do just as well as the boys in these courses (College Entrance Examination Board, 1974).

We see, then, that when it comes to education, the looking-glass self is indeed at work. When boys and girls are given different messages about their abilities, they see themselves differently, and as a result they do develop different abilities. The beliefs of parents, teachers, and counselors become a *self-fulfilling prophecy*. In other words, their perceptions lead them to behave in ways that make their expectations about boys and girls come true. When, however, boys and girls are given similar messages about their abilities, they develop similar abilities. Thus, sex-role socialization produces unequal opportunities for boys and girls, and elimination of some of these patterns of socialization could produce more equal opportunities. Although we have focused on subject channeling, much the same could be said of any of the other messages boys and girls get about themselves from significant others.

Modeling and Sex-Role Socialization

As we saw in Chapter 5, repeated and selective exposure to a particular behavior pattern leads to modeling of that behavior pattern. This is particularly true when children identify with the model, as they do with their parents. It is clear from the foregoing discussion that in nearly every aspect of their lives, children are exposed to images of men and women in very different roles. Does this selective exposure lead to modeling, as we would expect? Evidence suggests that it does.

Modeling and Occupations One example of modeling can be seen in the occupational aspirations of boys and girls. Despite all the recent changes in the roles of men and women, most boys and girls still plan on seeking jobs that have traditionally been held by people of their sex. A study of women in their twenties and early thirties by Barrett (1979), for example, showed that 80 percent of noncollege women and 75 percent of college women still aspired to traditionally female jobs, such as teacher, nurse, or secretary.

What happens when young people are *not* frequently exposed to sex-typed roles and behavior? Apparently, the answer is that they are less sex-typed in their own occupational plans. There is much evidence for this. In general, the more that children are exposed to sexual stereotypes at home or through the media, the more stereotyped their thinking is (Hoyenga and

Hoyenga, 1979, pp. 214–218; Coltrane, 1988). Robb and Raven (1982), for example, found that children of mothers who are employed full time see fewer sex-stereotyped roles in the home than other children, and that these children in fact become less stereotypical in their own thinking.

Structured Sexual Inequality

As was stated earlier, sex or gender roles, as they exist in the United States, are not just *different;* they are also *unequal.* Whether you consider power, income, or occupational status, men in the United States are an advantaged group compared to women. Let us consider each of these areas in greater detail.

Men, Women, and Power

Although we shall examine the concept of *power* in considerably greater detail in Chapters 9 and 10, we shall briefly introduce and define it here, because it is an important area in which men and women experience social inequality. Power can be defined as the ability to get other people to behave in ways that you desire. Power is often exercised through the political system. It frequently rises from *authority*—the right to make certain decisions that is attached to a certain social position. We shall focus on power as it relates to men and women in two key areas: positions of authority, and power within the family.

Men, Women, and Positions of Authority One way to judge the power of a social group is to gauge whether that group is well represented among people known to hold power. Clearly, power in the form of authority is held by people in certain positions in business and government. Chief executive officers (CEOs) of businesses, political officials, and certain public administrators such as city managers and school administrators have considerable power.

How well represented are women in these positions of power? Part of the answer can be found in Table 6.2. Even today, women are almost completely absent from the most important positions of power. Although approximately one in ten elected officials

TABLE 6.2
Percentage of Women in Elected Offices in the United States, 1979–1990

OFFICE	1979–80	1981–82	1983–84	1985–86	1987–88	1989–90
U.S. Senators	1.0	2.0	2.0	2.0	2.0	2.0
Governors	2.0	2.0	4.0	4.0	6.0	
U.S. Representatives	3.7	4.4	4.8	5.3	5.3	5.7
Lieutenant governors				4.0	8.0	
State treasurers				4.0	16.0	
Secretaries of state				4.0	22.0	
State legislators	10.3	12.4	13.5	14.8	15.0	

SOURCES: Taylor's *World of Politics; The New York Times;* U.S. Bureau of the Census, *Statistical Abstract of the United States.*

overall is female, the percentage declines considerably when we look at the most important positions such as governors and U.S. senators and representatives. When we consider the top political levels, we find that no woman has ever even been nominated for president by a major party, and no woman was nominated for vice president until Representative Geraldine Ferraro received the Democratic nomination in 1984 (her ticket lost in the general election). Women are almost totally absent from the ranks of CEOs of major corporations, as they are from corporate boards of directors. There has been some increase in the number of women in upper management in recent years, but very few of them have been selected for the *very* top positions.

SEX, AUTHORITY, AND POLITICS   It can no longer be said that women are underrepresented in positions of power because relatively few women seek them. Women are still less likely than men to run for political office, but the number of female candidates has risen sharply in recent years. Yet, they often have a harder time getting elected than men. Of the 13 women nominated to be governors or U.S. senators in 1986, only 3 won (Clements, 1987). One factor that perpetuates male dominance of politics is the advantage of *incumbency.* Incumbents usually win, and most incumbents are male. As a result, the limited number of women who are nominated to run for high offices usually run against male incumbents, and relatively few succeed in being elected. In addition, recent polls have indicated that many people are still reluctant to vote for a woman, though the number of people responding this way has fallen in recent years. Significantly, willingness to vote for women is greater when they are running for less-powerful positions such as city council and school board, but far lower when they seek more powerful positions such as governor, or president. In 1987 about one voter in four indicated an unwillingness to vote for *any* woman for president (ABC News, 1987). Popular attitudes toward women in politics are examined in more detail in the "Polls Apart" box.

SEX, AUTHORITY, AND THE BUSINESS WORLD   In the business world, the absence of women in part reflects the reluctance of male boards of directors to

In 1984, Geraldine Ferraro became the first woman to receive a major party's nomination for the vice presidency. As of 1990, no woman has ever been elected president or vice president in nearly 225 years of U.S. history.

POLLS APART

Attitudes toward Women in Politics

Despite the prominence of the women's movement over the past 2 decades, there are still only a handful of women in the U.S. Congress. Why is it that, although women represent over one-half the U.S. population, they fill only 6 percent of these elected offices? Polls suggest that the answer lies in deep-seated concerns about women's capacity to handle the responsibilities of public office.

Take a look at the responses below for a poll that asked:

"For each of these words and

SOURCE: "U.S. News and World Report Survey, 1986," *Issues and Reactions* (Washington, DC: U.S. News and World Report, 1987).

phrases, would you tell me if you associate it more with a woman running for public office or more with a man running for public office?"

As a sociologist analyzing these results, what would you ask yourself next? Well, you'd probably want to know how the male respondents as a group compared to the female respondents as a group. In other words, when *women* rate women, do they think that men would handle the Russian situation better? Yes, as a matter of fact, they do. Indeed, male *and* female respondents share the attitudes listed above. Both groups view women as more sympathetic but less decisive than men in dealing with public issues. No wonder that women are underrepresented in elective positions!

For even clearer findings, examine the data below that indicate the percentages by sex who would *not* vote for a woman for:

	% OF MEN	% OF WOMEN
Vice president of the U.S.	20	21
President of the U.S.	36	37

Does it come as a surprise to you that both men and women cling to certain long-standing perceptions of the sexes? How would you account for this? How rapidly do you think these attitudes will change in the coming years? What factors might encourage the change?

	% OF TOTAL GROUP WHO SAID		
	More With Woman	More With Man	No Difference
Compassion for the poor	63	11	23
Toughness	19	55	23
Effective in dealing with Russians	9	63	24
Effective in dealing with crises	14	50	34
Concerned about women's rights	78	7	12

These responses demonstrate that the traditional stereotypes of women as compassionate and men as practical problem solvers remain widespread in our society.

appoint women to top executive positions. Many men don't want to work under female supervisors, which may heighten this resistance. There are many women in lower- and middle-level management. Over half of all U.S. women, and almost 70 percent of women between the ages of 20 and 45, are in the labor force. By 1984 about 13 percent of full-time female workers were in executive or managerial work, compared to 16 percent of male workers (U.S. Bureau of the Census,

1985). Yet very few of these women have been appointed to the top management positions that have real decision-making power.

Women in the corporate world encounter barriers that inhibit their opportunities to gain real power. In corporations with relatively few women managers, women in management are often responded to more as women than as managers, thus being deprived of the full opportunity to be evaluated and responded to on the basis of the work they do (Kanter, 1977). As the number of women increases, male managers become more accustomed to women and treat them more as they would any other employee — up to a point. However, when the number of women begins to approach a majority, male workers often feel threatened, which may inhibit opportunities for the women workers (Weiss, 1983). Until such attitudes change, women are not likely to fill many positions of real power.

Men, Women, and Power in the Home   The relative powerlessness of women in the worlds of government and business is largely repeated in the home. Even in homes where both the husband and wife are employed full time, several realities give greater power to the husband. For one thing, even where both partners work full time, the husband typically provides 60 percent or more of the family's income, because men's wages substantially exceed those of women. Where the wife works only part time or not at all, this discrepancy is even greater (Sorensen and McCanahan, 1987). The power of the purse within the family, then, is disproportionately in the hands of the male. Even today, women must often seek money from their husbands for various types of purchases. Until recently, married women usually could not borrow money unless they applied jointly for credit with their husbands. Today, the law has changed, but women's incomes are often too low for them to get substantial credit lines on their own, so they must still sometimes depend on their husbands.

Also limiting the power of women in the home is the continuing influence of the norm that providing income through employment is the first responsibility of the husband, while taking care of the household is the first responsibility of the wife. For one thing, even women who have good jobs must often put their husband's jobs first when questions of relocation arise. Families are far more likely to move for the husband's career opportunities than for the wife's. In addition, the wife, not the husband, is expected to miss work for such household emergencies as taking care of sick children and letting in repairpersons. (For a discussion of both of these issues, see Duncan and Corcoran, 1984, pp. 156–161.)

Finally, the primacy of the woman's responsibility for the home means that full-time employed women have a longer work week than full-time employed men. According to one study (Peskin, 1982), the total (employment and home) work week of a typical full-time employed woman was 67 hours, compared to 63 hours for the typical male full-time employee. The difference: Women put in considerably more hours working around the house than men did. Translated to 1981 dollars, the value of the uncompensated housework of the average woman was $10,000 — compared to only $5,000 for the average man. Men *have* increased their work around the house, and such tasks as cooking, washing dishes, grocery shopping, and laundry are shared in far more households today than in the past. Thus, as women have entered the labor force, men have increased their share of household work. For many men, this is a dramatic role change from what they saw their fathers doing when they were children. In most households, however, men have still not increased their share of the household work to an *equal* share, even when both the husband and wife are employed full time.

The Income of Men and Women

As we saw earlier, the average woman who is employed full time receives slightly less than two-thirds

Men today have taken on a bigger share of household tasks such as cooking. However, they have not usually taken on an equal *share, even when both they and their wives work full time.*

the income of the typical full-time male worker. Moreover, as is shown in Table 6.3, this difference is not the result of differences in education between men and women. At every level of education, women's wages are only 60 to 70 percent of those of men (see also Bianchi and Spain, 1986). As shown in Table 6.4, income differences between male and female workers are smaller among younger workers and increase more or less steadily from age 25 to retirement. This fact could be interpreted in two ways. The optimistic interpretation is that sexual wage inequality is decreasing, and that young women now entering the labor market are receiving fairer treatment. However, we saw earlier in the chapter that declines in income inequality have been rather small since 1970. A less optimistic interpretation is that women do not get advanced to higher-paying jobs as quickly as men do. We have already seen that women are often excluded from the top managerial jobs. Even more important, many women work in clerical and service occupations that offer little chance for promotion to substantially higher-paying jobs. Finally, even though younger women do better relative to men than older women in terms of income, they still earn considerably less than men in their age group.

Causes of Women's Low Wages   Why do women continue to be paid so much less than men? A number of possibilities have been suggested, including the competing role of women in the home, wage inequality in the same job, hiring patterns, and occupational segregation. Let us consider each.

COMPETING EXPECTATIONS OF WORKING WOMEN   Certainly, part of the answer is to be found in women's role in the home. As we already saw, women are less able than men to move to take a job and are more likely to miss work because of household emergencies. Both of these things impede their ability to move up to better-paying positions. Moreover, women are more likely than men to leave the job market temporarily, especially to take care of young children. (Again, if anyone quits work for this reason in a family, it is usually the wife.) How important are these factors as a cause of low income? A national study by Duncan and Corcoran (1984) found that differences in work experience, work continuity, self-imposed restrictions on job hours and location, and

TABLE 6.3
Median Income of Male and Female Year-Round, Full-Time Workers, by Level of Education, 1986

LEVEL OF EDUCATION	MALE WORKERS	FEMALE WORKERS	PERCENT FEMALE OF MALE INCOME
All Workers	$25,894	16,843	65.0
Less than 8th grade	14,485	10,153	70.1
8th grade	18,541	11,183	60.3
1–3 years high school	20,003	12,267	61.3
4 years high school	24,701	15,947	64.6
1–3 years college	28,025	18,516	66.1
4 years college	34,391	22,412	65.2
5 or more years college	39,592	27,279	68.9

SOURCE: U.S. Bureau of the Census, 1987a, pp. 15, 16.

TABLE 6.4
Median Income of Male and Female Year-Round, Full-Time Workers, by Age, 1986

AGE	MALE WORKERS	FEMALE WORKERS	PERCENT FEMALE OF MALE INCOME
All Ages	$25,895	16,843	65.0
15–19	9,730	8,333	85.6
20–24	14,152	12,192	86.2
25–34	22,692	17,087	75.3
35–44	30,189	18,810	62.3
45–54	31,657	18,057	59.4
55–64	29,119	16,983	58.3
65 and over	27,326	17,180	62.9

SOURCE: U.S. Bureau of the Census, 1987a, pp. 15, 16.

absenteeism *combined* could explain only one-third of the difference in men's and women's income. Thus, these factors do make a difference in the income of women, but other factors make a considerably bigger difference. In addition, commitments of women to the home are probably declining in importance as a factor in women's wages. More employers are offering maternity leave (and in some cases paternity leave) as a standard practice, and women are taking it for shorter times (Mott and Shapiro, 1978). The practice of leaving the labor force to raise small children is also becoming less common (Mott and Shapiro, 1978). Thus, both employers and female employees are changing in ways that make home commitments less of an impediment to work advancement. Significantly, recent research has revealed that women actually devote *more* effort to their jobs than comparably situated men (Bielby and Bielby, 1988).

UNEQUAL WAGES   Even when they have similar experience and have taken no more time out of the labor force than men, women receive considerably lower pay than similarly educated men (England et al., 1988). One reason for this is that, even when they work in the same occupation, women are often paid less than men. Why is this true? First, women seem to have less access than men to on-the-job training that increases their skills, and thus their value to their employers. Although employers sometimes argue that they are reluctant to provide women with on-the-job training because they are more likely to leave the labor force to have children, Duncan and Corcoran (1984, p. 167) found that women get less on-the-job training, even compared to men who have been with the employer for the *same* amount of time.

HIRING PATTERNS   Another reason that men and women are paid differently in the same occupation is that some employers primarily hire men, whereas others primarily hire women. Firms that tend to hire men pay better than ones that primarily hire women. Currie and Skolnick (1984, p. 219), for example, have pointed out that some accounting firms hire women as accountants and pay them lower salaries than those paid by firms that hire men.

Finally, men are twice as likely as women to supervise other employees and be in positions to hire, promote, and fire. Employees who have this authority are paid better (see Hill and Morgan, 1979). Among men, education and job experience are more likely to increase the chance of having supervisory and hiring/firing authority than among women (Duncan and Corcoran, 1984, pp. 166–167). Perhaps because they fear that employees will object to being supervised by a woman, employers appear reluctant to give their female employees such authority. Besides depriving women of leadership opportunities, such policies help to keep their wages down.

OCCUPATIONAL SEGREGATION   Although women typically receive lower wages than men even in the same occupation, a major cause of income inequality is **occupational segregation.** This term refers to the concentration of men and women into different occupations, even when they have similar levels of skill and training. Occupational segregation has significant impacts, both in terms of the incomes of men and women and, more broadly, in terms of occupational choices and opportunities for men and women.

Considerable occupational segregation is evident even if we look at broad categories of jobs. Men are more likely to work in management and skilled labor (precision production and crafts), whereas women are more likely to work in clerical and service jobs. Significantly, management and skilled-labor jobs pay better than clerical and service jobs. In fact, managerial and executive workers are the best paid of any of the broad categories, while service workers are near the bottom.

However, even when men and women are evenly represented in one of these broad categories, they often work at different specific jobs *within* the category (Bielby and Baron, 1986). Women are slightly more likely than men to be employed in the "professional specialty" category, but within this category, they often work at lower-paying jobs than men. Most physicians, lawyers, engineers, dentists, and architects are men. These men are better paid than are nurses, teachers, and social workers—professional employees who are mostly women. As a result, the median income for a male with a professional job in 1986 was $35,143, while that for a female professional was $23,076—a difference of $12,000 (U.S. Bureau of the Census, 1987a, pp. 15–16).

Such differences can exist even within the same industry. Currie and Skolnick (1984, p. 222–223) have illustrated this point using the food and beverage industry. The highest-paid employees are brewery workers, who are 85 percent male. Their average pay in 1981 was $497 per week. At the opposite end are poultry workers, the majority of whom are women. Their average pay in 1981 was only $169 per week. In general, it has been shown that the greater the number of women in an occupation, the lower the pay of that occupation (England et al., 1988; Mellor, 1984).

Why do jobs typically held by men so often pay better than jobs typically held by women? There seem to be several reasons. First, unequal pay is probably a carry-over from the days when it was widely believed that men should be paid more because they were more likely to be supporting a family. This is no longer true today, when both men and women support families, and most two-parent families rely on both parents' incomes. Moreover, although deliberate sexual pay discrimination by an employer *within the same occupation* is illegal, there is nothing to stop unequal pay in *different* occupations. Thus, inequalities created in the past are perpetuated because employers do not want to raise pay in occupations that have historically had low pay.

Second, predominantly male occupations are more highly unionized than predominantly female occupations. As a result, their pay tends to be better. In part, these differences may reflect different attitudes among men and women toward unionization, but they probably also reflect the fact that, until recently, most unions were more interested in organizing predominantly male occupations.

Finally, the best-paid jobs have simply been seen as "men's jobs." Thus, until very recently, relatively few women sought to become doctors, lawyers, judges, airline pilots, dentists, managers, or engineers. The relative absence of women from high-paying occupations also reflects a related pattern we have already mentioned — the reluctance to place women in positions that involve hiring, firing, and supervision.

COMPARABLE WORTH   Clearly, occupational segregation is an important cause of male-female income inequality. Even when they require similar levels of skill and training, "men's jobs" usually pay better than "women's jobs." One short-term measure that has been proposed to address this income inequality is *comparable worth* legislation. Comparable worth states that men and women who work in different occupations that require similar skills and education should receive similar wages. To implement such a policy, an employer must first conduct a comparable worth study to evaluate the relative education, skill, knowledge, and responsibility required for different occupations. This study establishes sets of occupations that are similar in these regards. The employer must then adjust the pay scale so that people in occupations that fall within the same category receive similar or equal wages.

Comparable worth is a controversial policy that has aroused widespread opposition among employers. Most of the employers that have instituted such policies are state and local governments. Perhaps the classic case involved the state of Washington, where a 1974 comparable worth study revealed that female state employees were paid 20 percent less than male employees for jobs that involved equal responsibilities and skills. As a result, the American Federation of County, State, and Municipal Employees (AFCSME) filed suit against the state. A federal court ruled in favor of AFCSME in September 1983, although the state appealed the decision (Blau and Ferber, 1986, p. 270).

By the end of 1984, about half the states had conducted comparable worth studies, but only 12 had passed laws requiring equal pay for similar jobs. Even in these states, the laws applied only to state employees. At present, then, only a limited number of states and municipalities, and hardly any private employers, actually set wages on the basis of comparable worth. Thus, although comparable worth remains a promising way of reducing the income inequality that results from occupational segregation, only a tiny proportion of the nation's work force is presently covered by such policies.

Over the longer run, many people feel that to deal with income inequality we must address the question of occupational segregation itself. This view holds that occupational segregation would be a problem even if there were no inequalities in pay because it deprives women of opportunities to work in jobs that are more rewarding, challenging, and enjoyable. In general, jobs typically held by males offer greater autonomy and prestige than those held by women.

CAUSES OF OCCUPATIONAL SEGREGATION   This leads to the question, of course, of *why* women are so absent from many of these jobs. One reason turns out to be the effect of sex-role socialization — men and women are taught to aspire to different jobs and thus end up in different jobs. Another answer is that, until recently, open discrimination was common against women seeking to enter historically male occupations. This was true both of employers and of educational programs required for entry to an occupation. Although illegal today, such discrimination has lingering effects. An occupation composed primarily of members of one sex can be quite uncomfortable for a person of the opposite sex to enter. Thus, male nurses and secretaries and female firefighters and auto mechanics may face reactions ranging from ridicule to resistance to ostracism. These attitudes alone tend to perpetuate occupational segregation, particularly when they operate in combination with the effects of sex-role socialization. Also, as previously discussed, most young people still aspire to sex-typed occupations (Barrett, 1979; Bain and Fottler, 1980). As we would expect, occupational segregation appears to be most intense in the kinds of places where attitudes about sex roles are most traditional (Abrahamson and Sigelman, 1987).

Functionalist and Conflict Perspectives on Sex Roles

Thus far, our discussion of sexism has focused on the forces that maintain sexual inequality. Another fundamental question is: *Why does sexism exist in the first place?* As we have seen, the interactionist perspective is highly useful for understanding how sexism is perpetuated. To understand the more fundamental causes of sexism, however, we must use the functionalist and conflict perspectives. These perspectives ask such questions as:

1. What purpose or whose purpose is served by structured sexual inequality?
2. Why do societies establish social roles and social inequality along the lines of gender?
3. Why do societies teach these unequal roles to succeeding generations?

The Functionalist Perspective

Original Functions of Sex Roles One common school of thought among functionalist sociologists is that, whether or not sex roles perform any important functions for society today, they certainly did in the past. These sociologists note that until about a century ago, most women spent much of their young adult lives either pregnant or taking care of infants. Infant and child mortality was very high, and in order to have two or three children survive to adulthood, a woman

often had to give birth to five or six. In those days, of course, there was no baby formula, so having babies meant breast-feeding. In short, these necessities meant that women simply weren't available to do things away from the home much of the time, which probably explains, among other things, why hunting is one of the few activities that has quite consistently been performed by males across different societies.

A second consideration is physical strength. Because of their larger physical size, men are — on the average — more capable of tasks that involve heavy lifting or moving large objects. At a time when most work was physical in nature, this difference probably led to some sex-role specialization. Thus, frequent pregnancy and long periods of breast-feeding, together with differences in physical strength, explain why sex-role specialization was functional in the past. But what of today?

Sex Roles as Cultural Lag Some sociologists believe that sex roles exist today mainly as a result of *cultural lag*. Sex roles were functional in the past, but have no use to society today, according to this view. Nonetheless, they persist because society is slow to change. Sex roles, and the norms that support them, have become engrained in our culture, which is passed from generation to generation through the socialization process. Thus, they disappear only gradually. This viewpoint suggests that if sex roles are no longer functional, they will persist for some time but will become weaker with each new generation, because they have no use in today's society. A case can be made that this is in fact happening. As we shall see in more detail later, there have been major changes in the sex-role attitudes of Americans and people in many other modern societies. Nonetheless, many sociologists disagree with this interpretation. Some argue that sex roles are beneficial to society in other ways; others explain their existence from the conflict perspective. Let us consider the former group first.

Are Sex Roles Still Functional? Most functionalist arguments that support the usefulness of sex roles today focus on the family. Some argue that sex roles permit a desirable form of specialization within the family, and others argue that traditional sex roles are conducive to family cohesiveness.

SEX ROLES AND FAMILY SPECIALIZATION The notion that sex roles facilitate specialization within the family is largely associated with the writings of Talcott Parsons and Robert Bales (1955). They based their arguments on research showing that in organizations and groups performing tasks, two types of leaders typically emerge: *instrumental leaders,* whose main concern is getting the job done, and *expressive leaders,* whose role is to address the feelings of people in the group and the relations among those people. (This issue is addressed in greater detail in Chapter 7.) Parsons and Bales argued that, as a small group, the family needs both instrumental and expressive leadership. They saw the traditional male role as filling the family's need for instrumental leadership and the traditional female role as providing expressive leadership. Thus, a role division that emphasizes the man's getting the jobs done and providing income and the woman's taking care of social and emotional needs is seen as functional for the family.

Parsons and Bales's functionalist explanation of sex roles has been strongly criticized by other sociologists for two reasons. First, even though the family might need both instrumental and expressive leadership, there is no clear reason why the instrumental leadership must come from the male and the expressive leadership from the female. It could just as well happen the other way around. Second, this functionalist explanation does not consider the possible *dysfunctions* of restricting women to the expressive role, which will be addressed shortly.

SEX ROLES AND FAMILY COHESION A more contemporary functionalist argument centers around the cohesiveness of the family. This argument holds that traditional, male-dominated families experienced less divisiveness because women did not think and act independently of their husbands. Thus, as women have become more free and independent, family conflict has increased. Those who support this view often cite statistics showing that as women obtain work outside the home, the likelihood of their marriages ending through divorce rises. Finally, some people argue that when mothers work outside the home, their children suffer. These people claim that when children are in day care or must come home from school to an empty house, their mental health suffers, and they become high risks for juvenile delinquency, drug and alcohol abuse, and teenage pregnancy.

Although some of these issues will be addressed in later chapters, several important facts relevant to these arguments can be noted here. First, time-budget studies indicate that full-time working mothers interact with their children about as much as do full-time housewives (Goldberg, cited in Hodgson, 1979; Farley, 1977, pp. 197–202; Robinson, 1977), although housewives may spend more time on care-related tasks (Vanek, 1973, pp. 138, 172; Hodgson, 1979). Women's satisfaction with their roles, whether in the home or at work, seems to be a much better predictor: Women who are more satisfied spend more time interacting with their children (Hodgson, 1979). Sometimes there are problems of supervision of children, but as we shall see in greater detail in Chapter 13, these are largely the product of the limited availability of quality day care. In general, children in properly planned and supervised day-care centers do as well as children raised at home. There may, it is true, be an increasing tendency among adults to put their own concerns ahead of the welfare of their children. However, this tendency exists among both men and women and cannot simply be attributed to changing sex roles.

With respect to family cohesion, it is true that women who work outside the home are at greater risk of divorce than housewives. This may be partly due to the fact that dual-earner couples have less time to spend together (see Kingston and Nock, 1987). However, a more important reason is that working women are financially better able to leave an unhappy marriage. According to Thornton and Freedman (1983, pp. 27–28), social-science research provides no clear evidence that families with the wife in the labor force are any less happy than families where the wife remains at home. Thus, changing sex roles may have altered how women *respond* when they find themselves in an unhappy or troubled home situation, but there is no evidence that the actual incidence of such situations has increased.

Dysfunctions of Sex Roles Any functionalist analysis of sex roles must also consider their dysfunctions. In what ways do they *inhibit* the effectiveness of society, the family, or the individual? One area in which there is evidence of such dysfunctions is psychological well-being. Among both men and women, people with a *mix* of masculine and feminine personality traits have higher self-esteem and better mental health than those in whom traditional gender traits predominate (Spence et al., 1975; Deutsch and Gilbert, 1976; Lamke et al., 1982; Orlovsky, 1977; Major et al., 1981). Moreover, *androgynous* individuals—those with some of the traditional traits of each sex—display greater flexibility in various aspects of behavior (LaFrance and Carmen, 1980; Ickes and Barnes, 1978). These findings suggest that in terms of personal adjustment, self-esteem, and flexibility, adherence to a traditional sex role can be dysfunctional. These researchers conclude that women show better self-esteem, flexibility, and role performance when they have both masculine and feminine traits. Specifically in terms of roles, there is also evidence that women who are employed outside the home either part time or full time are happier on the average and less at risk of depression than those who are full-time home-makers (for a discussion of this research, see Hoyenga and Hoyenga, 1979, pp. 343–346).

From a broader functionalist perspective, one might raise serious questions about the benefits to society of denying half of its adult population the opportunity to develop fully their creativity, productive capacity, and freedom of choice. From a purely economic standpoint, the only thing that has saved the typical American family from a substantial decline in its standard of living over the past decade and a half has been the massive entry of women into the labor force. Productivity growth and real hourly wages (hourly pay adjusted for the effects of inflation) have generally lagged since the mid-1970s. Millions of wives and mothers entered the labor force in part to compensate for the resultant loss of income. Had this not occurred, the standard of living of many Americans would have declined substantially.

The Conflict Perspective

Male Gains from Sexism   The conflict perspective tells us that in order to understand any social arrangement, we must ask: Who benefits from this arrangement? So it goes for sex roles. Conflict theorists ask: Who benefits from sex roles as they exist in America? The answer, they believe, is that men benefit from them. (For a comprehensive statement of this view, see Collins, 1971.) Conflict theorists also ask: Does the group that benefits have disproportionate power, so that it can arrange society to its advantage? With respect to sex roles, they note the great power of men, something we have already discussed in reference to the political system, the family, and the world of work. Thus, sex roles persist because men use their power to maintain a system from which they benefit.

How do men benefit from traditional sex roles? We have already seen many ways in this chapter. Men receive higher wages than women and have a better chance of getting jobs that offer status, autonomy, and authority. Men enjoy greater mobility and freedom in choosing how to spend their time—their jobs take them outside the home, and if the family owns just one automobile, it is likely to be the husband's. Even in today's typical two-worker, two-car family, men still enjoy advantages. For example, when both husband and wife are employed full time, the total work week of men—on the job and in the home—is less than that of women. In a material sense—speaking in terms of income, wealth, status, power, and free time—all indications are that traditional sex roles work to the advantage of men. As shown in the box entitled "The Costs of Sexism to Men," there are other areas in which men pay a price for these benefits. Even so, the material benefits of sex roles to men are real. Thus, it is hardly surprising that men would use their power to maintain such sex roles.

Sources of Male Power   One question that conflict theorists ask is: How did males achieve unequal power in the first place? One explanation, which involves a combination of functionalist and conflict theory, is that male power is the outgrowth of a role specialization that was once useful to society. Although assigning roles to men that took them outside the home was originally useful, it also gave men certain power that women didn't have. It gave them greater freedom of movement and more contact with the outside world, and it made women dependent upon them for basic

The Costs of Sexism to Men

Although men benefit from sexism in terms of income, wealth, and power, sexism exacts some high costs in other areas of their lives. Men as well as women are denied certain freedoms by sexism. In fact, the pressure to "be a man" that males experience from early childhood probably exceeds anything that women encounter. Those who do not conform to this pressure are labeled "sissies" or "wimps," with all the negative consequences that such labels carry.

More specifically, men are supposed to be in control of every situation (which is not always possible) and to avoid any public display of emotion. Neither expressions of tenderness nor emotional breakdowns or outbursts have been acceptable male behavior. Such pressures on men exact a high cost in terms of mental and physical health.

In all likelihood, they are at least part of the reason why men are more likely than women to abuse alcohol and other drugs and are far more inclined to commit violence—the overwhelming majority of assaults and murders are committed by males, usually against other males. Many stress-related illnesses are also more common among men than among women, including heart disease, high blood pressure, and ulcers. Although men are often under less stress than women, they are expected to handle stress differently, always maintaining outward calm and control. Women, in contrast, have more opportunities to release the tension by expressing their emotions. This is probably one reason that women outlive men by 6 or 7 years on the average.

Thus, a move toward a more androgynous society could offer opportunities for men and risks for women. Men today undoubtedly feel freer to express their emotions than they did in the past. There is a growing recognition of the role of emotional expression in the mental health of both men and women. Conversely, as women move into traditionally male roles, they may experience some of the same pressures men feel. In 1987, for example, much was made of the fact that Representative Patricia Schroeder appeared to cry when she announced that she had decided not to run for president—a situation reminiscent of an earlier one when public tears lead to the breakdown of Senator Edmund Muskie's 1972 presidential candidacy. We see the presidency as a "male" role, and although it may now be more acceptable for women to seek that role, it seems that whoever seeks it is expected to play the role in a traditionally male manner.

---

food supplies obtained through hunting. All this translated into male power, and once males had this power, they began to use it to their advantage, setting up a society that became increasingly male-dominated.

Some conflict theorists add a second line of reasoning to this. They argue that size and physical strength were sources of power that males used to get what they wanted from women. In the United States, China, and many other societies, wives in times past were seen largely as their husbands' property. Certainly, the use or threat of violence is an important source of power, and it probably played a major role in the establishment of male dominance.

Today, of course, the law forbids violence by men against women, although even now the courts and police are often reluctant to intervene if such violence occurs within the family. Physical strength is largely irrelevant to most jobs, so occupational spe-

cialization by sex is far less functional than it once was. Yet today, there are other mechanisms by which men retain disproportionate power. To a large extent, we have already seen what these are: disproportionate political power and control of the purse strings within the family.

Feminism: A Challenge to Male Power Conflict theorists also hold, of course, that social inequality leads to conflict as disadvantaged groups struggle to improve their power and status in society. This, too, is true in the case of sex roles. In the United States and many other societies throughout the world (particularly those with higher levels of industrialization), one of the major social changes of recent decades has been the emergence of **feminism** on a large scale. Feminism can be defined as a social movement and an ideology in support of the idea that a larger share of scarce resources (wealth, income, power, status) should go to women. Essentially, the governing principles of feminism are that women should enjoy the same rights in society as men and that they should share equally in society's opportunities and in its scarce resources.

ORIGINS OF FEMINISM IN AMERICA   In the United States, feminism can be traced back nearly 150 years. The movement is generally regarded as having begun with a 1848 meeting in Seneca Falls, New York, which set forth a statement of women's rights modeled after the Declaration of Independence. For the next 70 years, the major objective of this movement was to obtain the vote for women (only men were allowed to vote in the national elections in the United States until 1920). The early feminist movement didn't succeed in changing other aspects of sex discrimination in America, however, for several reasons (Degler, 1980). First, women in that era saw advantages in the emerging housewife role. Second, just getting women the vote was a tremendous battle because opponents (as well as many supporters) of women's suffrage believed that if women got the vote, they would overturn the political order by voting in ways radically different from men. (They didn't.) After the suffrage battle was won, feminism as an issue faded for a time, only to resurface in the 1960s and 1970s in a form that amounted to a much wider and more fundamental challenge to traditional sex roles.

TWENTIETH-CENTURY FEMINISM   By the 1970s, U.S. feminists were challenging the housewife role in a way the earlier movement never did, and they had some real successes. For example, women have moved out of the home and into the paid labor force in unprecedented numbers over the past 2 decades. The notion that the woman's place is in the home, once taken for granted, is now rejected by most Americans — overwhelmingly so among younger and more educated Americans. As shown in Figure 6.3, a clear majority of married women are in the paid labor force. Even among women with young children, more than half work outside the home for pay. With less success, feminists also have united around the notion of equal pay for equal (or comparable) work and have sought to write a ban on sex discrimination (the Equal Rights Amendment) into the U.S. Constitution. In the home,

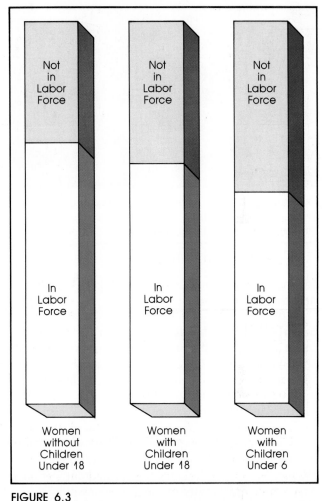

FIGURE 6.3
Labor Force Participation of Married Women, by Presence and Age of Children
SOURCE: U.S. Bureau of the Census, 1986a.

husbands have been challenged to take on a bigger share of household work as wives have moved into the labor force. In short, women in the past 2 decades have challenged sexism in more dramatic ways than at any previous time in our history.

Similar changes have occurred in many other countries, including virtually all of Europe and, in a somewhat different form, in China and the Soviet bloc. If not worldwide, the trend toward feminist thinking and toward new roles for women is at the

International Women's Conference in Mexico City. The trend toward the feminist viewpoint has been an important influence in many parts of the world.

least pervasive throughout all industrialized capitalist and socialist countries.

Social Origins of the New Feminism Why has feminism become so influential in the industrialized world since World War II? Although the reasons vary somewhat from country to country, certain conditions have appeared in a number of countries. First, traditional sex roles have become less functional in modern societies, for reasons noted earlier in this chapter. Conditions also developed in many countries that made women less satisfied with their traditional roles. Women were becoming more educated but were not getting the opportunity to use that education. During World War II, women were pressed into nontraditional roles in many countries, including performing manual labor in defense plants, and found out that they could be effective in those roles. They also found that under the right conditions, they could be well rewarded for work outside the home. Although many women were happy to return to their traditional roles after the war, they realized that they could succeed in other roles, and this may have had the long-term effect of making them more interested in nontraditional roles. Also during this time, the growth of mass media throughout the world enhanced communication, which made it easier for feminist leaders to transmit their message to other dissatisfied women.

Finally, the 1960s was a period of worldwide social upheaval that witnessed the antiwar and civil rights movements in the United States, the student and labor upheavals in France, the Cultural Revolution in China, the struggle for political freedom in Czechoslovakia, the separatist movement among French-Canadians, the religious conflict in Northern Ireland, and the beginnings of long struggles for majority rule in South Africa and Zimbabwe (then Rhodesia). Women were involved in all of these struggles, but they often found themselves relegated to such nonleadership roles as preparing meals, stuffing envelopes, and running errands. This had three effects. First, involvement in these movements made women realize that they, too, could create a movement. Second, the limited role allowed to women in many of these social movements heightened their dissatisfaction. Third, these movements brought dissatisfied women together, so they could communicate with each other and organize a movement of their own (Freeman, 1973). Together, these conditions greatly accelerated the development of feminist movements in many countries.

How Are Sex Roles Changing in America?

In this final section, I shall attempt to assess the meaning of recent changes in sex and gender roles in America and to address some information that may give us an idea where our society is headed. We shall begin by noting areas in which norms concerning relations between men and women have changed.

Sexual Double Standard

Society's views concerning the sexual freedom of men and women have also changed dramatically over the past few decades. The Victorian sexual double standard assumed that sex was to be enjoyed by men and that it was normal for unmarried men to want to "fool around." Women, however, were expected to remain pure and were considered "too good" to enjoy sex. As a result, sexual activity among unmarried males was largely taken for granted (even if somewhat disapproved of). For unmarried women, though, it was much more seriously forbidden, and a good deal less common. By the late 1960s, however, that system had changed (Christiansen and Gregg, 1970). Today, norms about sexual behavior are more similar for men and women than in the past, as are the behaviors themselves (Hunt, 1974).

Employment Discrimination

Another area in which there has been major change is the law. The Civil Rights Act of 1964 forbade deliberate discrimination against women in hiring and wages. Since then, it has been illegal to refuse to hire a person because of sex, unless the employer can prove that sex is a bona fide factor in a person's ability to perform a particular job, which is rarely the case. Similarly, you cannot pay an employee less (or, for that matter, more) than other employees in the same job with similar qualifications simply because she is a woman. Moreover, the government for a time interpreted this law as requiring employers to take affirmative action to ensure that women have the same opportunities as men to get the more desirable jobs. However, as we shall see in Chapter 11, there was a major reversal of such government support for affirmative action under the Reagan administration.

Sexual Assault

At the level of state law, there have been important changes in the rules of evidence concerning sexual assault. In the past, a rape victim practically had to

---

World War II pressed many former housewives to enter traditionally male manufacturing jobs, and they discovered that they could do so successfully.

prove to the court that she did not bring on the rape by her own behavior. She was asked questions about her past sexual behavior, as well as her past relationship with the person charged with raping her. Often, if a woman indicated that she had been sexually active in the past or had previously been involved with the accused, it was assumed that she really had engaged in sex voluntarily, or at least had misled the accused person into thinking she really wanted to have sex. In some cases, assumptions were made about the victim's sexual availability simply on the basis of how she dressed. In a sense, the victim was on trial, and if her past or present behavior was found wanting, judges and juries rejected the possibility that a crime might have taken place. Most states, however, have recently passed laws restricting the kinds of questions that can be asked of rape victims. It can no longer be assumed in most states that if a woman once wanted to have sex, she always will in the future, which is about what the old patterns of questioning assumed. Still, rape victims are often subjected to personal and embarrassing questioning, and as a result, many rapes still go unreported and thus unprosecuted.

Limitations of Change

Despite some changes, women's efforts to improve their status have met with only limited success. Most notable is the failure to ratify the Equal Rights Amendment (ERA), which reads in part:

> Equality of rights under the law shall not be denied or abridged by the United States or by any State on account of sex.

In 1972 this amendment passed in the U.S. Congress but was not ratified by the necessary number of states, even after a 3-year extension of a congressional deadline for ratification. Since the passage of that deadline in 1982, the ERA has not again been approved by Congress and thus has yet to become law.

The effect of civil rights legislation on the actual pay received by men and women, moreover, has been limited. We have seen that there have been changes, but only modest ones, in the wages of women relative to those of men and in occupational segregation. Thus, the biggest actual change in the status of women, so

Women in a shelter for the homeless. A growing share of poor people are either women or children in families with a female householder.

far, has been the movement of many women out of the housewife role and into the labor force. Although this movement has given women a measure of freedom and independence they did not enjoy in the past, the low pay of employed women remains a major barrier to full sexual equality. In fact, when combined with the increased divorce rate and changes in divorce law, this low pay has led to a new problem. As is discussed in the box "The Feminization of Poverty," being a woman has increasingly become associated with being poor in the United States. At present, the sex of the primary wage earner is the best predictor of whether a family's income will fall below the federal poverty level.

What Does the Future Hold?

What are the prospects for a move toward greater equality between American men and women in the future? There are a number of ways we can look for answers to this question. We can start with the attitudes of Americans. It does appear that, in many ways, American attitudes are supportive of gender equality. A poll by the Roper Organization (1980) showed that 72 percent of adult men and women believed that changes in American sex roles were of a permanent nature, and a smaller but still substantial majority of 57 percent said they *wanted* the changes to continue.

Of course, generalized support for equal opportunity does not always translate into the reality of equal opportunity. In the economic arena, for exam-

ple, true equality of opportunity for men and women would require fundamental social changes. One such change would be a major change in current patterns of occupational segregation. Is there any sign that this is happening? In keeping with the finding noted earlier that gifted girls are most likely to aspire to traditionally male occupations, there has been a sharp rise in the number of women training for certain prestigious fields such as law and medicine (see Figure 6.4). However, *overall* occupational segregation has declined only modestly, and many occupations remain overwhelmingly male or female. As late as 1980, for example, over 95 percent of nurses, secretaries, reception-

FIGURE 6.4
Percentage of Women among Degree Recipients, Selected Professions, 1974–1985
SOURCE: Carpenter, 1987, pp. 38, 40, 47.

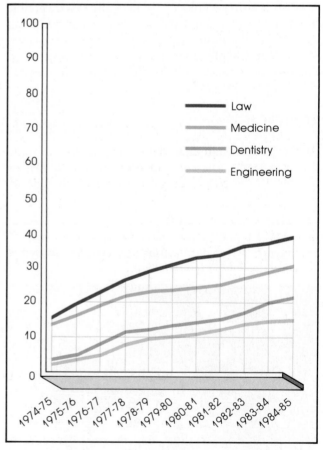

The Feminization of Poverty: A New Form of Sexism?

One highly disturbing trend in the United States is the *feminization of poverty* (Pearce, 1982). More than ever before in our history, being a woman has become associated with being poor. In 1986 the overall female poverty rate in the United States was 15.2 percent, compared to 11.8 percent among males (U.S. Bureau of the Census, 1987a, p. 30). Among adults, where virtually all the difference occurs, the poverty rate for women was 13.5 percent, compared to just 8.5 percent for men (computed from U.S. Bureau of the Census, 1987a, p. 30).

The difference becomes even more pronounced if we look at family data. Among families with a female householder, the poverty rate in 1986 was over 34 percent—more than three times the poverty rate among all families. Of course, the poverty rate among two-parent families is bound to be lower, because most of them have two earners. However, if we compare only single-parent families, the poverty rate was 11.4 percent among those with a male householder, compared to 34.6 percent among those with a female householder. In fact, the sex of the householder is more closely associated with family poverty than any other characteristic, including race, region of the country, or urban/rural location.

Why is being a woman, or living in a family with a female householder, so strongly associated with poverty today? Essentially, the reasons involve the high divorce rate, the resolution of divorce cases by the legal system, and—most importantly—the low pay of women. With our high divorce rate—about one marriage out of two ends in divorce—far more women today than in the past must support themselves and one or more children solely on their own incomes. Partly because women are more likely than men to seek custody of children, and partly because the courts often favor the mother in custody battles, over 90 percent of all children in one-parent households live with their mothers. Many more female households today are also created by out-of-wedlock births than was the case in the past.

The courts play a role in the feminization of poverty for several reasons. First, alimony is largely a thing of the past. Most judges today assume that women are employed and therefore can support their families, an assumption that is incorrect because of women's low wages.

Second, although child-support decrees are often awarded in divorce cases, they are poorly enforced. Thus, a large percentage of fathers stop paying child support rather quickly, and some never pay at all, despite court orders. Finally, any order to pay child support—much less enforcement—is very rare in cases of out-of-wedlock births. The result of all this is that the majority of fathers who do not live with their children do not contribute much, or anything, toward the support of those children.

All of these things might not make such a great difference if women's wages were as high as men's, and if quality, low-cost day care were as available in the United States as it is in most other industrialized countries. With women's wages so low, however, and with affordable day care so hard to find, the conditions described in the preceding paragraphs make a huge difference. The reality is that when a divorce occurs, the husband usually experiences a substantial *increase* in his standard of living, whereas the wife and children experience an even larger *decline* in theirs (Weitzman, 1985). The net result of all this is what sociologists call the feminization of poverty.

---

ists, and kindergarten teachers were female, but less than 5 percent of construction workers, engineers, firefighters, and airplane pilots were (Blau and Ferber, 1986, p. 167).

Although full work-place equality probably cannot occur as long as occupational segregation persists, major reductions of *income* inequality could occur even without a change in occupational segregation. For this to happen, however, something similar to comparable worth would have to be implemented. In other words, men and women with comparable skills, education, and experience would have to be paid equal wages, even when they work at *different* jobs. It has been estimated that although such a change would not eliminate *all* male-female income inequality, it would raise the real wages of the average woman worker by about 10 percent (Aldrich and Buchele, 1986), which is a very substantial difference.

Comparable worth is not likely to be implemented soon, however. It is unlikely to happen voluntarily in the private sector, because any company that decided to pay women the same as comparably skilled and educated men would experience an increase in labor costs, and therefore would be at a disadvantage vis-à-vis companies that had no such policy. In this sense, a conflict theorist could argue that our economic system, with its profit orientation, is inhibiting the move toward economic equality of the sexes.

In noneconomic areas the prospects for change also remain uncertain. Although men have changed their thinking concerning their role in the home, it is not clear that they are willing to share fully in domestic chores. Moreover, different patterns of communication continue to reflect inequalities between men and women. Although there are serious questions about the adequacy of her sample, Hite's (1987) survey of American women does strongly suggest that lack of communication is one of the biggest complaints women have about their husbands. In general, men interrupt far more than women (Zimmerman and West, 1975; Kollock et al., 1985), and women are expected to spend more time listening while men talk (Kollock et al., 1985). Women also are more likely than men to use gestures associated with low status, such as nodding, smiling, and holding their arms close to their bodies (see McKenna and Denmark, 1978). So long as these patterns exist, men and women will not interact as equals, and it is unlikely that women will attain equal access to desirable roles in life. Thus, although sex roles have changed considerably in some ways, they have not changed much in other ways. More important, sex roles remain not only different, but also *unequal.*

The likelihood that we will eliminate this inequality between the roles of men and women at any time in the foreseeable future appears dubious at best. Our society has moved in that direction, perhaps more dramatically in the past 2 decades than at any previous time in our history. However, it has a very long way to go before true sexual equality is attained.

Summary

Sex refers to the biological characteristic of being male or female, whereas *gender* refers to socially learned traits that are attached to sex in society. Most societies have a system of *sex roles,* in which men and women are expected to play different roles. In most societies, including the United States, these roles are unequal, and male dominance is the rule. Some societies, however, are androgynous, and a few are even female-dominant. Moreover, even though male dominance is widespread, its form varies from one society to another, and it changes over time. In the United States and other Western societies, for example, the housewife role that emerged with the Industrial Revolution faded in importance after World War II.

In the United States and other industrial societies, women are increasingly entering the paid labor force. However, women work at different jobs than men, usually for lower pay. Despite some improvements, the typical American woman still receives only two-thirds the wages of the typical man. Differences in the wages and salaries of men and women cannot be explained by differences in education or skills, or even by the greater tendency of women to work part time and to leave the labor force temporarily. Rather, they are a product of the different jobs of women, their lesser opportunity to be promoted into jobs with supervisory authority, and their frequent need to subordinate their own careers to those of their husbands.

Some of this inequality is also the result of sex-role socialization, the process by which men and women are taught to expect and seek different and unequal roles in life. Achievement, strength, and independence are stressed for boys, while girls are taught to be nice and to look attractive. Clothes, games, children's books, television, parents, and teachers all give these messages. Through the process of the looking-glass self, boys and girls are taught different self-images. They come to believe that their skills lie in different subjects, and by high school, this process has become a self-fulfilling prophecy. Children also see men and women in different jobs (in the media, in school materials, and in their own experiences), and as a result they aspire to different jobs themselves. As a result of all this, boys and girls who have little if any natural predisposition to develop different skills or adopt different roles end up doing so.

Some functionalists see sex roles as a case of cultural lag—something that was useful in the past but no longer is today. They predict that society will gradually move toward androgyny. Other functionalists, however, see sex roles as essential to the cohesiveness of the family and blame such problems as the soaring divorce rate on the declining influence of traditional sex roles. Conflict theorists argue that sex roles exist because men benefit from them. According to conflict theories, men use their disproportionate power to maintain a system of unequal sex roles. Feminism offers the possibility of changing this system of inequality. Conflict theorists also argue that families with traditional sex roles are no happier or more functional than are more androgynous families, and that the ability of working women to afford to get divorced may not be all bad.

Increasingly since World War II, women in a number of countries, including the United States, have challenged unequal sex roles through powerful feminist movements. These recent movements have been more broad-based and influential than earlier women's movements. They have been facilitated by the increased education of women, improved mass communication, and the participation of women in a number of other social movements. Feminism has not eliminated sex roles or sexual inequality, but it has brought significant legal changes in many countries, as well as some important changes in public opinion concerning the appropriate roles of men and women.

Glossary

sex The physical or biological characteristic of being male or female.

gender Socially learned traits or characteristics that are associated with men or women.

sex roles Social roles that people are expected to play because they are male or female, which often carry unequal status, rewards, and opportunities. Also called **gender roles**.

sexism Structured inequality between men and women, and the norms and beliefs that support such inequality.

institutional sexism Systematic practices and patterns within social institutions that lead to inequality between men and women.

sex-role socialization The process by which sex roles are taught and learned.

occupational segregation A pattern whereby two groups—most often men and women—hold different types of jobs.

feminism An ideology or a related social movement advocating the ideas that a larger share of scarce resources should go to women and that social roles should not be assigned on the basis of sex.

Further Reading

BERNARD, JESSE. 1981. *The Female World*. New York: Free Press. This book, already a classic, contrasts the female world of love and support with the male world of rational exchange. Because of male dominance, the male world has great impacts upon the female world. Bernard examines these impacts and how they affect women's options, and offers some important insights about how sociology must change in order to understand women and their lives better.

BIANCHI, SUZANNE, AND DAPHNE SPAIN. 1986. *American Women in Transition*. New York: Russell Sage Foundation. A comprehensive, data-based examination of the status of women in contemporary American society. A good source of statistical information on the relative positions of men and women with respect to income, employment, and family status.

DOYLE, JAMES A. 1983. *The Male Experience*. Dubuque, IA: William C. Brown. An examination of masculinity and the role of men in society, with emphasis on both historical development and cross-cultural comparison.

JONES, JAQUELINE. 1985. *Labor of Love, Labor of Sorrow: Black Women, Work, and the Family from Slavery to Present*. New York: Basic Books. Although sex roles exist within all racial and ethnic groups, the nature of those roles is greatly influenced by the experiences of each such group and by its position in the larger society. This book explores the female role as experienced by African-American women.

STOCKARD, JEAN, AND MIRIAM M. JOHNSON. 1980. *Sex Roles: Sex Inequality and Sex-Role Development*. Englewood Cliffs, NJ: Prentice Hall. An overview of the sociology of sex and gender, emphasizing the social roots and social meaning of sexism and the means by which unequal sex roles are taught and learned.

CHAPTER 7

Groups and Organizations

Think for a moment of the people you come into contact with over the course of a typical day. Depending on your living situation, you probably begin the day by interacting with a roommate, spouse, or parent. In class, you interact with your fellow students and your professor. After class, you may meet with a group of friends for lunch, then perhaps hurry off to work where you interact with co-workers and, perhaps, customers or clients. If you participate in sports or some other recreational activity, you likely interact with yet another group of people. Your daily experiences illustrate the very important point that people are social beings — much of what we do is done with groups of other people, and we come into contact with many such groups every day. Our need for groups is both practical and social. On the social side, we saw in Chapter 5 examples of the devastating consequences of being raised in isolation. On the practical side, we depend on the cooperative efforts of groups of people for everything from food and shelter to education and entertainment. In this chapter, we shall examine how and why people group together, along with the various types of human groups and their impacts on our lives.

S ociologists use the term *group* in a number of ways. Sometimes it is used to refer to a *status group,* a category of people who share some common, socially important status, such as race, ancestry, sex, or social class.

Groups and Organizations: What Is the Difference?

Groups

When sociologists use the term *social group,* however, they usually mean something a bit more specific. A **social group** can be defined as a set of two or more people who interact regularly and in a manner that is defined by some common purpose, a set of norms, and a structure of statuses and roles within the group. By this definition, a college class, a family, a softball team, and a work place all qualify as social groups. In contrast, people standing on a corner waiting for a stoplight do not qualify, even if they do interact. There is no regularity to these people's interaction, nor any division of roles and statuses. They share a common purpose only to the extent that they all want to cross the street, but once across, they will all go their separate ways. Sociologists refer to such a cluster of people as an *aggregate.*

Formal Organizations A particular kind of group that is of great importance in modern society is the **formal organization,** which is defined as a relatively large-scale group having a name, some official purpose or goals, and a structure of statuses and roles and set of rules designed to promote these goals. What distinguishes formal organizations from other kinds of groups is the official — and usually written — nature of the goals, rules, and status structure. The structure of a formal organization is sufficiently clear that it can be put on paper in the form of an organizational chart; in contrast, other kinds of groups are much less formal. Imagine, for example, making an organizational chart of your family or of a group of friends who meet once a week to bowl or swim.

Formal organizations can be grouped into three broad types, according to Etzioni (1975). Some organizations are *normative* or *voluntary organizations* — people choose to join them because they are interested in the group's purpose or activities. Examples are recreational clubs, political groups, and professional associations. Another type, overlapping somewhat with voluntary organizations, is the *utilitarian organization* — an organization designed to accomplish some task. Businesses and neighborhood improvement associations are examples of this type, as are large-scale organizations such as corporations, governments, and labor unions. Finally, there are *coercive organizations* — organizations that people are compelled to participate in. This category includes the total institutions discussed in Chapter 5 — prisons, the military, and mental hospitals, for example. However, for children, it includes a wider range of organizations, most notably schools and religious institutions. We now turn to a more detailed examination of groups and organizations, beginning with groups.

Group Characteristics and Dynamics

Group Size

One of the most important characteristics of a group is its size. The smallest possible group is a **dyad,** which consists of two people. In a dyad, only one interpersonal relationship exists in the group — that between the two members. If either member withdraws from interaction in a dyad — by daydreaming, for example — the group's interaction stops. Moreover, the group itself comes to an end if either member chooses to withdraw. The effects of group size on group dynamics can be seen by comparing the dyad to the **triad,** a group consisting of three people. In a triad, three relationships exist. In a group consisting of Bill, Mary, and

A college class and a baseball team are examples of social groups.

Sue, for example, there is one relationship between Bill and Mary, one between Bill and Sue, and one between Mary and Sue.

The presence of three relationships as opposed to one makes an important difference in several ways. First, one person can withdraw without stopping the group's interaction. Bill might daydream, but that would not stop interaction between Mary and Sue. Second, coalitions can be formed when disagreements arise within the group. Bill and Mary might, for example, form a coalition against Sue. They want to see one movie, while Sue wants to see another. In this situation, they would likely cooperate with each other to put pressure on Sue to go to the movie they want to see. And, in many cases, Sue will give in, in order to remain an accepted member of the group.

A third characteristic of triads is that they can be *balanced* or *unbalanced* (Heider, 1946, 1958; Zajonc, 1960). As long as Mary, Sue, and Bill remain friendly, the group is balanced: all of its relationships are positive. But suppose that one day Mary and Bill have a terrible fight and come to hate each other. The triad has now become unbalanced. Consider Sue's position: She likes both Bill and Mary, who hate each other. If she chooses to do something with Bill, Mary

will likely respond, "Why do you want to spend time with that jerk instead of me?" If she goes somewhere with Mary, she will likely get a similar response from Bill. Both Bill and Mary may try to get her to take "their side" in their conflicts. Sue is thus placed in an impossible position, and the likely result is that she will back away from her relationship with either Mary or Bill, thereby ending the triad.

Complexity and Group Size Obviously, the complexity of relationships in a triad is far beyond that of a dyad. This complexity continues to increase as small groups get larger, until eventually a size is reached where, rather than one small group, there is a large group with several smaller subgroups within it. At this point, which is reached at a group size of somewhere between about 7 and 12, several important changes occur. One is that it becomes commonplace to have two or more coalitions rather than one, as in a triad. The possibilities for the group to become unbalanced increase, although the pressures on individuals may decrease because they have more potential relationships to choose from. Another important difference is the need for a system of formal recognition of speakers—deciding who "has the floor." Often one or more side conversations go on while one person attempts to address the group. (You can probably observe this dynamic in your next sociology class.) Also, in this more formal situation, people speak differently:

Rather than talking to others, they address the group, using a different vocabulary and style of speech. At this point, the group has become less like a small group and more like a formal organization.

Primary and Secondary Groups

Another way that groups vary is in the degree of closeness of their members. Some groups, such as families and good friends, are very close. The people in such groups interact because they value one another — the interpersonal relationships are the primary purpose of the group's existence. This type of group is called a **primary group** (Cooley, 1929 [orig. 1909]). Primary groups are always small because intimate relationships cannot develop throughout a large network of people. Within large groups, interpersonal relationships are much less close and are secondary to some other purpose of the organization. This type of group is called a **secondary group.** Examples of secondary groups are businesses, schools, and political organizations. In these groups, interpersonal contacts occur for the purpose of conducting business, gaining an education, or influencing politics — not for the sake of the contacts themselves. A secondary group may be either large or small.

As is illustrated by Figure 7.1, the line between primary groups and secondary groups is not always clear, and real-life groups can be placed along a range or continuum from clear-cut primary groups through ambiguous cases to clear-cut secondary groups. Also, primary groups can and do form within a larger secondary group. In fact, a large secondary group typically includes many primary groups. Most formal organizations are secondary groups, but within them, primary groups often develop among members or co-workers.

Historically, secondary groups have proliferated as society has modernized. Prior to industrialization, people spent most of their time in small, informal primary groups centered around family, kin, neighborhood, and religious affiliation. Today we come into contact with far more people, and most of this contact is impersonal and centers around business, education, government, or some other large formal organization.

Although secondary groups have become much

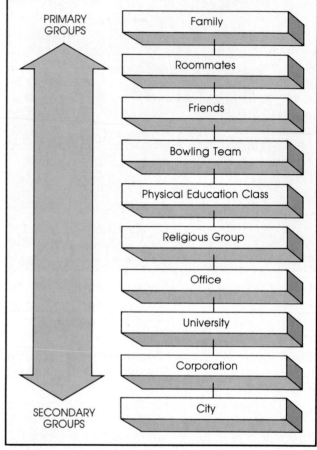

FIGURE 7-1
The Continuum from Primary to Secondary Groups

more important in modern society, they have *not* replaced primary groups. Rather, they have been added on, so that we come into contact with a far greater diversity of people than was the case in the past. Even in modern urban society, friends and families remain important to most people, and primary-group relationships still play an important role in people's lives (Fischer, 1982, 1984; Reiss, 1959).

Conflict and Cohesion within and between Groups

Conformity within Groups Pressures for conformity are present in any group. Observations of small groups show that if a clear majority holds a certain position at the start, the group generally will move toward consensus. Pressures on a dissenting individual are particularly strong, as was demonstrated by a fascinating experiment by Solomon Asch (1956, 1965). In this experiment, a group of eight people was asked, one by one, to choose which of three lines on a card matched the length of a line on another card. Actually, only one person in the group—the last to answer—was a subject of the experiment; the rest were *confederates*, that is, part of the experiment. After a few examples in which the confederates made the correct choice, they all gave an obviously wrong answer—such as choosing line B as the matching line in Figure 7.2. When it came time for the subject to answer, about one in three conformed to the obviously wrong opinion of the others and picked the incorrect line. (In a control group, only 1 percent answered incorrectly.) In most cases, the conformity was only outward, but for some, it was more than that. When debriefed afterward, the majority said they knew better but went along to avoid ridicule or ostracism from the rest of the group. However, some actually disbelieved what they were seeing, offering such explanations as "I guess I just couldn't see it right."

Outside Threats and Group Cohesion Despite the general tendency toward group consensus and conformity, conflicts of values, personality, or interest can lead to divisions within any group. Often, however, these divisions can be minimized through some outside threat or conflict with another group. In such situations, sociologists refer to the group to which a person belongs as the **ingroup** and to other groups as **outgroups.** Outgroups are often seen as threatening to the ingroup. They may be potential competitors, or they may simply do things differently. Because of the widespread tendency toward *ethnocentrism* discussed in Chapter 4, an outgroup that does things differently will often be seen as inferior. To acknowledge that an outgroup's way could be just as good would threaten the solidarity of the ingroup, so usually the opposite happens: The extent to which the outgroup is actually threatening or different is often exaggerated to promote ingroup unity.

The extent to which an outside threat can serve as a unifying force can be seen in the response of

people to natural disasters and wars. The usual tendency is to pull together to combat the threat or deal with the emergency. In the face of a flood, a blizzard, or an earthquake, people will forget their normal differences and work together. This tendency is so strong that leaders sometimes take advantage of it to strengthen their own position. On the societal level, national leaders sometimes encourage conflicts that lead to warfare in order to make people forget about divisive internal issues or about mistakes made by the leadership (Lang, 1972; Burrowes and Spector, 1973, p. 295). This process appears to have been part of the dynamic that led to World War I (Farrar, 1978, p. 169).

Despite this general tendency, some divisions

FIGURE 7-2
An Example of the Cards Used in Solomon Asch's Experiment
Although the standard line clearly corresponds to line B, many subjects were pressured into selecting the wrong choice. Adapted from Solomon Asch, 1955, "Opinions and Social Pressure," *Scientific American* (193): 31–35.

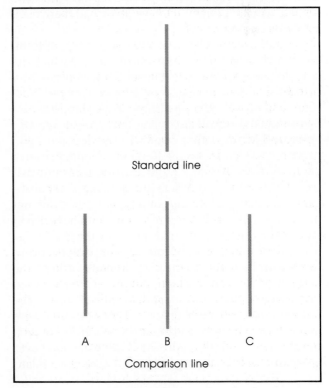

Standard line

A   B   C

Comparison line

within the group are too deep to be put aside, even in the face of an outside threat. In such cases, the outside threat may even deepen the conflict. The response of families to a crisis such as a major illness or a breadwinner's loss of employment serves as an example. If a family is relatively strong, a crisis of this type will usually bring it closer together. However, the crisis may be too much for a weak or deeply divided family, in which case it often leads to a divorce.

Groupthink   Certain processes and dynamics that occur in groups often result in dangerous or inappropriate decisions. Two such processes are *groupthink* and *group polarization.*

   Groupthink is a process whereby a group collectively arrives at a decision that individual members privately oppose but do not challenge. This usually happens in small, cohesive groups with powerful leaders. Although individual members of the group believe the decision to be unwise, they do not speak out against it because they do not want to break the group consensus or challenge the leader. The result is that the group makes an unwise decision with little debate, which it might not have made had there been more discussion.

   Two commonly cited examples of groupthink are the 1962 Bay of Pigs invasion of Cuba, in which the United States sponsored an unsuccessful attempt by a group of Cuban exiles to overthrow Premier Fidel Castro, and the 1986 *Challenger* space shuttle explosion. Social psychologist Irving Janis (1972; see also Janis and Mann, 1977) examined the decision-making process that led to the Kennedy administration's support of the Bay of Pigs invasion. It turns out that many of Kennedy's advisers privately saw the foolishness of what was being contemplated but did not speak up. The result was a resounding military defeat and a diplomatic embarrassment. In the *Challenger* case, some engineers who knew about potential problems with the component that ultimately caused the accident did try to speak up, but they were pressured into silence. Both NASA and Morton Thiokol, the manufacturer of the shuttle's rocket boosters, were under great pressure to have a launch on time. As a result, the doubts about the safety of the launch never got past Thiokol's management and were never heard by the NASA officials who could have postponed the launch.

Group Polarization   Closely related to groupthink is a process known as *group polarization,* in which a group moves toward a stronger position or more extreme course of action than its members individually favor. This process can lead to either excessively risky or excessively cautious courses of action.

   THE RISKY SHIFT   The effects of group polarizations were first discovered in the form of the *risky shift* (Stoner, 1961; Wallach, Kogan, and Bem, 1962). The risky shift can be illustrated by an incident that occurred in an organization to which I belong. A few years ago, I served for a year on the governing board of a ski club. One of the jobs of the board was to plan the club's ski trips for the coming year. Each trip has a group leader, and it so happens that one of these leaders (I'll call him "Wayne") was so popular that his trips filled quickly no matter where they went. Late in the meeting, someone suggested that we could fill a "mystery trip" with Wayne as the leader, listing on the brochure a price for the trip but not telling people the destination. After some further discussion, it was decided that it would be a clever idea to make this a trip to Florida, ending with a 1-day stop at a very small local ski area a few miles outside of our town, so we could legitimately call it a ski trip. People would have so much fun, we concluded, that they wouldn't really mind spending hundreds of dollars and their precious vacation time to go to Florida when they wanted, and had paid for, a ski vacation. After loading up their ski equipment, and lots of winter sweaters and coats, we thought they would react cheerfully to finding themselves in Florida without warm-weather clothes, and finally coming back to a place near home where they could ski any time they want for $20. We actually believed at the time that this was a good idea! Fortunately, we left the meeting without finalizing our plans, and once apart from the group, we individually realized the folly of our thinking.

   Why does a group move toward such risky decisions that individuals would probably never make? Often there is a feeling that "We need to do something bold and different." The group wants to think it is being dynamic and creative, rather than doing the same old thing. In addition, there is frequently a tendency to rally around an idea that seems clever and adventurous, without considering what could go wrong. I know that both of these things happened in the ski trip example. Recall, too, Oliver North's testimony that he and his White House colleagues thought it would be a "neat idea" to "take the Ayatollah's money and use it against the Sandinistas," despite the practical, legal, and ethical problems of selling weapons to hostage takers and using the money to do something explicitly forbidden by Congress. Finally, people may try to enhance their status in the group by going along with what others suggest, which tends to move the group toward whatever idea someone suggests first (Laughlin and Early, 1982).

Not all group shifts are risky, however. Some groups shift toward an overly cautious approach, shunning even moderate actions that the individual members of the group would take (Moscovici and Zavalloni, 1969). Thus, group polarization may lead a group toward a position that is either riskier or more cautious than individual members would take. This process has been shown to occur in a wide variety of groups, including such diverse examples as bargaining and negotiation groups (Lamm and Sauer, 1974), groups of gamblers (Blaskovich, Ginsburg, and Howe, 1975), juries (Meyers and Kaplan, 1976), and school discussion groups (Myers and Bishop, 1970).

Basic Characteristics of Organizations

Although their purposes vary widely, all formal organizations share certain characteristics. First, they have some *purpose* or *goal*, which just about any member of the organization can recognize. The purpose may be nothing more than to have fun (a social club, for example), but it is a *recognized* purpose. Sociologists describe this characteristic of formal organizations by saying that they are *instrumental*. Second, organizations are *self-perpetuating*. This means that they have a life above and beyond that of individual members. Old members may leave and new members may join, but the organization continues. Both of these characteris-

tics distinguish formal organizations from other kinds of groups. Many informal groups do not have a formally defined purpose (though they usually do have some informal purpose), and many informal groups continue to exist only as long as a given set of individuals continues to participate. A group of four people who meet to play cards on Saturday night, for example, may stop meeting if two of its members move out of town.

A third characteristic of organizations, which is shared with other kinds of groups, is the presence of a leader or leaders. Often organizations try to institutionalize the presence of leaders by creating an *authority structure,* a set of positions, each of which carries some recognized function and decision-making power. A formal authority structure, however, is not necessary for leadership to develop.

Oligarchy versus Democracy

We have already noted that even organizations that attempt to be leaderless usually end up with leaders. We can take this idea a step further. It turns out that even in organizations that consciously seek to be democratic, not only will leaders emerge, but very often these leaders will make the important decisions.

Michels's Iron Law of Oligarchy

This insight arises from the work of political sociologist Robert Michels (1967 [orig. 1911]; 1949 [orig. 1915]). Early in his life Michels was a member of political organizations that were strongly committed to democracy and social equality. He noticed that no matter what the organizations preached, they in fact were run by their leaders and not by the ordinary members. Michels became convinced that this tendency to be run by the leadership was a characteristic of all formal organizations, a principle that he called the **"iron law of oligarchy."**

According to Michels, there are clear reasons why all organizations exhibit this tendency. All organizations have certain tasks that members must *delegate* to their leaders. This delegation of work helps to

What Makes a Union Democratic?

The general membership has more influence relative to the leaders in some organizations than in others. A classic study by Lipset, Coleman, and Trow (1956) of the International Typographical Union shows some of the characteristics associated with democratic rather than oligarchic decision making. Lipset and his colleagues discovered that workers had distinctly more power relative to union leaders in the typographers' union than was the case in large-scale industrial unions such as the United Auto Workers. In other words, the typographers had much more influence over major decisions and day-to-day operations than did the autoworkers. Lipset accounted for this difference on the basis of the following characteristics of the typographers' union that made it different from many other unions:

- The small size of the typographers' union and its locals. This meant that most workers knew one another and their leaders fairly well, rather than just as faces at union meetings.
- The specialized nature of the typographer's work. This created a sense of community among the workers; a feeling that they constituted a distinct group of people.
- The tendency among typographers to socialize outside the job setting, so that the union members and leaders interacted in situations where their job and union status were irrelevant. This reduced the social distance between leaders and members.
- Limits on terms of office, especially on officers' serving successive terms. This institutionalized a rotation of leadership, which kept any one person from becoming too powerful.
- The development of organized political groupings, which became institutionalized within the union. Therefore, whoever was in office always faced an organized opposition.

These observations can be extended to other groups and organizations besides labor unions, including political systems. They partly explain why a two-party or multiparty system is usually more democratic than either a one-party or a nonpartisan system. The strong inference is that any group wanting to stay democratic should place strict limits on the amount of time its officers can serve and should encourage real elections, using an internal system of political parties if possible. Another inference is that the larger and more geographically dispersed a group or organization becomes, the harder it will be for that organization to remain truly democratic. In large organizations, the need for delegation is so great that the forces that led Michels to proclaim that "whoever says organization says oligarchy" are simply too strong to overcome.

---

concentrate power in the hands of leaders for several reasons. First, leaders gain access to information that others don't have. As will be discussed in Chapter 10, information is a source of power. Second, leaders benefit from a sense of obligation on the part of the organization's members. Because the leaders have spared the membership the burden of doing the work, most members feel obligated to cooperate with whatever policies the leaders suggest. As the leaders accumulate power, they frequently use it to advance or protect their own interests, sometimes even at the expense of the interests of the membership. Frequently, even in political organizations committed to social change, leaders become more conservative over time, more oriented to maintaining their own power, and thus more supportive of the status quo. As a result, when revolutions or new political movements succeed, they often have the ultimate result of merely replacing one group of powerful leaders with another because their original democratic ideals are lost or forgotten.

Oligarchy: Iron Law or Just a Tendency?

If Michels were entirely correct, his discovery would be depressing for anyone who favors democracy because it leads to the inevitable conclusion that democracy is an impossible ideal. Fortunately, Michels seems to have overstated his argument. Although leaders in all organizations do have disproportionate

Robert Michels outlined the iron law of oligarchy, which holds that no matter how democratic they attempt to be, all organizations are in reality run by their leaders.

power, that power is not unlimited. Many organizations have challenged and even removed their leaders. Moreover, as shown in the box entitled "What Makes for a Democratic Union?" we do know that certain elements can make organizations less oligarchic and more democratic.

A self-conscious effort to keep an organization democratic can sometimes succeed if the organization does not become too large. A recent example can be found in *cooperatives* and *collectives,* small organizations that provide goods or services and that are strongly committed to a democratic ideal. Rothschild and Whitt (1986) conducted field observations of five such organizations in California in the 1970s, all of which were made up of well-educated, middle-class people committed to liberal and democratic political principles. Among the features that kept these organizations democratic were avoidance of the written rules characteristic of most modern organizations, small size, and shunning of specialization. In effect, one way they prevented the leadership from gaining too much power was by eliminating formal positions of authority. Such organizations required a great deal of time for decision making because every decision had to be discussed and debated among the entire membership.

They had to keep to a narrow path between failure on the one side and "too much success" on the other. Organizations that failed often did so because of disorganization or conflict, which easily became personalized because every member was by definition deeply involved in it. Organizations that became "too successful" grew to the point that work had to be delegated and rules formalized, and at this point, oligarchic tendencies took over. Some organizations, though, were able to remain democratic and to continue to function effectively. We shall return to this issue later in this chapter.

Leadership in Groups and Organizations

Instrumental and Expressive Leadership

Although all groups and organizations have leaders, not all leaders have the same role and function within the group. Research on small groups by Bales (1953) and Slater (1955) uncovered two kinds of leaders, who

President Franklin Delano Roosevelt delivers a "fireside chat" concerning a census of unemployed Americans in 1937. Roosevelt was a rare example of a leader offering both instrumental and expressive leadership.

play different roles within the group. One type is the **instrumental leader,** also known as the *task leader.* This type of leader helps the group to define its job and determine how best to do it. The other kind of leader is the **expressive leader,** also known as the *socioemotional leader.* This leader helps to maintain the cohesiveness of the group and looks out for the emotional well-being of its members. He or she may tell a joke to relieve tension or help soothe the feelings of a member who was criticized.

A successful group needs both instrumental and expressive leaders. Groups that have only instrumental leaders are likely to bog down in dissension and lose their common identity. The members may feel that their leaders are insensitive to their concerns and cease to cooperate with the group (or, in extreme cases, cease to participate). Groups having only expressive leaders may get along very well but get nothing done. Even routine tasks essential to the maintenance of the group may go undone, thus threatening the group's very existence.

Although a group needs both types of leadership to be effective, it is rare to find both types in the same individual. Some groups initially rate the same person high on both qualities, but this estimation seldom lasts for long (Slater, 1955). Because instrumental leaders tend to upset people in the process of promoting their ideas, someone else must step forward to provide expressive leadership. Some societies have implicitly recognized this problem by institutionalizing separate roles for instrumental and expressive leadership. In constitutional monarchies such as Great Britain, Norway, and Sweden, the king or queen plays the expressive role, while the prime minister plays the instrumental role. The king or queen acts as a symbol of national pride and unity and performs a ceremonial function, while the parliament and the prime minister make the day-to-day political decisions.

Some sociologists believe that one of the characteristics of people who gain the reputation of being "great leaders" is their ability to offer both instrumental and expressive leadership. Franklin Roosevelt is sometimes cited as an example. As an instrumental leader, he developed a plan to get the country out of the Great Depression, and he got more legislation through Congress in his first 100 days in office than any of his predecessors. As an expressive leader, he soothed people with his fireside chats, assuring them that "The only thing we have to fear is fear itself." Most leaders, though, are clearly instrumental or expressive. Ronald Reagan, the "Great Communicator" who often couldn't keep his facts straight and left important decisions to subordinates, was clearly an expressive leader. Jimmy Carter and Richard Nixon, who planned and analyzed everything but ultimately failed to inspire much besides public distrust and ridicule, were examples of instrumental leaders.

Characteristics of Leaders

What are the personal characteristics of people who become leaders? The surprising answer is that it is not always easy to predict who will become a leader. Personality differences between people who become leaders and people who don't are rather small (Yukl, 1981). Leaders tend to be more intelligent, more extroverted, more psychologically balanced, more dominant, more self-confident, and more liberal than other group members (the last is true even in conservative groups), but the differences are minor, and many nonleaders have similar qualities (Mann, 1969; Hare, 1976; Stogdill, 1974; Yukl, 1981). Leaders also tend to be somewhat taller (Keyes, 1980) and more physically attractive than nonleaders. Becoming a leader, however, may be as much a product of a situation as of any individual characteristics, and different kinds of people emerge as leaders in different situations (Cooper and McGraugh, 1969). To some extent, becoming a leader is probably a product of being in the right place at the right time.

Styles of Leadership There are also important differences of style among leaders (Lewin, Lippitt, and White, 1939; White and Lippitt, 1960). Some leaders are *democratic;* they attempt to get the group to move on its own toward their ideas, but they do not force things. Ultimately, the decision is left to the group. Others are *authoritarian;* they tell the group what to do. Still others are *laizzez-faire;* they leave things up to the group, without providing any particular direction. Under ordinary circumstances, the democratic style of leadership seems to work best, at least in industrialized countries with democratic governments. Group members are happier, more group-oriented, and feel more involved, and consequently they are more cooperative and productive (Lewin, 1943; White and Lippitt, 1960). In some situations, however, such as emergencies and wartime, decisions must be made quickly. Then authoritarian decision making may be preferable, which may explain the authoritarian structure of such organizations as the military, police, prisons, and hospitals. In societies with a strong tradition of authoritarian government, such as dictatorships and traditional monarchies, the authoritarian style of leadership may also be more effective (Bass, 1960) because people may be unaccustomed to making decisions and may prefer to let someone else do so. The laizzez-faire style, in contrast, is rarely effective because it leaves the group without any form of instrumental leadership.

The Pervasiveness of Bureaucracy

Bureaucracy: What Is It?

The dominant type of formal organization in modern society is the **bureaucracy.** Although the term as commonly used often has negative connotations, sociologists employ it purely as a descriptive term. The best definition of bureaucracy is probably still to be found in Max Weber's (1968 [orig. 1922]) ideal-type bureaucracy. An **ideal type** is an abstract description that actual entities will fit to a greater or lesser extent. It lists a set of characteristics; the greater the extent to which something has those characteristics, the better it fits the ideal type. Weber's ideal-type definition of a bureaucracy includes six characteristics:

1. *Division of labor:* Different people specialize in different jobs. Each person has jurisdiction or responsibility for a given area of activity.
2. *Hierarchy:* Authority is specified according to a top-down chain of command. Each supervisor has specific authority, limited to specific people and areas of activity. A specific person is responsible for performance in each area of the organization.
3. *Formal rules and regulations:* Rules and policies are specific, official, and written rather than informal or oral. Records are kept in writing.

4. *Impersonality and universalism:* People are evaluated and rewarded on the basis of what they do, not who they are. Authority is linked to positions, not to individuals. Everyone in a given type of position is evaluated on the basis of a specified set of rules or performance factors; there are no special favors.
5. *Managerial or administrative staff:* There is an entire group of workers whose job is to keep the organization operating. They are not involved in producing whatever it is that the organization produces.
6. *Lifelong careers:* It is assumed that people will continue throughout life in the same general type of career. Although the reality is that people often switch employers (especially in the United States), the ideal is that people "work their way up" in a career within an organization.

Most large-scale organizations in industrialized countries fit this definition. Corporations, universities, government agencies, labor unions, and large religious denominations are all examples of bureaucracies. Large organizations will not have every one of the six traits to an equal extent and may be without one or more of them entirely (Hall, 1963–1964; Udy, 1959). However, most of the traits will be present in most large-scale formal organizations.

Why Bureaucracy?

Rationalization Nearly three-quarters of a century ago, Max Weber correctly predicted that bureaucracy would become the dominant form of organization in

An early Ford assembly line. The assembly line sought to apply the concept of rationalization to manufacturing; it coordinated large numbers of people and attempted to keep individual ideosyncracies from interfering with the manufacturing process.

modern society. How did he know this, and why has it happened as he predicted? The answer is to be found in what Weber called **rationalization.** By rationalization, he meant making all decisions purely on the basis of what will accomplish organizational goals. Weber saw rationalization as one of the most significant trends in modern society, and bureaucracy as the means by which it occurs. Bureaucracy facilitates rationalization in several ways. First, it eliminates tradition and personal favoritism as influences in decision making. Second, it identifies the various tasks that need to be done, assigns someone to do them, and provides a way of monitoring how well they get done. Third, it provides a way to coordinate the activities of a large number of people working on different tasks, so that each person's efforts contribute to some common task, goal, or product, rather than working at cross-purposes.

Bureaucracy and Large-Scale Tasks The larger the scale of an organization and its tasks, the more crucial these tasks become. Many tasks are of such a large scale that there is no other way to do them except through a bureaucracy. Consider the steps that are involved in manufacturing and selling an automobile. Natural materials must be obtained and shipped to some central location. Thousands of parts must be manufactured and then assembled to make the car. Market research must be conducted to determine what people want so the company doesn't produce a car nobody will buy. Thousands of workers must be hired, evaluated, and provided with benefits. Cars of various colors and design must be manufactured and shipped in accordance with customer orders, which in turn requires a large system of dealerships throughout the country. An extremely complex division of labor is necessary for any such task, and once a system of division of labor is devised, it becomes crucial to make sure that every part of the operation is working in a way that ultimately meets the organization's goals. Bureaucracy makes this possible, which is an important reason why it is so widespread.

Weber's thinking on the topic of bureaucracy reflects the functionalist perspective, though he never used that term. To Weber, bureaucracy would inevitably spread because it had to. Large-scale tasks required rationalization, and bureaucracy made rationalization possible. Weber even went a step further, arguing that bureaucracy was essential to democracy itself.

Bureaucracy and Democracy

How does bureaucracy make democracy possible? Consider a presidential election in the United States. Such an election requires decisions concerning who is to be on the ballot in 50 states and the District of Columbia and who is eligible to vote. There must be a way to resolve disputes about the eligibility of voters and the validity of votes. Someone has to operate hundreds of thousands of voting places throughout the country and enforce the voting laws. After the election, millions of votes must be reported to central locations, where they are counted. Someone must determine who has won every state and, ultimately, who has the most electoral votes. Can you imagine performing all these tasks without a division of labor? Can you imagine conducting an election without career officials who know how to run elections? Can you imagine doing it without a written set of rules concerning who is eligible to vote and how elections are to be run?

The need for bureaucracy to ensure democracy goes further than elections, however. According to Weber, every political and economic right requires a bureaucracy to enforce it. If people have the right of free speech, we need a court system to determine when that right has been violated. If workers have the right to join labor unions, we need a labor relations board to conduct elections to see if workers want a union. If we declare that financial security in old age is a right, we need a social security administration (or something like it) to collect taxes and distribute benefits according to a set of rules.

All of this might lead you to think that Max Weber considered bureaucracy to be a wonderful invention that would lead to the improvement of everyday life. He didn't. He actually looked upon it as a necessary evil. He perceived it as essential to accomplish tasks of any size and to protect democratic rights. At the same time, though, he saw it as depersonalizing. People would come to be treated as positions or numbers rather than as people. Many jobs would be repetitious and boring. People and their individual needs and concerns would become secondary to the goals of large, uncaring organizations. Weber did see some possibilities, such as charismatic movements (see Chapters 10 and 15), for humanizing bureaucracy somewhat. In the end, though, he saw no way for modern societies to avoid bureaucracy.

Karl Marx on Bureaucracy

Unlike Weber, Karl Marx saw bureaucracy as an *unnecessary* evil. Marx analyzed bureaucracy from a conflict perspective, arguing that it does not meet a *societal* need, only the needs of the rich and powerful. According to Marx, bureaucracy enables by which the owners of the means of production to maintain *control* of organizations. Through hierarchy, the ruling class assures that everyone in the organization works in a way that maximizes the owners' profits. If anyone in the organization fails to do this, the top-down chain of command assures that that person will be corrected or eliminated from the organization.

To the extent that maximizing efficiency maximizes profits, you could argue that Marx and Weber are saying much the same thing: bureaucratic organization exists because it works. You could argue further that efficient work organizations are in the interests of both the larger society and the ruling class. Indeed, very much like Weber, Marx (1967 [orig. 1867]) did emphasize the ruling class's need for efficient, low-cost labor that could mass-produce a variety of products with a minimum of training. However, modern Marxist social scientists have added a very important insight: What is most profitable to the owners of the means of production is *not always* what maximizes efficiency (Blumberg, 1973; Friedman, 1977; Gintis, 1974; Melman, 1983). In fact, productivity studies consistently find that giving workers more control of their work situation usually *increases* productivity (Bernstein, 1976; Blumberg, 1973; Melman, 1983, Chap. 13; Zwerdling, 1978; Le Boeuf, 1982; Chap. 6; Schooler and Naoi, 1988). This implies that reducing or eliminating the hierarchical features of bureaucratic organizations should raise an organization's productivity, not lower it. However, this does not mean that the business or factory will thereby become more profitable *for its owners*. If workers are made more powerful by eliminating hierarchical control, they may use

that power to bring about higher pay, more fringe benefits, better working conditions, and other workers' benefits. In short, because the most efficient organization is not always the most profitable one for the owners, owners often sacrifice efficiency in order to maintain control (Edwards, 1979; Gintis, 1974; Hecksher, 1980; Melman, 1983). From this perspective, then, bureaucracy is functional for a specific interest group (owners of the means of production) but dysfunctional for the larger society.

As we shall see in Chapter 9, Marx and his co-author Freidrich Engels believed that government bureaucracy would "wither away" once class inequalities were eliminated through common ownership of the means of production. Implicitly, at least, Marx appears to have believed much the same about private bureaucracies, because he saw them, too, as a tool by which the ruling class controls and dominates the masses. In fact, Marx even questioned the need for specialization, viewing it as a means by which the masses of workers were deprived of knowledge that could make them too threatening to the ruling class.

Evaluating Bureaucracy

It appears that functionalist and conflict viewpoints are both partially correct about the reasons bureaucracy has become so pervasive in the modern world. Every society that has industrialized has experienced the dramatic growth in organizations that fit Weber's definition of a bureaucracy. It is, in fact, very hard to see how any large-scale task could be accomplished without the coordination that bureaucracy makes possible. In every task from manufacturing to governing to waging war, organizations that fit Weber's general model appear more efficient than organizations that don't. Factories using division of labor and mass-production assembly lines (impossible without bureaucratic organization) are far more efficient than ones where each worker makes the whole product.

It therefore appears that the Marxian claim that bureaucracies will "wither away" is an impossible dream. Modern technology has made the need for specialization far greater today than it was over a century ago when Marx wrote. Moreover, attempts to level out socioeconomic inequalities and guarantee equal political and economic rights nearly always re-

Soviet President Mikhail Gorbachev's call for perestroika *represents an attempt to combat excessive bureaucratic control over the Soviet economy.*

quire more complex organization, not less. Thus, bureaucracies seem to be a growing feature of modern societies regardless of whether they are capitalist, socialist, or something in between.

Having said this, it must be acknowledged that some features of bureaucracy seem to have developed well beyond the point where they could be considered functional. Again, this is a feature of both capitalist and socialist societies, as those in charge seek to hold on to their power and economic advantage through hierarchical control. In the Soviet Union, the policy of centralized control has for years stifled the economy by insisting that decisions be made or approved in Moscow rather than by those who are closer to the local situation. This is one of the key problems that has been recognized by Soviet leadership under Mikhail Gorbachev, leading to his call for *perestroika,* or economic restructuring. In capitalist countries, a similar problem occurs when the owners of capital retain hierarchical control, even though granting their workers more autonomy would increase productivity. In these countries, too, the need for change is beginning to be recognized. In the United States, which has lost considerable ground economically to international competition, more and more companies are beginning to experiment with less centralized forms of work organization developed in Japan, Sweden, and elsewhere. These will be discussed later in this chapter.

The extent to which bureaucracy is an efficient form of organization also depends on the task being performed. In general, bureaucracy works better for complex but routine and repetitive tasks (such as

manufacturing and distributing automobiles) and less well for tasks that are nonroutine and require imagination (such as designing and building a space shuttle). Even with the most routine tasks, however, there are potential dysfunctions, which are addressed in the following section.

Dysfunctions of Bureaucracy

A bureaucracy, by definition, is a group. Therefore, it is subject to the same problems and dysfunctions as other groups, such as groupthink and group polarization. Bureaucracies are also subject to additional dysfunctions arising from their size, formality, complexity, and hierarchical organization.

Decision Avoidance One problem of bureaucracies is that they sometimes have a hard time making decisions. Most bureaucratic organizations are designed to handle routine matters according to a known set of guidelines. When they encounter a situation that falls outside the guidelines, they often have a hard time handling it. One reason is the tendency for each person in the organization to pass such decisions along to someone else because nobody wants to be responsible for a decision that might "go wrong" or be questioned later. If you have ever encountered a billing error, a lost file, or a "mistake on the computer," you have probably experienced this problem. It literally can be true that nobody knows what to do.

The USS Vincennes, *which in 1988 accidentally shot down an Iranian airliner, killing all 290 people aboard.*

Disaster over the Gulf: Tragic Consequence of Trained Incapacity

On July 3, 1988, the *USS Vincennes,* on patrol in the Persian Gulf, had just been involved in a skirmish with a fleet of small Iranian gunboats, two of which had been sunk in the fighting. Now its radar screens showed what the *Vincennes* crew thought was an Iranian F-14 jet fighter flying an attack pattern toward it. The *Vincennes* fired two missiles at the threatening plane, at least one of which hit it and destroyed it instantly. It turned out the plane was not a jet fighter, but an Iranian airliner on a regularly scheduled weekly flight across the Gulf. It was flying in a designated civilian air traffic corridor, climbing to cruising altitude just as it should have been. All 290 people aboard were killed.

How could such an accident happen? In large part, it happened because the situation that day was not one that was foreseen by those who designed either the defense system of the *Vincennes* or the civilian air traffic system. It was a tragic example of the consequences of *trained incapacity.* The *Vincennes* was equipped with the new, high-tech Aegis combat radar system. Its captain called it "the most sophisticated combat ship in the world, bar none" (*Newsweek,* 1988b). However, the system was designed for open-sea combat, not a crowded body of water no bigger than Lake Michigan with hundreds of airline flights

every day, in addition to hundreds of civilian ships, tankers, and launches, combined with gunboats, battleships, helicopters, and jet fighters from a dozen countries intermittently skirmishing with one another. To put it simply, neither the ship's high-tech combat system nor its sailors' training was designed for a situation in a confined area with a heavy mix of civilian and military air and sea activity. Therefore, things were not done that could have easily identified the plane as a civilian airliner. Had the ship monitored the correct frequency, it could have heard the communications between the airliner and the control tower and recognized the plane for what it was. Had the *Official Airline Guide*—in every travel agent's computer—been in the ship's computer, it would have shown that a commercial flight was scheduled to leave the airport and pass over the Gulf. As it was, the ship's crews hastily checked a printed airline schedule and missed the relevant flight. In short, the crew's training and the ship's defense system were designed for a very different situation than that encountered by the *Vincennes.* When it encountered that situation, the ship's crew did not know the correct actions to take.

Air controllers in Iran and the plane's destination, the United Arab Emirates, suffered from a similar type of trained incapacity. Being part of a

commercial operation, the air controllers in Bander Abbas, Iran, where the plane took off, did not monitor military activity in the Gulf and therefore did not know that there had been fighting half an hour before the plane took off. Later, the manager of the airport said, "If there is something like this, we would tell it not to take off." At the plane's destination, air controllers heard the *Vincennes*'s warnings to the airliner, but they didn't think to relay them. The plane's crew itself was so busy with routine air traffic information that it apparently did not hear the *Vincennes* warning. In short, the civilian air traffic system was no more designed to operate in a war zone than the *Vincennes* was designed to fight in a busy civilian air and sea corridor. The result of this trained incapacity on both sides was tragedy.

Unfortunately, such accidents have become fixtures of modern society (Perrow, 1986a). Other examples are the Soviet shootdown of a Korean airliner in 1983, the nuclear power plant accident at Chernobyl, USSR, in 1986, and the chemical leak in Bhopal, India, in 1984 that took 2,000 lives. Each of these disasters can be attributed at least in part to trained incapacity, the risks of which continue to increase as our technologies become more complex.

Trained Incapacity When faced with an unfamiliar situation, people in bureaucracies often try to fit the situation into an area for which they *do* have guidelines. Thus, if the postal service or the company you are paying loses your bill payment, you may be penalized for making the payment late. This tendency to "force" situations to fit the guidelines results in part from the tendency toward conformity in groups and organizations. For an individual to make a bold or innovative decision in such situations would implicitly challenge "the way we do things," a risk many people in organizations are unwilling to take. One result of all this is that, although bureaucratic organizations may be very rational and efficient in handling *familiar* situations, they often do not adapt well to change. New situations require new ways of doing things, but the old ways have a tendency to be self-perpetuating (Kanter, 1983, Chaps. 3, 4). This failure to adapt to new conditions—sometimes called *trained incapacity* (Veblen, 1921)—is a serious limitation of bureaucratic organizations. As shown in the box, it is also an important cause of many modern disasters.

Self-Perpetuation and Goal Displacement A U.S. senator once remarked that if he believed in reincarnation, he would pray to come back as a temporary Senate subcommittee, because he could then enjoy eternal life. Modern organizations do tend to persist, for several reasons. First, within any organization that has employees, a primary goal quickly becomes the preservation of the organization, which in turn preserves people's jobs (Selznick, 1957, p. 21). Sociologists refer to this process as *goal displacement*—whatever the original goals of the organization, its primary goal quickly becomes to preserve the organization. Consider the temporary Senate subcommittee. It has a staff whose jobs depend on the continued existence of the committee. Moreover, the senators who serve on the committee may gain status with other senators as a result of their role as committee members. They may also appear to constituents back home to be "doing something about the problem" the subcommittee was created to deal with.

The incentives for self-preservation are so strong that organizations often continue even when the problem that originally brought them into existence is gone. The American Lung Association, formerly the American Tuberculosis and Respiratory Association, was formed to reduce the incidence of tuberculosis in American society. It was successful in these efforts, to the point that very few Americans get tuberculosis today. Did the organization declare itself a success and disband? Not at all. It turned its attention to a new set of problems and works today to combat lung cancer.

Tendency to Expand Organizations tend not only to survive but also to grow. In a bureaucracy, a super-visor's prestige is largely determined by the number of people that he or she supervises. Thus, the manager of a large department has more prestige than the manager of a small department. It therefore becomes in every manager's interest to think of more things that "need" to be done and get authorization to hire more employees to do them. Once more workers are hired, more supervisors must be hired to supervise them, and more secretaries must be hired to keep track of their files. A principle called "Parkinson's Law" reveals why it is never any problem to keep them busy (Parkinson, 1957). According to Parkinson's Law, work expands to use the time or personnel available. If people are available, something will be found for them to do. A job can always be done in greater detail if more time is available.

PARKINSON'S LAW: AN EXAMPLE Nowhere is this principle clearer than in the case of computerization. Because computers are far more efficient than older methods of doing things, it would seem that computers could reduce the need for administrators and record keepers. Studies of organizations that have used computers to "automate their offices," however, have disproved this idea. (Heskiaoff, 1977). What actually happens is that new information is collected and processed. As one study of the American Broadcasting Company (ABC) revealed, computerization actually can lead to an *increase* in the number of administrators, as new people are hired to work with the additional information that is generated (Melman, 1983, p. 76).

Ritualism: The Bureaucratic Personality Another dysfunction of bureaucracies is the tendency of some workers to engage in *ritualism*—placing the procedures of the organization ahead of the purposes for which the procedures were designed (Merton, 1968). The main objective of such workers becomes following the correct rules and procedures rather than getting the job done properly. Workers who think and behave in this manner are sometimes said to have a *bureaucratic personality*. Supervisors sometimes encourage such behavior because following procedures is the "safe" thing to do. Fortunately, though, it appears that only a minority of workers in organizations develop such behavior (Kohn, 1978). Rather than devoting themselves to the rules, most workers develop

When the cabinet maker finishes her job, she can take pride in a visible product that she has designed and created. Can the assembly line worker say the same of the postage meters to which she has added one small part in a process designed by someone else?

an informal structure that bends the rules — a pattern that we shall explore in more detail shortly.

Alienation of Workers Worker **alienation** is a dysfunction that was recognized in different ways by both Marx and Weber. Marx was more explicit, defining alienation as the result of separating the worker from the product of his or her labor. In large, specialized organizations, each worker does only a small part of the job, and the finished product is not the product of any one worker's efforts. Contrast the auto assembly-line worker with the cabinet maker. When a car rolls off the assembly line, the autoworker cannot look at it and say "I made that" in the same sense that the cabinet maker can when he or she finishes handcrafting a piece of furniture. Modern workers in bureaucracies cannot see that they have produced an item of value, and as a result, they may come to doubt their own value (see Schooler and Naoi, 1988).

Weber also recognized this problem. He saw bureaucracy as an "iron cage," necessary yet inevitably trapping workers in a depersonalized situation. Both Marx and Weber recognized that lack of control over their work situation would be a key source of frustration to modern workers. In general, both men believed that alienation would make the life of modern workers miserable. Marx, in fact, believed that this would eventually sow the seeds of bureaucracy's de-

struction: Workers would rebel and replace bureaucracy with a new system of worker ownership. Although this has not happened (even in socialist countries), we do know that alienated workers are unproductive workers. We know, too, that some workers are far more alienated than others, and that women, minorities, and those with limited education are likely to end up in especially alienating roles. Fortunately, though, people in organizations have some ability to shape informally what really goes on in the organization, which partially offsets the alienating features of bureaucracy. We now turn to some of the ways they do this.

An Interactionist View of Bureaucracy

Formal and Informal Structure

We have seen, in Weber's ideal-type definition of bureaucracy, what the formal structure of complex organizations looks like. However, the symbolic-interactionist perspective reminds us that organizations also have an **informal structure** — the things people actually do on a day-to-day basis, in contrast to what the official rules say they are supposed to do (Blau and Meyer, 1971, Chap. 3). Although the formal structure of a bureaucracy consists of a complex set of positions with norms about how they are supposed to interact, these positions are filled by people, each of whom has his or her own personality, objectives, and understanding of the organization and his or her position within it. Each person acts on the basis of these factors (Blumer, 1969). Moreover, each person has a particular reaction to each of the other people with whom he or she works. Any two individuals will play a particular role in the organization differently and will thus evoke different reactions from co-workers. One boss might be identified as supportive and democratic, whereas another in the same position might be seen as authoritarian and critical. The former will likely inspire hard work from his or her subordinates, whereas the latter may get only loafing, avoidance, and "bitching." The degree to which a supervisor appears to know his or her job will also affect employee output and cooperativeness.

Whatever the official rules of the organization, workers have their own ideas and will collectively develop informal norms. Productivity, for example, is usually governed by such norms, as Rothlisberger and Dickson (1939) discovered in their famous study of production workers at the Hawthorne plant of Western Electric (see Chapter 2 for more details on this study). Workers who either exceed or fall below their co-workers' productivity norms will likely be made to feel uncomfortable. Those who work too hard relative to the group norm will be labeled as "rate-busters," and those who do not work hard enough will be labeled "lazy" or "goof-offs."

Flexibility Another reason for informal structure is that the formal rules don't always work. If everyone engaged in *ritualism*—following all the rules all the time—most organizations would grind to a halt. In fact, a familiar tactic of labor unions who want to pressure an employer without going so far as to strike is "working to rule"—following every regulation literally and exactly. Almost inevitably, this practice leads to a big drop in productivity as workers spend most of their time filling out forms and following procedures. Usually, though, workers follow informal norms rather than strictly obeying the official rules because that works best. Because no policy can cover every possibility, in order for the organization to work, employees must use their judgment and creativity in unusual situations. They often do so, deciding how to handle any given situation as it comes up, and the decision is not always "by the rules."

Similarly, the official channels of communication can be very slow and inefficient. The "official" way for a person in an organization to consult with someone in another department is to send a memo through his or her supervisor to the other person's supervisor, who then passes on the message to the person for whom it is intended. A simple phone call is much quicker. Similarly, you may know that you are "supposed to" communicate with one person concerning a given problem, but past experience tells you that someone else will be more helpful. Chances are, you will communicate with that "someone else."

Primary Groups and Informal Structure Finally, we have noted that primary groups frequently develop within large organizations, even though the organizations themselves are secondary groups. Friendship networks, "buddies," and cliques form within every organization, and whether any given worker is "in" or "out" of another worker's informal group will influence how the two workers relate to one another. Workers often protect and exchange favors with co-workers they consider friends, when they would treat someone else in the same situation differently.

Negotiated Order

These examples illustrate a key point: Regardless of the formal structure, people ultimately make the orga-

Workers in the lunchroom. Although work organizations are secondary groups, primary groups often form within them and can have an important impact on what happens in the larger work organization.

nization. These people, with their needs, objectives, and experiences of others in the organization, create a **negotiated order.** They push to get what they want, try things out, test the limits of the rules. This reality was illustrated in a now-classic study of mental hospitals by Anselm Strauss and his colleagues (1964). He found that the nature of the hospital at any given time was the outcome of pressures, actions, and reactions of the many people who made the organization: doctors, attendants, nurses, administrators, and patients. Each person in each of these groups had his or her own objectives, understandings of reality, and ideas about mental illness, which governed his or her behavior and relationships to others. Compromises, "looking the other way," and "agreements to disagree" were abundant, but they were always subject to change as the characters changed and new negotiations took place. Thus, "the hospital" today is not exactly the same as "the hospital" last month, even if the formal structure remains unchanged, because the process of negotiating order continues as long as the organization does. Although Strauss et al. used the mental hospital to illustrate this process, the evidence indicates that such negotiation occurs in most kinds of organizations (Lauer and Handel, 1983). The interaction of this process with the formal and informal structures of the organization and with the goals and objectives of organizational leaders produces an *organizational culture*. This culture is unique to each organization and cannot be understood merely by examining the organization's formal structure (Fine, 1984; Ouchi and Wilkins, 1985). As with any culture, new members must be socialized into organizational cultures, and new employees who do not become appropriately socialized usually experience a very difficult time.

Organizational Roles: Case Studies

Because each worker occupies a particular position within the work organization, each worker experiences the organization differently. This is in part a product of the worker's personality and desires, but it also reflects the worker's situation within the organization. According to Millman and Kanter (1975), an organization can be seen as an interrelated set of strata or groups, each with its own style, culture, norms, political allegiances, and internal hierarchy. As illustrated by the following case studies, portions of which draw largely on the research of Rosabeth Moss Kanter, different classes of workers experience and respond to the organization in different ways.

The Professional Professionals, such as doctors, scientists, professors, and engineers, generally enjoy a good deal more autonomy on the job than most workers. This is because their jobs require extensive, specialized training, and it is assumed that nobody else in the organization knows their work as well as they do (Parsons, 1947, 1951). Professionals tend to be supervised less closely than other workers. Unlike many other workers, they are not usually evaluated to any great extent on how well they follow established procedures. Rather, the evaluation is based mainly on the outcome — has a professional been successful in accomplishing what he or she was hired to do? Frequently, this judgment is arrived at through a process of *peer evaluation,* as when college professors judge their colleagues' worthiness for tenure or promotion (Blau and Meyer, 1971, pp. 76–77).

Professionals not only enjoy more autonomy than other workers, they *expect* it. When subjected to extensive bureaucratic rules and regulations, they are often the first to rebel. Moreover, they seek to secure their autonomy through the process of *professionalization*, in which they successfully complete certain procedures involving credentials and accreditation. These procedures serve to establish their expertise and justify their autonomy (Collins, 1979; Wilensky, 1964). The growing importance of professionals in our economy may be having the effect of reducing the influence of formal bureaucratic hierarchy in modern organizations.

Even with professionals, though, the organization makes a difference. Perrow (1979, pp. 50–55) points out that professionals in private corporations are more tolerant of hierarchy and regulations than are those in universities or research organizations. But even the latter institutions have broad rules and regulations within which professionals must operate. Perrow also notes that professionals with aspirations to move into management — where the best salaries frequently are — are often willing to sacrifice autonomy in exchange for upward mobility, money, and organizational prestige.

The Secretary   The role of the secretary stands in sharp contrast to that of the professional (Kanter, 1977a; Millman and Kanter, 1975). Typically, secretaries enjoy very little autonomy unless they work for a top executive. However, interaction with the boss, and not bureaucratic rules, determines the secretary's working conditions. This interaction is still more often than not a male-female relationship and is shaped heavily by societal norms governing such relationships (Mills, 1951). A male managerial worker may be judged on the attractiveness, educational level, and personality of his secretary, and having a private secretary is an important status symbol in many organizations (Burger, 1964). In a sense, secretaries are often treated as the personal property of their bosses, expected to do personal favors, to move within the organization when they move, and are evaluated on the basis of the boss's personal judgment rather than bureaucratic or procedural criteria. In many organizations, a promotion for a secretary does not mean new job responsibilities, but rather, a higher-status boss. A secretary's job status is not defined by anything the secretary does, but rather by what the boss does.

The Middle Manager   The middle manager, moving up in the organization, is probably the type of worker who conforms best to the formal bureaucratic model. Such workers seek to prove their worth by upholding the company's ways of doing things and by demonstrating their loyalty to their supervisors. This behavior is frequently successful because top managers— who actually deal with unpredictable market conditions outside the organization—are often uncertain about their decisions. To reduce their own uncertainty and to free them to deal with the external environment, these top managers need loyal, predictable subordinates (Kanter, 1977a). For the most part, middle managers with upward aspirations recognize this need, comply, and seek compliance from their employees.

What is good for individuals, however, is not always good for the organization. This tendency toward compliance in management can be so strong that it can prevent the company from adapting to changing conditions. In this sense, hierarchical command can be dysfunctional rather than serving the function of rationalization claimed by Weber. If blind obedience leads people to follow the unwise policies of an organization's leader, everyone can be led down a path of failure. As Blau and Meyer (1971, p. 35) put it, "To overcome bureaucratic inertia seems to require new organizations or new managers, unencumbered by traditions and personal loyalties, and not enmeshed in the social processes that characterize the interpersonal relations in the organization."

The Lone Minority   Yet another distinct role in the organization is that of the lone or token minority: the only woman on a board of directors; the only black professor in a university department. This individual will face issues that others entering the same role will not. In part, co-workers will react to this person as a woman or as a black person—a role they are not used to seeing in combination with the role of executive or professor (Kanter, 1977, Chap. 8). In their attempt to deal with this combination, colleagues may insist on fitting the lone minority into a role they associate with the person's group. They may treat a female colleague, for example, as they would their mother, or as a sex object, or as something akin to a mascot (Millman and Kanter, 1975). At the other extreme, some may view her as an "iron maiden," concluding that only a woman who fits the toughest male stereotype could rise to such heights (Kanter, 1977b). Others may mistake the person's role entirely, as when female executives or professors are mistaken for secretaries (Lynch, 1973). Finally, they may put such individuals on display as tokens, rewarding them for their *positions* ("our woman manager" or "our black vice president") but not for what they accomplish (Kanter, 1977, pp. 213–214).

All of this means that the lone minority must spend time working to define her or his role to colleagues in a way that others would not have to (Epstein, 1970). This burden diminishes the lone minority's ability to "take charge" of the job, makes interaction with colleagues clumsy, and leads to feelings of frustration and isolation. Ultimately, it means that until they become a substantial proportion of the work force, women and minorities may take longer than others to establish secure working relationships with colleagues based on their competence. This probably reduces the rate at which even the most capable women and minority-group members can move up the corporate ladder.

New Trends in Work Organization

We have seen that the bureaucratic form of organization has become pervasive in modern society because of its efficiency in handling large-scale tasks, but that bureaucracy has also tended to be more formal and hierarchical than what is required for such efficiency. Especially, but not only, in democratic societies, the informal structure is often as influential as the official, formal structure, and studies show that less hierarchy and more worker autonomy usually lead to better productivity. As more countries have modernized and industrialized in the second half of the twentieth century, the world economy has become more competitive. One result is greater pressure for efficiency, particularly in countries like the United States that have grown accustomed to occupying a dominant position in the world economy. Among the ways that some countries have sought to improve their position is by experimenting with new forms of work organization that offer greater efficiency than the traditional hierarchical model. Two such examples are Japan and the Scandinavian countries.

Japanese Work Organization

In recent decades, Japanese products have gained worldwide renown for their high quality and reasonable cost. Japanese manufacturers have achieved a healthy share of the automobile market in the United States and other countries, and their position in the electronics industry is even more prominent. In large part, Japan's strong position in the world economy is the result of innovations in work organization that were introduced as Japan rebuilt itself following World War II. Perhaps more than any other country, Japan has succeeded in developing a cooperative approach between workers and managers, where everyone's objective is to develop a better product at a lower cost, and where everyone is rewarded when this is accomplished. Two of the innovations that illustrate this are the *quality-control circle* and *lifetime employment*.

Quality-Control Circles   A quality-control circle (QC circle) is a small group of workers, usually numbering about five to ten, who meet regularly to assess the group's performance. The inventor of the circle claims that it serves three purposes (Ishikawa, 1984): It contributes to the improvement and development of the enterprise, it respects human relations and enhances worker satisfaction, and it utilizes the workers' full potential. QC circles often use statistical analysis to judge productivity. A key to the success of QC circles is that they focus on both productivity and worker satisfaction. These circles reflect the principle that workers will be more productive when they know that their ideas concerning working conditions will be respected and, where appropriate, implemented. In contrast to American philosophy, the QC circle is based on the principle that better productivity is achieved through a high-quality labor force, not automation that simplifies the worker's job (Cole, 1979).

Another governing principle of QC circles is that "the better the quality, the lower the cost." In other words, the objectives of quality-control circles include both lowering production cost *and* improving product quality. Neither is to be sacrificed for the other, and both are to be addressed at the same time (Karatsu, 1984, p. 9). In general, QC circles have been so effective that Japanese workers are rarely subjected to the inspections that are common in manufacturing plants in most countries. Moreover, because the QC circle often implements workers' suggestions, alienation in the sense used by Marx is far less common among Japanese workers than among workers in other societies.

The rewards of QC circles are financial as well as psychological. When a worker-initiated innovation saves the company money, workers frequently receive part of the savings in the form of bonuses or higher wages. As a result, Japanese wages quadrupled between 1969 and 1979, while prices for most Japanese products less than doubled (Karatsu, 1984, pp. 10–11). This means that the average Japanese worker made big gains against the cost of living. Significantly,

Work without Bosses: Organizational Democracy As the Alternative to Bureaucracy

My investigation into worker cooperatives was born, I suppose, out of my personal frustration with bureaucracy. Who has not encountered, in the daily course of events, some functionary telling us what can or cannot be done. If we respond that this makes little sense, that the proscribed or prescribed action runs contrary even to the stated goals of the organization, the bureaucrat remains undaunted: "I'm sorry, it is our rule, it is our policy."

About the time that I first started to consider the tremendous costs of running everything bureaucratically—the result of millions of employees who, surveys tell us, hold back their best energies and ideas because they feel they have no real voice in the workplace decisions that affect their lives—several social movements emerged that shed a new light on this issue. During my undergraduate years, antiwar activists defended the right of the Vietnamese people to decide their own fate. The women's movement was asserting the right of women to redefine their rights and roles in modern society. The civil rights movement had mobilized and experienced its first successes before I was old enough to appreciate it, but I understood that it was about the same thing. Everywhere people seemed to be demanding the opportunity to decide for themselves the fundamental conditions of their lives.

Joyce Rothschild *is Professor and Chair of the Department of Sociology, Anthropology, and Social Work at the University of Toledo. This account reports on her recent book with J. Allen Whitt,* The Cooperative Workplace: Conditions and Dilemmas of Organizational Democracy, *published by Cambridge University Press.*

The heated debates of the day, however, seemed to present a choice between the Soviet model of state-owned industry and the American model of private investor-owned industry. I reasoned that the socialist bureaucracy was not likely to be any more satisfying for the average working person than capitalist bureaucracy had been. Both located the centers of power way up in the hierarchy of organizations, far removed from the input of the average individual. If people wanted a voice in the decisions that affect their lives, I concluded that it is in their work places that they most needed to be heard. Any institution that absorbs this much of our time and energy as adults and that so shapes our sense of ourselves simply cannot be forfeited to hierarchal control.

In short, it seemed to me that a third path would have to be found in the world. Both socialist and capitalist economies would need to find a way to go beyond bureaucracy, or to dismantle bureaucracy if necessary, in order to include working people in decisions about the production process and product. This was a requirement if work organizations were to provide the sort of self-managed or autonomous work that people said they wanted, and if organizations were to remain responsive to their customer base and therefore competitive.

These observations led me to read about bureaucracy and to wondering whether a cooperative form of organization—one that was owned and run by its workers—might be a practical alternative. In my reading I discovered that bureaucracy and centralized control over organizations were accepted as a necessity, if not an inevitability, in social science. Weber had argued convincingly that bureaucratic authority would become a permanent and indispensible characteristic of modern society. Once firmly established, it would be revolution-proof. Modern societies could undergo changes in who controls the bureaucratic apparatus, but the structure of bureaucratic control would remain intact. Domination *(herrschaft),* in Weber's view, would always require an administrative apparatus to execute commands, and conversely, all administration would require domination. Robert Michels took Weber's philosophy one step further. His "iron law of oligarchy" asserted that organizational democracy inevitably yields to oligarchy. Michels's law became a cornerstone of twentieth-century social science, which subsequently dismissed the possibility of democracy in large organizations.

As I became immersed in the literature and traditions in organizational studies, I could not help but notice that right outside my window worker co-ops—or "collectives," as they were called—were appearing all over. These collectives were organized to do what the social-science literature said was impossible: to throw out accepted notions about bureaucracy with its chain of command, its written rules, and its strict separation of labor and management. In its place they wanted to create organizations where everyone had an opportunity to participate in decisions, where those who did the work of the organization also did the managing.

In their experimentation, the cooperatives offered a glimpse into how real-life functioning democracies would operate. I chose to examine a number of these organizations from different domains, to identify the key organizational structures and processes that are essential to democratic organizations. Just as Weber had identified the key characteristics of bureaucracy, we needed to learn if there were key characteristics of democracy. With this done, it became evident that the characteristic practices of democracies were made cohesive by the basic values of their participants (what Weber had called "substantive rationality"), just as the practices of bureaucracies are unified by their formal rules and procedures (which Weber calls "formal rationality"). In other words, to the three bases of authority put forward by Max Weber (traditional, charismatic, and legal-rational) would have to be added a fourth: value-rationality or substantive-rationality. In the bureaucratic model, authority resides in office incumbency that ideally is based in expertise; but in the cooperative-democratic model authority rests in the collectivity as a whole whose decisions are based on allegiance to their values or substantive purposes.

Beyond allowing us to see that a fourth basis of organization was possible, the very existence of the co-ops as participatory-democratic entities permitted us to search for the specific conditions that appeared to favor organizational democracy. We ended up identifying ten conditions that support democracy within an organization. There are inherent trade-offs, however, that go with the pursuit of democracy. For each condition we identify as supporting democracy, we show the problems that it raises for the organization in terms of productivity and efficiency. Cooperative enterprises must get a job done while retaining a democratic form. Although they do not always succeed, our study has shown that, contrary to the iron law of oligarchy, they do not always fail.

Thus, our research both specified the key characteristics of a whole new model of organization and identified some of the conditions that facilitate or undermine this model. Since this original research, many other worker-owned and worker-run enterprises have been developing around the United States that have added to the policy relevance of our study. Studies of these enterprises are also reported in our book. As a result of this research, any viable social science must now consider democratic forms of organization as legitimate alternatives to bureaucracy.

workers in QC circles are evaluated on the basis of group productivity rather than individual achievement, thereby encouraging workers to cooperate rather than compete.

Lifetime Employment Another innovation that has made Japanese work organizations more efficient is lifetime employment. In one sense, this practice probably brings the Japanese work organization closer to Weber's ideal-type bureaucracy because lifelong careers were part of his definition. However, lifetime employment in the Japanese sense is different from the norm for bureaucracies in the United States and other countries. Before being accepted for lifetime employment, a worker must successfully complete a probationary period. Those who cannot do so are expected to leave. After the early years are completed successfully, the worker and the company have obligations to each other. The worker is obliged not to leave for a better job offer elsewhere — a substantial obligation that is not, for example, expected of American workers. The employer is obliged not to cut costs by laying off workers or even, except in the worst emergency, by cutting the wages of production workers. When hard times occur, top management takes wage cuts, and workers are retrained and reassigned rather than being laid off.

This system offers advantages for both employers and workers in Japan. Employers don't have to increase wages to keep workers from leaving for another employer, and they don't have to worry about employees at any level leaving with company secrets. This presents a sharp contrast with the United States, where even top executives often jump to another employer if the offer is right. (Consider the case of Lee Iacocca, today so widely identified with Chrysler and its comeback from bankruptcy. Before going to Chrysler, he was president of the Ford Motor Company.) From the workers' standpoint, there is the guarantee of employment even in hard times. In the United States, thousands of autoworkers have been laid off in the face of economic downturns and technological innovations. Many more took wage freezes in the early 1980s, only to see their top managers get big raises when the economy turned around. In Japan, such situations have been largely avoided, as illustrated by the actions of Mazda during one economic

downturn. Top management took a 20 percent pay cut and middle management took a wage freeze, but layoffs were avoided and production workers even got a scheduled cost-of-living increase (Le Boeuf, 1982, p. 68). In short, the Japanese system makes layoffs and wage freezes for production workers a last resort in hard times, whereas under the American system, they are generally the company's first choices. As a result of both the lifetime employment philosophy itself and its productivity benefits, Japan enjoys the lowest unemployment rate of any major industrialized country.

The Limits of Japanese Innovations Although the Japanese work organization represents an important innovation, it has distinct limitations. As sociologist Robert Cole (1979) points out, it does not grant workers anything like unlimited power. The QC circle is intended to give workers more control of their specific work situation, but not more control in the central management of the company. As Cole put it, "Company representatives set the production goals for each work group; QC circles act to implement these goals whenever there is a gap between the goal and actual performance. In short, QC circles act in the framework of decisions determined by management."

Worker-Management Relationships It is also important to note that Japan does not have the history of worker-management conflict that Europe and North America do. Japanese culture, like other Asian cultures, emphasizes cooperation and group well-being, which, in the case of employees, means the *company*. Japanese companies effectively use slogans, company uniforms, company songs, and daily group rituals that would likely evoke ridicule in the United States. They also offer their employees housing, recreation, and group entertainment to a far greater extent than is typical in Western societies. Unlike the United States and Europe, there is a true sense of "worker for company and company for worker." Largely because of the cooperative and group-oriented character of Asian cultures, QC circles have spread quickly to other Asian countries like South Korea and Taiwan. Even China, which differs from Japan in that it is socialist and much less industrialized, has implemented similar mechanisms for worker input into the work process (Cole, 1979). To what extent these innovations would work in more individualistic Western societies remains uncertain. Many American companies have tried QC circles in recent years, but in some cases they have failed because managers have been reluctant to hand over real power to workers, even in the limited area of job redesign. As a result, American workers and unions have sometimes seen such reforms as management ploys to increase worker production or to undermine union influence. The more drastic reform of lifetime employment has not been tried out to any significant extent in the United States.

Scandinavian Work-Place Innovations

Important innovations in work organization have also been implemented in the Scandinavian countries, particularly Sweden and Norway. These countries may be more similar to the United States than Japan in that they have a tradition of unionism. In fact, class consciousness in Scandinavia is stronger than in Japan or in the United States. Swedish and Norwegian work redesign has much in common with Japanese work redesign, but it was implemented in a setting in which workers were unionized and did not trust management. As a result, the objective in Sweden and Norway was not only to redesign the job but "to achieve a fundamental change in the basic structure of the organization, with rather open-ended possibilities for worker influence" (Cole, 1979). Swedish work-place changes involved both the public and private sector and both white-collar and blue-collar workers. They were based on a widespread philosophy that workers should have some voice in shaping their working conditions and should share in the economic benefits of any changes they suggest. As a result, Scandinavian work-place innovations resulted more from national political decisions than was the case in Japan.

Cooperative Work Agreements One Scandinavian work-place innovation is the *cooperative work agreement* (Bowles, Gordon, and Weisskopf 1983). Much like the QC circle, this innovation arranges workers into small groups, called "work teams" or "autonomous work groups," that make important decisions about working conditions and assignments. Workers are guaranteed an economic return when their changes improve efficiency. This innovation has been applied at both the SAAB and Volvo automobile companies, whose products have a reputation for high quality. Thus, the Swedish and Norwegian experiences show that even where labor-management distrust exists (as in the United States, but not in Japan), work-place change can bring improved efficiency and product quality. However, issues of organizational control must be addressed, and management must be willing to share real power with workers in order for innovation to work in such a society.

Alternatives to Bureaucracy

As was mentioned earlier in this chapter, some people have sought to develop forms of organization completely different from bureaucracy, in the form of *cooperatives* and *collectives*. Although such organizations risk either failing for lack of decision making or evolving into bureaucracies, some of them do neither. These forms are probably not suitable for all types of tasks, but for some kinds of economic production they have been effective. In the following Personal Journey into Sociology vignette, sociologist Joyce Rothschild discusses how a democratic belief system can form the basis of a successful, nonbureaucratic organization.

Summary

We began this chapter by contrasting social groups and formal organizations. Formal organizations are different from other kinds of groups in that they have a stated purpose and an official role structure and set of rules. They are

self-perpetuating; that is, they have a life beyond that of their individual members. Formal organizations are but one example of secondary groups — groups that exist for some purpose beyond the group itself or the individuals that constitute the group. A primary group, in contrast, is a closer-knit group of people who interact for the sake of the interaction itself — for example, families and friends. Secondary groups and formal organizations have grown tremendously in importance as a result of modernization, but primary groups — once the main form of group life — remain important.

Groups and organizations usually have leaders, whether or not they are so designated. Some are instrumental leaders, who focus on the job to be done; and others are expressive leaders, who focus on the social and emotional needs of the group and its members. Groups and organizations usually tend to be oligarchic, that is, ruled largely by their leaders. Groups can do certain things to minimize this tendency, but as a group becomes larger, the tendency toward oligarchy increases. Groups also create strong pressures on their members to conform. Pressure to conform increases when the group comes into conflict with another group, referred to by social scientists as an outgroup.

The form of organization that has become most common in modern society is bureaucracy — a large, formal organization characterized by specialization, hierarchy, formal rules, impersonality, lifelong careers, and a specialized administrative staff. Max Weber developed what amounted to a functionalist analysis of bureaucracy, arguing that it has spread because it permits rationalization, making decisions on the basis of what best gets the job done. Conflict theorists, however, argue that bureaucracy also concentrates control over the organization in the hands of those at the top, which is one reason it is so widespread. Bureaucratic organization apparently is necessary for large-scale tasks, but most organizations are more formal and more hierarchical than is necessary in order to maximize efficiency. Bureaucratic organization also has many undesirable side effects, a reality that even Weber recognized.

Whatever the formal structure, there is always an informal structure — what people "really do" — that differs in significant ways from "official policy." In any organization, the reality of the situation is always the product of social negotiation among the people in the organization, each of whom has a different understanding of the organization and a different set of concerns and interests. A person's position and function in the organization, individual personality, and social characteristics such as sex, class, and race all influence the response to the organization. As a result, organizations are best understood as changing, rather than static, entities.

Glossary

social group A set of two or more people who interact regularly, share some common purpose, and have some structure of roles and statuses.

formal organization A relatively large, self-perpetuating social group with a name, an established purpose, a role structure, and a set of rules.

dyad A social group that consists of only two people.

triad A social group that consists of three people.

primary group A small, close-knit group whose members interact because they value or enjoy one another as people.

secondary group A social group, large or small, that exists for some purpose beyond the relationships among the group's members.

ingroup A social group that a person belongs to or identifies with.

outgroup A social group that a person does not belong to or identify with.

iron law of oligarchy A principle stated by Robert Michels that argues that in any organization, power will become concentrated in the hands of the leaders, who may then use that power to protect their own interests.

instrumental leaders People who exercise leadership in a group by focusing attention on the task to be done and by suggesting effective ways of completing that task.

expressive leaders People who exercise leadership by taking care of the social and emotional needs of people in their group.

bureaucracy A form of organization characterized by specialization, hierarchy, formal rules, impersonality, lifelong careers, and a specialized administrative staff.

ideal type An abstract definition based on a set of characteristics.

rationalization In Weberian sociology, the process by which tradition, faith, and personal relationships are set aside in the conduct of business, with decisions being made on the basis of what is expected to work best.

alienation As defined by Marx, the separation or isolation of workers from the products of their labor; more broadly, feelings or the experience of isolation, powerlessness, or loss of control.

informal structure The actual day-to-day norms, roles, statuses, and behaviors that exist within an organization, which differ from the official and formal structure of the organization.

negotiated order The character of an organization that is the product of fluid agreements arising from the ongoing interaction of its members.

Further Reading

KANTER, ROSABETH MOSS. 1977. *Men and Women of the Corporation.* New York: Basic Books. This award-winning book studies the modern corporation and the people who work in it. It critically examines the structure of roles and statuses within modern work organizations, and argues for decentralization, greater worker autonomy, and a more diverse work force at all levels of the corporate structure.

KANTER, ROSABETH MOSS. 1983. *The Change Masters: Innovations for Productivity in the American Corporation.* New York: Simon and Schuster. In this more recent work, Kanter presents us with a fine example of how sociology can be used to solve practical problems. Kanter uses sociological research to show why American productivity growth has lagged, how some work organizations have managed to counter that trend, and how more organizations can.

MELMAN, SEYMOUR. 1983. *Profits Without Production.* New York: Knopf. Operating from a conflict perspective, Melman argues that a major reason for poor productivity among American corporations is that it is often more profitable *not* to be productive. He illustrates, for example, some ways in which dependence on military contracts has led to massive short-term profits for American companies, yet has caused them to make decisions that have virtually destroyed their long-term competitiveness.

RIDGEWAY, CECELIA. 1983. *The Dynamics of Small Groups.* New York: St. Martin's Press. A textbook by an author who has conducted extensive research on dynamics in small groups. A good starting point for those who want more extensive knowledge about the small-group processes introduced in this chapter.

ROTHSCHILD, JOYCE, AND J. ALLEN WHITT. 1986. *The Cooperative Workplace: Potentials and Dilemmas of Organizational Democracy and Participation.* New York: Cambridge University Press. Another award-winning study, co-authored by the author of the vignette that appears in this chapter. This book presents numerous examples to show that democratic organization is possible. At the same time, democratic organization has its own distinctive set of risks and dilemmas, and these, too, are discussed, with real-life examples.

CHAPTER 8

Deviance, Crime, and Social Control

Think of the word deviance. What kind of behavior does it suggest to you? If you are like the students in my introductory sociology classes, you probably thought of prostitution, buying or viewing sexually explicit materials, engaging in homosexual behavior, or using illegal drugs. Some of you may have thought of men who dress like women or people who dye their hair bright colors. Many of you probably also thought of violent crimes, such as rape and murder, or property crimes, such as theft. I doubt that many of you thought of behaviors that destroy the environment, endanger the lives of workers or consumers, or illegally inflate the prices of products you buy. The students in my classes seldom mention these behaviors, yet, if I do and ask them if these behaviors are deviant, most students agree that they are.

What is it that makes these behaviors deviant? Is it the fact that they hurt someone? If so, who is hurt, for example, when two people of the same sex have a loving, lifelong sexual relationship? Who is hurt when a man dresses like a woman or a woman dyes her hair purple? And why is alcohol use, which contributes to tens of thousands of deaths in the United States every year, legal, while the use of marijuana—a substance that most experts agree is less dangerous than alcohol—remains illegal? Finally, if deviance is defined on the basis of inflicting hurt on someone else, why don't most people think of environmental, safety, and antitrust violations as examples of deviance, when these are among the most harmful and costly forms of illegal behavior?

Are things deviant because they are unnatural? If so, how do we explain the fact that what is deviant in one time and place is not deviant in another? For a single woman to have sexual intercourse was once seen as immoral in the United States; today we virtually take such behavior for granted. On the other hand, the United States today frowns on a variety of behaviors that other societies have regarded as normal, including homosexual behavior, prostitution, extramarital sex, and the use of various drugs.

What do the behaviors identified in the first paragraph have in common? The answer is that they are all disapproved of by a sizable segment of society. This, more than anything else, defines **deviance**: it is behavior that a large or powerful segment of society disapproves of. In other words, it is behavior that does not conform to the expectations and norms that exist within a society.

In this chapter, we shall examine how and why some behaviors come to be socially disapproved of — that is, how and why they come to be defined as deviant. We shall examine why and to what extent people engage in deviant behaviors, and how and why society attempts to control such nonconformity. We shall also examine the role of deviance in the larger society.

The Nature of Deviance

When they hear the word *deviance,* most people think of such behaviors as cross-dressing, prostitution, homosexuality, theft, assault, and murder. Many people consider these behaviors deviant because they believe that they violate a natural or absolute morality. Sociologists, however, tend to reject this reasoning because it ignores the social origins of deviance. For example, Peter Conrad and Joseph Schneider (1980:3) define deviance as "behavior that is negatively defined or condemned in our society." Kai T. Erikson (1987 [orig. 1962]:21) argues: "Deviance is not a property *inherent in* certain forms of behavior; it is a property *conferred upon* these forms by the audiences which directly or indirectly witness them."

How Sociologists View Deviance

Sociologists view deviance as defined by society rather than as a violation of absolute norms, for several reasons. First, cross-cultural analysis demonstrates that notions of right and wrong change from culture to culture. Among some *preindustrial societies* in warm climates, for example, wearing clothing, except perhaps for ornamental dress, was considered deviant. *Not* wearing clothing is deviant in the United States.

Second, historical analysis demonstrates that notions of deviance change over time. For example, women's rights advocate Susan B. Anthony was arrested and convicted for casting a ballot in the presidential election of 1872. Today, female voting is considered normal, if not a patriotic duty. In precapitalist Christian societies, lending money for interest (usury) was considered sinful. Modern societies consider such behavior not only moral, but necessary.

Third, observations of social interaction reveal that definitions of deviance tend to vary according to who performs the act. In other words, actions that when performed by one person are condemned as deviant, when performed by another are acceptable. For example, violent international behaviors such as bombings, invasions, assassinations, and espionage are often described as "heroic" when conducted by "our side," while similar activities by "the enemy" constitute "terrorism."

Notions about which behaviors are deviant change over time. In 1872, Susan B. Anthony, shown here, was arrested for voting, an act that was forbidden to women.

Finally, behavior is evaluated according to the context in which it appears. Few people in the United States recognize competitive boxing as assault, the forced removal of American Indians from their homelands as stealing, or killing by military personnel as murder. Did Lieutenant Calley commit murder at My Lai in Vietnam when he ordered scores of men, women, and children to be put in a trench and shot? Even fewer people equate capital punishment with murder. Under certain circumstances, assault, theft, and killing are not considered deviant.

Thus, whether a given behavior is considered deviant depends on the situation. Because of these considerations, sociologists tend to analyze deviance as violation of socially defined rules rather than of absolute moral standards. Kai T. Erikson (1966:5–6) summarizes this point:

> Definitions of deviance vary widely as we range over the various classes found in a single society or across the various cultures into which mankind is divided, and it soon becomes apparent that there are no objective properties which all deviant acts can be said to share in common — even within the confines of a given group. Behavior which qualifies one man for prison may qualify another for sainthood, since the quality of the act itself depends so much on the circumstances under which it was performed and the temper of the audience which witnessed it.

Types of Norms

As discussed in Chapter 4, *social norms* are rules that specify appropriate social behavior. Sociologists recognize three major categories of norms: folkways, mores, and laws. *Laws,* which are defined and enforced by the state, are the most serious and formal. Failure to conform to a law constitutes a **crime.**

The Sociology of Rule Making

Because rule breaking requires rule making, sociologists have studied history to learn how definitions of deviance develop. These studies suggest that what is defined as deviant is the outcome of political processes. In other words, notions of deviance are the consequence of struggle between competing ideas and interests. Political struggles occur in the form of moral crusades or interest-group politics. Whenever individuals or groups attempt to define a behavior as deviant for the "moral" good of the community, a moral crusade is under way.

In addition to moral crusades, group interests play an important role in defining what behaviors are considered deviant. As stressed by the conflict perspective, individuals and groups often seek to define behaviors of others as deviant so as to enhance their own political, social, or economic position. Interest groups are able to do this to the extent that they control significant political or economic resources.

Studies on the origins of law tend to focus on public order statutes and abuse of political (law-defining) power. Howard Becker (1963), in a study of the 1937 Marijuana Tax Act, discovered that the Bureau of Narcotics conducted a moral crusade to criminalize marijuana. The crusade utilized pseudoscientific language and assertions to argue that marijuana caused everything from madness to murder. (Concerning the actual effects of marijuana, see U.S. Department of Health, Education and Welfare, 1976.) These assertions were treated as fact by the popular press. Articles warning of death, insanity, and murder moved the U.S. Congress to pass the 1937 act. As Becker (1973:145) observed:

> Marijuana smokers, powerless, unorganized, and lacking publicly legitimate grounds for attack, sent no representatives to the (congressional) hearings and their point of view found no place in the record. . . . The subsequent enforcement would help create a new class of outsiders — marijuana users.

Joseph Gusfield's (1986 [orig. 1963]) study of alcohol prohibition concluded that the American Temperance Movement was an example of status politics. The movement was an attempt by a declining rural middle class to maintain its social dominance in a changing world. Because alcohol consumption was considered common among the foreign-born urban population that threatened the higher status of the rural middle class, it became symbolic of their divergent styles of life. Passage of the Eighteenth Amendment reinforced the notion that the middle class was morally superior.

In the 1970s, elite interests also helped to introduce laws lowering the penalties for first-offense mar-

This poster was widely circulated in the moral crusade against marijuana during the 1930s.

ijuana possession in a number of states. John Galliher (1983) found that the movement to reduce penalties reflected a desire to protect white middle-class youth from imprisonment and the label of felon. William Chambliss (1964) established that vagrancy laws were enacted to serve the interests of economic elites. When landowner interests dominated England, vagrancy laws were used to maintain a cheap supply of agricultural labor. As agricultural interests declined, vagrancy laws were seldom enforced. With the ascendance of commerce, however, they were revived to protect the interests of merchant elites engaged in transporting goods. Reconstructed vagrancy statutes made it possible to arrest people who had not committed a crime but were considered capable of doing so.

Social Control

Social control refers to all social processes used to minimize deviance from social norms. These processes can be divided into *indirect* and *direct control.* Indirect control is regulation through ideological or cultural manipulation. Direct control is regulation through enforcement of normative standards. Indirect techniques are the most pervasive and effective, and because indirect control is accomplished through *socialization,* social actors do not generally view it as repressive. The institutions of family, religion, education, and government present individuals with a relatively consistent definition of morality. People come to evaluate themselves in terms of their conformity to cultural expectations. They gain psychological pleasure from doing things "right" and experience guilt when they violate social norms. Social control becomes self-control. Thus, in most circumstances people conform to social expectations because they perceive them as legitimate constraints on their behavior, not because they are physically coerced. For example, it is not merely fear of getting caught that keeps people from stealing. Most people don't steal because they believe stealing is wrong. Effectively socialized people have difficulty perceiving, understanding, or accepting alternative ways of behaving.

Socialization can never entirely eliminate deviance, however. Therefore, direct control, or **sanctions,** are also necessary to ensure social conformity. Sanctions consist of rewards for conforming behavior and punishments for nonconforming behavior. They fall into four categories: informal-positive, informal-negative, formal-positive, and formal-negative.

Informal sanctions take the form of gestures, frowns, and smiles, locution (gossip and praise), companionship, avoidance, and, occasionally, violence. They are frequent, spontaneous reactions to behaviors that anyone can administer, and are applied to violations of folkways and, sometimes, mores. *Informal-negative* sanctions include the gossip and condemnation traditionally associated with unwed teenage motherhood, whereas the praise and attention connected with "legitimate births" constitute *informal-positive* sanctions.

Formal sanctions, in contrast, are well defined and can be applied only by people with proper institutional credentials, such as priests, police, and judges. Formal sanctions are far less frequently applied than informal sanctions. Receiving a diploma or winning a gold medal at a track meet are examples of *formal-positive* sanctions. Excommunication from a religious organization, expulsion from high school, and criminal punishment are types of *formal-negative* sanctions. Criminal sanctions constitute the most powerful negative sanctions a society can apply. Increased reliance on coercive criminal sanctions suggests that many citizens are questioning the legitimacy of social institutions or traditional social norms. The various forms of social control are illustrated in Table 8.1.

Crime

As previously explained, crime is any deviant act that violates a law. When the media, politicians, and citizens speak of "the crime problem," however, they are usually referring to street crime—illegal acts gener-

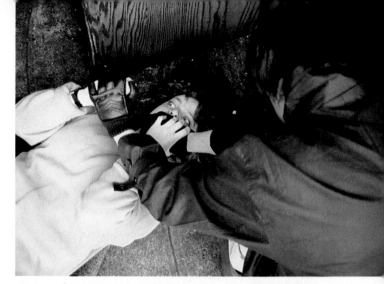

An assault against a woman. Every week, over 15,000 violent attacks occur somewhere in the United States.

ally carried out by members of lower classes. Nonetheless, white-collar crimes account for much larger economic losses and, in some instances, greater human misery.

Street Crime

The Federal Bureau of Investigation (FBI) divides **street crime,** or predatory crime, into two categories: violent offenses and property offenses. Violent offenses include murder, forcible rape, and assault and robbery; property crime includes burglary, larceny-theft, and motor vehicle theft.

Patterns in Street Crime Fear of street crime has been an ongoing issue in the United States for decades. This is not difficult to understand. In a typical year, 25 percent of U.S. households are touched by some form of street crime. Although citizens are roughly nine times more likely to be victimized by property than by violent offenses, rates of violent crimes are nonetheless staggering (NIJ, 1987:181). Approximately 365 people are murdered, 1,680 women raped, and 13,910 people assaulted *every week* in the United States. FBI statistics suggest that violent crime reached a record high in 1980 and then declined somewhat through the decade. Nonetheless, the violent crime rate in 1985 was higher than in any year preceding 1979. Property offenses have followed similar patterns (NIJ, 1987:243). Comparisons to other industrial societies testify to the seriousness of the "crime

TABLE 8.1
Messages That Illustrate Various Types of Social Control

INDIRECT SOCIAL CONTROL (SOCIALIZATION)	
"It is important to attend all your classes when you go away to college."	
"In college, you won't be able to keep up with your courses if you aren't there every day."	

DIRECT SOCIAL CONTROL (SANCTIONS)	
Positive	Negative
Formal	Formal
"You had five points added to your course grade because you were here for every class."	"Because you missed more than three classes, you have failed the course."
Informal	Informal
"I appreciate your willingness to be here even in this terrible weather."	"I'm sick of you skipping class."

problem." In 1984, for example, murder rates in the United States were approximately five times higher than in Europe. Similar differences existed for rape and robbery. Differences in property offenses (burglary, theft, and auto theft) were less pronounced. In fact, the reported U.S. burglary rate for 1984 was only 16 percent higher than Europe's. The U.S. rates for theft and auto theft, however, were roughly twice those of European nations (NIJ, 1988A:2).

Murder, the rarest of criminal offenses, and assault, the most common violent offense, are generally unplanned and unintended. Nonetheless, both crimes arise from similar circumstances. They tend to evolve out of spontaneous quarrels between neighbors, drinking partners, and family members. Roughly 60 percent of assaulters and murderers are relatives or acquaintances of their victims (NIJ, 1987:170, 262). One factor that contributes to the high rate of interpersonal violence in the United States is the availability of handguns. Morris and Hawkins (1970:72) contend that "easy access to weapons of this kind may not merely facilitate violence but may also stimulate, inspire, and provoke it."

Victims of Street Crime In our society certain groups are more likely than others to be victimized by street crime. Although white females and elderly people express the greatest fear of crime, they have relatively low levels of victimization. Victims of street crime are most likely to be poor, male, minority-group members (NIJ, 1987:184). Elliott Currie (1977:5) describes the relationship between poverty and victimization.

> A woman whose annual income is below $3,000 is roughly seven times as likely to be raped as a woman whose family income is between $15,000 and $25,000. A man with an annual income about $25,000 is only half as likely to be robbed as a man making less than $3,000, and less than one-third [as likely to be] injured in a robbery.

Victimless Crime

Victimless crime, or morals violations, refers to illegal acts in which all participants are consenting adults; in other words, crimes in which the only victims are the offenders. Examples are drug use, drunkenness, and prostitution. Why are such behaviors defined as criminal? The functionalist and conflict perspectives offer different answers to this question. From a functionalist perspective, they are defined as deviant because every society must have a set of behavioral expectations that help to define the character of that society (Durkheim, 1947 [orig. 1893]; 1964b [orig. 1893]). Thus, defining behaviors as deviant clarifies what it means to belong to a particular society. According to Durkheim, labeling certain behaviors deviant also promotes solidarity in society by uniting conformists against the threat represented by nonconformists. The functions of deviance and social control are discussed in greater detail later in this chapter.

The conflict perspective views the definition and punishment of victimless crimes differently. From this viewpoint, victimless acts are criminal only because politically powerful people or groups find such activities as drug use, gambling, prostitution, selling sexually explicit materials, and drunkenness undesirable

Kids "snorting coke." Drug laws eliminate legal sources of supply, but when demand for illegal drugs is high, illegal sources act to meet that demand.

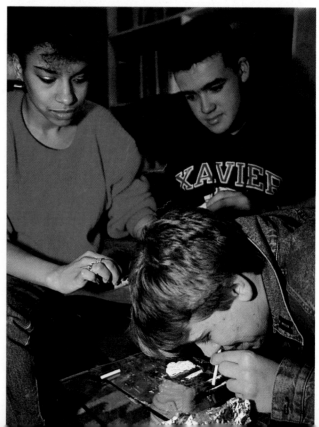

or offensive. Defining these behaviors as deviant also deflects attention from the destructive behaviors of the powerful, such as political bribery and selling unsafe products. Thus, social power, not societal need, is said to underlie the labeling of certain victimless behaviors as criminal.

However functional it may be in some regards to define such behavior as criminal, it is also clear that there are societal costs in doing so. To begin with, significant criminal justice resources (money, time, and personnel) are diverted to enforcing moral standards. Between 25 and 30 percent of all arrests made are for victimless crimes. In 1985, for example, 964,800 people were arrested for drunkenness (not counting the 1,788,400 arrested for driving under the influence of alcohol) and 811,400 for drug-abuse violations. By comparison, only 443,300 arrests were made for burglary, 133,900 for motor vehicle theft, and 136,870 for robbery (NIJ, 1987:291). In addition to consuming law enforcement resources, the massive numbers of people processed for victimless crime violations fill up local jails and clog the criminal courts. People convicted of such violations constitute over 8 percent of U.S. prison populations (NIJ, 1988B:3).

Second, because there are no victims to report violations, police must use highly intrusive and marginally legal measures, such as decoys, paid informers, no-knock raids, and buggings, to identify violations and offenders. Such methods encourage arbitrary and discriminatory law enforcement that furthers, especially among poor and minority people, a sense of persecution, powerlessness, and hostility toward the police and society in general.

Third, criminalizing victimless behaviors tends to increase rather than decrease deviant behavior. For example, drug laws destroy legal sources of supply but fail to reduce consumer demand. Consequently, market values (prices) of criminalized drugs increase. As the prices of illegal substances, and thus their profit potential, rise, more individuals and organizations begin to deal in them. For example, by the late 1980s, annual revenues from the illegal drug traffic were estimated at $100 billion to $150 billion (Handel, 1988). Additionally, criminalization and inflated prices force drug consumers (users) to engage in property offenses to raise money for drug purchases. Historically, when legal supplies of narcotics have been available, addic-

Ivan Boesky, who was found guilty of amassing vast sums of money through illegal "insider" stock trading. The cost of corporate and white-collar crime vastly exceeds that of street crime.

tion has not led to predatory crimes (Goode, 1981:255–256).

White-Collar and Corporate Crime

The term **white-collar crime** was coined by Edwin Sutherland (1940) to refer to illegal acts carried out by "respectable" members of the community. Sutherland's work exposed an inherent class bias in traditional explanations of criminality. As he pointed out, because white-collar crime is more prevalent than crimes committed by the lower classes, poverty or the consequences of poverty, such as mental illness, cannot explain the existence of crime. Thus, the notion of "white-collar crime" brought the middle and upper classes into the "crime problem."

Sutherland's (1983 [orig. 1949:7]) original conception of white-collar crime as an act "committed by a person of respectability and high status in the course of his occupation" has been modified to include almost any crime committed by high-status people. Thus, it is useful to distinguish between white-collar crimes motivated by individual interests and those motivated by organizational or corporate interests.

White-Collar Crime: Individual Offenders

Individually motivated white-collar crimes are nonviolent offenses carried out by people of relatively high social status who attempt to gain money, property, or personal benefit through deceit (Sykes, 1978:86). Employers, organizations, and the general public are victimized by these activities. White-collar crimes directed toward employers include larcenies of time (getting paid and not working), embezzlement (stealing money from employers), and padding expense accounts. Income tax evasion, insurance fraud, credit card fraud, and computer theft victimize organizations such as government and businesses. Consumer fraud in health care, real estate, and automotive sales victimize the general public (Bloch and Geis, 1970:301). The economic losses from white-collar offenses are far greater than those from street crimes. For example, conservative estimates of the cost of consumer fraud alone are five times higher than the combined economic costs of all street crimes (Hagan, 1985:103). In human terms, a California director of public health stated that medical quackery causes more deaths in the United States than all crimes of violence (in Geis, 1974:125). Nevertheless, the media, politicians, and enforcement agencies express little concern over white-collar offenses. Most go unnoticed or unreported, and when white-collar offenders are apprehended, they tend to avoid significant punishment (Eitzen and Timmer, 1985:196–199).

Corporate Crime

Corporate crimes are unique in that offenders are large organizations—corporations rather than individuals. Such crimes result from deliberate decisions made by corporate personnel to increase or maintain organizational resources or profits. The general public, employees, and organizations are victimized by predatory corporate activities. Crimes against the general public include multinational bribery (paying foreign officials to obtain business), price-fixing, the sale of unsafe products, and polluting the environment. Requiring people to work in an unhealthy or life-threatening environment and illegal or violent suppression of union activities are examples of corporate crimes against employees. Tax evasion and industrial espionage are examples of corporate offenses against other organizations. Even though the FBI does not collect data on corporate crimes, several studies suggest that corporate deviance is common (Sutherland, 1949; Clinard and Yeager, 1980). According to Marshall Clinard and Peter Yeager (1980:116–119), during 1976 and 1977 three-fifths of the largest manufacturing U.S. firms had at least one administrative, civil, or criminal action initiated against them. Forty-two percent faced multiple actions. A small percentage of corporations, however, committed a disproportionately high number of offenses. Large corporations accounted for nearly three-fourths of all serious corporate offenses. The annual economic impact of corporate crime likely exceeds $200 billion (Clinard and Yeager, 1980:8), over 14 times the cost of street crime. Human misery associated with corporate crime is no less dramatic.

Examples of serious corporate crimes abound. The A. H. Robins company, in the production of an intrauterine contraceptive device called the Dalkon Shield that was marketed during the 1970s, knowingly substituted less-expensive bacteria-conducive multifilament string for bacteria-resistant monofilament string. The cheaper component reduced the cost of production by 5 cents per unit. In the United States alone, this substitution, in conjunction with subsequent cover-up attempts, caused at least 20 deaths and almost 200,000 serious injuries. A total list of deaths and injuries is impossible to establish because many users of the device remain unaware of their victimization. Moreover, the product was vigorously marketed in Third-World countries where deaths and injuries associated with intrauterine infections likely go unreported (Eagan, 1988:23–30).

Punishment for corporate crimes is generally limited to fines. It is, after all, impossible to put a corporation in prison. Moreover, because offenses generally involve large numbers of corporate officials over extended periods of time, it is difficult to attach individual blame. Finally, because corporate offenders are white, middle class, and highly educated, they are generally not viewed as "criminal types." That label is reserved for street criminals. Thus, corporate law breakers, like other types of white-collar offenders, tend to go unpunished (Clinard and Yeager, 1980:272 – 298).

Organized Crime   *Organized crime* is similar to corporate crime in that it involves large-scale organizations rather than individuals, but differs in that these organizations exist mainly for the purpose of conducting illegal activity. Groups involved in organized crime are often also involved in legitimate businesses, but these activities are incidental to their large-scale illegal activities or serve as a cover or protection for them. Organized crime usually provides some type of illegal service for which there is a market, including the importation and distribution of illegal drugs, prostitution, gambling, and loan sharking (making loans at illegally high interest rates) (Cressey, 1969).

Organized crime gains control of these activities by a combination of threats and promises. People engaged in drug running or prostitution, for example, may be threatened with violence if they try to compete with organized crime or fail to make the required payoffs. On the other hand, organized crime provides protection from the law in exchange for the right to control such illegal activities. Such protection can be offered because of organized crime's substantial penetration of state and local governments, as well as elements of the federal government. So crucial is this political influence that organized crime probably could not exist without it (Barlow, 1987).

Historically, organized crime has been dominated by immigrant and working-class ethnic groups for whom more traditional means of upward mobility have been less available (Ianni, 1975, 1973). Through much of the mid-twentieth century, it was dominated by Italian and Sicilian Americans, largely because these groups happened to be the dominant group in organized crime when Prohibition was enacted after World War I. By creating a situation in which there was a huge market for an illegal commodity (alcohol), Prohibition led to a massive increase in organized crime activity and allowed the groups then in control to consolidate their power and amass tremendous illegal wealth.

The top leadership of American organized crime continues to be largely Italian and Sicilian. In earlier periods, Irish and Jewish Americans had substantial involvement in organized crime; in more recent years black, Hispanic, and Asian involvement has grown. In particular, Cuban Americans and immigrants from Central and South America have been heavily involved in the illegal drug trade, largely because Central and South America are such important sources of illegal drugs. It is important to stress, however, that among all the ethnic groups mentioned above, only a small minority have been involved in organized crime.

Political Crime   Related to both corporate and organized crime is *political crime* — the abuse of a government or political office or position, or crime carried out to gain office or political influence. Political crime includes a wide variety of activities. Some, such as bribery and influence peddling, are directed toward personal gain. After being accused of engaging in this type of activity as governor of Maryland, Spiro Agnew had to resign the vice presidency in 1973. Other political crimes, such as illegal wiretapping and political "dirty tricks," are aimed at gaining political office or influence. The Watergate burglary, which eventually led to the resignation of President Richard Nixon in 1974, is an example of this. Some political crime is ideological in nature: Illegal attempts are made to support some cause that officials favor. A recent example is the unlawful diversion of government funds to the Nicaraguan Contras under the Reagan administration.

A great deal of political crime is aimed at preventing or controlling dissent. Activities of this type range from wiretapping, opening mail, and other forms of illegal spying to the use of *provocateurs* to induce opponents to violate the law so they can be discredited. For example, some of the violence outside the 1968 Democratic convention in Chicago was initiated by an undercover police officer. FBI officials were involved in inciting several bombings and riots during the late 1960s and early 1970s (Jacobs, 1973). Often, illegal attempts to suppress dissent are more direct: Protestors are beaten, illegally arrested, or even shot. One instance occurred in 1969, when police attacked the Black Panthers' headquarters in Chicago, apparently while the people inside were sleeping, leading to two deaths (Farley, 1988, p. 159). Ultimately, those who survived the attack and relatives of those who were killed sued and received over $2 million in damages (Simpson and Yinger, 1985, p. 424).

The Nature of Criminals

Describing the "typical" criminal is an impossible task. Most people, regardless of their criminal record, conform to most norms. They tend to stop at traffic signals, get married, love their families, believe in private property, and respect human life. It is rare indeed to find an offender with no redeeming human qualities. The evil criminals portrayed on television and movie screens are intended to entertain, not to describe reality. Further, most people with no arrest record do violate laws at one time or another in their lives. Thus, human beings do not fit into distinct criminal versus noncriminal categories. Differences, where they exist, are of degree.

Only 21 percent of approximately 12 million arrests made in the United States each year are for street crimes (Uniform Crime Report Index offenses). Thus, the vast majority of people processed by the U.S. criminal justice system are not accused of predatory crimes (NIJ, 1988:67). The people described in arrest, jail, and prison statistics tend to be predominantly male and disproportionately young and black. Approximately 42 percent of all people arrested for street crime in 1985 were less than 20 years of age, and almost 80 percent were male. The majority (51 percent) of people arrested for violent offenses are white. Blacks, however, constitute 11 percent of the U.S. population but make up 48 percent of those arrested for violent offenses (NIJ, 1988c:41).

Crime Statistics: A Closer Look

There are some serious problems, however, with assuming that official statistics describe the majority of offenders. Surveys suggest that, with the exception of murder, only half of all incidents of street crime are reported to police. Additionally, most crimes known to police are never solved. Only 48 percent of violent crimes and 18 percent of property crimes are cleared by arrest (see Table 8.2). Finally, less than 67 percent of those prosecuted for violent crimes and 77 percent

TABLE 8.2
Most Crimes Are Not Cleared by Arrest

	PERCENTAGE OF REPORTED CRIMES CLEARED BY ARREST
Murder	72%
Aggravated assault	62
Forcible rape	54
Robbery	25
Larceny-theft	20
Motor vehicle theft	15
Burglary	14
Total of above	21%

SOURCE: FBI, *Crime in the United States*, 1985.

of those prosecuted for property violations are convicted (NIJ, 1988C:34–35, 68–69). Thus, the demographic traits of offenders in approximately 85 percent of criminal offenses can only be speculated upon.

Race, Class, and Crime Statistics Official statistics also reflect widespread class and racial bias (for an alternative account of the data discussed here, see Wilson and Herrnstein, 1985). In 1969, Chambliss summarized the findings of researchers who analyzed class bias in the U.S. criminal justice system.

> The lower class person is (1) more likely to be scrutinized and therefore be observed in any violation of the law, (2) more likely to be arrested if discovered under suspicious circumstances, (3) more likely to spend the time between arrest and trial in jail, (4) more likely to come to trial, (5) more likely to be found guilty, (6) if found guilty, more likely to receive harsh punishment than his middle- or upper-class counterpart (p. 86).

Later studies suggest that these biases continue to exist in many, if not all, geographic areas (Farley, 1988). For example, a study of Wing County, Washington, felony cases (Lotz and Hewitt, 1977) found that people with "unsteady" work histories were five times more likely to be imprisoned as those with "steady" work histories. Blacks and people with little formal education were most likely to be sentenced to prison. Some recent studies of juvenile processing have produced similar findings. Barry Krisberg and colleagues (1987:200) reported that minority youths were several times more liable to be arrested than white youths for the same delinquent behaviors. A study of juvenile offenders found that minority youths received harsher prison sentences than Anglo youths (Fagan et al., 1987:250):

> After controlling for a wide range of offense and offender characteristics, and despite the absence of differences between minority and Anglo offenders for factors other than race and social class, the disposition of minority offenders consistently was harsher and more punitive. And, at the "deepest" end of the system where the consequences are most serious, no factor other than race could be identified to explain the harsher response to minority youth.

Finally, criminals are not necessarily any less moral than noncriminals. It is difficult to imagine that corporate managers of Ford Motor Company were morally superior to prison inmates when they decided in 1972 that it was more profitable to subject customers to death or injury than to spend $11 to place a shield on an unsafe gas tank. In effect, Ford executives considered it "acceptable to kill 180 people and burn another 180 every year, even though they had the technology that could save their lives for $11 a car" (Dowie, 1977).

Explaining Deviance and Crime

There are numerous explanations, or theories, of deviance. Early thinkers tended to blame it on the work of evil spirits. Eighteenth-century classical theorists blamed deviance on unrestrained self-interest and irrational individuals. With the ascendance of science, twentieth-century theories of crime tended to emphasize biological, psychological, and sociological causes. Biological and psychological explanations attempt to ascertain why particular people become deviant. Sociological theories relate deviance to group behavior.

Classical Criminology

Classical criminology originated in the eighteenth century as a penal reform movement. Classical theorists were reacting to the corrupt and harsh legal systems of the day. By the end of the eighteenth century, for example, there were 350 capital crimes (hanging offenses) in England (Newman, 1978:138). In reac-

tion to this situation, classical thinkers argued that the legitimate purpose of punishment was to deter future criminal acts.

The central thesis of classical criminology was that criminal behavior represents rational decisions made by free-willed individuals. These individuals calculate the consequences of their behavior before acting to determine whether the pleasure to be gained from criminal behavior is worth the risk. Thus, classical reasoning suggests that states can deter crime through punishment. For state deterrents to be effective, however, they must be unavoidable, swift, and proportionate to the crime. Severity beyond what is necessary to deter future crime encourages rather than deters crime. Thus, Cesare Beccaria, a founder of classical criminology, argued for the abolition of capital punishment (Vold and Bernard, 1986:18–25).

Critique of Classical Reasoning The basic tenets of classical criminology continue to influence our attempts to understand and control deviant behavior. Sociologists, psychologists, and economists have produced a large volume of "deterrence research" that explores the relationship between punishment and criminal behavior. According to these data, severe punishments, as early classical theorists contended, have no deterrent effect. Capital punishment, for example, does not reduce rates of homicides (see Sellin, 1967; Bowers and Pierce, 1975; Bedau and Pierce, 1976:299–416).

Some studies do suggest that certainty of punishment is a more effective deterrent than severity of punishment (Blumstein, Cohen, and Nagin, 1978). However, this effect appears to be limited to property crimes, because violent crimes are often crimes of passion that involve little or no calculation of costs and benefits (Chambliss, 1967; Minor, 1978). Even for property crimes, however, there are some people for whom deterrence doesn't work, perhaps because they are impulsive in committing even these crimes. Therefore, if sanctions such as imprisonment do deter crime, the effect is minimal and inconsistent. Theodore Chiricos and Gordon Waldo (1970), in a study of homicide, robbery, assault, burglary, larceny, and auto theft, found no evidence to support the classical notion that increased certainty of punishment reduced crime rates. Further, the evidence suggests that it is fear of disapproval by significant others rather than fear of formal sanctions that deters delinquent and criminal behavior (Paternoster et al., 1983). The National Academy of Sciences in 1978 stated that the existing evidence on deterrence was extremely inadequate. Jack P. Gibbs (1981:143) noted that studies on deterrence were unable to establish any consistent relationships between punishment and crime rates.

These findings, in conjunction with the failure of the recent "get tough on crime" policy that increased U.S. prison populations by 68 percent between 1977 and 1985 (NIJ, 1986:1), lead to serious questions about the "commonsense" notion that severe punishments reduce crime. Thus, Elliot Currie (1985:28–29) argues that high crime rates in the United States are hard for deterrence theorists to explain.

Biological Theories of Crime

Biological explanations of criminal behavior evolved during the nineteenth century. Unlike religious and classical explanations, biological theories assume that human behavior is determined—humans lack free will. Accordingly, crime is the consequence of pathological defects in certain individuals. In other words, criminals are physically different from noncriminals.

Lombroso's Theory of Atavism At the end of the nineteenth century, Italian criminologist Cesare Lombroso argued that certain people were born criminals. Expanding on the evolutionary thought of the day, Lombroso theorized that criminals were throwbacks to earlier animallike forms of Homo sapiens. Lombroso further contended that physical degeneration, or *atavism,* made criminal types identifiable. He insisted, for example, that the heads of born criminals manifest the greatest disturbance and therefore the greatest number of anomalies (Lombroso-Ferrero, 1972 [orig. 1911]). Lombroso tested his theory by comparing the frequency of atavistic skull anomalies among Italian criminals and soldiers. He claimed that skull anomalies were more common among the criminals (Lombroso, 1900:273).

Twelve years later, Charles Goring (1913) raised serious questions about Lombroso's findings. Goring's comparative statistical study of 3,000 British recidivist (repeat) convicts, university undergraduates, hospital patients, and engineers in the British Army found no difference in head anomalies between criminals and noncriminals.

Body Type Theory The notion that physical traits cause criminal behavior did not end with the discrediting of Lombroso's theory. During the early 1940s, William Sheldon developed an explanation of criminal behavior based on general body types, called *somatotypes.* Sheldon reasoned that the three major body types—endomorphic, ectomorphic, and mesomorphic—are each characterized by a particular temperament. Endomorphs have short, tapering limbs and smooth, velvety skin. They are small-boned, obese, smooth, and rounded at various anatomical points. Psychologically, endomorphs are said to be calm, extroverted, and comfortable, with desires for the soft and opulent. Mesomorphs exhibit advanced muscle and bone development, and a solid, rectangular physique characterized by a large torso, chest, wrists, and hands. Psychologically, mesomorphic types are held to be active and aggressive in talk, walk, and gesture. Ectomorphs, on the other hand, are dominated by tissues of the skin and the nervous system. Consequently, they are tall, lean, and fragile. Their bodies exhibit little mass in relation to body surface. In temperament, they tend to be introverted and reclusive (Sheldon, 1949:14–30).

In a study comparing male delinquents living in a Boston reformatory with other male students, Sheldon discovered that delinquents exhibited disproportionately high mesomorphic scores. Thus, he concluded that mesomorphic structure was a cause of delinquent behavior. A later study by Glueck and Glueck (1956) duplicated Sheldon's findings.

CRITIQUES Sheldon's findings have been critiqued on methodological and theoretical grounds. The most serious criticism deals with the notion of scientific causality discussed in Chapter 2: the fact that two phenomena appear together does not mean that one causes the other. Thus, it is difficult to prove that body structure *causes* criminal activity. For example, tallness does not cause a person to be a basketball player. Lacking that trait, however, limits a person's potential to excel in the sport. In the same way, the absence or presence of mesomorphic traits may influence a person's ability to participate in certain deviant acts. Ectomorphs lack the physical strength to succeed in violent youth gangs, and endomorphs are unlikely to succeed at burglary. Thus, the physical requirements of delinquent tasks, rather than biological determinism, may account for any dominance of mesomorphic traits among identified delinquents.

XYY Theory During the 1960s, biological explanations of deviance shifted from physical structure to chromosomal structure. One such theory, the "supermale syndrome," contended that violence stemmed from an extra male (Y) chromosome (Jacobs et al., 1965). Supermales are characterized by XYY sex chromosomes; normal males have an XY chromosome pair. The popularity of the "supermale" theory no doubt stemmed from its "common-sense" appeal. Males account for 80 percent of people arrested for violent crimes, and most of them have a normal chromosomal structure, so an extra male (Y) chromosome would be catastrophic.

Common-sense appeal did not withstand the test of rigorous investigation. Although supermales exhibit slightly higher incidences of incarceration, they do not exhibit higher violence rates (Witkin et al., 1977). As with atavism and body-type explanations, the supermale syndrome does not explain the existence of crime in society.

Overview In summary, biological theories explain little, if any, criminal or delinquent behavior, and they have very little influence in sociology today. Exhaustive critiques of biological determinism were leveled by Gould (1981) and Lewontin, Rose, and Kamin (1984). Lewontin and associates (1984:23) also noted that biological theories serve a political purpose. Suppose, for example, we could convince ourselves that inner-city violence was the product of "bad genes" among the urban poor. We could then attribute such violence to the natural deficiencies of the poor rather than to their poverty in the midst of plenty. In short, we could blame the poor themselves for their violence. Perhaps it is because of this appeal that such theories continue to be popular, despite the lack of scientific support for them.

Psychological Explanations of Crime

Psychological theories attribute crime to the mental condition of individuals.

Psychoanalytic Explanations

Although Sigmund Freud himself said little specifically on this subject, psychoanalytic explanations of criminal behavior are based on his theories. In Chapter 5, we introduced the Freudian model of human behavior that focuses on three major components: the id, or pleasure-seeking instinctual base of personality; the ego, or rational mind; and the superego, an internalized set of values and expectations. According to the psychoanalytic school, a lack of balance between id and ego is one cause of criminal behavior. Id-dominated personalities are unrestrained, pleasure-seeking, and antisocial. Superego-dominated personalities suffer from ongoing and excessive feelings of guilt and anxiety, which they might try to resolve by committing crimes and purposefully leaving clues to aid in their apprehension.

Sociopathic Explanations

A number of personality patterns have also been linked theoretically to deviant behavior. One such pattern is the *sociopath*. A sociopath feels little or no guilt and is unable to empathize with others (McCord and McCord, 1964). In a Freudian sense, the sociopath could be said to lack a superego, or conscience.

The notion that violent crime is committed by people lacking a conscience has appeal in a society experiencing high rates of irrational violence. Closer inspection, however, suggests that the concept has little explanatory or predictive value. Attempts to identify sociopaths empirically have led psychoanalysts to group together people who have little in common except the label of "sociopath." The vast majority of sociopaths are not criminals, and the vast majority of criminals are not sociopaths (Cleckley, 1976:263). Moreover, the recidivism rates of sociopathic and nonsociopathic offenders are similar.

Thus, the label "sociopath" neither identifies serious offenders nor explains criminal recidivism (McCord et al., 1983).

Critique of Psychological Explanations Although psychological explanations may provide insights into why particular people commit crimes, psychological categories do not help criminologists to identify violent people before they act (Morris and Hawkins, 1970; Kozol et al., 1972). Further, psychology cannot explain the nature and cause of crime in the United States. Controlled studies find that criminals, as a category, experience no more mental illness than other social groups (Monahan and Steadman, 1983).

Societal Explanations of Deviance and Crime

Societal theories of deviance differ from biological and psychological explanations in that they locate the causes of crime in the social order rather than in individual psychologies or anatomies.

Anomie and Deviant Behavior

The term *anomie* was coined by Emile Durkheim to denote a societal state dominated by normlessness, a condition that prevents social control of individual behavior. Humans in anomic communities lack socially imposed restrictions on individual needs and desires; therefore, the more resources community members have, the more they want (Durkheim, 1952 [orig. 1897]). Because society does not contain enough resources to satisfy the infinite appetites of its members, criminality increases.

Merton and Anomie According to Robert Merton (1968), anomie develops when a society inculcates in its members certain needs and desires but fails to provide legitimate opportunities to satisfy them. In other words, a society creates appetites that it cannot or will not satisfy.

According to Merton's reasoning, deviance is prevalent in the United States because all social participants are taught to desire and strive for economic success, while individual variation and class structure prevent many from achieving that goal. Contrary to egalitarian ideology, Merton contends, socially approved means of achieving the American Dream—an education, a good job, inherited wealth—are structurally denied to lower-class and minority people. Assets of the lower classes, especially the ability and willingness to do hard physical labor, count for little.

Confronted with this anomic situation, excluded people come to realize the futility of their situation. Washing dishes at the local diner is not likely to provide the means to "drive the right car," "wear the right clothes," or "live in the right neighborhood." At this point, the internalized success ethic, confronted with unequal opportunity, generates a tendency toward deviance. An important implication of Merton's theory is that it is not poverty itself that generates deviant behavior, but poverty surrounded by wealth, in a society where wealth is the norm.

Merton identified five adaptations social actors make to the anxiety and frustration of anomic situations: conformity, innovation, ritualism, retreatism, and rebellion.

CONFORMITY According to Merton, *conformity*—the opposite of deviance—is a common response among people in anomic situations. This is true because people have internalized society's norms, even when conforming to those norms does not enable them to meet social expectations. Conformists accept both the goals and the means of society. Although conformity is common, people in anomic situations are less likely to conform than others. Many people who lack the means to attain what society expects them to attain turn to one of the four deviant responses outlined by Merton: innovation, ritualism, retreatism, or rebellion.

INNOVATION *Innovation* occurs when people remain committed to economic success but reject legitimate methods. Innovators use alternative methods, including criminal ones, to achieve legitimate ends. Thus, innovation often leads to crimes such as theft, burglary, and embezzlement, as well as such activities as drug dealing, illegal gambling, and prostitution. Although the ringleaders of these activities do not always come from disadvantaged backgrounds, those who directly provide them very often do. All these activities offer a means of economic advancement when conventional means are unavailable. From this perspective, such lucrative activities can appear attractive to those who cannot find a job or whose wages fall below the poverty level.

RITUALISM People who reject the success goal but retain allegiance to institutionalized means are exhibiting *ritualism*. This reaction is exemplified by the middle-level bureaucrat, unable to rise further in the hierarchy, who mindlessly follows organizational rules. Such people are concerned with neither the purpose of the rules nor with personal advancement. Ritualists simply want to put in their time, receive their pay, and ''punch out'' (go home). They follow every small detail of the rules but are uncommitted to the process.

RETREATISM People who practice *retreatism* reject and withdraw from both the goals and the means of society. In this category Merton places hobos, alcoholics, and drug addicts, among others. They are the ''dropouts'' of society. They are criminal only to the degree that society criminalizes victimless behaviors.

REBELLION The final adaptation, *rebellion,* is exhibited by people who, like retreatists, turn away from accepted goals and means of achieving them. However, unlike retreatists, rebels seek to substitute a different set of goals and means. They may use illegal tactics, either nonviolent (civil disobedience) or violent (rioting, sabotage, vandalism). Unlike innovators, their purpose in violating the rules is not to attain society's goals. Rather, rebels seek to change society, or at least to express a complaint about the unfairness of society. (The various adaptations to anomie are summarized in Table 8.3.)

Anomie and Gang Behavior Albert Cohen (1955) modified Merton's notion of rebellion to account for the nonutilitarian, negativistic, and violent behavior of lower-class youth. Cohen argued that these young people react to their shared frustration and resentment of the dominant society by forming subcultures that turn middle-class values upside down. For example, the middle-class value of delayed gratification is replaced by a commitment to short-term pleasure seeking. Deviant value systems allow socially disadvantaged youth to strike out at middle-class society and satisfy their status needs. Through violence, drug use, and theft, gang members earn the respect of their

TABLE 8.3
Typology of Adaptation to Anomie

	CONFORMITY TO GOALS	CONFORMITY TO INSTITUTIONALIZED MEANS
Conformity	+	+
Innovation	+	−
Ritualism	−	+
Retreatism	−	−
Rebellion	±	±

(+) ;eq acceptance

(−) ;eq rejection

± ;eq rejection and substitution

SOURCE: Modified from Robert K. Merton, 1968, *Social Theory and Social Structure* (New York: Free Press), p. 194.

peers, even though such behaviors are considered deviant by the dominant society.

Richard Cloward and Lloyd Ohlin (1960), expanding on Cohen's work, argued that delinquent gang behavior was determined by opportunity structures. Where environmental conditions allow criminal activities to be profitable, delinquent youths tend to form criminal gangs that are profit-oriented. This behavior is similar to Merton's notion of innovation. Where criminal profits are not probable, frustration increases, and delinquent youths tend to form conflict gangs, organized around nonutilitarian, malevolent behavior that operates as a form of rebellion. Cloward and Ohlin's third form of gang culture, retreatist, is organized around drug and alcohol use.

Critique of Anomie Theory Although anomie theory presents a plausible explanation for a good deal of deviance in the United States, its central assumption that all U.S. citizens are motivated by the desire for material goods is not supported by empirical observation. Moreover, the implicit assumption that deviance is fundamentally a lower-class phenomenon is inconsistent with empirical facts. Accordingly, although Merton's anomie theory is useful for understanding deviant behavior by people whose opportunities for advancement have been blocked, it does not tell us why there is so much deviant behavior among those who have ''made it'' in our society.

To the extent that anomie theory is correct, its social-policy implications are quite clear: If we con-

According to Durkheim, rapid social change often results in a breakdown of traditional norms, which in turn leads to an increase in nonconforming behaviors. This process can be illustrated by examining drug use by U.S. high-school students since the late 1970s.

As Figure 8.1 indicates, student drug use reached its peak at the end of the 1970s and declined throughout the 1980s. What accounts for this trend? Increased drug use in the 1970s was partly a product of the rapid social change and social conflict that characterized the 1960s and early 1970s. During this period, many behaviors traditionally labeled deviant — including drug and alcohol consumption, cohabitation, "psychedelic" music and art, and premarital sex — became more common. Thus, by 1979, 54 percent of high-school students reported that they had tried illegal drugs within the year.

By the 1980s, the pace of social change had slowed, and social conflict had become less evident. As might be expected, a new set of norms was established. As people embraced values such as wellness and self-fulfillment, they increasingly frowned on such behaviors as excessive drinking and sex with multiple partners (especially after the AIDS scare). A similar trend emerged with regard to drug use. As government, health officials, parents, and teachers warned students of the dangers associated with illicit drugs, students began to avoid those substances.

Figure 8.1 illustrates student use of marijuana, alcohol, and tobacco on a regular basis for the period 1975–1984. In all cases, these behaviors were declining by 1980. Similar trends existed for LSD, cocaine, and other illegal drugs. Moreover, these trends continued throughout the remainder of the decade. For example, by 1988, 39 percent of students reported that they had used some illegal drug that year (down 15 percentage points from 1979), while those reporting marijuana use had declined to 3 percent.

Interviews reveal that students have increasingly internalized the new social norms of the 1980s. For example, the percentage of students who disapproved of regular marijuana use rose from 65 percent in 1977 to 85 percent in 1984. During that same period the proportion of students who considered regular marijuana use to be dangerous doubled. In 1988, 62 percent of seniors believed that experimentation with crack was dangerous, an increase of 5 percent over the previous year.

These results, although dramatic, should not be interpreted as indicating a return to pre-1960s values. The current drug-use rate of 39 percent is still well above the level that prevailed before the late 1960s. In addition, student use of tobacco has not declined since 1984. The same could be said about other "deviant" behaviors. For example, although sex with multiple partners has become less acceptable, cohabitation has not. Thus, the prevailing norms of the 1990s are the product of a period of rapid change and one of relative stability.

SOURCE: Jerold G. Bachman, Lloyd D. Johnston, and Patrick M. O'Malley, 1986, "Lifestyles and Values of Youth," in Frank M. Andrews, ed., *Research on the Quality of Life* (Ann Arbor, MI: Institute for Social Research); *The New York Times*, March 1, 1989.

tinue to block the aspirations of certain groups to share in our wealth, we will continue to have high levels of crime and deviant behavior. In this regard, the trend throughout the 1980s of increasing economic inequality is a cause for concern.

Anomie and Social Change Whereas Merton saw anomie as arising from unachievable objectives, Emile Durkheim, as we saw in Chapter 3, argued that anomie often results from rapid social change and social conflict. When change occurs quickly, old norms break down, and behaviors once considered deviant spread. Thus, it is predicted that during periods of rapid social change, nonconforming behavior will increase. An example of this is the trend in drug use in the United States over the past 3 decades. This issue is discussed in more detail in the "Polls Apart" box.

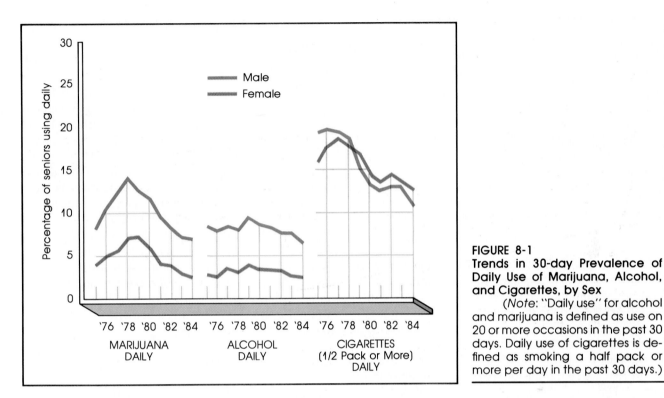

FIGURE 8-1
Trends in 30-day Prevalence of Daily Use of Marijuana, Alcohol, and Cigarettes, by Sex
(*Note:* "Daily use" for alcohol and marijuana is defined as use on 20 or more occasions in the past 30 days. Daily use of cigarettes is defined as smoking a half pack or more per day in the past 30 days.)

Subcultural Explanations of Deviance

Subcultural explanations contend that deviance arises from membership in one or more "deviant" groups. In other words, people are not deviant because they have antisocial or unsocialized personalities; rather, they are deviant because they learn and conform to the expectations of deviant or criminal subcultures instead of the norms and values of the dominant society.

Differential Association The subcultural school of deviance is indebted to the notion of **differential association** developed by Edwin Sutherland. Central to this notion is the assumption that deviance, like any behavior, is learned. People do not learn deviance through exposure to mass media (for example, violence on television). Rather, they learn attitudes within the context of intimate personal groups. The effect of contact with criminal behavior is determined by the intensity and duration of exposure of that con-

tact. People are more likely to be influenced by deviant attitudes of close friends or relatives than of strangers. Exposures occurring in childhood and adolescence have greater influence than those occurring later in life. Long-term associations with attitudes that condone lawbreaking have more influence than do brief exposures. If intimate contacts with criminal and noncriminal behaviors are equal in intensity and duration, people are less likely to participate in criminal behavior (Sutherland, 1947:5–9).

Lower-Class Culture and Crime Walter B. Miller (1958) contended that lower-class people in the United States constitute a unique subculture. He argued that the disproportionate number of female heads of households among poverty families forces lower-class males to develop masculine identities through peer-group association in gangs. These gangs promote "machismo," an exaggerated sense of maleness that encourages delinquent behavior. Whereas middle-class socialization encourages and rewards such values as achievement, lower-class youth culture encourages and rewards the following:

Trouble: getting into or avoiding it
Toughness: being a "tough guy"
Smartness: being able to dupe others
Excitement: seeking thrills
Fate: believing that what happens to people is beyond their control
Autonomy: not being "bossed around"

To Miller, lower-class deviance is the consequence of internalizing lower-class culture.

Subculture of Violence   Marvin E. Wolfgang and Franco Ferracuti (1981) used the subculture of violence to explain the high rate of unplanned and unintended murder among the lower classes. They argued that lower-class culture places more value on masculine honor than on human life. Consequently, lower-class males respond violently to trivial remarks and insults that are commonly disregarded in middle-class culture. Thus, according to the subculture-of-violence thesis, people become violent as they internalize lower-class culture.

Corporate Culture and Crime   Although the notion of criminal or deviant subcultures has most often been applied to the poor, it is equally applicable to some forms of corporate crime. In many cases, the attitude of corporate officials toward such crimes is "Everybody does it" or "You have to do it to make a profit." When a General Electric official was convicted of violating the antitrust laws, his response was: "Sure collusion was illegal, but it wasn't unethical" (Nader and Green, 1972).

Critique of Subcultural Explanations   A fundamental problem with subcultural theory is its failure to explain why some groups share deviant subcultures and others do not. A deviant subculture may perpetuate deviant behavior through differential association, but how did that subculture develop in the first place? Consider the case of the poor. A growing body of research suggests that criminal subcultures among the poor, if they exist at all, are a response to social conditions such as unemployment, poverty, and inequality. Thus, the ultimate cause of deviant behavior is to be found in these conditions (see Loftin and Hill, 1974; Braithwaite, 1979).

Sometimes, too, cultural characteristics believed to cause crime are misinterpreted. A cultural value is not always what it appears to be on the surface. This is illustrated by a classic study by Elliot Liebow in which, over time, he observed and gained the trust of a group of poor, inner-city black males. Liebow found that characteristics identified by social scientists as components of black or lower-class culture—for example, an exaggerated sense of masculinity—are actually "public fictions" offered by people to protect their self-concepts against failures at work, marriage, and life in general. These failures, according to Liebow's analysis, are the consequence of unskilled employment—hard work, low pay, low status, and limited opportunity for advancement—and not the cultural heritage of blacks.

Labeling Tradition

The *labeling tradition* represents a major shift in scientific explanations of human behavior. It arises largely from the symbolic-interactionist perspective, but it also utilizes important ideas from the conflict perspective. Earlier explanations of deviant behavior had accepted law as a reflection of a natural moral order or of social consensus. Deviants were seen as people who violate norms, and nondeviants as those who conform. **Labeling theory** has challenged these assumptions by arguing that deviance is defined by societal reaction to certain groups, individuals, and behaviors, and not by the behaviors themselves. Furthermore, messages given to deviant people—including punishment—enhance rather than decrease deviant behavior.

Relativism   The core of labeling theory is *relativism*, the contention that what is deviant in any society is the consequence of social or political processes. Laws that supported the Holocaust in Europe and racial discrimination in the United States illustrate this point. Though today we see these laws as morally indefensible, those who violated them were labeled as deviant and harshly punished. Thus, as is generally argued by

Juvenile court hearings inform youths accused of crimes of their devalued status, which often leads to stigma and labeling.

the interactionist perspective, social agreement, not some objective moral reality, defines what we experience as reality. In this case, social agreement defines who and what is deviant.

It is at this point where the conflict perspective influences labeling theory. Although there is agreement on what is deviant, this agreement is usually not complete, partly because different interest groups define reality differently and in ways consistent with their own interests. There is, for example, no single set of values or interests in the United States. Rather, society is composed of competing and conflicting values and interests. The Eighteenth Amendment, which prohibited the manufacture and sale of alcoholic beverages, reflected the values and interests of the Women's Christian Temperance Union and other reformist groups but contradicted the interests of many European immigrants. Currently, a number of criminal acts, such as homosexual behaviors, drug use, gambling, antitrust violations, and pornography, are not considered immoral by a significant proportion of the U.S. population. Thus, the labeling tradition argues that definitions of deviance reflect the ability of certain groups to legitimize and enforce their interests

over those of other groups (Schrag, 1984:1–2). Not surprisingly, those groups with the largest membership, greatest financial resources, and best internal organization will be able to enforce their definitions (Spector and Kitsuse, 1977).

Similarities between Deviants and Nondeviants

Labeling theory also contends that deviants are not fundamentally different from nondeviants. Deviants are products of social reaction rather than personal behavior. For example, although few people are arrested and processed as criminals, self-report surveys (studies that measure crime by asking people how many and what types of offenses they have committed) reveal that most people violate rules. In most such studies, more than 75 percent admit committing at least one illegal act (Barlow, 1987, p. 101). In a sample of several hundred Texas college students, Poterfield (1946) found that although all of them had engaged in delinquency, few had ever been involved with the police or courts. Short and Nye's (1958) self-report study of noninstitutionalized youth (midwestern and western high-school students) and institutionalized youth (delinquents in western training schools) found high rates of deviance among the high-school sample, and similarities in delinquency rates between the delinquent and high-school population. Although self-report methods have been legitimately critiqued for several methodological weaknesses (see Wilson and Herrnstein, 1985; Currie, 1985), the weight of the evidence continues to indicate that people cannot be divided into criminal and noncriminal categories. Social reaction, rather than behavior, often determines who is deviant.

The Consequences of Labeling

To understand the argument that social reaction creates deviants and increases the likelihood of future deviance, we must review the concepts of primary and secondary deviance (Lemert, 1978). **Primary deviance** is related to unique social, cultural, or psychological situations. It is not the result of labeling, nor is it associated with the basic psychic makeup of the offender. Taking money left unattended, shoplifting for a thrill, drinking alcohol before the age of 21, or smoking marijuana with college peers are examples of this type of behavior. Such behaviors are seldom repeated or cease with adult status, and they are only marginally related to the offender's self-concept. **Secondary deviance,** on the other hand, evolves out of an offender's self-concept. People engage in secondary deviance because they have come to identify themselves as deviant as a result of labeling by others. Secondary deviance occurs when people barter their sexuality because they think of themselves as prostitutes, steal because they think of themselves as thieves, or assault people because they think of themselves as "tough." Because such self-images have become internalized, secondary deviance often continues throughout adulthood.

DEVIANCE AND THE SELF-FULFILLING PROPHECY

Increasing involvement in deviant behavior follows the principles of the Thomas theorem (discussed in Chapter 3): If society defines a situation as real, it is real in its consequences. Thus, labeling theory holds that deviant behavior is often the result of a self-fulfilling prophecy. If society treats a person like a criminal, he or she will become a criminal. Being caught in an act of primary deviance sets in motion a process that develops its own momentum. Although the majority of identified offenders, through personal and class resources, can avoid being labeled as deviant, some cannot. For the latter group, a deviant label overrides all other personal characteristics and functions as a *master status*.

Alcohol plays an important role in the subculture of both college students and homeless people. Are these groups equally likely to be defined as deviant when they drink to excess?

For example, it matters little to other social actors that a homosexual is a Christian, a college student, a juvenile, or an athlete. Once the deviant label is attached, social interaction is fundamentally altered. Juvenile court hearings, for example, serve to inform offenders of their devalued status. Formal sanctions, if applied, further degrade self-esteem (see Zimbardo, 1972; Rosenhan, 1966). Stigmatized people are judged according to the stereotypical traits associated with their master status. Prostitutes, drug addicts, and thieves are condemned and avoided by "normal" (nonlabeled) people. Convicted criminals often lose their jobs and their families. The label "ex-con" tends to overshadow all other personal traits in the eyes of potential employers. Thus, systematic exclusion can force the labeled person to resort to crime in order to survive. Moreover, if the labeling becomes pervasive, it will be nearly impossible for the person to retain a positive self-image. At the extreme, some people come to view themselves wholly in terms of their deviant status—as nothing but thieves, prostitutes, or drug addicts. Then the self-fulfilling prophecy is complete. Actors have become what they were defined as being, thereby increasing the likelihood of deviance or crime (Schur, 1980:12–17).

Assigning Deviant Labels Labeling theorists further argue that this process is neither random nor haphazard. Access to power is a significant factor in distinguishing between those who take on deviant careers and those who avoid deviant identities. In addition to having a better chance of avoiding arrest in the

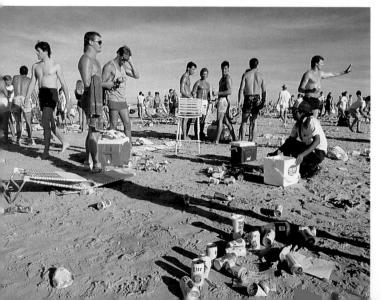

first place, people with greater resources who are arrested can obtain bail and secure private legal counsel, two factors that greatly reduce chances of conviction (Lizotte, 1978). Additionally, middle- and upper-class offenders are less likely to receive harsh punishments. They are less likely to go to prison, and if they are imprisoned, they serve less time (Sheldon, 1982:295).

William J. Chambliss (1984:135) succinctly described the dynamics and outcome of labeling in his study, "The Saints and the Roughnecks," which compared two delinquent youth gangs: the "Saints" and the "Roughnecks." The Saints were a middle-class gang; the Roughnecks came from low-income backgrounds. Both groups engaged in a variety of illegal activities, but only the Roughnecks were labeled as deviant. In the 2 years during which Chambliss carried out his observations, not one Saint was arrested, despite the fact that this group engaged in a number of dangerous and destructive activities, including vandalism, drunken driving, and removing barricades from street-repair sites. The Roughnecks, in contrast, were constantly in trouble with the police, in part because their deviant activities were more public and more visible to the police. Whereas the Saints could get in a car and drive out of town or to a secluded place, the Roughnecks drank, fought, and engaged in petty theft in public places. Thus, although the Saints actually caused more damage and endangered more people than the Roughnecks, the Roughnecks were labeled as deviant and consequently got in trouble.

The effects of these differences in labeling did not end in adolescence. Because the Saints were not labeled deviant, their deviant behavior ended when they outgrew the need to "sow their wild oats." The Roughnecks, in contrast, were steered toward careers of deviant behavior as a result of being labeled deviant. As Chambliss put it:

> When it's time to leave adolescence most [Saints] will follow the expected path, settling into the ways of the middle class, remembering fondly the delinquent but unnoticed fling of their youth. The Roughneck [lower-class deviant] and others like them may turn around, too. It is more likely that their noticeable deviance will have been so reinforced by police and community that their lives will be effectively channeled into careers consistent with their adolescent backgrounds.

Critique of the Labeling Tradition There are two clear policy implications of the labeling tradition. The first is to remove class and racial bias from the criminal justice system; the second is to make punishment more humane. A third implication is more radical: ignore much deviant behavior. Because the criminal justice system itself is a significant cause of crime, it should be used as sparingly as possible. To this end, many labeling theorists argue that victimless offenses such as prostitution, drug use, and pornography should be decriminalized (for a complete discussion of this issue, see Schur, 1973).

A number of criticisms can be directed at the labeling traditions. First, labeling theory cannot account for primary deviance. Labeling does not account for first-time serious offenders—murderers, rapists, robbers. Second, many people habitually smoke pot, steal, and commit sexually deviant acts without ever being exposed to formal punishment from the criminal justice system. Third, researchers in the labeling tradition have concentrated on less-serious offenses, even noncriminal behaviors, including mental illness. Findings in these studies may not be applicable to violent or serious property crimes or to white-collar crime. Finally, although the labeling tradition has historically been concerned with humanizing the deviant, labeling researchers, like other deviance researchers, may have actually helped label the powerless as deviant. This criticism is developed in the box entitled "An Argument against Studying 'Deviance.'"

Functionalist and Conflict Perspectives on Deviance

Within the discipline of sociology the functionalist and conflict schools provide competing explanations for the existence of deviance and social control. Functionalist views are best represented by the works of Emile Durkheim and Talcott Parsons. Conflict views are heavily influenced by the works of Karl Marx and Ralph Dahrendorf.

An Argument against Studying "Deviance"

C. Wright Mills left a rich legacy to sociology. One of his earliest, and best, contributions was "The Professional Ideology of Social Pathologists" (1943). In it, Mills argues that the small-town, middle-class background of writers of social problems textbooks blinded them to basic problems of social structure and power, and led them to emphasize melioristic, patchwork types of solutions to America's problems. They assumed as natural and orderly the structure of small-town America; anything else was pathology and disorganization.

Since Mills wrote his paper,

In a widely cited paper entitled "The Poverty of the Sociology of Deviance: Nuts, Sluts, and Preverts," sociologist Alexander Liazos argues that even sociologists who attempt to portray "deviants" in a sympathetic manner end up stigmatizing people we usually think of as deviant and ignoring more damaging forms of deviance. Liazos begins by explaining his rather unusual title.

The subtitle of this paper came from two sources. a) A Yale undergraduate once told me that the deviance course was known among Yale students as "nuts and sluts." b) A former colleague of mine at Quinnipiac College, John Bancroft, often told me that the deviance course was "all about those preverts." When I came to write this paper, I discovered that these descriptions were correct, and concise summaries of my argument. I thank both of them.

however, the field of social problems, social disorganization, and social pathology has undergone considerable changes.

The "deviant" has been humanized; the moralistic tone is no longer ever-present (although it still lurks underneath the explicit disavowals); and theoretical perspectives have been developed. Nevertheless, all is not well with the field of "deviance." Close examination reveals that writers of this field still do not try to relate the phenomena of "deviance" to larger social, historical, political, and economic contexts. The emphasis is still on the "deviant" and the "problems" *he* presents to himself and others, not on the society within which he emerges and operates.

I examined 16 textbooks in the field of "deviance," eight of them readers, to determine the state of the field. Theoretically, eight take the labeling-interactionist approach; three more tend to lean to that approach; four others argue for other orientations (anomie, structural-functional, etc.) or, among the readers, have an "eclectic" approach; and one is a collection of biographical and other statements by "deviants" themselves. A careful examination of these textbooks revealed a number of ideological biases. These biases became apparent as much from what these books leave unsaid and unexamined as from what they do say. The field of the sociology of deviance, as exemplified in these books, contains three

important theoretical and political biases.

1. All writers, especially those of the labeling school, either state explicitly or imply that one of their main concerns is to *humanize* and *normalize* the "deviant," to show that he is essentially no different from us. But by the very emphasis on the "deviant" and his identity problems and subculture, the opposite effect may have been achieved. The persisting use of the label "deviant" to refer to the people we are considering is an indication of the feeling that these people are indeed different.

2. By the overwhelming emphasis on the "dramatic" nature of the usual types of "deviance"—prostitution, homosexuality, juvenile delinquency, and others—we have neglected to examine other, more serious and harmful forms of "deviance." I refer to *covert institutional violence* (defined and discussed below) which leads to such things as poverty and exploitation, the war in Vietnam, unjust tax laws, racism and sexism, and so on.

3. Despite explicit statements by these authors of the importance of *power* in the designation of what is "deviant," in their substantive analyses they show a profound unconcern with power and its implications. The really powerful, the upper classes and the power elite, those Gouldner (1968) calls the "top dogs," are left essentially unexamined by these sociologists of deviance.

The Functionalist View

Durkheim and Deviance Although Durkheim regretted the negative consequences of deviant behavior, he considered a limited amount of crime to be a normal and necessary characteristic of all societies. He argued that deviance was so crucial to social order that societies lacking a given amount of it would redefine acceptable behavior to create deviance.

Without deviance, Durkheim contended, socie-

The lists and discussions of "deviant" acts and persons reveal the writers' biases and sentiments. These are acts which, "like robbery, burglary or rape [are] of a simple and dramatic predatory nature . . .'' (The President's Commission on Law Enforcement and the Administration of Justice, in Dinitz et al., 1969:105). All 16 texts, without exception, concentrate on actions and persons of a "dramatic predatory nature," on "perverts." This is true of both the labeling and other schools. The following are examples from the latter:

Ten different types of deviant behavior are considered: juvenile delinquency, adult crime, prison sub-cultures, homosexuality, prostitution, suicide, homicide, alcoholism, drug addiction and mental illness (Rushing, 1969: preface).

Traditionally, in American sociology the study of deviance has focused on criminals, juvenile delinquents, prostitutes, suicides, the mentally ill, drug users and drug addicts, homosexuals, and political and religious radicals (Lefton et al., 1968:v).

The list stays unchanged with the authors of the labeling school.

Homicide, suicide, alcoholism, mental illness, prostitution, and homosexuality are among the forms of behavior typically called deviant, and they are among the kinds of behavior that will be analyzed (Lofland, 1969:1). Included among my respondents were political radicals of the far left and the far right, homosexuals, militant blacks, convicts and mental hospital patients, mystics, narcotic addicts, LSD and marijuana users, illicit drug dealers, delinquent boys, racially mixed couples, hippies, health-food users, and bohemian artists and village eccentrics (Simmons, 1969:10).

As a result of the fascination with "nuts, sluts, and preverts," and their identities and subcultures, little attention has been paid to the unethical, illegal, and destructive actions of powerful individuals, groups, and institutions in our society.

In short, violence is presented as the exclusive property of the poor in the slums, the minorities, street gangs, and motorcycle beasts. But if we take the concept *violence* seriously, we see that much of our political and economic system thrives on it.

Moreover, we must see that *covert institutional violence* is much more destructive than overt individual violence. We must recognize that people's lives are violated by the very normal and everyday workings of institutions. We do not see such events and situations as violent because they are not dramatic and predatory; they do not make for as fascinating reading as the lives of preverts; but they kill, maim, and destroy many more lives than do violent individuals.

Here are some examples. Carmichael and Hamilton (1967:4), in distinguishing between *individual* and *institutional* racism, offer instances of each:

When white terrorists bomb a black church and kill five black children, that is an act of individual racism, widely deplored by most segments of the society. But when in that same city — Birmingham, Alabama — five hundred black babies die each year because of lack of proper food, shelter, and medical facilities, and thousands more are destroyed and maimed physically, emotionally and intellectually because of conditions of poverty and discrimination in the black community, that is a function of institutional racism.

This is surely much worse violence than any committed by the Hell's Angels or street gangs. Only these groups get stigmatized and analyzed by sociologists of deviance, however, while those good people who live in luxurious homes (fixing tax laws for their benefit) off profits derived from an exploitative economic system — they are the pillars of their community.

ties are unable to adjust to the demands of changing environments. Because of an unyielding commitment to outdated rules, rigid societies deteriorate and perish. By providing alternative ways of thinking, organizing, and behaving, deviance enables societies to adapt to new situations. To Durkheim, what is condemned as deviance today can become the norm of tomorrow. Civil rights activism of the 1960s offers a good example of this reasoning. The initial violators of "Jim Crow" laws were treated as criminals. Activists were

Doing Feminist Criminology

I can still vividly recall hearing a male researcher who, reporting on birth rates at a population meeting in Seattle, referred to his subjects using male pronouns throughout his presentation. Since his subjects were female (we are, after all, the only ones who can give birth), I was puzzled. As a graduate student attending my first national meeting and rather daunted by the setting, I waited until the break to ask him about his word choice. Without any embarrassment, he informed me that "I say *he* or *him* because to say *she* or *her* would trivialize my research."

For many years criminology was not haunted by this problem. Unlike demography, it was seen as an incontrovertibly male, even "macho" field. Crime has, in fact, sometimes been described as an ultimate form of masculinity. In Albert Cohen's words, "the delinquent is a rogue male" whose behavior, no matter how much it is condemned on moral grounds, "has at least one virtue: it incontestably confirms, in the eyes of all concerned, his essential masculinity."

The criminological fascination with male deviance and crime—which I have flippantly dubbed the "Westside Story Syndrome"—is not simply a reflection of the American crime problem. I suspect that it is also explained by Margaret Mead's observation that what men do, even if it is dressing dolls for religious ceremonies, has higher status and is more highly rewarded than what women do. For this reason, fields focus on male activities and attributes

by Meda Chesney-Lind
Meda Chesney-Lind is Associate Professor of Women's Studies at the University of Hawaii at Manoa. Author of over 50 articles, monographs, and reports on women and crime, she has served as a consultant to the United Nations on the topic. She was recently named a Fellow of the Western Society in Criminology for her work in this area.

wherever possible: studying them confers higher status on the researcher.

The question now is whether theories of delinquency and crime, which were admittedly developed to explain male behavior, can be used to understand female crime, delinquency, and victimization. My research experience convinces me that they cannot. About 15 years ago, when I was reading files compiled on youth who had been referred to Honolulu's family court during the

first half of this century, I ran across what I considered to be a bizarre pattern. Over half of all the girls had been referred to court for "immorality," and another one-third were charged with being "wayward." In reading the files, I discovered that this meant that the young women were suspected of being sexually active. Evidence of this "exposure" was vigorously pursued in all cases—and this was not subtle. Virtually all girls' files contained gynecological examinations (sometimes there were stacks of these forms). Doctors, who understood the purpose of such examinations, would routinely note the condition of the hymen on the form: "Admits intercourse, hymen ruptured," "Hymen ruptured," and "No laceration," as well as comments about whether the "laceration" looks new or old, were typical notations.

Later analysis of the data revealed the harsh sanctions imposed on those girls found guilty of these offenses. Thus, despite widespread repetitions about the chivalrous treatment of female offenders, I was finding in the then-skimpy literature on women's crime that girls referred to court in Honolulu in the 1930s were twice as likely as boys to be detained. They spent, on the average, five times as long as males in detention facilities, and they were three times as likely to be sent to training schools. Later research would confirm that this pattern was also found in other parts of the country and that similar, though less extreme, bias against girls existed well into the 1960s.

Reflecting on this pattern recently, it occurred to me that girls were being treated in this fashion as the field of criminology was developing. So while criminologists—mostly male—were paying a lot of attention to the male delinquent, large numbers of girls were being processed, punished, and incarcerated. Indeed, one of the classic excuses for neglecting female offenders—their relatively small numbers—did not hold during these years. I found, for example, that girls made up half of those committed to Hawaii training schools well into the 1950s.

One reason for this neglect of girls may have been the inability of researchers to identify with their problems or situations. By contrast, I was not able to distance myself from their lives. At that time, the women's movement was a major part of my life. For the first time, I was seeing the connections between my life and the lives of other women. I knew, first hand, about physical examinations, and I knew that even under the best circumstances they were stressful. I imagined what it would have been like to be a 13- or 14-year-old arrested on my family's orders, taken to a detention center, and forcibly examined by a doctor I didn't know. Later, I would also read of legal cases where girls, in other states, were held in solitary confinement for refusing such examinations, and I would talk to women who had undergone this experience as girls. Their comments and experiences confirmed the degradation and personal horror of this experience.

I bring up this particular point simply to demonstrate that the administration of a medical examination, the larger meaning of that medical examination in the girl's delinquent "career," and the harsh response to the girl so identified had no place in the delinquency theories I had studied.

Certainly, one can patch together, as I did, notions of stigma, degradation rituals, and labeling, but the job was incomplete and the picture imperfect. I have come increasingly to the conclusion that my own research results, in conjunction with the work of other feminist researchers, argue for a feminist revision of delinquency, crime, and criminal victimization—a feminist criminology.

Though I see the need for this, I am keenly aware that professional rewards for such an undertaking may be slow in coming. The work I just described on female delinquency was completed for my master's thesis. The sociology department where I did this research failed to perceive its import. In order to complete my work for the Ph.D., I was forced to abandon the topic of women and crime and venture into population research— that's how I got to Seattle to hear that even women's ability to give birth can be obfuscated.

Despite the professional liabilities, I would argue that an overhaul of criminological theory is essential. The extensive focus on disadvantaged males in public settings has meant that girls' victimization, the relationship between that experience and girls' crime, and the relationship between girls' problems and women's crime have been systematically ignored. Feminist research has established that many young women who run away from home, for example, are running from sexual and physical abuse in those homes. These backgrounds often lead to a street life, also rigidly stratified by gender, that frequently pushes girls further into the criminal world and, for some, into adult crime.

Also missed has been the central role played by the juvenile justice system in the sexualization of female delinquency and the criminalization of girls' survival strategies. In a very direct way, the family court's traditional insistence that girls "obey" their parents has forced young women, on the run from brutal or negligent families, into the lives of escaped convicts. It could be suggested that the official actions of the juvenile justice system should be understood as major forces in girls' oppression, as they have historically served to reinforce the obedience of all young women to the demands of patriarchal authority no matter how abusive and arbitrary.

And finally, a plea. Let's not see any more studies of "delinquency" and "crime" that either exclude female subjects or suggest that they will be considered in a future paper (which is often never written). If female behavior does not fit into the conceptual framework or the data on women "foul up" the results, then it's time to rethink the theory.

Police on crowd control duty. Functionalists view order as necessary for society to operate effectively, while conflict theorists see it as an outcome of suppression of competing interest groups.

recognized the positive consequences of deviance, he also warned that deviance beyond a certain level threatens social order and is dysfunctional. This point of view was echoed by Talcott Parsons. According to Parsons, the primary function of social control is to reduce tensions between different elements of the social system in order to ensure the cooperation necessary for a society to function reasonably well (Parsons 1962:58). Accordingly, all social participants benefit when society operates in a stable and harmonious fashion. Thus, deviance is counterproductive and reflects failure to understand the common social interests that bind all members of a society. Social control enables a society to move people into the different social roles required for its functioning. When socialization, rewards, and persuasion fail to accomplish this task, some form of coercion is required. Functional reasoning argues that this use of coercive social control is legitimate because laws are enacted by representatives of the people in the interest of the people. Moreover, these laws are applied equally to all members of society (Chambliss, 1976:7–9).

physically abused, even murdered, and subjected to legal sanctions. Twenty-five years later, few people consider civil rights organizers and participants as criminal. In fact, their demands for social, economic, and political equality are, at least nominally, supported by most major politicians and have been incorporated into law.

Durkheim also identified boundary maintenance and increased solidarity as positive consequences of deviance and social control. Identifying and punishing deviants clarifies the rules that society expects its members to obey. Defining and punishing deviance also demonstrates the consequences of breaking society's rules. Further, the use of social control reinforces a sense of righteousness and superiority among conformists and thereby strengthens social cohesion. Conformists are pushed together as they battle a shared threat, the deviants—be they criminals, witches, homosexuals, dope addicts, or communists (see Vold and Bernard, 1986:144–152).

The Dysfunctions of Deviance Although Durkheim

Alcohol and tobacco contribute to about 450,000 deaths every year. Why are these drugs legal when marijuana, though far less dangerous, is not?

The Conflict View

Conflict theorists deny the existence of a harmony of interests or value consensus in modern society. Rather, diverse groups, with varying degrees of social, economic, and political power, compete to have their interests and values protected and preserved in law. Rather than reflecting harmony and cooperation, social order reflects the suppression of competing interests (Vago, 1988:16–17).

Thus, conflict reasoning presents an alternative view of deviance and social control. Definitions of deviance and the enforcement of those definitions perpetuate the dominance of elites over the less powerful or powerless. To support this contention, conflict analysts point to the relative absence of legal restrictions against socially destructive elite behaviors. For example, alcohol consumption in the United States results in approximately 100,000 deaths per year and an economic cost of $120 billion. Tobacco is related to 350,000 deaths and $50 billion in economic costs every year. Although alcohol and tobacco cause more deaths and economic loss than all illegal drugs (marijuana, heroin, and cocaine) combined, enterprises that produce these drugs are allowed to advertise and market their goods. In the case of tobacco, the enterprise is supported with federal subsidies. Further, although the economic and human costs of corporate crime are greater than those of all other types of crime combined, few enforcement resources are directed against this problem (Simon and Eitzen, 1986:228–230). People almost never go to jail for violating antitrust laws, endangering their employees, damaging the environment, or selling products known to be dangerous. Thus, according to the conflict perspective, the laws that exist, the laws that are enforced, the methods, targets, and harshness of enforcement, all function to protect the interests of the ruling classes.

Some sociologists argue that such considerations also influence the study of deviant behavior. One example is pointed out in the box "An Argument against Studying Deviance": Most authors of social-problems textbooks in the 1950s came from a traditional rural background, and that background is reflected in their approach to deviance. Although this is no longer so, it remains true that most sociologists who study crime and deviant behavior are male. In her "Personal Journey into Sociology" criminologist Meda Chesney-Lind shares some insights on how that fact has affected the study of crime.

Summary

Deviance refers to behavior that violates social norms. Although the common-sense perspective frequently condemns such behavior as inappropriate or immoral, sociologists treat deviance as a label attached to certain behaviors by certain groups within society. They are aware that deviance is a relative and subjective concept; the behaviors that are labeled deviant vary both within a culture and among different cultures.

Social norms can be categorized as folkways, mores, and laws. A behavior that violates a law is referred to as a crime. Punishments of crime are formally specified and are carried out by state apparatuses. Crime is a broad term that can include the following categories: street crime, which refers to attacks against people and property; victimless crime, in which all participants are consenting adults; and white-collar crime, which involves illegal activities by "respectable" members of society. In general, people from lower-income backgrounds are more likely to commit street crimes, whereas higher-status people tend to commit white-collar crimes. Although our society generally focuses on the problems associated with street crime, the costs of white-collar crime in this country are enormous.

Theories of criminal behavior have changed over the centuries. Classical criminology treated crime as the result of rational decisions made by free-willed individuals and argued that crime could be deterred through punishment. Biological theories that prevailed in the nineteenth century portrayed criminals as suffering from pathological defects and therefore unable to control their behavior. Various psychological theories have focused on the mental processes of criminals, attributing crime to such phenomena as an imbalance between id and ego or an inability to experience guilt. All of these explanations assumed that criminals are different from the rest of society. More recent theories have defined crime in terms of social conditions, such as anomie or violent subcultures. Prominent among these is the labeling theory, which denies that deviants are inherently different from other people. Rather, deviance is defined as a label that powerful groups can impose on less-powerful groups and individuals. Labeling people as deviant often creates a self-fulfilling prophecy is which those people accept the deviant label and come to define themselves — and behave — accordingly. Although some of these various theories are more legitimate than others, none offers a complete explanation for crime.

The functionalist and conflict theories differ over the nature and role of deviance. Functionalists like Durkheim argue that a limited amount of deviance performs the positive role of providing a society with alternative ways of thinking, organizing, and behaving, thus facilitating adaption to changing conditions. When deviance becomes excessive, however, it threatens social cohesion and must be repressed. The conflict view, in contrast, argues that powerful groups use definitions of deviance to repress groups they perceive as threatening, thus enabling them to maintain their privileged position. Conflict theorists point to the relative lack of enforcement of laws against white-collar crimes as opposed to the national preoccupation with street crime as evidence that enforcement of social norms tends to protect the interests of the ruling classes.

Glossary

deviance Behavior that does not conform to the prevailing social norms of a society.

crime A deviant act that violates a law.

social control Those processes that minimize deviance from social norms.

sanctions A form of direct social control that uses rewards and punishments to encourage conformity to social norms.

street crime Illegal acts directed against people or property, including murder, robbery, and rape.

victimless crime Illegal acts in which the only victims are the offenders.

white-collar crime Illegal acts committed by members of high-status groups.

differential association A theory that explains criminal behavior as a product of long-term exposure to criminal activities.

labeling theory A theory holding that deviance is defined by societal reactions to certain behaviors, not by the behaviors themselves.

primary deviance Deviant behaviors that are short-term or cease with adult status.

secondary deviance Chronic deviant behavior by people who come to identify themselves as deviants.

Further Reading

BARLOW, HUGH D. 1987. *Introduction to Criminology*, 4th ed. Boston: Little, Brown. A readable, thorough, and well-referenced introduction to the study of crime and law enforcement, with attention to street crime, victimless crime, organized crime, and occupational crime.

BECKER, HOWARD S. 1963. *Outsiders: Studies in the Sociology of Deviance*. New York: Free Press. A classic statement of the interactionist perspective on deviant behavior, with a great deal of attention devoted to the labeling process. Much of this work is based on first-hand contacts with groups identified as deviant.

GOFFMAN, ERVING. 1963. *Stigma: Notes on the Management of a Spoiled Identity*. Englewood Cliffs, NJ: Prentice Hall. Another classic work on labeling. As the title suggests, this book focuses particularly on how people labeled as deviant respond to the many destructive consequences of receiving such a label.

GOODE, ERICH. 1984. *Deviant Behavior,* 2nd ed. Englewood Cliffs, NJ: Prentice Hall. An introduction to the study of deviant behavior, with two chapters devoted to theories of deviant behavior, including all of those introduced in this chapter. Each of the nine subsequent chapters examines a particular type of nonconforming behavior.

SCHUR, EDWIN M. 1984. *Labeling Women Deviant: Gender, Stigma, and Social Control*. New York: Random House. This book discusses issues and questions similar to those raised by Meda Chesney-Lind in this chapter's "Personal Journey into Sociology": How does the subordinate social status of women cause them to be stigmatized and labeled deviant, and how does this process perpetuate their unequal status in society?

SIMON, DAVID R., AND D. STANLEY EITZEN. 1982. *Elite Deviance*. Boston: Allyn and Bacon. An analysis of deviance and social control from the conflict perspective, focusing on white-collar, corporate, and political crime. Addresses the impact of these forms of deviant behavior on American consumers and workers.

PART 3

STRATIFICATION: STRUCTURED SOCIAL INEQUALITY

W e saw in Part 2 that social inequality is a key part of the structure of society. Indeed, Part 2 examined one form of structured social inequality, sexism. In Part 3, consisting of Chapters 9, 10, and 11, we shall examine social inequality in greater detail. Sociologists use the term stratification to refer to structured social inequality. More specifically, stratification can be defined as a systematic social pattern whereby scarce resources are distributed unequally among the people in a society.

Chapter 9 begins by describing some of the scarce resources that form the basis of stratification. One of the most important of these resources is wealth, and the major concern of Chapter 9 is with inequalities of wealth and income.

Chapter 10 concerns the political dimension of stratification. It examines how people get political power and asks who does and does not exercise power in the political system, and why. An important sociological debate addressed in this chapter concerns the relationship between economic wealth and political power: Are they one and the same, or is it possible to have wealth without power or power without wealth?

Both wealth and power, as well as other scarce resources, are often distributed unequally between racial and ethnic groups. As a result, many multiracial and multiethnic societies are marked by discrimination and conflict. These issues are addressed in Chapter 11. Because racial and ethnic problems are not unique to the United States, the chapter includes discussions of race and ethnic relations in a number of societies throughout the world, with the objective of understanding the underlying causes of racial inequality and conflict.

CHAPTER 9

Social Stratification: The Economic and Prestige Dimensions

In 1987, Jim Manzi, chairman of the board of Lotus Development Corporation, received a salary of $71,964. That was not his annual salary, however. That is how much he received per day. On an annual basis, Mr. Manzi received $26,297,000 in salary, bonuses, and long-term compensation (Business Week, 1988, p. 51). Although Jim Manzi was the highest-paid corporate executive in the United States, he was certainly not in a category by himself. Seven others were paid more than $10 million in 1987, and more than 2 dozen were paid over $5 million. Almost 300 made $1 million or more. Despite the stock market crash in October, 1987 was a very good year for corporate executives. Among 678 chief executive officers (CEOs) surveyed by Business Week, the average increase in total pay was 48 percent. Not bad in a year when the cost of living rose by 4 percent.

Unfortunately, millions of other Americans didn't fare so well against the cost of living. The median income among all black families failed to keep up with inflation, and Hispanic families fared even worse. The number of people living below the poverty level rose to 32.5 million. The immense contrast between the wealthiest CEOs and the poorest Americans is hard to imagine. The combined annual income of six families of four living at the poverty level would be less than Jim Manzi's daily pay in 1987.

somewhere between Jim Manzi and the family living at the poverty level are the great mass of middle-income Americans whose incomes have remained stable but whose share of the nation's total income has declined over the past decade or 2 (U.S. Bureau of the Census, 1988e). Between 1986 and 1987, the income of this group rose relative to inflation by only 1 percent (U.S. Bureau of the Census, 1988e).

Clearly, these figures indicate the existence of great inequality in American society. Although inequality may be more extreme in the United States than in other industrialized nations, the United States has no monopoly on social inequality. In this chapter, we shall examine the nature, causes, and consequences of social *stratification*: structured inequality in the distribution of scarce resources.

What Is Stratification?

In all societies, at least some scarce resources are distributed unequally. Thus, it could be said that some form of social stratification exists in all societies. In a sense, these patterns of stratification can be thought of as *ranking systems* within societies. People can be ranked on the basis of how much of the society's scarce resources they own and control. Those with a large share of scarce resources rank high; those with a small share rank low.

Dimensions of Stratification

Different kinds of scarce resources are distributed unequally in a society. You could rank people on the basis of how each kind of scarce resource is distributed. On the basis of his or her share of one resource, a person could hold a high rank, while on the basis of his or her share of another resource, the same person might rank low. These different ranking systems, based on the distribution of different scarce resources, have been referred to by sociologists as **dimensions of stratification.** A major contribution of the classic social theorist Max Weber (1968 [1922]) was his recognition that most societies have three major dimensions of stratification: an *economic dimension* (wealth and income), a *political dimension* (power), and a *social prestige dimension* (status). Let us consider each.

The Economic Dimension   The economic dimension of stratification concerns money and the things it can buy. It involves two key variables, *income* and *wealth,* which are related but are not the same thing.

INCOME   **Income** refers to the amount of money that a person or family receives over some defined period of time, usually a calendar year. Essentially, it is what you report on your income-tax form in April. Data on income in the United States are readily available because the Census Bureau asks people about their incomes each year in its current population survey. More detailed data on income are also collected every 10 years, as part of the decennial Census.

WEALTH   **Wealth** refers to the total value of everything that a person or family owns, minus any debts owed. It is similar in meaning to ''net worth.'' Thus, wealth refers not to what you *receive* over some time period, but to what you *have* at a particular point in time. Good information on the distribution of wealth in the United States is more difficult to collect than good information on income. Until very recently, there was no regular survey asking people about their wealth, nor are people required to report their wealth for taxation purposes (except the value of their house, land, and sometimes their vehicles, for property taxes). A few studies, however, have attempted to measure the distribution of wealth, and although they are less precise than most data on income, they do give us some useful information.

The Political Dimension   As we saw in earlier chapters, *power* can be defined as the ability to get people to behave as you want them to behave. Power is usually exercised through the political system, at least to some extent. Thus, voting, office holding, lobbying, contributing to campaigns, boycotting, striking, and demonstrating are all means by which people can exercise power. Because power is an abstract concept and can be exercised in many different ways, there is no simple way of measuring it. That does not mean that it cannot be measured at all. We shall see in Chapter 10 that sociologists have developed some rather sophisticated ways of examining the distribution of power. For now, however, our main concerns are the economic and social prestige dimensions of stratification. In Chapter 10 we shall explore the entire concept of power, as well as the relationship between the political and economic dimensions of stratification.

The Social Prestige Dimension The third dimension of stratification is social **prestige,** sometimes referred to as *status*. This dimension has to do with what people think of you. If people think highly of you and you are well known, you have a high level of status or prestige. If people think poorly of you, you have a low level of prestige. By definition, prestige is a scarce resource. Being ''well regarded'' is always a relative or comparative matter. It would be meaningless to be well regarded if everyone were equally well regarded. Then everyone would be the same, and nobody would stand out.

There are numerous ways to gain prestige or status. People can get status on the basis of their family name, if, for example, they happen to be a Rockefeller or a Kennedy, or, perhaps, a Fonda or an Osmond. They can get it on the basis of their education or occupation — as we shall see later, occupation is one of the most consistent determinants of status. Accomplishments, titles, and public exposure can all be sources of status or prestige. Ultimately, however, prestige is a matter of what people think. Thus, the best way to measure it is to ask. Surveys of occupational prestige, most admired person, most recognized name, and so forth are important ways of measuring prestige.

The Distribution of Wealth and Income in the United States

The Distribution of Income

In 1987, the median family income in the United States was $30,853 (U.S. Bureau of the Census, 1988). As you will recall from Chapter 2, median income refers to that value below which half of families have a higher income and above which half have a lower income. For individual adults not married or living with their parents, the median income in 1986 was $16,030. Income is distributed quite unequally in the United States. In 1987, the top one-fifth of families received 43.7 percent of all family income, or about *ten times* the share that went to the bottom fifth (4.6 percent). Among individuals, the top one-fifth got nearly half of all individual income, or *fourteen times* as much as the bottom fifth (U.S. Bureau of the Census, 1988). The total income divided among the wealthiest 20 percent of U.S. individuals is almost as much as the amount divided among the remaining 80 percent.

A limited number of families and individuals at the very top get an especially large share of the nation's income. For example, the richest 5 percent of American families divide among themselves about four times as big a share of the nation's income as is divided among the poorest 20 percent of families. In fact, this 5 percent actually divide among themselves a larger share of the nation's family income than the lowest 40 percent of families do.

Among individuals, the difference is even more

The opening of the Kennedy Library. How did the people in this photo gain prestige?

extreme: The richest 5 percent divide up five and one-half times as much income as the poorest (U.S. Bureau of the Census, 1987a, p. 13). 20 percent, and one and one-half times as much as went to the bottom 40 percent. Thus, it is clear that income differences within the United States are very large.

The Trend: More or Less Equal? Do these figures represent more or less inequality than in the past? The

answer is that, over the long run, there has not been a great deal of change, but since the mid-1970s, as is illustrated in Figure 9.1, the distribution has clearly shifted somewhat in the direction of inequality. Over the longer term of American history, there has been some limited change in the degree of inequality. There was some shift toward greater equality between about 1929 and 1944 (Fusfeld, 1976, p. 630)—a period roughly corresponding to Franklin Roosevelt's New Deal and World War II. For the next 30 years, there was little change. In the last 10 years, there appears to be some shift back to the pre-Roosevelt pattern, as the rich have gotten richer and the poor poorer. It is too early to tell whether this recent change represents the beginning of a trend or merely a short-term shift. It is, however, a fairly significant shift given the relatively small changes across the longer term of American history.

Income Inequality: A Comparative View How does the United States compare to other countries in its distribution of income? First, it is important to point out that *virtually all* industrialized countries distribute income more equally than most preindustrial, less economically developed countries (Fusfeld, 1976, p. 630). As countries industrialize and modernize, their inequality tends to decrease (Lenski, 1966). The appropriate standard of comparison for the United States, then, is other countries that have already industrialized.

Statistics reveal that the United States has greater income inequality than most of these countries. This can be seen by examining Table 9.1. The table shows that income inequality in the United States is above average for industrialized countries. The wealthiest 10 percent of Americans in 1980 received a slightly larger share of total income than the average for all of the countries, but the real difference was at the bottom end of the scale. There is not one country among the 17 shown in the table where the poorest 20 percent received a smaller share of total income than in the United States. Overall, the top 10 percent of Americans received 4.4 times as much income as the bottom 20 percent; this compares to an average of 3.6 for the other countries. Thus, in the United States, the wealthy receive more income relative to the poor than in most industrialized countries. Moreover, these fig-

FIGURE 9-1
Time Trend in the Distribution of Family Income, United States, 1958–1986

Top line: Share of family income going to top 5% of all U.S. families. Bottom line: Share of family income going to bottom 20% of all U.S. families.
SOURCE: U.S. Bureau of the Census, 1987a; 1985a.

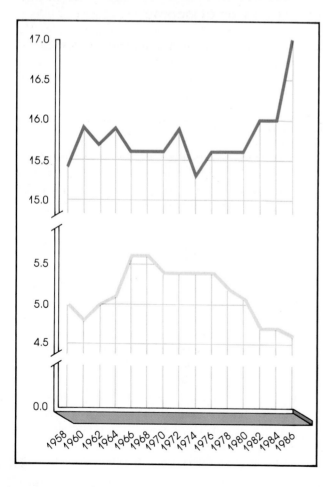

"The poor are getting poorer, but with the rich getting richer it all averages out in the long run."

SOURCE: *The New Yorker*, Sept. 26, 1988.

ures do not reflect the increase in income inequality that occurred in the United States during the 1980s, so the difference between the United States and other industrial countries may be even greater today.

The Distribution of Wealth

As unequal as the distribution of income is in the United States, wealth is even more unequally distributed. As noted earlier, the distribution of wealth is harder to measure than that of income, and fewer sources of good data exist. Nonetheless, several studies have examined the distribution of wealth, including two major ones that were released in 1986. A Census Bureau survey concerning household wealth found that just 12 percent of the population owned 38 percent of all household wealth (U.S. Bureau of the Census, 1986b). The study also showed that the average white household was ten times as wealthy as the average black household and that about one in ten white households and one in three black households had zero or negative net worth.

TABLE 9.1
Income Inequality in 17 Industrialized Countries

COUNTRY AND YEAR	PERCENT OF INCOME RECEIVED BY LOWEST 20% OF HOUSEHOLDS	PERCENT OF INCOME RECEIVED BY HIGHEST 10% OF HOUSEHOLDS	RATIO OF TOP 10% TO BOTTOM 20%
Ireland, 1973	7.2%	25.1	3.5
Spain, 1980–81	6.9	24.0	3.5
Italy, 1977	6.2	28.1	4.5
United Kingdom, 1979	7.0	23.4	3.3
Japan, 1979	8.7	21.2	2.4
Belgium, 1978–79	7.9	21.5	2.7
Finland, 1981	6.3	21.7	3.4
Netherlands, 1981	8.3	21.5	2.6
Australia, 1975–76	5.4	30.5	5.6
Canada, 1981	5.3	23.8	4.5
France, 1975	5.3	30.5	5.8
West Germany, 1978	7.9	24.0	3.0
Denmark, 1981	5.4	22.3	4.1
United States, 1980	**5.3**	**23.3**	**4.4**
Sweden, 1981	7.4	28.1	3.8
Norway, 1970	6.0	22.8	3.8
Average, 17 countries	6.3	23.0	3.6

SOURCE: Reprinted by permission from The World Bank, *World Development Report, 1988*. New York: Oxford University Press. Copyright 1988 by the International Bank for Reconstruction and Development/The World Bank.

POLLS APART

Government and Inequality

In this chapter, we have seen that inequality exists in all societies. Under these circumstances, a critical question for modern societies is: To what extent is government responsible for alleviating or eliminating the effects of inequality? Please answer the following questions that pertain to this issue. There are no "right" or "wrong" answers.

On the whole, do you think it should or should not be the government's responsibility to provide:

1. A job for everyone who wants one
2. Health care for the sick
3. A decent standard of living for the old
4. A decent standard of living for the unemployed

Within the past century, all industrialized nations have expanded the social-welfare role of government, to varying degrees. Generally speaking,

Europeans tend to believe more strongly than Americans that a government is responsible for the social and economic well-being of its people. This tendency probably reflects, in part, the much stronger socialist tradition in Europe. How do you stand on this question, compared both to your fellow Americans and to citizens of other industrial nations? Compare your responses with the table below.

	% ANSWERING "YES"				
	U.S.A.	Italy	U.K.	Austria	Germany
Provide a job for everyone who wants one	12.9	51.2	36.7	44.7	34.9
Provide health care for the sick	35.5	86.0	85.6	64.3	53.4
Provide a decent standard of living for the old	41.9	81.0	78.8	63.5	55.4
Provide a decent standard of living for the unemployed	14.7	38.7	42.8	16.2	23.2

A clear pattern emerges here, with Italy and the United Kingdom demonstrating the greatest support for the welfare state, the United States the least support, and Germany and Austria somewhere in between.

This trend appears in other poll questions as well. Consider the following question:

SOURCE: Tom W. Smith, 1987, "The Welfare State in Cross-National Perspective," *Public Opinion Quarterly* 51:404–421.

"On the whole, do you think it should or should not be the government's responsibility to reduce income differences between the rich and the poor?"

A similar pattern emerged in response to the question: Should the government provide assistance to college students whose parents have a low income? In all of the countries surveyed, over 90 percent of those questioned answered "yes." However, whereas a large majority of respon-

dents in Italy and the United Kingdom and a smaller majority in Germany favored grants, which students do not have to pay back, a majority of Americans favored loans, which must be repaid.

Which country's responses did yours most closely resemble? How do you think your friends and family would answer these questions? To what extent do you think that our responses to such questions are shaped by our social environment?

	U.S.A.	Italy	U.K.	Austria	Germany
Definitely should be	15.3%	46.0%	45.5%	37.8%	25.9%
Probably should be	20.6%	35.1%	24.6%	33.8%	37.1%
Probably should NOT be	25.0%	9.2%	13.7%	15.0%	23.6%
Definitely should NOT be	29.2%	5.4%	10.2%	5.2%	6.9%
Can't choose	9.9%	4.3%	6.0%	8.2%	6.6%

The other major study, conducted by staffers for the congressional Joint Economic Committee, considered all types of wealth, not just household wealth. This study, based on surveys by the Federal Reserve System, found even greater inequality: just 0.5 percent (that's one-half of 1 percent!) of all families were found to control 35 percent of all U.S. wealth (*St. Louis Post-Dispatch*, 1986). The top 10 percent of families controlled about three-quarters of all privately held wealth in the United States. Both of these studies — and all the earlier studies of wealth in the United States (Lampman, 1962; Blume, 1974; Gans, 1973; Projector and Weiss, 1966) — indicate that a small minority of the U.S. population owns most of the country's wealth. Certain types of wealth, such as stocks, are even more concentrated (Blume, 1974; U.S. Bureau of the Census, 1986b).

There is also evidence that wealth today is distributed *less* equally than it was in the past. The Joint Economic Committee compared the 1986 data to earlier years and found that the percentage of wealth controlled by the top 0.5 percent of families — 35 percent — was higher in 1986 than at any previous time since the 1920s. In 1929, the percentage had been almost as high as 32 percent, but it fell to 25 percent by 1963 and to 14 percent by 1976. Thus, this study indicates there was a very strong shift toward greater concentration of wealth in the decade 1976–1986. To put it succinctly, wealth in the United States is concentrated in the hands of a few, and it is apparently becoming even more concentrated.

Poverty in the United States

At the opposite end of the scale from the small group that controls most of America's wealth are America's poor. Generally, statistics on poverty are based on the federal government's poverty level. To make sense of these statistics, we must understand (1) what is meant by the term *poverty* and (2) how the federal poverty level is determined.

The New York Stock Exchange. Although many people own some corporate stock, the vast majority of stock is owned by a tiny percentage of the American population.

How Poverty Is Defined

Relative versus Absolute Concepts of Poverty **Poverty** can be defined as the condition of having a very low income and standard of living. However, such a definition immediately raises a question: What do we mean by low? Low could mean "low compared to almost everyone else," or it could mean "below the level sufficient to buy necessities." For this reason, poverty can be defined in either a relative (low compared to others) or an absolute (lacking necessities) manner. In the case of *relative poverty*, a person's standard of living is low compared to that of others who enjoy a higher standard of living. By this definition, every society with social inequality will have *some* poverty. However, some societies have greater degrees of poverty than others. In the United States, where the poorest 10 percent of the population has one-fifteenth the income of the richest 10 percent, poverty in a *relative* sense is more extreme than in Sweden, where the poorest 10 percent has one-seventh the income of the richest 10 percent (Thurow, 1977).

Now, consider the absolute definition of poverty. By this definition, poverty exists whenever people lack some basic necessities of life. Thus, it is possible, at least in theory, for a country to have no poverty at

Absolute poverty exists when people lack basic necessities.

all, even if it has considerable social inequality. If everyone gets all the basic necessities, there is no poverty.

The Official Definition of Poverty in the United States

The U.S. government's official definition of poverty is intended to delineate poverty in the *absolute* sense. In other words, it is meant to represent a level of income below which people are unlikely to be able to buy all of the necessities of life. The official definition of poverty in the United States originated in the 1950s, when the government estimated the cost of the minimum diet necessary to get a person or a family through a limited period of financial difficulty in good health. This diet, called the Economy Food Plan, became the basis for determining the official poverty level. As a result of a 1961 government study showing that the average low-income family spent one-third of its income on food, the poverty level was set at three times the cost of the Economy Food Plan. (Because of differences in their cost of living, this multiplication factor is a little more than three for individuals and smaller families, and a little less than three for rural families.) Since 1961, the poverty level has been adjusted upward each year to take account of inflation. In 1987, the poverty level for a family of four was approxi-

mately $11,600. For one nonelderly individual living alone, it was about $5,800. Questions have been raised about the extent to which this standard correctly measures poverty. Although some critics disagree, the dominant opinion among economists, home economists, and sociologists is that the official definition *fails* to include many people who are poor in the absolute sense. (See Rodgers, 1978; U.S Bureau of the Census, 1976).

Poverty in America: The Current Situation

In 1987, the most recent year for which data are available, 32.5 million Americans, or 13.5 percent of the population, were living below the poverty level (U.S. Bureau of the Census, 1988). This amounts to more than one person out of every eight living in the United States today. Just how large a group is this? It is nearly double the population of New York State and triple that of Illinois. Clearly, we are talking about a very large number of people.

Is the number of poor people growing or getting smaller? The answer to this question is found in Figure 9.2. This figure indicates that both the number and percentage of Americans living below the poverty level fell from 1960 until around 1970, reached a low point in 1973, and fluctuated irregularly from then until 1978. Between 1978 and 1983, poverty rose sharply. By 1983, there were again over 35 million poor people in the United States, the highest number since before 1964, when President Lyndon Johnson proclaimed his "War on Poverty." The poverty rate increased to over 15 percent. Between 1983 and 1986, poverty again declined modestly, but even the most recent numbers and percentages of poor people are well above those that prevailed through most of the 1970s. Moreover, the decline came to a halt after 1986, and the poverty rate among African and Hispanic Americans rose between 1986 and 1987 (U.S. Bureau of the Census, 1988).

In a direct sense, the rise in poverty after 1978 reflects two things. First is a general increase in social inequality in the United States. As we have already seen from the income and wealth data, the rich got richer and the poor got poorer during this period. To a

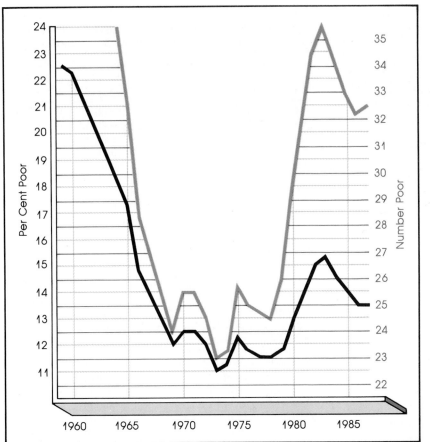

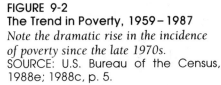

FIGURE 9-2
The Trend in Poverty, 1959–1987
Note the dramatic rise in the incidence of poverty since the late 1970s.
SOURCE: U.S. Bureau of the Census, 1988e; 1988c, p. 5.

very large extent, this trend resulted from policies of the Reagan administration: the deregulation of business, the decrease in tax rates for the wealthy, and cutbacks in government antipoverty programs. Second, the growth in poverty was partly the result of a lack of real economic growth and weak growth in productivity. Real (that is, adjusted for inflation) family incomes fell irregularly after 1973, and despite the entry of more women into the labor force to take up the slack, they were lower in 1984 than they had been in 1973 (*St. Louis Post-Dispatch,* 1985). Similarly, productivity growth has been poor since around 1973. Thus, there is a smaller "pie" to divide up among American families than there was in the early 1970s. When you combine that reality with the fact that the pie has been divided less equally in the 1980s, it is hardly surprising that we have more poor people today than we did in the 1970s.

Who Is Poor?

A number of social characteristics increase the risk that people will be poor. In general, the groups with disproportionate amounts of poverty are blacks, Hispanics, and American Indians; women; people living in female-headed families; children; and people who live in central cities and rural areas (as opposed to suburbs). The number of poor people and the poverty rates of people with various characteristics is shown in detail in Table 9.2. Note that although the poverty rate of blacks is three times that of whites and the Hispanic poverty rate is more than double that of non-Hispanic whites, the majority of all poor people in the United States are non-Hispanic whites. This is because the large majority of the population is white and non-Hispanic. The single biggest risk factor for poverty is living in a family with a female householder and no husband present. Just over half of all poor people live in such families, although only one American family out of six has a female householder. It is also significant that children have a relatively high risk of poverty. More than one in five were poor in 1986, and more than one in three will experience poverty at some time during their childhood (Ellwood, 1987).

Causes of Poverty

Poor People Themselves?

We can get some idea of the causes of poverty by a further examination of the characteristics of poor people. Popular culture claims that people often experience poverty as a result of their own actions or inactions — unwillingness to work, drunkenness, welfare dependency, and sexual promiscuity leading to out-of-wedlock births (Feagin, 1972; see also Kluegel and Smith, 1986; Schuman, 1975). A careful examination of the characteristics of the poor, however, indicates that these factors are relatively unimportant as causes of poverty.

Children in America are more likely than the population as a whole to live in poverty, and more than one American child out of every three will experience poverty sometime before reaching adulthood.

TABLE 9.2
Number of People below Poverty Level, and Poverty Rates For Selected Groups in the U.S. Population

POPULATION SUBGROUP	NUMBER OF PEOPLE BELOW POVERTY LEVEL	POVERTY RATE
Total U.S. Population	32.5 million	13.5%
White Americans	21.4 million	10.5
Black Americans	9.7 million	33.1
Americans of other races[1]	1.2 million	16.0
Hispanic Americans[2]	5.5 million	28.2
Children under 18	12.9 million	20.5
White children under 18	8.2 million	16.1
Black children under 18	4.1 million	43.1
Hispanic children under 18	2.5 million	37.7
Married-couple families	3.1 million	6.7
Female-householder families	3.6 million	34.0
People in female-house- holder families		34.2
White		27.9
Black		52.9
Hispanic[2]		51.3
Central-city residents	13.3 million	18.0
Suburban residents	9.4 million	8.4
Nonmetropolitan residents	9.7 million	18.1
People 22 to 64 years of age	13.6 million	10.2
People 65 years of age and over	3.5 million	12.4
People living in the Northeast	5.2 million	10.5
People living in the Midwest	7.6 million	13.0
People living in the South	13.0 million	16.1
People living in the West	6.4 million	13.2

[1] Does not include Hispanics. This group consists mainly of Asian Americans and American Indians.

[2] Hispanics are regarded by the Census Bureau as an ethnic group, not a race, and thus may be of any race.

SOURCES: Data for total population, whites, blacks, and Hispanics are from U.S. Bureau of the Census, 1988e. All other data are from U.S. Bureau of the Census, 1987a. Some statistics were computed from this source.

Work Experience of the Poor One relevant set of characteristics can be seen in Figure 9.3, which shows the work experience of poor people over age 15 in 1986. At first glance, the data in the figure appear to support the "unwillingness to work" explanation — over half of poor people over 15 did not, in fact, work during 1986. However, if we examine the *reasons* these people did not work, we get a different picture. To begin with, nearly two-thirds of those who did not work were ill, disabled, retired, or attending school — all of which are generally regarded as legitimate rea-

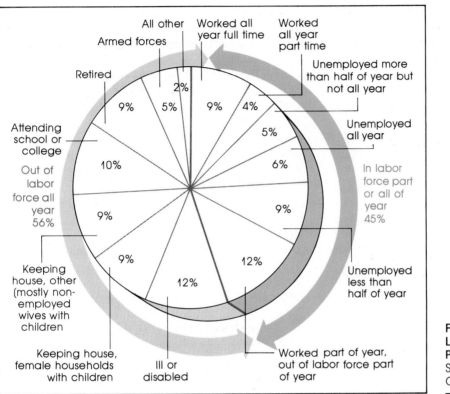

FIGURE 9-3
Labor-Force Status of Poor People 15 and Over, 1984
SOURCE: U.S. Bureau of the Census, 1985a, p. 27.)

Figure labels (clockwise from top):
- All other
- Armed forces
- Retired
- Attending school or college
- Out of labor force all year 56%
- Keeping house, other (mostly non-employed wives with children)
- Keeping house, female households with children
- Ill or disabled
- Worked part of year, out of labor force part of year
- Unemployed less than half of year
- In labor force part or all of year 45%
- Unemployed all year
- Unemployed more than half of year but not all year
- Worked all year part time
- Worked all year full time

Percentages: 2%, 5%, 9%, 4%, 5%, 6%, 9%, 12%, 12%, 9%, 9%, 10%, 9%, 5%, 9%

sons for being out of the work force. In fact, these groups combined account for about one-third of *all* poor people over 15.

Another sizable group (nearly 6 percent) of the nonworking poor had looked for work but were unable to find it. Almost all of the rest of the nonworking poor — 18 percent of all poor people — fell into the "keeping house" category. About half of these were female single parents with children, and most of the rest were nonemployed wives with children. In addition to the fact that a mother staying home to take care of her children has always been acceptable in American society (and until recently was the norm), we must consider here the cost of day care and medical care. As we shall see later, many poor people have no employment available except minimum-wage jobs, most of which include no medical benefits. By the time a poor mother pays for day care for her children (which can cost over $200 per month per child), she may already have used up all the income from a minimum-wage job. And in most states, once she goes to work, she must give up Medicaid, which means she must pay for medical care for herself and her family as well, or let her family go without needed care. In many cases, she literally can't afford to take a job — the costs of day care and medical care are simply too great.

We have now accounted for all but 2 percent out of the 58 percent of poor people who did not work in 1986. In other words, the number of poor people who did not work in 1986 and did not have what would generally be regarded as a good reason for not working was just 2 percent — hardly a great mass of people.

Out-of-Wedlock Births Female-headed families with no husband present are at a very high risk for poverty. Many female-householder families are the result of out-of-wedlock births, although many others are the result of divorces and separations. However, to say that out-of-wedlock childbearing (or, for that matter, divorce) is one of the most important causes of poverty is to ignore several key realities. First, the rate of out-of-wedlock births is far higher among people who are *already* poor or who grew up in poverty than among the general public. Thus, poverty appears to be at least as much a *cause* of out-of-wedlock births as a *consequence*. One reason for this is that poor people are less likely to be familiar with, or have access to, birth control, which increases their nonmarital birth rates. In addition, because of high unemployment, urban minority poor women—the ones most likely to give birth out of wedlock—have a strikingly small pool of employed, marriageable men (Wilson, 1987, pp. 95–100). As a result, a larger proportion of these women never marry, and those who do, marry later and wait longer to remarry after a divorce. This means that more of them are at risk of a nonmarital pregnancy. Like the great majority of nonmarried women of all socioeconomic levels, they are usually sexually active —but they are unmarried for a longer part of their lives, and they know less about contraception.

In addition, as is discussed in Chapter 6, the low wages of women are a major reason for the high poverty rate among female-householder families. This does not mean that out-of-wedlock births have *nothing* to do with poverty. Teenage pregnancy and childbirth lead many people down the path to poverty, although, again, these are probably as much a *result* of poverty as a *cause* of it. Moreover, as shown in the box entitled "Fighting Poverty by Fighting Teenage Pregnancy," there is much that we could do to prevent teenage pregnancy but have chosen not to for religious, political, and philosophical reasons.

Welfare Dependency   Some people have argued that the supposedly generous welfare benefits of the past 2 or 3 decades have made it too easy for people not to work, and that many people are poor simply because they would rather collect welfare than get a job. Although we have already seen that most non-working poor people have good reasons not to work, a further analysis of the welfare issue reveals several additional flaws in the welfare dependency argument. First, poverty is less often chronic and long-term than is commonly believed; relatively few poor people remain on welfare year after year. A long-term survey by Duncan et al. (1984), for example, showed that of all the people who were poor at some time between 1969 and 1978, about half were poor for 2 years or less. Only one in ten was persistently poor for 8 or more of the 10 study years, which amounts to less than 3 percent of the total U.S. population. Only about 4 percent of the U.S. population used welfare persistently over the decade, and of these, fewer than half used it as their main source of income. Thus, the number of people who consistently use welfare to avoid work is small, probably not larger than 2 percent of the entire population. Some people do use welfare chronically or go on and off it repeatedly over time. These poor people are the ones most likely to exhibit such poverty-related traits as female-householder families and minority-group membership (see Bane and Ellwood, 1983a, 1983b). In addition, a sizable share of the poor in *any given year* are people who are experiencing long periods of poverty (Bane and Ellwood, 1983a). However, there are other explanations that better account for this chronic poverty than the welfare incentive.

THE MURRAY THESIS   Charles Murray (1984) has made the argument in his controversial book *Losing Ground* that the expansion of welfare benefits has led to a growth in poverty by encouraging people to accept welfare benefits rather than to work. However, there are clear problems with this argument. One of the most important is that, during the period 1978 to 1983 when poverty grew most rapidly, real (inflation-adjusted) welfare benefits were *falling*, not rising (see, for example, Wilson, 1987). In fact, real welfare benefits fell steadily and substantially from 1972 on, and by 1984, the combined, inflation-adjusted value of welfare and Food Stamps was 22 percent *lower* than it had been in 1972 (Wilson, 1987, p. 94). According to Murray's argument, there should have been fewer poor people and less unemployment in 1984 than in 1972; in fact, exactly the opposite was true. There *was* an improvement in welfare benefits, as Murray argues, but it came earlier, at a time when poverty was on the way down, not up.

Research has been conducted on the extent to which the incentive to collect welfare leads people to have children, to avoid marriage, or to get divorced. Comparisons between states with high and low levels of welfare are instructive (e.g. Ellwood and Bane, 1984). In general, this research shows no effect of welfare levels on birth rates among the poor, and only

Fighting Poverty by Fighting Teenage Pregnancy

A teenager who has a baby is at an extremely high risk for experiencing poverty during much of her life, as is the child that is born to her. Just how high this risk is can be seen in some figures recently computed by Ellwood (1987). According to Ellwood's study, over 90 percent of all children who live in a single-parent home through the first 10 years of life will experience poverty. About two-thirds of these children will be poor for the entire 10 years. Is there anything that can be done to prevent this?

Comparisons with other industrialized countries suggest that there is. A study that compared teenage pregnancy in the United States with that in five other industrialized countries—Canada, France, Great Britain, the Netherlands, and Sweden—produced some startling results. The United States had by far the highest rates of pregnancies, births, and abortions of *any* of these countries (Jones et al., 1986). Although some of the difference was the product of the higher poverty rate

in the United States and the relatively high incidence of teenage pregnancy among American minority groups, these factors were not by any means the whole answer. White U.S. teenagers, for example, have pregnancy rates far above those found in any of the other countries. The differences could also not be explained by differences in sexual activity: U.S. teenagers are no more likely than teenagers in the other countries (except possibly Canada) to be sexually active.

Why, then, do American teenagers get pregnant so much more often than teenagers in other countries? At least part of the answer is that they are less likely to use contraceptives (Jones et al., 1986). Part of the reason for that, in turn, is that it is harder for American teenagers to get contraceptives. Americans believe that making contraceptives available to teenagers will encourage them to have sex, so we have avoided doing so.

What would happen if contraceptives were more available to U.S.

teenagers? We don't have all the answers, but we do have some. Experiments in cities such as Baltimore provided teenagers with contraceptives, along with information concerning human sexuality and advice that they did not *have* to be sexually active if they didn't want to (Hayes, 1987). In such a context, the provision of contraceptives did not increase teenage sexual activity; if anything, the total effect of the program was the opposite. Moreover, those teenagers who did have sex were more likely to use contraception, and the pregnancy rate fell—meaning fewer teenage births and fewer teenage abortions. Thus, we have clear evidence that we can lower the teenage pregnancy rate by making contraceptives more available to teenagers, and if the program is properly implemented, it will not lead to increased teenage sexual activity. However, because the American public tends to believe the contrary, an important opportunity to fight poverty by reducing teenage pregnancy is being largely missed.

very small effects on the divorce/separation rate (Wilson, 1987, pp. 77–81; Ellwood and Bane, 1984). If there is any effect, it is that where welfare levels are higher, young single mothers with children are more likely to live independently and less likely to live with *their* parents (Ellwood and Bane, 1984; Holden, 1987). The notion that poor people have more babies in order to collect welfare simply isn't supported by research findings. This is not surprising, as the costs associated with having and raising a child are *far* greater than the amount of additional welfare benefits that child might bring. (For further discussion of social policy on poverty, see Ellwood, 1987).

These findings clearly indicate that poor people

themselves are not, by and large, the cause of their own poverty. Most of them are either employed, looking for work, or have a good reason not to be working. Although they do have high rates of divorce, separation, and nonmarital childbearing—and thus a high incidence of female-householder families—this appears to be much more a *consequence* than a cause of poverty. Moreover, as we saw in Chapter 6, the economic situation of female-householder families would be far less difficult if women were simply paid at the same rate for their work as men are, and if day care and health care were publicly funded, as they are in nearly all other industrialized countries. As for the argument that drunkenness and other forms of substance abuse

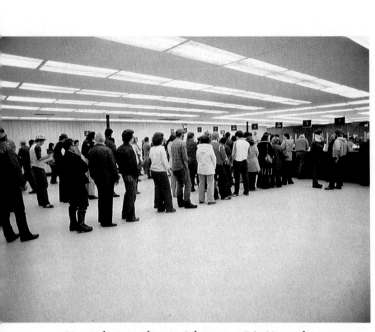

Unemployment line in Johnstown, PA. Unemployment contributed to the poverty of one out of four poor adults in the United States in 1986.

are major causes of poverty (Feagin, 1972), although there is some variation by social class in the incidence of alcoholism, it is not enough to be a major explanation of poverty. Much the same is true of other forms of substance abuse. Crack addiction is common among the inner-city poor, but dependency upon cocaine is also widespread on Wall Street, for example.

What, then, *are* the causes of poverty, and why has the incidence of poverty increased so much since the mid-1970s? Among the explanations are unemployment, low wages, and public policies that contribute to poverty or worsen its impact.

Unemployment

Consider again Figure 9.3. It indicates that fewer than 6 percent of all poor people were unemployed (that is, looking for work but unable to find a job) all year. However, if we look at the number of people who were employed for *part* of the year, we see a rather different picture. Among poor people, 12.5 percent were unemployed for more than half the year but not all year, and another 5.5 percent were unemployed for less

than half the year. Thus, about one poor adult out of four experienced some unemployment during 1986, and if we limit our discussion to those who actually looked for work, one out of two experienced some unemployment. Even these figures may understate the true amount of unemployment among the poor because they do not include people who are working part time only because they cannot find a full-time job. Certainly this group includes some of the 5.5 percent of poor people who worked part time all year.

Recent Trends Indications are that unemployment has become more important as a cause of poverty — particularly urban poverty — over the past 10 or 20 years. In the 1980s, the unemployment rate hovered around 6 or 7 percent, even in the most prosperous years, and soared to over 10 percent during the recession of the early 1980s. That was the highest rate of unemployment since the Great Depression of the 1930s. In general, the unemployment rate showed an upward trend from the 1960s to the 1980s. There are a number of reasons for the high unemployment rates of the 1980s. For one thing, a large number of people entered the labor force in the late 1970s and 1980s, as the Baby Boomers reached working age and more women entered the labor force — partly, it turns out, because of the falling **real wages** of their husbands. At the same time, however, the American manufacturing sector was shrinking because of international competition, automation, and relocation of jobs. Some of these jobs went to the suburbs, where black and Hispanic workers often could not follow because of segregation patterns (Farley, 1987b; Kasarda, 1980, 1985). Other jobs went to rural areas, other regions of the country, and overseas. Although foreign competition is often blamed for this loss of manufacturing jobs, the fact is that American companies often moved their assembly operations to foreign countries to take advantage of their cheap labor, depriving Americans of jobs in the process (Harrington, 1984).

In some cities, these employment losses were partly offset by growth of employment in the service and administrative sectors, but this did little for the unemployed for two reasons. First, these industries were highly automated and computerized and often did not employ as many people relative to their size as manufacturing had. Second, many of the jobs they did offer required a high level of education, so that they were not available to displaced industrial workers or the inner-city poor (Wilson, 1987, pp. 39–42). Moreover, the service jobs that did not have high educational requirements paid much lower wages than the industrial jobs that had been lost. As a result of these changes, portions of our older cities have increasingly become the home of a chronically poor and often unemployed *underclass* (Wilson, 1987). The underclass is discussed further in Chapters 11 and 18.

More broadly, the relatively high levels of unemployment in the United States in recent years as compared to the 1950s and 1960s are the result of poor productivity growth in the American economy since the early 1970s. As noted earlier in this chapter, real family income in the United States was lower in 1984 than in 1973. When productivity is poor, unemployment nearly always rises, and the result is an increase in poverty. Finally, we must recognize that today's relatively high unemployment is partly the result of government policy. In the 1980s, the government chose to place a higher priority on fighting inflation than on fighting unemployment. As a result, the rate of inflation fell, the unemployment rate rose, and more people slipped into poverty. By the late 1980s, unemployment had fallen to its pre-1980 level, but the poverty rate remained high, partly because of low wages, a subject to which we now turn.

Low Wages

One striking feature of Figure 9.3 is the number of people who worked but were poor anyway. In fact, about one poor adult in ten worked full time all year. How is it possible for these people to be poor? A little math will show you. Begin with the $3.35-per-hour minimum wage that prevailed through the 1980s. Assume that someone works at the minimum wage for 40 hours a week, 52 weeks a year. Such a person would earn $6,968. If this person is the sole source of support for a family as small as two people (including the wage earner), his or her earnings will not be enough to lift that family above the poverty level. In 1986, the poverty level for a family of two was $7,138; for a family of three, $8,737; and for a family of four, $11,203. Clearly, the minimum wage is not nearly enough for anyone who must support even one other person.

Two additional facts are relevant here. First, the minimum wage remained unchanged from 1981 through 1988, despite considerable inflation (about 30 percent, cumulative) during this period. Thus, the economic plight of anyone working for the minimum wage throughout that period steadily worsened. Second, low-wage jobs were among the fastest-growing areas of employment during the 1980s. In fact, most of the job growth during this decade occurred either in dead-end, low-wage jobs or in well-paid, high-tech jobs that required a high level of education. There was little job growth in between, which meant there were far fewer opportunities for a person with a limited education to get a decent-paying, stable industrial job.

Anyone who doubts the importance of unemployment and low wages as causes of poverty need look only as far as some research findings recently reported by Ellwood (1987, pp. 15–17, 33–36). Using the trends in wages and unemployment rates between 1970 and 1984, Ellwood was able to predict almost perfectly the trend in poverty over that time for both male- and female-headed families.

Job growth during the 1980s was mainly in low-wage, dead-end work, and in jobs requiring high levels of education.

Government Policy

We have already seen that both low wages and rising unemployment during the 1980s resulted partly from policies pursued by the federal government. Specifically, the government during this period chose to fight inflation rather than unemployment and refused for years to adjust the minimum wage for inflation. Also contributing to poverty during this period was a very substantial cutback in government antipoverty programs. Beginning in the late 1970s, and to a greater extent under the Reagan administration in the 1980s, benefits in government poverty programs were curtailed as part of an effort to reduce both federal spending and the budget deficit. (Actually, both government spending and the deficit increased because of a massive increase in military spending in the early 1980s.) Benefits in many programs were not adjusted to keep up with inflation, and standards of eligibility were tightened. Significantly, subsequent research has shown that those who were most severely hurt by these cutbacks were the working poor and the near-poor (Institute for Social Research, 1983). Many people were forced into poverty, and for many others, the impact of poverty became more severe as they were no longer able to supplement their meager incomes with government benefits such as Food Stamps.

Finally, it must be noted that the failure of the American public sector to provide certain necessities taken for granted in most industrialized countries also increases the extent and impact of poverty. Virtually all other industrialized countries, for example, use tax revenues to fund health care and child day care for all who need them. As is discussed in Chapter 16, the entire population seems to benefit from such programs; however, the benefits of such policies are greatest for lower-income people. In the United States, about one family in ten lacks health insurance of any kind, public or private. These people — mostly poor or near-poor, and largely unemployed — must beg, do without, or bankrupt themselves in order to get health care for themselves and their families. In contrast, lower-income people in Canada and Europe have no such problem. We have already discussed the limited availability and high cost of day care and how this problem contributes to poverty. Were the United States to provide or directly subsidize day care, as most other industrialized countries do, we could both reduce the impact of poverty and make it easier for the poor to work when they do manage to find a job.

Consequences of Poverty

If the causes of poverty are complex, its consequences are clear. In virtually every way imaginable, life is more difficult for poor people. They are ill more often, receive poorer and more limited medical care, and live shorter lives. They also have a higher rate of mental illness, particularly for the more serious illnesses such as depression, schizophrenia, and personality disorders (Dohrenwend, 1975; Warheit, Holzer, and Schwab, 1973). They also report lower levels of personal happiness than the nonpoor (Converse, Campbell, and Rogers, 1976). The children of the poor are at greater risk of dying in infancy, and if they survive, they have a greater risk than nonpoor children of getting in trouble with the law or of becoming pregnant as teenagers. They will receive a much poorer education than nonpoor children, and they are far less likely to complete high school. One recent study showed that in Chicago's public schools, where a large proportion of the students are from poverty-stricken families, fewer than half of all 1980 ninth-graders graduated on time in 1984 — and of those who did graduate, only one out of three could read at a 12th-grade level (Wilson, 1987, p. 57).

Poor people will spend more of their income on food and housing than the nonpoor, but they still will be less adequately fed and housed. A study of housing in southern Illinois by Quinn (1984) revealed that poor people were several times as likely as the general public to live in overcrowded housing, yet 80 to 90 percent of these poor people were paying more than the government standard of 25 percent of their incomes for rent. The ultimate housing problem, of course, is to have no home at all. In the 1980s, the incidence of homelessness surged in the United States. As Boston's Mayor Raymond Flynn put it: "The problem, folks, is just getting a lot worse each and every year" (*St. Louis Post-Dispatch,* 1987). The U.S. Conference of Mayors estimated that homelessness increased more than 20 percent between 1986 and

1987 alone, and that one-third of the homeless were children and their parents, indicating a great upsurge in homeless *families.*

Poor people are more likely both to commit street crimes and to be the victims of such crimes (Barlow, 1987). Crime rates are highest in poor neighborhoods, for criminals tend to victimize those who are close by and available. As a result, a highly disproportionate number of robbery, assault, and homicide victims are poor. So high is the incidence of crime in some poor neighborhoods that poor people are afraid to venture outside their homes (Rainwater, 1966). Summer after summer in several major cities, elderly poor people have died of the heat because they could not afford air conditioning and were afraid to open their windows because of crime.

In the winter, the risks become cold and fire. Dozens of poor people die every winter as a result of fires started by makeshift heating arrangements, some of which were attempted after their gas or electricity had been turned off because they could not pay the bill. In the icy January of 1988, a number of homeless people died of exposure to the cold. Even so, fear of crime in shelters led some of the homeless to remain outside.

The Cycle of Poverty?

Finally, poverty in one generation often begets poverty in the next. Although there is not as much persistent poverty as was once thought, those born into a poor family do have a greater risk of experiencing poverty at some time during adulthood. This is especially true for people who also face the disadvantages that come with minority racial or ethnic status or growing up in a family with a teenage mother.

Homelessness increased by as much as 20 percent per year in the 1980s.

Socioeconomic Mobility

Thus far, we have described the degree of economic inequality found in the United States, along with some of the consequences, particularly for those at the bottom of the distribution. A separate, although related, question about the *degree* of inequality concerns **socioeconomic mobility:** the frequency with which people move up or down in the society's economic hierarchy. In a society with very high socioeconomic mobility, it would not be unusual for a person to be born very poor and end up very wealthy as an adult — or the other way around. In sociological terms, a society such as this would have an **open stratification system.** In this type of system, *achieved statuses* have substantial influence over the social status a person attains in adulthood. In a society with very *low* mobility, those born poor nearly always stay poor, and those born wealthy nearly always stay wealthy. This type of society is said to have a **closed stratification system.** In a closed stratification system, *ascribed statuses* largely determine a person's social position throughout life.

If you consider all present and past societies, you would probably see a tendency toward greater mobility in societies with lesser degrees of inequality. Preindustrial societies, for example, have generally been characterized by rather great inequality and rather low mobility. However, in industrialized societies, the relationship has not been extremely strong and consist-

253

ent. Thus, among modern societies with similar levels of inequality, there is some variation in mobility. Similarly, in societies with similar degrees of mobility, there are significant variations in the degree of inequality.

Stratification and Mobility

Caste Systems Sociologists have defined three types of stratification system on the basis of social mobility. The least mobility is found in a **caste system.** A caste system has legally or formally defined groupings that are assigned by birth and are not subject to change. In other words, a person is born into a particular group, called a **caste,** and must remain in that caste throughout life. In sociological terms, a person's position throughout life is entirely determined by the ascribed status of the caste into which he or she was born; achieved statuses have *no* influence over a person's life situation in a caste system.

France under feudalism. Note the contrast between the landowning nobility and clergy on the one hand, and the landless peasants who worked the land on the other.

INDIA: A CASE STUDY Although caste has existed in some form in many societies throughout history, the two best-known examples of caste systems are those of India and South Africa. In India, a caste system based on religion has existed for thousands of years. Different roles have been assigned to different castes for centuries, ranging from the priestly religious functions of the highest, or Brahman, class to the common labor performed by the lowest caste. The lowest castes are defined as "untouchable" by people in the higher castes, with contact of all types — even looking at one another — being forbidden. Of course, the castes are also required to live separately. As is generally true of caste systems, the caste into which one is born has traditionally determined one's status throughout life, whom one can marry, and the status of one's children and grandchildren throughout their lives. The caste system in India was officially abolished in 1949, but it continues to have considerable influence on social behavior, particularly in rural areas. In urban areas, however, its influence has waned, partly because of the legislation, but also partly because cities house such a variety of people who must do business and come into contact with one another that regulating who may speak to whom is far more difficult. Not only in India, but everywhere, formal and rigid closed systems of stratification become harder and harder to maintain as society urbanizes and modernizes. (See Chapter 18 for further discussion of this point.)

SOUTH AFRICA AND APARTHEID About the same time that India was legally abolishing its caste system, South Africa was formally writing its caste system — called **apartheid** — into law. South Africa is an example of a **racial caste system,** in which the castes are defined on the basis of race. In South Africa, there are four racial castes: European (white), African (black), coloured (mixed European and African ancestry), and Asian. Political and educational rights, what jobs a person can hold, and where a person can live are all defined on the basis of these groupings. Until very recently, people of different races were forbidden to marry, have sexual contact, or even to *conspire* to have sexual contact. People had to carry passes identifying their race, which determined where and when they could go. Although the pass and marriage laws have been relaxed somewhat in recent years, the formal system of segregation, the gross educational and economic inequalities, and the denial of political rights to the black majority remain unchanged. The changes in the pass and marriage laws came as appeasements following years of violence beginning in the 1960s, in which over 2,500 people have died. The widespread and continuing upheaval over South Africa's racial caste system, and the appeasements made by the white government in an effort to curb that violence, again illustrate the extreme difficulty of maintaining a caste system in a modernizing, urbanizing society.

Estate or Feudal Systems The **estate system,** also called the *feudal system,* offers slightly more mobility than the caste system. In an estate system, status is determined on the basis of landownership, often accompanied by some type of formal title. In general, the high-status groups are those who own land, and the rest of the population generally works for them. Some variety of the estate system has been found in most of the world at some point in history, including the feudal systems of medieval Europe and of China and Russia in the nineteenth and early twentieth centuries, and the hacienda systems of Latin America, some of which remain largely intact today. The American South before the Civil War, where wealth and power were concentrated in the hands of large-scale plantation owners, is often regarded as a form of feudal or estate system, although slavery also made it a type of racial caste system.

In a feudal system, your position throughout life is usually determined by the *ascribed status* of whether you were born into the landowning class. Occasionally, however, titles that permit entry into this elite class may be conferred. In the European feudal system, for example, a peasant could occasionally be knighted or admitted to the clergy, which gave him the privileges associated with these landowning classes. However, this was the exception to the rule. Because of their link to landownership, estate systems are found in agricultural, preindustrial societies. When societies begin to urbanize, the feudal system almost inevitably breaks down.

Class Systems The highest degree of mobility is found in **class systems.** In a class system, both ascribed statuses and achieved statuses have significant effects on people's income, wealth, and social position. In other words, people who are born into affluent families generally enjoy a higher status as adults than people who are born into poorer families, but what people *do*—the amount of schooling they attain and the success of their personal and economic decisions—also influences their status as adults. Class systems are typically found in modern industrial societies. As we shall see in Chapter 12, class systems in different forms are found in both capitalist and socialist societies. The present-day United States, Canada, Australia, New Zealand, Israel, and the countries of Western Europe are all examples of class systems; Eastern Europe, the Soviet Union, and China are socialist countries with a somewhat different type of class system.

ACHIEVED AND ASCRIBED STATUSES IN CLASS SOCIETIES Many people have the misunderstanding that only achieved statuses matter in a class system. This is clearly *not* true; the difference between class systems and the other two systems (caste and estate) is not that ascribed statuses *don't* matter, but rather that achieved statuses *do*. This can be seen by examining studies of socioeconomic mobility in class societies. Most such studies look at **intergenerational mobility**; that is, they compare a person's status with that of his or her parents. The majority of these studies have compared the status of sons to that of their fathers, because in previous generations, mothers usually did not work outside the home and derived their social and economic status from their husbands. Recently, however, such studies have begun to include both women and men. What all these studies show is that mobility is quite limited in class systems. In other words, most men have statuses quite close to those of their fathers (Blau and Duncan, 1967; see also Featherman and Hauser, 1978). In most cases, the status of the son is slightly higher than that of the father, but this mainly reflects what sociologists call **structural mobility**—there has been growth in better-paying, more pleasant, higher-status, white-collar jobs, and a decline in the number of blue-collar jobs. Thus, in all class economies, more people are now working at the "better" jobs simply because there are more of them. This is why about half of all American men have higher statuses than their fathers, whereas only one out of five or six has a lower status (Featherman, 1979).

Although many people do move up slightly in

status and a good number of sons of blue-collar workers (about one in three) have moved up to white-collar employment, two facts show the continuing influence of ascribed statuses. First, although many people move up a little because there are more of the "desirable" jobs today than in the past, people usually do not change their *relative* status a great deal. A man who has a white-collar job in contrast to his father's blue-collar job may still have a job status and an income below those of 70 percent of the population, just as his father did. Sociologists refer to this situation as an absence of **exchange mobility**. People's absolute position may change, but their position *relative to others* is less likely to.

The second point to remember is that, even though people may move up or down slightly, they are not likely to move a great deal. We can see this by examining the proportion of sons of manual workers who attain *professional* employment—the more desirable jobs that require specific technical or professional education. In the United States, the most widely cited study of mobility found that only one out of ten sons of manual laborers attains professional employment—in contrast to *seven* out of ten sons of professional workers (Blau and Duncan, 1967). In other words, if your father is a professional worker, you have *seven times* as great a chance of getting that type of job as you have if your father is a laborer. Recently, research has indicated that exchange mobility has increased, but structural mobility has decreased in the United States; the result is little overall change in occupational mobility (Hout, 1988).

You should also remember that ascribed statuses such as race and sex also continue to be important in class societies. Women and racial or ethnic minorities receive lower pay and work at lower-status jobs than white males do, even when their parents have similar status. Thus, race and sex biases compound the influence of ascribed statuses in class societies. A final important point is that ownership of major, income-producing wealth is even more likely to be based on the luck of birth. For all these reasons, then, the status into which you are born makes a big difference, even in a class society.

MOBILITY IN THE UNITED STATES How does the United States compare to other class societies with regard to mobility? It is often argued that the greater

class inequality of the United States is offset by greater mobility. The actual findings of research suggest that this may be true, but only to a very limited extent. In general, there is little difference in the degree of mobility in different class societies (Lipset and Bendix, 1960; Tyree, Semyonov, and Hodge, 1979; Grusky and Hauser, 1984). All have some mobility, but in all of them, including the United States, movement from very low statuses to very high statuses is much more the exception than the rule. Movement within and out of the middle strata, in contrast, appears more common (Grusky and Hauser, 1984). Within this general observation, a case can be made that there is a little more mobility in the United States than in other industrialized countries. For example, the proportion of people who move from manual labor to professional occupations—although a tiny minority everywhere—*is* higher in the United States than in most other countries. This may reflect high *structural mobility* owing to white-collar job growth rather than high *exchange mobility* (see Slomczynski and Krauze, 1987, p. 605; but also Hauser and Grusky, 1988).

Whether the United States has more mobility than other countries, however, depends on how you measure mobility. Thus, although one recent study (Yamaguchi, 1986) found more mobility in the United States than in Great Britain, it could not make such a comparison between the United States and Japan. Although the two countries had become more similar over time, deciding which country has the greater mobility depends on what specific type of mobility you look at. By some measures, Japan has more mobility; by others, the United States does. Similarly, research by Slomczynski and Krauze (1987, p. 608) comparing 22 countries on two measures of exchange mobility found that the United States had above-average mobility according to one measure, but average mobility according to the other. At the very least, then, it would be inaccurate to say that the United States has *much* greater mobility than most other industrialized countries. The similarities are clearly greater than the differences, and different measures do not give highly consistent results.

Although the United States has little more mobility than most other industrialized societies, the fact remains that Americans *believe* we have considerable mobility. The Horatio Alger myth that anyone, no matter how poor, can succeed on a grand scale is alive and well. Seventy percent of Americans agree, for example, that ''America is the land of opportunity where everyone who works hard can get ahead'' (Kluegel and Smith, 1986, p. 44). Although over 80 percent agree that ''people who grew up in rich families'' have a better-than-average chance of getting ahead, two-thirds also thought that ''people who grew up in poor families'' have an average or better-than-average chance of getting ahead (Kluegel and Smith, 1986, p. 49). The majority also believed the same about blacks and women, and over 90 percent felt that way about ''people who grew up in working-class families.'' The fact is that all of these groups have a considerably poorer-than-average chance of getting ahead, yet most Americans persist in believing otherwise. In short, the reality is that there is significantly *less* mobility in American society than most Americans believe.

Social Class in American Society

Defining Social Class

Sociologists refer to a group of people who are similar in terms of level of income or wealth as a **social class.** Inequalities in income and wealth are called *class stratification,* and your position within that system of inequality is called your *social class.* A term similar in meaning to class is **socioeconomic status.** Social class and socioeconomic status are often taken to include not only your levels of income and wealth, but also the prestige of your occupation and the amount of education you have attained. Sociologists do not agree on the relative importance of these various factors in defining social class. Partly for this reason, they cannot agree on any uniform system for defining or identifying social classes. Marxist sociologists, for example, see wealth as the only key to defining social class. If you own the means of production, you are in the ruling class; if not, you are in the subordinate class. Other sociologists define class mainly on the basis of income, and still others see it as a composite of income, wealth, occupation, and education. The general public, too, has its ideas about social class, and sociol-

ogists have devoted major efforts to studying the relative effects of income, wealth, occupation, and education in shaping people's perceptions of their own social class. Let us consider some of the key formulations sociologists have used to identify social classes, recognizing at the start that none of these is accepted by all sociologists. We shall focus on three common formulations of social class: the Marxian definition, the composite approach, and subjective class.

The Marxian Definition of Social Class The social thinker who made the most important early contribution to thinking about social class and who made the study of social class a key item on the agenda for sociology was Karl Marx. Marx's entire analysis of society centers around social class. He believed that all aspects of a society are an outgrowth of—but also help to perpetuate—the society's **class structure.** To Marx, there were only two classes in any type of society that really mattered—the *ruling class,* who owned the means of production, and the *subordinate class,* who did not. In all societies that produce a surplus—that is, produce enough to provide more than a bare subsistence—the members of the subordinate class work for the members of the ruling class, and after they get their subsistence, they must turn over the surplus that they produce to the members of the ruling class.

In a feudal agricultural society, the landowners are the ruling class, and the subordinate class consists of peasants, serfs, tenant farmers, sharecroppers, or slaves—those who work land they do not own and turn over the products of their labor to the landowning class. When urbanization and industrialization arrive, such an economy is replaced by a new system with a new class structure. In a capitalist society—any industrial society where the means of production are privately owned—the ruling class is the bourgeoisie: the class that owns capital. By capital, we mean productive capacity—factories, mineral resources, land, or money that can be converted into these things.

Most of the population, however, belongs not to the bourgeoisie but to the proletariat: those who do not own capital but work for those who do. Thus, the only thing that really matters is ownership of the means of production. No matter how much money salaried employees earn, they still do not belong to the

American Social Classes in the 1980s

In the 1980s, Americans can be roughly classified into six social classes, each of which is described briefly below.

CORPORATE ELITE

Making up about 1 percent of the population, this is the group that owns the bulk of the country's corporate wealth. Usually owning assets in excess of $1 million, people in this group enjoy a standard of living far beyond that of the rest of the population. They are largely the "old rich," whose names alone are a source of great prestige, and who have been wealthy for generations. Such families include the Rockefellers, Fords, Carnegies, Mellons, and Danforths. A few in this elite are "new rich," having gained corporate wealth as a result of skillful investment, foresight, and often, an element of luck. Examples include Wal-Mart founder Sam Walton, with a net worth that stood at $7 billion *after* he lost $1 billion in one day in the 1987 stock market crash, and Apple computer founder Steven Jobs. Though the new rich are as wealthy as the old rich, the old rich do not accept them as members of the true elite, and their prestige remains a notch below that of the Fords and Rockefellers.

UPPER CLASS

Amounting to about 2 to 5 percent of the population, people in this group differ from the corporate elite in that they are less wealthy and more likely to have gained their wealth as a result of a high salary or investment of earned income than by ownership of key corporate capital. The successful rock singer and professional athlete would fall into this diverse group, as would many corporate executives and some owners of smaller-scale businesses. Although this group includes a good number of millionaires, it is made up mostly of "new rich," and to a significantly lesser extent than the corporate elite, its income comes from its own labor rather than from the labor of others.

UPPER-MIDDLE CLASS

Accounting for perhaps 15 to 20 percent of the U.S. population, this group is made up of better-paid management and professional employees: doctors, lawyers, airline pilots, middle and upper corporate management, and owners of the more successful small businesses. Most people in this group are college educated, and many have graduate or professional degrees. It is taken for granted that their children will attend college and, increasingly, graduate or professional school. This group is likely to live in bigger-than-average homes in the more prestigious suburbs. Incomes run above the median family income of $30,000, but generally not into the hundreds of thousands of dollars typical of the lower rungs of the upper class.

LOWER-MIDDLE CLASS

This group, amounting to about 25 to 30 percent of the population, holds the lower-status white-collar jobs, which may or may not require a college degree. Some of the best-paid blue-collar workers, such as skilled building crafts workers and auto workers, could also be included in this group, largely because of their

---

ruling class because they do not own the means of production and hence do not gain the benefits of wealth and income produced by the labor of others. At the time Marx wrote, most people who worked for wages or salaries had very low incomes, so the exclusion of this group from the ruling class was probably more obvious than it is today. Nonetheless, modern Marxist theorists argue that this definition continues to be appropriate for two reasons. First, even today most of those who work for wages and salaries have relatively low incomes compared to the owners of capital. Second, even those with high salaries do not receive most of their income from the work of others, unless they use their high salaries to purchase capital on a large scale.

According to this definition of social class, even today the ruling class is very small and the subordinate class is very large. One problem with using this definition is deciding how to classify what Marx called the *petit bourgeoisie;* people, such as "ma and pa" convenience store owners, who own small businesses that produce only marginal income. Most Marxist sociologists exclude this group from the true ruling class because their wealth produces a limited amount of in-

relatively high incomes. In general, the incomes in this group are fairly close to the median family income of about $30,000. People in this group tend to own their own homes and live in "good" suburbs, but not in the most prestigious areas. As in the upper-middle class, it is common for both the husband and wife to be employed full time, but here it is more likely that the wife will be working out of economic necessity and less likely that she will be "moving up" in her career. Though still diverse, this group tends to be a bit more conservative than the upper-middle class, particularly when it comes to "social issues" such as abortion, sexual freedom, and freedom of expression. The children of this group are often expected to attend college, but it is more likely to be a 2-year school or the local commuter university, and fewer go on to graduate or professional school.

WORKING CLASS

This group, around 30 to 35 percent of the population, works at blue-collar or clerical jobs and has incomes at or, more often, below the average level. More often than not, both the husband and wife must work in order to support the family. They typically have high-school diplomas but no college training. They often own homes in older and less prestigious suburbs, small towns, or the nonpoor areas of the central city, although many rent. They live an adequate, though by no means extravagant, lifestyle, but they must worry more often than middle- and upper-class people about how to pay their bills. Although their attitudes may be liberal on economic issues, they tend to be conservative socially and are sometimes fearful of losing economic ground to other groups. Their children are less likely to go to college. In some families, however, where education is seen as the hope for upward mobility for the next generation, the children do attend college, particularly 2-year and commuter schools in their local area. For this group, a crisis such as a divorce or the loss of a job can mean falling into poverty, and there is in general less feeling of security about life than in the middle class.

LOWER CLASS

Amounting to 15 to 20 percent of the population, this group is always struggling just to make it. Depending on such factors as being employed, marital status, and wage level, people in this group have incomes around the poverty level or a little above it. Finding adequate food, shelter, clothing, and medical care ranges from difficult to impossible for them. Many people in this group lack even a high-school education, and although their children have a better chance of completing high school than they did, many do not, and very few go on to college. Most rent rather than own their own homes, and they more frequently live in a central city, rural area, or small town than in the suburbs. Divorce and separation rates are high, as are the number of single-parent families. At the bottom of this group is the chronically poor and unemployed underclass, whose children rarely know anyone who has a stable job, a decent education, or the opportunity for upward mobility. Thus, they are psychologically prepared to be the next generation of poor and near-poor.

come and, usually, little additional wealth. Today, most wealth that generates income and additional wealth is to be found in the corporations — large-scale organizations with multiple owners. Moreover, although many people own *some* corporate stock, the great bulk of corporate wealth is held by a tiny fraction of the population. Recall, for example, the congressional Joint Economic Committee's 1986 study showing one-half of 1 percent of the population owning one-third of the nation's wealth. The great majority of the U.S. population work for those who do own capital, and even most of those with a relatively high in-

come have a standard of living far below that of the tiny elite that owns most of the corporate wealth. In this regard, the Marxian definition of social class continues to make sense, despite the great diversity in income and lifestyle among those who work for wages and salaries.

The Composite Definition of Social Class One problem with the Marxian definition of social class is that it places a salaried person receiving $100,000 a year in the same social class with a person working for the minimum wage (whose income, as we saw, would be less than $7,000 per year). Clearly, these two people would have very different life experiences, although neither would live in the style of a Ford or a Rockefeller. Moreover, income is not the only thing that defines social class. Should an assembly-line worker with a high-school degree and an income of $35,000 per year be placed in a higher social class than a college professor with a doctorate who earns $30,000? Many would say no, because the college professor has the advantage of a much greater education and enjoys far more freedom, autonomy, and opportunity for creativity on the job. In fact, this case illustrates the ambiguities of social class: the assembly-line worker enjoys an advantage in some areas of life, and the professor does in others.

Sociologists have attempted to deal with this problem by developing a *composite approach* to defining social class that considers wealth, income, prestige, education, job status, and other factors. This approach is consistent with Max Weber's view, discussed earlier in this chapter, that there are different dimensions of stratification that vary independently of one another. The composite approach does not use hard-and-fast rules for placing people into categories, and the boundaries between categories are often vague. What it does do is create groupings of people who, on the basis of a variety of considerations, are relatively similar. The first such effort, which has guided all subsequent efforts, was that of W. Lloyd Warner and colleagues (1949), in a study of a community they nicknamed "Yankee City." Warner's categories, defined on the basis of wealth, income, prestige, possessions, lifestyle, and community participation, defined six classes: upper-upper, lower-upper, upper-middle, lower-middle, upper-lower, and lower-lower. The majority of the population fell into the two lower groups, about 40 percent into the two middle groups, and just 3 percent into the two upper groups. Since then, sociologists have used a variety of classification systems, most of which have involved five or six classes, labeled in different ways, always with unclear boundaries. Some of these studies have indicated a shrinkage of the lower categories and a growth of the middle ones, partly as a result of the decline in blue-collar employment and the growth of white-collar employment. The truly wealthy elite, however, has changed little in size since the time of Warner's study.

Roughly speaking, the use of this type of classification system today would yield something like the six groupings shown in the box entitled "American Social Classes in the 1980s."

The Subjective Definition of Social Class A third way to approach social class is to let people define their own social class. We refer to this self-defined social class as **subjective class.** In the United States, people do not like to think in terms of class distinctions and tend to place themselves and nearly everyone else in or around the middle. Thus, most studies of subjective class, including a survey I have done in my own classes dozens of times, reveal that around 50 to 60 percent of Americans consider themselves "middle class," and about 30 to 40 percent "working class" (National Opinion Research Center, 1983; Hodge and Trieman, 1968). Very few—certainly under 10 percent—ever admit to being "upper class" or "lower class." In my own classes, I have had people who reported family incomes as high as $150,000 label themselves "middle class," even though such a figure puts them in the upper 2 or 3 percent of all families. Because nearly all Americans call themselves "middle class" or "working class," this method obviously has the disadvantage of classifying people less precisely than the composite method. However, it does tell us a good deal about how Americans think about class.

What factors determine how people define themselves? The answer appears to be a combination of income, education, and occupation. Those with high incomes, a college education, and a white-collar occupation nearly always answer "middle class," whereas those with a below-average income, a high-school education or less, and a blue-collar job generally answer "working class." Men and women define class in somewhat different ways. Men nearly always define their social class on the basis of their own characteristics, while married women define their social class partly according to their own characteristics and partly according to those of their husbands (Simpson, Stark, and Jackson, 1988). However, more women today define their class on the basis of their own characteristics (Davis and Robertson, 1988).

The least predictable answers come from those with *status inconsistencies*—people who rank high in

Example of high-, medium-, and low-prestige jobs. The prestige of an occupation depends heavily on the level of pay and the educational requirements.

one area but low in another. In my class survey, for example, people from blue-collar families with incomes at or above the median family income are about as likely to call themselves "middle class" as "working class." This is because while their parents' occupations are typical of the working class, their family income is typical of the middle class.

Another group experiencing status inconsistencies is the so-called new class, a rapidly growing group of young professionals who are well educated, but, partly because of a labor market flooded by Baby Boomers born in the 1950s and early 1960s, have experienced relatively low pay and a significant risk of unemployment or underemployment (Harrington, 1979, pp. 135–137). This group is said to have very middle-class tastes and expectations and the education to go with them. Moreover, the new class are people who deal in the production of ideas, such as professors, journalists, publishers, entertainers, planners, and policy makers. Thus, they tend to be independent thinkers and distrustful of conventional beliefs and traditions (Bruce-Briggs, 1979; Kristol, 1978). At the same time, their incomes are too small to live up to their high expectations, as illustrated by studies showing falling real family incomes among young workers (*St. Louis Post-Dispatch,* 1985). This background, combined with the fact that many of these people were in college during the tumultuous 1960s and early 1970s, has led some experts to predict that this group may become highly dissatisfied

and a major source of dissent in American society (Gouldner, 1979; Harrington, 1979).

Occupational Prestige Closely related to subjective class is occupational prestige. In fact, we already saw that occupation is one of the key factors that determines how people see their own social class. Different occupations clearly carry different levels of prestige, and the work people do has a major effect on the entire prestige or status dimension of stratification. Significantly, the relative prestige of various jobs has remained similar over time and across different places. Surveys done over half a century in the United States have consistently shown that the jobs that had high status in the 1920s and 1930s continue to have high status today; indeed, the relative status of a wide range of jobs has changed very little over the past 50 years (National Opinion Research Center, 1983; Hodge, Siegel, and Rossi, 1964). About the only source of change is in the creation of new jobs or the elimination of old ones. In 1920, for example, there was no such thing as a computer programmer or a television camera operator. Similarly, technology has largely eliminated other jobs, such as keypunch and elevator operators.

Additionally, studies comparing job status across different societies have shown that the relative status of different jobs is quite similar in a number of different industrialized societies (see Hodge, Trieman, and Rossi, 1966). Thus, a doctor, a lawyer, or an airline pilot has high status not only in the United States, but in Canada, Sweden, and Great Britain as well. A janitor or taxi driver, in contrast, has low status in all these societies. In addition, the relative status of these jobs in all these societies is about the same today as it was decades ago. Even in some less industrialized countries, the same patterns hold. Recent research by Nan and Wen (1988) has revealed that the prestige of jobs in China is very similar to the prestige of jobs in other countries.

What determines the prestige of a job? As is true of subjective class, several factors are relevant. In general, better-paid jobs have higher prestige. Prestige also depends on the educational requirements of the job and the amount of physical labor it entails. Thus, even though college professors are often paid less than many assembly-line workers, they consistently rank near the top in occupational prestige. The very highest ranked jobs, such as physician and airline pilot, are professional occupations associated with both high incomes and high levels of education. Similarly, the lowest-ranking jobs, such as garbage collector, janitor, and shoe shiner, involve hard physical work, require little or no education, and pay poorly. A list of some jobs and their occupational prestige ratings from a recent national survey is presented in Table 9.3.

Class Consciousness in America

One important aspect of class in America is the extent to which Americans are aware of, and identify with, the social classes to which they belong. We have already noted that nearly all Americans think of themselves as "middle class" or "working class." This contrasts with some other societies where, for example, the wealthy readily identify themselves as upper class. Our society was founded as a result of a rebellion against title and monarchy and was based on the principle that "all men are created equal." Although, as we have seen, the reality is that there is great social inequality in America, most Americans prefer not to acknowledge that openly. Rather, we prefer to believe that people have similar statuses and similar situations in life — that we are all pretty much alike.

Education and Class Identity Two other factors have contributed to this tendency to deny class differences. One is the American system of universal public education, based on the principle of the *common school* — the idea that everyone should have the opportunity to get an education and that social background should not influence the kind of education a child receives. Although America has never fully lived

TABLE 9.3
Occupational Prestige Ratings: United States Compared to 60-Country Average.

OCCUPATION	AVERAGE, 60 COUNTRIES	UNITED STATES
University president or dean	86	82.4
Physician	78	81.5
University professor	78	78.3
Physicist	76	73.8
Member, board of directors	75	71.8
Lawyer	73	75.7
Architect	72	70.5
Dentist	70	73.5
Chemist	69	68.8
Sociologist	67	65.0
Airline pilot	66	70.1
High-school teacher	64	63.1
Clergy member	60	70.5
Personnel director	58	57.8
Artist	57	57.0
Classical musician	56	55.0
Social worker	56	52.4
Journalist	55	51.6
Professional nurse	54	61.5
Secretary	53	45.8
Actor or actress	52	55.0
Union official	50	41.2
Real-estate agent	49	44.0
Professional athlete	48	51.4
Farmer	47	43.7
Motor-vehicle mechanic	44	35.8
Policeman or policewoman	40	47.8
Railroad conductor	39	40.9
Telephone operator	38	40.4
Jazz musician	38	37.2
Carpenter	37	42.5
Dancing teacher	36	32.3
Firefighter	35	33.2
Sales clerk	34	27.1
Truck driver	33	31.3
File clerk	31	30.3
Assembly-line worker	30	27.1
Construction worker	28	26.2
Gas-station attendant	25	21.6
Waiter	23	20.3
Janitor	21	16.1
Farm worker	20	21.4
Garbage collector	13	12.6
Shoe shiner	12	9.3

NOTE: In a limited number of instances, there were slight differences in job titles between Appendix A (worldwide average) and Appendix D (United States). In these instances, the closest job title was used.

SOURCE: Reprinted by permission from Appendices A and D in Donald J. Treiman, *Occupational Prestige in Comparative Perspective.* Copyright 1977, by Academic Press.

up to this ideal, we have created a society in which the great majority of people graduate from high school, and a higher percentage than elsewhere go on to college. Moreover, although we have great educational differences linked to class, we have not formalized and institutionalized these differences to the extent that other societies, such as Great Britain, have. Thus, our more common educational experiences as compared to other societies have led us to think of ourselves as being more similar to one another.

Structural Mobility and Class Identity The other relevant factor is the considerable structural mobility that occurred in the United States up to the early 1970s. An expanding economy enabled most Americans to experience upward mobility. In addition, the increasing number of white-collar jobs, combined with rising levels of education, meant that many Americans who grew up in blue-collar homes were able to move into white-collar employment. This made the American class structure seem more open and less rigid than those of other societies that experienced less economic growth. These realities have affected the thinking of people at every level of the American class structure. Many wealthy Americans, for example, tend to think of themselves as "middle class" and deny that they are really different from those who have less money. At the other end of the scale, many of those with low incomes identify with the "middle class" to which they aspire.

Class Consciousness and the Future We might close this section by noting the possibility that Americans will become more class conscious in the future. Over the past 15 years or so, the rapid growth of the American economy has stopped, closing off opportunities and solidifying the class structure as it exists. As we saw, inequality in the distribution of both wealth and income increased during the 1980s. Federal and state budget cuts during that decade made higher education less accessible to the working class and the poor. Taken together, these trends, should they continue, may force Americans to give more thought to where they stand in the nation's class structure. At the least, the current trends probably increase the social consequences of class, and that alone may make Americans more aware of the class distinctions that have always been present in their society.

Functionalist and Conflict Perspectives on Stratification

In this final section, we turn to the larger sociological issue of why economic inequality and poverty exist in society. As with other questions of this nature, the two macrosociological perspectives, functionalist and conflict theory, offer starkly different answers. Let us first consider the functionalist answer.

The Functionalist View: Davis and Moore

In one of the most widely cited and debated pieces ever to appear in a sociology journal, Kingsley Davis and Wilbert Moore presented a functionalist theory of socioeconomic inequality in their 1945 article "Some Principles of Stratification." Davis and Moore argued that economic stratification exists because it meets society's needs for productivity by motivating people. Davis and Moore started with the notions that some jobs are more critical to society's needs than others, and that some jobs — often the most critical ones — require longer and more difficult training than others. Such jobs also carry greater responsibility, are frequently very stressful, and often require people to work longer hours than other jobs. If the highly capable people needed to fill such jobs are to get the extra training and work the extra hours required, Davis and Moore argued, they must be motivated by the prospect of higher pay. Otherwise, why would people want these jobs with all the training, stress, and extra hours they entail? More specifically, would people sacrifice current income in order to get the years of training some of these jobs require? Suppose a person could get the same money as a doctor by working 7 or 8 hours a day sweeping streets — with no after-hours responsibility and no long, expensive period of training, including 4 years of college, 4 years of medical school, and 4 years of internship/residency. Would it not be harder to get people to become doctors if they could earn just as much money doing something much easier, and earn it now rather than 12 years from now?

The Conflict View

Although conflict theorists generally acknowledge that socioeconomic inequality occurs in nearly all societies, they do not think it exists because it meets a social need for productivity. They note, for example, that more economically developed and productive societies generally have *less* inequality than others, not more (see Lenski, 1966). In general, conflict theorists see socioeconomic inequality as existing because the wealthy and powerful—usually a small group in any society—benefit from it and have enough power to make the social system work to protect their interests.

Due to this great inequality, conflict theorists —in the tradition of Karl Marx—see a tendency in most societies for *class conflict.* It is in the interests of the wealthy to keep things as they are, whereas those without wealth have an interest in social change. Marx predicted that this conflict of interest would eventually lead to the overthrow of most capitalist societies, as the subordinate class realized its own interest and seized the wealth from the ruling class.

In fact, this has not happened, for many reasons. One of the most important is that the expansion of economies under capitalism, at least until recently, raised the standard of living of the working classes substantially, despite continued inequality. Another is that democratic reforms curtailed the more blatant excesses of the owners of wealth and afforded some protection to the rights of even those with little wealth and power. Marxists would argue that a third reason is that most people do not realize the extent to which wealth remains concentrated in modern industrial economies and how the wealthy use their influence over government, the media, and other key institutions to promote beliefs and ideologies that inhibit class consciousness. (The role of class conflict as a source of social change is explored in Chapter 20.)

According to the conflict perspective, then, the interests of the wealthy—not the needs of the society as a whole—are served by inequality. In an article that is also among the most widely cited in sociology, conflict theorist Melvin Tumin pointed out what he

saw as several shortcomings in the logic used by Davis and Moore (Tumin, 1953; see also Tumin, 1970).

Is Stratification Really Functional?

Tumin and others have cited at least four key shortcomings in Davis and Moore's functionalist theory of stratification. First, Tumin questioned whether some of the better-paying and more prestigious jobs are really more critical to society than others. For example, is the physician really more essential to the health of the public than the garbage collector? Without garbage collectors, the hazard of contagious disease would be tremendous. Significantly, historical demographers agree that public sanitation systems were able to increase people's life expectancies at an earlier point in history than were medical doctors. The treatment of illness was too unscientific to accomplish much before about 1900. Only then, for example, was the practice of washing one's hands before performing surgery becoming widespread. The establishment of garbage collection systems and sanitary sewers, however, had replaced the common practice of throwing garbage and human waste in the nearest street or river by around 1850 in many areas, and it was certainly a key factor in the steady fall in American and European mortality rates between 1800 and 1900. (For more discussion of the effects of medicine and public sanitation on mortality, see Thomlinson, 1976, pp. 98–107). In a similar vein, Tumin points out that if factories had all managers and engineers and no line workers, they could produce nothing. Thus, low-status, poorly paid workers can be as essential as those whose jobs carry status, power, and big paychecks.

Second, *wealth* is distributed more unequally than *income,* and a large share of wealth is inherited rather than earned. It is hard to see how inherited wealth could motivate people to do anything except be born into rich families, something that we have yet to figure out a way to control! In fact, most wealthy people became wealthy either through inheritance or through investment of inherited wealth (Barlow, Brazer, and Morgan, 1966; Lundberg, 1968). To the extent that wealth is concentrated through inheritance, it is very difficult to see how it could serve to motivate people to enter critical jobs. A related point is that parental income has a substantial effect on a person's ability to obtain the education necessary for the most demanding jobs. If stratification were really to work the way Davis and Moore argued it did, ability and motivation would have to be the main factors determining the amount of education obtained. In fact, family income plays a large role, making it easy for the wealthy to educate their children for the best jobs and hard for the poor to do so.

Third, the training required for getting better-paying jobs is often far from unpleasant; many people, for example, find college a highly rewarding time of their lives. In addition, attending college — and even more so, attending law, medical, or graduate school — gives a person a certain prestige. At the least, there is a good side as well as a bad side to the training that people must go through to get the better jobs, and that in itself can serve to motivate them.

Finally, Tumin points out that although the highest-paying jobs often require great training and long hours, they also carry considerable nonmaterial rewards, including autonomy, sense of accomplishment, prestige, and — in many cases — the ability to set your own hours. This has been confirmed by recent research by Jeucles, Perman, and Rainwater (1988), who found that there are many rewards to a good job besides high pay. We do, moreover, have no shortage of people in certain occupations that require great training but pay relatively poorly, for example, social workers and college professors. There are a number of jobs people with a high-school degree can get that pay as well as that of a college professor, which requires 4 years of college and, typically, 4 to 6 years after that to obtain a Ph.D. Even so, in the late 1970s, there were about two people obtaining doctorates for every job opening for college professors. At least when they started graduate school, most of these people intended to work as professors, although obviously many had to find employment elsewhere. Thus, despite the low pay relative to the training, we have not experienced shortages of professors in most fields. Clearly, the reason for this is that the job carries considerable nonmonetary rewards.

We might end by noting that medical doctors are better paid in the United States than in most industrialized countries. In spite of this, very few modern industrialized countries have ever experienced shortages of doctors. Ironically, the United States did experience a shortage of doctors in the 1950s and 1960s. However, this shortage had nothing to do with the number of qualified people seeking to become doctors. Rather, it reflected the power of the medical profession, which for many years used its lobby to limit the supply of physicians by limiting the size of medical schools (Tumin, 1953).

Synthesis

To conclude our discussion of the debate between functionalist and conflict sociologists about the causes of economic stratification, it may be useful to examine the relationship between social inequality and productivity among industrialized societies. This information is provided in Table 9.4. As a measure of inequality, the table shows the ratio of income going to the top 10 percent of the population to the share going to the bottom 20 percent. The larger this ratio, the greater the inequality of a society. As a measure of productivity, the table shows gross national product (GNP) per capita. These figures are shown for 2 recent years, 1982 and 1984. The table indicates there is little relationship between the inequality measure and the productivity measure. In 1982, for example, the countries with the least inequality were Japan, the Netherlands, and Sweden. In terms of productivity, Japan was a little below the middle (but improving rapidly), the Netherlands was near the middle, and Sweden was near the top. The greatest inequality was found in the United States, Canada, Australia, and France. All of these countries except the United States were near the middle in terms of productivity; the United States was toward the top. Overall, variations in inequality accounted for well under 1 percent of the variation in GNP per capita in either 1982 or 1984, and inequality was *negatively* correlated with productivity growth in those years. Thus, the conclusion is unavoidable that, among these industrialized countries, the degree of economic inequality has little to do with the level of productivity.

The Dysfunctions of Inequality From a functionalist viewpoint, we must also consider the possible dysfunctions of a condition such as social inequality along with its possible functions. Functionalists see a need

TABLE 9.4
Economic Inequality and Economic Productivity, Selected Industrialized Countries, 1982, 1984

COUNTRY	INEQUALITY. 1982	PRODUCTIVITY, 1982	INEQUALITY, 1984	PRODUCTIVITY, 1984	ECON. GROWTH
	Ratio of Income of Top 10% to that of Bottom 20%, Most Recent Data Available in 1982	Per Capita Gross National Product, 1982	Ratio of Income of Top 10% to that of Bottom 20%, Most Recent Data Available in 1984	Per Capita Gross National Product, 1984	Growth in Per Capita GNP, 1965–84
Ireland	3.49	$5,150	3.49	4,970	2.4%
Spain	4.45	5,430	3.55	4,440	2.7
Italy	4.53	6,840	4.53	6,450	2.7
United Kingdom	3.34	9,660	3.34	8,750	1.6
Japan	2.44	10,080	2.57	10,630	4.7
Belgium	3.16	10,760	2.72	8,610	3.0
Finland	3.12	10,870	3.44	10,770	3.3
Netherlands	2.73	10,930	2.59	9,520	2.1
Australia	5.65	11,140	5.65	11,740	1.7
Canada	7.08	11,320	4.49	13,280	2.4
France	5.75	11,680	5.75	9,760	3.0
W. Germany	3.04	12,640	3.04	11,130	2.7
Denmark	3.03	12,470	4.13	11,170	1.8
United States	7.26	13,160	4.40	15,390	1.7
Sweden	2.94	14,020	3.80	11,860	1.8
Norway	3.52	14,280	3.80	13,940	3.3
Switzerland	not available	17,010	3.59	16,330	1.4

SOURCE: The World Bank, 1984 and 1986, *1982 World Development Report* and *1986 World Development Report*. New York: Oxford University Press.

for order and cooperation in society—yet economic inequality is one of the most important causes of conflict and disorder in society (Tumin, 1953). Beyond this, those who are at the bottom often become hopeless and alienated and thus "drop out" of any economically productive role. Thus, whatever benefits inequality may have, it also clearly has its costs, to the larger society as well as to those at the bottom of the stratification system.

Does all this mean that the functionalist explanation of inequality is simply wrong? Probably not. For one thing, all of the countries in Table 9.4 do have a significant amount of inequality, although the levels vary widely. In Japan, with the least inequality, the wealthiest 10 percent still receive two and a half times as much income as the poorest 20 percent. The fact

that economic inequality exists in all modern countries—even socialist ones—is certainly consistent with the functionalist viewpoint. What the data do suggest, though, is that although inequality may be functional up to a point, most countries have far more of it than they need. This is especially true of the United States, which had over twice as much economic inequality (by the measure in Table 9.4) as either Norway or Sweden, yet did no better in terms of productivity in 1982. As Lenski (1966) put it, the functionalist theory probably explains a certain amount of stratification, but it cannot account for anywhere near all of it. Undoubtedly, much of the rest exists for the reasons outlined by conflict theorists—the disproportionate power of the wealthy, and their use of that power to keep their economic advantage.

Gans and the Functions of Poverty

A discussion of functionalist and conflict analyses of stratification could not be complete without a review of the writings of Herbert Gans (1971, 1972) concerning the functions of poverty. Gans's insights are useful not only for understanding poverty but also for seeing the similarities between functionalist and conflict theories. In an article titled "The Positive Functions of Poverty," Gans listed a number of ways in which poverty is "functional," some of which are given here:

> It provides people to do unpleasant "dirty work" that others don't want to do.
>
> It provides a source of employment for police and penologists, Pentecostal ministers, pawnshop owners, social workers, numbers runners, heroin pushers, and other legal and illegal occupations that depend upon the poor.
>
> It provides people to buy spoiled and damaged goods at a reduced price that otherwise would have to be thrown out.
>
> It provides a convenient group of people to punish in order to uphold society's rules.
>
> It reassures the nonpoor of their status and worth.
>
> It enhances educational opportunities for the middle class by assuring that a sizable part of the population will not compete with them.
>
> It is a source of popular culture that others enjoy and make money on. Jazz, blues, rock, gospel, and country music all had their origins among the poor.
>
> It provides people to absorb the costs of social change in the form of unemployment, cheap labor, and residential displacement—so others won't have to.

Although some people have interpreted this article as making a functionalist argument—and Gans certainly wrote it to sound that way—it has more commonly been seen as a spoof of functionalist theory written by someone who really identifies with the conflict perspective. An earlier and similar article by Gans, "The Uses of Poverty: The Poor Pay All" (1971), supports this interpretation. However, whether Gans identifies with functionalist theory or conflict theory, his articles make a key point: *A good many Americans —nonpoor and often wealthy—benefit from the continued existence of widespread poverty.* Thus, the fact that influential special interest groups benefit from poverty may be one reason that poverty persists. In essence, this is what conflict theorists have always argued: Inequality exists because some group benefits from it. It would appear that this is true to some extent, not only of overall socioeconomic inequality, but also of the widespread poverty existing amid affluence in the United States.

In conclusion, it may well be that both the functionalist and conflict theories of stratification are correct to some extent, although in some ways—such as by causing conflict and violence—stratification must be seen as dysfunctional even from the functionalist perspective. Poverty, in particular, seems to exist more because it benefits affluent interest groups than because it is of any great use to society as a whole.

Summary

Sociologists use the term *stratification* to refer to the unequal distribution in society of scarce resources. Stratification has an economic dimension (the distribution of income and wealth), a political dimension (the distribution of power), and a social prestige dimension, sometimes called *status*. In the United States, income (what a person receives annually) is distributed more unequally than in most other industrialized countries, and the distribution of wealth (the total value of everything a person owns) is even more unequal. Although the distributions of income and wealth in the United States have not changed dramatically over time, there has recently been a shift toward greater inequality.

Poverty can be defined in either a relative sense (being poor compared to others in the same society) or an absolute sense (lacking necessities). By either definition, there are a large number of poor people in the United States, despite its relative affluence, and this number has increased since the late 1970s. Most poor people are non-Hispanic whites, but blacks and Hispanics have disproportionately high poverty rates, as do female-headed families and people who live in either central cities or rural areas. Among the key causes of poverty are unemployment, low wages, and the inability of single mothers to earn sufficient wages to pay the costs of day care and medical care and support their families. It appears that relatively few people are poor because they prefer welfare to work. Although welfare dependency does occur, it is less widespread than is commonly believed, and most of the nonworking poor have good reasons to be out of the labor force. During the late 1970s and particularly the 1980s, government policies both raised the poverty rate (by allowing unemployment to increase in order to fight inflation) and made the impact of poverty more severe (by cutting back aid to the poor). The effects of poverty are devastating in nearly every aspect of life, ranging from educational opportunities to life expectancy to the likelihood of being a victim of crime.

Another area in which stratification systems vary is mobility. Open stratification systems have relative high mobility—people can move "up" or "down"—whereas closed systems have low mobility. The most closed type of stratification system is the caste system; the estate or feudal system has slightly greater mobility. The highest level of mobility is found in class systems, but even there, ascribed statuses—those into which we are born—play an important role. The mobility that does exist is frequently structural—that is, due to an increase in the number of better-paying jobs rather than to some people moving up while others move down. Although it is widely believed that the United States has high mobility compared to other class systems, the fact is that industrialized countries do not vary widely in their degree of mobility. The degree of mobility found in the United States is similar to that of most other industrialized societies.

Social class can be defined in a number of ways. To Karl Marx, there were only two classes: those who owned the means of production and those who did not. Many modern sociologists prefer a composite approach, which considers such factors as income, wealth, education, and occupational status. Another approach—subjective class—is to allow people to classify themselves. In the United States, most people call themselves "middle class" or "working class," because Americans don't like to divide themselves into classes, and thus tend to identify with the middle.

Functionalist and conflict theorists disagree about the causes of social stratification. In the view of functionalists, stratification exists because it is useful for society. It motivates people to get the training and work the long hours required for certain critical and difficult jobs. Conflict theorists, however, argue that stratification exists mainly because those with wealth and power benefit from it. At the least, it does appear that there is greater inequality in most societies than can be explained purely on the basis of the need for motivation. In the United States, with its particularly high degree of economic inequality, this seems to be especially true.

Glossary

dimensions of stratification The different bases on which people in a society are unequally ranked, including economic (wealth and income), political (power), and prestige (status).

income The dollar value of that which a person or family receives during a specified time period, including wages and return on investment.

wealth The total value of everything that a person or family owns, less any debts.

prestige The degree to which a person is respected and well regarded by others.

poverty The condition of having an extremely low income and standard of living, either in comparison with other members of society (relative poverty) or in terms of the ability to acquire basic necessities (absolute poverty).

real wages Wage and salary levels expressed in terms of purchasing power to adjust for the effects of inflation.

socioeconomic mobility The movement of people to higher or lower positions within the stratification system.

open stratification system A system of inequality in which opportunities to move to a higher or lower status are relatively great.

closed stratification system A system of inequality in which opportunities for mobility are relatively limited.

caste system A very closed stratification system in which the group or caste into which a person is born determines that person's status on a lifelong basis.

caste A grouping into which a person is born that determines that person's status in a caste system.

apartheid The official name for the racial caste system in South Africa, where political and economic rights are defined according to which of four official racial groupings — white, black, coloured, and Asian — a person belongs to.

racial caste system A closed stratification system in which castes are established on the basis of race.

estate system A relatively closed stratification system, also called a feudal system, found in agricultural economies, in which a person's status is determined on the basis of landownership and, frequently, formal title.

class system A system of social inequality, usually found in modern industrial societies, in which a person's position in life is influenced by both achieved and ascribed statuses.

intergenerational mobility Attainment by people of a socioeconomic status higher or lower than that of their parents.

structural mobility A type of socioeconomic mobility that occurs because of an increasing proportion of jobs in the higher-status, white-collar categories.

exchange mobility A type of socioeconomic mobility that occurs when some people move to higher positions in the stratification system, while others move to lower positions.

social class A group of people with similar socioeconomic status in an industrialized society.

socioeconomic status (SES) A person's overall position within the stratification system, reflecting such things as income, wealth, educational level, and occupational prestige.

class structure The distribution of wealth and other scarce resources in society.

subjective class The class to which people perceive that they belong.

Further Reading

DANZINGER, SHELDON, AND DANIEL H. WEINBERG (EDS.). 1986. *Fighting Poverty: What Works and What Doesn't.* Cambridge, MA: Harvard University Press. This is a collection of articles by experts on various aspects of poverty. It addresses the successes and failures of past efforts to fight poverty, and it lays out a research agenda to identify more effective ways to do so.

DUNCAN, GREG J., ET AL. 1984. *Years of Poverty, Years of Plenty: The Changing Economic Fortunes of American Workers and Families.* Ann Arbor: Institute for Social Research, The University of Michigan. This book presents the results of a study of family income conducted over a period of 10 years. It is written to be understood by people who do not have advanced training in sociology and statistics. Duncan and his colleagues present fascinating findings concerning family economic mobility, the extent of persistent poverty, and the causes of low wages among women.

EITZEN, D. STANLEY, AND MAXINE BACA ZINN (EDS.). 1989. *The Reshaping of America.* Englewood Cliffs, NJ: Prentice Hall. This book contains 42 articles by a variety of analysts examining how and why stratification is changing in the United States. Among the forces for change examined are electronic technology, the emergence of a worldwide economy, the increased mobility of capital throughout the nation and world, and the transition from an economy based primarily on manufacturing to one based primarily on information and services.

HARRINGTON, MICHAEL. 1984. *The New American Poverty.* New York: Penguin. This book examines the growth of poverty in the United States during the early 1980s. It identifies the diverse groups affected by this poverty, and it examines the various social, economic, and political conditions that led to the increase in poverty. The book is written from a conflict perspective by the author of *The Other America,* a 1962 book that made many Americans aware that they were living comfortably in the midst of poverty.

LANE, DAVID. 1982. *The End of Social Inequality: Class, Status, and Power Under State Socialism.* Winchester, MA: Allen and Unwin. The title of this book notwithstanding, Lane shows that there is social inequality in socialist countries. This paperback examines the extent, nature, and causes of that inequality.

TUMIN, MELVIN. 1985. *Social Stratification: The Forms and Functions of Social Inequality,* 2nd ed. Englewood Cliffs, NJ: Prentice Hall. A thorough and readable introduction to social stratification, written by a sociologist who is recognized as a leading theorist in this area.

CHAPTER 10

Stratification: The Political Dimension

For nearly 200 years the U.S. Supreme Court was America's most exclusive male club. After 101 male justices, Sandra Day O'Connor was named to the Supreme Court by President Reagan in 1981. At the time of her appointment, O'Connor was a 51-year-old state appellate court judge in Arizona. Justice O'Connor had no previous experience as a federal court judge, but she had the active support of Arizona's senior U.S. senator and Republican warhorse, Barry Goldwater. More importantly, she was a "she." Reagan was anxious to deflect attacks on his opposition to the Equal Rights Amendment and his failure to appoint many women in his own administration. As one Reagan aide put it: "This is worth 25 assistant secretaries, maybe more!" Feminist groups were forced to support the appointment, even though O'Connor's record in Arizona was moderately conservative.

Sandra Day grew up on her family's large Arizona ranch, graduated from Stanford with honors and then went on to Stanford Law School. She finished near the top of her class, along with Supreme Court Justice William Rehnquist (who was first in the class) and Forrest Shumway, chairman of the Signal Companies. She married John Jay O'Connor, a Phoenix attorney, and raised three sons. She entered Arizona politics about the time her youngest son entered school. She was appointed to the Arizona state senate in 1969 and was later elected twice to that body. She rose to majority leader in 1973. She left the Arizona legislature in 1975 to become a Phoenix trial judge. In 1979, she was appointed by a Democratic governor to the Arizona court of appeals. Work on this state intermediate court, however, does not involve major constitutional questions.

O'Connor has had some business experience: She was formerly a director of the First National Bank of Arizona and Blue Cross Blue Shield of Arizona. But until her appointment to the U.S. Supreme Court, O'Connor was an obscure state court judge. Her service as a Republican leader in the Arizona state senate

WHAT IS POWER?
SOURCES OF POWER
    Authority
    Voting
    Force and Coercion
    Control of Information
    Wealth and Income
ECONOMIC AND POLITICAL INEQUALITY:
HOW CLOSELY RELATED?
    Origins of the Debate: Marx and Weber
    The Debate Today
WHO HAS POWER IN AMERICA TODAY?
    Interest Groups in American Politics
    The Distribution of Power: The National Level
    The Distribution of Power: The Local Level
    The Importance of Local versus National
    Power

Reprinted by permission of the publisher from Thomas R. Dye, *Who Rules America? The Reagan Years*, 3rd ed. Copyright 1983 by Prentice Hall.

qualified her as a moderately conservative party loyalist. However, it appears as if her professional and political friendships had more to do with bringing her to President Reagan's attention than her record as a jurist. She had known Justice William Rehnquist since her law school days. She had known Chief Justice Warren Burger for a long time. And Barry Goldwater had been her mentor in Arizona Republican politics. When Reagan's political advisers told him during the presidential campaign that he was not doing well among women voters, the candidate responded by pledging to appoint a woman to the Supreme Court. Reagan's fulfillment of his campaign pledge was a politically popular decision.

A s Sandra Day O'Connor's experience shows, there are many routes to power. Wealth, connections, personal skill, and using the interaction of competing groups are all avenues to power. In Justice O'Connor's case, her background as the daughter of wealthy ranchers, combined with her own position as a bank director, was obviously helpful. So was her ability to cultivate the right political connections. Significantly, some of these connections were made during her years as a student in the Stanford Law School—one of a handful of prominent universities from which the nation's business and political leaders are regularly drawn. There are also lessons on power in Reagan's appointment of O'Connor. In trouble with feminists for opposing the Equal Rights Amendment, Reagan shrewdly appointed a woman to the highest court, an appointment feminists felt they had to endorse despite O'Connor's opposition to much of the feminist agenda.

In this chapter, we shall address the question of power: who has it, who doesn't, how evenly distributed it is in American society, and how closely it is related to wealth. We shall begin that discussion by explaining more clearly what we mean by power.

What Is Power?

When we talk about the political dimension of stratification or social inequality, we are, for the most part, talking about inequality in the distribution of **power.** What do sociologists mean when they use the word "power"? Simply put, they mean the ability to affect the actions of others, even when those others resist. If you can get people to do what you want them to do, you are exercising power (Dahl, 1957). Power may be exercised on an individual, a group, or a societal level. On the societal level, power means the ability to make

decisions that affect the direction in which the entire society moves.

To a large extent, power is exercised through the political system (Weber, 1946). However, there are many other ways people get and use power. In fact, many sociologists believe that in almost every situation in which people interact, unequal power exists. Proponents of exchange theory, for example, contend that even interpersonal relationships such as friendship and courtship display unequal power (Blau, 1964; Emerson, 1972; Molm, 1987). This unequal power leads to unequal exchanges, which shape every aspect of the social interaction, including who starts conversations, who gives in during disputes, who touches whom, and who terminates contacts.

In this chapter, our main concern is the use and distribution of power in the political system. However, before we can narrow our discussion to that extent, we must say a bit more about the various ways in which people get power.

Sources of Power

Recall that power means the ability to affect the actions of others. This includes the idea that if you have power over others, you can get them to do what you want even if that is not what *they* want to do. However, an even more effective form of power is getting people to *want* to do what you want them to do. If you can do this, you can exercise power without resorting to conflict. Thus, it is important to recognize that power is often exercised without any use of force, threat, or coercion. Sometimes the people involved do not even realize that they have been influenced by the will of another. Let us consider some of the ways that power is obtained and used.

Authority

One of the most important sources of power is **authority.** Individuals who have authority possess **legitimate power.** In other words, people accept the idea that it is proper for the individual with authority to have power. Hence, they will do what that person wants them to do, simply because he or she wants them to do it.

At about this point in my introductory sociology classes, I frequently ask my students to stand up. Every time I have done this, all of them or nearly all of them have done so. Because I am the professor, I have authority in the classroom. Hence, when I ask them to stand up, they do so—for no other reason than I wanted them to. This example also illustrates the fact that a given person's authority often exists only within a limited sphere of activity. In the classroom, I, as the professor, have authority, and my request to stand up is obeyed. Were I to make the same request of a group of strangers sitting on a bench at a bus stop, I would likely get a very different response because I have no authority in that situation.

There are at least four important ways in which people get authority. The first three—traditional authority, charismatic authority, and legal-rational authority—were first pointed out by Max Weber and have long been recognized by sociologists. The fourth —expertise—is largely a product of the important and growing role of science and technology in modern industrial societies.

Traditional Authority **Traditional authority** is based on long-standing, institutionalized, and largely unquestioned customs and practices. It often has a sacred element, so that the person who challenges it is defined as evil, heretical, or ungodly. The authority of a king or queen is perhaps the best example. It is obtained by birth and passed on to offspring according to a long tradition that says authority rests in a royal family, with a set procedure for succession to the throne. In many countries, monarchs play a key role in the established religion, and—at least in the past, when monarchs had much greater power than most do today—their rule was supposed to reflect the will of God.

Many religions also operate on the basis of traditional authority. In the Roman Catholic Church, for example, the pope is seen as a divinely inspired successor to St. Peter, who delivers the word of God and, under certain specified conditions, is infallible on matters of faith and morals.

Because this type of authority is based on tradition, it generally remains with the person once that person has attained the position of authority. Thus, because tradition specified that Queen Victoria was to be monarch and to rule the British Empire, she retained that title and the authority to rule from the time she ascended the throne to the end of her life.

Legal-Rational Authority Like traditional authority, **legal-rational authority** often has the backing of

Queen Victoria ruled the British Empire for life through traditional authority.

Margaret Thatcher, Prime Minister of Great Britain, derives her right to govern from legal rational authority.

law. However, law has a very different meaning in this case. Legal-rational authority is established to accomplish certain ends. In contrast to a king or queen, a prime minister or president — elected by a parliament or by the public — is chosen for the express purpose of carrying out policies desired by the people, as expressed by their votes. He or she will appoint numerous administrators who also have legal-rational authority, but their authority is derived from their appointment by a president or prime minister chosen to carry out the will of the people.

Legal-rational authority, then, is defined in terms of some purpose or objective. It is also tied to the position, not the person. Whereas a king, a pope, or an emperor normally rules for life, a president or a prime minister does not. When his or her policies are perceived as no longer meeting public objectives, a new leader is chosen, and the authority of the position transfers to the new leader. Unlike Queen Victoria, British Prime Minister Margaret Thatcher belongs to a political party that must face the voters periodically in order to continue to rule. When the majority of voters decide that some other political party could do a better job of running the country, Mrs. Thatcher's authority will disappear.

The anecdote about the professor's authority in the classroom is an example of legal-rational authority. I have authority in my classroom, given to me for the express purpose of teaching my students about sociology; I have no authority in matters unrelated to the class. Similarly, should I be perceived as failing in the objective for which I was given authority, I could be stripped of that authority. In this respect, legal-

rational authority is fundamentally different from traditional authority.

Charismatic Authority **Charismatic authority** derives from an individual's personal characteristics. Charismatic leaders have authority because they excite and inspire people. The Reverend Jesse Jackson, for example, has been able to gain a large political following in part because many people like not only what he has to say, but also how he says it. True, he is a well-educated minister, and as such exercises a certain amount of both legal-rational and traditional authority. However, the main basis of his appeal lies in the fact that he has "said things the other candidates aren't saying" and, as commentators observed after a debate prior to the 1988 Iowa caucuses, he "was a clear audience favorite" and "proved once again that he is the master of the one-liner." In other words, his style and substance created excitement in a political contest that, aside from his presence, seemed rather boring to many people.

CHARISMATIC LEADERSHIP AND SOCIAL CHANGE Charismatic leadership, which often arises during periods of social conflict, can be an important source of social change. It frequently offers a major challenge to traditional or legal-rational authority. Revolutions usually have charismatic leaders (Corazon Aquino and Mao Zedong, for example), as do many of the more successful social movements. Such movements always

Evita Peron influenced the politics of Argentina for many years through charismatic authority.

have underlying causes and grievances, of course, but their success is often due, at least partly, to a charismatic leader who can inspire and mobilize people.

Charismatic authority also occurs in nonpolitical settings. In the early 1970s, for example, Christianity in the United States — which had become dominated by large, formal, and bureaucratic religious organizations — was shaken up by such movements as the Pentecostals and the "Jesus freaks," some of whom referred to their movement as "charismatic renewal." An important feature of American religion during the 1970s and 1980s was the ability of a number of religious leaders to develop large personal followings, often through the use of television. Examples are Jerry Falwell, Jimmy Swaggert, Pat Robertson, Jim and Tammy Bakker, and Sun Myung Moon. The importance of charismatic leadership to these movements is shown by the fact that when the images of leaders such as Jim and Tammy Bakker and Jimmy Swaggert became tarnished by scandals, their movements quickly lost influence.

Because charismatic authority lies within the person and not the position, it differs from traditional and legal-rational authority in that it cannot be institutionalized. Attempts are sometimes made to do so, but they usually fail. When charismatic leaders die, for example, their leadership cannot be replaced simply by appointing another person to their position. For example, no civil rights leader could fill Martin Luther King's shoes at the time of his death, and the movement lost some of its dynamism as a result. The death of a charismatic national leader such as Gandhi in India or Mao in China almost inevitably leads to a period of power struggle, often followed by substantial changes in the direction of national policy.

Although charisma always involves exceptional leadership capabilities, charismatic leaders do not always use their power justly or wisely. Hitler most certainly was a charismatic leader, as was Iran's Ayatollah Khomeini. Such leaders have used their power brutally to suppress opposition. Hitler succeeded in convincing the German people that their problems were largely caused by Jews and other "non-Aryan" peoples and introduced a policy of genocide to wipe these peoples out. These cases illustrate the potential for danger in charisma. Because charismatic authority arises largely from the personal appeal of the leader, the change it brings about can be highly unpredictable. The nature of the change depends largely on the intentions and objectives of the leader. Charismatic leaders can either renew and revitalize a society or take it in self-destructive directions.

Expertise A final source of authority, not included in Weber's original formulation, is **expertise.** People often exercise authority because they possess special knowledge that others need or value. This is especially true in modern industrial societies that place a high value on scientific knowledge (Wilensky, 1967). As we shall see in more detail later in this chapter, social and natural scientists affiliated with universities, research institutions, and "think tanks" play a crucial role in the formulation of government policy in the United States. Expertise is also relied upon in the courts, private business, and virtually everywhere else that important decisions are made.

Another area where expertise has become an important source of power is political campaigns. Campaigns are increasingly dominated by the advice of pollsters, advertisers, and professional consultants. Moreover, when a campaign fails, as did Michael Dukakis's 1988 presidential campaign, defeat is often attributed to the failure of the candidate to "accept the advice of the experts" or to "run a professional campaign."

CREDENTIALS   A problem with expertise, of course, is how to decide who can legitimately claim it. Because of the power and prestige associated with expertise, many people claim to be experts when in fact they are not. For this reason, **credentials** have come to play a key role in distinguishing those with true expertise. Credentials include such indicators as graduate or professional degrees, occupation, reputation, professional certification, and evidence of acceptance in the form of scientific publications. Credentials, like expertise, are not universal but are subject-specific. That is, there are clear boundaries on the areas in which a person can claim expertise.

Voting

Besides authority, a key source of power in any democratic society is voting. Votes can be a source of power in several ways. First, voters do determine who gets

In any democratic society, voting is an important source of political power.

elected, and this is a direct exercise of power. To the extent that people vote on the basis of issues, this power also enables a group of people to elect someone they believe will represent their viewpoint. If the person elected does actually represent the constituents' viewpoint, then voters have exercised power not only in the choice of an elected official but also over the direction of public policy. Finally, after an official has been elected to office, his or her behavior can be influenced by the opinion of the voters. Politicians want to be reelected, and thus they do not usually say and do things that are likely to cost them votes. If they get a clear message that the majority of their constituents favor or oppose a given policy, they might vote accordingly (Burstein, 1981, pp. 293–294).

Do People Vote on the Basis of Issues?   The extent to which votes are actually translated into influence over public policy depends, of course, on the extent to which people vote on the issues. Clearly, many things besides the candidates' positions on the issues influence who gets elected. We have already seen that charisma can be important. More broadly, evidence indicates that people's personal reaction to a candidate can be at least as important as where that candidate stands on the issues. (For a discussion of research on factors influencing voter choice, see Beck, 1986.) Speaking ability, appearance, name recognition, and a perception that the candidate is or is not honest and competent influence the voters' personal reactions. Unfortunately, a good many people do not know

where the candidates stand on the major issues, or even what the key issues are. Given this situation, the extent to which votes are translated into influence over public policy is clearly limited.

Voting and Political Parties   One way in which people may indirectly vote on the basis of the issues is by voting on the basis of **political party**. Although differences between the political parties are smaller in the American two-party system than in European multiparty systems, the parties do represent somewhat different political viewpoints and somewhat different interest groups. In general, for example, support for the Republicans is greater among people with higher incomes (Drum, 1978, pp. 267–268), and the Republicans have long been perceived as the "party of business." Lower-income people, on the other hand, are more likely to support the Democrats,

FIGURE 10-1
American Voter Turnout: 1932–1988
SOURCE: U.S. Bureau of the Census, 1987, p. 243; Burnham, 1987; *New York Times*, 1988.

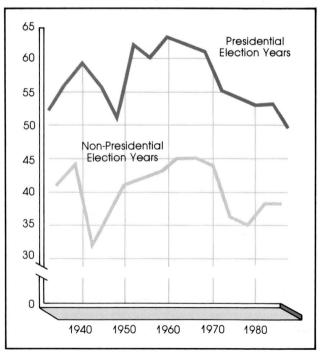

Why Don't Americans Vote?

Voting can operate as a source of power only if people actually vote. In fact, many Americans do *not* vote. Consider Ronald Reagan's "landslide" victory in the 1984 election. With over 60 percent of the popular vote, Reagan won by one of the most lopsided margins ever, and he took that victory as a great popular mandate for his agenda. There is, however, another way to look at it. Although Reagan won a big majority of *those who voted,* he, as well as all other recent presidents, got a distinct minority of *those who were eligible to vote.* In the 1984 presidential election, only 55 percent of voting-age citizens actually voted (Burnham, 1987). Of that 55 percent, only 60 percent, or about 33 percent of eligible voters, actually voted for Reagan. Thus, despite Reagan's landslide win, only one out of three voting-age Americans actually voted for him.

The 1984 voting pattern was not unusual. As shown in Figure 10.1, turnout in U.S. presidential elections has fluctuated between 50 and 65 percent over the past 50 years. In other words, one-third to one-half of all Americans have consistently not voted in presidential elections during the twentieth century. Congressional elections in nonpresidential years have drawn even lower turnouts; never in the past 50 years have as many as half the eligible voters turned out for such elections.

An interesting sidelight to this discussion is the effect on turnout of extending the vote to 18-year-olds. Note that when the voting age was lowered from 21 to 18 in 1972, voter turnout dropped. Young people are the least likely to vote, older people

the most likely. Thus, adding more young people to the voter rolls further lowered turnout on a percentage basis, though this merely accelerated a trend that was already under way. Finally, as shown in Figure 10.2, the low voter turnout in the United States is *not* typical of most industrial countries. In fact, it is easily the lowest of the 22 countries shown.

Why is turnout so low in the United States? Part of the answer is that registration or voting is mandatory in some other countries but optional in the United States. However, that is not the whole answer. It is more difficult to register in the United States than in some other countries, which maintain address registers and automatically update voter registration when people move. Here you must register each time you move, and in most states, voters are purged from the rolls if they do not vote within a certain period of time.

Other differences lie in the political and economic systems of the various countries. The United States, as we saw in Chapter 9, has proportionately more poor people than other Western democracies, and poor people vote at lower rates than the nonpoor. The American two-party system may also be partly responsible for the low turnout. When there are just two parties, each tries to appeal to a broad range of groups because no one group is big enough to furnish a majority. U.S. parties thus take a less ideological and more broad-based approach to politics. As a result of seeking "swing votes" in the middle, they become similar to each other. It therefore makes less difference who wins than it does in countries with

three, four, or five parties, each representing distinct viewpoints and interest groups (Downs, 1957). Thus, Americans in any given group have less incentive to vote. This may be especially true for poor people. In a two-party system, no party can win by appealing purely to the poor—they are too small a group to make up a majority. This is largely why the United States has no labor or socialist party like those found in most European democracies (Burnham, 1987; Hartz, 1955; Devine, 1972). Further evidence for this view can be seen in the fact that low income is more closely associated with low voter turnout in the United States than it is in other countries (Burnham, 1987, pp. 98, 101–102). In other words, poor Americans are much less likely to vote than poor people in other democracies.

Finally, it has been suggested that the U.S. Congress has a higher proportion of "safe seats" than the parliaments of many other countries (Bogdanor, 1987, p. 263). It is rare for a sitting representative to lose his or her seat—only 2 percent of those running for reelection did so in 1986, for example (Mann, 1987). Obviously, when a candidate's victory is certain, there is less reason to vote. Unfortunately, congressional districts are drawn by state legislatures, and the temptation is for each party to protect the seats of its sitting representatives—hence the tendency toward "safe districts." If you combine this fact with the advantages of name recognition and "favors owed" that a sitting representative enjoys, you can understand why few representatives are ever voted out of office.

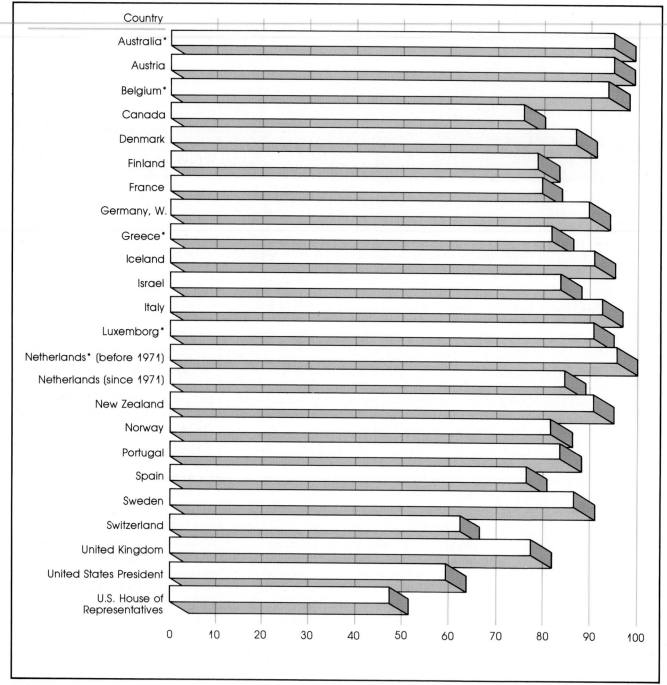

FIGURE 10-2
Voter Turnout in Selected Democratic Countries, Average, 1945–1980

All except United States are percentage of registered voters who vote. United States is percentage of voting-age population who vote. This distinction has little practical consequence because registration is mandatory in virtually all countries except U.S. and France. In general, 95 percent or more of voting-age population is registered in countries other than the United States, except France, where about 90 percent is registered (Bogdanor, 1987, p. 623).
SOURCE: Vernon Bogdanor, 1987, *The Blackwell Encyclopedia of Political Institutions* (New York: Basil Blackwell, p. 623.

who have historically been seen as the "party of the underdog." Although there are many issues on which the parties differ little, there are some on which they clearly disagree. In the 1988 presidential primaries, for example, every Republican candidate favored military aid to the Nicaraguan contras, whereas every Democratic presidential candidate opposed such aid. Thus, by choosing the party that comes closer to their viewpoints, people do vote on the basis of the issues to a certain extent, even if they do not actively consider a candidate's views on the issues. Having said this, however, it is also important to note that people's votes today are less influenced by a candidate's political party than was the case in the past.

Interest-Group Voting One situation in which votes do influence public policy occurs when large, organized interest groups vote as a bloc. This does not happen as often as most people believe, but it does occur in certain situations. One such example is the "ethnic vote." When a racial or ethnic group is concentrated in an area, it may choose its officials on the basis of their positions on issues of concern to the group, or it may seek power by electing its own members to public office. This influence is most important in local elections, where the concentration of a group is sometimes large enough to determine the outcome of an election. It is less important on the national level, where no one group is in a position to dominate. However, it can be important in close national elections. Were it not for the overwhelming support of black voters, for example, John Kennedy in 1960 and Jimmy Carter in 1976 would have lost narrowly instead of winning narrowly. However, the black vote did not influence the outcome of presidential elections in 1964, 1968, 1972, 1980, 1984, or 1988. At roughly 10 percent of the electorate, it simply was not large enough to determine the outcome.

Another example of interest-group power can be seen in the influence of "single-issue" voting groups. Like other interest groups, those who vote on the basis of one issue can influence the outcome of a close election. Most elections, however, are not close enough for single-issue voters to make much difference. In the 1988 Iowa Republican caucuses, for example, Pat Robertson did "better than expected," finishing second to Senator Robert Dole and ahead of the national frontrunner and ultimate nominee, Vice President George Bush. Newspapers noted that in one populous county where antiabortion sentiment was strong, Robertson actually won on the strength of that vote (*St. Louis Post-Dispatch,* 1988). However, as strong as that vote was in one geographic area, it was not strong enough statewide for Robertson to win — Dole's margin in the rest of the state was simply too big. Had Robertson and Dole been very close to begin with, the antiabortion vote could have been the deciding factor.

Force and Coercion

Another way to influence the behavior of others is through force and coercion. If I have the power to fail you in your introductory sociology course if you do not do what I tell you to do — and you see no way to prevent me from doing so — chances are you will do what I say. The reason is not that you really want to do what I say, but that I can impose real costs or harm on you if you do not. In effect, I have used **coercion** — I have created a situation where if you do not do what I want, you will suffer some undesirable consequence.

Legitimate versus Illegitimate Coercion Coercion, like some other forms of power, can be either *legitimate* or *illegitimate*. In general, people accept the principle that the police should be able to use coercion as a way of enforcing the law. Thus, if a person attempts to rob a bank, most of us would agree — as does the law — that a police officer has the right to use force (the threat of arrest and physical force, if necessary) to prevent that person from robbing the bank. This is a legitimate use of coercion. The bank robber, on the other hand, in threatening to shoot bank employees if they refuse to turn over the bank's money, is using a form of coercion that most of us would regard as illegitimate.

Governments, businesses, and private citizens all resort to coercion on occasion, and in each case, that coercion can be seen as either legitimate or illegitimate. In the case of government action, most of us would recognize the legitimacy of calling in the police to prevent a violent crowd from burning down a building or attacking an individual. However, what if the police are called in to shut down tables where students are peaceably handing out literature in a public place on a university campus? That happened at the University of California at Berkeley in 1964, and it was perceived by most of the students there as illegitimate coercion by the university aimed at stifling free speech. The result was the beginning of the "student protest" era of the 1960s.

We should not, however, think of coercion as something done only by governments. Businesses use coercion in a variety of ways, including the threat to fire employees or to close a plant and relocate to an area with a "friendlier business climate." Many businesses hire private security forces to coerce employees or customers, and the advent of the computer has produced a boom in electronic spying on employees, as bosses "listen in" to find out what their workers are saying and doing (Marx and Sherizen, 1987). The possibility that such spying may be going on, of course, is enough to prevent many employees from saying or doing anything they wouldn't want their bosses to know about. Finally, coercion has been extended to employees' private lives, as many employers have begun to require applicants to pass polygraph and drug tests in order to be hired. By 1988, for example, about one out of three major U.S. corporations required their employees or applicants to take drug tests (Finney, 1988).

When ordinary citizens lack or become frustrated with traditional channels of influence over either the political system or private businesses, they, too, turn to coercion. Coercion may occur in the form of legal activities such as strikes and boycotts, nonviolent civil disobedience such as sit-ins, or violent actions such as riots and sabotage. All of these actions are attempts to influence authorities by imposing costs upon them if they do not change their ways. Thus, a boycott threatens a company with the loss of income until it stops dumping raw sewage into a river; a restaurant that will not serve blacks is faced with a racially mixed crowd that refuses to leave until all are served; or a country occupying foreign territory is faced with continuous rioting until it gives up or democratizes that territory.

Limits of Coercion   In many cases, coercion — legitimate or otherwise — is regarded by those who use it as a last resort. With all forms of coercion, people comply not because they *want* to but because they *have* to. The problem is that as soon as the coercer loses the ability to coerce, he or she has lost power, and others may no longer behave as he or she wishes. Also, coercion nearly always requires more effort and energy than other ways of exercising power. Thus, authority, persuasion, voting, and other means of power are generally seen as preferable to coercion because they generally get people to *want* to do what the person exercising power desires them to do. In general, when the exercise of power is seen as legitimate, coercion is less likely. Legitimate authority, for example, is usually obeyed. Thus, there is little need for those holding such authority to resort to coercion. Those who oppose legitimate authority are also less likely to use coercion because even if they disagree with the policies being pursued by political authorities, they do recognize their *right* to pursue those policies.

Perhaps such considerations explain why coercion and attempts at coercion are more common in societies that are deeply divided. In such a situation, other forms of power are less likely to work, and people and governments turn to coercion as an alternative. South Africa, the Israeli-occupied Arab territories, Northern Ireland, Lebanon, Afghanistan, and Poland are probably all good examples of this principle. In less divided societies such as the United States, coercion is most likely to occur when divisive issues such as the Vietnam War arise, or when social movements fail to achieve their objectives through other methods, as was the case with the civil rights movement, which had little alternative to civil disobedience given the refusal of southern states in the 1950s to allow blacks to exercise their constitutional rights.

Control of Information

Particularly in modern societies with mass communications, the *control of information* is an important source of power. To some extent, everyone's behavior is influenced by the information available to him or her. Suppose, for example, that you have been told repeatedly that your chances of getting a job are better if you get a degree in business administration than if you get a degree in English, mathematics, or anthropology. To the extent that you are working toward a degree in order to get a job, you are likely to seek a degree in business administration. Thus, your behavior has been influenced by the information that you have been given. One important implication of this is that power or influence over your behavior has been exercised by those who have given you this information. Another is that it does not really matter, in terms of your behavior, whether the information you have been given is accurate. If you have consistently gotten the same message, you have probably trusted it and acted upon it. If it turns out to be right, you have been influenced in a way that will help you get what you want; if it turns out to be wrong, you have been what is commonly called a "victim of poor advice."

Who has control over the type of information that influences people's behavior? To help answer this question, think for a few moments about where you would look to find out which majors are most likely to land you a job. You would probably turn to placement counselors, and you might also choose to read a couple of studies of the job-finding experiences of recent college graduates. If you did these things, you would be influenced by expertise. Indeed, expertise is one important source of control over information. I suspect, however, that you might also try to find some magazine or newspaper articles on job prospects in different areas of employment. You might also watch the television schedule for any news specials dealing with this topic. In doing this, you would be obtaining information from the **mass media,** one of the most important sources of information in modern societies.

Media Control of Information   In what they choose to include and to exclude in their articles and programming, the mass media exercise great influence over the information that becomes available to the average citizen. Also, the tone and emphasis of media presentations of an issue or a topic have considerable influence over what people have the opportunity to learn. In presidential campaigns, for example, it is easy to find out who is three points ahead or behind in the polls in any given week. In fact, the media often treat the campaign as if it were a horse race, focusing mainly on who is ahead or behind and who is gaining or losing ground (Hunt, 1987, pp. 63–68; Patterson, 1980). However, try to find out by reading the paper or watching the television news which candidates

favor taxing capital gains at the same rate as wages and which ones favor different rates of taxation. If you want to choose your candidate on the basis of which one is thought to have a good chance to win, you can easily get that information. If, however, you want to choose on the basis of where the candidates stand on issues, that information is harder to get. Clearly, this makes it easier for people to choose on the basis of "Who's ahead?" than on the basis of the issues. Thus, the media exercise power over your choice by the kind of information they give you.

Many people legitimately ask whether this is really the media's fault. Media executives argue that they give the public what it wants. Because media income is determined by how many newspapers are sold or how many people watch television shows, they have little choice but to do so. However, the fact remains that people can only act on information that

Newscaster Sam Donaldson conducting an interview at the 1988 Democratic National Convention. The mass media in any society exercise considerable power by what they choose to report and not to report.

A Fresh Breath of Heresy

On the morning of June 24, Tenth-Grader Dmitri Predkov, 17, stood up to answer a question in his history class at Moscow's Middle School No. 734. The question: "Is *perestroika* [Gorbachev's economic and social reforms] a natural stage in the development of Soviet socialism?" Dmitri's answer: No, it is not. He added the tart opinion that some people say otherwise "only because Gorbachev is head of our party." A classmate, looking sporty in a black leather tie, was equally bold in discussing the loosening constraints on Soviet citizens. People of all stripes, "even fascists," he insisted, should have the legal right to form their own political parties to challenge the Communist Party. Said the openly skeptical Predkov: "We don't have any rights. They're just words on paper."

Just one year ago, such dialogue would have seemed pure heresy anywhere in the Soviet Union, let alone in a classroom, where doctrine has reigned and dissidence has been risky. Yet in the era of *glasnost,* talk like this is now allowed in schools all over the country. The stunning change came upon the insistence of Soviet Leader Mikhail Gorbachev for rapid reform in the education system. "We pin hopes for the future largely on the work of our schools," he told a meeting of the Communist Party Central Committee five months ago. The Soviet people, he said in another

—Adapted from Ezra Bowen, *Time*, July 25, 1988, p. 74.

speech, must learn history as it really happened (rather than as the party had long told it), "so as not to repeat the mistakes of the past."

In line with Gorbachev's calls for a more candid assessment of the past, the Soviet State Committee on Education in May canceled all traditional history exams, which are based on old-party-line texts. Instead, it ordered ungraded, open "discussion" groups of the sort held in Middle School 734, where teachers could judge their students' actual knowledge of the past. A June 10 editorial in the government daily *Izvestia* championed the decision and took the opportunity to blast the authors of old-line histories: "Immeasurable is the guilt of those who deluded generation after generation, poisoning their minds and souls with lies." (Never mind that the pre-*glasnost Izvestia* had long done the same.)

The old texts are indeed rife with distortions, deletions, and historical venom. Texts on Soviet history tend to celebrate triumph after triumph, from the success of the Revolution to victory in World War II to the launch of Sputnik. They gloss over Stalin's purges, the starvation of millions during the collectivization of farms, military blunders that nearly lost the war to Hitler, and corruption in the Brezhnev era. Meanwhile, an elementary primer claims,

Soviet educators worry that such skewed texts in history and other subjects may stifle creative thinking. Worse, the combination of bad books and ideologically rigid pedagogy may

put Soviets at a competitive disadvantage in the world arena. "I'm ashamed to say it, but my grandchildren study more or less from the textbooks that I used as a child before the war," one man wrote to *Pravda*.

In a rush to plug the knowledge gap, revised books are being churned out: 160 teams of authors recently submitted manuscripts in a competition for new texts.

In addition, teachers will for the first time be given the option to choose among texts and to diversify curriculums, which have long been dictated by the central government. "Three or four years ago, any variations in instruction methods were unthinkable," admits Vladimir Shadrikov, vice chairman of the state education committee. "Now all this has become a reality."

The impact is already apparent in the discussions in Yamburg's Moscow classroom, where 15-year-olds recently debated Stalin's role in Soviet history. "He had a lot to do with the industrialization and collectivization of our country," asserted one blond-haired boy. But a classmate countered, "Some consider him a criminal because he ruined our country's industrial system."

Yamburg beamed with pride at his students' lively performance. "I feel my chief task is to form nonconformist minds," says the veteran instructor and Communist Party member. Quite a change from the party line of yesteryear.

they get. Thus, in virtually all dictatorships, the government controls the media to prevent people from getting information that challenges the legitimacy or policies of the government. Democratic countries typically define a free press as a constitutional right, and any blatant attempt to regulate the press—such as censorship of programs about Northern Ireland on the government-owned British Broadcasting Corporation

(BBC) — instantly generates a major controversy. Both dictators and civil libertarians recognize that control of information is a source of power, and they act accordingly. Significantly, when a society moves toward democratization, information usually becomes more available. This is illustrated in the box entitled "A Fresh Breath of Heresy."

Government Control of Information Control of the press is not the only means by which governments can control information. Merely because they are in the center of the decision-making process, governments have access to a great deal of information that ordinary citizens do not. By choosing what to make public and by stressing the fact that they have more information than ordinary citizens, government decision makers are able to influence public perceptions of controversial issues. According to Wilensky (1967, p. 144), such secrecy "obscures great issues of public policy and permits sustained masking of blunders." Such a process was utilized during the Vietnam War. Presidents Johnson and Nixon repeatedly maintained that if the public had all the information that top government decision makers had, they would support the government's policy. The government insisted that such information couldn't be made public because it would provide the enemy with intelligence that might threaten the lives of American fighting men. As it turned out, this was not the only reason the information wasn't made public. Another key reason was that much of this information showed that the Viet Cong and North Vietnamese were stronger than widely believed, and that American prospects were poorer than the government publicly acknowledged (Karnow, 1983, pp. 423–426, 498–514). By keeping this information secret, government leaders were able to contain opposition to the war and to continue their policy longer than they would have had the true situation been understood by the American public. More recently, the Reagan administration withheld information from the public in the Iran-Contra scandal, again on the basis of "national security."

Wealth and Income

Another very important source of power is wealth and income. Money can be translated into political power in a number of ways. For one thing, it provides access to the mass media by enabling a person to buy advertising, publish books, and make movies and television programs. Such media access is important because it determines what information and viewpoints the public will and will not be exposed to. Thus, the people who control information are likely to be wealthy. Money is also of obvious importance in getting elected. In this era of media campaigns, running for public office is expensive. Campaigns for governor and U.S. senator inevitably cost *millions* of dollars, and it is increasingly common for candidates for the U.S. House of Representatives and for mayors in large cities to spend that kind of money. This is significant for two reasons. First, it means you usually need a lot of money to run for any major office. Note that between one-third and one-half of all U.S. senators are millionaires (Domhoff, 1983). Second, because even millionaires don't have enough personal wealth to finance an expensive campaign, candidates must raise a lot of money in campaign contributions in order to stand a chance of getting elected. Thus, people who are in a position to make large campaign contributions are also in a position to influence the votes, decisions, and policies of public officials.

How much does money influence the making of public policy? Social scientists have been debating this question for at least a century. One viewpoint — arising from the theories of Karl Marx — is that money and power are virtually synonymous: if you want to know who has power, find out who has money. Another view — based on the work of Max Weber — is that wealth and power, although not totally unrelated, can exist independently of each other. Wealth is no guarantee of power, and power is no guarantee of wealth. In the next section, we shall explore this debate in greater detail and evaluate it in terms of the findings of contemporary social research.

Economic and Political Inequality: How Closely Related?

Origins of the Debate: Marx and Weber

As noted, the debate about the relationship between wealth and power is a long-standing one, dating back to the early sociological writings of Karl Marx and Max Weber. Although these two important social thinkers lived in different generations, Weber's writings have been described as a "debate with the ghost of Marx," and both men have shaped subsequent sociological debates on the issue.

Marx: Wealth Determines Power Karl Marx saw wealth and power as essentially the same. Marx has often been described as an *economic determinist* because he felt that in any society, those who own the means of production determine virtually all the characteristics of that society. This group uses its wealth to control all social institutions—government, education, law, science, the arts, and the media. With respect to government policy, the wealthy use their power to assure that government operates in their interests. They can do this directly, by placing their own members in positions of power. An example was the feudal era, when landownership was the equivalent of wealth, and royal families always owned great amounts of land. The wealthy can also control policy indirectly by using their wealth either to put others in places of power to do their bidding or to influence whoever is in positions of power. Marx and his co-author Friedrich Engels believed so strongly that government was inevitably a tool of the wealthy that they predicted that after economic inequality was eliminated through common ownership of the means of production, government would "wither away."

Weber: Wealth and Power as Distinct Dimensions Writing about half a century after Marx, when the benefits of industrialization were beginning to spread beyond the owners of capital, Max Weber (1968 [orig. 1922]) saw wealth and power as distinct from each other. Although Weber did not deny that wealth often contributes to power, he argued that wealth, power, and social prestige are all distinct dimensions of stratification. Although your position along one of these dimensions can *influence* your position along another, it does not *determine* it. Thus, for example, being wealthy may increase your chance of having political power, but it is no *guarantee* of power (Orum, 1988, p. 398). According to Weber, some people have great wealth but little political power, and others have great political power but limited wealth. Rather than simply being an outgrowth or manifestation of wealth, power and prestige exist in their own rights, sometimes independently of wealth.

The Debate Today

Modern Weber: The Pluralist Theory A modern interpretation of Weber's thinking can be found in the **pluralist model** of power distribution, represented by such contemporary social thinkers as David Riesman (1951), Seymour Martin Lipset (1959), and Robert Dahl (1961, 1981, 1982). Pluralists argue, in effect, that the wealthy cannot have a monopoly on power in modern democratic societies because power is not concentrated in the hands of any one group, but rather is divided among many competing groups (Pampel and Williamson, 1988). These groups include business, labor, ethnic, racial, regional, and religious interests—all of which try to influence the decisions of political authorities. According to pluralists, *all* of these various groups (or at least their leaders) have some power, and *none* has complete power. Often they act as **veto groups;** that is, they are strong enough to prevent decisions that seriously threaten their interests, but not strong enough to bring about a decision that some other group opposes.

In one sense, the pluralist theory resembles the conflict perspective in that it addresses what happens when groups composed of people with opposing self-interests or policy orientations attempt to influence political decision making. However, in more important ways, the pluralist theory is functionalist, because it sees modern democracies as working well: They balance the interests of various groups so that every group gets some representation and some protection against harmful government decisions. Pluralism is also seen as functional in the sense that it keeps conflicts under control. Any one person may identify with several different interest groups depending on the issue. For example, the same person might at times identify with whites, females, born-again Christians, trade unionists, and environmentalists (Lipset, 1959). Hence people in a pluralist society enter into different coalitions on different issues, win some and lose some battles, and rarely, if ever, divide themselves into long-standing, hostile, opposing factions. Riesman even goes so far as to argue that what often protects the interests of a group is not the reality of its power, but the *perception* by others that it can exercise power through voting, lobbying, or other means. If politicians believe that a group has power, they will treat it as though it does, even if in reality it controls fewer votes than the politicians believe.

A final important point about pluralist theory is that it does not necessarily imply that a large number of ordinary citizens directly influence the political process. Rather, the idea is that they are represented by *leaders* of the interest groups they belong to (Knocke, 1981; see also Dahl, 1959; Riesman, 1951). Thus, the leadership of labor unions looks out for workers, the Chamber of Commerce looks out for small businesses, and leaders of civil rights organizations look out for the interests of blacks and Hispanics.

C. Wright Mills, pictured below, argued that the United States is ruled by a behind-the-scenes power elite composed of the top leaders of the executive branch of government, the military, and the largest corporations.

In this way, pluralists argue, everyone's interests are represented.

Modern Marx — Power-Elite Theory Standing in opposition to pluralist theory is a modern descendant of Marx's theory known as *power-elite theory*. The best-known modern American sociologists supporting this viewpoint are C. Wright Mills (1956) and G. William Domhoff (1967, 1978, 1983). Although this theory is not strictly Marxist, it does share many of Marx's assumptions. First, it directly opposes pluralist theory by arguing that real political power is concentrated among a small group (called the *power elite*), rather than divided up among competing groups. Second, it argues that this power elite is made up mainly or entirely of the very wealthy. Power-elite theory stresses that much of the real decision making is done behind the scenes, and that you therefore *cannot* necessarily judge who has power by looking at who holds elected offices or who lobbies public officials. Rather, real power and influence may lie with appointed officials who work quietly behind the scenes, or with research foundations that are funded by, and act on behalf of, specific wealthy interests, such as multinational corporations (Mills, 1956; Domhoff, 1983). According to power-elite theorists, these processes often go on without any appearance of public conflict. The power elite makes its important decisions behind the scenes so that they do not become controversial public issues. Because it portrays the political system as dominated by a small and wealthy interest group, power-elite theory is generally regarded as a type of conflict theory.

Power-elite theory also bears some similarity to a set of theories developed decades earlier by several European social theorists: Michels (1967 [orig. 1911]), Pareto (1935 [orig. 1915–1919]), and Mosca (1936 [orig. 1896]). Like Marxism and power-elite theory, these theories hold that societies tend to be dominated by a small ruling elite. However, unlike the other approaches, these theories argue that elite dominance is a product of the very nature of collective decision making, not of a particular distribution of wealth. Thus, Michels, Pareto, and Mosca maintained that power elites were inevitable. (The theories of Michels are discussed in greater detail in Chapter 7.) In contrast, both Marxists and the modern power-elite theorists see concentration of power as largely the product of concentration of wealth, and they deny that either type of concentration is inevitable.

Who Has Power in America Today?

Which theory comes closer to describing reality in the United States today—the pluralist theory or the power-elite theory? To answer this question, we must determine who really *has* power. This is not easy to do, because power is the type of abstract concept, or construct, that cannot be measured directly. Domhoff (1983) has proposed three questions to help sociologists determine who really has power.

- *Who Governs?* One possibility is that people in official decision-making positions have power. Thus, one way to measure power is to ask the question "Who governs?" In other words, what are the socioeconomic characteristics of the people who hold elective and appointive offices? (Remember that some of the most important decisions may be made behind the scenes by appointed rather than elected officials.)
- *Who Benefits?* A second question is "Who benefits from government decisions?" (Domhoff, 1983; Polsby, 1980). Presumably, if a group of people consistently benefits from government decisions, this group is exercising some degree of power in shaping those decisions.
- *Who Wins?* Finally, we can get an idea of who has power by asking "Who wins?" when controversial issues arise. Again, if the same group usually wins when various groups compete to influence public policy, we can assume that group is exercising power (Domhoff, 1983). If, however, different groups win on different issues, or if most decisions are actually compromises that take everyone's concerns into consideration, power is probably dispersed among a number of groups, as suggested by the pluralist theory (Banfield and Wilson, 1963; Banfield, 1962).

The U.S. Capitol. Although there is a great deal of influence over Congress by formal lobbyists, there may be even more influence by representatives of corporate interests who identify themselves as policy groups rather than as lobbyists.

- *Reputation.* Besides Domhoff's three ways of measuring power, there is the *reputational approach.* This approach assumes that when someone repeatedly exercises power, others know about it. Thus, one way to find out who has power is by *asking* people involved in politics who is powerful (Hunter, 1955, 1980). This method has two shortcomings: (1) People do not always *know* who has power. (2) Asking people "Who is powerful?" may lead them to assume that someone *must be* powerful and thus to answer the question in ways that confirm the existence of a power elite (Polsby, 1980; Cousins and Nagpaul, 1979; Walton, 1966, 1977).

Interest Groups in American Politics

The National Level To answer such questions as "Who governs?" or "Who wins?" we must have some sense of which interest groups are trying to influence public policy. There are literally thousands of such groups. On the federal level, there were about 2,000 official lobbying groups in the mid-1970s; if you counted other groups not officially registered but attempting to influence policy, the total swelled to around 5,000 (Lyons, 1975; Mintz and Cohen, 1976). This number has grown since. To attempt to rate the relative influence of all of these groups would require a lifetime of study. Fortunately, from the standpoint of research, many of these groups represent similar interests with similar policy orientations. In fact, Domhoff (1983) argues that the majority of these groups can be grouped under three broad coalitions, each of which represents a major identifiable interest group or coalition of interest groups: the multinational corporate interest group, the small-business interest group, and the labor-liberal coalition.

THE MULTINATIONAL CORPORATE-INTEREST GROUP The first group includes the largest **multinational corporations** and the families that own them. This group influences public policy through a variety of foundations, "think tanks," and "good government" groups. Included are the Ford, Rockefeller, and Carnegie foundations, the Committee for Economic Development (CED), the Council on Foreign Relations (CFR), the Trilateral Commission, and the Business Roundtable. Most of the members of these organizations have a direct link to one or more of the largest multinational corporations, and the foundations receive their funding from these same corporations. With a few exceptions, these organizations present themselves not as lobbyists ostensibly representing particular interests but rather as policy groups seeking to develop policies that are best for the nation as a whole. However, careful study of the positions advocated by this group reveals that:

1. Its positions and policy orientations follow a fairly consistent political or ideological orientation, which might be classified as "moderate conservative" or "middle of the road."

2. Its positions and policy orientations do relate to the interests of the groups that fund this coalition in that they are generally oriented toward making the nation and the world politically and economically "safe" for the major corporations. In other words, they are aimed at eliminating sources of upheaval and threats to the activities of the multinationals, preserving international free trade, and other policies that allow the multinationals to operate safely and profitably (Domhoff, 1983).

An example of the second point may be seen in the involvement of the Ford and Rockefeller foundations in the world population control movement. By supporting efforts of such groups as the Population Council, they seek to prevent the social upheaval — and threats to the business climate — created by runaway population growth (Dye, 1983 pp. 258–263).

THE SMALL-BUSINESS INTEREST GROUP The sec-

ond major interest group identified by Domhoff is small business. This group is represented by such organizations as the Chamber of Commerce and the national professional organizations that operate largely as small businesses — the American Medical Association (AMA), American Bar Association (ABA), American Dental Association (ADA), and the National Farm Bureau. It also includes some smaller corporations, but not generally the large multinationals. This group tends toward a more conservative political orientation, and unlike the multinational corporate group, it opposes virtually all governmental regulation of business. Although more openly a lobbying group and less supportive of research institutes and "good government" groups, the small-business interest group does have some involvement in this area. The most notable examples are the American Enterprise Institute and the Hoover Institute.

THE LABOR-LIBERAL COALITION The third group or coalition identified by Domhoff is the loosest coalition of the three and includes the widest variety of interest groups. It includes labor groups, minority groups, environmentalists, consumer groups, feminists, liberal intellectuals, and a variety of groups linked to the public sector, such as educators and public employees. It includes such organizations as the National Association for the Advancement of Colored People (NAACP), Urban League, National Organization for Women (NOW), National Education Association (NEA), the Ralph Nader organizations, and a variety of labor unions. Because of its greater variety, this group cannot always present a consistent and unified political front. However, there is sufficient cooperation and similarity of political orientation among the various elements of this coalition to identify it as a loose political alliance. Unlike the other two groups, this coalition is strongly oriented toward the Democratic party. However, it is more liberal in its orientation than most Democratic officeholders, and it is not necessarily better represented than the other two groups within Democratic administrations.

The Local Level The important interest groups at the local level vary, depending on the locality. However, certain types of groups are usually involved at this level. One such group consists of established, wealthy, and prestigious families in the community

(Lynd and Lynd, 1937; Levy, 1979). Such families exist in large and small cities. They may be founders of local industries (the most frequent type), families associated with major local cultural or educational institutions, or even descendants of the founders of the community. These families frequently overlap. A second important group, often overlapping with the first, consists of corporations and financial or industrial concerns with major operations in the locality. In many cities, ethnic groups and religious groups are organized and actively involved in city politics (Dahl, 1961). In some cities, too, poor people are well organized and seek to influence policy through groups such as ACORN (Association of Community Organizations for Reform Now), a poor people's organization with chapters in many medium-to-large cities.

Because issues related to development tend to dominate local politics, groups whose interests center around development are especially important. Banking and real estate interests depend upon growth and development for their profits, and in virtually every city they are actively involved in the promotion of "progrowth" policies. In fact, in many cities they dominate local politics to the point that city governments function as "growth machines." In other words, the primary consideration in the development of public policy is the promotion of growth and "economic development" (Molotch, 1976; Lyon et al., 1980). In some cities, however, antigrowth interests are also heavily involved in local politics. These groups represent citizens who see growth as a threat to the quality of life, bringing more crowds, noise, pollution, and traffic jams. In some cities, antigrowth lobbies have successfully challenged the notion that "bigger is better" and have succeeded in implementing policies that restrict growth. Most often this has happened in cities with affluent, educated, and highly involved citizens, located in rapidly growing areas such as California, Oregon, and parts of New England.

The Distribution of Power: The National Level

Now that we have identified the key interest groups in American politics, we are ready to examine the question of how power is actually distributed among these groups. We shall seek to discover this by considering the three questions raised by Domhoff that we introduced a few pages back: "Who governs?" "Who benefits?" and "Who wins?" When we turn to the local level, we shall also consider the findings of studies using the reputational approach.

Who Governs? There are two aspects to the question "Who governs?". One concerns who holds positions of power in government, and the other concerns who holds informal positions of power. When we look at the first aspect, it becomes clear that the wealthy are greatly overrepresented among those who hold public office. Mills (1956), for example, noted that top positions in the executive branch of government and the military were overwhelmingly in the hands of a power elite who shared a background of having served on large corporate boards of directors, to which they often returned after completing their public service. This group also had a common cultural and educational background. They went to a relatively small group of elite schools (recall our discussion of Supreme Court Justice O'Connor) and belonged to the same private clubs and organizations. Burch (1980–81) studied Cabinet members, diplomats, and Supreme Court appointees in every administration from George Washington's through Jimmy Carter's. His study defined the economic elite as executives or owners of large companies or law firms, or as members of families that were either very wealthy or were closely associated with corporate executive positions. By this definition, the elite held between 60 and 90 percent of Cabinet and diplomatic appointments throughout the entire period, except during Franklin Roosevelt's New Deal, when they held only 47 percent. From 1960 to 1980, the proportion remained between 60 and 70 percent. It is striking that presidents as politically divergent as Kennedy, Nixon, Carter, and Reagan chose their Cabinet officers from the same places (Domhoff, 1983). Thus, in virtually every administration in U.S. history, the great majority of top appointments have gone to the very wealthy (see also Mintz, 1975; Dye, 1983). Most people who get such appointments belong to the first of the three interest groups identified by Domhoff — the multinational corporations.

THE MAKEUP OF THE CONGRESS Congress is not a lot different. In recent years, about one-third of U.S.

Zbigenew Brezinski, National Security Advisor for Democratic President Jimmy Carter and campaign advisor for Republican President George Bush. Brezinski is a leader in the Trilateral Commission, one of the corporate-dominated organizations Domhoff identified as influential in American politics.

senators have been millionaires (cf. Domhoff, 1983). If the Senate were representative of the U.S. population in terms of wealth, there would be 1 or 2 millionaire senators instead of 30 or 40.

Of course, those who govern are unrepresentative, not only in terms of their wealth, but also in terms of race and sex. In the 1989–1990 Congress, there were 24 blacks in the House of Representatives. This was the highest number ever, but it still constituted only 5.5 percent of the House, not even half of the 12 percent of the U.S. population that is black. There have been no blacks in the U.S. Senate since 1978. Hispanics are similarly underrepresented. Although 7 percent of the population of the United States is Hispanic, less than 3 percent of House members and no senators were (*St. Louis Post Dispatch,* 1989). Most underrepresented of all are women. Although the majority of the voting-age population is made up of women, only 5.7 percent of U.S. representatives and just 2 senators—2 percent of the Senate—are women (*Taylor's World of Politics,* 1987; *St. Louis Post-Dispatch,* 1989). Blacks, Hispanics, and women have

also been extremely rare among Cabinet officers and top presidential advisers. Thus, the people who hold office at the national level are not only mainly wealthy but are, on the whole, wealthy white males, a large share of whom have direct connections to the nation's largest corporations. In this regard, the characteristics of top officeholders are much like what would be predicted by the power-elite theory.

If there is any exception to this, it is the House of Representatives. Compared to the Senate, the House has more blacks, Hispanics, and women, and fewer millionaires. Because it represents smaller districts, some of which vary greatly from one another, the House includes people from a wider range of backgrounds than either the Senate or the executive branch. Thus, the composition of the House conforms more closely to the pluralist model. Despite this greater diversity, however, white males and the wealthy are still greatly overrepresented. Moreover, to become law, bills must be approved not only by the House but also by the Senate, and they must be put into effect by the executive branch. Thus, the influence of the diverse population of the House can be offset to a large extent by the elite's highly disproportionate representation in the Senate and the executive branch.

THE MAKEUP OF ADVISORY GROUPS A look at those who have close access to policy makers is also revealing. Congresspersons do represent a variety of districts and constituencies, and the composition of their personal staffs largely reflects this reality. However, the advisers of executive-branch officials are distinctly less diverse. Also, congressional votes are influenced not only by the representatives' personal staffs but also by national lobbies and policy organizations. We shall discuss the influence of lobbies shortly when we address the question of "Who wins?" but first we must consider the effect of advice from policy groups in order to answer the question "Who governs?" The fact is that both the executive branch and the legislative leadership rely heavily on a fairly limited number of policy organizations, "think tanks," research centers, foundations, and professors from elite universities for advice on policy. These groups, in turn, have strong connections to the multinational corporate-interest group.

One sign of the influence of these organizations

is that they supply most of the members of governmental advisory commissions. The extent of corporate influence on such commissions is illustrated by a study of one ongoing government commission by Schwartz (1975). This study found that over half the professors who served on the President's Science Advisory Commission between 1957 and 1973 had been directors of large corporations. If you add consultants to large corporations and directors of smaller ones, the percentage rises to two-thirds. Because most professors do not serve on corporate boards of directors, it is clear that professors who directly influence government policy are far more connected to corporate interests than are professors as a whole.

Of course, the fact that most high officials and their advisers are drawn from the wealthy and the corporate elite does not mean they always support policies favored by that group. There are, for example, some very important differences between the political positions of millionaire Edward Kennedy and millionaire Ronald Reagan. Pluralists, in fact, argue that such fundamental differences over public policy prove that millionaires are not really a power elite (Dahl, 1982). Moreover, argue the pluralists, politicians have to worry about getting reelected, which limits their power to act on behalf of their own interest group (Riesman, 1969). Thus, although the answer to "Who governs?" at the national level seems to be more consistent with the power-elite view than with the pluralist view, we cannot definitively answer that question until we take up the questions "Who benefits?" and "Who wins?"

Who Benefits? The question of who benefits from government decisions is probably the hardest of Domhoff's three questions to answer. Sociologists who try to answer this question use such indicators as the distributions of wealth and income, the recipients of government money, and the share of income that people at different income levels pay in taxes. With respect to the distributions of income and wealth, we already saw in Chapter 9 that a large share of income, and an even larger share of wealth, are in the hands of a small minority of the American population. We also saw that income is distributed more *unequally* in the

United States than in most industrialized democracies. Still, it is very difficult to determine to what extent this concentration of income and wealth results from government policies as opposed to other influences. At the very least, however, we can say that the government has done nothing to break up this concentration, so in this sense it could be seen as acting on behalf of the wealthy.

Determining who benefits from government taxing and spending policies is a more difficult problem. With a budget exceeding *$1 trillion*, the federal government is collecting money from all segments of society and spending it on a wide variety of programs. Nonetheless, many of these expenditures clearly do benefit the wealthy.

THE MILITARY-INDUSTRIAL COMPLEX One example of spending that benefits the wealthy is the massive military budget. The United States, as a superpower, has a larger military budget than most industrialized countries, and a.large share of that budget goes to purchases of increasingly complex and expen-

The sales of the eight biggest Pentagon contractors exceed the entire gross national product of Norway.

sive weapons systems from the multinational corporations. Most of the largest corporations are involved in sales to the military; for some, military sales are the primary source of income. A study conducted in the late 1960s found over 25,000 private contractors that were sufficiently involved in the military business to operate under Pentagon security regulations (Raymond, 1971). The eight biggest Pentagon contractors had combined sales that exceeded the gross national product of the entire country of Norway in a recent year, and five of these companies were among the top 50 corporations in the United States (Currie and Skolnick, 1984). To put this a little differently, most of the 50 biggest U.S. companies had some degree of military involvement, and one in ten relied *primarily* on sales to the military. This is particularly significant in the context of Mills's (1956) finding that the top leaders of the military, the executive branch, and the major corporations have common backgrounds and often move back and forth among these three power centers.

Clearly, the government's expenditures are heavily influenced by the interests of this **military-industrial complex.** In many cases, such expenditures do more for the profits of these giant companies than for the country's true security needs. This is particularly true of expenditures for the procurement of weapons systems. Many experts, for example, have made this observation about the Strategic Defense Initiative (SDI), popularly known as "Star Wars." Though research and development costs alone for this project amount to billions of dollars, there is great doubt that it could ever stop a full-scale nuclear attack, and one panel of scientists recently estimated that not until 1995 will we even know whether we can build a workable system at any cost (Boffey, 1987). One member of that panel stated that he was "99.9 percent sure it won't work." Meanwhile, however, a great deal of public money will be received by those involved in the system's development.

ANTIPOVERTY PROGRAMS At the other end of the scale, we can learn something more about who benefits from government spending by examining the share of the budget that goes to antipoverty programs. Although it is widely believed that the government spends massive amounts of money on welfare, the actual share of the federal budget that goes to programs for low-income people is quite small. In 1984, for example, total means-tested assistance (assistance for which only low-income people were eligible) amounted to about $100 billion (Burtless, 1986, p. 22), or about 10 percent of the federal budget. If you add labor- and job-training programs, the total rises to around $115 billion (Burtless, 1986, p. 35), about 12 percent of the federal budget. Thus, it is *not* true that a massive share of the federal budget is going to antipoverty programs. In fact, the amount is quite small, and most of these programs suffered substantial cuts during the 1980s (Levitan, 1985).

FEDERAL TAXES On the surface at least, the federal tax is a somewhat different story. The federal income tax is, on paper, a **progressive tax:** The rates are designed so that the proportion of income paid in taxes increases as income increases. However, at least until the passage of the tax reform law in 1986, the system frequently did not work that way. Capital gains—which you can have only if you have capital—were taxed at a lower rate than money earned by working. Moreover, a collection of deductions, credits, tax shelters, and loopholes enabled those with high incomes to protect much of their incomes from taxation. As a result, there were many documented cases of individuals with incomes of over $1 million who paid *no* tax at all; the same was true of several major corporations. The 1986 tax reform brought five fundamental changes to the tax law, the net effect of which was probably to bring income taxation more in line with ability to pay. First, many deductions, tax shelters, and loopholes have been eliminated. Second, all income is now taxed at the same rate, regardless of whether it comes from work or capital gains. As a result of these changes, it is harder for the wealthy to avoid taxation. Third, the rates of taxation on higher incomes were lowered, on the theory that the wealthy would nonetheless pay more than before because of the elimination of loopholes and rate preferences. Fourth, personal exemptions and the standard deduction were increased, so people with very low incomes pay substantially less tax than they did under the old law. As an example, under the old law, a married couple with two children and an income of $11,360 (or less) would have had to pay $380. Under the new law, they pay no tax. Finally, the new law will shift about $120 billion in taxes from individuals to businesses between 1987 and 1992.

Early studies of the impact of the tax bill found that, as expected, corporate taxes rose and the taxes of low-income taxpayers fell. The taxes of upper-income people generally remained steady or rose somewhat. About half of taxpayers with incomes of $50,000 or more paid higher taxes in the first year following tax reform; most of the rest paid about the same (Klott, 1988). Corporate taxes also rose, from an average rate of 15 percent before tax reform to 22 percent afterward (*The New York Times*, 1988g). On the other hand, many two-earner couples were hurt by the loss of deductions (Klott, 1988), and some of these were middle-income, not upper-income couples. Moreover, many deductions favoring the affluent were retained. For example, interest on home mortgages of up to $1 million is still deductible. In the first year *after* tax reform, the amount of housing subsidy offered to middle- and upper-income taxpayers through this one tax deduction was more than all low-income housing subsidies *combined*. As a result, the 17 percent of the population with incomes of over $50,000 got 52 percent of all federal housing subsidies in 1987 (Mariano, 1988). Remember, too, that the other major federal tax, the Social Security tax, is regressive because income above a certain level is not taxed at all.

In summary, such indicators as the distribution of wealth and income and the beneficiaries of government spending suggest that government policies frequently benefit the wealthy. Federal tax laws have also largely favored the wealthy, but the interests of the poor, and possibly those of middle-income taxpayers, do appear to have been served by the 1986 tax reforms. Hence the answer to "Who benefits?" largely supports the power-elite model, but at least in the case of tax reform, there is some support for the pluralist view as well.

Who Wins? Perhaps most critical in assessing the nation's power structure is the question "Who wins when competing interest groups attempt to influence public policy?" Domhoff (1983) reviewed much of the research on this question, focusing on the relative influence of the three coalitions he identified — the multinational corporate group, the small-business group, and the labor-liberal coalition. His review showed that when there is substantial policy disagreement among these three groups, the corporate group nearly always gets its way (see also Neustadtl and Clawson, 1988). Over a period of about 5 decades, this group had only one clear defeat — the passage of the prolabor National Labor Relations Act in 1935. Even this case was not a total defeat, however, because the law was later modified to make it more acceptable to the corporations.

With respect to the other two groups, small business appears to have a fair amount of veto power; it could usually stop something that was threatening to it. It regularly defeated initiatives of the liberal group that it found threatening, and in some cases it was able to modify, although it could not block, initiatives of the corporate group. It fared less well with its own initiatives, usually winning only when it had the support of the corporate moderates.

Least powerful was the labor-liberal coalition. It could act as an effective veto group only when it had the support of the corporate group to stop an initiative of the small-business conservatives. Rarely did it succeed in passing its own initiatives, and when it did, it was usually with the support of the corporate group. Significantly, its power increased during periods of social conflict and upheaval, as the corporate group sought to maintain order by making concessions. Why, according to Domhoff, did this have the least ability to win? First, it was a looser and more diverse coalition, and thus suffered from less unity and more divisiveness. Second, it had fewer economic resources than either of the other groups. Third, it had less access to governmental officials.

Hence, the answer to the question "Who wins?" indicates limited pluralism. One group nearly always wins, another wins only sometimes, and the third usually can win only with help and under certain conditions. There is a power elite that has important advantages in any public policy conflict at the national level.

Much of what we know about the American

power structure has been discovered through the research of G. William Domhoff. In his "Personal Journal into Sociology," Domhoff tells us how he started out as a researcher on dreams and became a student of power structure.

The Distribution of Power: The Local Level

Measuring the distribution of power at the local level is even more difficult than doing so at the national level. Every locality is different and has its own distinct distribution of power. Thus, it is virtually impossible to make broad, sweeping generalizations about the distribution of power "at the local level."

Adding to these difficulties is the fact that the way you study local power distributions will influence the conclusions you reach. Even experts studying the same city cannot always agree on its distribution of power. In New Haven, Connecticut, for example, studies by Dahl (1961) and Polsby (1959) concluded that the city's power structure was pluralist, whereas a later study by Domhoff (1978) concluded that the city was dominated by a power elite. How did this happen? In this case, it happened partly because different researchers examined who was involved and who won *on different sets of issues.* Political nominations and school policies, two of the areas studied by Dahl, did not appear to be dominated by any one group, perhaps because the wealthy in New Haven made little effort to influence them. Their children attended private schools, and they appeared more concerned with influencing whatever policy was implemented than with who got elected. Domhoff, on the other hand, focused mainly on urban renewal, a development issue in which the affluent growth lobby dominated, as predicted by Molotch's (1976) "growth machine" theory. Domhoff's study emphasized an issue where the wealthy did have a clear economic stake, and on this issue they were both highly active and, according to Domhoff, successful in getting their way.

Who Wins? The general approach you choose in studying local power distributions can also affect your conclusions. Studies using the *reputational approach,* for example, tend to find a power elite: If you ask people who has power in a community, you will frequently get similar answers from many different people. Studies of *who wins* in controversial issues, however, frequently find a pluralist power distribution. Again, there may be a bias: Issues only become controversial when they are debated publicly and when two or more organized interest groups contend over them. If the power elite exercises its power behind the scenes, it might prevent issues of concern to it from becoming controversial (Molotch and Lester, 1973).

Who Governs? Studies of *who governs* may be biased toward a pluralist conclusion if, as some power-elite theorists argue, real power does not lie with elected officials. The elected officials may indeed represent a variety of backgrounds, but they may make their decisions under the influence of powerful unelected elites. This principle is vividly illustrated in the film *Poletown Lives,* which shows how a working-class Polish and black neighborhood in Detroit was destroyed to permit expansion of a General Motors plant. Despite the fact that the mayor and much of the city council had backgrounds in labor and civil rights activism, they were virtually unanimous in doing the bidding of the automaker.

Who Benefits? Finally, studies of *who benefits* often support the power-elite view. City after city offers massive *tax abatements* and other subsidies to industries to entice them to locate there. This means that large developers and corporations pay no property tax, or a much-reduced property tax, for a substantial period of time after building a new factory, business office, or apartment building. This policy is designed to encourage development and attract jobs, yet many studies have found that it is not very effective in doing so (Harrison and Kantner, 1978; Wolkoff, 1982, 1983; Kieschnick, 1981) and that its main result is to subsidize the wealthy through lower taxes. Abatements fail to attract jobs for several reasons. First, virtually every area offers such abatements to any company willing to locate there, so the policy does

PERSONAL JOURNEY INTO SOCIOLOGY

How I Became a Professor of Dreams and Power

Nothing about my background predisposed me to become a political sociologist interested in uncovering the power structure of American society. My family was average in every way and took no interest in politics. While growing up I played sports and wrote for the high-school newspaper, and I thought I might be a journalist when I left the Midwest to go to college in the South.

Still, I always had a strong dislike for injustice and unfairness. The poverty I saw as a child when we drove downtown always puzzled and upset me. But my inclination to question injustice manifested itself only in crusading articles in my high-school and college newspapers. Then, too, one of my early college term papers concerned the famous muckraking journalists of the Progressive Era. Their investigations into the rise of the "money trusts" and giant corporations fascinated me.

In college my interest in journalism slowly gave way to a liking for the mysteries of human psychology. I became interested in motivation, in what makes people tick. I read case histories of patients, interpretations of myths and rituals, and studies of the unconscious. After much hesitation and soul searching, I decided to go to graduate school to become a psychoanalyst or professor even though many aspects of psychology bored me. I had to steel myself for the fact that some of what I would study would not be enjoyable to me and that I would have to suffer through this material to attain my goal.

I gradually became involved in systematic studies of dreams, the revealing picture stories of the night.

G. William (Bill) Domhoff
G. William Domhoff is Professor of Psychology and Sociology at the University of California, Santa Cruz. He received his Ph.D. at the University of Miami and is the author of such books as Who Rules America?, The Higher Circles (1970), Fat Cats and Democrats (1972), The Bohemian Grove and Other Retreats (1974), The Powers That Be (1979), Who Rules America Now? (1983), *and* The Mystique of Dreams (1985).

This was because I had a chance to work with one of the few well-known psychologists who studied that almost-taboo topic, the late Calvin S. Hall, best known for such books as *Theories of Personality, The Primer of Freudian Psychology,* and *The Primer of Jungian Psychology.* My dissertation had the rather grandiose title "A Quantitative Study of Dream Content Using an Objective Indicator of Dreaming." That title sounds too strained to me now, for later research

showed that such objective indicators of dreaming as rapid eye movements (REM) and unique brain wave patterns were not as good as we originally thought they were.

But questions of power were creeping up on me, too, sometimes in very roundabout ways. Traveling in Europe the summer after my second year of graduate school, I met a woman from California, and the next summer we were married. It was her family that started me reading and thinking about power, for they were all political activists and avid readers. When I read a book by C. Wright Mills called *The Power Elite,* published in 1956, a year of complacency and celebration in America, I was more than interested, I was mildly hooked. Here was a world of power below the surface of society that was just as new and surprising to me as the private motives underneath our individual behavior.

Even so, I might not have switched my research interest from dreams to power if it had not been for the excitement and hopefulness stirred in me by the rising civil rights movement. That movement started to gain national attention just as I was finishing graduate school in Florida and taking my first teaching job in a state college in California. I was intrigued by the way the civil rights movement used research on local and national power structures to help its cause.

I still wouldn't have made the transition to power structure research if I hadn't come across another sociology book, this one by E. Digby Baltzell, *Philadelphia Gentlemen: The Making of a National Upper Class.*

Baltzell's book was crucial to me because it contained a list of "indicators" of upper-class standing, meaning that we could tell who was and was not part of the social elite by listings in the *Social Register,* attendance at expensive private schools, and membership in exclusive social clubs. His book enabled me to think in terms of systematic research that traced networks of power from the social upper class and the corporations to policy-forming groups, political parties, and government.

In other words, I immediately saw ways that I could use Baltzell's upper-class indicators to test the ideas of the aforementioned C. Wright Mills as well as those of various Marxists and pluralists. It has always been my tendency to try to test the most exciting ideas I can find with the most respectable and solid methods that can be used. I also like to synthesize the ideas of different people, so my first book, *Who Rules America?,* began by saying that it would build on the work of four very different people—Mills, Baltzell, the Marxist Paul Sweezy, and the pluralist Robert Dahl. It was written in a direct and graphic way, thanks to all that journalism experience in my background, and it was loaded with what we like to call empirical information. It also named names.

When I finished that book I honestly thought I would go back to dream research. I was not prepared for the book's great success. It had hit at just the right time, the late 60s, when civil rights activism had combined with antiwar and other movements to create tremendous ferment in the country. My book sold by the tens of thousands each year. It made sense to people because they were watching the power structure I described continue to fight the war in Vietnam even though growing numbers of people opposed it.

Even academic reviewers were not totally negative toward my book, which was surprising in an era when just about everyone in academia denied the existence of a power structure. Moreover, I felt that I could do more research to answer the kinds of questions that did get raised about the book. So I plunged back into research on power, writing more books, which in turn led critics to raise more questions. I was caught up in an exciting dialogue, and the result has been eight authored or co-authored books and three edited books in 25 years of research.

However, some of the fun went out of it for me in the late 1970s as the social movements of the 1960s disappeared and interest in the study of power structures declined. Moreover, a new breed of young Marxists began to claim that my books were part of the problem. I supposedly discouraged potential activists by writing that there is a power structure rooted in a small social upper class that owns and controls the large banks and corporations. I was making it seem hopeless. Thus, after being seen as useful in the 1960s, helping people to focus their actions and formulate the perspective within which they were operating, I now was viewed as a hindrance. This change from one decade to the next showed me that research such as mine has only a limited effect, and that it is often interpreted in terms of the atmosphere within which it is being read.

I think my research into power has been useful to democratic activists interested in opening up the power structure, but I also know from letters and conversations it has been used by upwardly mobile social climbers to find the "right" schools or summer resorts and by young members of the upper class who have not yet grasped the overall nature of the complex power structure they are destined to enter. My work has been of interest to these diverse people because it is first and foremost an attempt to describe and understand letting the chips fall where they may.

At the same time, even though there is little in my books that is judgmental or prescriptive, my research has been "radical" in that it attempts to get at the heart of the matter when it comes to understanding the great wealth and income inequality in the United States. It is also radical in a sense nicely stated by Mills in an answer to those hand-wringing social scientists who worried that he might be some sort of dangerous subversive rather than a proper sociologist. "When little is known," replied Mills, "or only trivial items publicized, or when myths prevail, then plain description becomes a radical fact—or at least is taken to be radically upsetting."

If my work has been radical, or radically upsetting, or useful, it is because so little is known about how power operates in a country where a mere one-half of one percent of the people own about 25 percent of *all* privately held wealth.

little to encourage development in any particular city. Second, considerations other than taxes generally play a bigger role in corporations' decisions about where to locate. Typically, local taxes are only 2 to 3 percent of the costs a company faces (Wolkoff, 1983). Third, many firms have little choice about where to locate because of established markets or business ties in local areas.

Some General Observations   If different studies tend to give different answers to the plualist versus power elite question, we do know that certain characteristics of cities predispose them toward either a pluralist or a power-elite orientation. Cities with partisan elections (except ones overwhelmingly dominated by one party) tend to conform more to the pluralist model (Aiken, 1970, p. 505) because there is always an organized opposition. Moreover, to some extent, one party may represent business and another labor, ethnic, or environmental concerns. In cities with nonpartisan elections, in contrast, the political and ideological orientations of the candidates are often less clear, and once elected, officials have no automatic opposition. This probably increases the behind-the-scenes influence of elites, because officials are less likely to be called to task for responding to special interests when there is no organized opposition. The city manager system also contributes to behind-the-scenes decision making, and cities with this system of government tend to resemble the power-elite model more closely than those with an elected mayor as the only executive leader (Aiken, 1970, pp. 499–500).

Cities with one major industry (like Detroit) have a tendency to operate according to the power-elite model, reflecting the great power of that industry. This is especially true if the industry is locally owned or headquartered, so that its leaders are present and concerned with city issues. In contrast, cities with diverse industries are more likely to follow a pluralist model, as are cities with absentee-owned or -operated industries, because the leaders live elsewhere and are thus less likely to become involved in local affairs (Aiken, 1970).

Cities with large, diverse, and well-organized ethnic or religious groups or labor unions are also more likely to operate according to the pluralist model (Alford, 1969; Aiken, 1970, pp. 501–505).

The Importance of Local versus National Power

Before concluding our discussion of the distribution of power in America, we should note one more important point. Regardless of the nature of the local power structure, the national power structure, which seems to come closer to the power-elite pattern, has important impacts at the local level.

One example of this can be seen in the federal government's treatment of poverty. As we saw in Chapter 9, American poverty today is heavily concentrated in large central cities. Federal decisions that have the consequence of increasing the poverty rate will have serious impacts on such cities regardless of their power structures. This impact will be compounded if the federal government simultaneously reduces aid to cities in order to finance a tax cut or a military buildup. This is not an academic example; it is exactly what happened in the early 1980s. The result was that in city after city across the country, the poverty rate rose and federal assistance fell at the same time. The rise in the poverty rate meant that cities could collect less in taxes and simultaneously had to pay more in costs associated with poverty, such as health services and crime control. Just when this happened, the cities lost some of their federal aid.

In many large cities, the results were devastating. City governments had to raise taxes and cut services at the same time. Aging streets and bridges could not be repaired, and sewers constructed a century ago collapsed and could not be replaced. In some cities, recent efforts to improve minority employment by hiring more blacks and Hispanics as city workers were largely undone when fiscal crisis forced layoffs according to seniority. Significantly, these things happened independently of the local power structure.

For cities dominated by a power elite at the local level, there is another significant consideration. Very often, local elites are closely linked to national elites (Domhoff, 1978; Hunter, 1980; Kourvetaris and Dobratz, 1982). One example of this that we have already seen is the power of the auto companies in Detroit. As members of the corporate coalition, they are part of the power elite at the national as well as the local level.

Thus, their influence on decisions made in Detroit is both indirect, through their influence over federal decision making, and direct, through their influence over local decision making.

Summary

Power can be defined as the ability to get others to behave as you want them to. When others accept a person's power as legitimate, that person is said to hold authority. Authority takes several forms. Legal-rational authority is attached to a position that a person holds and is linked to the tasks and responsibilities attached to that position. Traditional authority may also be linked to a position, but it is neither as limited nor as task-specific as legal-rational authority. Rather, it is based on long-standing and unquestioned ways of doing things, is often lifelong, and may have a sacred or mystical aspect. Charismatic authority arises out of the attractive or inspirational qualities of a particular individual and cannot be attached to a position. Finally, authority may be gained through expertise and credentials. Authority of this last type is linked not just to position but to knowledge, and it is limited to areas relevant to that knowledge.

There are several other important sources of power besides authority. One is voting, though the extent to which voting is translated into power depends on the extent to which people vote on the basis of issues (or, in fact, vote at all). Another form of power is coercion — attempting to force people to behave in a particular way by threatening them with undesirable consequences if they do not do so. Like other forms of power, coercion may be either legitimate or illegitimate. When coercion or any other form of power is legitimate, people accept the principle that the person exercising power has the right to do so. When power is illegitimate, people perceive its exercise as improper, unauthorized, or violating their rights.

Control of information is another important source of power. Those who possess or control information can manipulate public opinion by selectively making information public. They can also argue that they should make the decisions because they have information the general public doesn't.

Finally, wealth and income are important sources of power, largely because they can so easily be converted into influence over public officials and control of information.

One key issue is the relationship between money and power. To what extent do those with great wealth and high incomes hold power in the political system? A closely related issue is whether power is concentrated in the hands of a few or is widely dispersed among different groups. Power-elite theory holds that power is concentrated and that the few who hold it come mainly from the ranks of the very wealthy. An opposing theory holds that the power structure is pluralist, containing a number of competing centers of power arising from competing interest groups, many of which are outside the ranks of the very wealthy. In general, power-elite theory arises from assumptions made by the conflict perspective, and pluralist theory is more closely aligned with the functionalist perspective.

Sociologists have devoted considerable effort to studying power in the United States in an attempt to determine whether this country more closely resembles the power-elite or the pluralist model. Research has concentrated on discovering who governs, who benefits from government policy, and who wins when debates arise over alternative policies. In general, research at the national level is more supportive of the power-elite than the pluralist model, although it does not completely support either. A policy group dominated by large corporations has sought to influence national decision making throughout this century, has had more access to the policy-making process than anyone else, and has occasionally compromised but rarely lost. In contrast, policy groups dominated by small business and by a coalition of labor and liberal groups have had far less access and success. The labor-liberal group, in particular, has been able to win only when it has been supported by the corporate group.

At the local level, power structures are more variable, depending on such factors as the type of government of a city, its ethnic makeup, and the number and size of major businesses in the community. Regardless of a city's local power structure, two facts remain. First, the largely elite nature of the national power structure has important impacts at the local level because federal policy and federal spending have major consequences for virtually every major locality. Second, those who hold power at the local level are often the same groups who hold power at the federal level, which broadens the scope of their power and influence.

Glossary

power The ability of a person or group to get people to behave in particular ways.

authority A right to make decisions and exercise power that is attached to a social position or to an individual and is accepted because people recognize and acknowledge its legitimacy.

legitimate power Power that others accept as proper.

traditional authority Authority based on long-standing custom, often reinforced by a sacred element.

legal-rational authority Authority that is tied to a position rather than to an individual and is based on principles of law or on an individual's proper appointment to a position.

charismatic authority Authority that is based on the personal qualities of an individual, such as the ability to excite, inspire, and lead other people.

expertise An individual's specialized knowledge concerning some specific topic, issue, or scientific discipline.

credentials Items of information used to document or support the claim that an individual has certain capabilities.

political parties Organizations, usually with different viewpoints or ideologies, that run slates of candidates for elective office.

coercion An exercise of power that forces people to recognize and obey a group or an individual whose legitimacy they do not accept.

mass media Popular published and broadcast means of communication that reach a substantial segment of the population.

pluralist model A theory holding that power is dispersed among a number of competing power centers, each representing a different interest group.

veto groups Interest groups that possess the power to block policy changes or proposed laws that threaten their interests.

multinational corporation A large corporation that produces or sells its products, and usually owns property, in a large number of countries.

military-industrial complex A grouping of powerful individuals and organizations who share a common interest in large military expenditures.

progressive tax A tax that requires those with higher incomes to pay a greater percentage of their income in taxes.

Further Reading

DAHL, ROBERT. 1961. *Who Governs?* New Haven, CT: Yale University Press. This book, based on a study of the power structure of New Haven, is a classic and remains one of the most influential statements of the pluralist theory of local power distributions.

DOMHOFF, G. WILLIAM. 1983. *Who Rules America Now?* Englewood Cliffs, NJ: Prentice Hall. Probably the best place to get an overview of research on the American power structure by the author of the "Personal Journey into Sociology" box that appears in this chapter. This book addresses who has had power and influence at the national level in the United States under every president from Franklin Roosevelt through Ronald Reagan.

DYE, THOMAS R. 1983. *Who's Running America? The Reagan Years,* 3rd ed. Englewood Cliffs, NJ: Prentice Hall. An excellent introduction to research on the American power structure, updated to reflect changes and continuities that took place under Ronald Reagan. It addresses methodological issues in power research, describes the concentration of power in a variety of American institutions, and examines the social networks and interaction of leaders. Includes profiles of many leaders of the 1980s, such as the one that opens this chapter.

HUNTER, FLOYD. 1980. *Community Power Succession: Atlanta's Policy Makers Revisited.* Chapel Hill: University of North Carolina Press. An update of a highly influential reputational study of local power structure first published by Hunter in 1955; an influential statement of the power-elite viewpoint on local community power structures.

MILLS, C. WRIGHT. 1956. *The Power Elite*. New York: Oxford University. The classic American sociological work on power structure, this book remains one of the most influential statements of the power-elite thesis more than 30 years after its publication.

REISMAN, DAVID. 1961. *The Lonely Crowd*. New Haven, CT: Yale University Press. One of the more influential sociological descriptions of American society in the late 1950s, this work is also one of the most frequently cited examples of the pluralist view of power in industrial democracies.

CHAPTER 11

Race and Ethnic Relations

Over a century ago, the United States fought a bloody civil war partly over the issue of whether human beings could be held in slavery on the basis of their skin color. A few years later, in Los Angeles in 1871, mobs took to the streets, beating and killing people simply because they were Chinese. Between 1908 and 1921, similar mob actions against blacks occurred in dozens of cities, with over 125 deaths. In 1943, both blacks and Mexican Americans were the targets of white mobs. From the late 1950s to the mid-1960s, a massive civil rights movement challenged laws and regulations that required separate schools, bathrooms, lunch counters, and waiting rooms for nonwhites in the South. It was met with beatings, police dogs, thousands of arrests, and the murder of dozens of civil rights leaders, both black and white. Eventually, the movement succeeded in eliminating formal and official segregation, but no sooner had this happened than Black Americans in over 200 cities staged violent rebellions that took over 200 lives. (Most of the victims were black and died as a result of police attempts to put down the rebellions.) Most recently, in what many viewed as a sign of racial progress, the Reverend Jesse Jackson finished second in the 1988 campaign for the Democratic nomination, receiving — along with massive black support — the votes of millions of whites, and defeating six white candidates. Nonetheless, one of the reasons Jackson did not get the nomination is that, according to opinion polls, millions of other whites would not consider voting for him because he was black. In short, although the specifics have changed again and again, the realities of racial and ethnic conflict and inequality remain a dominant force in American life.

This issue, however, is not distinctly American. In the Soviet Union, violent outbreaks erupted in 1988 as Armenians and Azerbaijanis battled over control of disputed territories. Racial and ethnic conflict in South Africa and Northern Ireland have made headlines for decades. In Israel and the territories it occupies,

Palestinians have been relegated to a second-class status. In the occupied territories, they are confined to living in certain areas, and travel outside those areas is restricted much as it is for blacks in South Africa. In 1988 alone, the resultant conflict took hundreds of lives. In a deeper sense, this conflict arose from perhaps the worst case of ethnic conflict in world history. The drive to create a Jewish homeland in Israel — which led to the Jewish-Palestinian conflict — gained its impetus from attacks on Jewish people throughout history, culminating in the Holocaust — the Nazis' annihilation of 6 million Jews in the 1940s, two-thirds of Europe's Jewish population (Goren, 1980).

I n this chapter, we shall explore some of the reasons that racial and ethnic conflicts have been so widespread throughout history. In order to address this issue, we must first understand what is meant by race and ethnic group.

Racial and Ethnic Groups: What Is the Difference?

Some of the examples discussed above involve *racial* conflict and others involve *ethnic* conflict. There are similarities between a race and an ethnic group. Both are socially defined categories of people who share a common ascribed status. Membership in both is he-reditary. However, there are also differences. A **race** can be defined as a category of people who (1) share some socially recognized physical characteristic (such as skin color or facial features) that distinguishes them from other such categories, and (2) are recognized by themselves and others as a distinct status group (Cox, 1948, p. 402). An **ethnic group** in contrast, is a category of people who are recognized as a distinct status group entirely on the basis of social or cultural criteria such as ancestry or religion. There is no reliable way to identify a person's ethnic group by his or her physical appearance.

There are many different combinations of skin color, facial features, hair texture, and other physical characteristics among the human population. As a result, any system of racial classification involves making arbitrary distinctions.

How Many Races Are There?

Trying to classify people by race demonstrates the important role that social considerations play in the definition of race. Perhaps you have heard the common idea that there are three races: white (Caucasoid), black (Negroid), and yellow (Mongoloid). As popular as this notion is, there are several things wrong with it. First and foremost, it does not include everyone: There are some groups of people that cannot be placed in *any* of the three categories (Thernstrom, Orlov, and Handlin, 1980, p. 869). Second, there is tremendous variation within each category. Some people from India (considered "white"), for example, have darker skins than some Africans (considered "black"). Finally, many people and groups are of such mixed ancestry that they could be placed equally well in two or more categories. Relatively few people are "purely" of any one group. As a result, no matter what set of groups you use, there is a gradual range of appearances as you move along the continuum from people who clearly belong to one race to those who clearly belong to another, with a lot of people in between who cannot be clearly placed in any group.

Attempts have been made to classify races based on groups of people with similar physical appearance and common ancestry. Again, however, the number of "races" depends very heavily on which characteristics are considered. Genetics are of little use: There is no one gene for "race," and different genes determine different aspects of physical appearance commonly associated with race (Thernstrom, Orlov, and Handlin, 1980, p. 869). These different genes have different degrees of variation, so that how many "races" you find with this system depends on which gene you look at.

For these reasons, attempts to classify humanity into a set of races have never produced consistent results. Neither anthropologists, geneticists, nor sociologists have been able to agree on the number of races. Some have "found" only the three racial groups mentioned above. Others have identified over 100 races. The reality, though, is that there is no way to determine "scientifically" the number of races because the answer depends on which elements you pay attention to. Today most anthropologists, geneticists, and sociologists agree that race is largely a social concept with very little, if any, biological meaning.

The extent to which the definition of race is a *social* process is reflected in the fact that different societies use different classification systems. If you are a light-skinned African American, for example, you will be considered black in the United States, but in many other societies around the world, you will be placed in some mixed group, often called *colored* or *mulatto*. In many societies, people of mixed racial ancestry are regarded as members of mixed groups, whereas in the United States we do not recognize mixed groups. Usually, Americans with any visible non-European characteristics are regarded as members of the appropriate minority group (black, Asian, American Indian).

Although physical characteristics play a role in identifying races, race is much more a social concept than a biological one. A crucial part of the definition of *both* races and ethnic groups is that they must be *socially recognized* as distinct groups. Human societies choose to pay attention to a particular physical characteristic, which then becomes the basis for defining a race. Moreover, different societies use physical characteristics differently in defining races. The role of social considerations in the definition of race is shown in the box entitled "How Many Races Are There?"

For both races and ethnic groups, membership is usually involuntary and lifelong; in other words, it is an ascribed status. Moreover, it is usually passed from parent to child, although in some instances it may change for the offspring of marriages whose partners are of different races or ethnic groups. The characteristics used to define races are usually ones that are consistently and reliably passed from generation to generation, which explains, for example, why skin color is commonly used to define races and eye color is not.

Majority and Minority Groups

As we have seen, many societies that have two or more races or ethnic groups experience inequality and conflict. One or more groups are in an advantaged or dominant position with the power to discriminate, while other groups are in disadvantaged or subordinate positions and are often the victims of discrimination. Those in the advantaged or dominant positions are called **majority groups;** those in disadvantaged or subordinate positions are called **minority groups.** Often the majority group in this sociological sense is also a majority in the numerical sense, as with whites in the United States, people of British ancestry in Canada and Northern Ireland, and ethnic Russians in the Soviet Union. However, a numerical minority can be a majority group in the sociological sense, and vice versa. One example is South Africa, where about 5 million whites dominate more than 25 million native South Africans in politics, economics, and every other aspect of life. Hence, many sociologists believe the terms *dominant group* and *subordinate group* are more accurate, but the majority group/minority group terminology is still more commonly used.

Besides race, minority groups may be defined on the basis of other ascribed social characteristics such as sex, physical handicap, or sexual orientation.

Racism

Whenever prejudice, discrimination, or systematic social inequality occurs along the lines of race or ethnicity, we have an example of *racism*. Social scientists have used the term in so many ways that some have questioned its very usefulness (cf. Wilson, 1987, p. 12). Still, the reality of racial and ethnic conflict and inequality is so pervasive in the world that some underlying processes must be responsible for it. Thus, we shall select a broad definition of racism and then specify some distinct types of racism. For our purposes, **racism** is any attitude, belief, behavior, or social arrangement that has the intent or the ultimate effect of favoring one racial or ethnic group over another. As we shall see, this definition implies that although racism is often open, conscious, and deliberate, it can also exist in subtler forms. Sometimes, in fact, people can be racist without even being aware of it.

Ideological Racism

At one time, the term *racism* referred to the belief that one race or ethnic group is naturally superior (or inferior) to another. Today, in recognition of the variety of forms that racism can take, this type of belief is referred to as **ideological racism,** or *racist ideology*. It includes such notions as Hitler's concept of a "master race," the belief of slaveholders that blacks were uncivilized and incapable of anything more than physical labor (Jordan, 1968, Chap. 2; Wilson, 1973, pp. 76–81), and the conviction among Southwestern Anglos of the late nineteenth century that the partial Indian ancestry of Mexican Americans predisposed them to "savagery" and "banditry" (Mirande, 1987). Ideological racism can become institutionalized to the point where it has the status of an unquestioned "truth" that few people (in the majority group, at least) challenge.

An important function of ideological racism is to justify or rationalize the exploitation of the minority group (Cox, 1948). As Davis (1966) has pointed out, to enslave a human being like yourself is a terrible thing that most people in a supposedly democratic society cannot accept. If you can convince yourself and others that the one you are enslaving is less than fully human, however, then you can probably convince yourself and others that slavery is not so bad. This helps to explain why, for example, racist ideologies against blacks became more extreme and were invoked more frequently *after* lifelong black slavery was established in the U.S. South than *before* (Wilson, 1973, pp. 76–81).

Racial and Ethnic Prejudice

Still in the realm of racist *thinking* (as opposed to action) is racial and ethnic **prejudice:** any categorical and unfounded overgeneralization concerning a group. It can take the form of beliefs about a group, negative feelings toward a group, or the desire to discriminate against a group. In each of these cases, prejudice involves an automatic reaction to a group or to a person's group membership. If I automatically don't like you because you are white, if I want to discriminate against you because you are black, or if I think you are greedy because you are Jewish, I am prejudiced, because I am responding to you entirely on the basis of your race or ethnicity. I am choosing to ignore or disbelieve the influence of everything else about you except the fact that you are white, black, or Jewish.

Stereotypes One common type of prejudice is the **stereotype,** an exaggerated belief concerning a group of people. A stereotype assumes that anyone in a group is very likely to have a certain characteristic. American culture is full of stereotypes, such as the narrow-minded and authoritarian German, the greedy Jew, the lazy, musical, or sports-minded black, the hard-drinking Irish, the gang-prone Chicano, the bigoted southern white, and the hypocritical northern liberal who preaches integration while sending his or her own children to segregated private schools. Every one of these stereotypes, like all others, is a gross overgeneralization. Undoubtedly, some people in any group do fit the stereotype, but many others do not. The point is not that stereotypes do not apply to *anyone* in the group at which they are aimed, but that they are never true for *everyone* in that group.

Stereotypes can be positive or negative, but even the positive ones are a mixed blessing. It is, for example, undoubtedly good to be musical, athletic, or a good dancer, which are common stereotypes about African Americans. However, if whites believe that these are the only areas in which blacks can achieve, then they will probably behave in ways that close off opportunities for African Americans in professions other than sports and entertainment. Equally significantly, if young African Americans internalize the message that the areas for them to get ahead in are sports and music, they can be directed away from a variety of other areas in which they could be equally successful (see the vignette by Harry Edwards).

Individual Discrimination

Although prejudices of any type concern what people *think,* **discrimination** concerns what they *do.* **Individual discrimination** is any behavior that treats people differently or unequally on the basis of race, ethnicity, or some other group characteristic. Individual discrimination is usually, if not always, conscious and deliberate. Examples are a restaurant owner who refuses to serve a Chinese person, a taxi driver who passes a man by because he is black, and a sales clerk who takes longer to serve a customer because she is an American Indian. In the United States, most discrimination on the basis of sex, religion, or physical handicap is illegal. Nonetheless, some types of individual discrimination are hard to prove, and in some areas, such as the sale and rental of housing, this kind of discrimination remains common.

Institutional Discrimination

The most subtle form of racism, yet perhaps the one with the most serious consequences today, is **institutional racism,** or **institutional discrimination** on the basis of race (Carmichael and Hamilton, 1967; Feagin and Feagin, 1978; Farley, 1988). This form of discrimination occurs whenever widespread practices and arrangements within social institutions have the intent or effect of favoring one race (usually the majority group) over another (usually the minority group). Institutional discrimination can be very deliberate, as in the system of school segregation and denial of voting rights to blacks that existed throughout the U.S. South until the early 1960s. A more contemporary example of deliberate institutional discrimination is the widespread practice in the real estate industry of *racial steering*—showing white customers houses in white neighborhoods and black customers houses in racially mixed or all-black neighborhoods (Pearce, 1976; Lake, 1981).

Today, institutional discrimination is often unconscious and unintentional, though its consequences can be just as devastating as if it were deliberate. In the educational system, for example, teachers often expect less achievement from black and Hispanic students than they do from white students (Harvey and Slatin, 1975; Leacock, 1969; Brophy and Good, 1974; Hurn, 1978; Brophy, 1983; Moore and Pachon, 1985). In schools that are predominantly black or Hispanic, such low expectations often become generalized to the entire student body. When teachers *ex-*

A streetcar terminal in Oklahoma City, 1939. The segregation laws that existed throughout much of the United States until the 1960s are an example of deliberate and formalized institutional discrimination

pect less, they *demand* and *get* less, and achievement falls (Brophy, 1983). As a result, black and Hispanic students frequently learn less, are graded lower, get a poorer education, and consequently lose out on job opportunities when they grow up. Although none of this may be intentional discrimination, its consequences are every bit as serious. This issue is discussed in greater detail in Chapter 14.

Another important example of institutional discrimination is the movement of jobs out of predominantly black and Hispanic central cities and into predominantly white suburbs. This trend takes job opportunities away from the minority groups and gives them to whites (Squires, 1989). Evidence shows that where jobs have become suburbanized in this manner, both black and Hispanic men have higher unemployment rates than white men (Farley, 1987b; Lichter, 1988). To compound the problem, institutional discrimination within the real estate industry makes it very difficult for minorities to follow the jobs to all-white suburbs. In addition, the lack of automobiles in many black and Hispanic households, combined with poor mass transit, often makes commuting next to impossible (see Alexis and DiTomaso, 1983).

Causes of Racial and Ethnic Inequality

We now turn to a more detailed exploration of the *causes* of racial and ethnic discrimination, conflict, and inequality. Social scientists offer three general explanations for these behaviors. One set of theories is

based on social psychology, and the other two are sociological in nature, arising, respectively, from the functionalist and conflict perspectives. We turn our attention first to social-psychological theories.

Social-Psychological Theories of Race Relations

Most social-psychological theories about race relations center around the concept of prejudice (Wilson and See, 1988, p. 226). Recall that *prejudice* refers to unfounded and inflexible overgeneralizations concerning a racial or an ethnic group. Social-psychological theories argue that people's situations and social experiences influence their attitudes and beliefs. These experiences lead some people to develop prejudiced attitudes and beliefs, usually through *personality need* or *social learning.*

Personality Need The theory of **personality need** arises largely from the work of Theodor Adorno and his colleagues (1950), discussed in Chapter 2. In his content analysis of speeches and writings of rightwing extremists such as Nazis and Ku Klux Klan members, Adorno uncovered a number of themes that were not logically related but nonetheless appeared repeatedly. Sensing that these themes might reflect a certain personality type, he developed a personality measure to rate nine distinct attitudes and beliefs, including excessive respect for authority, superstition, aggression against nonconformers, cynicism, worry about sexual ''goings-on,'' opposition to looking inward to understand oneself, and a belief that the world is a dangerous place. Moreover, Adorno's research found that this personality type scored a good deal higher on anti-Semitic and antiblack prejudice than did other people. Thus, having a certain personality type — which Adorno called the **authoritarian personality** — does indeed appear to be associated with prejudice.

SCAPEGOATS Why are such people prejudiced? It appears that prejudice meets two kinds of personality need in such people. The first of these needs refers back to our discussion of Sigmund Freud in Chapter 5. Recall Freud's (1962 [orig. 1930]) theory that society's expectations, the superego, are in conflict with the child's natural drives, the id. If the superego is so powerful that it represses natural drives, these drives can surface later in other forms. Adorno applied this notion to prejudice. He found, from questions he asked his subjects, that adults with authoritarian personalities usually had experienced harsh discipline as children. As a result, they built up a good deal of frustration and aggression because they did not have the necessary outlets for their natural drives. However, because respect for authority was so deeply engrained in them, they could not take out their aggression on the true source of their anger—their parents and other authority figures. Instead, they took it out on **scapegoats**—racial, ethnic, or religious minorities, or other groups who displayed nonconformity in their dress or lifestyle. These scapegoats were not the true source of prejudiced people's anger, but they did serve as effective targets.

PROJECTION The second personality need met by prejudice is also related to childhood experiences. Prejudiced people had been taught that the world is made up of good and bad people, and you must always think, act, and behave as the good people do. People who adopt this good/bad world view cannot admit any fault in themselves, because to do so would be to put themselves in the "bad" category. Using open-ended questions, Adorno and his colleagues (1950) found that prejudiced people were much less willing than nonprejudiced people to admit faults in either themselves or their parents. Moreover, their prejudices helped them to deny their faults. By exaggerating the faults of others, they could deny or minimize their own. In particular, they tended to exaggerate the faults of minority groups. Thus, they could deny or minimize their own greed by pointing to "greedy Jews" or forget about their own violent tendencies by talking about "Mexican gangs." This process is called **projection.** As with scapegoating, other researchers besides Adorno have confirmed its presence among many prejudiced people (Allport, 1954, Chaps. 21 and 24; Simpson and Yinger, 1985, pp. 73–78).

Social Learning Although personality-need theories explain why some people are prejudiced, they do not explain all cases of prejudice. One need only look at the U.S. South during the 1950s to see this. Although the overwhelming majority of southern whites displayed relatively high levels of antiblack

prejudice, the incidence of authoritarian personalities in the South was not much higher than that found in the rest of the country (Prothro, 1952; Pettigrew, 1971, Chap. 5). Clearly, something other than personality need was responsible for antiblack feelings. A large part of the answer is to be found in culture and **social learning.** The social-learning theory of prejudice is much like the subcultural theory of deviance discussed in Chapter 8. According to this view, people are prejudiced because they grow up in prejudiced environments where they learn prejudice from their significant others. This learning occurs through the processes of selective exposure and modeling, reward and punishment, and identification that were introduced in Chapter 5. When your family, neighbors, and playmates are all prejudiced, you will probably be prejudiced, too. If you are exposed only to prejudiced attitudes and beliefs, they seem like unquestioned truths. You are informally rewarded when you express such attitudes but laughed at or teased if you express contrary attitudes. Finally, if all the people you respect and love hold prejudiced beliefs, could such beliefs really be wrong?

All of these social-learning processes do tend to produce prejudice. Research has shown that those whose parents and other childhood significant others were prejudiced tend themselves to be more prejudiced as adults (Ehrlich, 1973). However, this type of prejudice is different in an important way from prejudice based on personality need in that it is easier to change. Very often, when people whose prejudices are based on social learning move to environments where their significant others are relatively unprejudiced, their prejudice levels fall. In other words, people can conform to nonprejudice as well as to prejudice (DeFleur and Westie, 1958; Fendrich, 1967; Ewens and Ehrlich, 1969). For people who have a personality need to be prejudiced, however, that need remains regardless of their social environment.

Prejudice and Discrimination The relation between prejudice and discrimination is not always clear. As illustrated in Table 11.1, sociologist Robert Merton (1949) has shown that not everyone who is prejudiced discriminates, and some people who are *not* prejudiced do discriminate. Social pressures and the costs of discriminating or not discriminating de-

TABLE 11.1
Robert Merton's Typology on Prejudice and Discrimination

DOES NOT DISCRIMINATE	DISCRIMINATES
UNPREJUDICED	PREJUDICED
1. Unprejudiced nondiscriminator (all-weather liberal)	3. Prejudiced nondiscriminator (timid bigot)
2. Unprejudiced discriminator (fair-weather liberal)	4. Prejudiced discriminator (all-weather bigot)

SOURCE: John B. Farley (1988), *Majority-Minority Relations*, 2nd ed. Englewood Cliffs, NJ: Prentice Hall. Reprinted by permission of the publisher.

termine whether racial attitudes will be translated into behavior. If the costs of discriminating are great (complaints, legal hearings, and penalties), prejudiced people will often not discriminate. Similarly, relatively unprejudiced people may discriminate if pressured to do so by, say, the threat of losing white customers if they welcome black customers.

Attitudes may be changed by behavior. Prejudice, at least as measured by people's responses to questionnaires, fell considerably in the U.S. South after desegregation was ordered by federal law. In general, it was more satisfying for southerners to say "We know now that segregation is wrong" than to say "We did what those Yankee bureaucrats in Washington told us to do." This is very consistent with a social-psychological theory called **cognitive-dissonance theory,** which states that if behavior changes, attitudes will often change to become consistent with the new behavior (Festinger, 1957; Festinger and Carlsmith, 1959).

Thus, we cannot assume that behavior is always the result of attitudes. However, this does not mean that prejudiced attitudes are unrelated to actual racial discrimination. Prejudice has decreased considerably in the United States (R. Farley, 1984, 1977; Owen, Eisner, and McFaul, 1981; National Opinion Research Center, 1983; Firebaugh and Davis, 1988), but it has not disappeared. In fact, many researchers believe that modern prejudices have taken on a subtle form called **symbolic racism** (Kinder and Sears, 1981; McConahay et al., 1981; Kluegel and Smith,

1986, 1982). Rather than openly expressing prejudiced attitudes, whites argue that equal opportunity now exists, and therefore any disadvantage experienced by blacks today results from their own lack of motivation, ability, or hard work.

This theory is not supported by the facts. With 43 percent of all black children and 38 percent of all Hispanic children living below the poverty level — compared to just 16 percent of white children (U.S. Bureau of the Census, 1987a, p. 30) — black and Hispanic children do not grow up with the same opportunities as white children. Certainly, they are not to blame for the high poverty rates that deny them equal opportunity. Strapped by poverty and fighting against the types of institutional discrimination described earlier in this chapter, many of these children cannot enjoy the same benefits as the average white child unless the processes that place them at a disadvantage are changed. Yet, if whites believe, as most now do, that they have no further responsibility for reducing racial inequality, nothing will change, and unequal opportunity along the lines of race will be perpetuated (Sears and Allen, 1964).

Social-Structural Theories of Race Relations

Although attitudes continue to be relevant to race relations, there is a definite limit to how far you can go in explaining race relations by looking at individual attitudes. Individual factors, for example, cannot explain why entire countries have patterns of race relations that change over time, or why one country has racial harmony while another has racial conflict. To address questions such as these requires a social-structural approach, as reflected by the functionalist and conflict perspectives.

Functionalist Theories: The Role of Ethnocentrism Recall our discussion of the functions and dysfunctions of ethnocentrism, the tendency to judge other racial and cultural groups by the standards of your own group. Within a culturally homogeneous group, ethnocentrism performs the function of promoting solidarity, pride, and cooperation (Sumner,

The recitation of the Pledge of Allegiance at this graduation ceremony illustrates the process of assimilation, while this parade in Chicago celebrating Mexican Independence Day illustrates pluralism.

1906; Simpson and Yinger, 1985; Williams, 1977; Levin and Levin, 1982). Within a heterogeneous society, however, ethnocentrism is dysfunctional because it increases the likelihood of intergroup conflict and discrimination. Because functionalists believe that all societies have a tendency toward socioeconomic inequality, they argue that one important consequence of ethnocentrism is to structure this inequality along the lines of race or ethnicity. In other words, prejudice and conflict between groups usually enables one group to gain an advantaged position relative to another. Functionalists argue that this is why societies that are made up of diverse racial and ethnic groups so often have racial conflict and inequality.

How can such problems be minimized? Most functionalists see the answer in cultural **assimilation,** a process whereby various cultural groups in a society become more similar to one another, so that the differences that form the basis for discrimination are minimized or eliminated (Gordon, 1964). In practice, however, assimilation has often come to mean that minority groups are expected to accept the ways of the majority group, a process known as **forced assimilation.** In many instances they have resisted doing so. This has led many conflict theorists and others to advocate **pluralism.** Under this pattern, racial and ethnic groups remain culturally distinct from one another and from the larger society in some areas but share other elements of culture with the larger society.

Conflict Theories It is probably fair to say that the conflict perspective is the predominant approach today among sociologists specializing in race and ethnic relations. In fact, there are at least three important contemporary conflict theories about intergroup relations, which we shall explore shortly. These theories share certain elements. Unlike the functionalist approach, they do not see racial or ethnic inequality as resulting simply from cultural differences and ethnocentrism. Rather, they believe the critical factor is that *one group benefits by subjugating another.* When groups are in competition for scarce resources, or when one group has something (land, labor, wealth) that another wants, an essential condition for inequality exists. However, this by itself does not produce intergroup inequality. A second condition must also be present: *unequal power,* which means one group can take what it wants from another (Noel, 1968). Without this condition, inequality does not occur, and conflict may even be less likely, because groups often calculate their chances of winning before initiating a fight. However, when both competition or opportunity for gain *and* unequal power between groups exist, racial or ethnic inequality is likely to occur (Semyonov, 1988). This is especially likely when the conditions noted by functionalists—ethnocentrism and cultural differences—are also present.

Although conflict theorists share the belief that competition and unequal power play key roles in racial and ethnic inequality, they disagree about the nature of that competition. Most societies experience competition along both racial/ethnic and economic lines, and different conflict theories offer different ideas about the precise roles of race and economics.

Internal Colonialism Theory One conflict theory of race and ethnic relations is *internal colonialism.* Most of us are familiar with the concept of *colonialism* in its traditional meaning—a powerful country establishes control of a foreign area and its people.

Immigrants on a ship to the United States in 1920. Although immigrant minorities do often encounter discrimination, their experience is different from (and far more benign than) that of colonized minorities.

Typically, the native people of the colony are assigned a status lower than that of the colonizers. The natural resources of the colony are taken and used, often along with its people's labor, to enrich the colonizing country. In the case of internal colonialism, much the same thing happens, but within the borders of the colonizing country. In both cases, the colonized groups are placed under the colonizing country's control *involuntarily* (Blauner, 1972).

Once the colonized group takes on the status of a conquered people, certain things occur. Colonized minorities are subjected to intense attacks on their culture. Because they are defined as inferior, they are subjected either to isolation or to forced assimilation. They are also kept outside the mainstream of economic activity to ensure that they will not compete with members of the colonizing groups. Blauner (1972) points out that these experiences of colonized minori-

ties make them different from immigrant minorities. The latter enter a society voluntarily and are not subjected to the same levels of attack on their culture or economic isolation as are colonized minorities.

As we saw earlier in our discussion of American racial and ethnic groups, the four major groups who became "American" involuntarily are black Americans, Chicanos, Puerto Ricans, and American Indians. The experiences of these groups generally fit those of colonized minorities, which helps to explain why even today they occupy the most disadvantaged positions of all American racial and ethnic groups, including immigrant groups whose arrival is much more recent.

Internal-colonialism theory is different from other conflict theories of race and ethnic relations in one important regard — it focuses almost exclusively upon conflicts that occur between (rather than within) racial groups. Two other important conflict theories of intergroup relations focus in part upon economic conflicts *within the majority group,* pointing out that such conflicts may have an important effect on majority-minority relations. Let us examine these theories.

SPLIT-LABOR-MARKET THEORY The first such theory is *split-labor-market theory,* which lists three economic interest groups: employers (owners of capital), higher-paid labor, and lower-paid labor (Bonacich, 1972). In multiethnic or multiracial societies, higher-paid labor is often made up of majority-group members, while minority-group members are concentrated in the lower-paid labor category (Bonacich, 1976, 1975; Wilson, 1978). According to this theory, the majority-group members who hold the higher-paying jobs attempt to protect their position by demanding hiring discrimination against minorities. In the United States, for example, white workers have demanded discrimination against African Americans, Chicanos, and Asian Americans. Certain jobs were defined as "white men's work," and any minority person who aspired to them encountered blatant hostility from white workers. (For a personal account of such discrimination, see Wright, 1937, pp. 5–15.)

It is significant in this regard that the Ku Klux Klan and similar groups have always drawn the bulk of their support from working-class whites, who feel economically threatened by blacks and other minority groups. In the early twentieth century, labor unions demanded hiring discrimination (Wesley, 1927, pp.

254–281; Bonacich, 1975, p. 38), and in at least some instances, employers refused to hire blacks *because they were afraid of the reaction of white workers* (Brody, 1960, p. 186). Between 1850 and 1890, white workers in California rioted against Chinese, Japanese, and Chicano workers, protesting their presence in mining, shoemaking, and other industries (Barth, 1964; Kitano, 1985, p. 220; Ichihashi, 1969; Mirande, 1987, Chap. 3).

According to split-labor-market theory, majority-group workers demand and benefit from discrimination because it protects their favored position in the labor force. Employers, on the other hand, are often hurt by discrimination, both because it drives up wages by reducing the labor pool and because it deprives them of the opportunity to hire the best worker (on this point, see Becker, 1957).

How accurate is this view? Many white workers undoubtedly *believe* that discrimination works to their advantage. However, majority-group workers can only benefit from discrimination if they (rather than their employers) control the hiring process. To a certain extent, white workers did this in the late nineteenth and early twentieth centuries by threatening to "cause trouble" if minorities were hired. However, when the costs of discrimination became high enough, employers resorted to hiring tactics that used racism to the disadvantage of both majority- and minority-group members. The reality is that, except in occupations with union hiring halls, workers do not control the hiring process. Hence, most sectors of the economy operate more in accordance with a third theoretical model, to which we now turn.

MARXIST THEORY   The *Marxist theory of racism* holds that racism exists mainly because it benefits the ruling economic class (Cox, 1948). Today's Marxist theorists see two key economic interest groups, not three, as envisioned in split-labor-market theory. Marxist theory denies that there is any real conflict of interest between higher-paid and lower-paid labor. Rather, as wage laborers, both groups share a common interest that is in conflict with that of the owners of capital. Marxists believe that racial antagonisms are primarily a mechanism that is used by the owners of capital to divide the working class. Thus, they argue that employers encourage white workers to think that they are threatened by blacks and other minorities, because they then come to see the minority workers rather than the employer as their enemy. This divides the working class along the lines of race and ensures that employers will not have to confront a unified work force.

The labor history of the early twentieth century in the United States offers considerable support for this viewpoint. Between 1910 and 1920, all-white labor unions struck in the railroad, meat-packing, aluminum, and steel industries. The employers played upon racial antagonisms to break these strikes. Through a combination of deception (southern blacks were offered "good jobs up North" without being told they would be strikebreakers) and skillful exploitation of black antagonism toward all-white unions, thousands of blacks were recruited to break these strikes (Kloss et al., 1976; Bonacich, 1976; Rudwick, 1964; Foster, 1920). These tactics, of course, hurt both blacks and whites over the long run. White strikers were defeated, and black workers were restricted to low-paying nonunion jobs. These incidents of strikebreaking, along with a general fear of black economic competition, led to perhaps the worst wave of race riots in American history. Between 1906 and 1921, mobs of whites attacked and murdered African Americans in a number of cities, leading to at least 125 fatalities (Farley, 1988, p. 129).

By the 1930s, white workers increasingly realized that their approach of demanding discrimination was hurting them more than it was helping them. Industrial workers formed the Congress of Industrial Organizations (CIO), which, especially in the North, frequently supported policies, laws, and labor contracts forbidding racial discrimination. Even today the evidence suggests that racial inequality hurts white workers more than it helps them. Comparisons of states and metropolitan areas by Reich (1986, 1981) and Szymanski (1976) in 1970 and 1980 showed that those with greater racial inequality were also characterized by lower wages for white workers, higher profits, and weaker unions. With the exception of a very limited number of occupations that use union hiring halls, the Marxist theory appears today to be more accurate than the split-labor-market theory: Racial inequality benefits white owners of capital and hurts white workers. Of course, it hurts black, Hispanic, and other minority workers even more.

Racial and Ethnic Relations: An International Perspective

Ethnic Inequality and Conflict: How Universal?

Most societies with racial and ethnic diversity experience some degree of racial conflict and inequality. Discrimination and social inequality are encountered by Chinese in Vietnam, Aborigines in Australia, Catholics in Northern Ireland, Arabs in Israel, Jews and Baltic peoples in the Soviet Union, blacks, Pakistanis, and East Indians in Great Britain, Asians in several African countries, French-speaking people in Canada, and native Indians in several Latin American countries. In many places, violence has erupted between racial or ethnic groups. Recent examples are battles between Armenians and Azerbaijanis and between Uzbeks and Turks in the Soviet Union, Irish Catholics and British Protestants in Northern Ireland, Chinese and Malays in Malaysia, Palestinians and Jews in Israel, and a variety of ethnic and religious groups almost too complicated to enumerate in Lebanon.

Does this mean that ethnic inequality and conflict are inevitable whenever different groups come into contact? It does not. In Switzerland, a variety of ethnic and language groups have gotten along in relative harmony for years. In Hawaii, racial diversity is greater than anywhere else in the United States — no race is a majority there — and interracial relations, though far from perfect, are in general more harmonious than elsewhere in the United States. British Protestants and Irish Catholics, who hate one another in Northern Ireland, get along in the United States. Ethnic and racial conflict, then, are not inevitable; rather, they are the product of certain social conditions. We have already identified some of them. One is colonization, which, as shown in the box entitled "Colonized Minorities," is as evident in other societies as it is in the United States. Other examples of societies that must cope with racial and ethnic diversity are South Africa, Northern Ireland, and Latin America.

Racial Caste in South Africa

Recall from Chapter 9 our discussion of caste systems of stratification, including South Africa's racial caste system. In many regards, segregation in South Africa today is very similar to what existed in the U.S. South prior to the civil rights movement. Elaborate rules of segregation and effective denial of political rights to blacks were the rule there, too. In both South Africa and the U.S. South, urbanization and modernization brought a rising tide of protest by blacks and some white supporters. Both countries experienced prolonged periods of upheaval as protesters used both legal and illegal means to demand an end to segregation and the establishment of equal political rights.

Such upheavals demonstrate that caste systems are very difficult to maintain in modern urban societies without great conflict. The greater diversity and weaker social control of the city, along with mass communications, make it more likely that people will rise up in protest against their oppressed position (Blumer, 1965; Williams, 1977; Morris, 1984; Tilly, 1974). However, as Blumer (1965) has pointed out, this does not always lead to the same outcome. From a legal standpoint, the U.S. civil rights movement brought about dramatic change. Virtually all forms of deliberate or official segregation were banned, and the Voting Rights Act of 1965 guaranteed the right to vote to millions of southern blacks. In South Africa, however, no such thing has happened. True, there have been some reforms. To cite one example, a person can no longer go to jail for marrying or even "conspiring" to have sex with a person of another race. But the basic system of segregation and denial of political rights remains unchanged. As blacks have become more frustrated with the system's lack of change, their protest has grown increasingly violent. Violent incidents began as early as 1960 and increased in frequency in the 1970s and 1980s. In a 2-year period between the summers of 1984 and 1986, an estimated 2,100 people were killed (Cowell, 1986).

Why South Africa Hasn't Changed Why did change occur in the United States but not in South Africa? Two factors seem to have played a key role. THE SUBORDINATE GROUP AS A NUMERICAL MA-

Colonized Minorities: A Comparison of Mexican Americans and Baltic Peoples in the Soviet Union

The most powerless and oppressed minorities are very often colonized minorities. There is a striking similarity, for example, between Baltic peoples (Lithuanians, Estonians, and Latvians) in the Soviet Union and Mexicans in the United States, both of whom are colonized minorities. The Baltic groups live in regions that were involuntarily annexed by the U.S.S.R. after World War I, just as northern Mexico was annexed by the United States as a result of the Mexican-American War of the 1840s.

This common status as colonized minorities has led to some striking similarities in the experiences of Baltic Soviets and Mexican Americans. Baltic children are segregated from Russian children in the schools, just as Mexican children were long segregated from Anglo children in the United States. Baltic children are encouraged to speak Russian, but they cling to their own languages and fear being overwhelmed by Russian culture. Soviet authorities, in turn, worry that Baltic peoples will cling to their ways, fail to assimilate, and think of themselves as Baltic rather than Soviet. Again, the parallel to Mexican Americans is striking. The political and economic elite of the Baltic republics is overwhelmingly Russian, just as the elite of the U.S. Southwest is overwhelmingly Anglo. Anglos enjoy better jobs and higher incomes in the United States, just as do Russians in the Soviet Union.

With *glasnost* providing greater freedom, one of the serious problems the Soviet government will face is increased ethnic assertiveness by Baltic peoples and other groups. In 1988, thousands of Baltic nationals participated in mass demonstrations protesting past Soviet treatment of Baltic peoples, some of the first such demonstrations tolerated by the Soviet government. Again, there is a strong resemblance to protests by Chicanos in various parts of the United States.

Certainly there are also some differences between the experiences of Mexican Americans in the United States and Baltic peoples in the Soviet Union, but the parallels are striking, given the great differences between the Soviet and American economic and political systems. In both cases, the history of conquest and colonization has produced similar conflicts, problems, and social inequalities.

JORITY First, change is more threatening to whites in South Africa than it was to whites in the United States, and thus it is resisted more strongly. Without underestimating the fierce resistance of southern whites, the fact remains that white political control in the United States was never threatened to nearly the extent that it is in South Africa. Every southern state has a white majority who can outvote blacks if the voting divides along racial lines. In South Africa, by contrast, whites make up less than one-fifth of the population and would be easily outvoted. Thus, one-person, one-vote would mean a loss of white control. This suggests that where a sociological minority group is a numerical majority, the ruling minority will resist equality more vigorously (Blalock, 1967). More broadly, the larger the size of the minority group, the stronger the resistance to change will be.

ABSENCE OF OUTSIDE PRESSURE A second way in which South Africa differs from the U.S. South is the absence of effective outside pressure for change. What ultimately forced change in the South was the action of the federal government. Federal civil rights laws were passed in response to protest, the Supreme Court declared segregation illegal, and federal troops were sent into several states to enforce court orders for desegregated education. External pressure played a similar role in Zimbabwe, which as Rhodesia had a system of white minority rule similar to that in South Africa. There the reality of a growing civil war, along with strong pressure from the United States and Great Britain (which feared that the civil war would bring a pro-Soviet government into power), forced change. Today, Zimbabwe has majority rule, with some guarantee of representation for the white minority. However, in South Africa, there is no pressure comparable to that experienced by whites in the United States or

Zimbabwe. There is no pro–civil rights federal government and no neighboring country or insurgent movement strong enough to pose a military threat. There is not even any unified economic pressure from the rest of the world, despite limited sanctions by a handful of countries. Until greater pressure is brought to bear on the South African regime, the current bloody stalemate will likely continue.

Interethnic Conflict in Northern Ireland

Relations between Catholics and Protestants in Northern Ireland have sometimes been compared to relations between blacks and whites in the United States (Moore, 1972). There has been segregation, to the point that a wall had been built by the mid-1980s to separate the Catholic and Protestant sections of Belfast. The better jobs are held by Protestants, and poverty, though present in both groups, is more widespread among Catholics. Intergroup violence has been rampant for 2 decades and has claimed over 2,500 lives.

History of the Conflict   The Irish conflict is not simply a religious conflict but is also a conflict of nationalities that has its roots in conquest and colonialism (Moore, 1972; See, 1986). The Catholics are of Irish ancestry, and the Protestants are of British (either English or Scottish) ancestry. Furthermore, the British Protestants historically have been a colonizing group; the Irish Catholics, a colonized group. The British gained control over Ireland in the sixteenth century, and English colonists gradually established themselves as landlords over the native Irish population. The early English settlers were later joined by Scottish ones, who tended to be of a lower socioeconomic status. The English, however, retained their advantaged position by convincing the native Scots that they had a stake in the system because it protected them from competition by the native Irish (See, 1986). When Ireland gained its independence from England after a long and bloody conflict, Northern Ireland was created. It was made up of the six northern counties of Ireland, which were retained as a part of Great Britain to serve as a homeland for Protestants. However, a large share of this area's population were Catholics of Irish ancestry who did not want to move, and who resented British rule. Thus, a history of colonialism played a key role in the creation of ethnic conflict in Northern Ireland.

Ireland and Overlapping Cleavages   Besides being yet another example of the impact of colonialism, Northern Ireland illustrates a second principle, that of overlapping cleavages. We have already seen that nationality and religion divide people along the same lines: the Catholics are of Irish ancestry, the Protestants of British ancestry. Much the same is true of social class, though in a somewhat more complicated manner. The country's elite tend to be of English Protestant ancestry, its middle and working classes of Scottish Protestant ancestry, and its poor of Irish Catholic ancestry. Thus, social class divides the population along the lines of ancestry and religion. In short, whether divisions occur on the basis of ethnicity, religion, or social class, these divisions tend to be much the same. This condition usually increases social conflict (Lipset, 1959; Hunt and Walker, 1974). The opposite of this condition is cross-cutting cleavages, in which each division occurs along different lines. An example of this situation is Switzerland, where ethnicity, religion, and social class all divide the population differently. With people on different sides depending on the issue, conflict tends to be less intense. This may be one reason for Switzerland's relatively harmonious intergroup relations (Hunt and Walker, 1974).

Racial Assimilation in Latin America

A number of Latin American countries present a striking contrast to race relations in the United States. Like the United States, they were colonized by Europeans who imported blacks from Africa to serve as slave labor and who took land from the Indians (Van den Berghe, 1978, pp. 63–65). Yet, despite this history of colonialism, the outcome was ultimately very different. Both culturally and racially, such countries as Mexico and Brazil experienced a two-way assimilation that produced a new culture and ethnic group that are neither European, African, nor Indian (Harris, 1964). A key element of this process was **amalgamation** — repeated intermarriage and interbreeding between racial groups to the point that the various groups became largely indistinguishable. In both Mexico and Brazil, a large portion of the population is of mixed European, Indian, or African ancestry. As a result, relatively few people can be identified as strictly European, black, or Indian. The great majority belong to a mixed group that is often thought of as simply "Brazilian" or "Mexican."

Why did this happen in Mexico and Brazil and not in the United States? There are several reasons, which illustrate the variety of factors that can influence race relations in any given country. One such factor is population composition. The overwhelming majority of the Portuguese who came to the colony of Brazil were male. This led to widespread intermarriage early on, which became sufficiently accepted to continue when more European women did arrive. In the United States, by contrast, more English colonists came as families, which discouraged intermarriage. Whites in North America did, of course, have sexual contacts with Indians and black slaves—often highly sexist and exploitative ones. However, the children that resulted from these contacts were designated as part of the minority group, whereas in Brazil, they became part of the majority group.

Religious differences further contributed to these patterns (Kinloch, 1974). The Catholic religion of the Spanish and Portuguese emphasized conversion and the winning of souls (Harris, 1964). Thus, black slaves and especially Indians were incorporated into the dominant culture. In the United States, the Protestant religion of the early colonists placed a greater emphasis on predestination, the belief that people were either chosen to be saved or not, and not too much could be done for those who were not chosen. Thus, efforts to convert and integrate were less common, particularly in the case of Indians.

Other cultural attributes of both the dominant and minority groups also made a difference. In Brazil, many Portuguese of Moorish (North African) ancestry were dark-complexioned and viewed such a complexion as a standard of beauty (Pierson, 1942). This further encouraged intermarriage with Indians and Africans. In Mexico, the native Aztec Indians had a highly developed urban culture. Their largest city, with a population of 300,000, was one of the biggest in the world. Thus, in some ways, the Mexican Indians were culturally more similar to the Europeans, and therefore could more easily adjust to European ways.

In Mexico, the blend of European (Hispano) and native (Indio) culture became a symbol of national unity.

Although assimilation and amalgamation have been the rule in Mexico and Brazil, neither country is a racial paradise. In both countries, having a lighter skin is associated with a higher social and economic status (Mason, 1971; Bastide, 1965). Even so, the different cultural and demographic histories have produced very different patterns of race relations in Mexico and Brazil than in the United States.

Racial and Ethnic Groups in America

Because the United States is a nation of immigrants, it is one of the most diverse nations of the world in terms of race and ethnicity. No ethnic group in the United States accounts for more than about a quarter of the population, and—depending on how you count them—there are between 15 and 30 nationalities that are claimed by at least half a million Americans (see U.S. Bureau of the Census, 1983). About three-quarters of the U.S. population is of European ancestry; about one-fourth is of African, Asian, Latin American, or Native American ancestry. Although many of these groups entered American society voluntarily through immigration, some did not (Blauner, 1972). Africans were brought here as slaves, and the Mexican-American group was created by the conquest of a large area of northern Mexico (now California, Texas, Nevada, Colorado, New Mexico, and Arizona). Puerto Rico became a U.S. colony after the Spanish-American War of 1898, and the entire United States was Indian territory before the arrival of the Europeans. Because we have such great racial and ethnic diversity, and because a number of groups became "American" involuntarily, the United States has experienced greater racial and ethnic inequality and conflict than many other countries.

Minority Groups

African Americans The largest American racial and ethnic group that fits the definition of a minority is clearly Black (African) Americans. In 1987, there were 29.6 million Black Americans, or 12.2 percent of the U.S. population. The history of African Americans has been a history of exploitation, social inequality, and discrimination. Roughly speaking, it may be divided into three periods: slavery, segregation, and the modern era (Wilson, 1978, 1973).

SLAVERY The first period, slavery, dated from the arrival of blacks in 1619 until the end of the Civil War in 1865. During this period, most black Americans lived in the South and were slaves, although there were some free blacks, mainly in the North. Slavery was first and foremost a creation of the wealthy, landowning elite of the South, which sought a cheap and reliable source of labor to maximize profits in a highly labor-intensive plantation system. As Noel (1968), Boskin (1965), and Jordan (1968) have pointed out, blacks did not become slaves simply because the British colonists in America were prejudiced against them. Rather, Africans were one of many groups against whom the colonists were prejudiced, and antiblack prejudices became much stronger *after* slavery became institutionalized (Noel, 1972; Cox, 1948). Black slavery was a product of economic motivations and of the fact that blacks were in a weaker position to resist it than were other groups (Noel, 1968). The role of the economic interests and the power advantage of the southern ''planter class'' can be clearly seen by looking at what happened in the North. Slavery was, for a time, legal there too — but it never became widespread because no economic elite depended upon it for their wealth. Between 1780 and 1804, the northern states that had once allowed slavery outlawed it, but it took the Civil War to get rid of slavery in the South. This is a rather clear example of the conflict theorists' argument that social inequality occurs because it benefits a wealthy and powerful group.

SEGREGATION The second period in African-American history is often referred to as *segregation* because that was the dominant reality experienced by Black Americans during this period. Segregation is generally seen as lasting from shortly after the Civil War until the period following World War II, although it was the dominant pattern in the North even before the Civil War. Under segregation, forced separation of the races and social isolation of Black Americans was the rule. Segregation existed in both the North and the

South, although it broke down somewhat sooner in the North and was stricter and more formal in the South. Segregation meant separation of the races in everything from bathrooms, bus and theater seats, lunch counters, and waiting rooms to — in some places — fishing lakes and public baseball diamonds. By law, black and white children attended separate schools in many states, and housing segregation was enforced by federal policy and by deed covenants forbidding the sale of property to blacks (and in many cases, Jews, Asians, Hispanics, and other ''unwanted'' groups). The races actually became more separated from one another in the South after the end of slavery. Though the master-slave relationship disappeared with the Thirteenth Amendment, whites sought to preserve the role of a master race by excluding blacks entirely from their social and economic world.

THE MODERN ERA For a variety of reasons that are detailed in Chapter 19, a powerful black civil rights movement emerged in the 1950s and grew in the 1960s. Through legal action and civil rights demonstrations — often including nonviolent civil disobedience — African Americans attacked the system of segregation and eventually succeeded in making nondiscrimination the law of the land. In these actions, they had the support of a significant portion of the white population, and whites as well as blacks participated in the lawsuits, marches, sit-ins, and ''Freedom Rides.''

Despite the success of the civil rights movement in outlawing open and deliberate racial discrimination, Black Americans have not come even close to attaining social and economic equality in the United States (Farley and Allen, 1987). Open and deliberate discrimination has been replaced by subtler forms of institutional discrimination that perpetuate the old inequalities (Feagin and Feagin, 1978; Farley, 1988). In addition, many of the manufacturing industries that employed blacks in the 1950s and 1960s have cut back, closed down, or moved out (Wilson, 1987; Farley 1987b; Waquant and Wilson, 1989). As a result, the civil rights movement did not improve the day-to-day lives of Black Americans in the ways that many of them had expected.

Although the racial gap in incomes of *employed* workers has narrowed (but black workers still get only about three-fourths the wages of white workers), high black unemployment and differences in family structure have held black family incomes down to the point where there has been virtually no gain relative to whites (U.S. Bureau of the Census, 1987a, 1985; R. Farley, 1984; Bianchi, 1981). In the 1940s, median black family income was about half that of whites; by 1986, it had only reached 58 percent (U.S. Bureau of the Census, 1987a, p. 3). The black unemployment rate has been between two and two-and-one-half times the white unemployment rate ever since World War II, and the poverty rate of blacks has consistently been about three times that of whites.

Significantly, poor blacks have become poorer relative to the rest of the population and more isolated in urban ghettos during the 1980s (Wilson, 1987; Waquant and Wilson, 1989). As their poverty has worsened, federal programs to help them have been cut. Although the educational gap between blacks and whites has narrowed somewhat, whites remain twice as likely as blacks to obtain a college degree, and about one black youth in five fails to get a high school diploma by his or her early twenties (U.S. Department of Education, 1987b; Crews and Cancellier, 1988). Black college enrollment actually fell between the late 1970s and the mid-1980s, especially among males (*St. Louis Post-Dispatch,* 1989). Although housing discrimination is now illegal, the laws are not well enforced, and blacks and whites live almost as separately today as they did 30 years ago (Jakubs, 1986; Farley, 1987c; Massey and Denton, 1987, 1988; Denton and Massey, 1988; for a discussion of various aspects of this problem, see Tobin, 1987; and Momeni, 1986). Black people are more likely than whites to lack health insurance and to receive inadequate medical care, and they are at greater risk of malnutrition, infant mortality, on-the-job injury, and criminal victimization. For these reasons, the average black life expectancy is 5 to 6 years less than the average white life expectancy.

Hispanic Americans The rapidly growing segment of the American population known as Hispanics or Latinos is actually made up of several distinct groups that share Latin-American or Spanish ancestry. By 1988, the Hispanic population of the United States had reached 19.4 million, or 8.1 percent of the total U.S. population (U.S. Bureau of the Census, 1988f). This represented an increase of over 4 million just

since 1980. Of this total, 12.1 million, or nearly two-thirds, are Mexican Americans (see Figure 11.1). Other large groups are Puerto Ricans, Cubans, and Central and South Americans. Mexican Americans, or Chicanos, live mostly in the Southwest, though there are sizable numbers in the Midwest. Once primarily rural, Mexican Americans today, like other Hispanic groups and blacks, are heavily urban and live disproportionately in large central cities. Puerto Ricans are concentrated in the Northeast, especially in and around New York City, and Cuban Americans are concentrated in Florida. Because of their rapid growth rate, it is likely that sometime in the next century — and possibly within the next 50 years — the Hispanic population will surpass the black population, making Hispanics the nation's largest minority group. The Hispanic population is growing rapidly both because of a high birth rate and because of continuing high rates of immigration into the United States.

MEXICAN AMERICANS As noted above, both Mexican Americans and Puerto Ricans came under American rule through military conquest. As a result, both groups have experienced severe discrimination and disproportionate poverty. Chicanos were subjected to segregation and job discrimination much like

FIGURE 11-1
Nationality Composition of the U.S. Hispanic Population, 1988
SOURCE: U.S. Bureau of the Census, 1988f, p. 2.

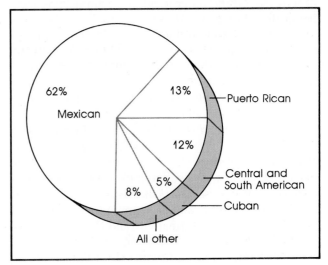

that experienced by blacks, and in many areas, non-Hispanic whites (often called Anglos) still look upon them primarily as a source of cheap labor. When northern Mexico was made a part of the United States by the treaty ending the Mexican-American War, many Mexicans in the territory were ranchers who owned large tracts of land. A protocol accompanying the treaty guaranteed that Mexican landowners would keep their land, but most lost it anyway. (Mirande, 1987). Afterward, many formerly wealthy ranchers were reduced to impoverished farmhands, working in one of the very few occupations to which U.S. federal law has never given the right to union representation and to which it has only recently extended minimum-wage protection. In some states, laws required school segregation for Mexican-American children, just as they did for blacks. White workers often saw Chicanos as a threat to their jobs, and they campaigned to stop immigration from Mexico and sometimes rioted against Chicanos. The worst instance of anti-Chicano rioting occurred in Los Angeles in 1943 and continued for about a week (McWilliams, 1949).

PUERTO RICANS AND CUBAN AMERICANS In the Northeast, some Puerto Ricans have experienced double discrimination. Because of their substantial African ancestry, they have been discriminated against not only as Hispanics but also as blacks. In general, Puerto Ricans are the poorest and most segregated of the various Hispanic groups. Their median income is less than half that of non-Hispanic whites. Cuban Americans, on the other hand, have fared somewhat better than either Chicanos or Puerto Ricans because many of them were affluent and educated refugees from Fidel Castro's communist revolution. Those who came in the Mariel boatlift of the 1970s are distinctly poorer.

Like Black Americans, many Hispanic Americans expected the civil rights movement to make substantial improvements in their lives. However, the same factors that have kept blacks disadvantaged have also worked against Hispanics. Even more so than blacks, Hispanics have suffered from a lack of educational opportunities. Half of all Hispanic adults lack a high school diploma, and even among people in their early twenties, who normally would benefit from recent advancements in education, one out of every three Hispanics lacks a diploma (U.S. Bureau of the Census, 1988f; U.S. Department of Education, 1987). Hispanics formerly were more likely to find good-paying jobs in heavy industry than anywhere else, but they lost many opportunities when those industries fled the central cities. Consequently, the unemployment rate of Hispanics is more than 50 percent above that of non-Hispanic whites. Their poverty rate has also risen steadily over the past decade; it is now two and one-half times that of white Anglos. In 1987, the typical Hispanic family's income was less than two-thirds that of the typical white Anglo family (U.S. Bureau of the Census, 1988f, p. 3).

American Indians When most Americans think of genocide, the first thing that comes to their minds is the extermination by the Nazis of millions of Jews during World War II. The fact is, though, that the United States has an equally clear case of genocide in its own history. Although we have no way of knowing for certain how many Indians were present when the first Europeans arrived in North America, most experts estimate a million or more (Collier, 1947; Josephy, 1968; Garbarino, 1976; Spicer, 1980a). By 1900, actions by white people had reduced that population to about 240,000 (Spicer, 1980a, p. 59). A number of Indian tribes were completely wiped out, and others lost up to 90 percent of their population. How and why did this happen? Many Indians died in wars with the whites, and many others were murdered. Many Indians died of European diseases to which they had no immunity. (In some cases, whites deliberately exposed them to such diseases.) In the early- to mid-1700s, colonial governments sometimes offered bounties for Indian scalps, including those of women and children. In a number of instances, whites who were victorious in battles with Indians killed them rather than taking them prisoner. Thousands of other Indian people died as a result of forced moves, such as the "Trail of Tears" between Georgia and Oklahoma.

The major reason for these attacks against Indian people was whites' desire for their land. As long as only limited numbers of whites were present in any given area, they usually coexisted peacefully with the Indians. However, when larger influxes of whites increased the demand for land, Indians were repeatedly attacked and pushed aside. Treaties were made specifying certain areas as "Indian territory," but whenever

"Trail of Tears," by Robert Lindneux. Thousands of Indian people died in this 1,000-mile forced march and in others like it.

farmland was in short supply or precious metals were discovered on those lands, the whites violated the treaties (Lurie, 1985; Spicer, 1980b). In 1871, Congress abolished the concept of treaties altogether. Official U.S. practice became one of placing Indian reservations on remote tracts of undesirable land that bore little ecological resemblance to the Indians' original homeland. As a result, farming, fishing, hunting, or gathering methods that worked in the original homeland often became useless.

FORCED ASSIMILATION   Once on the reservations, the surviving Indians were subjected to forced assimilation, particularly in the later nineteenth century. The idea was to remake the Indians in the image of white Americans. Their children were taken from them and placed in boarding schools, where they were forbidden to speak their native languages. A policy known as *allotment* was established in 1887 with the intent of giving each Indian a plot of land to become a small farmer, "just like the American family farmer." Although this policy may have been well intended, it was a miserable failure for several reasons. First, it was applied without regard to whether a tribe had a history and knowledge of agriculture, which many did not.

Second, it was based on white concepts of land ownership, which were different from Indian concepts of commonly owned land. Third, it was contrary to long-held patterns of sex roles in some tribes, which specified cultivation by women and hunting or warrior roles for men. Finally, whites widely encouraged Indian landowners who used the program to become indebted, then took their land for payment when they could not pay the debts. The result of this misguided attempt at assimilation was that Indians lost about two-thirds of their land (Lurie, 1985; Guillemin, 1978; Spicer, 1980b, p 117).

THE SITUATION TODAY   In general, the Indians showed remarkable tenacity in resisting attempts at assimilation, and many today continue to speak their native languages and to maintain their tribal traditions. Over the past century, the Indian population has recovered to the point that the 1980 Census counted 1.4 million Indians (U.S. Bureau of the Census, 1981). There are today about 200 different Indian tribes or nations, each with its own traditions and distinct social and economic history. Thus, even more so than Hispanic Americans, Indians are not one group but many. Although certain generalizations hold for most Indians (the nature of their experience with whites, for example), many aspects of culture and social structure vary widely from one Indian tribe or nation to another.

Indians remain the least urbanized of any major American racial or ethnic group, with just over half living in urban areas. Most rural Indians live on or near reservations. As of 1980, more than one American Indian out of four lived below the federal poverty level —about three times the white poverty rate for that year. On reservations, where Indian poverty is most intense, about half of the population lives below the poverty level. The 1980 unemployment rate for Indians was 13.2 percent, and on reservations it was higher yet.

Despite these difficulties, Indians have won some significant legal victories in recent years. Over the past decade, the courts have begun to take seriously the provisions of treaties that were negotiated long ago and then broken. Some tribes have been awarded monetary damages in the millions of dollars, and several states have been compelled to recognize Indian hunting and fishing rights guaranteed by treaties. Also, there has been growing recognition by non-

Indian Americans of the wrongs that have been done to Indian people. Undoubtedly, public awareness of the plight of American Indians was heightened by a series of militant Indian protests during the 1970s, including takeovers of closed federal institutions at Alcatraz Island in San Francisco Bay and Fort Lawton in Washington State that were based on an 1868 treaty stating that surplus federal property could be claimed by the Sioux. Perhaps the best-known incidents were a 1972 sit-in at the Bureau of Indian Affairs in Washington, D.C., and the 1973 occupation of Wounded Knee, South Dakota, which led to a confrontation with federal authorities and two fatalities.

One indicator of change in American thinking about Indian people is the fact that more Americans of mixed ancestry have come to identify with Indians as their racial or ethnic group. The number of people reporting their race as American Indian nearly doubled between the 1970 and 1980 Censuses. Not all of this change reflected real population growth; some of it occurred because people were more willing to identify themselves as Indians. On another Census question, over 6.7 million Americans listed American Indian as one of their two primary ancestry groups (U.S. Bureau of the Census, 1983).

Intermediate Status Groups

Although Black Americans, Hispanic Americans, and American Indians most clearly fit the sociological definition of a minority group, there are a number of other American racial and ethnic groups that occupy an intermediate status between a minority group and a majority group. Most of these groups can be gathered together under two broad groupings—Asian Americans and "white ethnics" from Eastern and Southern Europe. Jewish Americans are also an example of a group with an intermediate status.

Asian Americans The most rapidly growing segment of the American population since about 1970 has been Asian Americans. The Asian-American population increased from 1.4 million in 1970 to between 5 and 6 million, or a little over 2 percent of the population, in 1987. This rapid growth has taken place because of high rates of immigration and, to a lesser extent, relatively high birth rates. Like Hispanic

Americans, Asian Americans are not one group but several, each with its own distinct history, social structure, culture, and (unlike Hispanics) language. The six largest Asian-American groups are shown in Table 11.2. Asian Americans are concentrated very heavily on the West Coast and in Hawaii, although there are also significant numbers in a few large eastern and midwestern cities such as New York, Boston, Washington, and Chicago.

HISTORY OF ASIAN AMERICANS Unlike the groups discussed in the preceding section, most Asian Americans came to the United States voluntarily, which has given them advantages in American society that other minority groups have not enjoyed. At the same time, however, they have experienced considerable prejudice and discrimination. Like Mexican Americans, Asian Americans were valued in the nineteenth century primarily as a source of cheap labor. Chinese and Japanese were encouraged for a time to immigrate to the United States to meet labor needs in the railroad and mining industries. Before long, however, they were seen by white laborers as a threat to jobs and wages, and they became the victims of riots and lynchings. Whites resented the fact that Asians, who were often in debt for passage to the United States, were sometimes willing to work for less than whites, and vicious anti-Asian stereotypes and prejudices replaced earlier, more positive, stereotypes.

By the early twentieth century, anti-Asian racism had been written into law, as first Chinese and then Japanese were forbidden to immigrate to the United States. In 1924, the government adopted a quota system that forbade all Asian immigration, except by Filipinos, who were treated as Americans because the Philippine Islands at that time were an American territory. However, when the Philippines became inde-

TABLE 11.2
1980 Population of Asian-American Groups

Chinese Americans	806,040
Filipino Americans	774,652
Japanese Americans	700,974
Asian Indians	361,531
Korean Americans	354,593
Vietnamese Americans	261,729

SOURCE: U.S. Bureau of the Census, 1983b, p. 20.

pendent after World War II, Filipinos were also subjected to the quotas, which effectively banned Asian immigration until the mid-1960s.

INTERNMENT   One of the ugliest incidents of governmental racial discrimination in U.S. history occurred during World War II when 110,000 Japanese Americans were rounded up and put in prison camps after the government decided that they constituted a security threat because the United States was at war with Japan. They remained there for more than 2 years, even though very many of them were American citizens and there was no evidence that they had done anything to undermine the U.S. war effort. As a result of this imprisonment, many of them lost their jobs and all that they owned. The role that race played in this process can be seen by the fact that there was no such imprisonment of German Americans, even though the United States was at war with Germany at the same time. (For a viewpoint on the Japanese-American experience that is at once personal and sociological, see Harry H. L. Kitano's Personal Journey into Sociology.)

THE RECENT YEARS   Despite these very real and serious cases of abuse and discrimination, Asian Americans never experienced, on a prolonged basis, the isolation and powerlessness endured by black slaves or reservation Indians. Moreover, as noted, they entered American society voluntarily and thus have not been treated as a conquered people. Finally, since Asian immigration reopened in the 1960s, immigration laws have favored people trained in occupations in which labor shortages exist, including scientific, technical, and medical occupations. As a result, most Asian immigrants in recent decades, with the important exception of Vietnamese refugees, have been relatively well educated.

For all these reasons, as well as the high value most Asian cultures place on education, work, and achievement, Asian Americans have fared relatively well compared to other minority groups in recent years. Their educational attainment is the highest of any racial or ethnic group in American society, including whites. A large share of Asian Americans work in professional occupations and enjoy comfortable incomes. Nonetheless, there is also significant poverty among Asian-American groups, particularly the Vietnamese. Moreover, even middle-class Asian Americans still encounter prejudice and discrimination:

middle-class status is no guarantee of universal social acceptance. Where Asian-Americans are seen as competition by whites, prejudices still run strong. The Ku Klux Klan, for example, attacked Vietnamese shrimp-boat operators along the Texas coast in the early 1980s. Also in the 1980s, concerns arose in California as to whether "too many" Asians were attending top universities such as the University of California at Berkeley.

Jewish Americans   People of the Jewish faith have been present in the United States since 1654. Although there has been some immigration of Jews to the United States continuously for over 300 years, the major periods of immigration were from around 1880 until immigration quotas were imposed in 1924, and again around World War II (Goren, 1980). In the latter period, far more European Jews could have escaped Nazi genocide had the immigration quota been lifted. Before the Civil War, most Jewish immigrants came from Germany and Spain, but in the subsequent large-scale immigration, most came from Eastern Europe, with the largest numbers arriving from Poland and Russia, and from Germany around World War II.

Japanese Americans being processed in Salinas, California, for internment in prison camps, 1942. Why is it that, although we were at war with both Germany and Japan, Japanese Americans were imprisoned and German Americans were not?

Race, Ethnicity, and the Sociological perspective

I grew up in San Francisco, surrounded by a variety of different ethnic groups. My parents were from Japan, but I lived in Chinatown, which was also close to the Italian section. So I had acquaintances from a rich variety of backgrounds. Names that I can remember from early school days were Padilla, Derrivan, Wong, Francesconi, and Lee. I remember how we jeered a new student from France named Donat—he came to school in a shirt, tie, and knickers and therefore warranted the name of "frog." We practiced prejudice and discrimination, but we were totally unfamiliar with these terms.

Being Japanese in the middle of Chinatown certainly made for differences. There was an elementary school right across the street from where I lived, but it was for "Chinese students" only. I therefore had to walk to a school several blocks away. But although I had many contacts with children from a variety of backgrounds, my close friends were of Japanese ancestry. There were about a dozen Japanese families living in the area; birthday parties, family gatherings, and the like were with my own

Harry H. L. Kitano
Harry H. L. Kitano is Professor of Social Welfare and Sociology and Acting Director of the Asian American Study Center at UCLA. He was formerly a Visiting Professor of Sociology at the International Christian University in Tokyo. Professor Kitano was voted "Nisei of the Biennium" by the Japanese American Citizen's League in 1982.

ethnic group. Later, as I grew up, I joined a Boy Scout troop composed of Japanese Americans that was located in the Japanese section of San Francisco, a reasonable distance from my home. Concepts such as plural-

ism, acculturation, and integration had little meaning, although my behaviors were surely actual experiences of these terms.

The first time that I remember hearing the term *sociology* was in a World War II concentration camp for people of Japanese ancestry. It should be recalled that after the Japanese attack on Pearl Harbor in 1941, all people of Japanese ancestry residing along the West Coast, whether citizens or not, were sent to "relocation camps" scattered throughout the United States. I was a high-school student at the time, and during one of our endless discussions concerning our internment, I remember one fellow saying that a "sociological perspective" would give us insight into why we were imprisoned in such camps. My guess is that none of us knew what that meant, but, as was typical of many of our discussions, we all nodded wisely and agreed.

By that time I was dimly aware of terms such as *prejudice, discrimination,* and *racism,* but my main concern was to "gripe" about a system that put us into the camps. We blamed the Hearst press, greedy farmers, and "bad" politicians, as

The Jewish experience in the United States has been indelibly shaped by centuries of persecution in Europe. The Nazi Holocaust was only the most recent and violent of a series of systematic attacks that date back for about 1,000 years. In the thirteenth, fourteenth, and fifteenth centuries, Jews were expelled from England, France, and Spain (Goren, 1980). Many Christians viewed Jews as "Christ-killers," a view that only began to fade in the past century or so.

The exclusion of European Jews from most of the desirable jobs forced many of them to work at occupations other groups didn't want, such as tax and bill collection and lending, which only had the effect of further increasing resentment against them. Unfortunately, many of these prejudices carried over into the United States. As the Jewish population grew in the early twentieth century, colleges and universities imposed quotas limiting Jewish enrollment. Entire comwell as our parents, some members of our own ethnic community, the Japanese military, and even ourselves for our plight. We heard that university anthropologists, psychologists, and sociologists were studying the camps. Again, I didn't know what that meant, and only years later when monographs about the internment were published did I understand that these were "scientific studies" about us.

I was released with government clearance and relocated to the Midwest. Here I encountered racial and religious prejudice that differed from the West Coast variety where the Japanese were the main targets. I became a jazz musician and replaced a black musician in an all-white orchestra. At that time I must have thought that I was a better musician, but upon reflection, it is clear that the black player (who was one of the best musicians at his instrument and later gained fame with orchestras such as Duke Ellington's) was far superior, but that his color was less acceptable than mine. I was also surprised to hear violent discussions among my fellow musicians concerning anti-Semitism; one constant topic was to question the religion of Harry James, a famous trumpet player and band leader of the Big Band era. One young trumpet player argued that if Harry James was Jewish, then he would not serve as a role model, while there were constant jokes about Jews, Negroes (as they were politely referred to at that time), and Indians. I was sure that when I was not there, there would also be pointed jibes concerning Orientals (as we were known at that time).

These and other background experiences shaped my interest in questions of race and ethnicity. Although my initial training was in psychology, I found that psychological variables were limited in terms of understanding questions of racial stratification. I remember one argument that split the Japanese-American students while I was at the University of California in Berkeley. Evidently there was a house for Japanese-American students at that campus prior to the wartime evacuation; the house was to reopen, and the question was whether to retain it for the ethnic group or to provide a more open-door policy without ethnic restrictions. I tried to make some sense out of this dilemma through understanding some of the personalities that were involved, but it did not make any sense. However, if the question were framed in terms of an assimilation versus a pluralistic model, then the issue became clearer.

The most important influence on my concentration on ethnic groups, especially the Japanese and other Asian Americans, was a historian, Roger Daniels, who was also studying Asian-American groups, but through a historical perspective. We collaborated on a number of publications, starting with a book titled *American Racism,* then coediting (with Sandra Taylor) *Japanese Americans: From Relocation to Redress,* to *Asian Americans: Evolving Minorities.* My own writings attempt to cover issues of race and ethnicity through an "insider's" perspective; that is, I try to emphasize the experiences of an individual who has gone through many of the events that I write about. I believe that studying in areas where your own life experiences are involved can make for a meaningful career.

munities banned Jewish residents, and restrictive deed covenants forbade the sale of houses to Jews. Many hotels and other businesses were "restricted" —in other words, Jews and various other racial and ethnic groups were banned. Forms of discrimination against Jews that were once widespread were made illegal by the civil rights laws of the 1960s.

JEWS AND ASIAN AMERICANS The status of Jewish Americans today resembles that of Asian Americans in many ways. Educational levels among Jewish Americans are above the national average, and a high proportion of Jewish workers are in professional and managerial positions. Yet, like Asian Americans, Jewish Americans continue to encounter a good deal of prejudice and discrimination, and neither group has a major presence in the top echelons of American corporate or political life. Today there are about 6 million Jewish Americans, representing about 40 percent of

A sign that the status of white ethnics may be changing is the nomination of Michael Dukakis, a Greek American, for the president by the Democratic Party in 1988. Also significant is the fact that his closest competitor was the Reverend Jesse Jackson, an African American.

the world's Jewish population (Goren, 1980). The population growth rate of Jewish Americans is lower than that of the white population as a whole. Jewish Americans are one of the most urban ethnic groups, with over 95 percent living in cities or suburbs.

"White Ethnics"   The term *white ethnics* has been applied to a wide variety of groups from Eastern and Southern Europe, including Italian, Polish, Czech, Hungarian, Greek, and Ukrainian Americans. Besides their geographic origin, two other important features distinguish these groups from the rest of the white population. First, they are more recent immigrants. Most of them came between the late nineteenth century and the imposition of immigration quotas in 1924. Northern and Western European immigrants, in contrast, came a good deal earlier. Second, unlike earlier immigrants, almost none of the "white ethnics" was Protestant, the dominant religious group in the United States.

These differences had several significant impacts. First, because the earlier immigrants already held most of the desirable jobs, more recent immigrants had to "work their way up" from less desirable positions. Second, the newer immigrants were subjected to considerable prejudice and discrimination because they were seen as a threat both to the jobs of those already here and to the rural Protestant culture that predominated at the time of their arrival. In the mind of the "established" Americans of their time, they were associated with "rum, Romanism, and rebellion."

Most of the Eastern and Southern European groups settled in the Northeast and the industrial cities of the Great Lakes region. The booming growth of American industry in the first half of the twentieth century opened up opportunities despite widespread discrimination. Thus, the history of white ethnics in America has generally been one of upward mobility. Today the socioeconomic status of Americans of Eastern and Southern European descent is quite similar to that of Americans descended from "older" immigrant groups from Western and Northern Europe, with one important exception: White ethnics have not yet moved into the upper echelons of government or business. An important sign that this may be changing was the nomination in 1988 of a Greek American, Michael Dukakis, as the Democratic candidate for president. Because their healthy position in the American economy is newer and less secure than that of other groups, white ethnics have frequently perceived efforts to create opportunities for blacks and Hispanics as a threat.

The Majority Group

In the United States, the most advantaged societal position has always been occupied by whites from Northern and Western Europe. These groups include Americans of British, German, Irish, Scandinavian, French, and Dutch ancestry. They are predominantly Protestant, except for the Irish and French, most of whom are Catholic. Although virtually all of these groups except the British met with at least some prejudice and discrimination, it was less intense than that encountered by more recent immigrants, with the exception of Irish Catholics. Even they, however, are no longer the object of significant prejudice or discrimination, and they are thoroughly integrated into the population and culture of the United States. Northern and Western European groups have intermixed and intermarried so much that today most of them are of mixed ancestry and no longer identify exclusively with any one country of origin (U.S. Bureau of the Census, 1983, pp. 12–14).

Also contributing to the advantages enjoyed by these groups is the fact that, taken together, they are easily the majority of the American population. Just three groups—the English, Germans, and Irish—account for at least one-third, and possibly one-half, of the American population (Farley, 1988, p. 207). Significantly, however, there is very little growth in this population because of a low birth rate and because few people today immigrate from that part of the world. Thus, in the future, the numerically dominant position of these groups in American society will fade. Though once predominantly rural, these groups today overwhelmingly live in the suburbs and outer fringes of medium-to-large American cities, though they also constitute a large segment of America's shrinking farm population. Their children typically enjoy the benefits of suburbia, including the best public schools and, in some cases, private education. Besides enjoying high educational levels and desirable managerial and professional occupations, the majority group to a large extent controls the politics and business of the United States. Most corporate executives are males of Western and Northern European ancestry, as has been every president of the United States from George Washington to George Bush.

Current Issues in U.S. Race Relations

We shall conclude this chapter by examining two current issues concerning U.S. race and ethnic relations. The first is the growing debate over the relative importance of race versus class as causes of the disadvan-taged position of many African and Hispanic Americans. The second is the appropriateness of affirmative action as a means of improving opportunities for minority group members.

The Significance of Race versus Class

In 1978, William Julius Wilson published one of the most influential and controversial sociology books written in recent years, *The Declining Significance of Race*. In 1987, he elaborated on his ideas in another book, *The Truly Disadvantaged*. Wilson argued that current racial discrimination has become relatively unimportant as a cause of the disadvantages experienced by many blacks (and Hispanics). Rather, these groups are disadvantaged by their disproportionate presence in the **underclass,** a chronically impoverished group whose position has been worsened by recent changes in the American economy. So many blacks and Hispanics are part of this underclass largely because of disadvantages resulting from *past* racial discrimination. However, Wilson argues, their continued presence in this class results not so much from racial discrimination as from aspects of the American economy that make it hard for members of this class to escape.

Changes in the Job Market One of the key reasons that escape from the underclass is so difficult today is the fact that good-paying jobs that do not require an advanced education are disappearing from the American economy, especially from the inner cities of the Midwest and Northeast where blacks are most concentrated (Wilson, 1987, p. 148). At one time, heavy industry provided many such jobs and was an important source of mobility, first for immigrant groups, and more recently for blacks and Hispanics. However, in the 1970s, American industry began to lose jobs, and thus a promising opportunity for blacks and Hispanics with limited education was lost (Kasarda, 1989).

Such processes first create an underclass and then work to sustain it. As unemployment in the ghettoes and barrios rises, so does street crime, and many young males are arrested and imprisoned. Many more, of course, are not, but are unemployed. Wilson (1987, pp. 83–92) points out that this situation raises the incidence of separation and divorce and reduces the pool of appropriate marriage partners in the black community (see also Anderson, 1987; Schoen and Kluegel, 1988). This pattern has become much more pronounced over the past 20 years, and as a result, black women have far less opportunity to get married than white women. Moreover, because over 90 percent of unmarried adult women of either race are sexually active, many black children are born outside of marriage. This, of course, produces more female-householder black families, which have a very high risk of poverty for the reasons discussed in Chapter 6.

Finally, Wilson (1987, pp. 46–62) points out that black and Hispanic poor people are much more likely to live in neighborhoods with large concentrations of poor people than are poor whites. Thus, they are less exposed to successful role models and more prone to see illegal activities as their only hope for upward mobility.

For all these reasons, Wilson sees the growing disadvantage of poor blacks and Hispanics as a product of the lack of stable, good-paying job opportunities. He argues that we must create large numbers of decent-paying jobs and provide the support poor people need to get and keep such jobs. He also sees a need for job training and for providing day care and medical insurance to employed low-income workers.

Although Wilson has made a major contribution to our understanding of the forces that have perpetuated and worsened the conditions of poor blacks and Hispanics, there are reasons to question his claim that race is declining in significance (Willie, 1979; Hill, 1978). One is the concentration of the black and Hispanic poor, noted by Wilson, which is partly the result of racial housing segregation. As we saw, blacks and Hispanics are concentrated precisely where jobs are disappearing most rapidly, which means that jobs are growing most rapidly in places that are mainly white (Duster, 1988; Thompson, 1976). Blacks and Hispanics cannot readily move to many of these areas because of *racial* housing segregation and discrimination. This tends to elevate the black and Hispanic unemployment rates (Farley, 1987; Lichter, 1988; Kasarda, 1989). In short, both housing segregation and the movement of jobs from black and Hispanic areas into white areas are examples of *current institu-*

tional racism, a concept that Wilson does not bring into his theories.

Another concept that Wilson does not address is that of institutional discrimination in education. He notes, correctly, that lack of education is a key problem for the minority underclass, but he does not address the reasons for that lack of education, which, as we saw earlier in this chapter, are at least partly racial.

The Affirmative Action Debate

Racial inequality has persisted in the United States even though deliberate racial discrimination has been illegal for more than 20 years. This fact has convinced many Americans that steps beyond mere nondiscrimination are necessary to undo the effects of centuries of racial discrimination. One such step is affirmative action. In general, **affirmative action** refers to any special effort by an employer to increase the number of minority or female employees or to upgrade their positions, or by a college to increase the number of minority or female students. Affirmative action can include efforts to recruit more minority or female applicants, or it could involve hiring or admission preferences for underrepresented minorities or women.

Affirmative action efforts in student admissions have been particularly vigorous in law and medical schools. Often affirmative action involves the use of *goals and timetables;* for example, "By 1996 we will try to have 12 percent blacks and 8 percent Hispanics among our supervisory staff." Contrary to popular conception, however, affirmative action goals are *not* usually firm quotas, and affirmative action does *not* mean hiring, promoting, or admitting unqualified applicants to meet the goal. In fact, such goals are missed more often than they are met.

In 1965, the Johnson administration issued an executive order to government contractors requiring them to take "affirmative action" to make sure that they were not discriminating against women and minorities. From that time until the early 1980s, companies and universities having contracts with the federal government were required to establish goals and timetables. The Reagan administration, however, opposed any use of racial or sexual preferences and backed off

What Makes a Fair Footrace?

Imagine two runners in a 20-mile race. One of the runners must start with a 10-pound weight on each of her feet. As a result, she cannot run as fast, tires more quickly, and falls far behind. Almost anyone would agree that this is not a fair race. So, halfway through the race, the judges decide that she can take off the weights. Is this enough to make the race fair? Does she have any realistic chance to win from her present position? Would it not be fairer to allow her to move ahead to the position of the other runner to compensate for the disadvantage of wearing the weights for the first half of the race?

This analogy had been used to illustrate the reasoning behind affirmative action (Farley, 1988, pp. 265, 336). The runner represents a minority or female individual seeking a good job or entry into graduate or professional school. The weights represent the effects of both past discrimination and the institutional discrimination she encountered in her elementary and secondary education. Examples of such discrimination, which may or may not be intentional, include low teacher expectations, tracking, biased tests and classroom materials, lack of minority and female role models, and underfunded and segregated schools. Just as the runner is disadvantaged by the weights, the minority applicant is disadvantaged by poverty and institutional discrimination. Just as the other runner was not encumbered by weights in the first half of the race, the white male applicant was not burdened by these disadvantages in early life. Most people would agree that it would not be fair to expect the runner to catch up after having to run half the race with weights. Could the same argument be made in the case of the minority or female applicant who often has to run the first half of the "race" of life with the "weights" of poverty and educational disadvantage? Is it fair, when that minority person applies for college or employment, to say "Now the weights are gone, so it's a fair race?"

considerably on enforcement of affirmative action (for a history of affirmative action, see Weiss, 1985).

Reverse Discrimination? Affirmative action is controversial because many whites (especially white males) see it as reverse discrimination. Is a preference in hiring, promotion, or admission for minorities or women unfair to a white male who may have better qualifications? In some law and medical schools, white males with higher grade averages or admissions test scores have been turned down in favor of minorities with lower scores (Sindler, 1978). Because these white males are often not themselves guilty of discrimination, they are being made to pay unfairly for someone else's discrimination. Furthermore, it is argued, these policies hurt overall societal achievement by considering factors other than who is most qualified (Glazer, 1976).

The Only Remedy? Those who support affirmative action are equally strong in their belief that *not* to have affirmative action would be unfair to minorities and women. They argue that just getting rid of active discrimination is not enough to create truly equal opportunity, for two reasons. First is the lingering effects of past discrimination. Even those who see current black disadvantages as resulting from disproportionate poverty rather than from current discrimination acknowledge that this poverty itself is the effect of *past* discrimination (Wilson, 1978, 1987). Thus, people who are poor because of past discrimination find it harder to gain the qualifications necessary for admission or hiring. Second is the effect of current institutional discrimination, especially in elementary and secondary education. Factors such as segregation, low teacher expectations, tracking, and the use of biased tests prevent many minority students from learning and achieving on the same level as whites. In this context, to expect them to do so is unfair, and doing nothing to offset the effects of past and institutional discrimination perpetuates that discrimination. This point is illustrated in the box "What Makes a Fair Footrace?"

Some opponents of affirmative action say that reforming the schools so that they come closer to the ideal of creating equal opportunity is a better approach than affirmative action. In Chapter 14, some approaches to doing this, including desegregation of schools through busing, will be discussed. However, those who support affirmative action point out that school reform is a long-term effort that will not help the current generation of disadvantaged adults.

Supporters of affirmative action also contend that some of the tests used to assess people's qualifications contain racial or sexual biases. Moreover, these tests are not very accurate predictors of future success. Law school admission criteria, for example, typically explain only about 25 percent of the variation in first-year academic performance of law students (Sindler, 1978, pp. 115–116), and college admissions tests are only about half that accurate (Owen, 1985; Slack and Porter, 1980). Thus, determining who is "best qualified" is a haphazard process subject to great error.

Analysis Has affirmative action actually changed things to the point that minority group members and women enjoy an advantage over white males? Examination of income figures does *not* support this. Among young adults, white males continue to enjoy higher incomes than black and Hispanic males and women of any race, and black and Hispanic unemployment rates remain well above those of whites. Moreover, whites continue to graduate from college and enter medical, law, and graduate schools at double or more the rate of blacks and Hispanics. Women also remain underrepresented in law and medical schools, although their presence there has increased significantly. All these things suggest strongly that the effects of past and institutional discrimination outweigh any advantage affirmative action may bring to minorities or women. Even when we consider only those who complete college, minorities and women *still* do not appear to enjoy any overall advantage due to affirmative action. In 1980, young black male college graduates had greatly narrowed the income gap with white males, but they still earned 4 percent less. Among young college-educated women, blacks had a narrow lead over whites, but neither had anywhere near the income of white males (R. Farley, 1984).

Even so, it does appear that affirmative action has helped certain segments of the minority and female populations a good deal. A definite narrowing of the income gap between blacks and whites has occurred among people who do have jobs, particularly those with relatively high education levels. Law and medical schools are enrolling significantly more blacks, Hispanics, and women than they did before affirmative action, even though most of their students are still white males. Firms with government contracts, which are covered by federal affirmative action requirements, have nearly twice the percentage of minority employees as firms without government contracts (Pear, 1983).

Still, it is only the more educated segments of the minority and female populations that have truly benefited from affirmative action (Wilson, 1978). So far, affirmative action has done little for the chronically impoverished underclass, many of whom are lucky to get a high-school diploma. Affirmative action has probably contributed to a trend that was already under way in the black and Hispanic populations: The middle class is rising in status, while the situation of the poor is worsening (Wilson, 1978, 1987). This has produced increased social-class differences within the black and Hispanic populations. For this reason, Wilson (1978, 1987) has argued that to achieve racial equality we must implement policies to improve the situation of the chronically poor, which affirmative action does not do.

The Legal Status of Affirmative Action Between 1978 and 1987, the U.S. Supreme Court ruled on at least eight major cases concerning affirmative action. In all but one of these cases, the Court approved some form of preferences for underrepresented minorities or women. The one circumstance under which preferences were *not* approved was in the case of layoffs of present employees where there was no proof that the employer had previously discriminated against minorities. However, the Court approved the use of racial preferences (though not quotas) in public higher education in the 1978 *Bakke* case, and it approved hiring preferences for minorities and women in private industries in a series of cases such as *Weber* in 1979. In both public and private hiring decisions, the

Court has even approved the use of quotas under certain specified conditions. (More detailed discussion of the legal status of affirmative action can be found in Farley, 1988, pp. 340–343.)

In general, then, the U.S. Supreme Court until 1989 asserted that hiring and admissions preferences for underrepresented minorities and women were legal. The key was that they be *inclusionary* — their purpose must be to include the underrepresented or to make the student body or work force more diverse. It should be noted that many of these rulings were made by a five-vote majority of the Court — the bare minimum. The composition of the Court has changed since even the most recent of these rulings, and the Court has been known to reverse itself in the past. In 1989 the Court overturned the practice of setting aside a percentage of local government contracts for minority businesses (*Time,* 1989). Later that year, the court issued a series of decisions making it harder for minorities and women to prove discrimination and easier for white males to challenge affirmative action plans (Freivogel, 1989). Hence, it appears that in the 1990s, "affirmative action programs will be harder to justify" (Tribe, 1989).

Summary

Races are defined according to a combination of appearance and social criteria, whereas ethnic groups are defined on a purely social basis. Some of these groups occupy a dominant position in society and are called *majority groups,* while others occupy a subordinate position and are called *minority groups.* Racism takes a number of forms, including racist thought (racial prejudice) and racist behavior (racial discrimination). Ideological racism refers to the belief that one group is in some way naturally superior to another. The most subtle, but often the most important form of racism is institutional racism, which occurs when social institutions operate in ways that favor one group (usually the majority group) over another. This process is also called *institutional discrimination.*

Social psychologists emphasize prejudice in their studies of race and ethnic relations. For some people, prejudice meets personality needs that may date to childhood experiences, while other people are prejudiced largely out of conformity to the attitudes of significant others in their past or present social environment. The functionalist and conflict perspectives see prejudice and discrimination as arising from society rather than from the experiences of individuals. Functionalists view prejudice as largely the outgrowth of cultural diversity and ethnocentrism. They see assimilation as the solution because it eliminates the cultural differences that form the basis of prejudice and discrimination. Conflict theorists see racial inequality as an outgrowth of economic conflict, both within and between racial groups.

Much can be learned about the conditions that produce and alter patterns of racial and ethnic relations by examining other societies such as the Soviet Union, South Africa, Northern Ireland, and various Latin American countries. Each of these areas has its own set of social conditions that shape its pattern of intergroup relations.

The United States is one of the most diverse nations of the world in terms of race and ethnicity. The largest minority group in the United States is Black Americans, but the rapidly growing Hispanic-American population may soon catch up. Hispanic Americans are not really one group but several, of which Mexican Americans, or Chicanos, are the largest. Blacks, Chicanos, and Puerto Ricans, along with American Indians, have each in their own way endured conquest and internal colonization. As a result, they have experienced prejudice and discrimination far beyond that encountered by most American groups.

Groups that in some ways fit the minority group definition but in other ways do not include Asian Americans, Jewish Americans, and "white ethnics" from Eastern and Southern Europe. All have experienced discrimination, yet all are largely middle class today. The educational and professional achievement of Asian and Jewish Americans is particularly notable. Even so, most of America's political and economic elite continues to be drawn from the long-standing American majority group, whites from Northern and Western Europe.

In the United States, current sociological debates on race relations concern the relative importance of racial discrimination and social-class inequality, and the use of affirmative action as a means of bringing about racial equality.

Glossary

race A category of people who share some common physical characteristic and who are regarded by themselves and others as a distinct status group.

ethnic group A group of people who are recognized as a distinct group on the basis of cultural characteristics such as common ancestry or religion.

majority group A group of people who are in an advantaged social position relative to other groups, often having power to discriminate against those other groups.

minority group A group of people who are in a disadvantaged position relative to one or more groups in their society, and who are often the victims of discrimination.

racism Any attitude, belief, behavior, or institutional arrangement that has the intent or effect of favoring one race over another.

ideological racism The belief that one racial or ethnic group is inherently superior or inferior to another.

prejudice A categorical and unfounded attitude or belief concerning a group.

stereotype An exaggerated belief concerning a group of people that assumes that nearly everyone in the group possesses a certain characteristic.

discrimination Behavior that treats people unequally on the basis of an ascribed status such as race or sex.

individual discrimination Behavior by an individual that treats others unequally on the basis of an ascribed status such as race or sex.

institutional discrimination Behaviors or arrangements in social institutions that intentionally or unintentionally favor one race, sex, or ethnic group — usually the majority group — over another.

institutional racism Institutional discrimination on the basis of race.

personality need A psychological need for a particular attitude, belief, or behavior that arises from the particular personality type of an individual.

authoritarian personality A personality pattern believed by social psychologists to be associated with a psychological need to be prejudiced.

scapegoat A person or group against whom an individual displaces feelings of anger or frustration that cannot be expressed toward the true source of the individual's feelings.

projection A process by which a person denies or minimizes personal shortcomings by exaggerating the extent to which these same shortcomings occur in others.

social learning A process by which attitudes, beliefs, and behaviors are learned from significant others in a person's social environment or subculture.

cognitive-dissonance theory A social-psychological theory that claims that people often adjust their attitudes to make them consistent with their behavior in order to eliminate the stress that results when attitudes and behaviors are inconsistent.

symbolic racism A modern type of racial prejudice that does not express overtly prejudiced attitudes but does blame minority groups for any disadvantages they experience.

assimilation A process by which different ethnic or cultural groups in a society come to share a common culture and social structure.

forced assimilation A type of assimilation in which a minority group is required to adopt the culture of the majority group.

pluralism A process whereby different racial, ethnic, or cultural groups in a society retain some of their own cultural characteristics while sharing others with the larger society.

amalgamation A process whereby different racial or ethnic groups in a society gradually lose their identities and become one group as a result of intermarriage.

underclass Poor people who are chronically unemployed or underemployed and who lack the necessary skills to obtain stable, quality employment.

affirmative action Any effort designed to overcome past or institutional discrimination by increasing the number of minorities or females in schools, jobs, or job-training programs.

Further Reading

FARLEY, JOHN E. 1988. *Majority-Minority Relations*, 2nd ed. Englewood Cliffs, NJ: Prentice Hall. An introduction to the field of race and ethnic relations, written by the author of your textbook. Attention is given to the social-psychological and sociological perspectives on race and ethnic relations outlined in this chapter, as well as to the historical development of intergroup relations in the United States and the role of institutional discrimination today.

FEAGIN, JOE R., AND CLARECE BOOHER FEAGIN. 1978. *Discrimination American Style: Institutional Racism and Sexism.* Englewood Cliffs, NJ: Prentice Hall. An analysis and discussion of institutional discrimination as it exists in the post–civil rights era, focusing on both institutional racism and institutional sexism.

KITANO, HARRY H. L. 1985. *Race Relations,* 3rd. ed. Englewood Cliffs, NJ: Prentice Hall. This textbook, written by the author of the vignette in this chapter, devotes separate chapters to each of a variety of racial and ethnic groups in the United States.

SIMPSON, GEORGE EATON, AND J. MILTON YINGER. 1985. *Racial and Cultural Minorities: An Analysis of Prejudice and Discrimination,* 5th ed. New York: Plenum. Probably the most detailed and comprehensive textbook available on race and ethnic relations. Excellent reference source for issues concerning race and ethnic relations.

WILSON, WILLIAM JULIUS. 1980. *The Declining Significance of Race: Blacks and Changing American Institutions,* 2nd ed. Chicago: University of Chicago Press. A discussion of American race relations during the slavery era, the segregation era, and the modern era. Notes the effects of changing economic structures on race relations and posits the controversial view that social class has become more significant than race in defining the opportunities available to Black Americans.

WILSON, WILLIAM JULIUS (ed.). 1989. *The Ghetto Underclass: Social Science Perspectives.* Special issue of *The Annals of the American Academy of Political and Social Science,* Vol. 501. Newbury Park, CA: Sage Publications. Contains analyses of the social and economic conditions that perpetuate poverty among inner-city blacks and Hispanics by leading social science experts on race relations and poverty. Considerable attention is given to issues relating to social policy toward the inner-city minority poor.

PART 4

SOCIAL INSTITUTIONS

I n Part 4, we shall examine a number of social institutions. Although common usage of the term "institution" often refers to formal organizations (for example, "institution of higher education"), sociologists use the term differently. A social institution can be defined as a socially accepted pattern of organization, composed of many smaller groups with similar roles, statuses, and norms, that performs some key function in society. Examples include economic and political systems, the family, the educational system, religion, and the health-care system. Part 4 devotes one chapter to each of these institutions.

To clarify the meaning of an institution, consider education. An individual school is a formal organization, but on the societal level, education is an institution. The United States has hundreds of thousands of schools, all of which have certain similarities in function and role structure that are characteristic of the educational system in the United States. We recognize the functions that are performed by education and regard them as an integral part of our society.

In Part 4, Chapter 12 concerns economic and political systems, Chapter 13, marriage and the family, and Chapter 14, education. In Chapter 15 the focus is on religion, and in Chapter 16, on health and health care. Each of these chapters examines the relevant institution in the United States and compares it to institutions that play similar roles in other societies in the world. The chapters draw upon the insights of the functionalist, conflict, and symbolic-interactionist perspectives as they relate to the institution covered in each chapter.

CHAPTER 12

Economic and Political Systems

Home folks think I'm big in Detroit city
From the letters that I write, they think I'm fine
But by day I make the cars; by night I make the bars
If only they could read between the lines!

These were the words of a popular song in the early 1960s; the lament of the displaced country boy forced by economic reality to leave his beloved Kentucky hill country to find economic opportunity in the big city. A quarter of a century later, a similar lament could be heard in Houston, Texas — with an ironic twist. Many of the thousands who arrived weekly in Houston in the mid-1980s were children of the farmers and coal miners who had fled Appalachia a generation earlier, and some of these new economic refugees were desperately homesick for their beloved — you guessed it — Detroit!

How could the Detroit area change from a mecca of economic opportunity to a place that hundreds of thousands of people had to leave because they could not find a job in just 2 short decades? The answer to this question is to be found in changes and conflicts deeply rooted in the American and world economies—changes that have defined the situations of thousands of people like those in the "Detroit City" song and their children who found themselves displaced to Houston and other Sun Belt cities. In this chapter we shall examine economic systems and political systems and see how these institutions affect everyone's lives.

Economic Systems

Economic systems are the means by which scarce resources are produced and allocated within and (sometimes) between societies. They can be classified in two ways. One is on the basis of the *level of economic development*—how are scarce resources produced, and how much of them can the system produce? Systems at different levels of economic development are also characterized by different systems for the division of labor. A second way that economic systems can be classified is on the basis of who owns the means of production. We shall begin our discussion of economic systems by examining levels of development and then turn to the question of ownership of the means of production in modern societies.

Sectors of the Economy

At different levels of development, different sectors of the economy predominate. Economies contain up to three basic sectors: primary, secondary, and tertiary. The **primary sector** consists of the direct extraction of natural resources from the environment. It includes farming, fishing, mining, wood cutting, oil drilling, and generating solar or hydroelectric power. The **sec-**ondary sector** consists of making or manufacturing products, such as cars, airplanes, televisions, dishes, and computers. It includes not only mass production but also the hand-crafting of items such as furniture, carriages, and building fixtures, as well as the construction of buildings themselves. Generally, if a product is made by machines or by human hands rather than being taken directly from the environment, it is part of the secondary sector. The **tertiary sector** consists of producing and processing information and providing services. Rather than physical products such as cars or houses, the products of the tertiary sector are less tangible: knowledge, entertainment, and services. Examples of activities in the tertiary sector are teaching, research, broadcasting, entertainment, and writing. This sector also includes personal services, such as washing and repairing cars, cleaning houses, and providing medical care and legal assistance.

Economic Development and the Division of Labor

From one point of view, the plight of those who fled Kentucky for Michigan, and those who fled Michigan for Texas a generation later, resulted from the long-term evolution and development of the American economy. As the economy evolved from one level of development to another, different types of economic activity took place, different sectors of the economy predominated, and different regions of the country benefited. This process is but a small part of a much larger process of economic development going back to the origins of humankind. This process has led to great increases in the standard of living for much of the world's population, but as the above examples illustrate, it has also led to great upheavals and displacements. Moreover, it has left different parts of the world at very different levels of economic development, and, as we shall see in Chapter 17, has increased both world population and world consumption of natural resources to a point that might threaten human survival.

Hunting and Gathering Economies

The most basic level of economic development, with the simplest division of labor, is the **hunting and gathering economy.** This type of economy has no cultivation and no manufacturing. People live on what they can obtain directly from the natural environment by gathering wild fruit and vegetables, fishing, and hunting—the primary sector predominates in such economies. Societies with hunting and gathering economies are small (often 50 or fewer people) and are usually organized as a tribe or as a clan, a group in which everyone is related. Thus, the entire society could be characterized as a primary group. The small size of such societies is dictated by the nature of their economy: hunting and gathering can support only a very limited number of people. Indeed, even these small groups can support themselves only at a **subsistence level**, producing just enough food, clothing, and shelter to be able to survive. There is no **surplus** —in other words, there is nothing left over after people meet their basic needs.

Hunting and gathering societies are often **nomadic**—once they use up the available food in one area, they must move on to another. Generally, though, this movement occurs within a limited geographic range. Hunting and gathering societies have very little division of labor. Because of breast-feeding, women must remain with small children, and this largely shapes the division of labor. There may also be some division of labor on the basis of age, as people are assigned jobs in accordance with their physical capabilities. Some hunting and gathering societies assign a group of people to a military or war role to protect the society from other hostile groups. However, most of the time this is unnecessary: Because the environment can support so few people living in this manner, hunting and gathering societies usually remain separated from one another.

Because most people perform similar tasks, and because the society is isolated from other societies, the experiences of the people in a hunting and gathering society are very similar. Therefore, these small societies are characterized by a high level of consensus. Also, ownership is usually communal because the meager level of production dictates that everything be shared (Lee, 1984). People in such societies usually have a fair amount of time to spend interacting with one another and participating in group rituals because once they have collected enough food to meet group needs, they have little reason to collect more (Lee, 1984). Therefore, people in such societies frequently spend less time working than people in societies with more complex economic systems (Lee, 1984; Lee and Devore, 1968; Gowlatt, 1984).

From the origin of human societies several million years ago until around 10,000 B.C., all societies had hunting and gathering economies. Today, a limited number of such societies still exist, mostly in thinly populated tropical, Arctic, and desert areas remote from modern societies.

Agricultural Economies

The evolution of economic systems began with the transition from hunting and gathering economies to **agricultural economies.** This transition occurred gradually, with the intermediate steps of *horticultural* economies and *pastoral,* or herding, economies. Horticulture consisted of slashing and burning a small plot of forest, working the soil with a hoe or digging stick, and raising a crop. After a few years, when the soil was no longer fertile, horticulturalists moved on to another nearby location. Pastoral societies raised small herds of domesticated animals, also moving from place to place as forage was used up. Eventually, by around 5,000 or 6,000 years ago, these modes of production developed into true agriculture. Through the invention of the plow harnessed to animals such as oxen or horses, societies were able to raise crops on the same land year after year, because the plow could bring up nutrients from the subsoil and work weeds and leaves into the ground to act as fertilizers. Thus, people were no longer compelled to move from place to place to survive. Also, a much larger plot of land could be worked by one person, making the creation of a surplus possible for the first time (Lenski and Nolan, 1984).

The production of surplus food enabled societies to exist on a larger scale and in one location. It also freed some people to perform tasks other than food

The illustrations above contrast hunting and gathering economies (left) with agricultural economies (right). The primary sector predominates in both types of economy, but in agricultural economies people become attached to particular plots of land.

production. Towns and small cities became possible, and greater effort could be devoted to such secondary-sector activities as construction of temples and public buildings. The production of a surplus also added a critical new element to the economic system: inequality, or economic stratification. In a subsistence economy, everybody lived at a bare survival level, but in an agricultural economy, those with power and prestige accumulated more than the rest of the population.

The Feudal System   In agricultural societies, the means of production is land, and those who own the land obtain most of the wealth and power. Some agricultural societies are based on family farms, but more often a small elite — usually deriving its position from religious tradition or military power — owns the land, while the rest of the population works for them. The system is usually headed by a monarch, and those who own land often have some formal political or religious title that is passed on between generations (along with landownership). This type of system is referred to as a feudal system or an estate system, or sometimes simply as *feudalism.*

Agricultural societies gradually became dominant throughout the world and continued that way until 200 or 300 years ago. In various forms, feudal systems existed in Europe, Asia, Africa, and Latin America, and the southern U.S. plantation system bore an important resemblance to this system as well. As agriculture became more efficient, very large scale governments occasionally emerged, as in the Roman and Chinese Empires. More often, though, infighting among regional elites made warfare a constant reality. Such systems, though warlike and dramatically unequal, created enough surplus to allow the development of increasingly complex philosophy, art, religious institutions, architecture, and governments. Although the secondary and tertiary sectors were both larger than in less-developed economies, the primary sector still predominated in agricultural economies.

Industrial Economies

During the eighteenth and early nineteenth centuries, a new system of economic production based on manufacturing took hold in England and spread through the rest of Western and Northern Europe, as well as North America. Since that time, it has spread in varying degrees to virtually every part of the world. This new system, the **industrial economy,** was based on the use of machines to produce a variety of products ranging from military hardware to consumer goods to new machines that could produce more new products. Thus, the secondary sector became the sector of greatest economic importance. Beginning with the steam engine, a series of inventions made possible more and more efficient manufacturing. These inventions grew out of *technology* — the application of scientific knowledge to practical tasks. This new economic system so dramatically transformed society that we refer to its development as the Industrial Revolution.

The industrial mode of production was made possible not only by new technology, but also by the changes in social organization discussed in Chapter 7, including the rise of bureaucracy and the accompanying trend of rationalization. Tradition became less influential, and science, technology, and education more so. As we shall see later in this chapter, large-scale governments, based on *legal-rational authority* (see Chapter 10), replaced the *traditional authority* of monarchies.

Increased Standard of Living

With industrialization, the economy's ability to produce a surplus increased dramatically. This had a number of important consequences. One was a dramatic long-term rise in the standard of living, because the application of technology meant that far more could be manufactured per person (Rostow, 1965). In its early stages, however, industrialization did make life harder for many because of the long hours, low wages, and brutal working conditions it created. Over the long run, though, the increased productivity of industrial economies meant that people could have better diets, more adequate shelter, better health care, and more luxury goods. Life expectancy increased dramatically.

Greater Social Equality

Second, industrialization has been associated with *decreased* social inequality, at least with respect to income and standard of living (Lenski, 1966). Although the huge surplus it has created has allowed the wealthiest people to amass previously unheard-of, multibillion dollar fortunes (Bobbio, 1987), it has improved the standard of living of the masses more than that of the wealthy. Its surplus is

---

The emergence of industrial economies, a process that began in the eighteenth century, has led to major changes in nearly every aspect of society.

so great that the wealthy can have their wealth and still allow much more income to go to the bulk of the population, thereby avoiding a revolution that might deprive them of their wealth.

War and Revolution

Because of their high standard of living, industrialized societies seldom experience revolutions. The transition from an agricultural to an industrial economy has often been accompanied by a revolution, but once a society becomes industrialized, it is not likely to experience revolution. Similarly, industrialized societies are usually less warlike than other societies (Beer, 1981; Singer and Small, 1972; Sorokin, 1937) because they have too much of a stake in the industrial system they have built to risk its destruction through warfare. Moreover, they have developed such deadly weapons that war could mean the destruction of the entire society. When they do go to war, the results are catastrophic: over 40 million people, for example, died in World War II (Beer, 1981). Today, one nuclear war could destroy all of the world's industrialized societies.

In today's world, many societies have fully developed industrial economies, while others remain predominantly agricultural or even horticultural (Lenski and Nolan, 1984; 1986). Many Third-World societies are at intermediate stages between agricultural and industrial economies. The most industrialized areas of the world are Europe (both East and West), North America, the Soviet Union, Israel, Australia, New Zealand, and parts of Asia.

Postindustrial Economies

Around 1970, a group of sociologists, including Alain Touraine (1971 [orig. 1969]) and Daniel Bell (1973), raised the argument that the economies of the United States and Western Europe were moving into yet another level of development, which they referred to as a **postindustrial economy.** According to Bell, the main characteristics of the postindustrial economy are the transition from a manufacturing to a service economy, the growth of professional and technical occupations, the central role of theoretical knowledge as the source of innovation and policy formation, and a shift to decision making on the basis of problem-solving rules rather than intuitive judgments. In such economies, the tertiary sector has taken on greater importance than either of the other two sectors. Ownership of capital may become less important than control of information, the capability to develop new technologies, and the ability to provide services.

Many of the changes predicted by Bell, Touraine, and others in the early 1970s have indeed taken place in the most technologically developed societies. In the United States and Western Europe, heavy industry has declined as a source of employment. This happened partly because new technologies automated these industries, and partly because the core of economic growth shifted from manufacturing to services. Between 1950 and 1980, the proportion of American workers employed in industries that produce goods fell from 49 percent to 33 percent, while the share in service-producing industries rose from 51 percent to 66 percent (Clark, 1985, p. 22). Banking and investment, entertainment, accounting, health care, engineering, hotels and restaurants, and the electronics industry have been the growth areas — and all of these are either in the service sector or involve generating and processing information. This shift has generally hurt the industrial Midwest and Northeast and helped the South and West (Weinstein, Gross, and Rees, 1985; Sternlieb and Hughes, 1975). Unlike heavy industry, these businesses can locate to areas with a desirable climate and recreational amenities (see Morgan, 1976), rather than being tied to areas that have natural resources or transportation waterways.

Effects on the Labor Force   The transition to a postindustrial economy has resulted in the loss of hundreds of thousands of jobs in manufacturing, with job growth occurring in the professional and managerial sectors (as Bell predicted), but also in the service and clerical sectors. One consequence of this shift has been an increasing division of the labor force into two distinct and highly unequal segments. One segment, including doctors, lawyers, research workers, financial specialists, technicians, and engineers, is technologically educated, relatively well paid, and enjoys high prestige. The other segment, bigger and faster growing, is made up of service, clerical, and retail sales workers (Reich, 1986b). These workers are usually poorly educated and often work for very low wages.

Thus, in the United States at least, the develop-ment of the postindustrial economy appears to have contributed to greater socioeconomic inequality. The more advantaged segment of the population creates demand for increasingly diverse services as it spends its time and money in search of fun, good health, and self-fulfillment. The high educational level of these workers, along with the mobility and diversity that are typical of the postindustrial society, strengthens the forces for democratization already present in industrial societies. People demand to be informed, refuse to follow rules blindly, and object to discrimination based on race, sex, and religion. Women tend to be as well educated as men and to work outside the home.

The less-advantaged segment of society, although affected by these trends, has a much more difficult time than the middle and upper classes. This group provides the services the wealthier classes demand, but it often cannot afford to purchase many of them. Still, almost everyone is touched in some way by the information and entertainment industries, if only because of the low cost of televisions, radios, stereos, and other electronic diversions.

Science and Education   Because of the role of information in the postindustrial society, science and technology play a central role. Education is a key institution, for it is through the educational system that information is generated (in research universities) and taught. However, in some postindustrial societies such as the United States, privately funded and controlled research and development rival university research, as companies compete to discover for themselves the new technology that brings wealth.

This new role of science and education has its dangers. There is a tendency to believe that technology can solve any problem, including those that are produced by the new technologies themselves. The danger is that our ability to create risks — nuclear war, air pollution, hazardous chemicals, the "greenhouse effect" — may outstrip our ability to create knowledge to deal with those risks. Yet, we persist in creating risks because we believe that science and technology can solve any problems they create. To the extent that we miscalculate on this point, the very survival of humanity could be jeopardized.

An important feature of postindustrial economies is that they exist in a larger world, much of which has not even reached the industrial stage. This reality has contributed to the decline in manufacturing in the postindustrial societies: what cannot be automated can be moved. The owners of capital in developed countries have increasingly relocated their *labor-intensive* manufacturing operations to preindustrial countries where labor can be purchased more cheaply. Thus, many major American-owned firms have exported jobs from the United States to Mexico, Taiwan, Korea, Haiti, and other places where workers are paid far less than even the U.S. minimum wage.

Modern Economic Systems

Modern economic systems—industrial and post-industrial—vary in several important regards. One of the most important is the question of who owns capital, or productive capacity. In some modern economies, capital is for the most part privately owned; in others it is mainly publicly owned; and in yet others there is a mixture of public and private ownership.

Capitalism

An economy in which most of the productive capacity is privately owned is called a **capitalist economy.** This system of ownership is called *capitalism* or *private enterprise.* **Capital,** or productive capacity, includes manufacturing plants, distribution systems, land, raw materials, and money that can be converted into such things. Capital can be thought of as *income-producing wealth:* If you own something that produces income, you own capital. The larger the share of capital that is owned privately, the more capitalist an economy is said to be. In a purely capitalist economy—an *ideal type* that does not exist in real life—*all* productive capacity would be privately owned. The United States is one of the most highly capitalistic nations in the industrialized world. More of its productive capacity is privately owned than is the case in most European countries—but it is not completely capitalist. Certain important economic functions (highway construction, mail, education) are performed predominantly by government-owned organizations. Moreover, even economic activities that are *usually* privately owned

are not always so: The United States has publicly owned electric power companies, bookstores (on college campuses), campgrounds, marinas, and ski areas. Although capitalism is primarily found in industrialized economies, its basic characteristics have been adopted by countries in various stages of industrializing, such as South Korea, Taiwan, and Brazil.

Individual and Corporate Capitalism Capitalist economies can be further subdivided into two types: individual capitalism and corporate capitalism. In *individual capitalism,* income-producing wealth is owned by individuals or families. In *corporate capitalism,* most income-producing wealth is owned by **corporations,** large organizations whose ownership is shared by a number of people, called *stockholders.* A share of ownership in a corporation is called *corporate stock.* Corporations exist as separate legal entities. The corporation itself, and not any individual, assumes responsibility for the consequences of corporate decisions. Corporations enjoy various legal rights and must meet certain legal responsibilities; they can be sued and penalized if they fail to do so.

As industrial societies grow and modernize, the tendency is for individual capitalism to be replaced by corporate capitalism. In the United States, this happened quite rapidly, between about 1890 and 1905 (Roy, 1983). By 1905, corporations accounted for 74 percent of domestic production (Roy, 1983). The amount of capital required to produce, market, distribute, and sell products in today's large national and international markets is so great that even the wealthiest individuals lack sufficient means to own or finance the entire operation. Therefore, large numbers of individuals pool their wealth and jointly own the corporation. Corporate stock is usually bought and sold on public markets. Although a good many people own some stock, *most* stock is owned by a very small, wealthy segment of the population (see Chapter 9). In fact, because a corporation's rights include ownership of stock in other corporations, a large share of corporate stock in the United States is owned by corporations rather than by individuals.

CORPORATE MANAGEMENT Rather than being run directly by their owners, corporations are run by boards of directors elected by the owners and by managers hired by these boards of directors. Whereas in

Harvest time at a state farm in the Soviet Union. In socialist economies, productive capacity is publicly owned.

individual capitalism the owner actually operates the business, in corporate capitalism the owners hire someone else to do so. As a practical matter, the control of the corporation lies with its board of directors and managers, not its owners (Mintz and Schwartz, 1985). Boards of directors are effectively self-perpetuating: Although their members are elected by stockholders, most stockholders vote by *proxy;* that is, they allow someone else to vote for them. The board of directors makes recommendations to the stockholders concerning its membership, and the proxies ratify these recommendations. The only major exception to this rule is a "hostile takeover," in which a group of investors (which may include other corporations) buys the majority of the stock over the objection of the board of directors.

The American economy in the twentieth century is best classified as a corporate capitalist system. Although many individual enterprises remain today, the bulk of wealth is owned, produced, and sold by corporations. The 500 largest manufacturing corporations — a tiny percentage of all businesses — account for 42 percent of the U.S. gross national product and two-thirds of after-tax profits (Guzzardi, 1988). Even retailing, once dominated by small, family-owned

stores, is today dominated by big corporations such as K-Mart, J. C. Penney, Sears, Wal-Mart, and Dayton-Hudson.

Socialism

A system in which capital is publicly owned is called a **socialist economy.** Sometimes, to emphasize the major role of government, this system is referred to as *state socialism* (Edwards, Reich, and Weisskopf, 1986). Examples of countries with a socialist economy are the Soviet Union, China, Cuba, and most East Europe nations. This system is also found in a number of developing countries, such as Mozambique, Nicaragua, and Vietnam. Just as there is no such thing as a purely capitalist economy, so is there no purely socialist economy. In each of the countries mentioned above, *some* income-producing wealth is privately owned. Both the U.S.S.R. and China, for example, permit farmers to have privately owned plots and sell what they produce, as long as they meet production quotas for their collective farm or commune. Moreover, many socialist countries have *black markets* — illegal private sales of goods and services.

Americans often think of the Soviet Union and China as communist, but that label is not appropriate, at least as Karl Marx used the term. The ideologies of these countries may be communist, but their economic systems are not, as we shall see shortly.

Capitalism, Socialism, and Cultural Values

Capitalism and socialism both reflect and produce dramatically different value systems. Capitalism depends upon a **norm of maximization** that assumes that people will seek to get as much wealth and income as they can. Undoubtedly, some of you are thinking right now, "Of course — that's human nature." In fact, it is *not* human nature. It only seems to be because the norm of maximization is so deeply engrained in the culture of capitalist societies.

Early capitalist economists such as Adam Smith (1910 [orig. 1776]) believed that the norm of maximization would benefit all groups in a society. By rewarding greater efficiency with higher profits, they argued, capitalism would improve overall productivity and thus make everyone's life better. However, Smith was writing about individual capitalism; modern corporate capitalism operates differently from what he envisioned. Smith would probably no more recognize capitalism in the United States today than Marx would recognize "communism" in the Soviet Union.

Socialist Values Socialism is based on a very different set of values than those that sustain capitalism. Central to socialism is the belief that nobody should become wealthy if someone else must do without necessities, such as food, shelter, clothing, health care, or the opportunity for meaningful employment. Thus, the first priority of a socialist economy is to meet basic needs, even if that means operating at a loss, using government subsidies, or maintaining unprofitable enterprises. Rather than competition for wealth, the ideal value of socialist economies is cooperation for the common goal of leaving nobody's basic needs unmet.

Communism

As Marx saw it, **communism** — or what he called the "classless communist society" — was the final stage of economic evolution that could only come after capitalism and socialism (see Figure 12.1). In communism, as defined by Marx, capital would be controlled not by government but by collectives of workers who would own and operate the establishments at which they work. The role of government would fade away because the people would act collectively and democratically at the local level. Individuals would contribute according to their talents and abilities and receive according to their needs. Because people would con-

trol their work situation, they would be able to perform to their fullest potential.

Marx's utopian ideal has never been achieved. Some features of this system have been incorporated in Yugoslavia and China, but even these countries fit the pattern of state socialism far more closely than that of Marxian communism. Given the need for some degree of bureaucracy, along with the tendency toward oligarchy in all large organizations (see Chapter 7), it is very doubtful that Marx's ideal of communism could ever be attained in an industrial society. Although the Soviet Union still claims to aspire to it, that country has not evolved beyond state socialism nearly three-quarters of a century after the Russian Revolution. Although it once set dates for attaining the goal of becoming a classless communist society (all of which have passed), it no longer does. All industrialized economies are either capitalist, socialist, or some mix of the two — a pattern to which we now turn.

Mixed Economies

The final modern economic system that we shall discuss is the **mixed economy,** sometimes called *democratic socialism*. In this system, characteristic of most of Western Europe, some means of production are privately owned and some are publicly owned. Great Britain, France, and Sweden are prime examples of this system. In the developing world Zimbabwe can be cited as an example.

Railroads, airlines, and utilities such as gas and

FIGURE 12-1
Stages of Economic Evolution, according to Karl Marx.

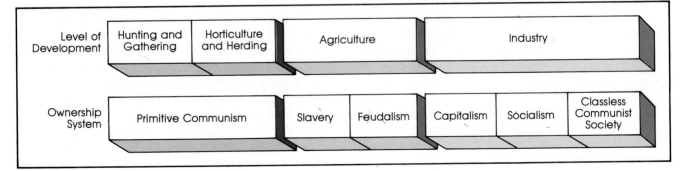

electricity are nearly always publicly owned in a mixed economy, although there may be private competition. Day care for children, which is mainly a private industry in the United States, is run by government on a nonprofit basis in virtually all mixed economies. Health care is publicly financed, although doctors may or may not be government employees. Certain manufacturing industries are state-owned. Shipbuilding, mining, and petroleum are also frequently public enterprises. At the same time, there is a great deal of for-profit private economic activity, and even government-operated firms often try to maximize profits. Private firms compete with government-owned ones, and some industries are entirely private, although they are typically more regulated than in more capitalist countries such as the United States.

The mixed economy is sometimes called democratic socialism because the governments that run the publicly owned enterprises are elected. The prevailing political trends can and do influence the precise mix of public and private control. Especially in Great Britain and France, there was a trend toward privatization in mixed economies in the 1980s, reflecting in part the election of more conservative governments under Margaret Thatcher and Jacques Chirac (until 1988). This trend primarily took the form of selling off part or all of the stock in some government-owned industries. Even so, the role of the public sector in these economies remains far greater than in the United States. The key difference is that most European public-service functions, such as health care, utilities, child care, and domestic transportation, remain in the public sector, whereas they are usually in the private sector in the United States.

Mixed economies combine the values underlying capitalism and socialism. The norm of maximization is clearly present, but it is tempered by the norm of trying to meet everyone's needs. In a sense, the mixed economy represents an attempt to balance the values and goals of capitalism with those of socialism.

Convergence Theory

There are many who believe that the future lies with mixed economies, and that over time capitalist and socialist economies have each adopted certain features of the other and will continue to do so. This viewpoint is called **convergence theory** (Form, 1979). State socialist economies, for example, are clearly becoming more capitalistic. The extent of private ownership has been greatly increased in China in recent years, as small shops and businesses have been allowed to operate and communal farmers have been permitted to farm private plots and sell the produce. The result of both of these innovations has been excellent growth in productivity, particularly in the agricultural sector, where private production has gone the furthest. By 1985, almost half of all farm products were marketed through a free-market system, which led to a "national network of wholesale markets with private merchants dealing in free-market goods" (Watson, 1988). In the 1980s the Soviet Union began to move in a similar direction as its leader, Mikhail Gorbachev, sought to improve the nation's productivity through *perestroika,* which, roughly translated, means "economic restructuring." At a party congress in 1986, Gorbachev expressed support for the idea of family farms (Shlapentokh, 1988). In doing so, he was endorsing what is clearly a form of private enterprise. Both the Soviet Union and China have increasingly accepted consumer goods and entertainment, which were once viewed as wasteful and decadent excesses of capitalism. Blue jeans, bright shirts, and rock music are replacing the drab dress and quiet lifestyles of earlier generations. It is possible, however, that the suppression of dissent that took place in China in 1989 could lead to a reversal of these trends there.

Convergence Theory and the U.S. Economy The role of the public sector in the United States has increased significantly during the twentieth century. Americans realized that a purely capitalist system could not meet such basic needs as economic and medical security in old age or protection against the ravages of unemployment. Thus, the government now operates a pension system (social security) and insurance systems to meet the medical needs of the elderly (Medicare) and to protect people from impoverishment during periods of unemployment (unemployment insurance). Moreover, this trend may go further. In 1988, Massachusetts became the first state to provide comprehensive health insurance coverage, through a combination of mandated employer coverage and state coverage for the unemployed. On the federal level, strong legislative efforts were under way by the late 1980s to establish a similar health insurance program as well as federally funded day care for children of working parents. During the decades after World War II, there was also a considerable increase in governmental regulation of private enterprise for the purposes of protecting the environment, preventing price fixing, guaranteeing a minimum wage, and protecting workers from unreasonable risk of injury on the job. However, the more conservative federal administrations of the 1980s reversed certain aspects of this trend, as several industries were deregulated and domestic spending was curtailed. As noted, similar reversals occurred in several countries in Western Europe, most notably Great Britain. Thus, if there is a trend toward convergence, it is an irregular one.

Concentration in Economic Systems

Another important way that modern economic systems vary is in their degree of concentration. In a **concentrated economy,** the means of production in any given industry are centrally owned and controlled, so there is little or no competition. In a **deconcentrated economy** there are many different producers in each industry, so there is a great deal of competition. In different ways, the issue of concentration is relevant to both capitalist and socialist economies. In fact, concentration is probably a major reason that modern capitalist and socialist economies vary so much from the visions of Adam Smith and Karl Marx.

Concentration in Corporate Capitalism

Modern American capitalism is for the most part corporate capitalism. As corporations have come to dominate production in the American economy, that economy has become more concentrated. Many major industries today take the form of a **monopoly** (controlled by just one producer) or, more commonly, an **oligopoly** (controlled by just a few producers). For a number of products less than five producers control half or more of the American market (see Table 12.1).

As private enterprise has become more concentrated, it has moved further away from the model of Adam Smith. A deconcentrated, individual capitalist economy can operate as a *free enterprise system,* in which anyone with a reasonable amount of capital can start a business, many businesses compete, and the market rewards those that are most efficient. This is very much the way the American economy operated for its first century or so (see Gordon, 1976). A concentrated economy, however, cannot work this way. The scale of production is so large that it is virtually impossible for anyone to acquire sufficient capital to start a new company that could seriously compete, for example, with Ford or General Motors. Moreover, if this did happen, the established firms could temporarily reduce prices to drive the new company out of business.

In the late nineteenth century, large American producers began to combine into trusts, thereby eliminating competition and creating oligopoly in industry after industry. In the early twentieth century, the growing concern about the effects of concentration in the U.S. economy led to the passage of *antitrust laws.* However, these laws have rarely been strictly enforced, and current statistics reveal that the American economy has remained concentrated—indeed, many industries have become more concentrated—throughout the twentieth century. In this concentrated economy, there is little real competition (except from imported goods), and without competition, the market forces noted by Adam Smith cannot set the price. Compounding this problem is the growth of *conglomerates*—massive corporations that own companies that dominate a number of different industries. An example of this can be seen in the box entitled ''Conglomerates: A Case Study,'' which illustrates the range of businesses owned by one corporation. As we shall see later in the chapter, this tendency has affected both the efficiency of the American economy and the distribution of economic resources in the United States.

Interlocking Directorates A feature closely related to concentration, which has also reduced the degree of competition in modern capitalism, is the **interlock-**

TABLE 12.1
Concentration in the American Economy: Selected Industries, 1982.

INDUSTRY	NUMBER OF FIRMS IN INDUSTRY, 1982	DOMESTIC MARKET SHARE OF FOUR LARGEST PRODUCERS, 1982
Breakfast cereal	32	86%
Pet food	222	52%
Cookies and crackers	296	59%
Chocolate products	77	75%
Chewing gum	9	95%
Beer	67	77%
Soap and detergents	642	60%
Tires	108	66%
Guns (small arms)	138	51%
Household cooking equipment	71	52%
Home refrigerators & freezers	39	94%
Home laundry equipment	15	91%
Household vacuum cleaners	29	79%
Electric lamps	113	91%
Radios and televisions	432	49%
Records and tapes	548	61%
Telephones	259	76%
Motor vehicles & car bodies	284	92%
Aircraft	139	64%
Motorcycles and bicycles	269	59%
Watches and clocks	227	51%
Burial caskets	270	52%

SOURCE: U.S. Bureau of the Census, 1986c, Table 5.

ing directorate. This occurs when the same individual serves on the board of directors of more than one corporation. In effect, it means that the same people may have a hand in the operation of numerous legally automonous corporations. The overwhelming majority of major U.S. corporations have interlocking directorates with other corporations. In fact, interlocks have been widespread ever since the U.S. economy shifted from individual to corporate capitalism around the turn of the century (Roy, 1983). Of 1,131 corporations studied by Mintz and Schwartz (1985, p. 145), 998 were part of a continuous network of interlocking directorates. Almost all of these corporations could communicate with a director of any other one in the network via a chain of communication involving three or fewer directors. At the center of the network, and connected directly to nearly all of the largest corporations, were banks and insurance companies. Thus, a relatively small group of people has vast power over the economy, and great opportunities and pressures exist for producers who are supposed to compete to

collude instead (Mintz and Schwartz, 1981; Burt, 1983). Another very important effect of interlocking directorates is that they help large corporations act on behalf of their political self-interests by enabling them to operate as a relatively unified political force (Useem, 1984; Zeitlin, 1974).

Multinational Corporations

A particular feature of concentrated corporate capitalism is the **multinational corporation,** a giant business that is headquartered in one country but operates in many. Multinational corporations engage in production, resource extraction, and marketing in different parts of the world, locating each operation wherever it will best contribute to the corporation's profitability. Such corporations may dominate markets not just in their home country, but in many other countries as well. To some extent, multinational operations may be necessary in today's world economy. In dollar value, about one-fifth of what is manufactured

Conglomerates: A Case Study

We can learn several things about conglomerates by looking at America's nineteenth-largest corporation, RJR Nabisco. First, this conglomerate is, on several levels, a product of mergers between formerly independent corporations. RJR Nabisco was created when Nabisco Brands merged with R. J. Reynolds Tobacco. In turn, Nabisco Brands itself was the result of an earlier merger between Nabisco and Standard Brands. Each of these three corporations was in turn composed of a number of smaller companies and brand names, some of which had been developed by the parent companies and some of which had been purchased. The result is that many products, often in unrelated industries, that we *think of* as being produced by different companies in fact come from one great conglomerate. The RJR-Nabisco merger brought the following brands and companies under common ownership:

- Winston, Salem, and Camel cigarettes
- Hublein liquors*
- Kentucky Fried Chicken*
- Del Monte fruits and vegetables
- Grey Poupon Dijon mustard
- Patio frozen foods*
- Morton frozen foods*
- Hawaiian Punch
- Harry & David, Inc.
- Planter's nuts
- Blue Bonnet margarine
- Baby Ruth candies
- Ritz crackers
- Nabisco biscuits
- Oreo cookies
- Fleischman's margarine
- Royal gelatin desserts
- A-1 Steak Sauce
- Nabisco Shredded Wheat
- Milk Bone pet treats

* Subsequently sold.

- Life Savers
- Almaden Vineyards*
- Triscuits
- Butterfingers candy bars

Note that several of these companies were later sold, some to other conglomerates. Kentucky Fried Chicken, for example, was sold to PepsiCo, which also owns Taco Bell and Pizza Hut. In late 1988, the entire RJR Nabisco conglomerate was itself bought by Kohlberg Kravis Roberts & Co. for nearly $25 billion in the largest corporate buyout in U.S. history. As often happens, so much money was borrowed for the buyout that at least $6 billion worth of companies owned by the conglomerate were to be sold off to service the debt. One problem with such mergers and buyouts is that resources that could be put into modernizing a company and improving its operations are often put instead into bidding wars to buy it.

---

in the United States today is sold elsewhere, and more than one-fifth of what is sold here is manufactured elsewhere. Both markets and sources of essential natural resources are often located far from a company's home country. A product of a given corporation may be produced or sold in a place far from the country where the corporation is headquartered. American Levi's are partially manufactured in Mexico; Toyota now has manufacturing operations in the United States. Another common pattern is for a corporation based in one country to be absorbed into one based in another; RCA televisions are today the product of a French government-owned corporation.

Although multinational operations may be necessary in today's world economy, operating on such a scale gives corporations great power, which is easily abused. If a segment of the operation in any country is regulated to the corporation's dislike, or if it is simply too costly, it can be moved elsewhere, regardless of the consequences for employees and others. Capital is neither patriotic nor respecting of international boundaries. In recent years, many American multinationals have shifted their operations from the United States to Third-World countries where wages are a fraction of what American workers receive. Thus, the popular villain "foreign competition" is in fact often the creation of American-owned corporations seeking to cut costs.

Problems of Multinationals Although multinational corporations often do pay higher wages than Third-World workers might otherwise receive, their activities in the developing world are in many ways detrimental. For one thing, they take the profits from

McDonald's in Bangkok, Thailand. Multinational corporations market their products in parts of the world far from the country where they are headquartered.

what they produce out of the Third-World country, depriving it of the opportunity to invest and grow. Bribery and coercion are also rampant. Since congressional investigations of business and political corruption began in 1976, hundreds of American corporations have admitted making payments to foreign government officials to gain favors. Payments totaling hundreds of millions of dollars were made by various American corporations (particularly in the aerospace industry) to government officials in South Korea, Bolivia, Japan, the Netherlands, Turkey, Italy, Pakistan, and Colombia, among others (Barlow, 1987, p. 261). Since World War II, corporations have been involved — with the assistance of the American government — in overthrowing the governments of Chile, Guatemala, and Iran.

Multinational operations are by their very nature exceedingly difficult to regulate. Every country has different rules, and the corporation can simply move around until it finds either rules it likes or officials willing to bend or ignore the rules. The very threat to move usually discourages enforcement of the rules, for fear of losing jobs. Thus, to a large extent, multinational corporations can operate outside the law.

Concentration in Socialist Economies

In a different way, the issue of concentration is also relevant to socialist economies. Most state socialist economies are highly concentrated because government owns the means of production, and decisions are therefore made by government officials in the capital city. Thus, the market has little effect on what is produced or the price at which it is sold.

Some socialist economies, however, are less concentrated. The best example of this is Yugoslavia, where plants are run at the local level by management personnel selected by worker councils. These plants, though all government-owned, in effect compete with one another because the market is largely allowed to set the price, and the most efficient plants are rewarded by the market (Lane, 1979). This has led some analysts to refer to the Yugoslav economy as "market socialism" (Fusfeld, 1976, pp. 811–814). China and Cuba have also moved in this direction, although centralized planning continues to play a major role in both countries. Most recently, Soviet leader Mikhail Gorbachev has also proposed an increased role for market forces in the Soviet economy. Although Soviet plant managers lost autonomy when Leonid Brezhnev centralized planning in the 1970s, the reverse has been true under Gorbachev. In recent years plant managers have had increased opportunities to make decisions at the local level (Linz, 1988).

Economic Systems, Productivity, and Equality

Productivity and Equality: A Comparison

As we have already seen, proponents of capitalism argue that it is more productive than any other economic system. In contrast, the chief advantage of a socialist system is said to be that it does a better job of meeting everyone's basic needs and of sharing scarce resources equitably. How valid are these arguments?

Capitalism, Socialism, and Productivity With respect to productivity, capitalism appears to be superior to state socialism, but the productivity of mixed economies is similar to that of capitalist ones. In 1987, the gross national product per capita — a rough indicator of productivity — among industrialized socialist countries ranged from $2,010 in Yugoslavia to $7,400 in the Soviet Union, well below that of either capitalist or mixed economies in the industrialized world (Population Reference Bureau, 1988). This lack of productivity in a purely socialist economy has been recognized by both China and the Soviet Union over the past decade or so, which is why both countries have permitted an increase in private economic activity. It also seems to be true that many industries in the mixed economies of Western Europe have been more profitable since they have been privatized, partly because they can raise money for investment through stock sales rather than by borrowing.

Although they clearly outproduce socialist economies, capitalist economies are not necessarily more efficient or productive than mixed ones. Among Western and Northern Europe's mixed economies, the GNP per capita in 1987 ranged from $8,920 in Great Britain to $15,480 in Norway (Population Reference Bureau, 1988). Among the more capitalist countries, the GNP per capita ranged from $11,910 in Australia to $17,840 in Switzerland. Thus, the typical productivity advantage of capitalist over mixed economies is rather small, and the most productive mixed economies, such as Norway, exceed the average for more capitalist economies.

Capitalism, Socialism, and Equity Although capitalist economies have an advantage over socialist ones with respect to productivity, the reverse may be true when it comes to meeting basic needs and distributing resources equitably. In industrialized socialist countries, nobody goes without such basic needs as medical care and adequate food and shelter. In the United States, in contrast, there are at least several hundred thousand homeless people, and more than one person in ten lacks any medical insurance. Moreover, there is less inequality between higher-paid and lower-paid workers in socialist countries than in capitalist countries. Even so, there is still significant inequality in socialist countries: The very highest paid industrial employees in China and Eastern Europe receive incomes many times greater than those of the average worker (Lane, 1976, p. 178).

Although socialist countries probably do better at meeting everyone's basic needs than the most capitalist countries, they do not necessarily do better than the mixed economies. These societies, too, have government policies and programs aimed at meeting everyone's basic needs. All of them have universal, publicly funded health coverage and do a great deal to provide other necessities. A large share of the population in some mixed economies lives in public housing (as in Great Britain) or cooperative housing (as in Sweden).

Unemployment and the Economic Cycle

Two closely related problems in modern economies are *unemployment* and the economic cycle. By and large, these are problems of capitalist and mixed economies, though they probably exist in different forms in socialist economies. Unemployment occurs when people who want to work are unable to find jobs. Usually, unemployment as such does not exist in socialist economies because people are hired and given something to do even if nothing needs to be done. However, such economies do suffer from a lack of

Unemployment line in New York City, 1932. The cycle of "boom" and "bust" affects all industrialized societies, particularly relatively unregulated capitalist economies such as the United States up to the time of the Great Depression.

meaningful employment. In capitalist and mixed economies, unemployment rises and falls along with an *economic cycle,* a periodic movement of the economy between "boom" and "bust." During boom periods, jobs are plentiful, wages rise, businesses grow, and unemployment is low. During bust periods— called *recessions* or *depressions,* depending on their severity—unemployment rises, wages fall, and businesses shrink in size.

The Functionalist Perspective There are many reasons for the business cycle and for unemployment, some of which are beyond the scope of this book. We will simply note how differently these phenomena are viewed from the functionalist and conflict perspectives.

The functionalist perspective sees the economic cycle as a means by which the economy corrects itself. When demand outstrips supply, a boom period occurs, until prices rise high enough that people cannot pay them, or people borrow so much that they have trouble handling the debt. At that point, people stop buying, loans are not paid back, and the economy goes into a "bust" period. Eventually, prices fall or stop rising, people learn to live within their means, and a new upturn occurs.

Ups and downs of the economy may also be the result of outside forces. A new technology may eliminate jobs in one area and create them in another. Until an adjustment is made, unemployment rises. Groups who lack the skills for which there is demand may experience especially high levels of unemployment, as is the case with inner-city blacks and Hispanics, particularly youths. The answer to this problem, according to the functionalists, is not to restructure the economy, but to train those who lack skills and establish policies that prevent the cycle from going out of control. Thus, a certain level of government regulation has come to be accepted in the United States as a means by which a necessary and unavoidable economic cycle is kept under control.

The Conflict Perspective Conflict theorists view the economic cycle and unemployment as means by which some people gain at the expense of others. In most capitalist countries, if it is profitable to lay workers off, it will be done. In mixed and socialist economies, workers' welfare is more likely to be considered in decisions regarding layoffs. This clearly makes the employer less profitable in hard times, and it is one reason that government-owned companies in Western Europe have sometimes been less profitable than private ones. In these countries, an additional consideration is that laid-off workers may vote against the government.

Some conflict theorists believe that the economic cycle itself is useful to the owners of capital. The idea dates to Marx (1967 [1867–1894]) and a concept he called the *reserve army of the unemployed.* According to Marx, this reserve army serves an important function for the owners of capital: It reminds workers that they can easily be replaced and keeps them from demanding too much in the way of higher wages and benefits. Modern conflict economists and sociologists have applied this argument to the economic cycle. They argue that when a boom economy creates pressures for increased wages, a recession is actually useful to employers because it raises the unemployment rate and this allows employers to threaten their workers with replacement if they demand too much (Lekachman, 1982). Sometimes they deliver on this threat, as happened with increasing frequency in meatpacking, the airlines, and other industries in which workers struck during the 1980s. Unions were eliminated, and strikers were replaced with nonunion employees by TWA and Continental Airlines, Iowa Beef Processors, and Hormel Meats. One reason the strategy succeeded was the presence of large numbers of unemployed workers, over 11.5 million at one point. In fact, recessions can be very profitable. During the twentieth century, the share of American corporate income going to profits, as opposed to wages, has generally been higher *after* recessions than before. (For further discussion of these and related issues, see Gordon, 1975, and Heilbroner, 1978).

Productivity and Equality: Effects of Concentration

Concentration and Productivity How an economic system works depends not only on the mix of public and private ownership, but also on the degree of concentration. The incentives for productivity noted by Adam Smith (1910 [orig. 1776]) can work

Eastern Airlines employees on strike in 1989, protesting cutbacks in pay and benefits. The deregulation of the airline industry led to fierce price competition and to widespread labor strife as airlines sought to cut costs by reducing employee's pay and benefits.

only when an economy is competitive. One problem in the concentrated U.S. economy has been the failure to update aging manufacturing plants to the extent that some international competitors have. Partly as a result of this, productivity growth in the United States has lagged sharply since about 1973. Despite periodic spurts, U.S. productivity has been growing at a slower rate than in the past, and at a slower rate than in many competitor nations (Le Boeuf, 1982; Bowles, Gordon, and Weisskopf, 1983; Bain, 1982; U.S. Bureau of Labor Statistics, 1988).

Economies of Scale   Although concentration retards productivity, the increasing size of producers may help productivity, at least up to a point. That is because as manufacturing operations get larger, they can take advantage of *economies of scale*. In other words, they can benefit by using mass-production techniques to produce more goods relative to fixed costs such as land and machinery. However, there are limits to the economies of scale, and most American manufacturing operations grew beyond these limits several decades ago (Moroney, 1972, pp. 23–26). Thus, at the level of concentration found in the United States, re-

ductions in productivity caused by concentration probably outweigh any advantage arising from economies of scale.

Concentration and Equality   By definition, concentration in either a capitalist or a socialist economy places considerable power and wealth in the hands of a few. In so doing, it clearly contributes to inequality. However, the actual effect of concentration on inequality is more complicated than this formula suggests. Under certain conditions, strong competition can lead to lower wages. In the nineteenth century, when the U.S. economy was characterized by individual capitalism and intense competition, wages were very low. The reason was that producers tried to outsell the competition by keeping prices—and hence wages—low. To a large extent, concentration eliminated this incentive to pay low wages by reducing the incentive to cut prices—monopolies and oligopolies involve little or no price competition. More recently, competition was introduced into the airline industry through deregulation, and again the result was declining wages. As described earlier, unions were broken at TWA and Continental, and throughout the airline industry employees were asked to work for less money and fewer benefits (Salpukas, 1988). Thus, intense competition can lead to increased inequality by reducing workers' wages and benefits.

Although concentration does reduce pressures for wage cuts, it leads to inequality in other ways. In the absence of price competition, prices generally rise. Employers may pay higher wages than in a competitive economy, high enough to keep workers from striking or "causing trouble." However, these wages often do not proportionately reflect the greater corporate profits that occur in a concentrated economy.

Political Systems

Although national governments are taken for granted today, it is important to recognize that they are relatively recent creations. Throughout most of European history, for example, national governments existed only "on paper." The real power during the era of feudalism was held by titled landowners, each of whom ruled a relatively small area. Nominally, these landowners paid allegiance to the king or queen, but real power belonged to the local noble. Another common arrangement in parts of the world that had at least an agricultural economy was the city-state. Under this arrangement, a government based in a city ruled the surrounding territory. Sometimes, as in ancient Greece, city-states formed alliances over areas as large as a modern nation, but these alliances were temporary and unstable. In those parts of the world with hunting and gathering, horticultural, or pastoral economies, the tribe or clan was usually the largest unit of government. There were exceptions to these rules in some agricultural societies, notably the Roman, Chinese, Russian, and Egyptian Empires (Lenski and Lenski, 1982). However, much smaller units of rule were more common, and government on the scale of today's national governments was quite exceptional.

The Rise of the Modern Nation-State

As societies began to move from the agricultural to the industrial level, all this began to change. Real wealth came to be concentrated in the city, weakening the position of rural landowners. Industrialization required regional governments to promote trade and commerce and supply raw materials. The need for government services over a wide area grew. Feudal and tribal systems became dysfunctional and were replaced by national governments. Gradually, the *nation-state* became the dominant political system. A **nation-state** is a legally recognized government that rules a relatively large geographic area and provides such services as military protection, law enforcement, transportation, and the regulation of commerce. In a few centuries the nation-state has gone from a rarity to the chief form of government in the world (Skocpol, 1979, pp. 20–22). After developing in Europe, it was exported and imposed on the Third World through colonialism. One problem arising from this process is that diverse tribal societies, some of which had been traditional enemies, were lumped together into nations that reflected the ideas of European colonialists rather than local realities. In many cases, these nations were unnatural groupings, and some have been torn by bitter internal conflict.

Authoritarian and Democratic Governments

Present-day political systems can be categorized in a number of ways, but the most critical distinctions are between **democratic governments** and **authoritarian governments.** Under democratic governments, leaders are elected periodically. Although these leaders have considerable leeway in making and enforcing laws and policy, their power is limited in three important ways. First, they must periodically stand for reelection. Second, there are traditional or constitutional limits to their power. The president of the United States, for example, cannot shut down the Supreme Court or dismiss its justices because it makes a ruling the president doesn't like. Third, leaders must respect broadly guaranteed rights of free speech, freedom of the press (including free access by the press to information), and, usually, freedom of religion (Coulter, 1975). The basic assumption of all democratic governments is that the power of government is derived from the will of the people, and that when the people wish to change the government, they can do so.

Authoritarian governments, in contrast, give much greater power to their leaders. The people have no real say over who their leaders will be. Leaders may be chosen by heredity or by decisions of a small clique who do not have to answer to a larger public, or they may install themselves in power through military actions. They typically rule for life, unless someone with more power or influence displaces them. Usually, the leaders' power is absolute. There is no broad guarantee of freedom of speech, press, or religion. Although some authoritarian governments guarantee such freedoms "on paper," the reality is that those who express ideas the leaders don't like are quickly silenced.

Democracy is, by and large, a modern phenomenon. Although its origins can be traced to the ancient Greeks, it did not become widespread until around the time of the Industrial Revolution. Even today, only a relatively small minority of the world's population lives under truly democratic governments. Why do so few countries have democratic governments? This is one issue we shall explore further as we consider the various forms of authoritarian governments and the conditions under which they tend to develop.

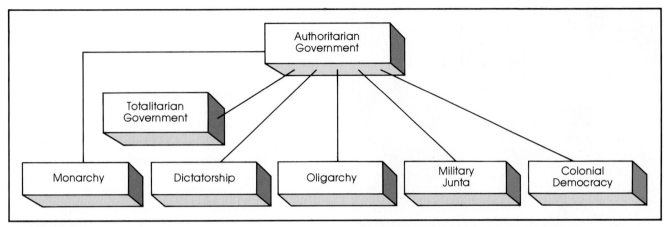

FIGURE 12-2
Forms of authoritarian governments

Authoritarian Governments

Traditional Authoritarian Governments: Monarchies The oldest form of authoritarian government is the **monarchy.** In a monarchy leadership is hereditary, being passed from generation to generation in a royal family. It is based on traditional authority (see Chapter 10). The leader, or *monarch,* has a royal title, such as king, queen, or emperor. Often the monarch is also the leader of a national religion, which reinforces his or her position. In such societies, rights and freedoms are granted to the population only to the extent the monarch wishes. In some cases — a recent example is King Juan Carlos of Spain — monarchs have formally given their power over to legislative bodies, which has led to a transition from authoritarian to democratic rule.

Historically, monarchies have most commonly occurred in agricultural societies with some form of feudalism (see Skocpol, 1979, pp. 47–49). Traditional monarchies are less common today than in the past, but some still exist. This form of government is especially common in the Middle East, where Jordan, Kuwait, Saudi Arabia, and other countries continue to be ruled by royal families with close to absolute power.

Modern Authoritarian Governments Most present-day authoritarian governments are not monarchies. Rather, they take the forms of *dictatorships, oligarchies, military juntas,* and *colonial democracies.* All except the last are very similar in that they involve absolute rule by one person or a small group, based on criteria other than heredity.

DICTATORSHIP A **dictatorship** is a government in which one person rules with absolute power. Examples are Libya under Muamar Ghadafi, Panama under

---

Libya's Col. Muamar Ghadafi. Libya under Ghadafi is an example of a dictatorship.

King Juan Carlos of Spain. Following the death of dictator Francisco Franco, Juan Carlos called for elections, and Spain was transformed from a dictatorship to a constitutional monarchy with an elected parliament.

Manuel Noriega, and the Philippines under Ferdinand Marcos. The Soviet Union, when it was ruled by Josef Stalin, was also a clear example of this type; however, it has evolved more recently into a slightly different form.

OLIGARCHIES The Soviet Union today since Stalin has functioned as an **oligarchy,** a society in which a small group of people have absolute power. Although the Soviet premier or party chairman does have enormous power, that power is shared with the Politburo, a small ruling council (Deutsch, 1974). If the leader falls out of favor with the Politburo, as happened with Nikita Khrushchev in the 1960s, that leader may be removed and replaced. Officially, the Soviet legislative body is the Supreme Soviet, or parliament, but at least until the late 1980s, that body simply ratified the decisions of the leaders. Recently, Soviet leader Mikhail Gorbachev has made changes in that system, and the parliament may now evolve into a real policy-making body (see box entitled "Is the Soviet Union Moving Toward Democracy?").

Another example of an oligarchy is Iran under Ayatollah Khomeini. Although Khomeini was the absolute ruler and all policies had to be approved by him, he was influenced by a small group of religious and parliamentary leaders. The influence of this group was clear in Khomeini's 1988 decision to seek a cease-fire

after a long and bitter war with neighboring Iraq (*Newsweek*, 1988c). As in the Soviet Union (at least until Gorbachev) the Iranian parliament acts as a rubber stamp for policies proposed by the ruling oligarchy.

MILITARY JUNTAS Another arrangement that can overlap closely with either dictatorship or oligarchy is the *military junta.* This is a group of military leaders (with power sometimes concentrated in the hands of one individual) who seize power from another government in an act known as a *coup d'état,* or simply a *coup.* A coup is different from a revolution because it involves a power grab by a small group within the military. A *revolution,* in contrast, is a broad-based uprising that has the participation or support of a substantial segment of the population. Sometimes a military junta rules for many years, as in Chile, where General Agusto Pinochet has ruled ever since he gained power in a 1973 military coup (carried out with undercover support from the U.S. government) that resulted in the death of Chile's elected president, Salvador Allende. In other cases, one coup after another leads to a series of short-lived military juntas, as has occurred during much of the recent history of Argentina.

COLONIAL DEMOCRACIES The least common type of authoritarian government is the *colonial democracy.* This form occurs when a small group of colonizers establishes power over a much larger native population. The colonizers hold elections among themselves and may allow members of their group a fair amount of freedom, but they deny these rights to the much larger native population. In other words, there is democracy for the few but authoritarian rule for the many. A limited amount of free speech may be permitted within the colonizer group, but even its members face repression if they challenge the fairness of the system. Examples of this system are Rhodesia (until it became Zimbabwe in 1979) and South Africa. This pattern is also characteristic of the Israeli-occupied Arab territories in the West Bank and the Gaza Strip, though in Israel itself Arabs do enjoy political rights.

Authoritarianism and Ideology Authoritarian governments are not linked to any particular ideology. There are leftist authoritarian governments, such as

Is the Soviet Union Moving toward Democracy?

Since Mikhail Gorbachev took over as leader of the U.S.S.R. in 1985, he has spoken a great deal about *glasnost,* or "openness." Is this just for show, or is he genuinely leading the Soviet Union in a more democratic direction? The question is hard to answer, but because of his actions, the Soviet Union today appears more democratic and less autocratic than it was a decade ago, and it may be moving even further in that direction. Consider the level of dissent that is now permitted in the Soviet Union. Street demonstrations have become much more common. Although they are still sometimes broken up by police, they are sometimes left alone, and it has become rare for protesters to be held by police for more than a few hours. As was noted in Chapter 11, *glasnost* has allowed ethnic conflicts to come out into the open. Thus, in the provinces of Armenia and Azerbaijan, massive ethnic protests involving hundreds of thousands of demonstrators occurred repeatedly in 1988. Much of Armenia was shut down for months by general strikes, and protestors even closed an airport briefly by staging a sit-in. Such actions would have been unthinkable in the Soviet Union just a year or two earlier.

Moreover, Gorbachev proposed, and the ruling Communist Party approved, changes in Soviet government and Communist Party rules that would clearly make the country more democratic. Officials of the party and those who serve in the legislatures (called *soviets*) are to be elected in contested elections and by secret ballot. Thus, for the first time since the Russian Revolution, voters are being given a choice. A new elected legislative body called the Congress of People's Deputies has been created, and the nation is to be governed by a new Supreme Soviet elected by the Congress. The term of office for most officials is to be 5 years, and officials will only be allowed to serve two terms in most cases. (A 75 percent vote by secret ballot will waive this restriction.) The national and regional parliaments are also to be given additional policymaking authority, and will no longer merely rubber-stamp decisions made by the Communist Party's small leadership group. Gorbachev's proposals also included extending additional rights to defendants in criminal cases and giving judges greater independence (Taubman, 1988). If these proposals are fully put into practice, they will likely have the real effect of giving citizens greater

influence over their government and greater protection against arbitrary prosecutions.

When the first elections under the new plan took place in 1989, however, only a minority of races were actually contested. (However, in several of the uncontested elections, many people voted "no.") There is, moreover, no guarantee of how fully or for how long these proposals will remain in effect. They are likely to encounter strong resistance from bureaucrats and party officials who do not want their power diminished (Taubman, 1988). Earlier proposals for change, even ones that have been approved by the Politburo, have not yet been fully implemented. Finally, there is the risk that after Gorbachev dies or leaves office, his successor could reverse direction. This has happened after moves toward democratization in many other countries that, like the Soviet Union, lack longstanding traditions of democracy. On the other hand, by giving the voters a choice, limiting terms of office, and creating a more independent judiciary, the proposals do seem to create some of the conditions that are necessary for democratization.

---

the Soviet Union's, that claim to represent the interests of working people and to guarantee equality. There are religious authoritarian governments, such as Iran's, that justify their rule as carrying out God's will. There are rightist authoritarian governments, such as that of the German Nazis and Pinochet in Chile, that claim to be protecting their countries from the "red menace" of communism. Finally, there are authoritarian governments, such as some traditional monar-

chies, that seem to exist mainly for the purpose of preserving the wealth of a small, privileged elite. What all these types have in common is not ideology, which varies widely, but rather the principle that power lies with those who govern, not those who are governed.

Totalitarian Governments Those authoritarian governments that exert the most stringent control over their people are called **totalitarian govern-**

ments. Such governments have total control over all aspects of life, even those that do not involve political activity (Berger, 1986, p. 83). They have highly developed secret police forces with the power to arrest, punish, and in many cases torture anyone whom they suspect of dissenting from the official government line. They have massive propaganda systems that bombard the populace with a continuous message glorifying the government and its policies. Only newspapers and publishers sympathetic to (or under the direct control of) the government are permitted to operate, and opposition to the ruling political party is forbidden. Organizations that are independent in democratic societies, such as churches and universities, are permitted to operate only to the extent that they are controlled by, or agree not to offend, the government. The most extreme feature of totalitarian governments is the use of what Hitler called the "final solution"—mass extermination of those who dissent or who belong to groups the government considers threatening.

The clearest examples of totalitarian governments in this century are Nazi Germany, the Soviet Union in the Stalin era, and Cambodia (Kampuchea) in the 1970s under Pol Pot. In each of these cases, millions of people were exterminated, either because of suspected disloyalty or because they belonged to ethnic groups hated by the rulers. Many authoritarian governments, however, display totalitarian tendencies. Chile, Cuba, South Africa, Libya, and Iran, for instance, suppress dissent and imprison thousands without trial merely on suspicion of disloyalty. China moved in the direction of totalitarianism in 1989 to repress a massive student movement for democracy begun by college students. Thousands died when the military put down the uprising, and a police state was put into effect during the following weeks, accompanied by mass arrests.

Democratic Governments

Democracy literally means "rule by the people." In a *direct democracy* every issue of importance would be voted upon directly by the general public. This is essentially how the New England town meeting works: The people of the town meet periodically and collectively decide the policies of their town government. It is also the method of decision making used in some preindustrial tribal societies. However, on any scale larger than that of small towns or tribes, direct democracy becomes impossible. Even in a small city, with a population of 50,000 or 100,000, it would be quite impossible to get everyone together every time a decision of importance had to be made. Imagine the difficulty of doing this in the case of the U.S. government, which governs a population of 245 million people spread out over an area thousands of miles wide!

Representative Democracy Because of the impracticality of direct democracy on anything but the smallest scale, almost all democratic governments use *representative democracy* (Dahl, 1982, Chap. 2). The political decisions are made not by the people themselves but by representatives elected by the people to serve in legislatures or parliaments. Occasionally, an important issue may be put to the popular vote, as in a *referendum,* but routine decision making (and in some representative democracies, all decision making) is left to the elected representatives. The idea underlying this system is that if representatives make decisions that are contrary to the will of the people, they will be voted out of office.

Power in Representative Democracies   The reality, though, is that elected representatives reserve a good deal of power to themselves. As we saw in Chapter 10, in some representative democracies, such as the United States and Switzerland, less than half of the eligible public commonly votes. Further, when people *do* vote, they often vote on the basis of the candidate's personality rather than the issues. In Chapter 7, we discussed Robert Michels's *iron law of oligarchy,* which holds that any organization in which authority is delegated will tend to be ruled by its leaders. Such delegation occurs by definition in a representative democracy, and all representative democracies have some tendency to operate like oligarchies because representatives have considerable information that the general public lacks.

This process can be illustrated by the results of a 1983 survey (Clymer, 1983) that asked Americans whether their government was attempting to support or overthrow the governments of El Salvador and Nicaragua. Do you know the answer? If not, you are not alone. Only 25 percent of Americans knew that their

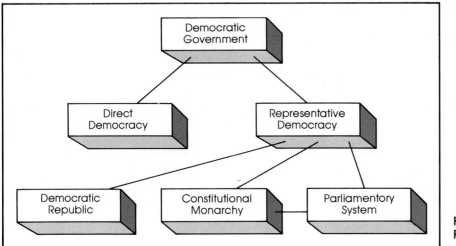

FIGURE 12-3
Forms of democratic governments

government was giving military aid to the government of El Salvador, and only 13 percent knew the American government was aiding guerrillas attempting to overthrow the government of Nicaragua. A tiny 8 percent knew about both alignments, even though these facts could have been obtained from almost any newspaper or television newscast on almost any day. With a public this poorly informed, political representatives obviously have a lot of latitude to do what they want. A tendency closely related to the iron law of oligarchy is that of politicians to represent an affluent power elite rather than the average citizen (Mills, 1956b). This issue is discussed at length in Chapter 10.

CONSTITUTIONAL MONARCHIES   There are several common forms of representative democracies. One is the *constitutional monarchy,* in which the monarch serves an important and ceremonial function but has no real power over government decision making. The monarch's claim to his or her position is hereditary and is defined by traditional authority. There is, for example, a clear set of rules about who is entitled to succeed to the British throne, and in what order. Monarchs in this system play a very important expressive leadership role as symbols of national unity. Events such as the Wimbledon tennis tournament in England and the Holmenkollen ski jumping championship in Norway derive part of their prestige from the presence of the nation's royal family.

THE PARLIAMENTARY SYSTEM   Although their

monarchs play an important symbolic role, the day-to-day governing of England, Norway, and other constitutional monarchies is the responsibility of elected officials. Most constitutional monarchies, and some other representative democracies, use a *parliamentary system* of government. Under this system, members of the parliament, or national legislature, are elected from slates that run for office under the banner of two or more political parties. The chief executive of the country, often called the *prime minister,* is the legislative leader of the majority party in the parliament. He or she is chosen by the parliament rather than directly elected by the people. If no one party has a majority (50 percent of the parliament plus one vote), a coalition government may be formed: Two or more parties combine so that they can claim a majority of the legislature and elect a prime minister from their membership. If this cannot be accomplished, or if an existing coalition breaks down, a new parliament must be elected. In general, countries with this system of government have elections every time the ruling party or coalition loses a major vote. Alternatively, the ruling party or coalition may choose to call elections; in any case, there is certain minimum time (for example, 5 years in Great Britain) after which an election must be held.

Parliamentary systems, in combination with a constitutional monarchy, exist in Great Britain and other Commonwealth countries, which, though independent, formally owe allegiance to the British monarchy. This combination is also found in the Scandinavian countries (Sweden, Norway, and Denmark), the Netherlands, Spain, and several smaller European countries. Other countries, such as Israel, have parliamentary democracies without monarchs.

DEMOCRATIC REPUBLICS Another form of representative democracy is the *democratic republic,* of which the United States is an example. The main feature that distinguishes this system from the parliamentary system is a *popularly elected chief executive.* Unlike the British or Israeli prime minister, the president of the United States is elected by the public instead of by the legislature. This makes for several important differences. First, it is possible — and not unusual — for the president to be of one party and the majority of the legislature (Congress) to be of another. In fact, this was the case for the majority of the time between 1954 and 1988. Second, political parties make less difference. In a parliamentary system, where the leader is chosen by the parliament, parties can reward those who are loyal to the party position with increasingly influential parliamentary and ministerial positions. In democratic republics, where chief executives are popularly elected, the way to move to the top is not necessarily to please legislators but to gain popular appeal and experience, often through some form of service outside the national legislature. A number of U.S. presidents (Reagan, Carter, Roosevelt) were governors of states before being elected president; others, like Eisenhower, converted military fame into a successful run for the presidency.

In democratic republics, there is also less difference between the political parties. Each party has to appeal to the middle in order to get its candidate elected president. Therefore, the parties tend to take positions very similar to one another (Cummings and Wise, 1981; Wilson, 1980). In general, there is greater class consciousness in parliamentary democracies, and parties often represent distinct social classes.

These tendencies are enhanced by the fact that the political systems of parliamentary democracies often encourage the formation of more than two major political parties. One such feature of some parliamentary systems, such as that of Sweden, is *proportional representation,* in which each party gets representation in parliament proportionate to its share of the popular vote. In the American form of the democratic republic, in contrast, whoever gets the most votes in any congressional district wins that whole district. This discourages the formation of third parties, which have little chance of winning a majority. Thus, American politics has always been dominated by two major parties, even though particular parties have come and gone. (Neither of the current major parties dates to the beginning of the United States.) As the box in Chapter 10 explained, having two parties further increases the "middle of the road" tendencies of the American republic (Lowi, 1976, p. 293).

Some representative democracies combine features of parliamentary systems and republics. Germany and France are examples, having both elected chief executives and prime ministers chosen from the parliament. Regardless of its form, however, a democratic government can only emerge when certain conditions are present.

Necessary Conditions for Democracy

Freedom of Expression As we have already noted, democracy is impossible unless people are guaranteed freedom of expression (Shils, 1962; Pennock, 1979; Berger, 1986). This includes free speech, freedom of the press, freedom to travel and associate, and freedom of religion. There must be political organizations and a mass media that are independent of the government and free to criticize it (Dahl, 1982, p. 11). To protect these rights, there must also be a court system that is largely independent of the government, so that people have some means of redress when they feel their rights have been violated.

In practice, all societies, including the United States, place some restrictions on freedom of expression, sometimes illegally. Groups espousing positions critical of the U.S. system, such as the Black Panthers, the Students for a Democratic Society (SDS), and the Communist Party, USA, have been penalized in various ways that are forbidden by the law, including break-ins of offices, illegal wiretaps and searches, and arrests without evidence. Informal pressures can also

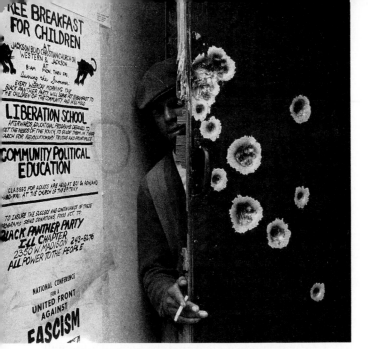

Bullet holes left in door of Chicago Black Panthers' headquarters after a 1969 police raid. Do groups such as the Black Panthers enjoy the same freedom of expression as other groups less critical of the system?

strongly limit a person's freedom of expression. Just consider what would happen if you were to sit during the national anthem at your college's next athletic event.

Informed Citizens and Access to Information

In order to have a workable democracy, people must be sufficiently informed to vote intelligently. Of course, citizens themselves bear a large amount of responsibility for being uninformed, and even in the most stable democracies the knowledge of the average citizen is limited. However, the problem becomes vastly greater in societies where most of the population cannot read and many lack such sources of information as televisions or radios. Although innovations such as portable radios are becoming commonplace in even the least-developed nations, this is a recent development. Mass illiteracy was widespread in almost every human society until the past century or two. This is certainly one of the reasons that democracy is so much a product of the modern era.

Technology and literacy are not the only things that affect citizens' access to information, however. Even if people can read and do have radios or televisions, democracy is impossible if the government denies them the information they need in order to make choices. In any country where most major decisions are made secretly, democracy is impossible (Bobbio, 1987, p. 18). Moreover, unless a country has a free press, people will get no information except what the government wants them to have. In such a situation, democracy is impossible, because even the most informed citizens cannot make real choices.

Willingness to Cooperate

Ultimately, democracy depends upon people's willingness to observe certain fundamental rules. Democracy cannot work, for example, if a party responds to an election loss by overthrowing the government. If a society is divided to the point that different groups view each other as bitter enemies, democracy is unlikely to work.

Industrialized Economy

The final feature associated with democratic governments is an industrialized economy. Although industrialization is no guarantee of democracy—Hitler's Germany and Stalin's Soviet Union were both industrialized countries—stable democracy is rare in countries that have not reached at least the industrial stage of economic development. In the following section, the reasons for this will be explored further, as will other ways that economic and political systems are related to each other.

Economic Systems and Political Systems

Political Systems and Levels of Economic Development

As noted just above, an industrial economy appears to be essential for the development of democracy (Lenski, 1966; Lipset, 1959; Almond and Coleman, 1960). Preindustrial countries usually cannot sustain the necessary conditions for democracy. One such condition is a degree of equality. The great inequalities associated with preindustrial economies are often based largely on coercion, and if the coercion is removed, the result is often a revolution or other conflict in which one group "wins" and imposes its will on all others. Another necessary condition is information. Prior to industrialization and the emergence of mass media, there was no way to keep a citizenry informed on a large scale, and traditional rulers had no desire to do so. Often, too, preindustrial countries have strong traditions of monarchy, which only break down under the pressures for rationalization that accompany modernization (Weber, 1968 [1922]; Pennock, 1979, p. 228). With industrialization, the educational level of the public rises, and people feel a greater sense of control over their lives and therefore want to control their governments as well.

Capitalism, Socialism, and Political Systems

Authoritarian political systems are found in every type of economic system. Capitalist South Korea and South Africa are authoritarian, as are China and the Soviet Union with their socialist economies and Iraq with its mixed economy. Democracy, on the other hand, has been typically associated with either capitalist or mixed economies. Most of today's authoritarian capitalist and mixed economies are in less industrialized countries, such as South Korea and Chile. The absence thus far of democratic governments in countries with strongly socialist economies has led some observers, such as Berger (1986), Usher (1981), Friedrich (1972), and Downs (1957), to argue that state socialism is incompatible with democracy. Even when industrialized, state socialist countries thus far have not adopted democratic political systems.

State Socialism and Democracy Critics maintain that several features of state socialist economies make them unlikely candidates for democracy. According to Berger (1986, p. 79), the state is so big and powerful in all modern societies that a countervailing center of power is needed to offset it. Private owners of the means of production serve this function in capitalist and mixed economies, but there is nobody to serve it in a socialist economy. Moreover, for a society to remain socialist, the government must restrict the economic activities of its citizens — in other words, tell them there are many things they cannot do. If the majority want to engage in private enterprise, then a choice must be made between democracy and socialism.

Current trends in the Soviet Union could, depending on your viewpoint, be seen as either supporting or contradicting Berger's argument. If Mikhail Gorbachev's current proposals to allow contested elections with secret ballots and an independent judiciary are genuinely put into practice and given constitutional protection, the Soviet Union would become distinctly more democratic than it is today. Gorbachev has, however, made it clear that the Soviet Union will remain predominantly a state socialist country. Thus, it may be turning more democratic while remaining state socialist. On the other hand, it could be argued that the Soviet Union is becoming more capitalist: The same proposals that contained the political reforms also included "giving private business expanded freedom to hire workers, set prices, and engage in foreign trade" (Taubman, 1988). In other words, as the Soviet Union moves toward democratic reforms, it may also adopt more elements of capitalism, even if its economy remains *predominantly* socialist. Such a trend might not be at all inconsistent with the arguments of Berger, Downs, Usher, and others.

Whether or not a strongly socialist country can be democratic, it is clear that mixed economies where *part* of the means of production are publicly owned can be. No society is any more democratic or protective of freedom of expression than Sweden, and the means of production there are partly public-owned and partly private. If anything, the trend in Sweden in recent decades has been to enlarge the public sector and move toward worker ownership of industries (Himmelstrand et al., 1981). Thus far, this development has posed no threat to democracy in Sweden's government; in fact, it has extended the principle of democracy to Swedish industry. Thus, trends in Sweden and elsewhere suggest that democracy can prosper in economies where public ownership plays a major role, though it is not clear that it can exist in economies that have *only* public ownership of the means of production.

Summary

The economic system of any society is partly a product of that society's level of economic development and partly a result of who owns the means of production. The simplest level of economic development is the hunting and gathering society—a small nomadic tribe or clan. Its economy produces no surplus, and property is usually communally owned. People in such societies live at a bare subsistence level, yet they enjoy considerable leisure time and engage in common activities that hold the group together. Eventually, the group may learn to cultivate crops or raise animals. Such horticultural and pastoral societies are an intermediate between hunting and gathering and agricultural economies. Agricultural economies farm larger plots of land using plows and draft animals, which enables them to produce a surplus. This surplus allows a certain portion of the population to live in permanent towns and engage in activities other than food production; it also creates socioeconomic inequality.

In agricultural societies, the means of production is land, and the wealthy are those who own land. Typically, they develop a feudal system, which is characterized by a landowning gentry and a large peasant class who work for the landowners. When society reaches the industrial stage, the means of production becomes capital, or productive capacity. In industrial societies, manufacturing—made possible by new technologies and by bureaucratic organization—is the most important economic activity and a key source of employment. Industrial societies tend over the long run to produce a large increase in the standard of living and some leveling of inequalities.

A new form emerging in some of the most highly developed countries is the postindustrial economy. In this system, the provision of services becomes the predominant activity, as industry becomes more automated and a relatively affluent population demands more services. Application and control of new technology become the route to economic growth, and possession of information may become almost as important as ownership of capital for the accumulation of wealth.

Whereas agricultural economies were generally organized on feudalist lines, new systems of ownership emerged in industrial societies. Most such systems are either capitalist, with private ownership of the means of production; socialist, with public ownership of the means of production; or some mix of the two. Capitalist economies are highly efficient but produce greater inequality than socialist ones.

Socialist economies place a high priority on meeting everyone's basic needs, but they are less efficient and productive than capitalist ones. An intermediate type is the mixed economy, where part of the means of production is publicly owned and part is privately owned. Some analysts feel that mixed economies combine the best features of capitalist and socialist economies: They are more efficient than socialism and do a better job of meeting everyone's basic needs than capitalism.

Another dimension along which modern economies vary is the degree of concentration. In a concentrated economy, ownership and power are in the hands of a few, with little competition. A deconcentrated economy, in contrast, has many competing producers. As economies have modernized, they have become more concentrated, which has reduced incentives for efficiency.

Along with the development of industrial economies came the modern nation-state. A declining number of these nation-states are monarchies, a traditional form of authoritarian government that is an outgrowth of the feudal system. Modern forms of authoritarian governments include dictatorships, oligarchies, military juntas, and colonial democracies. Some modern governments are democratic. Democratic leaders are freely chosen by their people, serve limited terms, and have constitutional limitations on their power that protect citizens' basic rights.

There are various forms of democratic systems. Most modern democracies are representative democracies rather than direct democracies. In other words, people elect representatives who make the laws and form policy. Some representative democracies use a parliamentary system, whereas others are republics, with popularly elected chief executives. Political parties tend to be stronger, and diverse interests better represented, under parliamentary systems. However, consensus is easier to achieve in republics, especially if there are just two major parties. The tendency in such systems is to appeal to the middle rather than to distinct constituency groups.

Authoritarian governments are found in all types of economic systems. They are particularly common in less-industrialized societies. Democratic governments, in contrast, are usually found in societies with a high level of economic development and a capitalist or mixed economy. The degree to which democracy is possible in societies with more strongly socialist economies is a matter of debate among sociologists.

Glossary

economic systems Systems that determine the production and distribution of scarce resources.

primary sector That part of an economy consisting of the direct extraction of natural resources from the environment.

secondary sector That part of an economy consisting of the making or manufacturing of tangible physical products.

tertiary sector That part of an economy consisting of producing and processing information and providing services.

hunting and gathering economy A level of economic development in which people live on what they can collect, catch, or kill in their natural environment.

subsistence level A level of economic production that meets a population's minimum needs but produces no surplus.

surplus Whatever an economy produces in excess of the minimum needed to keep everyone alive.

nomadic A society in which members move from place to place rather than living permanently in one place.

agricultural economy A system of production based primarily on raising crops through the use of plows and draft animals.

industrial economy A level of economic development in which machines are used to manufacture things of value.

postindustrial economy A modern economy dominated by services, technical knowledge, and information rather than by industry.

capitalist economy An economic system, found primarily in industrialized countries, in which the means of production are privately owned.

capital Productive capacity in an industrialized economy, including manufacturing and distribution capacity, raw materials, and money.

corporation A large-scale private company with multiple owners (called *stockholders*) that is legally independent and has legal rights and responsibilities separate from either its owners or managers.

socialist economy An economic system, normally found in industrialized countries, in which the means of production are publicly owned.

norm of maximization A value in capitalist countries of trying to derive maximum benefits from scarce resources.

communism As used by Karl Marx, a utopian society, to date not attained in the real world, in which all wealth is collectively owned, workers control the work place, and government is unnecessary.

mixed economy An economic system in which the government provides extensive social services and performs some major economic functions, while manufacturing and other industries are at least in part privately owned. Also called *democratic socialism*.

convergence theory A theory that holds that capitalist and socialist economies are becoming more similar to one another as the role of the public sector grows in capitalist societies and the roles of private ownership and the market increase in socialist societies.

concentrated economy An economy in which competition is limited or absent because there are very few producers of any given product (in a capitalist economy) or because decisions are made centrally by government officials (in a socialist economy).

deconcentrated economy An economy characterized by competition resulting from a large number of producers.

monopoly A condition in which there is only one producer of a given product, thereby eliminating competition.

oligopoly A condition in which there are only a few producers of a given product, so that competition is limited or nonexistent.

interlocking directorate The presence of some of the same people on the boards of directors of different corporations.

multinational corporation A large corporation that produces and sells its products, and usually owns property, in a large number of countries.

nation-state A legally recognized government that effectively rules a relatively large geographic area and provides services, including military protection, law enforcement, and the regulation of commerce.

democratic government A system in which government is chosen by the people, who enjoy freedom of expression and the right to vote for their leaders.

authoritarian government A government in which the leaders have virtually unrestricted power and the people have limited or no freedom of expression.

monarchy A form of authoritarian government with a hereditary ruler whose absolute power is based on traditional authority.

dictatorship A modern form of authoritarian government in which one person rules by absolute power.

oligarchy A form of authoritarian government in which a small group rules with absolute power. Also refers to the tendency of large-scale organizations to be ruled by their leaders, even if they are formally democratic.

totalitarian government An extreme form of authoritarian government that takes total control over all aspects of life.

Further Reading

BELL, DANIEL. 1973. *The Coming of Post-Industrial Society: A Venture in Social Forecasting.* New York: Basic Books. An early and influential analysis of the shift from industrial to postindustrial economies. Examines the causes and social consequences of the declining importance of the secondary sector and the rising importance of the tertiary sector.

BERGER, PETER. 1986. *The Capitalist Revolution.* New York: Basic Books. A sociological analysis of capitalism, which takes a procapitalist stance. Berger argues that capitalism enhances productivity and personal freedom to a greater extent than socialism, and that as a result, people in capitalist societies enjoy a better quality of life than those who live in socialist ones.

BLUESTONE, BARRY, AND BENNETT HARRISON. 1982. *The Deindustrialization of America.* New York: Basic Books. An analysis, by two of the most respected experts in the field, of the transition from an industrial to a postindustrial economy that is taking place in the United States.

MARX, KARL. 1964. *Selected Writings in Sociology and Social Philosophy.* Thomas B. Bottomore and Maximilien Rubel, eds. and trs. New York: McGraw Hill. Excerpts from Marx's major writings. A good place to begin if you want to learn about Marxian theory first hand. Selections address such issues as the nature of social class, alienation, and the relationship between economics and politics.

ORUM, ANTHONY. 1989. *Introduction to Political Sociology,* 3rd ed. Englewood Cliffs, NJ: Prentice Hall. An overview of the field of political sociology, with attention to both theory and research. Addresses issues relevant both to this Chapter and to Chapter 10.

USEEM, MICHAEL. 1984. *The Inner Circle.* New York: Oxford University Press. Discusses the network of business leadership under American and British corporate capitalism, and how this corporate leadership has come to play a major role in defining and acting upon the political interests of big business. Includes an extensive analysis of interlocking directorates.

CHAPTER 13

Marriage and the Family

In this chapter, we will examine the most basic of all social institutions — the family. Every human society has had some sort of family system. A stable family unit is necessary because, unlike many other species, human babies require an extended period of parental attention and socialization in order to survive and become functioning members of their society. A stable family unit is also made more likely by the fact that human sexual relations are not restricted to a breeding season, as is the case with other species.

Although we will focus primarily on the American family today, we will also explore the diversity of family arrangements and the different functions that the family performs in other societies. The structure of the family varies to a great extent from one society to another. The reasons for this variation have to do with other aspects of the culture and the need to fulfill basic needs within this context. Members of every society generally believe that their particular society's marriage and family patterns are the most appropriate.

Unlike many other subjects studied in colleges and universities, the family is one subject students often believe they already know all about. After all, the vast majority of people have had first-hand experience of at least one family. In fact, most people have only limited knowledge of families, because their beliefs about the family are formed largely from their own experiences. Their personal background does little to prepare them for the wide diversity of families, even within their own society.

Try, for example, to answer the following questions. Do marriages in which the bride is pregnant have a higher risk of divorce? Are the majority of American families married couples with children? Has love always been the main reason for marriage? Do the majority of American children today live with stepparents? In the past, did the majority of adult Americans live with other *relatives besides their spouse and children? When it comes to marriage, do "opposites attract"? Although common beliefs could lead a person to answer "yes" to each of these questions, the correct answer to all of them is "no." Thus, much of what many people think they know about families is not true.*

Many people still cling to the nostalgic image of the American family as being composed of a breadwinner father, a stay-at-home mother, and two or three children. This is *not* a realistic description of the majority of American families today. In truth, only 7 percent of families currently fit that picture (VanderZanden, 1988). The other 93 percent are made up of many other types: dual-earner families in which both the husband and wife provide financial support; single-parent households in which either a mother or, less frequently, a father has primary responsibility for dependent children; married couples who have chosen not to have children; unmarried couples who live together; homosexual couples; and countless other variations. Some of these variations, and the numbers of families they represent, are shown in Figure 13.1. Furthermore, one out of four households in the United States today is not a family at all, but is composed of one unmarried person.

Neither was the family ever a "golden" institution that fulfilled the needs of all its members while providing them with security and love. In fact, many marriages in past eras were little more than economic arrangements in which men were usually the primary beneficiaries. Although some families were characterized by considerable warmth and emotional support, the socioemotional functions of marriage were generally seen as secondary to its economic functions until fairly recently.

Family and Marriage Defined

Although the exact meaning of *family* and *marriage* can vary from one society to another, these institutions do share certain key features in *all* societies. The **family** is a social group of people related by ancestry, marriage, or adoption who live together, form an economic unit, and cooperatively rear their young. Of course, this definition says nothing about the psychological bonds between family members, which, to some people, is what family is all about. **Kinship** also

refers to people related by ancestry, marriage, or adoption, but kin can live independently from one another. Societies exhibit tremendous diversity in determining who are kin.

Marriage is a socially approved arrangement between a male and a female that involves an economic and a sexual relationship. Children born to a married couple are said to be "legitimate," whereas those born to a woman not married to the father are often labeled "illegitimate." Society has generally disapproved of births outside of marriage, in part because such children are more likely to need support from the larger society.

FIGURE 13.1
Types of Families in the United States, 1987
SOURCE: U.S. Bureau of the Census, 1988d, pp. 3, 96, 111, 115.

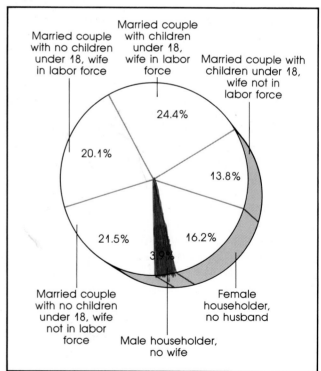

Married couple with no children under 18, wife in labor force — 20.1%

Married couple with children under 18, wife in labor force — 24.4%

Married couple with children under 18, wife not in labor force — 13.8%

Married couple with no children under 18, wife not in labor force — 21.5%

Female householder, no husband — 16.2%

Male householder, no wife — 3.9%

Homosexual couples like these gay women are one of the many new types of marriage and family relationships that have emerged in American society.

Extended and Nuclear Families

All family systems can be divided into one of two basic types: extended and nuclear families. The **extended family** is based on blood ties. It is made up of more than two generations who generally live together, contribute to the economic well-being of the household, and share housekeeping and child-rearing responsibilities. Extended families can include a large number of people, such as grandparents, aunts, uncles, and cousins. The **nuclear family** is based on marital ties. It is made up of two or fewer generations who live together, and it generally includes a husband, a wife, and their dependent children.

Although in many other cultures extended families have been and continue to be common, the most common form of the family is and probably always has been the nuclear family. This has become even more true than in the past among modern societies. Few families in such societies consist of more than two generations living together in the same residence. When this does occur, it often involves an aging parent living with a grown child and his or her family. This is referred to as "the sandwich generation" because the adult child has responsibilities for both a parent and children.

Even though few Americans live in extended families, extended family members may interact frequently, and they are often important in terms of providing assistance of various types, such as child care and financial help. Holidays and other social occasions are often spent with extended kin.

Growth of Nuclear Families in the United States
Although nuclear families have always been the primary family form, the extended family was more common in the past than it is today. With the spread of industrialization, extended families have become rare. Several reasons account for this transition. First, although "many hands" are economic assets in preindustrial societies in which agriculture and cottage industries shape the economy, they become "more mouths to feed" in industrial societies. In addition, highly industrialized economies require a trained, mobile work force. Because it has fewer people to move, the nuclear family makes it easier for workers to go where the jobs are. Also, social mobility was less frequent in the past, making it more likely that extended family members would have much in common. Today, social mobility has made required contact with extended family members, with whom there may be little in common, less useful. Finally, nuclear families today are able to get services from other institutions, such as social security and schools, which makes them less dependent on extended family members.

A family in Jordan. Extended families are more common in preindustrial societies than in industrial societies, although the majority of families in both types of societies are usually nuclear families.

Your family of orientation is the family into which you are born. It is the one family relationship about which you have no choice.

Family Memberships

Most Americans will belong to at least three different families in the course of their lifetime. When you are born, you become a member of your **family of orientation,** which consists of your father, mother, and any brothers or sisters. This is the only family membership about which you have no choice.

The second family that most people have is the **family of procreation.** This family is formed when you marry, and it includes your spouse and children. Because over 90 percent of people in our society marry at some point, most people have a family of procreation. When a divorced person remarries, he or she forms a second family of procreation. Given the current high divorce rate, many people will have more than one family of procreation.

When you marry, you become a member of yet a third family, the *in-law family.* As discussed earlier, even though most people in our culture reside in a nuclear family, they often have frequent contact with members of their extended families. In American cul-

ture, we have terms to refer to these relationships with a spouse's family, including mother-in-law, father-in-law, sister-in-law, and brother-in-law. Beyond this, however, we have only fairly awkward means of referring to in-law family members, such as "my wife's grandmother" or "my husband's uncle." Although technically we choose our in-law families, many people feel they have little choice in the matter. They choose a spouse, and the in-law family comes with that choice. Perhaps this forced relationship explains the existence of "mother-in-law jokes." There are no clear-cut rules as to what happens to the in-law family when a couple divorces. Although marriage creates the tie, divorce does not necessarily terminate it, especially when strong feelings of attachment exist between a divorced person and an ex-spouse's family, or when there are children who create a grandparent-grandchild relationship.

Marriage Patterns

The only legally recognized form of marriage today in the United States is **monogamy,** the marriage of one husband to one wife. In practice, our particular type of monogamy has been called **serial monogamy** because many people will have more than one spouse in their lifetime, although only one at a time.

In some societies, marriage practices have allowed, or even required, people to have more than one spouse at a time. This system is referred to as **polygamy.** When males have more than one wife, the arrangement is called **polygyny.** Although this practice is most common in preindustrial societies, it has been practiced in the United States. For example, Mormons practiced polygyny until 1890, when the Utah territory sought acceptance into the Union. The federal government made the outlawing of polygyny a condition of statehood. In some instances, males may be required to have the first wife's approval before marrying another wife; in others, a man may marry sisters. Both patterns are thought to reduce jealousy between wives. **Polyandry** is the pattern of women having more than one husband. Although numerous societies have practiced polygyny, few have allowed polyandry.

Although many—perhaps most—societies permit polygamy under at least some circumstances, the reality is that most marriages have been monogamous. There are several reasons for this. To begin with, the number of males and females in most populations is roughly equal. Whenever a male takes more than one wife, he effectively deprives another male from having any wife. Beyond this is the issue of cost. The financial costs of supporting multiple wives and the large number of children that might be born would be great. Traditionally, only the wealthiest, most powerful males have had more than one wife.

Mate Selection

Age Restrictions The United States today has an open mate-selection system. With two exceptions, one having to do with age and the other with kinship, a person may legally marry any unmarried person of the opposite sex. Regarding age, although we have no upper-age restriction (a 90-year-old may legally marry), we do have minimum-age requirements. Because each state has its own laws governing marriage and divorce, the minimum age for marriage varies. There are usually two age standards for marriage — one with and one without the parents' consent.

The Incest Taboo The other primary exception to our open marriage system has to do with kinship. The **incest taboo,** a near-universal feature of all family systems, prohibits sexual relations or marriage between people who are related to one another. Societies vary in defining which relationships violate the incest taboo. In the United States, no state permits marriage between parent and child, brother and sister, uncle or aunt and niece or nephew, or grandparent and grandchild. Marriages between first cousins are illegal in many states. The incest taboo reduces potential jealousy between family members, fosters alliances with other families, and may keep the gene pool healthier. Historically, only a few societies have made exceptions to the incest taboo. Marriages between brothers and sisters from royal families, such as in ancient Egypt and early Hawaii, have been the most common exception to this rule.

Exogamy versus Endogamy Until 1967, when the United States Supreme Court ruled them unconstitu-

tional, *miscegenation laws* existed in some states, especially in the South, to prohibit marriage between the races. These laws represented an attempt to prohibit **exogamy,** which is marriage between people from different groups, such as racial, religious, or ethnic groups. On the other hand, exogamy may be required in some societies that desire to cement relations between certain groups, such as between two potentially hostile tribes.

Endogamy is the pattern followed when marriage partners are required or expected to be from the same groups. For example, a particular religious faith might prohibit its members from marrying members of other religions. Many societies attempt to prohibit marriages between partners from different social groups. The United States has no legal prohibitions to such marriages. In practice, however, most American marriages tend to be between people of the same race, ethnic background, religion, and social class, and are therefore endogamous. Interracial marriages, especially between whites and blacks, are particularly rare in the United States.

A Jewish wedding. Most of us marry people who are similar to us with respect to religion, race, age, education, and other social characteristics.

Spouses: How Similar? How Different? Researchers have found that similarities between marital partners go beyond race, religion, and ethnic background. Most husbands and wives tend to be similar in terms of social-class background, educational attainment, intelligence, physical characteristics such as attractiveness and age (although husbands tend to be slightly older than wives), personality traits, and values. This pattern is referred to as **homogamy,** or the idea of "like marrying like." Homogamy occurs partially because people often marry on the basis of *propinquity,* or geographical nearness. The people we live near and associate with are often similar to us in social background. These people serve as a pool of potential marriage partners: People usually marry someone they live near, work with, go to school with, or otherwise have associated with. At the same time, homogamy also reflects the greater ease with which people with similar values and interests interact.

Those who ultimately marry are likely to be very closely matched, creating balanced relationships that tend to be stable. Unbalanced relationships tend to be less stable and produce higher rates of divorce. Stable relationships are more likely to develop when both partners feel that they are getting something out of the relationship as well as giving to it. The partner who believes he or she is giving too much feels angry; the one who believes he or she is getting too much feels insecure and guilty.

Romantic Love and Mate Selection

We use the word *love* to refer to many different types of feelings and emotions. Many people use the word freely, claiming to "love" such things as ice cream, skiing, or a favorite movie. Others reserve the word to describe their feelings for the important people in their lives, such as their wife, brother, or mother. Although we tend to think and write about love a great deal (*Bartlett's Familiar Quotations* contains 769 different listings under love), our ideas are often contradictory. Compare, for example, "Absence makes the heart grow fonder" with "Out of sight, out of mind."

Romantic love is a unique type of love. It involves physical and emotional attraction, as well as *idealization,* which means seeing the person in an entirely positive light and failing to recognize any negative

qualities or traits. If you were to ask most Americans on their wedding day why they were marrying their soon-to-be wife or husband, they would likely answer that they are "in love." In fact, if they said they were marrying for money, power, or some equally unromantic reason, many people would view the marriage as a sham.

Limits of Romantic Love In our culture, movies, television plots, and novels support romantic love as the basis for marriage. Infrequent attention is given to the fact that this type of love does not last more than a few years, at most. In long-term marriages, romantic love develops into a different type of love based on other factors such as companionship and shared goals. Unfortunately, many people believe that marriage without the type of romantic love depicted in the movies lacks a critical element. As a result, they may become disenchanted with their relationship.

Love has not always played such an important role in the selection of a spouse or in marriage. In the past, marriages were often arranged by parents or others, and love either developed later or was not seen as an essential part of marriage. Even today in many other, especially non-Western, cultures, the selection of a marriage partner is considered too important to be based on love. People in love are considered too emotional to make such a critical decision. Love is often viewed with suspicion, and attempts may be made to prevent its occurrence. For example, young males and females may be isolated from one another, and chaperones may monitor the activities of their charges to ensure that no inappropriate relationships develop. In such societies, an unmarried woman's virginity is a valuable commodity, and a sexually experienced young woman is not considered a desirable marriage partner. In some cultures, girl and boy babies may be betrothed to one another at birth, or even before. In such societies, love is not a prerequisite for marriage. Community elders or parents decide who should marry whom, basing their decisions on such issues as cementing ties between two families, maintaining power, or increasing wealth. (See the box entitled "Mate Selection in India" for a description of arranged marriage in India today.) The young couple may eventually grow to love each other, but the failure to do so is not considered important. In our culture, because

Mate Selection in India

In India today, marriages are still often arranged by parents. Even among the highly educated, it is considered appropriate for young people to rely upon the judgment of their elders in making such an important decision.

One young woman working toward a Ph.D. degree who had been married only a few months described her relationship with her new husband. She said that she did not love him, but that she found him to be a very kind man who should prove to be a good husband. He, too, was working toward an advanced university degree.

Here is the process that led to her marriage. Her father asked if she was interested in marrying. He was somewhat liberal, because taking a daughter's feelings into account at all is somewhat unusual in India. When

she told her father she would like to marry, he placed an ad in the local newspaper stating his interest in finding an appropriate husband for his daughter. The ad listed requirements, including family background, caste, religion, social characteristics, and educational expectations.

The next week the father, mother, and daughter spent Sunday afternoon at a local hotel where the father had rented a suite. He spent hours interviewing young men who had answered the ad. Meanwhile, the daughter sat with her mother to the side, quietly observing the interviews. At the end of the day, the father informed his daughter of his top choices. Again, although many fathers would not have done this, he asked her for preferences among those men he found acceptable.

The following Sunday the hotel

suite was again rented. The daughter and the man she would marry were allowed to spend an hour or two together discussing their values and hopes for the future while both sets of parents sat across the room discussing the future relationship between the two families.

On the third Sunday the couple were married. Asked whether she resented the fact that her husband had been selected for her and that she had little control over the matter, this highly intelligent and well-educated woman expressed only gratitude that she was not responsible for making this difficult and important decision. Of course, had she been raised in another culture where individual choice is expected, her feelings would undoubtedly have been different.

many necessary services are performed by institutions other than the family, love may be required to hold the family unit together.

Dating Considering how many people each of us gets to know, just how do we ultimately select a mate? In the United States today, mate selection occurs primarily through dating or the informal system of "getting together." Dating allows people to become acquainted and to determine whether they want to spend more time together.

Dating can serve a number of other functions as well. For younger adolescents and those with no immediate interest in marriage, dating can be an enjoyable recreational activity involving the companionship of another person. Dating also allows young people an opportunity to learn more about the opposite sex and about themselves. It can also provide an opportunity for sexual experience and satisfaction.

Finally, dating can help some people improve their status or prestige by being seen with someone who is popular, attractive, or wealthy.

Patterns within Marriages

Although selecting a mate and getting married can be viewed as the end of a long process, they are also the first steps in another long process. Every married couple must address and resolve certain issues in order to develop a viable, long-term relationship. Among these issues are decision making, residency, and inheritance. Although each individual couple exercises some control over these questions, their choices are often determined by larger cultural patterns.

Power and Authority

Who dominates the decision making in a marriage varies from one culture to another. The most common pattern throughout history has been **patriarchy.** In patriarchal societies, husbands have the right to control their wives and children and are expected to do so. In a **matriarchy,** women are given the power and right of decision making. There are no known cultures that could be described as being matriarchal by preference. In the United States, some family systems have been classified as matriarchal, but such patterns typically occur when the husband is not present because of death, divorce, separation, or desertion. Such families have sometimes been described as dysfunctional and unstable. For example, efforts have been made to link male juvenile delinquency to the lack of a male role model in the household. The sociological debate over the effects of living in female-headed families will be discussed later in this chapter.

The United States is in the process of moving from a primarily patriarchal pattern to an *egalitarian* one, in which neither males nor females necessarily control or dominate one another. This transformation is largely the result of changing sex roles. Later in this chapter we will discuss the changes that have occurred in male-female relationships over the past decades.

Residency Patterns

Most newly married couples in the United States prefer to establish their own residence away from the control and scrutiny of their parents. Sociologists use the term **neolocality** to refer to a residency pattern in which married couples form a separate household and live in their own residence. For most young people, getting married and moving out on their own represents independence from parental control. A couple who marries but continues to live with one spouse's parents continues to be dependent to some extent, and their decisions must take the parents into account. In other cultures, a newly married couple might be expected to take up residence with the husband's family, called **patrilocality,** or with the wife's family, called **matrilocality.**

The relative wealth of a society and the availability of affordable housing can affect residency patterns. Historically, couples in the United States often delayed marriage until they could afford a home of their own. Happily, most couples did not have to wait very long. More recently, there has been increasing concern that the price of housing has risen faster than the purchasing power of young married couples. As a result, some couples are forced to share their parents' residence or rent apartments, although they would prefer their own home.

Inheritance and Descent Patterns

Societies differ in their practices that determine how property is inherited and how descent is traced. In a **patrilineal system**, wealth is handed down to males but not to females. This system has contributed to the high birth rates of many developing countries, including India, Korea, Pakistan, and Egypt: No matter how many daughters they have, couples continue trying to have children until they have a son (Weeks, 1986, pp 113–114). Furthermore, kinship is traced through male kin, not female. In other words, a child would be considered related to his father's extended family, but not to his mother's. In a **matrilineal system,** the reverse is true; wealth and descent are passed through female family members. This system is much less common than the patrilineal system.

Like other industrialized societies, the United States has, with one exception, a **bilineal system.** Americans consider themselves to be related both to their father's and their mother's families, and wealth is generally passed down to the children regardless of their sex. This pattern increases the independence of the nuclear family by reducing deference to either the husband or the wife's family. The exception to this bilineal system is the nearly universal practice of giving children their father's last name. Some pioneering couples have decided not to follow this pattern and have given their children a combination of both parents' last names. Because U.S. society is so used to the patrilineal naming pattern, however, such a decision often results in much confusion.

A Functionalist Analysis of the Family

The fact that all societies have some type of family system leads us to consider what the family does for a society. After all, if the family did not do something that was not or could not be done elsewhere, it would probably cease to exist. In the 1930s and early 1940s, writers such as Ogburn (1933) suggested that the family's functions were decreasing and that the family would cease to exist in the near future. As we know, that prediction has not come true. The vast majority of people still marry and raise a family. Of those who divorce, a high proportion remarry. A future for the family seemed unlikely to Ogburn because many of its activities were being taken over by other institutions. What he failed to see was that the family's functions were not really decreasing, they were just changing. The following section examines how several key functions of the family have changed over time.

Changing Functions

Economic   As noted earlier, families in the past were economically more independent than they are today. A higher proportion of the population lived on family farms where they grew their own food and produced much else of what they needed. Home-based businesses and cottage industries also allowed families to be economically productive. Industrialization transformed the economic function of the family from production to consumption. Most families became dependent on outside employers for their income, which allowed them to purchase, rather than produce, the things that they needed. Grocery stores replaced the garden plot and barn, department stores replaced the sewing rooms, and laundries and dry cleaners replaced the washrooms. The family's economic function did not cease to exist, it just changed.

Status Transferral   *Status transferral* refers to the way in which a person acquires his or her social status or social class. The family used to be the primary source of a person's social position. People inherited social status just as they inherited material goods. Today, however, social status is partly inherited and partly a product of market forces. Although many personal characteristics are still determined by family background, and predictions about a person's future based upon family factors are still fairly accurate, modern societies frequently place as much or more emphasis on people's achieved statuses as on their ascribed statuses. In traditional societies such as India, however, a person's entire lifestyle is still dictated by the social status of his or her family.

Religious, Educational, Protective, and Recreational   Although the family used to be the primary source of religious training, much of this responsibility has been turned over to churches, synagogues, Sunday schools, and other organizations supported by religious institutions. Nevertheless, people generally adopt the same religion as their family, and many families still give their children religious training.

Before schools were available on a widespread basis, the family often taught its children to read and write at home. Fathers also taught their sons the work skills they would need to provide for their families. Education now is the responsibility of school systems, colleges, and universities, and relatively few people

Schools and day-care centers have replaced families as the primary educators of their children. However, parental attitudes toward education still have an important effect on children's educational accomplishments.

follow in the occupational footsteps of their parents. Still, the family is critical in supporting and encouraging the education of children. Parents send their young children to preschools and provide them with lessons and camps. Whether a teenager graduates from high school is largely determined by parental attitudes toward the importance of education. Furthermore, many parents sacrifice financially so they can send their children to college.

Protection refers to the provision of food, shelter, and care. It used to be entirely the responsibility of nuclear or extended family members or neighbors. Although the family still cares for children, the sick, the elderly, and others in need of help or care, it is greatly supported by hospitals, pension plans, police and fire departments, nursing and retirement homes, and day-care centers.

In the past, families often spent their limited leisure time together. Recreation today often takes family members in different directions to movie houses, golf courses, and video arcades. However, family-oriented entertainment is still a high priority.

Socialization and Emotional Support

Talcott Parsons and R. F. Bales (1955) identified two "basic and irreducible functions" of the family: "the primary socialization of children so that they can truly become members of the society into which they have been born; second, the stabilization of the adult personalities of the population of the society." The family provides children with the necessary socialization to allow them to become functioning, contributing members of society, and it gives adults the emotional support they need to function in a depersonalizing world.

As discussed in Chapter 5, socialization means that family members provide children with the training that equips them to exist as members of a particular society. Families teach children the behaviors, beliefs, and customs necessary to function within their culture.

Perhaps the emotional value of the family can be appreciated by considering to whom most people turn in times of sickness, sorrow, joy, or financial setback. Although most people have close friendships that give them emotional support, family members generally play a larger role in this area. Most people feel a particular bond with family members that is unlike that felt in any other social relationship.

Affectional

For all the functions discussed so far, the family's role still exists, though in an altered fashion. One function that has become *more* the domain of the family than in the past is the *affectional* function. The family has been referred to as the "shock absorber of society" in that it offers support for the individual who must cope in a difficult world (Toffler, 1972). As the family has become less important as a unit of economic production and the notion of romantic love has become more influential, the affectional function of the family has received greater emphasis.

A Conflict Analysis of the Family

Role Inequality within the Family

Whereas functionalists view the family as a cooperative arrangement between its members and the larger society, conflict theorists see the family as a microcosm of the larger society in which groups who possess wealth and power exploit those who do not. In the family, men dominate women and exploit them both economically and sexually (Marx and Engels, 1969/1848).

Patriarchy and Inequality

The predominance of patriarchal authority patterns underscores the fact that women have traditionally been considered the property of their fathers and husbands. In some cultures, a groom pays a "bride price" to his future wife's father. Even in our society, it is common for a bride to be given away by her father to a man whom she promises to "obey." Fewer women are willing to agree to this condition today; instead they make the same promise as their husband, "to love, honor, and cherish." Still, the majority of women take their husband's last name at marriage, although it is increasingly acceptable for women to keep their unmarried name (which is usually their father's name).

When a couple marries, the agreement is more than a two-party arrangement. The couple is bound by the rights and responsibilities dictated by the state in which they reside. In the United States, this has meant, until recently, that when a woman married, she lost control of her property, both inherited and earned. She also could not sign a contract without her husband's permission and, until 1970, could not get a credit rating in her own name. Until 1985, there had never been a provision in the law that would allow the prosecution of a husband for raping his wife. The presumption was that a husband has the legal right of sexual access to his wife. There are still a number of states in which a husband is immune from such prosecution and others in which he can only be prosecuted under specified conditions. In addition, in many jurisdictions, it is much more difficult to prosecute a husband for assaulting his wife than if a stranger were the offender. This is of particular concern because research has found that the family is one of the most violent institutions, surpassed only by the police and the military (and then only in times of war) (Gelles and Straus, 1979).

Violence and the Family

Although violence in the family was not recognized as a social problem in the academic literature until 1970 (O'Brien, 1971), violence between family members has always been a feature of family life. The closeness and dependency created in the family unit can breed anger, hostility, and physical abuse. Family violence ranges from the physical punishment of a child to physical assault and it frequently results in serious injury. The fact that the abuse takes place in the context of the family makes it especially difficult to prevent, detect, and control.

Child Abuse Physical violence against children has traditionally been viewed as a necessary part of child rearing, as indicated by the expression "Spare the rod and spoil the child." Extreme physical violence against children is one form of **child abuse.** Although child abuse has always existed, it has only received serious recognition during the last few decades. Today it is unfortunately all too common for news stories to report the death of a child as a result of abuse, often at the hands of a parent, or the arrest of an adult, again often the parent, for sexual abuse of a child. Research estimates that 1.5 million children are physically abused each year (Straus and Gelles, 1986).

Parents who are under a great deal of stress are more likely to abuse their children, as are those with limited knowledge of child development. Children who cause family stress, such as the physically or mentally handicapped, are likely targets of abuse, as are babies and very young children, who are too young to tell anyone. Although the cases that most frequently come to public attention are from lower-class families, child abuse occurs among all social classes. Middle-class families may be more successful at keeping violence hidden. There is some evidence, however, that lower-class people may not be as aware of child development or of more appropriate ways of dealing with stress, and may therefore resort to violence more readily than middle-class people. Also, because stress increases the risk of abuse, and poverty itself is a major stressor, there may be a relationship between social class and increased risk of abuse. The "cycle of violence" refers to the fact that abused children often grow up to be abusing parents, modeling their child-rearing practices after those of their own parents. This fact underscores the need to break the cycle through education, counseling, and training.

Courtship Violence Violence also occurs between many dating couples. Most cases involve slapping, punching, and hitting, but some involve sexual attacks. In one recent study, three out of four college women reported that they had been the victims of sexual aggression, with 15 percent actually being raped (Muehlenhard and Linton, 1987). This has been referred to as *date rape* or *acquaintance rape,* and it accounts for a large proportion of all rapes.

Makepeace (1981) found that females were more likely to be the victims of courtship violence. In half of the cases, violence occurred on multiple occasions. Following these incidents, only about half of the relationships were terminated. Another study found that the most frequent abusers were traditionally masculine males and that less traditionally feminine females were the most likely targets (Bernard, et al., 1985). These men may feel psychologically threat-

A battered wife and child do chores in a group home for victims of family violence. As awareness of the problem of abuse has risen, such shelters have been opened in numerous cities and towns.

ened by such women. Of significant concern is the fact that violence that begins in courtship generally continues into marriage (Roscoe and Benaske, 1985).

Spouse Abuse   Although some husbands are abused by their wives (Gelles, 1983), violence inflicted by husbands against wives tends to be more frequent and more intense. Researchers estimate that about 2 million cases of spouse abuse occur each year and that 1 out of every 20 couples will experience severe abuse. Again, there is the cycle of violence — males who were abused as children or whose fathers beat their mothers are more likely to become abusers than other men. Although some social scientists have predicted that as women's status improves, the incidence of wife beating will decline, one study found that high-status wives may actually threaten insecure males, thus resulting in *greater* levels of abuse (Yllo, 1983).

Children who are abused are usually too immature to escape the situation, but battered women often stay in abusive situations by choice. The reasons range from economic dependency and an inability to see alternatives to low self-esteem resulting in perceived helplessness. Some wives are committed to their husbands and their marriage regardless of the situation; others blame themselves for bringing on the abuse.

The Family in the Larger Social Structure

The conflict perspective is also relevant to the role and position of the family within the larger society. Specifically, when the needs of other institutions conflict with those of the family or its members, the family must generally conform or adapt. For example, in order to compete for jobs, families often must be prepared to go where the work is. To pull up roots and move to a distant location for a breadwinner's job can be an unpleasant experience. Social ties may be difficult to break, and if the other spouse is employed, he or she might not want to quit a good job with no firm prospects in the new location. Significantly, women give up their jobs when their husbands get better offers out of town much more often than the reverse.

There are many other situations of potential conflict between the family and other institutions. Parents often experience conflict between the need to provide child care and the demands of work; school schedules fail to conform to vacations from work; family members who are ill must get treatment when medical personnel are available, regardless of the inconvenience; and even religious services may conflict with family schedules.

Changing Patterns of Marriage and the Family

During the 1960s, social movements such as women's liberation, the sexual revolution, and gay rights transformed many of our traditional concepts concerning marriage and the family. As we enter the 1990s, new trends are again emerging.

Changing Roles within Marriage

Undoubtedly, the most fundamental change in American marriage and family life revolves around the changing roles of men and women. Women have entered the labor force in record numbers, a trend that is expected to continue. In fact, a 1986 Gallup Poll found that more than 70 percent of full-time housewives and mothers would like to be employed outside the home. In addition, three-quarters of working mothers claimed that they would continue to work even if they did not need the money (Kantrowitz, 1986). There have also been significant increases in the actual labor force participation of women with children. In 1987, 68 percent of married women with children between 6 and 17 years of age worked, as well as 54 percent of those with children under 6.

Both women and families have benefited from this movement of wives and mothers into the work force. The additional revenue helps meet family expenses, provide for children's education, and avoid poverty in old age. No longer entirely dependent on their husbands for financial support, working wives exercise increased power within the marriage, which helps to create a more equal relationship (Sorensen and McLanahan, 1987; see also Plutzer, 1988).

Men's Contributions to Housekeeping and Child Care Although in many ways the movement of women into the labor force has been positive, some studies have shown that women have had new responsibilities thrust upon them but have not been relieved of any of their traditional duties. Despite significant changes in the roles women play outside the home, there has not been a major shift in the allocation of tasks within the home between males and females during the past 20 years (Coverman and Sheley, 1986). Many women who now work full time still get little help with housework or child care. A large percentage of fathers are present at the birth of their children and have taken on additional child-care responsibilities. Many of the duties they perform, however, tend to be those that are less routine and more "fun" (Pleck, 1985).

Men's housekeeping responsibilities may be limited because of their often feigned incompetence in this area. They have learned that when they exhibit an inability to carry out household chores, they are often relieved of them by wives who would rather do the chores themselves than accept poor housekeeping. One study found that men married to nonworking spouses spent about 45 minutes per day on housekeeping duties, whereas men married to working wives added only an extra 5 to 14 minutes (Michelson, 1985). A more recent study, however, finds that the smaller the gap between the husband's and wife's earnings, the more time the husband spends on household tasks (Ross, 1987). Similar findings have been obtained in international comparative studies (Coltrane, 1988). There are also indications that younger males may be increasingly receptive to changing sex-role expectations. Also, men are begin-

ning to take into account a woman's earning potential when choosing a spouse.

Because women continue to assume the bulk of child-care and housekeeping responsibilities, even when both spouses work full time, men have more time to devote to their careers than do working mothers. As a result, women who become financially successful frequently are unmarried or married without children, which is not true of men. Thus, 51 percent of top female executives are unmarried and 61 percent are childless, compared to 4 percent and 3 percent for men (Fraker, 1984). In general, women with children earn about 20 percent less than those who remain childless (Bloom, 1986). Unlike men, women frequently must choose between home and career.

The increased number of families where both parents work has also required adjustments in child-care and child-rearing arrangements, which has had important consequences for children as well as their parents. This issue is addressed in the box entitled "Latchkey Children."

Although men have taken on a larger share of household tasks, they still do not spend as much time on these tasks as women, even when both husband and wife are employed full time.

Latchkey Children

Every day during the school year, about 10 million children arrive home after school to an empty house or apartment. Some of these "latchkey kids"—so called because they carry keys to let themselves in—are the children of a single parent who must support the entire family. Others have two parents in the home, but both work.

The situation of latchkey kids raises problems both for the children and for the larger society. One 12-year-old girl wrote the following:

I hate being alone. It gets real lonely and depressing. Sometimes if I have trouble on my homework I would forget by the time my parents get home. A lot of the basic stuff I have to learn on my own, like cooking.*

The child who wrote this lives in a safe, middle-class suburban neighbor-

* Written by Kelly D. Wagner, age 12, and used by permission of parent.

hood and comes home to an empty house about 2 days out of 3. Her concerns are shared by all latchkey children, but for some, the problem is greater. In rough city neighborhoods, for example, there are serious risks to the safety of children who must get home on their own and stay there by themselves for hours. In all cases, there is increased danger from hazards such as fire. Because there is also a daily time period in which children know they will be unsupervised, there is also greater opportunity for them to experiment with drugs, alcohol, smoking, and sex—all of which have been more common among teens and preteens during the past 2 decades.

The increasing number of latchkey kids has created problems for the larger society as well. One issue is the tendency of children and parents to use settings not intended for baby-sitting for that purpose. An example is libraries. In many cities, large numbers of children are told by their parents to go to the library after school. Parents know that the

children will be relatively safe, somewhat supervised, and in an "educational" setting. To librarians, however, this practice creates problems, including noise, fights, vandalism, injuries, and in some cases, drug use. Library staff have neither the training nor the numbers needed to handle such problems. In some cities, this use of the library has been forbidden.

Part of the problem is that our institutions have not kept up with societal changes. Schools close at 2:30 or 3:00, and they offer no routine care or activity after that time. This may be starting to change. Recently, Boston University began to assist the school board of one Massachusetts city in setting up after-school care and programming for any students who wish it. The program involves no new construction; some school buildings will simply be used after the normal hours. It will cost money, but this must be balanced against the real cost of leaving children unsupervised several hours a day through most of their later childhood years.

Delayed Marriage and Permanent Singlehood

About one out of every four households in the United States today is made up of one person living alone. In comparison, just 30 years ago only about one out of every ten households was made up of a single person. These households come about in a number of ways.

First, some people are unmarried, and of these, some may never marry, an increasingly common and socially acceptable pattern. Currently, about 5 to 10 percent of the population never marries, and this percentage has been slowly increasing.

There has also been a trend to delay marriage. The average age at first marriage is now 25.5 years for men and 23.3 for women, the highest since the beginning of the century (see Figure 13.2). Women are delaying marriage to complete academic degrees and establish careers. In addition, because premarital sex has become more acceptable, people no longer need to marry in order to enter into a sexual relationship.

Single-person households are also created when a married person becomes widowed or divorced. Although younger people in this category frequently remarry, people widowed or divorced later in life frequently do not. Because women significantly outnumber men by age 60, widowed women are especially unlikely to find another partner.

Finally, there are more single-person households because it is more common today than in the

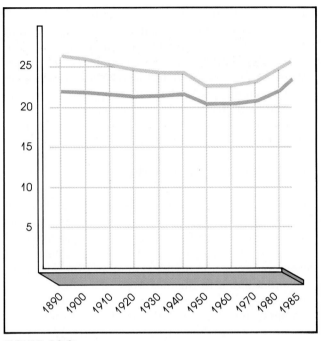

FIGURE 13.2
**Median Age of U.S. Men and Women at First Marriage,
1890–1985**
Note that the age for both sexes has risen steadily since
1960. The recent trend to delay marriage has been more
pronounced among women than among men. According to Oppenheimer (1988), this trend reflects in part
women's greater economic independence: They no
longer have as great a need as in the past to enter a
relationship in order to get economic support. Oppenheimer argues that this change allows women to wait for
a better match, which could result in happier marriages.

past for young unmarried adults to live independently
rather than with their parents (Goldscheider and
Goldscheider, 1987).

Cohabitation

According to census data, the incidence of **cohabitation,** an unmarried male-female couple living together, has tripled since 1970. Four percent of all U.S.
households fall into this category. This involves more
than 2 million households, or over 4.5 million individ-

uals, 60 percent of whom are under 35 years of age
(U.S. Bureau of the Census, 1988d). Half of these people have been previously married, and 30 percent
have children in the household. Because Census
workers do not inquire about the details of a couple's
living arrangement, we don't know the proportion of
cohabiters who are sharing a household but not a sexual relationship. One study found that the proportion
of applicants for marriage licenses who listed the same
address rose from 13 percent in 1970 to 53 percent in
1980 (Gwartney-Gibbs, 1986). Other research during
the first half of the 1980s has found that 44 percent of
all couples who ultimately married had lived together
(Bumpass and Sweet, 1988).

Cohabitation and Marriage In some cases, cohabitation is another stage of "courtship" leading to
marriage. Couples may want to test the relationship
under more realistic conditions than dating allows. In
fact, cohabitation is similar in some respects to marriage, and the lives of couples who live together are not
much different from those of married couples. Cohabiters generally are committed to an exclusive sexual
relationship, although they may be less committed to a
long-term relationship with that person. Women still
perform a disproportionate share of the housework,
and men still make more of the decisions.

Living together, however, does not always lead
to marriage. The couple can enter the relationship
with this understanding, or they can arrive at this
decision after living together for a while. Misunderstandings can occur, however, when partners have
different expectations about the arrangement.

Recently, a number of sociologists have conducted research to find out whether couples who live
together before marriage have better or worse marriages, or a greater or lesser risk of divorce, as compared to couples who do not live together before marriage. At first, such studies found little or no difference
(Olday, 1981; Newcomb and Bentler, 1980). However, more recent studies in the United States, Canada, and Sweden have found that couples who live
together before marriage appear to experience a
higher rate of divorce and report lower levels of marital happiness (DeMaris and Leslie, 1984; Balakrishnan et al., 1987; Bennett, Blanc, and Bloom, 1988). A
possible reason for such differences is that those who

cohabit before marriage are less committed to the institution of marriage and are more hesitant to make a long-term commitment. This suggests that it may not be cohabitation itself that leads to later divorce, but rather that people who are willing to cohabit are also more willing to divorce.

Gay and Lesbian Couples

Homosexuals have a sexual preference for persons of the same sex, whereas *heterosexuals* prefer sexual partners of the opposite sex. Homosexuals, especially male homosexuals, often are identified as *gay*. Homosexual females may be referred to as *lesbians*. Ford and Beach (1951) found that in 64 percent of tribal societies, homosexuality was approved. In the United States, our Judeo-Christian religious foundation has condoned only sexual acts that can lead to conception within marriage, making homosexual relations unacceptable. Although some churches have begun to perform "marriage" ceremonies for homosexual couples, there is no state that legally recognizes marriage between partners of the same sex.

In most respects, homosexual couples are quite similar to heterosexual couples. One significant difference, however, is that homosexual relationships frequently do not receive the social sanctions extended to heterosexual relationships, including legal recognition, support from family and community, and rituals such as a marriage ceremony. For these reasons, and because homosexual couples face most of the same problems as heterosexual couples, homosexual relationships may have an even higher rate of instability than heterosexual relationships. Nevertheless, many older homosexuals remain with the same partner for a number of years. Compared to heterosexuals, homosexual relationships tend to be more egalitarian (Harry, 1982). There is also less gender-based role playing in homosexual relationships (Maracek et al., 1982).

Studies by both Peplau (1981) and Blumstein and Schwartz (1983) have revealed that, although more than half of homosexual men in committed relationships have had sex with someone other than their partner during the previous 2 months, this was true for only 13 percent of lesbians. Although homosexuals are less inclined to keep their sexual preference hidden than in the past, there is still significant discrimination against homosexuals in our society. The recent AIDS epidemic that initially affected primarily the homosexual community has increased negative attitudes toward homosexuals. It has also bolstered monogamous relationships. With the development of artificial insemination, more lesbian couples have children. Courts today are willing to consider granting custody of children to homosexual fathers.

Fewer Children, No Children

Large families are no longer considered ideal. In a poll taken in 1941, about 70 percent of the respondents thought that three or more children would make an ideal-size family. Today, 60 percent consider two or fewer children to be the ideal number (Roper, 1985).

In addition to the economic changes discussed previously, one reason for the trend toward smaller families is the rejection of the belief that an only child will grow up lonely and spoiled. In fact, recent research has found that only children are happy, mentally healthy, and tend to be high achievers (McCoy, 1986), although children raised in larger families do tend to be more outgoing and sociable.

Until recently, childless couples were pitied because it was assumed that they could not have children. The belief was that all married couples wanted children, so those who did not have them must be bitterly disappointed. A decision not to have children was considered selfish because communities and countries wanted to see their populations grow. Today there is more concern about the problems of overpopulation, and many couples admit that they are voluntarily childless. Recent evidence estimates that up to one in five married women might ultimately remain childless. Couples who voluntarily remain childless are often highly educated and career-oriented. They may have been previously married or have married later in life, and their relationships are more egalitarian. Women who are heavily involved in demanding careers often believe that advancement on the job will be slowed if they have children. Couples sometimes argue that their lives are fulfilling without children and that they are reluctant to change an already satisfying situation. With the skyrocketing costs of child rearing, financial considerations may also play a part in the decision to remain childless. Research has shown that couples without children are happier than couples with children, although, paradoxically, they also have a greater risk of divorce (Morgan, Lye, and Condran, 1988), perhaps because couples with children often try to stay together for the sake of the children.

Some couples "drift" into childlessness. They keep delaying having children until they are entrenched in an enjoyable lifestyle or until the wife is too old to become a mother.

Involuntary Childlessness Couples with fertility problems who want to have children now have options that were not available even a few years ago. Medical technology has developed various innovative means of allowing couples to produce a child, including *in vitro fertilization* and *artificial insemination*. Surrogate mothers are bearing children for couples with fertility problems, provoking intense debate. Many people perceive surrogate motherhood as "selling babies." In addition, because surrogate mothers often act out of economic need, the practice raises questions of lower-income women serving as "breeders" for the wealthier classes. Adoption has always been a possibility, but with the legalization of abortion and with more single mothers choosing to keep their babies, there are fewer children available for adoption.

Marital Disruption and Divorce

Americans depend heavily on marriage for their psychological well-being (Glenn and Weaver, 1981). If the choice of a spouse is a good one, the result can be a happy, satisfying future. If the choice is poor, however, the unhappiness of the marriage can penetrate other areas and reduce the overall quality of a person's life.

Divorce in the United States

The United States has one of the highest marriage rates in the world, but it also has the highest level of divorce. In 1987, there were 1,160,000 divorces, meaning that 2,320,000 people ended their marriages (National Center for Health Statistics, 1987). According to Glick (1984), about half of all recent marriages will end in divorce, and the divorce rate for remarriages is even higher (Becker, 1981).

Although the most recent figures show a slight downturn, the incidence of divorce in the United States has risen significantly since the turn of the century (Huber and Spitze, 1988). Just over 100 years ago, about one divorce would occur for every 21 marriages. During World War I, there was one divorce for every 9 marriages. In the 1960s, the divorce rate increased again to one divorce for every 3.5 marriages. Now in the 1980s, there is nearly one divorce for every 2 marriages (Glick and Sung-Ling, 1986). Recent trends in the divorce rate are shown in Figure 13.3.

Who Gets Divorced? The risks of divorce are highest in the early years of marriage, with the average divorce occurring in the seventh year. The longer a marriage has been intact, the lower the chance of divorce. There is also an increased risk for divorce when a person has previously been divorced or comes from a family with a history of divorce. A couple is also more likely to divorce if they married very young. Because those who marry younger have a higher probability of divorce, the recent increase in the age at first marriage should help reduce this risk. Couples who knew each other less than 6 months before they married have higher rates of divorce, as do those in which the wife had a child prior to marriage (Bumpass and Sweet, 1972; Teachman, 1983). On the other hand, research shows that the incidence of divorce is no longer elevated by premarital pregnancy (Teachman, 1983). The relationship between socioeconomic factors and divorce has also been documented. Couples with low income, limited educational attainment, and unemployment tend to have a higher risk of divorce.

Causes of Divorce

Longevity Some people interpret the growing divorce rate as evidence that many people are making poor decisions regarding their choice of a mate. Others believe that greater life expectancy almost inevitably leads to more divorces. In the past, when people had much shorter life expectancies, couples who married until "death us do part" frequently didn't have to wait very long to be parted. The *combined* risk

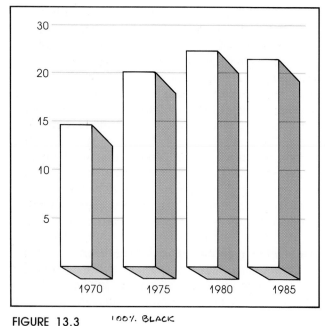

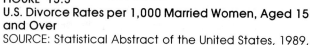

FIGURE 13.3
U.S. Divorce Rates per 1,000 Married Women, Aged 15 and Over
SOURCE: Statistical Abstract of the United States, 1989, Table 126.

of marital disruption from either death or divorce was only modestly lower then than now (Sweetser, 1985; Cheslin, 1981). However, marriages were more likely to be ended by death and less likely to be ended by divorce. Today, with average life expectancy exceeding 70 years (U.S. Bureau of the Census, 1987d), a couple who marry in their early twenties could, in the absence of divorce, expect their marriage to last 50 or more years. It may be unrealistic to expect that the right mate for a person of 20 will still be the best choice 20, 40, or 60 years later. People continue to change throughout life, and spouses often find that they are not changing in parallel ways.

Economic Independence of Women Other circumstances have also contributed to the increasing rate of divorce. As women have become better educated and have entered the labor force, they have become less economically dependent upon their husbands. As a result, a woman in an unhappy marriage has the op-

tion of leaving the marriage because she is, or can become, economically self-sufficient.

Unrealistic Expectations Another factor is the high level of expectations people have for marriage. With the decline of the extended family, husbands and wives increasingly look to each other for needs that had previously been met by other family members. It may be unrealistic to expect any marital relationship to be able to meet all the diverse needs of both partners at all times.

Maintaining a Bad Marriage Not all bad marriages end in divorce. Many of the same factors that contribute to high divorce rates also create stress in marriage, producing unhappy, unsatisfying marriages that remain outwardly intact but are internally broken. Sometimes these relationships have been termed ''empty-shell'' marriages.

Cuber and Harroff (1965) contrasted *intrinsic marriages,* in which the relationship always takes top priority, with *utilitarian marriages,* which are established or maintained for purposes other than to express an intimate relationship. A couple who expected an intrinsic relationship might seek a divorce if significant problems exist in the marriage, whereas a couple involved in a utilitarian marriage might choose to remain married for many reasons, none of which involve the quality of their relationship. Cuber and Harroff

As divorce has become more commonplace in America, it has also become a big business, as illustrated by this photo.

also described *devitalized marriages,* which are characterized by an initial closeness that is lost, and *conflict-habituated marriages,* which are characterized by pervasive incompatibility, constant conflict, and an atmosphere of tension. Again, although divorce can occur in either type, it might not. People might accept the devitalized quality of their marriage, or they may be so emotionally dependent on their conflict-habituated relationship that they do not consider divorce a realistic option.

Of course, many marriages are happy and remain so throughout life. What is it that distinguishes these successful and rewarding marriages from ones that end in divorce or drag unhappily on? Sociologists Jeanette and Robert Lauer conducted research on this question, and they tell us what they discovered in their ''Personal Journey into Sociology.''

Changing Divorce Laws

Until recent decades, divorce was a cause of public censure and personal humiliation. With divorce so common today, however, the emphasis is now on reducing the negative impacts on the divorcing spouses and especially on the children. Social and legal accommodations have been made to ease the trauma.

Divorce laws have been significantly liberalized. No longer do spouses have to accuse each other of adultery, alcoholism, or physical cruelty to get a divorce. In almost every state, couples can now be granted divorces because of *irreconcilable differences.* Such change has been slow in coming, however. For example, in New York State, adultery was the only legal grounds for divorce until 1973. In 1970, California became the first state to eliminate any requirement of fault in cases of divorce in its much-copied no-fault divorce law. The majority of states now have statutes allowing no-fault divorce. Just as no-fault automobile insurance seeks to save court expenses by eliminating the need to determine responsibility, so no-fault divorce seeks to allow divorce without requiring that one spouse prove the other was at fault. In no-fault divorce, marital partners agree that the marriage has broken down and that they have irreconcilable differences. This reduces potential hostility between

spouses and saves children much trauma. It is also a more realistic perspective. In only a minority of divorce cases is one of the partners entirely at fault.

Although many people hail this trend as humane and farsighted, others fear that it has made divorce too easy. They argue that such laws have contributed to the increase in the divorce rate in the United States, and they speculate that if divorce were harder, more people would stay married. Of course, this would not guarantee that the marriages would be any happier.

There have been other legal changes regarding divorce. Custody of dependent children almost always went to the mother in the past. Although the mother still gets custody about 90 percent of the time (Weitzman, 1985), the courts today increasingly try to determine which parent would make the better custodial parent, often taking into account the wishes of the children, especially if they are older. Joint custody has become increasingly common as well.

Effects on Women Some evidence indicates that liberalized divorce laws may actually be harming women in some instances (Weitzman, 1985). For example, when a woman who has been a full-time homemaker is divorced and the court orders that the couple's assets be divided, it may be necessary for the home to be sold to allow this division, thereby displacing the ex-wife and children. Furthermore, a woman who has not been on the job market in years, or perhaps ever before, may have a difficult time supporting herself. At the same time, she is less likely to receive alimony. Now that women are more often able to take care of themselves financially, courts are awarding alimony much less frequently, in less than 15 percent of divorces. Even when awarded, alimony is paid only three-quarters of the time, and the average alimony payment is only about $4,000 per year. Child support is awarded only about half the time, and it is actually paid in full in only half of the cases in which it was awarded. The average amount of child support paid is only $2,300 per year (Bureau of the Census, 1987). Following a divorce, a woman's standard of living declines by about 73 percent on the average, while her ex-husband's rises by 42 percent (Weitzman, 1985, p. 339; see also Weiss, 1984). Not surprisingly, research has shown that children of di-

Background of 'Til Death Do Us Part: How Couples Stay Together

Ideas for research come in various ways. Some of the research we have done has been stimulated by unanswered questions or ambiguous findings or suggestions made in the literature. Our study of long-term marriages, however, grew out of a technique that we urge our own students to use—introspection. Think about your own experiences. What questions are raised? In reflecting on and questioning your experiences, you may find a rich source of research ideas.

The idea for long-term marriages came to us as we were running together one day. We were concerned that so many of our friends' marriages seemed to be breaking apart. In each case, we knew the reasons they gave. Then the conversation took a different turn. We jokingly said that we were going to be one of the last married couples in our group of friends. Then we seriously asked the question of why. What keeps a marriage going? Why do some marriages *not* fail? What is the cement that makes some relationships not only lasting but thriving?

At that moment we agreed to research the topic. We had a personal as well as a professional interest in the outcome. Our first step was to re-

Jeanette C. Lauer and Robert H. Lauer

Robert and Jeanette Lauer are co-authors of Watersheds: Mastering Life's Unpredictable Crises, chosen as the main selection of the *Psychology Today* Book Club. Each has written numerous other books dealing with human behavior. Both received doctorates from Washington University in St. Louis, and both currently teach at U.S. International University in San Diego.

search the literature. We were stunned. At the time, there were no books and only a handful of articles that addressed the question of what keeps a marriage together. At least, they didn't address it by looking directly at marriages that had

succeeded. We immediately went to work to design an instrument. We decided to use the Dyadic Adjustment Scale, a widely used measure of marital satisfaction. But again using introspection, we thought about our own relationship and decided that the scale did not capture all of the important ingredients. We added six items that reflected our own experience. We also used some open-ended questions to probe such things as our subjects' perceptions of why their marriages had lasted, their methods of dealing with conflict, and how they maintained vitality in their relationships.

Using doctoral students and friends, we eventually made contact with 351 couples in various parts of the country who had been married 15 years or more. We chose 15 as a reasonable number of years for "long-term" because the median number of years of marriage among those who eventually break up is 7. Thus, our couples had been married slightly more than twice as long as the median.

Initially, we assumed that anyone married so long in this day would be happy. We were wrong. In 51 of the couples, one or both spouses was unhappy with the rela-

vorced parents are less prone to problem behavior when they receive adequate economic support from their noncustodial fathers (Furstenberg, Morgan, and Allison, 1987).

Effects on Children Some research has found that "a divorced family per se is neither more nor less beneficial for children than an unhappy marriage" (Wallerstein and Kelly, 1980). Although children of divorcing parents are psychologically and emotionally affected by the stress over the short term, the long-term effects of divorce do not seem to be as great. Other research on the impact of divorce on children has found that children actually fare better with di-

tionship. This unexpected finding gave us useful data for comparisons. Not only could we now say what factors seemed to be involved in stable marriages, but we could also determine how stable and satisfying marriages differ from those that are stable but unsatisfying.

We asked each individual to look at 38 factors (32 on the Dyadic Adjustment Scale and the 6 we added) and identify those most responsible for the stability of their marriage. We also asked them to volunteer any other factors that they perceived as important. For couples where one or both partners was unhappy, the most frequent reasons for staying together were commitment (for religious reasons or family tradition) and children. In a sense, they said that they were determined to keep the marriage intact no matter how dissatisfied they were. The marriage itself, and not their personal happiness, had priority.

For those in happy marriages, an interesting thing happened. First, although men and women were interviewed and filled out the questionnaires separately, the first seven factors most frequently listed were identical for husbands and wives. Four of the seven were items

from the six that we had added to the scale, underscoring our conviction that introspection can frequently be an important part of the research process. The seven factors identified by people as important to long-term, happy marriages are listed below.

1. Their spouse is their best friend.
2. They like the spouse as a person.
3. They are committed both to the spouse and to the institution of marriage.
4. They believe in the sanctity of marriage.
5. They agree with the spouse on aims and goals.
6. They believe that the spouse has grown more interesting over the years.
7. They strongly want the relationship to succeed.

Perhaps the central factor was captured well by one wife who said of her husband: "I like him. I like the kind of person he is. Even if he weren't my husband, I would want to have him as a friend." Like those in unhappy unions, the happy spouses were committed. But there was a difference. Whereas the unhappy people were committed to the marriage

no matter how miserable they were personally, the happy people were committed in the sense of being determined to confront any problems and work through them. Unhappy spouses may ignore or avoid or simply endure problems. Happy spouses are not willing either for themselves or their mates to be unhappy in the relationship.

Although not in the top seven, humor was also one of the factors frequently mentioned. Respondents often said that humor is very important in maintaining a vital relationship. Some people consciously work at maintaining humor in the relationship. For example, one woman said that she saves cartoons and shares them with her husband so they can laugh together.

Finally, we are pleased to report that a follow-up study was done by a doctoral student who used our questionnaire to interview 200 couples married 45 years or more. Her results were virtually identical to ours. We feel some confidence, therefore, in saying that we have been able to identify the factors that are necessary for a marriage to be both long-term and satisfying to both husband and wife.

vorce than they do in a home characterized by conflict, tension, and, sometimes, violence (Zill, 1984; Cooper, Holman, and Braithwaite, 1983). This refutes the frequently cited belief that parents should stay together for the sake of the children. Of course, divorce is a major cause of one-parent families, and there has been a great deal of debate concerning the

effects on children of living in such families. This debate will be discussed later in this chapter.

Remarriage

Although divorce rates are high, remarriage rates are also high. According to 1980 statistics, 83 percent of divorced men and 78 percent of divorced women eventually remarry (Schoen, Woodrow, and Baj, 1985). Americans may be disenchanted with their current marital partners, but they do not seem to be disenchanted with the institution of marriage. Males tend to have higher rates of remarriage than females. As women grow older, the number of males in their age range diminishes rapidly, reducing their chances of finding a second husband. Also, divorced men often marry women considerably younger than they are, further reducing the pool of potential partners for divorced women, who less frequently marry younger males. Women with higher educational attainment levels also remarry less frequently (Glick and Lin, 1986), demonstrating the *marriage gradient,* that is, the pattern of women marrying ''up'' (men with more education and higher incomes) and men marrying ''down.'' Although most divorced people do remarry, the percentage who do so has been falling, and people have been waiting longer after a divorce before they remarry. Between 1970 and 1980, for example, the median amount of time between divorce and remarriage doubled for both men and women in the United States (National Center for Health Statistics, 1988).

Second marriages have about the same risk of divorce as first marriages, except that those with children tend to have somewhat higher rates (White and Booth, 1985). When children are involved and a ''blended'' family is created, the remarriage experience is considerably different from a first marriage. Today, about one child in ten lives with a stepparent, and two-thirds of these have stepsiblings, halfsiblings, or both (Huber and Spitze, 1988, p. 434). There are few established norms or rules to guide relationships between stepparents and stepchildren, stepbrothers and stepsisters. This often results in uncertainty, confusion—and a higher divorce rate.

Women who are widowed later in life have low rates of remarriage because of the lack of eligible males. Only 9 percent of males between the ages of 65 and 74 are widowed, whereas 39 percent of females are. For those 75 and older, the difference is even greater, with 23 percent of males, but 68 percent of females, widowed (U.S. Bureau of the Census, 1986).

Single-Parent Families

According to the most recent figures, at any given point in time, about one out of every four children in this country is living in a one-parent household. Forty-two percent of white children and 86 percent of black children will live in a single-parent household at some point before reaching the age of 18 (Bumpass, 1984). Almost 90 percent of single-parent households are headed by a female (Bureau of the Census, 1988e).

The number of single-parent, female-headed households has increased for several reasons. One is the rising rates of divorce and separation, discussed above. Another is the rapid increase in the birth rate among unmarried people. One out of every five babies in this country is born to a single mother (Bureau of the Census, 1987d), many of whom are teenagers. This should not be surprising considering that the vast majority of sexually active American teenagers fail to use birth control regularly. Today only 10 percent of single mothers choose not to keep their babies.

More than half of all children in families with no father present live in poverty, with their mothers often dependent upon welfare (Bureau of the Census, 1987d). Children from single-parent households exhibit rates of delinquency double those for children from two-parent homes, but this may be related to poverty as much as to living arrangements. Often having lower educational and economic levels to begin with, single parents must then cope with living on only one income while playing both mother and father to their children.

The goal of one recent children's book is to let children know that ''It doesn't matter what kind of family you live in, it's still your family. . . . [W]hatever it looks like, wherever it lives, whomever it contains, each family is very real and precious to the people in it'' (Thomas, 1987). Children cannot *choose* the family in which they are raised any more than they can choose to be born male or female, black or white, rich or poor. But how children experience each of these realities is determined by the way adults act on often unexamined assumptions about different personal attributes or family compositions. Just as children suffer from sexism and racism, they suffer when their families are discredited—either directly or by inference or innuendo. Children internalize social criticism. They feel personally stigmatized. They blame themselves for not living "Dick and Jane" lives.

Race, Poverty, and the One-Parent Family

For more than 2 decades, sociologists and policy makers have debated the importance of the growing number of one-parent families as a cause of poverty. This debate has often taken on racial overtones. The statistics concerning race, poverty, and family type are clear, but their meanings are not. The incidence of one-parent, female-headed families is much higher among the poor than among the nonpoor population for all races (U.S. Bureau of the Census, 1988d, p. 64, 85). This is illustrated in Table 13.1. However, the incidence of such families is lowest among whites, higher among Hispanics, and highest of all among African Americans, as shown in Figure 13.4. Nonetheless, there have been substantial increases in the proportion of one-parent families among all racial and income groups since the late 1960s.

The Moynihan Report and Black Families The high incidence of single-parent families among blacks and poor people has led some sociologists to argue that the structure of the black family is an important cause of disproportionate black poverty. These sociologists, operating largely from a functionalist perspective, see danger in any group having a family structure too different from the standard nuclear family. The best-known proponent of this viewpoint is Daniel Patrick Moynihan, who in 1965 published a very controversial report on the subject (U.S. Department of Labor, 1965). Moynihan's report was controversial not because of the statistics it cited, but because of its interpretation of those statistics (Rainwater and Yancey, 1967). Although the debate today is much less centered around the Moynihan Report than it once was, the controversy over the importance of the single-parent family as a cause of minority inner-city poverty continues. The Moynihan interpretation and others like it have been criticized on several points.

First and foremost, the single-parent family is at least as much a product of poverty as a cause of it. Poverty breaks up the family in several ways. When husbands and fathers cannot fulfill their role expectations of supporting their family because of unemployment or low pay, they sometimes retreat from that role by deserting their families. The stresses of poverty increase the risk of conflict, violence, and substance abuse within the family. Welfare laws create an economic incentive for the family to break up, because the presence of a father, no matter how low his income, prevents the family from receiving certain kinds of support. Many single-parent families result from nonmarital pregnancies, and these, too, are very much a product of poverty. Poor teenagers, for example, are much more likely to become teenage mothers than are nonpoor ones, for a variety of reasons discussed in Chapter 9. All of these facts point to the interpretation that single-parent families are a *consequence* of urban

TABLE 13.1
Percentage of Female Householder Families, by Race, Hispanic Origin, and Income Above or Below Poverty Level, 1986.

	WHITE FAMILIES	BLACK FAMILIES	HISPANIC FAMILIES
Families of All Income Levels	13.0%	41.8%	23.4%
Families Above Poverty Level	10.2%	28.4%	15.2%
Families Below Poverty Level	42.4%	74.9%	48.7%

SOURCE: U.S. Bureau of the Census, 1988d, pp. 64, 85.

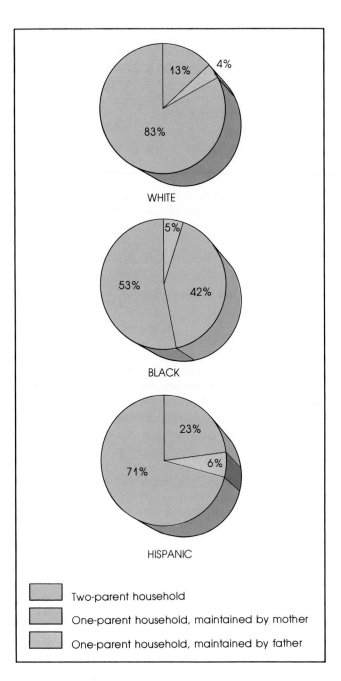

13% 4%

83%

WHITE

5%

53%   42%

BLACK

23%

71%   6%

HISPANIC

☐ Two-parent household

☐ One-parent household, maintained by mother

☐ One-parent household, maintained by father

FIGURE 13.4
Proportion of Single-Parent Households among All Family Households, 1986
SOURCE: Statistical Abstract of the United States, 1988, Table 58.

poverty and unemployment. If this is the case, the logical policy direction is to address the direct causes of poverty, discussed in Chapter 9, rather than to try to reduce poverty by changing families.

With respect to black families, several other issues have been raised in this debate. It is commonly argued that *matriarchy* is part of African-American culture, and that the disproportionate number of female-headed families has roots that can be traced at least to slavery. There is a problem with this argument, however. Most evidence suggests that the vast majority of black families were two-parent families until the mid-twentieth century, and that female-headed families only became common among Black Americans when the black population began to urbanize on a large scale (Gutman, 1976; Fursterberg, Hershberg, and Modell, 1975; Lammermeier, 1973; Wilson, 1987). This further suggests that the urban poverty experienced by Black Americans is an important factor in shaping black family structure.

Another problem is the portrayal by Moynihan and others of "the black family." Actually, there is no one black family pattern, just as there is no one white family pattern or Hispanic family pattern. At the time Moynihan wrote his report, only 23 percent of black families were headed by women; so "the black family" then could hardly be characterized as "female-headed." Even today there are about as many husband-wife families among African Americans as there are female-headed families. Finally, Moynihan used some highly value-laden terminology in his report. He referred to the black family as a "tangle of pathology" and "the fundamental source of weakness in the Negro community at this time." Many people felt that this led to blaming the victim: it implied that poverty resulted not from racism or from the operation of the American economy, but rather from characteristics of blacks themselves (Ryan, 1971).

Family Structure: A Cause of Poverty? A final criticism of the Moynihan Report was that it made no real attempt to test its assumption that single-parent families are an important cause of poverty (Gans, 1967b; Ryan, 1967). Since that report was published, a good deal of research and analysis on this topic has taken place. Some research has indicated that the rising incidence of female-headed households has been accompanied by increases in poverty and a worsening of the position of the urban *underclass* (Bianchi, 1981; Wilson, 1987; Reimers, 1984). In one sense, single-parent families would seem to be at greater risk of poverty. They have only one potential earner and thus cannot take advantage of the trend in the American family toward having two sources of income. However, an even larger problem is related to the low pay of women. As shown in Table 13.2, the median income of one-parent *male-headed* families is very near that of all U.S. families and is also very close to that of the "traditional" family where the husband is employed and the wife is a homemaker. Thus, if women's incomes were the same as those of men, living in a female-headed family would be much less likely to mean living in a poor family. (The causes of women's low wages are discussed in Chapter 6.) In short, the low wages of women are a major cause of whatever economic disadvantages female-headed families suffer. Among black and Hispanic women, this condition is worsened by relatively low levels of education, which further depress wages.

Of course, part of the argument made by Moynihan and others is that other disadvantages of growing up in a female-headed family can lead to the perpetuation of poverty into successive generations. Until recently, research findings provided relatively little support for this viewpoint. Lieberson (1980, pp. 183–193), for example, found that very little of the black-white gap in educational attainment could be explained by differences in family structure. More recent research, though, indicates that growing up in single-parent families can have long-term effects for both blacks and whites (McLanahan and Bumpass, 1988), including a greater risk of early and premarital childbearing, a greater risk of divorce, and lower education and income. Research by Sampson (1987) also found that black family disruption led to increased rates of juvenile crime. Undoubtedly, some of these effects are the result of teenage pregnancy, which has become widespread among poor Americans of all racial and ethnic groups.

Although growing up in single-parent families does appear to be detrimental in some ways, it also appears that one-parent families are here to stay in the United States. Moreover, virtually all studies agree on certain points. First, people with low incomes—black, Hispanic, *and* white—are more likely than others to form one-parent families either by premarital childbearing or by divorce/separation. Second, an important source of problems among people in female-headed families is the low income of their wage earners (Reimers, 1984). Therefore, dealing with such causes of poverty as low wages and high unemployment will likely reduce the number of urban single-parent families, and taking steps to eliminate wage inequalities based on sex and to enforce payment of child support by absent fathers would alleviate many of the disadvantages of female-headed families.

The Family and Sexuality

Unlike other species whose sexual activity is limited to specific periods of time, human beings have no such

TABLE 13.2
Median Family Income, by Race, Hispanic Origin, and Type of Family, 1986

	ALL FAMILIES	MARRIED-COUPLE FAMILIES		MALE HOUSEHOLDER, NO WIFE	FEMALE HOUSEHOLDER, NO HUSBAND
		Wife in Paid Labor Force	Wife Not in Paid Labor Force		
U.S. Total	$29,458	$38,346	$25,803	$24,962	$13,647
White	30,809	38,972	26,421	26,247	15,716
Black	17,604	31,949	16,766	18,731	9,300
Hispanic	19,995	30,206	17,507	20,894	9,432

SOURCE: U.S. Bureau of the Census, 1988g, pp. 28–30.

limitations. We are sexual creatures throughout our lifetime. Whereas sex between most other species is motivated solely by reproductive instincts, our sexuality is not limited to those times during which the female can conceive. Although sex may be desired for purely physical reasons, it often reflects a desire for emotional closeness, and it can enhance intimacy in a relationship.

The Family As a Regulator of Sexual Behavior

Human sexual preferences and practices are primarily learned through the process of socialization. All societies control sexual behavior in some manner. In fact, three cultural universals or patterns relating to the family are found in all societies. The first is the incest taboo, discussed earlier in this chapter. The next universal is marriage. Societies have typically encouraged sex within marriage and discouraged or regulated it outside of marriage to provide a stable environment for the nurturance of children. The final cultural universal is heterosexuality, which is necessary for the perpetuation of the species.

Outside of these expectations, however, a great deal of variety exists in what practices different societies require, encourage, permit, ignore, discourage, or condemn. Some cultures encourage premarital sex; others discourage it. Some societies condemn homosexuality, others ignore it, and some approve of it for certain groups. These values can change over time. Although a sexual relationship is expected of couples when they marry, the details of that relationship can vary significantly between cultures, social classes, or religions, and from one couple to another. Unlike in other species, human sexuality is quite diverse.

Similarly, standards of beauty vary from one society to another. Females traditionally have been judged by their physical appearance, although a woman considered highly attractive and sexually desirable in one culture might be considered repulsive in another. Males have been valued for their wealth or power rather than their physical attractiveness. In fact, men have traditionally been judged by the beauty of their wives (Zetterberg, 1966). As women become more economically independent, however, this system may change, and males may be judged more on physical attractiveness. Already we have seen a growing interest on the part of men in cosmetics, hair restoration, and plastic surgery.

Nonmarital Sex *Nonmarital sex* refers to any sexual activity outside of a marital relationship. Within this category, *premarital sex* is sexual activity prior to marriage and *extramarital sex* refers to a married person's sexual relations with anyone other than his or her spouse. Although sex outside of marriage has never been socially supported in the United States, premarital sex has become increasingly common and acceptable since the turn of the century.

Sex outside of marriage has been discouraged for various reasons, including disease, pregnancy, and social and religious disapproval. When effective means of treating most sexually transmitted diseases were found and contraception became widely available, much of the resistance to premarital sex broke down. Extramarital sex, however, is still frowned upon by most people.

THE SEXUAL REVOLUTIONS Before World War I, approximately three-quarters of all new brides and half of grooms were virgins. During World War I and the 1920s, however, a little-recognized sexual revolution occurred that involved significant changes in sexual behavior. By the mid-1920s, only half of brides and one-third of grooms were sexually inexperienced on their wedding day. Because of the lack of social support for sex outside of marriage, however, these new behavior patterns were not discussed. When Alfred Kinsey (1948; 1953) conducted his monumental studies of sexual behavior in the late 1940s and early 1950s, he noted that 85 percent of males had engaged in premarital sex, as had about half of all women. Furthermore, half of males and one-quarter of females had engaged in extramarital sex. Not until the second sexual revolution, from the mid-1960s to mid-1970s, however, did people openly espouse the sexual values that had, to a great extent, already taken hold. Although the figures are somewhat lower for college students, studies now consistently find that on their wedding days more than 80 percent of brides and 90 percent of grooms are nonvirginal.

The increase in premarital sexual activity has been greater for women than for men. Male rates have been less affected because men have traditionally had sex with prostitutes. There has been a move away from the double standard in which premarital sex was condoned for men but condemned for women. Although promiscuous sexual behavior—that is, having sex with a number of different partners—is still particularly frowned upon among females, society today is much more tolerant of a woman having sex with a partner with whom she is emotionally involved. The changing role of women is partially responsible for this shift, as is the availability of effective contraception. The availability of birth-control pills beginning in the mid-1960s enabled women to control their reproductive behavior.

Certain remnants of the traditional moral stance remain visible in U.S. society. One prominent example is the hesitancy to make birth control freely available to unmarried teenagers. Those who support this position mistakenly believe that limiting access to birth control will in turn limit sexual activity. As a result, the United States has one of the highest rates of teenage pregnancy among industrialized countries (Jones et al., 1986). One-fourth of all brides are either pregnant or mothers when they marry. The United States also has a relatively high abortion rate, in large part because of its high rate of teenage pregnancy.

We have moved away from another double standard that required people to say that they believed in abstinence before marriage when, in fact, most of them were behaving differently. Christensen (1960) found that when people valued chastity and yet engaged in premarital sex, they were more likely to feel guilty about their behavior. If they saw nothing inappropriate in engaging in sexual relations before marriage, however, their behavior provoked no guilt.

AIDS Fear of contracting AIDS (acquired immune deficiency syndrome) has caused many people to alter their sexual behavior. Both homosexuals and heterosexuals are limiting the number of their sexual partners, a trend that was already underway before AIDS became widespread but has been accelerated by the fear of AIDS. In addition, more people today are engaging in safer sex practices, such as the use of condoms. Studies suggest that teenagers, however, do not view themselves as being at risk for AIDS and therefore still fail to take basic precautions. As a result,

they may be more likely to contract the disease. Generally, however, some people believe that AIDS has contributed to a swing of the pendulum back toward traditional values.

Marital Sex Sexuality within marriage has also been undergoing change. Years ago women were not expected to enjoy sex. In fact, a woman who did was considered to be highly unusual and undesirable. Sex was viewed as a "wifely duty." This is no longer the case. Today sexual pleasure is considered to be equally important and desirable for males and females. A woman's sexual role is no longer defined as simply to satisfy her husband's sexual needs. Apparently reflecting these changes, studies have reported increased frequency of marital sex. At the same time, many dual-career couples find that between their jobs, children, and household responsibilities, they don't have much time or energy for sex. Women, especially, state that fatigue reduces their interest in sex.

The Future of Sexuality, Marriage, and the Family

"Surrogate Mother Refuses To Give Up Baby"

"One Quarter of Conceptions End In Abortion"

"Working Moms Lobby Legislature For Day Care Assistance"

"Half Of All Marriages End In Divorce"

"AIDS Education In The Schools Is Encouraged"

"Father Sentenced To Prison For Sexual Abuse Of Daughter"

"Researchers Find Higher Cancer Risk With More Sexual Partners"

"Gay Rights Activists Want Health Benefits For Partners"

Headlines such as these reflect our growing concern, disagreement, and even anger over issues such as homosexuality, abortion, and artificial conception. Only 25 years ago, things were quite different. Surrogate mothers and AIDS were unknown, abortion was illegal in most states, and openness about sexuality still made many people uncomfortable. Fewer women worked outside the home, and more couples stayed married for a lifetime. The scope of the changes that have affected marriage and the family in this relatively brief period of time is almost overwhelming. What will families be like 25 years from now, and what problems will they face?

Just as sociologists 50 years ago feared the disintegration of the family because it was losing its traditional functions, today some social observers point to sexual permissiveness, smaller families, higher divorce rates, single-parent households, teenage pregnancy, family violence, increasing numbers of people postponing marriage or not marrying at all, and the prevalence of alternative family structures as evidence that the family is a decaying institution. Others look at these same developments and proclaim that the family is a resilient institution that is "here to stay" (Bane, 1976). Ninety percent of Americans think that marriage is the best way to live. Most people still ultimately marry and, if they divorce, later remarry.

Ideally, the changes we are undergoing in the area of sex roles will allow people to choose what is right for them individually rather than conform to predetermined roles. However, the options available today, especially to women, make it increasingly difficult to know what to do or to be content with our choices. This often produces a situation of *anomie*—a lack of effective norms that can lead to confusion and alienation. At the same time, people are less likely to be stigmatized for the personal choices that they make. American society has become increasingly tolerant of alternative forms of marital and family life. Choices about personal lifestyles reflect the diversity in the rest of the culture. People are choosing family systems to complement their social and economic situations. As these institutions have changed, so has the family.

Summary

The family is the most basic and universal of all human social institutions. A family can be defined as a group of related people who live together as a unit. The precise form and functions of the family vary from culture to culture. The most basic family types are the nuclear family and the extended family; the latter is the predominant type in the United States. The family you are born into is called your family of orientation; the family you create when you marry and have children is called the family of procreation. Although monogamy is the only legally recognized form of marriage in Western societies, many cultures have practiced different forms of polygamy.

Because the family is a cultural universal, functionalists assume that it must perform certain roles that other institutions cannot. The key functions of the family can be divided into general categories, including economic, status transferral, religious and educational, affectional, socialization, and emotional support. In modern societies, the family must share these functions with outside institutions, but it continues to play a critical role in all of them.

Conflict theorists argue that the family reflects the inequalities of the larger society. They point to such social realities as role inequality and violence within the family to argue that family structure and behavior are designed to promote the well-being of the dominant group in the society, males.

As with most institutions, the family has changed in response to larger societal and cultural changes. As women have increasingly entered the work force, many have chosen to delay marriage and childbirth. More women and men than in the past do not marry, and among those who do, the percentage of couples who choose to remain childless has increased. Cohabitation, in which an unmarried couple live together, has become acceptable. Married and cohabiting couples divide household responsibilities more equally than in the past, although the woman still assumes a disproportionate share of such responsibilities in most relationships.

As a result of women's increased economic independence and related legal and ideological changes, divorce has become more common and acceptable in U.S. society. On the one hand, this change has benefited people, especially women, by allowing them to escape from unhappy marriages. On the other hand, increased divorce rates have created many one-parent families and placed severe economic hardships on many women. One consequence of this trend has been the feminization of poverty.

Despite all these changes, the family remains a viable unit, and warnings of the "demise of the family" are unfounded. Most people still marry and have families. If divorce rates are high, so are remarriage rates. Although the family must change to adapt to changes in other social institutions, it will continue to play a crucial role in modern societies.

Glossary

family A group of people related by ancestry, marriage, or adoption who live together, form an economic unit, and cooperatively rear their young.

kinship A pattern in which people are related by ancestry, marriage, or adoption but can live independently from one another.

marriage A socially approved arrangement between a male and a female that involves an economic and a sexual relationship.

extended family A family consisting of more than two generations who live together and share responsibilities for the maintenance of the family.

nuclear family A family that is restricted to a parent or parents and their unmarried children.

family of orientation The family into which a person is born.

family of procreation The family a person forms by marrying and having children.

monogamy The marriage of one husband to one wife.

serial monogamy A system in which people engage in a series of monogamous relationships; it usually occurs as a result of divorce and remarriage.

polygamy Any form of marriage that involves more than two partners.

polygyny A form of marriage in which a man has more than one wife.

polyandry A form of marriage in which a woman has more than one husband.

incest taboo Societal rules that prohibit marriage or sexual relationships between people defined as being related to each other.

exogamy Marriage between people from different racial, ethnic, or religious groups.

endogamy Marriage between people from the same racial, religious, and ethnic groups.

homogamy "Like marrying like"; marriage between people of similar backgrounds and social characteristics.

patriarchy A form of society in which males possess power and the right of decision making.

matriarchy A form of society in which females possess power and the right of decision making.

neolocality A residency pattern in which married couples form a separate household and live in their own residence.

patrilocality A residency pattern in which married couples live with the husband's family.

matrilocality A residency pattern in which married couples live with the wife's family.

patrilineal system A system in which wealth and kinship are passed on through males.

matrilineal system A system in which wealth and kinship are passed on through females.

bilineal system A system in which wealth and kinship are passed on through both males and females.

child abuse Extreme or sustained physical or psychological violence directed against children.

cohabitation An arrangement in which an unmarried couple form a household.

Further Readings

BLUMSTEIN, PHILIP, AND PEPPER SCHWARTZ. 1983. *American Couples*. New York: William Morrow and Company. An important book based on studies of hundreds of heterosexual, homosexual, and lesbian couples from different parts of the country. A good source of information on relationships in today's society.

GLENN, NORVAL D., AND MARION TOLBERT COLEMAN. 1988. *Family Relations: A Reader*. Chicago: Dorsey Press. A series of essays on marriage and the family. The early sections examine the family from a comparative and historical perspective; the bulk of the readings focus on contemporary issues.

HAVEMANN, ERNEST, AND MARLENE LEHTINEN. 1990. *Marriages & Families: New Problems, New Opportunities*, 2nd edition. Englewood Cliffs, NJ: Prentice Hall. A useful overview of marriage and the family written specifically for college students. The authors emphasize the variety of arrangements that can exist in a pluralistic society.

HOCHSCHILD, ARLIE. 1989. *The Second Shift: Working Parents and the Revolution at Home*. New York: Viking Penguin. Hochschild conducted unstructured interviews and participant observation in homes where both spouses were employed full time. She finds that wives employed full time are virtually forced to become "supermoms."

CHAPTER 14

Education

Could you find Egypt on a map of the world? How about the Persian Gulf? Do you know the name of the country where the Sandinistas and contras have battled throughout much of the 1980s? If not, you're not alone. In 1988, the Gallup Organization gave a test of geographic literacy to 18- to 24-year-olds in Sweden, West Germany, Japan, Canada, Italy, France, the United Kingdom, Mexico, and the United States. How did young Americans score compared to their counterparts in other countries? Dead last! The average American in this age group got 6.9 of 16 questions right — compared to scores elsewhere ranging from 8.2 in Mexico to 11.9 in Sweden (Newsweek, 1988d).

Further evidence of the poor knowledge levels of young Americans was provided by another test administered in 1988 to high-school students in the greater St. Louis area. Thirty percent of the students did not know that Lyndon Johnson became president after John Kennedy was assassinated, and fewer than one in four could correctly place five major world cities on a map. However, the students did know certain things — some related to entertainment, a few concerning current affairs and history. For example, 90 percent could identify television star Vanna White, and 94 percent recognized rock star Jon Bon Jovi. Over 90 percent also knew what had happened to the space shuttle Challenger and could identify the Reverend Jesse Jackson. Significantly, all the items the students got high scores on could be learned by watching a lot of television. Apparently, St. Louis area youngsters are retaining quite a bit of what they see on television, but not much of what they hear in the classroom. Unfortunately, although television has considerable educational potential, much of what young people watch gives them little information of value. Evidently, they don't watch many news programs because only 43 percent of the students could identify an anchorperson on any St. Louis television newscast (Regional Research and Development Services, 1987).

The St. Louis study revealed one other significant finding, which illustrates a principle demonstrated by dozens of other studies over the past 3 decades: socioeconomic status is still closely tied to what students learn. In the affluent suburban Parkway district, the mean score on the test was 70. In East St. Louis, Illinois, where 43 percent of the population lives below the poverty level, the mean score was only 40.

These two 1988 tests demonstrate what many other tests have also shown:

1. *American students score lower on tests of knowledge than students in many other countries.*
2. *Because students learn far more from television than from school, much of what they know has little educational value.*
3. *There are vast differences in knowledge and achievement between students from affluent and poor backgrounds.*

F indings of studies like these raise profound questions about American education. Why, for example, do young people from Japan, Sweden, and even Mexico — where the average young person gets far less education than in the United States — know more about world geography and current events than the average young American? Why do race and social class have so much to do with how much students learn in U.S. schools? Do the causes of these patterns lie in the schools or in the larger society? Is it true, as some people argue, that our schools teach other things — such as work habits and democratic values — that are more important than learning how to read maps or recall names? If so, how successful are they at teaching these things? Finally, *whose* values do the schools teach? These are the kinds of questions that sociologists of education attempt to answer, and all of them will be addressed in this chapter.

Education As a Social Institution

How often, when discussing some social problem, have you heard the phrase "Education is the answer"? You have probably heard it said many times, in reference to many different problems. This phrase reveals the extent to which education has become institutionalized in postindustrial societies such as the United States. In such societies, the importance of education is virtually unquestioned. Through education we gain knowledge, and through knowledge we gain the capacity to create new products, achieve new accomplishments, and find new ways to solve our problems. Yet, although this is very much taken for granted today, the institutionalization of education is something that has happened fairly recently. Through most of human history, truth consisted of that which was handed down from God or a set of gods, as interpreted by some human religious leader. Thus, "truth" could be taught in the home, by religious organizations, or by tribal elders, and no formal schools were required. Some societies deviated from these patterns — for example, the ancient Greek, Roman, and Arabic civilizations. However, the belief that all children should attend school existed in only a few societies.

Luther and Mass Education

One of the first advocates of mass public education was Martin Luther (1497–1560), whose views about education were an outgrowth of his revolutionary ideas about religion. The Catholic Church, which dominated Europe in Luther's time, asserted that its religious leadership offered the only true interpretation of scripture, and, therefore, individual Catholics had no need to read the Bible themselves. Luther, in contrast, believed that it was the right — indeed, the duty — of every Christian to interpret the Bible for himself or herself. In order to do this, everyone had to learn to read, which required mass education.

Universal public education did not emerge during Luther's lifetime, however. In fact, until little more than a century ago, education in Europe and America was limited primarily to members of the wealthier classes. Although some U.S. colonies established schools early on, their purpose was mainly religious training, including reading the Bible. Moreover, not all children got even this type of education. In both the United States and Europe, as well as in most other societies, most learning and socialization occurred in the family, not the school.

Mass Education in the United States

The real spread of mass education in the United States began with the movement to establish *common schools* prior to the Civil War. Common schools are available free to everyone, based on the concept that all children should be educated, regardless of their social

Martin Luther, one of the first advocates of mass education.

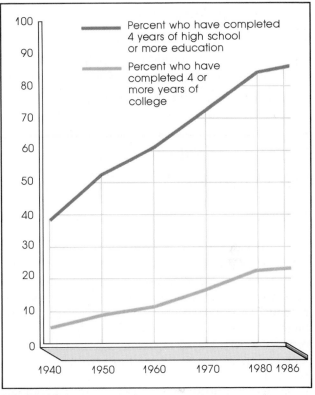

FIGURE 14.1
Percent with 4 or More Years of High School and 4 or More Years of College, 1940–1986, People 25 to 29 Years Old, United States
SOURCE: U.S. Bureau of the Census, 1988a, p. 25.

class or background. In 1852, Massachusetts became the first state to require children to attend school; by 1900, 30 states had done so (Johnson et al., 1982, p. 255). The notion that public education should be both free and mandatory for all children was only accepted about a century ago in the United States and even more recently in Europe. In the United States, for example, the proportion of young people who graduate from high school has risen during this century from about 6 percent to over 85 percent (U.S. Bureau of the Census, 1975, p. 379; U.S. Department of Education, 1987). The trends in high-school and college graduation rates since 1940 are shown in Figure 14.1.

To understand why mass education developed so recently and why it developed to a greater extent in the United States than elsewhere, we must examine the functions of education as it exists in the United States today. Sociologists of different perspectives disagree on exactly what functions education serves and why it has become so widespread. These debates involve nearly every important issue concerning the role of education in society.

The Functionalist Perspective on Education

Manifest Functions of Education

Functionalists see education as meeting basic societal needs. Some of these needs are obvious; they constitute the manifest functions of education. In today's society they include a technically trained population, a means of assigning people to jobs in accordance with their abilities, and a citizenry sufficiently educated to make democracy work. Let us explore each in a bit more detail.

Technical Training Clearly, a modern, technologically advanced society needs a better-educated population than a preindustrial society. Simply to function in such a society requires literacy. Imagine trying to shop, drive a car, or perform even the simplest jobs if you could not read, write, add, or subtract. Although most Americans take these skills for granted, the fact is that for most of human history the great majority of people lacked these skills. Today's society also demands skills that go far beyond mere reading and writing. Many occupations require elaborate scientific, quantitative, and technological capabilities. The relatively high standard of living in the United States and other industrialized societies is directly the result of the development of such knowledge. To sustain this standard of living, our educational system must continue to produce people with the skills necessary to take advantage of the advances that have been made and to make new advances (Porter, 1965; Callahan, 1962; Hurn, 1978, pp. 30–31). This pool of trained individuals is sometimes referred to as **human capital**, or *human resources* (Schultz, 1961; Becker, 1964).

Selection and Allocation Of course, not everyone has equal capacity to learn any given skill or area of knowledge. Thus, another important function of education is to *select* those who have the ability to learn, *teach* them in accordance with that ability, and *allocate* them to positions that match their capabilities (Hunter, 1988). Traditional wisdom maintains that people have different overall capacities to learn—some are better learners than others. Thus, "good learners" have been encouraged to get more education, and "poor learners" to get less. Today, however, educational research has shown that different people have capacities to excel in different kinds of skill and knowledge. Some people excel in the long-recognized verbal or mathematical dimensions of intelligence, but we know today that there are several other dimensions of intelligence that were not recognized in the past (Guilford, 1988, 1985; Sternberg, 1986a, 1986b). Some people, for example, have a great capacity for understanding physical relationships; other people have a greater ability to perceive and respond correctly to the feelings of others; still others have the capacity to excel in the fine arts, such as drama, music, and dance.

As a result, a modern view of education is that although it must still select and allocate people in accordance with their abilities, it is no longer appropriate to select some and exclude others. Rather, successful education identifies each student's strengths and capacities, helps that individual to develop those strengths and capacities, and assists in allocating that individual to a life role that allows him or her to make the most of those capacities.

CREDENTIALING AND MERITOCRACY Part of the process of allocating people to tasks and roles that fit their ability involves identifying who is and who is not capable of doing any given task (Hurn, 1978, pp. 30–31). This is accomplished through **credentials**—items of information, such as school grades and educational degrees, that document or support a claim of expertise, such as an M.D. or a Ph.D. (Chesler and Cave, 1981, pp. 60–61). Ideally, these selection, allocation, and credentialing processes work as a **meritocracy**, which literally means "merit rules." In other words, people are allocated to jobs in accordance with their abilities and what they have learned. When education operates as a true meritocracy, it acts as a source of mobility. It is not your background that matters, but how much you learn (Parsons, 1959; Goslin, 1965; Rehberg and Rosenthal, 1978; Ravitch, 1983). A skilled surgeon who grew up in a poor family is just as valuable as one from a wealthy family. However, ideals and reality are not the same: few people who grow up in poverty ever become surgeons. (For critical discussions of the notion of meritocracy, see Chesler and Cave, 1981, pp. 282–292; and Bastian et al., 1985, pp. 20–22.)

Education for Democracy The final manifest function of American education is to prepare people to participate in a democratic society. This means, for one thing, that people must understand how the political system works. They must, for example, know which political officials have the power to make particular decisions. A state legislator's position on the nation's nuclear arsenal might be interesting, but it is not relevant to the office he or she holds: Decisions relating to national defense are made at the federal level. An educated citizenry can make much more useful contributions to good public policy than an uneducated one. A candidate may, for instance, claim that he or she will deal effectively with the problem of drug abuse. How do you know whether such a claim is valid? You don't, unless you know something about the conditions associated with drug abuse, or at least how to find out about those conditions. Without knowledge, you can act only on the basis of prejudice or guesswork, which hardly contributes to effective democracy (Gutman, 1987, pp. 48–52; Gabriel, 1963).

Latent Functions of Education

Socialization and Cultural Transmission As was noted in Chapter 5, the school is an important agent of socialization. Part of this socialization function is to help build consensus and solidarity, or a sense of common interest (Durkheim, 1956 [orig. 1922]). According to functionalists, consensus and solidarity form a basis for cooperation, which is essential if the social system is to prosper. Also, if a culture is to be sustained, each generation must pass it on to the next.

Thus, schools engage in rituals, such as the Pledge of Allegiance, that are intended to build feelings of patriotism, consensus, and respect for the social system. In elementary and secondary schools, at least, there is a tendency to accentuate the positive aspects of the national identity and history and downplay the negative aspects. In short, the schools teach children to be proud of their society and to view it positively rather than critically (Bourdieu and Passeron, 1977 [orig. 1970]; Apple, 1982; Chesler and Cave, 1981).

Americans readily recognize this characteristic of schools in societies with values different from our own, such as the Soviet Union or China. When speaking of such societies, we refer to this function as "indoctrination" or "propaganda." However, in our own society, because the values taught in the schools are the same ones most of us hold, we do not see this function as indoctrination. Yet, the reality is that every modern society uses education to socialize children to the beliefs of their culture.

ACCULTURATION A closely related social integration function of schools is the **acculturation** of immigrants and minority groups. As we saw in Chapter 11, functionalists see ethnic divisions and cultural distinctions as a threat to societal consensus (Porter, 1972). Thus, they view education as performing a special integrative function in societies with large numbers of immigrants, such as the United States and Canada, or in societies where outside powers drew boundaries that combined disparate tribal and ethnic groups into one nation, such as in many African countries. Functionalists believe that the schools in such societies must teach the national language and culture to the children of immigrants and minorities. In short, the goal is to get people to think of themselves as Americans or Canadians rather than immigrants from Germany or Japan; as Zambians rather than Bantus.

The Hidden Curriculum To the extent that schools perform this integrative function, they are teaching values as well as academic content. The values and work habits taught in the schools make up the **hidden curriculum** of the educational system (Jackson, 1968). Sociologists of all theoretical orientations agree that, in addition to skills and factual information, the schools teach values. Critics of American education ranging from conservative religious fundamentalists to Marxists have criticized the schools for just that reason. However, what they usually mean is that they disagree with the values being taught rather than with the idea that the schools should teach values. In fact, value-free education is probably impossible. As long as teachers, students, administrators, parents, and school boards have values, these values will likely be reflected in what is taught and how it is taught (Purpel and Ryan, 1976; Gutman, 1987, pp. 53–54). So, although sociologists agree that the hidden curriculum exists, they disagree on the usefulness of its content, and they also disagree on the reasons why the schools teach the values they do. We shall return to the hidden curriculum later in this chapter when we consider the conflict perspective on education.

Weakening Parental Control An important part of growing up is becoming independent of your parents. Until fairly recently, most young children spent the day at home, usually with their mothers, until they reached kindergarten age. Thus, up to that age, the parents were far more important than any other agent of socialization. Entering school meant encountering new agents of socialization whose expectations sometimes differed from those of parents. This experience offered children new choices and was an important part of growing up — the first step in the process of becoming independent. Today, this process begins earlier than in the past, as most children are cared for by someone other than their parents for a substantial part of the time. Some — about 15 percent of the children of working mothers — are in day care (Lueck, Orr, and O'Connel, 1982). More are cared for by friends or relatives. In either case, preschool children are encountering agents of socialization besides their parents to a greater extent than they did in the past.

Gaining Experience in Secondary Groups In addition to helping children achieve independence, education prepares them for the situations they will encounter as adults. School or day care is the first important secondary-group experience most children have. For the first time, they encounter a major life situation where they are "one of a crowd" rather than "someone special." In contrast to home, where children are rewarded and valued for *who they are,* the

reward system of the school is based on *what they do.* Making this transition successfully is an important part of learning to function in the work environment of a modern industrial society. Learning how to function in a secondary-group situation, then, is another important part of education's hidden curriculum.

The School as Baby-Sitter One latent function of education is to care for children, especially if the parents work. The school not only serves as a baby-sitter, it also gives children something to do during the day, which relieves their boredom and keeps them out of trouble. Although these functions have been served by the school for many years, their importance has grown as fewer and fewer children have a parent at home during the day.

Building Peer Relations As we discussed in Chapter 5, it is essential as children get older that they establish independence from their family of orientation — the family in which they grew up. One of the most important latent functions of education is to create opportunities for children to establish that independence by building relationships with their peers.

Although teachers and parents often decry the great influence that peers exercise over adolescents, the fact is that children in this age group develop important social skills through peer interactions, skills that they will use later in their relationships with co-workers. It is also through peer interactions that young people learn the skills of dating and developing romantic relationships (Lefrancois, 1981, pp. 233–234). In fact, mate selection itself often occurs in the context of college or, in some cases, high school. Thus, most sociologists agree that the latent functions of education include not only the development of social skills, but also the creation of a pool from which marriage partners can be selected.

PEER CULTURE AND CLIQUES Adolescent peer groups tend to be dominated by **cliques** — relatively close and exclusive groups ranging in size from about three to nine (Dunphy, 1963, 1972). Acceptance in cliques is gained in part through conformity to the clique's values and norms, and in part through achievement. In this case, achievement refers to interpersonal skills and sexual attractiveness, not school achievement. There is a status hierarchy among adolescent cliques, largely linked to one's prowess with the opposite sex (Grinder, 1978). In order to remain part of a clique, a person must conform to its culture and maintain interpersonal skills and sexual attractiveness appropriate to its status. Not all adolescents have sufficient skills to be accepted by a clique. For those who do not gain such acceptance, life can be very difficult—not only in adolescence, but in some cases, later in life as well. A young person rejected by peers may have a very hard time learning interpersonal skills because he or she has been excluded from the group in which such skills are taught (Lefrancois, 1981, p. 234).

The Schools and Equal Opportunity

As we saw earlier, functionalists believe that one purpose of education is to operate as a meritocracy. To do so, schools must create *equal opportunity*. Serious questions have been raised, even by functionalists, about whether the schools really work this way. Certainly, the schools do *not* produce *equal results*: Middle-class children on the average get more years of school and higher-quality education than poor children; white children similarly get more and better education than African-American or Hispanic children. The reasons for these unequal results—and whether they reflect unequal opportunity—are at the core of the debate between functionalists and conflict theorists about education. According to functionalists, children must have certain basic abilities, as well as certain cultural attributes, if they are to learn. Functionalists believe that children from low-income families generally do not get the opportunity during their childhood to develop these basic abilities and cultural attributes, and as a result they cannot compete when they enter school. They refer to this condition of poor children as **cultural deprivation**, which is one of the most important and controversial concepts in the sociology of education.

The Coleman Report   Much of the reasoning behind the concept of cultural deprivation arose from a massive study of American education commissioned by the federal government during the 1960s, called the Coleman Report for its chief author, James S. Coleman

(see Coleman et al., 1966). The Coleman Report, which included over 570,000 students and 10,000 teachers nationwide, was the most comprehensive study of the factors influencing student achievement that had ever been done. Its findings were striking. Perhaps the key finding was that regardless of the amount spent on education, the personal attitudes and social background of the student—not the apparent quality of the school—were most closely linked to student achievement. The characteristics of the school accounted for only about 5 percent of overall variation in student achievement, whereas personal and background variables accounted for one-third of the overall variation. In general, students who had healthy self-concepts and positive attitudes toward learning and success learned a lot; students with the opposite characteristics learned far less. Similarly, students from homes with well-educated parents who took an active interest in their education and who had considerable educational resources in the home did well; students with the opposite background did poorly. Generally, middle-class students were far more likely than poor students to possess the background and personal characteristics associated with success in school.

Coleman and other educational sociologists of his time concluded that it was not the school, but the student, that determined educational success. From a functionalist perspective, this made a good deal of sense. After all, one function of the school is to socialize students in the attitudes and habits that bring success. Therefore, the functionalists reasoned, it is hardly surprising that students from backgrounds that did not transmit these attitudes and habits did less well in school. Significantly, some, though not many, students from low-income backgrounds did do well. Generally, Coleman argued, these students had developed the attitudes associated with educational success. In other words, they were poor but *not* culturally deprived. As we shall see shortly, the entire concept of cultural deprivation has been sharply disputed by conflict theorists and others, and a strong case can be made that the concept reflects the cultural biases of social scientists and educators more than any social reality. However, the concept of cultural deprivation was a driving force behind most of the educational policies of the 1960s and 1970s.

The Functionalist View and Educational Policy

The Coleman Report encouraged two new thrusts in educational policy, both intended to eliminate the condition of cultural deprivation. One of these thrusts was *compensatory education,* the other was *desegregation through busing.*

Compensatory Education The compensatory education movement was actually under way before the Coleman Report was published. The federal program Head Start, for example, had been established to offer children from disadvantaged backgrounds an opportunity to develop healthy educational habits and an appreciation for learning before they entered primary school. The Coleman Report provided new support for these programs.

Unfortunately, the results of the initial studies that tested the effectiveness of Head Start and other compensatory education programs seemed to show that compensatory education made little difference in later student achievement (Cicirelli et al., 1969; White, 1970; Little and Smith, 1971; Stanley, 1973). This led many conflict theorists to argue that compensatory education could not succeed because the cause of educational inequality was not cultural deprivation (Baratz and Baratz, 1970; Bowles and Gintis, 1976; Ogbu, 1978). However, as research continued, achievement measurement became more sophisticated, and measurement over longer time periods became possible. Generally, these more recent studies have painted a much more optimistic picture (Brown, 1985). By 1978, a review of 96 studies of preschool compensatory education revealed that children who had received such education clearly did better than similar children who had not (Brown, 1978). In general, children who receive compensatory education score higher on IQ and achievement measures (at least in the early grades), are less likely to be placed in special education or to fail a grade, have better achievement self-images, and receive more encouragement from their parents to get a good education (Consortium for Longitudinal Studies, 1979, 1983; Lazar et al., 1977, 1982). At least one study found the

Recent research has shown that compensatory education programs such as Head Start have positive educational effects that can continue into adulthood.

effects of compensatory education lingering through adolescence and early adulthood, including lower rates of unemployment, delinquency, and teenage pregnancy (Berrueta-Clement, 1984; see also Weber et al., 1978; Lazar, 1981). These studies were so encouraging that Head Start was expanded during the 1980s at a time when educational and social-service programs in general were being cut back (Farley, 1988, p. 319).

Desegregation through Busing The other major policy thrust emerging from the Coleman Report was a nationwide trend toward school desegregation through busing. The impetus for this policy arose from another finding of the Coleman Report: Low-income black students who attended racially and socioeconomically integrated schools showed higher achievement than low-income black students attending predominantly poor black schools (Coleman et al., 1966, pp. 307–312, 330–331). Coleman attributed this to the tendency of low-income and black students to pick up good study habits and an optimistic outlook on education from the middle-class white students in integrated schools. In other words, by teaching such habits and outlooks, integrated schools were undoing the effects of cultural deprivation. Coleman's data also showed that white middle-class students did just as well in schools with black and poor students as they did in schools where everyone was white and middle class.

These findings led social scientists to argue — often before the courts in school segregation cases — that equal educational opportunity was impossible in cases of **de facto segregation** — that is, segregation resulting from housing patterns rather than from deliberate policy. If segregated schools denied equal opportunity — as the Coleman data appeared to show — then they were illegal and should be integrated. In many cases, neighborhoods were so segregated that the only way to desegregate the schools was by busing children to schools in other neighborhoods. By the 1970s, busing had been implemented on some scale in virtually every racially mixed medium-to-large city in the United States. Sometimes, school boards themselves set up a busing program, but more often busing resulted from a court order or the threat of one.

DOES BUSING WORK?   Does busing work as its proponents envisioned it would? The answer seems to be that it depends on various aspects of each situation (Praeger, Longshore, and Seeman, 1986). Sometimes, for example, busing leads to resegregation of the schools through "white flight" to the suburbs or to private schools (Coleman, 1975; Armor, 1978). This consideration led Coleman himself to oppose busing publicly by the 1970s. However, the long-term effect of busing on white enrollment is small, and it occurs mainly in cases of city-only busing (as opposed to city-suburb) in largely black central cities surrounded by heavily white suburbs (Farley, Richards, and Wurdock, 1980; Wilson, 1985). In other situations, busing causes relatively little white flight.

In those instances where busing does not cause a great deal of white flight (probably the majority of cases), it does — under certain specified conditions — lead to significant improvements in learning and educational aspirations among minority students. In general, black and Hispanic students in predominantly white schools score higher than similar students in racially segregated schools (Mahard and Crain, 1983; St. John, 1975; Weinberg, 1977; Krol, 1978). However, improved performance by minority

students does not happen in every instance of school desegregation. As predicted by Coleman (1966), it occurs primarily in schools where the whites are of relatively high socioeconomic status. Thus, *socioeconomic* integration may be as important as *racial* integration (Mahard and Crain, 1983). Interestingly, the benefits of desegregation may not arise from the learning of values or study habits, because in some desegregated schools the achievement of black students appears to be unrelated to the extent of their contact with white students (Patchen, Hofmann, and Brown, 1980; Patchen, 1982; Maruyama and Miller, 1979). Other characteristics of integrated schools might account for these benefits (Mahard and Crain, 1983; see also Miller, 1980).

A FORMULA FOR SUCCESS   The extent to which black and Hispanic students benefit from any given instance of racial or socioeconomic desegregation varies widely. In general, the benefit appears to be greatest when:

> Desegregation occurs during the early grades. Desegregating kindergarten or the first grade is far more effective than desegregating at the second grade or above (Mahard and Crain, 1983, p. 110).
>
> The school is internally integrated. In some cases, especially where students are grouped according to their supposed ability, some classes within supposedly desegregated schools are virtually all-black (or Hispanic), and others are nearly all-white (Pettigrew, 1969a, 1969b; Eyler, Cook,

---

African-American students and their parents as busing begins in Cleveland. If properly implemented, busing can be educationally beneficial, though it remains very controverisal among both blacks and whites.

and Ward, 1983). When such internal resegregation occurs, it may widen rather than reduce racial inequalities in achievement (Yinger, 1986, p. 242).

Desegregation is metropolitanwide, so black and Hispanic students from the central city gain access to suburban schools (Mahard and Crain, 1983, p. 118).

The end result of desegregation is to produce schools between 10 and 30 percent black (Mahard and Crain, 1983, p. 120; Yinger, 1986). In many cities, where school enrollment is 70 to 95 percent black or Hispanic, the racial mix that maximizes achievement is impossible to attain unless busing occurs between the city and the suburbs (see Pisko and Stern, 1985; Farley, 1988, p. 324).

Teachers and students are adequately prepared for desegregation, and the school is free of other practices (discussed later in this chapter) that produce racial inequality in education.

The desegregation does not produce conflict sufficiently severe to disrupt school, as happened, for example, in Boston in the mid-1970s. Such conflict is less likely when local political, economic, and religious leaders urge cooperation with desegregation, and it is more likely when they encourage people to oppose it (U.S. Commission on Civil Rights, 1976).

Finally, it is important to stress that improved educational achievement is not the only benefit associated with school desegregation. If desegregation is implemented properly, racial and ethnic relations in the school will often improve through increased intergroup contact. Moreover, there is increasing evidence that the educational benefits to black and Hispanic students can be long-lasting. Blacks who attend integrated schools appear more likely to go on to college (Crain and Weisman, 1972), to enter integrated work and educational settings later in life (McPartland and Braddock, 1981), and to get good jobs (Crain and Weissman, 1972; see also Granovetter, 1986).

Although desegregation and compensatory education do seem to reduce racial and economic achievement differences in many cases, they are not the only ways to accomplish this. Moreover, conflict theorists and symbolic-interactionists point out that many processes in the schools that produce inequality remain untouched by either desegregation or compensatory education. Both desegregation and compensatory education operate from the basic assumption that the schools are generally working well, but that certain groups need help "fitting in" if they are to enjoy equal opportunity. Conflict theorists and many symbolic-interactionists in the sociology of education do not share this positive view of the schools.

The Conflict and Interactionist Perspectives on Education

Reproducing, Transmitting, and Justifying Inequality

The Coleman Report concluded that the social and economic background of students is strongly correlated to how much students learn and the amount of education that they ultimately get. To conflict theorists these results indicate the absence of equality of opportunity in the schools. Conflict theorists argue that the main function of education is to pass economic, racial, and sexual inequality from one generation to the next (Bowles and Gintis, 1976). They have identified a number of ways in which the educational system encourages learning and advancement in children from certain backgrounds and discourages it in children from other backgrounds:

> Unequal funding of schools by social class.
> Processes of symbolic-interaction in the schools that encourage achievement in some children and discourage it in others.
> Effects of the hidden curriculum.

Conflict theorists believe that the educational system serves other functions for the more economically advantaged segments of society. One such function, they argue, is to justify educational inequalities along the lines of social class, sex, and race. In other words, educators convince poor, working-class, minority, and female students that their limited advancement in the educational system is a result of their own shortcomings and not of biases built into the educational system (Bourdeiu, 1966; Bourdeiu and Passeron, 1977). Another closely related function is to teach children attitudes and beliefs that support the economic and political system. Functionalists see this process as necessary for cooperation, which benefits everyone. Conflict theorists, however, believe that the wealthy have the greatest stake in keeping the system as it is. Thus, they are the ones who benefit when children are taught to see the social system as basically fair.

Schools and Mobility

Before addressing the mechanisms by which conflict theorists claim that education perpetuates inequality, it may be useful to examine briefly some statistics concerning educational mobility. What are the chances, for example, that the child of parents with an eighth-grade education will receive a college degree? And how does that child's chance of getting a college education compare to that of another child whose parents were college-educated? The answers to these questions can be seen in Table 14.1. Clearly, the differences are great. A child who scores well on standardized intelligence tests but comes from a low socioeconomic background has a much lower chance of attending college than a student with low intelligence but a high socioeconomic background. In general, research has shown the parents' educational level to be one of the best predictors of a person's educational attainment (see Kerbo, 1983, pp. 358–363). If you combine parental education with other aspects of socioeconomic status, the effect on educational attainment is even greater (Alwin and Thornton, 1984; Teachman, 1987). Thus, the amount of education you get is closely associated with the socioeconomic status and particularly the education of your parents—a finding consistent with the view that education transmits inequality from generation to generation (Bidwell and Friedkin, 1988). Let us now examine some of the explanations conflict theorists offer for these findings.

Unequal Funding of Schools

About half of the funding for public schools in the United States comes from state revenues, and most of the rest comes from the local property tax (Pisko and Stern, 1985). To the extent that schools rely on the local property tax, the tendency is for schools in more affluent areas to be better funded. Property taxes raise more money per child in affluent areas than they do in

TABLE 14.1
Percent Attending College, by Social-Class Background and Intelligence*

SOCIAL CLASS BACKGROUND	TOTAL	INTELLIGENCE LOW	INTELLIGENCE HIGH
Low	20.8%	9.3%	40.1%
High	84.2%	58.0%	91.1%

* "Intelligence" in this table is measured by scores on standardized tests.
SOURCE: William Sewell and Vimal Shah, 1968, "Parents' Education and Children's Education Aspirations and Achievements," *American Sociological Review* 33:191–209.

poor ones because the value of the property is higher. Poor communities often have very high tax rates but raise only small amounts of money because there is so little to tax. A study by the Illinois Capital Development Board (1977) of East St. Louis illustrates this. The study found that tax rates, relative to income, were *six and one-half times* higher in East St. Louis than in the surrounding county, yet the city and its schools teetered on the brink of bankruptcy.

In recent years, inequalities in funding between wealthy and poor school districts have been reduced somewhat because the states have been picking up an increasing share of school costs (Pisko and Stern, 1985). However, some states offer aid in proportion to what is raised locally, a formula that again favors wealthier districts. Since the 1970s, some states have offered more state aid to poorer districts, but the extent of this adjustment has varied widely among the states (Brown et al., 1978).

Funding: How Important? Although funding inequalities exist, their impact on student achievement is unclear. Remember, the Coleman Report found that school characteristics, including funding levels, explained only about 5 percent of the variation in student achievement. To say that funding makes relatively little difference is not, however, to say that it makes *no* difference. If the level of funding falls so low that basics such as current textbooks, adequate lighting and heating, safe school buildings, and minimally qualified teachers cannot be provided, student learning will inevitably suffer. Significantly, school characteristics make more difference in the achievement of black, Hispanic, and Indian children than they do for white Anglo children (Coleman et al., 1966).

Clearly, though, inadequate funding does not explain the low achievement levels of minority students. The real message of the Coleman Report is that if *all* we do is spend more on education, the results will likely be disappointing. Research since the Coleman Report has reaffirmed that a bigger influence on student achievement is the interaction between students and teachers. To see how this interaction inhibits the education of poor, minority, and (in some subject areas) female students, we must combine the insights of the conflict perspective with those of the symbolic-interactionist perspective.

Symbolic-Interaction and Educational Inequality

There are a number of ways in which student-teacher interactions differ along the lines of social class, race, and sex. In some cases, individual teachers treat students differently; in others, the different treatment is institutionalized and occurs throughout the school. In yet other cases, students from different backgrounds may encounter similar situations but interpret their meaning differently because they bring different experiences and world views to the classroom. Three of the most important issues relating to interaction in the schools are *teacher expectations, tracking,* and *testing.*

Teacher Expectations In the 1960s, social psychologists Robert Rosenthal and Lenore Jacobson (1968) conducted an experiment that led to a dramatic reassessment by social scientists of the forces that affect student learning in the classroom. In a California elementary school, Rosenthal and Jacobson gave a test to all of the students at the beginning of the school year. They then told the teachers that the test had identified certain children as "spurters"—children who could be expected to make especially rapid progress in school that year. The key to the experiment was that these students had in fact been chosen *randomly*, but the teachers didn't know that. In reality, the test had been an ordinary IQ test, not a test designed to identify "spurters." Rosenthal and Jacobson returned to the

school at the end of the year to give the IQ test again, and in the first and second grades the results were dramatic. Although the "spurters" had been randomly chosen and were no different from other students, their IQ scores had increased 10 to 15 points more than those of other students. Rosenthal and Jacobson concluded that a self-fulfilling prophecy was operating in the classroom: When teachers were told that a particular student was likely to do well—even if there was no basis for such a statement—the teachers treated that student in ways that assured that he or she *would* do well.

Although there were certain methodological problems with the Rosenthal and Jacobson study (Thorndike, 1969), and attempts to replicate its results precisely have failed (Boocock, 1978), a broad range of research has supported the basic idea of a self-fulfilling prophecy in education. In general, students who are *expected* by their teachers to do better than other students generally do learn more (Beez, 1968; Brophy and Good, 1974; Nash, 1976, Chap. 3; Rist, 1970). In a review of the literature on the self-fulfilling prophecy in education, Brophy (1983) estimated that teacher expectations account for 5 to 10 percent of student achievement, though this percent can vary widely depending on the situation. Although these effects are greatest in the early grades, they can linger throughout a person's schooling (Leiter, 1974; Rist, 1970).

Teacher expectations concerning student achievement have important effects on how much students actually do achieve.

FACTORS AFFECTING TEACHER EXPECTATIONS
Evidence also indicates that social characteristics of students such as race and socioeconomic status influence teachers' expectations of their achievement, although the extent to which this is true varies widely (Brophy and Good, 1974; Hurn, 1978; Leacock, 1969; Weinberg, 1977; Wasserman, 1970; Brophy, 1983; Harvey and Slatin, 1975; Rist, 1970). Teachers of high social status often have particularly low expectations of minority and poor students (Alexander, Entwisle, and Thompson, 1987). Counselors also play a role in this process by encouraging white and middle-class students to prepare for college, while discouraging minority and low-income students from doing so. This process occurs even when students' academic performances are similar (Cicourel and Kitsuse, 1963; see also Erickson and Shultz, 1982). Sex also influences teacher expectations. Boys are often expected to excel in certain subjects and activities, while girls are expected to excel in others (see Stacy, Bereaud, and Daniels, 1974; Frazier and Sadker, 1974; Safran, 1988).

Teacher Expectations: The Schoolwide Level The problem of teacher expectations and student achievement does not occur just in the case of individual students. Teachers sometimes form negative expectations about the achievement potential of an entire class or even an entire school. Low expectations are especially likely to develop in central-city schools with a large proportion of low-income, black, and Hispanic students. Teachers develop the attitude that "Students like ours can't be expected to learn too much." Such teachers demand less of their students; in turn, the students learn less (Hallinan and Sorensen, 1985).

Tragically, this situation need not exist. In schools with overwhelmingly black or Hispanic populations — even ones where most of the students are from low-income families — high levels of student achievement are possible *if* certain conditions are present. The most important requirement is that teachers *expect* and *demand* high levels of achievement (Edmonds, 1979). For this to happen, teachers must believe that their students are capable of such achievement. As one teacher in an all-black Chicago school with high achievement levels put it, "The belief that

children can succeed is half the battle" (Fuerst, 1981). In some of these all-black inner-city schools, Fuerst found achievement levels that exceeded those of the mostly white and middle-class schools in Chicago's suburbs. Dramatic evidence of how much students from "disadvantaged" backgrounds can learn was provided by a Department of Education report (1987a) of certain schools in poor neighborhoods. In these schools, high expectations and demands for achievement were producing dramatic results, as is illustrated in the box entitled "Schools That Work."

Another recent source of data is the nationwide *High School and Beyond* study. That study found that students in Catholic high schools on the average show higher achievement and more rapid growth than students in public high schools, and that black, Hispanic, and low-income students in Catholic schools on the average achieve at levels closer to that of white middle-class students (Greeley, 1982; Coleman, Hoffer, and Kilgore, 1982; Hoffer, Greeley, and Coleman, 1987). While there is debate about how big these differences are (Alexander and Pallas, 1987; Willms, 1987), such differences do show up consistently in a variety of analyses of the data (Haertel, 1987). Why do Catholic schools produce better achievement than public schools? An important reason seems to be that they assign more homework, expect higher student achievement, and are more likely to expose minority and low-income students to advanced, college-preparatory materials. Importantly, some public high schools have similar characteristics, and these schools have similar levels of achievement to the Catholic schools. As Hoffman, Greeley, and Coleman (1987, p. 87) put it:

> Catholic schools are especially beneficial to the least-advantaged students: minorities, poor, and those whose initial achievement is low. For these students, the lack of structure, demands, and expectations found in many public schools is especially harmful. *Our analyses show that those public schools which make the same demands as found in the typical Catholic school produce comparable achievement.* [emphasis added]

Thus, the level of achievement expected and demanded by the schools has a real influence on how much students achieve. This is particularly true for students from social backgrounds that teachers often

Schools That Work

Schools with overwhelmingly poor or minority student bodies can and do produce excellence. That is the finding of the Department of Education's 1987 report, *Schools That Work: Educating Disadvantaged Children.* Consider the following examples:

Edison Primary School, Dayton, Ohio. In this inner-city school, 70 percent of the students are black, and 95 percent come from low-income families. Many are malnourished. Yet, when Principal Brenda Lee instituted certain changes, student achievement improved dramatically. Lee believes that "all students can succeed," that they can "speak fluently and precisely in complete sentences . . . have a solid foundation in the basic skills . . . and realize their own worth." Under her leadership, the percentage of students performing at grade level in math rose from 40 to 64 percent in 3 years, and in reading, from 65 to 78 percent. Student attendance rose to 95 percent.

George Washington Preparatory High School, Los Angeles. The addition of the word "Preparatory" to the title of this high school by Principal George McKenna says it all. Despite the fact that two-thirds of its students are from low-income families, this school determined to prepare them for something better— higher education. To offset rampant gang violence, vandalism, and drug use, McKenna incorporated training in the principles of nonviolence embraced by Martin Luther King and Mahatma Gandhi into the school's curriculum. He required parents and students to sign contracts in which they agreed not only to obey school rules and see that homework was done, but also to abstain from verbal or physical abuse against one another in the home. The results? When McKenna took over, half the school's students were asking to be bused elsewhere. Today, the school is one of the city's best, and although it has 1,000 more students than it had in the past, it has a waiting list to get in. There is a good reason for this: 70 percent of the school's students go on to college, which is well above the national average.

Hales Franciscan High School, Chicago. Founded 45 years ago as the nation's first Catholic high school for young black men, this school has remained true to its principles that poverty is no barrier to achievement. Over half of its students come from families with incomes below the poverty level, including many one-parent families. The school stresses effective communication in speech and writing. Although it is Catholic, many of its students are not, and it stresses moral judgment and social responsibility in its religion classes. Its principal, Father Mario Di-Ciccio, notes that "Inside and out, [it] is a beautiful building, cared for and developed because it attempts to be a model of cleanliness and good order for the students." Despite its badly deteriorated surroundings, the school building is rarely vandalized because neighbors "respect this building as a symbol of great pride and great caring for the black community." Nine out of ten of its graduates go on to college; three-quarters to 4-year schools.

These are exceptions, you might say. One great principal can do this in one school, but can it be done in an entire city's school system? Yes! The Jacksonville, Florida, school district has enjoyed such successes citywide. It eliminated "social promotion" (promoting students regardless of achievement, on the presumption that they can't achieve and they shouldn't be discouraged when they fail) and established a "Blacks for Success in Education" program, assisting students in test-preparation skills and helping them buy books to improve their critical-thinking skills. Students are urged by their advisers to think about their future academic plans—just the reverse of what usually happens in schools with large minority enrollments. When the program was begun, about three-fourths of the nation's high-school students scored above the average Jacksonville black student on the Stanford Achievement Test. By 1985, the typical Jacksonville black student got a score close to the national average.

---

associate with low levels of achievement. Unfortunately, expectations remain too low in the vast majority of public schools in areas with low-income or minority populations. Fuerst (1981), for example, found that about 20,000 black students in Chicago were attending all-black schools with high expectations and were generally doing well. Another 10,000 were attending racially integrated schools and were also generally doing well. However, another 145,000 of Chicago's black students—over 80 percent of the total—were attending schools where both expectations and achievement were low.

Tracking In many schools, students are placed into groups or classes according to their teachers' assessments of their abilities. This practice is called **tracking.** The idea behind tracking is to allow students to proceed at their own pace. Thus, more-capable students will not be held back and bored; less-capable students will not be overwhelmed or left behind. However, as it is actually practiced, tracking raises several problems. The most fundamental are the effects of tracking itself on the educational attainment of students, and the tendency to track students largely on the basis of social class, race, ethnicity, and other irrelevant characteristics. Half to three-quarters of all U.S. elementary schools today use some form of tracking (Eyler, Cook, and Ward, 1983), and some begin it as early as the first week of kindergarten (Leiter, 1974; Rist, 1970). Once a student is placed in a given track, he or she can rarely move to another one (Rosenbaum, 1976; Bidwell and Friedkin, 1988). Among students of comparable ability, those placed in higher tracks learn more and ultimately complete more years of education than those placed in lower tracks (Hauser, Sewell, and Almin, 1976; Schafer, Olexa, and Polk, 1972; Esposito, 1973; Rosenbaum, 1978; Vanfossen, Jones, and Spade, 1987; Gamoran, 1987; Gamoran and Mare, 1989). Students placed in low tracks also do more poorly than students of similar ability who are not tracked but instead are placed in classes or groups with higher-ability students (Froman, 1981; Marascuilo and McSweeney, 1972). When they reach high school, students are placed in either vocational or college-preparatory tracks. Again, this has a substantial effect on the amount of education that students ultimately get. A study by Alexander, Cook, and McDill (1978) found that "enrollment in a college-preparatory track increases by about 30 percent the probability that students will plan in their senior year to continue their education in comparison to equally able, motivated, and encouraged youth in nonacademic programs."

In general, lower-income and minority children are overrepresented in lower-ability tracks (Boocock, 1978; Brischetto and Arciniega, 1973; Shafer, Olexa, and Polk, 1972; U.S. Commission on Civil Rights, 1974; Harnischfeger and Wiley, 1980; Larkins and Oldham, 1976; Jencks et al., 1972; Carter and Segura, 1979; Vanfossen, Jones, and Spade, 1987). Numerous studies indicate that social class affects track placement, even among students of similar ability (Rist, 1970; Findley and Bryan, 1971; Lunn, 1980; Haller and Davis, 1980; Alexander, Cook, and McDill, 1978; Gamoran and Mare, 1989). Placement into tracks is often haphazard. One national study, after considering every factor that might influence placement, could explain only 30 to 40 percent of the variation in track placement (Alexander, Cook, and McDill, 1978).

OPTIONS WITHIN TRACKING Would class and racial inequality in education be decreased if tracking were eliminated? A strong case can be made that it would. It has been argued, for example, that one reason for the greater achievement and more equal achievement in Catholic high schools is that they are less likely to use tracking, and when they do use it, they include a larger share of their students in college-preparatory tracks (Coleman, Hoffer, and Kilgore, 1982; Hoffer, Greeley, and Coleman, 1987).

Rather than eliminating tracking, however, educators might make the system more flexible by routinely reevaluating track assignments. This was done by many of the successful all-black schools in Chicago studied by Fuerst (1981). Of course, this is possible only if there is some similarity among the subject matter taught to students in different tracks, which is frequently not the case (Bidwell and Friedkin, 1988). Yet another possibility is to track students separately for each subject, rather than placing them in the same track for all subjects. Even with these alternatives, some educational sociologists argue that the practice of tracking is inherently unsound (Eyler, Cook, and Ward, 1983, p. 132).

Testing Even standardized tests do not eliminate biases in tracking. In fact, achievement testing has been identified by educational sociologists and psychologists as another important mechanism by which class and racial inequalities are often perpetuated by education. Any test directly measures only what a stu-

Although IQ tests are used to make inferences about student ability, there is no way to measure ability directly.

dent knows or can do at any given time. Test results are used to make inferences about student ability, but these are only educated guesses. Moreover, what students know or can do—indeed, even how they understand a given question—will always be influenced by their background or culture (MacKay, 1974). Because most tests are designed primarily for a white, middle-class population, they tend to test knowledge, beliefs, and tasks that are familiar to that group. Such factors as language models in the home, strictness of upbringing, and family emphasis on achievement and independence influence test scores (Marjoribanks, 1972; Wolf, 1966; Radin, 1972; Hanson, 1975), as do test anxiety and the formality of the test situation (Kirkland, 1971; Palmer, 1970; Zigler Abelson, and Seitz, 1973; Golden and Burns, 1968). Children from poor neighborhoods who see little hope for success may see less reason for trying to do well on tests (Ogbu, 1978, 1986). All of these factors work to produce lower scores among low-income and minority students, and race and social class do correlate with test scores (Sexton, 1961). However, this does not prove that such factors influence student's natural abilities; rather, the differences appear to be social in origin (Bidwell and Friedkin, 1988).

Because the schools reward responses similar to the "right answers" on the tests, such tests are fair predictors of school success in our educational system as it operates. However, they are not valid measures of student ability, and they should not be used as the basis for grouping students. As one expert on testing —who favors the continued use of standardized tests —put it:

Assessment should focus on discovering ways to help children. The aim should be getting knowledge about children, on improving instruction, and on helping children best develop their potentials. Eliminating the focus on screening, classification, and selection and replacing it with these aims may reduce some of the objections to intelligence and achievement testing (Sattler, 1982, p. 384).

It is clear that to change the patterns described above, teachers must become convinced that more of their students—even those from "disadvantaged" backgrounds—can learn. Institutional change, such as the modification or elimination of tracking and more appropriate use of testing, is also probably a prerequisite to truly equal opportunity. However, there is yet another issue that conflict theorists raise concerning inequality.

The Hidden Curriculum: A Conflict Analysis

The final issue raised by conflict theorists of education is the hidden curriculum. Whereas functionalists see the hidden curriculum as teaching all children valuable habits and beliefs, the conflict perspective sees it as a mechanism to perpetuate inequality by teaching *different* values, beliefs, and habits to children of different social classes.

Social Class and Socialization Content In general, children being prepared for more desirable and better-paying jobs are taught to work independently, although within the framework of a hierarchical, bureaucratic structure. Other children, in contrast, are taught simply to obey rules (Bowles and Gintis, 1976). As conflict theorist Randall Collins (1971b, p. 1011) described it, the functions of the educational system are to "select new members for elite positions who share elite culture, and, at a lower level of education, to hire lower and middle employees who have acquired a general respect for these elite values and styles."

Social Class and School Orientation Studies of schools in working-class and poor neighborhoods reveal an emphasis on order and conformity rather than achievement (Bowles and Gintis, 1976; Leacock, 1969; Sharp and Green, 1975; Gouldner, 1978).

These schools also teach students to feed back a predetermined "right" answer rather than to analyze new situations independently. Schools in middle-class areas, in contrast, allow their students more autonomy, place a greater emphasis on independent work, and have fewer rules.

SOCIALIZATION CONTENT   Significantly, the teaching of different values in the schools reflects a similar process in the home. As sociologist Melvin Kohn (1969) has shown, middle-class families are more likely to instill such values as achievement and independent thinking in their children, whereas working-class and poor families stress obedience and conformity. These differences are based on the different job situations of the two groups. In general, parents socialize their children in ways that reflect their own experiences of autonomy or conformity on the job (Kohn, 1969). Thus, the schools do not *originate* this process, but they do *reinforce* it (Miller, Kohn, and Schooles, 1986). As a result, middle- and upper-class students are inculcated with the values necessary for managerial and professional occupations, while working-class and poor students are prepared for lower-level or less-skilled positions. These processes that pass inequalities from generation to generation occur in all industrialized countries, not just the United States. A vivid example can be seen in the box entitled "Letter to a Teacher."

The same differences in the hidden curriculum occur at different levels of the educational system. The further you advance, the more the schools resemble the upper-middle-class, independent-thinking model rather than the working-class obedience model. Significantly, the further you go, the more upper middle class the student bodies become. In addition, as more students from working-class and poor backgrounds have attended college, the colleges themselves have become more differentiated. Community colleges, teachers' colleges, and many commuter universities —all of which are more working class in character than other types of colleges—have more rules and a greater emphasis on "right" and "wrong" answers and following directions (Bowles and Gintis, 1976). Major state universities and elite private universities —with more upper-class student bodies—place a greater emphasis on autonomy, flexible task orientation, and leadership qualities (Binstock, 1970). Is it

any surprise, then, that graduates of different colleges get very different types of employment?

Schooling and Job Status   Another trend that, according to conflict theorists, inhibits mobility is rising educational requirements for most jobs. At a time when more students from lower socioeconomic backgrounds are completing high school, jobs that in the past required a high-school diploma require a college degree; jobs for which a college degree would once have sufficed now require a graduate or professional degree. In fact, Bowles and Gintis (1976) have amassed a good deal of evidence suggesting that the key variable in securing a good job is not what you know or can do, but rather, how many years you stay in school. Indicators such as IQ, grade point average, and standardized test scores have little to do with income or job success among people with any given level of education. What matters is mainly how many years of school you have. (For evidence and a review of studies, see Bowles and Gintis, 1976, pp. 111–113, 294–297.) Collins (1979) argues that raising educational requirements enables the upper classes to keep their hold on better jobs, because their children have always been able to go further in the educational system than the children of the working class and the poor.

Significantly, the relatively few schools that do not fit the usual pattern often produce strikingly successful results. Some schools, even in working-class areas, do give students greater responsibility—and these schools tend to be more effective (Rutter et al., 1979). In these schools expectations are high and more time is spent on instructional tasks than on following rules. Thus, the educational system does not *have* to reinforce social-class inequalities, but as it presently operates, that is what it usually does.

Higher Education

Consider the following quotation, written by a professor concerning college students:

The student regards a professor's course simply as a credit. Of these he is compelled to purchase with his time a certain number necessary for a degree. Occasionally he discovers a

Letter to a Teacher

The educational system can serve to perpetuate inequality in societies other than the United States. The following excerpts are taken from *Letter to a Teacher*, a book written by a group of eight Italian rural, working-class teenagers. The book chronicles their experiences in the Italian public schools. It discusses, from the students' viewpoint, how they were held back and programmed for failure by the school system. Some of you might ask, If the system is such a failure, how did they learn to write so well? The answer is that, after being failed out of the public schools, they were given a second chance in a small private school for underprivileged youngsters. The school had one room, few books, and a tiny budget — but it had one crucial

---

* *Magistrale*: a four-year high school leading to a diploma for elementary school teachers [Translators' note].
SOURCE: Reprinted by permission from *Letter to a Teacher,* by the School Boys of Barbiana, translated by Norma Rossi and Tom Cole. Copyright 1970 by Random House, Inc., Vintage Books.

---

element: a teacher who believed that his students could succeed.

DEAR MISS,

You won't remember me or my name. You have flunked so many of us.

On the other hand I have often had thoughts about you, and the other teachers, and about that institution which you call "school" and about the kids that you flunk.

You flunk us right out into the fields and factories and there you forget us.

Two years ago, when I was in first *magistrale*,* you used to make me feel shy.

At first I thought it was some kind of sickness of mine or maybe of my family. My mother is the kind that gets timid in front of a telegram form. My father listens and notices, but is not a talker.

Later on I thought shyness was a disease of mountain people. The farmers on the flat lands seemed surer of themselves. To say nothing of the workers in town.

Now I have observed that the workers let "daddy's boys" grab all the jobs with responsibility in the political machines, and all the seats in Parliament.

So they too are like us. And the shyness of the poor is an older mystery. I myself, in the midst of it, can't explain it. Perhaps it is neither a form of cowardice nor of heroism. It may just be lack of arrogance.

The Mountain People

During the five elementary grades the State offered me a second-rate schooling. Five classes in one room. A fifth of the schooling that was due me.

It is the same system used in America to create the differences between blacks and whites. Right from the start a poorer school for the poor.

Some of the children may have left school for lack of money, which is not your fault. But there are some workers who will support their children through ten or eleven years of schooling just to get them through third intermediate.

---

bargain, technically known as a "snap," whereat he rejoices, despising however as "easy" the teacher from whom he can buy a credit so cheap. When, on the other hand, . . . he finds himself in a course which requires more than the average amount of study, he feels that he has been sold. . . . That professor is a "skinflint;" he sells a credit too high.

This piece could have been written by any number of my colleagues, who frequently complain that college students today are mainly interested in getting a degree and a job and not in learning for the sake of learning. This quote, however, was written by George

C. Cook in 1912. It illustrates the important point that both change and continuity characterize American higher education.

The Changing Role of College in American Society

Increasing Access to College   One of the biggest changes in higher education is the increasing proportion of young Americans who attend and graduate from college. About 45 percent of Americans today

They have spent every bit as much money as Pierino's daddy, but Pierino by the age of their children has already received his high-school diploma.

Born Different?
You tell us that you fail only the stupid and the lazy.

Then you claim that God causes the stupid and the lazy to be born in the houses of the poor. But God would never spite the poor in this way. More likely, the spiteful one is you. It was a Fascist who defended the theory of "differences by birth" at the Constituent Assembly: "The Honorable Mastroianni, referring to the word 'compulsory,' points out that certain children have an organic incapacity to attend schools."

And a principal of an intermediate school has written: "The Constitution cannot, unfortunately, guarantee to all children the same mental development or the same scholastic aptitude." But he will never admit it about his own child. Will he fail to make him finish the interme-

diate? Will he send him out to dig in the fields? I have been told that in the China of Mao such things are happening. But is it true?

Even the rich have difficult offspring. But they push them ahead.

Children born to others do appear stupid at times. Never our own. When we live close to them we realize that they are not stupid. Nor are they lazy. Or, at least, we feel that it might be a question of time, that they may snap out of it, that we must find a remedy.

Then, it is more honest to say that all children are born equal; if, later, they are not equal, it is our fault and we have to find the remedy. One of your colleagues (a sweet young bride who managed to fail ten out of twenty-eight kids in first intermediate —both she and her husband Communists, and quite militant) used this argument with us: "I did not chase them away, I just failed them. If their parents don't see to it that they return, that's their worry."

A teacher with the *Sports Gazette* sticking out of his pocket gets

along very well with a laborer-father who also has the *Sports Gazette* in his pocket, while they talk about a son who carries a ball or a daughter who spends hours at the hairdresser.

Then the teacher puts a little mark in the grade book and the laborer's children have to go to work before they have learned to read. But the teacher's children—they will go on with their studies to the last, even if they "don't feel like it" or "don't understand a thing."

Selection Is Useful to Some
Here someone will start blaming it all on fate. To read history as keyed to fate is so restful.

To read it as keyed to politics is more disturbing: fashions then turn into a well-calculated scheme to assure that the Giannis are left out. The apolitical teacher becomes one of the 411,000 useful idiots armed by their boss with a grade book and report cards. Reserve troops charged with stopping 1,031,000 Giannis a year, just in case the sway of fashion is not sufficient to divert them.

take at least some college courses by the time they reach their late 20s, and nearly one out of four graduates from college by then (U.S. Department of Education, 1987). Some students, of course, enroll and graduate much later. In fact, the proportion of college students outside the traditional 18-to-24 age group has risen greatly in recent years. Today, 38 percent of college students are older than 24 (U.S. Department of Education, 1987b, p. 122–123). Based on these statistics, it is reasonable to assume that more than half of all Americans now in their late teens or twenties will eventually attend college. In contrast, in 1900 just 4

percent of the traditional college-age group were enrolled in college (Veysey, 1965, p. 269).

At the turn of the century, almost all college students came from upper socioeconomic backgrounds, and almost none (except at a few colleges) were Catholic, Jewish, or black. In a 1902 poll conducted at the University of Michigan, two-thirds of the respondents reported that their fathers held the kind of upper-level positions (business and professional) that accounted for only 10 percent of the nation's jobs (Ellsworth, 1903; U.S. Bureau of the Census, 1975, p. 139).

The 1950s and Beyond: Increased Diversity In recent decades, more working-class and even poor people have been attending college. After World War II, the GI Bill of Rights permitted many young men who otherwise could not have afforded it to enroll in college. (It also had the effect of making financial aid more available to males than to females.) Many mobility-conscious working-class parents saw a college degree as the passport by which their children would gain greater opportunities than they had enjoyed.

The 1960s and early 1970s witnessed increasing pressure from civil rights organizations and students themselves to increase the proportion of minority and working-class college students. At the City University of New York (CUNY), students struck in support of open admissions, and at the University of Michigan, strikers demanded that the school's black enrollment be increased to 10 percent. Many of the students who protested in support of more open access were white and middle class. At about the same time, the federal government was pressing universities to adopt affirmative action programs for colleges and professional schools.

The Growth of Community Colleges Another important trend during the 1960s was the growth of community colleges. Many of these 2-year schools were opened during the 1960s, and their enrollment increased rapidly through the 1970s and 1980s. Today, about 45 percent of college students attend community colleges (Monk-Turner, 1988). As a group, community colleges are more diverse than 4-year schools (Hodgkinson, 1986). More of their students come from lower-income families, and the proportion of black and Hispanic students is higher than in the 4-year schools.

The original purpose of community colleges was to open higher education to poor and working-class students who were being largely ignored by the 4-year schools. The community colleges have enabled many people who would not otherwise have done so to continue their education beyond high school. For some, they have been a route to a 4-year college degree. Even the majority who do not go on to 4-year schools get significantly better jobs than they could have without a community college education.

On the other hand, community colleges clearly prepare students for a different type of employment than do the 4-year colleges and universities—often technical or clerical jobs, with mid-level pay. Management and professional jobs, in contrast, usually require 4 years of college. Recent research has confirmed that a year in a community college pays fewer dividends both in income and job status than a year in a 4-year school (Monk-Turner, 1988). This finding, combined with the fact that most lower-income college students attend 2-year rather than 4-year schools, has led some critics to categorize community colleges as part of the process by which inequalities are perpetuated. From this perspective, the channeling of working-class and poor people into community colleges rather than 4-year schools places an upper limit on their occupational opportunities (Bowles and Gintis, 1976; Pincus, 1980).

College Today: Who Goes? Who Graduates? The cumulative effect of the changes we have discussed has been an increase in the socioeconomic, racial, and ethnic diversity of the overall population of college students since the 1950s. However, working-class and minority youths are still far less likely to attend college than are youths from the upper classes. Moreover, the proportion of working-class and minority youths among college students began to fall in the late 1970s and continued to do so during the 1980s. Two major factors appear to account for this: cutbacks in government grant and loan programs, and declining pressures from students and the government to increase minority and working-class enrollment.

BLACKS IN COLLEGE The proportion of black college students peaked at 10.8 percent in 1977 (U.S. Bureau of the Census, 1983) and has not reached that point since. In recent years, it has fluctuated around 10 percent, which represents considerable underrepresentation, as more than 13 percent of the college-age population is black. Moreover, about one black student in three attends a predominantly black college. For many black students, this option offers support during a challenging period of life that would not be present in the less-familiar atmosphere of the predominantly white college. The rising number of racial incidents at many predominantly white schools in the 1980s also led some black students to select black schools. At the same time, white colleges have in-

A science class at Tuskeegee Institute. Some young African Americans prefer predominantly black colleges like Tuskeegee because they offer more support than predominantly white colleges.

creased their recruitment of black students, although blacks still remain underrepresented in most schools.

As shown in Table 14.2, black and Hispanic young people are about one-third less likely to attend college today than are white young people. The black-white gap has widened because between 1978 and 1985, the proportion of whites going to college rose, while the proportion of blacks going to college fell slightly. The gap in graduation rates is even larger. Whites in their late 20s are more than twice as likely as either blacks or Hispanics to have college degrees. In large part, this is because blacks and Hispanics are more likely to attend 2-year colleges.

Why Do Students Go to College?

As suggested by the quotation at the beginning of this section, getting a good job has always been an important reason for attending college, yet it is not and never has been the *only* reason. Students go to college in order to gain general knowledge and to learn more about themselves. Some also attend partly to have a good time or to meet a mate. In general, vocational motivations have become more important reasons for college attendance over the past 2 decades. During the 1960s, motivations related to personal development were about as important as job-related ones; today job-related objectives are by far the most important reason students give for attending college (Boyer, 1987; Chiet, 1975).

College and Employment As previously noted, educational requirements for many jobs have risen — in some cases even beyond an undergraduate degree. As a result, there are more educated young people competing for jobs. Consequently, college graduates have increasingly experienced unemployment or have settled for jobs that do not utilize their education. Many college graduates today work as taxi drivers, store clerks, or secretaries — a situation that would have been rare a few decades ago. In addition, more and more students go on to graduate or professional school after finishing college. About 80 percent of today's college students report that they plan to enroll in graduate school at some time; one-third to one-half actually do so (Boyer, 1987; U.S. Bureau of the Census,

TABLE 14.2
College Enrollment and Graduation Rates among Young American Adults, by Race and Spanish Origin

	PERCENT OF 18- TO 24-YEAR-OLDS ENROLLED IN COLLEGE			PERCENT WITH 4 YEARS COLLEGE, PERSONS AGES 25–29
	1978	1982	1985	1980
White	25.7	27.2	28.7	23.9
Black	20.1	19.8	19.8	11.4
Hispanic	15.2	16.8	16.9	9.0

SOURCES: U.S. Bureau of the Census, 1984; U.S. Department of Education, 1987a.

University Education in the 1980s

In the early 1980s I served on a campuswide committee at Southern Illinois University at Edwardsville. This experience brought me into direct contact with many of the trends in higher education that are discussed in this chapter. The committee was created in response to a genuine risk that the state would have to implement major program cuts in light of its inability, at the height of the 1982 recession, to come up with sufficient funding for the school's programs. A second reason for the convening of the committee was to reduce costs after the university had been identified by the Illinois Board of Higher Education as "overfunded"; in other words, its programs cost more per student-hour than those in other state universities. The committee was charged with examining each of the university's programs to recommend whether its funding be increased, maintained, or decreased. These recommendations were to be made on the basis of four criteria: program demand, program cost, program quality, and an underlying need to preserve a strong curriculum in the basic arts and sciences.

During the committee's deliberations, a number of things became clear. First, student demand was concentrated in the professional programs, not in the arts and sciences. Together, business, nursing, engineering, and computer-science majors accounted for close to half of the university's undergraduate students. Moreover, because these programs had such high enrollments, they were inexpensive on a per-credit-hour basis. Thus, they looked *very* good on two of the four criteria—demand and cost.

The programs in the arts and sciences were a very different story. Not only were few students majoring in such subjects as English, biology, or sociology, but students in the professional programs were discouraged from taking courses in these areas because their major requirements took up most of their time. Only when a course was required by a professional program, such as sociology for nursing students or physics for engineering students, did the students in these programs take it. The result, of course, was that the demand for arts and sciences programs was low, and the cost per credit hour was high.

There was considerable debate concerning the other two criteria: quality and maintaining a strong background in the arts and sciences. Ultimately, however, nearly all of the programs that were recommended for decreased funding were in the arts and sciences. Conversely, the programs recommended for increased funding were almost entirely professional programs. Thus, the university adhered to the national trend of funding the programs the students wanted at the expense of a basic education in the arts and sciences.

Is this sound educational policy? Evidence suggests that it is *not*. Although employers often prefer to hire people with specific job-related training, such people do not always make the best employees. A study commissioned by the Bell Telephone Companies (Beck, 1981) illustrated this point. Most of the people the company hired for its management positions came from professional programs in schools of business. However, some people with backgrounds in the arts and sciences did get hired. The study found that the people with this more diverse background outperformed those from the professional programs, perhaps because of their broader general knowledge.

SOURCE: Adapted from John E. Farley, *American Social Problems: An Institutional Analysis* (Englewood Cliffs, NJ: Prentice Hall, © 1987), p. 455. Used by permission of the author.

1987c). Finally, more students now major in professional programs such as nursing, engineering, business, or social work, as opposed to arts and sciences programs such as English, mathematics, physics, or history. (Ironically—as shown in the box entitled "University Education in the 1980s"—students trained in professional programs do not necessarily make more productive employees!)

According to the Carnegie Foundation, one result of increased student job orientation has been greater emphasis by colleges on training students for specific jobs, at the expense of giving them a sound general education (Boyer, 1987). This trend is unfortunate, for several reasons. First, many jobs are learned primarily through on-the-job training, and attempts to teach them in college may be a waste of time. Second, most people today change occupations one or more times during their lives, and they would thus be better served by learning broad knowledge and skills that could be applied to a variety of jobs. Finally, the emphasis on vocational education has lessened the effectiveness of colleges in preparing people for the nonvocational aspects of their lives (Boyer, 1987).

Does College Pay? A final implication of rising educational levels is that as college degrees have become more commonplace, the income advantage of attending college, though still considerable, is less than in the past. This point can be illustrated by looking at the incomes of young adult workers with and without college degrees. Such data are presented in Figure 14.2. In general, college *does* pay: The incomes of people with a college degree run about one-quarter to one-third higher than those of people without one. However, the *extent* to which it pays has declined over time. Between 1970 and 1980, for example, the difference between the incomes of people with college degrees and those with only high-school diplomas fell for both men and women (Guinzberg, 1983).

It is also important to point out that the income value of a college degree differs by race and sex. On the one hand, college-educated women and minorities enjoy a relatively large advantage relative to high-school–educated women and minorities. However, the incomes of women and minorities with college degrees are lower than those of white males with college degrees. In this regard, minorities seem to be doing better than women. Among *recent* black male college graduates in 1980, hourly earnings were 96 percent of those of white males (Farley, 1984), although the gap in annual income is slightly greater because black college graduates are a little less likely to find full-time work. Recent black female college graduates actually have slightly higher incomes than recent white female college graduates, but both have incomes only about three-quarters as great as those of recent white male graduates.

Of course, the rewards of college are not all economic. Studies of college students have indicated that their verbal, mathematical, and reasoning skills do improve as a result of college attendance (Bowen, 1977; Anderson, Farley, and McReynolds, 1986). A

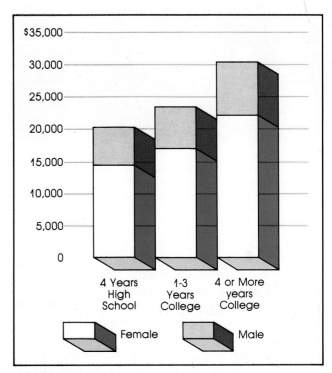

FIGURE 14.2
Median Incomes of Year-Round, Full-Time Workers, 25 to 34 Years Old, by Sex and Educational Level, 1986
Note that the average male with a high-school diploma made more money than the average female with 1 to 3 years of college.
SOURCE: U.S. Bureau of the Census, 1988a, pp. 133, 137.

college education also enhances interest in learning, stimulates a positive self-image, improves interpersonal skills, and leads to greater tolerance and respect for civil liberties (Hyman and Wright, 1979; Hyman, Wright, and Reed, 1975; Astin, 1977).

The Functions of Higher Education

The Production of Knowledge

In addition to teaching, a second key function of higher education has been the production of knowl-

Dream research at Stanford Universtiy. Do you think the research function of colleges and universities supports or conflicts with their teaching function?

edge through research. Many key advances in the natural sciences, new discoveries in the social sciences, and important literary and artistic creations have been produced by college and university professors. This function has been particularly important for the elite private universities such as Harvard, Stanford, Yale, and MIT, and for top state universities such as Michigan, Wisconsin, and California. To a great extent, the prestige of colleges and universities is determined by the number of faculty publications and research grants they generate (see Webster, Conrad, and Jensen, 1988; Webster, 1986). Moreover, the knowledge that is created in colleges and universities has been put to a number of important uses. Research is an important criterion for faculty tenure, promotion, and salary decisions almost everywhere except in the community colleges.

Research and Role Conflict Although the creation of knowledge is important, it is also a source of considerable role conflict for many professors. Colleges and universities claim to stress good teaching, but they usually offer greater rewards for the professor with a good publication record than for the professor with a good teaching record. Thus, colleges penalize the professors who put most of their energy into teaching rather than research. Being involved in research, of course, does keep a professor more up-to-date and informed about his or her field. Thus, that professor may have more current and complete knowledge to pass along to students. Sometimes, however, the pres-

sures of time and work lead professors to avoid interacting with students or to devote minimal effort to teaching so that they can get the research grants and publications they need for promotions and salary increases. Sometimes, too, professors are frustrated because those who evaluate them are more interested in how much they publish and the prestige of the journals they publish in than in the knowledge they produced by their efforts. Most professors experience at least some conflict between their roles as researchers and as teachers, and it is not clear that the pressure to "publish or perish" does much to enhance the quality of teaching and learning (Boyer, 1987).

Innovation and Social Criticism

It has also been argued that an important role of colleges is to foster innovative ways of dealing with issues and problems in the larger society and to promote a healthy degree of societal self-examination and social criticism. Toward this end, colleges have traditionally protected *academic freedom* — the right of professors and students to explore and advocate ideas and theories that may be unpopular with the larger population because they challenge conventional wisdom (Gutman, 1987, pp. 175–181). One means by which academic freedom is protected is academic *tenure,* which guarantees that after successfully completing a probationary period of 5 to 7 years, a professor cannot be dismissed except for serious failure to perform duties, financial exigency, or a decision to eliminate a program of study.

Because they foster skepticism and intellectual freedom, colleges and universities have sometimes helped to generate social movements that have brought significant social change. In the 1950s and 1960s, a great deal of civil rights activity was planned and organized on college campuses — especially, but not only, on predominantly black campuses. In the 1960s and early 1970s, the campuses were the most important center of activity in the movement against the war in Vietnam. Both of these movements brought important and long-lasting changes in American public policy and social and political beliefs (Yankelovich,

1981; *Newsweek*, 1988x). More recently, college students have been involved in the movement supporting U.S. disinvestment in South Africa as a means of opposing apartheid.

Limits on Academic Freedom The freedom of scholars to search for truth is not unlimited. Both public and private colleges and universities depend on outside sources for much of their financial support (state government, religious organizations, private donors). Ultimately, they are governed not by the faculty, but by lay governing boards and by administrators chosen by these boards. These boards, in turn, answer to political, religious, or other officials who appoint them, or to the public who elects them. Thus, they can and sometimes do penalize faculty who challenge the existing order or popular wisdom, often by denying tenure, sometimes by eliminating or curtailing programs.

Even greater control is exerted by those who fund research projects. Most projects are funded by government agencies, corporations, and private foundations (most of which are, in turn, funded by major corporations, as discussed in Chapter 9). By deciding which projects to fund, these agencies exert control over the kinds of research that will be conducted. In general, they support research that suits their purposes and do not pay for research that does not. Professors often serve as advisers and consultants to government and corporations, but those who challenge the prevailing viewpoints within these institutions find their services are not required (Domhoff, 1983).

Ties between universities and industries have increased in recent years. As enrollments have leveled off or fallen owing to the declining size of the college-age population, universities have looked for other activities besides teaching. Because of concerns about job loss in much of the country, one area of promise has been economic development activities. Many universities have opened research parks in cooperation with private industries, established programs to help local governments attract new industries, and promoted cooperative research projects with industries (Kenney, 1987). In some cases, part or all of the results of such research are not made available to other

scholars, as has been the case traditionally, but are treated instead as "proprietary"— the property of the company or agency that paid for the research. In fact, most universities now have policies outlining the conditions under which proprietary research is permitted. The relationships that universities establish with business and government substantially reduce their ability to serve as dispassionate social analysts.

Is the Quality of American Education Declining?

Several reports on the American educational system that appeared in 1983 brought to the forefront concerns that the American education system is doing a less-effective job of educating American students today than in the past (College Board, 1983; Twentieth Century Fund, 1983; Task Force on Education for Economic Growth, 1983). The most influential of these reports was *A Nation at Risk,* published by the National Commission on Excellence in Education (1983). All these reports agreed that American students in the 1980s were less knowledgeable than students with the same amount of education a generation

Scores on college entrance tests have fallen, but one reason for the decline is that more students, with a wider range of achievment and educational background, take these tests today than in the past.

earlier or students in most other industrialized countries. Subsequent studies have supported these conclusions (Stevenson, Lee, and Stigler, 1986). Average American scores on most achievement tests have improved slightly since around 1980, but they remain well below average scores in the 1950s and 1960s.

We must be careful when interpreting studies such as these. As noted earlier in this chapter, a higher percentage of Americans today attend high school (and take college entry tests) than was the case in the past or is the case in many other countries. Thus, if we compare *all* Americans at any given age (that is, not just students or graduates) to the comparable age group in the past, they come out better educated, not worse. Still, the fact that those who graduate from our schools know less than those who graduated in the past is a cause for concern. Moreover, some of the international comparisons are not limited to students; entire age groups in some other countries outperform the same age group in the United States (*Newsweek,* 1988x). Some people who graduate from American high schools are *functionally illiterate:* They cannot read, write, add, or subtract well enough to read a newspaper, fill out a form, balance a checkbook, or determine the best buy in a store (Kozol, 1986).

Have Educational Changes Reduced Achievement?

The declining scores have led educators and sociologists to ask what, besides the changing composition of the population taking the tests, accounts for the declines. Some of their answers are discussed below.

Less Time Spent Teaching Core Subjects   As the educational institution has been asked to deal with an increasing number of social problems and issues, courses outside the traditional areas of academic achievement (language, writing, reading, math, the natural and social sciences, speech, and the fine arts) have proliferated. Examples are driver training, cooking, marriage training, drug and sex education, and health and physical education. However important such courses may be, they are taught at the expense of time spent on traditional subjects. In some states,

more than half a student's time in school is spent on nonacademic courses. In some cases, the effect of this trend has been compounded by shifts to a shorter school year or school day. At higher levels of education, declining attention to core subjects has also resulted from increased emphasis on vocational education.

The Influence of Television   By the time the typical child graduates from high school, he or she will have spent a good deal more time in front of the television than in the classroom. Although television and video technology offer a great deal of educational material, most television viewing involves entertainment-oriented material. This comes at the expense of reading, and sometimes of homework. Moreover, watching television is a passive activity that emphasizes watching rather than doing. In general, the more time a child spends watching television, the poorer he or she performs in school (Hodge and Tripp, 1986, pp. 162–166).

Reduced Expectations of Student Achievement   We addressed this issue in our discussion of inequality in education, but expectations have been reduced not only for individual students or in individual schools, but also for the educational system as a whole. One piece of evidence is *grade inflation:* Even as the mea-

By the time these children graduate from high school, it is likely that they will have spent a good deal more time watching television than attending school.

sured achievement of American students has fallen, the average grades they are given have risen. Thus, it takes less knowledge to get an "A" in the average school or college today than it did 25 years ago.

Changes in the Home Background of Students

More students today come from single-parent homes or homes where both parents work. Thus, they are often subject to less supervision. In many cases, too, child rearing is more permissive, which means that children may be learning less self-discipline. These changes do not necessarily prevent students from learning, but they may place a greater burden on the schools to stimulate student interest and commitment to learning. Clearly, part of the problem is that our society has failed to provide quality, stimulating day care for children whose parents are employed. Where this is done, achievement is usually higher.

Lower-Quality Teaching

For a number of reasons, more teachers today than in the past lack either a sound knowledge of the subjects they teach or the interpersonal skills needed to teach effectively. Education majors have lower average college admissions test scores than people majoring in most other subjects, and a sizable number of teachers have been unable to pass basic-skills tests. In part, this has happened because the pay of teachers is relatively low compared to other occupations that require comparable (or even less) training. Moreover, talented women and minorities for whom teaching was one of the few open professions a generation ago today go into more lucrative fields. Thus, teaching has experienced a "brain drain."

Recently, there has been considerable effort to improve the quality of education in the United States. Moreover, average student scores on some standardized tests have improved somewhat. However, the declining test scores are to a large extent the result of long-term social trends, and some of the forces responsible for them (television, changing student background and attitudes, reduced attractiveness of the teaching profession) are unlikely to change in the forseeable future.

Summary

Sociologists of education are concerned with a variety of issues relating to education, including who goes to school, for how long, and why; the role of schooling in society; and international differences in the kind and amount of schooling. In the United States, education has become firmly institutionalized—probably more so than in any other country. Elementary and secondary schooling are free and compulsory up to about the age of 16. Americans believe that, ideally, everyone should be educated regardless of social background.

Functionalists see education as serving many key functions, including technical training, the development of human capital, and matching people to appropriate jobs. They also see it as providing people with the necessary knowledge to be informed citizens of a democracy, and as an important part of the socialization process. Education promotes consensus and solidarity by emphasizing the positive aspects of the national identity and by teaching children the rituals of patriotism. An important aspect of education is the hidden curriculum, which functionalists see as teaching children the beliefs and work habits they will need to be successful in the world of work.

Functionalists believe that schools promote social mobility by rewarding students on the basis of what they do rather than who they are. However, many students from low-income backgrounds do experience difficulty in school, which functionalists attribute to cultural and behavioral characteristics associated with their disadvantaged background. Functionalists believe that if such children are socialized to the values of middle-class children, they will have greater opportunities. Some functionalists have suggested compensatory education and school desegregation as ways of doing this. Properly executed, both methods appear to improve the achievement of economically disadvantaged students without hurting the achievement of others.

Conflict theorists, in contrast, see the schools primarily as a mechanism by which inequalities are perpetuated. They point to mobility studies showing that social-class background is strongly correlated to the amount of education a person gets, which in turn is the strongest determinant of future income and job status. Although schools in more affluent areas are better funded, this is not the main reason for inequality. Drawing from symbolic-interactionist theory, conflict theorists argue that schools give their students messages about who will do well and who will not, based largely on socioeconomic background. These messages are transmitted to students through such processes as teacher expectations, tracking, and testing. Importantly, schools where expectations are uniformly high produce higher achievement. Student achievement is less influenced by socioeconomic background in such schools.

Conflict theorists also see the hidden curriculum as part of the problem, in part because it varies according to a student's social background. For students of lower socioeconomic status, the message is primarily to conform to authority, whereas for those of higher status, it is to work independently, though within a framework of hierarchical authority. This process reinforces differences in socialization that have already occurred in the home, and it prepares students for distinctly different kinds of jobs.

More young Americans enter higher education today than at any time in the past. More college students today are older adults, and more are attending community colleges. There was some increase in college attendance by working-class and minority students during the 1960s and early 1970s, but rising tuition and decreasing pressure on colleges to admit such students reversed that trend during the 1980s. Besides education, a key function of colleges and universities is the production of knowledge through research. This function sometimes clashes with the teaching function. In some regards, the academic freedom necessary for the production of knowledge encourages colleges to be centers of innovation and change, but in other regards, colleges work to support the status quo.

Concerns have been raised in recent years about the quality of education in America. Although Americans are getting more education than ever, test scores of American students have fallen and are below those of students in many other countries. Possible causes of this trend include the changing composition of secondary-school students, reduced time spent teaching core subjects, the influence of television, reduced expectations of achievement, and changes in the home background of students. It has also been suggested that the quality of teaching has declined, perhaps because teaching has become less attractive compared to other professions.

Glossary

human capital The pool of trained workers necessary for productivity in modern industrial and postindustrial economies.

credentials Items of information used to document or support the claim that an individual has certain capabilities or expertise.

meritocracy A reward system based on ability and achievement rather than social background.

acculturation A process in which immigrant minority groups are expected to adopt the dominant culture of the host country.

hidden curriculum The values, beliefs, and habits that are taught in the schools in addition to factual content and skills.

cliques Relatively close and exclusive informal groups with distinct boundaries, usually consisting of about three to nine people.

cultural deprivation A condition that functionalist theorists believe commonly exists among lower-income groups, whereby such groups suffer disadvantages in education and economics because they lack cultural characteristics associated with success.

de facto segregation Racial school segregation that is brought about as a result of housing and neighborhood segregation patterns.

tracking An educational practice in which students are grouped according to their teachers' judgments of their ability.

Further Reading

BALLANTINE, JEANNE. 1989. *The Sociology of Education: A Systematic Analysis,* 2nd ed. Englewood Cliffs, NJ: Prentice Hall. A thorough and well-written introduction to the sociology of education. Each chapter contains a concluding section titled "Putting Sociology to Work" that applies sociological theories to practical educational problems.

BOWLES, SAMUEL, AND HERBERT GINTIS. 1976. *Schooling in Capitalist America.* New York: Basic Books. A highly influential analysis of American education from the conflict perspective. It documents a number of ways in which education is used to pass inequalities from generation to generation, and it employs a variety of data to argue that it is not what you know but rather how well socialized you are in the ways of the middle-class work world that enables you to get ahead in American society.

COHEN, ARTHUR, AND FLORENCE BREWER. 1982. *The American Community College.* San Francisco: Jossey-Bass. An examination of the role, structure, and processes of the community college in the United States.

COLEMAN, JAMES S., THOMAS HOFFER, AND SALLY KILGORE. 1982. *High School Achievement: Public, Catholic, and Private Schools Compared.* New York: Basic Books. This study, based on the *High School and Beyond* project, compares public, Catholic, and private schools in terms of (1) overall achievement of their students, and (2) the extent to which student achievement is influenced by ascribed statuses such as race, social class, and ethnicity. It shows how our schools can produce higher levels of achievement and how we can move toward the goal of truly equal educational opportunity.

KOZOL, JONATHON. 1985. *Illiterate America.* Garden City, NY: Anchor-Doubleday. This book discusses the problem of functional illiteracy—a problem that is shockingly widespread considering that the overwhelming majority of young Americans graduate from high school.

U.S. DEPARTMENT OF EDUCATION. 1987. *Schools That Work: Educating Disadvantaged Children.* Washington, DC: U.S. Government Printing Office. This short book should be required reading for anyone who doubts the educability of low-income, inner-city children. It gives examples from throughout the country of both public and private schools where children considered "uneducable" by many people are being successfully educated, and it discusses some of the ways that this is being accomplished.

CHAPTER 15

Religion

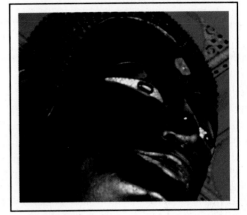

Humanity's fascination with the supernatural spans the ages. This shared fascination reflects universal and timeless efforts to explain the mystery of life, human suffering, and death. Greek mythology vividly portrays the relationships between gods and mortals. Beginning with an account of how Prometheus formed man from moistened clay in the image of the gods, we learn that the gods' willingness to protect humanity in return for homage was threatened by the deceit of Prometheus in stealing fire from heaven to give to humankind. In response to this deceit, Zeus cast his wrath upon humanity in the form of Pandora's box. Thus, we see a theme that is common among many religions — divine punishment of evil behavior:

> *. . . and now misery in countless forms filled the earth, the air, and the sea. By day and by night sicknesses prowled among men, secretly and silently, for Zeus had not given them a voice. A flock of fevers beleagued the earth and Death, who had been coming to mortals on slow reluctant feet, now walked with winged steps (Schwab, 1974).*

This example not only illustrates the presence of common religious themes in Greek mythology, it also calls our attention to a basic question: Just what is religion? There is debate among scholars, for example, on the extent to which Greek mythology fits the definition of a religion. Max Muller argued that

> *. . . belief in Zeus was religious in so far as the Greeks considered him the supreme God, father of humanity, protector of laws, avenger of crimes, etc.; but all that which concerned the biography of Zeus, his marriages and his adventures, was only mythology (quoted in Durkheim, 1965 [orig. 1915]).*

T he criteria used to identify religions have caused some scholars to question not only the proper classification of Greek mythology, but also such seemingly diverse phenomena as Marxism, Alcoholics Anonymous, EST groups, and Weight Watchers.

What Is Religion?

In search of an answer to the elusive question "What is religion?" Emile Durkheim undertook a study of Australian aborigines, arguing that elementary forms of religion could best be studied in tribal cultures. He later presented his conclusions in his seminal work on religion, *The Elementary Forms of the Religious Life* (1965 [orig. 1915]). In this work, Durkheim distinguished the aspects of everyday life, which he called the **profane,** from those things, often associated with the supernatural, that inspire awe, reverence, fear, or deep respect, which he called the **sacred.** Durkheim thus defined religion as formalized behavior that is directed toward the sacred. Such behavior usually involved **ritual,** a system of established rites and ceremonies. Durkheim thus developed the following definition of **religion:**

> A religion is a unified system of beliefs and practices relative to sacred things, that is to say, things set apart and forbidden — beliefs and practices which unite into one single moral community called a Church, all those who adhere to them (1965).

Classifying Religion

Durkheim's study of the religion of Australian aborigines set the stage for sociologists of religion, who continued to examine different religions in search of common fundamental concepts. In his article "Religious Evolution" (1964), Robert Bellah classified religions according to five typical stages: primitive, archaic, historic, early modern, and modern. Defining evolution

as a process in which more-complex forms develop from less-complex ones, Bellah compared the religious symbolization, action, and organization, as well as the social implications, of these five stages.

According to Bellah, the *primitive* stage was characterized by ritualized worship of ancestral figures, who were not considered gods. An example of this type of religion would be Chinese ancestor worship. In contrast, the mythical beings of *archaic religions* were gods who actively involved themselves in human affairs. People communicated to these gods through worship and sacrifice. Because these societies had developed a system of social stratification, the upper class assumed the priestly function. Greek, Roman, and Norse mythology typify this pattern. *Historic religions* retained the idea of a deity but added the crucial concept of *salvation.* This emphasis on achieving life after death encouraged people to stress their spiritual life rather than the material world. Islam and Roman Catholicism, particularly in their more traditional forms, are examples of this pattern.

As religions moved into the *early modern* stage, people continued to focus on salvation, but they no longer attempted to withdraw from the material world. Rather, they believed they could achieve salvation through involvement in worldly affairs. In addition, early modern religions stressed a direct relationship with God as opposed to mediation through a priestly class. Protestantism, particularly the Calvinist variety, is an example of this type of religion. The final stage, *modern religions,* reflects the complexities and accumulation of knowledge associated with the twentieth-century world. These religions place a greater emphasis on the physical world, stressing individual and social reform, and are less likely to adopt a formal, hierarchical organization. Unitarians and Quakers practice this type of religion.

Types of Organized Religion

When we discuss organized religions, we use many terms, such as *church, denomination,* and *sect.* Although the distinction among these terms is not always clear, each term does refer to a particular type of religious organization. The broadest of these, the **church,** is a religion with a formal hierarchy and an established set of rules and practices. Similar to the church is the **denomination,** which is one of several major religions in a given society. Denominations, like churches, have formalized rules and hierarchies. Although they might compete for members, they usually are tolerant of one another. Churches and denominations share several key characteristics. Perhaps most importantly, both attempt to accommodate themselves to the larger society. Although some of their teachings may conflict with certain social norms, these institutions usually do not challenge basic cultural rules and beliefs, and generally seek to avoid major conflicts with the society. In addition, churches and denominations tend to distinguish between those with special religious authority, called **clergy,** and the general membership, or **laity.**

In contrast to the church and denomination is the sect (Iannoccone, 1988). A **sect** is a relatively dogmatic religious group that is not well integrated into society. Sects usually challenge, rather than accept, the basic norms of the larger society. Thus, sects find themselves in conflict with society far more frequently than churches do. Sects usually claim that they alone possess religious truth; therefore, they are far less tolerant than denominations. They tend to reject pluralism and compromise with the larger society. They are also less formal and usually more egalitarian than churches. Sects frequently arise from breaks, or *schisms,* with churches. Some sects that achieve success lose some of their intensity and become more formalized and socially acceptable. In such cases, a sect can develop into a denomination.

Church-Sect Typologies
Although churches and sects differ in several respects, no clear line separates one from the other. In fact, sociologists of religion have wrestled for about a century with the question of how to distinguish a church from a sect.

TROELTSCH ON CHURCH VERSUS SECTS Although Max Weber introduced the concepts of church and sect, it was his student, Ernst Troeltsch, who first developed a system to classify various religions ac-

cording to these concepts. Troeltsch's theory was based entirely on his analysis of Christianity in Europe before 1800. He argued that over the course of many centuries, established Christian churches had abandoned the more radical teachings of Jesus Christ in order to accommodate themselves to the secular world. Among the characteristics of these churches were a formal hierarchy, involuntary membership (you were baptized into the church your parents belonged to), and a set of rituals and sacraments that reinforced the authority of the clergy. Certain small groups of Christians, however, guided by a more literal reading of the New Testament, established communities that separated themselves from the larger society. These communities, or sects, denied the authority of both the state and the ruling classes, espoused the ideals of poverty and frugality, and rejected the separation between clergy and laity (see Troeltsch, 1932).

LATER TYPOLOGIES Because Troeltsch's typology was based exclusively on an analysis of one religion during a particular historical period, some of his distinctions between a church or denomination and a sect did not apply in many other cases, including several in the United States. For example, although the Amish practice involuntary membership, they are considered a sect, not a religion. Conversely, many Protestant groups that lack a system of sacraments are still classified as churches (Johnson, 1963). As a result, many scholars have attempted to modify Troeltsch's system.

One major modification was proposed by the American theologian H. Richard Niebuhr. In *The Social Sources of Denominationalism* (1929), he denied that most religions could be neatly categorized as either sects or churches. Rather, he proposed a continuum in which church and sect were at opposite polls, with most religions falling somewhere in between.

Niebuhr further argued that the major force that drove various sects to break from established religions was not religious differences, but rather class conflict. According to Niebuhr, church membership was primarily middle and upper class, whereas most sect members came from the lower classes. Thus, the reason that churches sought accommodation with society was that their members wished to justify their success in the secular world. Similarly, members of sects found comfort in religions that rejected this world and taught that the faithful will be rewarded in the next world. As sect members became more successful, the sects became more like churches, and the poorer members frequently broke away to form new sects.

Since Niebuhr proposed his church-sect theory, many sociologists have attempted to modify it (Wilson, 1959, 1961, 1970; Wallis, 1975). For example, Johnson (1963) retained Niebuhr's model of the continuum, but he argued, like earlier sociologists, that a religion's classification depended on its acceptance of the larger cultural environment, not the class background of its members. Thus, Johnson's continuum ranged from complete rejection of the environment (sect) to complete acceptance (church). In his words:

> . . . since a sect tends to be in a state of tension with its surroundings, we are safe in supposing that religions that have totally withdrawn from participation in a society or that are engaged in open attack on it are likely to fall close to the sect end. . . . Churches, on the other hand, are comparatively at ease with the established values and practices of a society. Therefore we will probably be justified in classifying as churches those religions that comprehend the entire society or at least its dominant classes. (1963)

The idea of *tension* between the religion and the larger society is central to the theories of many other sociologists of religion (see, for example, Stark and Bainbridge, 1981). Some of the key differences between churches and sects are summarized in Table 15.1.

Cults A **cult** is a religion that is totally withdrawn from, and often at odds with, the religious traditions of a society. Although there is a great deal of similarity between cults and sects, there are also important differences. Sects often arise from established denominations and attempt to renew a society's traditional religious values. Cults, in contrast, promote values and behaviors that deviate greatly from established norms (Stark, 1985). Because cults reject many basic societal values, they sometimes isolate their converts from the larger society to maintain their influence. Consequently, some cults have been accused of "kidnapping" and "brainwashing" their members. In some cases, relatives have had members forcibly removed from the cult and "deprogrammed." Examples of current and recent cults in the United States are Scientology, the People's Temple, the Children of God, the

TABLE 15.1
Comparison of the Sect and the Denomination

CHARACTERISTIC	SECT	DENOMINATION
Size	Small	Large
Relationship with other religious groups	Rejects—feels that the sect alone has the truth	Accepts other denominations and is able to work with them in harmony
Wealth (church property), buildings, salary of clergy, income of members	Limited	Extensive
Religious services	Emotional emphasis—try to recapture conversion thrill; informal, extensive congregational participation	Intellectual emphasis—concern with teachings; formal, limited congregational participation
Clergy	Unspecialized; little if any professional training; frequently part-time	Specialized, professionally trained, full-time
Doctrines	Literal interpretations of Scriptures; emphasis upon otherworldly rewards	Liberal interpretations of Scriptures; emphasis upon this-worldly rewards
Membership recruitment	Conversion experience; emotional commitment	Born into group or ritualistic requirements; intellectual commitment
Relationship with secular world	"At war" with the secular world, which is defined as evil	Endorses prevailing culture and social organization
Social class of members	Mainly lower class	Mainly middle class

SOURCE: Glenn Vernon, 1962, *Sociology and Religion* (New York: McGraw-Hill), p. 174.

History, Beliefs, and Practices of the Major Religions

Weber addressed a number of other issues, including some ideas similar to those found in Durkheim's *Elementary Forms of the Religious Life*. In addition, Weber analyzed religious roles (magicians, priests, prophets), links between social stratification and religion (for example, the caste system of Hinduism), differences in what was required for salvation, and the relationship of religion to other aspects of life (politics, economics, sexuality, and art). We shall now consider some of the major religious groups studied by Weber, examining their history, growth, and beliefs.

Hinduism   Hinduism, a polytheistic religion, is recognized as the religion of India, where it originated thousands of years ago. Although most of the basic beliefs of Hinduism solidified about 2,000 years ago, some of the *Vedas* (sacred writings), as well as the gods whom Hindus worship today, date back 4,000 years. Unlike other religions, Hinduism claims no founder and lacks any form of structured organization (that is, a hierarchy of religious leaders). Hindus acknowledge the existence of hundreds of gods, but they recognize Brahman as the greatest deity, the creator of all who, as an everlasting spirit, contains all the lesser gods. Some of the best known of these gods are Vishnu, Rama, and Krishna. The Vedas were originally passed from one generation to the next by bards who, it is believed, received them from Brahman. Today gurus (teachers) transmit these sacred beliefs. The *Bhagavad-Gita,* part of a lengthy epic (100,000 verses), is perhaps the most famous of Hindu scriptures, and it may come closest to capturing the central truths of Hinduism.

Reincarnation, a fundamental concept of Hinduism, links together explanations of the meaning of life, inequalities in this world, and our fate after death. Reincarnation is the belief in a cycle of births and rebirths. According to this belief, the human soul does not die. Rather, after death the soul goes to heaven, purgatory, or hell until it is reborn. Central to this belief is *karma*, the idea that a person's behavior in this life will determine his or her position in the next life. Those who follow the rules of *dharma*, the proper conduct expected for a given caste, will be reborn into a higher position; those who do not will be reborn into a lower position. With the hope of reducing the amount of suffering that their ancestors might endure in hell or purgatory, Hindus may perform special rites and pilgrimages.

Special Hindu rites also exist for each of the major transitions in life—birth, puberty, marriage, and death. Thus, a special ceremony for birth occurs before the umbilical cord is cut, and a naming rite is performed about 10 days after birth. When a boy reaches puberty, he is invested with a sacred thread, which he wears across one shoulder for the remainder of his life. During a marriage ceremony a bridal couple walks around a sacred fire with their clothing knotted together, reciting vows. Funeral rites involve cremation and the scattering of the ashes in either the Ganges or another sacred river. In the days following cremation, the family of the deceased may give offerings of rice balls and milk to ward off harm from the deceased's ghost.

Buddhism   In the sixth century B.C., Siddhartha Gautama (c. 563 B.C.–483 B.C.) founded Buddhism in India. Although it arose from a rejection of orthodox Hinduism, Buddhism retained reincarnation as a fundamental concept. By 200 B.C., Buddhism had split into two major forms—Hinayana and Mahayana. Hinayana Buddhism, which is based on Buddha's teachings, is a sacred philosophy and code of ethics. Distinguishing itself from Mahayana by the belief that Buddha was human and not divine, the focus of Hinayana is not upon deities, but rather upon the attainment of *nirvana*—a state of perfect bliss in which the self, freed from suffering and desire, loses individual awareness and is merged into the universal. A person achieves this state by practicing a number of virtues, including humility, mercy, charity, and most importantly, self-control. In Mahayana Buddhism, which regards Buddha as divine, followers may worship many gods and stress faith, and not good works, as the key to salvation. Mahayana Buddhists perceive nirvana not as a total loss of individual awareness, but as a state of passionless peace.

Buddha ("the Enlightened One") rejected the

authority of both the Vedas and the Brahmin priests, teaching that salvation could be attained through knowing and living by "Four Noble Truths." These truths maintain that suffering arises from a desire for objects and ideas that are not permanent; this desire — and thus suffering — can be overcome by following the "Noble Eightfold Path."

Buddha's concept of the self was central to his rejection of the Vedas. In place of sacrificial rites to gods, Buddha emphasized the purification of the self, which he claimed occurred through proper thoughts and actions. He advocated a love for all creation, which would reduce human frustrations.

Although Buddhism spread into Central and East Asia, its influence in India lasted only until about A.D. 500. Today Hinayana is practiced in Burma, Ceylon, Thailand, Laos, and Cambodia; Mahayana is practiced in China, Tibet, Vietnam, Japan, and Korea.

Confucianism   Regarded as the major traditional religion of China, Confucianism is a sacred philosophy or ethical doctrine that provides rules for the proper conduct of family, community, and political affairs. The principles of this religion are based upon the teachings of Confucius, who lived around 551 to 479 B.C. Although Confucianism became the ethic of the mandarin class — the elite group — Confucius himself came from a poor but well-respected family. The principle upon which he built his philosophy has been compared to the Golden Rule. Considered central to producing ideal relationships, it is recorded in the *Analects,* a collection of Confucius's most famous sayings, and in other works.

> "Tzu-kung asked, saying, "Is there one word which may serve as a rule of practice for all one's life?" The Master said, "Is not Reciprocity (*shu*) such a word? What you do not want done to yourself, do not do to others." (Noss, 1980)

In addition to this fundamental principle, Confucius taught the importance of many other virtues, including loyalty, wisdom, self-control, filial piety, and self-development. Confucius used the family as the model for society. Those in power should rule for the well-being of the people, while the rest of society should obey and respect their rulers, as children do their parents.

Unlike other major world religions, Confucianism is not oriented to the metaphysical. Confucius did not speculate about the afterlife or salvation. Characterizing Confucianism as an ethical doctrine that values proper conduct for its own sake, Parsons noted that in this religion there is no such thing as sin, only error. He described Confucius's view of the perfect gentleman in the following way:

> The rational man will avoid display of emotion, will be always self-controlled, dignified, polite. He will always observe the proprieties of any situation most punctiliously. His basic aim is to live in harmony with a social order which is generally accepted and to be an ornament to it (1937).

Judaism   Historians trace the beginnings of the Jewish faith to a period somewhere between 2000 and 1600 B.C. Taking its name from Jacob's fourth son, Judah, Judaism was the religion adopted by the descendants of Jacob and Benjamin who claimed Jerusalem as the capital of their kingdom. Central to Judaism is the belief that salvation cannot be attained simply by adhering to a set of beliefs. Rather, true believers must act in accordance with their faith in Yahweh, the sole creator and ruler of the universe.

Influenced by the cultures of Canaan and Babylonia, Judaism evolved from a polytheistic to a monotheistic religion based on ethical ideas. No divine leader is recognized as the founder of Judaism, but several historical leaders are credited with establishing and maintaining the principles and practices of the Jewish faith. It was with Abraham (c. 2000 B.C.) that God established his covenant. Yahweh instructed Abraham that every male should be circumcised as a symbol of that covenant. Abraham's descendants trace their lineage directly to Judah, who was the grandson of Isaac, Abraham's son, whereas Muslims trace their history back to Abraham through his son Ishmael, whose mother was Hagar, an Egyptian handmaid of Abraham's wife, Sarah.

Moses (c. 1500 B.C.) is recognized as the greatest Jewish leader. He is credited with the Torah, the first five books of the Bible — Genesis, Exodus, Leviticus, Numbers, and Deuteronomy — that contain the Jewish law. These works include an explanation of creation (Genesis), the Ten Commandments, and the Golden Rule. The prophets, special messengers sent by God, also exerted a tremendous influence on the Jewish faith. Teaching an ethical monotheism, the prophets fought against the idolatry and pagan rites of other religions and taught, instead, a religion that emphasized social justice and belief in Yahweh.

TENETS OF JUDAISM Although they believe in only one God, Jews view God as having many roles — creator, ruler, helper, friend, father, liberator, and saviour. Believing that God is the creator of good as well as evil, Jews maintain that the human soul is immortal. Thus, if good acts are not rewarded in this world, they will be rewarded in the hereafter.

The ethical nature of Judaism is reflected in its core beliefs, which include, above all, love of God. This love will lead people to do good everywhere. Teachings about good and evil also include the belief in a free will. Jews believe that we are free from sin at birth and consciously choose to do evil. Atonement for sin must be sought directly with God through prayers, reflection, and good works. Judaism's emphasis upon social justice is clearly recognized in the Golden Rule: "Love thy neighbor as thyself." Because we are all created in God's image, all people are equal. Judaism also teaches that the world is good, and that the blessings of this world are to be enjoyed. This does not, however, signify a life oriented to pleasure: Jews emphasize a person's duty to family and community.

The special rites of Judaism are associated with major life transitions. As noted earlier, males are circumcised at birth to symbolize Abraham's covenant with God. At puberty boys have a Bar Mitzvah and girls have a Bat Mitzvah to signify their entrance into the world of adult responsibilities. Marriage rites include the use of a special canopy for the wedding ceremony, drinking together from a wine cup, placing of the ring on the bride's finger during the recitation of promises, and the breaking of a glass following the ceremony. For Jews death is a time for a person's confession to God. Funeral rites include the recitation of a prayer honoring the dead, the Mourner's Kaddish, the lighting of a memorial candle, and the dressing of the dead in a white shroud.

Christianity Christianity began as a sect of Judaism nearly 2,000 years ago. The distinctive feature of Christianity is its focus upon Jesus Christ, who is regarded as a divine being who came into this world to achieve salvation for all people. He achieved this by dying on the cross and rising from the dead 3 days later. Following his resurrection, he spent a brief period with his followers during which he established his church, and then he ascended into heaven.

Unlike the mythical figures of many other religions, Jesus is a historical figure who lived in Israel during the period of the Roman occupation. He led a brief ministry lasting somewhere from 1 to 3 years, during which he preached and performed miracles, such as healing the sick and raising people from the dead. Though his teachings were not organized or written down during his life he did assemble a group of *apostles* to whom he entrusted the responsibility of spreading his teachings. Thus, Christianity spread rapidly, and in the fourth century it was proclaimed the official religion of the Roman Empire.

Somewhere between A.D. 50 and 100, the 27 documents that were incorporated into the Christian Bible as the New Testament were compiled. Included among these writings are four accounts of the life of Jesus, called the *Gospels;* a history of the early Church, called the *Acts of the Apostles;* and a series of letters, called *epistles,* many of which are credited to St. Paul. The Sermon on the Mount is possibly the best known of Jesus's teachings, containing both the Lord's Prayer and the Beatitudes. Jesus's life and teachings centered around the love of God and the Golden Rule.

Although St. Paul was not among Jesus's original 12 apostles, he is recognized as one of Christianity's greatest missionaries. His ability to attract many followers may have been due to his position against enforcing Jewish customs such as circumcision and dietary laws. It should be no surprise, therefore, that many of the reasons that Jews reject Christianity are related to Paul's teachings.

DIVISIONS WITHIN CHRISTIANITY By the Middle Ages most people in Europe had been converted to Christianity. As the Christian Church grew larger, however, it experienced numerous internal conflicts, which eventually led to formal divisions and the establishment of different denominations. In the first major schism two distinct branches of Christianity emerged: the Roman Catholic Church, headed by the Pope, in the West; and the Orthodox Church in the East. The Catholic Church remained supreme in most of Europe until the sixteenth century, when Martin Luther inspired the Protestant Reformation, which rejected the authority of the Pope and insisted upon the authority of the Bible. Among the many Protestant denominations that emerged from the Reformation were Lutheranism, Calvinism, Anglicanism (Episcopalianism in the United States after the Revolution), Methodism, and the Society of Friends (Quakers). As shown in Figure 15.2, the great majority of the American population identifies itself as Christian, with well over half considering themselves Protestant and more than another quarter considering themselves Catholic.

Christian rituals that mark the major transitions in a person's life are called *sacraments*. Different Christian denominations observe some or all of the following: Baptism, Confirmation, Communion, Marriage, Extreme Unction ("last rites"), Penance, and Ordination.

Islam Of all the world's major religions, Islam has existed for the shortest period of time. It was founded in Arabia by Muhammad (A.D. 570–632), whom Muslims regard as a prophet. Islam is linked historically to both Judaism and Christianity, which were established religions by the time Muhammad began to preach. Although Islam recognizes the validity of both of these religions, it maintains that the followers of Abraham, Moses, and Jesus Christ altered these figures' original teachings, thereby producing the religions we see today. Thus, Islam claims that only Mu-

hammad's teachings represent the true words of God, whom they call *Allah*.

The *Koran,* which contains the sacred writings of Islam, consists of 114 chapters, or *suras*. Muslims believe that God revealed these words to Muhammad and therefore regard them as holy truths. Muhammad, like Jesus, did not organize or write these truths down; this task was left to his followers, who assembled his teachings in the Koran after his death.

The set of beliefs that best characterize the Islamic faith are the following:

1. God is great, meaning greater than anyone or anything possible. He is the ruler of the world and universe, and He is viewed as both compassionate and merciful.
2. There will be a Judgment Day when good will be rewarded and evil punished.
3. Muhammad was a prophet to whom God revealed His truths for all men.
4. The Koran contains the truths that God revealed to Muhammad.
5. Islam is a faith for all who believe, and it restricts no one on the basis of race, color, nationality, or social status.

In addition to these beliefs, Muslims are expected to fulfill certain duties referred to as the *Five Pillars of Islam*:

1. Recitation of the creed that "There is no god but God."
2. Worship and prayer five times daily and in the mosque on Fridays. A ritual washing must precede the offering of these prayers, and a Muslim must pray while facing in the direction of Mecca.
3. During *Ramadan* (the sacred month when Muhammad first received his revelation from God) Muslims must abstain from eating, drinking, and sexual activity from dawn to dusk.
4. All Muslims must practice almsgiving (donating money to the poor).
5. All Muslims must make a pilgrimage to Mecca before they die.

Like Christianity, Islam has multiple denominations. The two largest and most important are the Sunni and Shi'ite branches. The schism between these two groups began in the earliest days as a political struggle over who was to succeed to the rule of the Prophet Muhammad. Their religious disagreement concerns the role of the imam, or spiritual leader of the commu-

FIGURE 15-2
Religious Preferences in the United States, 1989
SOURCE: *Statistical Abstracts,* 1988, Table #75.

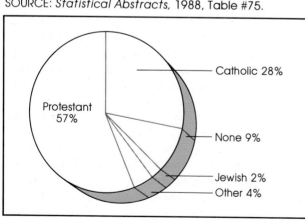

Catholic 28%

Protestant 57%

None 9%

Jewish 2%

Other 4%

nity. Shi'ites see imams as inspired interpreters of Islamic principles; Sunnis do not. In general, Shi'ite Muslims tend to be stricter and more fundamentalist in their beliefs than Sunni Muslims. However, there is considerable variation in this regard among the Sunnis, who are by far the larger of the two denominations. In Saudi Arabia, for example, Sunni Muslims are far more traditional and puritanical than Sunni Muslims elsewhere (Philipp, 1980). Shi'ites are also more opposed to modern and Western influences than most Sunnis, a reality that has been reflected in the political stance of the Islamic Republic of Iran.

Religion: The Sociological Perspective

Because religion exists in some form in all societies, it is of great interest to sociologists. Sociologists study religion within the framework of the *social construction of reality,* discussed in Chapter 3; that is, they treat religion as a social institution created by human beings. In so doing, they do not pass judgment on the truth or validity of any religion. Rather, they maintain that, whatever the *source* of religious beliefs, the forms and roles that a religion assumes within a society are determined by human actions. Thus, religion can be examined from the *sociological perspective.*

In the area of religion, as in most areas, the functionalist and conflict schools espouse different views. We will examine the functionalist perspective first and then proceed to the conflict school.

A Functionalist Analysis of Religion

Functionalists assume that society tends to be a stable and integrated system, and they argue that the interrelated parts of this system (the family, the military, religion) maintain the stability of society by teaching and reinforcing the same set of basic values. Our examination of the world's major religions referred to several of the functions performed by religion. As we saw earlier, Durkheim cited many of religion's functions in his analysis of the religion of Australian aborigines, and this work inspired later sociologists, who

built upon his theory to make it relevant to modern-day religion. Sociologists tend to agree on six basic functions of religion that are inextricably linked: social solidarity, meaning, social control, identity, psychological support, and social change (see O'Dea and Aviada, 1983; Chalfant, Berkely, Palmer, 1987).

Social Solidarity Religious beliefs and practices operate jointly to bond members into an integrated community. This idea was central to Durkheim's functionalist analysis of religion. In short, Durkheim claimed that religion *was* society; he explained the meaning of this statement by referring to the functions of religious beliefs and practices.

The Christian practice of receiving Holy Communion (the Eucharist) illustrates Durkheim's argument. This sacrament, which is often referred to as the Lord's Supper, represents the central beliefs regarding Jesus's mission, death, and resurrection. In Jesus's time a shared meal signified peace, trust, and community (social solidarity); today the term *communion* connotes a very similar meaning—a sharing of thoughts and emotions, which is often simply conceived as fellowship or community.

Meaning Parsons (1965) claimed that religion provides answers to our questions concerning the meaning of our relations to others, of existence, of happiness and suffering, and of good and evil. The importance of providing meaning was clearly recognized in Buddhism; thus, the meaning of suffering was fully explained in the "Four Noble Truths." Religions that fail to provide answers to questions about the ultimate meaning of life will frequently lose members. Kelly (1977) used this argument to explain why conservative churches are growing in the United States. According to Kelly, liberal churches placed themselves in serious competition with nonreligious organizations by offering incentives that are not unique to religion (for example, fellowship, entertainment, and knowledge). Conservative churches, in contrast, kept their focus on salvation, with its attendant answers to questions about the meaning of life, and thereby stimulated growth in their memberships. One could add to this analysis the fact that the liberal churches often define truth as a matter to be individually reasoned or interpreted, whereas the more fundamentalist churches offer clear answers through their more dogmatic beliefs.

Social Control In addition to explaining the supernatural, religions offer prescriptions for life in this world — those things a person must do (virtue) or avoid (sins) in order to attain salvation (Glock and Stark, 1965). Although civil authorities frequently share responsibility for enforcing moral behavior (by punishing such offenses as murder, theft, and improper sexual conduct), religion's use of a normative power — whose source of legitimacy is usually rooted in a supreme authority — is often the most effective means of exercising control over society's members. Moral prescriptions are usually contained in a religion's sacred writings. Thus, the Bible contains the Ten Commandments, which enumerate what Jews and Christians must do in order to attain salvation. Because socialization is the means by which people learn right and wrong, religion plays an important part in the socialization process in most societies.

Identity By providing an answer to the question "Who am I?" religion gives people a sense of security, a feeling of acceptance and belonging. As we saw, the role that the identity function plays in Hinduism is especially important, because recognition and acceptance of the identity assigned at birth determines a person's position in the next life.

Psychological Support Religion serves as a source of psychological support during the trying times of a person's life. Not only do religious rites mark the most stressful and major transitions throughout a person's lifetime, but they offer tremendous support during unexpected crises.

Social Change Although religion creates social solidarity and provides support during uncertain times, it can also serve as a catalyst for social change. One recent example is the civil rights movement in the United States. Among the most prominent leaders were the Reverend Martin Luther King and other ministers, many of whom were associated with the Southern Christian Leadership Conference (SCLC). In addition, representatives of religious groups throughout

Dr. Martin Luther King, Jr., (front center), Reverend Ralph Abernathy, and others leading the Selma-to-Montgomery march of 1965. The civil rights movement was a major example of how religion can promote social change.

the country participated in various ways, including marching and demonstrating, lobbying for civil rights laws, and teaching about racial justice. At the local level, black churches played a critical role in the organization of these civil rights activities (Morris, 1984).

The Iranian Revolution provides a more dramatic example of religion as a source of social change. The revolution was, in part, a reaction to the modernization and secularization that had been introduced into Iran by the Shah. Under the leadership of a major religious figure, the Ayatullah Khomeini, the revolution led to the creation of an Islamic state based on strict enforcement of Shi'ite Islamic law.

A Conflict Analysis of Religion

Conflict theorists view religion as they do other social institutions: as a mechanism that allows an elite minority to dominate a relatively powerless majority. Conflict theories concerning religion center around the writings of Karl Marx, whose beliefs about religion were heavily influenced by the Young Hegelians, a group of German philosophers who viewed religion as an oppressive force in German society (Coser, 1977). Between 1835 and 1841 three of these Young Hegelians — David Strauss, Bruno Bauer, and Ludwig

Feuerbach—published books that claimed that Christian beliefs were based on fiction. In his *Essence of Christianity* Feuerbach used the concept of alienation to argue that people are ruled and oppressed by a force of their own creation—religion (Coser, 1971). Feuerbach's focus on the social conditions that caused people to turn to religion for support heavily influenced Marx. This influence can be seen in Marx's best-known statement regarding religion:

> The basis of irreligious criticism is this: man makes religion; religion does not make man. Religion is indeed man's self-consciousness and self-awareness so long as he has not found himself or has lost himself again. But man is not an abstract being, squatting outside the world. Man is the human world, the state, society. This state, this society, produce religion which is an inverted world consciousness, because they are an inverted world. . . . Religious suffering is at the same time an expression of real suffering and a protest against real suffering. Religion is the sigh of the oppressed creature, the sentiment of a heartless world, and the soul of soulless conditions. It is the opium of the people (1978).

In his theory of economic determinism, Marx argued that the economic base of society influenced the rest of society—its laws, government, education, and religion. Because the dominant class controlled the economic resources, it was able to control all of the social institutions. By claiming that religion was the opium of the people, Marx meant that the dominant religion in society was the religion of the ruling class, who formulated and maintained beliefs that justified the inequalities of the social order. Rooted in beliefs about eternal rewards and punishments, this form of social control was extremely effective. By teaching people to look forward to happiness in the next life, religion led them to accept their lot in this life, no matter how bad or unfair it might be. Thus, argued Marx, religion encouraged people to accept unfairness and inequality rather than fighting for change.

Religion and Inequality The degree to which religion can maintain inequalities and injustices to serve the interests of the ruling class is illustrated by Hinduism, which has for centuries effectively maintained a caste system in India. As we discussed, the rules of *dharma* specify different behaviors to be followed by members of each caste. An attempt to move out of one's caste constitutes a violation of dharma that will be punished by rebirth into a lower position. Thus has Hinduism prohibited the social mobility that has become a central tenet—although often not a reality—of Western thought.

In writing about slavery in America, Gary Marx claimed that although there was some controversy among slaveholders over religion's effect upon slaves, most of them eventually saw religion as an effective means of social control (1974). In support of this claim, he cited historian Kenneth Stampp:

> Through religious instruction the bondsmen learned that slavery had divine sanction, that insolence was as much an offense against God as against the temporal master. They received the Biblical command that servants should obey their masters, and they heard of the punishments awaiting the disobedient slave in the hereafter. They heard, too, that eternal salvation would be their reward for faithful service (1956).

Religious Conflicts Conflict theory explains not only how religion legitimizes and maintains inequalities in a given social order, but also how different religious faiths come to conflict. Thus, for example, wars such as the Crusades, which appear to have been motivated by religious convictions, have been explained in terms of economic motives: The European

This 1988 Russian Orthodox ceremony celebrated the 1,000th anniversary of the introduction of Christianity into Russia. Although all communist countries are officially atheistic, many people in these countries retain their religious beliefs.

nobility had a serious economic interest in gaining control over the trade routes to the East. Similarly, we noted in Chapter 11 that conflict theorists view the conflict in Northern Ireland as a class struggle rather than a religious conflict.

✳ Weber and the Protestant Ethic

Although Marx's theories enjoy widespread support, many critics contend that not all religious conflicts can be classified as simply class struggles. In *The Protestant Ethic and the Spirit of Capitalism* Max Weber proposed a more complex theory concerning the relationship between religion and social structure than the cause-and-effect model introduced by Marx (Weber, 1958).

Weber's work focused around those factors that gave rise to capitalism. Although he acknowledged the important roles played by increased agricultural production, industrial technology, and improvements in transportation and sanitation, he considered the decisive factor to be neither science nor technology, but rather the emergence of new values associated with the rise of Protestantism. According to Weber, Calvinism — the form of Protestantism developed by John Calvin — taught that God had determined in advance who was to be saved and who was not. Although we could never be certain as to whom God had chosen, success in this world, coupled with a "moral" lifestyle, might be interpreted as a sign that a person was among the "elect." Thus, while maintaining a focus on God and religion, Calvinism encouraged people to place greater emphasis on material success. This success was to be achieved through the **Protestant Ethic** of individualism, hard work, and frugality. In promoting this more secular view of the world, Calvinism paved the way for a major restructuring of economic life.

Weber's analysis of the conditions that gave rise to the development of capitalism was not limited to Europe. He also examined Eastern societies and religions, noting where conditions matched or differed from those in the West. He argued, for example, that although trade and manufacture had reached fairly high levels in both India and China, the religious beliefs and practices in those societies inhibited the development of capitalism. Regarding India, Hinduism stressed the importance of a frugal and ascetic lifestyle, much as did Calvinism. However, the purpose of this lifestyle was not to enable a person to attain wealth, as in Calvinism, but rather to separate the Hindu from the material world. Likewise, in China, the ethical principles embodied in Confucianism did not promote the pursuit of wealth and material success.

Weber's explanation of why capitalism emerged in the West focused on, but was not limited to, religious factors. He identified a number of socioeconomic factors that he also considered necessary for the development of capitalism. These factors included the following:

The rational capitalistic organization of free labor

A physical separation (independence) of business from the household

A rational form of bookkeeping

Rational structures of law and administration

Impact of Weber's Theory Weber's theory created a great deal of controversy. Some of this controversy arose from misunderstandings regarding his fundamental theoretical position. Other critics questioned his accuracy in describing different religions and claimed that he lacked empirical evidence for his arguments and that he distorted his concept of "modern capitalism" so that it would fit specific features of Calvinism. Nevertheless, Weber's thesis on the Protestant Ethic and the spirit of capitalism is a seminal work in the sociology of religion. According to Andrew Greeley:

Weberian theory . . . is the most influential antecedent of contemporary sociological theorizing about the nature of religion and society and also . . . a classic example of the caution with which a sociological thinker ought to approach the complex issue of the relationship between religion and society (1972).

Weber's theory that religion and society mutually influence each other represents a complex theoretical model. This complexity has hindered efforts to devise a conclusive test of his hypothesis. There are, for example, a variety of alternative explanations that may account for the rise of Calvinism and capitalism during the same general period in history (Johnstone,

1988, pp. 148–151). Even so, there are clearly a number of ways in which Calvinism could have facilitated the rise of capitalism (Rachfall, quoted in Samuelsson, 1961). For this reason, Weber's work has remained influential in the sociological study of both religion and economics.

If the specific relationship between Calvinism and capitalism continues to be debated, the notion of a two-way relationship between religion and the nature of society is not a matter of debate among sociologists. In the United States, one of the first comprehensive studies of this relationship, *The Religious Factor,* was published by Gerhard Lenski in 1958. Lenski demonstrated that religion was linked to economics, politics, family life, education, and science in the United States.

On the other hand, the distinctive features of Protestant theology that may have given rise to capitalism are no longer so distinctive, at least within industrial societies. The theological differences between American Protestants and Catholics, for example, have narrowed, and the two groups no longer vary significantly in their work-related values. As a result, Protestants and Catholics today have similar income and education levels, although various Protestant denominations vary widely in this regard (Roof, 1979; Greeley, 1977).

Church and State in America

Although Lenski was the first American to measure comprehensively the mutual influences between religion and other major social institutions, the idea that a fine line existed between religion and politics has long been a part of American thought. In formal recognition of the potential influence that the church and the state could exert upon one another, the First Amendment of the Bill of Rights (1791) forbade Congress from passing any law "respecting an establishment of religion, or prohibiting the free exercise thereof." John Wilson (1978) has identified the key motives underlying this amendment:

1. The United States was originally settled in part by groups such as Mennonites, Catholics, and Puritans who were seeking freedom from the religious persecution they had suffered in Europe.

2. The dominant values in the infant nation—liberalism and pluralism—both emphasized freedom of choice and individual responsibility, an emphasis that extended into the area of religion.

3. Most of the earliest immigrants came from England, where (after the Revolution of 1688) religious toleration was practiced to a greater degree than in most other European countries.

4. The sheer number and variety of religious groups present by the time of the founding of the independent nation made some sort of accommodation to pluralism necessary if a united nation was to be established and preserved. In addition, the voluntarism of these groups paved the way for religious pluralism and militated against a church in which citizenship and religious affiliation would be synonymous.

5. At the time of the framing of the Constitution, only one in eight Americans was a church member. This made it necessary to make provision in the Constitution for tolerance of irreligion.

6. The colonial experiences of states such as Rhode Island, Pennsylvania, and Virginia, which had successfully practiced some degree of religious toleration, acted as a model for the nation as a whole.

7. The First Great Awakening, a religious revival that began in 1734, strengthened the nonconformist spirit in the United States and helped break down the constraints of the old parish system upon which the Anglican Church (Church of England) largely depended.

8. The need to attract settlers and trade made it economically advantageous to prohibit religious barriers to migration.

9. The framing of the Constitution was much influenced by French pre-Revolutionary ideas of egalitarianism and deism, which stated that God had created the world and then left it to function according to natural laws.

10. Freemasonry, popular among many moving spirits of the American Revolution, strongly advocated religious toleration.

Religion and Politics

Although the First Amendment prevented the government from establishing or prohibiting any one religion, it did not ensure the complete separation of religion and politics. In fact, throughout U.S. history many people have participated in political movements as a result of their religious and ethical values.

The Nineteenth Century In 1831, the French scholar Alexis de Tocqueville visited America and documented his observations in a book entitled *De-*

In 1960, John Kennedy became the first Catholic to be elected president of the Unites States. Although religion was an issue in 1960, being Catholic is no longer viewed as a barrier to being elected.

mocracy in America. Aware that the First Amendment ensured the separation of church and state, Tocqueville nonetheless maintained that religion "contributed powerfully to the establishment of a republic and a democracy in public affairs" (1948).

In the decades leading up to the Civil War, the United States experienced a period of humanitarian and social reform that evolved from the major religious movements of that time. Proponents of such reforms as temperance, women's rights, peace, and the humane treatment of prisoners and the mentally ill drew much of their inspiration from religious revivalism (Unger, 1989, pp. 318–329). Perhaps the most significant of these movements was the drive to abolish slavery. Many of the leading abolitionists, including Theodore Weld, Henry Ward Beecher, and Elijah Lovejoy, were closely associated with liberal Protestant denominations.

The Twentieth Century The interaction of religion and politics has continued into this century. This activity has included the full range of political orientations: radical, liberal, conservative, and reactionary. One example of the last can be seen in the activities during the 1930s and 1940s of Father Charles Coughlin, a Detroit priest. He broadcast on a national radio program and published a newspaper entitled *Social Justice* in which he espoused extreme anticommunism and anti-Semitism. Among other things, he stated his support in 1938 for the Nazi persecution of Jews, arguing that it was necessary to stop the spread of communism (Goren, 1980, p. 591). His position was endorsed by several diocesan Catholic newspapers, although other Catholics vigorously opposed it.

Another example of the interaction between religion and politics occurred in the 1960s, when religious values contributed to a period of social reform, as they had before the Civil War. As discussed in the box "The Black Church in America," religion played a major role in the movement for racial equality. Many religious leaders were also active in opposing U.S. involvement in the Vietnam War. For example, Daniel and Philip Berrigan were Catholic priests who engaged in many antiwar protests. In the 1980s, religious figures were among those who called for an end to the nuclear arms race and for increased aid to the poor and homeless. Also in the 1980s, the National Conference of Catholic Bishops took the position that the American economic system inherently produces social injustice—a position that angered Catholic conservatives and was openly criticized from the pulpit by a few Catholic priests.

The church has played an important role in the culture and society of African Americans, serving as a base of both community and social action, as in the civil rights movement.

The Black Church in America

The black church serves as a home to many of its members. It cooks suppers, plans outings, arranges picnics, conducts bingo games, provides day care for children, and lends money. All of this has a cosy, small-town quality, even when it occurs within the inner city. In Lenski's terms, the black church forms a strong communal bond. Homey or not, the black church contains tensions and contradictions.

In fact, many scholars question whether we should use the term "black church" at all. There is no single black church in the United States. Rather, the term refers to a collection of mainly Protestant denominations that emerged in response to racial discrimination and the need of black Americans to achieve some measure of self-identity and independence. Most of these denominations can be described as *evangelical;* that is, they accept the Bible as the word of God, emphasize salvation in the next life, and stress emotional expression in their services. Critical to many black denominations is the idea of a personal conversion and a direct relationship with God. As a regular

SOURCE: Ezra E. H. Griffith, Thelouiz English, and Violet Mayfield, 1980, "Possession, Prayer, and Testimony: Therapeutic Aspects of the Wednesday Night Meetings in a Black Church," *Psychiatry* 45: 120–128; Gerhard Lenski, 1961, *The Religious Factor* (Garden City, NY: Doubleday); Ronald L. Johnstone, 1988, *Religion in Society,* 3rd ed. (Englewood Cliffs, NJ: Prentice Hall); Suzanne T. Ortega et al., 1983, "Race Differences in Elderly Personal Well-Being: Friendship, Family, and Church," *Research-on-Aging* 5: 101–118; and Aldon Morris, 1980, *The Origins of the Civil Rights Movement: Black Communities Organizing for Change* (New York: Free Press).

participant in the Wednesday evening prayer services in a southern church explained, when troubled worshippers "testify" and wail and speak in tongues, "They go and leave their burdens at the altar. It's like a service station. You go there 'to get filled up.'"

How and why did the black church emerge as a separate entity? The answer lies in the history of the racial caste system in the United States. By the early 1800s, U.S. slaveowners had decided that slaves should be converted to Christianity but should also remain in bondage. To justify this apparent contradiction, they argued that the Christian's duty was to obey God, and the slave's duty was to obey his or her master. All of the faithful would then be rewarded in the next life.

At first, owners and slaves worshipped together, although blacks were usually forced to sit in the church balcony. Gradually, however, blacks splintered off from the white congregations. In the North, the first all-black denominations were the African Methodist Episcopal Zion Church (organized in 1796) and the African Methodist Episcopal Church (1816). Not surprisingly, black Christianity adopted certain distinctive features. Perhaps the most significant was identification with the Israelites of the Old Testament. Many black prayers and hymns expressed the same hope of liberation from bondage and suffering that was so common in the nation of Israel.

The transition from interracial to all-black congregations increased dramatically following the abolition of slavery in 1865. As society became segregated (see Chapter 11), so did religion. In addition to their religious function, black churches offered the ex-slaves an opportunity to learn to read, to vote (at least for church officials), and to find some personal dignity in a racist society. As time passed, the role of the church in promoting education became especially important. The church was deeply involved in building schools, and ministers were among the best-educated members of the black community.

Not surprisingly, given its prominent position within the black community, the black church played a vital role in the struggle for racial equality in the twentieth century. Many black religious figures—including Martin Luther King, Jr., Malcolm X, and Jesse Jackson—became leaders in the movement for black equality. The Southern Christian Leadership Conference (SCLC), an association of black ministers that was created during the Montgomery bus boycott of 1955–1956, became one of the major civil rights organizations of the 1960s. Churches often served as meeting places, and civil rights marches frequently were accompanied by the sounds of hymns and gospel music.

As the black church moves into the 1990s, it faces many challenges. Some young blacks are now turning to secular organizations for help in overcoming barriers to mobility and equality. At the same time, the success of the civil rights movement in eliminating legal segregation has raised questions concerning the appropriateness of racially separate churches. If and when the United States achieves racial justice and equality, will blacks and whites worship together as one community? Until that time, however, the black church will continue to be a core institution in the black community, playing many important roles.

Jesse Jackson and Pat Robertson

During the 1980s two religious leaders campaigned for their parties' nomination for president of the United States—Jesse Jackson and Pat Robertson.

In 1984, Jesse Jackson, the first black candidate to amass a large number of delegates to a presidential nominating convention, successfully organized the support of black Protestant ministers who assisted him in registering many black voters. Jackson's style, which reflected his training as a minister and the influence of Reverend Martin Luther King, Jr., was remarkably successful and won him acclaim as an inspirational speaker. Jackson's success in the 1984 Democratic primaries led him to seek the nomination again in 1988. In that year, he ran a strong second to the eventual nominee, Michael Dukakis, and outlasted a number of other candidates.

By 1988, the tendency for American religious leaders to seek a more political role had increased. Thus, despite remarks he made in the early 1980s rejecting active political involvement as a means for solving economic, social, and political problems, television evangelist Pat Robertson became a candidate for the Republican presidential nomination after resigning from the ministry. Robertson had gained national attention as the host of "The 700 Club," a 90-minute television program that had addressed issues such as abortion and prayer in the schools.

Robertson made a strong showing in the Iowa caucuses, the first test in the 1988 campaign. He finished second, behind Senator Robert Dole and ahead of the ultimate nominee, then-Vice President George Bush. However, Robertson's strategy of turning out members of fundamentalist churches was better suited to the Iowa caucuses—with their small overall turnout—than to the primary system in most states. When the campaign moved into the primary states, Robertson quickly faded.

Although Robertson had gained wide audience recognition through television, he received more negative than positive ratings as a presidential candidate. In a Gallup Poll conducted in 1987, 4 percent of Republican supporters who were familiar with Robertson said he would make an excellent president, 11 percent indicated good, 16 percent indicated fair, and 54 percent indicated poor. Gallup did not explore the

In 1988, television evangelist Pat Robertson resigned from the ministry and campaigned unsuccessfully for the Republican nomination for the presidency.

reasons for Robertson's poor ratings, but he did suggest that they might have been linked to Americans' reactions to the widely publicized sex scandal of the Reverend Jim Bakker, another television evangelist (Gallup, 1987).

Fundamentalism and the New Religious Right

Robertson's candidacy illustrates an important recent trend in the relationship between religion and politics: increased political activism by and support for religious *fundamentalists*. **Fundamentalism** can be defined as a form of religion characterized by strict and unambiguous rules, and by literal and dogmatic acceptance of scriptures exactly as written. In the United States, fundamentalist Christians became increasingly involved in politics during the 1980s, through such organizations as the Reverend Jerry Falwell's Moral Majority and Robertson's 700 Club. To a large extent, fundamentalism has been a Protestant movement, supported largely by Southern Baptists and by members of a variety of evangelical churches and sects. However, there is a comparable movement among conservative Catholics, who have provided much of the support for groups such as the Eagle Forum. The political agenda of religious conservatives has centered on a limited number of issues: opposition to legal abortion, support for prayer in the public schools, opposition to laws forbidding discrimination against homosexuals, and opposition to school-based family-planning clinics and to sex education in the schools.

These groups also generally oppose the teaching of evolution in the schools, because they believe that this is contrary to a literal interpretation of the first book of the Bible, *Genesis,* which states that God created the world in 6 days.

Televangelism This movement, sometimes referred to as the New Religious Right, has used three major approaches, two of which reflect modern technology and partially account for its increased influence in the electronic era.

One technique is *televangelism* — religious programming broadcast over television. Although televangelism has existed for as long as television (in fact, religious broadcasting goes back to the early days of radio), its influence has increased recently, for two reasons. First, cable television has facilitated such specialized types of telecasting by making it economically feasible to broadcast to an audience that may be limited in any locality, yet sizable on a national scale. Second, religious organizations have increased their ownership of television and radio stations; by 1980, they had 1,400 radio stations and 60 television stations (Johnstone, 1988, p. 130). In addition, several nationwide cable television networks are also owned by religious organizations. It has been estimated, on the basis of Nielsen television ratings, that the audience for religious programming in the United States is around 7 to 10 million (Martin, 1981).

According to sociologists Jeffrey Hadden and Charles Swann (1981), the television preachers appeal to many people because they present simple, certain, and clear-cut answers. By so doing, they offer a refuge from the confusion, uncertainty, and ambiguity associated with modern society. Television, of course, is a two-edged sword. In the mid-1980s, the influence of television evangelists was sharply curtailed by widely publicized scandals involving televangelists Jim and Tammy Bakker and Jimmy Swaggert.

Direct Mail The second modern technique used by the religious right is direct mail, especially computerized files of supporters and computerized label generation. This technology permits various organizations to share lists of supporters, and it allows for quick appeals for funds, votes, and signatures on preprinted letters to politicians. Direct mail has been used both by religious organizations themselves and by political organizations that work closely with them, such as NCPAC (National Conservative Political Action Committee) and the National Right to Life Committee.

Mobilizing Congregations The third technique used by the religious right is mobilization of congregations. Issues such as abortion, school prayer, evolution, and homosexuality are regularly addressed from the pulpit, and congregations are sometimes mobilized for political actions, such as right-to-life marches or attendance at presidential caucuses. The weekend before the 1988 election, parking lots of Catholic and fundamentalist Protestant churches were leafleted in support of Republican George Bush by right-to-life organizations. Sometimes the effort was enhanced by sermons inside the church on the abortion issue.

Assessing the Fundamentalist Revival

To what extent has this fundamentalist revival influenced American politics? This question is difficult to answer. In 1980, five of six U.S. senators targeted by the Religious Right went down to defeat (Johnstone, 1988, p. 132), but since that time, the New Right has

Muslims demonstrating against Salmon Rushdie's book, The Satanic Verses. *The widespread banning of Rushdie's book indicated the political strength of fundamentalist movements throughout the world.*

Liberation Theology

For centuries, the Catholic Church has ministered *to* the poor; now, a movement within the Church is fighting *for* the poor. More precisely, this movement is mobilizing the poor to fight for themselves. Liberation theology, a major current in Catholicism, opposes all kinds of oppression: social, economic, political, and racial. It is a movement that starts at the grass roots by creating "base communities" within the urban barrio or the rural village. Here, the priests gradually hope to demonstrate to the poor that by working with, rather than against, one another, they may actually achieve some of the rights that they have been denied for so long.

Liberation theology became a major force for social change after the second Latin American Bishops' Conference in Medellín, Colombia, in 1968, where a liberal group found support for a series of documents stating that the Church had a duty to lead people out of the enslavement of poverty. When Father Gustavo Gutiérrez of Peru produced the phrase "theology of liberation," the new movement had a name.

SOURCES: "A Lesson on Liberation," *Time,* April 14, 1986, p. 84; Deane William Ferm, 1986, *Third-World Liberation Theologies* (Maryknoll, NY: Orbis); Jane Kramer, 1987, "Letter from the Elysian Fields," *The New Yorker,* March 2, pp. 40–75; Penny Lernoux, 1982, *Cry of the People* (New York: Penguin Books); Ninian Smart, 1989, *The World's Religions* (Englewood Cliffs, NJ: Prentice Hall); and Peter Steinfels, 1989, "Vatican Document Condemns All Forms of Racism As Sinful," *The New York Times,* February 11, p. A1.

It is not surprising that liberation theology has found its major support in Latin America, where a rigid and corrupt class system has kept the poor powerless for centuries. Catholicism is the dominant religion of Latin America, but the "People's Church" is distinctive from traditional Catholicism in many ways. By combining Roman Catholic doctrine with local traditions, liberation theology produces some exotic results. Imagine, for example, churchgoers singing through the sacraments or dancing during the Mass. Imagine a priest walking through the community in blue jeans, or villagers attending church and then going home to wield charms and magic to ward off evil spirits.

What has liberation theology accomplished in these settings? The clergy hope they have raised the consciousness of the poor in concrete ways. People who never had the opportunity to learn to read are now being given the chance to do so. Many communities have schools and medical facilities for the first time. There are even lunch kitchens for the schoolchildren—and their parents. Some communities have managed to buy land for farming or to purchase their own fishing boats. None of this has been easy. People who have long been told they are lazy or incompetent can only slowly change their negative self-images. But people who once didn't dare question the authority of the ruling classes are now gaining the courage to do so.

Of course, these changes have not gone unchallenged, and many

courageous priests, bishops, and nuns have been arrested, tortured, and executed. In a move that recalls the early period of Christianity, some liberation theologians seem to measure their success by keeping an ever-growing roster of martyrs.

The Vatican is uneasy about this movement because it raises many difficult questions concerning the role of religion in the secular world. What *is* the proper boundary between religion and politics? In the fervor for social reform, have the liberation leaders moved too far toward a Marxist analysis of society? In the continuing battle for material welfare, are the private and spiritual aspects of religion being neglected? The Vatican has wavered in its stance. In 1985, for example, it banned Brazilian Franciscan Father Leonardo Boff from public speaking, claiming that he had endangered the faith by describing the relation between the Church hierarchy and laity as a Marxist class struggle. The ban was later rescinded.

In February 1989, the Vatican published a formal condemnation of all forms of racism. Drawn up at the request of Pope John Paul II, the document specifically alludes to the enslavement of Latin American natives and avows that they must have the right to land and the means to preserve their cultural identity. At the same time, however, the Church leadership continues to oppose Marxism. What implications will this have for the future of liberation theology? At this point, no one is sure.

---

been unsuccessful at the local and state levels. After his surprise second-place finish in the Iowa caucuses, Pat Robertson finished near the bottom in subsequent primaries. The New Right has backed Republican presidential candidates and these candidates have won, but the tendency for Republicans to win presidential elections was under way before the emergence of the New Religious Right. It is true, however, that there is substantial political support for the agenda of the Religious Right. Sociologist John Simpson (1981) demonstrated that about 30 percent of Americans agree with all four of the Moral Majority's key positions: opposition to legal abortion, opposition to homosexuality, support of organized prayer in public schools, and support for a traditional female role. Moreover, about 70 percent of the public agrees with the Moral Majority on at least two of these issues.

Despite the substantial support for these positions, we cannot conclude that all religious political activism reflects fundamentalist values. Millions of Americans, including many religious leaders, feel that attempts to legislate sexual behavior and mandate prayer in school represent a dangerous move toward legally institutionalized religion, which is forbidden by the Constitution as a threat to religious freedom. If one set of religious beliefs is given the backing of the law, these leaders warn, other beliefs (or the choice

Archbishop Oscar Romero of El Salvador. An outspoken proponent of the rights of the poor, Romero was assassinated while saying mass in March 1980.

not to be believers) may be penalized. Groups such as the National Council of Churches have campaigned against religious attempts to regulate personal behavior. More broadly, a variety of Protestant, Jewish, and Catholic leaders have campaigned against New Right positions on many issues. Religious leaders overall have probably been just as involved on the liberal side as on the conservative side, as illustrated by a number of examples we have already mentioned, such as the Berrigans, Dr. Martin Luther King, Jesse Jackson, and the Catholic bishops' statement on the U.S. economy.

As we complete our discussion of the relationship between religion and politics, we must stress that the debates revolving around this issue are not limited to the United States. The box entitled "Liberation Theology" illustrates how the issue has arisen in Latin America and led to a major debate within the Roman Catholic Church.

Civil Religion

At a 1966 conference on American religion, sociologist Robert Bellah addressed a sensitive and controversial subject — the issue of a national religion. Responding to the arguments of conservative religious and political groups claiming that Christianity was the national faith, Bellah dismissed the idea that people can belong to only one religion at a time. He proposed, instead, that alongside the many religions in America there existed an institutionalized **civil religion.**

Bellah traced the origin of the phrase *civil religion* to the French philosopher Jean Jacques Rousseau, who identified the major tenets of such a religion as belief in the existence of God, the life to come, the reward of virtue and the punishment of evil, and the need to exclude religious intolerance. Although Bellah did not link the influence of Rousseau or the term *civil religion* directly to America's founders, he did argue that similar ideas existed in the United States during the late eighteenth century. For example, he cited Benjamin Franklin:

> I never was without some religious principles. I never doubted, for instance, the existence of the Deity; that he made the world and govern'd it by his Providence; that the most acceptable service of God was the doing of good to men; that our souls are immortal; and that all crime will be

punished, virtue rewarded either here or hereafter. I esteemed the essentials of every religion (Bellah, 1970).

As Franklin's remarks suggest, this "civil religion" was related to Christianity, though clearly not identical with it. Bellah builds this argument by focusing on the central concept of civil religion—God. Thus, he notes that although speeches by American presidents on solemn occasions almost invariably contain references to God, these references are not to Christ nor to any specific deity. The meaning of "God" remains vague in civil religion, but Bellah claims that this God is "unitarian" and "much more related to order, law, and right than to salvation and love" (1970).

As this statement implies, civil religion plays a crucial political role within a society. By referring to the sovereignty of God, civil religion teaches that the laws and traditions of U.S. society are sanctioned by God and are therefore good. President Dwight Eisenhower expressed this view when he asserted that "our government makes no sense unless it is founded in a deeply felt religious faith—and I don't care what it is" (quoted in Nash et al., 1986, p. 895). Even today, a president who is being inaugurated takes the oath of office with one hand on the Bible, implying that the chief executive must answer to a higher authority than even the will of the people. Thus, civil religion serves as a means of social control (Chapter 8) by promoting nationalism and conformity to prevailing social norms.

A good illustration of this function occurred in the 1950s when Congress voted to add the phrase "under God" to the Pledge of Allegiance and "In God We Trust" to all U.S. currency. Congress took these actions during the height of the Cold War to emphasize the distinction between the "God-fearing" United States and "atheistic communism." The implication was that God was supporting the United States in this conflict.

You might ask how the concept of God can play any role in the political realm given the separation of church and state. According to Bellah, the separation of church and state did not deprive politics of a religious dimension. Although personal religious beliefs are regarded as strictly private, Americans have since the beginning of the republic shared certain religious beliefs, symbols, and rituals. Thanksgiving, a day that "serves to integrate the family into the civil religion," and Memorial Day, which serves "to integrate the local community into the national cult," are both occasions for the public expression of Americans' civil religion (Bellah, 1970).

Those who argue that God has no place in politics must recognize the function that civil religion serves and, what is more, the value Americans place upon that function. In fact, belief in God appears to be a prerequisite for those seeking the presidency of the United States. According to a 1987 Gallup Poll, only 44 percent of Americans would vote for an atheist for president.

Current Trends: Secularization or Fundamentalist Revival?

An important debate today in the sociology of religion revolves around the issue of whether religion is gaining or losing influence in the modern world. Sociologists who believe that *secularization* is occurring hold that religion is losing influence, and sociologists who believe that a *fundamentalist revival* is taking place see a growing influence of religion in the 1980s and 1990s, at least in the United States.

Secularization

Most definitions of **secularization** include two central ideas: (1) people increasingly rely on science rather than religion to explain reality; and (2) the distinction between the religious and the profane (secular) becomes greater, with important ideas increasingly coming from the secular rather than the religious realm (Johnstone, 1988, pp. 272–273; Hargrove, 1979). Some sociologists see secularization as a long-term social trend that necessarily accompanies modernization, urbanization, and industrialization. The term itself dates to the Renaissance period, when it was used to describe the transfer of church property to the state or private owners.

Secularization theories developed a wide audience during the 1960s and 1970s. Many theologians proclaimed "God is dead" to signify that traditional religious beliefs and practices were no longer relevant to contemporary Americans. Increased scientific knowledge — including our greater understanding of the genetic code, space travel, new theories in physics, and the growth of social science — all challenged religion as the source of knowledge and interpretation of life and the universe. According to Hargrove (1979), science provided us with an "increased ability to explain what was previously mysterious." As people learned to rely more on science to understand their lives, secularization theorists predicted, their interest in religion would decline.

Some statistics on church membership and attendance seemed to support this conclusion. Roozen and Carrol (1979), for example, demonstrated that church attendance declined for most of the liberal Protestant denominations from the mid-1960s through the mid-1970s. Hout and Greeley (1987) similarly showed that there was a large falloff in church attendance among Catholics during that same time period. The latter study found that the major reasons for this decline were opposition to the church's traditional sexual teachings and disenchantment with its authoritarian system of rules and beliefs. One could argue that science had something to do with both of these factors. Technology made it possible to have sex without producing unwanted children, which eliminated one of the traditional reasons for opposing premarital sex. Similarly, as knowledge is increasingly obtained from science, people become less likely to accept ideas solely on the authority of church officials.

Fundamentalist Revival

Despite these findings, secularization theories have been widely challenged in the 1980s (Sasaki and Suzuki, 1987). Some of the challenges are methodological: It has been noted, for example, that statistics on church membership are not very reliable. Different denominations use different methods to record membership, and any conclusions drawn from these figures must be approached with caution.

More critically, some sociologists argue that the influence of religion has expanded in the past decade, as reflected in the rapid growth of a number of fundamentalist denominations and the ascending political influence of fundamentalism discussed earlier in this chapter. This growth led to an increased emphasis on such issues as abortion, school prayer, and pornography. Moreover, as shown in Figure 15.3, recent data indicate that church membership and attendance have stabilized in the 1980s, and may even have increased (Gallup, 1987; *World Almanac,* 1988, p. 591; Hout and Greeley, 1987). According to Hout and Greeley, the decline in Catholic Church attendance ended after 1975, and *overall* Protestant attendance remained stable from the 1960s through the mid-1980s.

This stability masks an important fact, however: Even when attendance among Catholics and liberal Protestant denominations was declining, membership was rising among fundamentalist denominations (Kelly, 1977; Doyle and Kelly, 1979). During the 1960s and 1970s, for example, the Seventh-Day Adventists, Church of the Nazarene, Jehovah's Witnesses, Christian Reformed Church, Southern Baptist Church, and Assemblies of God all enjoyed rapid growth. As Hout and Greeley (1987) put it: "The center doesn't hold." In other words, some Catholics and liberal Protestants stopped going to church (though most continued to think of themselves as Catholic, Episcopal, Lutheran, or whatever), but other people were joining the fundamentalist churches and sects. Because these religious organizations offered clear answers and continued to focus on salvation, they appealed to people in a way that many of the larger churches didn't (Kelly, 1977). These trends put the Catholic and liberal Protestant denominations in a bind. If they continued to emphasize traditional rules and beliefs, they would alienate their more liberal, educated, and science-oriented members, who would then stop going to church. If, on the other hand, they tried to "keep up with the times," they would alienate those seeking salvation and clear-cut answers, who would switch to more conservative denominations.

Overview

However much church attendance patterns may have changed in the United States, America remains a very religious society in many regards. In a December 1988 Gallup Poll, for example, 94 percent of respondents expressed a belief in God and 77 percent in heaven

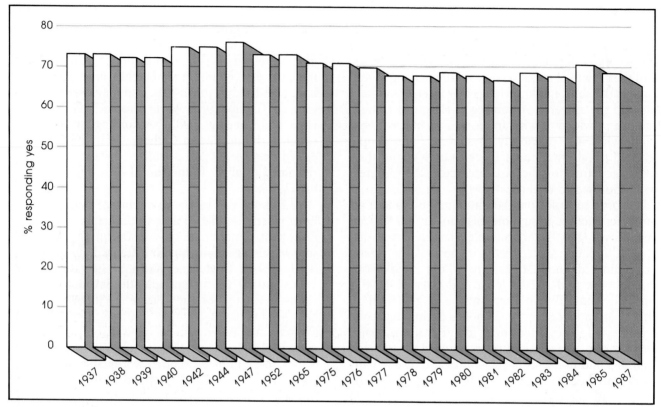

FIGURE 15-3

In response to the question: "Do you happen to be a member of a church or synagogue?"

Note that the number of people stating that they are church members peaked during World War II (a time of national crisis), returned to its prewar level by 1952, then changed little until the mid-1960s. Between 1965 and 1982, there was a modest decline in church membership, which then leveled off or rose irregularly thereafter. The statistics here indicate people who say they are members of a church. Many other people who do not say that they are members nonetheless do identify with a denomination or sect.

SOURCE: George Gallup, Jr., 1987, *The Gallup Poll: Public Opinion 1987* (Wilmington, DE: Scholarly Resources, Inc.).

(Woodward, 1989, p. 53). A year earlier, over 60 percent claimed to have a "great deal" of confidence in the church or organized religion (Gallup, 1987). In 1986, only 8 percent of Americans answered "none" when asked their religious beliefs (U.S. Bureau of the Census, 1987d, Table 75). Finally, as is illustrated in the "Polls Apart" box, the majority of Americans continue to favor organized prayer in public schools.

At the same time, questions must be raised about the extent to which American trends are typical of modern industrialized societies. For one thing, the United States is more religious than most industrialized nations. On a given Sunday, about 50 percent of Catholics and 40 percent of Protestants attend church (Hout and Greeley, 1987). These percentages are higher than those for most other industrialized societies, and more people in the United States than elsewhere say God is important in their lives (Jones et al., 1986, p. 223). Thus, the United States is not typical of industrialized countries as a whole, and it seems clear that secularization has gone further in many other countries. Sasaki and Suzuki (1987) compared a number of indicators of religious participation and beliefs in the United States, Holland, and Japan. They found that secularization had clearly taken place in Holland, but that there was mixed evidence in the case of the

POLLS APART

School Prayer: Church and State in Conflict

A lthough the United States technically adheres to the concept of separation of church and state, conflicts involving religious practices and public institutions are common. Perhaps the most publicized conflict focuses on the question of prayer in the public schools. Until 1960, Bible readings and prayers were acceptable practices in many public schools. At that point, the U.S. Supreme Court ruled these practices unconstitutional.

Public opinion polls since the 1960s suggest that, despite the Court's ruling, a majority of Americans continue to support prayer in the schools. An examination of data from some of these polls conducted between 1974 and 1982 provides important lessons concerning the use of polls as research tools.

One crucial point concerning polls that researchers must learn is that the very wording of a question can affect the nature of the response. For example, a 1980 poll asked whether schools should be allowed to begin each day with a prayer. The respondent's options were: Should allow; Depends; Does not belong; Other. How would you answer this question? If you answered "Should allow," you are in agreement with 72 percent of the respondents. Now answer this question. "The Supreme Court ruled that it is unconstitutional to require the reading of the Lord's Prayer or Bible verses in public schools. Do you agree or disagree with this ruling?" In 1982, 60 percent of the respon-

dents favored the required readings.

Note that a significantly higher percentage of respondents agreed with the first question. Why is this so? Look again at the two questions. The first question is more general. It asks whether prayer should be allowed, not required; it also refers only to prayer and *not* to a specific prayer or religion. The second question, then, comes closer to requiring the observation of a particular religion within the schools. Although a majority of respondents did answer "Yes" to this question, many people who agreed with the first item disagreed with the second one.

Composite figures concerning public support for school prayer do not, of course, tell us much about who supports this practice and who does

Age	
Under 30	66%
Over 30	76%
Education	
Less than high school	91%
High school only	79%
Beyond high school	60%
Race	
Nonwhite	83%
White	71%
Political Views	
Conservative	74%
Moderate	70%
Liberal	49%
Religion	
Protestant	81%
Sects	93%
Southern Baptist	85%
Methodist	78%
Presbyterian	64%
Catholic	76%
Jewish	26%

SOURCE: Kirk S. Elifson and C. Kirk Hadaway, 1985, "Prayer in Public Schools: When Church and State Collide," *Public Opinion Quarterly*, 49:317–329.

not. For this reason the polls collect certain demographic data to identify centers of support and opposition. The statistics in the table refer to people who answered "Yes" to question #1; that is, they believe that schools should be allowed to begin each day with a prayer.

What do these numbers tell us? For one thing, we learn that supporters of school prayer tend to be older, conservative, less educated, and to belong to the Catholic Church or to certain Protestant denominations. (Other polls point out that support for school prayer is greater in the South than in the North.) Jewish opposition stems from their experience as a religious minority. Historically, the prayers recited in school have reflected Christian (especially Protestant) beliefs. (Remember that a majority of respondents in 1982 supported the reciting of the Lord's Prayer or Bible readings.)

Sociologists would also point out that many of the categories examined in this poll are interrelated. For example, older people tend to have less formal education and to be more conservative politically than younger people; the Baptist population includes large numbers of nonwhites. Were these variables to conflict rather than to correspond with each other, sociologists would be forced to question the validity of the poll.

Can you think of other questions that these polls raise but do not answer? How would you go about answering them? What other issues concerning attitudes toward school prayer need to be addressed? Can you suggest other possible relationships between the different categories listed above?

United States. Japan, on the other hand, showed no evidence of secularization. Thus, secularization appears to have occurred in some modern societies but not in others. For this reason, Sasaki and Suzuki concluded that secularization is not a global trend that automatically occurs with modernization.

For all these reasons, some sociologists have argued that, like the family, religion has not so much declined as adapted to a changing environment (Wilson, 1985; Swatos, 1983; Hammond, 1985). Their arguments resemble those of Bellah (1964), discussed early in this chapter, that religion takes different forms during different periods of history. According to these sociologists, most people today clearly rely less on mystical explanations of events in the physical world,

a basic tenet of secularization theory. At the same time, they continue to turn to religion for values and spiritual support and for consolation in times of crisis. In some cases, religion has assumed a secular form. For example, the great emphasis in the 1980s on "self-fulfillment" (see Chapter 4), which often involves self-help and therapy groups that stress the metaphysical, is frequently cited as a form of religious behavior. Many sociologists would therefore agree with the analysis of Emile Durkheim (1965 [orig. 1915]): "There is something eternal in religion which is destined to survive all the particular symbols in which religious thought has successively enveloped itself."

Summary

Religion reflects a universal human concern with the meaning of life and the supernatural. According to Durkheim, societies distinguish between the aspects of everyday life, called the *profane*, and those things that inspire awe or deep respect, called the *sacred*. He defined religion as a system of beliefs and behaviors involving the sacred. This is a broad definition, and the nature of religious beliefs and practices varies considerably from culture to culture.

Sociologists classify religions according to several broad categories. Churches and denominations are established religions with formal rules and hierarchies. Such religions usually distinguish between those with religious authority, called *clergy*, and the general membership, called *laity*. A sect is a smaller, more dogmatic group that is not well integrated into the larger society. Some sects gain acceptance and develop into denominations. A religion that is totally withdrawn from the larger society is called a *cult*.

In his study of the beliefs of the world's major religions, Max Weber distinguished between religions that worship only one God, called *monotheism*, and those that worship two or more gods, called *polytheism*. Some religions, however, do not worship any deities; instead, they emphasize spiritual or moral principles on which their members base their behavior. These faiths are referred to as *sacred philosophies*. Judaism is an example of monotheism; Hinduism of polytheism; and Confucianism of a sacred philosophy. Among the other major world religions are Christianity, Islam, and Buddhism.

Functionalists and conflict theorists disagree as to the social roles of religion. Functionalists argue that religion

contributes to the well-being of a society by encouraging social solidarity, providing meaning and identity to society's members, and allowing for a degree of social change while maintaining basic social control. Conflict theorists respond that religion, like all social institutions, serves the interests of the ruling classes. By focusing people's attention on salvation in the next world, religion distracts them from the injustices of this world. For this reason, Marx called religion the "opium of the people." Weber maintained that the interaction between religion and social structure was too complicated to be classified simply as class conflict. He argued that changes in people's views of the world brought about by the Protestant Reformation made possible the rise of capitalism in the West.

The United States officially practices separation of church and state in the sense that the Constitution forbids the government to establish or prohibit any religion. In fact, religion and politics interact regularly, and people's political behavior is frequently influenced by their religious and moral beliefs. This applies to the antislave and social reform movements of the nineteenth century as well as to the civil rights and antiwar movements of the twentieth century. One current example of religious activism is the "Religious Right," which pursues a conservative agenda that opposes abortion, gay rights, and pornography while supporting prayer in the public schools.

Scholars debate the current and future state of religion in the United States. Some adhere to secularization theory, arguing that as people accept scientific explanations of reality, religion will become less important to them.

Others contend that the United States is in the midst of a fundamentalist revival as people turn to religion to cope with an increasingly complex world. Significantly, two Protestant ministers, Jesse Jackson and Pat Robertson, ran in the 1988 presidential primaries. One possibility is that, as with the family, the role of religion is changing, but the institution itself will remain strong.

Glossary

profane Aspects of everyday life, which are not usually associated with religion.

sacred That which inspires awe, reverence, fear, or deep respect in people.

ritual A system of established rites and ceremonies that is often religious in nature.

religion Formalized beliefs and practices that are directed toward the sacred elements in a culture.

church A religion with a formalized hierarchy and set of rules that accommodates itself to the larger society.

denomination One of several major religions in a society that usually tolerates other religions.

clergy Religious officials with special authority to conduct ceremonies, establish rules, and administer sacraments.

laity The general membership of a religion, who play a limited, and often passive, role in religious activities.

sect A religious group, often created through a schism with an established church, that is not well integrated into the larger society.

cult A religious group that is withdrawn from, and often at odds with, the religious traditions of a society.

monotheism A religion that teaches the existence of one God.

polytheism A religion that teaches the existence of two or more gods.

sacred philosophy A form of religion that does not revolve around a deity but does have a concept of the sacred from which moral and philosophical principles and behavioral norms are derived.

Protestant Ethic A belief in hard work, frugality, and material success that Max Weber associated with the emergence of Protestantism and capitalism in Europe.

fundamentalism A form of religion characterized by strict rules and by literal and unquestioning acceptance of sacred writings and teachings.

civil religion A series of beliefs, not associated with any single denomination, that portray a society's institutions and structure as consistent with the will of God.

secularization A process in which the influence of religion in a society declines.

Further Readings

CHALFANT, H. PAUL, ROBERT E. BECKLEY, AND C. EDDIE PALMER. 1986. *Religion in Contemporary Society,* 2nd ed. Palo Alto, CA: Mayfield Press. A good overview of the sociology of religion in the United States. Among the topics discussed are theoretical perspectives, leadership and participation in religious organizations, new expressions of Christiantiy, and nontraditional religions.

GREELEY, ANDREW. 1982. *Religion: A Secular Theory.* New York: Free Press. A valuable book that examines the rise of formal religious institutions in complex societies. The author contends that the boundaries between the secular and sacred are often vague.

HARGROVE, BARBARA. 1979. *The Sociology of Religion: Classical and Contemporary Approaches.* Arlington Heights, IL: AHM Publishing Corp. A survey of the sociology of religion divided into four major sections: the nature and functions of religion, the cultural basis of religious organizations, function and process in institutionalized religions, and religion as structure and movement.

HUGHEY, MICHAEL W. 1983. *Civil Religion and Moral Order.* Westport, CT: Greenwood Press. This overview discusses civil religion in both traditional and modern societies. It contrasts the views of several prominent sociologists, including Weber, Durkheim, Parsons, and Bellah.

SMART, NINIAN. 1989. *The World's Religions.* Englewood Cliffs, NJ: Prentice Hall. An in-depth analysis of the major religions by a recognized expert in the field. Each chapter focuses on a particular historical period or geographical area.

VERNON, GLENN M. 1962. *Sociology and Religion.* New York: McGraw-Hill. Vernon explores the social impact of religion by using a symbolic-interactionist approach. He focuses on the relationship between religion and other societal institutions.

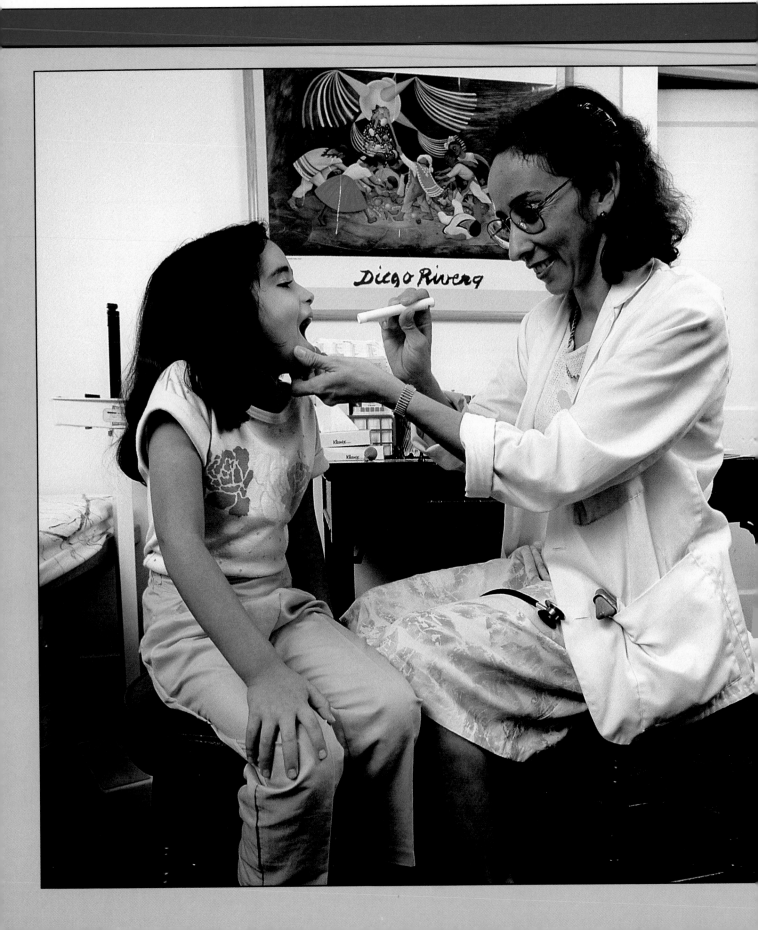

CHAPTER 16

Health and Health Care

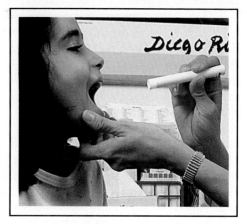

Think about the images you had of sociologists and what they do before you took this course. Did sickness, health, and health care come to mind? Would you be surprised to learn that medical sociology is the largest specialty among sociologists in both the United States and Europe? In the United States, more than one in ten members of the American Sociological Association (ASA) belongs to the Medical Sociology Association, making it the largest of the ASA's 23 specialty groups. In Europe, medical sociology is even larger. In West Germany, for example, the German Society for Medical Sociology had more members in 1985 than the German Sociological Association (Cockerham, 1988, p. 575).

Why are sociologists so interested in health and medicine? Although health and illness are commonly considered biological conditions — you get sick because some abnormal condition develops in your body — it turns out that society influences both who gets sick and how sick people are treated. We know that social factors have a lot to do with sexually transmitted diseases such as AIDS, but we often do not realize that they can have an equally great influence on more common diseases such as heart disorders and cancer. In preindustrial societies, for example, people almost never die of heart disease or cancer, and in modern societies like our own, lifestyle, diet, and environment — all products of human behavior — play a major role in determining who contracts these diseases. Regardless of what disease you get, your social situation makes a big difference in your treatment and your chances of recovery — perhaps more so in the United States than in most industrialized societies.

Health and illness affect a society significantly. Consider how people's behaviors have been changed by the fear of AIDS. Children with the AIDS virus have been driven from their schools, homes of AIDS victims have been burned by people afraid of getting the disease, and discrimination against homosexuals has increased. All of this has happened in spite of the fact that AIDS cannot be transmitted by casual everyday contacts. Because AIDS can be transmitted by sexual contact, changes in sexual mores and behaviors have occurred in a number of countries.

Now imagine the impact on human behavior of an equally deadly disease that could be transmitted through casual contact. Actually, you don't have to imagine it—you can read about it in history books. Various plagues and epidemics have occurred intermittently throughout human history. The responses to these outbreaks have resembled the responses of many Americans to AIDS, but they were even more extreme because the actual danger was far greater. During the Black Death, a plague in fourteenth-century Europe, parents abandoned their children, husbands abandoned their wives, and entire cities were deserted as people fled in panic. In some places, the entire social order came to an end. This is not surprising when you consider that a force that nobody really understood suddenly killed one-quarter to one-half of the population (Gottfried, 1983; Thomlinson, 1976, pp. 88—93).

T his chapter will examine both society's influence on health and illness and the influence of health and illness on society. It will pay special attention to the institution of **medicine:** the system developed for the purpose of treating illness. We shall see that this system itself has a major impact on public health, and that it reflects and maintains the patterns of the larger society.

Health and Society: A Functionalist View

The Sick Role

From a functionalist standpoint, the normal and natural state of affairs is for people to be healthy and to contribute to their society. The opposite situation, ill health, is a form of *deviance*. When people are not healthy, they cannot contribute. Therefore, sickness is dysfunctional for both the individual who suffers an illness and for the larger society (Parsons, 1951, 1977). Because illness is dysfunctional for the social system, societies must establish boundaries that define who can legitimately claim to be sick and who cannot. It is equally essential that those who are sick make efforts to get better so that they can again contribute to the operation of the social system.

For these reasons, according to Talcott Parsons,

all societies define a **sick role.** Like many other roles, the sick role is determined by a set of rules that outline who can and cannot play it. In general, a person can only enter the sick role by showing some evidence, visible to others, that he or she is suffering from ill health. Precisely what these rules are vary among different types of societies. Externally visible symptoms, such as an obvious serious injury, a high fever, vomiting, or a severe rash, allow a person to play the sick role in most societies. Other indicators vary with the nature of the society. In modern industrial societies, you must be recognized as sick by a medical professional in order to play the sick role for any length of time. Even there, however, what doctors regard as sufficient cause to play the sick role varies widely from one society to another, and even from one doctor to another in the same society. In preindustrial societies, in contrast, evidence of exposure to generally recognized evil spirits might place a person in the sick role.

The sick role is best understood by combining the insights of the functionalist and symbolic-interactionist perspectives. The functionalist perspective — specifically Parsons's theory — tells us why society has a sick role. The symbolic-interactionist perspective gives us important insights into how that role is defined and applied. How the sick role is defined in any society depends on societal agreements about the causes, meanings, and consequences of illness. Furthermore, whether any individual may play the sick role is the result of a process of social negotiation based on agreements about the nature of that role.

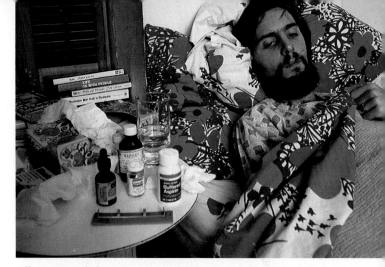

All societies define some type of sick role, which exempts the sick person from normal role obligations but carries its own set of obligations.

Although the sick role is a deviant role, it is different from many other deviant roles (prostitute, robber, crooked politician) in that it is not usually seen as voluntary. That perception, however, is highly conditional. It does not apply to certain illnesses that are socially defined as the product of a person's own behavior. For example, because AIDS is most often transmitted sexually or as a result of taking illegal drugs intravenously, AIDS victims are often severely stigmatized. Some religious fundamentalists have even suggested that AIDS is God's way of punishing evil behavior. Society has similar reactions to other sexually transmitted diseases (herpes, gonorrhea, syphilis), all of which are far more common (though far less deadly) than AIDS. To a lesser extent, the notion that people are responsible for their own illness is also applied to diseases resulting from excess drinking, overeating, and smoking. Also, an individual who is seen as making inadequate efforts to get out of the sick role may be stigmatized as a "malingerer" or "hypochondriac." This labeling process can occur with a wide range of ailments.

As the preceding sentence suggests, the sick role, like all roles, carries a specific set of expectations. It excuses a person from the normal obligations of his or her other roles. However, it also brings some new obligations. In general, people are expected to do their best to get out of the sick role. Specifically, they are expected to want to get well and to seek technically competent treatment. Moreover, they are expected to do what their doctor tells them. If they fail at any of these things, they will no longer be seen as entitled to play the sick role (Parsons, 1951). This is illustrated by such statements as "If you had gone to bed, followed your diet, and taken your medicine, you wouldn't still be sick. It's your own fault."

Health: The Individual's Responsibility This formulation of the sick role by Parsons, as well as the functionalist view of health and illness in general, has been controversial because it places so much responsibility for illness upon sick people themselves (Crawford, 1981). Conflict theorists criticize it for neglecting ways in which the actions of other people may cause someone to be ill. Some people, for example, become sick after being exposed to hazardous substances, through no fault of their own. Others suffer injury or illness because of unsafe conditions at work, over which they have no control. Yet others are sick because they lack the income to purchase adequate food or shelter. None of these conditions is the responsibility of the sick person; all of them result from situations created by others or from which others benefit. To define illness, as Parsons did, simply as the result of either "bad luck" or individual irresponsibility, is to cover up an important source of illness.

The Case of AIDS

The individual-responsibility model can also lead to the stigmatization of any unpopular group that becomes ill. This is vividly illustrated by the public's reaction to the spread of AIDS. AIDS is a fatal disease that attacks the immune system. It was first recognized in 1981; by 1984, the virus that causes it had been identified. One reason AIDS is so deadly is that it destroys the body's ability to fight off a wide range of diseases. Ultimately, AIDS victims die of some disease their bodies cannot resist, usually within 3 to 5 years of being diagnosed as having AIDS.

The Extent of the Disease There are far more people who have the AIDS virus in their systems than who actually have the disease. An unknown number of these people will eventually develop AIDS. Although nobody really knows how many Americans carry the AIDS virus, a common estimate is 1 to 2 million—possibly as many as one American out of every 100. Several hundred thousand of these people have *AIDS-related complex (ARC)*, a milder form of the disease that

AIDS victims have been commemorated with the AIDS Quilt. Each design on the quilt is dedicated to one of the more than 27,000 people who have died of the disease.

may or may not develop into the deadly form. The number of confirmed cases of AIDS in the United States at the beginning of 1988 was about 50,000, of which 40 percent had been diagnosed in 1987. By mid-1988, another 20,000 new cases had been diagnosed (National Center for Health Services Research 1988: 1). As you can see, the number of cases was nearly doubling every year. Keep in mind, though, that these people came into contact with the virus in the early 1980s, since it usually takes years after exposure for the disease to develop. If people have altered their behavior in ways that decrease their risk, as appears likely, the rate of increase will probably decline in the future. Public Health Service projections indicate that by 1992 there may be about 365,000 confirmed AIDS cases. (National Center for Health Services Research, 1988). A total of over 27,000 Americans had died of AIDS as of the beginning of 1988, 8,000 of them in 1987 alone (National Center for Health Statistics, 1988).

Even those who get AIDS may carry the virus for years before they become sick. In fact, the average length of time between exposure and symptoms is nearly 8 years (National Center for Health Services Research, 1988). Anyone who has the virus in his or her system can give the disease to someone else, though the ways by which it can be spread are very limited. AIDS can be transmitted only through exchange of body fluids, primarily blood or semen. The most common modes of transmission are anal, genital, or oral sex with an infected person, and sharing of hypodermic needles by intravenous drug users. Much more rarely, people have gotten AIDS from receiving a transfusion of infected blood, which caused a significant number of AIDS cases among hemophiliacs, who receive frequent transfusions. By the mid-1980s, however, it became possible to test the blood supply for the AIDS virus, and since then it has been very rare to get AIDS from a transfusion. You *cannot* get the disease from casual contact, dishes, toilet seats, mosquito bites, or closed-mouth kissing. There is no known case of anyone having contracted the disease from open-mouth kissing. You are not endangered by attending work or school with an AIDS victim, or by eating in the same restaurant as an AIDS victim. Even so, fears of the disease have been widespread and irrational, and a number of people have been fired from work and banned from school because they are known to carry the AIDS virus. One such unfortunate example is discussed in the box entitled "Take a Lonely Walk to School in Jason's Shoes."

The Response to AIDS In the United States, the societal reaction to AIDS reflects the fact that the disease has been largely confined to people who are socially devalued by many in the larger population: male homosexuals and bisexuals, intravenous drug users, and, in the early stages of the epidemic, Haitian immigrants. Over 90 percent of all U.S. AIDS cases thus far have occurred among people in one or more of these groups (mainly the first two), though the percentage is falling. (see Figure 16.1). Two factors seem responsible for the high incidence of AIDS among homosexuals and bisexuals. First, the disease is more easily spread through anal sex than other kinds of sex, and that form of sex is more common among homosexuals. Second, prior to the AIDS scare, the average active homosexual had more sexual partners than the typical active heterosexual. However, high-risk behavior has declined significantly among the gay population (Martin, 1987), and this may be slowing the spread of the disease in that population.

AIDS, however, is neither a homosexual disease nor a drug user's disease. In fact, there are some societies in which most AIDS victims are heterosexual and do not use intravenous drugs. The people who get AIDS in these societies usually have a large number of sexual partners or are prostitutes or have sex with prostitutes (Serrill, 1987). In some societies, the use of unsterilized needles by healers has contributed to the

Take a Lonely Walk to School in Jason's Shoes

Last spring, when 7-year-old Jason Robertson left the mobile classroom in which he had been instructed and entered a regular classroom at Prather Elementary School in Granite City [Illinois], he was escorted by his mother, family members, friends—down a sidewalk lined with people holding placards telling him to go back to his lonely and isolated mobile unit.

We all saw it on television news shows, the big-eyed child whose expression reflected wariness, puzzlement, fear. Jason, as we all know by now, suffers from AIDS-related complex, probably contracted through a blood transfusion. Jason is a hemophiliac.

The Robertsons have since left Granite City, alleging threats and harassment. Jason's mother, Tammie, reportedly was struck in the head by a man in a quick-stop shop there.

The family moved to the Roxana area and efforts are now under way to enroll Jason in a South Roxana Elementary School. And there are apparently a lot of parents there who don't want him in a regular classroom.

I, for one, hope not to see again a small boy being escorted to class down an aisle of hostile adult faces. Once was enough.

At the time, the scene reminded me of something else, something I

Adapted from Carol Clarkin in *Edwardsville Journal*, September 28, 1988.

couldn't quite put my finger on. Then I remembered, recently, memory spurred by present controversy. The "something else" was a Norman Rockwell painting on the cover of a *Look* magazine back in 1964.

You know Norman Rockwell, the painter who so often depicted us the way we *wish* we all looked, or imagine Americans as looking. The man whose illustrations reminded us of Mom and apple pie, Thanksgiving and Christmas, young love and elderly devotion.
The *Look* cover wasn't very endearing. It portrays a small pig-tailed black girl in a white dress, carrying her ruler and school books. She is escorted by four deputy Federal marshals and she looks straight ahead, not at the wall she's passing on which are scrawled the words "KKK" and "Nigger," and against which a tomato has been hurled. It's a well-done but ugly, ugly picture, inspired by events at Little Rock, Ark.

According to news stories last week, Tammie Robertson is optimistic about her family's reception in her new neighborhood, as well as hopeful about her young son's admission to school. She's apparently found supportive neighbors and churches in her new home, certainly a credit to the community itself. She's also finding that a large number of her fellow parents have been willing to listen to her, to meet with her. Whether Jason is placed in a regular

classroom or in a special facility remains to be seen, but one has a sense that the ugly scenes in Granite City will probably not be duplicated.

There have been, however, a couple of troubling reports from the Roxana situation. One, of course, is that in spite of support groups, there are numbers of parents who feel their own children's well-being and health are threatened by Jason's presence and who are threatening to take their children out of school if he enters a regular classroom.

As I write this, the latest information is that Jason will have started school this week somewhere in the Roxana district and that a meeting will have been held with concerned parents by school officials who will discuss exactly how the particular case is being handled and what steps are being taken to protect Jason's classmates.

To parents in that district, I would say, "Listen. Learn. And believe that school officials will do nothing that will harm your own child.

And use your imagination. Ask yourself how you would feel if this unfortunate boy were your own child . . . how would you want him treated . . . what would you want for him?

Take a walk in someone else's Reeboks or mocs or pumps. And don't repeat a scene which reflects an Ugly American adult, bereft of compassion—that quality with which we so pride ourselves."

---

spread of the disease, as has the use of anal intercourse as a means of birth control.

As we noted, AIDS is often attributed by Americans to irresponsible behavior among socially unpopular groups. In this case, the individual-responsibility

model of illness has produced certain negative results. First, it caused the victims of the disease, already socially unpopular, to be blamed for their illness and to be treated unsympathetically. This occurred even though the early victims could do nothing to prevent

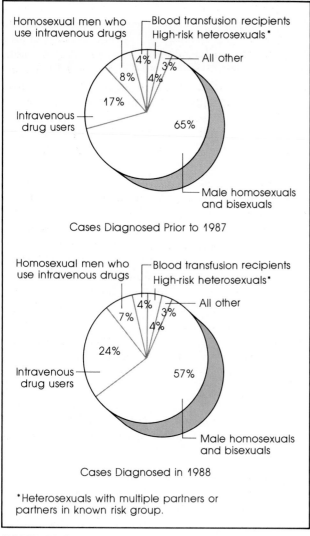

Homosexual men who use intravenous drugs

Blood transfusion recipients
High-risk heterosexuals*

All other

4%
8%
3%
4%
17%

Intravenous drug users

65%

Male homosexuals and bisexuals

Cases Diagnosed Prior to 1987

Homosexual men who use intravenous drugs

Blood transfusion recipients
High-risk heterosexuals*

All other

4%
7%
3%
4%
24%

Intravenous drug users

57%

Male homosexuals and bisexuals

Cases Diagnosed in 1988

*Heterosexuals with multiple partners or partners in known risk group.

FIGURE 16-1
Characteristics of People with AIDS, by Time of Diagnosis

getting AIDS, since the disease had been spreading for 4 or 5 years before it was recognized. Second, it caused society at large to understate the problem because the disease was at first believed to threaten only groups whose lifestyles were socially disapproved of. Third, when AIDS began to threaten non-Haitian heterosexuals who don't use drugs, the groups that initially suffered from the disease were blamed by some Americans for spreading it among the larger population. In such a context, it is easy to see how fear of AIDS could lead to an increase in prejudice and discrimination against homosexuals. There is already some evidence that this is happening: The percentage of Americans favoring laws against homosexual behavior between consenting adults jumped 15 points between 1982 and 1986, and more than one out of three Americans in 1986 said their views about homosexuals had "changed for the worse" (Gallup, 1987). Some homosexuals—or even people merely suspected of being homosexual—have been physically assaulted.

The Sick Role: An Evaluation

In addition to the critique of the individual-responsibility model, many other criticisms have been leveled at Parsons's concept of the sick role. One is that the sick role is more applicable to some types of illness than to others. It best fits **acute disorders:** illnesses of limited duration from which the victim recovers or dies. Examples are influenza, pneumonia, and appendicitis. It does not apply as well to **chronic disorders,** long-term or permanent conditions, such as arthritis, allergies, and muscular distrophy, that may or may not be fatal. Because these diseases cannot be "cured," obliging the victim to try to get well makes less sense. The sick role concept has also been criticized for reflecting a middle-class bias and for emphasizing treatment over prevention. However, these facts do not negate its importance or usefulness in medical sociology. The sick role may be defined differently by different groups (Zola, 1966), but virtually all definitions contain the notion of wanting to get well (Twaddle, 1979).

Modernization and Health Status

To functionalists, then, good health is important to the operations of society. For this reason, they hold that a well-functioning social system will maximize health and minimize illness among its members. As we shall see in Chapter 20, many functionalists see society as undergoing a process of *social evolution*—a gradual process whereby society becomes more complex and better functioning, and the quality of life improves.

Modernization and industrialization contribute to this process by providing benefits to both the individual and society. This is evident in the relationship between modernization and health: In general, modernization and industrialization are associated with longer lives and fewer illnesses.

The Health Benefits of Modernization Massive outbreaks of deadly epidemics have generally been eliminated from industrial societies (the present epidemic of AIDS is a recent exception). Modernization and economic development have brought dramatic changes in health and *life expectancy* — the length of time the average person lives. Although these changes and the reasons for them will be explored in greater detail in Chapter 17, we can note here three great changes that have taken place over the past 2 to 3 centuries. First, people are living much longer. The life expectancy in most industrialized countries today is over 70, compared to between about 25 and 35 as recently as the eighteenth century (Population Reference Bureau, 1988; Thomlinson, 1976, p. 84). Second, people are healthier than they were in the past, and they do not get as seriously ill when they do get sick. Conditions that were once life-threatening, such as influenza and diarrhea, are usually little more than a temporary nuisance today. Third, as the preceding sentence suggests, the causes of death have changed. In industrialized societies, heart disease, cancer, and strokes account for most deaths — partly because our lifestyles and social conditions have made us more susceptible to such illnesses, but more importantly, because in the past people simply didn't live long enough to acquire these illnesses. Rather, most deaths were from contagious diseases that frequently took the form of epidemics like those described at the beginning of the chapter. Directly or indirectly, malnutrition was another important cause of mortality until a century or 2 ago. In industrialized countries, that too has declined greatly as a cause of death. Diet remains a factor in illness and mortality, but in the United States, too much food and the wrong kinds of food are the most serious dietary problems for much of the population.

Changes in health and longevity have not been limited to industrialized countries. Malnutrition and contagious diseases are more serious problems in the less-developed countries, but there, too, dramatic changes have taken place. The average life expectancy in nonindustrial countries had reached 57 by 1988, which is much higher than people enjoyed *anywhere* 200 years ago (Population Reference Bureau, 1988).

Thus, the nature and development of society have had worldwide effects on health, illness, and longevity. Although so far these effects have been primarily good, there have been some negatives.

The Health Risks of Modernization As we have seen, people live longer today than in the past, but death rates from cancer, strokes, and heart disease have risen dramatically. This increase results partly from changes associated with modernization.

CASE STUDY: THE EPIDEMIOLOGY OF CANCER One serious dysfunction of modernization and industrialization is the considerable damage done to the environment, which in turn has created new health risks (see Catalano, 1989, pp. 93–94). This can be illustrated by examining the **epidemiology** of cancer. Epidemiology is the measurement of the extent of medical disorders and the social, demographic, and geographic characteristics of those who become ill. Cancer, the second most common cause of death in the United States, has clearly increased as a result of damage to the environment and is linked by epidemi-

In the United States, diet is an important source of health difficulties. Unlike preindustrial societies, the main dietary problems in the United States today are too much food and the wrong kinds of food.

ological studies to environmental pollution. Consider the following:

- In 1978, a group of researchers estimated that 13 to 18 percent of cancer deaths were the result of exposure to one *carcinogen* (substance that causes cancer): asbestos (U.S. Department of Health et al., 1978). Asbestos was widely used in construction during the 1950s and 1960s because of its flame-retardant capacities, but it was later discovered to cause cancer. It remains in many buildings today, including thousands of schools.

- In 1988, malignant melanoma, a potentially fatal skin cancer, was expected to kill 6,000 Americans, and the overall incidence of skin cancer was *doubling* every 12 to 20 years. The suspected reason: destruction of the earth's ozone layer, which filters out carcinogenic ultraviolet sun rays. The ozone layer is being destroyed by chlorofluorocarbons (for example, Freon) that are used in air conditioners, spray cans, and fast-food containers.

- Dioxin and other hazardous waste has been blamed for the high incidence of cancer among residents of Love Canal, a subdivision near Niagara Falls that was unknowingly built on top of an illegal hazardous waste dump. Abnormally high rates of cancer have also been observed among farm workers who are regularly exposed to agricultural pesticides. Also many homes pose a cancer threat to those who live in them because of the presence of radon and other hazardous substances.

- Cancer mortality is abnormally high in counties with large numbers of petroleum refineries (Blot et al., 1977), and some recent evidence indicates that the highest incidence of cancer occurs among those who live closest to the petroleum installations (Meyerson, 1988).

- The release of radioactive substances, both intentional (as in above-ground nuclear tests and the bombing of Hiroshima and Nagasaki, Japan, in World War II) and unintentional (as in the Chernobyl nuclear power accident in the Soviet Union), has caused a large number of cancers among those exposed.

Although cancer may be the most deadly disorder resulting from environmental contamination, it is not the only one. A variety of nerve, liver, skin, and respiratory conditions, as well as birth defects, have been linked to various environmental contaminants.

Environment and Health: The Social Side It is important to stress that although environmentally induced disease has been a byproduct of modernization, this development is *not* inevitable. The amount of disease-causing contaminants placed in the environment varies widely, even among societies with similar

levels of production (Organization for Economic Cooperation and Development, 1979). *Some* pollution from industrialization is inevitable, but the *amount* depends on a variety of social factors, among them legal restrictions on pollution, the location of the population relative to the sources of pollution, and the extent to which the safety of various substances and practices is determined beforehand.

PUBLIC OPINION   Culture and public opinion also make a difference. When people are concerned about environmental risks, they are more likely to demand protection of the environment. For example, environmentalism has been a major issue in the United States both in the early 1970s and in the late 1980s.

POPULATION DISTRIBUTION   Finally, the distribution of population relative to sources of pollution makes a difference. Per-capita emissions of pollutants in Europe are relatively low, but the population is nonetheless exposed to a good deal of risk. In some areas, the levels of contaminants are higher than in the United States. A major reason for this is that Europe has a higher overall population density. With more people per square mile, there is as much or more pollution per square mile — and thereby a greater risk of sickness.

Health and Society: A Conflict View

Whereas the functionalists focus on the functions of health, the sick role, and the relationship between societal evolution and health, conflict theorists examine ways in which the distribution of wealth and power in society influences health. Because we have already discussed the relationship between environmental quality and health, we shall begin with that issue.

Environmental Quality and Health

Conflict theorists do not see health-threatening pollutants as merely an unfortunate byproduct of industrial growth. And although they agree that the values of a society concerning environmental quality are important, they believe these values are frequently set by the power elites. Moreover, the elites may use their power to circumvent the public will concerning environmental quality, just as they do on many other issues. Conflict theorists point out that manufacturers and producers have an important stake in pollution (Commoner, 1982; Epstein, 1981). It is usually cheaper or more profitable (at least in the short run) to dump pollutants into the environment than to dispose of them safely. Similarly, products that are known pollutants — detergents as opposed to soaps, plastic fast-food containers as opposed to paper ones, Freon-propelled spray cans as opposed to other kinds — may be cheaper or more profitable to produce than safer products. Because producers are out to maximize profits, they can be expected to take the cheapest and most profitable route, unless they are prevented by regulation from doing so (Commoner, 1982).

Politics and Regulation To support these contentions, conflict theorists point out that, on a per-capita basis, more pollutants are released into the environment in the relatively *capitalistic* United States than in most of the *mixed economies* of Western Europe (Organization for Economic Cooperation and Development, 1979), where industry is more regulated. In the United States, air and water quality stopped deteriorating, and might have improved, in the middle and late 1970s, when environmental regulation was strengthened (Council on Environmental Quality, 1984; U.S. Environmental Protection Agency, 1984). In the 1980s, however, enforcement of environmental regulations was relaxed, and that — together with continued national and world growth and economic development — resulted in new problems. Among the most serious are acid rain, the potential for worldwide heating from the "greenhouse effect" (the burning of more and more fossil fuels increasingly retains the heat of the sun), and the effects of too much artificial (polluted) ozone at ground level and the loss of natural ozone from the upper atmosphere. The loss of natural ozone in the upper atmosphere has caused a sharp increase in skin cancer in recent years; the increase in artificial ozone in the lower atmosphere is associated with a variety of respiratory problems.

Environmental damage is also widespread in nations with concentrated state socialism. Societies such as the Soviet Union, where (at least until recently)

The damaged nuclear power plant at Chernobyl, USSR. The fact that until very recently the entire Soviet leadership was unelected minimized the impact of public concerns about the environment, which increased the risk of accidents like Chernobyl.

public concerns about the environment have had little effect on unelected leaders, often have serious pollution problems. One of the major causes of the Chernobyl accident, for example, was the lax safety procedures in Soviet nuclear plants. The United States and the Soviet Union together have only about one-tenth of the world's population (Population Reference Bureau, 1988), but they produce 45 percent of the *entire world's* emission of carbon dioxide (CO_2), the substance considered largely responsible for the greenhouse effect.

Social Inequality and Health

Conflict theorists are also greatly interested in the effects of social inequality on health. In virtually all societies, people of higher socioeconomic status live longer and healthier lives than people of lower socioeconomic status (see Cockerham, 1988; Lundberg, 1986; Thomlinson, 1976). There are many reasons for this difference, some related to the individual and others to the social system. Conflict theorists stress those causes related to the social system, arguing that unequal access to the resources needed for a healthy life inevitably leads to inequalities in health and mortality. They also argue that the health-care system often provides better care to those with more money.

Income and Health Many of the reasons for social-class differences in health are related to income. People with higher incomes enjoy better food and shelter. Senate investigations in the late 1960s uncovered shocking amounts of hunger in the United States. The incidence of hunger was subsequently reduced by the federal Food Stamp program, but in the early 1980s that and other federal nutrition programs absorbed cuts of over $12 billion (*St. Louis Post-Dispatch,* 1985b). In the mid-1980s, a group of physicians who conducted an investigation of hunger concluded that up to 20 million Americans suffered malnutrition at some time each month (Physician's Task Force on Hunger in America, 1985). In the developing countries, of course, malnutrition and inadequate shelter are more serious problems than in the United States, and class differences in health are even greater.

Poor and working-class people also face a greater risk of injury or exposure to contaminants on the job. Poor people are more likely than others to be victims of violent crime, and they are more likely to live in locations where pollution, flooding, and other hazards threaten their health and safety. Makeshift heating and cooking arrangements, inadequate electrical wiring, and older housing all increase the danger of fire for poor people. Poor people also experience more divorce, separation, and unemployment, which raise their levels of stress significantly above those of the more affluent. Although we often think of ulcers, high blood pressure, and heart attacks as perils for the overworked business executive, the rates of these diseases are actually higher among the poor (Susser, Hopper, and Richman, 1983; Cockerham, 1988).

Race, Ethnicity, and Health

In the United States, race and ethnicity are related to both illness and mortality (Farley, 1988, pp. 216–217; 242–243). African Americans and American Indians live an average of 5 to 7 years less than whites (National Center for Health Statistics, 1986; Farley, 1988, p. 216). Twice as many black babies as white babies die in the first year of life, and both blacks and Hispanics are sick more days per year than whites (National Center for Health Statistics, 1986). Blacks are about one-third more likely than whites to be handicapped or disabled. These variances are not the product of innate differences in susceptibility to disease, though such differences do exist for some diseases such as sickle-cell anemia (much more common among blacks) and multiple sclerosis (more common among whites).

Rather, they are related to social conditions that are largely associated with social class.

As we saw in earlier chapters, African Americans, Hispanic Americans, and American Indians are all far more likely to live below the poverty level than whites. Therefore, they experience more stress. For example, the incidence of high blood pressure is 17 times as high among blacks as among whites (Cockerham, 1978, p. 34). Evidence that this is largely the result of poverty comes from research by Livingston (1985), which found that high blood pressure is more common among low-income blacks than among either middle-class or upper-class blacks. Because of their high poverty rate and frequent lack of medical insurance, blacks, Hispanics, and Indians are also less likely to get adequate prenatal care than whites, which largely explains their high infant mortality rates. The risks of injury or death from criminal victimization, accident, and fire are far greater for these groups than for whites, and all these risks are of social origin.

Education and Health

The poorer health of lower-income people may also result from their relative lack of education. People with less education are less likely to know the value of a healthy diet and lifestyle in preventing illness (Harris and Guten, 1979), which symptoms require medical attention (see Koos, 1954; Cockerham et al., 1986), and how to take care of themselves when they are sick. Therefore, it is not

Recent research indicates that efforts to achieve good health through lifestyle have become commonplace among Americans of all social classes.

surprising that even among people with similar incomes, those with less education are less healthy (Grossman, 1982; Williams, 1986).

Recent research, however, indicates that people of different income and education levels may be getting *more* similar in the extent to which they seek to prevent illness by adopting healthier lifestyles. In analyzing data from a statewide survey in Illinois, Cockerham and associates (1986) found little difference among the social classes in food habits, exercise, smoking, or alcohol use. Virtually everyone, for example, attempted to engage in some form of exercise, and most people tried to eat food with good nutritional value, avoid chemical additives, and so on.

On the other hand, important social-class differences, probably linked to education, have emerged in the ways people use doctors. These differences will be explored next, when we examine health from the interactionist perspective. Overall, it is fair to say that both income and education have significant effects on health, not including access to health care.

Health and Society: An Interactionist View

The Meaning of Health, Sickness, and Illness

How do you know when you are sick? The answer is that you have learned from others what it means to be sick, and when the way you feel fits your understanding of what it means to be sick, you decide that you are sick. In sociological terms, you adopt the sick role. From an interactionist standpoint, the important fact is that illness is socially defined: you learn from others how to decide that you are sick. You may sometimes decide you are sick when others do not believe that you are sick. Sociologists, for example, distinguish between **illness**—a condition that occurs when *you* perceive that you are suffering from a bodily disorder—and **sickness**—a condition that occurs when *others* perceive that you are suffering from a bodily disorder (Twaddle and Hessler, 1977; Clark, 1988). Even if you believe you are ill when others don't—or

vice versa—the basis of that belief is a set of cues about sickness that you have learned from others (Lewis, 1953).

Suppose you have a headache—an objective physical condition. Does this condition mean that you are ill? You have to decide, and you decide on the basis of messages you have gotten from others in the past: "A headache means you have a fever"; "After the day I've had, no wonder I've got an Excedrin headache"; or "If you drink any more beer, you'll have a hangover tomorrow." Your decision on the meaning of your headache will partly depend on the context or situation in which you got it (Locker, 1981). In addition, you may check out the impressions of others (Berger and Luckmann, 1966)—"Mom, do you think I'm getting a cold?" Ultimately, you make a subjective decision as to whether or not you are ill, based on current and past messages from others, in the context of the current situation.

Ultimately, if you think you are or may be sick, you may go to a doctor. The doctor may or not diagnose a **disease**—a specific condition defined by a medical practitioner as a cause of illness. Here again, a subjective judgment is being made of your condition, this time by a doctor in accordance with his or her medical training and experience. This judgment may or may not accord with your own or others' about your health status. Although the doctor's judgment is based on medical training, it is still subjective—as anyone who has gone to two different doctors and gotten two different diagnoses of the same symptoms will tell you. Doctors' diagnoses of disease are based on messages they have received about what conditions indicate what disease—or even whether a given condition indicates any disease.

Doctors socialized in different schools and different countries can and do define disease differently. For example, you have probably never heard of a mild cardiac disorder known as *Herzinsuffzienz*. Yet if you visit Germany, you might: This disorder is frequently diagnosed by German doctors but is virtually unrecognized anywhere else (Payer, 1988). The reason is not that the disease is unique to the German environment, but rather that doctors trained in German medical schools learn to recognize a certain condition and classify it as *Herzinsuffzienz*.

Culture and the definition of Illness: A Case Study

A case in a children's psychiatric hospital illustrates not only the effects of *individual* behavior in producing disease, but also the effects of the social organization of medicine in failing to discern it. (It should be pointed out that this hospital served 56 patients with a staff of 120 at a cost of medical and psychiatric care of approximately $14,000 per year.) One of the patients, age 11, suddenly became unexplainably ill. He had nausea, loss of appetite, generalized weakness, and a slight fever. The hospital turned its battery of technologies to him without success. After a week or ten days he was sent to the major general hospital in the community for a diagnostic workup. Nothing definitive was uncovered, so his tonsils were removed and he was returned to the psychiatric treatment center. The identical symptoms reappeared and he was transferred to the state communicable disease hospital where an effort was made to isolate the problem. Again, nothing was found. So his adenoids were removed and he was returned once again to the institution and there the symptoms persisted. After some three months of this fruitless technical search, the psychiatric hospital interns were rotated, and an intern trained in India joined the staff. He examined the patient quickly and immediately announced, "This boy has typhoid fever." This diagnosis proved to be

correct, and the condition was corrected. Now, two questions arise: Why typhoid fever in a patient at a high-technology hospital? And why was the medical establishment unable to diagnose it? Now, the State Epidemiology Division began its work on the question of what *behavior* this individual engaged in to contract such a "rare" disease. The answer is as bizarre as it is both social and psychological.

One of the behavioral aberrations to which this boy was prone was to consider himself a dog. He would drop down on all fours, hop around barking, refuse to eat unless a plate of food were placed on the floor, and occasionally nip at staff members' heels. How did he "catch" typhoid? A group of child patients had, in the early part of the summer, been taken on an overnight trip to a well-known resort area. During this outing the patient at issue "became a dog" and lapped water from a polluted mud puddle!

Why the inability of three high-technology hospitals correctly to diagnose a simple case of typhoid fever? The answer is simple but important; physicians and medical institutions generally, when confronting patients, tend to entertain a limited number of hypotheses concerning what may conceivably be "wrong" with the patient. These hypotheses entertained are usually generated out of the individual practitioner's prior experience with cases handled in the past that have exhibited similar symptoms. That is, most medical institutions encounter

and recognize those diseases and illnesses that are common to their practices. This, however, is deceptive because of the twin processes of "differential diagnosis" on the one hand, and "treatment of choice" on the other.

With the possible exception of diagnosis by means of X rays, exploratory surgery, and a handful of other visual means of inspection, physicians often make a diagnosis on the basis of the utterances that patients make about their body sensations. People report symptoms verbally and the physician makes a judgment as to what these mean in terms of body lesion. The problem with this is that reported symptom A may in fact reflect either condition 1, 2, 3, or 4. However that might be, the doctor—like a baseball umpire—*does* make a diagnosis. This is differential diagnosis. Following that, a curative or palliative prescription is made. If diagnosis 1 has been made, the doctor may prescribe treatment a, b, c, or d, each of which may be remembered to have had some effect on lesion A, if that is what in fact ails the patient. This is known as the "treatment of choice." In short, in the vast number of cases with which physicians deal, they rely upon their *recollection* of similar symptoms reported by patients in the past, their further recollection of what diagnosis they made in most such cases, their additional recollection of what the prescribed intervention was, and their memory about its effects.

SOURCE: William R. Rosengren, *Sociology of Medicine: Diversity, Conflict, and Change.* New York: Harper and Row. Copyright 1980 by William R. Rosengren

Because culture, training, and experience influence their judgments, doctors sometimes make the "wrong" diagnosis, even when there is a clear medical explanation for a condition. For an example of this, see the box. In other cases, there may be no clear-cut "right" diagnosis; the meaning of a given set of signs and symptoms is simply viewed differently by doctors from varying backgrounds.

Illness, sickness, and disease, then, are *all* socially defined, and for this reason vary from one culture to another. Thus, not only do German doctors diagnose different diseases than American doctors, but people of different countries, social classes, and ethnic groups use different rules to define themselves as ill or others as sick. In the United States, Italian and Jewish Americans are more expressive and emotional about pain than Anglo-Saxons and Irish Americans, who tend to maintain a "stiff upper lip" (see Zborowski, 1969; Croog, 1961; Mechanic, 1963; Sternbach and Tursky, 1965). American women also acknowledge and respond to illness more quickly than American men (Lennane and Lennane, 1973). So what you have learned about how to decide when you are ill is a product of your particular social situation.

As significant as such differences are among industrialized societies and among different groups within those societies, they are far greater between industrial and preindustrial societies. A condition recognized as a virus in the United States might, in another time or place, be defined as possession by the devil, the presence of evil spirits, witchcraft, bad blood, a malfunctioning organ, or an imbalance between the individual and the environment.

Health

At the opposite end of the scale from illness, sickness, and disease is **health.** One way to view health is as the absence of these negative conditions. However, most contemporary definitions take a broader view, defining health in terms of ability to function (Cockerham, 1989, p. 2). Following the World Health Organization (1946), we can define *healthy* as the ability to function effectively — physically, mentally, and socially.

This definition makes three important points. First, health has physical, social, and psychological dimensions: The truly healthy person is one who functions well in all of these areas. Second, such effective functioning does not merely depend on the absence of disease or sickness. You can be free from any recognized disease or illness and yet not function well in one or more of the three areas. Or you can have a disease and yet function well, either because the disease is being medically managed or because you have successfully adapted to it. Third, what constitutes effective functioning is socially defined and therefore can change over time and among societies. People viewed as healthy in the United States, for example, might be seen as less healthy in other societies that place a greater value on physical fitness. As with sickness, we define ourselves as healthy or not healthy largely on the basis of messages we get from others about how well we are functioning.

Personal Outlook and Health

Thus far, in considering health from an interactionist standpoint, we have seen that a person's response to a given physical condition is a product of social interaction. There are also similar influences on the physical conditions themselves. To a certain extent, a *self-fulfilling prophecy* operates when it comes to illness. People who believe that they have little control over their health are more likely to get sick than people with a more positive attitude (Seeman and Seeman, 1983). If you believe that you have some control over your health, you are more likely to exercise, avoid overeating, smoking, and excessive drinking, and try harder to eat a balanced diet and to protect yourself from environmental contaminants. This process suggests another reason why socioeconomic status influences health status. Recall from Chapters 9 and 14 that people of lower status experience less control over their lives in general (Kohn, 1969). As a result, they are less likely to *believe* that they can control their health and may therefore be less likely to adopt health-enhancing behaviors (Ross, Mirowsky, and Cockerham, 1983; Seeman and Evans, 1962).

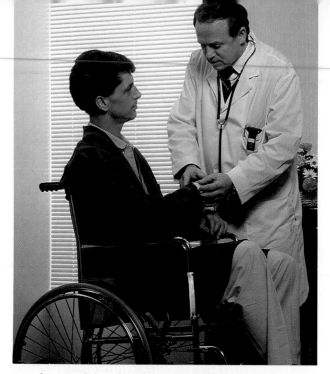

Social research has found that the different ways that people use doctors are one source of social class differences in health.

Personal Outlook and Physician Use The same forces that influence people's health behavior also influence the ways in which they use the health-care system. Although the poor in both Great Britain and the United States now visit doctors more often than the nonpoor because of government assistance programs, substantial differences in health and illness persist between the two groups (Susser, Watson, and Hopper, 1985; Susser, Hopper, and Richman, 1983). According to Cockerham (1988), one reason for this is that people of different social classes use doctors differently. Because they have less confidence in their ability to control their life situations, poor people are more likely to turn responsibility for managing their health over to their doctors. They are equally likely to go to the doctor whether their symptoms indicate a possible serious illness or not, and they are more likely to follow the doctor's instructions blindly.

This behavior has several negative consequences. First, low-income patients take "the doctor's word" even if they don't understand what it means, and therefore have a poorer understanding of their disorder. Moreover, if the doctor does make mistakes, or if the condition changes after a visit to the doctor, they are more likely to continue following "doctor's orders" anyway.

Middle-class patients, in contrast, have adopted a consumer orientation toward medical care—a certain healthy skepticism that allows them to be less dependent on physicians and thus quicker to respond on their own to symptoms (Haug and Lavin, 1981, 1983). Cockerham (1988) argues that the medical profession encourages "a healthy lifestyle"—exercise, balanced diet, no smoking or heavy drinking—but discourages the consumerism that leads to patients' asking for explanations or questioning the doctor's judgment. Poor people have developed a healthier lifestyle, but they still have not become skeptical consumers of medicine.

The Medical Institution

Some kind of health-care system—a social institution known as *medicine*—exists in every society. The form of that institution varies widely among societies, depending on culture, level of technology, and the economic system. What is less variable is the relatively high status accorded to medical practitioners—an indication of the value that most societies place on good health (Twaddle and Hessler, 1977, p. 140). As has been suggested, societal beliefs about the causes of sickness play a big role in determining the nature of medicine. In societies where sickness is thought to be caused by evil spirits or witchcraft, for example, medicine is the domain of spiritual healers who perform ceremonies aimed at driving the offending spirits or curses away.

Traditional and Scientific Medicine

Traditional Medicine Spiritual healing is one of several types of *traditional medicine*. Such practices are common in preindustrial societies, where they take a variety of forms. Besides blaming witchcraft and evil spirits for their ills, preindustrial societies frequently view sickness as a punishment from God or the gods for evil behavior or as the result of the soul leaving the body (Twaddle and Hessler, 1977, p. 141). When people believe in these causes of illness, they often turn to prayer, repentance, and faith healing, so that medicine becomes largely the domain of religious figures. Another common belief is that illness results from the presence of foreign substances within the body or from an imbalance of forces affecting the body. In societies with this belief, medicine centers around a combination of magical ceremonies and preparation of herbs aimed at restoring balance or helping the body fight off the offending agent.

Scientific Medicine Industrialized societies subscribe to a scientific notion of the nature of sickness and disease. They believe that some identifiable malfunction of the body underlies all illness. Sickness is often caused by the invasion of the body by some microscopic living organism—bacteria or a virus. It may also stem from the failure of some bodily organ to work as it should, the growth of abnormal body tissue, or an injury. The underlying assumption of scientific medicine is that the cause of a sickness can be identified through observation and treated scientifically. Medicine in industrialized societies is the domain of scientifically trained physicians who use technology to treat and cure illness. A key element of scientific medicine is the *hospital*, the setting where the diagnosis and treatment of relatively serious illnesses takes place.

Blends of Traditional and Scientific Medicine
Although scientific medicine is generally associated with industrialized societies and traditional forms of medicine with preindustrial societies, the distinction is not really that clear-cut. Many preindustrial societies have, in fact, combined scientific methods of medicine with more traditional methods. One of the clearest examples is American Indian medicine. In preindustrial America, medicine among both American Indians and Americans of European ancestry was a blend of science and superstition. It could be argued that Indian medicine was at least as scientific as European medicine. Among the medical advances made by American Indian tribes were effective oral contraceptives (first used by Indians over 100 years ago, but not "rediscovered" by modern American medicine until the 1950s), stimulant and anesthetic drugs, isolation of sick people, surgery, antibiotic drugs, and a cure for scurvy (Twaddle and Hessler, 1977, pp. 152–156). These techniques, developed through a process of trial and error much like modern scientific experimentation, were combined with religious rituals.

Similarly, traditional forms of medicine continue to coexist with scientific medicine. Millions of Americans, along with people in many other societies, believe in faith healing. *Curanderismo,* a time-honored form of Latin American folk medicine, is practiced by significant numbers of Chicanos and Latinos in the United States. It is based on the assumption that sickness results largely from an imbalance of forces, such as heat and cold, in the human body, and it relies on herbs and foods aimed at restoring the balance, in combination with the use of religious or magical symbols (Twaddle and Hessler, 1977; Willard, 1972; Clark, 1970).

Although traditional forms of medicine such as faith healing and *curanderismo* are based on different assumptions than modern scientific medicine, the reality is that significant numbers of people rely on both kinds of medicine. For example, thousands of American cancer patients spent great amounts of money during the 1970s to travel to other countries to get Laetrile, a substance extracted from apricot pits that was rumored to cure cancer, despite the absence of any scientific evidence that it worked and some evidence that it could be harmful. (It was banned in the United States for these reasons.) Significantly, most people who used Laetrile also used such conventional therapies as radiation. Similarly, most people who go to faith healers or *curanderos* also go to regular doctors.

Does Traditional Medicine Work? In some cases, traditional medicine may "work" in the same way as a **placebo,** a nonmedicated substance prescribed by a doctor to a patient who wants a "cure" for an incurable illness. When people *believe* that they are being treated by something that works, their personal outlook improves, which may actually make them feel better (Mechanic, 1978, p. 429). *Are* they really better? In some cases, yes. Actual physiological changes have been documented in people given placebos and in people treated by traditional medicine. Warts and stomach ulcers, for example, have healed at above-average rates among people given placebos (Frank, 1959). However, placebos also can have side effects, and the effectiveness of both placebos and traditional medicine varies widely, depending upon the patient's personality, illness, and social situation (Mechanic, 1978, pp. 427–430).

Modern Medicine: The Medicalization of Everything?

Although traditional medicine does persist in industrialized societies, by far the dominant medical institution in such societies is scientific medicine. Over time, scientific medicine has grown dramatically in industrialized countries (see Table 16.1) and has defined as diseases an increasing number of problems and conditions. The presumption is that these problems are the result of bodily malfunctions, and that the answer to them is medical treatment. Sociologists call this **medicalization.** The trend to medicalization has been most pronounced since World War II, and it has been applied especially to human behaviors defined as causing problems (Clark, 1988). Those who eat too much have a compulsive eating disorder; those who eat too little, *anorexia nervosa*. Drug addiction, alcoholism, childhood hyperactivity ("attention deficit disorder" or "hyperkinetic impulse disorder"), and insomnia have all been defined as diseases or medical problems. Problems of personal adjustment are grouped together under the label *mental illness*—despite the fact that diagnosis of any given disorder (for example, schizophrenia) is often highly subjective and not very reliable (Clausen, 1979; Scheff, 1975; World Health Organization, 1973). One of the most recently defined illnesses is *hysteroid dysphoria,* or "love addiction"—a compulsive rush from one love relationship to another (Clark, 1988).

Reasons for Medicalization Although behaviors like those just described can be serious problems, it is questionable whether they are diseases. The reasons for the growing medicalization of industrialized societies are probably more social than scientific (Schneider and Conrad, 1980). In many cases, no specific bodily condition that would lead to certain behavior problems can be identified. Health providers have encouraged the medicalization of these problems because it has greatly increased their authority and domain of activity. Major industries have developed to treat eating disorders, alcohol and drug dependence, smoking, childhood hyperactivity, and so forth (Schneider and Conrad, 1980). That these industries are clearly part of the medical establishment is shown by their dominance by doctors and hospitals.

Medicalization is seen as more humane and effective than the alternatives. Formerly, many behavior problems currently defined as diseases were viewed as immoral behavior, bad habits, or delinquency. Thus, the person with the problem was placed at fault. With medicalization, it is possible to say, "It's not your fault, you have a disease" (Clark, 1988; Illich, 1976). Removing the stigma encourages the person to acknowledge the problem and do something about it. Moreover, medical treatment is usually more effective than threats and punishment (Clark, 1988). Sociologists point out, though, that medical treatment is still a form of social control (Schneider and Conrad, 1980; Ehrenreich and Ehrenreich, 1975). For example, the mandatory alcoholism treatment program becomes a functional substitute for the "drunk tank."

Limits of Medicalization Unfortunately, medicalizing a problem does not always remove the stigma attached to it. Labels such as "alcoholic," "drug addict," "schizophrenic," or "hyperactive child" can still be considerably damaging. For this reason, some social scientists argue that although the disease model has been helpful in getting some people to seek treatment, it has inhibited others from doing so. The individual's response depends upon his or her personality and culture. Another criticism of the medical model is that, like earlier models, it stresses individual characteristics rather than the social situation as the source of the problem (Conrad, 1975). In fact, problems such as over- or undereating, substance abuse, and excessive activity in children arise from a mixture of psychological, sociological, and biomedical influences that varies from person to person. Thus, although the medical model has become the most common approach to such problems, its appropriateness continues to be debated, and its value probably varies widely.

Medicalization of Nondisease Conditions In addition to behavior problems, a variety of routine life events have become medicalized. Births occur in hospitals; they have become an expensive event that involves a large number of medical workers. This was not always so; it came about as a result of vigorous efforts by physicians over the course of the nineteenth and twentieth centuries to gain control of the birthing process (Savage, 1986; Zola, 1972; Mehl, 1977).

Pregnancy today is defined as a medical condition, with the expectant mother encouraged to adopt a role similar to the sick role. Medicine has become the answer to a range of problems in other areas of life, ranging from dissatisfaction with one's sex (the sex-change operation) to dissatisfaction with one's appearance (plastic surgery).

The medicalization of these conditions brings both costs and benefits. Childbirth is one example. The medicalization of birth has meant there will be rapid detection of, and treatment for, any problems that arise. Fetal monitoring during labor, for example, may have contributed to the substantial decline in infant mortality that occurred in industrialized countries during the 1980s. Yet a strong case can be made that for standard births, medicalization has been excessive. Routine fetal monitoring, for example, may *increase* the risk of infant mortality from unnecessary Caesarean deliveries (Banta and Thacker, 1979). In the Netherlands, nearly half of all births occur in the home, under the supervision of a midwife rather than a doctor, and the infant mortality rate is 23 percent *lower* than in the United States (Sagor and Brodsky, 1984; Population Reference Bureau, 1988). As Americans in general, and women in particular, have sought to exert greater control over their own health, midwifery and home birth have become more popular

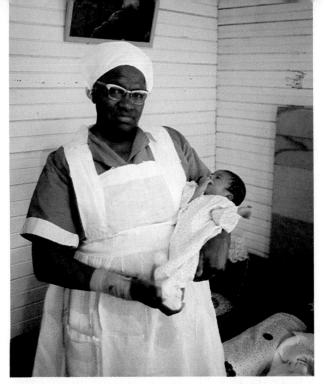

A midwife with a newborn baby. For a time, the trend toward the medicalization of childbirth threatened to put an end to midwifery, but recent efforts by women toward greater control of their health have led to its resurgence.

(Weitz and Sullivan, 1986; Ruzek, 1980). Though the costs and benefits of medicalization are mixed for the general public, there is no such mix for the medical establishment, as illustrated by the growth of medicine shown in Table 16.1.

TABLE 16.1
The Growth of Medicine in the United States during the Twentieth Century: Selected Indicators

YEAR	NUMBER OF PHYSICIANS	PHYSICIANS PER 10,000 POPULATION	NATIONAL EXPENDITURE ON HEALTH CARE[1]	PERCENT OF GNP SPENT ON HEALTH CARE
1929			3.6	3.5
1935			2.9	4.0
1940			4.0	4.0
1950	219,900	14.1	12.7	4.4
1955			17.7	4.4
1960	247,300	14.0	26.9	5.2
1965			41.9	5.9
1970	326,500	15.6	75.0	7.4
1975	384,500	17.4	132.7	8.3
1980	457,500	19.7	248.1	9.1
1983	501,200	21.1	357.2	10.5
1985	534,800	22.0	422.6	10.6
1986			458.2	10.9

[1] In billions of dollars.
SOURCE: National Center on Health Statistics, 1987, pp. 128, 149.

Roles and Stratification in the Medical Institution

Because of such trends as the advancement of medical technology, the growth of scientific medicine, and the medicalization of a widening variety of problems and conditions, medicine has become an increasingly large and complex institution (Loft and Kletke, 1989). It is made up of a structure of roles that are both specialized and stratified.

Physicians   At the top of the stratification hierarchy is the *physician*. Traditionally, physicians, once they have completed periods of supervised hospital practice known as *internship* and *residency,* have been all-powerful in medicine. This is because of their professional status (Rasmussen, 1975). Thus, nurses, paramedics, orderlies, and patients are all expected to follow "doctor's orders." The hospital, which has become the primary place where medical care is given, has traditionally been ruled by physicians. Because only doctors are assumed to have the professional training and scientific knowledge necessary to identify and cure disease, they make their decisions independently from any supervision by, for example, hospital administrators.

The rewards of being a doctor go beyond power. In 1986, the average income of an American medical doctor was $119,500, compared to $25,256 for men and $16,232 for women in the general population (Cockerham, 1989, p. 172).

As we shall see shortly, recent efforts to control the cost of medicine in the United States have curtailed the power of doctors. Those who pay for health care—government, insurance companies, and employers—have demanded and gotten greater power to decide how much and what kind of care will be given (Light, 1989).

Nurses and Other Health Providers   As the institution of medicine became larger and more complex, a variety of roles other than that of physician developed. In the early twentieth century, medicine was often practiced in the patient's home and usually involved only the doctor and the patient (Rosenberg, 1987; Loft and Kletke, 1989, p. 419). Today, care occurs much more often in the hospital and involves a much wider variety of providers, including nurses, paramedics, emergency medical technicians, physician's assistants, and physical therapists.

Still, the physician continues to reign supreme. Many medical sociologists argue that the sharp distinction between the doctor and other medical providers creates a number of difficulties. One problem is that the doctor does not always know the most about a patient's condition. A nurse, for example, interacts regularly with a hospitalized patient over the course of his or her shift. The doctor, in contrast, may see the patient only once a day while "making rounds," and even then may evaluate the patient's condition partly on the basis of data (body temperature, blood pressure, heart rate) collected by the nurse. Nevertheless, the norm is for the physician to manage the patient's care. This can lead to mistakes, as well as to an elaborate and potentially demeaning ritual, sometimes called "the doctor-nurse game" (Stein, 1967), in which the doctor indirectly elicits suggestions from the nurse, and the nurse in turn gives indirect answers.

The much lower status of nurses and other medical personnel relative to doctors is reflected in their salary structures. Nurses are relatively poorly paid workers, reflecting the tendency, described in Chapter 6, for predominantly female occupations to have low rates of pay. Moreover, low pay may not be the only thing about the profession that is influenced by gender. A recent study by Floge and Merrill (1986) revealed that male nurses do not have to play the "doctor-nurse game": They are asked for and make direct recommendations concerning treatment.

The nursing occupation has therefore become less attractive to women, particularly with the opening of other employment opportunities that offer better pay, higher status, and greater autonomy. As a result, nursing shortages have become a perennial problem. The nursing profession has responded by attempting to gain more authority and autonomy, largely through expanding into hospital administration and a variety of specialties such as anesthesia and cardiac care (Cockerham, 1989, p. 224). Particularly significant has been the emergence of the category of nursing known as *nurse practitioner*. The nurse practitioner has taken over a number of routine medical-care tasks

ple still see the doctor less than nonpoor people. The Americans now least likely to see the doctor are those *just above* the poverty level, who typically have neither Medicaid nor private insurance (Davis and Schoen, 1978). In 1986, people with family incomes of $10,000 to $20,000 were more likely to have gone two or more years without seeing a doctor than those with either lower or higher incomes (National Center for Health Statistics, 1988, p. 104).

Setting Price and Demand

The final feature of the American health-care system that distinguishes it from those of other industrial societies is the ability of American physicians to set their own prices. In many other countries the initiation of third-party payment was accompanied by *cost controls* that limited the fees that could be charged and reviewed the necessity of proposed medical procedures. In the United States, this did not happen until the 1980s. Analyzing American medicine from a conflict perspective, sociologist Paul Starr (1982) has attributed this difference to the great power of doctors and hospitals in the United States.

The key fact underlying Starr's analysis is that, until recently, most third-party payers in the United States were under the control of health providers—doctors and hospitals. When third-party payment spread in the United States, it was primarily under the auspices of Blue Cross and Blue Shield. Blue Cross, which covers hospitalization, was created and controlled by hospitals, and Blue Shield, which pays doctor bills, was created and controlled by doctors. Moreover, doctors and hospitals used their powerful political lobbies to ensure that these organizations would be the dominant third-party payers (Starr, 1982, pp. 295–298).

The result was that doctors and hospitals could define their own demand *and* set their own prices. Blue Cross and Blue Shield generally paid for whatever procedures were done at whatever fee was charged, as long as it fell within the vague guidelines of "usual, customary, and reasonable." Under this system, new doctors with no record of past fees would test the

standard by billing a higher fee than that charged by their colleagues to see what would happen. Usually they got paid, and more-experienced doctors would then match these higher rates and also get paid (Starr, 1982, p. 385). The result was rampant inflation in medical costs.

When Medicare was proposed in the 1960s, doctors vehemently opposed it at first, but later they successfully lobbied to retain fee-for-service payment and the "usual, customary, and reasonable" standard. Thus, the medical profession soon "not only accepted Medicare, but discovered that it was a bonanza" (Starr, 1982, p. 370).

For these reasons, there was simply no force for restraint on the amount or cost of health care in the United States. Inevitably, the cost of medicine sky-rocketed. As we saw in Table 16.1, the share of the U.S. gross national product devoted to medical expenses soared from under 5 percent in the early 1950s to nearly 11 percent in the mid-1980s, the highest in the industrialized world. In dollar terms, the cost of health care rose from $13 billion to over $450 billion. One reason for the increase was the development of new and more expensive technology. Another was the rise of *defensive medicine*: the ordering of medical tests and procedures by doctors to head off malpractice suits. A third was the cost of malpractice insurance, which rose enormously in recent decades. And a fourth reason was an aging (and therefore sicker) population. But all of these factors added together do not explain our soaring medical expenditures.

Cost spirals are inevitable any time incentives operate the way they did in American medicine between 1950 and 1980. Providers could set their own prices and demand, and patients didn't have to pay directly—"the boss," the "government," or "insurance" took care of it. Clearly, such a situation could not go on indefinitely, and change came with a vengeance in the 1980s.

Crisis and Change in American Medicine

Somebody, of course, had to pay for these spiraling costs, and by the early 1980s, it was becoming in-

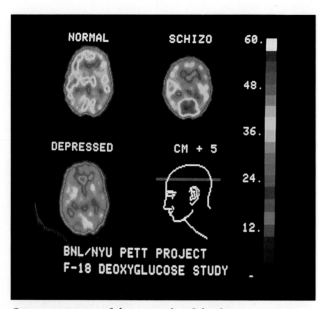

NORMAL   SCHIZO   60.

48.

36.

DEPRESSED   CM + 5

24.

12.

BNL/NYU PETT PROJECT
F-18 DEOXYGLUCOSE STUDY

One consequence of the unregulated fee-for-service system has been the duplication of expensive equipment such as PET Scanners, as hospitals seek to attract physicians and patients. Often localities have two or three expensive scanners when one would be sufficient.

creasingly clear who that someone was—*everyone*. More and more of the costs of producing anything involved health-care expenses. Lee Iacocca pointed out that $600 was added to the cost of every Chrysler to pay for automobile workers' health care (Starr, 1984). A few years earlier, General Motors reported that it was paying more to Blue Cross/Blue Shield than to U.S. Steel, its primary metal supplier (Fox and Crawford, 1979). More and more employers found that the cost of health benefits for their employees was severely cutting into their profitability. At about the same time, the government began to feel the pinch of medical expenditures. The costs of Medicare and Medicaid had far outstripped original projections, and record federal budget deficits created pressure to contain them. Both employers and the government took strong steps to control the costs of medicine. Among the most important were the following.

Prospective payment: Rather than paying whatever was charged, Medicare began to pay hospitals a standard amount for any given medical condition. Medical conditions were identified as *diagnostic related groups (DRGs)*, and the hospital was paid a fixed amount for a patient in any given DRG. If the hospital spent less than the average amount to treat a patient, it made money; if it spent more, it lost money. This payment system has been adopted by a number of private insurance companies, and in some instances it has been extended to payments of doctors. It has saved money, but it has also been criticized for leading hospitals to favor "simpler" cases that are more profitable and to discharge some patients too soon when Medicare "runs out."

Utilization reviews: Health-care personnel employed by insurance companies or employers review each proposed operation or day in the hospital to determine whether it is necessary. If the reviewer decides it isn't necessary, the insurance does not pay. This system has been praised for eliminating unnecessary procedures and hospitalizations, but it has been criticized for putting cost ahead of medical considerations. Another common practice is to require a second doctor's opinion before any expensive procedure or operation is undertaken.

HMOs: As mentioned earlier, many employers are covering their workers under HMOs rather than traditional fee-for-service plans. In some areas, Medicaid has also turned to HMOs. Moreover, HMOs are but one part of a related pattern: the growth of payment plans not controlled by doctors and hospitals. The proportion of workers covered under traditional Blue Cross/Blue Shield plans has fallen significantly.

Deductibles and copayments: Many insurers have tried to regulate use of doctors and hospitals by requiring patients to pay more of their own bills. The most common methods are *deductibles* (the patient pays the first $200, $500, or whatever) and *copayments* (the patient pays 10 or 20 percent of the total bill). These procedures have been criticized on the basis that they make the availability of medicine more dependent on the ability to pay.

Bans on cost shifting: As noted above, cost controls have made "charity care" less available. This is because hospitals and doctors used to charge "paying" patients a bit extra to cover the cost of treating those who could not pay—a practice known as *cost shifting*. Today, most insurance plans forbid cost shifting and reduce payments to doctors and hospitals if they find evidence that it is being done.

Increased use of proprietary hospitals: During the 1980s, *proprietary* or for-profit hospitals became increasingly popular with employer-paid medical plans. In general, these hospitals are able to hold costs down by limiting patients to those who are insured and who have relatively simple medical problems, which cost less to treat. (An exception to this rule is expensive but highly visible "high tech" procedures like heart transplants that generate favorable publicity for the hospital.) Between 1960 and 1985, the percentage of U.S. hospital beds in proprietary hospitals rose from about 5 percent to nearly 10 percent (National Center for Health Statistics, 1988, p. 135), and continued increases are projected.

For all these efforts at cost control, the American medical system remains the most expensive in the world. The share of the gross national product that is spent on health care in this country is higher than in other industrial societies, and per capita expenditures on health care are the highest in the world. Even so, it cannot be said that Americans are healthier than people in many other countries that spend less on health care. As of 1988, 21 countries had lower infant mortality rates, 10 had longer life expectancies, and 12 more had the same life expectancy (Population Reference Bureau, 1988). Besides the relative inefficiency and high cost of the U.S. system, a key problem is unequal access to care, which is particularly evident in the infant mortality statistics.

For the reasons outlined above, it is commonly suggested that the United States consider adopting a health-care system more like that of other industrialized countries. Virtually all other industrialized countries have either national health insurance or a national health service. We shall conclude this chapter by considering these alternatives.

Alternatives to the U.S. Health-Care System

National Health Insurance

The most common form of health-care system in industrialized countries is **national health insurance.** This is a system in which health-care providers remain in the private sector but are paid through a nationwide insurance system supervised and, to varying degrees, financed by government. Among the countries with this form of health system are Canada, France, West Germany, Norway, Japan, Denmark, and Australia.

Although some Americans refer to national health insurance as "socialized medicine," national health insurance actually retains the basic capitalistic nature of medicine. Doctors and hospitals remain in the private sector, and in most cases the fee-for-service system is retained. The difference is a legal requirement that *everyone* be covered by health insurance. There are two basic variants on this system: public insurance and private but legally mandated insurance. In the public version, as in Canada, the insurance is financed through taxes and administered by government or by private organizations hired by government to do the job. In the private version, employers are required to provide insurance to all employees and their families. Some countries have a mix of the two, using private insurance for employed workers and public insurance for people who are unemployed or not in the labor force (students, retirees). One U.S. state, Massachusetts, adopted a statewide health insurance program of this type in 1988, and that same year the Democratic Party proposed a system of this type on a national scale.

Questions Concerning National Insurance There are two key issues involved in national health insurance. The first is care for people who are unemployed or out of the labor force. If national health insurance is financed by a payroll tax or mandated employer-paid private insurance, special provisions must be made for those not working.

The second issue is cost. As the Blue Cross/Blue Shield and Medicare experiences indicate, national health insurance must be accompanied by cost controls. Without them, third-party, fee-for-service payment will almost surely lead to soaring costs and excessive use of the health-care system. However, France and Canada have shown that cost controls can be effective. In both countries, controls such as fee regulation and utilization reviews have held per-capita medical expenses well below those in the United States (Marmor and Tenner, 1977; Sandier, 1983). In

Canada, physican fees are negotiated between the government and doctors, after which they remain in force for a specified time. When national health care was adopted in the early 1970s, per-capita medical expenses were as high as those in the United States, but they are now significantly lower (Marmor and Tenner, 1977; U.S. Bureau of the Census, 1987d, p. 804).

The fear of such regulation of fees has led the American Medical Association (AMA) to block national health insurance ever since it was first proposed by President Harry Truman in the 1940s (Starr, 1982). Even milder reforms such as Medicare were strongly opposed until it became evident that they would pass with or without AMA support. At that point, lobbying efforts shifted to ensuring that doctors would retain control over price and demand. Now that even private insurance companies have invoked cost controls, national health insurance may look less threatening to doctors. It can be assumed, however, that they and hospitals will lobby vigorously against cost controls should national insurance seem inevitable. The success or failure of this lobbying will have a major impact on whether national health insurance ends up controlling the cost of health care or making it even more expensive (Mechanic, 1978).

National Health Service

The other major alternative to the American health-care system is the **national health service,** sometimes referred to as the *public health care system.* This system exists in Great Britain, New Zealand, and most socialist countries, including the Soviet Union. The label *socialized medicine* applies more appropriately here than to national health insurance, because under a national health service system, doctors are public employees. Rather than being paid on a fee-for-service basis, they receive either salaries or capitation payments. Supporters of this system claim that it has two major advantages over national health insurance. First, it treats everyone the same, because coverage is not linked to payroll taxes or employer-paid insurance. Thus, the unemployed, retired, and college stu-

dents all get the same coverage as working people. Second, it is significantly less expensive. Without fee-for-service, there is no incentive for unnecessary procedures and hospitalizations. In this regard, a national health service works in much the same way as an HMO. (Indeed, it has been referred to as "one big HMO.")

The pros and cons of the national health service are much the same as the pros and cons of the HMO. On the positive side, it is clearly less expensive than other systems of health care, and it carries less risk of harm from unnecessary medical procedures. On the negative side, patients are sometimes assigned a doctor rather than allowed to choose one, and they may feel that they are being deprived of care they need. In Great Britain, for example, coronary bypass surgery is only one-sixth as common as in the United States, and computerized axial tomography (CAT) scanners are hardly used at all (Payer, 1988). Again, whether this trend is good or bad depends on one's individual perspective.

It is hard to make a clear-cut case for any one system over another on the basis of overall health, as Table 16.2 shows. The United States with its ability-to-pay system, Canada and France with their national health insurance, and Great Britain with its national health service all have rather similar health status, except for higher infant mortality in the United States. The adoption of a national health service in Great Britain did improve the health of the poor as well as others, but socioeconomic inequality in health persisted for reasons not entirely related to the health-care system (Hollingsworth, 1981; Cockerham, 1988).

What is clear from Table 16.2 is the difference in cost: the American system is the most expensive, the British system the least. There are also substantially greater socioeconomic inequalities under the American system than in any of the others. Because of these shortcomings, recent polls reveal that Americans are less satisfied with their health system than are Canadians and Britons, and that a majority would prefer the Canadian system to the present American system (see Polls Apart: "How Americans View Their Health-Care System").

TABLE 16.2
Selected Indicators of Health Expense and Health Status, Industrialized Countries with Various Health-Care Systems

Country[1]:	Percent of GNP Spent on Health Care		HEALTH EXPENSE INDICATORS		HEALTH STATUS INDICATORS	
			Per Capita Health Expenditure, 1980			
	1980	1984	Based on Exchange Rate	Based on Purchasing Power	Life Expectancy	Infant Mortality Rate[2]
U.S. (AP)	9.5	10.7	$1,087	1,087	75	10.0
France (NHI)	8.5	9.1	1,036	837	75	8.0
Canada (NHI)	7.3	8.4	747	853	76	7.9
Great Britain (NHS)	5.6	5.9	530	468	75	9.5

SOURCES: Expenditure data are from U.S. Bureau of the Census, 1987d. Health status data are from Population Reference Bureau, 1988.

[1] AP ;= Health care based on ability to pay; NHI ;= national health insurance; NHS ;= national health service.

[2] Infant Mortality Rate ;= Deaths to children under age 1 per 1,000 live births.

Case Study: Sweden

We can learn more about alternative systems of health care by looking at an example of one. Sweden has an employer-paid health-care system that is a blend of national health insurance and a national health service. Health care is one of several benefits provided through this system; others include basic and supplemental old-age pensions and parental leave. Social benefits are paid for by employers; the costs amount to 35 to 40 percent of each employee's salary, which is paid into the national social insurance systems. Most of the money goes to county councils (local governments), which operate hospitals and clinics; some of it goes to the federal government for the portion of the programs it directly funds. These payments are treated by employers as business expenses. Self-employed people pay 32.5 percent of their income for the social insurance programs; this amount is treated as a deduction for income tax purposes. (For comparison purposes, self-employed people in the United States pay 13 percent of their income in Social Security taxes—not deductible for income tax purposes—and in addition must purchase their own health insurance and supplemental retirement plans.)

From the social insurance payments made by employers and self-employed people, all Swedes— employees, retirees, children, and the unemployed— receive a wide range of benefits when they become ill. When people are sick or must stay home to care for sick children, they receive a daily allowance of 90 percent of their lost income. With the exception of small fees, the national health insurance program pays all hospitalization costs, prescription drug costs, and laboratory and diagnostic test costs. If people obtain their health care at public outpatient clinics, all of their expenses are paid for (Swedish Institute, 1988a).

The doctors who work in these clinics are employees of the county councils who operate them. The clinics are funded by the social insurance payments described above, and the doctors are salaried rather than paid on a fee-for-service basis (Cockerham, 1989, pp. 289–291). In this regard, the Swedish system resembles Britain's national health service. However, there are also private doctors, and Swedes who choose to use them have most, but not all, of the cost paid by national health insurance. These doctors operate on a fee-for-service basis, but the fees are set by the national government. In this regard, the Swedish system is similar to the Canadian system.

In effect, Swedish medical consumers are free to choose between a national health service (the public clinics) and a national health insurance system based on fee-for-service (the private physicians). Besides medical expenses, the Swedish system also pays 40 percent of dental care costs.

POLLS APART

How Americans View Their Health-Care System

Think back to the health-related services you used within the past year. Were you satisfied with the care you received? What did you think of the expenses involved? As we learned in this chapter, the United States has a private fee-for-service system. In contrast, Canada has national health insurance, in which the government pays for all health costs and regulates fees, and Britain has a national health service, in which medical practitioners work for the government. Which of these systems would you prefer? Why?

If you feel that the British or Canadian system might work better than the U.S. system, you are not alone. According to a 1989 national survey, the majority of Americans are disenchanted with the U.S. system of health care. Only 35 percent, for example, were "very satisfied" with

SOURCE: "Poll: Americans Dislike Health-Care System," *St. Louis Post-Dispatch*, February 15, 1989, p. 16A.

the medical services they had received in the previous year, compared to 39 percent in Britain and 67 percent in Canada. As the chapter mentions, one problem with the fee-for-service system is that many people cannot afford good medical treatment. This is reflected in the survey, which revealed that over 7 percent of Americans felt that financial considerations prevented them from receiving adequate medical care, compared to less than 1 percent of British and Canadians.

Of course, the fact that most Americans are disappointed with the health care they have been receiving does not automatically mean they would support an alternate system. It is interesting to note, therefore, that in the same survey, 61 percent of the respondents expressed a preference for a system based on the Canadian model, and 29 percent supported a national health service modeled after the British system. In contrast, only 4 percent of Canadian and 12 percent

of British respondents indicated a preference for the U.S. system.

At this point, you might conclude that support for national health insurance comes primarily from lower-income people who lack insurance and cannot afford doctors' fees. In fact, as the following table reveals, support for the Canadian model was high among all income groups. Just what do these numbers mean? Robert Blendon, chairman of the Department of Health Policy and Management at Harvard University, analyzed the results as follows: "This survey puts an end to the myth cited by a lot of policy makers that Americans believe they have the best health-care system in the world. It also puts an end to the myth that others believe we have the best health care."

Questions: Do you agree with Blendon's conclusions? If so, how do you explain the fact that the United States is the only industrialized nation, outside of South Africa, that does not have some system of national health care? If not, how do you interpret the survey results?

How did your responses compare to those of the general public? Were you surprised at the public response? Would you answer the same questions differently now that you are aware of these results?

PERCENTAGE OF RESPONDENTS FAVORING CANADIAN SYSTEM	
Upper-income	56%
Middle-income	68%
Lower-income	58%
Insured	61%
Uninsured	62%

This system has given Sweden both good health and reasonable health-care costs. Sweden enjoyed the second-longest life expectancy in the world in 1988, tied with Iceland and Switzerland at 77, and just behind the leader, Japan, which had a life expectancy of 78. Sweden also had the fourth-lowest infant mortality rate in the world (5.9 per thousand), trailing only Japan, Iceland, and Finland. These figures compare to a life expectancy of 75 and an infant mortality rate of 10.0 per thousand in the United States (Population Reference Bureau, 1988a). At the same time, Swedes spend less on health care than Americans: 9 percent of the Swedish gross national product went to health care in 1986, compared to 11 percent of GNP in the United States (Cockerham, 1989, pp. 291, 296).

Summary

In this chapter, we have explored ways in which society influences health and medicine, and ways in which health and medicine influence society. The functionalist, conflict, and symbolic-interactionist perspectives have all made important contributions to our understanding of the relationship between health and society.

Perhaps the functionalists' major contribution has been the concept of the sick role, reflecting the notion that good health is normal and functional for society, but not always attainable. The sick role is a deviant one, but unlike many other deviant roles, it is not usually adopted by choice. Thus, it is less stigmatized. Although sociologists debate the individual-responsibility model and other aspects of the sick role proposed by the functionalists, most accept the basic concept of a sick role. Another major contribution of the functionalist perspective to medical sociology has been analysis of the relationship between modernization and health. Industrialization and modernization have brought great improvements in health and longevity, but, there have also been some costs in the form of environmentally induced illness.

Conflict theorists focus on the inequalities in health and medicine and on the question of who, if anyone, benefits from them. They emphasize the strong link between environmental pollution and certain disorders such as cancer, and note that certain interest groups have an economic stake in polluting the environment. Conflict theorists also point out that there is a near-universal relationship between income and health status, noting the health consequences of inadequate food, shelter, and job safety among the poor, as well as their unequal access to health care. Poor education and the risk of criminal victimization also endanger the health of the poor.

The symbolic-interactionist approach to medical sociology stresses two main issues. The first is the meaning of health or the lack of it. Interactionists distinguish between illness (your own belief that you are not well), sickness (the judgment of others that you are not well), and disease (a doctor's judgment about what is wrong with you). Each is the result of a subjective judgment about the meaning of what is observed — feelings in the case of the patient; signs and symptoms in the case of the doctor and others. All these judgments are made on the basis of meanings learned through interaction with others. Medical cultures vary among societies, as do doctor's judgments about the meaning of signs and symptoms. A second area stressed by interactionists is personal outlook and its effect on health and the use of medicine. Different groups of people approach and use doctors and hospitals differently. Differences in their life experiences influence the degree to which people become involved in their own treatment, which in turn influences the outcome.

Another major concern in medical sociology is the institution of medicine — the system by which sickness is treated in a society. All societies have medicine, but its nature varies widely. In some societies, traditional medicine dominates: illness is believed to be the result of spiritual forces, punishment for evil, or imbalances of natural forces. Scientific medicine, in contrast, assumes that every illness has a cause that can be identified through scientific observation, and that, with sufficient knowledge and experimentation, an effective treatment can be devised.

The tendency of scientific medicine has been to grow by defining an increasing number of problems and conditions as medical in nature. Sociologists refer to this as *medicalization*. As medical care has expanded, it has become more costly. From a conflict standpoint, both of these trends reflect the power and self-interest of medical providers. This has been especially true in the United States, which has a private medical-care system based on ability to pay. Within this system, unrestricted third-party payment became the rule for most Americans during the mid-twentieth century. For the majority who have insurance, this system has meant good health care, but spiraling costs (for employers, insurance companies, and government). However, many of the working poor and unemployed lack any health insurance and must depend on "charity care." A limited number of poor Americans are covered by Medicaid. This system has provided them with previously unavailable medical care, though they are often treated in less-desirable settings than the rest of the population.

As costs have soared, government, employers, and the insurance companies have tried a variety of cost-cutting techniques, among them prospective payment, utilization reviews, HMOs, deductibles and copayments, and increased use of proprietary hospitals. Unfortunately, these changes have made things even harder on those without health insurance — a group that grew dramatically during the 1980s. Problems such as these have led many analysts of American medicine to suggest the United States consider adopting one of two alternative systems common among industrialized countries: national health insurance or national health service. In countries that have these systems, health and longevity are equal to, or better than, in the United States, and costs are lower.

Glossary

medicine An institution found in all societies, whose purpose is to treat illness.

sick role A social role played by people who are recognized by others as having a sickness, which exempts them from normal role obligations.

acute disorder A medical disorder of limited duration, which is followed either by rapid recovery or death.

chronic disorder An extended or ongoing medical disorder from which a patient cannot expect to recover.

epidemiology The measurement of the extent of medical disorders in a population, and the social, demographic, and geographic characteristics of those with such disorders.

illness The condition that occurs when an individual believes that he or she has a medical disorder.

sickness A condition in which a person is recognized by others as having a medical problem or disorder.

disease A condition defined by a medical practitioner as the cause of an illness.

health A condition in which a person can function effectively on the physical, mental, and social levels.

placebo A nonmedicated substance that can provide relief against an illness because patients believe that their condition is being treated.

medicalization A trend whereby an increasing number of conditions and problems are defined as diseases and treated by the institution of medicine.

medically indigent The condition of lacking health insurance and not having sufficient resources to pay for one's own health care.

fee-for-service payment A method of payment for health care in which providers receive a set amount of money (fee) for each service that they provide.

health maintenance organization (HMO) A medical coverage plan in which members prepay their health care and receive services as needed without a fee.

third-party payment A system of health-care payment in which providers of health care are paid by someone other than the patient, usually government or an insurance company.

national health insurance A governmentally mandated system of health insurance for the entire population, based on fee-for-service payment, that is funded through taxes or through a combination of taxes and employer-paid insurance.

national health service A system of health care operated by the government, in which doctors become salaried employees of the government or are paid a fixed amount per patient.

Further Reading

COCKERHAM, WILLIAM C. 1989. *Medical Sociology,* 4th ed. Englewood Cliffs, NJ: Prentice Hall. A comprehensive introduction to the sociology of medicine. Cockerham discusses the social aspects of health and illness, the medical and nursing professions, the hospital, and the health-care systems in the United States and other countries.

CONRAD, PETER, AND JOSEPH W. SCHNEIDER, 1980. *Deviance to Medicalization: From Badness to Sickness.* St. Louis: Mosby. Examines the medicalization trend that was discussed in this chapter. Conrad and Schneider show how various problems and behaviors have come to be defined as illnesses or diseases and to be treated accordingly. The book explores the causes of this medicalization trend, as well as its consequences, not only for the medical profession, but also for the larger society.

CORLESS, INGE B., AND MARY PITTMAN-LINDEMAN. 1987. *AIDS: Principles, Practices, and Politics.* New York: Hemisphere. A collection of essays by experts in various specialties related to AIDS. These essays provide information on the medical, social, and political aspects of the disease.

PAYER, LYNN. 1988. *Medicine and Culture.* New York: Holt. Writing with the nonprofessional audience in mind, Payer examines ways in which cultural differences influence how illness is defined and treated in different societies. She demonstrates that these differences exist even among industrialized countries, all of which practice scientific medicine.

STARR, PAUL. 1982. *The Social Transformation of American Medicine.* New York: Basic Books. This award-winning book examines major trends in American medicine during the twentieth century, largely from a conflict perspective. It shows how the medical profession gained control of third-party payment, which led to uncontrolled inflation in American medicine, and ultimately to a situation in which government and business acted to limit their medical costs, with some loss of power and autonomy for the medical profession.

TWADDLE, ANDREW C., AND RICHARD HESSLER. 1977. *A Sociology of Health.* St. Louis: Mosby. An introduction to the field, with special attention to the interactionist perspective. Addresses such issues as the social construction of health and illness and the differences and similarities between modern and traditional medicine.

PART 5

SOCIAL CHANGE

I n this final part of the book, we examine a number of the ways in which human societies undergo change. In Chapter 17, we examine population and aging. Over the past several hundred years, dramatic changes have taken place in the size, composition, and age structures of human populations. As the chapter shows, these changes are both the causes and consequences of other important social changes, such as urbanization, modernization, and industrialization.

Chapter 18 addresses urbanization — the transition from a predominantly rural society to a predominantly urban one, along with the consequences of living in an urban society. Urban lifestyles, urban power, and urban problems are all addressed in this chapter.

Although technology, population change, and urbanization are important sources of social change, there are other more abrupt and dramatic sources of change, which are addressed in Chapter 19. Often, social change is the product of sudden and seemingly unpredictable actions on the part of massive numbers of people acting collectively. The full range of such actions is discussed in Chapter 19, Collective Behavior and Social Movements.

Finally, in Chapter 20, we shall see how the forces discussed throughout the book combine to bring change to society. Most social changes are not the product of one event of social condition, but many. In this chapter, we shall also examine various theories about the direction of social change.

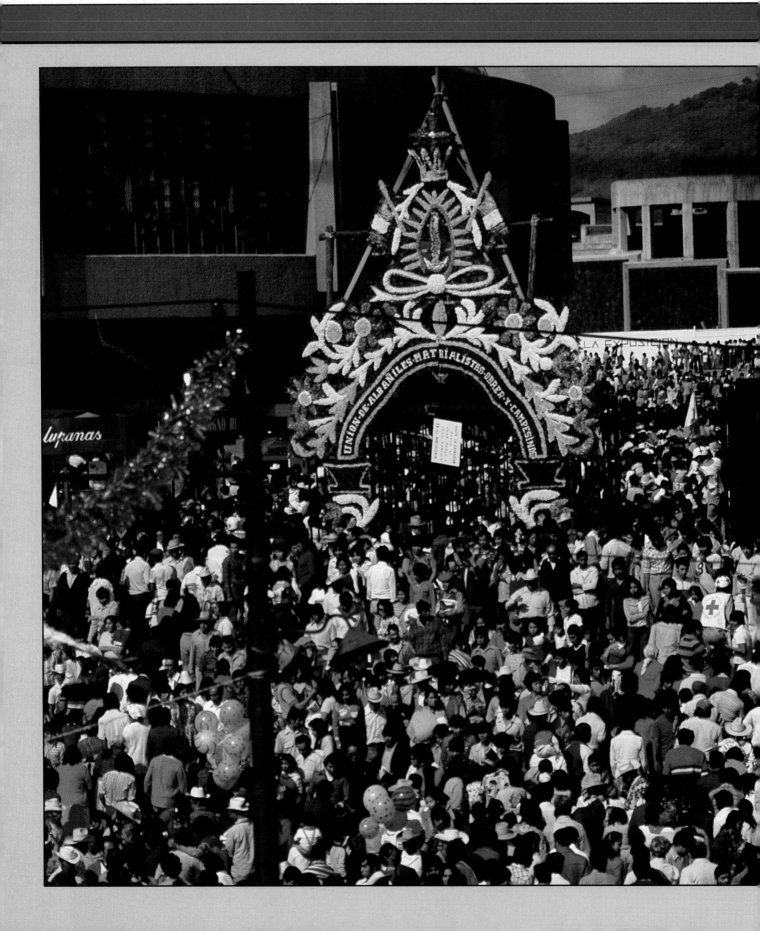

CHAPTER 17

Population and Aging

Consider the following situations:

- *You want a career that will enable you to help people, but you also want to be sure of finding a job. Would you be better off going into a health-related field or teaching?*

- *You hear two politicians making competing claims about whether it will be necessary either to raise social security taxes or to cut social security benefits. Is there any way to tell who is right?*

- *You want to open a second branch of your business, and you have the choice of doing so in two different communities. Is there any way to tell which community would give you more customers?*

- *You wonder whether your children will face a better economic future than your own, or whether they will fare no better, or possibly worse.*

- *You are divorced or widowed at the age of 45 and want to remarry. How easy will it be for you to find a new partner?*

- *You have heard some people say that the world's future is threatened by a ''population explosion''—population growth so rapid that the world's resources will run out, and mass starvation and international conflict will threaten human survival. How great is this risk?*

A lthough these situations concern a variety of seemingly unrelated questions, they share one important element. All raise a question that concerns the study of human populations, known as **demography.** The answer to the first question, for example, depends in part on likely changes in the *age structure* of the population in coming years. If a large increase in the number of children is expected, opportunities in teaching will improve. If, instead, the most rapidly growing segment of the population is the elderly, the health fields would be a good choice, because the elderly are relatively high users of health care. The answer to the question about Social Security depends greatly on *future population changes.* The ratio of the working-age to the retirement-age population at any given time in the future is especially critical. If there are more retired people relative to the number of workers, then either each worker must pay more or each retiree must get less (unless money is taken or borrowed from some other source).

The answers to all the other questions also depend, at least partially, on demography. Some places are more desirable than others to locate any given business, because they have more of the kind of people likely to buy the products sold by that business, or because they are likely to become "growth markets." Your children's economic future will depend in part on whether they enter a crowded or uncrowded employment market when they finish school, and that will depend largely on whether they are graduating with a lot of other people or only a few. If you are 45 and looking for a marriage partner, your chances will depend in part on whether there are more or fewer single people of the opposite sex in your age group. Thus, although only the last question (concerning the "population explosion") is explicitly about population, population is part of the answer to every one of these questions.

Because of its many practical applications, demography is one of the areas of sociology most in demand today. Businesses, government, educational institutions, labor organizations, and a curious public have all turned to *demographers* to provide information and advice (Merrick and Tordella, 1988). In this chapter, we shall see what kind of information demographers use, and some of the key ways they use it. We shall give special attention to one aspect of demographic change: the aging of the population of the United States and other industrialized countries. In so doing, we shall examine how roles are attached to age, and, in particular, the roles of the growing number of older people in industrial societies.

The Three Basic Demographic Variables

The size, growth, and characteristics of all human populations are determined by three basic forces, referred to by sociologists as the *three basic demographic variables.* These variables are *fertility,* or birth rates; *mortality,* or death rates; and *migration.* Because these basic variables are the building blocks of all studies of population, we shall describe each in more detail.

Mortality

In one sense, mortality might not be thought of as a variable; after all, everyone dies once and only once. Yet, in a *population* great variations occur in the number of deaths, and these variations are what demographers mean by **mortality.** One way that mortality varies is in the number of deaths that occur each year relative to the size of the population. This aspect of mortality is measured by the **crude death rate** — the number of deaths in a year per 1,000 people. This measure, however, is influenced by the age structure of the population: A population with a higher proportion of older people will have a higher crude death rate. Another aspect of mortality is measured by **life expectancy,** the length of time the average person can be expected to live. Life expectancy is computed on the basis of the current risk of death in each year of life from infancy through old age. Thus, it is based on present mortality, but it is not influenced by the mix of old and young people in a population. Hence, if you want to compare mortality in populations with different age structures, life expectancy is the statistic to use. The average worldwide life expectancy in 1988 was 63 years. Life expectancy varies widely among different countries, ranging from a low of 35 in Sierra Leone to a high of 78 in Japan. Life expectancy in 1988 was 75 in the United States and 76 in Canada (Population Reference Bureau, 1988).

A concept different from life expectancy is *life span.* This term refers to the maximum number of years a form of life is capable of living. Life expectancy is never as great as life span because accidents, malnutrition, and inadequate medical care all lead to deaths that are, theoretically, avoidable. The human life span cannot be measured precisely because we have no way of determining the upper limit of life. The longest any human has been *known* to live is 119 years; that record was achieved by Shigechiyo Izumi of Japan (McWhirter, 1985). Although we cannot precisely know the human life span, we do know that beyond a certain age the human body suffers physical degeneration, which places some upper limit on how long human beings are capable of living. As societies modernize, life expectancy rises closer to life span.

Infant Mortality Another important measure of mortality is the **infant mortality rate** — the number of deaths in a year of children less than 1 year old per 1,000 live births. The infant mortality rate is especially important for two reasons. First, it is a sensitive measure of nutrition and access to health care, because newborn infants are among the most vulnerable members of the population. Second, it has a disproportionate effect on life expectancy, because the death of an infant means the loss of many years of potential life. In 1988 the average worldwide infant mortality rate was 77. The variation in infant mortality is tremendous, ranging from a high rate of 183 (in other words, almost one baby out of every five) in Afghanistan to a low of 5.2 in Japan. The infant mortality rate of the United States in 1988 was 10.0; in Canada it was 7.9 (Population Reference Bureau, 1988).

Fertility

Fertility refers to the number of births occurring in a population. It means the number of actual births, in contrast to *fecundity,* which refers to the number of births a woman is *capable* of having. Fertility is more complicated to measure than mortality because (1) only some people — women of childbearing age — are capable of having babies, and (2) the same person can have more than one baby. One measure of fertility is directly comparable to the crude death rate. It is the **crude birth rate,** which is the number of births in a year per 1,000 population. Like the crude death rate, this measure is influenced by the age structure of the population: It will be higher in a population where more of the women are in the childbearing ages, roughly 15 to 49. It may also be influenced by the sex composition: If there is a higher percentage of women in the population, the crude birth rate might be higher.

For this reason, demographers often use another measure of fertility. This measure, the *total fertility rate,* is the number of babies that the average woman can be expected to have over her entire lifetime, based on current patterns of fertility. As with life expectancy, total fertility rate is a better figure to use if you are comparing different populations or groups that have different age structures. Worldwide, the total fertility rate in 1988 was 3.6. In other words, the average woman in the world can be expected to have 3.6 children over her lifetime if fertility rates remain as they are now. The countries with the highest total fertility rate, 8.5, are North Yemen and Rwanda, East Africa. The world's lowest total fertility rate, 1.4, is found in three European countries: West Germany, Austria, and Italy. The total fertility rate of the United States is 1.8; in Canada it is 1.7 (Population Reference Bureau, 1988).

Migration

The third basic demographic variable is **migration,** which occurs whenever people change their places of residence from one location to another. Migration may be broken down into two components: *in-migration,* which refers to the number of people moving into some geographic area during a fixed period of time;

and *out-migration,* which refers to the number moving out. These components can be combined to produce *net migration,* which is the total gain or loss of population in an area due to migration. Net migration simply equals in-migration minus out-migration. In-migration, out-migration, and net migration statistics may be expressed as numbers (how many people move) or rates (the number of movers per 1,000 population).

Migration can be an important force in the growth or decline of populations. In the early to mid-1980s, net migration into the United States accounted for between one-quarter and one-third of the growth of the American population (Bouvier and Gardner, 1986). The rest of the growth occurred because births exceeded deaths. For smaller areas, the impact of migration was greater. It is the main reason why cities gain or lose population over time.

The Basic Demographic Equation and Population Projections

As the preceding example suggests, the growth or decline of a population is determined by mortality, fertility, and migration. This is summarized by the following equation, called the *basic demographic equation:*

Population change = births − deaths + in-migration − out-migration

Another way to say the same thing is:

Population change = births − deaths + net migration

Although this equation seems simple, it is in fact very powerful and serves as the basis of all *population projections.* **Population projections** are estimates of the future size of a population based on assumptions about mortality, fertility, and migration. Importantly, population projections themselves are not predictions, but rather are statements of what will occur in a population under given levels of mortality, fertility, and net migration. The key to the accuracy of population projections, therefore, lies in the accuracy of our assumptions about what will happen to these variables. The difficulties involved in making accurate assumptions vary among the three variables. Mortality is

the easiest to determine. Modern demographic techniques enable us to predict the number of deaths in a population if we know its age structure and current patterns of mortality. Except in the case of catastrophes, mortality changes only gradually. Fertility is harder to predict, because we do not know if women will choose to have more or fewer babies in the future. Migration is the hardest of the three demographic variables to predict because it depends on economic and political forces that are hard to foresee.

The usefulness of population projections is not so much in making predictions about future population size as in answering "what if" questions. For example, how much would the population grow if life expectancy increased by 10 years? What would be the consequences if women suddenly decided to have twice as many babies as they are having now? What if immigration doubled, or suddenly stopped?

Moreover, population projections can answer specific questions about subgroups in a population as well as the population as a whole. We know, for example, that if anticipated fertility, mortality, and immigration patterns hold, by 2040, 42 percent of the U.S. college-age population will be either black, Hispanic, or of Asian ancestry, compared to less than 25 percent today (U.S. Bureau of the Census, 1986c, 1984b). This projection is likely to be fairly accurate because it is based largely on the mortality rates of people already born: Those who will be of college age through about half the period of this projection are already alive. Even this projection could be misleading, however, if birth rates or migration rates for the various groups deviate drastically from expectations.

Although such projections are only as good as the assumptions about fertility, mortality, and migration they rest on, projections are a tremendously important tool for any type of planning for the future, including social-services planning, business and investment decisions, political strategies, and estimating tax revenues and expenses. To continue the education example, projections like those above give college administrators and teachers some idea of the number of students in the future, as well as their social characteristics. They may also suggest new strategies—for example, recruiting students outside the traditional college ages when these age groups seem likely to shrink.

World Population Growth

Throughout most of human history, the population of the world grew only very slowly. Then, rather suddenly around 250 years ago, it began to increase, until in recent years it has reached levels that would have seemed unimaginable just a few centuries ago. In this part of the chapter, we shall examine how and why such a dramatic change has taken place.

A History of Population Growth

The growth of the world's population is illustrated in Figure 17.1. From the beginnings of humanity until about 10,000 years ago—a period of more than 1 million years—the world's population grew only to about 8 million (Cipolla, 1965; Coale, 1974). That is less than the present population of Michigan or Florida. From about 10,000 years ago until around A.D. 1750, the world's population increased from 8 million to about 800 million. This was a much more rapid rate of growth, but it has been dwarfed by growth rates of the last 250 years. The world's population first reached 1 billion around 1820. By 1930 it reached 2 billion. Three billion was achieved in 1960, 4 billion in 1976, and 5 billion in 1987. Thus, it now takes only about 10 years to add 1 billion people, in contrast to the 1 to 3 million years it took to add the first billion. Recall that 10,000 years ago the world's population had just reached 8 million; today it takes about 5 weeks for the world's population to grow by that amount. This rapid world population growth has been referred to as the *population explosion.*

Why has the world's population grown so dramatically in the past few hundred years? The answer to this question revolves around two factors—

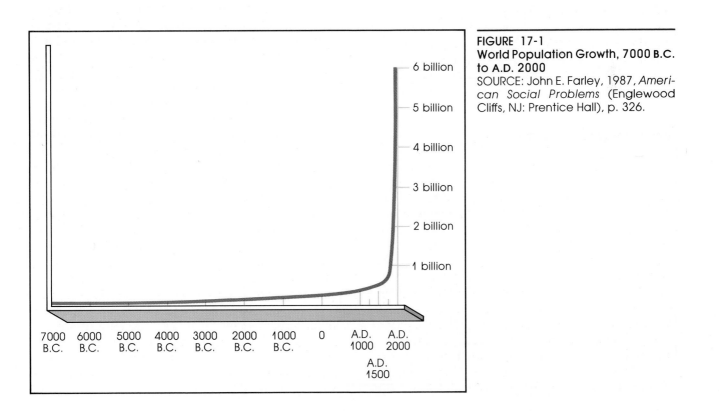

FIGURE 17-1
World Population Growth, 7000 B.C. to A.D. 2000
SOURCE: John E. Farley, 1987, *American Social Problems* (Englewood Cliffs, NJ: Prentice Hall), p. 326.

exponential growth and the demographic transition. We will examine both in more detail.

Exponential Growth

Exponential growth is defined as growth at a fixed percentage rate, which results in greater growth in numbers each year. This concept can be illustrated by comparing the world's population in 1950 and 1985 (Weeks, 1986, p. 56). In both years, population was growing at a rate of 1.7 percent per year. In 1950, the world's population was about 2.5 billion. Thus, a 1.7 percent growth rate meant that 43 million people were being added each year. By 1985, the world's population was 4.9 billion; a 1.7 percent growth rate now meant an annual increase of 83 million people.

When populations grow exponentially, they double at certain intervals. This *doubling time* is estimated by dividing 70 by the percentage growth rate (Weeks, 1986, p. 54). Thus, at the current rate of population growth of 1.7 percent, it takes the world's population about 41 years to double. A growth rate of 2 percent would imply a doubling time of 35 years; a growth rate of 3 percent 23 years; a growth rate of 4

percent about 17 years; and so forth. If the world population were to grow indefinitely at its present rate, it would reach 10 billion in 2028, 20 billion in 2069, 40 billion in 2110, and so forth. Obviously, it could not continue to grow at this rate for very long because an upper limit would be quickly reached.

The Demographic Transition

The exponential nature of the growth of human populations shows why they can grow so rapidly, but it does not tell us much about the underlying forces that drive that growth. To do this, we must return to the basic demographic equation outlined above: population growth equals births minus deaths plus net migration. Because we are talking here about world population, we can disregard net migration. Basically, as long as births and deaths each year are roughly in balance, the world's population will remain constant. When births exceed deaths, it will grow.

The recent experience of rapid world population growth is explained by a process called the **demographic transition,** which is depicted in Figure 17.2.

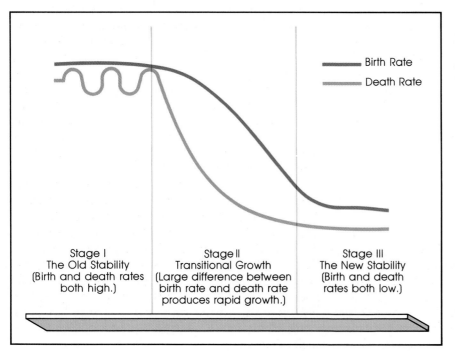

| | Birth Rate |
| | Death Rate |

Stage I
The Old Stability
(Birth and death rates both high.)

Stage II
Transitional Growth
(Large difference between birth rate and death rate produces rapid growth.)

Stage III
The New Stability
(Birth and death rates both low.)

FIGURE 17-2
The Demographic Transition
SOURCE: John E. Farley, 1987, *American Social Problems* (Englewood Cliffs, NJ: Prentice Hall), p. 331.

The demographic transition has three distinct stages. In the first stage, birth and death rates are both high. Because they are in balance, there is little or no population growth. In the second stage, the death rate falls, but the birth rate remains high. This produces rapid population growth. In the third stage the birth rate falls and returns to a new balance with the death rate. In this stage, birth and death rates are both low, and because they are again in balance, population growth slows or ends.

How does the demographic transition explain the world's population explosion? To answer this question, we must consider industrialized and preindustrial societies separately. Most societies that are today industrialized have gone through the entire process of the demographic transition. They began to do so around 250 to 300 years ago, which explains why the world's population began to grow rapidly around that time. Although they have completed the demographic transition and now generally have low growth, the situation is very different elsewhere. The less-industrialized countries of the world, which account for over three-fourths of the world's population, are today in the middle stage of the demographic transition. Their death rates have fallen, but their birth rates remain high. Thus, their population is growing rapidly, and because they represent the majority of the world's population, the world's population is also growing rapidly. Will they follow the experience of Europe and North America, or will they be different? To address this question, we must consider the forces that brought about the demographic transition in the industrialized countries and compare them to the social forces currently at work in the Third World.

The Demographic Transition in Europe and North America

Declining Mortality   Until about 250 or 300 years ago, mortality was very high. The typical life expectancy ranged from 20 to 30 years, and to have two or three children who would live to be adults, a woman typically had to have from four to six babies (Weeks, 1986, p. 55). Mortality varied sharply from year to year owing to famines and epidemics, but over the

long run, the numbers of births and deaths per year were fairly close.

In Europe and North America, this pattern began to change about the same time industrialization began to occur: the death rate started to fall. It fell enough so that a substantial gap was opened between births and deaths: every year more people were born than died. This trend developed, not because women had more babies, but because more babies lived to adulthood and had babies of their own. Thus, a family who might have once had two of their children survive to adulthood now had three or four survive to adulthood, and each of these in turn gave birth to three or four children who survived to adulthood.

In Europe and North America, this decline in mortality occurred gradually, beginning around 1700. At that time, the main causes of death were malnutrition and contagious diseases. Over the next 2 centuries, these conditions claimed fewer and fewer lives for a variety of reasons, including increased food supply, better shelter, improved transportation to get food to people, and the development of vaccinations against contagious diseases. Many of these changes were the result of rising standards of living, brought about by new technologies. Especially important, though, were improvements in sanitation. As recently as the eighteenth century, it was commonplace to throw garbage (including human waste) into the street or the nearest stream, which also served as the source of drinking water. The importance of washing one's hands was not understood, even by surgeons. Thus, advances such as sanitary sewers, trash collection systems, water pumping and filtration, and simple knowledge of the importance of cleanliness and sanitation were major causes of the decline in mortality (Thomlinson, 1976, pp. 97–99).

You will notice that I have not mentioned the treatment of illness as a cause of declining mortality. This is because medicine was not very scientific until after about 1900, and many historians believe that doctors killed more people than they saved until about that time (Conant, 1952). Since then, however, the effects of medicine on mortality have been substantial, and a mortality decline that began through better sanitation and rising standards of living has been reinforced by increasingly sophisticated medical technology.

Declining Fertility   As noted above, the decline in mortality in the industrialized countries led to a period of rapid population growth. Gradually, though, fertility also declined, and today birth rates are only slightly above death rates in most industrialized countries. The trend in the total fertility rate of the United States illustrates this point. In 1800, the average American woman had more than seven children over her lifetime, compared to less than two today (Coale and Zelnick, 1963; Population Reference Bureau, 1988). The one exception to this downward trend was the baby boom of the 1950s and early 1960s, a temporary but large surge in fertility that occurred in most industrialized countries. By the 1960s, however, the downward trend had resumed, and birth rates today are well below those of the period just before the baby boom. As illustrated in the box, there are even a few countries, like West Germany, where birth rates are *lower* than death rates (van de Kaa, 1987).

Birth rates in the United States, Europe, and other industrialized countries have fallen for a number of reasons. One factor is the decline in mortality itself. As more children survived into adulthood, the pressure to give birth to a large number of offspring diminished. Also important, though, were social and economic changes that came with a rising standard of living. People began to feel greater control over all aspects of their lives, including the number of children

they had (Tabah, 1980). Gradually, "as many as God provides" was replaced with "as many as I want." Also, people increasingly put off having children in order to attain such goals as more education and a higher standard of living (Coale, 1973). Postponement of childbearing usually means having fewer children, because the number of years during which a woman can give birth is limited.

The movement of women into higher education and the labor force has also helped to lower the birth rate, because employed women have fewer babies than nonemployed women, and because women's birth rates decline as their education and job status increase (U.S. Bureau of the Census, 1984c; Hallouda, Amin, and Farid, 1983). As society modernizes and industrializes, the costs and benefits of having children change. In agricultural societies, children are often an important source of labor; in industrialized societies, they are mouths to be fed, and the cost of educating them is substantial (Caldwell, 1982). Finally, of course, birth-control techniques improved dramatically and became available to more women.

Third-World Demographic Transition

As noted above, the death rates of most preindustrial countries of the Third World have fallen, while their birth rates remain high. In 1988, for example, the overall crude death rate for the world's less developed countries, which contain over three-fourths of the world's population, was 10. This was almost as low as the rate for the more-developed countries, which was

---

American family portraits, 1900 and 1989. These portraits illustrate the downward trend in fertility in the twentieth century.

Zero Population Growth: Present and future

Zero population growth—a situation in which a population stops growing—has already been attained in Austria, Denmark, East and West Germany, Hungary, and Italy. In all these countries, the birth rate is at or below the death rate, and the population is stable or—in the case of West Germany—declining. In West Germany, for example, the 1988 population was 61.2 million; at current mortality, fertility, and immigration rates, that number will decline to 59.6 million by the year 2000 and 51.5 million by 2020 (Population Reference Bureau, 1988a).

If we disregard for a moment the effects of migration, we can see that zero population growth will occur whenever the birth rate is at or below the death rate. Over the long run, this will happen when the total fertility rate remains at or below the *replace-ment level* of 2.1. This represents the number of children the average woman must have over her lifetime in order for each generation to replace itself exactly. The number is 2.1 rather than 2.0 because some women die before they reach childbearing age, and others must have slightly more children to compensate for this.

Although only those countries noted above have attained zero population growth, dozens of others have total fertility rates below the replacement level of 2.1, including the United States. Why, then, haven't these countries reached zero population growth? One reason, of course, is that some, like the United States, have a good deal of immigration. However, even without immigration, the United States would not yet have zero population growth. The reason is *age structure*: Because of the high birth rates of the 1950s and early 1960s, there are now a large number of women of childbearing age (15 to 44). Moreover, the number of people in this age group has grown over the past few decades. Thus, there are huge numbers of women having babies—more than enough to offset the number of deaths. This is true even though each woman is having fewer babies than women had in the past.

Over the long run, though, the United States and many other countries will attain zero population growth if their fertility remains below the replacement level, once the irregularities of age structure have "smoothed out." In the United States, for example, the population would grow until about the year 2030 and then begin to decline, if fertility and mortality remained at their current levels and there were no immigration (Weeks, 1986, p. 233).

---

9. Fertility, however, is another story: The crude birth rate of the less developed countries was 31 in 1988, compared to just 15 in the more developed countries (Population Reference Bureau, 1988). There are various ways to interpret this statistic.

Demographic Transition Theory One interpretation is offered by demographic transition theory. Demographers of this school believe that most Third-World countries are currently in the middle stage of the demographic transition, and they predict that the birth rates in these countries will fall over time and thereby create a new balance between births and deaths, as happened in the industrialized world. Evidence in support of this viewpoint can be found in the fact that the worldwide growth rate has fallen from a little over 2 percent in the late 1960s to 1.7 percent today. Also, the birth rate in a number of preindustrial countries has already fallen by one-third or more since the early 1960s (Merrick, 1986). Demographic transition theorists predict a continuing decline in the world's population growth rate (Tsui and Bogue, 1979; Merrick, 1986). A closely related argument is that new technology will lead to heightened productivity that will at least partially offset the effects of population growth, and therefore the degree of growth anticipated need not be a cause for alarm (Simon, 1981; Simon and Kahn, 1984). Demographic transition theory is sometimes associated with the functionalist perspective because it views societies as tending naturally to adjust to ensure their long-term survival.

Malthusian Theory A very different and more pessimistic interpretation is offered by Malthusian theory, reflected in the writings of Coale and Hoover (1958), Meadows and colleagues (1972), and in a 1980 report of the U.S. Council on Environmental Quality. Malthusian theory is named for Thomas Robert Malthus, a prominent English population theorist who wrote around 1800 (see Malthus, 1965 [orig. 1798], 1872). Malthus believed that while population increases exponentially, food production could grow only by a fixed annual amount. For this reason, he thought that a worldwide crisis resulting from overpopulation was inevitable. Present-day Malthusians recognize that many other factors besides food supply limit growth. In general, they see the current rapid growth of the world's population as potentially catastrophic. They argue that the current and probable future growth rates will carry the world's population beyond what the earth can support, and they note that the numbers of people being added are dramatically greater now than when Europe and North America were in the middle stages of the demographic transition. They also argue that important differences exist between the experiences of European and Third-World countries that will make it harder for the latter to restore their population balance as easily as the Europeans

did. As a result, they predict that the birth rates of Third-World countries are unlikely to fall enough to avert disaster unless extreme measures are taken. We shall explore these differences shortly, but first we turn our attention to a third theory about world population growth.

Marxist Population Theory Marxist population theory emphasizes *maldistribution,* rather than the danger of running out of natural resources, as the main cause of suffering in the world. Traditionally, Marxists denied any risk of overpopulation. They claimed instead that there would be sufficient resources for everyone if some people did not consume far in excess of what they need. However, rapid population growth has led to some alteration of that view, so that today most Marxist countries in the Third World have sought to reduce their birth rates. Indeed, the most dramatic case of success in doing so is the People's Republic of China, where the total fertility rate has declined from somewhere in the range of 6 or 7 in the early 1960s to just 2.4 in 1988 (Lavely, 1984; Merrick, 1986; Population Reference Bureau, 1988). Today, Marxists point out that maldistribution greatly worsens the effects of overpopulation and can create great suffering even when there is no overpopulation. They also note that if scarce resources are redistributed so as to improve the standard of living of the poor, birth rates will fall (Ahmad, 1977). Importantly, Marxists agree with demographic transition theorists on one point: an improving standard of living will lead to a decline in the birth rate. However, the two approaches disagree on how to bring about an improvement in the standard of living.

Evaluating the Theories Each of the three theories about the population future of the Third World might offer part of the answer. Demographic transition theorists are almost certainly right to predict a continuing decline in the world's rate of growth. By the turn of the century this decline could lead to a leveling off, and eventual decline, in the *number* of people being added each year (Merrick, 1986; United Nations, 1985). Nonetheless, several differences exist between the situation in the Third World today and that in Europe when it experienced its demographic transi-

---

The one-child family is a matter of public policy in China. Although Marxist theory argues that maldistribution, not overpopulation, is the cause of human misery, most developing countries with Marxist governments are trying to reduce their birth rates.

tion. Among the most important of these differences are the following:

- The decline in mortality has occurred much more quickly in the Third World than it did in Europe, which has given people less time to adjust their fertility patterns to the new situation. Mortality declines that took over 200 years to occur in Europe and America have happened in a far shorter time in the Third World. In Mexico, for example, mortality has fallen as much in 50 years as it did over 500 years in Europe (Weeks, 1986, p. 171).

- The decline in mortality in the Third World has been due to imported technology rather than domestic economic development. Thus, it has not been accompanied by the rising standard of living that took place in the industrialized countries. It is a rising standard of living (and people's response to it) that drives down fertility. Without it, there has been less downward pressure on birth rates in the Third World.

- In part because they have not yet industrialized, many Third-World countries have extremely unequal distributions of wealth and income. As Marxists argue, this means that even when the resources exist for a rise in the standard of living, only a few people benefit, and thus only a few share in the experiences that led to lower fertility in the industrialized countries. Although these conditions also prevailed in Europe at the start of the Industrial Revolution, they began to break down with fuller industrialization and the growth of an urban trading class. Today, in the Third World, much of the wealth produced by industrialization goes to foreign investors.

- Education remains highly limited in many Third-World countries, and education is one of the main forces that lowers fertility. In the small number of Third-World countries that do have well-developed educational systems, such as China, Taiwan, Korea, and Sri Lanka, birth rates have fallen dramatically (see World Bank, 1988, pp. 276–281).

- In many Third-World countries, the role of women remains traditional, though great variation exists from one country to another. In general, where women are more educated and more involved in the labor force, fertility falls.

For all these reasons, fertility in the preindustrial Third World is likely, at best, to fall into balance with today's lower mortality only very gradually. Thus, the truth falls somewhere between the optimism of the demographic transition theorists and the pessimism of the Malthusians, but precisely *where* is hard to say.

It is important to realize that women must *want* to have fewer children if they are to lower their birth rates. In many Third-World countries, strong cultural values continue to support large families. In some countries, for example, only males can inherit property, which leads people to keep having babies until they have a boy. In other countries, a family's social status is determined largely by the number of children. The World Fertility Survey found that in the early 1980s the elimination of all unwanted pregnancies in 20 preindustrial countries would still have produced a birth rate more than twice as high as the death rate (Lightbourne, Singh, and Green, 1982).

POPULATION GROWTH AND THE FUTURE   One critical source of predictions concerning population growth is the United Nations population projections. These projections, shown in Table 17.1, are based on the assumption—which some regard as overly optimistic—that fertility will fall to about the replacement level by around 2040. If this process takes just 25 years longer, the world's population in the year 2100 will be over 14 billion rather than 10 billion (Merrick, 1986, p. 14). Note also that these projections show much larger growth in the less-developed regions than in the industrialized countries. By the year 2100, more than 85 percent of the world's population will be in what today are the less-developed regions of the world.

World Population Growth and Resources

Is the world in imminent danger of overpopulation? The answer seems to be that there is indeed a very substantial danger, but how great a danger is difficult to assess. Although we are fairly sure that the world's population will at least double during the next century (barring nuclear war), we do not know precisely how great the growth will be because we do not know how much and how fast the birth rate will fall. We know that the expected growth will create some problems, but just how severe those problems will be depends on a number of factors, which are discussed below.

Food Supply   One key factor is the level of agricultural production. A recent study predicted that in a "worst case" situation, in which all of the less-developed countries would have only traditional subsistence farming techniques, half of them would be unable to feed their populations without food imports by the year 2000. In the "best case" situation, where

TABLE 17.1
United Nations "Middle" Projections of the World's Population

| | ACTUAL POPULATION | | PROJECTED POPULATION FOR | | | | | |
| | 1988 | | 2000 | | 2025 | | 2100 | |
	Number (in millions)	Percent	Number	Percent	Number	Percent	Number	Percent
World total	5,128	100.0	6,122	100.0	8,206	100.0	10,185	100.0
Less developed regions	3,931	76.7	4,837	79.0	6,799	82.9	8,748	85.9
Africa	623	12.1	872	14.2	1,617	19.7	2,591	25.4
Asia (minus Japan)	2,872	56.0	3,419	55.8	4,403	53.7	4,919	48.3
Latin America	429	8.4	546	8.9	779	9.5	1,238	12.2
More developed regions	1,198	23.4	1,284	21.0	1,407	17.1	1,437	14.1
Europe, USSR, Japan, Australia, New Zealand	932	18.2	987	16.1	1,062	12.9	1,055	10.4
North America	272	5.3	297	4.9	345	4.2	382	3.8

SOURCE: Thomas W. Merrick, "World Population in Transition," *Population Bulletin* 41 (April 1986), pp. 12–13.

all countries would develop agricultural techniques like those of the United States, only about 15 percent would be unable to do so (Higgins et al., 1982). Almost certainly, the reality will fall somewhere in between, but even that case could be disastrous. In 1988, the Worldwatch Institute warned that the world's food supply had fallen dangerously low because of the combination of droughts, loss of farmland to erosion and urbanization, and continued population growth (*Newsweek*, 1988f).

PROBLEMS OF FOOD DISTRIBUTION Another key factor has to do with the social and economic systems of less-developed countries. Marxists correctly point out that inequalities greatly worsen supply problems. When one group consumes more than it needs, there is less for others. Thus, what is theoretically adequate food production does not feed everyone. Most experts agree that food production today is adequate to feed the world's population (Zopf, 1984), yet over 1 million people died of starvation in African famines during the 1980s. The reasons had to do with maldistribution and with the inability of many countries to pay for food, or even to distribute it when it is given to them for free. Another major barrier to feeding the hungry is warfare. Throughout history wars have prevented the delivery of food to people in areas suffering famines. For example, warfare between rebels and the government in Ethiopia has prevented food from reaching thousands of starving people (*Newsweek*, 1987, p. 56).

Because of overpopulation, maldistribution, and warfare, starving children are an all-too-common reality in today's world.

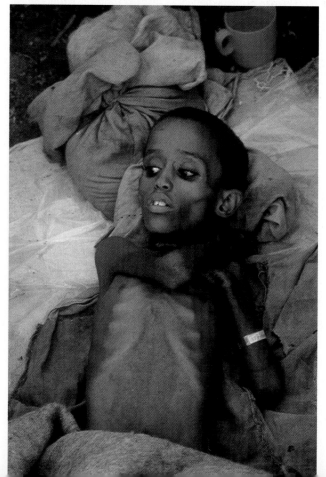

The Supply of Energy and Mineral Resources Besides food, the world could run out of various energy and mineral resources. Because today's standard of living depends so heavily on modern production and transportation techniques, running out of these resources could be as serious as running out of food. It could, in fact, lead to a food shortage by preventing the production and transportation of food. The potential consequences of such shortages were illustrated in the 1970s, when a short-term shortage of oil led to a worldwide economic recession.

The risk of depleting energy sources does not come simply from rising population. At least as crucial is the amount of energy consumed per person. The industrialized countries, because their standard of living depends on it, consume far more energy, as well as mineral resources per capita, than do the preindustrial countries. Moreover, as countries industrialize, their energy consumption inevitably increases. Consequently, world energy consumption has risen much more rapidly than world population. As recently as the 1970s, world energy consumption was increasing at an annual rate of 7 percent, which implied a doubling of consumption every 10 years (Turk et al., 1978). The oil crisis forced an end to that rate of growth, but world energy consumption is still increasing faster than population. The average annual rate of increase between 1983 and 1986 was 2.76 percent (computed from United Nations, 1988, p. 3). This rate implies that world energy consumption will double every 25 years. Thus, although the rate of increase has declined, a further decline might be difficult to attain, if the standards of living of the less-developed countries are to be raised. Raising these standards of living requires industrialization, which in turn requires energy.

FUTURE PROJECTIONS Does this mean that the world will soon run out of energy and mineral resources? We do not know the answer to this question. We can reasonably assume three things. First, new energy reserves will be discovered, although we do not know how much. Second, new technologies for generating energy will be developed. Third, both new technology and conservation measures offer the opportunity to do more with the energy we have. All of these facts mean that energy will last longer than current projections would indicate. The problem is that we don't know *how much longer*. An optimistic view is that the three factors outlined above will allow us to get by *for a very long time* (Simon, 1981). A pessimistic view is that these developments will not be enough, and that only drastic conservation measures can prevent a genuine, long-term world energy crisis (Council on Environmental Quality, 1980). An especially disturbing aspect of this view is that people are likely to resist such conservation measures because they would mean a lower standard of living.

There is clearly some upper limit to energy supplies that can eventually be reached, but we do not know what that limit is. We do know that if it is ever reached—especially if at a time when energy consumption is growing rapidly—a catastrophic situation could develop very quickly. Consider that at current rates energy consumption will double every 25 years. An implication of this is that once we have used half the world's resources, it will take only 25 years to use up the rest (see Turk et al., 1978, p. 210).

POSSIBLE STRATEGIES Two relatively painless courses of action can help to reduce (though probably not eliminate) this real, if unknown, risk. One is for the industrialized countries to hold down energy use through better efficiency. In 1986, for example, Japan used less than half as much energy per person as the United States, despite its high standard of living. Switzerland actually enjoyed a higher standard of living than the United States but used 44 percent less energy per person (World Bank, 1988, p. 241). Canada and Norway, on the other hand, squandered away 20 percent *more* energy per person than the United States. Clearly, increased efficiency in countries like the United States, Canada, and Norway could help.

The second course of action that could reduce the threat is a slowing in the rate of population growth. The desires of less-developed countries to industrialize and of industrialized countries to remain prosperous will create pressures for rising energy consumption. Yet, if population grows more slowly, there will be fewer people to consume the scarce resources. Fortunately, economic growth does tend to reduce population growth, which offsets some of the tendency to consume more energy. Still, to minimize the risk of a world energy crisis, it will be necessary simultaneously to hold down population growth rates and to maximize efficiency in the use of energy.

There are indications that people are finally rec-

As illustrated by this photo, Switzerland enjoys the highest standard of living in the world. Yet, per-capita energy consumption in Switzerland is barely more than half that of the United States.

ognizing these realities. According to the Population Reference Bureau (1988), 67 of the world's governments—including most in Africa, Central America, and southern Asia—view their fertility rates as too high; 69 view them as satisfactory; and only 22 view them as too low. Thus, many governments in parts of the world where fertility is too high *are* making efforts to lower it. Many of these efforts have been successful. Similarly, energy conservation measures are beginning to pay off. In the industrial market economies, the average annual increase in energy consumption from 1980 to 1986 was just 0.4 percent—compared to 3.0 percent from 1965 to 1980. Thus, the doubling time has increased from 23 years to 175 years.

The Population of the United States

Over the past few decades, the population of the United States has undergone a number of major changes. These changes, all of which are the products of mortality, fertility, and migration patterns, have affected the population's size, age structure, geographic distribution, and ethnic composition. Indirectly, these changes have affected crime rates, economic opportunity, product markets, and national politics.

Decreasing Mortality

One of the most consistent trends in the United States has been a decrease in mortality. As shown in Figure 17.3, life expectancy has increased steadily for men

FIGURE 17-3
Life Expectancy at Birth, According to Race and Sex: United States, Selected Years 1900–1985
SOURCE: National Center for Health Statistics, Division of Vital Statistics, National Vital Statistics System.
NOTE: Until 1940, all nonwhites were classified under "all other." The overwhelming majority of people in this category were black.

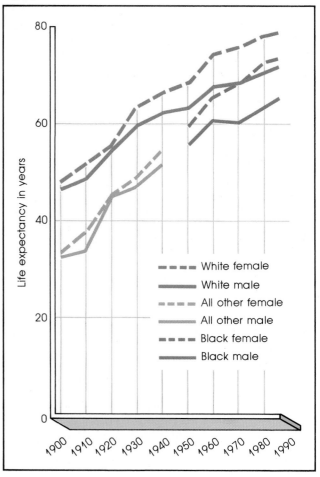

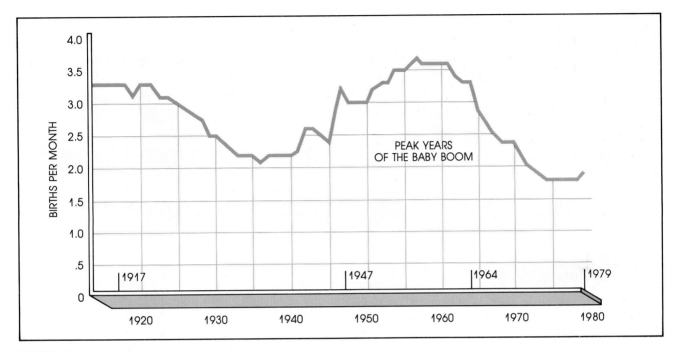

FIGURE 17-4
Total Fertility Rates for U.S. Women: 1917–1987
SOURCES: 1917–1975: Selma Taffel, *Trends in Fertility in the United States,* Vital and Health Statistics, Series 21: Data from the National Vital Statistics System, No. 28 (Hyattsville, MD: National Center for Health Statistics, 1977), Table 13; 1976–1977: U.S. Bureau of the Census, *Statistical Abstract of the United States, 1979,* Table 82; 1978: U.S. Bureau of the Census, "Population Profile of the United States: 1978," *Current Population Reports,* Series P-20, No. 336, Table 3; 1979: National Center for Health Statistics, Natality Division, personal communication, April 1980. Portion of figure pertaining to 1917–1979 is reprinted from *Population Bulletin* 35, 1, p. 5, published by Population Reference Bureau.

and women of all races throughout the twentieth century. This is one reason why the average age of Americans alive today is the highest ever recorded and continues to rise. Although life expectancy is rising in the United States, there are several countries in which people live longer, and the United States is not even among the lowest 20 countries in terms of infant mortality. Although mortality has fallen significantly, changes in fertility and migration have had greater impacts on the size and composition of the American population.

Changing Fertility: Baby Boom, Baby Bust

Although mortality influences the age structure of a population, the long-run effects of fertility are much greater (Weeks, 1986, p. 214; United Nations, 1954). Whenever a nation's birth rate moves sharply up or down, that movement will shape that nation's age structure for years. This has been the case in the United States during the twentieth century. We have already mentioned the *baby boom,* the major surge in the birth rate that occurred in the United States and other industrialized countries just after World War II. The baby boom was preceded and followed by the two periods of *lowest* fertility on record: the "baby busts" of the Great Depression of the 1930s and the Oil Crisis era of the 1970s. (See Figure 17.4.)

Birth Cohorts: The Baby Boom These sharp variations in fertility have produced great fluctuations in

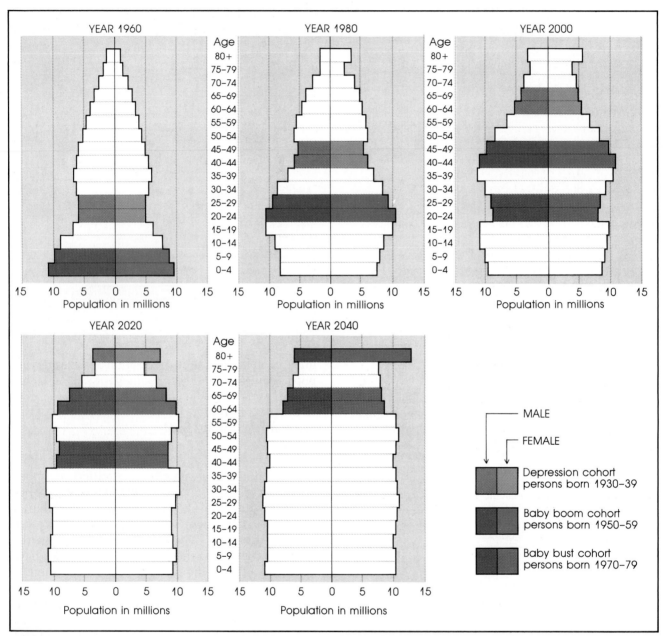

FIGURE 17-5
Age-Sex Pyramids for the United States: 1960–2040
SOURCES: 1960–1970: U.S. Bureau of the Census, *1970 U.S. Census of Population: General Population Characteristics, United States Summary,* Vol. I, PC(1)-B1, 1972, Table 52; and 1980–2050: Special unpublished tabulations prepared by Leon F. Bouvier for the Select Commission on Immigration and Refugee Policy, 1980.
a Includes survivors of Depression cohort.

b Includes survivors of baby boom cohort.
NOTE: 1980–2050 projections assume a total fertility rate rising to 2.0 births per woman by 1985 and constant thereafter; life expectancy at birth rising to 72.8 years for males and 82.9 years for females by 2050; net immigration constant at 750,000 persons per year.
Figure is reprinted from *Population Bulletin* 35, 1, p. 19, published by Population Reference Bureau.

the age structure of the United States (Bouvier, 1980). These fluctuations are depicted, in 20-year intervals from 1960 to 2040, in the age-sex pyramids shown in Figure 17.5. The baby boom *birth cohort* is shown in green. A **birth cohort** is a group of people who were born during some given time period. In the case of these age-sex pyramids, the birth cohort of the baby boom is defined as the 1950s.

Look at the changes shown in the pyramids, and consider their consequences. In 1960, there was a shortage of young adults in their twenties, but a sizable number of children under 10. The 1960s were a decade of prosperity, in part because young adults faced uncrowded job markets (Easterlin, 1968, 1978). The decade also began with overcrowded elementary schools and ended in a state of social upheaval led largely by a huge and restless cohort of college students. Throughout the country, new elementary and secondary schools—and later, new colleges—were opened to accommodate the mass of baby boomers.

Now look at the pyramid for 1980. By this year, the elementary-school children of the 1960s were the young-adult generation. They crowded the job market, and they did so precisely when the world economy was greatly strained by the oil crisis. As a result, they encountered much harder times: unemployment and inflation soared through most of the 1970s (Easterlin, 1978). Moreover, many of these young adults had experienced the student rebellions and the antiwar and civil rights movements, and they were less optimistic and family-oriented than their parents. Therefore, they waited longer to get married, and when they finally did marry, they had far fewer children. Between 1957 and 1973, the total fertility rate fell by 50 percent. In other words, the typical woman was having half as many babies over her lifetime.

As the 1980 pyramid shows, the job market had become overcrowded, and the schools were relatively empty. One congressional study found that by 1985 the typical 30-year-old male earned 25 percent *less* than his counterpart in 1973, after adjustment for inflation (*St. Louis Post-Dispatch*, 1985). In many cities, schools built just 20 years earlier to accommodate the baby boom were closed for lack of students. Colleges increasingly turned to "adult students" rather than the traditional college-age group. These changes haven't just influenced job opportunity or the demand for schooling. They have also influenced product markets, as the "growth" industries shifted from baby food in the 1950s through stereos and rock music in the 1960s, apartments and singles bars in the 1970s, and VCRs, single-family homes, cable television, and travel in the 1980s. (If you had money to invest, what industry would you select for the 1990s?) Another example where the effects have been quite significant is the crime rate, as is illustrated in the box entitled "Demographics and the Crime Rate."

The projected pyramids for 2000, 2020, and 2040 forecast a surge in the middle-aged population, followed by a dramatic increase in the proportion of the population over 65. The implications of this trend will be discussed later in the chapter.

Migration within the United States

Between 1980 and 1986, there were wide variations in the growth rates of the different states. Some, like Illinois and Pennsylvania, experienced very little growth. Others, like Florida and Arizona, grew by more than 15 percent. Four states—Iowa, Michigan, Ohio, and West Virginia—actually lost population (Crews and Cancellier, 1988). For the most part, these changes did not occur because of differences in mortality and fertility. Rather, they happened because people moved. This process can be illustrated by looking at Iowa. Between 1980 and 1986, there were 103,000 *more* births than deaths in Iowa, which by itself would have resulted in a 4 percent population increase. However, Iowa *lost* population because so many people moved out: the number of out-migrants exceeded the number of in-migrants by 166,000 during this same time period. As a result, Iowa's population declined by 63,000.

Migration and the U.S. West In general, the recent migration trends in the United States have been away from the Midwest and East (except New England) and toward the West and South. Between 1980 and 1986, all the midwestern states had more people move out than in, as did all of the more populous northeastern states, except New Jersey. The experience in the South and West was just the opposite: 13 out of 16 southern states had more in-migrants than out-migrants, as did 9 of 13 states in the West. The

Demographics and the Crime Rate

Throughout the 1960s and 1970s, the incidence of street crime in the United States rose. Between 1969 and 1981, for example, the overall rate of FBI Index Crimes rose from under 3,700 crimes per 100,000 population to more than 5,700 (Federal Bureau of Investigation, 1979, 1983). Many people interpreted this development as a sign that American society was falling apart. America was getting soft on crime, and the old values of honesty and respect for the rights of others were on the decline. After about 1981, the crime rate leveled off, and even declined in some years. This, it was said, proved that the new "get tough on crime" approach advocated by Ronald Reagan was working.

It turns out, though, that there is a simpler explanation for much of the variation in the U.S. crime rate. If arrest statistics are any indication of the ages at which people commit crimes, then it is clear that a very large share of street crime is committed by people between the ages of 15 and 24. Thus, an increase in the share of the population in this age group will produce an increase in the crime rate, and a decrease in their share will produce a decline in crime. The share of the population in this age group *did* increase between 1970 and 1980, because the peak wave of the Baby Boom birth cohort moved from the 5–14 age group in 1970 to the 15–24 age group in 1980. For the same reason, it began to decline thereafter.

How much of the changes in the crime rate did these changes in the age structure cause? Demographer John Weeks (1986, pp. 230–232) found part of the answer by using arrest rates for each age group in 1970 and computing what the change in the overall arrest rate *would* have been had the arrest rates remained constant *within each age group* until 1980. This represents the change in arrest rates that would have been produced by age structure changes alone. He then compared this to the actual changes in the number of arrests and found that 43 percent of the increase was the result of age-structure change. This suggests that nearly half of the increase in street crime happened because more people were in the crime-prone age groups. This result was highly consistent with an earlier study of crime increases conducted in the early 1960s by the National Crime Commission, which estimated that 40 to 50 percent of the increase then was attributable to changes in the age structure. The leveling off of crime rates after 1980 is also partly the product of age structure, because the share of the population in the crime-prone age groups has fallen since 1980 and will continue to do so through the early 1990s (Cohen and Land, 1987).

---

westward portion of this migration reflects a long-standing trend: The population center of the United States has shifted toward the West every year since the first U.S. Census in 1790. However, the impact of this shift on the Midwest and Northeast is greater now than in the past because of changes in foreign immigration. Throughout much of U.S. history, immigrants entered the United States through New York or other eastern ports and settled mainly in the Northeast and Great Lakes states. Thus, as Americans moved west, they were replaced by new Americans arriving as immigrants, and population growth in the East was sustained. Today, however, most immigrants are arriving in the South and West, particularly California, Texas, and Florida. This shift reinforces rather than offsets the internal migration patterns, because the states receiving the most immigrants are the ones that are already growing most rapidly.

Migration and the U.S. South   Although migration to the West has been going on throughout U.S. history, the shift toward the South is more recent. In the late nineteenth and early twentieth centuries, the South was economically depressed compared to the rest of the country. It was less industrialized, and had more poverty and lower levels of wages and education. As a result, people moved away to seek opportunity in other parts of the country (Hamilton, 1965). Blacks had another reason for moving out of the South: the desire to escape the blatant racial discrimination that was pervasive there. With time, however, the economy of the South began to grow, and federal laws banning deliberate racial discrimination and segregation were passed in the 1960s. By the 1950s, more whites were moving into the South than out, and by the 1970s, the same was true for blacks (Biggar, 1979).

Reasons for Migration   Today's migration within the United States reflects, in large part, shifts in the U.S. economy (Wilson, 1988). The economy of the Northeast and Midwest depends substantially on heavy manufacturing and agriculture. Both have suffered as factories have closed or automated and farms have gone out of business or consolidated. The result has been especially devastating in cities strongly dependent on one industry, such as Detroit and Flint, Michigan (auto manufacturing); Pittsburgh, Pennsylvania, Gary, Indiana, and Granite City, Illinois (steel mills); and Waterloo, Iowa, and Peoria, Illinois (tractor manufacturing).

At the other end, of course, are the receiving areas. With more diversified, service-oriented economies, states like California, Arizona, Colorado, and Florida have fared better. Their climates and recreational amenities have also attracted both people and businesses. The aging of the population—and the relative affluence of today's older Americans—has accelerated this trend. Retired people who want a pleasant climate with good recreational opportunities have migrated to states such as Florida and Arizona. For a time, areas like Texas, Oklahoma, and Wyoming enjoyed a gigantic boom because of their oil and energy resources, although this trend slackened abruptly when the price of oil fell in the mid-1980s (Crews and Cancellier, 1988). Wyoming, Oklahoma, and Louisiana, for example, all *lost* population between 1987 and 1988 despite their earlier rapid growth (Population Reference Bureau, 1988b). Although such short-term trends will influence the precise amount of migration into specific areas, the long-term prospect is for a continued, if possibly slower, movement of population from the Midwest and Northeast to the West and South. Both agriculture and manufacturing are becoming less labor-intensive, with machines doing more of the work, which means that job growth is at best likely to be slower in the Midwest and Northeast than elsewhere. Although these areas will make vigorous attempts to attract the growing service industries

—and have already had some success in doing so—they are at some disadvantage in terms of noneconomic factors such as climate, scenery, and recreational opportunities. Though these factors were once unimportant in determining where people moved (people went where they knew someone or had a job lined up), their importance has grown and is likely to continue to do so (Thomlinson, 1976, p. 318). For these reasons, little or no population growth is projected for the Midwest by the year 2010, and only modest growth is projected for the Northeast. In contrast, the populations of the South and West are projected to grow by 25 and 32 percent, respectively (Population Reference Bureau, 1988b).

Immigration into the United States

Throughout U.S. history, immigration has played a varying role in the growth of the nation's population. In the first decade of the twentieth century, immigration accounted for 40 percent of population growth, continuing the heavy immigration pattern of the nineteenth century. After that, the Asian exclusion laws of 1907 and 1917 and the immigration quota acts of 1921 and 1924 greatly reduced immigration; the Great Depression temporarily stopped it altogether. When the immigration laws were reformed in 1965 to eliminate quotas that prevented most immigration from the Third World, the portion of growth accounted for by immigration rose to around 20 percent, and by the 1980s, it was nearly 30 percent. Between 1980 and 1985, annual legal immigration into the United States averaged just under 600,000 people (computed from Bouvier and Gardner, 1986, p. 44).

One reason that a bigger share of the nation's growth today comes from immigration is that low birth rates have reduced the rate of growth from the excess of births over deaths. Another reason, though, is that the rapidly growing population of the Third World is increasing immigration pressure on *all* industrialized countries. Although we think of the United States as having a great deal of immigration, its rate of immigration relative to its population is in fact near the average for major industrialized countries. In the 1980s, for example, the percentage of foreign-born people in the American population was 6.2, compared to 1981 figures of 7.5 in West Germany, 6.8 in France, 5.0 in Sweden, and 3.9 in the United Kingdom (van de Kaa, 1987). These figures, of course, include only legal, or documented, immigration. We know that there is also a significant amount of undocumented immigration (and emigration, because some people come only temporarily), but we do not know how much. Informed estimates of annual net illegal immigration (immigrants minus emigrants) range from about 100,000 to 500,000 (Bouvier and Gardner, 1986; Passel, 1986).

Not surprisingly, immigration is bringing about important changes in the racial and ethnic composition of the U.S. population. Between 1981 and 1985, for example, 48 percent of legal immigrants came to the United States from Asia, and another 35 percent came from Latin America (Bouvier and Gardner, 1986). However, immigration is just one force that is changing the ethnic face of America.

The Changing Composition of the U.S. Population

In Chapter 11, we noted that the populations of African Americans, Hispanic Americans, Asian Americans, and American Indians are all increasing faster than the overall U.S. population. As a result, the percentage of all these groups in the U.S. population is growing and will continue to do so for some time. The combined percentage of the American population in these four groups rose from 13.6 percent in 1950 to 22.4 percent in 1987, and it should exceed 30 percent by 2020 (Crews and Cancellier, 1988). By that time, it is projected that 14.3 percent of the U.S. population will be black, 11.1 percent Hispanic, and 5 percent Asian and American Indian.

The reasons for the increases vary from group to group. Both blacks and non-Hispanic whites are relatively scarce among current immigrants, but the black population is growing modestly faster than the white population because the black birth rate is about 30 percent higher (U.S. Bureau of the Census, 1981, p. 3; 1983, pp. 29–35). In general, the American Indian population appears to be growing at a pace similar to that of the black population, given that it has similar or somewhat higher birth rates and no immigration. However, it is hard to say precisely how fast the American Indian population is growing because many people of mixed ancestry who identified themselves as white in the 1970 Census identified themselves as Indian in 1980. Thus, the 50 percent increase in the Census Indian population between 1970 and 1980 was more than could possibly have taken place through births alone.

The fastest-growing groups in the United States are Hispanic and Asian Americans. On a sheer percentage basis, Asians are the fastest growing: Their population more than doubled between 1970 and 1980, and may have nearly doubled again since then. This growth is due to high rates of immigration: More legal immigrants during the 1980s have come from Asia than anywhere else. As a result, it was estimated that the combined Asian and American Indian population (over 80 percent of which is Asian) had reached 7.9 million by 1987 (U.S. Bureau of the Census, 1988a). Fertility is *not* a major factor in that growth: The Asians' birth rate is lower than that of other racial groups. The Hispanic population, in contrast, is growing rapidly because of both high immigration rates and high birth rates. Between 1980 and 1988, the Hispanic population of the United States rose from 14.6 million to 19.4 million, or 8.1 percent of the population (U.S. Bureau of the Census, 1988b).

The Aging of the U.S. Population

One of the most important changes within the U.S. population is that it is getting older. This trend is occurring in all industrialized countries, for two reasons. One is related to the increases in life expectancy that have taken place in recent years. Much more important, however, are the low birth rates that have predominated since the early 1970s (Soldo and Agree, 1988). Whenever the birth rate falls, the population gets older on the average, because the percentage of young people declines. Moreover, as long as the birth rate remains low, the population will continue to get older until the baby boom generation dies off, which will likely occur between about 2030 and 2040.

Today, about 12 percent of the American population is 65 years old or older. This reflects an increase from around 9 percent in 1970 and 4 percent in 1900. The present percentage will hold steady until around 2010, but after that time it will increase sharply as the baby boomers begin to reach old age. By 2020, the percentage will be about 17 percent, and from 2030 through 2050 it will hover around 21 to 22 percent, reaching 60 million people (double the present total) by 2040 (Soldo and Agree, 1988; Bouvier, 1980). In countries where the birth rate has fallen even further than in the United States, these trends are still more pronounced. In West Germany, which has the world's lowest fertility rate, more than 15 percent of the population is already over 65, and by 2025 it is projected that 22.5 percent will be (van de Kaa, 1987). Sometime between now and then, West Germany will become the first country in the history of the world to have more elderly people than children.

Implications of an Aging Population The implications of such changes are enormous. To cite one, political support for education could decline, particularly in places that rely heavily on property taxes to pay for it. Product markets will change significantly, and the crime rate may well continue to fall. Because older people are more likely to vote, and because they vote differently than younger people, there will be major political effects as well. There will also be new pressures on the health-care system, which may increase the already rising costs of health care, discussed in Chapter 16. But perhaps most important of all will be the impact upon private and public pension systems, and—very likely—upon society's conceptions of the role of the elderly.

Both social security and some private pension systems have been funded on the premise that funds collected from today's workers pay for today's retirees, and funds collected from future workers will pay for future retirees. Until recently, this worked well because high birth rates meant that the labor force was sufficiently replenished with young workers to take care of the growing number of retirees. However, the soaring number of elderly people has affected this balance, and a real crunch will occur when the baby boomers begin reaching retirement age around 2010.

By that date, there will be significantly fewer people paying into social security and private pension systems for each person drawing benefits. In the case of social security, Congress has responded by implementing a gradual increase in the social security tax, raising the income level above which there is no social security tax, and reducing or delaying some benefits. Whether these changes will succeed in averting a financial crisis in the social security system in the next half century is uncertain. If they do not, further benefit reductions or tax increases may be necessary. One factor that affects the viability of social security and other pension systems is the age at which people retire. The need for further tax increases and benefit cuts may therefore be alleviated by eliminating expectations that people stop working by the age of 65.

Although the changing age structure of the population will require changes in pension systems, it is a mistake to think of older people simply as a dependent population who must be supported by others. In fact, older people create an important and growing product market, and as such serve as an important stimulant to the economy. Many Americans are employed in industries that provide a variety of goods and services to senior citizens, and as the older population grows, such employment will likely also grow.

Aging and Ageism

Aging As a Biological Process

On one level, aging can be seen as a biological process. Up to a certain age, around late adolescence, the body grows and develops. During this part of life, there is a steady increase in both intellectual and physical capabilities. At that point, the human body reaches something of a physical peak. Once the peak is attained, the body remains relatively unchanged for a time, until a very gradual and often quite irregular process of physical degeneration sets in. Ultimately, this process of degeneration leads to death, even if disease or accident does not intervene prematurely. Degeneration includes wrinkling of the skin, a reduction of height and muscle mass, reduced sensations of taste, smell, touch, vision, and hearing, and changes in the circulatory system. Women typically lose the ability to have babies between the ages of 40 and 50, but their sex drive does not go away; it may even intensify (Weg, 1985). The rate at which the physical changes associated with aging occur varies widely from one person to another (Kart, 1976). At any given age, some people

Aging in America

The 1980 Census reports that approximately 1.3 million elderly people in this country now live in old-age institutions. As gerontological researchers have made us aware, the risk of an aged person being institutionalized during his or her lifetime is about one in four. Estimates are that the number of elderly people requiring institutional care will grow by more than 70 percent by the end of the century.

In the face of these expected dramatic increases in the long-term care needs of the elderly, concern continues to be expressed about whether health-care resources are being used efficiently to meet the needs of the elderly population. Some people argue that those who could be cared for in nursing homes or at home remain in hospital beds, and that people in nursing homes could be cared for at home with proper supportive services. The unnecessary use of hospitals and nursing homes that occurs all too frequently is seen as a shortcoming of current governmental programs and policies for the aged.

Identifying the causes of this overuse is difficult. For example, does overuse simply reflect a lack of availability of a wide range of services in a community so that people have to make do with what is available — such as nursing home care — even

Cary S. Kart is Professor of Sociology at the University of Toledo. He received his Ph.D. from the University of Virginia in 1974. He is a Fellow of the Gerontological Society of America. The third edition of his gerontology text, The Realities of Aging (Allyn & Bacon), will appear in 1990. He is also co-author (with E. and S. Metress) of Aging, Health and Society (Jones and Bartlett, 1988).

when home care would be adequate? Determining the causes of overuse of nursing homes is made more difficult by our general lack of knowledge about the process by which older people enter this segment of the health-care system and are assigned to different levels of care within old-age

institutions. My own research has explored this placement process. In addition, I have experienced it first-hand.

After the death of my maternal grandmother, some 25 years or so ago, my grandfather and uncle moved from Brooklyn to an apartment in Queens, New York, located across the street from where I was living. My uncle had never married and, devoted to his parents, had resided with them for most of his adult life, although he was employed full time. The new proximity to us allowed my mother (and, to some extent, my father, sister, and me) to stop in, say hello, run errands, and carry out assorted household chores for my grandfather while my uncle was at work. My grandfather did not walk very well and was generally apartment-bound. This was especially the case during the winter season. After he experienced several falls, it became apparent that he could not be left alone in the apartment for any length of time. Increasingly he spent his days on our living-room couch and, with equal attention, watched television and observed the family activities around him. His health deteriorated, at first slowly, but then more speedily. My recollection is of several hospitalizations before we decided to look for a nursing home.

are heavily affected by these processes, whereas others are affected hardly at all. Moreover, these changes do not necessarily represent a steady, irreversible process (Riley and Bond, 1983). Changes in diet or lifestyle, for example, can significantly alter

these processes, and even halt or reverse some of them for varying amounts of time.

Moreover, some processes thought natural to aging do not occur in most individuals. It is often believed, for example, that memory and intellectual

Today, we would be defined as family caregivers, or even as an informal social-support system. In recent years, a large body of research has developed that describes the role of family members in the decision to institutionalize an elderly relative. This work suggests that presence of family may be an important factor in delaying, if not preventing, the institutionalization of a chronically ill elderly person. In much of this research, the family is seen as a mediating social support that helps the individual cope with the vagaries of old age and reduces the immediate need for institutionalization.

For a long while, and for reasons not unrelated to the personal experience cited above, I have been interested in the process by which older people are placed in old-age institutions. In a recent work (carried out with Neil M. Palmer) I asked: How do we explain the level of care received by the institutionalized elderly? Do those institutionalized elderly people who have the greatest impairment receive the most intensive care? Or do alternative social factors, such as age, gender, or the presence or absence of family caregivers, provide a better explanation of the distribution of aged persons across available levels of care inside nursing homes?

Analyzing data from the 1977 National Nursing Home Study, we found that a number of influences affect the way care is distributed in U.S. nursing homes. Demographic variables, including age, gender, and marital status, along with the source of payment for institutional care (government assistance versus payment by personal funds) and need (measured by the number of chronic illnesses diagnosed), had direct effects on the level of care received by institutionalized elderly people.

Of particular interest is the finding that factors seemingly unrelated to illness or impairment influence the level of care received by older people in nursing homes. It seems easy enough to understand why those elderly who are most ill would be more likely than those less ill to receive intensive nursing care, but why would those with a spouse present be more likely than those who had never married to receive intensive nursing care? One explanation is that spouses can provide (and/or organize) lower-level care in the residential home setting, thus postponing entry into the nursing home until it is absolutely necessary for intensive nursing care. Absent such family resources, those elderly who have never married might

employ the nursing home as an alternative, more secure, long-term residential site.

Should we expect greater congruence between the needs of the institutionalized elderly and the services offered in nursing homes? Perhaps an expectation of rationality in this sector of the health-care system is unreasonable for at least three reasons. First, 25 years ago there were no guidelines to assist families such as mine with a nursing-home placement decision, and this remains true today. Second, approximately 75 percent of nursing homes are in the private sector—this is, after all, a free enterprise system. The care of institutionalized older people for profit, coupled with cost-plus reimbursement formulas to fund care for the poor, have encouraged pervasive and acknowledged exploitive practices by some nursing-home operators. As a result, patients in need only of personal care, for example, find themselves placed in high-level, skilled nursing facilities. Finally, government efforts to control nursing home abuses have been aimed primarily at reducing costs rather than at improving quality and providing a more efficient match between patient need and level of care.

functioning fail as we get older; the term *senility* is used to describe this process. We now know, however, that much of what was once called senility is the result of disease. One such illness is *Alzheimer's disease,* a fatal, degenerative brain disorder that is present for years but generally does not show visible symptoms until after the age of 50 or 60. Only a small minority of older people have this disease, however; among the healthy majority, intellectual functioning is not usually affected by age. Even up to the age of 80, most healthy individuals show no decline in intellectual functioning, and when decline does set in, it can often be reversed by changes in the social environment (Riley, Foner, and Waring, 1988). This suggests that the decline is social rather than biological in origin.

Aging As a Social Process

The Social Construction of Age Groups   Although humans do undergo a physical process of aging, the meaning of that process is socially determined. In every society, there are **age groups**—social categories of people based upon age. These groups are not the result simply of the biological process of aging, and the precise age groups found in any society have little biological basis. Rather, age groups are *socially constructed*. The age groups that are familiar to us— infancy, childhood, adolescence, young adulthood, middle age, and old age—are creations of industrial society. In earlier ages, the norm was for people to work, marry, and have children at much younger ages than today. Marriage and childbearing often began around the age of 13, particularly in non-European societies (Hajnal, 1965). In Europe and the United States, work sometimes began as young as 6 or 7, and full-time work was the norm for people in their teens (Demos, 1970; Smelser, 1968). In such a society, the concept of adolescence makes little sense, and no such concept existed prior to industrialization.

The concept of old age is also largely an invention of the industrial era. With the high mortality that existed before industrialization, the death of relatively older workers (that is, people in their thirties, forties, or fifties) opened spaces for new workers, and these new workers needed little or no special training. As life expectancy increased, society was forced to open up spots for new, young workers while older people were still alive and working. This need led to the creation of both adolescence and old age as social categories. A retirement age, at which a person would be expected to leave the work force, was established in order to make room for new workers (Foner and Schwab, 1981). That the "normal retirement age" became established at 65 instead of some other age is probably a matter of historical chance; there is nothing distinct about that age (as opposed to, say, 60 or

A young boy at work in an American cannery in the early 1900s. When labor began as young as 7, there was no recognition of the age group we call adolescence.

70) in terms of human capability. Once established, however, the concept of a retirement age created a new age group, with a role very distinct from that of younger adults.

Likewise, the category of adolescence was developed to delay entry into the work force. Adolescence was also the product of the rising educational requirements of jobs under industrialization: Education delayed entry into the work force and created a new category of people sharing common experiences.

As you may have recognized, the preceding analysis is essentially functionalist: different sets of age groups are functional in different types of societies. In societies where there is no labor surplus and little technical knowledge is required for work, the age groups of adolescence and old age make little sense. With labor surpluses and advanced technology, however, these age categories become highly functional.

Age Stratification   As is true for other social categories such as race or sex, there is **age stratification,** or social inequality, between different age groups in all societies (Riley, Johnson, and Foner, 1972). In most societies, for example, children are relatively powerless. Throughout much of human history, children were treated terribly (DeMause, 1975). They were beaten in virtually all known societies before the twentieth century, often with whips, sticks, or closed fists. They were coerced into compliance with adult wishes through methods that today would be seen as "thought control." These included terrifying them with stories about witches and ghosts that punished bad children and taking them to see public hangings to show them what happened to "bad people." If they were the "wrong" sex (which usually meant female), they were frequently killed in infancy.

In modern industrialized countries, childhood is seen very differently, as a special or "protected" time of life (Aries, 1962). Parents try to give their children every opportunity and to shelter them from the ugly side of life (see Gronoval, 1984, pp. 8–9). (Can you imagine a school class being taken to witness an execution today?) Yet, children are still powerless, and vestiges of the old thinking remain. Many adults still endorse the biblical adage "Spare the rod, spoil the child," and, as Chapter 13 discussed, few children escape family violence altogether. Industrial societies generally agree that children should have few or no political rights. They cannot vote or hold office, and their rights of self-expression are severely limited. The U.S. Supreme Court ruled in 1988, for example, that high-school student newspapers do not enjoy freedom of the press in the same sense that newspapers owned and published by adults do (*St. Louis Post-Dispatch*, 1988d). Moreover, American children today may be suffering new disadvantages. They are more likely than any other age group to live in poverty, and half or more of them can expect to have at least one parent absent by the time they reach the age of 18.

STRATIFICATION AND THE ELDERLY Whereas children have consistently been a powerless group throughout history, the power and status of older people has varied dramatically over time and place. In many preindustrial societies, older people enjoyed an honored and powerful status (Cowgill, 1974). Where knowledge was passed on by verbal tradition rather than through a written scientific literature, older people were the main teachers. There is a tendency among some people in modern industrial societies to look back on this era with nostalgia, but like any other arrangement, it had its disadvantages as well as its advantages. The great power held by the elderly in many preindustrial societies meant that other,

younger adults had less power. Can you imagine a woman today being a servant to her mother-in-law as long as she lives, as was the case in ancient China? Can you imagine a man having to wait to own property, marry, and have children until his father dies, as was the case in medieval Ireland?

AGE GROUPS: THE CONFLICT PERSPECTIVE From a conflict perspective, the standing of an age group is determined by its power and resources. When one group gains power, another usually loses some. Thus, the greater power of the elderly in ancient China and medieval Ireland meant that younger people had less power than they have today. Today, the power of the elderly, and even of middle-aged adults, has declined because the younger, recent products of higher education are likely to have the most current scientific knowledge. This resource strengthens the position of the young: A recently trained professional has a big job-market advantage over a professional over the age of 50 who loses his or her job and must look for a new one. Even if such a person was laid off for reasons totally unrelated to performance, it can be difficult, even impossible, to find a job in his or her profession. The reasons: The middle-aged employee is seen as having fewer "years to give" and as being less up-to-date on the field than those with more recent training.

Because modern industrial society places such a high value on work, those who are out of the work force tend to be devalued by society. This leads to the devaluation of an entire age group—the elderly, who come to be seen as a dependent population, much like children. In fact, the terms *childlike* and *second childhood* are often applied to older people, implying that they are regressing to an earlier developmental stage (Arluke and Levin, 1985). The low esteem in which older people are held can be seen in results from a 1984 Roper Poll, which showed that fewer than 8 percent of the people in any age group under 60 viewed the retirement years as the best part of life— fewer than for any other age group, including childhood. (In contrast, it was the most frequently chosen period of life by people over 60, which might reflect either a tendency to pick one's own age as the best time of life or the discovery that the pleasures of retirement are a well-kept secret!)

Aging, Role Change, and Socialization

Age Roles You have all heard the expression "Act your age." This message illustrates what sociologists call **age roles:** the belief that people in different age groups should behave in different ways (Riley, Foner, and Waring, 1988). Age roles work in two ways. First are broad expectations about how people of a given age are expected to behave: "Big girls don't cry"; "You're too young to drink"; "People your age shouldn't dress that way." Second are age-related expectations about the other roles that people are expected to play, as reflected in such expressions as *preschool, school age, college age, working age,* and *retirement age.* Although society determines which age groups are appropriate for roles such as student, worker, parent, and retiree, these roles are sequential, and if you miss part of the sequence, you must often "pick up where you left off." This is illustrated by a study of former nuns who withdrew from society to enter a convent during their adolescence. When they returned to the lay world, they had to learn such roles as consumer, worker, and lover the same way any other high-school graduate would have to—except that they were much older than the typical high-school graduate (San Giovanni, 1978).

It is important to stress that age roles, like age groups, are socially constructed. Different societies have very different ideas about what is appropriate behavior for a particular age group, even if they do recognize the same age groups. To cite one example, sexual activity among teenagers is socially disapproved of in the United States but widely accepted in Sweden (Jones et al., 1986, pp. 222–223).

Like any other social role, age roles are learned through socialization (Mortimer and Simmons, 1978). We learn from others what behavior is expected of people in any given age group, and behavior that conforms to role expectations is rewarded, while other behavior is ridiculed or punished.

Rites of Passage Society often establishes rituals, called **rites of passage,** to mark the transition from one age role to another. Rites of passage abound in preindustrial societies, where they frequently involve elaborate ceremonies and painful rituals, such as cir-

cumcision. Rites of passage are also commonplace in industrialized societies, albeit in a different form. Examples are religious ceremonies such as the Catholic Confirmation and the Jewish Bar Mitzvah or Bat Mitzvah, which mark the transition from childhood to adolescence, and graduation ceremonies, which mark the transition from adolescence to adulthood. Weddings and retirement parties are also rites of passage. An important tradition associated with all of the examples listed above is the giving of gifts. These gifts serve as symbols of the person's new status (as in the case of the wedding gift), and sometimes as reminders of the age role that has been given up (as in the case of the gold watch that is often given at retirement).

Less-formal rites of passage also exist in our society, particularly for the transition into adult roles. These include such things as the first drink and the first sexual encounter. In fact, the status of such occurrences as rites of passage often leads adolescents into them. They drink or have sex not necessarily because they want to, but because our society identifies drinking and sex as normal adult behaviors, and they want to think of themselves as adults (see Ensminger, 1987). Some evidence suggests that for certain teenagers, particularly in areas of concentrated poverty, becoming a parent is a similar rite of passage. Thus, they have a baby not because they really want a child, but because being a parent will allow them to think of themselves as grown up (Wilson, 1987; Clark, 1965).

The Role of Older Americans Today

Old age brings on a number of changes in a person's social situation. In a sense, however, this transition is different from all the others that have gone before it. In industrial societies, moving into old age means giving up roles that are highly valued by society and moving into new roles that are less valued. Among the most important role changes associated with aging are the "empty nest," retirement, and widowhood.

The Empty Nest Old age usually involves giving up the role of parent. When the last child grows up and leaves home, parents no longer have the responsibilities, the activities, or the company associated with having children in the home. This probably represents a greater change today than in the past, and it also

When the youngest child leaves home in order to attend college, the "empty nest" age role begins for the parents.

comes earlier in life. In the early part of the twentieth century, it was commonplace for adults to live in their parents' homes at least until marriage, and often afterward. Today, the majority of young people leave their parents' homes shortly after high-school graduation. Many go to college, and those who do not frequently find their own homes. Many unmarried adults in their twenties live either by themselves, with a roommate, or with a lover. Whereas at one time it was common for older people to live with their married children, today this rarely happens except in the case of illness. As a result, the proportion of older people who live with their adult children has fallen dramatically (Thornton and Freedman, 1984). In one regard, however, this trend toward separate households for parents and adult children may be reversing: Very recently, there has been an upturn in the percentage of young adults living with their parents, to the point that in 1987 about half of all unmarried adults in their 20s lived with their parents (compiled from U.S. Bureau of the Census, 1988h, p. 9).

Although most older people seem to value the independence and free time that come when their children leave home, the transition to the empty nest can still be stressful. It reminds people that they are growing old, and they may feel ignored by their children, who are now kept busy juggling dual careers and children of their own (Williamson, Munley, and Evans, 1980, p. 107). It may be especially stressful for older people who were heavily involved with their children, and for older women who identify strongly with the traditional female role (Williamson, Munley, and Evans, 1980; Bart, 1973).

Old age does not, however, mean a loss of con-

tact with adult children. Although few older people live *with* their children, most live *near* their children and see them on a regular basis (Riley, Foner, and Waring, 1988; Shanas, 1979; Shanas et al., 1968; Cicerelli, 1983).

Widowhood For some elderly people, particularly older women, the loss of children in the home is followed by the loss of a spouse. Many more women than men will experience this loss. In 1987, for example, over one-third of women between the ages of 65 and 75 were widowed—compared to less than 10 percent of men (U.S. Bureau of the Census, 1988h, p. 3). At the age of 75, fewer than one out of four men is widowed, compared to two-thirds of all women (U.S. Bureau of the Census, 1988h, p. 3). There are two reasons for this difference. First, women live about 7 years longer than men on the average. Second, the man is older than the woman in the majority of marriages and that makes it even more likely that he will die before his wife. This tendency has become even more pronounced with today's high divorce rates, because the age difference between husband and wife is typically greater in second marriages than in first marriages (Riley, Foner, and Waring, 1988, p. 277).

Becoming widowed is stressful not only because of the grief of losing a loved one, but also because it represents a major role change and often leads to social isolation. One-third of all women 65 to 74 and 45 percent of those 75 and over live alone, mainly as a result of being widowed (Hess, 1985). People suddenly placed in a situation of living alone are at risk of experiencing severe effects of loneliness and isolation. Moreover, both men and women must learn to do the things that were formerly done by the spouse.

Retirement For those who spent much of their lives in the paid labor force—which is to say the great majority of older men and a rising proportion of older women—one of the biggest changes associated with growing old is retirement. Retirement as we now know it is a relatively new social invention. The notion of an age at which one is expected to quit working dates to the early days of industrialization, for the reasons discussed earlier. However, life expectancies in those times were short enough so that relatively few people lived to retirement age, and many of those who did were in ill health. As recently as 1900, the typical length of retirement for an American male was only about 1 year; by 1980, it was about 14 years (Riley, Foner, and Waring, 1988, p. 271). Thus, the lengthy retirement is a very recent phenomenon.

The portion of life spent in the retirement years is increasing for two reasons. First, people are living longer. Not until 1940 did the average American woman live to the age of 65; for men, that did not happen until 1950. By contrast, current life expectancies are about 78 for American women and 71 for American men (National Center for Health Statistics, 1988, p. 44). However, people who manage to survive to retirement age live longer than that. The typical 65-year-old American can expect to live another 17 years (Ehrlich and Garland, 1988, p. 120). The other reason retirement lasts longer is that people are retiring earlier. Three-fourths of men and over four-fifths of women who apply for social security retirement benefits do so before the age of 65; about half of all men are out of the labor force by the age of 62 (Parnes and Less, 1985). As a result of these trends, the retirement years are growing longer, and the working years shorter. For workers who take early retirement at 58, retirement commonly lasts for at least half as long as their working life (Ehrlich and Garland, 1988).

RETIREMENT: GOOD OR BAD? As was suggested earlier, the notion of retirement has been seen as functional in industrial society, because space must be made for new people entering the work force. However, as our discussion of social security and pension funds earlier indicated, this view may change with the aging of the baby boom generation, followed by the small "baby bust" cohort born in the 1970s. Rather than overcrowded labor markets, America could face a shortage of workers (Ehrlich and Garland, 1988). Certainly, social security and some pension funds will experience funding difficulties if the baby boomers retire around the age of 62. Moreover, there is no clear work-related reason for most people to retire at any given age. Overall productivity is just as high among workers in their sixties and seventies as among younger workers (Riley and Bond, 1983; Robinson, Coberly, and Paul, 1985; Special Committee on Aging, 1980), and problems such as drug and alcohol abuse are less common. In some fields, such as writing, philosophy, science, and politics, many people attain the peak of their accomplishments in their sixties or later. Ronald Reagan was 73 when reelected to the presidency in 1984. In the sciences and humanities, some studies have found that one-third or more of total lifetime productivity occurs after the age of 60. For further examples of achievement after the age of 65, see the box entitled "Achievement after 65."

Whether retirement is good or bad for people depends largely on what they are retiring from and what they are retiring to. Those who enjoy their work, work in a stimulating environment, and control their work situation can experience a real loss with retirement. Even "voluntary" retirement often occurs out of conformity to the social expectations of co-workers, friends, or family, as in "It's time for you to get out" (Williamson, Munley, and Evans, 1980, pp. 151–157; 159–162). However, people who view their jobs merely as a source of income eagerly anticipate retirement because it provides a reliable income while giving them the freedom to do what they "really want." Moreover, people with a number of interests and activities unrelated to work generally enjoy retirement and adjust to it very well (Williamson, Munley, and Evans, 1980, pp. 156–157, 160). Finally, retirement income makes a difference: Those with sufficient money to support themselves and their interests have better mental and physical health in retirement (see Crowley, 1986; Parnes and Less, 1985).

Maggie Kuhn, who at age 66 founded the Gray Panthers.

Achievement after 65

How productive can people be at work after the traditional retirement age of 65? Consider the following cases.

Eubie Blake: Retired at the age of 66, but made comeback to ragtime jazz career around the age of 80. Subsequently performed frequently at Newport Jazz Festival and on television specials. Performed at New York Philharmonic at age of 89 and issued three new LP record albums (and reissued two old ones) at age of 90. Was awarded Medal of Freedom at age of 98; died a few days after gala celebration held on his 100th birthday.

George Burns: At the age of 80, received the Academy Award for Best Supporting Actor. Later starred in seven movies, hosted a television series (as well as a special celebrating his 90th birthday), made two LP record albums, and was the author of two books.

Maggie Kuhn: At the age of 66, founded the Gray Panthers, a national organization concerned with the rights of senior citizens as well as a wide range of issues pertaining to peace and social justice. Subsequently wrote two books, maintained national speaking schedule, served as adviser to television series *Over Easy.* Won numerous awards and served on a variety of task forces, advisory boards, and committees. Continues these activities at age of 85.

Anna Mary (Grandma) Moses: Began a career in painting at the age of 78 that continued until her death at the age of 101. Painted more than 800 pictures that were displayed in over 65 exhibitions; won major art awards at the ages of 80 and 86.

Claude Pepper: Served in U.S. Congress until his death at the age of 89; chaired Florida delegation to 1984 Democratic National Convention at age of 81. Was a nationally recognized leader in writing of legislation pertaining to issues of concern to senior citizens.

Pablo Picasso: Created scores of paintings and sculptures between the age of 65 and his death at the age of 91, including massive sculpture in front of Chicago City Hall. At 80, was praised by *London Times Literary Supplement* for publishing "one of the greatest illustrated books of all time."

Income   Retirement typically means a decrease in income (Crowley, 1986). This does not necessarily mean that older people are at high risk of poverty; their expenses are typically lower than other age groups, and they also enjoy the protections of social security and Medicare (although these sources alone are not sufficient to meet most people's needs). Prior to these programs and to the growth of employer-paid pension funds, the poverty rate among older Americans was quite high, but it has since fallen dramatically. Cohort effects have also contributed to the decline. Today's generation of older Americans were children during the Great Depression, but they enjoyed prosperous times through most of their working years. Both because of the prosperity and because growing up in the Depression taught them to be cautious, they tended to save and invest, and some of them became affluent. In 1986, the poverty rate of people over 65 was 12.4 percent, lower than the over-

People who remain active and develop interests unrelated to work generally adjust well to retirement and old age.

all rate of 13.6 percent (U.S. Bureau of the Census, 1988c).

Even so, some elderly people are poor. The poverty rate is especially high among single and widowed older women. Because of their lower incomes, nonmarried women who retire may experience more financial difficulties than other retirees (Szinovacz, 1985). In some cases, the death of a husband means the partial or complete loss of pension income. As a result, the incidence of poverty among older women is well above the incidence of poverty in the overall population. For all women 65 and over, the poverty rate in 1986 was 15.2 percent; for single, widowed, and divorced women 65 and over, the poverty rate was over 20 percent (U.S. Bureau of the Census, 1988c, p. 33).

Disengagement versus Activity

All of the role changes we have discussed share one common element: leaving behind an important role that people have played through most of their adult life — parent, spouse, worker. Typically, both social scientific and popular views about aging have centered around such *disengagement,* or giving up of roles. The social-scientific version of this view is **disengagement theory** (Cummings and Henry, 1961). This theory is essentially a more sweeping version of the functionalist explanation of the role of retirement in industrial society: To sustain the society, space must be made for new people to take on roles and statuses essential for the preservation of society. For this to happen, older people must step aside and society must have a set of norms and rituals (like retirement parties) through which this occurs. It is also argued that disengagement from role obligations gives older people more opportunity to do the things they want to do.

Until recently, disengagement theory has been the dominant paradigm in the sociology of aging. Today, however, sociologists have been moving away from this theory, for several reasons. First, on the basis of capabilities, there is no good reason for disengagement at any given age. Second, the norm of disengagement is applied to all kinds of areas where it makes no

sense. Older people, for example, have traditionally been expected to lose interest in sex. There is no good reason, however, for the elderly not to have sex, and many are interested in sex and continue to engage in it, even if less often than when they were younger (Garza and Dresel, 1983; Weg, 1985).

Finally, considering today's demographic reality, the original reasons for disengagement may be waning. As we have seen, there will be a surplus of retired people and a potential shortage of working people in the coming decades. For all these reasons, and because older people are clearly better off when they participate in *some* socially valued activities, many social scientists today are paying increasing attention to **activity theory,** which holds that activity is essential to the positive self-esteem of older people and thus is good for their physical and mental health (Havighurst and Albrecht, 1953; Hochschild, 1975). According to this view, older people who wish to do so should be allowed to hold onto such roles as worker and lover, and that when they do give up a role, they should substitute a new one for it. Because it stresses the effect of role expectations on self-esteem, and the benefits of interaction with others, activity theory is generally associated with the symbolic-interactionist perspective (Friedman and Havighurst, 1954). In general, research has shown that older people who remain active experience better morale, greater adjustment, and higher personal satisfaction (Palmore, 1970; 1979; Havighurst, Neugarten, and Tobin, 1968). However, different people have different needs (Maddox and Campbell, 1985), so the relative appropriateness of disengaging, learning new roles, and continuing in old ones will depend on health status, personality, and other individual characteristics.

Ageism

By now, it is clear that there are considerable inequalities along the lines of age, and that people have distinct ideas about what is and is not appropriate for people of different ages. These realities in large part reflect the phenomenon of **ageism,** or prejudice and discrimination on the basis of age. Like racism and sexim, ageism may occur in thought, behavior, or ideology. It includes stereotypes about older people —"They can't remember," "They're bad drivers," or "They're conservative and stuck in their ways." Like any other stereotype, these beliefs are true for some people and false for others. What makes such stereotypes a form of prejudice is that they are often automatically applied to all older people. One of the most destructive forms of ageism is *ideological ageism* — the belief that certain age groups are inferior, which is then used to justify placing them in a socially disadvantaged position. An obvious example is the once widespread conviction that the work-related abilities of older people decline; for years this was used to justify mandatory retirement ages. The notion of the "second childhood" was similarly used to deprive older people of the opportunity to make their own choices. This mistaken notion has sometimes led people to engage in degrading behaviors such as talking about older people in their presence as if they aren't there, or talking down to them as if they cannot understand normal adult conversation.

Although older people are the major victims of ageism, no age group escapes it entirely. The so-called generation gap, though exaggerated, reflects the stereotyped thinking of adolescents and adults against one another. In the 1960s and early 1970s, a popular saying among rebellious college students was "Never trust anyone over 30."

People who are in socially devalued age groups often display ageism toward their own age group, wishing they were older or younger. Teenagers frequently exaggerate their age in order to gain access to some role, such as employment, that is forbidden to people below a certain age. Middle-aged adults approaching old age often understate their age, or refuse to state it at all. This practice is especially common among middle-aged women, which reflects a response to both ageism and sexism. Appearance is more important to women than men because society has traditionally rewarded women more on the basis of how they look and less on the basis of what they do. At the same time, the dominant view is that you have to be young to be attractive. Not only has this view led many women to conceal their ages; it has also made

the restoration of youth into a multimillion-dollar industry, including cosmetic products such as skin creams, medicines, and vitamin therapies, and a burgeoning business in cosmetic surgery.

Death and Dying

The Changing Meaning of Death

The final step in the aging process is death. Although we think of death as a natural or biological event, many aspects of death are social in nature. We have already seen some examples of this. One is the postponement of death through a rising standard of living and the application of technology to lengthen life. Another is the great variation in the risk of death among social groups, such as classes and races, even within the same society. Moreover, the meaning of death has changed over time as society has changed. It has gone from being a commonplace social experience to something we rarely encounter and do our best to avoid.

In preindustrial societies, when life expectancies were short and medicine was practiced in the home, death was a regular part of the human experience (Blauner, 1966). Most people had to deal with the death of one or more of their siblings and of their children, as well as that of their parents, other relatives, and friends. These deaths occurred at home, with family and sometimes friends gathered together.

Today, few people in industrial societies die before old age, and most die in a hospital or a nursing home. Many Americans, even adults, have never seen anyone die, except on television. Because of these changes, we have far less direct experience of death than people in a preindustrial society, who, by the ages we regard as young adulthood, would have personally witnessed any number of deaths (Blauner, 1966). Death has, in effect, been isolated from the rest of society (Aries, 1981). Consequently, death is a much feared and poorly understood event that most of us would rather avoid. We have even developed a lan-

A Buddhist monk is cremated in South Korea. Death is accompanied in most societies by religious rituals, because religion offers people a way of understanding and dealing with death.

guage of avoidance: "dying" becomes "passing away"; "dead" becomes "deceased" or "no longer with us." We have learned to stave off death through modern technology. Ultimately, however, we can only postpone death, not prevent it—a fact that is contrary to the entire modern industrial and scientific notion of "humanity over nature."

Of particular concern to Americans today is "premature death," death at ages younger than is typical. In the past, premature death was routine, and it was usually understood in religious terms. The notion of a young person going to his or her eternal reward provided comfort to the bereaved (Marshall, 1986, p. 134). Today death is no longer a routine event before old age, and premature death is experienced as "unfair" and abnormal: Why did this person have to die when so many like him or her live on? At the same time, religious understandings of reality have, at least in part, given way to scientific understandings, which makes religion a lesser source of solace for many than it once was.

When death occurs at the "normal" time in life —old age—the fear and shock to the survivors may be lessened by a tendency to view it as the normal conclusion of the life cycle (Marshall, 1986). Even then, however, death can be dreaded. In the past, death came quickly, often as a result of plague, pneumonia, smallpox, or some other contagious disease, and within hours or a few days of getting sick. Today, death more often follows a much longer period of chronic illness, gradual physical deterioration, and hospitalization (Marshall, 1986, p. 132). This process is referred to by sociologists as **dying,** and it is not only a physiological process, but a psychological and social one as well. Thus, people can see their deaths coming for some time. To some, death represents freedom from pain and suffering, the end to a long and successful life, or a passage to an eternal reward. To most of us, though, it is an unwanted and inescapable reality to which we must adjust as best we can.

Stages in the Process of Dying

Becoming a dying person is the final role transition in most people's lives, and it can be one of the most difficult. Our understanding of the process of dying has been greatly enhanced by the research of Elisabeth Kübler-Ross (1969, 1981), who observed and interviewed a number of dying people. She discovered a series of stages that people often go through in the process of dying. The first of these stages is *denial:* There must be some kind of mistake; I'm not really going to die. The second is *anger:* Why me? What did I do to deserve this? The third stage is *bargaining* with God, fate, or the disease: If only I can live until Christmas or until my child graduates next spring, I'll go willingly. Next comes *depression,* a form of grief at the upcoming loss of one's own life. The final stage is *acceptance:* the person has made peace with the reality of death and uses the remaining time to get his or her affairs in order. Not everyone moves through all these stages, and some people cross back and forth between them, but many people do experience the stages roughly in the order outlined by Kübler-Ross. Obviously, the circumstances of the process of dying influence how the process will be played out. A person dying prematurely, for example, might experience a longer and more intense period of anger than a person dying "on schedule." The latter person might even welcome death, because it frees him or her from a state of incapacity and being a burden on others (Marshall, 1986, p. 141).

Significantly, people close to the dying person go through a similar process. Indeed, some research indicates that the process of dying is actually more stressful for those left behind than for the dying person (Riley, Foner, and Waring, 1988, p. 253; Riley, 1983; Hyman, 1983). Those close to a dying person, for example, engage in denial through such behaviors as not telling friends and relatives about a serious illness in the family or refusing to talk about the illness. A more problematic form of denial occurs when relatives refuse to tell the dying person his or her illness is fatal. This practice was once common, but today most doctors believe that the dying person has a right to know, and that both the dying person and those close to him or her will adjust to the death better the sooner they can get past the denial phase (Despelder and Strickland, 1983). Moreover, the great majority of people answering surveys say that they would want to be told if they were dying (Kalish and Reynolds, 1976). To do otherwise is to deny people the opportunity for what Marshall (1986) calls "authoring"— controlling and shaping the process of dying.

Summary

Demography is the study of human populations. It is based on three variables—fertility, mortality, and migration—that determine population growth, composition, and age structure. The different mortality patterns of men and women lead to different mixes of males and females in different age groups, and the size and growth of various racial and ethnic groups are determined by their distinct patterns of fertility, mortality, and migration. An increasingly important activity of demographers has been to make population projections based on assumptions about the three basic variables.

Populations grow exponentially, or on the basis of a percentage rate of increase. They grow especially fast when there are substantially more births than deaths. On a worldwide basis, births and deaths were relatively in balance throughout most of human history, so the world's population grew only slowly. However, around 250 years ago, that trend changed, owing to a process known as the *demographic transition*. This process, which accompanied industrialization, involved a gradual decline in the death rate, followed only later by a decline in the birth rate. During the lag between the two declines, the world population grew rapidly.

Today in most industrialized countries, the birth rate has fallen back into balance with the death rate, so the rate of population growth is slow. But in the majority of the world that has not completed industrialization, population growth remains rapid. Because of imported technologies, the death rate has fallen rapidly, while the birth rate remains high; this has led to a "population explosion." In just the past 60 years the world's population has gone from 2 billion to 5 billion, with 1 billion now being added about every decade. The birth rate is now falling in the less-developed countries, but only slowly. As was historically true for Europe and North America, the best chance for a declining birth rate is through a rising standard of living and improved education. However, current population growth rates make these ideals difficult to attain in some areas. Therefore it is likely that the world's population will at least double over the next century or so.

In industrialized countries such as the United States, low birth rates are leading to an aging population. This effect will be enhanced after about 2010 by the aging of the massive baby boom birth cohort, followed by the much smaller "baby bust" cohort born in the 1970s. Thus, the share of the population that is over 65 is at a record high in most industrialized countries and will be sharply higher still in about 25 years. This trend will affect many areas, including the funding of private and public pensions, the demand for health care and education, political trends, and even the crime rate.

Because social roles are linked to age, the aging of the population has other important implications for both society and individuals. Age groups and age roles are socially constructed and partly reflect the needs of society. Adolescence and retirement age, for example, are social inventions of the industrialized era.

The delineation of age groups is typically accompanied by ageism, prejudice and discrimination on the basis of age. Adolescents and, especially, old people are more affected by ageism than other age groups. Many of our negative ideas about the roles of older people and their need to disengage are more the product of ageism than of social need. Retirement in the 60s may actually be dysfunctional for society because of the continuing growth in the old-age group and the projected decline in the traditional working-age group.

The final role most human beings play is that of a dying person. Dying is a more difficult process in modern society than in earlier ages because we have less experience of death and dying is more drawn out than it was in the past. Typically, the process of dying involves a series of steps, starting with denial and ending in acceptance. An individual's personality and social environment, as well as the timing of death, influence his or her adjustment to the role of dying person.

Glossary

demography The scientific study of human populations.

mortality The number of deaths occurring in a society.

crude death rate The number of deaths occurring in a year per 1,000 population.

life expectancy The number of years that the average person in a society can be expected to live, based on current patterns of mortality.

infant mortality rate The number of deaths in a year of people under 1 year of age per 1,000 births.

fertility The number of births occurring in a population.

crude birth rate The number of births occurring in a year per 1,000 population.

migration Large-scale movement of people to different neighborhoods, areas, or countries.

population projections Estimates of the future size and composition of populations, based on scientific assumptions about future fertility, mortality, and migration.

exponential growth Growth based on a percentage rate of increase that results in larger numerical growth in each successive year.

demographic transition A historic process whereby declines in mortality are not immediately followed by declines in fertility, thereby creating a period of rapid population growth.

birth cohort The set of all people who were born during a given time period.

age groups Socially defined categories of people based on age; for example, childhood, adolescence, old age.

age stratification Social inequality among age groups.

age roles Roles that are associated with age and carry the expectation that people of different ages should behave differently.

rites of passage Formal or informal rituals marking the passage from one age group or age role to another.

disengagement theory A theory, drawing largely on the functionalist perspective, that supports older people's giving up their role obligations to create opportunities for younger people.

activity theory A theory arguing that activity is beneficial to the health and self-esteem of older people, and that there is no need for them to give up socially valued roles and activities.

ageism Prejudice and discrimination based on age.

dying A process of physical deterioration and preparation for death.

Further Reading

BOGUE, DONALD I. 1985. *The Population of the United States: Historical Trends and Future Projections.* New York: Free Press. As the title suggests, this overview of American population patterns and trends includes analyses and discussions of past and possible future trends. In addition to fertility, mortality, and migration, the book discusses the socioeconomic, racial, and ethnic composition of the U.S. population.

FORNOS, WERNER. 1986. *Gaining People, Losing Ground: A Blue-*

print for Stabilizing Population Growth. Washington DC: The Population Institute. Fornos, the director of The Population Institute, examines the risks inherent in current rates of world population growth and examines some of the likely consequences if such growth continues unchecked. He also suggests policies aimed at averting these consequences by controlling world population growth.

HOOYMAN, NANCY R., AND H. ASUMAN KIYAK.1988. *Social Gerontology: An Interdisciplinary Perspective.* Needham Heights, MA: Allyn and Bacon. An up-to-date introduction to the field of aging, co-authored by a sociologist/social worker and a psychologist. As the subtitle suggests, the authors draw upon the perspectives of a number of disciplines, including sociology, psychology, social work, nursing, health education, and other health professions to help the reader learn about the many facets of the aging process.

JACKSON, JAQUELINE JOHNSON.1980. *Minorities and Aging.* Belmont, CA: Wadsworth. This book examines the aging process as experienced by racial and ethnic minorities. Attention is given both to the many aspects of aging that are similar for different ethnic groups and to aspects that differ by race and ethnicity. Demographic, social, physiological, and psychological aspects of the aging process are discussed, as well as policies toward aged minorities.

KART, CARY S., AND BARBARA MAHARD.1976. *Aging in America: Readings in Social Gerontology.* Port Washington, NY: Alfred. A broad and diverse set of readings concerning the aging process, co-edited by the author of this chapter's "Personal Journey into Sociology." Excellent reference source.

WEEKS, JOHN R.1989. *Population: An Introduction to Concepts and Issues,* 4th ed. Belmont, CA: Wadsworth. A thorough and up-to-date introduction to population studies, written by a highly regarded demographic researcher. Contains detailed discussions of all three demographic variables, with attention to both world and domestic population issues. Much of the book concerns the relationship between population and contemporary social issues.

CHAPTER 18

Urban Society

Think for a moment about the place where you grew up. For about three out of every four Americans, that place was either a city of 50,000 or more, or a suburb of such a city. Chances are that encounters with crowds and strangers were among your experiences from the day you were born. Chances are, too, that from a very early age you were warned about avoiding certain kinds of people who are "not like us." In fact, these things are probably so much a part of your experience that you long ago learned to take them for granted, and you probably haven't given them much thought for some time.

A minority of you, of course, did not grow up in an urban environment. You grew up in a small town, away from a major city, or perhaps in the country. Even to you, however, the urban environment is not completely foreign. The majority of you probably travel to a large city or its suburbs for entertainment, business, or shopping. There you encounter the same strangers, crowds, and "kinds of people" the urban dweller does all the time. But even if you are one of the relatively few people who have had no direct experience of the city, you probably still know something about it and have been influenced by its values and realities, whether you realize it or not. The mass media, for example, are almost entirely a product of the city; indeed, American television, movies, and many major magazines are based largely in just three cities: New York, Washington, and Los Angeles.

Consider television images. Although some shows do depict rural life (usually in a nostalgic, idealized way), you can hardly spend any amount of time watching television without being exposed to an urban setting. This is true of the network news, children's programs (Sesame Street, Mr. Rogers' Neighborhood), situation comedies (Cheers, The Cosby Show), adventure/action series (Cagney & Lacy, Miami Vice), and soap operas (Dallas). In fact, we take this setting so much for granted that we don't even *think of these shows as being about city life — but they are. The mass media not only show us images of the city, but also reflect the beliefs, experiences, and values of people who live in urban areas, because they are almost without exception the product of urban writers, actors, producers, and networks. Nothing about this strikes us as strange, nor should it, because these products reflect the experiences of the great majority of Americans.*

All of this seems so ordinary, in fact, that you are probably wondering why so much space has been devoted to it. The reason is that what seems so ordinary to Americans in the 1990s is in fact quite extraordinary in a historical and global sense. Throughout most of human history (including even that of the United States), the human experience has not been primarily an urban one. Most people did not live in cities or suburbs. In fact, many people never visited a city even once in their lives, and, of course, they had no television or movies to bring the city to them. Thus, the experiences that we regard as an ordinary part of life would have been totally foreign to most people in the past.

I n this chapter, we shall explore the reasons for the transformation from rural to urban life and the ways in which that transformation has altered our lives. Our new urban life has been both praised and condemned. We shall see that although both the glorification and the villification of the city contain an element of truth, both are extreme over-simplifications.

The Growth of Cities throughout the World

What Is a City?

To describe the growth of cities, we must begin by defining what we mean by the term *city*. Probably the most widely used definition is that of Louis Wirth (1938), who defined a city as "a relatively large, dense, permanent settlement of socially heterogeneous individuals." Note that this definition contains four elements: size of population, density of population, permanence of settlement, and social heterogeneity (diversity). Note, too, that it is *relative*; that is, a city has these characteristics as compared to other settlements. Thus, what was considered a city in the past might not be today. In past eras, a settlement of 10,000 people would have qualified as a city; today it would not because such a population is *relatively small*.

Moreover, a settlement of 10,000 people during certain past eras would certainly have been a highly specialized and complex place; more so than a town that size today, and certainly more so than most human settlements at the time. Finally, it would have had a much *higher* population density (people per square mile) than a town of 10,000 today.

Wirth's definition leaves room for debate as to whether a given settlement is or is not a city, but it continues to be widely used because it makes two important points. First, what is or is not a city is relative and must be considered in the context of any given society. Second, a city is not defined merely on the basis of size, but also on the basis of the diversity of its inhabitants and the complexity of their activities. This point was later elaborated upon by Childe (1950), who pointed out that cities are associated with such things as specialization, monumental public buildings, trade, and the development of writing and the arts and sciences.

The History of Urbanization

Large-scale urbanization is a recent phenomenon. **Urbanization** can be defined as the process by which an increasing share of a population lives in cities (Choldin, 1985, pp. 150–152). Urbanization does not mean merely that cities are growing; that is *urban growth*. We say that urbanization occurs when cities not only grow, but grow to a greater extent than rural areas or grow when rural areas do not.

It is only within the past 2 centuries that any sizable proportion of the human population has lived in cities. Only the Roman Empire and the Inca, Aztec, and Mayan Indians of Central and South America were able to attain urbanization levels of as much as 10 or 20 percent (Hawley, 1981; Childe, 1946; Davis, 1955; Kornberg, 1975; Rivet, 1960). Most early cities had small populations, usually under 40,000 and often well under 10,000. The largest early cities were ancient Rome, which probably had a population of 350,000 to 600,000, and the Central and South American Indian cities, the largest of which had populations

of around 200,000 — hardly large cities by today's standards (Chandler and Fox, 1974; Russell, 1958; Kornberg, 1975; Rivet, 1960). As shown in the box entitled "A Portrait of the Preindustrial City," these early cities differed from cities in today's industrialized societies in a number of ways besides size.

After around A.D. 500, cities grew somewhat larger, but truly large cities remained rare for another thousand years or more. As shown in Table 18.1, only a handful of cities in the world had populations exceeding 150,000 at any time between A.D. 800 and 1600, and none had populations that even came close to 1

TABLE 18.1
Estimated Populations of Major World Cities, A.D. 800–1600

Population	YEAR				
	800	1000	1200	1400	1600
900,000					
800,000	Sian, China				
700,000	Baghdad, Persia				Peking, China Istanbul, Turkey
600,000					
500,000					
		Cordoba, Spain Istanbul, Turkey		Cairo, Egypt	
400,000		Kaifeng, China			Cairo, Egypt Osaka, Japan Tokyo, Japan Kyoto, Japan
				Peking, China	
300,000	Istanbul, Turkey	Sian, China		Paris, France	Naples, Italy Paris, France
			Istanbul, Turkey Fez, Morocco		
200,000	Alexandria, Egypt Kyoto, Japan	Kyoto, Japan	Cairo, Egypt	Kyoto, Japan	London, England
	Cordoba, Spain	Cairo, Egypt	Kamakura, Japan 4 cities*	Sian, China Fez, Morocco	3 cities**

* Palermo, Italy; Peking, China; Kaifeng, China; Sian, China
** Venice, Italy; Potasi, Mexico; Sian, China
SOURCES: Chandler and Fox, 1974; Bardo and Hartman, 1982.

A Portrait of the Preindustrial City

Most of the earliest cities would be almost unrecognizable to anyone living in a modern city. Certain features appeared independently in the earliest cities in Mesopotamia, China, and Central America, and, with minor variations, these features characterized most preindustrial cities throughout history.

One major way preindustrial cities differed from modern ones was in the nature of the city center. Rather than centering on a downtown commercial district, early cities were built around a religious center: a temple, tower, or pyramid in the earliest cities; a cathedral in medieval cities. Usually, this religious center was on a hill in the middle of the city. In the earliest cities, the temple was more than just a religious center. It also served as "a place for meditation and research, a warehouse, an accounting and distributing agency" (Comhaire and Cahnman, 1959, p. 2). Records of animal herds and crop yields were kept there; grain and treasures were stored there; loans were made there—all, of course, under the supervision and control of a high priest or a king who was often believed to be divine. In medieval cities, the economic function of the religious center itself declined, but it was taken over by open-air markets that typically located close to the cathedral.

Another difference between preindustrial and modern cities had to do with who lived where. The wealthiest and most powerful people in virtually all preindustrial cities lived near the center, for two reasons. First, it was desirable to live near the religious center, and such a privilege was reserved for priests, military leaders, kings, and their courts. Second, it was safer to live near the center. City-states were frequently at war with one another, and living near the city wall was riskier than living near the center. Thus, the further from the center, the lower the social and economic status of the population —just the opposite of what we find in the modern American city. Cities sometimes outgrew the area enclosed by their walls, so that some people had to live outside the walls, at least until new ones could be built. As you might expect, this unhappy fate befell those with the lowest social status. Social status, moreover, was an *ascribed status*: Most early cities had what we would call a caste system.

Early cities were denser and more compact than today's cities. When the main mode of transportation is walking, nobody wants to be too far from anything. The ancient city of Uruk, for example, may have had a population of about 29,000 per square mile (computed from Spates and Macionis, 1987, p. 37), and Ur's population density may have been as great as 125,000 per square mile (Thomlinson, 1976, p. 403). These figures compare to about 12,000 per square mile in present-day Boston and under 10,000 in Washington, D.C. (U.S. Bureau of the Census, 1986d, pp. 42, 418). When these early cities grew, their density usually increased, as more and more people crammed into the space inside the city walls.

Closely related to high density was the absence of a distinction between work and home (Sjoberg, 1955, 1960). People worked at home, and they often have sold their products on the street outside their homes or through a window in their houses. Both people and businesses were frequently segregated by occupation. In medieval London, for example, streets and neighborhoods were named for the occupational group that resided there. There was a Beer Street, where the breweries were located, and a Baker Street, where the city's bakeries were located.

---

million. Today, in contrast, the industrialized societies have become overwhelmingly urban, and the rest of the world is urbanizing rapidly. The United States alone had 39 metropolitan areas with populations of more than 1 million as of the 1980 Census. (The term *metropolitan area* refers to a city and its suburbs.) At least 23 cities and 43 metropolitan areas in Europe have populations of 1 million or more (Lane, 1983, pp. 473–558; Thomlinson, 1976, pp. 414–415). In both Europe and North America, the population today is about 75 percent urban (Population Reference Bureau, 1988a; Hawley, 1981, p. 73).

Technology, Industrialization, and Urbanization This rapid urbanization was the result of both technological and social innovations. On the technological side, industrialization was the driving force. When inventions such as the steam engine, the spinning jenny, and the automatic weaving machine made mass production possible, the place of work shifted

These reproductions of ancient Nineveh (above, left) and of medieval London (above, right), respectively, illustrate the grand palaces and temples of the earliest cities and the high population density of most preindustrial cities.

from the home to the factory. Mass production also created a demand for a substantial labor force. Outside the cities, better roads and inland canals made the movement of both people and food from the countryside to the city far more feasible. Agriculture, too, was transformed by technological changes associated with the Industrial Revolution. In the eighteenth and nineteenth centuries, such innovations as crop rotation, selective breeding of animals, and new tools led to dramatic improvements in productivity (Wrigley, 1969; Mumford, 1938). This meant that a larger agricultural surplus could be produced, and therefore a larger urban population could be supported.

Social Change and Urbanization At the same time, important social changes that encouraged urban growth were emerging. One was the development of effective national governments. In contrast to the feudal era, when violent disputes among nobles discouraged travel and trade, national governments created an environment in which national and international trade flourished. National governments also brought about a common monetary system, greater consistency of laws, and uniform systems of weights and measures—all of which are vital to trade. Increased trade led to a growth in manufacturing, which in turn further stimulated urbanization. These trends were reinforced by world exploration, trade, and colonization, which created new demand and supplied new raw materials.

Gradually, the urban business-owning class, called the *bourgeoisie*, replaced the rural lords and barons as the dominant group in society. In the city, craftsmen who formerly had owned their own businesses began to work in factories for the bourgeoisie. This change created a new form of social stratification in the city, and power became more concentrated in the hands of the bourgeoisie, who used it to institute national policies that favored urban growth.

The Demographic Transition and Urbanization
The *demographic transition*, described in Chapter 17,

also contributed dramatically to urbanization. As death rates fell, more children survived to adulthood and rural areas became overpopulated. To avoid the splitting of farmland into ever-smaller pieces, many societies had laws dictating that parents had to pass on a plot of land only to one child. Most children, therefore, had no source of economic support in the rural areas, but there was a great demand for industrial workers in the cities. Thus, the *push* of overpopulation in rural areas and the *pull* of employment opportunities in cities led increasing numbers of young people in Europe and North America to leave the countryside and head for the city.

Urban life was hard for most people in the early stages of industrialization. Industrial laborers, who in many cases were only 10 years old, worked 13 hours per day, 7 days per week (Choldin, 1985, pp. 100–102). They had no health insurance, workers' compensation, or government-mandated safety rules. In many cities sanitation remained deplorable through much of the nineteenth century. As a result, death rates in cities were higher than in rural areas (Thomlinson, 1976). In fact, urban death rates were so high during the earlier stages of the Industrial Revolution that some of the fastest-growing cities would actually have *lost* population had it not been for in-migration.

Urbanization in the United States

As in Europe, industrialization was a major source of urban growth in the United States. When the first U.S. Census was taken in 1790, the American population was only 5 percent urban, despite the fact that any town with a population of 2,500 or more was regarded as urban. By 1840, the urban population had risen to about 10 percent. The Civil War was a major stimulus to industrialization in the United States, and it accelerated an already rapid urbanization. By 1870, the United States population was one-quarter urban; by 1900, it was 40 percent urban. By 1920, the majority of the American population lived in cities, and the percentage continued to increase rapidly (except during the Great Depression) until 1960, when it reached about 70 percent. Since then, it has risen only slowly to about 74 percent in 1980 (U.S. Bureau of the Census, 1983c).

Economics of Urban Growth   The growth of different cities at different points in U.S. history reflects the various stages in the development of the U.S. economy (Hawley, 1981; Duncan and Lieberson, 1970; Glaab and Brown, 1976; Glaab, 1963). As Table 18.2 shows, the most rapidly growing cities in early American history were seaports. During the nineteenth century, New York became the preeminent American city because it had a great natural harbor, water access to the interior, and a central location relative to early America's population. A key to its development was the construction of transportation systems: first the Erie Canal in 1825, which connected the city to the Great Lakes shipping routes, and later the railroads (Palen, 1987, p. 67).

The next surge of growth, before and during the Civil War, took place in the "inland ports"—cities located at *transshipment points,* that is, at the junction of two rivers, or where water routes ended and land transportation took over. Chicago is the leading example: between 1850 and 1890, its population at least doubled every 10 years. From 1880 to 1900, the most rapid growth occurred in cities whose economies were based almost entirely on manufacturing. Most of these cities, like Cleveland, Buffalo, and Detroit, were located on the Great Lakes. To the west, new port and transshipment cities were also growing, like Minneapolis–St. Paul and San Francisco. From 1900 until the beginning of World War II, the automobile was the dominant force shaping the growth of American cities. Rapid growth continued in Detroit and other auto-manufacturing cities in Michigan and Ohio, as well as in cities near oil fields, such as Los Angeles and Houston. Since World War II, the fastest-growing American cities have been in the Sun Belt—the South and the West. These cities have had diversified economies that benefited from tourism, energy extraction, military spending, and service industries.

Functional Specialization   An important point about cities that arises from this discussion is their **functional specialization**—different cities specialize in different kinds of economic activity. Detroit specializes in auto manufacturing, Pittsburgh in steel, Minneapolis and San Francisco in regional trade, Seattle in aircraft manufacturing, and Hartford and

TABLE 18.2
Period of Emergence of Major Urban Centers in the United States

BEFORE 1850	1850 TO 1880	1880 TO 1900	1900 TO 1940	1940 TO PRESENT
New York	Chicago	Buffalo	Los Angeles	Dallas
Charleston, SC*	St. Louis	Cleveland	Houston	Atlanta
Boston	Cincinatti	Detroit		Miami
Philadelphia	San Francisco	Milwaukee		Seattle
Baltimore	Washington	Minneapolis–St. Paul		Denver
New Orleans	Pittsburgh	Kansas City		San Diego
				San Antonio
				Phoenix

* Failed to grow rapidly after 1850, and no longer regarded as major urban center.

SOURCES: James E. Vance, 1976, "Cities in the Shaping of the American Nation," *Journal of Geography* (January): 41–52; Beverly Duncan and Stanley Lieberson, 1970, *Metropolis and Region in Transition* (Beverly Hills, CA: Sage); and U.S. Bureau of the Census, 1913, *Thirteenth Census of the United States: 1910.*

Des Moines in finance and insurance (Duncan and Lieberson, 1970; Getis, Getis, and Fellman, 1981). Houston's economy is based largely on oil; New Orleans is a major seaport. Some cities, of course, are more diversified, and this protects them to some extent from economic fluctuations. Los Angeles, Boston, and Dallas have relatively diversified economies (see Getis, Getis, and Fellman, 1981), and they have not experienced the sharp "busts" that have hit Seattle during declines in the aircraft industry, Detroit when imports hurt domestic car sales, or Houston when the price of oil fell. A few cities, including Washington, Los Angeles, Chicago, and, above all, New York, are *national metropolises.* In other words, they are the centers of economic activities that are national or international in scope. Many national and multinational corporations have their headquarters in or near these cities; national organizations are headquartered there; network television originates there (Hawley, 1981, pp. 244–248). Washington, of course, is virtually guaranteed such a status by its position as the national capital. With the rise of the Sun Belt cities, Atlanta also appears to be developing some of the characteristics of a national metropolis.

Urban Hierarchy The United States, like other industrialized countries, has developed a system called an *urban hierarchy* within which different cities, depending on their size and level of economic activity, may supply goods and services to less-populated areas on the one hand, and be dependent on larger cities for goods and services on the other hand (Hawley, 1981; Golden, 1981; Simmons, 1978). Those products and services for which a nationwide market is required tend to be concentrated in the national metropolises. For other goods and services, the market is regional. Cities such as Minneapolis, Kansas City, and San Francisco do not provide goods and services just for the people who live in them, but also for the *hinterland:* a surrounding area that is dependent on the city for goods, services, and markets. Another step down the scale are smaller cities like Peoria, Illinois; Bakers-

This picture of the Cincinnati riverfront in 1838 illustrates the importance of water transportation routes in the early growth of American cities.

field, California; Knoxville, Tennessee; and Springfield, Massachusetts. These cities are part of the hinterland of larger cities and rely on those larger cities for certain specialized goods and services. Yet, these cities provide other products and services (local television stations, regional shopping malls, smaller-scale wholesaling) for hinterlands of their own (Bourne and Simmons, 1978). This hierarchy continues until you reach the level of the very smallest towns that can support only a gas station, a convenience store, and perhaps a grain elevator.

Urbanization in the Third World

Since World War II, many Third-World countries have experienced rapid urbanization. This process results from some of the same social forces that produced urbanization in Europe and North America, although the *push* factors forcing people out of rural areas have been more important than the *pull* factors attracting them to the cities. As discussed in Chapter 17, the decrease in mortality rates that accompanies the demographic transition has happened much more quickly in the Third World than it did in the West. As a result, rural overpopulation has been more sudden and severe, and millions of people around the world have left their rural homes for the city.

Unfortunately, many Third-World countries have not industrialized to the extent that Europe had when the demographic transition took place there, so millions of people in Third-World cities have no useful economic role to play. Lacking any real means of support, they live by the thousands — sometimes by the millions — in shantytowns, or squatter settlements, on the fringes of major cities. The squatter population of Mexico City, for example, has been estimated at 4 million, and estimates for Calcutta, India, reach 2 million (Palen, 1987, p. 342). The squatters live crowded together in makeshift structures built from cardboard, scrap wood, or metal, without running water, flush toilets, or electricity.

Although the deplorable conditions of today's Third-World shantytowns may not be any worse than those of nineteenth-century European working-class neighborhoods, there are some important differences. First, today's Third-World urbanization is occurring on a far larger scale. Mexico City's population, for example, is 20 million — six times that of Paris in 1900. Second, urbanization in many Third-World countries is running ahead of industrialization, whereas in Europe it tended to follow or accompany industrialization. Thus, urban populations in these countries have grown far beyond what the economy can support. This condition is known as **overurbanization.** The term does not mean that the population in these countries is "too urban" — usually the urban standard of living exceeds that of rural areas, even in the poorest nations — but rather that the economy has not developed enough to employ the urban population (Wellisz, 1971; Palen, 1987; Sovani, 1964; Gugler, 1982).

This problem is especially severe in the least-industrialized countries, such as Mexico, India, Peru, Indonesia, and Thailand. Many of these countries lack the *urban hierarchy* of industrialized countries. Instead, they are characterized by *primate cities* (Portes, 1977). A primate city is one large city into which the great share of the country's population and economic growth is channeled. The extreme example is probably Bangkok, Thailand, which has 33 times the population of the country's next largest city, and more than half of the entire urban population of Thailand (Spates and Macionis, 1987, p. 272). Many theorists argue that primate cities hinder economic development in two ways. First, they are said to retard economic growth in the rest of the country because the perception develops that the only place where there is opportunity is "the big city" (London and Smith, 1988; Bradshaw, 1987). Second, they are especially subject to overurbanization because people flock to the primate city in hopes of bettering their lives.

We must, however, be careful in generalizing about Third-World cities. Some countries have primate cities (especially those with long histories of colonial domination), but others do not. The concept of overurbanization is far more applicable to some countries than to others. A number of Third-World nations are rapidly industrializing, and for them overurbanization is not such a problem. Several of the "Pacific Rim" countries, such as Taiwan, South Korea, and Hong Kong, have industrialized to such an extent that they are able to employ most of their urban populations. In China overurbanization has been prevented by governmental controls on migration to the city, a

With a population of over 20 million, Mexico City has become the largest city in the history of the world. It is also a superb example of a primate city.

solution that would probably only work under China's centralized economic and political system.

Overurbanization Despite the problems in many Third-World cities, the urban population continues to soar. Overall, about two-thirds of the population of Latin America is urban, as is about one-third in Asia and Africa (Population Reference Bureau, 1988a). These figures represent a sharp increase since World War II. In fact, there are *50 times* as many people living in Third-World cities of over 1 million today as there were in 1950. In 1950, seven of the world's ten largest cities were in industrialized countries. By 2000, according to a 1985 United Nations projection, only two of the world's ten largest cities (Tokyo and New York) will be in what today are industrialized countries. The two largest cities, Mexico City and São Paulo, Brazil, will have a combined population of 50 million. Consider that number in comparison to the historic urban populations shown in Table 18.1.

Urban Life

Rural versus Urban Societies

The large-scale growth of cities has generated intense debates about the relative merits of urban and rural life. As was previously noted, the city has been both praised and condemned: praised as the cradle of civilization, and condemned as impersonal, brutal, and corrupt. Early sociological theories about the city reflected both views. Sociologists sought to identify what it was about city living that seemed, for example, to spur both creativity and deviance. As noted in Chapter 1, urban problems associated with industrialization were a major focus of early sociology in both Europe and the United States. More recently, sociologists have used empirical research to test systematically the accuracy of popular and sociological perceptions about the city. This research has shown such perceptions to be right in some ways and wrong in others.

Toennies on Urban Life Probably the earliest systematic sociological comparison of urban and rural life was that of the German sociologist Ferdinand Toennies (1963 [orig. 1887]). It is important to understand that Toennies's theory, like others that followed it, was not *simply* a comparison of rural and urban life, but rather a comparison of traditional, preindustrial society — which is rural in nature — and modern industrial society — which is urban. It is, therefore, difficult to sort out the effects of modernization, industrialization, and urbanization in this and other theories.

Toennies referred to the traditional rural society as **gemeinschaft,** a German word that, roughly translated, means *community.* In this society, relations between people were close and personal, behavior was governed by widely accepted traditions, and contact with strangers was rare. People were closely bound together by kinship, friendship, and neighborliness. They recognized "common goods — common evils; common friends — common enemies" (Toennies, 1963 [orig. 1887]). They trusted one another and were careful to fulfill their mutual obligations. Modern, industrial, urban society, or **gesellschaft,** presented a sharp contrast, according to Toennies. Gesellschaft, roughly translated, means *association,* a term that captures the more formal, instrumental nature of this society. According to Toennies, people in modern urban societies follow their own individualistic agendas, which are often driven by economic self-interest. As a result, they are less likely to know and care about one another. The city becomes an impersonal arena where everyone looks out only for himself or herself. Common identity and consensus based on tradition disappear, and people become isolated and alienated.

SIMMEL'S THEORY As another German sociologist, Georg Simmel (1964 [orig. 1905]), pointed out, part of the reason for these differences is that the city simply contains more people and more situations than any one person can possibly become familiar with. As a result, Simmel believed, urbanites protect themselves from overstimulation by withdrawing and developing what he called a "blasé attitude," which involves tuning out most of what is going on and paying attention only to that small part that is interesting or useful in terms of personal concerns and goals. According to Simmel, this is why urbanites so often "don't want to get involved." (For a modern elaboration of Simmel's viewpoint, see Milgram, 1970.)

Wirth on Urban Life   In the United States, the most influential sociological theory about urban life has been that of Louis Wirth, presented in a 1938 article entitled "Urbanism as a Way of Life." Wirth was a product of the "Chicago School" that was so influential in early American sociology (see Chapter 1), and like his colleagues at the University of Chicago, he had a strong interest in understanding the social problems that were evident in American cities in the early twentieth century. Wirth pointed to three specific characteristics of the city that he believed produced the type of urban life pictured by Toennies and Simmel: *size, density,* and *heterogeneity.* The large population size of cities, Wirth argued, produces a need for specialization. When this happens, people begin to interact in terms of their particular roles in a situation, rather than with one another as people. In the terminology introduced in Chapter 7 of this book, *primary-group* relations are replaced by *secondary-group* relations. As a result, relationships become "impersonal, superficial, transitory, and segmental" (Wirth, 1964, p. 71).

The high population density leads to the type of overstimulation discussed by Simmel, and people respond to it not only by "tuning out" but also by simplifying and stereotyping. Thus, people's images of the city are organized (but simplified) into "Little Italy," "the Gold Coast," "the ghetto," and so forth, and the residents of these areas are psychologically lumped into categories: "immigrants," "Yuppies," "the underclass." According to Wirth, this process leads to a greater tolerance of differences in the city, but it also leads to depersonalization, stereotyping, and withdrawal in order to avoid contact with those who are "not like us." A common variation on Wirth's arguments is the notion that high population densities are

Louis Wirth, a leading urban sociologist of the "Chicago School," authored the widely cited article "Urbanism as a Way of Life."

stressful and lead to pathological behaviors such as violence, crime, conflict, and withdrawal from normal human interaction (Hall, 1966). Evidence for this line of reasoning is provided in part by studies of animals showing that they behave abnormally when crowded beyond some limit (Calhoun, 1962).

Perhaps the most important of all the characteristics of the city, to Wirth, is heterogeneity. It is easy for urbanites to stereotype and avoid one another because they are, in fact, far more diverse than people who came into contact with one another in preindustrial rural societies. Different professions, different racial, ethnic, and religious groups, different social classes, and different personality types are all mixed together in a relatively confined space. The city also enhances physical and social mobility, so that people interact with different sets of neighbors and coworkers at different times in their lives—an experience far different from that of traditional villagers. As a result, people resist the tendency to "get too close," knowing that soon they will be associating with a new set of people. (How many of your current classmates will you be close to 5 years from now?) Consequently, Wirth saw urbanites as isolated and alienated, using one another to advance their own personal interests, and largely devoid of close, meaningful primary-group relationships.

The Isolated Urbanite: Myth or Fact?

In the half century since Wirth wrote his influential article, there has been a great deal of research on the experiences, lifestyles, attitudes, and behaviors of people living in cities. We know today that important points Toennies, Simmel, and Wirth made about the city are true, but we also know that some of their views were overly pessimistic. It *is* true that urbanites spend much more of their time in secondary-group relationships than the rural people or villagers of the past, or even the farm population of today (Reiss, 1959). It is also true that city residents do not and cannot interact with most of the people they encounter, and that they engage in a variety of mechanisms to avoid unwanted interaction. They also think in a stereotyped manner, as Wirth argued, but urbanites have no monopoly on this type of thinking.

Urban Life and Interpersonal Relationships
Nonetheless, certain aspects of the Toennies-Simmel-Wirth viewpoint have been disproved. First, most urbanites are *not* lacking in close, interpersonal relationships. Rather, they typically have family and friends with whom they share relationships that are as close and personal as anything found in the traditional gemeinschaft-type society (Fischer, 1982; Wellman, 1979; Bell, 1968). Often, though, the friends of urbanites are not neighbors; they may live miles away, but they interact regularly on the basis of common interests, work, or family background (Wellman, 1979). Second, there is no evidence that people living in cities are more alienated or suffer more mental illness than people living in rural areas (Srole, 1972, 1980; Srole et al., 1962; Fischer, 1984). If anything, mental illness is slightly more common in rural areas than in urban areas (Fischer, 1973; Srole, 1972). It is hard to judge accurately just how much mental illness existed in preindustrial rural societies, but there is good reason to believe that there was a significant amount. Today, in the societies that most closely re-

semble preindustrial societies, mental illness is not unusual. Eaton and Weil (1955), for example, studied the Hutterites, a very traditional religious organization whose members live in rural communities in the northern plains, in a manner that closely approximates Toennies's concept of gemeinschaft. The researchers found their rates of mental illness to be just as high as those in highly urban New York State. The only difference was that the Hutterites cared for their own members when they were mentally ill, rather than hospitalizing them or sending them to a mental-health professional.

Population Density and Crowding On the whole, research has also found no substantial relationship between population density and mental illness or other pathologies, after controlling for other factors such as poverty (Choldin, 1978; Baldassare, 1979; Booth, Johnson, and Edwards, 1980; Farley, 1982). Some urban lifestyles even thrive on density, such as that of ethnic neighborhoods where interaction is based on kinship. There are some studies showing that *feeling* crowded is associated with problems, but feeling crowded is not always associated with real crowding, and it may even be a consequences of family conflict (Booth, 1976). Although crowded cities were blamed by some observers for the riots and the rising crime rates of the 1960s, there is a serious flaw in this reasoning: Urban population densities have fallen throughout most of the twentieth century, and they were lower in the 1960s than they had been at any previous time in U.S. history! There is one qualification to the general conclusion that population density does not *by itself* cause problems. Crowding *within houses or apartments* may cause some adverse effects, especially if it is combined with poverty and the presence of small children (Baldassare, 1981; Gove, Hughes, and Galle, 1979).

Urban Life and "Getting Involved" Sociologists also question whether urbanites are as uncaring as they are portrayed to be. To be sure, certain dramatic incidents appear to support this portrayal. In New York City in 1964, for example, a woman was attacked and repeatedly stabbed in the view of dozens of people. Nobody intervened; indeed nobody even called the police until after she had died. In 1984, a virtually identical incident occurred in Brooklyn, and in St. Louis a woman was attacked in front of a crowd of people filing out of Busch Stadium after a baseball game (Spates and Macionis, 1987, p. 107). Again, nobody intervened or even notified the police — they just kept walking by. Certainly such incidents are very disturbing, and they have often been used as evidence that urbanites don't care about one another.

REASONS FOR NONINVOLVEMENT   There are, however, alternative explanations. For one thing, direct intervention can be dangerous. Around the time of the St. Louis incident, an off-duty fireman in nearby Alton, Illinois, was killed when he saw a man beating a woman in the front yard of a house and tried to stop him. Of course, this doesn't explain why people do not even call the police in such situations. Here sociologists refer to the concept of *diffused responsibility*. It is significant that the fireman in this example was the *only* person who witnessed the event, and he *did* try to do something about it. In the other three instances a large crowd of people saw the event, and no one person felt individually responsible for doing something about it. Instead, everyone who correctly recognized the situation as an emergency assumed that someone else had called the police, but tragically, nobody had.

Besides the fact that nobody felt responsible, it also appears that many people misidentified the situations as nonemergencies, such as lovers' quarrels. This, too, happens more often when a number of people witness an event, because each person interprets the nonparticipation of others as a cue that the situation is not really an emergency. This phenomenon has been referred to as *pluralistic ignorance* (Latane and Darley, 1970; Penrod, 1986, p. 395). Dozens of studies have demonstrated that as the number of people who witness an emergency increases, the chances that anyone will help decrease (Latane, Nida, and Wilson, 1981). These studies suggest that, rather than not caring, urban crowds either do not realize that the situation is an emergency or they assume that someone else is already taking care of it.

Gans's Theory of Urban Residents   One other important consideration that was underemphasized by Wirth and his intellectual predecessors is that, because cities are highly diverse, the experiences of one group of urban residents can be very different from those of others. Herbert Gans (1972), for example, has identified several distinct groups of people who live in central cities and at least one distinct group in the suburbs. These groups are summarized below.

COSMOPOLITES   These are well-educated and affluent people who like the cultural and entertainment opportunities of the city. Though they may be unmarried or childless if married, they typically have a number of friends with whom they share interests. Often, however, these friends are not neighbors. Like other groups in the city, cosmopolites often develop a *subculture* based on their similar interests. Cities facilitate this process by providing a *critical mass* of people with similar interests (Choldin, 1985, pp. 50–52).

UNMARRIED   These people live in the city for some of the same reasons as the cosmopolites, but they may reside there only during certain periods of their lives, such as young adulthood before marriage, or after a divorce. Also included in this group is the substantial gay population that lives in some central cities. Usually their lives and friendships center around work or common interests rather than the neighborhood, but they are hardly isolated or friendless. Although this group was once associated with central cities, it is today also a sizable portion of the suburban population, particularly in the large apartment complexes that have become common in American suburbs.

ETHNIC VILLAGERS   This group is composed of families with children who live in ethnically segregated neighborhoods, often near their relatives (Gans, 1962). They are working class, but not poor. Gans called their neighborhoods "urban villages" because they have many of the characteristics of a traditional rural village. Extended family relationships are important, relatives often live near one another, and neighborhood interaction is strong. This group is probably the most removed from the urbanites portrayed by Wirth. Many Italian, Puerto Rican, Jewish, and Mexican neighborhoods fit this description, as do some of the newer communities of Asian immigrants and some black and Irish working-class neighborhoods. City officials and people from elsewhere in the city sometimes label these neighborhoods slums because of their working-class character, but this label is inaccurate. As Gans (1962) and William Foote Whyte (1981) found in studies of one such neighborhood in Boston, these areas are often the most stable and cohesive neighborhoods in the city. Frequently, their residents are strongly attached to the neighborhood and wouldn't move to a "better" one even if they could (Terkel, 1967, p. 198).

THE DEPRIVED, THE TRAPPED, AND THE DOWN-WARDLY MOBILE These groups (which Gans treated as several distinct, though similar, groups) are made up of the poor and the unemployed. They chronically constitute what has come to be called the *underclass* (Wilson, 1987). Many of them have experienced downward mobility because of the loss of industrial jobs from many of our cities. They are relatively uneducated and often live in families that consist of a mother and her children. Because their financial situation is desperate and because their neighborhoods are crime-ridden and unsafe, this is the one set of urbanites for whom most of Wirth's more pessimistic views about city life hold true. However, their difficult life is not the product of living in the city; rather, it is the product of living in poverty. Even so, these groups have become increasingly concentrated in the older central cities (Wilson, 1987). In fact, some sociologists now argue that cities such as Newark, New Jersey; Gary, Indiana; and East St. Louis, Illinois, are being made into ghetto reservations for the poor, where they are confined and isolated from the rest of society (Sternleib, 1977; Conforti, 1972).

SUBURBANITES The final group identified by Gans was suburbanites. This group has become increasingly diverse since Gans wrote his article, and it will be discussed at some length in a later section of this chapter concerning suburbanization.

The City and Tolerance Despite the growth of the urban population and the homogenizing effects of the mass media, important differences between cities and rural areas continue to exist. One difference that has been confirmed by research is that people in cities *are* more tolerant of diversity and of nonconforming lifestyles, including alcohol use, nonconforming sexual behaviors, and marijuana use (Fischer, 1975, 1971; Tuch, 1987) than people in rural areas. They are also more tolerant toward different racial, ethnic, religious, and cultural groups (Tuch, 1987). These differences have long been recognized by urban theorists. Simmel, though pessimistic about other aspects of city life, saw this as a great advantage. He argued (1964 [orig. 1905]) that the metropolis "assures the individual of a degree and type of personal freedom to which there is no analogy in other circumstances." Importantly, though, there are wide differences in tolerance within both cities and rural areas: In each kind of area, some people are far more tolerant than others.

Cities and Social Conflict

Think of the last time you heard about a riot, strike, or political assassination. Whether it took place in the United States or in another country, chances are it happened in an urban area. Most outbreaks of conflict do. The United States, for example, has a long history of urban rioting. The bloodiest urban riot in the United States did not happen in the 1960s, as many people would suspect, but in New York City in 1863. It began as a protest against the draft that had been established to provide soldiers to fight in the Civil War. Its participants came from the ethnic working class, the group least able to avoid the draft. It was in part racially motivated: Whites did not want to fight to free black slaves, and not only the draft office but also the Colored Orphan Asylum was burned. Estimates of the number killed vary widely; it could have been more than 1,000 (McCague, 1968). Other major riots occurred in San Francisco and Los Angeles in the 1870s; Chicago, East St. Louis, and Springfield in the 1910s; Tulsa in the 1920s; Detroit, New York City, and Los Angeles in the 1940s; in hundreds of American cities in the 1960s and early 1970s; and in Miami in 1980 and 1989. Notably, there have been far more of these events in urban areas than in rural areas, though rural areas have hardly been free of violent conflict (lynchings, for example). This is to say nothing of the strikes, nonviolent protests, and other forms of routine conflict that go on in cities all the time. Such widespread and consistent patterns of conflict and violence in cities, both in the United States and elsewhere, have led some sociologists to argue that the city is a *crucible of conflict,* that living in cities *causes* conflict. It has been suggested, for example, that city living is stressful, and people respond to that stress by engaging in conflict.

The Arena of Conflict   The reality, however, is quite different. Rather than causing conflict, the city acts as an *arena of conflict.* In other words, it serves as the place where societal conflicts are fought out. As conflict theorists point out, social inequality and the existence of competing interest groups work to create conflict in *all* societies. Notably, virtually all of the riots described in the preceding paragraph involved groups who felt threatened or were relatively powerless. These conflicts are fought out in the cities, for several reasons. First, the most important political and corporate decisions are made in the cities because that is where governments, corporations, and organizations are headquartered. Thus, the conflicts that affect cities are often national in character, but the city is where they are fought out.

CRITICAL MASS   Three other phenomena cause cities to be arenas of conflict: critical mass, relative deprivation, and the costs and benefits of dissent. The concept of *critical mass,* applied earlier to the notion of subcultures, also applies to conflict. If 1 percent of the population in a city of 1 million is dissatisfied, the result will be 10,000 dissatisfied people, which is enough to form an organization or a sizable demonstration. The same percentage of dissatisfied people in

a rural area with a widely scattered population of 100 people would translate to one dissatisfied person—isolated in his or her dissatisfaction, with nobody of like mind to get together with.

RELATIVE DEPRIVATION   The second consideration is *relative deprivation,* which is discussed in greater detail in Chapter 19. The basic point here is that people are more likely to engage in conflict when they feel they have been disadvantaged or mistreated *relative to* someone else. Obviously, such feelings can develop more easily in a big, diverse city, where the wealthy and poor regularly come into contact with each other, than in a homogeneous rural area or village, where even if you are poor, most of the people you see and associate with are equally poor (see Williams, 1977, p. 28).

COSTS AND BENEFITS OF DISSENT   The third consideration, costs and benefits of dissent, has to do with the greater personal freedom of the city. In the city, where you can be anonymous if you choose, you are simply less likely to ''get in trouble'' for dissenting than you would in a small town. In a big city, for example, your employer need never know if, after work, you protest against abortion, contra aid, or nuclear weapons. In contrast, in a village setting where everyone knows everyone else, you might be quickly labeled a ''troublemaker'' and shunned by others, perhaps even at the cost of your job. Thus, it is less costly to you to engage in conflict in the urban setting, and the benefits of conflict may also be greater because there is a better chance of finding the critical mass necessary for an effective movement.

A Conflict Perspective on the City

Urban conflict is the product of the same basic social forces that produce conflict in the larger society. Conflict theorists point out that cities, just like the societies in which they exist, are greatly shaped by the interests of dominant social groups. Feminists, for example, point out that the structure of the city has traditionally reflected male interests (Wekerle, 1980). The industrial city was built around the notion of males leaving the home for the workplace and women staying behind to tend the home and children. Thus, for the workday at least, the downtown business and financial center became a male domain, the home and

Violence erupts in Capetown, South Africa, as police attack protestors attempting to march against apartheid. Conflict occurs in cities because that is where national conflicts are usually played out.

neighborhood a female domain. Today, with two-car and two-worker families more common, this has changed to some extent. However, Lopata (1980) and Wekerle (1980) have found that the city still imposes difficulties upon women that it does not on men. The most serious is the limited availability of child care, discussed in Chapter 6.

Marxist urban sociologists argue that the structure of the city has always reflected the needs of the capital-owning class (Castells, 1977, 1985; Gottdiener, 1985; Harvey, 1973; Tabb and Sawers, 1978). They point out, for example, that urban land use is in large part determined by what is profitable for banks, corporations, and real-estate interests (Molotch, 1979). The exercise of political power by these groups in urban politics is discussed in Chapter 9 (on this point, see also Whitt, 1982; Feagin, 1983, 1985; Logan and Molotch, 1987).

It is not just through politics, however, that the owners of capital shape the city. Such decisions as the opening or closing of a factory, for example, have tremendous impact on a city. Capitalists determine urban growth patterns largely through their decisions about where to locate. The way this process works is illustrated by historical analyses by Gordon (1978, 1977a, 1977b). Gordon's basic premise is that capitalists put their plants where they can make the most money, which in part involves locating where workers' wages can be kept low.

The Structure of the City

Human Ecology

One of the most influential approaches among sociologists who study the city has been **human ecology,** also sometimes called *urban social ecology.* Human ecology is concerned with the distribution of people over territory (see Park and Burgess, 1921) and with how people adjust and adapt to their environment (Hawley 1981, pp. 9–10; 1950). Specifically, it is concerned with the growth and decline of cities and city neighborhoods and with the distribution within the city of people with different social characteristics, such as race, social class, and marital and family status. It is also concerned with the economic processes that shape population distributions and with the distribution of different land uses within urban areas. Duncan (1959) has described human ecology as the study of relationships among *population, organization, environment,* and *technology*—a combination sometimes referred to as the *P.O.E.T.* complex. Because the patterns of interest to human ecologists largely concern population characteristics and are an outgrowth of migration, the ecological orientation is closely related to the sociological specialization of *demography,* discussed in Chapter 17.

One of the most important contributions of human ecology has been to improve our understanding of how different land uses and different groups of people are distributed within urban areas, and why they are so distributed. Human ecologists have developed three distinct theories concerning these questions: the *concentric-zones* model, the *sectoral* model, and the *multiple-nuclei* model. Each of these theories seems to fit some cities better than others, or even different characteristics of the same city.

The Concentric-Zones Model One basic premise of human ecology is that virtually every city has a center. In industrial and postindustrial cities, this center is known as the *central business district,* or "downtown." It is usually near the site where the city was originally settled. As the city grows over time, populations and land uses expand outward from the center. As a result, at any given time, the outer part of the urban area is the newest. The **concentric-zones model,** developed by Ernest W. Burgess of the University of Chicago in 1925, is based on this reality. It holds that population and land-use characteristics change as you move away from the center of the city. Thus, urban areas can be characterized as a set of rings around the center, each of which has different population characteristics and land-use patterns.

The concentric-zones model is depicted in the first part of Figure 18.1. In reality, the rings do not always have distinct boundaries, and they are not precisely circular. However, Burgess did find in his studies of Chicago and certain other industrial cities that the model fit reality fairly well. At the center was the business district, which was surrounded by what he called a "zone in transition," containing warehouses.

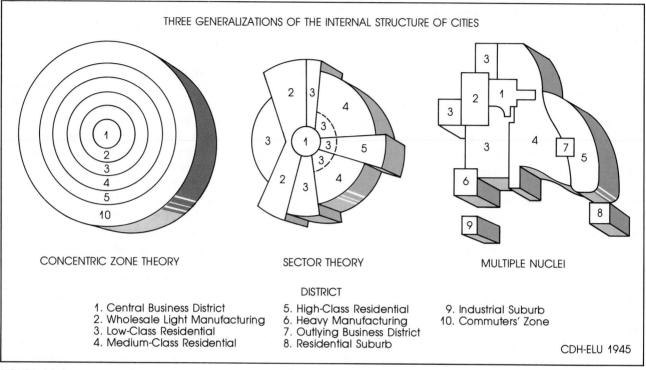

THREE GENERALIZATIONS OF THE INTERNAL STRUCTURE OF CITIES

CONCENTRIC ZONE THEORY

SECTOR THEORY

MULTIPLE NUCLEI

DISTRICT

1. Central Business District
2. Wholesale Light Manufacturing
3. Low-Class Residential
4. Medium-Class Residential

5. High-Class Residential
6. Heavy Manufacturing
7. Outlying Business District
8. Residential Suburb

9. Industrial Suburb
10. Commuters' Zone

CDH-ELU 1945

FIGURE 18-1
—Generalizations of Internal Structure of Cities
The concentric-zone theory is a generalization for all cities. The arrangement of the sectors in the sector theory varies from city to city. The diagram for multiple-nuclei represents one possible pattern among innumerable variations.

Although this area might formerly have been residential, residents were steadily being displaced by expanding businesses. Most of these residents were poor people. Moving out farther from the center, you would encounter working-class neighborhoods, then neighborhoods of gradually higher status. The newest housing and lowest population density were found on the fringe, where people could afford new houses, big lots, and the costs of commuting. As automobiles became commonplace, the population density of the fringe areas further diminished, giving rise to the low-density commuter suburbs that are so familiar today. Another change occurring as you moved away from the center was an increasing percentage of married couples,

families, and children. It should be noted that the concentric-zones model, which was originally based largely on Chicago, is applicable primarily to cities in industrial capitalist countries (Shibutani, 1986). Preindustrial cities have very different patterns (Sjoberg, 1955), and cities in socialist economies may also be very different because land use and housing locations are determined by government planning rather than by market forces and capitalist economic interests.

The Sectoral Model Although cities always grow outward, this outward growth does not always produce the concentric-zones pattern discussed by Burgess, even in industrialized capitalist countries. Homer Hoyt (1939) studied a broader range of American cities than Burgess and discovered that many of them were better described by a **sectoral model,** depicted in the second part of Figure 18.1. Sectors are pie-shaped segments of the city that extend outward from the center in different directions. These patterns develop because different social groups originally settle on different sides of the center of a city. As their populations grow, they expand outward, often along transportation routes such as streetcar lines or, more recently, expressways.

The Multiple-Nuclei Model   The third model of urban population distribution was developed by Harris and Ullman (1945). Their **multiple-nuclei model,** depicted in the third part of Figure 18.1, is based on the principle that some urban areas have not one center of activity, but many. Some cities, such as Boston, developed as a number of nearby communities and towns grew together into one great urban center. Because each community had its own center, the city contained a number of distinct centers. The multiple-nuclei model also reflects the tendency of some activities, such as heavy industry, to cluster together in certain areas of the city. Chicago, for example, has two distinct industrial areas: one along the southwest shore of Lake Michigan, south of the downtown area, and another one to the southwest along the railroad tracks (Choldin, 1985, p. 179). These industrial areas have historically been surrounded by working-class neighborhoods of people who are employed by the industries. Finally, another factor that produces the multiple-nuclei pattern is the tendency of some suburbs to grow into secondary commercial centers. Clayton, Missouri, a suburb of St. Louis, has become such a center, boasting a cluster of gleaming skyscrapers that you would expect to find "downtown," and not in the suburbs.

Most cities do not neatly fit any one of these models, but represent combinations of the three. Attempts to place cities into clear-cut categories usually involve an oversimplification of complex realities. Different social characteristics can be distributed differently even within the *same* urban area, as has been discovered by sociologists who study *urban social segregation.*

Urban Social Segregation

The models discussed above are all partly based on a pattern sociologists call **social segregation,** in which people with similar social characteristics live together in the same neighborhoods. Social segregation occurs largely because people with similar lifestyles prefer to live together, and some neighborhoods are better suited to a given lifestyle than others (Michelson, 1976, 1977). However, it also develops because people in one group try to keep people in other groups *out* of their neighborhoods, particularly different racial groups. Sociologists who study urban social segregation ask two main questions about the city: "What are the characteristics on which people are segregated in cities?" and "How are people with a given set of characteristics distributed in urban areas?" Sociologists interested in the second question have drawn heavily upon the concentric-zones, sectoral, and multiple-nuclei models, and they have developed sophisticated techniques using computers and census data to test the accuracy of these models for particular social characteristics. One factor that has made such studies possible is the availability of a wide range of data for *census tracts,* small neighborhood areas within cities, each of which has a population of about 3,000 to 6,000.

Social-Area Analysis   Using a technique they called *social-area analysis,* sociologists Ehsref Shevky and Wendell Bell (1955) argued that urban social segregation occurs on the basis of three fundamental social characteristics: socioeconomic status, family status, and race or ethnicity. They then identified specific variables from the 1940 and 1950 Censuses that they thought captured each of these concepts. Family status, for example, was ranked "high" in census tracts with many children, a high percentage of single-family houses, and few women in the labor force. (Because of the massive entry of married women into the labor force since Shevky and Bell published their research, the last variable would probably no longer be a good indicator.) They found that, at least in Los Angeles and San Francisco, the sets of variables they chose to represent each of the three fundamental characteristics did cluster closely together. They also found that people were indeed segregated on the basis of each of the three fundamental characteristics (Shevky and Bell, 1955; Shevky and Williams, 1949). Later research confirmed that the patterns discovered in West Coast cities by Shevky and Bell generally held true for cities in other parts of the country (Anderson and Bean, 1961; Van Arsdol, Camilleri, and Schmid, 1958).

Factorial Ecology Around the time Shevky and Bell were introducing social-area analysis, researchers began to use computers to study human ecology. Through a technique known as *factorial ecology,* researchers were able to take large data sets of 100 or more census variables and identify clusters of similar variables that represent underlying dimensions or concepts. Using this method, researchers have discovered that in most urban areas a broad range of census variables can be reduced to three basic dimensions: socioeconomic status, family status, and race/ethnicity (Rees, 1979; see also Perle, 1981; Elgie and Clark, 1982). Significantly, these are the same three bases of segregation that were identified by Shevky and Bell in their social-area analysis. In many of these studies, up to 75 percent of the variation in as many as 100 variables can be reduced to these three underlying concepts (Farley, 1985).

Factorial ecology can also be used to map the three dimensions to see whether each better fits the concentric-zones, sectoral, or multiple-nuclei patterns (Murdie, 1976; Boal, 1976). In general, family status fits the concentric-zones model, with unmarried people, childless couples, and renters living near the city's center, and families, children, and homeowners living farther away (Berry and Rees, 1969). However, the rise of apartment complexes near suburban "beltline" freeways may now be changing this pattern (Farley, 1985). Socioeconomic status is often distributed according to both the concentric-zones and sectoral models: It is higher going in some directions from the center than others (in other words, sectoral), but it also increases as you move from the center (concentric).

Racial Segregation The most pervasive form of urban social segregation in the United States is racial segregation, particularly between blacks and whites. Levels of segregation in American cities have declined since 1960, but not much. Most blacks still live in neighborhoods that are overwhelmingly black, and most whites live in neighborhoods that are overwhelmingly white (Massey and Denton, 1987, 1988; Jakubs, 1986; Farley, 1987c). Older cities in the Midwest and Northeast, with their long-established patterns of segregation, are the most rigidly segregated (Massey and Denton, 1987; Jakubs, 1986).

Unlike some other forms of urban social segregation, racial segregation is mainly the product of discrimination. It is *not* the product of black preferences, because study after study has shown that most blacks prefer to live in racially mixed rather than all-black neighborhoods (Farley et al., 1978; Farley, Bianchi, and Colasanto, 1979; Lake, 1981; Pettigrew, 1973). Neither is it a product of affordability. Although most blacks cannot afford to live in the wealthiest white neighborhoods, a large portion of the black population can afford to live in many white neighborhoods — but they don't. Studies based on the 1980 Census have found that if affordability were the only consideration, our urban areas would be only about one-quarter as segregated as they actually are (Farley, 1986b; Darden, 1987; Kain, 1987; see also Denton and Massey, 1988). This finding is consistent with earlier findings from the 1970 and 1960 Censuses (Hermalin and Farley, 1973; Taeuber and Taeuber, 1965).

RACIAL STEERING   Housing discrimination occurs in three important ways: racial steering, blockbusting, and redlining. *Racial steering* is a practice whereby real estate agents direct whites toward housing in all-white neighborhoods and blacks toward housing in all-black or racially mixed neighborhoods (Pearce, 1976; Lake, 1981). This perpetuates segregation, because in order for integrated neighborhoods to remain integrated, *both* races must move into them.

BLOCKBUSTING   The second form of housing discrimination is *blockbusting*: Real estate speculators attempt to scare white homeowners into selling their houses for less than they are worth by exploiting their fear of racial change in their neighborhoods. They then sell the house above market price to blacks, who can choose housing only in limited areas because of segregation. Because this practice blatantly violates the 1968 fair housing law, it has been largely replaced by the much subtler practice of racial steering.

REDLINING   The third form of racial discrimination is *redlining*: a practice whereby lenders and insurance companies refuse to make loans or sell insurance in certain neighborhoods, usually ones that are racially mixed or predominantly black. Redlining transforms housing in such neighborhoods from owner-occupied to renter-occupied, prevents upkeep of buildings, and contributes to abandonment of homes, apartment buildings, and businesses, whose owners cannot obtain loans or insurance. Moreover, by setting these processes in motion, redlining make whites more reluctant to buy in mixed neighborhoods. In spite of redlining and racial steering, survey data indicate that a sizable segment of the white population is willing to (and in some cases actively desires to) buy homes in racially mixed neighborhoods (Farley et al., 1978, 1979; Lake, 1981). The problem is that racial steering and redlining make it nearly impossible for them to do so. (In the "Personal Journey into Sociology" vignette for this chapter, sociologist Juliet Saltman discusses her studies of efforts to combat these practices and keep neighborhoods integrated.)

The Changing City in Postindustrial America

As the United States has gradually undergone the transition from an industrial economy to a postindustrial economy (see Chapter 12), America's urban areas have been profoundly affected. The declining role of industry, the shift toward a service economy, the changing distribution of wealth and income, and the pervasiveness of the automobile have all brought dramatic changes to American cities since World War II. These changes include the rise of the suburbs, the decline of the central city, the increasing concentration of urban poverty, joblessness, and homelessness, and the shift of urban growth from the "Frost Belt" of the Midwest and Northeast to the "Sun Belt" of the South and West. We shall begin our examination of these changes with a discussion of suburbanization.

The Rise of the Suburbs

As illustrated by Table 18.3, the percentage of Americans living in the suburbs has risen dramatically since World War II. The statistics in the table are based on a concept known as the **metropolitan statistical area (MSA)**. This concept was developed by the Census Bureau to reflect the fact that by the end of World War II, the population of urban areas was beginning to expand beyond the legal boundaries of the city. Using counties as building blocks, metropolitan statistical areas are intended to include the full extent of the

TABLE 18.3
Percent of Population in Central Cities, Suburban Areas, and Outside Metropolitan Areas, 1950–1980

YEAR	1950	1960	1970	1980
Total in Metropolitan Areas	62.4%	66.7	68.6	74.8
In Central Cities	35.4	33.4	31.4	30.0
In Suburban Areas	27.0	33.3	37.2	44.8
Outside Metropolitan Areas	37.5	33.3	31.4	25.2

SOURCE: 1980 data are from U.S. Bureau of the Census (1983), *Statistical Abstract of the United States, 1982–83*, p. 15. Data for earlier years are from U.S. Bureau of the Census (1972), *Statistical Abstract of the United States, 1972*, p. 16.

Note: Data are based on metropolitan area boundaries as they were defined in each census year. New areas were added to metropolitan areas in each census, both because new areas grew large enough to be defined as metropolitan, and because new counties were added to existing areas to reflect the expansion of these areas.

metropolitan area, both city and suburbs. Each MSA consists of one or more *central cities,* which must have a combined population of 50,000 or more, and a *suburban ring,* which consists of the rest of the county or counties containing the central cities plus any adjoining counties that are largely urban in character and economically linked to the central cities. As an example, the Memphis MSA consists of Shelby County, Tennessee (which contains the city of Memphis), and adjoining Tipton County, Tennessee, Crittendon County, Arkansas, and DeSoto County, Mississippi. As

The growth of suburbs has been the most prominent trend in metropolitan America since World War II. Today, more Americans live in suburbs than in either central cities or rural areas.

Sociologist at Work

Writing a book on the neighborhood stabilization movement (*A Fragile Movement: The Struggle for Neighborhood Stabilization,* Greenwood/Praeger 1989) grew out of my experience of living in Akron's west side for over 30 years. Neighborhood stabilization is an organized effort to prevent "white flight" and thus maintain racially integrated neighborhoods. My earlier book (*Open Housing: Dynamics of a Social Movement,* Praeger 1978) had stemmed from my experience with the fair housing movement in Akron, Ohio. Both movements are composed of people who believe that it is possible and desirable for people of different races to live together as neighbors. My participation in both local movements prompted me to search for further knowledge about racial integration elsewhere in the nation. Was what I saw in Akron typical of what was happening in other communities?

When I analyzed the 20-year struggle for fair housing and integration maintenance in Akron, I slowly and painfully came to realize that it is easier to *attain* racial integration than to *maintain* it. i thus became curious as to whether racial integration in this society was merely a transitional stage on the way to total resegregation, as other people had claimed. Was integration just a brief step in the

Juliet Saltman is Professor Emerita of Sociology at Kent State University, where she has been nominated several times for the Distinguished Teaching Award. She has also been involved in the open-housing and stabilization movements at all levels and has received national and local awards for her work. She is the author of Open Housing: Dynamics of a Social Movement *(Praeger, 1978) and* A Fragile Movement: The Struggle for Neighborhood Stabilization *(Greenwood/Praeger, 1989).*

transition of neighborhoods from all-white to all-black? Were there any examples of really successful stable integrated neighborhoods in this country? I had to find out.

When I began this research, I thought that I would not find any success stories. For this reason I was

surprised and delighted when I did. My research questions then changed from "What happened to the Neighborhood Stabilization movement?" and "*Can* racially integrated neighborhoods remain integrated?" to "Can we identify the factors that lead to success or failure in maintaining racial integration?"

I answered "Yes" to the last two questions, using comparative in-depth examples of success and failure in the development and maturation of the stabilization movement in a number of neighborhoods in various U.S. cities. I analyzed the movement on two levels — community and national — through a study of movement organizations on each level and their interaction. The analysis of the national level offered a detailed study of the only national organization devoted solely to this movement's goal of integration maintenance — National Neighbors, now based in Washington, D.C. Here I examined not only the national group's development over time, but also the interaction between the national organization and the local groups. We see many of the organizational struggles on the local level repeated on the national level, and we recognize that the national climate affects both levels in the same way and significantly affects the whole movement. If federal fair housing laws

this example shows, MSAs can cross state lines. As of 1980, there were about 320 MSAs in the United States.

The population in an MSA can be divided into two parts: those who live in the central cities and those who live in the suburbs. Since World War II, the pro-

portion of people living in the central cities has fallen steadily, and the proportion living in the suburbs has risen steadily. Today, more people live in the suburbs than anywhere else, a complete reversal of the situation that existed just 50 years ago. As more people

are not enforced, for example, integrated neighborhoods will be harder to maintain.

Based on field research, census data, review of documents, historical analysis, and some participant observation, I considered the success and failure of neighborhood stabilization at the local level. The clearly successful cases are those where the neighborhood remained integrated and the organization remained active throughout the time period I studied. The clear failures are cases where the organization died and the neighborhood did not remain integrated. Finally, some cases were *conditional;* in these, the organization continued to be active, but the neighborhood shifted from racially mixed to predominantly black.

Case studies offered as examples of success were Indianapolis, Rochester, and Milwaukee, supplemented with briefer profiles of urban neighborhoods in Nashville, Denver, and Philadelphia. Suburban efforts in Shaker Heights, Ohio; Teaneck, New Jersey; and Oak Park, Illinois, were also examples of success. The example offered of failure was a neighborhood in Hartford, Connecticut. Conditional examples were in the case study of Akron, Ohio, and briefer profiles of urban neighborhoods in Brooklyn, New York; Washington, D.C.; and

Philadelphia. All together, I examined 12 neighborhoods in 11 different cities, and also 3 suburbs with movement programs sponsored and supported by their local government.

What did I find? I found some common factors that accounted for the formation of the stabilization movement in each local community, such as racial concentration and urban-renewal dislocation. I found many of the same obstacles and institutional forces in each community that each movement organization had to confront, such as real-estate blockbusting and bank redlining. These common factors explain the similarity of programs each group developed, long before they knew of each other's existence.

Significantly, I was finally able to identify some of the factors that lead to success or failure in this movement. I concluded that a neighborhood organization is necessary, but it cannot by itself guarantee the maintenance of racial integration. After reviewing internal and external factors relevant to movement achievement, I found that four critical external factors are related to success or failure:

1. The amenities of the neighborhood
2. The role of the city
3. School desegregation

4. Public housing deconcentration

Of these, the "killer variables" are the schools and public housing. In the examples I found of successful neighborhood stabilization, none had a concentration of public housing in the target neighborhood, and all had a system-wide school desegregation program. These are essential for the successful affirmative marketing of the target neighborhood because they increase the chances that whites as well as blacks will continue to move into the neighborhood, thus maintaining racial integration. If all neighborhoods in a city have racially balanced schools, for example, one neighborhood cannot be singled out by whites as "the one with the black schools."

Finally, based on my findings, I developed 13 hypotheses concerning neighborhood stabilization that I hope other scholars will test and research further. I suggest some policy implications of this study, and I offer a comprehensive strategy for maintaining racial integration in urban neighborhoods.

Even when integration maintenance has been attained, the success is a fragile one, and all gains could be quickly eroded. Eternal vigilance is necessary to counteract the massive institutional forces that hasten neighborhood instability and resegregation.

have moved to the suburbs, jobs, retail businesses, office complexes, warehouses, and factories have all followed (Choldin, 1985, pp. 363–369). In most metropolitan areas, the majority of the population is suburban (the average is about 60 percent), and in

some areas the majority of economic activity is also suburban. Moreover, despite much talk about a "return to the city" in the 1970s and 1980s (discussed below), the movement of people and economic activity from central cities to the suburbs continues. In part, this is because people or businesses who move to a new urban area tend to locate in the suburbs rather than the central city.

Causes of Suburbanization

There are a number of reasons for the tremendous surge of people and economic activity into the suburbs. One is human preference. People want the open space, peace, and quiet of rural areas, but they depend on cities for jobs, services, and a variety of amenities. The suburbs offer the best compromise between these two competing sets of needs and desires (see Claab, 1963, pp. 233–234). Moreover, for those who want and can afford a large house and a big yard, the open space of the urban fringe is the obvious choice of location. The generally healthy growth of the economy after World War II made the suburbs affordable to growing numbers of Americans.

Suburbanization is not entirely the product of people's choices, however. Government policy, technology, demographic trends, and economic interests all contributed to the growth of the suburbs (Palen, 1987, pp. 182–187). The U.S. government encouraged and subsidized homeownership through such mechanisms as the home mortgage tax deduction and, after World War II, substantial subsidies of mortgage interest through loan programs administered by the Federal Housing Administration (FHA) and Veterans Administration (VA). These subsidies enabled millions of middle- and lower-middle-income Americans to purchase their own homes. Although these policies were undoubtedly popular because people *wanted* to buy homes in the suburbs, it should be stressed that they also served the interests of large-scale real-estate developers, who were able to amass great fortunes by mass-producing standardized, relatively low-cost suburban housing.

Another government policy that contributed to suburbanization was the construction of the interstate highway system. The freeways enabled people to commute up to 50 miles within an hour. Finally, the 1950s were the years of the baby boom, which meant a massive surge in families with children—the group with the lifestyle best suited to the suburbs. In short, a number of factors worked together to produce the suburban transformation of the United States after World War II.

Life in the Suburbs

Like cities, suburbs have been both praised and condemned. On the one hand, they are praised as the ideal place to raise children—quieter, safer, and roomier than the city, but with all the urban amenities close by. On the other hand, they are condemned as uninteresting places of conformity where "they all live in little boxes, and all look just the same." As usual, both the praisers and the condemners overstate their case. In the whole, suburbanites are somewhat more affluent and less heterogeneous than central-city residents, and there are fewer blacks and Hispanics in the suburbs than in the city. However, the socioeconomic differences are not great, and the suburbs have become more diverse as different groups of people have moved there. Research published in the early 1960s showed little difference between city and suburban residents of similar socioeconomic status with respect to organizational participation and cultural and recreational interests (Berger, 1960; Cohen and Hodges, 1963), but more recent research has uncovered some differences. Choldin (1980), for example, found that suburban women are more involved in neighborhood and community organizations than are city women of the same race and socioeconomic status.

There are other ways in which suburbanites differ *on the average* from city residents. Partly because they more often own their homes and thus have a greater investment in their neighborhoods, suburbanites interact more with their neighbors and are in general more involved with their neighborhoods (Fava, 1959; Gans, 1967; Choldin, 1980; Fischer and Jackson, 1976). Another reason for this interaction is that suburbanites are more likely than city residents to have children, and adult neighbors often become better acquainted because their children are playmates. On the other hand, research results conflict on the question of whether suburbanites' lives are more centered around their children (Gans, 1967; Berger, 1960). Gans (1972b) has characterized suburban neighbors as "quasi-primary groups" because their relationships are typically closer than the secondary-group relationships of the business and commercial world but not as close as the bond between close friends and family members. To a large extent, the neighbor relationship seems to be one of mutual assistance, which is one of the characteristics Toennies

As retailing has shifted from the city to the suburbs, suburban malls have replaced downtown areas as centers of activity for many Americans. For these young people, the mall is a place to meet friends and have fun as much as it is a place to shop.

associated with the rural gemeinschaft. In general, suburbanites like their place of residence better than city dwellers do, but this partly reflects their higher average socioeconomic status.

The claim that the suburbs produce a certain type of lifestyle appears to be an overstatement. Michelson's (1977) study of people moving into city and suburban neighborhoods in Toronto offers a better analysis. Michelson found that people largely choose a neighborhood and housing type that fits their lifestyle at a given point in their lives. The city fits the lifestyle of unmarried people and childless couples, especially those who are cosmopolitan in outlook, whereas the suburbs fit the lifestyle of families with children. The only people who are likely to feel real dissatisfaction with their environment are those who for some reason — such as cost — cannot get the kind of housing that fits their lifestyle or aspirations.

A final note that should be stressed is that, as they age, some suburbs are becoming more like the central city, specifically in terms of problems. During the 1980s, increasing numbers of suburbs experienced loss of jobs, housing abandonment, racial conflict, rising poverty rates, and population decline. It is in the central cities, however, where these problems have been most severe, a pattern to which we now turn our attention.

The Crisis of the Central Cities

While the suburbs have experienced booming growth, the central cities have experienced steady decline since World War II. Despite a few bright spots, such as the rejuvenation of the downtown area in many cities, the dominant condition of the larger, older central cities has been deepening crisis. This has been manifested in a number of ways.

Population Decline The majority of large cities have lost a substantial portion of their population through outmigration. This trend has been particularly pronounced in the Midwest and Northeast: between 1950 and 1980, St. Louis lost nearly half of its population; Detroit, Cleveland, Boston, Minneapolis, and Cincinnati all lost between one-quarter and one-third; and New York, Chicago, Baltimore, and San Francisco lost between 10 and 20 percent. Even some cities in the South and West have begun to lose population; Atlanta and Denver are examples.

The Urban Underclass As those who could afford to relocate to the suburbs did so, an increasing concentration of the minority poor was left behind in the central cities. Sociologists refer to these poor people as the *underclass* (see Chapter 11). Wilson (1987, p. 50) uses a study of Chicago to illustrate the growing concentration of poverty in the cities. Between 1970 and 1980, the population of the city fell by 11 percent, but the number of poor people living in the city *grew* by 24 percent. The major reason a number of people living in Chicago (and other central cities) became poor during the 1970s was increased joblessness (Wilson, 1987). This rise in joblessness occurred for several reasons that are discussed elsewhere in this book: loss of jobs from the central city (Chapter 9), housing segregation that excludes minorities from areas with the greatest job growth (Chapter 11), and limited educational opportunities combined with rising educational requirements for many jobs (Chapter 14). Another factor is the increasing proportion of female-headed households in the central cities; these women literally cannot afford to work in the absence of subsidized day care and health care (Chapters 6 and 13).

The Urban Fiscal Crisis The combination of an overall population decline and a rise in the number of poor residents is affecting cities in a number of ways. First and foremost, it means a sharp increase in the *proportion* of the city's population that is poor. Poor populations require more services, particularly in the areas of health, welfare, and police protection; however, they pay less in taxes. The consequence is that city governments have had to do more with less, a reality further aggravated by cutbacks in federal aid to cities in the 1980s. City after city has had to curtail needed services; in the worst cases, cities such as New York, Cleveland, and East St. Louis have experienced financial emergencies. Besides cutting back on services, cities have been unable to maintain their aging and overused *infrastructures:* roads, sewers, mass transit, water systems, and bridges. Thus, the collapse of bridges and sewers has become an increasingly common event in American cities. Any American who lives in or near a major city has experienced the frustrations and delays that result from inadequate transportation systems.

Homelessness One effect of the increasing amount and concentration of poverty has been an increase in homelessness. Hundreds of thousands—perhaps millions—of Americans no longer have a permanent place to live. The homeless are found on streets, in parks, in subway stations, in shelters, in "welfare hotels," even in campgrounds, in swelling numbers. Just as the poverty rate soared in the early 1980s, budget cutbacks curtailed federal housing programs. There were more poor people, and fewer dollars available to house them. That homelessness increased is hardly surprising.

Growing up in the Underclass The growth of the urban underclass has major implications for the future of the United States. Historically, the cities have served as a launching ground for upward mobility and assimilation for both the native poor and immigrants (Bradbury, Downs, and Small, 1982). With today's unprecedented concentration of poverty, cities may be losing that function. Poor urban dwellers are more likely than ever to live in neighborhoods where nearly everyone is poor or near-poor. Millions of children today are growing up in neighborhoods where jobs are scarce, in families where nobody can find a job, and in areas where key institutions have left along with the middle class (Wilson, 1987, pp. 140–146). In such an environment, the traditional work ethic doesn't

pay, but a "fast buck" can be made through drug dealing, theft, or prostitution. The result today is youth gangs, and the result tomorrow could be an *entire* generation of inner-city residents outside the legitimate work force.

Gentrification

During the 1970s and 1980s, the popular press has written extensively about "urban revitalization" in the older central cities. Many neighborhoods experiencing revitalization are undergoing what sociologists call **gentrification.** This term, first coined in London, refers to the return of the upper class ("gentry") to older and formerly deteriorating central-city neighborhoods. Many observers have argued that gentrification will rescue the inner cities by bringing back a more stable and affluent population, improving the tax base, attracting new investment, and reducing the concentration of the poor in the central city.

Although gentrification has upgraded the housing stock in certain areas, its potential benefits are limited. The most important reason for this is that, except in a few cases like Washington, D.C., gentrification is occurring on too small a scale to offset the outmigration of the middle class from the central city (Farley, 1984; Gale, 1980; Spain, 1980; Sternlieb and Hughes, 1983). It affects a limited number of neighborhoods, mostly those near the center of the city that have large, architecturally interesting houses that have fallen into disrepair. Most of the gentrifiers are either single or married couples without children; families with children continue to prefer the suburbs. Moreover, gentrification often involves not a "back-to-the-city" movement, but a movement from one part of the city to another (Clay, 1980). For all these reasons, average family incomes in the city have continued to fall relative to those in the suburbs (Long, 1980), despite gentrification.

Displacement of the Poor One criticism of gentrification is that it displaces the poor, either *directly* through eviction or, more commonly, *indirectly* by raising their taxes and rents beyond what they can afford. A particular problem is that the poor are least able to afford the costs of displacement, which include moving expenses and, usually, higher rent in their new home. A particularly disturbing fact is that, although public funds are often used to encourage gentrification, there is no public subsidy of these expenses for the displaced poor. Moreover, no public housing has been built in recent years, and housing subsidies for the poor have been curtailed. Of course, some displacement occurs even without gentrification as landlords abandon their buildings when their tenants' incomes become so low that they cannot pay enough rent for the building to be profitable (Mendelson and Quinn, 1977). This has led some to argue that the real problem is not gentrification, but rather that the supply of subsidized housing is far too small.

Downtown Redevelopment Gentrification is not the only kind of redevelopment occurring on the urban scene. Downtown redevelopment projects have been undertaken on a dramatic scale in many cities, including Harborplace in Baltimore, Union Station in St. Louis and Indianapolis, Renaissance Center in Detroit, and the area around Faneuil Hall in Boston. These spectacular developments and others like them have brought new vitality to the centers of cities that were well on the way to becoming deserted. In many central cities, banks, corporate offices, insurance

companies, and other service-oriented activities have led to dramatic downtown building booms. However, there are definite limits to the benefits of such redevelopment. In general, downtown redevelopment has not provided jobs for city dwellers who need them, because these people lack the necessary education. Thus, redevelopment has done little or nothing to lower inner-city unemployment (Levine, 1987). A related criticism is that large downtown developments siphon off resources that might have been invested elsewhere in the city.

Uneven Development of American Cities

Although suburbanization and urban decline have occurred to some extent in all parts of the United States, these trends have been far more pronounced in the Midwest and Northeast (the "Frost Belt") than in the South and West (the "Sun Belt"). In general, Sun Belt metropolitan areas are growing; Frost Belt metropolitan areas are not. Sociologists refer to such regional differences in urban growth as **uneven development** (Watkins and Perry, 1977; Frisbie and Kasarda, 1988, pp. 657–658). This term is also sometimes used to describe the differences in growth between cities and suburbs, or between downtown and residential neighborhoods. Sociologists have two fundamental disagreements over the meaning of uneven development among cities in different regions. The first concerns whether Frost Belt and Sun Belt cities are simply at different stages of a similar process of growth and decline or whether they are following fundamentally different courses of development (Frey, 1987). The second concerns whether regional differences in urban development reflect differences in the efficiency and effectiveness of different kinds of cities (the functionalist view) or whether they are the product of fundamental societal inequalities in power and wealth (the conflict view).

Different Processes or Different Stages? One view about the uneven development of American cities is that "Frost Belt" and "Sun Belt" cities are in

Baltimore's Harborplace. This project, stimulated by substantial public investment, has changed the face of Baltimore's waterfront and contributed to the development of downtown Baltimore. However, it did little or nothing to help the many poor and unemployed people in the city.

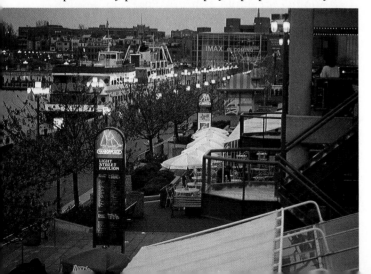

different stages of a similar process of growth and decline. According to this view, Frost Belt cities like New York, Philadelphia, Pittsburgh, Chicago, Detroit, St. Louis, and Cleveland are losing population and becoming increasingly poor because they are older cities. The quality of housing is deteriorating, people are moving out, and the cities are losing population. They cannot do much about it, because they are surrounded by established suburbs and cannot expand their boundaries by annexing these growing areas. Sun Belt cities like Houston, Phoenix, San Diego, Los Angeles, Tampa, San Antonio, and San Jose are at an earlier stage of development. They are still growing, they have considerable new housing within their boundaries, and they can expand those boundaries outward to accommodate growth (Fleischman, 1977). In all these ways, they are similar to the Frost Belt cities in the early twentieth century. At that time, the major cities of the Midwest and Northeast were all experiencing rapid growth.

This view that Sun Belt and Frost Belt cities are in different stages of the same process of growth and decline predicts that the now-growing cities of the West and South will eventually age, become surrounded by suburbs, and begin to lose population. In fact, this is already happening in a number of the older cities of the South and West. Denver, San Francisco, Atlanta, Fort Worth, and Portland all lost population between 1970 and 1980, and Los Angeles barely grew during that decade.

An opposing view about uneven development emphasizes the transition from an industrial to a post-industrial economy in the United States. As was discussed in Chapter 12, the postindustrial economy is based largely on services, such as commerce, finance, tourism, and real estate, as well as on high-technology industries, such as electronics, aircraft, and energy (see Sale, 1975). From this standpoint, the South and West, with their warmer climates, greater recreational amenities, and abundant energy supplies, are the natural locations of new growth. Proponents of this viewpoint note that even though some Sun Belt cities have lost population recently, the overall growth of MSAs has been far greater in the South and West than in the Northeast and Midwest. In the latter two regions, even

some inner suburbs have lost population; in the former two regions, the majority of central cities have gained population, and suburban growth has been even more dramatic.

Metropolitan statistical areas like New York, Chicago, Detroit, Philadelphia, and St. Louis barely grew, or even lost population, between 1970 and 1980 because suburban growth was at best just sufficient to offset central-city decline. In contrast, the growth rates of the Dallas, Houston, Atlanta, and San Diego MSAs averaged about 45 percent in that same period. Thus, this view holds that uneven development does not just involve the situation of the central city, but also the overall rate of metropolitan growth reflecting the various economic specializations of different areas (Watkins and Perry, 1977).

The Conflict Theory of Uneven Development
Conflict theorists argue that uneven development reflects inequalities of wealth and power (Sawers and Tabb, 1984). More-powerful interest groups and more-powerful cities erect barriers to ensure their own growth and to prevent growth elsewhere that might threaten their interests (Watkins and Perry, 1977, p. 26; Gordon, 1977b; Squires et al., 1988; see also Molotch, 1976). Many examples can be used to illustrate this process. Federal taxing and spending policies have for a number of years generally favored the South and West over the Northeast and Midwest. In other words, Frost Belt cities pay more in taxes and get less back in federal expenditures than cities in the South and West (Watkins and Perry, 1977, p. 50). One important reason for this is that military spending has gone heavily to the West and South.

Another example concerns uneven development within cities. Large real-estate companies, banks, and corporations use their influence with city officials to get such benefits as abatement of property taxes on new developments or local money to upgrade streets, sidewalks, and lighting in neighborhoods where new businesses or expensive housing are being located. In more and more instances businesses secure the land for their projects free or at very low prices through government use of the right of *eminent domain*. This right allows government to take land from its owners "for the greater good" and "at a fair market price" even when owners don't want to sell it. In Detroit, this right was used to force over 1,000 families out of the Poletown neighborhood, at a cost to the government of $200 million—after which the land was sold to General Motors for $8 million (Palen, 1987, p. 281). Finally, although substantial public money was used to stimulate downtown development in Baltimore, the poor and unemployed did not share in the benefits (Levine, 1987). The project contributed to the development of the downtown area and aided the financial interests of downtown businesses, but it did little for anyone living in the neighborhoods. Thus, uneven development in Baltimore (1) was clearly the product of government policies, and (2) benefited certain interest groups who had disproportionate power over the decision-making process. In general, conflict theorists see uneven development as resulting from cooperative actions between governments and wealthy private interests that have disproportionate influence over government (Jaret, 1983).

Summary

Cities are defined on the basis of population size, density, and heterogeneity. They were made possible by production of an agricultural surplus, the development of regional transportation systems, and growth in demand for urban products. Yet, these same factors also acted as limits on urban growth, and cities accounted for only a small share of the population in virtually all societies until the Industrial Revolution. The demographic transition added another impetus to urbanization: As rural populations grew beyond what these areas could support, people migrated to the city. The population of cities grew tremendously, in some cases to tens of millions. Thus, today's urbanization in much of the world is on a scale utterly unheard of until the past century or so.

In the United States, rapid urbanization began in the mid-nineteenth century and continued until around 1960. In the Third World, urbanization has been more recent, and in some areas the majority of the population is still rural. In many countries, urbanization has exceeded the ability of the economy to support an urban population, resulting in massive urban poverty and shantytowns. Even so, the fastest-growing cities in the world today are in the less-economically developed countries.

Since the surge of urbanization that accompanied industrialization, sociologists have been interested in the effects of urban living on society and human behavior. Early theorists such as Toennies, Simmel, and Wirth were generally pessimistic, arguing that urban life resulted in social isolation, impersonal relations, and other problems. However, actual research on urban populations has cast doubt on most of these arguments. Although urbanites may have a greater number of impersonal contacts and client relationships than people in rural areas, they generally do not lack friends and close family relationships, and their levels of mental health equal those of rural populations. Moreover, there is no such thing as the "typical urbanite": there are many different groups of people in urban areas, with many different lifestyles. Some groups have very close relationships with neighbors and kin; others have relationships that are more wide-ranging and are based on common activities and interests rather than neighborhood or kinship. Because of this diversity, urbanites tend to be somewhat more tolerant and enjoy greater personal freedom than people in rural societies.

A key aspect of urban sociology concerns human ecology, the study of relationships between population and territory. Social segregation, a pattern whereby people with similar characteristics live together, is found in all cities. Depending on its history, a particular city can exhibit various combinations of three common patterns of population distribution: concentric zones, sectors, and multiple nuclei. The most important factors influencing where people live and how they group together are social class, family status, and race or ethnicity. Racial and ethnic segregation has been especially persistent in American cities and, in the case of racial segregation, has often been the product of deliberate discrimination.

Since World War II the bulk of the urban population of the United States, and a good deal of its economic activity, have shifted from the central cities to the suburbs.

Transportation innovations, preferences for more space, government policy, and economic trends have all contributed to this development. The suburbs tend to have higher-income populations than cities, a higher percentage of families with children, and a higher percentage of whites.

Glossary

urbanization The process whereby an increasing share of a population lives in cities.

functional specialization The tendency of different cities or metropolitan areas to specialize in different types of economic activity.

hinterland The area around a city that is dependent upon the city for goods, services, and markets.

overurbanization A situation, common among less-developed countries, in which the population of cities expands beyond what can be supported by the economy of these cities.

gemeinschaft According to Toennies, a traditional community in which relations between people are close and personal, behavior is governed by tradition, and contacts with strangers are rare.

gesellschaft According to Toennies, an urban society in which personal goals come before community objectives, relations are impersonal, and tradition is weak.

human ecology An area of sociology that is concerned with the relationships of people and their activity to territory and the physical environment.

concentric-zones model A theory in urban sociology holding that population characteristics and land use change systematically as you move away from the center of the city,

such that they are arranged roughly as a series of rings around the center of the city.

sectoral model A theory holding that urban population groups and land use are arranged in pie-shaped segments extending outward in different directions from the center of the city.

multiple-nuclei model A theory holding that population groups and land use in urban areas tend to concentrate in distinct and scattered clusters, often around a number of distinct centers of activity scattered around an urban area.

social segregation The tendency for people with similar social characteristics to live together in the same neighborhoods.

metropolitan statistical area (MSA) An area consisting of a central city or cluster of up to three central cities, the remainder of the county containing the central cities, and any adjacent counties that are urban in character and linked to those cities.

gentrification The movement of the upper class into older central-city neighborhoods, leading to renovation of buildings and a turnover in neighborhood population.

uneven development The tendency of some cities or neighborhoods to grow and prosper while others stagnate or decline.

Further Reading

CHOLDIN, HARVEY M. 1985. *Cities and Suburbs: An Introduction to Urban Sociology*. New York: McGraw Hill. A readable and thorough introduction to urban sociology, written by a leading researcher on urban and suburban social environments. Topics addressed include the histories of urban development, urban social ecology, urban community and interaction in the city, suburbanization, and urban problems.

GANS, HERBERT J. 1967. *The Levittowners*. New York: Random House; and Herbert J. Gans. 1962. *The Urban Villagers*. New York:

Free Press. Both of these books, written by one of America's best-known urban sociologists, are classics in the field. Both are products of long-term participant observation and in-depth interviews that Gans conducted while living in the neighborhoods he studied. *The Levittowners* is a study of life in a mass-produced lower-middle-class suburb, while *The Urban Villagers* is a study of an Italian working-class neighborhood in Boston that was subsequently destroyed by urban renewal because it had been mislabeled a slum.

SALTMAN, JULIET. 1989. *A Fragile Movement: The Struggle for Neighborhood Stabilization.* New York: Greenwood/Praeger. Written by the author of this chapter's "Personal Journey into Sociology," this book explores the movement to keep neighborhoods racially integrated. Saltman combines the methods and insights of an urban sociologist with experiences she gained as a participant in that movement.

TOBIN, GARY. 1987. *Divided Neighborhoods: Changing Patterns of Racial Segregation.* Urban Affairs Annual Reviews, Vol. 32. Newbury Park, CA: Sage Publications. A series of chapters addressing the extent, causes, and consequences of racial housing segregation in the 1980s, written by experts on various aspects of the problem.

WILSON, WILLIAM JULIUS. 1987. *The Truly Disadvantaged: The Inner City, the Underclass, and Public Policy.* Chicago: University of Chicago Press. A current insightful analysis of contemporary urban poverty, by a winner of the prestigious MacArthur Prize fellowship. Wilson shows how the loss of stable, good-paying jobs in the central city has led to increasing concentration of the urban minority poor, thus depriving them not only of job opportunities, but also of role models for employment and upward mobility.

CHAPTER 19

Collective Behavior and Social Movements

On the evening of March 11, 1974, a crowd of about 5,000 students assembled on the "Diag" at the center of the University of Michigan campus. Repeatedly, the throng made sudden surges to the left or right, as everyone in the crowd ran in the direction the people ahead of them were running. Each surge was triggered by two or three people running naked past the edges of the crowd. In the midst of the crowd, utterly ignored, wandered one man wearing nothing but a Nixon mask.

At the same place, on October 15, 1969, there were 20,000 or more. There may have been some Nixon masks in that crowd, but there were no naked people, and the mood was far more serious. This crowd heard a series of speeches about the horrors of the Vietnam War. When this crowd began to move, it was not to chase naked people, but to march, sing, and chant in opposition to the war.

The first crowd described above was participating in a brief college fad known as "streaking." Similar incidents took place at about 800 college campuses around the United States in 1974, most of them within 1 week in early March (Aguirre, Quarantelli, and Mendoza, 1988). The second crowd was participating in the Moratorium, a nationwide 1-day protest against the war in Vietnam. In this case, too, similar events took place on hundreds of college campuses around the country and involved between 1 and 3 million people.

bviously, there are both similarities and differences between streaking and the Moratorium. These events are examples of two related but distinguishable phenomena known as *collective behavior* and *social movements.* What the two events had in common is that both involved people acting *collectively* rather than as individuals. With respect to purpose, however, streaking and the Moratorium were entirely different. The streaking crowd had no clear purpose other than to "have fun," and perhaps to "outstreak" other nearby campuses. Those who participated in the Moratorium, however, had a very clear purpose: to oppose U.S. participation in the war in Vietnam. The presence of a clear purpose is what distinguishes a social movement from the broader concept of collective behavior.

Collective Behavior

Collective behavior can be defined as large numbers of people acting together in an extraordinary situation, in which usual norms governing behavior do not apply. In some instances, people make up new norms as they go along. Collective behavior occurs in a great variety of forms, including crowds, rumors, panics, riots, "urban legends," fashions and fads, mass hysteria, and mass suicide. As different as these things are, they all involve behaviors or beliefs by sizable numbers of people that deviate from normal or past norms (Lofland, 1986, p. 37).

Causes of Collective Behavior

One way that collective behavior differs from other social behavior is that it does not normally occur in ongoing *social groups,* that is, groups that interact regularly and share a common purpose (see Chapter 7). Rather, collective behavior occurs among *aggregates* or *collectivities:* sets of people, often large in number, who interact only in a temporary or superficial way. These sets of people may be *localized* in one place, in

which case they are called **crowds,** or they may be *dispersed,* as in the case of rumors, urban legends, and fashions (Turner and Killian, 1987). Dispersed collectivities are called **masses.**

There are two important characteristics of aggregates or collectivities that lead to behavior that does not occur in ordinary, ongoing social groups. First, as the distinction implies, collectivities themselves interact only temporarily, even though they often include many small clusters of friends and acquaintances. In many cases the interaction in collectivities is superficial and at a distance. Second, unlike groups, collectivities do not have clear *boundaries:* in other words, it is not clear who belongs to a collectivity and who doesn't. Consider an outdoor rally at the center of a college campus. Some people are clearly participating; others are "just watching"; still others are "passing through" on their way to somewhere else. Are all of these people part of the crowd? Or does the crowd consist only of those who are participating or who stopped to watch? Or, perhaps, only those who actively participate? There is no obvious answer.

Because of these differences, some of the usual norms that govern human behavior can break down in collectivities, and people in collectivities therefore frequently behave in different ways than they otherwise would. Neil Smelzer (1962) developed what he called a *value-added theory* to identify conditions that increase the likelihood of such collective behavior. Among the key elements of his theory are social control, structural conduciveness and structural strain, and precipitating incidents.

Breakdown of Social Control Clearly, *social control* (Chapter 8) is weaker in collectivities than in groups. This is because the individual has no ongoing relationship with the collectivity to be concerned about. At the same time, however, the collectivity frequently develops norms of its own, often on the spot. Because the collectivity is temporary and ill defined, it is not fully governed by usual societal norms, and therefore the collectivity's norms often do not conform to the usual norms of society. Instead, they offer an alternative set of guidelines for behavior or beliefs. Thus, when interacting with a collectivity, people sometimes do things they would never do either when alone or when part of their everyday, ongoing social groups.

Structural Conduciveness Although a collectivity (either localized or dispersed) is a necessary condition for collective behavior, it does not always result in collective behavior. Rather, collective behavior occurs when there is **structural conduciveness**—that is, when the situation in some way encourages collective behavior. Just what this means depends on the type of behavior. In the case of a rumor, fear, suspicion, and incomplete information are often underlying causes: People spread rumors concerning things they are afraid of or suspect, but about which they lack direct information (Rosnow and Fine, 1976). In the case of a riot, some collective grievance is often (though not always) present (Smelser, 1962). Smelser referred to the conflicts of interest that produce such grievances as *structural strain*. As we discuss various types of collective behavior, we shall explore further the kinds

---

Elvis Presley in concert. In the late 1980s, repeated rumors surfaced that Presley, who died in 1977, was in reality still alive.

of situations that are conducive to different types of collective behavior.

Precipitating Incident Finally, there is usually a **precipitating incident** that triggers some type of collective behavior (Smelser, 1963). In the case of fashion, it could be a particular style of clothes or hair worn by a famous person. Figure skater Dorothy Hamill, British Crown Princess Diana, and former U.S. First Lady Jacqueline Kennedy Onassis each triggered a major fashion trend in hair style when she was at the peak of her popularity. In the case of riots, a fight or an arrest often acts as a precipitating incident; in the case of rumors, it may be the broadcast of the rumor by a television or radio station that makes it widespread, even when it has been around but generally ignored for years. Such was the case in 1969, when a Detroit radio station broadcast the false rumor that Beatle Paul McCartney was dead—a rumor that dated at least to 1967. A similar but ironically opposite rumor occurred in 1988, when several radio stations announced that Elvis Presley, dead since 1977, was really alive. Again, the rumor had been around for years, but suddenly it became much more widely circulated and believed.

Types of Collective Behavior

As has already been noted, one way to classify the various types of collective behavior is by the type of collectivity involved: crowd or mass. Another is by the predominant type of emotion expressed. According to Lofland (1985), three emotions are commonly expressed by collective behavior: fear, hostility, and joy. Other emotions may also drive collective behavior, such as grief (Plutchik, 1962). Table 19.1 classifies various types of collective behavior according to the type of collectivity involved and the dominant emotion expressed. Our discussion of collective behavior is organized around this classification system. It should be stressed that the types of collective behavior described in Table 19.1 are not always distinct. Rather, they are ideal types that are only approximated in social reality. It is quite common, for example, for a crowd to represent something of a mixture of two or more of the types of crowd behavior shown in the table.

TABLE 19.1
Types of Collective Behavior

Type of Collectivity	DOMINANT EMOTION			
	Fear	Hostility	Joy	Mixed or Other
Localized (crowd behavior)	Panics	Mobs Riots Protest crowds	Expressive crowds	Mass suicides Public grief
Dispersed (mass behavior)	Mass hysteria	Villification	Fads Fashions	Rumors Urban legends

SOURCE: Adaption of Figure 1.1 in John Lofland, 1985, *Protest: Studies of Collective Behavior and Social Movements* (New Brunswick, NJ: Transaction Books), p. 43. The "fear," "joy," and "hostility" categories were formulated by Lofland; the "mixed or other" category was added by the author of this book.

Collective Behavior in Crowds

As stated earlier, the mere presence of a crowd does not always produce collective behavior. Two types of crowds that do not usually produce collective behavior are casual crowds and conventional crowds (Blumer, 1969). *Casual crowds* are large numbers of people who are present in some place, such as a downtown sidewalk. Their attention becomes temporarily drawn together by some event such as an accident, but the action of the crowd does not go beyond viewing — nor is the presence of the crowd essential to the activity being viewed (Wright, 1978, p. 71). When the event is over (for example, an ambulance takes the injured person away), the people quickly return to their previous activities. *Conventional crowds* do share a common focus, but at a scheduled event such as a lecture, concert, or religious service. These events occur with some regularity and have a well-understood set of norms, so the crowd is neither normless nor makes up norms on the spot, as happens in the case of collective behavior. This type of crowd *is* essential to the event being viewed. Wright (1978, p. 40) uses the Tournament of Roses Parade to illustrate this; without the audience, the parade would have no purpose.

Conditions Conducive to Collective Behavior by Crowds Under conditions of *structural conduciveness,* however, crowds do engage in collective behavior. Even casual and conventional crowds can be changed into the types of crowds that engage in collective behavior. Structurally conducive conditions produce the emotions described in Table 19.1. A real or imagined danger, for example, produces fear. A threat can produce hostility, as happened in East St. Louis, Illinois, in 1917, when whites came to believe that their jobs were being given away to blacks who were willing to work for less pay and without unions (Rudwick, 1964). As a result, whites stormed into black neighborhoods, killing, beating, raping, and burning. Forty-eight people died in the violence. Conditions that produce joy can also turn a crowd to collective behavior, as in the case of the violent celebrations that have occurred in several cities after their baseball teams won the World Series. Any time a crowd is present in a situation that produces strong emotions such as fear, hostility, or joy (or a combination), collective behavior is possible.

Crowd Dynamics When the situation is conducive in this way, there are at least three distinct dynamics that can lead to the spread of collective behavior. One, which has been known to sociologists for nearly a century, is **contagion** (Le Bon, 1960 [orig. 1895]). An individual or small group of people in a crowd urges a course of action, or begins to move, chant, sing, or behave in some other visible way, and the behavior rapidly spreads through the crowd (Turner and Killian, 1987, p. 21). Probably the basic dynamics of contagion involve nonverbal communication and imitation (Wright, 1978, p. 135). Once the behavior has been modeled, restraints against it may be reduced, leading others to behave the same way (Wheeler, 1966). The crowd behavior may *begin* spontaneously as a product of the dominant emotion in the crowd.

More often, it will be triggered by organized behavior by a few people in the crowd, by a speaker urging some action upon the crowd, or by an external stimulus such as an activity going on at the edge of the crowd. Given that the emotion is shared and that the norms of the crowd are supportive, others in the crowd quickly imitate the behavior. Thus, people in the crowd forget their usual behavioral tendencies and are taken over by the emergent behavior of the crowd. It is this aspect of crowd behavior that renders it capable of sudden changes and often leads to the appearance that crowd behavior is unpredictable.

However, although it can change quickly, crowd behavior is not necessarily *irrational.* Crowds do not do everything that is urged upon them, they do not imitate everything that some people in the crowd do, and they do not respond to every incident that occurs in their midst or near them (Rose, 1982, pp. 7–8). Rather, they are selective. Moreover, not everyone in the crowd adopts the most visible crowd behaviors (McPhail and Wohlstein, 1983, p. 581). In virtually every crowd action, some people are merely spectators. Moreover, even participants do not always behave in the same way. In crowd situations where violence occurs, for example, usually only a minority of those present participate in the violence. Others cheer them on, and still others just watch (Lewis, 1972, Turner and Killian, 1987). These facts have led some sociologists to reject the contagion explanation of crowd behavior. Even sociologists who still emphasize imitation and contagion no longer see the crowd as a mindless collectivity but believe, rather, that behaviors are suggested to the crowd through verbal and nonverbal communication (Wright, 1978). Sometimes the crowd follows these suggestions, sometimes it does not, and even when it does, not everyone in the crowd participates.

The second important crowd dynamic is **convergence** (Berk, 1974; Turner and Killian, 1987). This concept refers to the sharing of emotions, goals, or beliefs by many people in a crowd. As Allport (1924) put it, "The individual in the crowd behaves just as he would alone, *only more so.*" In other words, people in the crowd are influenced by common emotions or desires, as we have already seen. When they get in the crowd situation, they *act* upon these common emotions in a way they might not otherwise,

because usual norms do not apply. Importantly, though, the behavior of the crowd is not irrational and would not be unpredictable to someone who understood the emotions of the people in the crowd.

One problem with this viewpoint is that the attitudes of those who participate in crowd behavior are not always distinguishable from those of nonparticipants. McPhail (1971), for example, was able to find little attitudinal difference between participants and nonparticipants in urban riots. One answer to this issue may be found in Rose's (1982, p. 97) notion of "protesters as representative." He argues that certain groups among whom protest occurs (he cites inner-city blacks and college students in the 1960s as examples) *do* share attitudes conducive to collective behavior, and these attitudes *are* different from those of others in their society. When these groups come together in crowds, the convergence process can lead to collective behavior. On the other hand, within such groups, the attitudes of participants and nonparticipants in collective behavior may not be much different. From this viewpoint, convergence may explain why collective behavior occurred among blacks and college students much more than among other groups in the 1960s. However it may not be of much use in explaining why some blacks and college students participated in collective behavior and others did not.

The third important crowd dynamic is **emergent norms,** the process whereby the crowd collectively and interactively develops its own definition of the situation and norms about how to behave. If the crowd comes to some agreement on such definitions and norms, they then come to dominate the behavior of people in the crowd. If it does not, collective behavior will not occur. Turner and Killian (1987, p. 27) argue that the more unfamiliar and uncertain the situation, the more easily members of a crowd mutually influence one another, which increases the likelihood that the crowd will come to such agreement.

Crowd Dynamics: Two Examples Contagion theory, convergence theory, and emergent-norms theory began as mutually exclusive theories (Wright, 1978, p. 133). In reality, however, all three theories can tell us something about the processes that influence crowd dynamics. This can be illustrated by crowd dynamics in two protest crowds observed by the author. The first, observed in 1971, was a campus protest against the Vietnam War. Several thousand people had turned out for a march around the campus, which was to have been followed by a march to the nearby state Capitol, a common site of antiwar protests. The city council, however, had recently passed an ordinance forbidding "parading without a permit" and had denied a permit for the march to the Capitol. Following the first march, the protesters debated whether to parade to the Capitol anyway. As the debate went on for perhaps an hour, the crowd dwindled to only about 500. At that point, a speaker asked a question that suddenly altered the mood of the crowd: "Do you have to ask your oppressors' *permission* in order to exercise your constitutional rights?" The crowd responded with the chant "March, march!" Shortly thereafter, people began to move in the direction of the Capitol, in what one observer described as "the most spirited demonstration I've seen in years."

This example illustrates some important points about crowd dynamics. The speaker's rhetoric had been followed quickly by the rapid spread of the idea of marching, even among people who up to the time of the speech had not intended to march. Thus, there was a *contagion* process. However, the crowd did not blindly follow the speaker's exhortation in some irrational manner, nor was it inevitable that a march would occur just because the speaker urged it. Rather, the speaker was able to tap a common emotion that was present in the crowd—the desire to protect its right of free assembly—that made that contagion possible. Thus, contagion was not the *cause* of the march, but rather the means by which the idea and the behavior of marching spread. The underlying condition that made the rapid spread of that idea possible was *convergence*: common attitudes in the crowd about the right to march and about the larger issue of the Vietnam War. These attitudes had existed all along, even among those who had not originally intended to march to the Capitol.

A similar demonstration the following year at another campus illustrates how opposing norms can divide a crowd at least temporarily. In this instance, a particularly angry crowd, protesting a sudden escalation of the war (the bombing of Hanoi), had marched around the campus and arrived at the ROTC building, viewed by the protesters as a symbol of military pres-

ence on the campus. Despite the anger of the crowd, its behavior changed abruptly when a small group behaved in a way that violated the norms of most people in the crowd. This group broke into the building and began throwing chairs and typewriters through the windows. At that point the bulk of the crowd suddenly fell silent, a few began to shout "Stop!" and others walked away. Within minutes, almost the entire crowd of about 2,000 had turned its back on those vandalizing the building and walked over and sat in a nearby street. Dramatically, the crowd had rejected the behavior of the vandals and said "Civil disobedience yes, violence no." In this case, there was no contagion leading to imitation, and neither convergence nor an emergent norm in support of the violent behavior of would-be leaders. Rather, the emergent norm was to reject that behavior, and substitute the more acceptable behavior of peacefully blocking traffic. Thus, it is clear that although crowds often follow, they do not necessarily do so blindly.

Types of Crowd Behavior

Although collective behavior in crowds usually spreads as a result of one or more of the three dynamics discussed above, the emotions that lead to that behavior vary widely among different types of crowds. Again referring to Table 19.1, the two examples presented above can best be classified as cases where the dominant emotion expressed by the crowd is hostility. This emotion typically produces either *protest crowds* like the ones in the examples (McPhail and Wohlman, 1983), or the more violent *acting crowds,* such as mobs and riots (Blumer, 1969). If the dominant emotion is fear, the likely result is a *panic*. Joy leads to *expressive crowds,* illustrated by the example of a World Series celebration (Blumer, 1969). Various other emotions or mixtures of emotions can produce other types of crowd behavior, of which *public grief* and *mass suicide* are examples. As noted earlier, these crowd types are ideal types; real crowds may only roughly approximate them, or may show characteristics reflecting two or more of these types.

Protest Crowds We have already seen several examples of *protest crowds:* crowds whose purpose is to achieve political goals (McPhail and Wohlstein, 1983)

The throngs of students who filled Beijing's Tianenman Square in the spring of 1989 are a dramatic example of a protest crowd.

and whose dominant emotion is often hostility or anger (Lofland, 1985). The Moratorium and the two antiwar demonstrations previously discussed were all protest crowds. More recent examples of protest crowds include the 20,000 demonstrators who converged on Forsyth County, Georgia, in 1987 to protest Ku Klux Klan activity there, the "right to life" marches in Washington that occurred each year during the 1980s on the anniversary of the Supreme Court ruling legalizing abortion, and the massive mobilization of students and workers in Beijing, China, in 1989. The activities of protest crowds include rallies, marches, picket lines, and sometimes **civil disobedience**—actions such as sit-ins, blocking traffic, and mass trespassing that violate the law but are nonviolent. Although the vast majority of protest crowds remain nonviolent (Eisinger, 1973; Gamson, 1975), they do occasionally turn violent, at which point the protest crowd has been converted into an *acting crowd.*

Expressive Crowds *Expressive crowds* are crowds whose predominant action is to express some emotion, usually joy, excitement, or ecstasy. Examples of expressive crowds are audiences at sports events and at rock music concerts and festivals, and people attending religious revivals. In each of these examples, people collectively express their emotions in ways that they would not in other situations. Such behaviors include cheering, booing, and throwing streamers at sports events; moving with the music, clapping, and holding up lighted matches at rock concerts; and shouting, singing, arm waving, and "speaking in tongues" at religious revivals. The streaking crowd

described at the beginning of the chapter is also an example of an expressive crowd.

Although expressive crowds are most often moved by joy or exuberance, they can also express other emotions, such as grief. The thousands of people who lined the streets for the funerals of John and Robert Kennedy and Martin Luther King were expressing a common emotion. *Public grief,* however, can be either a crowd behavior or a mass behavior. Although the crowds at these funerals were feeling and expressing grief, so were millions of others nationwide and worldwide who were watching the funerals on television at home.

According to Turner and Killian (1987), both collective and individualistic forces are at work in expressive crowds. At the collective level, there is the widely shared emotion that produces the behavior, often triggered by an event such as a winning goal in a soccer or hockey game, or by the death of a well-loved public figure. Also, the behavior of the crowd exerts pressures on others to conform. When everyone around you is clapping, chanting, or moving in a particular direction, you may feel very out of place if you stand there and do nothing. At the individual level, there is *personality need.* Many people find everyday life repetitive and boring, so they enjoy the change of pace and excitement of cheering, singing, shouting, or dancing in an expressive crowd. The crowd makes such behavior acceptable when it would otherwise be regarded as strange or immoral (Turner and Killian, 1987). Some people also find that participating in the emotional behavior of an expressive crowd gives them a sense of being "part of things"; of gaining the approval of the crowd. Thus, joining with the crowd is helpful to their self-esteem.

Acting Crowds: Riots, Mobs, and Panics Protest crowds, expressive crowds, and even casual or conventional crowds can, under the right circumstances, be transformed into *acting crowds.* Acting crowds are crowds that engage in violent or destructive behavior. There are three main types of acting crowds, all of which overlap somewhat: mobs, riots, and panics.

MOBS A **mob** is an extremely emotional acting crowd that directs its violence against a specific target. This target can be a person, a group of people, or a physical object. Mob violence is often of short dura-

As in this mob action in Marion, Indiana in 1930, lynchings were a common form of racial violence used by whites against African Americans from the Civil War to the early 1930s.

tion, because once the mob has vented its anger against its target, it often views its work as finished and breaks up.

A type of mob behavior that has been particularly common in the history of the United States (much more so than elsewhere) is the *lynch mob,* which captures and kills, often by hanging, a person suspected or accused of a crime or other social transgression. In the United States, lynching has frequently been a form of racial violence. It was particularly common in the South between the end of the Civil War and about 1930 (Franklin, 1969, p. 439). Some reports estimate that 2,500 lynchings occurred during the last 16 years of the nineteenth century. The majority of the victims were black males. Although many of them were accused of murder or rape (often without evidence), many others were killed for real or imagined violations of Jim Crow segregation practices (Raper, 1933). These "violations" included such things as being in an area reserved for whites, "talking smart" to whites (especially white women), or simply being too prosperous or well educated.

Lynchings were also fairly common in the West, particularly in the nineteenth century. There, more of the victims were white, although a disproportionate number were of Mexican or Asian ancestry (Mirande,

1987). The nature of these mob actions is captured in the following excerpt from Pitt (1966, p. 77) concerning one mob during the Gold Rush days in California:

> Miners gathered at nearby Devil Springs and vowed to "exterminate the Mexican race from the country." Thereupon, some Yankees seized one Mexican each at Yaqui's Camp and at Cherokee Ranch for extraneous reasons and strung them up immediately. Hundreds of miners thrust guns and knives into their belts, roamed angrily over the 5-mile region from San Andreas to Calaveras Forks, and methodically drove out the entire Mexican population—as prospectors had done in previous seasons—and confiscated all property.

Although lynchings may be distinctively American, mob violence is not. In 1988, for example, a number of Soviet soldiers were killed while trying to protect Soviet Armenians hiding in their homes from death at the hands of angry mobs of Soviet Azerbaijanis. Historically, mob action has been a precipitating event for revolution on a number of occasions, as when the storming of the Bastille (a French prison where political prisoners were held) marked the start of the French Revolution.

RIOTS   The main difference between a mob and a riot is that a riot is less focused on a particular target. A **riot** can be defined as violent crowd behavior, aimed against people, property, or both, which is not directed at one specific target. As with mobs, the emotions that most often underlie riots are anger and hostility. Sometimes these emotions are the result of competition between two groups, each of which feels it is being treated unfairly. When this occurs, rioting often takes the form of mass street fighting between opposing groups, or of attacks by crowds of one group against people in another group. Earlier chapters described the frequent history of this type of violence in the United States; similar violence has occurred between Chinese and Malays in Malasia, Sikhs and Hindus in India, and Armenians and Azerbaijanis in the Soviet Union.

On other occasions, underlying resentment and feelings of unfair treatment among one group lead that group to rise in violent rebellion. This is often triggered by a precipitating incident, such as an arrest (U.S. National Advisory Commission on Civil Disorders, 1968). In this type of riot, most of the crowd violence is directed against property rather than people, except for violence between the crowd and police or troops. This pattern of violence, marked by rebellion rather than street fighting, was the typical form of violence in the so-called ghetto riots of the 1960s. With respect to violence between the crowds and police, studies of several of these riots have shown that deadly violence is vastly more likely to be used by the police than by members of the crowd, in some cases because police mistook gunfire from other police for shots fired from the crowd (Conot, 1967).

In some instances, riots occur when protest crowds get out of hand (as in the example of the march on the ROTC building described earlier) or when agents of the state seeking to control a protest crowd themselves get out of control. The best-known cases of the latter are the "police riot" outside the 1968 Democratic National Convention in Chicago (U.S. National Commission on the Causes and Prevention of Violence, 1968), and the actions of the Birmingham, Alabama, police against civil rights demonstrators in May 1963. In both of these instances, police repeatedly beat protesters in front of television cameras, sending shocking images of the violence around the world.

In all of the preceding examples, hostility or anger was the dominant emotion in the crowd. Sometimes, however, joy, exuberance, or the desire to have fun can convert expressive crowds into acting crowds and lead to a riot. In 1988, for example, crowds got out of control at Veisha Days, an annual celebration that had been held for years without major incidents at Iowa State University. Similar trouble occurred that same year at an annual Halloween Party in Carbondale, Illinois, near the campus of Southern Illinois University. In these outbreaks, dozens of people were arrested for fighting with others in the crowd or with police, or for damaging property. A favorite "stunt" at the Carbondale event was throwing full cans of beer into the crowd, which led to a number of injuries. In these events, like the annual spring-break rowdiness in Florida and the out-of-hand World Series celebrations that have taken place in several cities, nobody was protesting anything—beyond, perhaps, the attempts of the police to control the revelers. Rather, the dominant emotion was exuberance and the desire for excitement—often helped along by excessive amounts of alcohol.

Even in protest crowds, however, excitement and fun can sometimes become the dominant crowd emotion. This may occur in conjunction with riots, but also with civil disobedience or mere protest. Rose (1982, p. 103) describes this as the "Roman Holiday" phase of the protest: protesters revel at having "conquered the street," at least for a time. He argues that in this phase, the protest action comes to resemble a sporting event, as the crowd revels in its sense of victory. An example of this can be seen in the jubilation of Chinese student demonstrators in Beijing in May 1989, after troops sent in to disperse them were stopped for a time by crowds blocking streets on the outskirts of the city. Rose also notes that this phase is nearly always a temporary situation, followed by fierce suppression by forces of social control angered at the embarrassment it has caused them. Tragically, this was very much the case in Beijing, as thousands of students and workers were killed when the army moved in to crush the protest.

PANICS Another type of crowd action is the **panic.** Panics occur when crowds react suddenly to perceived entrapment or exclusion, resulting in spontaneous and often self-destructive behavior. There are two common types of panic. In the most common, people seek to escape some perceived danger, such as a fire, an earthquake, or a military attack. They perceive themselves as entrapped and react accordingly. This reaction is especially likely when the danger is

Ann Arbor, 1989: student celebrations of the University of Michigan's victory in the NCAA basketball tournament turn destructive. How does crowd behavior based on joy and exuberance become violent?

sudden and unexpected and the escape routes are limited. The other type of panic occurs when a crowd is seeking to gain access to an event or a location and perceives itself to be in danger of being excluded. In both types of panic, surging and pushing occur, and deaths often result from suffocation and trampling. Examples of the first type of panic are fires at the Iroquois Theater in Chicago (1902, 602 deaths), the Coconut Grove Nightclub in Boston (1942, 491 deaths), and the Beverly Hills Supper Club in Southgate, Kentucky (1980, 164 deaths). Examples of the second type of panic are stampedes at the entrance to a concert by the rock band The Who in Cincinnati (1979, 11 deaths) and at a soccer match in Sheffield, England (1989, 94 deaths).

Turner and Killian (1987, p. 81) list four main factors that are characteristic of the panic-producing situation:

> Partial entrapment   There are limited escape routes in the case of escape panics, and limited entrance routes in the case of panics directed toward entry. In the nightclub panics mentioned above, some exits were locked or inoperable, and in the Sheffield soccer match and the Cincinnati Who concert, the number of entrances open was far too small to accommodate the crowd. Moreover, in the soccer incident, a major factor was the presence of a "crowd-control" fence aimed at keeping the crowd off the field, which caused lines to back up outside the stadium.

> Perceived threat   There is a generalized belief, usually sudden, that there is a danger of entrapment or exclusion. This belief acts as an *emergent norm,* which becomes the basis of the crowd's behavior. In the case of the nightclub fires, the fire was the perceived threat. In the case of the concert and the soccer game, it was a sudden perception by the crowd that the event had started and those outside were missing it. The concert crowd heard the band tuning its instruments, and the soccer crowd heard that the kickoff had taken place. In both cases, the crowd immediately surged forward.

> Breakdown of escape route   Whatever limited escape route there is becomes jammed or blocked, and there is no way for the people in front to get out. In the soccer panic, the crowd-control fence blocked any escape route for those in front when the pushing began from behind, and most of those who died were crushed against the fence or trampled near the front of the crowd.

> Failure of front-to-rear communication   People in the rear continue to press forward because they do not know that people in the front have blocked their escape routes. In fact,

the reverse appears to be true. The rear of the crowd continues to move forward because people in the front are being pushed and jammed more tightly together.

Mintz (1951) notes one additional factor in most panics: Although the behavior of the crowd seems entirely irrational, what is rational at the crowd level may not always be what is rational for the individual. He wrote:

> Cooperative behavior at a theater fire is likely to deteriorate progressively as soon as an individual disturbance occurs. If a few individuals begin to push, the others are apt to recognize that their interests are threatened: They can expect to win through to their individual rewards only by pressing their personal advantages at the group's expense. Many of them react accordingly, a vicious circle is set up, and the disturbance spreads.

At this point, the panic behavior has become the norm. Smelser (1963) has referred to this as the *derived phase* of the panic.

Mass Suicide   One of the rarest but most frightening forms of crowd behavior is *mass suicide.* Mass suicide illustrates the extremes to which collective behavior can go under certain circumstances. The best-known modern case of mass suicide occurred in a jungle camp called Jonestown in the South American country of Guyana in 1978, where more than 900 Americans died in one day after knowingly drinking from a vat of Kool Aid poisoned with cyanide. How could such a thing happen? Many analysts at the time focused on the bizarre personality of the group's leader, the Reverend Jim Jones. Such analyses miss some important points about how the *situation* can lead to such events. Can you, for example, imagine *anyone,* no matter how unusual or persuasive, convincing everyone in your introductory sociology class to commit suicide?

Rather than looking merely at the personality of Jim Jones, we must examine the background of the Jonestown tragedy. Jones's group, the People's Temple, had been active in the San Francisco area for more than 20 years. Most of its adherents were poor, not well educated, black, and disillusioned with the American system. Jones's blend of fundamentalist Christian ritual, liberal Christian "social gospel," and

Marxism therefore appealed to his audience. However, several other elements added to the structural conduciveness of the situation. First, Jones had persuaded a large portion of his congregation to leave San Francisco to establish a utopian religious community in the jungle of Guyana. This move had two important effects. First, it narrowed the group to those who were willing to commit themselves totally to Jones's movement. Second, it isolated the members from any outside influences (Turner and Killian, 1987, p. 360). In effect, it converted what had been a religious organization into a *total institution,* as described in Chapter 5. Groups of friends and kin within Jonestown were systematically broken up, and people were continually required to demonstrate their commitment to Jones by giving him their personal property and having sex with him (Coser and Coser, 1979, pp. 160–162; see also Hall, 1979). Clearly, this background set the stage for people's compliant behavior when ordered by Jones to commit suicide.

Like other forms of collective behavior, though, a *precipitating incident* acted as a trigger to the mass suicide. In this case, it was the murder of a U.S. congressman from California, Leo Ryan, and four other people who had come to investigate conditions at the camp. This incident gave reality to the long-standing belief by members of the group that the governments of the United States and Guyana were "out to get" the organization. In the eyes of People's Temple members, the killing of Ryan had now given these governments the excuse they needed, and apparently few of

them doubted that doom was at hand. Jones assembled the group and urged them to "die with dignity" by drinking the poison—a behavior that they had rehearsed many times. They did so (including Jones), giving it first to their children and then taking it themselves. Apparently, only a few resisted and were forced to drink the poison; most willingly poisoned themselves and their own children.

The elements of total commitment to a movement or a leader, isolation from and conflict with the outside world, and a perception of impending doom appear to be common to other instances of mass suicide. Turner and Killian (1987, pp. 356–357) offer two similar examples: the suicide of up to 50,000 members of a Chinese movement in 1864, and the mass suicide (and killing of their children) by an Israeli religious group known as the Zealots in 66 B.C. In both instances, the groups in question had waged military warfare with the larger society and had become hopelessly surrounded by their enemies. Rather than grant their enemies a victory, they killed themselves.

SUICIDE PACTS AND COPYCAT SUICIDES Two other patterns of suicide appear closely related to mass suicide. One is the *suicide pact,* in which two or more people agree to commit suicide. Although not the same, it shares certain elements with mass suicide. For example, the norms of the group of people committing suicide are substituted for ordinary norms that prevent suicide, just as happened at Jonestown. Apparently, the number of suicide pacts taking place is rising, particularly among teenagers. The other related phenomenon is "copycat suicides," which occur when people commit suicide following the widely reported death or suicide of a famous or admired individual (Gundlach and Stack, 1988). Research by Wasserman (1984), for example, has shown that suicides increase during the month after the suicide of a famous celebrity. Fictional suicides, as on soap operas and television movies, however, do *not* seem to cause an increase in the incidence of suicide (Kessler and Stipp, 1984; Phillips, 1987). "Copycat suicides" are a form of collective behavior, but they are best classified as mass behavior rather than crowd behavior because they occur among people who are separated from one another, yet subject to the same collective influences. We now turn to an analysis of some more common forms of mass behavior.

Over 900 people died in the mass suicide in Jonestown, Guyana, in 1978.

Mass Behavior

As noted above, *mass behavior* is collective behavior that takes place among *dispersed collectivities* — people who are separated from one another yet share some common source of information or communication and respond with similar forms of collective behavior. The most important types of mass behavior are *rumors, urban legends, mass hysteria, fashions,* and *fads.* It is important to stress that although these behaviors are treated as mass behaviors, some of them can also occur in crowds. Rumors and the streaking fad are two examples. Rumors can and do sweep through crowds, although they can also travel in the absence of crowds. Streaking was usually a crowd behavior, but it spread quickly from place to place by means of communication that did not involve crowds. In fact, the peak of the behavior occurred the day after all three television networks reported it on the evening news (Aguirre, Quarantelli, and Mendoza, 1988).

Types of Mass Behavior

Rumors **Rumors** are unconfirmed items of information that spread by word of mouth and, in some cases, unconfirmed media reports. Rumors can be partially based on fact; however, in all cases, they tend to change as they are spread. Rumors, like other collective behavior, occur when the situation is structurally conducive. Generally, this means that complete, unambiguous, and confirmed information is unavailable; people are distrustful of sources of information; and people either *want* to believe something is true or *fear* that something is true.

Rumors often begin in a context where something unusual is happening. One example is a situation in which some other form of collective behavior has taken place or is expected to take place. Thus, for example, whites fearful of black violence in cities during the 1960s often believed rumors such as the one that blacks had decided to meet at some specified time and march into the downtown area to attack whites and burn stores. Blacks similarly believed rumors that white gangs or police had beaten, raped, or castrated innocent blacks. A few years later, alienated and angry students on various campuses circulated rumors fol-

lowing the Kent State killings that National Guard troops had been massed at some site near their own campuses and were ready to take over the campus at a moment's notice.

Almost none of these rumors were true. However, in all of these cases, all the conditions conducive to rumors were present. Unrest had taken place or was taking place, which put the situation outside people's experiences. Moreover, real information concerning the rumors was hard to come by. Whites and blacks, in their separate neighborhoods, knew very little about each other's actions, and students were equally unaware of the true actions of the National Guard. In both cases, people believed that the information contained in the rumors was being kept secret by authorities to avoid inflaming an already tense situation. Finally, the rumors confirmed people's worst fears: the fear by whites that they or their businesses would be attacked by angry blacks; the fear by blacks of being brutalized by whites, particularly the police; and the fear by students that their campus would be overrun by armed troops who had already killed students elsewhere. In the absence of such fears, these rumors would have been far less believable. Because of such rumors, rumor-control centers were established in many cities and on many college campuses during the turmoil of the 1960s. Not surprisingly, they received thousands of calls.

NONLOCALIZED RUMORS   The rumors described above were localized in nature — that is, they tended to concern one campus or one city — though there was an element of mass behavior in that very similar rumors swept dozens of campuses and cities. In some instances, however, a single rumor will rapidly sweep an entire country. These rumors often involve famous personalities. Examples have already been mentioned: the rumor in 1969 that Beatle Paul McCartney was dead, and the rumor in 1988 that Elvis Presley, dead for 11 years, was in fact still alive. In each case, people who believed the rumors could find all kinds of "evidence." "Clues" such as a barefoot Paul McCartney on the cover of the *Abbey Road* album (people are often buried without shoes) and the words "Turn me on, dead man" when the Beatle song "Revolution Number Nine" is played backward, were discovered by radio disc jockeys and broadcast to the public. Among the disillusioned and skeptical youth of 1969, these clues were readily interpreted as hidden messages from the surviving Beatles. Similarly, radio stations broadcast reports of "sightings" of Elvis, giving hope to the many people who wanted to believe that he remained alive.

Rumors have also circulated nationwide concerning certain products and companies. In the late 1970s and early 1980s, it was rumored that various fast-food chains were diluting their hamburgers with foreign substances—kangaroo meat, according to one version of the rumor; worms, according to another. Enough people believed these rumors that several chains began to advertise that their hamburgers contained only "100 percent pure American beef." People believed such rumors for a variety of reasons: a recognition that fast food is neither dietarily beneficial nor prepared with great care, and perhaps a twinge of guilt about taking their children out instead of going to the trouble of cooking at home. Another element is the uncertainty that always feeds rumors: We really *don't* know exactly how fast food is produced, which makes

This logo, used in various versions by Procter and Gamble since 1882, became the object of one of America's most persistent rumors in the early 1980s. The logo was removed from most products in 1985.

the rumor believable. Another rumor that circulated for years was that the corporate logo of Procter and Gamble was a symbol of devil worship. Actually, the logo, which had been used in various versions since 1882 and in its current version since 1930, represented something very different. The man in the moon was a popular design in the early days of the company in the late nineteenth century, and the 13 stars represented the original American states.

Urban Legends Consider the following story. Perhaps you've heard it, or something like it:

> A Bergen citizen who several days a week drives a ready-mix cement truck as a second job the other day came by his own residence and saw a friend's car with a sun roof parked there. He stopped the cement truck and went in the apartment building to say hello. But sounds from the bedroom gave him to understand it wasn't him but rather his wife that the fellow had come to visit. Without disturbing the couple in the bedroom, the man went back out of the building and over to his friend's car. He pulled the sun roof back, and backed the cement truck alongside it. Then he switched on the delivery system and filled the parked car with about two cubic meters of cement. When the lover came back for his car, the cement was completely hard.

Though this story appeared in a Norweigian newspaper in 1973, local versions of it circulated throughout all the Scandinavian countries, as well as Germany, England, and Kenya. Its origin, however, was in the United States, not Norway, and it dates back at least to 1960. By 1961, 43 distinct versions had circulated in various parts of the United States, most of which claimed that the event had taken place in the local area where the story was being circulated (Brunvand, 1981, pp. 126-132). This story is an example of an **urban legend:** an unsubstantiated story containing a plot that is widely circulated *and believed*. Urban legends are very similar to rumors, except that they are more complex. Like rumors, they are based on fears and concerns that people have—such as what your partner is up to when you aren't around. Like rumors, they change as they are circulated. The Norwegian version of the concrete car story involved a Volkswagen, whereas the American version usually involved a Cadillac. Like rumors, they may be partially based in fact. This story, for example, may have been partially based on a 1960 publicity stunt by a Denver concrete company, in which a car (a 14-year-old De Soto) was filled with concrete and publicly displayed (Brunvand, 1981). However, the story was already in circulation before that incident, and most versions of the legend bore little resemblance to the real incident.

In some cases, the themes of urban legends are very similar to the themes of rumors. Unexpected problems with fast food or mass-produced food are a common theme, as are stories about mice in soft-drink bottles or about people eating fast-food fried chicken in the dark, deciding that it "tastes funny," and turning on the light to discover they are really eating a batter-fried rat that somehow "went through the process." This story carries the same moral as the "worm-burger" rumor: If you shirk your responsibilities by opting for fast food, you will be at risk. A particular aspect that highlights this is the fact that it is usually a *woman* who supposedly eats the rat, suggesting that if she had attended to the traditional female role and cooked dinner, she would have avoided her awful fate (Fine, 1979).

The key point about urban legends (which are not limited to cities) is that they are not only told but believed. I have heard convincing versions of all the stories mentioned above, in some cases recounted by fellow sociologists who believed every word of them. Typically, they happened to a "friend of a friend," and some of them (like the cement car) even get reported in newspapers. However, they can never be fully verified, or if they are verified, it turns out that what actually happened is quite different from what is reported in the story (Brunvand, 1981, 1984, 1986). However, they are believed because they call up fears or concerns that are real, because they describe embarrassing situations that we could imagine happening to ourselves, or because they relate to some aspect of modern life that we accept yet find at least mildly disturbing. Often, like true fictional stories, they contain a moral: Don't become involved with your friend's wife; don't eat too much fast food.

Mass Hysteria **Mass hysteria** occurs when many people in a sizable geographic area perceive and respond frantically to some danger. Often the danger is not real or, if real, is not as great as people believe. As was discussed in Chapter 16, contagious diseases often lead to such hysteria. The plagues of medieval Europe, the worldwide influenza epidemic of the early twentieth century, and the current AIDS epidemic have all provoked mass hysteria. Although the danger of disease is real, the hysteria leads people to behave in ways that either heighten the danger or create other problems while doing nothing to curtail the spread of the disease. This happened in the case of the plagues: People spread the disease by fleeing from the cities where it broke out, and doctors refused to treat sick people for fear of contracting the disease themselves. Scapegoats were common: Such diverse groups as Jews, deformed people, and nobles were persecuted for creating this suffering (Thomlinson, 1976, p. 90).

There are some striking parallels between these responses and the current AIDS hysteria, even though AIDS is far less contagious. As described in Chapter 16, the AIDS scare has in some instances led to increased prejudice against homosexuals, and AIDS victims have been abandoned by their families and friends and banned from school and work—despite the fact that the disease cannot be caught through casual contact.

WAR OF THE WORLDS   Sometimes real or imagined events lead to short-term outbreaks of mass hysteria. These incidents resemble panics, except that they do not take place in crowds, but rather among dispersed masses who become agitated as a result of rumors or media broadcasts. The best-known example occurred on the night before Halloween in 1938, when Orson Welles broadcast a radio play, *The War of the Worlds*. Made to sound like a news report about an invasion by Martians, Welles's program was believed by many people who—despite a disclaimer at the midway point that it was only a play—flooded police switchboards with frightened calls. Others gathered in groups to discuss the frightening invasion, and still others jumped in their cars to flee, which created massive traffic jams in some areas. Just how many people really believed the report is a disputed point: It may have been only a tiny percentage (Rosengren et al., 1975), or it may have been as many as a quarter of those who heard it (Cantril, 1940). However many it was, public manifestations of the hysteria were quite visible in some areas and attracted a good deal of media attention (Rosengren et al., 1975).

Undoubtedly, part of the reason that this radio play about an invasion by hostile Martians led to mass

The Great Los Angeles Air Raid

On the night of February 26, 1942, less than 3 months after the Japanese attack on Pearl Harbor, word spread that Los Angeles was under attack by foreign airplanes. For 2 hours, searchlights filled the sky, and antiaircraft guns blasted away at the invaders. *The Los Angeles Times* reported it this way:

> Roaring out of a brilliant moonlit western sky, foreign aircraft flying in both large formation and singly flew over Southern California early today and drew heavy barrages of antiaircraft fire — the first ever to sound over United States continental soil against an enemy invader.

While the army fired away at the invaders, the Los Angeles County Sheriff's Department and the FBI

The above material is based primarily on Mauricio Mazon, 1984, *The Zoot Suit Riots: The Psychology of Symbolic Annihilation* (Austin: University of Texas Press).

moved quickly to round up a number of Japanese gardeners and nursery workers, who had purportedly been caught in the act of sending signals to the invaders.

It turns out that this entire event was a false alarm. The secretary of the navy, in an effort to prevent panic, made a public announcement to this effect the next day. Yet, surprisingly, Los Angeles had not experienced any of the panic that is common when a city comes under a bombing attack. Exuberant excitement would better describe the public mood during the incident. *Los Angeles Times* columnist Jack Smith (1976) wrote, "There were no bombs. There was no raid. But it was a glorious night, if only a dream."

Even more surprisingly, the public response to the secretary's announcement was not relief, as one might expect. Rather, it ranged from anger to outright disbelief. Many people felt pride in being attacked and refused to believe that no attack had occurred. The war was, after all, distant, and they wanted to feel that

they were contributing to it. By coming under attack and fighting off the invaders, they could become participants in the war. Meanwhile, the soldiers and sheriff's deputies reacted angrily to the news that they were blasting away at nothing and arresting nonexistent spies.

According to Mazon (1984), emotions similar to these also account for some of the domestic rioting that occurred during World War II. In Los Angeles, nonconforming Chicano youth (the so-called Zoot Suiters) were attacked by young servicemen and other whites. If these attackers could not fight the Japanese, at least they could strike a blow against "unpatriotic youth gangsters" in their hometown, who were perceived as "having fun" while others were "fighting a war." Thus, the same war psychology that led to bizarre collective behavior such as the "Great Los Angeles Air Raid" was a contributing factor to racial violence at home. And indeed, widespread outbreaks of domestic violence did occur during both World War I and World War II

---

hysteria was that the world was on the brink of World War II. People felt insecure and afraid; events seemed to be out of control. Concerns about war brought a very different type of mass behavior in another incident, the "Great Los Angeles Air Raid," which occurred a few years later. This incident, along with some of its social and psychological underpinnings, is discussed in the box.

Fashions and Fads

FASHIONS Two closely related types of collective behavior among masses are *fashions* and *fads*. A **fashion** is a style of appearance or behavior that is

favored by a large number of people for a limited amount of time. The most common fashions concern dress and hair style (Lofland, 1985, p. 67), although there are also fashions in automobiles, home decoration, landscaping, and city neighborhoods. Even activities are sometimes governed by fashion; for example, surfing, tennis, Transcendental Meditation, and stamp collecting (Irwin, 1977). Language, too, is the subject of fashion. Lofland (1985, p. 67) illustrates this point with the changing terms used by young people to show approval: "Swell!" in the 1930s, "Neat!" in the 1950s, "Right on!" in the 1960s, and "Really!" in the 1970s. By definition, fashions change over time. In this regard, fashions are a product of modern industrialized society. In preindustrial societies, dress and behavior are governed by long-standing traditions that do not change as long as the same society persists (Lofland, 1973). Popular dress in Morocco today, for example, is the same as it was 200 years ago. Contrast this to the United States, where styles of dress today bear little resemblance to those at the time of the American Revolution.

Like other aspects of collective behavior, fashions reflect people's values. During the 1960s, when sexual freedom and new experiences were valued, the miniskirt was popular. However, in the 1970s that style changed, reflecting two shifts in values: the rise of feminism and a more conservative sexual climate.

FADS **Fads** are amusing mass involvements or activities, usually somewhat unconventional, that are temporary in nature. They are similar to fashions, except that they are of shorter duration and are typically adopted by a smaller number of people. The short duration of fads is illustrated by streaking, which came and went within a period of about 2 months, with a peak of intensity that lasted only 1 week (Aguirre, Quarantelli, and Mendoza, 1988). Fads typically are less serious and more frivolous than fashions, and are much less likely to be linked to core values or lifestyles. Besides being more frivolous, fads are often limited to one item or behavior. According to Lofland (1985, p. 69), there are four common types of fads: object fads, such as Hula-Hoops, bumper stickers, pet rocks, and smiley-face buttons; idea fads, such as the practice of astrology; activity fads, such as streaking and people stuffing themselves into phone booths; and fads centered around personalities, such as Pee Wee Herman, Ernest P. Worrell, "the Fonz" (actor Henry Winkler), and Vanna White.

Perspectives on Collective Behavior

Before we turn our attention to social movements, we need to discuss the role of collective behavior in society. Insights into the role of collective behavior can be gained from both the functionalist and conflict perspectives.

The Functionalist Perspective

Functionalists point out that collective behavior does a number of things that are useful for society. Expressive crowds, for example, can promote social unity and solidarity (Turner and Killian, 1987), as in the case of sports celebrations that unite people in the local community or campus. When the St. Louis Cardinals made three appearances in the World Series during the 1980s, for example, local boosters cheered them on with the slogan "What a team! What a time! What a town, St. Louis!" A similar function occurs at the national level during events such as presidential inaugurations and Veterans Day parades. These celebrations "combat the tendency of the social order to degenerate into an uninspired enactment of daily routines without imagination or sense of purpose" (Turner and Killian, 1972, p. 423). Another important function of collective behavior is what has been called the "safety-valve function." Collective behavior such as streaking, wild spring-break celebrations, and even rumors allows people to dissipate their tensions in a relatively harmless way. If not thus released, these tensions could lead to more serious consequences.

The Conflict Perspective

From a conflict perspective, collective behavior can work to advance the interests of various groups in society. Changes in fashion, for example, encourage people to buy more clothes, cosmetics, cars, and toys. Fads can serve a similar function, for those lucky enough to invent a fad product that catches on, such as the game Trivial Pursuit. More fundamentally, some conflict theorists argue that by focusing their attention on fun, fashion, and celebration, many forms of collective behavior distract people from real social problems. Thus, they will not do anything to solve these problems that might threaten the interests of the wealthy. Consider again the St. Louis World Series celebrations. These took place in a city that, by any objective measure, had social problems rivaling those of any American city: widespread poverty, racial segregation and inequality, unemployment, crime, and teenage pregnancy. To solve these problems would involve a massive commitment of time, energy, and money. It might mean a redistribution of power, wealth, and income that would be to the disadvantage of the community's elite. From their point of view, then, it is better to get people excited about the World Series than to let them focus on the city's problems.

In a more extreme way, collective behavior can be a mechanism by which a group maintains its advantaged position in society. The clearest examples of this are the race riot and the lynch mob, in which members of an advantaged racial or ethnic group seek to maintain their position by attacking members of minority groups.

Collective Behavior and Disadvantaged Groups

Collective behavior can also be used to advance the interests of disadvantaged groups. Much of the collective behavior of the 1960s and early 1970s — crowds, fashions, rumors, and entertainment — centered around widespread feelings that the system was unfair. This is illustrated by the popularity of blue jeans, symbolizing the rejection of high fashion in favor of traditional working-class attire. More dramatic forms of collective behavior, such as protests and riots, are also commonly used by dissatisfied groups to publicize their plight. In some instances, even violent protest achieves short-term results. Widespread rebellions in American cities between 1964 and 1968 unquestionably drew attention to the plight of inner-city blacks; a host of government programs and laws were passed during or shortly after this period. Survey research by Campbell and Schuman (1968) revealed that more blacks felt that their situation had been helped than hurt by the riots. However, most of the programs were short-lived, suffering cutbacks or elimination almost as soon as the violence died down. Twenty years later, most experts agreed that the conditions of urban ghettoes were worse than before the rioting (Wilson, 1987).

Social Movements

A **social movement** can be defined as a large number of people acting together on behalf of some objective or idea. Often the objective or idea either promotes or opposes a social or cultural change. Social movements involve substantial numbers of people and usually continue for an extended length of time (Blumer, 1974).

Social movements are more organized and more purposeful than collective behavior. Collective behavior can occur spontaneously, but a social movement requires organization. Sometimes collective behavior does occur spontaneously on behalf of an objective or idea. An example is the 1969 police raid on the Stonewall Bar, a gay nightclub in New York City's Greenwich Village (Altman, 1982, p. 113), that resulted in a spontaneous protest by homosexuals who felt that they were being unfairly persecuted simply because of their sexual preference. This event is generally regarded as the beginning of the gay rights movement in the United States. However, this event alone did not make a social movement. Rather, by focusing attention on the problem, it led people to form organizations, which then adopted goals and organized a variety of activities to promote those goals. Once these organizations had been formed, the Stonewall event had been transformed from a spontaneous outbreak of protest activity into a social movement.

Social movements are more common in industrialized countries than in preindustrial countries, and they are more common in relatively democratic societies than in authoritarian ones. With industrialization, interest groups become far more diverse, and social control weaker, which makes it easier for people to organize against conditions or ideas they oppose. Democracy has similar effects, whereas authoritarian regimes view social movements as a threat and use such techniques as surveillance and imprisonment to immobilize them before they can achieve a popular following. Industrialization makes this more difficult to do, however, and countries such as the Soviet Union and Poland have changed with respect to both the incidence of, and response to, social movements. They have had to contend with increasingly large and numerous movements, such as the Solidarity union in Poland, and Armenian, Azerbaijani, and Baltic nationalists as well as Jewish "refuseniks" in the Soviet Union. As these movements have grown, both the Soviet Union and Poland have somewhat liberalized their approach to them, although this process has been irregular, has suffered reversals, and has depended in large part upon the personalities in leadership positions.

Types of Social Movements

There are five common types of social movements: protest movements, regressive movements, religious movements, communal movements, and personal cults. Although these are classified as different kinds of movements, they do overlap, and a particular movement may contain elements of more than one of the five types. Let us consider each in some detail.

Protest Movements   *Protest movements* are movements whose objective is to change or oppose some current social condition. This is the most common type of social movement in most industrialized countries; examples in the United States are the civil rights movement, the feminist movement, the gay rights movement, the antinuclear movement, the environmental movement, and the peace movement.

REFORM MOVEMENTS   Protest movements can be classified as reform movements or as revolutionary movements. Most protest movements are *reform movements* aimed at achieving certain limited reforms, not remaking the entire society. They urge a new policy toward the environment, foreign affairs, or a particular racial or ethnic group. They do not urge the wholesale elimination or remaking of basic social institutions, such as the system of government or the economy.

Revolutionary movements   Occasionally, however, protest movements take the form of *revolutionary movements,* which seek to remake an entire society through eliminating old institutions and establishing new ones. Revolutionary movements develop when a government repeatedly ignores or rejects the wishes of a large portion of its citizens or uses what people widely view as illegal means to suppress dissent. They can also form among a colonized racial or ethnic minority. Often a revolutionary movement develops after a series of related reform movements are unable to achieve the objectives they seek. Generally, revolutionary movements become successful only when a substantial share of the population comes to believe that their system of government cannot meet their basic needs. Although successful revolutions are rare, they do occur. Countries as diverse as the United States, the Soviet Union, France, China, Iran, Mexico,

Zimbabwe, and the Philippines have this in common: In every one of these countries, the current system of government is directly or indirectly the product of a revolution at some time in the past.

Regressive Movements   *Regressive movements* are social movements whose objective is to undo social change or to oppose a protest movement. An example of a regressive movement would be the antifeminist movement that opposes recent changes in the role and status of women, urging them to remain at home and take care of their children rather than seek outside employment. Other regressive movements include the Moral Majority, which opposes recent trends toward greater sexual freedom, and the Citizens' Councils, which have opposed school desegregation. More extreme forms of regressive movements include the Ku Klux Klan and various neo-Nazi groups, which believe in white supremacy and favor a return to strict racial segregation.

Sometimes a regressive movement forms directly in response to a protest movement. This type of regressive movement is called a *countermovement.* The movement against the Equal Rights Amendment and Anita Bryant's anti–gay rights movement, which advocated repeal of a law forbidding discrimination against homosexuals in Miami, are examples of countermovements. Almost any protest movement that becomes large and influential can generate a countermovement (McAdam, McCarthy, and Zald, 1988, pp. 721–722). Countermovements develop among groups whose interests, values, or ways of life are challenged by the original protest movements. Once they have emerged, protest movements and their countermovements often engage in efforts to capture the support of public opinion (McAdam, 1983). An example of this can be seen in the efforts of opposing sides in the abortion debate to label themselves "prochoice" and "prolife" and to label their opponents as oppressors of women or killers of babies.

Religious Movements   *Religious movements* can be defined as social movements relating to spiritual or supernatural issues, which oppose or propose alternatives to some aspect of the dominant religious or cultural order (see Lofland, 1985, p. 180; Zald and Ash, 1966; Zald and McCarthy, 1979). This broad category includes many sects, and even some relatively institutionalized churches that nonetheless oppose some element of the dominant religion or culture. Examples are the Jehovah's Witnesses, Christian Scientists, and Mormons. This category includes movements that combine a religious message with political protest, such as the Nation of Islam (once popularly called the "Black Muslims") in the United States and "liberation theology" among Latin American Catholics. Also included in the category of religious movements are the so-called cults, such as the Unification Church (Moonies), the Hare Krishnas, and the Scientologists, as well as movements within major religious organizations, such as the Pentecostal movement within several Protestant denominations and the Catholic Church. Because these types of movement are discussed in Chapter 15, they will not be further explored here.

MILLENARIAN MOVEMENTS One important variant on the religious movement is the *millenarian movement,* which forecasts an impending cataclysmic upheaval, as in "the end is near." Although millenarian movements are more common in preindustrial than in industrial societies (which tend to be more optimistic concerning the future), some millenarian themes are present in modern Christianity, especially among the more fundamentalist sects. Moreover, some modern religious movements, such as the Jehovah's Witnesses, are clearly millenarian in origin.

Communal Movements *Communal movements* attempt to bring about change through example by building a model society among a small group. They seek not to challenge conventional society directly, but rather to build alternatives to it. This is done in various ways. Some seek to create *household collectives,* popularly known as *communes,* in which people live together, share resources and work equally, and base their lives on principles of equality (Kanter, 1972, 1979). Others develop *work collectives,* in which people often live separately but jointly own, govern, and operate an organization that produces and sells some product (Rothschild-Whitt, 1979). They prefer this approach to the hierarchy and inequality that characterize more typical work organizations.

Personal Cults A final type of movement, which usually occurs in combination with one of the others,

In China, a personal cult centered around Mao Zedong developed in the 1960s. It included wearing Mao suits, posting his picture nearly everywhere, and mass distribution of the "little red book" of quotations from Chairman Mao.

is the *personal cult.* This kind of social movement centers around a person as much as around an idea, and that charismatic individual is revered by the people in the movement and elevated to a godlike status. Personal cults seem particularly common among religious and revolutionary political movements. We have already seen one example of a religious personal cult in our discussion of Jim Jones and his People's Temple. Another recent example is the cult that developed around the Bagwan Shree Rajneesh in the northwestern United States during the 1980s.

The Causes of Social Movements

Early Theories

Until fairly recently, sociologists often treated social movements as a form of collective behavior (McAdam, McCarthy, and Zald, 1988; for examples of this approach see Park, 1967; Park and Burgess, 1921; Blumer, 1946, 1955). It was believed that, like collective behavior, mass movements developed when conditions were structurally conducive and spread through such means as contagion and convergence. Social movements were considered an outgrowth of people's psychological response to social conditions. Let us briefly examine some prominent early theories concerning the origins of social movements.

Personality and Mass-Society Theories

The *personality theory* of social movements holds that people participate in movements to satisfy a personality need rather than to address a real grievance (Adorno et al., 1950; Carden, 1978; Feuer, 1969). This theory locates the cause of social movements, not in society, but in the individual, thus labeling movement participants as personally troubled. Similarly, *mass-society theory* (Arendt, 1951; Selznick, 1952; Kornhauser, 1959) holds that people often join social movements because they feel isolated and alienated in today's large-scale and often impersonal society.

One major flaw of both theories is that, according to most studies, movement participants are not very different from the rest of the population in terms of personality or psychological makeup. They are no more "alienated" than other people and are often drawn into these movements by friends and family (Drum, 1972; McAdam, 1986; McAdam, McCarthy, and Zald, 1988; Snow, Zurcher, and Ekland-Olson, 1980). Moreover, assuming that human personalities are fairly constant, these theories do not explain why social-movement activities vary so much over time and among different societies.

Relative-Deprivation Theory

Relative-deprivation theory holds that social movements emerge when people feel deprived or mistreated relative either to how others are treated or to how they feel they should be treated (Gurney and Tierney, 1982; Geschwender, 1964). Although this theory also refers to a psychological state or feeling, that state is clearly the product of certain kinds of social conditions. The important point here is that *absolute* deprivation does not cause social movements. In fact, more-affluent societies have more social movements than less-prosperous ones (McCarthy and Zald,

1973). In a country where everyone is poor, there is great absolute deprivation, but no relative deprivation. Nobody knows anything but poverty, so nobody feels unfairly treated (de Toqueville, 1955 [orig. 1856]).

In a society where wealth and poverty exist side by side, however, the poor are very conscious of their different situation and may well come to feel deprived. Similarly, when people are led to believe that their lot is going to improve and it does not, they are more likely to feel deprived. This is sometimes called the *revolution of rising expectations* (Davies, 1962). Social movements and revolutions often occur when conditions have improved but then either stop improving or don't improve as fast as people expect. This fact, along with the fact that more affluent societies have more social movements (McAdam, McCarthy, and Zald, 1988), provides some evidence in support of the relative-deprivation theory. However, it is hard to measure precisely how people *feel,* and studies that have correlated feelings of deprivation with participation in social movements have not generally revealed strong relationships (Mueller, 1980; Wilson and Orum, 1976). Thus, relative-deprivation theory can often predict *when* social movements are likely to emerge but cannot predict *who* is likely to participate.

Recent Theories

Since the 1960s, theories about the causes of social movements have become less psychological and more macrostructural. The relative-deprivation theory has remained influential, although some sociologists have reformulated it to emphasize its structural aspects rather than its psychological aspects. Smelser (1963), for example, emphasizes the notion of *structural strain:* conflicts or inequalities in society that are the source of feelings of dissatisfaction. This can include the types of social inequality that cause relative deprivation, but it can also include such things as gaps between what leaders preach and what they do.

In addition, social conditions must be conducive to the formation of a social movement. People seeking to organize movements must have resources available to organize with, and people must see some usefulness in forming a social movement. Two newer theories of social movements, *resource-mobilization theory* and *political-process theory,* explore the social conditions under which these things happen.

Resource-Mobilization Theory **Resource-mobilization theory** argues that social movements emerge when people have access to resources that enable them to organize a movement. This theory assumes that some discontent is always present in a society, but that the resources necessary to form social movements are not always available (McCarthy and Zald, 1973, 1977). Money, communication technology, and intellectual elites (from which leaders emerge) are all resources that can be used to organize a social movement (Zald and McCarthy, 1975). Because these resources are more available in a prosperous economy, we now see another reason why growing prosperity is associated with growing protest. How well a movement taps these resources also influences its chances of success. The black civil rights movement of the 1960s was able to gain strength, for example, by tapping significant resources offered by sympathetic whites, including money, legal representation, and direct participation. The mobilization of these resources did not *generate* the civil rights movement, but it did help to sustain and strengthen the movement once it had become large and influential (Morris, 1984; McAdam, 1982; Jenkins and Eckert, 1986). One of the most important resources any movement can mobilize is interpersonal contacts. These contacts are the major source of new recruits, as well as of money and other kinds of assistance (Snow et al., 1986; Bolton, 1972). Clearly, such activities as recruitment and fund raising are also facilitated by modern communication technology (McAdam, McCarthy, and Zald, 1988, pp. 722–723), by a concentration of like-minded people in the same place (Morris, 1984, pp. 4–12; Wilson, 1973, pp. 140–151; Lofland, 1985, Chapter 3; D'Emillio, 1983), and by any other situation that brings like-minded people into contact with one another (Freeman, 1973; 1979).

Political-Process Theory Closely related to resource-mobilization theory is **political-process theory.** This approach stresses opportunities for movements that are created by larger social and political processes (Tilly, 1978). The absence of repression that is associated with democratic societies, industrialization, and urbanization, for example, makes it easier for social movements to emerge. When people realize that the system is vulnerable to protest, movements are much more likely to develop (Jenkins and Perrow, 1978). People often make cost-benefit assessments of their potential participation in a social movement: Will the movement, or their participation in it, make any difference? One comparative study (Nelkin and Pollack, 1981) demonstrates how social movements are more likely to develop in the proper political environment. It compared the development of the anti–nuclear power movement in West Germany and France. The movement started similarly in both countries, but it grew and prospered in Germany, while it atrophied in France. The reason: The German governmental review procedures provided opportunities for intervention by those opposed to nuclear power plants; the French procedures did not.

Necessary Conditions for Social Movements

Taken together, these theories identify a number of important social conditions that must be present in order for a social movement to emerge. First, as pointed out by the relative-deprivation and structural-strain approaches, people must be *dissatisfied.* Second, as the resource-mobilization approach emphasizes, people who are dissatisfied must be able to *communicate with one another.* Third, as the political-process model suggests, the movement must be able to *survive any attempts at repression,* and it must be *seen by potential participants as having a reasonable chance for success.* This condition is a product both of its actual chances and of people's sense of their ability to make a difference. Finally, the movement must have *adequate resources,* including leadership, money, and supporters, to grow and develop. Any one of these by itself is not sufficient to generate a social movement, but when all of them occur together, the likelihood of a movement is greatly increased.

On the Way to Revolution

At Harvard in the 1940s and 1950s, four remarkable teachers guided me to historical studies of conflict, collective action, state formation, and revolution. Pitirim Sorokin, veteran and victim of the Russian Revolution, was a hard taskmaster, but he showed his students the value of confronting large theories of social change with systematic evidence. Samuel Beer, a specialist in British politics, taught generations of undergraduates (not to mention the graduate assistants, myself among them, who worked in his famous lecture course on Western Thought and Institutions) how and why to confront political thought, social-scientific analysis, and major historical crises such as the English Revolution. George Homans combined sociology, history, and poetry in his own work, and he demonstrated the possibility of addressing pressing problems of sociological theory by means of analyses that would stand up to the scrutiny of professional historians. Barrington Moore, Jr., exemplified the restless, committed, independent scholar who undertakes large comparisons in order to seek answers to urgent contemporary questions such as the social foundations of tyranny. All four of them did me the enormous favor of letting me make my own mistakes and stumble toward my own definitions of the problems worth pursuing.

Charles Tilly received a Ph.D. in sociology from Harvard University in 1958. He is Director of the Center for Studies of Social Change at the New School for Social Research in New York City. He has received numerous scholastic honors and awards, including an honorary doctorate in social sciences from Erasmus University in Rotterdam. He has become one of the leading scholars of social change and has published numerous books and articles on that subject.

Over many years, those problems came to be: How and why do large processes of structural change such as urbanization, industrialization, and the formation of national states occur, and what impact do they have on the lives of ordinary people? Under what conditions, and with what outcomes, do ordinary people act together on behalf of common interests? How do large structural changes alter the conditions for collective action? As a result of my own experiences and the influence of my teachers, I was skeptical from the beginning about prevailing functionalist theories, in which social order was normal, deviations from social order the result of system breakdowns and excessively rapid social change, and intense collective action a symptom of system overload. Much of my work has combatted those theories and attempted to develop valid alternatives.

Early in my career, I approached these problems in two different ways: through studies of migration and population change in contemporary American cities such as Wilmington, Delaware, and through an examination of rural conflicts during the French Revolution. The two studies converged in a series of empirically based attacks on the common notion that rapid social change disorganizes people and therefore produces both individual disorders and collective protests. It took me a long time to work out positive alternatives to these negative ideas. Eventually I constructed a series of models of class formation, state formation, collective action, and relative social processes. In attempt-

The Life-Course of Social Movements

Thus far, we have focused largely on social conditions that lead to the *emergence* of social movements. This is only the first in a series of stages that movements pass through over time (Blumer, 1969, 1974; Tilly, 1978; Zald and Ash, 1966). Social movements go through a phase of *organization,* followed by *bureaucratization* or *institutionalization.* Finally, many movements sooner or later reach a period of *decline.*

ing to test these models and make them empirically workable, my collaborators (mostly advanced graduate students at the University of Toronto, the University of Michigan, and the New School for Social Research) and I developed methods for standardizing tangled historical evidence into comparable events, especially strikes, violent conflicts, and "contentious gatherings": occasions on which a number of people gathered publicly and made claims bearing on someone else's interests. Our painstaking definitions and procedures made it possible to create large computerized files of events such as our descriptions of about 6,000 contentious gatherings that occurred somewhere in Great Britain between 1828 and 1834, the period of the first successful popular mobilization for reform of Parliament and expansion of suffrage. This work involved me in organizing sizable research teams and inventing techniques for transcribing bulky, complicated historical material. A number of other researchers have since improved these methods in studying such subjects as ethnic conflicts in the United States, coffee growers' politics in Brazil, and industrial conflicts in post-war Italy.

As my research groups worked on models and methods, the nation entered a period of intense social conflict over civil rights, the Vietnam War, educational reform, and other salient issues of the 1960s and 1970s. That wave of struggle undoubtedly helped inspire my effort and probably made its results more credible to students, other researchers, and the general public. On the whole, analyses of collective action were moving away from ideas of breakdown, disorder, and protest toward ideas of organized claim making. It is hard to know how much my work merely reflected the temper of the times and how much it actually made an independent difference to shared understanding of collective action. Some of each, no doubt.

In recent years, my collaborators and I have continued to analyze industrial conflict, violent encounters, and routine contention, but have also spent more and more time examining transformations of state power in the past and in the contemporary world. I am now, for example, trying to explain the rise of military power and of the military coup as a form of succession in the world's poorer countries. All this work echoes a theme that has reverberated in my research and writing for 30 years: the relations, in both directions, between large structural changes and the experiences of ordinary people.

I have yielded to an ever-present temptation. Looking back on our complicated lives, most of us feel an urge to make them tell coherent stories, as if they spelled out a plan that worked from the beginning. Someone else could easily make the same events tell a much more contingent story. When I was writing my book on the Vendée's counterrevolution, for example, Harry Eckstein was starting a project on "internal war" at Princeton. Harry's invitation to submit a fellowship proposal led me to lay out a research program on "urbanization and political upheaval" in France that now seems naive, but that started me on a series of studies I have never abandoned. What if no invitation to spend a year at Princeton had come along? I might easily have ended up much more heavily involved in the study of contemporary cities and urbanization, the other main topic on which I was working at the time. All I can honestly claim is that my great teachers taught me to watch for theoretical problems and research opportunities in which systematic evidence spread over considerable blocks of time and space could help narrow our uncertainty about the connections between large structural changes such as state formation, revolution, and urbanization, on the one hand, and alterations in the experiences—especially the collective experiences—of ordinary people, on the other.

Organization During the *organization* phase, the emphasis is on mobilizing people, recruiting new participants, and attracting media attention. At this stage, events such as protest marches, picket lines, petition campaigns, boycotts, and efforts to pass legislation are common. Frequently, there are attempts to build coalitions with other groups with related or similar goals. Building a viable organization is crucial at this stage.

Institutionalization When a social movement has

reached the stage of *bureaucratization* or *institutionalization,* it has begun to cross the boundary from something "out of the ordinary" to an accepted part of the political, religious, or cultural patterns of society. Offices and bureaucratic structures are created to complete the tasks of the movement, and if the movement's goals are widely accepted in a society, the movement becomes an ordinary part of the society's social structure. Civil rights legislation and commissions, the National Labor Relations Board and similar state-level agencies, and modern large-scale bureaucratic religious organizations all reflect this transition. What began as a labor movement driven by such protest tactics as sit-down strikes, for example, has been turned into an ordinary part of the social structure. A risk for every movement is that once the movement reaches this stage, it will become a part of the social structure that it originally opposed and take on some of the characteristics of this structure. In fact, it is a common tactic of institutions challenged by social movements to offer leaders of the movements positions within the institution they are challenging. In so doing, they give protest leaders "a stake in the system" and often succeed in getting them to moderate their criticisms. This process is called **cooptation.** Many universities, for example, created "student trustee" positions during the student protests of the 1960s and early 1970s, and corporations and govern-

ments hired civil rights leaders for such positions as "community-relations specialist."

Decline   Eventually, a movement may *decline.* This may happen for a number of reasons: the loss of a charismatic leader, internal dissent, loss of support, or perhaps because the movement achieved its goals and did not succeed in developing new ones. Although decline is listed last, it may occur at any point in the development of a social movement. Unless it is later reversed, it usually signals the end of a social movement. In a fair number of cases, however, the decline is eventually reversed, as social conditions become conducive to a new round of movement activity.

The dynamics of these various stages can be illustrated by looking at the U.S. civil rights movement. (The early stages of the feminist movement, discussed in Chapter 6, provide another example.)

The Civil Rights Movement

Emergence   Civil rights movements by Black Americans have occurred repeatedly in various forms throughout American history (Farley, 1987, pp. 140–141). In this sense, then, the civil rights movement of the 1950s and 1960s was not unique. However, in other ways, it was something very new: it was utterly unprecedented in size, scope, and influence. A number of recent studies have shed considerable light on how this movement developed (Morris, 1984; Jenkins and Eckert, 1986; McAdam, 1982; Killian, 1984; see also Orum, 1972; Geschwender, 1964; Wilson, 1978, 1973). The movement emerged through the efforts of leaders who took advantage of the opportunity created by urbanization and economic growth. Organization played a key role. Legal attacks on racial discrimination planned and undertaken as early as the 1930s had laid the groundwork for subsequent activities. Conditions, of course, were favorable: Urbanization had heightened blacks' sense of relative deprivation, as had the experience of many African-American soldiers who fought for their country in World War II, only to return to a society that did not regard them as full citizens. The concentration of African Americans in urban ghettos facilitated communication and organization. When a black woman named Rosa Parks was arrested for refusing to give up her seat to a white

As the civil rights movement passed from the organization stage to the institutionalization, Andrew Young evolved from protest leader to mayor of one of the nation's largest cities — Atlanta.

person on a bus in Montgomery, Alabama, in 1955, black churches were largely responsible for organizing the massive bus boycott that followed. In fact, Parks had discussed her plans and their possible consequences with church leaders and leaders of civil rights organizations. The Montgomery bus boycott helped to bring about a legal decision forcing the bus system to desegregate, brought Martin Luther King to national prominence, and marked the beginning of the direct-protest phase of the movement.

Organization From this point on, the civil rights movement could be said to be in the organizational phase. A citywide organization was developed to coordinate the bus boycott under the leadership of Dr. King. Later, national coordination of the movement was handled by the Southern Christian Leadership Conference (SCLC) under Dr. King's direction. This illustrates an important point about social movements: both local and national organization and coordination are needed (McAdam, McCarthy, and Zald, 1988, p. 717). As described earlier, outside support was sought and mobilized. The SCLC was only one of a number of national organizations involved in the movement.

A critical phase of the organization stage of any movement is the development of new goals and tactics in response to changing conditions and changing strategies of opponents (Zald and Useem, 1987). In a number of cases, the civil rights groups were effective in using the brutal tactics of their opponents to mobilize new support — with the assistance of technologies such as television, which showed shocked Americans vivid images of southern police turning fire hoses on small children. New tactics are often invented by new organizations, and in the civil rights movement as in other movements, these various organizations cooperated in many ways, yet competed for supporters' acceptance of their goals and tactics (Morris, 1984; Barkan, 1986). The Student Nonviolent Coordinating Committee (SNCC), for example, emerged as a major force after the SCLC and carried out an effective new strategy of lunch-counter sit-ins. Blacks or mixed groups of blacks and whites would sit at "whites only" lunch counters and refuse to leave until they were served. One of the most memorable highlights of the organization phase of the civil rights movement was a massive march on Washington by over 250,000 people in 1963, at which Dr. King gave his famous "I Have a Dream" speech.

Institutionalization By 1964, the influence of the civil rights movement had become sufficient to lead to the passage of major civil rights laws. The most important of these were the Civil Rights Act of 1964, the Voting Rights Act of 1965, and the Fair Housing Act of 1968. These laws, along with a series of Supreme Court rulings, effectively forbade virtually all forms of formal and deliberate racial discrimination and segregation. The courts and civil rights commissions took responsibility for enforcement, and a number of former civil rights leaders such as Andrew Young were elected or appointed to public office. The SCLC, NAACP, and other civil rights organizations became an accepted part of the political landscape, coming to be viewed more as political lobbies than as protest organizations.

These changes did not come easily. Before this stage could be reached, fierce opposition had to be overcome. A number of civil rights workers were killed, and on two occasions reluctant presidents sent federal troops to southern states to enforce the law in the face of local defiance. President Eisenhower sent troops to Little Rock, Arkansas, when Governor Orval Faubus used the state's national guard to block integration of the city's high school. President Kennedy did the same in Mississippi after rioters attacked federal marshalls sent to desegregate the University of Mississippi when Governor Ross Barnett refused to do so. Two of the marshalls had been killed by the mob before the troops arrived.

Decline In the 1970s, civil rights activity temporarily declined, probably for two main reasons. First, the assassination of Martin Luther King in 1968 created the type of confusion and power vacuum that often follows the loss of a charismatic leader. Second, the movement had succeeded in removing the visible villains of segregation laws and police attacks on nonviolent demonstrators. Now the villain was an abstract set of processes, not well understood and not even recognized by most whites (Schuman, 1975; Kluegel and Smith, 1982, 1986), that continued to keep blacks disproportionately poor and unemployed.

From a recruitment standpoint, blacks saw *less* point in getting involved, because their previous successes had made so little difference in their everyday lives.

By the 1980s, however, the civil rights movement was enjoying a resurgence of support. Once again, it had a charismatic leader, the Reverend Jesse Jackson. Moreover, policies pursued under the Reagan administration were seen as clearly harmful to blacks and galvanized growing numbers of them to action. Finally, the growth of overtly racist incidents, such as a 1987 Ku Klux Klan attack on civil rights marchers in Forsythe County, Georgia, and the repeated burning of a black church near Alton, Illinois, in 1988, had important effects. They made the enemy more visible, and they acted as precipitating incidents that mobilized many concerned citizens. In the Forsythe County case, for example, 20,000 Americans from nearly every state came to the county and staged a mass march just 1 week after the incident.

Terrorism

Occasionally, either social movements or their opponents turn to **terrorism:** the use of violence, usually against civilian targets, as a means of intimidation through fear. Terrorism can be committed either by clandestine organizations or by governments, or by the two in cooperation. Clandestine organizations that commit terrorism are usually associated with *insurgent groups,* militant and highly ideological protest groups that are generally, but not always, revolutionary in nature. Significantly, these groups tend to be made up of relatively well-educated rebels, not the very poor (Radu, 1987, p. 300). Usually, they are acting on behalf of an ideology, and they tend to be both "true believers" and "ideological purists" who see their own views as "correct" and those who disagree with them as being "in need of education." In many cases, terrorist groups form among ethnic separatists or nationalists who seek to create their own state separate from the larger society in which they live. Examples of separatist or nationalist movements that have led to terrorism are French-speaking separatists in Quebec, Basque separatists in Spain, and Palestinians seeking to create a homeland in the Middle East.

In some cases, such as the Ku Klux Klan and various neo-Nazi organizations in the United States, countermovement groups also use tactics of terrorism. In fact, groups of this type have probably been the most important source of terrorist actions within the United States in recent years (Oakley, 1986, p. 22). In contrast to insurgent groups, members of these groups tend to be poor and relatively uneducated, although their leaders might have somewhat higher levels of education.

Terrorist groups tend to be limited in the types of violence in which they engage. The most common forms of terrorism by insurgent groups are bombings, assassinations, armed assaults, kidnappings, hostage taking, and hijackings (Jenkins, 1982). Countermovement groups engage in assassinations, kidnappings, and lynchings.

Governments and Terrorism

Terrorism is also committed by *governments.* Most often government terrorism takes the form of countermovement terrorism: an attempt to intimidate its opponents or critics. Obviously, government terrorism is most common in authoritarian and totalitarian governments (see Chapter 12). The most common kinds of terrorism by governments are political executions, death squads, torture, imprisonment without trial, and military attacks against civilian targets. In El Salvador, for example, 37,000 political murders were documented by human rights organizations affiliated with the Archdiocese of San Salvador during the period from 1979 to 1984 (Neier, 1985). These murders were committed by government security forces and by paramilitary organizations working with them. Government terrorism against civilians also occurred on a substantial scale during the 1980s in Guatemala, Argentina, Chile, Nicaragua, Iran, and a number of other countries. Moreover, there is no question that the largest-scale terrorism is committed by governments. Millions of people were killed by the Hitler regime in the 1930s and 1940s, by the Stalin regime from the 1930s to 1953, and by the Pol Pot regime in Cambodia in the 1970s.

Governments can also assist insurgent groups in other countries (as, for example, Iran has in Lebanon),

Is One Person's "Terrorist" Another Person's Freedom Fighter"?

An important issue in any discussion of terrorism is the question of who gets labeled a terrorist. As Jenkins (1980, p. 1) points out, *terrorist* is generally a perjorative term that you apply to your opponents while applying a different label, such as *freedom fighters,* to your allies:

> What is called terrorism thus seems to depend on one's point of view. Use of the term implies a moral judgment; and if one party can successfully attach the label *terrorist* to its opponent, then it has indirectly persuaded others to adopt its moral viewpoint. Terrorism is what the bad guys do.

Thus, to the Israelis, the Palestine Liberation Organization (PLO) is a terrorist organization, killing innocent women and children on behalf of its goal of eliminating Israel. Attacks on

PLO camps by Israel are seen as entirely justifiable retributions for that terrorism. Yet from the Palestinian view, the PLO consists of freedom fighters seeking the return of land illegally taken by the Israelis. Palistinians argue that Israeli "retributions" take the lives of innocent women and children in refugee camps, not of those who carry out the attacks. Moreover, far more lives are lost in these attacks than in any of the PLO attacks. Thus, from the Palestinian view, the Israelis were the terrorists, and from the Israeli view, the Palestinians were the terrorists.

Jenkins (1980, p. 2) argues, however, that, in reality, the distinction between "terrorists" and "freedom fighters" is clear: Attacks on civilian rather than military targets, carried out for political motives, are terrorist acts no matter who commits them. Attacks against strictly military targets may be classified as freedom fighting. Even war has its

rules, such as not killing or harming civilian prisoners. According to Jenkins (1980, p. 2), freedom fighting usually follows these rules; terrorism does not. By his criteria, both the PLO attacks and the Israeli reprisals are terrorism (Jenkins, 1980, p. 5). Similarly, the Nicaraguan Contras, labeled "freedom fighters" by Ronald Reagan, have also engaged in terrorism, in the form of assassinations of public officials and violence against villagers sympathetic to the Sandinista government. In another case, the United States went even further when it labeled as "freedom fighters" a group that by Jenkins's definition would have to be considered terrorists: In an ironic twist, it proposed in 1984 to make payments to the Salvadoran army to "fight terrorism"—just months after units of that army had massacred 80 unarmed civilians near the town of Los Llanitos (Treisman, 1985).

---

but they do not usually engage directly in insurgent terrorism. Governments also engage in terrorism when they attempt to intimidate their military opponents by bombing entirely civilian targets. Significantly, this rarely has the intended effect. For example, Germany's saturation bombing of London appears only to have intensified British resolve and hatred of the Nazis; much the same appears to have been true in the case of Allied saturation bombing of German cities such as Dresden (U.S. Strategic Bombing Survey, 1947).

A final point is that the word *terrorism* is an emotionally charged term. For this reason, both governments and advocacy groups tend to characterize their opponents as "terrorists" and their supporters as "freedom fighters." The validity of this distinction is

discussed in the box entitled "Is One Person's 'Terrorist' Another Person's 'Freedom Fighter'?"

The Growth of Terrorism

Both insurgent terrorism and government terrorism occurred at least as long ago as the first century A.D., when the Zealots in Palestine used terrorism to try to throw off Roman rule (Oakley, 1986, p. 21), and the Romans attempted to intimidate the rebels by mass crucifixions of political dissenters. Even the car bomb is not a new invention: Cart bombs were used by terrorists in the days of Napoleon (Oakley, 1986).

Terrorism in the Modern World Although terrorism has a long history, it has become more common

Wreckage of Pan Am Flight 103, brought down by a bomb over Lockerbie, Scotland, killing 270 people. In the 1980s, more terrorist attacks were aimed at killing large numbers of innocent people than in earlier decades.

and deadly since about 1970. Not only has the number of terrorist incidents risen dramatically, but they are increasingly directed against people rather than property. In the 1980s, about half of all terrorist attacks were directed against people, far more than in the early 1970s. Moreover, the number of attacks indiscriminately aimed at innocent bystanders, such as large bombs in cars and airport lockers, has increased (Jenkins, 1987), for several reasons. First, today's international economy requires world travel and world trade on a massive scale. This makes it virtually impossible to screen out every potential terrorist. Second, the development of modern mass media gives terrorists a means by which they can get attention and instill fear — much of what they do is done for the benefit of the television cameras. The effectiveness of terrorism in instilling fear can be seen by the massive drop in U.S. tourism to Europe during the summer of 1986. In fact, any individual's risk of becoming a victim of terrorism was tiny, and Americans were actually safer traveling in Europe than walking the streets of many American cities or even driving on many American highways. However, because Americans *believed* it was dangerous to travel in Europe, they canceled trips there. Third, the relative openness of today's industrial democracies makes them especially vulnerable to terrorism. You cannot prevent people from committing terrorism without curtailing personal freedom. For example, we now accept personal searches as part of the cost of making air travel safer.

In spite of all this, terrorism must be kept in perspective. At least four out of five terrorist incidents

involve no deaths (Jenkins, 1987, p. 353), and the number of incidents that result in many deaths is surprisingly small. Between 1900 and 1985, only seven incidents involved 100 or more deaths, and only a dozen or so more involved 50 to 99 deaths (Jenkins, 1987, p. 353). The consequences of terrorism have been substantial in two regards, however. First, many public officials have been killed by political assassins, including the prime ministers or presidents of India, Sweden, Egypt, and Pakistan, in just the past decade. Thus, an individual or a small group of terrorists can and often does overrule established law in the choice of government leaders. Second, terrorism invokes fear, which does influence people's behavior.

Who Is Vulnerable to Insurgent Terrorism?

In general, the countries that have been most vulnerable to insurgent terrorism are those that are either relatively democratic (Western Europe) or that lack effective central governments (Lebanon). Countries that routinely have a large number of foreign visitors are particularly vulnerable to international terrorism. This analysis helps to explain the relative lack of terrorism within the United States. Although the United States is the target in about half of all incidents of insurgent terrorism (Jenkins, 1982), most of these attacks have taken place in overseas offices and headquarters, mainly in Europe and the Middle East. The United States is relatively isolated, sharing borders with only two foreign countries. European countries have far more foreign visitors relative to their population, and thus are more frequently infiltrated by international terrorists.

The countries that have been most free of insurgent terrorism have been authoritarian and totalitarian countries that systematically and effectively repress dissent. Until recently, the Soviet-bloc socialist countries have been relatively free from insurgent terrorism for these reasons. However, this may be changing with *glasnost,* indicating that a greater risk of insurgent terrorism may be one of the costs of democratization. In recent years, incidents such as hijackings and lynchings have occurred in the Soviet Union; along with ethnic violence and unrest in many areas, they have led military leaders and other "hardliners" to argue that *glasnost* has produced a decline in public order in the Soviet Union. Moreover, the Soviet Union, like the United States, has been the victim of a good deal of terrorism outside its boundaries, such as kidnappings and assassinations of diplomats and bombings of embassies (Alexander, 1987).

Can Terrorism Be Combated?

Can anything be done about terrorism? Briefly, the answer is yes, but at a cost. Effective dictatorships do not usually have problems with terrorism, as we already noted. However, a free government, unwilling to engage in terrorism itself, probably cannot entirely prevent terrorism. Arresting terrorists reduces the incidence of terrorism (Laqueur, 1987). Yet, if only some of the terrorists are arrested, the result may be reprisals by their collaborators. Acts of retaliation against terrorists may convince them that the costs of their actions are too great, as may well have happened when the United States made raids against Lybia's Gadaffi in reprisal for his support of anti-American

terrorists. Still, reprisals can lead to new incidents of terrorism, as is illustrated by the cycle of violence between Israelis and Palestinians. Experts do agree on one thing: It is clearly unwise to threaten acts of reprisal and then fail to carry them out (Whitaker, 1985).

There is an expert consensus on two other points. First, the opportunities for terrorism should be decreased, by instituting better security at airports and potential targets such as embassies, and by improving intelligence gathering (Whitaker, 1985). Second, although negotiations with terrorists are essential in many cases, it is unwise to give in to their demands because this only gives them an incentive to commit more terrorism. However, when government leaders are genuinely concerned about freeing hostages, the temptation to make concessions to terrorists can be great, as even Ronald Reagan came to discover when he sold arms to Iran in an effort to free American hostages held by pro-Iranian groups in Lebanon.

Although terrorism can be reduced, the reality is that in democratic societies operating in a worldwide economy, it cannot be eliminated entirely.

Summary

Collective behavior occurs when large numbers of people act together in extraordinary situations, where usual norms do not apply. It can take place in either crowds or masses; in both cases, the temporary norms of the collectivity permit or encourage behavior that would not normally occur. Collective behavior emerges when the situation is structurally conducive — in other words, one that generates feelings of fear, anger, happiness, excitement, sorrow, or some other strong emotion. But even when the situation is conducive, collective behavior does not occur until some precipitating incident triggers it.

The main kinds of crowd behavior are panics, mobs, riots, protest crowds, expressive crowds, and public grief. Obviously, different kinds of conditions generate these various types of collective behavior. A most extreme type of crowd behavior, fortunately very rare, is mass suicide. This behavior illustrates the extent to which the collectivity's norms can replace society's usual norms when conditions are conducive.

The main forms of mass behavior are rumors, urban legends, mass hysteria, fads, and fashions. As with crowd behavior, these different forms of mass behavior reflect different predominant emotions and are generated under different social conditions. Here, too, a precipitating incident, such as a radio broadcast of a rumor, can often trigger widespread collective behavior — but, again, only when the conditions are otherwise conducive.

A phenomenon related to, but different from, collective behavior is social movements. Social movements can trigger or use events of collective behavior, such as protest crowds or riots. However, movements are more planned and goal-oriented than collective behavior. In addition, they require sustained and often complex organization. Collective behavior does not; in fact, it is typically characterized by a *lack* of such organization.

The main kinds of social movements are protest movements (which may seek either reform or revolutionary change), regressive movements (including countermovements), religious movements, communal movements, and personal cults. Movements tend to develop when people experience relative deprivation, when they have the necessary resources to organize themselves, and when the situation creates opportunities to alter the conditions that led to dissatisfaction. Dissatisfaction, the ability of dissatisfied people to communicate, and a belief that "something can be done" are all critical to the emergence of a social movement. In order to grow, a movement must avoid or survive attempts at repression. Often, unsuccessful attempts at repression become an important organizing tool, as was the case with the Black American civil rights movement.

Occasionally, either movements or countermovements (including governments) may turn to terrorism: violence against civilians aimed at intimidation. Although terrorism has been around for centuries, it has been getting more common in recent decades. The most serious form of terrorism in terms of loss of life is government terrorism against its own citizens. Other forms take relatively few lives, but they have had significant effects in terms of changing people's routines and creating fear. They have also led to the loss of a number of important world leaders through assassination. Short of creating dictatorships that lead to government terrorism, insurgent terrorism probably cannot be entirely prevented, although certain actions can be taken to reduce its impact and frequency.

Glossary

collective behavior Large numbers of people acting together in an extraordinary situation, in which usual norms governing behavior do not apply.

crowd A large number of people who are localized in one place and whose interaction is only temporary.

mass A large number of people who are physically separated yet interact and are subject to common social influences.

structural conduciveness A condition in which the social situation is favorable for the emergence of a particular behavior, such as collective behavior or a social movement.

precipitating incident An event, often dramatic, unexpected, or highly publicized, that acts as a trigger for collective behavior under conditions of structural conduciveness.

contagion A process through which a proposed or initiated action is rapidly adopted or imitated by a crowd or mass.

convergence A dynamic in which a crowd acts as one because many people in the crowd share emotions, goals, or beliefs.

emergent norms A process whereby a crowd collectively and interactively develops its own norms about how to behave.

civil disobedience Nonviolent protest actions that violate the law.

mob An extremely emotional acting crowd that directs its violence against a specific target.

riot An outbreak of violent crowd behavior, aimed against people, property, or both, that is not focused on one specific target.

panic An acting crowd that is suddenly swept by fear and responds with spontaneous and often self-destructive behavior.

rumor An unconfirmed item of information spread by word of mouth and sometimes by unconfirmed media reports.

urban legend An unsubstantiated story containing a plot, which is widely circulated and believed.

mass hysteria A behavior in which people dispersed over a sizable geographic area perceive and respond to a threat, either real or imagined.

fashion A style of appearance or behavior that is favored by a large number of people for a limited amount of time.

fad An amusing mass involvement or activity, usually somewhat unconventional, that is temporary in nature.

social movement A large number of people acting together on behalf of a shared objective or idea.

relative-deprivation theory A theory holding that social movements emerge when people feel deprived or mistreated relative to others, or relative to what they feel they should be receiving.

resource-mobilization theory A theory arguing that social movements grow when they are able to obtain and use available resources successfully.

political-process theory A theory arguing that social movements arise in response to opportunities created by political and social processes, such as modernization, democratization, and economic growth.

cooptation A process whereby leaders of social move- ments are led to adopt more moderate positions by being given positions of status or authority in institutions.

terrorism The use of violence, usually against civilian targets, as a means of intimidation or social control.

Further Reading

BRUNVAND, JAN HAROLD. 1984. *The Choking Doberman and Other "New" Urban Legends.* New York: W. W. Norton. You'll have so much fun reading this book that you may not realize you are learning something important about sociology in the process. Brunvand spins the latest yarns and then proceeds to show that they aren't as new as we think. He also analyzes why they spread and why people believe them.

GITLIN, TODD. 1987. *The Sixties: Years of Hope, Days of Rage.* New York: Bantam. This book was written by a sociologist, but for a wider audience than just sociology students and teachers. Gitlin describes and analyzes the social movements and collective behaviors of the 1960s, combining his perspectives as a sociology professor today and as a nationally recognized leader in the movements of the 1960s when he was in college.

HALL, JOHN R. 1987. *Gone From the Promised Land: Jonestown in American Cultural History.* New Brunswick, NJ: Transaction Books. Hall's analysis of the causes of the Jonestown tragedy is a fine example of the use of the sociological imagination. Hall bases his analysis on a combination of content analysis of original documents concerning the tragedy, reviews of what others have written, and interviews with people with first-hand experience of the People's Temple. Hall shows how the People's Temple used organizational practices that are totally commonplace in American life to bring about a most uncommon and disastrous result.

LUKER, KRISTIN. 1984. *Abortion and the Politics of Motherhood.* Los Angeles: University of California Press. A case study of an issue that illustrates the interaction between movement and countermovement. Luker also examines the very different social characteristics that lead people to become involved in the "prochoice" and "prolife" movements, offering important insights into their social meaning.

MORRIS, ALDON. 1984. *The Origins of the Civil Rights Movement: Black Communities Organizing for Change.* New York: The Free Press. Like Charles Tilly's vignette in this chapter, Morris shows how responses by people to the oppressive situations they encounter give rise to social movements—in this case, the black civil rights movement in the United States.

TURNER, RALPH H., AND LEWIS M. KILLIAN. 1987. *Collective Behavior,* 3rd ed. Englewood Cliffs, NJ: Prentice Hall. An up-to-date, comprehensive discussion of both collective behavior and social movements by two widely recognized sociologists. It includes over 60 items by a variety of authors, presenting information on actual cases of collective behavior and social movements.

WRIGHT, SAM. 1978. *Crowds and Riots.* Beverly Hills, CA: Sage. A superb discussion of crowd dynamics. A particularly appealing feature of this book is the author's extensive experience in observing crowd behavior.

CHAPTER 20

Social Change

It was the summer of 1972. I had recently received my Master's degree in anthropology and had been hired to teach at Navajo Community College on the Navajo Nation at Many Farms, Arizona. At that time the college was a novel experiment in Native American self-determination in which Navajos ran their own school, which was oriented toward Navajo needs. I was on Black Mesa with a vanfull of students I had brought to see the Peabody Coal strip-mining operation first hand. We were watching an excavating machine take house-sized bites of coal from the earth and load them into huge trucks that carried them to electricity generating stations across the desert.

Even then, I was trying to make sense of a number of puzzles: How was it that "traditional" Navajos could be displaced from their land by fellow tribesmen in order to strip-mine coal that would be used to generate electricity for such things as airconditioning the sidewalks of the Las Vegas strip? How was it that Navajo and Hopi coal was sold to finance cultural and educational centers to preserve native "traditions"? Why was Navajo Community College dedicated to preserving such "Navajo traditions" as silversmithing, rug weaving, sheepherding, and religious traditions, many of which had originally come from outsiders? I was also pondering how an Anglo anthropologist could teach Navajo students about culture and ethnocentrism.

Less than a year later, I found myself back in Los Angeles, paying double prices to fuel my little VW bug to visit friends in the Navajo Nation and worrying about something bug drivers seldom fretted over—getting a speeding ticket for exceeding suddenly lower speed limits. On that trip I pondered how OPEC, half a world away, shaped events even on the remote Navajo reservation, changing the price of oil, and therefore of coal, and therefore Navajo tribal politics, and even the funding situation at Navajo

T his is how one sociologist described the origins of his interests in social change. His curiosity led him to write a book, *Social Change in the Southwest, 1350-1880* (Hall, 1989), tracing the patterns and processes of social change in this region. This example could be repeated many times, showing how and why sociologists study social change. All such examples would share the same curiosity about how distant events shaped the world we live in today.

What Is Social Change?

Probably the most difficult aspect of social change is defining the term. We will define **social change** as any alteration of behavior patterns, social relationships, or social structure over time. For the Navajo tribe the adoption of sheepherding, the development of a college, and shifts in its relationship with the United States government are all examples of social change. Each of these is somewhat different, with distinct causes and consequences.

Each of those changes also has potential consequences for other aspects of Navajo culture and society. Thus, social change has no clear limits and frequently affects all aspects of a society. This makes the study of social change at once fascinating and difficult. In fact, tracing the interconnections between different aspects of social change is one way in which sociologists synthesize (reassemble) the various aspects of society that have been analyzed (taken apart) separately in previous chapters of this text.

History and Social Change

It is useful to distinguish between history and social change. Sociologists use the term *history* to refer to a specific sequence of events and processes as they actually occur in a society. The study of *social change* is a search for *patterns and causes*. Every topic discussed in this book can be the focus of a study of social change. Other disciplines also study social change, each using its own tools and theories. For these reasons and be-

cause virtually the entire history of human existence involves some degree of social change, it is useful to describe the different perspectives, sources, and problems associated with this subject.

Theories and Rates of Social Change

As with the other topics we have studied, social change can be examined through the functionalist and conflict perspectives. Functionalist theories focus on stability, whereas conflict theories focus on change. Despite their emphasis on stability, functionalist theories can be used to study change by examining equilibrium-maintaining processes.

Equilibrium Theory

An *equilibrium* is a state of balance in a system of two or more parts. Any system that functions to maintain a balanced, steady condition is called *homeostatic* (from Greek roots meaning *same state*). Familiar examples are the way a human body maintains a constant temperature and the way a heat pump maintains a constant temperature in a room. On the societal level, it is not a temperature that is maintained, but a condition in which the society functions smoothly. Thus, in sociology **equilibrium** refers to a condition in which the components of society — institutions, classes, political parties, families — function together.

Most functionalist theories of change examine how a society restores equilibrium after a disturbance (Parsons, 1951). According to this view, such an equilibrium is necessary because of the interdependency of the various parts of society. When society is in equilibrium, each part performs its function and works in harmony with other parts. However, changes in the external environment can alter the old equilibrium, and society must then change just enough to establish a new one. For example, a society might adjust to a sudden increase in the price of oil by producing more-efficient automobiles, reducing driving, and seeking other sources of energy. This illustrates an important point about functionalist theories: they view change as something that usually comes from the *outside*. Thus, in our example, a worldwide change in the oil price forces a particular society to adapt. If the disturbance or change is very severe, the society might be destroyed unless it is able to adapt to the shock and produce a new equilibrium (Parsons, 1966).

Conflict Theory

Conflict theories study the role of conflict — between individuals, classes, groups, institutions, or all of these — in producing change. Karl Marx is the classic conflict theorist who emphasized competition between classes as the major source of social change. Most conflict theories use some parts of Marx's theory and add other elements.

Conflict theories see change as normal, because any type of conflict or competition can lead to change. Stability is most frequently explained as a temporary balance between competing groups, or as a product of false consciousness on the part of subordinate groups (see Chapter 9). Conflict theorists disagree about the number, kind and mix of factors that they believe contribute to competition and conflict. Because conflict and competition are major sources of change, conflict theories of social change are more common than functionalist theories.

Both perspectives are used to study social change, but in different ways. Conflict theories tend to emphasize the social origins of *change*, whereas functionalist theories emphasize the social origins of *stability*. In reality, actual social change does not fit neatly into the functionalist or conflict perspectives, as the following example explains.

Real-Life Social Change: Rock Groups Consider the changing popularity of rock groups. From the view of the music industry, which particular band or song is hot is not as important as the fact that there are *some* hot bands for the company to sell. From a functionalist perspective, rock groups provide entertainment, employment, and an avenue of upward (and sometimes downward) mobility. From a conflict perspective, rock bands are in competition with one another for listeners, and with managers, promoters, and recording studios for shares of earnings — not to mention the conflict between parents and teenagers over what constitutes music! Indeed, generational conflict is functional for the music industry. As each new generation seeks to define itself apart from its parents, it creates a ready market for whatever is ''new'' and more outrageous in music. As that generation ages its music becomes acceptable. This keeps the music industry going. Ask your parents about the reaction to the Beatles when they first appeared in America and compare that with current reactions on your local ''oldies'' station.

CURTIS by Ray Billingsley

When the Beatles first toured the United States in 1964, their "long" hair, "loud" music, and "outrageous" behavior upset many people. How do you react to this photo today?

Rates of Change

Social change occurs at different rates. Changes in fads and fashions (Chapter 19), changes in marriage and divorce patterns (Chapter 13), and changes in the economic and political organization (Chapter 12) are all examples of social change. However, fads and fashions change on a weekly, sometime even daily, basis; family patterns change over generations; change in economic and political organization can take hundreds, or even thousands, of years. The faster changes, called *micro changes,* typically involve small or individual alterations and are readily observable. Who has not noticed the rapid rise and fall in the popularity of some particular rock band? Somewhat slower changes are not so easily seen. For example, many college students have not personally observed changes in family structure. Most, however, have probably read about them or heard about them from their parents or grandparents. The slowest and largest-scale changes, called *macro changes,* are the most difficult to observe. In fact, they are only noticeable in rare moments when the change is spectacular, as in a revolution. But even then, they are often not obvious until they are over.

Micro and macro changes occur at the same time, each shaping the other. Most times micro changes, like the changing popularity of any given rock group, are of little consequence to slower changes. Other times micro changes build to macro change, as is the case with the gradual increase of the number and percentage of married women working outside the home. Thus, as we saw in Chapters 6 and

13, many individual family decisions have added up to a major change in marriage patterns and gender roles. Generally, though, macro changes are so slow that they are a more-or-less stable context for micro changes.

But what about 150 years ago? There were no rock bands, and indeed, there were no superstars of any sort in the entertainment field. In hunting and gathering societies there were no bands, at least in our sense of the term. People did make music, but there was no way to reach a mass audience. Rock bands could not exist without electronics and mass markets. Where did these changes come from?

Sources of Social Change

Social change can come from many sources. Some of these sources originate outside of the society; others develop from processes occurring within the society. Those that come from outside the society are called *exogenous* sources; those that originate within the society are called *endogenous.* Functionalist theories focus on exogenous sources and how societies adapt to the resulting changes. Conflict theories tend to emphasize endogenous sources of change, focusing on how society itself creates change.

This difference, however, is at best a rule of thumb — that is, a difference that is typical but does not always hold true. It is an especially tricky distinction when two societies are in contact. To what extent is *perestroika* a response to Russian citizens' exposure to, and desires for, Western goods? To what extent is it a response to internal Soviet politics? We may never know. How should we categorize the social movements that are forming in response to the "greenhouse effect"? Regardless of whether the earth is actually warming, the anxieties and social movements arising in response to this perceived threat are potential sources of social change.

There are many sources of social change. Among them are the *physical environment* and *contact with other societies,* which are usually exogenous changes. Another is the invention and discovery of *technology,* which can be either endogenous or exogenous. Finally, some are usually endogenous, including *internal conflict* and *planned change.* Let us examine each of these in a bit more detail.

Physical Environment   The physical environment can be a major source of social change. When climate changes, which it has from time to time (Lamb, 1982), or when a group moves to a new climate, social life must adjust accordingly. Sometimes human activities can change climate, as in the expansion of deserts due to overgrazing of animals and overharvesting of firewood (Thomas, 1956). In general, the physical environment limits the types of production systems a society can develop. Would it be possible to practice agriculture north of the Arctic Circle? People living in a terrain that is made up of mountains, rivers, and valleys are much more difficult to unify into one society than are those living on a large plain. For a dramatic example of how changes in the physical environment can affect human society, see the box entitled "Laplanders and Bavarians."

The traditional Lapp way of life centering around reindeer herding was suddenly changed by the Chernobyl nuclear accident.

Contact and Diffusion   Contact between societies, whether hostile or friendly, intense or slight, can bring about changes. New ideas, new objects, new weapons, new crops, or new animals can be exchanged. Some exchanges are easier than others. For example, horses that escaped from early Spanish colonists in what is now New Mexico spread to many Indian societies. Horses enabled the Indians to hunt buffalo more easily and to chase them further out onto the Great Plains. Several formerly sedentary horticultural societies became nomadic hunting societies. Domestication of the horse also led to increased fighting between groups who raided one another to acquire horses (Lowie, 1954; Row, 1955). Spanish colonists also exposed the Indians to diseases to which they had no immunity. The result was a series of plagues that decimated many Indian populations (Thornton, 1987). These examples show that contact doesn't need to be intense or regular to cause important social changes.

The spread of ideas and objects from one culture to another is known as **cultural diffusion.** Diffusion, however, is at best only an intermediate explanation (as opposed to source) of social change. It fails to address certain basic questions: Why did a specific object or idea spread? How was it received? Why was it accepted? In the case of the horse and North American Indians, horses were originally used as food and only later used as a means of transportation. In other cases, societies have repelled attempts to conduct trade, thereby blocking diffusion. This happened in fifteenth-century China when the emperor forbade further overseas trade and exploration. Although this policy sheltered traditional Chinese society from outside influences for several centuries, it was also a major reason China eventually lagged behind the West in technological innovation.

Technology   As you no doubt noticed in the discussion of rock bands, technology can be an important source of social change. **Technology** refers to the application of scientific knowledge to a practical task. New technologies can create new occupations (rock star) or make formerly inaccessible or unusable resources valuable. The development of irrigation systems greatly expanded human capacities for farming. The acquisition of horses changed the Great Plains from a barely accessible hunting ground to a rich envi-

Laplanders and Bavarians: How the Environment Brought Unwanted Social Change

For more than 2,000 years, the Laplanders (or Sami, as they prefer to be called) of northern Sweden, Finland, and Norway have earned a living by herding reindeer. Each year, a small portion of the half million reindeer are removed from the herd and eaten or sold for food. Although the Sami have boosted their economy by developing a major international gourmet food industry to market their product, the importance of the reindeer harvest has changed little over the centuries for the 10 percent of today's Sami who are directly involved in it.

Far to the south, in Germany's Bavarian Alps, another long-standing culture revolves around the growing and herding of dairy cattle. The picture is familiar: cows being milked in an Alpine pasture with spectacular, snow-capped mountains in the background. It would seem that no way of life could be more removed from the environmental hazards of modern life than that of the Sami reindeer herders north of the Arctic Circle, or that of the Bavarian dairy farmers high in the Alps. Unfortunately, nothing could be farther from the truth, and the traditional way of life of both groups was suddenly threatened in 1986 by one environmental disaster far removed from both Lapland and Bavaria: the nuclear accident at Chernobyl in the Soviet Union.

The Bavarian dairy farmers suddenly found their product dangerous and unmarketable: The pastures in which their cows grazed had been contaminated by radiation, and their milk had three to six times the amount of radiation regarded as safe for human consumption (Tagliabue, 1987). But it was not just the Bavarians who were affected—what to do with the milk became an issue that affected national German politics. This happened after a company that had purchased some of the milk devised a plan to dilute the contaminated milk and ship it off to Egypt and Angola. Provincial officials in Bremen, where the milk had been shipped, discovered the plan and sent the milk back to Bavaria. Because different political parties predominated in Bremen and Bavaria, the disposal of the milk became a national issue, with one side claiming the milk was perfectly safe once diluted and the other side claiming that milk deemed too toxic for Germans was being dumped on unknowing victims in the Third World. (The plan to sell the milk was eventually dropped when the German government agreed to buy and destroy it.)

The most devastating effects of Chernobyl outside the Soviet Union, though, were not on the Bavarians but on the Sami reindeer herders of Lapland. Fully 97 percent of the reindeer herd was contaminated to the point of being unfit for human consumption, again because they grazed on plant life contaminated by radioactive fallout. Some reindeer had ten times the safe level of radiation (Clines, 1986). At first, the Swedish government planned to destroy all the contaminated reindeer in that country and try to rebuild the herd gradually, but that plan was dropped because it would have utterly destroyed the traditional Sami way of life. Instead, a plan was devised to allow the reindeer to be herded, then sold as food for mink and fox that are raised for fur and are outside the human food chain. Yet, such help from governments could not undo all the harm to the Sami culture and economy (Clines, 1098; Paine, 1987). Without reindeer, the gourmet food export industry could no longer thrive as it had before, and an even greater loss was described by a Sami who said the following: "You must imagine what it is like now with all these doubts when before you would just step outside your doorstep and take what you need for the table." Thus, one environmental event brought changes to the Sami of Lapland, the dairy farmers of Bavaria, and the politicians of Germany's cities—as well as thousands of others in a dozen or more other countries.

ronment for Plains Indians.

Changes initiated by a new technology can be far-reaching. Consider, for example, what happened when the automobile replaced horse-drawn transportation in the United States. It resulted in the demise of certain occupations—blacksmith, buggy maker, and livery man—and the development of numerous industries connected with the use of cars—automobile manufacturers, motels, drive-ins, filling stations, and parking lots. Another result was increased government activity in such areas as highway and bridge maintenance, drivers' licenses, fuel and transporta-

A crowd gathers to listen to music on a cassette player in Kashi, China. What changes have modern communication technologies brought to rural China?

tion taxes, and various forms of vehicle registration. It has also contributed to some existing health problems such as emphysema and has created new ones such as automobile fatalities and injuries. The automobile also played an important role in the development of suburbs, and it has given young people greater mobility when socializing and more privacy when dating, facilitating sexual activity.

INVENTION AND DISCOVERY Besides diffusion, new technologies can originate in invention and discovery. But a society will benefit from the discovery or invention of a new technology only if it is prepared to use that technology. History is full of examples of new technologies that were not recognized or were actively shunned because people either feared change or could see no practical use for them.

For many years, the steam engine was used in England only to pump water out of coal mines. It was considered to have no other practical use until the late eighteenth century, when Scottish inventor James Watt improved its efficiency and applied it to running textile machinery. The application of steam power to the textile industry helped to bring about the Industrial Revolution in Britain.

MASS MEDIA A great deal has been written about mass media: television, films, radio, newspapers, and magazines. They are both criticized and praised as agents of social change. Much of this is overstated in the sense that media more often respond to changes than cause them. Still, there is one aspect of mass media that does contribute to social change: the speed with which information travels. Information travels so fast today that the entire world has come to resemble a "global village" in which everyone instantly knows

what everyone else is doing (McLuhan, 1964). Increases in communication have shrunk the world.

One consequence of the speed of information flow is that the media themselves become an instrument used by social movements. Consider the prodemocracy movement that erupted in China in the spring of 1989. Students assembled in Tiananmen Square in Beijing to prod their government into making democratic reforms. Throughout the time they occupied the square they played to the international media, using symbols like the Statue of Liberty. At the same time, of course, the media played an important role in the diffusion of such symbols into the Chinese culture. Thus, one important effect of the media on social change is that they greatly facilitate and accelerate the process of diffusion.

When the government violently suppressed the movement, news of the massacre spread around the world within hours, and into much of China from radio networks broadcasting from outside China. Shortly thereafter the Chinese government began a countercampaign in the Chinese media, claiming no students had been shot when Tiananmen Square was cleared. Both claims may be partially correct. Many students were killed by government troops, but most of the deaths probably occurred outside the central part of Tiananmen Square.

Although it may be years before we know the effects of the student demonstration and its repression, we did learn quite a bit about it as it happened. Even 100 years ago this would not have been the case. The mass media, which grew out of several basic technological changes, have greatly increased the rate of diffusion. Their roles in social change are only now beginning to be understood.

Internal Conflict Internal conflicts and failures are another major source of social change. The functionalist perspective tends to stress failures or dysfunctional processes as a source of change, whereas the conflict perspective stresses conflicts. Conflicts frequently serve as the focal point for social movements, which are discussed in Chapter 19. Social movements and the conflicts in which they originate are major sources of change.

It is interesting to note that many movements originate in an attempt to preserve past traditions. The

The Haymarket Riot in Chicago, 1886. Internal conflict is an important source of social change. The rights and protections American workers take for granted today were in many instances established as a result of bloody conflicts like this one.

English working-class and early union movements emerged from attempts by workers to preserve their rights as independent skilled craftsmen that they had enjoyed in preindustrial times (Thompson, 1963). The Right-to-Life movement originated in an attempt to preserve what movement members see as traditional religious values. Other movements have led to revolutions, the most dramatic, if also one of the rarest forms of social change.

Revolutions **Revolutions** are attempts to change the nature of a government, and to restructure an entire society: its economic system, its ideology, and its distribution of wealth (stratification system) (Skocpol, 1979). **Rebellions,** in contrast, are attempts to change specific officeholders or policies. Although they are sometimes expressions of very broad-based dissatisfaction, they do not seek to change the structure of the government. The agitation in the thirteen American colonies started out as a rebellion in which colonists demanded the same rights as other British citizens. It turned into a revolution when the colonists

sought to form an independent state and to eliminate all vestiges of monarchy.

The Russian (1917), Chinese (1949), Cuban (1959), and Iranian (1979) Revolutions are all examples of social revolutions. Here the revolutionary leaders sought to transform the entire society, in the first three cases to some form of socialism, in the last to an Islamic republic. These examples illustrate another common feature among most twentieth-century revolutions: The resulting government is frequently more centralized and often more authoritarian than the one it replaced (Goldstone, 1986). The evidence remains unclear as to whether revolutions succeed in achieving other goals such as land reform or greater equality.

THEORIES OF REVOLUTION   Theories of revolutions are notoriously difficult to evaluate. On the one hand *successful* revolutions are rare. The fundamental question is: Why under broadly similar conditions do revolutions occur in one setting and not another? One explanation is *widespread discontent*: a large number of people become dissatisfied often over the distribution of scarce resources. Closely related is *loss of legitimacy*: people no longer view their government as having the right or authority to rule. Another explanation of revolution is the *theory of rising expectations,* which is closely linked to the relative-deprivation theory of social movements discussed in Chapter 19. This theory argues that as conditions improve a little, people expect them to improve a lot more and become disillusioned when they do not. Another theory links revolution to the spread of revolutionary *ideology* that challenges the social, political, and economic system. Revolution is also more likely when alternative means for change are blocked. However, none of these conditions *usually* leads to revolution: revolutions are relatively rare events. It is possible that all these events must occur simultaneously for a revolution to occur, but even this does not always lead to revolution. Researchers are exploring all these theories and questions, but no consensus has emerged (Goldstone, 1986).

There are, nonetheless, certain things we *do* know about revolution. One is that when revolution does occur, it is not usually the most disadvantaged and oppressed elements of society that are in the forefront. Rather, revolutions are led by relatively educated and affluent people and often draw much of their support from these groups. We also know that, contrary to Marx's predictions, most revolutions do not happen in industrialized capitalist systems (Skocpol, 1979). Rather, they most often occur in predominantly agricultural societies in the early stages of industrialization, usually under a feudal system or monarchy. Some, as in Russia, China, and Cuba, have led to socialist economic systems; others, as in France and the United States, have led to capitalist systems.

One condition that may be particularly important when it occurs in conjuncture with the other conditions outlined above is *military breakdown:* the inability or unwillingness of the military to put down the uprising. Most modern societies have sufficient military power to put down revolutions if they choose to do so and the military cooperates. However, the mili-

tary may refuse to act, or they may switch sides and join the rebels. If the military does not at some point act to put down the revolution, it has a good chance to succeed. The recent attempts at "people power" revolution in the Philippines (1986) and in China (1989) illustrate this. In the Philippines, the military never intervened, and the revolution succeeded in ending the Marcos dictatorship and establishing democracy. In China, the uprising ended with the army's bloody assaults on protesters in Beijing, and despite the temporary spread of rumors to the contrary, the army throughout the country acted to restore the threatened authority of the central government.

War War is often associated with revolution because of the presence of armies and violence, but the two are different. Revolutions are *internal* conflicts, whereas **war** is an organized conflict between two or more societies over a significant amount of time. The one major exception is **civil war,** an armed conflict among different factions within the same country. Like revolution, civil war is a major internal conflict that can lead to major social change. The U.S. Civil War, for example, led to the abolition of slavery and the expansion of an industrial economy.

Since the development of horticultural societies, human societies have been marked by more-or-less constant warfare. This is not to say that all societies have been at war for all that time, but that for most of the last 9,000 years, wars have been occurring somewhere.

WAR AND SOCIAL CHANGE The changes that result from warfare are dramatic and far-reaching. Wars have redefined political boundaries; they have given rise to many technological discoveries and inventions; they have helped bring about new forms of government; they have led to redistribution of wealth; and they have forced the relocations of millions of people. Among the consequences of World War II, for example, were the deaths of tens of millions of people, the political division of Germany, Soviet domination of Eastern Europe, the nuclear arms race, the economic rebuilding of Japan and Germany, the Cold War between the United States and the Soviet Union, and the rise of Third-World nationalism and revolution.

The nature of war itself has changed in the twentieth century. Massive civilian deaths have become

The storming of the Bastille in 1789. The French Revolution, like most revolutions, occurred in an agricultural society in the early stages of industrialization. This revolution was a critical step in the transition from feudalism to capitalism in France.

common. Indeed, it is now possible that a war could kill every human being, a danger made possible by technological developments in the field of nuclear power. In the twentieth century alone, two-thirds of the world's countries (97 percent of its population) have been involved in at least one war, and over 80 million people have been killed (Sivard, 1987).

Planned Change Planning social change is always difficult. Sometimes the intended changes bring about unforeseen and unwanted changes. As was noted in Chapter 17, the Chinese government sought to control its rapid population growth by restricting every couple to one child. How well this policy is working is not entirely clear. The policy, though, has had some unintended and unforeseen consequences. With only one child, children receive far more attention than they did when families were large. Consequently, it has become more difficult to operate schools. Teachers complain of children being spoiled. More troublesome is a possible reappearance of female infanticide. Because Chinese society is strongly patrilineal, sons are highly desired as heirs. If the first child is a girl, there is considerable pressure either to have a second child or to kill the girl and try for a boy.

In the longer term, a successful one-child policy could create other problems such as a labor shortage in the next generation as many older people retire, but not enough new workers are born to replace and support them. Because this type of change takes place over a long time, it is not clear whether these problems will develop or how serious they might become.

Problems in the Study of Social Change

Data Identifying the sources of change is only one of the special challenges posed by the study of social change. Among the other challenges are the problems arising from lack of good data. Sometimes data are missing; other times they are unclear. For instance, in studies of trade between Eastern and Western Europe in the fifteenth and sixteenth centuries, shipping records note the number of *lasts* of grain transported. A *last* is best translated as a "sackful." By studying these records, can we determine precisely the amount of trade that occurred during that period? Unfortu-

nately, we cannot — the records do not specify the *size* of the sack! However, we can make an informed estimate of *changes* in the grain trade (Anderson, 1974; Malowist, 1958; O'Brien, 1982; Wallerstein, 1974b).

Ethnocentrism Another source of difficulty is ethnocentrism, the tendency to judge other cultures by our own standards (Chapter 4). The more distant the subject matter of the study, the greater the danger of misinterpretation. A specific version of this problem is reading present processes and institutions into the past. For instance, the term "family" refers to quite different human arrangements in second-century China than in the twentieth-century United States.

The Problem of Time Defining the time period to be studied is also a problem. If there are regular patterns or cycles of change that occur over long periods, it is possible to discover two different directions of change depending on which parts of the cycle you study. Figure 20.1 shows how the choice of points for comparison would lead to very different conclusions about trends. Only by comparing points B and E would the overall trend of change be discovered. Comparing points D and E would suggest that the overall trend was almost opposite of what the figure shows (down rather than up).

Figure 20.1 also demonstrates another important aspect of social change: Different processes of social change, which occur at different rates, all occur *simultaneously*. Thus, in studying social change we must be careful to specify the scale of time we are using. For example, a comparison of points A and E could lead to several different interpretations. If we were only interested in that time period, we might reasonably say there was no real change, only cyclical movement up and down. If we were interested in shorter time periods, we might say this was a chaotic period in which there was a decrease, followed by an increase, followed by another decrease which left us back where we started. That is, we might claim this change was only cyclical. If we were interested in a much longer period, we might say that there is a long-term *trend* toward gradual increase that occurs simultaneously with a shorter cyclical process. In fact, it is very common for such long-term events to overlap

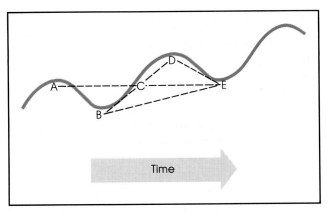

FIGURE 20-1
A Trend with Embedded Cycles.
This stylized diagram shows how the choice of points for comparison could lead to different estimations of the average change over a long period.

with short-term cycles, and sometimes with one-time shifts or changes as well (Moore, 1974).

When long-term processes are very gradual but measured only over a very short period of time, they may be very hard to detect. This is precisely the type of problem climatologists face in trying to decide whether the earth is warming: temperatures vary in daily, annual, and longer cycles (Lamb, 1982). Fortunately, climatologists can measure temperatures very precisely and can use sophisticated statistical techniques to remove the cycles and make a reasonable assessment of long-term changes. Sociologists, however, have very few variables they can measure so precisely. In many cases, the best we can do is be aware of this problem.

When social processes and social structures change, the boundaries of a society frequently change too. For example, the United States was a very different country in 1800 than in the 1840s (when Texas, California, and New Mexico were annexed from Mexico), or in 1990. Even greater changes have occurred in the nature of trade and markets from the time of Buddha or Christ to the late twentieth century. Can these different periods even be compared? Some sociologists would argue they cannot (Polanyi, 1944). The point is that depending on the scope of time being studied, nearly everything undergoes change, making comparisons difficult.

Long-Term Social Change

For students of social change, a fundamental question is: "How did we human beings get from a large number of very small hunting and gathering societies to today's so-called global village?" One basic answer involves the process of evolution.

Evolutionary Theories

The precise meaning of *evolution* has varied through time. When applied to human cultures, the word generally refers to nineteenth-century models of change, such as Lewis Henry Morgan's sequence of savagery, barbarism, and civilization, or Karl Marx's sequence of primitive communism, feudalism, capitalism, socialism, and communism. These and all other similar models of evolution suffer from two major defects. First, they are all *unilinear*, meaning that they see the stages as a simple one-line progression through which every society must pass. Second, the authors of these theories all see the endpoint of evolution as an ideal form that resembles their own society (or in Marx's case, a predicted society). They also share a third major feature: the available evidence does not support many of their conclusions. Some writers equate all evolutionary theories with these nineteenth century *unilinear* evolutionary theories. We will see shortly that this is a mistake, but first we will look at an alternative kind of theory of change.

Cyclical Theories

Several theorists have noted that historical civilizations rise and fall or change in cycles. Some see these as endless oscillations, others as a cycle in the sense of a life-cycle from birth to death. Oswald Spengler drew an analogy between cultures and the human life-cycle: youth was followed by maturity, old age, and death. In 1918 he wrote a book that predicted *The Decline of the West*. So far his prediction has failed.

Another prominent cyclical theorist is the historian Arnold Toynbee. He argued (1945) that all civilizations rise and fall, but he saw this cycle in terms of challenge and response to the environment. Briefly, he argued that if the challenge was not too severe, and if the response was sufficiently creative, then the civilization would continue. In fact, to the extent that each civilization built upon the accomplishments of earlier civilizations, a higher stage of development could be attained in each cycle. However, if a civilization's response to its challenges was not sufficiently creative, it could die.

Human History in 1 Hour

Suppose we made a time-lapse film of human history over the last 4 million years such that the film lasted exactly 24 hours. Suppose we start the film just at midnight and it runs until the next midnight. In the film the events we have discussed and some other important historical dates would take place at the following times.

FILM TIME	EVENT
00:00	Film begins
11:42–48 PM!	Modern humans appear (50–35,000 years ago)
11:56:36	Neolithic Revolution: Planting begins (9,000 years ago).
11:58:12	Agricultural societies: first civilizations (5,000 years ago).
11:58:45	Time of Moses (*circa* 1500 B.C.)
11:59:17	Time of Jesus Christ (1 A.D.)
11:59:29.3–30.7	Time of Mohammed (570–632 A.D.)
11:59:40.1	Norman Conquest of England (1066)
11:59:49.2	Columbus arrives in America (1492)
11:59:53.7–55.9	Industrial Revolution begins (1700–1800)
11:59:58.7	1929 Stock crash
11:59:59.3	Sputnik launched (1957)
11:59:59.6	Most college freshman born (1972)

Obviously, most of the important events occur very late in the film. If you blinked slowly at the end you would have missed the entire industrial era!

Finally Pitrim Sorokin, a sociologist, argued that civilizations oscillated between two major forms: ideational culture and sensate culture. *Ideational culture* emphasized faith as the key to knowledge and encouraged spirituality; whereas *sensate culture* emphasized empirical evidence as the path to knowledge and encouraged a practical and hedonistic way of life. He argued that societies shifted from one to the other due to an unclearly described inner logic (Sorokin, 1941).

All three of these cyclical theories fail on the evidence. None could account for the rise of industrial societies, nor could they account for the continued prominence of the West.

Sociocultural Evolution

Today the kind of evolutionary theory that is taken most seriously by sociologists and anthropologists is **sociocultural evolution,** that is, the study of how hunting and gathering societies changed into other types of societies. Here it is useful to recall the discussion in Chapter 1 about the difference between general patterns and specific events. Emile Durkhiem could predict *general* suicide rates accurately, but he could not predict which *individuals* would try to kill themselves. Sociocultural evolution follows the same principle: It provides an account of general patterns within which there are many individual variations.

Looking back over the last 10,000 to 15,000 years of human history, we can discern a general pattern, summarized in Chapter 12 as hunting and gathering to horticultural to agricultural to industrial societies (Lenski, 1966; Lenski and Lenski 1987; Fried, 1967; and Service, 1971, 1975). It is useful to review this sequence briefly.

From about 50,000 to 10,000 years ago, all humans lived in hunting and gathering societies. Around 9,000 years ago in Mesopotamia, some humans took up purposeful planting and began living in permanent villages. As the ability to produce a surplus increased, agriculture became more common. This period, which began about 5,000 years ago, is sometimes referred to as the "dawn of civilization." With permanent agricultural settlements came such "modern" cultural elements as monumental architecture, writing, and the state as a form of government. Then, about 200 years ago, humans began to use machines to produce goods, beginning the industrial era.

Lessons From the Long-Term Perspective

This brief summary of sociocultural evolution suggests the value of a long-term perspective. It teaches us that the rate of change has itself changed several times in the last 15,000 years and that most of history—the period for which we have written records—was an era of relatively slow social change. This was an era where empires expanded, contracted, were conquered, or were replaced (Wilkinson, 1987). This is one source of the cyclical theories of Spengler, Toynbee, and Sorokin. Most of human history was characterized by the rise and fall of "civilizations."

Finally, the long-term perspective informs us that our own era is distinctive, for several reasons. First, it is an era of extremely fast social change. Second, the rate of social change gives no indication of slowing down. Obviously, some things, like population growth (see Chapter 17), cannot continue to change indefinitely at current rates. Still, sociologists cannot predict with any accuracy when and how the rate of change will slow down.

This unprecedented rate of social change is itself an additional difficulty for the study of social change. It means that when looking at any period before our own we must be extremely cautious about reading current processes into the past. In the perspective of long-term social change, the industrial era is new, but we take it for granted because we have never experienced any other type of society. That is why it is hard not to be ethnocentric and why the long-term perspective is a helpful antidote to ethnocentrism.

The Industrial Revolution and Modernization

The process of development from agricultural to industrial societies is frequently referred to as **modernization.** There is considerable controversy about this process, and social scientists even disagree over what it should be called. But before exploring these controversies, let's summarize the changes that have occurred in the last 200 to 300 years. According to eco-nomic historian Phyllis Deane (1969), the Industrial Revolution included:

> Widespread application of modern science to the processes of production for the market
>
> Specialization of the economic activity directed toward production for the market
>
> Movement of population from rural to urban communities
>
> Shift in production toward corporate or public enterprise and away from the family
>
> Movement of labor from production of raw materials (primary production) to manufacturing (secondary) and eventually to services (tertiary)
>
> The use of capital resources as a substitute for human labor
>
> The emergence of new classes determined by ownership of, or relationship to, the means of production, especially capital as opposed to land

Other associated changes discussed in earlier chapters include: a 600 percent increase in global population; a decline in birth rates and an even faster decline in death rates; tremendous increase in the size and number of cities; changing economic roles for women, children and the family; a major rise in literacy rates; a vast increase in per capita production and consumption of goods; sharp decreases in the cost and time for transportation of bulk goods; the appearance of new economic and political ideologies, including capitalism, socialism, and representative democracy; and the technical capability to destroy the entire human race.

These changes are especially astounding when we realize they have occurred in the last 200 to 300 years. The *modern societies* that have experienced all these changes are often contrasted with *traditional societies,* which lack all or most of these changes (Bendix, 1967). This change from tradition to modernity has been the most dramatic social change in human history.

Modernization as an Intellectual Problem

The Industrial Revolution began in England during the late eighteenth century and later spread to the rest of Europe and its colonies. It prompted many thinkers to try to explain how and why things were changing. As we saw in Chapter 1, one result of this process was the emergence of sociology. To a large extent, making sense of these changes is still the major task of sociology. Because Karl Marx was one of the first writers to study these changes in detail, almost all sociological theory is "a debate with Marx's ghost" (I. Zeitlin, 1987). Many of the later social theorists have sought to "correct," modify, or add to Marx's works, but most have dealt with some aspect of modernization.

Drawing on this brief summary and on the long-term perspective, we can learn a few more lessons from the study of social change. First, many of the issues discussed in earlier chapters—increased divorce rates, changing gender roles, changing marriage patterns, decreasing respect for the aged, changing attitudes toward religion, the population explosion, increasing anomie—are rooted in the transition from traditional to modern society. Indeed, the very speed with which these changes have occurred is itself a problem. We have not had much time to adjust to these changes, and even when we have adjusted we find society has changed even more.

Rapid Social Change   Rapid social change gives a distinct advantage to young people over older people.

The Industrial Revolution, which began in the late eighteenth century, is an ongoing process that has transformed every aspect of life in modern societies.

In an era of rapid change, older people must constantly learn new things and "unlearn" old ones. This is one reason for the decreasing respect for the elderly. Living a long time no longer means you are especially capable, and experience is not all that valuable when it occurred in a different setting. Young people, however, only-need to learn what is current. Of course, what they learn as current soon becomes obsolete. This is especially true in technical areas, such as engineering, where change is especially fast. For these reasons many people now long for older, simpler times. Of course, the "good old days" were not typically all that good, but they *were* more familiar.

The longing for simpler times is one source of religious fundamentalism both in Iran and in the United States. In Iran, the Shah's program of rapid modernization disturbed old patterns and produced a high level of anomie. In the United States, the many changes that occurred during the 1960s also disturbed many people's sense of security by undermining prevailing norms. In both places, people sought security and reduction of anomie by returning to rules of behavior with which they were more familiar.

Rapid social change also increases the general level of anomie in society. Things are changing so fast that people do not know what to do, how to behave. They literally do not know what the norms are. For example, rapid changes in the roles of men and women, discussed in Chapters 6 and 13, have led to a certain amount of anomie, which in turn has contributed to increased divorce rates. As more women work outside the home the household division of labor is changing. For many young couples this is a major source of stress. We learn how to behave as marriage partners largely by observing our own parents, but for many of us our parents had a different type of marriage than we will or do have. Consequently, we have not learned how to be marriage partners in a dual-career marriage. Contrary to the arguments of those who long for a simpler past, it is not that the new system is "bad," but that we do not understand it (yet) and have not yet developed a workable set of norms to guide our behavior. It is in this sense that the speed of change is a source of social problems and further change.

It remains unclear where all this change is leading. On street corners, in airports, in the popular press, and in science-fiction literature, we find all sorts of people trying to tell us—and frequently sell us—"the answer." But in a fundamental sense, there is no answer because the Industrial Revolution is not over. The change from an industrial to a postindustrial society discussed in Chapter 12 can also be seen as a movement from primary through secondary to tertiary economic activity. Where it may go is uncertain.

The speed and uncertainty of future change is one reason why sociology is a valuable discipline and why most colleges require students to take a course in sociology (or a related discipline). It is also why many employers now prefer broadly trained liberal arts majors over students with specific training. The specialized student is immediately productive but soon obsolete; the liberal arts student takes longer to "learn the job" but has knowledge that will enable her or him to adjust to changes.

Finally, there is another sense in which the Industrial Revolution is a social problem: it has not spread evenly throughout the world. We will now examine this issue in more detail.

The Industrial Revolution and Uneven Development

Many of you probably wonder why some countries modernized before others. Why haven't Third-World countries followed the patterns of the industrialized countries? Here the long-term perspective gives some insight. Based on the "neolithic revolution"—the change from hunting and gathering to agriculture—we have no reason to expect that the entire world *should* industrialize at the same time. But the fact that some societies have industrialized while others have not is a major source of conflict in the world today.

Categories and Terms for Development

Sociologists frequently place different countries in categories that reflect different degrees of economic development. *Developed countries* are those that have modern political institutions, industrial economies, high standards of living, high literacy rates, and good medical care. Examples are the United States, Japan, and the Scandinavian countries. The less-developed,

or *developing countries* lack some or all of these things and have low standards of living. Many countries in Africa, Asia, and South America fall into this category.

Other sociologists classify countries based on a combination of economic, political, and historical characteristics. Developed countries with democratic institutions, and except for Japan, a history linked to Western Europe or its former colonies constitute the *First World.* The *Second World* is made up of communist countries, some of which are industrialized (the Soviet Union), and some that are only beginning to industrialize (China). The remaining countries, primarily the less-developed countries—many of which were former colonies of First-World countries—constitute the *Third World* (Worsley, 1984). Neither of these classification systems provides a fully adequate description of the modern world: many countries fall in between. Still, they do make reasonable divisions among countries.

Development is often used in two senses in the literature. The narrow sense refers to *economic development,* the economic changes associated with the Industrial Revolution. In the broad sense, *development* refers to all the changes that have occurred in the last 200 to 300 years. In this sense the term is used interchangeably with modernization. In this chapter we will use the term *development* for this broad meaning and *economic development* for the narrow meaning.

Conflict versus Functionalist Perspective

Theories concerning uneven development fall into two broad categories that generally correspond to the functionalist and conflict perspectives. Functionalist theories tend to portray development as inevitable and positive; conflict theories see it as a cause of inequality and suffering.

Functionalist theorists stress that developed societies support more people, at a higher standard of living, with less inequality than traditional ones. They also have lower birth and death rates, higher literacy rates, and a much greater degree of urbanization, which enables more people to enjoy the fruits of modern technology.

Conflict theories emphasize the conflict between developed countries and all other countries.

They do recognize the superior adaptation of developed societies, but they see this as the root cause of the lack of development elsewhere. They explain differences in rates of development in terms of competition between developed and less-developed countries over raw materials, international trade, and the changing uses of labor and capital.

Modernization Theories

The major functionalist approach to uneven development is **modernization theory,** which argues that developing countries are striving to achieve the benefits of development. Modernization theory holds that, as the process of modernization or development spreads to the developing countries, they will benefit from it in much the same ways that the industrialized countries have. Some theorists emphasize macro factors in modernization. W. W. Rostow, in *Economic Growth: A Non-Communist Manifesto* (1960), attempted to provide an explanatory alternative to Karl Marx. He argued that economic growth occurs in five stages: (1) traditional society; (2) preconditions for take-off; (3) take-off; (4) drive to maturity; and (5) age of high mass-consumption. Progress from one stage to the next depends on the right mix of factors: population; technology; entrepreneurship; distribution of income among consumption, savings, and investment; and the balance of production between consumer and capital goods. The first countries to develop had a nearly optimal mix of ingredients; other countries did not. Through time, as many of the necessary factors diffuse to less-developed countries, they, too, are expected to move through these stages.

Other theorists emphasize psychological factors, such as a spirit of individualism and self-reliance, ability to delay gratification, and the need for achievement in modernization. David McClelland (1961) argued that people in less-developed countries did not have a sufficiently strong need for achievement to impel them to work hard. In effect, he was arguing that they lacked the Protestant Ethic discussed in Chapter 15.

Thus, according to modernization theories, development is due to a society's possession of an optimal mix of financial, productive, and cultural factors. Differences in the distribution of these factors explain differences in development.

To the extent that these factors are favorable, less-developed countries will follow the same general path of modernization as the developed countries. Modernization theorists believe that this may be facilitated through a variety of conditions: imitation of developed countries, adoption of cultural values thought to be favorable to modernization, aid from developed countries, and importation of capital and technology from developed countries.

Criticisms of Modernization Theories Modernization theory has been criticized on a number of grounds. The most damaging criticism is that many of the arguments made by these theories are not supported by data. None of the less-developed countries has gone through the stages that Rostow describes. Phyllis Deane (1969) showed that many twentieth-century Third-World countries (India, Nigeria, Brazil, and Mexico) were less well prepared for industrialization than England was in the mid-eighteenth century. England was one of the three wealthiest countries in the world, produced an agricultural surplus, and already had a dynamic and somewhat integrated national economy. This is not to deny that eighteenth-century England resembled a traditional society much more than it did an industrial society. It does explain, however, why England was better prepared for "take-off" over 200 years ago than many Third-World countries were at the time Rostow wrote his book.

In addition, research has *not* demonstrated that the need for achievement is any less in developing countries. Moreover, the emphasis on internal factors amounts to "blaming the victim" on an international level rather than examining international relations for possible cause of uneven development. For these reasons, sociological criticisms of modernization theory have increased (Chirot, 1981; Wallerstein, 1976).

It should be noted that many of the lesser claims of modernization theory do, indeed, appear to hold. Virtually every country that does develop becomes increasingly rationalized and bureaucratized, although sometimes in different ways. There does appear to be a significant degree of convergence among modern, industrial countries. There is considerable urbanization, a decline in birth and death rates, a movement toward secular and away from religious values, increasing change toward the nuclear family and away from the extended family, a general increase in the importance of formal education, and a nearly global agreement on the relative rankings of various occupations. What is missing is a theory that adequately explains *why* countries participate in these changes to different degrees and describes the effect on less-developed countries of their interaction with more-developed countries.

Lenin and Imperialism

Russian revolutionary V. I. Lenin applied Marx's theories on inequality and class to the international arena. In 1916, he published *Imperialism, the Highest Stage of Capitalism*. **Imperialism** can be defined as a system in which one country uses the resources of another to its own advantage while not giving the other country a fair return for its contribution. Imperialism frequently involves some form of coercion or violence. Lenin argued that as markets in industrialized countries begin to saturate, banks and corporations use their influence to encourage their governments to engage in colonial expansion to secure sources of raw materials and new markets for their products (goods and capital investments). The race for colonies leads to intense rivalry, and eventually to war, among developed countries.

Since 1916, there have been many modifications and elaborations of Lenin's theory. One of the major debates about development centers around the extent to which imperialism contributed to the initial development of the First-World countries. A second debate centers on the extent to which continued imperialistic relationships are necessary to preserve the advantages of the developed countries. This debate is similar to that between conflict and functionalist theorists concerning inequality.

Dependency Theories

Some conflict theories argue that First-World countries have developed at the expense of less-developed countries and have even pushed these countries backward. This process is called *the development of underdevelopment,* a name popularized in North America by Andre Gunder Frank (1969). These theories are called **dependency theories** because they claim that the activities of the industrialized countries keep the Third-World countries in a dependent position, rather than enabling them to develop on their own. Some dependency theories argue that the "help" provided by the First World to the Third World is either disguised benefits for its own international corporations or political blackmail used to force Third-World countries to support First-World political goals.

World-System Theory

In North America, the most widely accepted version of dependency theory is **world-system theory,** associated with the work of Immanuel Wallerstein (1974a, 1974b, 1979, 1980, 1989; Chirot 1981; Chirot and Hall, 1982). Wallerstein defined *world-system* as a self-contained division of labor and a self-sufficient political and economic system. He argued that the "modern world-system" began in what he called the "long sixteenth century," which ran from about 1450 to 1650 in Western Europe. During the last few centuries, this world-system expanded to encompass the entire planet. The appearance and growth of this world-system is the fundamental context for the spread of capitalism, the Industrial Revolution, and modernization.

As the modern world-system grew, it produced a division of labor that divided the countries of the world into three major, interrelated groups. At the center are *core countries,* characterized by industrialization, economic diversification in secondary and tertiary production, heavy investment in foreign areas, and considerable political and economic autonomy in pursuing their own interests. In 1990, the leading core countries are the United States, West Germany, and Japan. *Peripheral countries,* in contrast, have little or no industrialization, specialize in primary production, are heavily invested in by foreign countries, and experience frequent outside interference in their political and economic affairs. Core countries use the resources of peripheral countries to enhance their own development and consequently retard the development of peripheral countries. (This is Lenin's imperialism.) Examples of peripheral countries are Sri Lanka, El Salvador, and Zimbabwe. In between core and periphery are *semiperipheral countries* that are more developed than peripheral countries but less developed than core countries. Because semiperipheral countries exploit peripheral countries even as they are exploited by core countries, they (or at least their economic elites) have a vested interest in keeping the entire system stable. Brazil, Spain, and Greece are semiperipheral countries.

It should be noted that the division of labor in this context refers to differences across the entire world rather than within a particular society. It is only within this world-system that the rise and fall of states, relative rates of development, and social relations in general can be fully understood. Although the system has always had core countries, which countries have been in the core has varied through time. Similarly, world-system theory sees the origin of the modern nation-state as a result of the expansion of the international system. Semiperipheral countries are especially volatile because they are typically declining former core countries or rising former peripheral countries.

Relationships within the World-System   Some simple accounts present the world-system as an international class system, equating core, semiperipheral, and peripheral countries with upper, middle, and lower classes. Such summaries overlook a basic tenet of this theory: The world-system is the context within which all other social units, states, ethnic groups, classes, and so on are formed and changed. There is no simple one-way causal link between the system and its parts. Rather, world-system theory studies both how the makeup of a country shapes its role within the system and how the role of a country within the system transforms its social structure. This approach helps us to understand why apparently similar social processes, such as stratification, work in different ways in core and peripheral countries.

The basic arguments of world-system theory are that relations between core countries and peripheral countries are imperialistic and that core development and continued economic growth occur at the expense of the underdevelopment of peripheral and semiperipheral countries. Core countries use peripheral countries as sources of cheap raw materials and, increasingly, cheap labor. Thus, the objective of investment by core countries in peripheral countries is to increase profits in core countries and not to assist peripheral countries. Specifically, a large proportion of the profits generated in peripheral countries are taken out of those countries by the *multinational corporations* of the core countries, as discussed in Chapter 12.

These kinds of investments and economic relations distort class stratification in peripheral countries. They lead to the development of a small, wealthy class that owes its position to the economic relations with core countries. In order to maintain their class position, members of the wealthy class must continue to support core investment and related policies.

In addition, investment in primary production (that is, the extraction of natural resources) does not lead to economic development. Primary production creates relatively few jobs, and those it does create are unskilled and low-paying. Consequently, a large, relatively poor working class, or, in the case of agricultural production, a large class of peasants develops. In either case the gap between rich and poor in peripheral countries *increases* with development—just the opposite of what happened in core countries.

Why Socialist Revolutions?   These conditions can lead to revolution. Because they trace their problems to the policies of core nations, working-class and peasant rebels are often attracted to socialist and communist philosophies and ask for—and sometimes receive—aid from communist countries. The Soviet Union in particular frequently serves as a model of development because from a peripheral point of view, it has been very successful in modernizing. In 1917, Russia was a declining semiperipheral country; today it is a major world power. This fact contributes to the appeal of socialism as a route to development for peripheral countries. For these reasons, most peripheral and semiperipheral revolutions are leftist, working toward socialist or communist governments. However the underlying goal is modernization.

Because socialism is perceived as the enemy of capitalism and because Third-World revolutions seek to reverse the relationship between core and peripheral countries by seizing control of local resources and forcing out core investors (or at leaast controlling them tightly), these revolutions are almost universally opposed by core countries. This is a major reason why the United States intervened in 1973 to help over-throw Salvador Allende, the elected socialist president of Chile (see Chapter 12). This is also one reason why the United States, a country born in revolution, always seems to oppose revolution, except for some revolutions against socialist regimes. American opposition is almost always justified by an appeal to democracy and freedom. The freedom, though, often refers not to people in peripheral nations, but rather to the freedom of major international corporations to do business anywhere. For example, although evidence indicates greater repression and human rights violations in El Salvador than in Nicaragua, the United States continues to support the Salvadoran government and oppose the Nicaraguan government. Why? The key reason is that El Salvador is capitalist and friendly to American economic and political interests, whereas Nicaragua is socialist and much less open to the multi-

A hospital under construction in Cuba. Although most twentieth-century revolutions in developing countries have been leftist, they have also shared the goal of modernization.

nationals. Even revolutions against socialist regimes may not gain American support if American economic interests are substantially involved in a socialist country. In 1989, President Bush initially responded in a relatively low-key manner to the repression of dissent in China, stating that he wanted to preserve the economic relationship with China that had been opened in the 1970s and 1980s.

Foreign Aid and International Loans In this perspective, foreign aid, loans from the International Monetary Fund (IMF), and development loans from private banks are all forms of imperialism because they require the recipient to buy goods and supplies from the loaning country and to follow certain economic and political policies. Thus, foreign aid ensures large markets for core firms. To some extent, it is also designed to ensure large profits for banks in the form of interest on development loans. This is the root of the current debt crisis. So much money has been loaned to developing countries that failure to repay the loans will lead to the collapse of major core banks. Their lack of development, however, has made many of them unable to pay these loans. Ironically, this crisis gives some control to debtor countries and forces core countries to take some interest in peripheral development to protect their money.

Another way that international corporations take advantage of the global division of labor is to move labor-intensive operations — such as assembly-line production — to peripheral countries where labor costs are lower. This policy can harm both core and peripheral countries, but in different ways. In core countries, it leads to the loss of jobs and plant closings. In peripheral countries, the new jobs do not pay enough to allow sufficient savings for investment in further development.

World-System Theory: An Analysis A good deal of empirical research supports some aspects of world-system theory. Snyder and Kick (1979) analyzed international networks of trade, military intervention, diplomatic ties, and treaty memberships to see if they could verify the existence of the global division of labor postulated by world-system theory. They found that countries did fall into three groups, and that each of the three groups of countries had development patterns described by world-system theory.

Heavy foreign investment, presence of international corporations, and concentration on raw material production (especially in agriculture) do seem to slow development (Bornschier and Chase-Dunn, 1985). Core countries are developing faster than peripheral countries. Capitalist countries are growing faster than communist countries, and communist countries are growing faster than most noncommunist peripheral countries. Thus, the gap between rich and core countries continues to widen (Breedlove and Nolan, 1988). This is consistent with the view that international relations work to the advantage of the First and Second Worlds and to the disadvantage of the Third World. Development also has the predicted effects on internal inequality. In core countries, as we saw in Chapter 12, development has led to a *decrease* in inequality. In peripheral countries, however, inequality has *increased* (Nolan, 1987; Chirot, 1986).

CRITIQUES OF WORLD-SYSTEM THEORY Dependency theories are not without criticism. Bairoch (1986) and O'Brien (1982) challenge the argument that imperialism was necessary for the origin of the capitalist world-system. They find that, at most, the raw materials taken from early colonies sped up the development of the core countries but were not crucial to it. They do not, however, dispute the contention that colonization may have had some harmful effects on the development of colonial areas. This suggests that Lenin's theory, and hence a major portion of world-system theory, may describe what happened but not *why* it happened.

World-system theory has also been criticized for an overemphasis on economic factors and a relative neglect of class, politics, culture, and gender (Brenner, 1977; Denemark and Thomas, 1988; Zeitlin, M., 1984; Evans, et al., 1985; Ward, 1984, 1988). Despite these criticisms, a major contribution of this theory has been to prompt sociologists to look carefully at historical and international aspects of social change. It has also raised important questions about the assumption that the importation of capital and technology leads to economic development, even if many of these questions remain less than fully answered.

New Directions in the Study of Social Change

There are many new directions in the study of social change. As you read about these topics, think about how new knowledge in these areas would affect your view of social change and the world.

The causes of modernization and development remain an important research topic. Some researchers are tracing the origins of the Industrial Revolution further back in history (Chase-Dunn, 1988; Abu-Lughod, 1989). Others are looking at the role of technology, education, and population (Meyer and Hannan, 1979; Chirot, 1986). Studies of the micro and macro processes of social change converge in the analysis of the revolutions and social movements, as depicted in Charles Tilly's box in Chapter 19. Another fascinating area of research is the study of various long cycles of change (Goldstein, 1988; Bergesen, 1983; Boswell, 1989).

How can we use the sociological imagination in the study of social change? First, we can note that long-term processes can only be slightly altered (not created or reversed) by individual activities during our lifetimes. Next we can note that much of the social change going on in the world today is out of any one leader's direct control, whether that leader is George Bush, Margaret Thatcher, Mikhail Gorbachev, or Deng Xiaoping. Within these restrictions, however, a great deal can be shaped by human actors. Figuring what can be affected by individual effort helps us direct our energies. To paraphrase Marx we make our own history, but we don't make it any way we please.

At a more direct level, all of you will contribute to the newly emerging patterns of family relations, relations between the sexes, relations among social groups, and relations between humans and technology. We have a great deal in common with the Navajo Tribe because we, too, are trying to solve the same basic problems. How can we preserve what is good from our past and use it to build a positive future? Although sociology cannot supply "all the answers," it does give us some valuable suggestions about where to look for them and how to apply our energies usefully in promoting desirable social changes.

Summary

Social change can be defined as any alteration of behavior patterns, social relationships, or social structure over time. Certain cultural patterns, like fads and fashions, change very quickly; others, like political and social institutions, usually change very slowly. According to the functionalist perspective, societies tend toward equilibrium, a condition in which the various components of the culture function together. Change, therefore, is usually a response to exogenous forces, those originating outside the society. Conflict theorists, in contrast, view change as the norm. Change arises from endogenous factors, especially internal conflicts over the unequal distribution of scarce resources. Among the major sources of social change recognized by sociologists are the physical environment, contact with other societies, technology, internal conflict (including revolution and civil war), and planned change.

Early theories of social change were either evolutionary, which often stressed a unilinear progression from a traditional to an industrial society, or cyclical, which sometimes referred to the life-cycle of a civilization. These theories are no longer accepted by most sociologists. More widely accepted is the theory of sociocultural evolution, which examines how hunting and gathering societies changed into other types of societies. Sociocultural evolution focuses on general patterns, within which there are many individual variations.

Although we live in a period of rapid social change, the long-term perspective teaches us that throughout most of human history, change occurred very slowly. Rapid social change is basically the product of the Industrial Revolution, which began only a few centuries ago. Within that period, traditional agricultural societies have been transformed into technologically advanced industrial (and post-industrial) societies. Sociologists refer to this process and the accompanying political and social changes as modernization. Although many of these changes have increased life expectancy and raised the overall standard of living, the rate of change has led to increased anomie and other social problems as skills and behavioral norms quickly become obsolete.

Despite the rapid rate of change, different countries remain at different levels of development. Sociologists have developed systems for classifying countries according to a variety of factors related to economic development, as well as diverse theories to account for differences among countries. Modernization theories, which draw heavily from the functionalist perspective, argue that the less-developed nations will pursue a path similar to that of the developed nations and will enjoy similar benefits. Dependency theories, which reflect the conflict perspective, maintain that the imperialistic policies of the developed nations keep the less-developed nations in a dependent state in which they serve as markets and sources of raw materials for the developed nations. One form of dependency theory, the world-system theory, sees all the world's economies as part of a worldwide system dominated by the developed, or core nations. Dependency theories help to explain the preponderance of socialist revolutions in the Third World, and they argue that traditional foreign policies such as investment and foreign aid to less-developed countries will increase rather than solve their problems.

Glossary

social change The alteration of behavior patterns, social relationships, institutions, and social structure over time.

equilibrium A condition in which the components of a society function together in a state of balance.

cultural diffusion A process whereby a belief, value, norm, symbol, or practice spreads from one culture into another, or from a subculture into the larger culture.

technology The application of scientific knowledge to a practical task.

revolution A rapid fundamental change in the basic institutions, relationships, and ideologies within a society.

rebellion A movement to change specific officeholders or policies forcibly without changing the structure of the government.

war Armed conflict among different nations.

civil war An armed conflict among different groups or factions within the same nation.

sociocultural evolution The process whereby hunting

and gathering societies develop into more technologically advanced societies.

modernization The process of development of industrial societies from agricultural societies, and the accompanying social, economic, and cultural changes.

modernization theory A theory holding that developing countries will follow the same general pattern of development as industrial nations.

imperialism A system in which a more-powerful country uses the resources of a less-powerful country to its own advantage, often by controlling that country's economic or political system.

dependency theories A group of theories holding that industrial nations keep Third-World nations in a dependent position to maintain the advantages of the industrial nations.

world-system theory A form of dependency theory that divides all countries into core, peripheral, and semiperipheral nations, in which the more-developed nations keep the less-developed ones in a weak and dependent position.

Further Reading

APPELBAUM, RICHARD P. 1970. *Theories of Social Change*. Chicago: Markham. Though an older book, it is still one of the best summaries of the various approaches to social change.

CHASE-DUNN, CHRISTOPHER. 1989. *Global Formation: Structures of the World-Economy*. London: Basil Blackwell. This is the best, most up-to-date summary of research that is based on world-system theory.

GOLDSTEIN, JOSHUA. 1988. *Long Cycles: Prosperity and War in the Modern Age*. New Haven, CT: Yale University Press. This book summarizes the empirical evidence and the major theoretical interpretations of cyclical social change that has occurred in the last 500 years.

GOLDSTONE, JACK A., ED. 1986. *Revolutions: Theoretical, Comparative, and Historical Studies*. New York: Harcourt, Brace Jovanovich. This collection, as its subtitle suggests, summarizes much of the recent research on revolutions.

WALLERSTEIN, IMMANUEL. 1979. *The Capitalist World-Economy*. Cambridge University Press. This collection of essays covers most of the major points of world-system theory.

APPENDIX 1

Careers in Sociology

The kinds of jobs that people with sociology degrees obtain vary widely according to the level of the degree. Those with a bachelor's degree obtain a wide variety of jobs, and many go on to graduate or professional school in other disciplines. Most of those who get Ph.D. degrees in sociology, end up in teaching, research, or some combination of the two. Let us consider the opportunities at each level.

Careers for Those with a Bachelor's Degree

Although a bachelor's degree in sociology does not prepare a student for any specific job in the sense that a nursing or accounting degree does, there are many jobs for which the knowledge and skills of a sociology major are useful and in which sociology majors are working. About 15 percent of sociology graduates in the early 1980s were employed in management, a percentage that has steadily increased over the past 2 decades (Kinloch, 1983). A sociology major might have to work harder to find a job in management than a business major would, but employers are increasingly recognizing the benefits of the broad substantive training and analytical skills that students in sociology obtain. In fact, a study commissioned in the late 1970s by Bell Telephone found that students who majored in the arts and sciences (including sociology) outperformed those with professional majors such as business administration in managerial employment (Beck, 1981). One important reason for this was the broader general knowledge the arts and sciences majors possessed compared to business students.

Chris: Personnel Manager in a Small Manufacturing Firm Chris C_ _ _ _ is viewed by most of her friends as a business executive rather than a sociologist. Nevertheless, she owes her start in the firm to her background in industrial sociology and social psychology. Starting as a lower-level assistant in the personnel department, Chris now has a post with considerable control over her company's personnel policies — that is, strategies and programs for hiring, training, supervising, and promoting. Eventually, she may be promoted to a higher executive position within the firm or she may seek advancement by joining another organization. Chris received a B.A. in sociology and did not go on to graduate school. In fact, she has not really kept up with sociological research for the past 10 years, and now thinks of herself more as a practitioner than a scholar. However, she does read specialized publications on organizational behavior and industrial and business practices, and here her sociological training is especially helpful. Although the company does not consider Chris's position to be that of a sociologist, like many firms, it is beginning to realize that sociological training is worthwhile for administrators and executives.

Teaching, planning, and wholesale and retail trade are also common careers for sociology majors. With the bachelor's degree, teaching jobs in sociology are most likely to be found at the high-school level and usually require sufficient education courses to obtain teacher certification. Some sociology graduates who go into retail or wholesale trade have jobs, such as textbook sales representative, that require both academic knowledge (in order to communicate intelligently with the professors to whom they are trying to sell books) and skills in interacting with people, both of which can be obtained through majoring in sociology. Increasingly, sociology majors are finding jobs in areas such as planning and market analysis where they can apply their research skills. At the same time, areas such as social work and counseling, which were once important career opportunities for those with B.A.'s in sociology, have been largely closed off because of the requirements for professional degrees in these fields. Most of the jobs in these areas now go to students with such degrees. Although sociologists today less frequently provide direct services such as counseling to clients, they do commonly work in administrative, planning, and analytic positions within social-service agencies. (An example of this can be seen in the vignette about Wally.) Finally, about one in ten sociology majors goes directly into graduate school, either in sociology or some other subject. Others choose to take time off from school and enter a graduate program at a later date. The substantial majority of people who major in sociology either find a job in a related career or enter graduate school.

Wally: Staff Administrator in a Public Assistance Agency

Throughout his studies, Wally W____ was interested in using his knowledge to serve people. Unlike many students who go into sociology to become teachers or researchers, Wally saw sociology as a field that could be used to provide services. He now works for his city's Department of Social Service as a program coordinator. In this position, he draws on his studies in such areas as the family, social stratification, urban communities, and group dynamics. His work includes routine processing of reports and legal forms, but it also includes much contact with agency clients and direct involvement with the problems of the poor, disabled, aged, and minorities. He also works with other employees, most of whom are professional social workers who deal with individual families and clients. Wally brings a unique perspective and special resources to his job. He has mixed feelings about the possibility of taking on more administrative responsibility, because this would mean less time available to work with families directly. He often serves as a kind of trouble-shooter by providing help in the personal crises of his clients. This, in turn, requires him to maintain contacts with various other public and private agencies that affect the lives of the poor. For example, one of his fellow undergraduate majors is now working on the staff of a large community mental-health center, and another is involved in supervising rehabilitation for state penitentiary inmates. Like Wally, these two are using their undergraduate sociology as a basis for social-service positions. All three take satisfaction in day-to-day accomplishments in their work. Their salaries are commensurate with the general wage scales of public agencies. Wally could progress through civil service channels to a career of relative security. However, he still thinks about going back to school to earn a graduate degree, which would give him a considerable boost along the way.

Careers for Those with a Master's Degree

Generally, 2 to 3 years of graduate school are required to obtain a master's degree in sociology. This degree is available at over 250 universities throughout the United States, although a few of them offer it only as a steppingstone toward the doctorate. Research, analysis, planning, administration, and community college teaching are among the most common positions filled by sociology M.A.'s. The jobs held by recent graduates of the masters program in which I teach are probably illustrative. Several of our recent graduates are employed by state governments. Two of them work for the state of Illinois criminal justice system—one as a researcher and the other as an administrator (the administrator was promoted to that position after having begun as a researcher). Another recent graduate serves as a researcher at the regional planning agency for the St. Louis metropolitan area. Still another found a job with a private research and consulting firm. Other graduates have been employed as community-college teachers—a profession that generally requires the master's degree, but not the Ph.D., to enter. (For an example of this type of employment, see the vignette about Francis.) Several of our recent M.A. graduates hold administrative positions in public or private social-service agencies. One works in an agency serving alcoholics, another in an agency providing assistance to the disabled. Because sociology graduate programs frequently provide considerable training in the use of the computer as a research tool, some graduates find jobs in areas that primarily involve working with computers. One of our recent graduates, for example, is working as a programmer/analyst for a major aerospace firm.

Francis: Teaching Sociology in a State Community College

Francis F_____ teaches in a 2-year community college located 50 miles from the university where he received his B.A. and M.A. degrees. He chose not to pursue a Ph.D. Francis enjoys teaching, which is good because he does a great deal of it. He teaches five classes a semester. Although at least two of them are sections of the same course, the burden is heavy. This was particularly true when Francis was a new faculty member. However, courses become less demanding as they are repeated from semester to semester, even though it is important continually to seek out new and up-to-date materials and teaching techniques. Although many people think that teaching consists primarily of time spent in the classroom, this is often only a fraction of a teacher's total responsibilities. Other requirements include preparing for courses, serving on college committees, and meeting with individual students. These students have questions about the courses they are taking, the courses they should take, and their longer-range educational and occupational goals. Student counseling often goes beyond the formal rounds of regular office hours. Meanwhile, Francis also must devote time to reading so that he can keep up with new developments in sociology and related fields. In fact, he is a member of the Behavioral Science Department, and his colleagues include anthropologists, economists, political scientists, and psychologists. His salary is competitive with that of other state workers and with that of sociologists who teach in 4-year colleges. This represents a fairly recent improvement in the salaries at 2-year community (or junior) colleges. After several years of adequate service, Francis should receive *tenure,* which amounts to almost a guarantee of continued employment. Francis is a member of a union that represents community college teachers in bargaining with the state for cost-of-living raises and step increases with greater seniority. Actually, most community colleges are now reevaluating their admissions and programs. For example, as traditional college-aged populations have begun to decline, many colleges now seek to serve a new sort of student by emphasizing continuing education programs geared to the needs of adults in their community.

Many people who hold jobs in areas related to sociology obtain a master's degree in order to develop skills useful to them in their employment. Among our current graduate students, for example, is a college admissions officer (who has a particular interest in opening opportunities in his college to minority students), a parole officer, and an employee of a job-training agency.

Marion: Staff Member of a Research Institute

Marion M_____ is a member of the staff of a private research institute that conducts sociological studies on specific problems of interest to government agencies, businesses, and political groups. The institute is located in a large metropolitan center, and many of the studies concentrate on the city and the surrounding region. Marion began the job with a B.A. in sociology. She had focused her studies around courses in research methods and statistics. Since joining the institute she has returned to graduate school for an M.S. degree. She has also accumulated considerable on-the-job training. During her first several years, she was a "research assistant," but she is now an "associate project director" with responsibility for developing new research projects as well as for supervising the actual research process. She has developed a sense of how clients' problems can be met by appropriate research studies. She is learning to write research proposals and then to follow them through discussion and revision to actual funding. Her work schedule is basically 9 to 6, but she sometimes puts in considerable evening and weekend work, especially when she is conducting interviews, supervising an interviewing staff, or doing the statistical analysis and writing that go into a final report to a client. Her salary is now somewhat above average for those in her graduating class. With success in obtaining contracts and advising clients, her income will probably increase considerably in a short period of time. Marion may stay here or move to another research firm, or she may consider starting her own agency. Some research agencies are run on a nonprofit basis and are associated with an educational or a governmental institution. If Marion were to open a research firm for profit, she would be facing the same substantial risks involved in launching any new business.

Careers for Those With a Doctorate (Ph.D.)

To obtain a Ph.D. in sociology generally requires about 2 to 3 additional years of study beyond the master's degree, or a period of 4 to 5 years if you enter a doctoral program directly out of undergraduate school. There are about 130 doctoral programs in sociology in the United States. The time required to complete the Ph.D. varies somewhat because a major requirement is to write a *dissertation*—an original piece of research or theory that adds new knowledge to the field of sociology. The dissertation is longer and more rigorous than the thesis sometimes required of master's students, and the time taken to complete it varies widely. In many programs, students must also take some kind of qualifying examination before they begin their dissertation to demonstrate that they have a sufficient knowlege of sociology in general and of their special field in particular. Once they have received their Ph.D.'s, nearly all sociologists enter either college or university teaching or a full-time research position with a government agency, a research institute, a research/consulting firm, or a corporate employer. The majority of sociology Ph.D.'s go into college or university teaching, and for those who want a permanent teaching job in a 4-year college or university, a Ph.D. is a must. Major universities also require research as a condition of keeping one's job, and many other 4-year colleges and locally oriented universities encourage research by making it an important criterion for promotions and salary increases. (The vignette concerning Shelly illustrates the role of sociologists in major research universities, and that of Clyde illustrates a sociologist working in a 4-year liberal arts college.)

Shelly: Professor in a University Department of Sociology Shelly ____ is an assistant professor of sociology in a large university. Her department teaches both undergraduate and graduate students. It offers the M.A. and the Ph.D. degrees, as well as the B.A. Shelly recently received her Ph.D. from a different university, where she served as an instructor before she completed her dissertation. During her first year in her new job, she worked on her doctoral project evenings, weekends, and every other spare moment. Shelly has ample company and stimulation from her new faculty colleagues. After all, the department has 25 faculty members handling the department's 400 undergraduate majors and 75 graduate students. Five of these faculty members are also assistant professors. In one sense, they are competing with Shelly for promotion to associate professor and the award of tenure. Shelly teaches five, sometimes six, courses a year, including two advanced seminars for graduate students. As important as teaching is to Shelly, research and writing might be even more important to her career development. In fact, at the graduate level, she teaches largely through her research. She has hired two graduate students as research assistants on a study financed by a grant from a federal research agency in Washington. Shelly's tenure decision will be made in her sixth year at the university, and her chances will be improved considerably if she is able to publish a number of scholarly articles and perhaps a book before then. But these are the kinds of activities that attracted Shelly into sociology and academic life in the first place. Although her salary does not compete with financial compensation in the business world, she considers it more than adequate, especially when combined with that of her husband, who teaches in the physics department of the same university. Shelly has avoided summer-school teaching supplements to work on a book that could produce some additional income in the form of royalties, although she is aware that scholarly books rarely make much money.

Clyde: Faculty Member of a Liberal Arts College While working on his doctoral dissertation, Clyde C____ received an invitation to join the faculty of a liberal arts college located in a small town. Because he considered teaching his major goal in life, he accepted the position, despite some warnings from his adviser that he might find it difficult to complete his dissertation while teaching full time. It took him 2 hard years to do so, but now he has been at the college for 6 years, has been promoted to associate professor, and has received tenure. This is an important source of security for Clyde, because it means that his job is virtually guaranteed (unless he commits some major moral offense or the college suffers a major economic catastrophe). Tenure is an important safeguard of a teacher's academic freedom. Clyde's major activity is teaching, usually four courses each semester, which amounts to 12 hours per week. Occasionally he teaches during the summer for additional pay. His teaching is primarily oriented to students for whom sociology is part of their education for citizenship, and he helps them make choices among various occupational goals. He spends a lot of time with students in various campus activities and is active in community programs. Because college programs emphasize general liberal education, Clyde works with faculty members from other disciplines. He has learned to work with other social scientists and with the faculty in the biological and physical sciences. He knows that his salary may continue to be lower than that of his colleagues in universities or in some state institutions, but he also knows that life in this college town is relatively inexpensive, and he is doing what he really enjoys — working closely with young people.

Statistics in Sociology

Dispersion

In Chapter 2 we saw how measures of central tendency — more specifically, the mean, median, and mode — could be disproportionately affected by a small number of scores that deviate significantly from most of the population that is being studied. Does this tendency render statistical measurement useless? Fortunately, it does not. Statisticians have developed formulas for measuring and assessing those results that deviate greatly from the norm. This area of statistics is known as *dispersion*.

Consider two high schools. In each of the schools, 250 seniors take a college entrance test. In Jefferson High School the mean score is 520. In Lincoln High School the mean score is 570. Can we state that, in general, students in Lincoln High did better than students in Jefferson High?

The answer is "no" for several reasons. First, because we're talking about mean scores, Lincoln's mean could be higher mainly because a few students scored very high, while the rest of the students had the same distribution of scores as those in Jefferson High. But what if we looked at the median scores, which are *not* influenced by extreme values, and found that Lincoln High still came out 50 points higher? *Now* could we conclude that students in Lincoln scored higher as a whole than students in Jefferson? We'd be on better grounds than before, but such a conclusion still wouldn't be very sound. Why not? The answer can be found in Figure A1.

Figure A1 shows two examples. *In both examples, Lincoln High has a mean and median score of 520, and Jefferson High has a mean and median of 570.* However, even a casual glance indicates that the two examples are quite different. They are different because the degree of *dispersion* is different. In Example 1, nearly everyone in each school got close to the average score. Thus, almost everyone in Lincoln High School got a higher score than nearly everyone in Jefferson High School. The area of overlap in scores between the schools is shaded, and there is obviously very little overlap. In this example, the observation that students in Lincoln generally did better than students in Jefferson would hold true.

Now consider Example 2. In this example, the scores are much more spread out from the middle. Here, some people in both schools scored far above the average, and others scored far below. In this example, there is a great deal of overlap between the distributions of scores in the two schools, again shown shaded. This area represents an area in which some students from Jefferson High outscored some students from Lincoln High, despite the higher *average* score in Lincoln. Clearly in this example the dominant feature is overlap, and it would not be true to say that, in general, students in Lincoln outscored students in Jefferson — for a good many pairs of students in the two schools, the result was just the opposite.

This example illustrates the need to look at more than a measure of central tendency. We also need to look at a measure of dispersion when comparing any

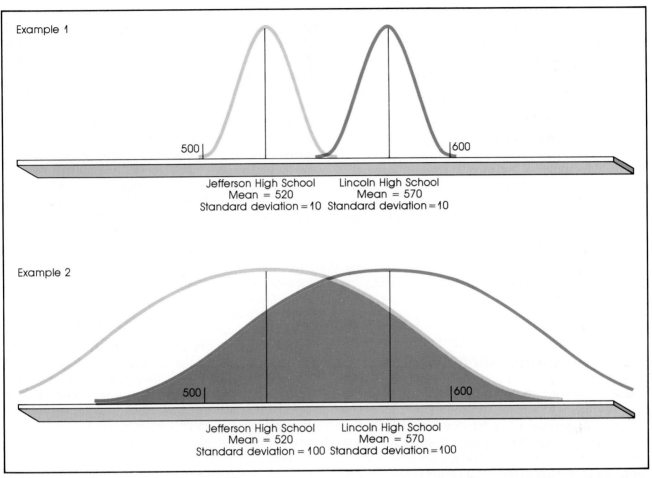

Example 1

500 | | 600

Jefferson High School
Mean = 520
Standard deviation = 10

Lincoln High School
Mean = 570
Standard deviation = 10

Example 2

500 | | 600

Jefferson High School
Mean = 520
Standard deviation = 100

Lincoln High School
Mean = 570
Standard deviation = 100

FIGURE A1

numerical distribution between two groups. The most common such measure is the *standard deviation*.

Standard Deviation

Although its computation is beyond the scope of this book, the *standard deviation* is an important concept for beginning sociology students to understand. The standard deviation is a statistic computed in a manner such that—subject to certain assumptions—about two-thirds of scores will fall within one standard deviation above or below the mean. In Example 1 in Figure A1, the standard deviation is 10. This means that about two-thirds of the 250 people taking the test will have scores within 10 points of the mean. In other words, in Jefferson High School, around 167 people will score between 510 and 530, and in Lincoln High School about the same number will score between 560 and 580. In contrast, the scores vary much more widely in Example 2. There about 167 people will score between 470 and 670 in Lincoln—a much wider range. About 95 percent will fall within two standard deviations, and 99 percent within three standard deviations. Thus, in Example 1, almost everyone (all but two or three people) will likely score between 540 and 600 in Lincoln High.

In general, when you compare two groups, you can regard the groups as being quite different if the difference between their means is a good deal more than either of the standard deviations, and as not very different if the difference is less than either of their standard deviations. This is a very rough guideline, and you should know that more rigorous standards are used in scientific research. However, this at least alerts you to the fact that standard deviation is an important concept to consider whenever a sociologist compares two groups.

Other Measures of Dispersion

Although the standard deviation is the most important measure of dispersion, social scientists also use other methods. One is the *variance,* which is simply the standard deviation squared. Another is the *range.* The range is the difference between the highest score and the lowest score. Although the range is easy to understand and compute, it suffers from the same weakness as the mean—it is influenced disproportionately by extreme high or low scores.

The Correlation Coefficient

Chapter 2 explained that some tables are different from the ones we discussed, which show numbers of people with particular combinations of characteristics. Other kinds of tables show measures of statistical correlation. Some tables of this type are well beyond the scope of this book, but one measure is so common that even beginning students will encounter it. That measure is the *correlation coefficient,* also sometimes called "Pearson's r" and abbreviated as "r" in tables. The correlation coefficient can be used any time you are working with two variables that can each be expressed as a number. It tells you the *strength* and *direction* of the correlation between the two variables. The correlation coefficient can range anywhere from 1 through 0 to −1. The sign indicates the direction of the relationship between the variables. If the sign is positive, it is a *positive* or *direct* relationship: When one variable increases, the other also tends to increase. If the sign is negative, it is a *negative* or *inverse* relationship: When one variable increases, the other decreases. The stronger the relationship is, the closer the correlation coefficient will be to 1 or −1. The weaker the relationship is, the closer the correlation coefficient will be to 0. A correlation coefficient of 1 or −1 means a perfect relationship. In cases where this occurs, you are really measuring the same variable two different ways. An example would be the perfect correlation of −1 between the percentage of males in the classes at your college and the percentage of females in those classes. (Both measures are measuring the same variable, the sex composition of the classes.) A correlation coefficient of 0, however, means there is absolutely no relationship between the two variables—as one increases, the other will show no tendency either to increase or to decrease.

As a very general guideline in sociology, correlations between .2 and −.2 are considered weak; correlations of .2 to .6 and −.2 to −.6 are moderate, and correlations stronger than .6 or −.6 are considered strong. However, exactly what is considered a strong correlation depends somewhat on the researcher's purpose. A researcher trying out a new IQ test, for example, would probably want to show more than a .6 correlation to existing IQ tests; after all, the new test is supposed to measure the same concept as the existing tests. However, a researcher testing a theory about a relationship between distinct variables—say, education and prejudice—would probably be delighted to be able to show a correlation as strong as .6 or, in this case, −.6.

acculturation A process in which immigrant minority groups are expected to adopt the dominant culture of the host country.

achieved status Any status that a person has attained at least in part as a result of something that the person has done.

acting crowd A crowd that engages in violent or destructive behavior.

activity theory A theory arguing that activity is beneficial to the health and self-esteem of older people, and that there is no social need for them to give up socially valued roles and activities.

acute disorder A medical disorder of limited duration, which is followed either by rapid recovery or death.

affirmative action Any effort designed to overcome past or institutional discrimination by increasing the number of minorities or females in schools, jobs, or job-training programs.

age groups Socially defined categories of people based on age; for example, childhood, adolescence, old age.

age roles Roles that are associated with age and carry the expectation that people of different ages should behave differently.

age stratification Social inequality among age groups.

ageism Prejudice and discrimination based on age.

agents of socialization People and institutions that carry out the process of socialization; they act as important influences on the individual's attitudes, beliefs, self-image, and behavior.

agricultural economy A system of production based primarily on raising crops through the use of plows and draft animals.

alienation As defined by Marx, the separation or isolation of workers from the products of their labor; more broadly, feelings or the experience of isolation, powerlessness, or loss of control.

amalgamation A process whereby different racial or ethnic groups in a society gradually lose their identities and become one group as a result of intermarriage.

androgenous society A society in which men and women are not assigned distinct sex roles.

anomie A situation in which social norms either do not exist or have become ineffective.

apartheid The official name for the racial caste system in South Africa, where political and economic rights are defined according to which of four official racial groupings — white, black, coloured, and Asian — a person belongs to.

ascribed status Any status that a person receives through birth, including race, sex, and family of origin.

assimilation A process by which different ethnic or cultural groups in a society come to share a common culture and social structure.

authoritarian government A government in which the leaders have virtually unrestricted power and the people have little or no freedom of expession.

authoritarian personality A personality pattern believed by social psychologists to be associated with a psychological need to be prejudiced.

authority A right to make decisions and exercise power that is attached to a social position or to an individual and is accepted because people recognize and acknowledge its legitimacy.

bilineal system A system in which wealth and kinship are passed on through both males and females.

birth cohort The set of all people who were born during a given time period.

bourgeoisie In a capitalist economy, those who own capital, who constitute the dominant group or ruling class.

bureaucracy A form of organization characterized by specialization, hierarchy, formal rules, impersonality, lifelong careers, and a specialized administrative staff.

capital Productive capacity in an industrialized economy, including manufacturing and distribution capacity, raw materials, and money.

capitalist economy An economic system, found mainly in industrialized countries, in which the means of production are privately owned.

caste A grouping into which a person is born that determines that person's status in a caste system.

caste system A very closed stratification system in which the group or caste into which a person is born determines that person's social status on a lifelong basis.

cause and effect A relationship in which some condition (the effect) is more likely to occur when some other condition (the cause) is present than it otherwise would be.

central tendency A measure of where the center of a distribution lies, or where the middle, average, or typical person falls in some distribution of scores or characteristics.

charismatic authority Authority that is based on the personal qualities of an individual, such as the ability to excite, inspire, and lead other people.

child abuse Extreme or sustained physical or psychological violence directed against children.

chronic disorder An extended or ongoing medical disorder from which a patient cannot expect to recover.

church A religion with a formalized hierarchy and set of rules that accommodates itself to the larger society.

civil disobedience Nonviolent protest actions that violate the law.

civil religion A series of beliefs, not associated with any single denomination, that portray a society's institutions and structure as consistent with the will of God.

civil war An armed conflict among different groups or factions within the same nation.

class A grouping of people with similar socioeconomic status in an industrialized society.

class consciousness A situation in which a group of people with a common self-interest correctly perceive that interest, and develop beliefs, values, and norms consistent with advancing that interest.

class structure The distribution of wealth and other scarce resources in society.

class system A system of social inequality, usually found in modern, industrial societies, in which a person's position in life is influenced by both achieved and ascribed statuses.

clergy Religious officials with special authority to conduct ceremonies, establish rules, and administer sacraments.

cliques Relatively close and exclusive informal groups with distinct boundaries, usually consisting of about three to nine people.

closed stratification system A system of inequality in which opportunities for mobility are relatively limited.

coercion An exercise of power that forces people to recognize and obey a group or an individual whose legitimacy they do not accept.

cognitive-developmental theories Theories of socialization that emphasize the development of reasoning ability.

cognitive-dissonance theory A social-psychological theory that claims that people often adjust their attitudes to make them consistent with their behavior to eliminate the stress that results when their attitudes and behaviors are inconsistent.

cognitive processes Mental processes involved in learning and reasoning.

cohabitation An arrangement in which an unmarried couple form a household.

collective behavior Large numbers of people acting together in an extraordinary situation, in which usual norms governing behavior do not apply.

common schools Schools intended to educate everyone, regardless of social background.

communal movement A social movement that attempts to bring about social change through example, by building a model society within a group of limited size.

communism As used by Karl Marx, a utopian society, to date not attained in the real world in which all wealth is collectively owned, workers control the work place, and government is unnecessary.

concentrated economy An economy in which competition is limited or absent because there are very few producers of any given product (in a capitalist economy) or because decisions are made centrally by government officials (in a socialist economy).

concentric-zones model A theory in urban sociology holding that population characteristics and land use change systematically as you move away from the center of the city, such that they are arranged roughly as a series of rings around the center of the city.

conflict perspective A macrosociological perspective based on the key premise that society is made up of groups that compete, usually with unequal power, for scarce resources; conflict and change are seen as the natural order of things.

constructs Abstract concepts that cannot be measured directly; examples are intelligence, happiness, and power.

contagion A process through which a proposed or initiated action is rapidly adopted or imitated by a crowd or mass.

content analysis A research method based on the systematic examination of the content of some message or communication.

control group In experimental research, a group that experiences no manipulation of the independent variable; it is used for purposes of comparison to the experimental group.

control variable A variable that is introduced into an experiment to determine whether correlation between an independent and a dependent variable is the product of some other influence operating on both of them.

convergence A dynamic in which a crowd acts as one because many people in the crowd share emotions, goals, or beliefs.

convergence theory A theory that holds that capitalist and socialist economies are becoming more similar to one another as the role of the public sector grows in capitalist societies and the roles of private ownership and the market increase in socialist societies.

cooptation A process whereby leaders of social movements are led to adopt more moderate positions by being given positions of status or authority in institutions.

corporation A large-scale private company with multiple owners (called stockholders) that is legally independent and has legal rights and responsibilities separate from either its owners or managers.

correlation A relationship between two variables in

which a change in one is accompanied by a change in the other.

counterculture A subculture that has developed beliefs, values, symbols, and norms that stand in opposition to those of the larger culture.

credentials Items of information used to document or support the claim that an individual has certain capabilities, or expertise.

crime A deviant act that violates a law.

cross-cutting cleavages Situations in which divisions or issues of conflict divide a society in different ways on different issues.

crowd A large set of people who are localized in one place and whose interaction is only temporary.

crude birth rate The number of births occurring in a year per 1,000 population.

crude death rate The number of deaths occurring in a year per 1,000 population.

cult A religious group that is withdrawn from, and often at odds with, the religious traditions of a society.

cultural deprivation A condition that functionalist theorists believe commonly exists among lower-income groups, whereby such groups suffer disadvantages in education and economics because they lack cultural characteristics associated with success.

cultural diffusion A process whereby a belief, value, norm, symbol, or practice spreads from one cultural into another, or from a subculture into the larger culture.

cultural lag A pattern whereby some aspect of culture that was once functional persists after social or technological change has eliminated its usefulness.

cultural relativism A view that recognizes cultures other than one's own as different, but not odd or inferior; other cultures are not judged by the standards of one's own.

culture A set of knowledge, beliefs, attitudes, and rules for behavior that are held commonly within a society

deconcentrated economy An economy characterized by competition resulting from a large number of producers.

de facto segregation Racial school segregation that is brought about as a result of housing and neighborhood segregation patterns.

democratic government A system in which government is chosen by the people, who enjoy freedom of expression and the right to vote for their leaders.

demographic transition A historic process whereby declines in mortality are not immediately followed by declines in fertility, thereby creating a period of rapid population growth.

demography The scientific study of human populations.

denomination One of several major religions in a society that usually tolerates other religions.

dependency theories A group of theories holding that industrialized nations keep Third-World nations in a dependent position to maintain the advantages of the industrialized nations.

dependent variable A variable that is assumed by the researcher to be the effect of some other variable, called the independent variable.

deviance Behavior that does not conform to the prevailing norms of a society.

dictatorship A modern form of authoritarian government in which one person rules by absolute power.

differential association A theory that explains criminal behavior as a product of long-term exposure to criminal activities.

dimensions of stratification The different bases on which people in a society are unequally ranked, including economic (wealth and income), political (power), and prestige (status).

disease A condition defined by a medical practitioner as the cause of an illness.

discrimination Behavior that treats people unequally on the basis of an ascribed status such as race or sex.

disengagement theory A theory, drawing largely on the functionalist perspective, that supports older people's giving up their role obligations to create opportunities for younger people.

division of labor A characteristic of most societies in which different individuals or groups specialize in different tasks.

dramaturgical perspective A theory arising from the symbolic-interactionist perspective that holds that human behavior is often an attempt to present a particular self-image to others.

dyad A social group that consists of only two people.

dying A process of physical deterioration and preparation for death.

dysfunction A consequence of a social arrangement that is in some way damaging or problematic to the social system.

economic structure In Marxian terminology, those aspects of social structure that relate to production, wealth, and income.

economic systems Systems that determine the production and distribution of scarce resources.

ego In Freudian theory, that part of the personality that mediates between the id and the superego.

emergent norms A process whereby a crowd collectively and interactively develops its own norms about how to behave.

endogamy Marriage between people from the same racial, religious, and ethnic groups.

epidemiology The measurement of the extent of medical disorders in a population, and the social, demographic, and geographic characteristics of those with such disorders.

equilibrium A condition in which the components of a society function together in a state of balance.

estate system A relatively closed stratification system, also called a feudal system, that is found in agricultural economies, in which a person's status is determined on the basis of landownership and, frequently, formal title.

ethnic group A group of people who are recognized as a distinct group on the basis of cultural characteristics such as common ancestry or religion.

ethnocentrism A pattern whereby people view their own culture as normal, natural, and superior, and judge other cultures accordingly.

ethnomethodology A theory arising from the symbolic-interactionist perspective that argues that human behavior is a product of how people understand the situations they encounter.

exchange mobility A type of socioeconomic mobility that occurs when some people move to higher positions in the stratification system, while others move to lower positions.

exchange theory A theory holding that people enter a relationship of any kind because each participant expects to gain something from it.

exogamy Marriage between people from different racial, ethnic, or religious groups.

experiment A research method in which the researcher manipulates the independent variable while keeping everything else constant in order to measure the effect on the dependent variable.

experimental group In experimental research, the group that experiences some manipulation or change of the independent variable.

expertise An individual's specialized knowledge concerning some specific topic, issue, or scientific discipline.

exponential growth Growth based on a percentage rate of increase that results in larger numerical growth in each successive year.

expressive crowd A crowd whose dominant action is to express some emotion, usually joy, excitement, or ecstasy.

expressive leaders People who exercise leadership by taking care of the social and emotional needs of people in their group.

extended family A family consisting of more than two generations who live together and share responsibilities for the maintenance of the family.

fad An amusing mass involvement or activity, usually somewhat unconventional, that is temporary in nature.

false consciousness A condition in which people, usually in groups that are relatively powerless, accept beliefs that work against their self-interests.

family A group of people related by ancestry, marriage, or adoption who live together, form an economic unit, and cooperatively rear their young.

family of orientation The family into which a person is born.

family of procreation The family a person forms by marrying and having children.

fashion A style of appearance or behavior that is favored by a large number of people for a limited amount of time.

fee-for-service payment A method of payment for health care in which providers receive a set amount of money (fee) for each service that they provide.

feminism An ideology or a related social movement advocating the ideas that a larger share of scarce resources should go to women and that social roles should not be assigned on the basis of sex.

fertility The number of births occurring in a population.

field observation A research method in which the researcher observes human behavior as it occurs in natural, "real-life" situations.

folkways Relatively minor informal norms that carry only informal sanctions such as mild joking or ridicule, when they are violated.

forced assimilation A type of assimilation in which a minority group is required to adopt the culture of the majority group.

formal organization A relatively large self-perpetuating social group with a name, an established purpose, a role structure, and a set of rules.

function A consequence of a social arrangement that is in some way useful for the social system.

functional illiteracy The inability to read, write, add, or subtract well enough to perform everyday tasks.

functional specialization The tendency of different cities or metropolitan areas to specialize in different types of economic activity.

functionalist perspective A macrosociological perspective stressing the basic notion that society is made up of interdependent parts that function together to produce consensus and stability.

fundamentalism A form of religion characterized by strict rules and by literal and unquestioning acceptance of sacred writings and teachings.

game stage According to George Herbert Mead, a stage of socialization at which organized activity becomes possible.

gemeinschaft According to Toennies, a traditional community in which relations between people are close and personal, behavior is governed by tradition, and contacts with strangers are rare.

gender Socially learned traits or characteristics that are associated with men or women.

gender roles *See* **sex roles.**

generalized other Classes of people with whom a person interacts on the basis of generalized roles rather than on individual characteristics.

gentrification The movement of the upper class into older central-city neighborhoods, leading to renovation of buildings and a turnover in neighborhood population.

gesellschaft According to Toennies, an urban society in which personal goals come before community objectives, relations are impersonal, and tradition is weak.

group See **social group.**

group polarization A process by which a group moves toward a more extreme or more cautious position than its individual members would take.

groupthink A process by which a group arrives, by apparent consensus, at a decision with which many individual members privately disagree.

hawthorne effect A source of error in social research, in which the people being studied attempt to please the researcher or otherwise respond to the attention they receive from the research rather than to the condition that the researcher is attempting to study.

health A condition in which a person can function effectively on the physical, mental, and social levels.

health maintenance organization (HMO) A medical coverage plan in which members prepay their health care and receive services as needed without a fee.

hidden curriculum The values, beliefs, and habits that are taught in the schools in addition to factual content and skills.

hinterland The area around a city that is dependent upon the city for goods, services, and markets.

homogamy "Like marrying like"; marriage between people of similar backgrounds and social characteristics.

human capital The pool of trained workers necessary for productivity in modern industrial and post-industrial economies.

human ecology An area of sociology that is concerned with the relationships of people and their activity to territory and the physical environment.

hunting and gathering economy A level of economic development in which people live on what they can collect, catch, or kill in their natural environment.

hypothesis A testable statement about reality, usually derived from a theory and developed for purposes of testing some part of that theory.

id In Freudian theory, that part of the human personality that is a product of natural drives such as hunger, aggression, and sexual desire.

ideal culture The norms and beliefs that people in a society accept in principle.

ideal type An abstract definition based on a set of characteristics.

ideational superstructure A Marxian term for ideology; so named because Marx considered ideology an outgrowth of the economic structure.

identification A process whereby an individual develops strong positive feelings toward a person acting as an agent of socialization.

ideological racism The belief that one racial or ethnic group is inherently superior or inferior to another.

ideology A system of beliefs about reality that often serves to justify a society's social arrangements.

illness The condition that occurs when an individual believes that he or she has a medical disorder.

imperialism A system in which a more-powerful country uses the resources of a less-powerful country to its own advantage, often by controlling that country's economic or political system.

incest taboo Societal rules that prohibit marriage or sexual relationships between people defined as being related to each other.

income The dollar value of that which a person or family receives during a specified time period, including wages and returns on investment.

independent variable A variable that is presumed by the researcher to be the cause of some other variable, called the dependent variable.

individual discrimination Behavior by an individual that treats others unequally on the basis of an ascribed status such as race or sex.

industrial economy A level of economic development in which machines are used to manufacture things of value.

infant mortality rate The number of deaths in a year of people under 1 year of age per 1,000 births.

informal structure The actual day-to-day norms, roles, statuses, and behaviors that exist within an organization, which differ from the official and formal structure of the organization.

ingroup A social group that a person belongs to or indentifies with.

institution A form of organization, with supporting sets of norms, that performs basic functions in a society, is strongly supported by that society's culture, and is generally accepted as an essential element of the society's social structure.

institutional discrimination Behaviors or arrangements in social institutions that intentionally or unintentionally favor one race, sex, or ethnic group — usually the majority group — over another.

institutional racism Institutional discrimination on the basis of race.

institutional sexism Systematic practices and patterns within social institutions that lead to inequality between men and women.

institutionalization A process whereby a condition or social arrangement becomes accepted as a normal and necessary part of a society.

instrumental leaders People who exercise leadership in a group by focusing attention on the task to be done and by suggesting effective ways of completing that task.

intergenerational mobility Attainment by people of a socioeconomic status higher or lower than that of their parents.

interlocking directorate The presence of some of the same people on boards of directors of different corporations.

iron law of oligarchy A principle stated by Robert Michels that argues that in any organization, power will become concentrated in the hands of the leaders, who may then use that power to protect their own interests.

kinship A pattern in which people are related by ancestry, marriage, or adoption but can live independently from one another.

labeling theory A theory holding that deviance is defined by societal reactions to certain behaviors, not by the behaviors themselves.

laity The general membership of a religion, who play a limited, and often passive, role in religious activities.

language A set of symbols though which the people in a society communicate with one another.

latent function A function of a social arrangement that is not evident and is often unintended.

laws Officially stated social norm that carry formal, specific, and publicized sanctions when violated, and which are enforced through formal agencies of social control.

legal-rational authority Authority that is tied to a position rather than to an individual, and which is based on principles of law or on an individual's proper appointment to a position.

legitimate power Power that others accept as proper.

life expectancy The number of years that the average person in a society can be expected to live, based on current patterns of mortality.

linguistic relativity A theory holding that language not only reflects, but also helps to shape, people's perceptions of reality.

looking-glass self A self-image based on an individual's understanding of messages from others about what kind of person that individual is.

macrosociology Those areas of sociology that are concerned with large-scale patterns operating at the level of the group of society.

majority group A group of people who are in an advantaged social position relative to other groups, often having the power discriminate against those other groups.

manifest function A function of a social arrangement that is evident and, often, intended.

marriage A socially approved arrangement between a male and a female that involves an economic and a sexual relationship.

mass A large number of people who are physically separated yet interact and are subject to common social influences.

mass hysteria A behavior in which people dispersed over a sizable geographic area perceive and respond to a threat, either real or imagined.

mass media Popular published and broadcast means of communication, including television, radio, newspapers, magazines, and motion pictures, that reach a substantial segment of the public.

master status A status that has a dominant influence in shaping a person's life and identity.

material culture Physical objects that are the product of a group of society.

matriarchy A form of society in which females possess power and the right of decision making.

matrilineal system A system in which wealth and kinship are passed on through females.

matrilocality A residency pattern in which married couples live with the wife's family.

mean The arithmetic average of a set of numbers or scores, dividing the sum of the scores by the number of scores.

means of production Those goods or services, including land in an agricultural society and capital in an industrial society, that a person must own to produce things of value.

median The middle score or number in a distribution of scores or numbers.

medically indigent The condition of lacking health insurance and not having sufficient resources to pay for one's own health care.

medicalization A trend whereby an increasing number of conditions and problems are defined as diseases and treated by the institution of medicine.

medicine An institution found in some form in all societies, whose purpose is to treat illness.

meritocracy A reward system based on ability and achievement rather than social background.

metropolitan statistical area (MSA) An area consisting of a central city or cluster of up to three central cities, the remainder of the county containing the central cities, and any adjacent counties that are urban in character and linked to those cities.

microsociology An area of sociology that is concerned with interaction of individual with larger societal influences.

migration Large-scale movement of people to different neighborhoods, areas, or countries.

military-industrial complex A grouping of powerful individuals and organizations who share a common interest in large military expenditures.

minority group A group of people who are in a disadvantaged position relative to one or more groups in their society, and who are often the victims of discrimination.

mixed economy An economic system in which the government provides extensive social services and performs some major economic functions while manufacturing and other industries are at least in part privately owned. Also called democratic socialism.

mob An extremely emotional acting crowd that directs its violence against a specific target.

mode The most frequently occurring number or score in a distribution of numbers or scores.

modeling A process whereby the behavior of a significant other is observed and imitated.

modernization The process of development of industrial societies from agricultural societies, and the accompanying social, economic, and cultural changes.

modernization theory A theory holding that developing countries will follow the same general pattern of development as industrial nations.

monarchy A form of authoritarian government with a hereditary ruler whose absolute power is based on traditional authority.

monogamy The marriage of one husband to one wife.

monopoly A condition in which there is only one producer of a given product, thereby eliminating competition.

monotheism A religion that teaches the existence of one God.

mores informal but serious social norms, violations of which result in strong sanctions.

mortality The number of deaths occurring in a society.

multinational corporation A large corporation that produces or sells its products, and usually owns property, in a large number of countries.

multiple-nuclei model A theory holding that population groups and land use in urban areas tend to concentrate in distinct and scattered clusters, often around a number of distinct centers of activity scattered around an urban area.

nation-state A legally recognized government that effectively rules a relatively large geographic area and provides services, including military protection, law enforcement, and the regulation of commerce.

national health insurance A governmentally mandated system of health insurance for the entire population, based on fee-for-service payment, that is funded through taxes or through a combination of taxes and employer-paid insurance.

national health service A system of health care operated by the government, in which doctors become salaried employees of the government or are paid a fixed amount per patient.

natural sciences Those sciences that are concerned with the natural or physical world, including chemistry, biology, physics, astronomy, geology, oceanography, and meterology.

negotiated order The character of an organization that is the product of fluid agreements arising from the ongoing interaction of its members.

neolocality A residency pattern in which married couples form a separate household and live in their own residence.

nomadic A society in which members move from place to place rather than living permanently in one place.

nonmaterial culture Abstract creations, such as knowledge or values, that are produced by a society.

norm of maximization A value in capitalist countries of trying to derive maximum benefits from scarce resources.

norms Socially defined rules and expectations concerning behavior.

nuclear family A family that is restricted to a parent or parents and their unmarried children.

occupational segregation A pattern whereby two groups—most often men and women—hold different kinds of jobs.

oligarchy A form of authoritarian government in which a small group rules with absolute power. Also sometimes refers to the tendency of large-scale organizations to be ruled by their leaders, even if they are formally democratic.

oligopoly A condition in which there are only a few producers of a given product, so that competition is limited or nonexistent.

open stratification system A system of inequality in which opportunities to move to a higher or lower status are relatively great.

operational definition A precise statement of the meaning of a variable or categories of a variable for the purpose of measurement.

organized skepticism A norm or principle specifying that scientists will be required to support their claims about reality through observed evidence.

outgroup A group that a person does not belong to or identify with.

overlapping cleavages Divisions or issues of conflict in society that divide people along generally similar lines on different issues.

overurbanization A situation, common among less-developed countries, in which the population of cities expands beyond what can be supported by the economy of these cities.

panic An acting crowd that is suddenly swept by fear and responds with spontaneous and often self-destructive behavior.

participant observation A form of field observation in which the researcher participates in some way in the behavior that is being studied.

patriarchy A form of society in which males possess power and the right of decision making.

patrilineal system A system in which wealth and kinship are passed on through males.

patrilocality A residency pattern in which married couples live with the husband's family.

peers People who share a similar age and social position.

personal cult A social movement primarily centered around a charismatic individual, which elevates that individual to a revered status.

personality need A psychological need for a particular attitude, belief, or behavior that arises from the particular personality type of an individual.

perspective A general approach to a subject, including a set of questions to be addressed, a theoretical framework, and, often, a set of values.

placebo A nonmedicated substance that can provide relief against an illness because patients believe that their condition is being treated.

play stage According to George Herbert Mead, a stage of *socialization* in which the child acquires language, recognizes the self as a separate entity, and learns norms from significant others.

pluralism A process whereby different racial, ethnic, or cultural groups in a society retain some of their own cultural characteristics while sharing others with the larger society.

pluralist model A theory holding that power is dispersed among a number of competing power centers, each representing a different interest group.

political parties Organizations, usually with different viewpoints or ideologies, that run slates of candidates for elective office.

political-process theory A theory arguing that social movements arise in response to opportunities created by political and social processes, such as modernization, democratization, and economic growth.

polyandry A form of marriage in which a woman has more than one husband.

polygamy Any form of marriage that involves more than two partners.

polygyny A form of marriage in which a man has more than one wife.

polytheism A religion that teaches the existence of two or more gods.

population projections Estimates of the future size and composition of populations, based on specific assumptions about future fertility, mortality, and migration.

postindustrial economy A modern economy dominated by services, technical knowledge, and information, rather than industry.

poverty The condition of having an extremely low income and standard of living, either in comparison with other members of society (relative poverty), or in terms of the ability to acquire basic necessities (absolute poverty).

power The ability of a person or group to get people to behave in particular ways.

power elite A relatively small group that holds a disproportionate share of power in a society or a political system.

precipitating incident An event, often dramatic, unexpected, or highly publicized, that acts as a trigger for collective behavior under conditions of structural conductiveness.

prejudice A categorical and unfounded attitude or belief concerning a group.

prestige The degree to which a person is respected and well regarded by others.

primary deviance Deviant behaviors that are short-term or cease with adult status.

primary group A small, close-knit group whose members interact because they value or enjoy one another as people.

primary sector That part of an economy consisting of the direct extraction of natural resources from the environment.

profane Aspects of everyday life, which are not usually associated with religion.

progressive tax A tax that requires those with higher incomes to pay a greater percentage of their income in taxes.

projection A process by which a person denies or minimizes personal shortcomings by exaggerating the extent to which these same shortcomings occur in others.

proletariat In a capitalist economy, the class who work for wages or salaries and who are employed by the owners of capital.

Protestant ethic A belief in hard work, frugality, and material success that Max Weber associated with the emergence of Protestantism in Europe.

protest crowd A crowd whose purpose is to achieve political goals, and whose dominant emotion is often anger or hostility.

protest movement A social movement whose objective is to oppose or change some existing social or political condition.

race A category of people who share some common physical characteristic and who are regarded by themselves and others as a distant status group.

racial caste system A closed stratification system in which castes are established on the basis of race.

racism Any attitude, belief, behavior, or institutional arrangement that has the intent or effect of favoring one race over another.

rationalization In Weberian sociology, the process by which tradition, faith, and personal relationships are set aside in the conduct of business, with decisions being made on the basis of what is expected to work best.

reactivity The tendency of people being studied by social scientists to react to the researcher or to the fact that they are being studied.

real culture The norms and principles that people in a society actually practice.

real wages Wage and salary levels expressed in terms of purchasing power to adjust for the effects of inflation.

rebellion A movement to change specific officeholders or policies forcibly without changing the structure of the government.

regressive movement A social movement whose objective is to change things back to the way they were in the past or to oppose the efforts of a protest movement.

relative-deprivation theory A theory holding that social movements emerge when people feel deprived or mistreated relative to others, or relative to what they feel they should be receiving.

reliability The ability of a measurement process to produce consistent results when the same variable is measured several times.

religion Formalized beliefs and practices that are directed toward the sacred elements in a culture.

religious movement A social movement relating to spiritual or supernatural issues, which opposes or offers alternatives to some aspect of the dominant religious or cultural order.

research The process of systematic observation used in all sciences.

resocialization A process occuring in *total institutions* designed to undo the effects of previous socialization and teach an individual new and different beliefs, attitudes, and behavior patterns.

resource-mobilization theory A theory arguing that social movements grow when they are able to obtain and use available resources successfully.

revolution A rapid fundamental change in the basic institutions, relationships, and ideologies within a society.

riot An outbreak of violent crowd behavior, aimed against people, property, or both, that is not focused on one specific target.

rites of passage Formal or informal rituals marking the passage from one age group or age role to another.

ritual A system of established rites and ceremonies that is often religious in nature.

role See **social role.**

role conflict Conflicting or opposing expectations attached to *roles.*

role model A significant other from whom a child learns to play a role.

role set A set of related roles attached to one social position or status.

role strain A condition in which one role contains conflicting expectations.

ruling class In Marxist terminology, the class that owns the means of production and therefore enjoys a dominant economic and political position in society.

rumor An unconfirmed item of information spread by word of mouth and sometimes by unconfirmed media reports.

sacred That which inspires awe, reverence, fear, or deep respect in people.

sacred philosophy A form of religion that does not revolve around a deity but does have a concept of the sacred from which moral and philosophical principles and behavioral norms are derived.

sample A subset of some larger population that is studied for the purposes of drawing conclusions about that larger population.

sanctions A form of direct social control that uses rewards and punishments to encourage conformity to social norms.

scapegoat A person or group against whom an individual displaces feelings of anger or frustration that cannot be expressed toward the true source of the individual's feelings.

scarce resources Material goods, statuses, and other things that people want, but that do not exist in sufficient quantities to satisfy everybody's needs or desires.

science An approach to understanding the world based on systematic observation and generalization, which is used to generate theories to explain what is observed and to predict future results under similar conditions.

secondary deviance Chronic deviant behavior by people who come to identify themselves as deviants.

secondary group A social group, large or small, that exists for some purpose beyond the relationships among the group's members.

secondary sector That part of an economy consisting of the making or manufacturing of tangible physical products.

sect A religious group, often created through a schism with an established church, that is not well integrated into the larger society.

sectoral model A theory holding that urban population groups and land use are arranged in pie-shaped segments extending outward in different directions from the center of the city.

secularization A process in which the influence of religion in a society declines.

self A distinct identity attached to a person; an awareness of that person's existence as a separate entity.

self-esteem One's positive or negative judgment of oneself.

self-fulfilling prophecy A process in which people's belief that a certain event will occur leads people to behave in such a way that they cause the expected event to happen.

self-image The totality of the type of person that one perceives oneself to be.

serial monogamy A system in which people engage in a series of monogamous relationships; it usually occurs as a result of divorce and remarriage.

sex The physical or biological characteristic of being male or female. See also **gender.**

sexism Structured inequality between men and women, and the norms and beliefs that support such inequality.

sex roles Social roles that people are expected to play because they are male or female, which often carry unequal status, rewards, and opportunities. Also called **gender roles.**

sex-role socialization The process by which sex roles are taught and learned.

sickness A condition in which a person is recognized by others as having a medical problem or disorder.

sick role A social role played by people who are recognized by others as having a *sickness,* which exempts them from normal role obligations.

significant others Specific individuals with whom a person interacts and who are important in that person's life.

social change The alteration of behavior patterns, social relationships, institutions, and social structure over time.

social channeling A process whereby socialization prepares an individual for a particular role in life.

social class See **class.**

social construction of reality A process in which people's experience of reality is largely determined by the meanings they attach to that reality.

social evolution A gradual process of social change whereby a society develops, increases in complexity, and offers its members a better quality of life.

social group A set of two or more people who interact regularly, share some common purpose, and have some structure of roles and statuses.

social learning A process by which attitudes, beliefs, and behaviors are learned from significant others in a person's social environment or subculture.

social movement A large number of people acting together on behalf of a shared objective or idea.

social psychology An important subspecialty of both sociology and psychology that is concerned with the interaction of the individual with larger societal forces.

social role A set of behavioral expectations that are attached to a social position or status.

social segregation The tendency for people with similar social characteristics to live together in the same neighborhoods.

social sciences Those sciences that are concerned with the study of human behavior, including sociology, anthropology, psychology, economics, political science, and, by some definitions, history.

social structure The organization of society, including institutions, social positions, the relationships among social positions, the groups that make up the society, and the distribution of scarce resources within the society.

socialist economy An economic system, normally found in industrialized countries, in which the means of production are publicly owned.

socialization The process by which new members of a society are taught to participate in that society, learn their roles, and develop a self-image.

society A relatively self-contained and organized group of people who interact under some shared political authority within some reasonably well-defined geographic area.

sociocultural evolution The process whereby hunting and gathering societies develop into more technologically advanced societies.

socioeconomic mobility The movement of people to higher or lower positions within the stratification system.

socioeconomic status (SES) A person's overall position within the stratification system, reflecting such things as income, wealth, educational level, and occupational prestige.

sociological imagination A series of insights or perspectives toward society that is achieved through the study of sociology.

sociology The systematic study of society, human social behavior, and social groups.

sociopath A personality type characterized by a poorly developed right and wrong and the absence of guilt for harm caused to others.

solidarity A sence of oneness or common interest that encourages cooperation among members of a society.

status Any position within a social system. The term *status* is also sometimes used to refer to *prestige*.

status quo The existing set of arrangements within a society.

stereotype An exaggerated belief concerning a group of people that assumes that nearly everyone in the group possesses a certain characteristic.

stratification A pattern whereby scarce resources, such as wealth, income, power, and prestige, are distributed unequally among the members of a society.

street crime Illegal acts directed against people or property, including murder, robbery, and rape.

structural conductiveness A condition in which the social situation is favorable for the emergence of a particular behavior, such as collective behavior or a social movement.

structural mobility A type of socioeconomic mobility that occurs because of an increasing proportion of jobs in the higher-status, white-collar categories.

subculture A set of knowledge, beliefs, attitudes, symbols, and norms held by a group sharing some common experience or situation within a larger society.

subjective class The class to which people perceive that they belong.

subsistence level A level of economic production that meets a population's minimum needs but produces no surplus.

Sun Belt A term referring to the combined South and West regions of the United States, which have experienced rapid population growth and economic development in recent decades.

superego In Freudian psychology, that part of the personality that internalizes the norms and expectations of society and of significant others.

surplus Whatever an economy produces in excess of the minimum needed to keep everyone alive.

survey research Any research in which a population is asked a set of questions by a researcher, who then analyzes the responses.

symbol Anything including words, signs, and gestures, that is used to represent something else.

symbolic-interactionist perspective A major microsociological perspective stressing the importance of messages from others and from society, how people understand and interpret these messages, and how this process affects people's behaviors.

symbolic racism A modern type of racial prejudice that does not express overtly prejudiced attitudes but does blame minority groups for any disadvantages that they experience.

technology The application of scientific knowledge to a practical task.

terrorism The use of violence, usually against civilian targets, as a means of intimidation or social control.

tertiary sector That part of an economy consisting of producing and processing information and providing services.

theory A set of interrelated statements about reality, usually involving one or more cause-and-effect relationships.

third-party payment A system of health-care payment in which providers of health care are paid by someone other than the patient, usually government or an insurance company.

Thomas theorem A sociological principle that states that situations defined by people as real, are real in their consequences.

total fertility rate The average number of children that a woman can be expected to have over her entire lifetime, based on current patterns of fertility.

total institution An organization or group that has complete control over an individual and that usually engages in a process of resocialization.

totalitarian government An extreme form of authoritarian government that takes total control over all aspects of life.

tracking An educational practice in which students are grouped according to their teachers' judgments of their ability.

traditional authority Authority based on long-standing custom, often reinforced a sacred element.

triad A social group that consists of three people.

underclass Poor people who are chronically unemployed or underemployed and who lack the necessary skills to obtain stable, quality employment.

uneven development The tendency of some cities or neighborhoods to grow and prosper while others stagnate or decline.

unobtrusive observation A type of field observation in which the researcher does not interact with the people being studied, participate in the behavior being studied, or reveal his or her identity as a researcher.

urbanization The process whereby an increasing share of a population lives in cities.

urban legend An unsubstantiated story containing a plot, which is widely circulated and believed.

validity The ability of measurement process to measure correctly that which it is intended to measure.

values Personal preferences, likes and dislikes, or judgments about what is good and desirable or bad and undesirable.

variable Any concept that can take on different values or be classified into different categories.

veto groups Interest groups that possess the power to block policy changes or proposed laws that threaten their interests.

victimless crime Illegal acts in which the only victims are the offenders.

war Armed conflict among different nations.

wealth The total value of everything that a person or family owns, less any debts.

white-collar crime Illegal acts committed by members of high-status groups.

world-system theory A form of dependency theory that divides all countries into core, peripheral, and semiperipheral nations, in which the more-developed nations keep the less-developed ones in a weak and dependent position.

REFERENCES

ABC News. 1987. *World News Tonight.* September 27.

Aberle, D. F., et. al. 1950. "The Functional Prerequisites of a Society." *Ethics* 60: 100–101.

Abrahamson, Mark, and Lee Sigelman. 1987. "Occupational Sex Segregation in Metropolitan Areas." *American Sociological Review* 52: 588–597.

Abu-Lughod, Janet. 1987. "The Shape of the World-System in the Thirteenth Century." *Studies in Comparative International Development* 22, 4: 3–25.

Abu-Lughod, Janet. 1989. *Before European Hegemony: The World System A.D. 1250–1350.* New York: Oxford University Press.

Acuna, Rodolpho. 1972. *Occupied America: The Chicano's Struggle for Liberation.* San Francisco: Canfield Press.

Aday, Lu Ann. 1976. "The Impact of Health Policy on Access to Medical Care." *Milbank Memorial Fund Quarterly* 54: 215–233.

Adorno, Theodor W., Else Frenkel-Brunwick, D. J. Levinson, and R. N. Sanford. 1950. *The Authoritarian Personality.* New York: Harper and Row.

Aguirre, B. E., E. L. Quarantelli, and Jorge L. Mendoza. 1988. "The Collective Behavior of Fads: The Characteristics, Effects, and Career of Streaking." *American Sociological Review* 53: 569–584.

Ahmad, S. 1977. "Population Myths and Realities." *Race and Class* 19, 1: 19–29.

Aiken, Michael. 1970. "Distribution of Community Power: Structural Bases and Social Consequences." Pp. 487–525 in Michael Aiken and Paul E. Mott (eds.), *The Structure of Community Power.* New York: Random House.

Aldrich, Mark, and Robert Buchele. 1986. *The Economics of Comparable Worth.* Cambridge, MA: Ballinger.

Alexander, Jeffrey C. 1988. "The New Theoretical Movement." Pp. 77–101 in Neil J. Smelser (eds.), *Handbook of Sociology.* Newbury Park, CA: Sage.

Alexander, Jeffrey C. 1985. *Neofunctionlism.* Beverly Hills, CA: Sage.

Alexander, Karl, Doris R. Entwisle, and Maxine S. Thompson. 1987. "School Performance, Status Relations, and the Structure of Sentiment: Bringing the Teachers Back In." *American Sociological Review* 52: 665–682.

Alexander, Karl L., Martha Cook, and Edward L. McDill. 1978. "Curriculum Tracking an Educational Stratification: Some Further Evidence." *American Sociological Review* 43: 47–66.

Alexander, Karl L., and Aaron M. Pallas. 1987. "School Sector and Cognitive Performance: When is a Little a Little?" Pp. 89–112 in Edward H. Haertel, Thomas James, and Henry M. Levin (eds.), *Comparing Public and Private Schools,* Volume 2: School Achievement. New York: Falmer.

Alexander, Yonah. 1987. "Some Perspectives on Terrorism and the Soviet Union." Pp. 350–357 in Walter Laqueur and Yonah Alexander (eds.), *The Terrorism Reader,* rev. ed. New York: NAL Penguin.

Alexis, M., and Nancy Di Tomaso. 1983. "Transportation, Race, and Employment: In Search of the Elusive Triad." *Journal of Urban Affairs* 5: 81–94.

Alford, Robert R. 1969. *Bureaucracy and Participation: Political Culture in Four Wisconsin Cities.* Chicago: Rand McNally.

Allport, Floyd H. 1924. *Social Psychology.* Boston: Houghton-Mifflin.

Allport, Gordon W. 1954. *The Nature of Prejudice.* New York: Addison-Wesley.

Almond, Gabriel A., and James S. Coleman (eds.). 1960. *The Politics of Developing Areas.* Princeton, NJ: Princeton University Press.

Altman, Dennis. 1982. *The Homosexualization of America; The Americanization of the Homosexual.* New York: St. Martin's Press.

Alwin, Duane F., and Arland Thornton. 1984. "Family Origins and the Schooling Process: Early Versus Late Influence of Parental Characteristics." *American Sociological Review* 52: 548–557.

American Sociological Association. 1977. *Careers in Sociology.* Washington, DC: American Sociological Association.

Ames, Van Meter. 1973. "No Separate Self." Pp. 43–58 in Walter Robert Corti (ed.), *The Philosophy of George Herbert Mead.* Winterthur, Switzerland: Amriswiler Bucherei.

Anderson, Elijah. 1989. "Sex Codes and Family Life Among Poor Inner-City Youths." *The Annals of the American Academy of Political and Social Science* 501: 59–78.

Anderson, Perry. 1974. *Passages from Antiquity to Feudalism.* London: New Left Books.

Anderson, Robert, John Farley, and Janet McReynolds. 1986. "Southern Illinois University at Edwardsville." Pp. 35–43 in American Association of State Colleges and Universities (ed.), *Defining and Assessing Baccalaureate Skills: Ten Case Studies.* Washington: American Association of State Colleges and Universities.

Anderson, Ronald, and Odin W. Anderson. 1979. "Trends in the Use of Health Services." Pp. 371–391 in Howard E. Freeman, Sol Levine, and Leo G. Reeder (eds.), *Handbook of Medical Sociology,* 3rd ed. Englewood Cliffs, NJ: Prentice Hall.

Anderson, Theodore R., and Lee L. Bean. 1961. "The Shevky-Bell Social Areas: Confirmation of Results and a Reinterpretation." *Social Forces* 40: 119–124.

Apple, Michael. 1982. *Education and Power: Reproduction and Contradiction in Education.* London: Routledge and Kegan Paul.

Appelbaum, Richard P. 1970. *Theories of Social Change.* Chicago: Markham.

Apthorpe, Raymond. 1985. "Modernization." Pp. 532–533 in Adam and Jessica Kuper (eds.), *Social Science Encyclopaedia.* London: RKP.

Arendt, Hannah. 1951. *The Origins of Totalitarianism.* New York: Harcourt, Brace.

Aries, Philippe. 1981. *The Hour of Our Death.* New York: Knopf.

Aries, Philippe. 1962. *Centuries of Childhood: A Social History of Family Life.* New York: Alfred A. Knopf.

Arluke, Arnold, and Jack Levin. 1985. " 'Second Childhood': Old Age in Popular Culture." Pp. 151–158 in Beth B. Hess and Elizabeth W. Markson (eds.), *Growing Old in America: New Perspectives on Old Age.* New Brunswick, NJ: Transaction Books.

Armor, David J. and Donna Schwartzbach. 1978. "White Flight, Demographic Transition, and the Future of School Desegregation." *The Rand Paper Series* No. P-5931. Presented at annual meeting of the American Sociological Association, San Francisco.

Asch, Solomon E. 1965. "Effects of Group Pressure upon the Modification and Distortion of Judgements." Pp. 393–401 in Harold Proshansky and B. Seidenerg (eds.), *Basic Studies in Social Psychology.* New York: Holt, Rinehart, and Winston.

Asch, Solomon E. 1956. "Studies of Independence and Conformity: A Minority of One Against a Unanimous Majority." *Psychological Monographs* 70, 9 (whole No. 416).

Astin, Alexander W. 1977. *Four Critical Years.* San Francisco: Josssey-Bass.

Babbie, Earl. 1989. *The Practice of Social Research,* 5th ed. Belmont, CA: Wadsworth.

Backman, Carl W., and Paul F. Secord. 1968. "The Self and Role Selection." In Chad Gordon and Kenneth J. Gergen (eds.), *The Self in Social Interaction.* New York: Wiley.

Bain, David. 1982. *The Productivity Prescription: The Manager's Guide to Improving Productivity and Profits.* New York: McGraw-Hill.

Bain, Trevor, and David Fottler. 1980. "Male-Female Professionals: A Model of Career Choice." *Industrial Relations* 19, 3: 366–370.

Bairoch, Paul. 1986. "Historical Roots of Economic Underdevelopment: Myths and Realities." Pp. 191–216 in Wolfgang Mommsen and Jürgen Osterhammel (eds.), *Imperialism After Empire: Continuities and Discontinuities.* London: Allen and Unwin.

Balakrishnan, T. R., R. V. Rao, Evelyne Lapierre-Adamcyk, and Karol J. Krotki. 1987. "A Hazard Model of the Covariates of Marital Dissolution in Canada." *Demography* 24: 395–406.

Ballentine, Jeanne. 1983. *The Sociology of Education: A Systematic Analysis.* Englewood Cliffs, NJ: Prentice Hall.

Baker, M. A. 1980. *Women Today: A Multidisciplinary Approach to Women's Studies.* Monterey, CA: Brooks, Cole.

Baldassare, Mark. 1981. "The Effects of Household Density on Subgroups." *American Sociological Review* 46: 110–118.

Baldassare, Mark. 1979. *Residential Crowding in Urban America.* Berkeley: University of California Press.

Bales, Robert F. 1953. "The Equilibrium Problem in Small Groups." Pp. 111–162 in Talcott Parsons et al. (eds.), *Working Papers in the Theory of Action.* Glencoe, IL: Free Press.

Bales, Robert F., and P. E. Slater. 1955. "Role Differentiation in Small Decision-making Groups." Pp. 259–306 in Talcott Parsons, Robert Bales, et al., *Family, Socialization, and Interaction Process.* Glencoe, IL: Free Press.

Balswick, Jack O., and Charles W. Peek. 1971. "The Inexpressive Male: A Tragedy of American Society." *The Family Coordinator* 20: 363–368.

Bandura, Albert. 1977. *Social Learning Theory.* Englewood Cliffs, NJ: Prentice Hall.

Bane, Mary Jo. 1976. *Here to Stay: American Families in the Twentieth Century.* New York: Basic Books.

Bane, Mary Jo, and David T. Ellwood. 1983a. "The Dynamics of Dependency: Routes to Self-Sufficiency." Unpublished paper supported by U.S. Department of Health and Human Services Grant, contract no. HHS-100-82-0038.

Bane, Mary Jo, and David T. Ellwood. 1983b. "Slipping Into and Out of Poverty: The Dynamics of Spells." Working Paper No. 1199, National Bureau of Economic Research, Cambridge, MA.

Banfield, Edward C. 1968. *The Unheavenly City.* Boston: Little, Brown.

Banfield, Edward C. 1962. *Political Influence.* New York: Free Press.

Banfield, Edward C., and James Q. Wilson. 1963. *City Politics.* Cambridge, MA: Harvard University and M.I.T. Press.

Banta, David, and Stephen B. Thacker. 1979. *Costs and Benefits of Electronic Fetal Monitoring: A Review of the Literature.* DHEW Publication No. (PHS) 79-3245. Washington DC: National Center for Health Services Research.

Baratz, Steven S., and Joan C. Baratz. 1970. "Early Childhood Education: The Social Science Base of Institutional Racism." *Harvard Educational Review* 40: 29–50.

Barber, Bernard. 1971. "Function, Variability, and Change in Ideological Systems." Pp. 244–265 in Bernard Barber and Alex Inkeles (eds.), *Stability and Social Change.* Boston: Little Brown.

Barkan, Steven E. 1986. "Interorganizational Conflict in the Southern Civil Rights Movement." *Sociological Inquiry* 56: 190–209.

Barlow, Hugh D. 1987. *Introduction to Criminology,* 4th ed. Boston: Little, Brown.

Barlow, Robin, Harvey E. Barzer, and James M. Morgan. 1966. *Economic Behavior of the Affluent.* Washington DC: Brookings Institution.

Bart, Pauline. 1973. "Portnoy's Mother's Complaint." Pp. 222–228 in Helena Z. Lopata (ed.), *Marriages and Families.* New York: D. Van Nostrand.

Bart, Pauline, and Linda Frankel. 1986. *The Student Sociologist's Handbook,* 4th ed. New York: Random House.

Barth, Gunther. 1964. *Bitter Strength: A History of the Chinese in the United States.* Cambridge, MA: Harvard University Press.

Barrett, Nancy. 1979. "Women in the Job Market: Occupations, Earnings, and Career Opportunities." In Ralph Smith (ed.), *The Subtle Revolution.* Washington DC: Urban Institute.

Bass, Bernard. 1960. *Leadership, Psychology, and Organizational Behavior.* New York: Harper & Row.

Bastian, Ann, Norm Fruchter, Marilyn Gittell, Colin Greer, and Kenneth Haskins. 1985. *Choosing Equality: The Case for Democratic Schooling.* Philadelphia: Temple University Press.

Bastide, Roger. 1965. "The Development of Race Relations in Brazil." Pp. 9–29 in Guy Hunter (ed.), *Industrialisation and Race Relations.* London: Oxford University Press.

Bauer, Raymond A. 1957. "Brainwashing: Psychology or Demonology?" *Journal of Social Issues* 13, 3: 41–47.

Beach, Stephen W. 1977. "Religion and Political Change in Northern Ireland." *Sociological Analysis,* 38: 1, 37–48.

Beck, Paul Allen. 1986. "Choice, Context, and Consequence: Beaten and Unbeaten Paths Toward a Science of Electoral Behavior." Pp. 241–283 in Herbert F. Weisberg (ed.), *Political Science: The Science of Politics.* New York: Agathon.

Beck, Robert E. 1981. "Career Patterns: The Liberal Arts Major in Bell System Management." Paper presented at conference on "Quality in Liberal Learning—and How to Improve It," sponsored by Association of American Colleges. Reprinted by Association of American Colleges.

Becker, Gary. 1981. *A Treatise on the Family.* Cambridge, MA: Harvard University Press.

Becker, Gary S. 1971. *The Economics of Discrimination,* rev. ed. Chicago: University of Chicago Press. (Originally published in 1957.)

Becker, Gary S. 1964. *Human Capital.* New York: Columbia University Press.

Becker, Howard. 1932. *Systematic Sociology.* New York: Wiley.

Becker, Howard. P. 1950. *True Values to Social Interpretation: Essays on Social Context, Actions and Prospects.* Durham, North Carolina: Duke University Press.

Becker, Howard S. 1973. *Outsiders.* New York: The Free Press.

Becker, Howard S. 1963. *Outsiders: Studies in the Sociology of Deviance.* New York: Free Press.

Becker, Howard S., et. al. 1961. *Boys in White.* Chicago: University of Chicago Press.

Bedau, Hugo Adam, and Chester M. Pierce (eds). 1976. *Capital Punishment in the United States.* New York: AMS Press.

Beer, Francis A. 1981. *Peace against War: The Ecology of International Violence.* San Francisco: W. H. Freeman.

Beez, W. V. 1968. "Influence of Biased Psychological Reports on Teacher Behavior and Pupil Performance." *Proceedings of the 76th Annual Convention of th American Psychological Association* 3: 605–606.

Beigel, H. G. 1951. "Romantic Love." *American Sociological Review* 16: 326–334.

Bell, Daniel. 1976. *The Cultural Contradiction of Capitalism.* New York: Basic Books.

Bell, Daniel. 1973. *The Coming of Post-Industrial Society: A Venture into Social Forecasting.* New York: Basic Books.

Bell, Wendell. 1968. "The City, The Suburb, and a Theory of Social Choice." Pp. 137–143 in Scott Greer et al., (eds.), *The New Urbanization.* New York: St. Martin's Press.

Bellah, Robert. 1970. *Beyond Belief.* New York: Harper & Row.

Bellah, Robert N. 1964. "Religious Evolution." *American Sociological Review,* 29 (3), June, 358–374.

Bellah, Robert N. 1988. *Britannica Book of the Year.* Chicago: Encyclopaedia Britannica Inc.

Benbow, Camilla, and Julian Stanley. 1980. "Sex Differences in Mathematical Ability: Fact or Artifact?" *Science* 210: 1262–1264.

Bendix, Reihard. 1967. "Tradition and Modernity Reconsidered." *Comparative Studies in Society and History* 9, 3: 292–346.

Bennett, Neil G., Ann Klimas Blanc, and David E. Bloom. 1988. "Commitment and the Modern Union: Assessing the Link Between Premarital Cohabitation and Subsequent Marital Stability." *American Sociological Review* 53: 127–138.

Bensman, Joseph, and Arthur J. Vidich. 1984. *American Society, the Welfare State and Beyond,* rev. ed. South Hadley, MA: Bergin and Garvey.

Bensman, Joseph, and Arthur J. Vidich. 1987. *American Society: The Welfare State & Beyond, Revisited.* South Hadley, Massachusetts: Bergin and Garve.

Berger, Bennett. 1960. *Working-Class Suburb.* Berkeley: University of California Press.

Berger, Peter. 1986. *The Capitalist Revolution.* New York: Basic Books.

Berger, Peter. 1963. *Invitation to Sociology: A Humanistic Perspective.* New York: Doubleday Anchor.

Berger, Peter, and Thomas Luckmann. 1966. *The Social Construction of Reality: A Treatise in the Sociology of Knowledge.* Garden City, NY: Doubleday.

Bergesen, Albert. 1983. "Modeling Long Waves of Crisis in the World-System." Pp. 73–92 in *Crises in the World-System.* A. Bergesen, (ed.). Volume 6, Political Economy of the World-System Annuals. Beverly Hills, CA: Sage.

Berk, Richard A. 1974. *Collective Behavior.* Dubuque, IA: William C. Brown.

Bernard, J. L., S. L. Bernard, and M. L. Bernard. 1985. "Courtship Violence and Sex-Typing." *Family Relations* 34: 573–576.

Bernard, Jesse. 1981. *The Female World.* New York: Free Press.

Berndt, Harry. 1979. "Displacement and Relocation Practices in Five Midwestern Cities." Paper presented at annual meeting of the Society for the Study of Social Problems.

Bernstein, Paul. 1976. *Workplace Democratization: Its Internal Dynamics.* Kent, OH: Kent State University Press.

Berscheid, E., K. Dion, E. Walster, and G. W. Walster. 1971. "Physical Attractiveness and Dating Choice: A Test of the Matching Hypothesis." *Journal of Experimental Social Psychology* 7: 173–189.

Berreman, Gerald. 1975. "Himalayan Polyandry and the Domestic Cycle." *American Ethnologist* 2: 127–138.

Berrueta-Clement, J. R., C. J. Schweinhart, W. S. Barnett, A. S. Epstein, and D. P. Weikart. 1984. "Changed Lives: The Effects of the Perry Preschool Program on Youths Through Age 19." *Monographs of the High/Scope Educational Research Foundation 8.*

Berry, Brian J. L., and Philip H. Rees. 1969. "The Factorial Ecology of Calcutta." *American Journal of Sociology* 74: 445–491.

Best, Raphaela. 1983. *We've All Got Scars: What Boys and Girls Learn in Elementary School.* Bloomington: Indiana University Press.

Bettelheim, Bruno. 1959. "Feral Children and Autistic Children." *American Journal of Sociology* 54: 455–467.

Bettman, Otto L. 1974. *The Good Old Days—They Were Terrible.* New York: Random House.

Beuf, A. 1974. "Doctor, Lawyer, Household Drudge." *Journal of Communication* 24, 2: 142–145.

Bianchi, Suzanne. 1981. *Household Composition and Racial Inequality.* New Brunswick, NJ: Rutgers University Press.

Bianchi, Suzanne M., and Daphne Spain. 1986. *American Women in Transition.* Report for the National Committee for Research on the 1980 Census. New York: Russell Sage Foundation.

Bidwell, Charles E., and Noah E. Friedkin. 1988. "The Sociology of Education." Pp. 449–471 in Neil J. Smelser (ed.), *Handbook of Sociology.* Newbury Park, CA: Sage.

Bielby, Denise D., and William T. Bielby. 1988. "She Works Hard for the Money: Household Responsibilities and the Allocation of Work Effort." *American Journal of Sociology* 93: 1031–1059.

Bielby, William T., and James N. Baron. 1986. "Men and Women at Work: Sex Segregation and Statistical Discrimination." *American Journal of Sociology* 91: 759–799.

Biggar, Jeanne C. 1979. "The Sunning of America: Migration to the Sunbelt." *Population Bulletin* 34, 1.

Binstock, Jeanne. 1970 "Survival in the American College Industry." Unpublished Ph. D. dissertation, Brandeis University.

Blalock, Hubert M. 1967. *Toward a Theory of Minority Group Relations.* New York: Wiley.

Blascovich, Jim, Gerald P. Ginsberg, and René C. Howe. 1975. "Blackjack and the Risky Shift, II: Monetary Stakes." *Journal of Experimental Social Psychology* 11: 224–232.

Blasi, Augusto. 1980. "Bridging Moral Cognition and Moral Action: A Critical Review of the Literature." *Psychological Bulletin* 88: 1–45.

Blau, Francine D., and Marianne A. Ferber. 1986. *The Economics of Women, Men, and Work.* Englewood Cliffs, NJ: Prentice Hall.

Blau, Peter M. 1964. *Exchange and Power in Social Life.* New York: Wiley.

Blau, Peter M., and Otis Dudley Duncan. 1967. *The American Occupational Structure.* New York: Wiley.

Blau, Peter M., and Marshall W. Meyer. 1971. *Bureaucracy in Modern Society,* 2nd ed. New York: Random House.

Blau, Zena Smith. 1961. "Structural Constraints of Friendship and Old Age." *American Sociological Review* 36: 429–439.

Blauner, Robert. 1972. *Racial Oppression in America.* New York: Harper & Row.

Blauner, Robert. 1966. "Death and Social Structure." *Psychiatry* 29: 378–394.

Blendon, Robert J., Linda H. Aiken, Howard E. Freeman, Bradford L. Kirkman-Liff, and John W. Murphy. 1986. "Uncompensated Care by Hospitals or Public Insurance for the Poor?" *New England Journal of Medicine* 314: 1160–1163.

Block, Herbert A. and Gilbert Geis. 1970. *Man Crime and Society,* 2nd ed. New York: Random House.

Bloom, D. E. 1986. "Women and Work." *American Demographics* 8, 25–30.

Blot, William, L. A. Brinton, J. F. Fraumeni, and B. J. Stone. 1977. "Cancer Mortality in U.S. Counties with Petroleum Industries." *Science* 198: 51–53.

Blumberg, Paul. 1973. *Industrial Democracy: The Sociology of Participation.* New York: Schocken.

Blume, Marshall E. 1974. "Stock Ownership in the United States: Characteristics and Trends." *Survey of Current Business* (U.S. Department of Commerce) 54: 16–40.

Blumer, Herbert. 1966. "Sociological Implications of the Thought of George Herbert Mead." *American Journal of Sociology* 71: 535–544.

Blumer, Herbert G. 1974. "Social Movements." In R. Serge Denisoff (ed.), *The Sociology of Dissent.* New York: Harcourt, Brace, Jovanovich.

Blumer, Herbert G. 1969a. *Symbolic Interactionism: Perspective and Method.* Englewood Cliffs, NJ: Prentice Hall.

Blumer, Herbert G. 1969b. "Collective Behavior." Pp. 65–121 in Alfred McClung Lee (ed.), *Principles of Sociology,* 3rd ed. New York: Barnes and Noble.

Blumer, Herbert G. 1965. "Industrialisation and Race Relations." Pp. 220–553 in Guy Hunter (ed.), *Industrialisation and Race Relations: A Symposium.* London: Oxford University Press.

Blumer, Herbert G. 1955. "Social Movements." Pp. 99–220 in Alfred McClung Lee (ed.), *Principles of Sociology.* New York: Barnes and Noble.

Blumer, Herbert G. 1946. "Collective Behavior." Pp. 167–219 in Alfred McClung Lee (ed.), *A New Outline of the Principles of Sociology.* New York: Barnes and Noble.

Blumstein, Alfred, Jacqueline Cohen, and Daniel Nagin (eds.). 1978. *Deterrence and Incapacitation.* Washington, DC: National Academy of Sciences.

Blumstein, Alfred, Jacqueline Cohen, and Daniel Nagin (eds.). 1962. "Society as Symbolic Interaction." In Arnold M. Rose (ed.), *Human Behavior and Social Process.* Boston: Houghton Mifflin.

Blumstein, Philip, and Pepper Schwartz. 1983. *American Couples.* New York: William Morrow.

Boal, F. W. 1976. "Ethnic Residential Segregation." Pp. 41–79 in D. T. Herbert and R. J. Johnson (eds.), *Social Areas in Cities, Vol. 1: Spatial Processes and Form.* London: John Wiley.

Bobbio, Norberto. 1987. *The Future of Democracy: A Defence of the Rules of the Game.* Roger Griffin (tr.). Minneapolis: University of Minnesota Press. [Originally published in Italian in 1984.]

Boffey, Philip M. 1987. "Physicists Express Star Wars Doubt; Long Delay Seen." *New York Times,* April 23, pp. 1, 6.

Bogdanor, Vernon. 1987. *The Blackwell Encyclopedia of Political Institutions.* New York: Basil Blackwell.

Bolce, Louis Henri, III, and Susan Gray. 1979. "Blacks, Whites, and Race Policies." *The Public Interest* 54: 61–75.

Bolton, Charles D. 1972. "Alienation and Action: A Study of Peace Group Members." *American Journal of Sociology* 78: 537–561.

Boocock, Sarene Spence. 1978. "The Social Organization of the Classroom." Pp. 1–28 in Ralph H. Turner, James Coleman, and Renee C. Fox (eds.), *Annual Review of Sociology, 1978.* Palo Alto, CA: Annual Revieews.

Booth, Alan. 1976. *Urban Crowding and its Consequences.* New York: Praeger.

Booth, Alan, David R. Johnson, and John N. Edwards. 1980. "In Pursuit of Pathology: The Effects of Human Crowding." *American Sociological Review* 45: 873–878.

Bonacich, Edna. 1976. "Advanced Capitalism and Black/White Relations in the United States: A Split Labor Market Interpretation." *American Sociological Review* 41: 34–51.

Bonacich, Edna. 1975. "Abolition, the Extension of Slavery, and the Position of Free Blacks: A Study of Split Labor Markets in the United States, 1830–1863." *American Journal of Sociology* 81: 601–628.

Bonacich, Edna. 1972. "A Theory of Ethnic Antagonism: The Split Labor Market." *American Sociological Review* 37: 547–559.

Bornschier, Volker, and Christopher Chase-Dunn. 1985. *Transnational Corporations and Underdevelopment.* New York: Praeger.

Boskin, Joseph. 1965. "Race Relations in Seventeenth-Century America: The Problem of the Origin of Negro Slavery." *Sociology and Social Research* 49: 446–455.

Boswell, Terry. 1989. "Colonial Empires and the Capitalist World-System: A Time Series Analysis of Colonization, 1640–1960." *American Sociological Review* 54, 2: 180–196.

Bourdieu, Pierre. 1966. "L'Ecole Conservatrice: Les Inegalities Devant L'ecole et Devant la Culture." *Revue Francaise de Sociologie* 7: 325–347.

Bourdieu, Pierre, and Jean Claude Passeron. 1977. *Reproduction in Education, Society, and Culture.* Beverly Hills, CA: Sage Publications. [Originally published in French in 1970.]

Bourne, Larry S., and James W. Simmons (eds.). 1978. *Systems of Cities.* New York: Oxford University Press.

Bouvier, Leon F. 1980. "America's Baby Boom Generation: The Fateful Bulge." *Population Bulletin* 35, 1.

Bouvier, Leon F., and Robert W. Gardner. 1986. "Immigration to the United States: The Unfinished Story." *Population Bulletin* 41, 4.

Bowen, Howard R. 1977. *Investment in Learning: The Individual and Social Value of American Higher Education.* San Francisco: Jossey-Bass.

Bowers, William J. and Glenn L. Pierce. 1975. "The Illusion of Deterrence in Issac Ehrlich's Research on Capital Punishment." *The Yale Law Journal* (85): 187–207.

Bowles, Samuel, and Herbert Gintis. 1976. *Schooling in Capitalist America.* New York: Basic Books.

Bowles, Samuel, David M. Gordon, and Thomas E. Weisskopf. 1983. *Beyond the Waste Land: A Democratic Alternative to Economic Decline.* Garden City, NY: Anchor-Doubleday.

Boyer, Ernest L. 1987. *College — The Undergraduate Experience in America.* New York: Harper & Row.

Bradbury, Katherine L., Anthony Downs, and Kenneth A. Small. 1982. *Urban Decline and the Future of American Cities.* Washington: Brookings Institution.

Braithwaite, John. 1979. *Inequality, Crime, and Public Policy.* London: Routlege and Kigan Paul.

Breault, K. D. 1988. "Beyond the Quick and Dirty: Problems Associated with Analyses Based on Small Samples of Large Aggregates: Reply to Girard." *American Journal of Sociology* 93: 1479–1486.

Breault, K. D. 1986. "Suicide in America: A Test of Durkheim's Theory of Religion and Family Integration." *American Journal of Sociology* 93: 1479–1486.

Breedlove, William L. and Patrick D. Nolan. 1988. "International Stratification and Inequality 1960–1980." *International Journal of Contemporary Sociology* 25, 3–4: 1005–123.

Brenner, Robert. 1977. "The Origins of Capitalist Development: A Critique of Neo-Smithian Marxism." *New Left Review* 104: 25–93.

Brint, Steven. 1984. " 'New Class' and Cumulative Trend Explanations of

Liberal Political Attitudes of Professionals." *American Journal of Sociology* 90: 30–77.

Brinton, Crane. 1959. *The Anatomy of Revolution*. New York: Vintage.

Brischetto, Robert, and Tomas Arciniega. 1973. "Examining the Examiner: A Look at Educators' Perspectives on the Chicano Student." In Rudolph O. de la Garza, Z. Anthony Kruzezewski, and Tomas A. Arciniega (eds.), *Chicanos and Native Americans: The Territorial Minorities*. Englewood Cliffs, NJ: Prentice Hall.

Britain, C. V. 1963. "Adolescent Choices and Parent-Peer Cross-Pressures." *American Sociological Review* (June): 385–391.

Brodeur, Paul. 1974. *Expendable Americans*. New York: Viking.

Brody, David. 1960. *Steelworkers in America: The Nonunion Era*. Cambridge, MA: Harvard University Press.

Brophy, Jere E. 1983. "Research on the Self-Fulfilling Prophecy and Teacher Expectations." *Journal of Educational Psychology* 75: 631–661.

Brophy, Jere, and Thomas Good. 1974. *Teacher-Student Relationships*. New York: Holt, Rinehart, and Winston.

Broverman, Inge K., S. R. Vogel, D. M. Broverman, F. E. Clarkson, and P. S. Rosenkrantz. 1972. "Sex-Role Stereotypes: A Current Appraisal." *Journal of Social Issues* 28: 59–78.

Brown, Bernard. 1985. "Head Start: How Research Changed Public Policy." *Young Children* 40: 9–13.

Brown, Bernard. 1978. *Found: Long-Term Gains from Early Intervention*. Boulder, CO: Westview.

Brown, Lawrence L., Alan L. Ginsberg, J. Neil Killalea, and Esther O. Tron. 1978. "School Finance Reform in the Seventies: Achievements and Failures." Pp. 57–110 in Esther O. Tron (ed.), *Selected Papers in School Finance*. Washington, DC: U.S. Department of Health, Education, and Welfare.

Brown, Roger. 1954. "Mass Phenomena." In Gardner Lindzey (ed.), *Handbook of Social Psychology*, vol. 2. Cambridge, MA: Addison-Wesley.

Bruce-Briggs, B. 1979. "An Introduction to the Idea of the New Class." Pp. 1–18 in B. Bruce-Briggs (ed.), *The New Class?*. New Brunswick, NJ: Transaction Books.

Brunvand, Jan Harold. 1986. *The Study of American Folklore*. New York: W. W. Norton.

Brunvand, Jan Harold. 1984. *The Choking Doberman and Other "New" Urban Legends*. New York: W. W. Norton.

Brunvand, Jan Harold. 1981. *The Vanishing Hitchhiker: American Urban Legends and Their Meanings*. New York: W. W. Norton.

Bryan, James H., and Nancy H. Walbek. 1970a. "Preaching and Practicing Self-Sacrifice: Children's Actions and Reactions." *Child Development* 41: 329–353.

Bryan, James H., and Nancy H. Walbek. 1970b. "The Impact of Words and Deeds Concerning Altruism Upon Children." *Child Development* 41: 747–757.

Buckley, Walter. 1967. *Sociology and Modern Systems Theory*. Englewood Cliffs, NJ: Prentice Hall.

Bumpass, Larry, and James Sweet. 1988. "Preliminary Evidence on Cohabitation." Paper presented to the Population Association, New Orleans.

Bumpass, Larry, and James Sweet. 1984. "Some Characteristics of Children's Second Families." *American Journal of Sociology* 90: 608–622.

Bumpass, Larry, and James Sweet. 1972. "Differentials in Marital Instability: 1970." *American Sociological Review* 37: 754–766.

Burch, Philip, Jr. 1980–81. *Elites in American History*, vols. 1–3. New York: Holmes and Meier.

Burger, Chester. 1964. *Survival in the Executive Jungle*. New York: MacMillan.

Burgess, Ernest W. 1925. "The Growth of the City." Pp. 47–62 in Robert E. Park and Ernest W. Burgess (eds.), *The City*. Chicago: University of Chicago Press.

Burnham, Walter Dean. 1987. "The Turnout Problem." Pp. 97–133 in A. James Reichley (ed.), *Elections American Style*. Washington, DC: The Brookings Institution.

Burrowes, R., and B. Spector. 1973. "The Strength and Direction of Relationships Between Domestic and External Conflict and Cooperation: Syria, 1961–67." Pp. 294–324 in J. Wilkenfeld (ed.), *Conflict Behavior and Linkage Politics*. New York: McKay.

Burstein, Paul. 1981. "The Sociology of Democratic Politics and Government." Pp. 291–319 in Ralph H. Turner and James F. Short, Jr., (eds.), *Annual Review of Sociology*, vol. 7. Palo Alto, CA: Annual Reviews.

Burt, Ronald. 1983. *Corporate Profits and Cooptation: Networks of Market Constraints and Directorate Ties in the American Economy*. New York: Academic Press.

Burtless, Gary. 1986. "Public Spending for the Poor: Trends, Prospects, and Economic Limits." Pp. 18–49 in Sheldon H. Danzinger and Daniel H. Weinberg (eds.), *Fighting Poverty: What Works and What Doesn't*. Cambridge, MA: Harvard University Press.

Business Week. 1988. "Who Made the Most—And Why." *Business Week*, May 2, pp. 50–91.

Caldwell, John. 1982. *Theory of Fertility Decline*. New York: Academic Press.

Calhoun, John C. 1962. "Population Density and Social Pathology." *Scientific American* 206: 139–148.

Callahan, Raymond E. 1962. *Education and the Cult of Efficiency: A Study of the Forces That Have Shaped the Administration of Public Schools*. Chicago: University of Chicago Press.

Campbell, Angus, and Howard Schuman. 1968. "Racial Attitudes in Fifteen American Cities." Pp. 1–67 in *Supplemental Studies for the National Advisory Commission on Civil Disorders*. Washington, DC: U.S. Government Printing Office.

Campbell, Angus, Philip E. Converse, and William L. Rogers. 1976. *The Quality of American Life: Perceptions, Evaluations, and Satisfactions*. New York: Russell Sage Foundation.

Campbell, Joseph. 1988. *The Power of Myth*. New York: Doubleday.

Cantril, Hadley. 1940. *The Invasion from Mars*. Princeton, NJ: Princeton University Press.

Carden, M. L. 1978. "The Proliferation of a Social Movement." *Research in Social Movements, Conflict, and Change* 1: 179–196.

Carmichael, Stokeley, and Charles V. Hamilton. 1967. *Black Power*. New York: Random House.

Carmichael, Stokeley, and Charles V. Hamilton. 1967. *Black Power: The Politics of Liberation in America*. New York: Vintage Books.

Carpenter, Judi. 1987. *Trends in Bachelors and Higher Degrees, 1975–1985*. Center for Education Statistics Report. Washington, DC: U.S. Government Printing Office.

Carter, Thomas P., and R. D. Segura. 1979. *Mexican Americans in School: A Decade of Change*. New York: College Entrance Examination Board.

Castells, Manuel. 1985. "High Technology, Economic Restructuring, and the Urban-Regional Process in the United States." Pp. 11–40 in

Manuel Castells (ed.), *High Technology, Space, and Society*. Beverly Hills, CA: Sage.

Castells, Manuel. 1977. *The Urban Question: A Marxist Approach*. (Alan Sheridan, tr.) Cambridge, MA: MIT Press. [Originally published in Spanish, 1972.]

Catton, William J., Jr. 1961. "The Functions and Dysfunctions of Ethnocentrism: A Theory." *Social Problems* 8: 201–211.

Chalfant, H. Paul, Robert E. Beckley, and C. Eddie Palmer. 1987. *Religion in Contemporary Society*, 2nd ed. Palo Alto, CA: Mayfield Publishing Company.

Chambliss, William. 1969. "Types of Deviance and the Effectiveness of the Legal Sanction." *Wisconsin Law Review*: 703–799.

Chambliss, William J. 1984. "The Saints and the Roughnecks." In William J. Chambliss, (ed.), *Criminal Law in Action*. New York: John Wiley and Sons.

Chambliss, William J. 1964. "A Sociological Analysis of the Law of Vagrancy," *Social Problems* (12): 46–67.

Chambliss, William and Milton Mankoff (eds). 1976. *Whose Law What Order?: A Conflict Approach to Criminology*. New York: John Wiley & Sons.

Chandler, Tertius, and Gerald Fox. 1974. *3000 Years of Urban Growth*. New York: Academic Press.

Charon, Joel. 1985. *Symbolic Interactionism: An Introduction, an Interpretation, an Integration*. Englewood Cliffs, NJ: Prentice Hall.

Chase-Dunn, Christopher. 1989a. *Global Formation: Structures of the World-Economy*. London: Basil Blackwell.

Chase-Dunn, Christopher. 1989b. "Comparing World Systems: Toward a Theory of Semiperipheral Development." *Comparative Civilizations Review* 19: 29–66.

Cherlin, Andrew. 1981. *Marriage, Divorce, Remarriage*. Cambridge, MA: Harvard University Press.

Chesler, Mark A., and William M. Cave. 1981. *A Sociology of Education: Access to Power and Privilege*. New York: Macmillan.

Chiet, E. F. 1975. *The Useful Arts and the Liberal Tradition*. New York: McGraw-Hill.

Chilcote, Ronald H. 1984. *Theories of Development and Underdevelopment*. Boulder, CO: Westview Press.

Childe, V. Gordon. 1950. "The Urban Revolution." *Town Planning Review* 21: 3–17.

Childe, V. Gordon. 1946. *What Happened in History*. London: Penguin.

Chiricos, Theodore G. and Gordon P. Waldo. 1970. "Punishment and Crime: An Examination of Some Empirical Evidence." *Social Problems* XVIII: 1–18.

Chirot, Daniel. 1986. *Social Change in the Modern Era*. New York: Harcourt Brace Jovanovich.

Chirot, Daniel. 1986. *Social Change in the Modern Era*. San Diego: Harcourt Brace Jovanovich.

Chirot, Daniel. 1985. "The Rise of the West." *American Sociological Review* 50: 181–195.

Chirot, Daniel. 1981. "Changing Fashions in the Study of the Social Causes of Economic and Political Change." Pp. 259–282 in James Short (ed.), *The State of Sociology*. Beverly Hills, CA: Sage.

Chirot, Daniel, and Thomas D. Hall. 1982. "World-System Theory." *Annual Review of Sociology* 8: 81–106.

Choldin, Harvey M. 1980. "Social Participation in Suburban Apartment Enclaves." Chapter 8 in Clare Underson and Valerie Karn (eds.), *The Consumer Experience of Housing*. Westmead, England: Gower.

Choldin, Harvey M. 1985. *Cities and Suburbs: An Introduction to Urban Sociology*. New York: McGraw Hill.

Choldin, Harvey M. 1978. "Urban Density and Pathology." Pp. 91–113 in Alex Inkeles et al., (eds.), *Annual Review of Socioloty*, Vol. 4. Palo Alto, CA: Annual Reviews.

Christensen, H. T. 1960. "Cultural Relativism and Premarital Sex Norms." *American Sociological Review* 25: 31–39.

Cicerelli, Victor G. 1983. "Adult Children and Their Elderly Parents." Pp. 31–46 in Timothy H. Brubaker (ed.), *Family Relationships in Later Life*. Beverly Hills, CA: Sage.

Cicerelli, Victor G., J. W. Evans, and J. S. Schiller. 1969. *The Impact of Head Start: An Evaluation of the Effects of Head Start on Children's Cognitive an Affective Development*, vols. 1 and 2. Athens, OH: Westinghouse Learning Corporation and Ohio University.

Cicourel, Aaron, and J. Kituse. 1963. *Educational Decision Makers*. Indianapolis: Bobbs-Merrill.

Cipolla, Carlo M. 1965. *The Economic History of World Population*. Sussex: Harvester Press.

Clark, Candace. 1988. "Sickness and Social Control." Pp. 471–491 in Candace Clark and Howard Robboy (eds.), *Social Interaction: Readings in Sociology*, 3rd ed. New York: St. Martin's Press.

Clark, Candace. 1987. "Sympathy Biography and Sympathy Margin." *American Journal of Sociology* 93: 290–321.

Clark, Daniel. 1985. *Post-Industrial America: A Geographic Perspective*. New York: Methuen.

Clark, Kenneth. 1965. *Dark Ghetto: Dilemmas of Social Power*. New York: Harper and Row.

Clark, Margaret. 1970. *Health in the Mexican-American Culture: A Community Study*, 2nd ed. Berkeley: University of California Press.

Clarke-Stewart, Alison. 1985. Quoted and cited in *New York Times*, May 29, Section 3, p. 15.

Clay, Phillip. 1980. "The Rediscovery of City Neighborhoods: Reinvestment by Long-Time Residents and Newcomers." Pp. 13–26 in Shirley B. Laska and Daphne Spain (eds.), *Back to the City: Issues in Neighborhood Renovation*. New York: Permagon.

Clausen, John A. 1979. "Mental Disorder." Pp. 97–112 in Howard E. Freeman, Sol Levine, and Leo G. Reeder (eds.), *Handbook of Medical Sociology*, 3rd ed. Englewood Cliffs, NJ: Prentice Hall.

Cleckley, Hervey. 1976. *The Mark of Sanity*. St. Louis: Mosby.

Clelland, Donald A., and Ian Robertson. 1974. "Social Stratification." Pp. 194–221 in Dushkin Publishing Group (ed.), *The Study of Society*. Guilford, CT: Dushkin Publishing Group.

Clements, John. 1987. *Taylor's Encyclopedia of Government Officials: Federal and State*, Vol. XI, 1987–1988. Dallas, TX: Political Research.

Clinard, Marshall. 1974. *Sociology of Deviant Behavior*, 4th ed. New York: Holt, Rinehart, and Winston.

Clinard, Marshall B. and Peter C. Yeager. 1980. *Corporate Crime*. New York: The Free Press.

Clines, Francis X. 1986. "Chernobyl Shakes Reindeer Culture of Lapps." *New York Times*, September 14, pp. 1, 20.

Close, David, and Carl Bridge (eds.) 1985. *Revolution: A History of the Idea*. Totowa, NJ: Barnes & Noble.

Cloward, Richard A. and Lloyd E. Ohlin. 1960. *Delinquency and Opportunity: A Theory of Delinquent Gangs*. New York: Free Press.

Clymer, Adam. 1983. "Poll Finds Americans Don't Know U.S. Positions on Central America." *New York Times*, July 1, pp. 1, 2.

Coakley, Joane. 1972. "Attitudes of Guidance Counselors." Appendix E in

Report of the Massachusetts Governor's Commission on the Status of Women. Boston: Massachusetts Governor's Commission.

Coale, Ansley J. 1974. "The History of the Human Population." *Scientific American* 231, 3: 40–51.

Coale, Ansley J. 1973. "The Demographic Transition." Pp. 53–72 in *Proceedings of the International Population Conference, Liege,* Vol. 1.

Coale, Ansley J., and Edgar Hoover. 1958. *Population Growth and Economic Development in Low-Income Countries.* Princeton, NJ: Princeton University Press.

Coale, Ansley J., and Melvin Zelnick. 1963. *New Estimates of Fertility and Population in the United States.* Princeton, NJ: Princeton University Press.

Cockerham, William. 1989. *Medical Sociology,* 4th ed. Englewood Cliffs, NJ: Prentice Hall.

Cockerham, William C. 1988. "Medical Sociology." Pp. 575–599 in Neil J. Smelser (ed.), *Handbook of Sociology.* Newbury Park, CA: Sage.

Cockerham, William C. 1978. *Medical Sociology.* Englewood Cliffs, NJ: Prentice Hall.

Cockerham, William C., Guenther Lueschen, Gerhard Kunz, and Joe L. Spaeth. 1986. "Social Stratification and Self-Management of Health." *Journal of Health and Social Behavior* 27: 1–14.

Coe, Rodney. M. 1978. *Sociology of Medicine,* 2nd ed. New York: McGraw Hill.

Cohen, Albert, and Harold M. Hodges, Jr. 1963. "Characteristics of the Lower Blue Collar Class." *Social Problems* 10: 303–333.

Cohen, Albert K. 1955. *Delinquent Boys: The Culture of the Gang.* New York: Free Press.

Cohen, Arthur, and Florence Brewer. 1982. *The American Community College.* San Francisco: Jossey-Bass.

Cohen, Lawrence E., and Marcus Felson. 1979. "Social Change and Crime Rate Trends: A Routine Activity Approach." *American Sociological Review* 44: 588–608.

Cohen, Lawrence E., and Kenneth C. Land. 1987. "Age Structure and Crime: Symmetry Versus Asymmetry and the Projection of Crime Rates Through the 1990s." *American Sociological Review* 52: 170–183.

Colby, Anne; Lawrence Kohlberg; John Gibbs; and Marcus Lieberman. 1983. "A Longitudinal Study of Moral Development." *Monographs of the Society for Research in Child Development* 48, 200.

Cole, Robert. 1979. *Work Mobility and Participation: A Comparative Study of American and Japanese Industry.* Berkeley: University of California Press.

Cole Stephen, and Robert Lejeune. 1972. "Illness and the Legitimation of Failure." *American Sociological Review* (June): 347–356.

Coleman, James S. 1975. "Racial Segregation in the Schools: New Research with New Policy Implications." *Phi Delta Kappan* 57: 75–78.

Coleman, James S. 1961. *The Adolescent Society.* New York: Free Press.

Coleman, James S., Ernest Q. Campbell, Carol J. Hobson, James McPartland, Alexander Mood, Frederick D. Weinfield, and Robert L. York. 1966. *Equality of Educational Opportunity.* Washington DC: U.S. Government Printing Office.

Coleman, James S., Thomas Hoffer, and Sally Kilgore. 1982. *High School Achievement: Public, Catholic, and Private Schools Compared.* New York: Basic Books.

College Board. 1983. *Academic Preparation for College: What Students Need to Know.* New York: College Board.

Collier, John. 1947. *The Indians of the Americas.* New York: W. W. Norton.

Collins, Randall. 1988. "The Conflict Tradition in Durkheimian Sociology." In Jeffrey C. Alexander (ed.), *Durkheimian Sociology: Cultural Studies.* New York: Cambridge University Press.

Collins, Randall. 1988. *Theoretical Sociology.* San Diego: Harcourt Brace Jovanovich.

Collins, Randall. 1987. "Looking Forward or Looking Back?: Reply to Denzin." *American Journal of Sociology* 93: 180–184.

Collins, Randall. (ed.) 1985a. *Three Sociological Traditions: Selected Readings.* New York: Oxford University Press.

Collins, Randall. 1985c. *Three Sociological Traditions.* New York: Oxford University Press.

Collins, Randall. 1985b. *Sociology of Marriage and the Family: Gender, Love, and Property.* Chicago: Nelson-Hall.

Collins, Randall. 1981. "On the Microfoundations of Macrosociology." *American Journal of Sociology* 86: 984–1014.

Collins, Randall. 1979. *The Credential Society.* New York: Academic Press.

Collins, Randall. 1974. *Conflict Sociology: Toward an Explanatory Science.* New York: Academic Press.

Collins, Randall. 1971a. "A Conflict Theory of Sexual Stratification." *Social Problems* 19: 3–12.

Collins, Randall. 1971b. "Functional and Conflict Theories of Educational Stratification." *American Sociological Review* 36: 1002–1019.

Collins, Randall, and Michael Makowsky. 1984. *The Discovery of Society,* 3rd ed. New York: Random House.

Coltrane, Scott. 1988. "Father-Child Relationships and the Status of Women: A Cross-Cultural Study." *American Journal of Sociology* 93: 1060–1095.

Comhaire, Jean, and Werner J. Cahnman. 1959. *How Cities Grew: The Historical Sociology of Cities.* Madison, NJ: Florham Park Press.

Committee on the Budget, U.S. House of Representatives. 1976. *Working Papers on Major Budget and Program Issues in Selected Health Programs.* Washington, DC: U.S. Government Printing Office.

Commoner, Barry. 1982. "The Economic Meaning of Ecology." Pp. 290–296 in Jerome H. Skolnick and Elliott Currie (eds.), *Crisis in American Institutions,* 5th ed. Boston: Little, Brown.

Conant, James B. 1952. *Modern Science and Modern Man.* Garden City, NY: Doubleday.

Conforti, Joseph M. 1972. "Newark: Ghetto or City?" *Society* 9: 20–32.

Conrad, Joseph W. and Joseph W. Schneider. 1980. *Deviance and Medicalization: From Badness to Sickness.* St. Louis: The C. V. Mosby Company.

Conrad, Peter. 1975. "The Discovery of Hyperkinesis: Notes on the Medicalization of Deviant Behavior." *Social Problems* 23: 12–21.

Consortium for Longitudinal Studies. 1983. *As the Twig is Bent: Lasting Effects of Preschool Programs.* Hillsdale, NJ: Erlbaum.

Consortium for Longitudinal Studies. 1979. *Lasting Effects After Preschool, Summary Report.* Washington DC: U.S. Department of Health, Education, and Welfare, Human Services Administration for Children, Youth, and Families.

Cooley, Charles Horton. 1964. *Human Nature and the Social Order.* New York: Schocken. [Originally published in 1902.]

Cooley, Charles Horton. 1929. *Social Organization.* New York: Scribner's. [Originally published in 1909.]

Cook, George C. 1912. "The Third American Sex." *Forum* 50: 447.

Cooper, J., and J. C. McGaugh. 1969. "Leadership: Integrating Principles of Social Psychology." In C. A. Gibb (ed.), *Leadership.* Baltimore: Penguin.

Coser, Lewis. 1977. *Masters of Sociological Thought: Ideas in Historical and Social Context,* 2nd ed. New York: Harcourt Brace Jovanovich.

Coser, Lewis. 1956. *The Functions of Social Conflict.* New York: The Free Press.

Coser, Lewis A. 1956. *The Functions of Social Conflict.* Glencoe, IL: Free Press.

Coser, Rose Laub, and Lewis Coser. 1979. "Jonestown as a Perverse Utopia." *Dissent* (Spring): 158–163.

Council on Environmental Quality. 1984. *Environmental Quality 1983.* 14th Annual Report of the Council on Environmental Quality. Washington, DC: Council on Environmental Quality.

Council on Environmental Quality. 1980. *The Global Report to the President of the United States, Entering the 21st Century.* New York: Permagon.

Coulter, Philip. 1975. *Social Mobilization and Liberal Democracy.* Lexington, MA: Heath.

Cousins, Albert N., and Hans Nagpaul. 1979. *Urban Life: The Sociology of Cities and Urban Society.* New York: John Wiley and Sons.

Coverman, S., and J. Sheley. 1986. "Change in Men's Housework and Child-Care Time, 1965–1975." *Journal of Marriage and Family* 48: 413–22.

Cowell, Alan. 1986. "Three Blacks Reported Slain in South African Violence." *New York Times,* July 29, Section 1, p. 2.

Cowgill, Donald O. 1974. "The Aging of Populations and Societies." *The Annals of the American Academy of Political and Social Science* 415: 1–18.

Cox, Oliver Cromwell. 1948. *Caste, Class, and Race.* Garden City, NY: Doubleday.

Crain, Robert L., and C. Weisman. 1972. *Discrimination, Personality, and Achievement: A Survey of Northern Blacks.* New York: Seminar.

Crawford, R. 1981. "Individual Responsibility and Health Politics." Pp. 468–481 in Peter Conrad and Rochelle Kern (eds.), *The Sociology of Health and Illness: Critical Perspectives.* New York: St. Martin's Press.

Crews, Kimberly A., and Patricia Cancellier. 1988. *U.S. Population: Charting the Change.* Washington, DC: Population Reference Bureau.

Croog, S. H. 1961. "Ethnic Origins, Educational Level, and Responses to a Health Questionnaire." *Human Organization* 20, 2: 65–69.

Crowley, Joan E. 1986. "Longitudinal Effects of Retirement on Men's Psychological and Physical Well-Being." Pp. 147–173 in Herbert S. Parnes et al. (eds.), *Retirement Among American Men.* Lexington, MA: Lexington Books/D. C. Heath.

Cuber, John F., and Peggy B. Harroff. 1965. *Sex and the Significant Americans.* New York: Penguin Books.

Cummings, Milton C., and David Wise. 1981. *Democracy Under Pressure: An Introduction to the American Political System,* 4th ed. New York: Harcourt Brace Jovanovich.

Cunningham, Frances C., and John W. Williamson. 1980. "How Does the Quality of Health Care in HMOs Compare to that in Other Settings?" *Group Health Journal* (Winter): 4–13.

Curran, Libby. 1980. "Science Education: Did She Drop Out or Was She Pushed?" Pp. 22–41 in Brighton Women and Science Group (eds.), *Alice Through the Microscope: The Power of Science Over the Lives of Women.* London: VIRAGO.

Currie, Elliot. *Confronting Crime: An American Challenge.* New York: Pantheon Books.

Currie, Elliot, and Jerome H. Skolnick. 1984. *America's Problems: Social Issues and Public Policy.* Boston: Little, Brown.

Curtis, Lynn A. 1975. *Violence, Race, and Culture.* Lexington, MA: Heath.

Curtiss, Susan. 1977. *Genie: A Linguistic Study of a Modern-Day "Wild Child."* New York: Academic Press.

Dahl, Robert. 1967. *Pluralist Democracy in the United States: Conflict and Consent.* Chicago: Rand McNally.

Dahl, Robert A. 1982. *Dilemmas of Pluralist Democracy: Autonomy vs. Control.* New Haven: Yale University Press.

Dahl, Robert A. 1981. *Democracy in the United States,* 4th ed. Boston: Houghton-Mifflin.

Dahl, Robert A. 1961. *Who Governs?* New Haven: Yale University Press.

Dahl, Robert A. 1957. "The Concept of Power." *Behavioral Science* 2: 201–215.

Dahrendorf, Ralf. 1959. *Class and Class Conflict in Industrial Society.* Stanford, CA: Stanford University Press.

Danzinger, Sheldon, and Daniel Weinberg. (eds.) 1986. *Fighting Poverty: What Works and What Doesn't.* Cambridge, MA: Harvard University Press.

Darden, Joe T. 1987. "Choosing Neighbors and Neighborhoods: The Role of Race in Housing Preference." Pp. 15–42 in Gary A. Tobin (ed.), *Divided Neighborhoods: Changing Patterns of Racial Segregation.* Urban Affairs Annual Reviews, vol. 32. Newbury Park, CA: Sage.

Davies, James C. 1962. "Toward a Theory of Revolution." *American Sociological Review* 27: 5–19.

Davis, David Brion. 1966. *The Problem of Slavery in Western Culture.* Ithaca, NY: Cornell University Press.

Davis, Karen, and Cathy Schoen. 1978. *Health and the War on Poverty.* Washington DC: Brookings Institution.

Davis, Kingsley. 1955. "The Origin and Growth of Urbanization in the World." *American Journal of Sociology* 60: 429–437.

Davis, Kingsley. 1940. "Extreme Social Isolation of a Child." *American Journal of Sociology* 45: 554–565.

Davis, Kingsley, and Wilbert E. Moore. 1945. "Some Principles of Stratification." *American Sociological Review* 10: 242–249.

Davis, Nancy S., and Robert Robertson. 1988. "Class Identification of Men and Women in the 1970s and 1980s." *American Sociological Review* 53: 103–112.

Deane, Phyllis. 1969. *The First Industrial Revolution.* Cambridge: Cambridge University Press.

Deaux, Kay, and L. Laurie Lewis. 1984. "Structure of Gender Stereotypes: Interrelations among Components and Gender Label." *Journal of Personality and Social Psychology* 46: 991–1004.

Deaux, Kay, and L. Laurie Lewis. 1983. "Components of Gender Stereotypes." *Psychological Monographs* 13, 25.

de Chauliac, Guy. 1890. *Great Surgery.* Latin-English Translation.

De Fleur, Melvin L., and F. R. Westie. 1958. "Verbal Attitudes and Overt Acts: An Experiment on the Salience of Attitudes." *American Sociological Review* 23: 667–673.

Degler, Carl N. 1980. *At Odds: Women and the Family in America from the Revolution to the Present.* New York: Oxford University Press.

De Maris, A., and Gerald R. Leslie. 1984. "Cohabitation With the Future Spouse: Its Influence upon Marital Satisfaction and Communication." *Journal of Marriage and the Family* 46: 77–84.

De Mause, Lloyd. 1975. "Our Forebears Made Childhood a Nightmare." *Psychology Today* (April): 85–87.

D'Emillio, John. 1983. *Sexual Politics, Sexual Communities.* Chicago: University of Chicago Press.

Denton, Nancy, and Douglas S. Massey. 1988. "Residential Segregation of Blacks, Hispanics, and Asians by Socioeconomic Status and Generation." *Social Science Quarterly* (December): 797–817.

Denzin, Norman K. 1989. *The Research Act: A Theoretical Introduction to Sociological Research Methods,* 3rd ed. Englewood Cliffs, NJ: Prentice Hall.

Denzin, Norman K. 1987. "The Death of Sociology in the 1980s: Comment on Collins." *American Journal of Sociology* 93: 175–180.

De Prete, Thomas A., and Whitman T. Soule. 1988. "Gender and Promotion in Segmented Job Ladder Systems." *American Sociological Review* 53: 26–40.

Despelder, Lynne Anne, and Albert Lee Strickland. 1983. *The Last Dance: Encountering Death and Dying.* Palo Alto, CA: Mayfield.

Deterrence and Incapacitation: Estimating the Effects of Criminal Sanctions on Crime Rates. 1978. Washington, DC: National Academy of Sciences.

de Tocqueville, Alexis. 1988. *Democracy in America.* J. P. Mayer (ed.), George Lawrence (tr.). New York: Harper & Row. [Originally published in French, 1835.]

de Tocqueville, Alexis. 1955. *The Old Regime and the French Revolution.* (Stuart Gilbert, tr.) Garden City, NY: Doubleday Anchor. [Originally published in French in 1856.]

de Tocqueville, Alexis. 1948. *Democracy in America.* New York: Alfred A. Knopf.

Deutsch, Connie J., and Lucia A. Gilbert. 1976. "Sex-Role Stereotypes: Effects on Self and Others and on Personal Adjustment." *Journal of Counseling Psychology* 23: 373–379.

Deutsch, Karl W. 1974. *Politics and Government: How People Decide Their Fate.* Boston: Houghton-Mifflin.

Devine, Donald J. 1972. *The Political Culture of the United States: The Influence of Member Values on Regime Maintenance.* Boston: Little, Brown.

Dicker, Marvin. 1983. "Health Care Coverage and Insurance Premiums of Families, United States, 1980." *National Medical Care Utilization and Expenditure Survey,* Preliminary Report No. 3. DHHS Publication No. 83-20000. Washington, D.C.: U.S. Government Printing Office.

Diebold, John. 1985. *Making the Future Work.* New York: Simon and Schuster.

Dinitz, Simon, Russell R. Dynes, and Alfred C. Clarke (eds.) 1969. *Deviance.* New York: Oxford University Press.

Dixon, Marlene. 1971. "Why Women's Liberation?" In Elsie Adams and Mary Louise Briscoe (eds.), *Up Against the Wall, Mother* . . . Beverly Hills, CA: Glencoe.

Dobzhansky, Theodosius. 1962. *Mankind Evolving.* New Haven, CT: Yale University Press.

Dohrenwend, Bruce P. 1975. "Sociocultural and Social-Psychological Factors in the Genesis of Mental Disorders." *Journal of Health and Social Behavior* 16: 365–392.

Domhoff, G. William. 1983. *Who Rules America Now? A View for the Eighties.* Englewood Cliffs, NJ: Prentice Hall.

Domhoff, G. William. 1978. *Who Really Rules? New Haven and Community Power Reexamined.* New Brunswick, NJ: Transaction Books.

Domhoff, G. William. 1967. *Who Rules America?* Englewood Cliffs, NJ: Prentice Hall.

Dowie, Mark. 1982. "Pinto Madness." Pp. 21–37 in Jerome H. Sholnick and Elliot Currie (eds.), *Crisis in American Institutions,* 5th ed. Boston: Little, Brown, and Company.

Downs, A. Chris, and Sheila K. Harrsion. 1985. "Embarassing Age Spots or Just Plain Ugly? Physical Attractiveness Stereotyping as an Instrument of Sexism on American Television Commercials." *Sex Roles* 13: 9–19.

Downs, Anthony. 1957. *An Economic Theory of Democracy.* New York: Harper.

Doyle, H., and D. M. Kelley. 1979. "Comparison of Trends in Ten Denominations 1950–75." In D. R. Hoge and D. A. Roozen (eds.), *Understanding Church Growth and Decline: 1950–1978.* New York: Pilgrim Press.

Doyle, James A. 1983. *The Male Experience.* Dubuque, IA: William C. Brown.

Driedger, L., and G. Church. 1974. "Residential Segregation and Institutional Completeness: A Comparison of Ethnic Minorities. *Canadian Review of Sociology and Anthropology* 11: 30–52.

Duncan, Beverly, and Stanley Lieberson. 1970. *Metropolis and Region in Transition.* Beverly Hills, CA: Sage.

Duncan, Greg J., with Richard Coe, Mary E. Corcoran, Martha S. Hill, Saul D. Hoffman, and James N. Morgan. 1984. *Years of Poverty, Years of Plenty: The Changing Economic Fortunes of American Workers and Families.* Ann Arbor: Institute for Social Research, University of Michigan.

Duncan, Greg J., with Mary E. Corcoran. 1984. "Do Women ;osDeserve' to Earn Less than Men?" Pp. 153–172 in Greg J. Duncan, et al. (eds.), *Years of Poverty, Years of Plenty: The Changing Economic Fortunes of American Workers and Families.* Ann Arbor: Institute for Social Research, University of Michigan.

Dunphy, D. C. 1972. "Peer Group Socialization." Pp. 200–217 in F. J. Hunt (ed.), *Socialization in Australia.* Sydney: Angus and Robertson.

Dunphy, D. C. 1963. "The Social Structure of Urban Adolescent Peer Groups." *Sociometry* 26: 230–246.

Durkheim, Emile. 1965. *The Elementary Forms of the Religious Life.* New York: The Free Press. Originally published in 1915.

Durkheim, Emile. 1964. *Suicide.* Glencer, IL: Free Press. [Originally published 1897.]

Durkheim, Emile. 1964. *Suicide, A Study in Sociology.* (J. A. Spaulding and George Simpson, trs.) Glencoe, IL: The Free Press. Originally published in French, 1897.

Durkheim, Emile. 1964b. *The Rules of the Sociological Method.* New York: Free Press. [Originally published in 1893.]

Durkheim, Emile. 1956. *Education and Society.* Glencoe, IL: Free Press. [Originally published in French in 1922.]

Durkheim, Emile. 1953. "Individual and Collective Representations." In D. F. Pocock (tr.), *Sociology and Philosophy.* Glencoe, IL: Free Press. Originally published in French, 1898.

Durkheim, Emile. 1947. *Division of Labor in Society.* (George Simpson, tr.) Glencoe, IL: The Free Press. Originally published in French in 1893.

Dushkin Publishing Group. 1985. *Encyclopedic Dictionary of Sociology,* 3rd ed. Guilford, CT: Dushkin Publishing Group.

Duster, Troy. 1988. "From Structural Analysis to Public Policy: Review of William Julius Wilson, *The Truly Disadvantaged: The Inner City, the Underclass, and Public Policy.*" *Contemporary Sociology* 17: 287–290.

Duvall, Evelyn M., and Brent C. Miller. 1985. *Marriage and Family Development,* 6th ed. New York: Harper & Row.

Dye, T. 1983. *Who's Running America? The Reagan Years.* Englewood Cliffs, NJ: Prentice Hall.

Eagan, Andrea Boroff. 1988. "The Damage Done: The Endless Saga of the Dalkon Shield." *Village Voice,* July 5.

Easterlin, Richard. 1978. "What Will 1984 Be Like? Socioeconomic Implications of Recent Trends in Family Structure." *Demography* 15: 397–432.

Easterlin, Richard. 1968. *Population, Labor Force, and Long Swings in Economic Growth.* New York: National Bureau of Economic Research.

Edmonds, Ronald. 1979. "Some Schools Work and More Can." *Social Policy* 9, 5: 28–32.

Edwards, Richard. 1979. *Contested Terrain.* New York: Basic Books.

Edwards, Richard C., Michael Reich, and Thomas E. Weisskopf. 1986. "Introduction." Pp. 1–4 in Richard C. Edwards, Michael Reich, and Thomas E. Weisskopf (eds.), *The Capitalist System,* 3rd ed. Englewood Cliffs, NJ: Prentice Hall.

Ehrenreich, B., and J. Ehrenreich. 1975. "Medicine and Social Control." Pp. 138–167 in B. R. Mandell (ed.), *Welfare in America: Controlling the "Dangerous" Classes.* Englewood Cliffs, NJ: Prentice Hall.

Ehrlich, Elizabeth, and Susan B. Garland. 1988. "For American Business, A New World of Workers." *Business Week* 3070 (September 19): 112–120.

Ehrlich, Howard J. 1973. *The Social Psychology of Prejudice.* New York: Wiley Interscience.

Eisenstadt, S. N. 1985. "Macro-Societal Analysis-Background, Development and Indication." Pp. 7–24 in S. N. Eisenstadt and H. J. Helle (eds.), *Macro-Sociological Theory: Perspectives on Sociological Theory,* vol. 1. London: Sage Publications Ltd.

Eisenstadt, S. N. 1973. *Tradition, Change, and Modernity.* New York: Wiley.

Eisinger, Peter K. 1973. "Conditions of Protest Behavior in American Cities." *American Political Science Review* 67: 11–28.

Eitzen, D. Stanley, and Maxine Baca Zinn. 1989. *The Reshaping of America: Social Consequences of the Changing Economy.* Englewood Cliffs, NJ: Prentice Hall.

Eitzen, Stanley D., and Doug A. Timmer. 1985. *Criminology.* New York: John Wiley and Sons.

Ekerdt, D. J., and R. Bosse. 1982. "Change in Self-Reported Health with Retirement." *International Journal of Aging and Human Development* 15: 213–223.

Elgie, Robert A., and Alex Rees Clark. 1980. "The Metropolitan Structure of Southern Metropolitan Areas: A Comparative Analysis." *Urban Geography* 1: 317–334.

Elkin, Frederick, and Gerald Handel. 1984. *The Child and Society,* 4th ed. New York: Random House.

Ellsworth, R. N. 1903. "Tables and Charts Showing the Occupations of the Fathers of the Students in the University of Michigan, November, 1902." James Burrill Angell Papers, The University of Michigan.

Ellwood, David T. 1987. *Divide and Conquer: Responsible Security for America's Poor.* Occasional Paper 1, Ford Foundation Project on Social Welfare and the American Future. New York: Ford Foundation.

Ellwood, David T., and Mary Jo Bane. 1984. "The Impact of AFDC on Family Structure and Living Arrangements." Working Paper prepared for U.S. Department of Health and Human Services, grant no. 92A-82.

Ellwood, Robert S., Jr. 1987. *Many Peoples, Many Faiths.* Englewood Cliffs, NJ: Prentice Hall.

Emerson, Richard M. 1972. "Exchange Theory. Part I: A Psychological Basis for Social Change, and Part I: Exchange Relations and Networks." Pp. 38–87 in J. Berger, M. Zeldich, and B. Anderson (eds.), *Sociological Theories in Progress,* vol. 2. Boston: Houghton-Mifflin.

England, Paula, George Farkas, Barbara Stanek Kilbourne, and Thomas Dou. 1988. "Explaining Occupational Sex Segregation and Wages: Findings From a Model with Fixed Effects." *American Sociological Review* 53: 544–558.

Entwisle, Doris R., and David P. Baker. 1983. "Gender and Young Children's Expectations for Performance in Arithmetic." *Developmental Psychology* 19: 200–209.

Ensminger, Margaret E. 1987. "Adolescent Sexual Behavior As It Relates to Other Transition Behaviors in Youth." Pp. 36–55 in Sandra L. Hofferth and Cheryl D. Hayes (eds.), *Risking the Future: Adolescent Sexuality and Childbearing. Vol. II: Working Papers and Statistical Appendixes.* Washington: National Academy Press.

Epstein, Cynthia Fuchs. 1970. *Women's Place: Options and Limits on Professional Careers.* Berkeley: University of California Press.

Epstein, S. S. 1981. "The Political and Economic Basis of Cancer." Pp. 75–82 in Peter Conrad and Rochelle Kern (eds.), *The Sociology of Health and Illness: Critical Perspectives.* New York: St. Martin's Press.

Epstein, S. S. 1978. *The Politics of Cancer.* San Francisco. Sierra Club Book.

Equal Employment Opportunity Commission. 1972. "A Unique Competence: A Study of Employment Opportunity in the Bell System." *Congressional Record* 17: E1243–E1268.

Erickson, F., and S. Schultz. 1982. *The Counselor as Gatekeeper.* New York: Academic Press.

Erickson, Kai T. 1966. *Wayward Puritans: A Study in the Sociology of Deviance.* New York: John Wiley.

Erikson, Erik H. 1982. *The Life Cycle Completed: A Review.* New York: Norton.

Erikson, Erik H. 1950. *Childhood and Society.* New York: Norton.

Erikson, Kai T. 1987. "Notes on the Sociology of Deviance." Pp. 21–23 in *Deviance: The Interactional Perspective,* 5th ed. Earl Rubington and Martin S. Weinberg (eds.), New York: Macmillan.

Esposito, D. 1973. "Homogeneous and Heterogeneous Ability Grouping: Principal Findings and Implications for Evaluating and Designing More Effective School Environments." *Review of Educational Research* 43: 163–179.

Etzioni, Amitai. 1982. *An Immodest Agenda: Rebuilding America Before the Twenty-First Century.* New York: McGraw Hill.

Etzioni, Amitai. 1975. *A Comparative Analysis of Complex Organizations,* rev. and enl. ed. Glencoe, IL: Free Press.

Evans, Christopher. 1979. *The Micro Millennium.* New York: Viking.

Evans, Peter, Dietrich Rueschmeyer and Theda Skocpol (eds.) 1985. *Bringing the State Back In.* Cambridge: Cambridge University Press.

Ewens, William L., and Howard J. Ehrlich. 1969. "Reference Other Support and Ethnic Attitudes as Predictors of Intergroup Behavior." Revised version of paper presented to the joint meetings of the Midwest Sociological Society and Ohio Valley Sociological Society, Indianapolis, May.

Eyler, Janet, Valerie J. Cook, and Leslie E. Ward. 1983. "Resegregation: Segregation Within Desegregated Schools." Pp. 126–162 in

Christine H. Rossell and Willis D. Hawley (eds.), *The Consequences of School Desegregation*. Philadelphia: Temple University Press.

Fagan, Jeffrey, Ellen Slaughter, and Eliot Hartstone. 1987. "Blind Justice? The Impact of Race on the Juvenile Justice Process." *Crime and Delinquency* 33, 2: 224–258.

Fairweather, Hugh. 1976. "Sex Differences in Cognitive Tests." *Cognition* 4: 231–275.

Faris, Robert E. L. 1979. *Chicago Sociology: 1920–1932*. Chicago: University of Chicago Press.

Farley, John E. 1988. *Majority-Minority Relations*, 2nd ed. Englewood Cliffs, NJ: Prentice Hall.

Farley, John E. 1987a. *American Social Problems: An Institutional Analysis*. Englewood Cliffs, NJ: Prentice Hall.

Farley, John E. 1987b. "Excessive Black and Hispanic Unemployment in U.S. Metropolitan Areas: The Roles of Racial Inequality, Segregation, and Discrimination in Male Joblessness." *American Journal of Economics and Sociology* 46: 129–150.

Farley, John E. 1987c. "Segregation in 1980: How Segregated Are America's Metropolitan Areas?" Pp. 95–114 in Gary Tobin (ed.), *Divided Neighborhoods: Changing Patterns of Racial Segregation*. Urban Affairs Annual Reviews, vol. 32. Newbury Park, CA: Sage.

Farley, John E. 1986. "Health Care." Pp. 43–47 in Ann R. Ruwitch (ed.), *St. Louis Currents: The Community and its Resources*. St. Louis: Leadership St. Louis.

Farley, John E. 1986b. "Segregated City, Segregated Suburbs: To What Extent Are They Products of Black-White Socioeconomic Differentials?" *Urban Geography* 7, 2: 180–187.

Farley, John E. 1985. "The Factorial Ecology and Social Areas of Metropolitan St. Louis, 1980." Paper presented at Annual Meeting of the Midwest Sociological Society, St. Louis, April.

Farley, John E. 1984. "Characteristics of Movers To, From, and Within St. Louis City, 1975–1980." Paper presented at Annual Meeting of the Illinois Sociological Association, Chicago, October.

Farley, John E. 1983. "Metropolitan Housing Segregation in 1980: The St. Louis Case." *Urban Affairs Quarterly* 18: 347–359.

Farley, John E. 1982. "Effects of Higher-Density Living on Children." Pp. 50–60 in *Proceedings: The Impact of Energy Policy and Technology on the Family*. Knoxville: University of Tennessee.

Farley, John E. 1977. *Effects of Residential Setting, Parental Lifestyle, and Demographic Characteristics on Children's Activity Patterns*. Ph.D. dissertation, University of Michigan.

Farley, Reynolds. 1984. *Blacks and Whites: Narrowing the Gap?* Cambridge, MA: Harvard University Press.

Farley, Reynolds. 1980. "Homicide Trends in the United States." *Demography* 17: 177–188.

Farley, Reynolds. 1977. "Trends in Racial Inequalities: Have the Gains of the 1960s Disappeared in the 1970s?" *American Sociological Review* 42: 189–208.

Farley, Reynolds, and Walter Allen. 1987. *The Color Line and the Quality of Life in America*. New York: Russell Sage.

Farley, Reynolds, Suzanne Bianchi, and Diane Colasanto. 1979. "Barriers to the Racial Integration of Neighborhoods: The Detroit Case." *The Annals of the American Academy of Political and Social Science* 441: 47–113.

Farley, Reynolds, Toni Richards, and Clarence Wurdock. 1980. "School Desegregation and White Flight.: An Investigation of Competing Models and Their Discrepant Findings." *Sociology of Education* 53: 123–129.

Farley, Reynolds, Howard Schuman, Suzanne Bianchi, Diane Colasanto, and Shirley Hatchett. 1978. "Chocolate City, Vanilla Suburbs: Will the Trend Toward Racially Separate Communities Continue?" *Social Science Research* 7: 319–344.

Farrar, L. L. 1978. "The Causes of World War I." Pp. 171–180 in L. L. Farrar (ed.), *War: A Historical, Political, and Social Study*. Santa Barbara, CA: ABC-Clio.

Fausto-Sterling, Anne. 1985. *Myths of Gender: Biological Theories About Women and Men*. New York: Basic Books.

Fava, Sylvia F. 1959. "Contrasts in Neighboring: New York City and a Suburban County." Pp. 122–131 in W. M. Dobriner (ed.), *The Suburban Community*. New York: Putnam.

Feagin, Joe R. 1985. "The Global Context of Metropolitan Growth: Houston and the Oil Industry." *American Journal of Sociology* 90: 1204–1230.

Feagin, Joe R. 1983. *The Urban Real Estate Game*. Englewood Cliffs, NJ: Prentice Hall.

Feagin, Joe R. 1972. "Poverty: We Still Believe That God Helps Those That Help Themselves." *Psychology Today* 6: 101–110.

Feagin, Joe R., and Clarice Booher Feagin. 1978. *Discrimination American Style: Institutional Racism and Sexism*. Englewood Cliffs, NJ: Prentice Hall.

Featherman, David L. 1979. "Opportunities are Expanding." *Society* 13: 4–11.

Featherman, David L., and Robert M. Hauser. 1978. *Opportunity and Change*. New York: Academic Press.

Federal Bureau of Investigation. 1989. *Uniform Crime Reports: Crime in the United States, 1988*. Washington, DC: U.S. Government Printing Office.

Federal Bureau of Investigation. 1983. *Uniform Crime Reports: Crime in the United States, 1983*. Washington: U.S. Government Printing Office.

Federal Bureau of Investigation. 1979. *Uniform Crime Reports: Crime in the United States, 1979*. Washington: U.S. Government Printing Office.

Federbush, Marsha. 1974. "The Sex Problems of School Math Books." Pp. 178–184 in Judith Stacey, Susan Bereaud, and Joan Daniels (eds.), *And Jill Came Tumbling After: Sexism in American Education*. New York: Dell.

Fendrich, James M. 1967. "Perceived Reference Group Support: Racial Attitudes and Overt Behavior." *American Sociological Review* 32: 960–970.

Festinger, Leon. 1957. *A Theory of Cognitive Dissonance*. Stanford, CA: Stanford University Press.

Festinger, Leon, and J. Merrill Carlsmith. 1959. "Cognitive Consequences of Forced Compliance." *Journal of Abnormal and Social Psychology* 58: 203–210.

Feuer, Lewis. 1969. *The Conflict of Generations: The Character and Significance of the Student Movement*. New York: Basic Books.

Findley, W. G., and M. M. Bryan. 1971. *Ability Grouping, 1970: Status, Impact, and Alternatives*. Athens: University of Georgia, Center for Educational Improvement.

Fine, Gary Alan. 1984. "Negotiated Order and Organizational Cultures." Pp. 239–262 in Ralph H. Turner (ed.), *Annual Review of Sociology*, vol. 10. Palo Alto, CA: Annual Reviews.

Fine, Gary Alan. 1979. "Cokelore and Coke Law: Urban Belief Tales and the Problem of Multiple Origins." *Journal of American Folklore* 92: 477–482.

Finney, Martha I. 1988. "The Right to be Tested." *Personnel Administrator* (March): 74–75.

Firebaugh, Glenn, and Kenneth E. Davis. 1988. "Trends in Antiblack Prejudice, 1972–1984: Region and Cohort Effects." *American Journal of Sociology* 94: 251–272.

Fischer, Claude S. 1984. *The Urban Experience,* 2nd ed. New York: Harcourt, Brace, Jovanovich.

Fischer, Claude S. 1982. *To Dwell Among Friends: Personal Networks in Town and City.* Chicago: University of Chicago Press.

Fischer, Claude S. 1975. "Toward a Subcultural Theory of Urbanism." *American Journal of Sociology* 80: 1319–1341.

Fischer, Claude S. 1973. "Urban Malaise." *Social Problems* 52: 221–235.

Fischer, Claude S. 1971. "A Research Note on Urbanism and Tolerance." *American Journal of Sociology* 76: 847–856.

Fischer, Claude S., and Robert M. Jackson. 1976. "Suburbs, Networks, and Attitudes." Chapter 11 in Barry Schwartz (ed.), *The Changing Face of the Suburbs.* Chicago: University of Chicago Press.

Fleischman, Arnold. 1977. "Sunbelt Boosterism: The Politics of Postwar Growth and Annexation in San Antonio." Pp. 151–168 in David C. Perry and Alfred J. Watkins (eds.), *The Rise of the Sunbelt Cities.* Urban Affairs Annual Reviews, vol. 14. Beverly Hills, CA: Sage.

Floge, Liliane, and Deborah M. Merrill. 1986. "Tokenism Reconsidered: Male Nurses and Female Physicians in a Hospital Setting." *Social Forces* 64: 925–947.

Floyd, H. Hugh, Jr., and Donald R. South. 1972. "Dilemma of Youth: The Choice of Parents or Peers as a Frame of Reference for Behavior." *Journal of Marriage and the Family* 34: 627–634.

Foner, Anne, and Karen Schwab. 1981. *Aging and Retirement.* Monterey, CA: Brooks-Cole.

Ford, Clellan S., and Frank A. Beach. 1951. *Patterns of Sexual Behavior.* New York: Harper.

Ford, Clellan S., and Frank A. Beach. 1951. *Patterns of Sexual Behavior.* New York: Harper and Row.

Form, William. 1979. "Comparative Industrial Sociology and the Convergence Hypothesis." In Alex Inkeles, James Coleman, and Ralph H. Turner (eds.), *Annual Review of Sociology,* vol. 5. Palo Alto, CA: Annual Reviews.

Foster, William Z. 1920. *The Great Steel Strike and Its Lessons.* New York: Huebsch.

Fox, Daniel M., and Robert Crawford. 1979. "Health Politics in the United States." Pp. 392–411 in Howard E. Freeman, Sol Levine, and Leo G. Reeder (eds.), *Handbook of Medical Sociology,* 3rd ed. Englewood Cliffs, NJ: Prentice Hall.

Fraher, S. 1984. "Why Women Aren't Getting to the Top." *Fortune,* pp. 40–45.

Frank, Andre Gunder. 1969. "The Development of Underdevelopment." Pp. 3–17 in *Latin America: Underdevelopment or Revolution?* New York: Monthly Review Press.

Frank, Jerome. 1959. "The Dynamics of a Psychotheraputic Relationship." *Psychiatry* 22: 17–39.

Franklin, John Hope. 1969. *From Slavery to Freedom: A History of Negro Americans,* 3rd ed. New York: Vintage Books.

Frazier, Nancy, and Myrna Sadker. 1974. *Sexism in School and Society.* New York: Dell.

Freeman, Jo. 1979. "The Women's Liberation Movement: Its Origins, Organization, Activities, and Ideas." In Jo Freeman (ed.), *Women: A Feminist Perspective.* Palo Alto, CA: Mayfield.

Freeman, Jo. 1973. "The Origins of the Women's Liberation Movement." *American Journal of Sociology* 78: 792–811.

Freivogel, William H. 1989. "A New Majority: Shift on Court Endangers Precedents." *St. Louis Post-Dispatch,* June 14, Section B, p. 1.

Freud, Sigmund. 1970. *Beyond the Pleasure Principle.* New York: Bantam. Originally published, 1920.

Freud, Sigmund. 1962. *Society and its Discontents.* New York: Norton. Originally published in German, 1930.

Freudenheim, Milt. 1988. "Prepaid Programs for Health Care Encounter Snag." *New York Times,* September 25, Section 1, pp. 1, 32.

Fried, Morton. 1967. *The Evolution of Political Society.* New York: Random House.

Friedan, Betty. 1963. *The Feminine Mystique.* New York: Dell.

Frieden, Eliot. 1975. *Doctoring Together: A Study of Professional Social Control.* New York: Elsevier.

Friedland, Robert B. 1987. "Introduction and Background: Private Iniatives to Contain Health Care Expenditures." In Frank B. McArdle (ed.), *The Changing Health Care Market.* Washington: Employee Benefit Research Institute.

Friedman, Andrew. 1971. *Industry and Labor: Class Struggle at Work and Monopoly Capitalism.* New York: MacMillan.

Friedman, E. A., and H. L. Orbach. 1974. "Adjustment to Retirement." Pp. 609–645 in Silvane Arieti (ed.), *American Handbook of Psychiatry,* vol. 1. New York: Basic Books.

Friedrich, Carl J. 1972. "In Defense of a Concept." In Leonard Schapiro (ed.), *Political Opposition in One-Party States.* London: MacMillan.

Frieze, I., Jacquelyn Ecles Parsons, P. Johnson, D. Ruble, and G. Zellman. 1978. *Women and Sex Roles: A Social-Psychological Perspective.* New York: Norton.

Frisbie, W. Parker, and John D. Kasarda. 1988. "Spatial Processes." Pp. 629–666 in Neil J. Smelser (ed.), *Handbook of Sociology.* Newbury Park, CA: Sage.

Froman, R. D. 1981. "Ability Grouping: Why Do We Persist and Should We?" Paper presented at annual meeting of the American Educational Research Association, Los Angeles.

Frueh, Terry, and Paul E. McGhee. 1975. "Traditional Sex-Role Development and Amount of Time Spent Watching Television." *Developmental Psychology* 11: 109.

Fuerst, J. S. 1981. "Report Card: Chicago's All-Black Public Schools." *The Public Interest* 64: 79–91.

Funk and Wagnalls. 1976. *Funk and Wagnalls Standard Desk Dictionary.* New York: Funk and Wagnalls.

Furstenberg, Frank F., Theodore Hershberg, and J. Modell. 1975. "The Origins of the Female-Headed Black Family: The Impact of the Urban Experience." *Journal of Interdisciplinary History* 6: 211–233.

Furstenberg, Frank F., S. Philip Morgan, and Pual P. Allison. 1987. "Paternal Participation and Children's Well-Beiing After Marital Dissolution." *American Sociological Review* 52: 695–701.

Fusfeld, Daniel R. 1976. *Economics,* 2nd ed. Lexington, MA: Heath.

Gabriel, Ralph. 1963. *Traditional Values in American Life.* New York: Harcourt, Brace, Jovanovich.

Gale, Dennis E. 1980. "Neighborhood Resettlement: Washington, D.C." Pp. 95–115 in Shirley B. Laska and Daphne Spain (eds.), *Back to the City: Issues in Neighborhood Renovation.* New York: Permagon.

Galliher, John F., and John R. Cross. 1983. *Morals Legislation Without Morality.* New Brunswick, NJ: Rutgers University Press.

Gallup, George. 1984. *The Gallup Poll: Public Opinion, 1983.* Wilmington, DE: Scholarly Resources.

Gallup, George, Jr. 1988. *The Gallup Poll: Public Opinion, 1987*. Wilmington, DE: Scholarly Resources.

Gallup, George, Jr. 1987. *The Gallup Poll: Public Opinion, 1987*. Wilmington, DE: Scholarly Resources, Inc.

Gallup, George, Jr. 1987. *The Gallup Poll: Public Opinion, 1986*. Wilmington, DE: Scholarly Resources.

Gallup Organization. 1987. "Confidence in Institutions." *The Gallup Report* 263: 2–11.

Gamoran, Adam. 1987. "The Stratification of High School Learning Opportunities." *Sociology of Education* 60: 135–155.

Gamson, William. 1975. *The Strategy of Political Protest*. Homewood, IL: Dorsey.

Gans, Herbert J. 1973. *More Equality*. New York: Pantheon.

Gans, Herbert J. 1972. "The Positive Functions of Poverty." *American Journal of Sociology* 78: 275–289.

Gans, Herbert J. 1972b. "Urbanism and Suburbanism as Ways of Life: A Re-Evaluation of Definitions." Pp. 184–200 in J. John Palen and Karl H. Flaming (eds.), *Urban America*. New York: Holt, Reinhart, and Winston.

Gans, Herbert J. 1971. "The Uses of Poverty: The Poor Pay All." *Social Policy* (July/August).

Gans, Herbert J. 1967. *The Levittowners*. New York: Random House.

Gans, Herbert J. 1967b. "The Negro Family: Reflections on the Moynihan Report." Pp. 445–457 in Lee Rainwater (ed.), *The Moynihan Report and the Politics of Controversy*. Cambridge, MA: MIT Press.

Gans, Herbert J. 1962. *The Urban Villagers*. New York: Free Press.

Garbarino, Merwin S. 1976. *American Indian Heritage*. Boston: Little, Brown.

Garfinkel, Harold. 1967. *Studies in Ethnomethodology*. Englewood Cliffs, NJ: Prentice Hall.

Garrett, C. S., P. [374]. Ein, and L. Tremaine. 1977. "The Development of Gender Stereotyping of Adult Occupations in Elementary School Children." *Child Development* 48: 507–512.

Geiger, H. Jack. 1975. "The Causes of Dehumanization in Health Care and Prospects for Humanization." Pp. 11–36 in J. Howard and Ansalem Strauss (eds.), *Humanizing Health Care*. New York: Wiley-Interscience.

Geis, F. L., Virginia Brown, Joyce J. Walstedt, and Natalie Porter. 1984. "TV Commercials as Achievement Scripts for Women." *Sex Roles* 10: 513–525.

Geis, Gilbert. 1974. "Upperworld Crime." Pp. 114–137 in Abraham S. Bluberg (ed.), *Current Perspectives on Criminal Behavior*. New York: Alfred A. Knopf, pp. 114–137.

Gelles, Richard J. 1983. "The Myth of Battered Husbands and New Facts about Family Violence." In O. Pocs and R. H. Walsh (eds.), *Marriage and Family 83/84*. Guilford, CT: Dushkin.

Gelles, Richard J., and Murray A. Straus. 1979. *"Violence in the American Family."* *Journal of Social Issues* 35: 15–39.

Gerlach, Luther P., and Virginia Hine. 1973. *LifeWay Leap: The Dynamics of Change in America*. Minneapolis: University of Minnesota Press.

Germani, Gino. 1981. *The Sociology of Modernization*. New Brunswick, NJ: Transaction Books.

Gerth, Hans. 1940. "The Nazi Party: Its Leadership and Composition." *American Journal of Sociology* 45: 517–541.

Geschwender, James A. 1964. "Social Structure and the Negro Revolt: An Examination of Some Hypotheses." *Social Forces* 43: 250–256.

Getis, Arthur, Judith Getis, and Jerome Fellman. 1981. *Geography*. New York: MacMillan.

Gibbs, Jack P. 1981. *Norms, Deviances, and Social Control*. New York: Elsevier.

Giddens, Anthony. 1985. *The Constitution of Societies*. London: MacMillan.

Giddens, Anthony. 1978. *Central Problems in Social Theory*. Berkeley: University of California Press.

Giele, Janet Z. 1988. "Gender and Sex Roles." Pp. 291–323 in Neil J. Smelser (ed.), *Handbook of Sociology*. Newbury Park, CA: Sage.

Gilligan, Carol. 1982. *In a Different Voice: Psychological Theory and Women's Development*. Cambridge, MA: Harvard University Press.

Gintis, Herbert. 1974. "Sociology of Economics." Unit 21 in Dushkin Publishing Group (ed.), *The Study of Society*. Guilford, CT: Dushkin Publishing Group.

Gitlin, Todd. 1987. *The Sixties: Years of Hope, Days of Rage*. New York: Bantam.

Glaab, Charles N. 1963. *The American City: A Documentary History*. Homewood, IL: Dorsey.

Glaab, Charles N., and A. Theodore Brown. 1976. *A History of Urban America*, 2nd ed. New York: MacMillan.

Glazer, Nathan. 1981. "Black English and Reluctant Judges." *The Public Interest* 62: 40–54.

Glazer, Nathan. 1976. *Affirmative Discrimination*. New York: Basic Books.

Glenn, Evelyn Makano. 1980. "Dialectics of Wage Work: Japanese-American Women and Domestic Service, 1905–1940." *Feminist Studies* 6: 432–471.

Glenn, Norvall, and C. N. Weaver. 1981. "The Contribution of Marital Happiness to Global Happiness." *Journal of Marriage and Family* 43: 161–168.

Glick, Paul. 1984. "Marriage, Divorce, and Living Arrangements: Prospective Changes." *Journal of Family Issues* 5: 7–26.

Glick, Paul C., and L. Sung-Ling. 1986. "Recent Changes in Divorce and Remarriage." *Journal of Marriage and Family* 48: 737–747.

Glock, Charles Y. and Rodney Stark. 1965. *Religion and Society in Tension*. Chicago: Rand McNally and Co.

Glueck, Sheldon, and Eleanor Glueck. 1956. *Physique and Delinquency*. New York: Harper.

Goddard, Henry. 1914. *Feeble Mindedness: Its Causes and Consequences*. New York: Macmillan.

Goffman, Erving. 1963. *Stigma: Notes on the Management of a Spoiled Identity*. Englewood Cliffs, NJ: Prentice Hall.

Goffman, Erving. 1961. *Asylums: Essays on the Social Situation of Mental Patients and Other Inmates*. Chicago: Aldine.

Goffman, Erving. 1959. *The Presentation of Self in Everyday Life*. Garden City, NY: Doubleday.

Goldberg, P. 1968. "Are Women Prejudiced against Women?" *Trans-action* 5: 32–38.

Goldberg, R. (no date). "Maternal Time-Use and Pre-School Performance." Graduate Faculty of Education, University of Pennsylvania. Cited in Susan Hodgson, "Childrearing Systems: The Influence of Shared Childrearing on the Development of Competence." Pp. 96–178 in William Michelson, Saul V. Levine, and Anna-Rose Spina (eds.), *The Child in the City: Changes and Challenges*. Toronto: University of Toronto Press.

Golden, Hilda H. 1981. *Urbanization and Cities*. Lexington, MA: D. C. Heath.

Golden, Mark, and B. Birns. 1968. "Social Class and Cognitive Development in Infancy." *Merrill-Palmer Quarterly* 14: 139–149.

Goldfarb, William. 1945. "Psychological Privation in Infancy and Subsequent Development." *American Journal of Orthopsychiatry* 15: 247–253.

Goldscheider, Calvin, and Frances K. Goldscheider. 1987. "Moving Out and Marriage: What Do Young Adults Expect?" *American Sociological Review* 52: 278–285.

Goldstein, Joshua. 1988. *Long Cycles: Prosperity and War in the Modern Age*. New Haven: Yale University Press.

Goldstone, Jack A. (ed.) 1986. *Revolutions: Theoretical, Comparative, and Historical Studies*. New York: Harcourt, Brace Jovanovich.

Goode, Erich. 1984. *Deviant Behavior,* 2nd ed. Englewood Cliffs, NJ: Prentice Hall.

Goode, Erich. 1972. "Drugs and Crime." Pp. 227–272 in Abraham Blumberg (ed.), *Current Perspectives on Criminal Behavior*. New York: Alfred A. Knopf.

Goodenough, Ward H. 1957. "Cultural Anthropology and Linguistics." In Paul Garvin (ed.), *Report of the Seventh Annual Round Table Meeting on Linguistics and Language Study*. Georgetown Monograph Series, 9. Washington, DC: Georgetown University Press.

Gordon, David. 1978. "Capitalist Development and the History of American Cities." In William Tabb and Larry Sawers (eds.), *Marxism and the Metropolis*. New York: Oxford University Press.

Gordon, David. 1977a. "Capitalism and the Roots of the Urban Crisis." Pp. 82–112 in Roger E. Alacly and David Mermelstein (eds.), *The Fiscal Crisis of American Cities*. New York: Vintage.

Gordon, David. 1977b. "Class Struggle and the Stages of American Urban Development." Pp. 55–82 in David C. Perry and Alfred J. Watkins (eds.), *The Rise of the Sunbelt Cities*. Urban Affairs Annual Reviews, vol. 14. Beverly Hills, CA: Sage.

Gordon, David. 1975. "Recession Is Capitalism As Usual." *New York Times Magazine,* April 27.

Gordon, Michael. 1978. *The American Family: Past, Present, and Future*. New York: Random House.

Gordon, Milton M. 1964. *Assimilation in American Life*. New York: Oxford University Press.

Gordon, Robert. 1976. "Prevalence: The Race Datum in Delinquency Measurement and Its Implications for the Theory of Delinquency." Pp. 201–284 in Malcohm Klein (ed.), *The Junvenile Justice System*. Beverly Hills, CA: Sage.

Goren, Arthur A. 1980. "Jews." Pp. 571–598 in Stephan Thernstrom, Ann Orlov, and Oscar Handlin (eds.), *Harvard Encyclopedia of American Ethnic Groups*. Cambridge, MA: Harvard University Press.

Goring, Charles. 1913. *The English Convict*. London: His Majesty's Stationary Office, reprinted by Patterson Smith, Montclair, NJ, 1972.

Gortmaker, Steven. 1979. "Poverty and Infant Mortality in the United States." *American Sociological Review* 44: 280–297.

Goslin, David A. 1965. *The School in Contemporary Society*. Glenview, IL: Scott, Foresman.

Gottdiener, Mark. 1985. *The Social Production of Urban Space*. Austin: University of Texas Press.

Gottfried, Robert S. 1983. *The Black Death: Natural and Human Disaster in Medieval Europe*. New York: Free Press.

Gould, Stephen Jay. 1981. *The Mismeasure of Man*. New York: W. W. Norton and Company.

Gouldner, Alvin W. 1979. *The Future of Intellectuals and the Rise of the New Class*. New York: Seabury.

Gouldner, Alvin W. 1976. *The Dialectic of Ideology and Technology: The Origins, Future, and Grammar of Ideology*. New York: Seabury.

Gouldner, Alvin W. 1968. "The Sociologist As Partisan: Sociology and the Welfare State." *American Sociologist* 3, 2: 103–116.

Gouldner, Helen, with Mary Symons Strong. 1978. *Teachers' Pets, Troublemakers, and Nobodies*. Westport, CT: Greenwood Press.

Gove, Walter R. 1985. "The Effect of Age and Gender on Deviant Behavior: A Biopsychological Perspective." Pp. 115–144 in Alice S. Rossi (ed.), *Gender and the Life Course*. Hawthorne, NY: Aldine.

Gove, Walter R., Michael Hughes, and Omer R. Galle. 1979. "Overcrowding in the Home: An Investigation of Its Possible Consequences." *American Sociological Review* 44: 59–80.

Gover, Robert. 1981. *One Hundred Dollar Misunderstanding*. New York: Grove.

Gowlett, John. 1984. *Ascent to Civilization*. New York: Knopf.

Graham, James M. 1972. "Amphetamine Politics on Capital Hill." *Society,* 9, 3: 14–23.

Granovetter, Mark. 1986. "The Micro-Structure of School Desegregation." Pp. 81–100 in Jeffrey Prager, Douglas Longshore, and Melvin Seeman (eds.), *School Desegregation Research: New Directions in Situational Analysis*. New York: Plenum.

Greeley, Andrew. 1977. *The American Catholic: A Social Portrait*. New York: Basic Books.

Greeley, Andrew M. 1982. *Catholic High Schools and Minority Students*. New Brunswick, NJ: Transaction Books.

Greeley, Andrew M. 1981. "Minority Students in Catholic Secondary Schools." Paper presented at conference on "High School and Beyond," National Center for Educational Statistics, Washington, DC.

Greeley, Andrew M. 1972. *The Denominational Society*. Glenview, IL: Foresman and Company.

Grier, George, and Eunice Grier. 1980. "Urban Displacement: A Reconnaissance." Pp. 252–268 in Shirley B. Laska and Daphne Spain (eds.), *Back to the City: Issues in Neighborhood Renovation*. New York: Permagon.

Grinder, Robert E. 1978. *Adolescence,* 2nd ed. New York: John Wiley.

Gronval, Karin. 1984. "The Physical and Psychological Environment of Children in Sweden." *Current Sweden* 33.

Grossman, Michael. 1982. "Government and Health Outcomes." *American Economic Review* 72, 2: 191–195.

Grusky, David B., and Robert M. Hauser. 1984. "Comparative Social Mobility Revisited: Models of Convergence and Divergence in 16 Countries." *American Sociological Review* 49: 19–38.

Guellemin, Jeane. 1978. "The Politics of National Integration: A Comparison of United States and Canadian Indian Administrations." *Social Problems* 25: 319–332.

Gugler, Joseph. 1982. "Overurbanization Reconsidered." *Economic Development and Cultural Change* 31: 173–189.

Guinsberg, Suzanne. 1983. "Education's Earning Power." *Psychology Today* 1, 7: 20–21.

Gundlach, James H., and Steven J. Stack. 1988. "The Impact of Hyper Media Coverage of Suicide: New York City, 1910–1920." Paper presented at annual meeting of the American Sociological Association, Atlanta, August.

Gurney, Joan N., and Kathleen T. Tierney. 1982. "Relative Deprivation and Social Movements: A Critical Look at Twenty Years of Theory and Research." *Sociological Quarterly* 23: 33–47.

Gusfield, Joseph R. 1986. *Symbolism Crusade,* 2nd ed. Urbans and Chicago: University of Illinois Press.

Gutman, Amy. 1987. *Democratic Education.* Princeton, NJ: Princeton University Press.

Gutman, Herbert. 1976. *The Black Family in Slavery and Freedom, 1750–1925.* New York: Pantheon.

Guzzardi, Walter. 1988. "Can Big Still Be Beautiful?" *Fortune* 117: 50–64.

Gwartney-Gibbs, Patricia A. 1986. "The Institutionalization of Premarital Cohabitation: Estimates from Marriage License Applications, 1970 and 1980." *Journal of Marriage and Family* 48: 423–434.

Haan, N., M. B. Smith, and J. Block. 1968. "Moral Reasoning of Young Adults: Political-Social Behavior, Family Background, and Personality Correlates." *Journal of Personality and Social Psychology* 10: 183–201.

Hacker, Sally L. 1979. "Sex Stratification, Technology, and Organizational Change: A Longitudinal Case Study of AT&T." *Social Problems* 26: 539–557.

Hadden, Jeffrey K., and Charles E. Swann. 1981. *Prime Time Preachers.* Reading, MA: Addison-Wesley.

Haertel, Edward H. 1987. "Comparing Public and Private Schools Using Longitudinal Data from the HSB Study." Pp. 9–32 in Edward H. Haertel, Thomas James, and Henry M. Levin (eds.), *Comparing Public and Private Schools,* vol. 2: Student Achievement. New York: Falmer.

Hagan, Frank E. 1986. *Introduction to Criminology.* Chicago: Nelson-Hall.

Hagan, John, John Simpson, and A. R. Gillis. 1987. "Class in the Household: A Power-Control Theory of Gender and Delinquency." *American Journal of Sociology* 92: 788–816.

Hajnal, John. 1965. "European Marriage Patterns in Perspective." In D. V. Glass and D. E. C. Eversly (eds.), *Population in History.* London: Edward Arnold.

Hall, Edward T. 1966. *The Hidden Dimension.* Garden City, NY: Doubleday.

Hall, John R. 1987. *Gone From the Promised Land: Jonestown in American Cultural History.* New Brunswick, NJ: Transaction Books.

Hall, John R. 1979. "Apocalypse at Jonestown." *Society* 16: 52–61.

Hall, Richard H. 1987. *Organizations: Structures, Processes and Outcomes,* 4th ed. Englewood Cliffs, NJ: Prentice Hall.

Hall, Richard H. 1963–64. "The Concept of Bureaucracy: An Empirical Assessment." *American Journal of Sociology* 69: 32–40.

Hall, Thomas D. 1989. *Social Change in the Southwest, 1350–1880.* Lawrence, KS: University Press of Kansas.

Haller, Emil J., and Sharon A. Davis. 1980. "Does Socioeconomic Status Bias the Assignment of Elementary School Students to Reading Groups?" *American Educational Research Journal* 17: 409–418.

Hallinen, M., and Aage B. Sorensen. 1985. "Ability Grouping and Student Friendships." *American Educational Research Journal* 22: 485–499.

Hallouda, A. S. Amin, and S. Farid. 1983. *The Egyptian Fertility Survey 1980,* Vol. 2, Fertility and Family Planning. Cairo: Central Agency for Public Mobilization and Statistics.

Hamblin, Dora Jane. 1973. *The First Cities.* New York: Time-Life.

Hamilton, C. Horace. 1965. "Continuity and Change in Southern Migration." Pp. 53–78 in John C. McKinney and Edgar T. Thompson (eds.), *The South in Continuity and Change.* Durham, NC: Duke University.

Hammond, Phillip E. 1985. *The Sacred in a Secular Age: Toward Revision in the Scientific Study of Religion.* Berkeley: University of California Press.

Handel, Warren. 1982. *Ethnomethodology: How People Make Sense.* Englewood Cliffs, NJ: Prentice Hall.

Handel, Warren. 1979. "Normative Expectations and the Emergence of Meaning As Solutions to Problems: Convergence of Structural and Interactionist Views." *American Journal of Sociology* 84: 855–881.

Handlin, Oscar, and Mary F. Handlin. 1950. "Origins of the Southern Labor System." *William and Mary Quarterly* 7: 199–222.

Hanson, R. A. 1975. "Consistency and Stability of Home Environment Measures Related to IQ." *Child Development* 46: 470–480.

Hare, A. Paul. 1976. *Handbook of Small Group Research,* 2nd ed. New York: Free Press.

Hargrove, Barbara. 1979. *The Sociology of Religion: Classical and Contemporary Approaches.* Arlington Heights, IL: AHM Publishing Corporation.

Harlow, Harry F. 1958. "The Nature of Love." *American Psychologist* 13: 673–685.

Harlow, Harry F., and Margaret Kuenne Harlow. 1970. "The Young Monkeys." In P. Cramer (ed.), *Readings in Developmental Psychology Today.* Del Mar, CA: CRM Books.

Harlow, Harry F., and Margaret Kuenne Harlow. 1962. "Social Deprivation in Monkeys." *Scientific American* 207, 5: 137–146.

Harlow, Harry F., and R. R. Zimmerman. 1959. "Affectional Responses in the Infant Monkey." *Science* 130: 421–423.

Harnischfeger, A., and D. E. Wiley. 1980. "A Merit Assessment of Vocational Education Programs in Secondary Schools." Statement to the Subcommittee on Elementary, Secondary, and Vocational Education of the Committee on Education, U.S. House of Representatives, September.

Harrington, Michael. 1984. *The New American Poverty.* New York: Holt, Rinehart, and Winston.

Harrington, Michael. 1979. "The New Class and the Left." Pp. 123–138 in B. Bruce-Briggs (ed.), *The New Class?.* New Brunswick, NJ: Transaction Books.

Harris, Chauncy D., and Edward L. Ullman. 1945. "The Nature of Cities." *The Annals of the American Academy of Political and Social Science* 242: 7–17.

Harris, Daniel M., and Sharon Guten. 1979. "Health-Protective Behavior: An Exploratory Study." *Journal of Health and Social Behavior* 20: 17–29.

Harris, Marvin. 1980. *Cultural Materialism: The Struggle for a Science of Culture.* New York: Vintage.

Harrison, Bennett, and Sandra Kantner. 1978. "The Political Economy of States' Job Creation Efforts." *Journal of the American Institute of Planners* 44: 424–435.

Harry, Joseph. 1984. *Gay Couples.* New York: Praeger.

Hartley, Ruth E. 1974. "Sex-Role Pressures and the Socialization of the Male Child." Pp. 185–198 in Judith Stacey, Susan Bereaud, and Joan Daniels (eds.), *And Jill Came Tumbling After: Sexism in American Education.* New York: Dell. (Reprinted from *Psychological Reports* 5 (1959).

Hartley, Ruth E. 1970. "American Core Culture: Changes and Continuities." In Georgene H. Seward and Robert C. Williamson (eds.), *Sex Roles in a Changing Society.* New York: Random House.

Hartmann, Heidi I., Patricia A. Roos, and Donald J. Treiman. 1985. "An Agenda for Basic Research in Comparable Worth." Pp. 3–33 in

Heidi I. Hartmann (ed.), *Comparable Worth: New Directions for Research.* Washington: National Academy Press.

Hartz, Louis. 1955. *The Liberal Tradition in America: An Interpretation of American Political Thought since the Revolution.* New York: Harcourt, Brace.

Harvey, Dak G., and Gerald T. Slatin. 1975. "The Relationship As Hypothesis." *Social Forces* 54: 140–159.

Harvey, David. 1973. *Social Justice and the City.* Baltimore: Johns Hopkins University Press.

Haskell, Martin R., and Louis Yablonsky. 1978. *Crime and Delinquency,* 3rd ed. Chicago: Rand McNally College Publishing Company.

Haug, Marie, and Bebe Lavin. 1983. *Consumerism in Medicine.* Beverly Hills, CA: Sage.

Haug, Marie, and Bebe Lavin. 1981. "Practitioner or Patient: Who's in Charge?" *Journal of Health and Social Behavior* 22: 212–229.

Hauser, Robert M., William H. Sewell, and Duane F. Alwin. 1976. "High School Effects on Achievement." Pp. 309–341 in William H. Sewell, Robert M. Hauser, and David L. Featherman (eds.), *Schooling and Achievement in American Society.* New York: Academic Press.

Hauser, Robert M., and David B. Grusky. 1988. "Cross-National Variation in Occupational Distributions, Relative Mobility Chances, and Intergenerational Shifts in Occupational Distributions." *American Sociological Review* 53: 723–741.

Hawley, Amos. 1981. *Urban Society,* 2nd ed. New York: Random House.

Hayes, C. D. (ed.) 1987. *Risking the Future: Adolescent Sexuality, Pregnancy, and Childbearing.* Report of the Panel on Adolescent Pregnancy and Childbearing, National Research Council, vol. 1. Washington, DC: National Academy Press.

Hecksher, Charles. 1980. "Worker Participation and Management Control." *Journal of Social Reconstruction* (January—March).

Heider, Fritz. 1958. *The Psychology of Interpersonal Relations.* New York: John Wiley and Sons.

Heider, Fritz. 1946. "Attitudes and Cognitive Organization." *Journal of Psychology* 21: 107–112.

Heilbroner, Robert L. 1982. *Beyond Boom and Crash.* New York: W. W. Norton.

Helsing, K. J., and M. Szklo. 1981. "Mortality after Bereavement." *American Journal of Epidemiology* 114, 1: 4–52.

Henslin, James M. 1975. *Introducing Sociology.* New York: The Free Press.

Hermalin, Albert I., and Reynolds Farley. 1973. "The Potential for Residential Integration in Cities and Suburbs: Implications for the School Busing Controversy." *American Sociological Review* 38: 595–610.

Heskiaoff, Heskia. 1977. "Computers and Productivity in Production and Administrative Functions in Manufacturing Industries in the United States." Ph. D. dissertation, Columbia University.

Hess, Beth B. 1985. "America's Elderly: A Demographic Overview." Pp. 3–21 in Beth B. Hess and Elizabeth Markson (eds.), *Growing Old in America: New Perspectives on Old Age.* New Brunswick, NJ: Transaction Books.

Higgins, G. M., et al. 1982. *Potential Population-Supporting Capacities of Lands in the Developing World,* Technical Report of Land Resources for Population of the Future Project. Rome: United Nations Food and Agriculture Organization.

Hill, Martha S., and James N. Morgan. 1979. "Dimensions of Occupation." Pp. 293–334 in Greg J. Duncan and James N. Morgan (eds.), *Five Thousand American Families: Patterns of Economic Progress.* Ann Arbor: Institute for Social Research, University of Michigan.

Hill, Robert B. 1978. *The Illusion of Progress.* Washington: National Urban League.

Himmelstrand, Ulf, Goran Akrne, Leif Lundberg, and Lar Lundberg. 1981. *Beyond Welfare Capitalism: Issues, Actors, and Forces in Societal Change.* London: William Heinemann.

Hite, Shere. 1987. *Women and Love: A Cultural Revolution in Progress.* New York: Alfred A. Knopf.

Hochschild, Arlie. 1987. *The Second Shift: Working Parents and the Revolution at Home.* New York: Viking Penguin.

Hodge, Robert W., Paul M. Siegel, and Peter H. Rossi. 1964. "Occupational Prestige in the United States, 1925–1963." *American Journal of Sociology* 70: 286–302.

Hodge, Robert W., and Donald J. Treiman. 1968. "Class Identification in the United States." *American Journal of Sociology* 73: 286–302.

Hodge, Robert W., Donald J. Treiman, and Peter H. Rossi. 1966. "A Comparative Study of Occupational Prestige." Pp. 309–321 in Reinhard Bendix and Seymour Martin Lipset (eds.), *Class, Status, and Power: Social Stratification in Comparative Perspective,* 2nd ed. New York: Free Press.

Hodge, Robert, and David Tripp. 1986. *Children and Television: A Semiotic Approach.* Stanford, CA: Stanford University Press.

Hodgkinson, Harold L. 1986. "Reform? Higher Education? Don't be Absurd!" *Phi Delta Kappan* 68: 271–274.

Hodgson, Susana. 1979. "Childrearing Systems: The Influence of Shared Childrearing on the Development of Competence." Pp. 96–178 in William Michelson, Saul V. Levine, and Anna-Rose Spina (eds.), *The Child in the City: Changes and Challenges.* Toronto: University of Toronto Press.

Hoffer, Thomas, Andrew M. Greeley, and James S. Coleman. 1987. "Catholic High School Effects on Achievement Growth." Pp. 67–88 in Edward H. Haertel, Thomas James, and Henry M. Levin (eds.), *Comparing Public and Private Schools.* Volume 2: Student Achievement. New York: Falmer.

Hoffer, Thomas, Andrew M. Greeley, and James S. Coleman. 1985. "Achievement Growth in Public and Catholic Schools." *Sociology of Education* 58: 74–97.

Hoffman, Laurie. 1982. "Empirical Findings Concerning Sexism in Our Schools." *Corrective and Social Psychology and Journal of Behavior Technology, Methodology, and Therapy* 28, 3: 100–108.

Holden, Constance. 1987. "Is the Time Ripe For Welfare Reform?" *Science* 238: 607–609.

Hollingshead, August B. 1949. *Elmtown's Youth.* New York: John Wiley.

Hollingsworth, J. Rogers. 1981. "Inequality in Levels of Health in England and Wales, 1891–1971." *Journal of Health and Social Behavior* 22: 268–283.

Homans, George. 1984. *Coming to My Senses.* New Brunswick, NJ: Transaction.

Homans, George C. 1961. *Social Behavior: The Elementary Forms.* New York: Harcourt, Brace, Jovanovich.

Homans, George C. 1950. *The Human Group.* New York: Harcourt, Brace, Jovanovich.

Hooton, Ernest A. 1939. *The American Criminal: An Anthropological Study,* Cambridge, MA: Harvard.

Hout, Michael. 1988. "More Universalism, Less Structural Mobility: The

American Occupational Structure in the 1980s." *American Journal of Sociology* 93: 1358–1400.

Hout, Michael, and Andrew Greeley. 1987. "The Center Doesn't Hold: Church Attendance in the United States, 1940–1984." *American Sociological Review* 52: 325–345.

Howard, Michael C., and Patrick C. McKim. 1983. *Contemporary Cultural Anthropology.* Boston: Little, Brown.

Hoyenga, Katherine Blick, and Kermit T. Hoyenga. 1979. *The Question of Sex Differences: Psychological, Cultural, and Biological Issues.* Boston: Little, Brown.

Hoyt, Homer. 1939. *The Structure and Growth of Residential Neighborhoods in American Cities.* Washington: Federal Housing Administration.

Huber, Joan, and Glenna Spitze. 1988. "Trends in Family Sociology." Pp. 425–448 in Neil Smelser (ed.), *Handbook of Sociology.* Newbury Park, CA: Sage.

Humphreys, Laud. 1970. *Tearoom Trade: Impersonal Sex in Public Places.* Chicago: Aldine.

Hunt, Albert R. 1987. "The Media and Presidential Campaigns." Pp. 52–74 in A. James Reichley (ed.), *Elections American Style.* Washington, D.C.: The Brookings Institute.

Hunt, Chester, and Lewis Walker. 1974. *Ethnic Dynamics: Patterns of Intergroup Relations in Various Societies.* Homewood, IL: Dorsey.

Hunt, Morton. 1974. *Sexual Behavior in the 1970s.* New York: Dell.

Hunter, Alfred A. 1988. "Formal Education and Initial Employment: Unraveling the Relationships between Schooling and Skills over Time." *American Sociological Review* 53: 753–765.

Hunter, Floyd. 1980. *Community Power Succession: Atlanta's Policy Makers Revisited.* Chapel Hill: University of North Carolina Press.

Hunter, Floyd. 1955. *Community Power Structure.* Chapel Hill: University of North Carolina Press.

Hurn, Christopher. 1978. *The Limits and Possibilities of Schooling: An Introduction to the Sociology of Education.* Boston: Allyn and Bacon.

Huston, A. 1983. "Sex-Typing." In E. M. Hetherington (ed.), *Socialization, Personality, and Social Development.* New York: Wiley.

Hyman, Herbert H. 1983. *Of Time and Widowhood: Nationwide Studies of Enduring Effects.* Durham, NC: Duke University Press.

Hyman, Herbert, and Charles Wright. 1979. *Education's Lasting Influence on Values.* Chicago: University of Chicago Press.

Hyman, Herbert, Charles Wright, and John Shelton Reed. 1975. *The Enduring Effects of Education.* Chicago: University of Chicago Press.

Iannoccone, Lawrence R. 1988. "A Formal Model of Church and Sect." *American Journal of Sociology* 94: S241–S268.

Ichihashi, Yamato. 1969. *Japanese in the United States.* New York: Arno Press and the *New York Times* (originally published by Stanford University Press in 1932).

Ickes, William J., and Richard D. Barnes. 1978. "Boys and Girls Together—and Alienated: On Enacting Stereotyped Sex Roles in Mixed-Sex Dyads." *Journal of Personality and Social Psychology* 36: 669–683.

Illich, Ivan. 1976. *Medical Nemesis.* New York: Pantheon.

Illinois Capital Development Board. 1977. *The East St. Louis Area: An Overview of State Capital Projects and Policies.* Springfield: Illinois Capital Development Board.

Insko, Chester A., and W. H. Melson. 1969. "Verbal Reinforcement of Attitude in Laboratory and Nonlaboratory Contexts." *Journal of Personality* 37: 25–40.

Institute for Social Research. 1983. *The Impact of OBRA Policies on Welfare Women and their Children, 1981–82.* Ann Arbor: Institute for Social Research, The University of Michigan.

Irwin, John. 1977. *Scenes.* Beverly Hills, CA: Sage.

Ishikawa, Kaoru. 1984. "Quality Control in Japan." Pp. 1–5 in Naoto Sasaki and David Hutchins (eds.), *The Japanese Approach to Product Quality: Its Applicability to the West.* Oxford: Permagon Press.

Issel, William. 1985. *Social Change in the United States, 1945–1983.* New York: Schocken Books.

Jackson, Phillip W. 1968. *Life in Classrooms.* New York: Holt, Rinehart, and Winston.

Jacobs, P. A., M. Brunton, and M. M. Melville. 1965. "Aggressive Behavior, Mental Subnormality, and the XYY Male." *Nature* 208 (December): 1351–1352.

Jakubs, John F. 1986. "Recent Racial Segregation in U.S. SMSAs." *Urban Geography* 7: 146–163.

Jaret, Charles. 1983. "Recent Neo-Marxist Urban Analysis." Pp. 499–525 in Ralph H. Turner and James F. Short, Jr. (eds.), *Annual Review of Sociology,* Vol. 9. Palo Alto, CA: Annual Reviews.

Jencks, Christopher, Marshall Smith, Henry Ackland, Mary Jo Bane, David Cohen, Herbert Gintis, Barbara Heyns, and Stephan Michelson. 1972. *Inequality: A Reassessment of the Effect of Family and Schooling in America.* New York: Basic Books.

Jenkins, Brian M. 1987. "Will Terrorists Go Nuclear?" Pp. 350–357 in Walter Laqueur and Yonah Alexander (eds.), *The Terrorism Reader,* rev. ed. New York: NAL Penguin.

Jenkins, Brian M. 1982. "Statements About Terrorism." *The Annals of the American Academy of Political and Social Science* 463: 11–19.

Jenkins, Brian M. 1980. "The Study of Terrorism: Definitional Problems." *Rand Paper Series,* No. P-6563.

Jenkins, J. Craig, and Craig M. Eckert. 1986. "Channeling Black Insurgency: Elite Patronage and Professional Social Movement Organizations in the Development of the Black Movement." *American Sociological Review* 51: 812–829.

Jenkins, J. Craig, and Charles Perrow. 1977. "Insurgency of the Powerless: Farm Workers' Movements (1946–1972)." *American Sociological Review* 42: 249–268.

Jiobu, Robert. 1988. "Ethnic Hegemony and the Japanese of California." *American Sociological Review* 53: 353–367.

Johansen, Elaine. 1984. *Comparable Worth: The Myth and the Movement.* Boulder, CO: Westview Press.

Johnson, Benton. 1963. "On Church and Sect." American Sociological Review 28: 539–549.

Johnson, J., and T. Davidson. 1981. *The Persistence of Effects: A Supplement to An Evaluation of "Freestyle": A Television Series to Reduce Sex Role Stereotypes.* Ann Arbor: Institute for Social Research, University of Michigan.

Johnson, J., J. Ettema, and T. Davidson. 1980. *An Evaluation of "Freestyle": A Television Series to Reduce Sex Role Stereotypes.* Ann Arbor: Institute for Social Research, University of Michigan.

Johnson, James A., Harold W. Collins, Victor L. Dupuis, and John H. Johansen. 1982. *Introduction to the Foundations of American Education.* Boston: Allyn and Bacon.

Johnstone, Ronald L. 1988. *Religion in Society: A Sociology of Religion,* 3rd ed. Englewood Cliffs, NJ: Prentice Hall.

Jones, Elise F., Jacqueline Darroch Forrest, Noreen Goldman, Stanley Henshaw, Richard Lincoln, Jeannie I. Rosoff, Charles F. Westoff, and Deirdre Wulf. 1986. *Teenage Pregnancy in Industrialized Countries: A Study Sponsored by the Alan Guttmacher Institute.* New Haven: Yale University Press.

Jones, Jaqueline. 1985. *Labor of Love, Labor of Sorrow: Black Women, Work, and the Family From Slavery to the Present.* New York: Basic.

Jordan, Winthrop D. 1968. *White Over Black.* Chapel Hill: University of North Carolina Press.

Josephy, Alvin M., Jr. 1968. *The Indian Heritage of America.* New York: Alfred A. Knopf.

Kain, John F. 1987. "Housing Market Discrimination and Black Suburbanization in the 1980s." Pp. 68–94 in Gary A. Tobin (ed.), *Divided Neighborhoods: Changing Patterns of Racial Segregation,* Urban Affairs Annual Reviews, Vol. 32. Newbury Park, CA: Sage.

Kalisch, P. A., and B. J. Kalisch. 1984. "Sex Role Stereotyping of Nurses and Physicians on Prime-Time Television: A Dichotomy of Occupational Portrayals." *Sex Roles* 10: 533–553.

Kalish, R. A., and D. K. Reynolds. 1976. *Death and Ethnicity: A Psychocultural Study.* Los Angeles: University of Southern California Press.

Kanter, Rosabeth Moss. 1979. "Communes in Cities." In J. Case and R. Taylor (eds.), *Co-ops, Communes, and Collectives.* New York: Pantheon.

Kanter, Rosabeth Moss. 1977. *Men and Women of the Corporation.* New York: Basic Books.

Kanter, Rosabeth Moss. 1972. *Commitment and Community: Communes and Utopias in Sociological Perspective.* Cambridge, MA: Harvard University Press.

Kantrowitz, B. 1986. "A Mother's Choice." *Newsweek,* pp. 46–51.

Karatsu, Hajime. 1984. "Quality Control: The Japanese Approach." Pp. 9–14 in Naoto Sasaki and David Hutchins (eds.), *The Japanese Approach to Product Quality: Its Applicability to the West.* Oxford: Pergamon Press.

Karnow, Stanley. 1983. *Vietnam: A History.* New York: Viking Press.

Kart, Cary S. 1976. "Some Biological Aspects of Aging." Pp. 179–183 in Cary S. Kart and Barbara Manard (eds.), *Aging in America: Readings in Social Gerontology.* Port Washington, NY: Alfred.

Kasarda, John. 1989. "Urban Industrial Transition and the Underclass." *The Annals of the American Academy of Political and Social Science* 501: 26–47.

Kasarda, John D. 1985. "Urban Change and Minority Opportunities." In P. E. Peterson (ed.), *The New Urban Reality.* Washington, D.C.: Brookings Institution.

Kasarda, John D. 1980. "The Implication of Contemporary Redistribution Trends for National Policy." *Social Science Quarterly* 61: 373–400.

Kasper, Judith A., Daniel C. Walden, and Gail Wilensky. 1980. *NCHSR National Health Care Expenditures Study.* "Data Preview 1: Who Are the Uninsured?" Hyattsville, MD: National Center for Health Services Research.

Kelly, Dean. 1977. *Why Conservative Churches Are Growing.* rev. ed. New York: Harper & Row, Publishers.

Kelly, Dean. 1972. *Why Conservative Churches Are Growing.* New York: Harper & Row.

Kennedy, Paul. 1988. *The Rise and Fall of the Great Powers: Economic Change and Military Conflict from 1500–2000.* New York: Random House.

Kenney, Martin. 1987. *Biotechnology: The University-Industrial Complex.* New Haven, CT: Yale University Press.

Kenniston, Kenneth. 1970. *Youth and Dissent: The Rise of a New Opposition.* New York: Harcourt, Brace, Jovanovich.

Kenyon, Kathleen. 1970. *Archaeology in the Holy Land.* New York: Praeger.

Kerbo, Harold R. 1983. *Social Stratification and Inequality: Class Conflict in the United States.* New York: McGraw-Hill.

Kessler, Ronald, and Horst Stipp. 1984. "The Impact of Fictional Television Suicide Stories on U. S. Fatalities: A Replication." *American Journal of Sociology* 90: 151–167.

Key, Mary Ritchie. 1975. "The Roles of Males and Females in Children's Books: Dispelling All Doubt." Pp. 56–70 in Rhoda Kesler Unger and Florence L. Denmark (eds.), *Woman Dependent or Independent Variable?* New York: Psychological Dimensions.

Keyes, R. 1980. *The Height of Your Life.* Boston: Little, Brown.

Kieschnick, Michael. 1981. *Taxes and Growth: Business Incentives and Economic Development.* Washington, DC: Council of State Planning Agencies.

Killian, Lewis M. 1984. "Organization, Rationality, and Spontaneity in the Civil Rights Movement." *American Sociological Review* 49: 770–783.

Kinder, D. R., and D. O. Sears. 1981. "Symbolic Racism versus Racial Threats to the Good Life." *Journal of Personality and Social Psychology* 40: 414–431.

Kingston, Paul William, and Steven L. Nock. 1987. "Time Together Among Dual-Earner Couples." *American Sociological Review* 52: 391–400.

Kinloch, Graham C. 1983. "Undergraduate Sociology Majors and the Job Market." *The Southern Sociologist* 14: 20–21.

Kinsey, Alfred C., Wardell B. Pomeroy, and Clyde E. Martin. 1949. *Sexual Behavior in the Human Male.* Philadelphia: Saunders.

Kinsey, Alfred C., et al. 1948. *Sexual Behavior in the Human Male.* Philadelphia: W. B. Saunders.

Kinsey, Alfred C., et al. 1953. *Sexual Behavior in the Human Female.* Philadelphia: W. B. Saunders.

Kirkland, M. C. 1971. "The Effects of Tests on Students and Schools." *Review of Educational Research* 41: 303–350.

Kitano, Harry H. L. 1985. *Race Relations,* 3rd ed. Englewood Cliffs, NJ: Prentice Hall.

Kitsuse, John I. 1978. "Societal Reaction to Deviant Behavior," Pp. 15–24 in Earl Rubington and Martin S. Weinberg (eds.), *Deviance,* 3rd ed, New York: Macmillan.

Klemesrud, Judy. 1981. "The Voice of Authority Is Still Male." *New York Times,* February 2, p. 16.

Kloss, Robert Marsh, Ron E. Boberts, and Dean S. Dorn. 1976. *Sociology with a Human Face.* St. Louis: C. V. Mosby.

Klott, Gary. 1988. "Tax Watch: Some Surprises for the Affluent." *New York Times,* April 25, Section D, p. 2.

Kluegel, James R., and Eliot R. Smith. 1986. *Beliefs About Inequality: Americans' Views of What Is and What Ought to Be.* Hawthorne, NY: Aldine de Gruyter.

Kluegel, James R., and Eliot R. Smith. 1982. "Whites' Beliefs About Blacks' Opportunity." *American Sociological Review* 47: 518–532.

Knocke, D. 1981. "Power Structures." Pp. 275–332 in S. Long (ed.), *Handbook of Political Behavior.* New York: Plenum.

Kohlberg, Lawrence. 1986. "A Current Statement on Some Theoretical Issues." Pp. 485–546 in Sohan Modgil and Celia Modgil (eds.), *Lawrence Kohlberg: Consensus and Controversey.* Philadelphia: Falmer Press, Taylor and Francis.

Kohlberg, Lawrence. 1984. *The Psychology of Moral Development: Moral Stages and the Life Cycle,* Volume 2. San Francisco: Harper and Row.

Kohlberg, Lawrence. 1981. *The Philosophy of Moral Development: Moral Stages and the Idea of Justice,* Volume 1. San Francisco: Harper and Row.

Kohlberg, Lawrence. 1975. "Moral Education for a Society in Moral Transition." *Educational Leadership* 33: 46–54.

Kohlberg, Lawrence. 1969. "Stage and Sequence: The Cognitive-Developmental Approach to Socialization." Pp. 347–380 in D. A. Goslin (ed.), *Handbook of Socialization: Theory and Research.* Chicago: Rand McNally.

Kohn, Melvin L. 1969. *Class and Conformity.* Homewood, IL: Dorsey.

Kolbe, R., and J. C. LaVoie. 1981. "Sex Role Stereotyping in Pre-School Children's Picture Books." *Social Psychology Quarterly* 44: 369–374.

Kollock, Peter, Philip Blumstein, and Pepper Schwartz. 1985. "Sex and Power in Interaction: Conversational Privileges and Duties." *American Sociological Review* 50: 34–46.

Koos, Earl. 1954. *The Health of Regionville.* New York: Columbia University Press.

Kornburg, W. 1975. "A Pre-Columbian Metropolis." *Mosaic* (Sept.—Oct.): 26–33.

Kornhauser, William. 1959. *The Politics of Mass Society.* Glencoe, IL: The Free Press.

Kouvetaris, George A., and Betty A. Dobratz. 1982. "Political Power and Conventional Political Participation." Pp. 289–317 in Ralph H. Turner and James F. Short, Jr., (eds.), *Annual Review of Sociology,* vol. 8. Palo Alto, CA: Annual Reviews.

Kozol, Harry L., Richard J. Boucher, and Ralph T. Garofalo. 1972. "The Diagnosis and Treatment of Dangerousness." *Crime and Delinquency* 18: 371–392.

Kozol, Jonathan. 1986. *Illiterate America.* New York: Anchor-Doubleday.

Krichbaum, Daniel H. 1973. "Masculinity and Racism—Breaking Out of the Illusion." *The Christian Century,* January 10.

Krisberg, Barry, Ira Schwartz, Gideon Fishman, Zvi Eisikovits, Edna Guttman, and Karen Joe. 1987. "The Incarceration of Minority Youth." *Crime and Delinquency.* 33, 2.

Kristol, Irving. 1978. *Two Cheers for Capitalism.* New York: Basic Books.

Krol, R. A. 1978. "A Meta Analysis of Comparative Research on the Effects of Desegregation on Academic Achievement." Ph. D. dissertation, Western Michigan University. *Dissertation Abstracts International* 39: 6011A.

Kubler-Ross, Elizabeth. 1981. *Living With Death and Dying.* New York: MacMillan.

Kubler-Ross, Elizabeth. 1969. *On Death and Dying.* New York: MacMillan.

Kuhn, Thomas. 1962. *The Structure of Scientific Revolutions.* Chicago: University of Chicago Press.

Kutnick, Peter. 1986. "The Relationship of Moral Judgement and Moral Action: Kohlberg's Theory, Criticism, and Revision." Pp. 125–148 in Sohan Modgil and Celia Modgil (eds.), *Lawrence Kohlberg: Consensus and Controversy.* Philadelphia: Falmer Press, Taylor and Francis.

Kuykendall, Jack L. 1970. "Police and Minority Groups: A Theory of Negative Contact." *Police* 15: 47–56.

LaFrance, Marianne, and Barbara Carmen. 1980. "The Nonverbal Display of Psychological Androgyny." *Journal of Personality and Social Psychology* 38: 36–49.

Lake, Robert. 1981. *The New Suburbanites: Race and Housing in the Suburbs.* New Brunswick, NJ: Center for Urban Policy Research, Rutgers University.

Lamb, H. H. 1982. *Climate History and the Modern World.* London: Methuen.

Lamke, Leanne. 1982. "The Impact of Sex-Role Orientation on Self-Esteem in Early Adolescence." *Child Development* 53: 1530–1535.

Lamm, Helmut, and C. Sauer. 1974. "Discussion-Induced Shift Toward Higher Demands in Negotiation." *European Journal of Social Psychology*

Lammermeier, P. J. 1973. "The Urban Black Family in the Nineteenth Century: A Study of Black Family Structure in the Ohio Valley, 1850–1880." *Journal of Marriage and the Family* 35: 440–456.

Lampman, Robert J. 1962. *The Share of Top Wealth-Holders in National Wealth: 1922–1956.* Princeton, NJ: Princeton University Press.

Landes, David S. 1969. *The Unbound Prometheus.* Cambridge: Cambridge University Press.

Lane, David. 1982. *The End of Social Inequality: Class, Status, and Power Under State Socialism.* Winchester, MA: Allen and Unwin.

Lane, David. 1979. *The Socialist Industrial State: Toward a Political Sociology of State Socialism.* London: Allen and Unwin.

Lane, Hana Umlauf (ed.). 1983. *The 1984 World Almanac and Book of Facts.* New York: Newspaper Enterprise Association.

Lang, Kurt. 1972. *Military Institutions and the Sociology of War: A Review of the Literature with Annotated Bibliography.* Beverly Hills, CA: Sage Publications.

Langer, William L. 1973. "The Black Death." Pp. 106–111 in *Scientific American's Cities: Their Origin, Growth, and Human Impact.* San Francisco: W. H. Freeman.

Laqueur, Walter. 1987. "Reflections on Terrorism." Pp. 378–392 in Walter Laqueur and Yonah Alexander (eds.), *The Terrorism Reader,* rev. ed. New York: NAL Penguin.

Larkins, G. A., and S. E. Oldham. 1976. "Patterns of Racial Segregation in a Desegregated High School." *Theory and Research in Social Education* 4, 2: 23–28.

Lasch, C. 1977. *Haven in a Heartless World: The Family Beseiged.* New York: Basic Books.

Lasswell, Harold. 1958. *Politics: Who Gets What, When, How.* New York: Harcourt.

Laughlin, Patrick R., and Early, P. Christopher. 1982. "Social Combination Models, Persuasive Arguments Theory, Social Comparison Theory, and Choice Shift." *Journal of Personality and Social Psychology* 42: 273–280.

Lavely, W. 1984. "The Rural Chinese Fertility Transition: A Report From Shifang Xian Sichuan." *Population Studies* 38: 365–384.

Lazar, Irving. 1981. "Early Childhood Education is Effective." *Educational Leadership* 38: 303–305.

Lazar, Irving, R. Darlington, H. Murray, J. Royce, and A. Snipper. 1982. "Lasting Effects of Early Childhood Education." *Monographs of the Society for Research in Child Development* 47 (1, 2, Serial No. 194).

Lazar, Irving, V. R. Hubbel, H. Murray, M. Rosche, and J. Royce. 1977. *The Persistence of Pre-School Effects: A Long-Term Follow-up of Fourteen Infant and Pre-School Experiments, Summary.* Washington D.C.: U.S. Department of Health and Human Services, Administration for Children, Youth, and Families.

Leacock, E. B. 1969. *Teaching and Learning in City Schools.* New York: Basic Books.

Le Boeuf, Michael. 1982. *The Productivity Challenge: How to Make it Work for America and You.* New York: McGraw Hill.

Le Bon, Gustave. 1960. *The Crowd: A Study of the Popular Mind.* New York: Viking. [Originally published in 1895.]

Lee, Richard B. 1984. *The Dobe !Kung.* New York: Holt, Rinehart, and Winston.

Lee, Richard B., and Irven DeVore. 1968. *Man the Hunter.* Chicago: Aldine.

Lefrancois, Guy. 1981. *Adolescents,* 2nd ed. Belmont, CA: Wadsworth.

Lefton, Mark, J. K. Skipper, and C. H. McCaghy (eds.) 1968. *Approaches to Deviance.* New York: Appleton-Century-Crofts.

Leiter, K. C. W. 1974. "Ad Hocing in the Schools: A Study of Placement Practices in the Kindergartens of Two Schools." Pp. 17–75 in Aaron Cicourel, K. Jennings, S. Jennings, K. Leiter, R. MacKay, H. Mehan, and D. Roth (eds.), *Language Use and School Performance.* New York: Academic Press.

Lekachman, Robert. 1982. "The Specter of Full Employment." Pp. 68–74 in Jerome H. Skolnick and Elliott Currie (eds.), *Crisis in American Institutions,* 5th ed.

Lemert, Edwin M. 1978. "Primary and Secondary Deviation" In Earl Rubington and Martin S. Weinberg (eds.), *Deviance,* 3rd ed. New York: Macmillan.

Lenin, V. I. 1939. *Imperialism, the Highest Stage of Capitalism.* New York: International Publishers. [Originally published in 1916.]

Lennane, K. Jean, and R. John Lennane. 1973. "Alleged Psychogenic Disorders in Women: A Possible Manifestation of Sexual Prejudice." *New England Journal of Medicine* 288: 288–292.

Lenski, Gerhard. 1988. "Rethinking Macrosociological Theory." *American Sociological Review* 53: 163–171.

Lenski, Gerhard. 1976. "History and Social Change." *American Journal of Sociology* 82, 3: 548–64.

Lenski, Gerhard. 1966. *Power and Privilege: A Theory of Social Stratification.* New York: McGraw Hill.

Lenski, Gerhard. 1963. *The Religious Factor.* Garden City, NY: Doubleday.

Lenski, Gerhard, and Jean Lenski. 1987. *Human Societies: An Introduction to Macrosociology,* 5th ed. New York: McGraw-Hill.

Lenski, Gerhard, and Jean Lenski. 1982. *Human Societies,* 4th ed. New York: McGraw-Hill.

Lenski, Gerhard, and Jean Lenski. 1963. *The Religious Factor: A Sociological Study of Religion's Impact on Politics, Economics, and Family Life,* rev. ed. Garden City, NY: Anchor Books.

Lenski, Gerhard, and Patrick D. Nolan. 1986. "Trajectories of Development: A Further Test." *Social Forces* 64: 794–795.

Lenski, Gerhard, and Patrick D. Nolan. 1984. "Trajectories of Development: A Test of Ecological-Evolutionary Theory." *Social Forces* 63: 1–23.

Leonard, Jonathon S. 1987. "The Interaction of Residential Segregation and Employment Discrimination." *Journal of Urban Economics* 21: 323–346.

Levin, Jack, and William C. Levin. 1982. *The Functions of Prejudice,* 2nd ed. New York: Harper and Row.

Levine, Marc V. 1987. "Downtown Redevelopment As an Urban Growth Strategy: A Critical Appraisal of the Baltimore Renaissance." *Journal of Urban Affairs* 9: 103–123.

Levitan, Sar A. 1985. *Programs in Aid of the Poor,* 5th ed. Baltimore: Johns Hopkins University Press.

Levy, Maury Z. 1979. "The Powers That Be." *Philadelphia* (September): 159–172; 255.

Levy, Mickey D. 1984. "Achieving Financial Solvency in Social Security." Pp. 3–58 in Colin Campbell (ed.), *Controlling the Cost of Social Security.* Lexington, MA: D. C. Heath/Lexington Books.

Lewin, Kurt. 1943. "Forces behind Food Habits and Methods of Change." *Bulletin of the National Research Counil* 108: 35–65.

Lewin, Kurt, Ronald Lippitt, and Ralph K. White. 1939. "Patterns of Aggressive Behavior in Experimentally Created 'Social Climates.'" *Journal of Social Psychology* 10: 271–299.

Lewin, Tamar. 1984. "A New Rush to Raise Women's Pay." *New York Times,* January 1, pp. F1, F15.

Lewis, Aubrey. 1953. "Health as a Social Concept." *British Journal of Sociology* 4: 109–124.

Lewis, Jerry M. 1972. "A Study of the Kent State Incident Using Smelser's Theory of Collective Behavior." *Sociological Inquiry* 42: 87–96.

Lewontin, R. C., Steven Rose, and Leon J. Kamin. 1984. *Not in Our Genes.* New York: Pantheon Books.

Liazor, Alexander. 1972. "The Poverty of the Sociology of Deviance: Nuts, Sluts, and Perverts." *Social Problems.* 20: 103–120.

Lieberson, Stanley. 1980. *A Piece of the Pie: Blacks and White Immigrants Since 1880.* Berkeley: University of California Press.

Liebow, Elliot. 1967. *Talley's Corner: A Study of Negro Streetcorner Men.* Boston: Little, Brown.

Light, Donald W. 1989. "Social Control and the American Health Care System." Pp. 456–474 in Howard E. Freeman and Sol Levine (eds.), *Handbook of Medical Sociology,* 4th ed. Englewood Cliffs, NJ: Prentice Hall.

Lightbourne, Robert, Jr., Susheela Singh, and Cynthia P. Green. 1982. "The World Fertility Survey: Charting Global Childbearing." *Population Bulletin* 37, 1.

Linz, Susan J. 1988. "Managerial Autonomy in Soviet Firms." *Soviet Studies* 40: 175–195.

Lipset, Seymour Martin. 1959. *Political Man.* Garden City, NY: Doubleday, Anchor Books.

Lipset, Seymour Martin, and Reinhard Bendix. 1960. *Social Mobility in Industrial Society.* Berkeley: University of California Press.

Lipset, Seymour Martin, Martin A. Trow, and James S. Coleman. 1956. *Union Democracy.* Glencoe, IL: Free Press.

Linton, Ralph. 1936. *The Study of Man.* New York: Appleton-Century-Crofts.

Little, Allan, and George Smith. 1971. *Strategies of Compensation: A Review of Educational Projects for the Disadvantaged in the United States.* Paris: Organization for Economic Cooperation and Development.

Livingston, Ivor L. 1985. "The Importance of Socio-Psychological Stress in the Interpretation of the Race-Hypertension Association." *Humanity and Society* 9: 168–175.

Lizotte, Alan J. "Extra-Legal Factors in Chicago's Criminal Courts: Testing the Conflict Model of Criminal Justice." *Social Problems.* 25, 5: 564–580.

Locker, David. 1981. *Symptoms and Illness: The Cognitive Organization of Disorder.* London: Tavistock.

Lofland, John. 1985. *Protest: Studies of Collective Behavior and Social Movements.* New Brunswick, NJ: Transaction Books.

Lofland, John. 1969. *Deviance and Identity.* Englewood Cliffs, NJ: Prentice Hall.

Lofland, Lyn H. 1973. *A World of Strangers: Order and Action in Public Space.* New York: Basic Books.

Loft, John D., and Phillip R. Kletke. 1989. "Human Resource Trends in the Health Field." Pp. 419–436 in Howard E. Freeman and Sol Levine (eds.), *Handbook of Medical Sociology,* 4th ed. Englewood Cliffs, NJ: Prentice Hall.

Loftin, Colin, and R. H. Hill. 1974. "Regional Subculture and Homicide." *American Sociological Review* 39: 714–25.

Logan, John R., and Harvey L. Molotch. 1987. *Urban Fortunes: The Political Economy of Place.* Berkeley: University of California Press.

Lombroso, Cesare. 1889. *Liuomo delinquent (The Criminal Man),* 4th ed. In Enrico Ferri, *Criminal Sociology,* in George Vold and Thomas Bernard, (eds.) 1986, *Theoretical Criminology,* 3rd ed. New York: Oxford University Press.

Long, 1985. "Industrialization and Deindustrialization." Pp. 386–387 in Adam and Jessica Kuper (eds.), *Social Science Encyclopedia.* London: RKP.

Long, Larry H. 1980. "What the Census Will Show about Gentrification." *American Demographics* 2: 18–21.

Lopata, Helena Z. 1980. "The Chicago Woman: A Study of Patterns of Mobility and Transportation." *Signs: Journal of Women in Culture and Society* 5, 3: S161–S169.

Lorber, Judith. 1975. "Good Patients and Problem Patients: Conformity and Deviance in a General Hospital." *Journal of Health and Social Behavior* 16: 213–225.

Lorenz, Konrad. 1966. *On Aggression.* New York: Harcourt, Brace, Jovanovich.

Lotz, Roy, and John D. Hewitt. 1976. "The Influence of Legally Irrelevant Factors on Felony Sentencing." *Sociological Inquiry* 47, 1: 39–48.

Lowenthal, Marjorie F., and Betsy Robinson. 1976. "Social Networks and Isolation." Pp. 432–456 in Robert H. Binstock and Ethel Shanas (eds.), *Handbook of Aging and the Social Sciences.* New York: D. Van Nostrand.

Lowi, Theodore. 1976. *American Government: Incomplete Conquest.* New York: Dryden.

Lowie, Robert H. 1954. *Indians of the Plains.* Garden City, NY: Natural History Press.

Lueck, Marjorie, Ann Orr, and Martin O'Connell. 1982. "Trends in Child-Care Arrangements of Working Mothers." *Current Population Reports,* Series P-23, No. 117. Washington, DC: U.S. Government Printing Office.

Luft, Harold S. 1978. "How Do Health Maintenance Organizations Achieve Their Savings?" *New England Journal of Medicine* 298: 1336–1343.

Luker, Kristin. 1984. *Abortion and the Politics of Motherhood.* Los Angeles: University of California Press.

Lundberg, Ferdinand. 1968. *The Rich and the Super-Rich.* New York: Lyle Stewart.

Lundberg, Olle. 1986. "Class and Health: Comparing Britain and Sweden." *Social Science and Medicine* 23: 511–517.

Lunn, Joan C. 1970. *Streaming in the Primary School.* London: National Foundation for Educational Research in England and Wales.

Lurie, Nancy Oestreich. 1985. "The American Indian: Historical Background." Pp. 136–149 in Norman R. Yetman, *Majority and Minority,* 4th ed. Boston: Allyn and Bacon.

Lynch, Edith M. 1973. *The Executive Suite: Feminine Style.* New York: AMACOM.

Lynd, Robert, and Helen Lynd. 1937. *Middletown in Transition.* New York: Harcourt, Brace, and World.

Lyon, Larry, Lawrence Felice, and M. Ray Perryman. 1980. "Community Power and Population Increase: An Empirical Test of the Growth Machine Model." *American Journal of Sociology* 86: 1387–1400.

Lyons, Richard D. 1975. "Revisions Seen in Lobbying Law." *New York Times,* April 20.

Maccoby, E. E., and C. N. Jacklin. 1980. "Sex Differences in Aggression." *Child Development* 51: 964–980.

Maccoby, Eleanor. 1980. *Social Development: Psychological Growth and the Parent-Child Relationship.* New York: Harcourt, Brace, Jovanovich.

Maccoby, Eleanor, and Carol Nagy Jacklin. 1974. *The Psychology of Sex Differences.* Stanford, CA: Stanford University Press.

MacKay, Robert. 1974. "Standardized Tests: Objective/Objectified Measures of Competence." In Aaron Cicourel (ed.), *Language Use and School Performance.* New York: Academic Press.

Macklin, Carole, and Richard H. Kolbe. 1984. "Sex Role Stereotyping in Children's Advertising: Current and Past Trends." *Journal of Advertising* 13: 34–42.

Madans, Jennifer, and Joel C. Kleinman. 1980. "Use of Ambulatory Care by the Por and Non-Poor." Pp. 43–50 in National Center for Health Statistics, *Health, United States, 1980.* Washington, DC: U.S. Government Printing Office.

Mahard, Rita E., and Robert L. Crain. 1983. "Research on Minority Achievement in Desegregated Schools." Pp. 103–125 in Christine H. Rossell and Willis D. Hawley (eds.), *The Consequences of School Desegregation.* Philadelphia: Temple University Press.

Maine, Sir Henry. 1870. *Ancient Society.* London: John Murray.

Major, Brenda, Key Deaux, and Peter J. D. Carnevale. 1981. "A Different Perspective on Androgyny: Evaluations of Masculine and Feminine Personality Characteristics." *Journal of Personality and Social Psychology* 41: 988–1001.

Makepeace, J. M. 1981. "Courtship Violence Among College Students." *Family Relations* 30: 97–102.

Malinowski, Bronislaw. 1967. *A Diary in the Strict Sense of the Term.* London: Routledge and Kegan Paul.

Malinowski, Bronislaw. 1948. *Magic, Science and Religion and Other Essays.* Glencoe, IL: Free Press.

Malinowski, Bronislaw. 1926. *Crime and Custom in Savage Society.* New York: Harcourt, Brace.

Malinowski, Bronislaw. 1922. *The Argonauts of the Western Pacific.* New York: Dutton.

Malowist, Marian. 1958. "Poland, Russia and Western Trade in the 15th and 16th Centuries." *Past & Present* 13: 26–41.

Malthus, Thomas Robert. 1965. *An Essay on Population.* New York: Augustus Kelly. [Originally published in 1798.]

Malthus, Thomas Robert. 1872. *An Essay on the Principle of Population,* 7th ed. London: Reeves and Turner.

Mann, Richard D. 1959. "A Review of the Relationship Between Personality and Performance in Small Groups." *Psychological Bulletin* 56: 241–270.

Mann, Thomas E. 1987. "Is the House of Representatives Unresponsive to Political Change?" Pp. 261–282 in A. James Reichley (ed.), *Elections American Style.* Washington, D.C.: The Brookings Institute.

Mannheim, Karl. 1936. *Ideology and Utopia.* New York: Harcourt. Originally published in German in 1929.

Maracek, J., S. E. Finn, and M. Cardell. 1982. "Gender Roles in the Relationships of Lesbians and Gay Men." *Journal of Homosexuality* 8: 45–49.

Marascuilo, Leonard A., and Maryellen McSweeney. 1972. "Tracking and Minority Student Attitudes and Performance." *Urban Education* 6: 303–319.

Mare, Robert D. 1982. "Socioeconomic Effects on Child Mortality in the United States." *American Journal of Public Health* 2, 6: 539–547.

Mariano, Ann. 1988. "Affluent Get Thousands in Subsidies." *Washington Post,* October 15, Section E, p. 1.

Marjoribanks, Kevin. 1972. "Environment, Social Class, and Mental Abilities." *Journal of Educational Psychology* 63: 103–109.

Mark, Vernon and Frank Ervin. 1970. *Violence and the Brain.* New York: Harper & Row.

Marmor, Theodore, and Edward Tenner. 1977. "National Health Insurance: Canada's Path, America's Choice." *Challenge* 20: 13–21.

Marshall, Susan E. 1985. "Ladies Against Women: Mobilization Dilemmas of Antifeminist Movements." *Social Problems* 32: 348–362.

Marshall, Victor W. 1986. "A Sociological Perspective on Aging and Dying." Pp. 125–146 in Victor W. Marshall (ed.), *Later Life: The Social Psychology of Aging.* Beverly Hills, CA: Sage.

Martin, Thomas, and K. Berry. 1974. "Competitive Sport in Post-Industrial Society." *Journal of Popular Culture* 8: 107–120.

Martin, William. 1981. "The Birth of a Media Myth." *The Atlantic* 247, 6: 7–16.

Marty, Martin. 1979. "Foreword to Dean R. Hoge and David A. Roozen (eds.), *Understanding Church Growth and Decline, 1950–1978.* New York: Pilgrim.

Maruyama, G., and N. Miller. 1979. "Reexamination of Normative Influence Processes in Desegregated Classrooms." *American Educational Research Journal* 16: 273–283.

Marx, Gary T., and Sanford Sherizen. 1987. "Corporations that Spy on Their Employees." *Business and Society Review* (Winter): 32–37.

Marx, Gary T. 1974. "Religion: Opiate or Inspiration of Civil Rights Militancy among Negroes?" In William M. Newman (ed.), *The Social Meanings of Religion.* Chicago: Rand McNally College Publishing Co.

Marx, Karl. 1978. *The Marx-Engels Reader,* 2nd ed. Robert C. Tucker, ed. New York: W. W. Norton.

Marx, Karl. 1967. *Capital: A Critique of Political Economy.* Friedrich Engels ed., Samuel Moore and Edward Aveling (trs.) New York: International Publishers. Originally published in German in 1867, 1885, and 1894.

Marx, Karl. 1964. *Selected Writings in Sociology and Social Philosophy.* Thomas B. Bottomore and Maximilien Rubel, (eds. and trs.) New York: McGraw Hill.

Marx, Karl, and Friedrich Engels. 1969. *The Communist Manifesto.* Baltimore: Penguin. Originally published in German in 1848.

Mason, Philip. 1971. *Patterns of Dominance.* London: Oxford University Press.

Massey, Douglas S., and Nancy A. Denton. 1988. "Suburbanization and Segregation in U.S. Metropolitan Areas." *American Journal of Sociology* 94: 592–626.

Massey, Douglas S., and Nancy A. Denton. 1987. "Trends in the Residential Segregation of Blacks, Hispanics, and Asians: 1970–1980." *American Sociological Review* 52: 802–825.

Masters, J. C., and A. Wilkinson. 1976. "Consensual and Discriminative Stereotypes of Sex-Type Judgments by Parents and Children." *Child Development* 47: 208–217.

Masters, William H. and Virginia E. Johnson. *Human Sexual Response.* Boston: Little, Brown, 1969.

Mayer, A. J., J. J. Lindsay, J. Fineman, S. McGuire, J. Kirsch, and M. Reese. 1980. "A Tide of Born-Again Politics." *Newsweek,* September 15, pp. 28–36.

Mazon, Mauricio. 1984. *The Zoot-Suit Riots: The Psychology of Symbolic Annihilation.* Austin: University of Texas Press.

McAdam, Doug. 1986. "Recruitment to High-Risk Activism: The Case of Freedom Summer." *American Journal of Sociology* 92: 64–90.

McAdam, Doug. 1983. "Tactical Innovation and the Pace of Insurgency." *American Sociological Review* 48: 735–754.

McAdam, Doug. 1982. *Political Process and the Development of Black Insurgency, 1930–1970.* Chicago: University of Chicago Press.

McAdam, Doug, John D. McCarthy, and Mayer N. Zald. 1988. "Social Movements." Pp. 695–737 in Neil J. Smelser (ed.), *Handbook of Sociology.* Newbury Park, CA: Sage.

McArthur, Leslie A., and Susan V. Eisen. 1976. "Achievements of Male and Female Storybook Characters as Determinants of Achievement Behavior in Boys and Girls." *Journal of Personality and Social Psychology* 33: 467–473.

McCague, James. 1968. *The Second Rebellion: The Story of the New York City Draft Riots of 1863.* New York: Dial.

McCarthy, John D., and Mayer N. Zald. 1977. "Resource Mobilization and Social Movements: A Partial Theory." *American Journal of Sociology* 82: 1212–1241.

McCarthy, John D., and Mayer N. Zald. 1973. *The Trend of Social Movements in America: Professionalization and Resource Mobilization.* Morristown, NJ: General Learning Press.

McClanahan, Sara, and Larry Bumpass. 1988. "Intergenerational Consequences of Family Disruption." *American Journal of Sociology* 94: 130–152.

McClelland, David C. 1961. *The Achieving Society.* New York: Van Nostrand.

McConahay, J. B., B. B. Hardee, and V. Batts. 1981. "Has Racism Declined in America? It Depends on Who Is Asking and What Is Asked." *Journal of Conflict Resolution* 25: 563–579.

McConkie, Bruce. 1966. *Mormon Doctrine,* 2nd ed. Salt Lake City, UT: Brookcraft.

McCord, William, and Joan McCord. 1964. *The Psychopath.* In R. Martin Hackell and Lewis Yablonsky, 1978, In *Crime and Delinquency,* 3rd ed. Chicago: Rand McNally College Publishing Company.

McCoy, E. "Your One and Only." *Parents,* 1986, pp. 118–121, 236.

McKenna, Wendy, and Florence Denmark. 1978. "Women and the University." *International Journal of Group Tensions* 5: 226–234.

McLanahan, Sara, and Irwin Garfinkel. 1989. "Single Mothers, the Underclass, and Social Policy." *The Annals of the American Academy of Political and Social Science* 501: 92–104.

McLuhan, Marshall. 1964. *Understanding Media: The Extensions of Man.* New York: McGraw-Hill.

McNeill, William H. 1976. *Plagues and Peoples.* Garden City, NY: Anchor Press.

McPartland, J., and J. Braddock. 1981. "Going to College and Getting a Good Job: The Impact of Desegregation." In Willis D. Hawley (ed.), *Effective School Desegregation.* Beverly Hills, CA: Sage.

McPhail, Clark. 1971. "Civil Disorder Participation: A Critical Examination of Recent Research." *American Sociological Review* 36: 1058–1073.

McPhail, Clark, and Ronald T. Wohlstein. 1983. "Individual and Collective Behaviors within Gatherings, Demonstrations, and Riots." Pp. 579–600 in Ralph H. Turner and James f. Short, Jr. (eds.), *Annual Review of Sociology,* vol. 9. Palo Alto, CA: Annual Reviews.

McWhirter, Norris. 1985. *Guinness Book of World Records.* New York: Bantam.

McWilliams, Carey. 1949. *North From Mexico.* Philadelphia: Lippincott.

Mead, George Herbert. 1934. *Mind, Self, and Society.* Chicago: University of Chicago Press.

Mead, George Herbert. 1925. "The Genesis of the Self and Self-Control." *International Journal of Ethics* 35: 251–277.

Mead, Margaret. 1950. *Sex and Temperament in Three Primitive Societies.* New York: NAL Mentor.

Mead, Margaret. 1935. *Sex and Temperament in Three Primitive Societies.* New York: Dell.

Meadows, Donnella H., et al. 1972. *The Limits to Growth.* New York: New American Library.

Meadows, Donnella H., Dennis L. Meadows, Jorgen Randers, and William W. Behrens. 1972. *The Limits to Growth: A Report for the Club of Rome's Project on the Predicament of Mankind.* New York: Universe.

Mechanic, David. 1978. *Medical Sociology,* 2nd ed. New York: Free Press.

Mechanic, David. 1963. "Religion, Religiosity, and Illness Behavior." *Human Organization* 22, 3: 202–208.

Mechanic, David, and Linda H. Aiken. 1989. "Access to Health Care and Use of Medical Care Services." Pp. 166–184 in Howard E. Freeman and Sol Levine (eds.), *Handbook of Medical Sociology,* 4th ed. Englewood Cliffs, NJ: Prentice Hall.

Mehl, Lewis E. 1977. "Options in Maternity Care." *Women and Health* 2: 11–23.

Mellor, Earl F. 1984. "Investigating the Differences in Weekly Earnings of Women and Men." *Monthly Labor Review* 107: 17–28.

Melman, Seymour. 1983. *Profits without Production.* New York: Knopf.

Melton, J. Gordon. 1978. *Encyclopedia of American Religions.* Wilmington, NC: McGrath.

Mendelson, Robert, and Michael Quinn. 1977. *The Demise of an Urban Real Estate Entrepreneur.* Edwardsville, IL: Center for Urban and Environmental Research and Services, Southern Illinois University at Edwardsville.

Merrick, Thomas W. 1986. "World Population in Transition." *Population Bulletin* 41, 2.

Merrick, Thomas W., and Stephen J. Tordella. 1988. "Demographics: People and Markets." *Population Bulletin* 43, 1.

Merton, Robert. 1973. *The Sociology of Science: Theoretical and Empirical Investigations.* Chicago: University of Chicago Press.

Merton, Robert. 1968. *Social Theory and Social Structure,* 2nd ed. New York: Free Press.

Merton, Robert. 1967. *On Theoretical Sociology.* New York: Free Press.

Merton, Robert. 1949. *Social Theory and Social Structure.* New York: Free Press.

Merton, Robert. 1948. "Discrimination and the American Creed." Pp. 99–128 in Robert M. MacIver (ed.), *Discrimination and National Welfare.* New York: Harper.

Merton, Robert. 1938. "Social Structure and Anomie." *American Sociological Review* 3: 672–682.

Merton, Robert K. 1968. *Social Theory and Social Structure,* 2nd ed. New York: Free Press.

Merton, Robert K. 1957. *Social Theory and Social Structure.* New York: Free Press.

Meyer, John W. and Michael T. Hannan (eds.) 1979. *National Development and the World System: Educational, Economic, and Political Change, 1950–1979.* Chicago: University of Chicago Press.

Meyerson, Rebecca. 1988. "The Distribution of Cancer Incidence in Madison and St. Clair Counties in Southwestern Illinois." Masters Thesis, Soouthern Illinois University at Edwardsville.

Michels, Robert. 1967. *Political Parties: A Sociological Study of the Oligarchical Tendencies in Modern Democracy.* New York: Free Press. [Originally published in 1911.]

Michels, Robert. 1949. *First Lectures in Political Science.* Alfred de Grazia (tr.). Minneapolis: University of Minnesota Press. [Originally published in 1915.]

Michelson, William. 1985. *From Sun to Sun — Daily Obligations and Community Structure in the Lives of Employed Women and Their Families;* Totowa, NJ: Rowman and Allanheld.

Michelson, William. 1977. *Environmental Choice, Human Behavior, and Residential Satisfaction.* New York: Oxford University Press.

Michelson, William. 1976. *Man and His Urban Environment: A Sociological Approach,* with revisions. Boston: Addison-Wesley.

Milgram, Stanley. 1970. "The Experience of Living in Cities." *Science* 167: 1461–1468.

Miller, Karen A., Melvin L. Kohn, and Carmi Schooler. 1986. "Educational Self-Direction and Personality." *American Sociological Review* 51: 372–390.

Miller, M. M., and B. Reeves. 1976. "Dramatic TV Content and Children's Sex-Role Stereotypes." *Journal of Broadcasting* 20: 35–50.

Miller, N. 1980. "Making School Desegregation Work." In W. Stephan and Joe R. Feagin (eds.), *School Desegregation: Past, Present, and Future.* New York: Plenum.

Miller, Walter. 1958. "Lower-Class Culture as a Generating Milieu of Gang Delinquency." *Journal of Sociological Issues* 14: 5–19.

Millman, Marcia, and Rosabeth Moss Kanter. 1975. *Another Voice.* New York: Doubleday, Sociological Inquiry.

Mills, C. Wright. 1961. *The Sociological Imagination.* New York: Grove Press.

Mills, C. Wright. 1956. *The Power Elite.* New York: Oxford University Press.

Mills, C. Wright. 1951. *White Collar: The American Middle Classes.* New York: Oxford University Press.

Minor, W. William. 1978. "Deterrence Research: Problems of Theory and Method." Pp. 21–45 in James a. Cramer (ed.), *Preventing Crime.* Beverly Hills, CA: Sage.

Mintz, Beth. 1975. "The President's Cabinet, 1897–1972." *Insurgent Sociologist* (Spring).

Mintz, Beth, and Michael Schwartz. 1985. *The Power Structure of American Business.* Chicago: University of Chicago Press.

Mintz, Beth, and Michael Schwartz. 1981a. "Interlocking Directorates and Interest Group Formation." *American Journal of Sociology* 48: 851–869.

Mintz, Beth, and Michael Schwartz. 1981b. "The Structure of Intercorporate Unity in American Business." *Social Problems* 29: 87–103.

Mintz, Morton, and Jerry F. Cohen. 1976. *Power, Inc.* New York: Viking.

Mirande, Alfredo. 1987. *Gringo Justice*. Notre Dame, IN: University of Notre Dame Press.

Molm, Linda S. 1987. "Linking Power Structure and Power Use." Pp. 101–129 in Karen S. Cook (ed.), *Social Exchange Theory*. Newbury Park, CA: Sage Publications.

Molotch, Harvey. 1979. "Media and Movement." Pp. 71–93 in Mayer N. Zald and John B. McCarthy (eds.), *The Dynamics of Social Movements*. Cambridge, MA: Winthrop.

Molotch, Harvey. 1979b. "Capital and Neighborhood in the United States: Some Conceptual Links." *Urban Affairs Quarterly* 14: 289–312.

Molotch, Harvey. 1976. "The City as a Growth Machine: Toward a Political Economy of Place." *American Journal of Sociology* 82: 309–333.

Molotch, Harvey, and Marilyn Lester. 1973. "Accidents, Scandals, and Routines: Resources for Insurgent Methodology." *Insurgent Sociologist* (Summer).

Momeni, Jamshid A. (ed.) 1986. *Race, Ethnicity, and Minority Housing in the United States*. Westport, CT: Greenwood Press.

Monahan, John, and Henry J. Steadman. 1983. "Crime and Mental Disorder: An Epidemiological Appraisal." in Michael Tonry and Norval Morris. (eds.), *Crime and Justice*. Pp. 4, Chicago: University of Chicago Press.

Monette, Duane R., Thomas J. Sullivan, and Cornell R. Dejong. 1986. *Applied Social Research*. New York: Holt, Rinehart, and Winston.

Monk-Turner, Elizabeth. 1988. "Educational Differentiation and Status Attainment: The Community College Controversy." *Sociological Focus* 21: 141–152.

Moore, Joan, and Harry Pachon. 1985. *Hispanics in the United States*, 2nd ed. Englewood Cliffs, NJ: Prentice Hall.

Moore, Joan W., with Harry Pachon. 1976. *Mexican Americans*. Englewood Cliffs, NJ: Prentice Hall.

Moore, Kristin A., and S. B. Caldwell. 1977. "The Effect of Government Policies on Out-of-Wedlock Sex and Pregnancy." *Family Planning Perspectives* 9: 164–169.

Moore, Robert. 1972. "Race Relations in the Six Counties: Colonialism, Industrialization, and Stratification in Ireland." *Race* 14. Reprinted in Norman R. Yetman and C. Hoy Steele (eds.), *Majority and Minority: The Dynamics of Racial and Ethnic Relations*, 2nd ed. Boston: Allyn and Bacon, 1975.

Moore, Wilbert E. 1974. *Social Change*, 2nd ed. Englewood Cliffs, NJ: Prentice Hall.

Morgan, David. 1986. *The Mongols*. London: Blackwell.

Morgan, David J. 1976. *Patterns of Population Distribution in a Residential Preference Model and its Dynamic*. Chicago: University of Chicago Department of Geography.

Morgan, S. Philip, Diane N. Lye, and Gretchen A. Condran. 1988. "Sons, Daughters, and the Risk of Marital Disruption." *American Sociological Review* 52: 278–285.

Moroney, J. R. 1972. *The Structure of Production in American Manufacturing*. Chapel Hill: University of North Carolina Press.

Morris, Aldon. 1984. *The Origins of the Civil Rights Movement: Black Communities Organizing for Change*. New York: The Free Press.

Morris, N., and G. Hawkins. 1970. *The Honest Politician's Guide to Crime Control*. Chicago: University of Chicago Press.

Mortensen, Dale. 1988. "Gifts as Economic Symbols and Social Symbols." *American Journal of Sociology* 94: S180–S214.

Mortimer, Jeylan T., and Roberta G. Simmons. 1978. "Adult Socialization." Pp. 421–454 in Alex Inkeles et al. (eds.), *Annual Review of Sociology*, vol. 4. Palo Alto, CA: Annual Reviews.

Mosca, Gaetano. 1939. *The Ruling Class*. Hannah D. Kahn (tr.). New York: McGraw Hill. [Originally published in Italian in 1896.]

Moscovici, Serge, and Marisa Zavalloni. 1969. "The Group as a Polarizer of Attitudes." *Journal of Personality and Social Psychology* 12: 125–135.

Mott, Frank, and David Shapiro. 1978. "Pregnancy, Motherhood, and Work Activity." In Frank Mott (ed.), *Women, Work, and Family*. Lexington, MA: Lexington Books.

Muehlenhard, C. L., and M. A. Linton. 1987. "Date Rape and Sexual Aggression in Dating Situations: Incidence and Risk Factors." *Journal of Counseling Psychology* 34: 186–196.

Mueller, Edward N. 1980. "The Psychology of Political Protest and Violence." Pp. 69–99 in Ted Robert Gurr (ed.), *Handbook of Political Conflict*. New York: Free Press.

Mumford, Lewis. 1938. *The Culture of Cities*. New York: Harcourt, Brace.

Murdie, Robert A. 1976. "Spatial Form in the Residential Mosaic." Pp. 237–272 in D. T. Herbert and R. J. Johnson (eds.), *Social Areas in Cities, Vol. 1: Spatial Processes and Form*. London: John Wiley.

Murdock, George Peter. 1965. *Culture and Society*. Pittsburgh: University of Pittsburgh Press.

Murdock, George Peter. 1960. *Social Structure*. New York: Macmillan.

Murdock, George Peter. 1945. "The Common Denominator of Cultures." Pp. 123–142 in Ralph Linton (ed.), *The Science of Man in the World Crisis*. New York: Columbia University Press.

Murdock, George Peter. 1935. "Comparative Data on the Division of Labor by Sex." *Social Forces* 15: 551–553.

Murray, Charles. 1984. *Losing Ground: American Social Policy, 1950–1980*. New York: Basic Books.

Myers, David G., and G. D. Bishop. 1970. "Discussion Effects on Racial Attitudes." *Science* 169: 778–789.

Myers, David G., and M. F. Kaplan. 1976. "Group-Induced Polarization in Simulated Juries." *Personality and Social Psychology Bulletin* 2: 63–66.

Myrdal, Gunnar. 1944. *An American Dilemma: The Negro Problem and Modern Democracy*. New York: Harper and Row.

Naisbett, John. 1982. *Megatrends: Ten New Directions Transforming Our Lives*. New York: Warner Books.

Nan Lin and Wen Xie. 1988. "Occupational Prestige in Urban China." *American Journal of Sociology* 93: 793–832.

Nash, Gary B., et al. (eds.). 1986. *The American People: Creating a Nation and a Society*. New York: Harper & Row.

Nash, Roy. 1976. *Teacher Expectations and Pupil Learning*. London: Routledge and Kegan Paul.

National Center for Health Statistics. 1988. *Health, United States, 1988*. DHHS Publication No. (PHS) 88–1232. Washington, DC: U.S. Government Printing Office.

National Center for Health Statistics. 1987. *Monthly Vital Statistics Report: Births, Marriages, Divorces, and Death for 1987*.

National Center for Health Statistics. 1986. *Current Estimates from the Health Interview Survey, United States, 1985*. Series 10, No. 160. Washington, DC: U.S. Government Printing Office.

National Center for Health Statistics. 1984. *Health, United States, 1984*. Washington, DC: U.S. Government Printing Office.

National Commission on Excellence in Education. 1983. *A Nation at Risk:*

The Imperative for Educational Reform. Washington, DC: U.S. Government Printing Office.

National Institute of Justice. 1988A. "International Crime Rates." Washington, DC: U.S. Government Printing Office.

National Institute of Justice. Special Report. 1988B. "Profile of State Inmates, 1986. Washington, DC: U.S. Government Printing Office.

National Institute of Justice. 1988C. "Report to the Nation on Crime and Justice," 2nd ed. Washington, DC: U.S. Government Printing Office.

National Institute of Justice. 1987. "Sourcebook of Criminal Statistics." Washington, DC: U.S. Government Printing Office.

National Institute of Justice. 1986. *Prisoners in 1985.* Washington, DC: U.S. Government Printing Office.

National Institute of Mental Health. 1982. *Television and Behavior: Ten Years of Scientific Progress and Implications for the Eighties.* Washington, DC: U.S. Government Printing Office.

National Opinion Research Center. 1983. *General Social Surveys, 1972–1983: Cumulative Codebook.* Chicago: National Opinion Research Center.

Neckerman, Kathryn M., Robert Aponte, and William Julius Wilson. 1988. "Family Structure, Black Unemployment, and American Social Policy." In Ann S. Orloff and Theda Skopkol (eds.), *The Politics of Social Policy in the United States.* Princeton, NJ: Princeton University Press.

Neier, Aryeh. 1985. "No One is Safe." Pp. 11–16 in Gary E. McCuen (ed.), *Political Murder in Central America: Death Squads and U.S. Policies.* Hudson, WI: Gary E. McCuen Publications.

Nelkin, Dorothy, and Michael Pollak. 1981. *The Atom Beseiged.* Cambridge, MA: MIT Press.

Neumann, Sigmund. 1971. "The International Civil War." Pp. 110–123 in Clifford T. Paynton and Robert Blackey (eds.), *Why Revolution? Theories and Analysis.* Cambridge, MA: Schenkman.

New York Times. 1988. "Tax Act's Corporate Effect." *New York Times,* September 23, Section D, p. 18.

New York Times. 1988b. "New York Times/CBS News Poll: Portrait of the Electorate." November 10, Section B, p. 6.

New York Times. 1987. "Washington Talk: Briefings. A Surge of Sorts." December 1, Section A, p. 16.

New York Times. 1987b. "Does 1987 Equal 1929?" October 20, Section A, p. 1.

New York Times. 1984. "Auto Union Seeks Big Economic Gain." March 7, Section A, p. 14.

New York Times. 1982. "Librarians Say ;osGo Ask Alice' Censored Most in Schools." November 28, Section 1, p. 73.

New York Times. 1977. "Assembly Draws Bill to Regulate 'Medicaid Mills' and Limit Abuse." February 15, p. 35.

Newcomb, Michael, and P. M. Bentler. 1980. "Assessment of Personality and Demographic Effects of Cohabitation and Marital Success." *Journal of Personality Assessment* 44, 1: 11–24.

Newcombe, Nora, Mary M. Bandura, and Dawn C. Taylor. 1983. "Sex Differences in Spatial Abilities and Spatial Activities." *Sex Roles* 9: 377–386.

Newman, Graeme. 1978. *The Punishment Response.* Philadelphia: L. B. Lippencott Company.

Newstadtl, Alan, and Dan Clawson. 1988. "Corporate Political Groupings: Does Ideology Unify Business Political Behavior?" *American Sociological Review* 53: 172–190.

Newsweek. 1988. "Saving One High School." May 2, pp. 56–65.

Newsweek. 1988b. "Seven Minutes to Death." July 18, pp. 18–24.

Newsweek. 1988c. "More Deadly Than Poison." August 1, pp. 28–31.

Newsweek. 1988d. "Lost on the Planet Earth: American Adults Know Shockingly Little Geography." August 8, p. 31.

Newsweek. 1988e. "Decade Shock." September 5: 14–16.

Newsweek. 1988f. "The Threat of a Global Grain Drain." August 15, p. 36.

Newsweek. 1987. "Attacking the Victims: The Rebels Cut Food-Supply Lines in Ethiopia." November 9, p. 56.

Newton, George D., and Franklin E. Zimring. 1969. *Firearms and Violence in American Life.* Consultant report to the National Commission on the Causes and Prevention of Violence. Washington, DC: U.S. Government Printing Office.

Niebuhr, H. Richard. 1929. *The Social Sources of Denominationalism.* New York: Henry Holt and Company.

Nisbet, Robert A. 1969. *Social Change in History.* New York: Oxford.

Nisbet, Robert. 1969. *Social Change and History: Aspects of the Western Theory of Development.* New York: Oxford University Press.

Noel, Donald L. 1972. "Slavery and the Rise of Racism." Pp. 153–174 in Donald L. Noel (ed.), *The Origins of American Slavery and Racism.* Columbus, OH: Charles E. Merrill.

Noel, Donald L. 1968. "A Theory of the Origins of Ethnic Stratification." *Social Problems* 16: 157–172.

Nolan, Patrick D. 1987. "World System Status, Income Inequality, and Economic Growth: A Criticism of Recent Criticism." *International Journal of Comparative Sociology* 28, 1–2: 69–75.

Noss, John B. 1980. *Man's Religions,* 6th ed. New York: Macmillan.

Oakley, Robert. 1986. "Terrorism: Overview and Developments." Pp. 18–32 in Steven Anzovin (ed.), *Terrorism.* New York: H. W. Wilson.

O'Brien, J. E. 1971. "Violence in Divorce-Prone Families." *Journal of Marriage and the Family* 33: 692–698.

O'Brien, Patrick. 1982. "European Economic Development: The Contribution of the Periphery." *Economic History Review,* 2nd. ser. 35,1:1–18.

O'Dea, Thomas and Janet O'Dea Aviada. 1983. *Sociology of Religion,* 2nd ed. Englewood Cliffs, NJ: Prentice Hall.

Office of Civil Rights, U.S. Department of Health, Education, and Welfare. 1976. *Racial and Ethnic Enrollment Data From Institutions of Higher Education.* Washington, D.C.: Office of Civil Rights.

Ogbu, John U. 1986. "Structural Constraints in School Desegregation." Pp. 21–45 in Jeffrey Prager, Douglas Longshore, and Melvin Seeman (eds.), *School Desegregation Research: New Directions in Situational Analysis.* New York: Plenum.

Ogbu, John U. 1978. *Minority Education and Caste: The American System in Cross-Cultural Perspective.* New York: Academic Press.

Ogburn, William F. 1966. *Social Change with Respect to Culture and Original Nature.* New York: Dell. Originally published in 1922.

Ogburn, William F. 1938. "The Changing Family." *The Family* 19: 139–143.

Ogburn, William F. 1933. "The Family and Its Functions." *Recent Trends in the U.S.,* Report of the President's Research Committee on Social Trends.

Ogburn, William F. 1922. *Social Change with Respect to Culture and Original Nature.* New York: Viking.

Olday, David E. 1981. "Premarital Cohabitation: An Assessment of the

Consequences for Marriage.'' Paper presented at annual meeting of the Midwest Sociological Society, Minneapolis.

Oppenheimer, Valerie Kincaide. 1988. ''A Theory of Marriage Timing.'' *American Journal of Sociology* 94: 563–591.

Organization for Economic Cooperation and Development. 1979. *The State of the Environment in OECD Countries.* Paris: Organization for Economic Cooperation and Development.

Orlofsky, Jacob. 1977. ''Sex-Role Orientation, Identity Formation, and Self-Esteem in College Men and Women.'' *Sex Roles* 3: 561–575.

Orum, Anthony. 1988. ''Political Sociology.'' Pp. 393–423 in Neil Smelser (ed.), *Handbook of Sociology.* Newbury Park, CA: Sage.

Orum, Anthony. 1978. *Introduction to Political Sociology: The Social Anatomy of the Body Politic.* Englewood Cliffs, NJ: Prentice Hall.

Orum, Anthony. 1972. *Black Students in Protest.* Washington: American Sociological Association.

Ouchi, William G., and Alan L. Wilkins. 1985. ''Organizational Culture.'' Pp. 457–483 in Ralph H. Turner and James F. Short (eds.), *Annual Review of Sociology,* vol. 11. Palo Alto, CA: Annual Reviews.

Owen, Carolyn, Howard C. Eisner, and Thomas R. McFaul. 1981. ''A Half-Century of Social Distance Research: National Replication of the Bogardus Studies.'' *Sociology and Social Research* 66: 80–98.

Owen, David. 1985. *None of the Above: Behind the Myth of Scholastic Aptitude.* Boston: Houghton Mifflin.

Packard, Vance. 1983. *Our Endangered Children: Growing Up in a Changing World.* Boston: Little, Brown.

Paine, Robert. 1987. ''Accidents, Ideologies, and Routines: Chernobyl Over Norway.'' *Anthropology Today* 30, 4: 7–10.

Palen, J. John. 1987. *The Urban World,* 3rd ed. New York: McGraw-Hill.

Palmer, Francis H. 1970. ''Socioeconomic Status and Intellective Performance Among Negro Preschool Boys.'' *Developmental Psychology* 3: 1–9.

Paludi, M. A., and Lisa Strayer. 1985. ''What's in an Author's Name? Differential Evaluations of Performance as a Function of Author's Name.'' *Sex Roles* 12: 353–361.

Pampel, Fred. 1988. ''Welfare Spending in Advanced Industrial Democracies, 1950–1980.'' *American Journal of Sociology* 93: 1424–1456.

Pareto, Vilfredo. 1935. *The Mind and Society,* Vols. I—-IV. London: Jonathan Cape. [Originally published in Italian in 1915–1919.]

Park, Robert E. 1967. *On Social Control and Collective Behavior.* Ralph H. Turner (ed.). Chicago: University of Chicago Press.

Park, Robert E. 1927. ''Human Nature and Collective Behavior.'' *American Journal of Sociology* 32: 733–741.

Park, Robert E., and Ernest W. Burgess. 1921. *Introduction to the Science of Sociology.* Chicago: University of Chicago Press.

Parkinson, C. Northcotte. 1957. *Parkinson's Law.* New York: Houghton-Mifflin.

Parnes, Herbert S., and Laurence J. Less. 1985. ''Introduction and Overview.'' Pp. 1–29 in Herbert S. Parnes et al. (eds.), *Retirement among American Men.* Lexington, MA: Lexington Books/D. C. Heath.

Parnes, Herbert S., and Gilbert Nestel. 1981. ''The Retirement Experience.'' In Herbert S. Parnes (ed.), *Work and Retirement: A Longitudinal Study.* Cambridge, MA: MIT Press.

Parsons, Jacquelynne Ecles, Terry F. Adler, and Caroline M. Kaczala. 1982. ''Socialization of Achievement Attitudes and Beliefs: Parental Influences.'' *Child Development* 53: 310–321.

Parsons, Talcott. 1977. *The Evolutions of Societies.* Jackson Toby, ed. Englewood Cliffs, NJ: Prentice Hall.

Parsons, Talcott. 1977. *Social Systems and the Evolution of Action Theory.* New York: Free Press.

Parsons, Talcott. 1971. *The System of Modern Societies.* Englewood Cliffs, NJ: Prentice Hall.

Parsons, Talcott. 1966. *Societies: Evolutionary and Comparative Perspectives.* Englewood Cliffs, NJ: Prentice Hall.

Parsons, Talcott. 1962. ''The Law and Social Control.'' Pp. 56–72 in *Law and Sociology: Exploratory Essays,* William M. Evans, New York: Free Press.

Parsons, Talcott. 1959. ''The School Class As a Social System: Some of Its Functions in American Society.'' *Harvard Educational Review* 29: 297–318.

Parsons, Talcott. 1951. *The Social System.* Glencoe, IL. Free Press.

Parsons, Talcott. 1951. *The Social System.* New York: Free Press.

Parsons, Talcott. 1947. ''Introduction.'' In Max Weber, *The Theory of Social and Economic Organization.* A. M. Henderson and Talcott Parsons (trs.). New York: Oxford University Press.

Parsons, Talcott. 1937. *The Structure of Social Action.* New York: McGraw-Hill.

Parsons, Talcott, and Robert F. Bales. 1955. *Family, Socialization, and Interaction Process.* Glencoe, IL: The Free Press.

Parsons, Talcott, Robert Bales, et al. 1955. *Family, Socialization, and the Interaction Process.* Glencoe, IL: Free Press.

Passel, Jeffrey S. 1986. ''Immigration to the United States.'' Presentation at Census Table, Honolulu, HI, August.

Patchen, Martin. 1982. *Black-White Contact in the Schools: Its Social and Academic Effects.* West Lafayette, IN: Purdue University Press.

Patchen, Martin, G. Hofmann, and W. R. Brown. 1980. ''Academic Performance of Black High School Students Under Different Conditions of Contact with White Peers.'' *Sociology of Education* 53: 33–50.

Paternoster, Raymond, Linda Saltzman, Gordon Waldo, and Theodore Chiricos. 1983. ''Perceiv[365]d Risk and Social Control: Do Sanctions Really Deter?'' *Law and Society Review.* 17,3: 478.

Patterson, Thomas E. 1980. *The Mass Media Election: How Americans Choose Their President.* New York: Praeger.

Payer, Lynn. 1988. *Medicine and Culture.* New York: Holt.

Pearce, Diana. ''Women in Poverty.'' Pp. 7–32 in Arthur I. Blaustein (ed.), *The American Promise: Equal Justice and Economic Opportunity.* New Brunswick, NJ: Transaction.

Pearce, Diana. 1976. ''Black, White, and Many Shades of Gray: Real Estate Brokers and Their Racial Practices.'' Ph. D. Dissertation, The University of Michigan, Ann Arbor.

Pennock, J. Roland. 1979. *Democratic Political Theory.* Princeton, NJ: Princeton University Press.

Pennsylvania Crime Commision. 1980. ''A Decade of Organized Crime: 1980 Report.'' In Frank E. Hagan, 1986, *Introduction to Criminology: Theories, Methods and Criminal Behavior.* Chicago: Nihon Hall.

Penrod, Steven. 1986. *Social Psychology,* 2nd ed. Englewood Cliffs, NJ: Prentice Hall.

Peplau, L. A. 1981. ''What Homosexuals Want in Relationships.'' *Psychology Today* 15: 28–38.

Perle, Eugene D. 1981. ''Perspectives on the Changing Ecological Structure of Suburbia.'' *Urban Geography* 2: 237–254.

Perolle, Judith A. 1987. *Computers and Social Change: Information, Property, and Power.* Belmont, CA: Wadsworth.

Perrow, Charles. 1986a. *Normal Accidents: Living with High-Risk Technologies.* New York: Basic Books.

Perrow, Charles. 1979. *Complex Organizations: A Critical Essay,* 2nd ed. Glencoe, IL: Free Press.

Persell, C. H. 1977. *Education and Inequality: A Theoretical and Empirical Synthesis.* New York: Free Press.

Peskin, Janice. 1982. "Measuring Household Production for the GNP." *Family Economics Review* (Summer): 16–25.

Pettigrew, Thomas F. 1973. "Attitudes on Race and Housing: A Social Psychological View." Pp. 21–84 in Amos H. Hawley and V. P. Rock (eds.), *Segregation in Residential Areas.* Washington, DC: National Academy of Sciences.

Pettigrew, Thomas F. 1971. *Racially Separate or Together.* New York: McGraw-Hill.

Pettigrew, Thomas F. 1969a. "Race and Equal Educational Opportunity." Pp. 69–79 in Harvard Educational Review Editors (eds.), *Equality of Educational Opportunity.* Cambridge, MA: Harvard University Press.

Pettigrew, Thomas F. 1969b. "The Negro and Education: Problems and Proposals." Pp. 49–112 in Irwin Katz and Patricia Gurin (eds.), *Race and the Social Sciences.* New York: Basic Books.

Pfohl, Stephen J. 1985. *Images of Deviance and Social Control: A Sociological History.* New York: McGraw-Hill Book

Philipp, Thomas. 1980. "Muslims." Pp. 732–733 in Stephan Thernstrom, Ann Orlov, and Oscar Handlin (eds.), *The Harvard Encyclopedia of American Ethnic Groups.* Cambridge, MA: Harvard University Press.

Phillips, David P. 1987. "The Impact of Televised Movies About Suicide: A Replication." *New England Journal of Medicine* 317, 13: 809–811.

Physicians' Task Force on Hunger. 1985. *Report of the Physicians' Task Force on Hunger in America.*

Piaget, Jean. 1956. *The Origins of Intelligence in Children.* New York: Norton.

Piaget, Jean. 1932. *The Moral Judgment of the Child.* London: Routledge and Kegan Paul.

Piaget, Jean. 1926. *The Language and Thought of the Child.* New York: Harcourt, Brace.

Piaget, Jean, and Barbel Inhelder. 1969. *The Psychology of the Child.* New York: Basic Books.

Pierson, Donald. 1942. *Negroes in Brazil.* Chicago: University of Chicago Press.

Pincus, Fred L. 1980. "The False Promises of Community Colleges: Class Conflict and Vocational Education." *Harvard Educational Review* 50: 332–361.

Pines, Maya. 1982. "Behavior and Heredity: Links for Specific Traits are Growing Stronger." *New York Times* (June 29): 19, 22.

Pines, Maya. 1981. "The Civilizing of Genie." *Psychology Today* (September): 28–34.

Pinkney, Alphonso. 1976. *Red, Black, and Green: Black Nationalism in the United States.* New York: Cambridge University.

Pisko, Valena White, and Joyce D. Stern (eds.). 1985. *The Condition of Education, 1985 Edition.* Statistical Report, National Center for Education Statistics. Washington, DC: U.S. Government Printing Office.

Pitt, Leonard. 1966. *The Decline of the Californios: A Social History of the Spanish-Speaking, 1846–1890.* Berkeley: University of California Press.

Plutchik, Robert. 1962. *The Emotions.* New York: Random House.

Plutzer, Eric. 1988. "Work Life, Family Life, and Women's Support of Feminism." *American Sociological Review* 53: 640–649.

Polany, Karl. 1944. *The Great Transformation.* Boston: Beacon Press.

Polsby, Nelson W. 1980. *Community Power and Political Theory.* New Haven: Yale University Press.

Polsby, Nelson W. 1959. "Three Problems in the Analysis of Community Power." *American Sociological Review* 24: 796–803.

Population Reference Bureau. 1988. *1988 World Population Data Sheet.* Washington, DC: Population Reference Bureau.

Population Reference Bureau. 1988b. *The United States Poulation Data Sheet of the Population Reference Bureau, Inc.,* 7th ed. Washington, DC: Population Reference Bureau.

Population Reference Bureau. 1988c. "Take a Number: Childbearing USA." *Population Today* 16, 7/8: 10.

Porter, John. 1972. "Dilemmas and Contradictions of a Multiethnic Society." Royal Society of Canada, *Transactions* 10: 193–205.

Porter, John. 1965. *The Vertical Mosaic.* Toronto: University of Toronto Press.

Postel, Sandra. 1987. "Stabilizing Chemical Cycles." Pp. 157–176 in Lester R. Brown (ed.), *State of the World 1987.* New York: W. W. Norton & Co.

Poston, Dudley L. and Mei-Yu Yu. 1985. "Quality of Life, Intellectual Development and Behavior Characteristics of Single Children in China: Evidence from a 1980 Survey in Changsha, Hunan Province." *Journal of Biosocial Science* 17, 2: 127–136.

Potterfield, Austin L. 1943. "Delinquency and Its Court and Collage." *American Journal of Sociology,* 49: 199–208.

Prager, Jeffrey, Douglas Longshore, and Melvin Seeman. 1986. "Introduction: The Desegregation Situation." Pp. 3–20 in Jeffrey Prager, Douglas Longshore, and Melvin Seeman (eds.), *School Desegregation Research: New Directions in Situational Analysis.* New York: Plenum.

Price, Richard, and Edwin S. Mills. 1985. "Race and Residence in Earnings Determinations." *Journal of Urban Economics* 17: 1–18.

Projector, Dorothy, and Gertrude Weiss. 1966. *Survey of Financial Characteristics of Consumers.* Federal Reserve Technical Papers. Washington, DC: U.S. Government Printing Office.

Prothro, E. Terry. 1952. "Ethnocentrism and Anti-Negro Attitudes in the Deep South." *Journal of Abnormal and Social Psychology* 47: 105–108.

Purpel, David, and Kevin Ryan. 1976. "It Comes With the Territory: The Inevitability of Moral Education in the Schools." Pp. 44–54 in David Purpel and Kevin Ryan (eds.), *Moral Education . . . It Comes With the Territory.* Berkeley, CA: McCutchan.

Quinn, Michael. 1984. *Housing Quality Trends in Metro East.* Center for Urban and Environmental Research and Services Report No. 20. Edwardsville, IL: Southern Illinois University.

Quinney, Richard. 1979. *Capitalist Society: Readings for a Critical Sociology.* Homewood, IL: Dorsey.

Radcliffe-Brown, A. R. 1952. *Structure and Function in Primitive Society.* Glencoe, IL: The Free Press.

Radcliffe-Brown, A. R. 1950. "Introduction." Pp. 1–85 in A. R. Radcliffe-Brown and D. Forde (eds.), *African Systems of Kinship and Marriage.* London: Oxford University Press.

Radcliffe-Brown, A. R. 1935. "On the Concept of Functionalism in the Social Sciences." *American Anthropologist* 37: 394–402.

Radin, Norma. 1972. "Three Degrees of Maternal Involvement in a Preschool Program: Impact on Mothers and Children." *Child Development* 43: 1355–1364.

Radu, Michael S. 1987. "Terror, Terrorism, and Insurgency in Latin America." Pp. 298–302 in Walter Laqueur and Yonah Alexander (eds.), *The Terrorism Reader,* rev. ed. New York: NAL Penguin.

Rainwater, Lee. 1966. "Fear and the House-As-Haven in the Lower Class." *Journal of the American Institute of Planners* 32: 23–31.

Rainwater, Lee, and William L. Yancey (eds.). 1967. *The Moynihan Report and the Politics of Controversey.* Cambridge, MA: MIT Press.

Raper, Arthur. 1933. *The Tragedy of Lynching.* Chapel Hill: University of North Carolina Press.

Rassmussen, Howard. 1975. "Medical Education—Revolution or Reaction?" *Pharos* 38: 53–59.

Ravitch, Diane. 1983. *The Troubled Crusade: American Education, 1945–1980.* New York: Basic Books.

Raymond, Jack. 1971. "Free Enterprise and National Defense." Pp. 71–76 in Seymour Melman (ed.), *The War Economy of the United States.* New York: St. Martin's Press.

Redfield, Robert. 1947. "The Folk Society." *American Journal of Sociology* 52: 293–308.

Rees, Philip H. 1979. *Residential Patterns in American Cities: 1960.* Research Paper No. 189, Department of Geography, University of Chicago.

Rees, Philip H. 1970. "Concepts of Social Space: Toward an Urban Social Geography." Pp. 306–394 in Brian J. L. Berry and Frank Horton (eds.), *Geographic Perspectives on Urban Systems.* Englewood Cliffs, NJ: Prentice Hall.

Rehberg, Richard A., and Evelyn R. Rosenthal. 1978. *Class and Merit in the American High School.* New York: Longman.

Reich, Michael. 1986. "The Political-Economic Effects of Racism." Pp. 304–311 in Richard C. Edwards, Michael Reich, and Thomas E. Weisskopf (eds.), *The Capitalist System: A Radical Analysis of American Society,* 3rd ed. Englewood Cliffs, NJ: Prentice Hall.

Reich, Michael. 1986b. "The Proletarianization of the Labor Force." Pp. 122–131 in Richard C. Edwards, Michael Reich, and Thomas E. Weisskopf (eds.), *The Capitalist System: A Radical Analysis of American Society,* 3rd ed. Englewood Cliffs, NJ: Prentice Hall.

Reimer, Rita Ann. 1986. "Work and Family Life in Sweden." *Social Change in Sweden,* vol. 34. New York: Swedish Information Service.

Reimers, Cordella W. 1984. "Sources of the Family Income Differential Between Hispanics, Blacks, and White Non-Hispanics." *American Journal of Sociology* 89: 889–903.

Reis, H. T., and S. Wright. 1982. "Knowledge of Sex-Role Stereotypes in Children Aged 3 to 5." *Sex Roles* 8: 1049–1056.

Reiss, Albert J. 1959. "Rural-Urban and Status Differences in Interpersonal Contact." *American Journal of Sociology* 65: 182–195.

Reskin, Barbara F., and Heidi I. Hartmann. 1986. *Women's Work, Men's Work.* Washington, DC: National Academy Press.

Reskin, Barbara F. and Heidi I. Hartmann, eds. 1986. *Women's Work, Men's Work: Sex Segregation on the Job.* Washington, DC: National Academy Press.

Reynolds, Paul D. 1982. *Ethics and Social Research.* Englewood Cliffs, NJ: Prentice Hall.

Riesman, David. 1961. *The Lonely Crowd.* New Haven, CT: Yale University Press.

Riesman, David, with Nathan Glazer and Reuel Denney. 1969. *The Lonely Crowd,* abridged edition with a 1969 preface. New Haven: Yale University Press.

Riley, John W. 1983. "Dying and the Meanings of Death: Sociological Inquiries." Pp. 191–216 in Ralph H. Turner and James F. Short (eds.), *Annual Review of Sociology,* vol. 9. Palo Alto, CA: Annual Reviews.

Riley, Matilda White, and Kathleen Bond. 1983. "Beyond Ageism: Postponing the Onset of Disability." Pp. 243–252 in Matilda White Riley, Beth B. Hess, and Kathleen Bond (eds.), *Aging in Society: Selected Reviews of Recent Research.* Hillsdale, NJ: Lawrence Erlbaum.

Riley, Matilda White, Anne Foner, and Joan Waring. 1988. "Sociology of Age." Pp. 243–290 in Neil J. Smelser (ed.), *Handbook of Sociology.* Newbury Park, CA: Sage.

Riley, Matilda White, and Anne Foner, with Mary E. Moore, Beth B. Hess, and Barbara K. Roth. 1968. *Aging and Society: An Inventory of Research Findings,* vol. 1. New York: Russell Sage Foundation.

Riley, Matilda White, Marilyn Johnson, and Anne Foner. 1972. *Aging and Society, Vol. III: A Sociology of Age Stratification.* New York: Russell Sage Foundation.

Rist, Ray C. 1970. "Student Social Class and Teacher Expectations: The Self-Fulfilling Prophecy in Ghetto Education." *Harvard Educational Review* 40: 411–451.

Rivet, Paul. 1960. *Mayan Cities.* Miriam Kochan and Lionel Kochan (trs.). New York: Putnam.

Robb, Barbara, and Michael Raven. 1982. "Working Mothers and Children's Perceptions." *Research in Education* 27: 75–83.

Robert Wood Johnson Foundation. 1983. *Special Report: Updated Report on Access to Health Care for the American People.* Princeton, NJ: Robert Wood Johnson Foundation.

Robinson, John. 1988. "Who's Doing the Housework?" *American Demographics* 10, 12: 24–28, 63.

Robinson, John. 1977. *How Americans Use Their Time: A Social Psychological Analysis of Everyday Behavior.* New York: Praeger.

Robinson, Pauline K., Sally Coberly, and Carolyn S. Paul. 1985. "Work and Retirement." Pp. 503–527 in Robert H. Binstock and Ethel Shanas (eds.), *Handbook of Aging and the Social Sciences.* New York: Van Nostrand Reinhold.

Rodgers, H. R. 1978. "Hiding versus Ending Poverty." *Political Sociology* 8: 253–266.

Rodgers, Roy H. 1973. *Family Interaction and Transaction.* Englewood Cliffs, NJ: Prentice Hall.

Roe, Frank G. 1955. *The Indian and the Horse.* Norman: University of Oklahoma Press.

Roethlisberger, Fritz J., and William J. Dickson. 1939. *Management and the Worker.* Cambridge, MA: Harvard University Press.

Roman, Tsilia. 1986. "Role Conflict in the Portrayal of Female Heroes of Television Crime Dramas: A Theoretical Conceptualization." *Interchange* 17: 23–32.

Roof, Wade Clark. 1979. "Socioeconomic Differentials among White Socio-Religious Groups in the United States." *Social Forces* 58, 1: 280–289.

Roozen, David A., and Jackson W. Carroll. 1979. "Recent Trends in Church Membership and Participation: An Introduction." In D. R. Hoge and D. A. Roozen (eds.), *Understanding Church Growth and Decline: 1950–1978.* New York: Pilgrim Press.

Roozen, David A., and Jackson W. Carroll. 1979. "Recent Trends in Church Membership and Participation: An Introduction. In Dean

R. Hoge and Davod A. Roozen (eds.), *Understanding Church Growth and Decline, 1950–1978.* New York: Pilgrim.

Roper Organization. 1985. *Virginia Slims Poll.* New York: Richard Weiner.

Roper Organization, Inc. 1980. *The Virginia Slims American Women's Poll.*

Roscoe, B., and N. Benaske. 1985. "Courtship Violence Experienced by Abused Wives: Similarities in Patterns of Abuse." *Family Relations,* 34: 419–424.

Rose, Jerry D. 1982. *Outbreaks: The Sociology of Collective Behavior.* New York: Free Press.

Rose, Peter I. (ed.) 1979. *Socialization and the Life Cycle.* New York: St. Martin's Press.

Rosenbaum, James E. 1976. *Making Inequality: The Hidden Curriculum of High School Tracking.* New York: John Wiley.

Rosenberg, Charles E. 1987. *The Case of Strangers.* New York: Basic Books.

Rosengren, Karl, P. Arvidson, and D. Sturesson. 1975. "The Barseback 'Panic'." *Acta Sociologica* 18: 303–321.

Rosenhan, D. L. 1973. "On Being Sane in Insane Places." *Science* 179: 250–258.

Rosenthal, R., and D. B. Rubin. 1982. "Further Meta-Analytic Procedures for Assessing Cognitive Gender Differences." *Journal of Educational Psychology* 74: 708–712.

Rosenthal, Robert, and Lenore Jacobson. 1968. *Pygmalion in the Classroom: Teacher Expectation and Pupils' Intellectual Development.* New York: Holt, Rinehart, and Winston.

Rosnow, Ralph L, and Gary Allen Fine. 1976. *Rumor and Gossip: The Social Psychology of Hearsay.* New York: Elsevier.

Ross, Catherine E. 1987. "The Division of Labor at Home." *Social Forces* 65: 816–833.

Ross, Catherine, John Mirowsky, and William C. Cockerham. 1983. "Social Class, Mexican Culture, and Fatalism: Their Effects on Psychological Distress." *American Journal of Community Psychology* 11: 383–399.

Rossi, Alice S. 1985. "Gender and Parenthood." Pp. 161–191 in Alice S. Rossi (ed.), *Gender and the Life Course.* Hawthorne, NY: Aldine.

Rostow, Walt W. 1960. *The Stages of Economic Growth: A Non-Communist Manifesto.* Cambridge: Cambridge University Press.

Rostow, Walter. 1965. *The Stages of Economic Growth.* London: Cambridge University Press.

Roszak, Theodore. 1969. *The Making of a Counter-Culture: Reflections on the Technocratic Society and its Youthful Opposition.* New York: Doubleday.

Rothschild-Whitt, Joyce. 1979. "The Collectivist Organization: An Alternative to Rational-Bureaucratic Models." *American Sociological Review* 44: 509–527.

Rothschild, Joyce, and J. Allen Whitt. 1986. *The Cooperative Workplace: Potentials and Dilemmas of Organizational Democracy and Participation.* New York: Cambridge University Press.

Roy, William G. 1983. "The Unfolding of the Interlocking Directorate Structure of the United States." *American Sociological Review* 48: 248–257.

Rubin, J. Z., F. J. Prevenzano, and Z. Luria. 1974. "The Eye of the Beholder: Parents' Views on Sex of Newborns." *American Journal of Orthopsychiatry* 44: 512–519.

Rudwick, Elliott M. 1964. *Race Riot at East St. Louis, July 2, 1917.* Carbondale, IL: Southern Illinois University Press.

Rushing, William A. (ed.) 1969. *Deviant Behavior and Social Processes.* Chicago: Rand McNally.

Rushton, J. Philippe. 1975. "Generosity in Children: Immediate and Long-Term Effects of Modeling, Preaching, and Moral Judgment." *Journal of Personality and Social Psychology* 31: 459–466.

Russell, J. C. 1958. *Late Ancient and Medieval Population.* Philadelphia: American Philosophical Society.

Rutter, Michael, et al. 1979. *Fifteen Thousand Hours.* Cambridge, MA: Harvard University Press.

Ruzek, Cheryl Burt. 1980. "Medical Response to Women's Health Activities: Conflict, Accommodation, and Cooptation." Pp. 335–354 in Julius A. Roth (ed.), *Research in the Sociology of Health Care: A Research Annual,* Volume 1 - 1980: Professional Control to Health Services and Challenges to Such Control. Greenwich, CT: Jai Press.

Ryan, William. 1976. *Blaming the Victim,* rev. ed. New York: Vintage Books.

Ryan, William. 1971. *Blaming the Victim.* New York: Vintage.

Ryan, William. 1967. "Savage Discovery: The Moynihan Report." Pp. 445–457 in Lee Rainwater (ed.), *The Moynihan Report and the Politics of Controversey.* Cambridge, MA: MIT Press.

Safran, Claire. 1988. "Hidden Lessons: Do Little Boys Get a Better Education than Little Girls?" Pp. 35–37 in Paula S. Rothenberg (ed.), *Racism and Sexism: An Integrated Study.* New York: St. Martin's Press.

Sagor, Stanley E., and Archie Brodsky. 1984. "The Issue of Safety." Pp. 17–49 in Stanley E. Sagor, Richard I. Feinbloom, Peggy Spindel, and Archie Brodsky (eds.), *Home Birth: A Practitioner's Guide to Birth Outside the Hospital.* Rockville, MD: Aspen Systems.

St. John, Nancy H. 1975. *School Desegregation: Outcomes for Children.* New York: John Wiley.

St. Louis Post-Dispatch. 1989. "Demographics of the 101st Congress." *St. Louis Post-Dispatch* (January 4).

St. Louis Post-Dispatch. 1989b. "Help More Black Men Reach Campus." *St. Louis Post-Dispatch,* January 28, Section B, p. 2.

St. Louis Post-Dispatch. 1988b. "Deficit Leads List of Concerns in Poll." September 25, p. 7a.

St. Louis Post-Dispatch. 1988c. "Dukakis Backs Insurance for All Workers." September 21, pp. 1, 12.

St. Louis Post-Dispatch. 1988d. "Court Rules Against School Paper: Censoring Allowed at Hazelwood." January 14, p. 1.

St. Louis Post-Dispatch. 1987. "Homelessness Rocks Families, Mayors Report." December 17, pp. 1, 10.

St. Louis Post-Dispatch. "Educators Weigh Idea to Lengthen College Year." August 23, 1987, pp. 1C, 4C.

St. Louis Post-Dispatch. 1986a. "Super Rich Even Richer." July 26, p. 2.

St. Louis Post-Dispatch. 1986b. "Tax Bill Effects." August 18, p. 8a.

St. Louis Post-Dispatch. 1985. "Baby Bust: Middle Class Caught in Squeeze, Study Says." December 8, p. 1.

St. Louis Post-Dispatch. 1985b. "Hunger Reported Epidemic in U.S., Hitting 20 Million." February 27, pp. 1, 10.

Sale, Kirkpatrick. 1975. *Power Shift: The Rise of the Southern Rim and Its Challenge to the Eastern Establishment.* New York: Random House.

Salpukas, Agis. 1986. "Eastern's Battle over Wages." *New York Times,* January 22, Section D, p. 1.

Sampson, Robert J. 1987. "Urban Black Violence: The Effect of Male Joblessness and Family Disruption." *American Journal of Sociology* 93: 348–382.

Samuelson, Kurt. 1961. *Religion and Economic Action: A Critique of Max Weber.* (E. Geoffrey French, tr.) New York: Harper & Row.

Sandier, Simone. 1983. "Comparison of Health Expenditures in France and the United States, 1950–1978." Vital and Health Statistics, Series No. 21, DHHS Publication No. (PHS) 83-1405. Washington, DC: U.S. Government Printing Office.

San Giovanni, Lucinda. 1978. Ex-nuns: A Study of Emergent Role Passages. Norwood, NJ: Ablex.

Sapir, Edward. 1921. Language: An Introduction to the Study of Speech. New York: Harvest Books.

Sasaki, Masamichi, and Tatsuzo Suzuki. 1987. "Changes in Religious Committment in the United States, Holland, and Japan." American Journal of Sociology 92: 1055–1076.

Sattler, Jerome M. 1982. Assessment of Children's Intelligence and Special Abilities, 2nd ed. Boston: Allyn and Bacon.

Savage, Wendy. 1986. A Savage Enquiry. London: Virago.

Savin, Theodore R., and Jeffery E. Miller. 1970. "Demonism Revisited: The XYY Chromosomal Anomaly." Issues in Criminology, 5, 2: 199–207.

Sawers, Larry, and William K. Tabb (eds.). 1984. Sunbelt/Snowbelt: Urban Development and Regional Restructuring. New York: Oxford University Press.

Sayers, Janet. 1980. "Psychological Sex Differences." Pp. 42–62 in The Brighton Women and Science Group (eds.), Alice Through the Microscope: The Power of Science Over Women's Lives. London: VIRAGO.

Schafer, Walter E., Carol Olexa, and Kenneth Polk. 1972. "Programmed for Social Class: Tracking in High School." Pp. 34–54 in Kenneth Polk and Walter E. Schafer (eds.), Schools and Delinquency. Englewood Cliffs, NJ: Prentice Hall.

Scheff, Thomas J. 1975. Labeling Madness. Englewood Cliffs, NJ: Prentice Hall.

Schein, Edgar H., with Inge Schneier and Curtis H. Barker. 1961. Coercive Persuasion: A Socio-psychological Analysis of the "Brainwashing" of American Civilian Prisoners by the Chinese Communists. New York: Norton.

Schein, Edgar H. 1957. "Reaction Patterns to Severe Chronic Stress in American Army Prisoners of War of the Chinese." Journal of Social Issues 13,3: 21–30.

Schlapentokh, Vladimir. 1988. "The XXVII Congress: A Case Study in the Shaping of a New Party Ideology." Soviet Studies 40: 1–20.

Schneider, Joseph W., and Peter Conrad. 1980. "The Medical Control of Deviance: Conquests and Consequences." Pp. 1–53 in Julius A. Roth (ed.), Research in the Sociology of Health Care: A Research Annual, Volume 1 - 1980: Professional Control of Health Services and Challenges to Such Control. Greenwich, CT: Jai Press.

Schell, Jonathan. 1982. The Fate of the Earth. New York: Knopf.

Schoen, Robert, and James R. Kluegel. 1988. "The Widening Gap in Black and White Marriage Rates: The Impact of Population Composition and Differential Marriage Propensities." American Sociological Review 53: 895–907.

Schoen, Robert, Karen Woodrow, and John Baj. 1985. "Marriage and Divorce in Twentieth Century American Cohorts." Demography 22: 101–114.

Schooler, Carmi, and Atushi Naoi. 1988. "The Psychological Effects of Traditional and Economically Peripheral Job Settings in Japan." American Journal of Sociology 94: 335–355.

Schrag, C. Crime. 1984. Crime and Justice: American Style. Rockwell, MD: National Institute of Mental Health, 1971, pp. 90–92. Quoted in William J. Chambliss (ed.), Criminal Law in Action 2nd ed. New York: John Wiley & Sons.

Schur, Edwin M. 1980. The Politics of Deviance. Englewood Cliffs, NJ: Prentice Hall, Inc.

Schur, Edwin M. 1973. Radical Nonintervention: Rethinking the Delinquency Problem. Englewood Cliffs, NJ: Prentice Hall (Spectrum Books).

Schultz, Theodore W. 1961. "Investment in Human Capital." American Economic Review 51: 1–17.

Schuman, Howard. 1975. "Free Will and Determinism in Public Beliefs About Race." Pp. 375–380 in Norman R. Yetman and C. Hoy Steele (eds.), Majority and Minority: The Dynamics of Race and Ethnic Relations, 2nd ed. Boston: Allyn and Bacon. (Earlier version appeared in TransAction 7, 2 (1969): 44–48.)

Schur, Edwin. 1984. Labeling Women Deviant: Gender, Stigma, and Social Control. New York: Random House.

Schwab, Gustav. 1974. Gods and Heroes: Myths and Epics of Ancient Greece. New York: Pantheon Books.

Schwartz, Charles. 1975. "The Corporate Connection." Bulletin of the Atomic Scientist (October).

Sears, David O., and Harris M. Allen. 1984. "The Trajectory of Local Desegregation Controversies and Whites' Opposition to Busing." Pp. 123–151 in Norman Miller and Marilyn Brewer (eds.), Groups in Contact: The Psychology of Desegregation. New York: Academic.

Sears, Robert K., Maccoby, E. E., and H. Lewin. 1957. Patterns of Child Rearing. Evanston, IL: Row and Peterson.

See, Katherine O'Sullivan. 1986. First World Nationalisms: Class and Ethnic Politics in Northern Ireland and Quebec. Chicago: University of Chicago Press.

Seeman, Melvin, and J. W. Evans. 1962. "Alienation and Learning in a Hospital Setting." American Sociological Review 22: 772–783.

Seeman, Melvin, and Teresa E. Seeman. 1983. "Health Behavior and Personal Autonomy: A Longitudinal Study of the Sense of Control in Illness." Journal of Health and Social Behavior 24: 144–160.

Seifer, Nancy. 1973. Absent from the Majority: Working-Class Women in America. New York: American Jewish Committee.

Sellin, Thorsten (ed.) 1967. Capital Punishment. New York: Harper & Row.

Selznick, Philip. 1957. Leadership in Organizations. Evanston, IL: Row, Peterson.

Selznick, Philip. 1952. The Organizational Weapon. New York: McGraw Hill.

Semyonov, Moshe. 1988. "Bi-Ethnic Labor Markets, Mono-Ethnic Labor Markets, and Socioeconomic Inequality." American Sociological Review 53: 256–266.

Serrill, Michael S. 1987. "In the Grip of the Scourge." Time, February 16, pp. 58–59.

Service, Elman R. 1975. Origins of the State and Civilization. New York: Norton.

Sivard, Ruth Legger. 1987. World Military and Social Expenditures, 1987. Washington, D.C.: World Priorities.

Sexton, Patricia. 1961. Education and Income. New York: Viking.

Shah, Saleem A., and Laren H. Roth. 1974. "Biological and Psychophysiological Factors in Criminality." In Daniel Gloser (ed.), Handbook of Criminology. Chicago: Rand McNally.

Shanas, Ethel. 1979. "Social Myths as Hypothesis: The Case of Family Relations of Old People." Gerontologist 19: 2–9.

Shanas, Ethel, Peter Townsend, Dorothy Wedderburn, Hennig Friis, P. Milhj, and Jan Stehouwer. 1968. *Old People in Three Industrial Societies.* New York: Atherton Press.

Sharp, Rachel, and Anthony Green. 1975. *Education and Social Control.* London: Routledge and Kegan Paul.

Sheldon, Randall L. 1982. *Criminal Justice in America: A Sociological Approach.* Boston: Little, Brown and Company.

Sheldon, William. 1949. *Varieties of Delinquent Youth: An Introduction to Constitutional Psychiatry.* New York: Harper.

Shevky, Eshref, and Wendell Bell. 1955. *Social Area Analysis: Theory, Illustrative Application, and Computational Procedures.* Stanford, CA: Stanford University Press.

Shevky, Eshref, and Marilyn Williams. 1949. *The Social Areas of Los Angeles.* Berkeley: University of California Press.

Shibutani, Tamatsu. 1986. *Social Processes: An Introduction to Sociology.* Berkeley: University of California Press.

Shils, Edward. 1962. *Political Development in the New States.* The Hague: Monton.

Shockley, William. 1967. "A Try Simplist Cases' Approach to the Heredity-Poverty-Crime Problem." Proceedings of the National Academy of Sciences 57, 6: 1767–74.

Short, James F., Jr., and Ivan F. Nye. 1958. "Extent of Unrecorded Delinquency: Tentative Conclusions." *Journal of Criminal Law, Criminology and Police Science.* 49: 296–302.

Shultz, T. R., D. Wells, and M. Sarda. 1980. "Development of the Ability to Distinguish Intended Actions from Mistakes, Reflexes, and Passive Movements." *British Journal of Clinical and Social Psychology* 19: 301–310.

Silk, Leonard. 1987. "The Global Financial Circus: Everyone is Growing Frantic." *The New York Times,* April 5, p. 3.

Silverstein, Brett, Lauren Perdue, Barbara Peterson, and Eileen Kelly. 1986. "The Role of the Mass Media in Promoting a Thin Standard of Bodily Attractiveness for Women." *Sex Roles* 14: 519–532.

Simmel, Georg. 1971. "Fashion." In Donald N. Levine (ed.), *Georg Simmel: On Individuality and Social Forms.* Chicago: University of Chicago Press. [Originally published in 1904.]

Simmel, Georg. 1964. "The Metropolis and Mental Life." Pp. 409–424 in Kurt Wolf (ed. and tr.), *The Sociology of Georg Simmel.* New York: Free Press. [Originally published in 1905.]

Simmons, J. L. 1969. *Deviants.* Berkeley, CA: Glendessary.

Simmons, James W. 1978. "The Organization of the Urban System." Chapter 1.4 in Larry S. Bourne and James W. Simmons (eds.), *Systems of Cities.* New York: Oxford University Press.

Simmons, Rosa, and Susan G. Broyler. 1983. *Fall Enrollment in Colleges and Universities, 1980.* Washington: National Center for Education Statistics.

Simon, David R., and D. Stanley Eitzen. 1986. *Elite Deviance.* Boston: Allyn and Bacon.

Simon, Julian L. 1981. *The Ultimate Resource.* Princeton, NJ: Princeton University Press.

Simon, Julian L., and Herman Kahn. 1984. *The Resourceful Earth: A Response to Global 2000.* New York: Basil Blackwell.

Simpson, George Eaton, and J. Milton Yinger. 1985. *Racial and Cultural Minorities: An Analysis of Prejudice and Discrimination,* 5th ed. New York: Plenum.

Simpson, John H. 1981. "Is There a Moral Majority?" Paper presented at joint annual meeting of the Society for the Scientific Study of Religion and the Religious Research Association, Baltimore, MD, October 30.

Sindler, Allan P. 1978. *Bakke, DeFunis, and Minority Admissions: The Quest for Equal Opportunity.* New York: Longman.

Singer, Joel David, and Melvin Small. 1972. *The Wages of War, 1816–1965: A Statistical Handbook.* New York: John Wiley.

Sivard, Ruth Leger. 1987. *World, Military and Social Expenditures 1987–1988,* 12th ed. Washington DC: World Priorities.

Sivard, Ruth Legger. 1987. *World Military and Social Expenditures, 1987* Washington, D.C.: World Priorities.

Sjoberg, Gideon. 1960. *The Preindustrial City.* Glencoe, IL: Free Press.

Sjoberg, Gideon. 1955. "The Preindustrial City." *American Journal of Sociology* 60: 438–445.

Skinner, B. F. 1971. *Beyond Freedom and Dignity.* New York: Alfred A. Knopf.

Skinner, B. F. 1968. *The Technology of Teaching.* New York: Appleton, Century, Crofts.

Skinner, B. F. 1938. *The Behavior of Organisms.* New York: Appleton, Century, Crofts.

Skinner, G. William. 1985. Presidential Address: "The Structure of Chines History." *Journal of Asian Studies* 64, 2: 271–292.

Skocpol, Theda. 1979. *States and Social Revolutions: A Comparative Analysis of France, Russia, and China.* Cambridge: Cambridge University Press.

Skolnick, Jerome H. 1969. *The Politics of Protest.* New York: Simon and Schuster.

Slack, W. V., and Douglas Porter. 1980. "The Scholastic Aptitude Test: A Critical Appraisal." *Harvard Educational Review* 50: 154–175.

Slater, Philip E. 1970. *The Pursuit of Loneliness.* Boston: Beacon Press.

Slater, Philip E. 1955. "Role Differentiation in Small Groups." Pp. 498–515 in A. Paul Hare (ed.), *Small Groups: Studies in Social Interaction.* New York: Knopf.

Slomczynski, Kazimierz M., and Tadeusz K Krauze. 1987. "Cross-National Similarity in Social Mobility Patterns: A Direct Test of the Featherman-Jones-Hauser Hypothesis." *American Sociological Review* 52: 598–611.

Smart, Ninian. *The World's Religions.* 1989. Englewood Cliffs, NJ: Prentice Hall.

Smelser, Neil J. 1988. "Social Structure." Pp. 103–129 in Neil J. Smelser (ed.), *Handbook of Sociology.* Newbury Park, CA: Sage.

Smelser, Neil J. 1963. *Theory of Collective Behavior.* New York: Free Press.

Smith, Adam. 1910. *The Wealth of Nations.* London: J. M. Dent. [Originally published in 1776.]

Smith, David A. and Roger J. Nemeth. 1988. "An Empirical Analysis of Commodity Exchange in the International Economy: 1965–1980." *International Studies Quarterly* 32, 2: 227–240.

Smith, Jack. 1976. "The Great Los Angeles Air Raid." In John Caughey and La Rue Caughey (eds.), *Los Angeles: Biography of a City.* Los Angeles: *Los Angeles Times.*

Snow, David A., E. Burke Rochford, Jr., Steven K. Worden, and Robert D. Benford. 1986. "Frame Alignment Processes, Micromobilization, and Movement Participation." *American Sociological Review* 78: 537–561.

Snyder, David and Edward L. Kick. 1979. "Structural Position in the World System and Economic Growth, 1955–1970: A Multiple-

Network Analysis of Transnational Interactions." *American Journal of Sociology* 84: 1096–1126.

Soldo, Beth J., and Emily M. Agree. 1988. "America's Elderly." *Poulation Bulletin* 43, 3.

Sorauf, Frank. 1976. *The Wall of Separation: The Constitutional Politics of Church and State.* Princeton, NJ: Princeton University Press.

Sorensen, Annemette, and Sara McLanahan. 1987. "Married Women's Economic Opportunity, 1940–1980." *American Journal of Sociology* 93: 659–687.

Sorokin, Pitirim A. 1941. *The Crisis of Our Age.* New York: E. P. Dutton.

Sorokin, Pitirim A. 1937. *Social and Cultural Dynamics.* New York: American Book.

Sorokin, Pitirim A. 1937. *Social and Cultural Dynamics, Vol. 3: Fluctuation of Social Relationships, War, and Revolution.* New York: American Book.

Sovani, N. V. 1964. "The Analysis of Over-Urbanization." *Economic Development and Cultural Change* 12: 113–122.

Spain, Daphne. 1980. "Black-to-White Successions in Central City Housing: Limited Evidence of Urban Revitalization." *Urban Affairs Quarterly* 15: 381–396.

Spates, James L., and John J. Macionis. 1987. *The Sociology of Cities,* 2nd ed. Belmont, CA: Wadsworth.

Special Committee on Aging, U.S. Senate. 1980. *Developments in Aging, 1980.* Washington, DC: U.S. Government Printing Office.

Spector, Malcolm, and John I. Kitsuse. 1977. *Constructing Social Problems.* Menlo Park, CA: Cummings.

Spence, Janet T., Kay Deaux, and Robert L. Helmreich. 1985. "Sex Roles in Contemporary American Society." Pp. 149–178 in Gardne Lindzey and Elliot Aronson (eds.), *Handbook of Social Psychology,* vol. 1. New York: Random House.

Spence, Janet T., Robert L. Helmreich, and Joy Stapp. 1975. "Ratings of Self and Peers on Sex Role Attributes and their Relations to Self-Esteem and Conceptions of Masculinity and Feminity. *Journal of Personality and Social Psychology* 32: 29–39.

Spence, Janet T., Robert L. Helmreich, and Joy Stapp. 1974. "The Personal Attributes Questionnaire: A Measure of Sex Role Stereotypes and Masculinity-Femininity." *JSAS Catalog of Selected Documents in Psychology* 43, Ms. No. 617.

Spengler, Oswald. 1962. *The Decline of the West.* New York: Knopf. [Originally published in 1918, 1922.]

Spengler, Oswald. 1932. *The Decline of the West.* New York: Knopf.

Spicer, Edward H. 1980a. "American Indians." Pp. 58–114 in Stephan Thernstrom, Ann Orlov, and Oscar Handlin (eds.), *Harvard Encyclpedia of American Ethnic Groups.* Cambridge, MA: Harvard University Press.

Spicer, Edward H. 1980b. "American Indians, Federal Policy Toward." Pp. 114–122 in Stephan Thernstrom, Ann Orlov, and Oscar Handlin (eds.), *Harvard Encyclopedia of American Ethnic Groups.* Cambridge, MA: Harvard University Press.

Spitz, Rene A. 1945. "Hospitalism: An Inquiry into the Genesis of Psychiatric Conditions in Early Childhood." In Anna Freund et al., (eds.), *The Psychoanalytic Study of the Child.* New York: International Universities Press.

Squires, Gregory D. 1989. "Runaway Factories Are Also a Civil Rights Issue." Pp. 179–181 in D. Stanley Eitzen and Maxine Baca Zinn (eds.), *The Reshaping of America: Social Consequences of a Changing Economy.* Englewood Cliffs, NJ: Prentice Hall.

Srole, Leo. 1980. "Mental Health in New York." *The Sciences* 20, 10: 16–29.

Srole, Leo. 1972. "Urbanization and Mental Health: Some Reformulations." *American Scientist* 60: 576–583.

Srole, Leo, Thomas Langer, Stanley Michael, Marvin Opler, and Thomas Rennie. 1962. *Mental Health in the Metropolis: The Midtown Manhattan Study.* New York: McGraw Hill.

Stacy, J., S. Bereaud, and J. Daniels. 1974. *Sexism in American Education.* New York: Dell.

Stampp, Kenneth. 1956. *The Peculiar Institution.* New York: Alfred A. Knopf.

Stanley, Julian C. (ed.). 1973. *Compensatory Education for Children Ages 2 to 8, Recent Studies of Environmental Intervention.* Baltimore: Johns Hopkins University Press.

Star, Jack 1984. "Putting a Clamp on Your Medical Costs." *Chicago* (June): 166–171, 192–193.

Stark, Rodney. 1985. "Church and Sect." In P. Hammond, ed., *The Sacred in a Secular Age.* Berkeley: University of California Press.

Stark, Rodney and W. S. Bainbridge. 1981. "American-Born Sects: Initial Findings." *Journal for the Scientific Study of Religion* 20: 130–149.

Stark, Rodney and W. S. Bainbridge. 1979. "Of Churches, Sects, and Cults: Preliminary Concepts for a Theory of Religious Movements." *Journal for the Scientific Study of Religion* 18: 117–133.

Starr, Paul. 1982. *The Social Transformation of American Medicine.* New York: Basic Books.

Stein, Leonard I. 1967. "The Doctor-Nurse Game." *Archives of General Psychiatry* 16: 699–703.

Sternbach, R. A., and B. Tursky. 1965. "Ethnic Differences Among Housewives in Psychophysical and Skin Potential Responses to Electric Shock." *Psychophysiology* 1, 3: 241–246.

Sternlieb, George, and James W. Hughes. 1983. "The Uncertain Future of the Central City." *Urban Affairs Quarterly* 18: 455–472.

Sternlieb, George, and James W. Hughes. 1975. *Post-Industrial America: Metropolitan Decline and Interregional Job Shifts.* New Brunswick, NJ: Center for Urban Policy Research, Rutgers University.

Stevenson, Harold W., Shin-Ying Lee, and James W. Stigler. 1986. "Mathematics Achievement of Chinese, Japanese, and American Children." *Science* 231: 693–699.

Stockard, Jean, and Miriam M. Johnson. 1980. *Sex Roles: Sex Inequality and Sex Role Development.* Englewood Cliffs, NJ: Prentice Hall.

Stogdill, Ralph M. 1974. *Handbook of Leadership: A Survey of Theory and Research.* New York: Free Press.

Stoner, J. A. F. 1961. "A Comparison of Individual and Group Decisions Involving Risk." Masters thesis, Massachusetts Institute of Technology, School of Industrial Management.

Stouffer, Samuel A., A. A. Lumsdaine, M. H. Lumsdaine, M. R. Williams, M. B. Smith, Irving L. Janis, S. A. Star, and L. S. Cottrell. 1949. *The American Soldier. Vol II: Combat and its Aftermath.* Princeton, NJ: Princeton University Press.

Straus, Murray A., and R. J. Gelles. 1986. "Societal Change and Change in Family Violence From 1975 to 1985 as Revealed by Two National Surveys." *Journal of Marriage and the Family* 48: 465–479.

Strauss, Anselm, Leonard Schatzman, Rue Bucher, Danuta Ehrlich, and Melvin Sabslim. 1964. *Psychiatric Ideologies and Institutions.* New York: Free Press.

Sumner, William Graham. 1906. *Folkways.* Boston: Ginn.

Sumner, William Graham. 1896. *Folkways.* Boston: Ginn.

Sundquist, James L. 1982. *Dynamics of the Party System: Alignment and Realignment of Political Parties in the United States,* rev. ed. Washington, DC: Brookings Institute.

Susser, Mervyn W., Kim Hopper, and Judith Richman. 1983. "Society, Culture, and Health." Pp. 23–49 in David Mechanic (ed.), *Handbook of Health, Health Care, and the Health Professions.* New York: Free Press.

Susser, Mervyn W., William Watson, and Kim Hopper. 1985. *Sociology in Medicine,* 3rd ed. New York: Oxford University Press.

Sutherland, Edwin H. 1983. *White-Collar Crime.* NewHaven, CT: Yale University Press.

Sutherland, Edwin H. 1947. *Criminology,* 4th ed. Philadelphia: Lippencott.

Sutherland, Edwin H. 1940. "White-Collar Criminality." *American Sociological Review* 5: 1–12.

Swatos, William H. 1983. "Enchantment and Disenchantment in Modernity: The Significance of 'Religion' As a Sociological Category." *Sociological Analysis* 44: 321–38.

Swedish Institute. 1988. "Fact Sheets on Sweden: General Facts on Sweden." Stockholm: Swedish Institute.

Sweetser, D. A. 1985. "Broken Homes, Stable Risk, Changing Reasons, Changing Forms." *Journal of Marriage and Family,* 47: 709–715.

Sykes, Gresham M. 1970. *Criminology.* NY: Harcourt, Brace and Jovanovich.

Szinovacz, Maximiliane. 1985. "Beyond the Hearth: Older Women and Retirement." Pp. 327–353 in Beth B. Hess and Elizabeth W. Markson (eds.), *Growing Old in America: New Perspectives on Old Age,* 3rd ed. New Brunswick, NJ: Transaction Books.

Szymanski, Albert. 1976. "Racial Discrimination and White Gain." *American Sociological Review* 41: 403–414.

Tabah, Leon. 1980. "World Population Trends: A Stocktaking." *Population and Development Review* 6: 355–390.

Tabb, William, and Larry Sawers (eds.). 1978. *Marxism and the Metropolis.* New York: Oxford University Press.

Taeuber, Karl E., and Alma F. Taeuber. 1965. *Negroes in Cities.* Chicago: Aldine.

Tagliabue, John. 1987. "A Nuclear Taint in Milk Sets Off German Dispute." *New York Times,* January 31, pp. 1, 4.

Tan, Alexis S. 1979. "TV Beauty Ads and Role Expectations of Adolescent Female Viewers." *Journalism Quarterly* 56: 283–288.

Task Force on Education for Economic Growth, Educational Commission of the States. 1983. *Action for Excellence: A Comprehensive Plan to Improve Our Nation's Schools.* Denver: A. B. Hirschfield Press.

Taubman, Philip. 1988. "Soviet Moves to Curtail Communist Party's Power." *New York Times,* May 27, pp. 1, 9.

Taylor, Ian, et al. 1973. *The New Criminology: For a Social Theory of Deviance.* Boston: Routledge & Kegan Paul.

Taylor's World of Politics. 1987. "Changes Across the Nation Resulting From the 1986 Elections." *Taylor's World of Politics* (April): 5.

Teachman, Jay. 1983. "Early Marriage, Premarital Fertility, and Marital Dissolution." *Journal of Family Issues* 4: 105–126.

Teachman, Jay D. 1987. "Family Background, Educational Resources, and Educational Attainment." *American Sociological Review* 52: 548–557.

Teich, Albert H., ed. 1986. *Technology and the Future,* 4th ed. New York: St. Martin's Press.

Thernstrom, Abigail. 1980. "E Pluribus Plura: Congress and Bilingual Education." *The Public Interest* 60: 3–22.

Thernstrom, Stephan, Ann Orlov, and Oscar Handlin (eds.). 1980. *Harvard Encyclopedia of American Ethnic Groups.* Cambridge, MA: Harvard University Press.

Thomas, Marlo. 1987. *Free To Be . . . a Family.* New York: Bantam.

Thomas, W. I. 1966. *W. I. Thomas on Social Organization and Personality.* (Morris Janowitz, ed.) Chicago: University of Chicago Press.

Thomas, William L., (ed.) 1956. *Man's Role in Change the Face of the Earth,* vol. 1. Chicago: University of Chicago Press.

Thomlinson, Ralph. 1976. *Population Dynamics: Causes and Consequences of World Population Change,* 2nd ed. New York: Random House.

Thompson, E. P. 1963. *The Making of the English Working Class.* New York: Vintage Books.

Thompson, Wilbur. 1975. "Economic Processes and Employment Problems in Declining Metropolitan Areas." Pp. 187–196 in George Sternlieb and James W. Hughes (eds.), *Post-Industrial America: Metropolitan Decline and Interregional Job Shifts.* New Brunswick, NJ: Center for Urban Policy Research, Rutgers University.

Thompson, William R. 1983. "Introduction: World System Analysis With and Without the Hyphen." Pp. 7–24 in Thompson, William R., ed., *Contending Approaches to World System Analysis.* Beverly Hills, CA: Sage.

Thorndike, Robert B. 1969. "Review of *Pygmalion in the Classroom.*" *Teachers College Record* 70: 805–807.

Thornton, Arland. 1983. "Changing Attitudes toward Divorce with Children: Evidence from an Inter-generational Panel Study." Paper presented at annual meeting of the Population Association of America, Pittsburgh.

Thornton, Arland, and Deborah Freedman. 1984. "The Changing American Family." *Population Bulletin* 38, 4.

Thornton, Russell. 1987. *American Indian Holocaust and Survival: A Population History since 1492.* Norman: University of Oklahoma Press.

Thurow, Lester C. 1977. "The Myth of the American Economy." *Newsweek,* February 14, p. 11.

Tilly, Charles. 1978. *From Mobilization to Revolution.* Reading, MA: Addison-Wesley.

Tilly, Charles. 1974. "The Chaos of the Living City." Pp. 86–108 in Charles Tilly (ed.), *An Urban World.* Boston: Little, Brown.

Tilly, Charles, Louise A. Tilly, and Richard Tilly. 1975. *The Rebellious Century: 1830–1930.* Cambridge, MA: Harvard University Press.

Tilly, Louise A., and J. W. Scott. 1978. *Women, Work, and the Family.* New York: Holt, Rinehart, and Winston.

Time. 1989. "A Blow to Affirmative Action." *Time,* February 6, p. 60.

Tobias, Sheila. 1978. *Overcoming Math Anxiety.* New York: Norton.

Tobin, Gary (ed.). 1987. *Divided Neighborhoods.* Urban Affairs Annual Reviews, vol 32. Newbury Park, CA: Sage Publications.

Toennies, Ferdinand. 1963. *Community and Society.* New York: Harper and Row. [Originally published in German as *Gemeinschaft und Gesellschaft* in 1887.]

Toennies, Ferdinand. 1957. *Community and Society: Gemeinschaft and Und Gesellschaft.* Charles P. Loomis. (tr. and ed.) East Lansing: Michigan State University Press.

Toffler, Alvin. 1980. *The Third Wave.* New York: William Morrow.

Toffler, Alvin. 1970. *Future Shock.* New York: Random House.

Toynbee, Arnold. 1962. *A Study of History.* New York: Oxford.

Tolchin, Martin. 1988. "House Backs Conference Bill on Major Illness." *New York Times,* June 3, p. 32.

Touraine, Alain. 1971. *The Post-Industrial Society.* Leonard F. X. Mayhew (tr.). New York: Random House. [Originally published in French in 1969.]

Toye, J. F. J. 1985. "Economic Development." Pp. 223–225 in Adam and Jessica Kuper (eds.). *Social Science Encyclopaedia.* London: RKP.

Toynbee, Arnold. 1946. *A Study of History.* New York: Oxford University Press.

Treisman, Daniel. 1985. "Terror Error." *The New Republic* 193(16): 16–18.

Tribe, Lawrence. 1989. Quoted in *Time,* "A Blow to Affirmative Action," February 6, p. 60.

Troeltsch, Ernst. 1932. *The Social Teaching of the Christian Churches* Olive Wyon (tr.). New York: Macmillan.

Tsui, A. O., and Donald J. Bogue. 1979. "Declining World Fertility: Trends, Causes, Implications." *Population Bulletin* 33, 4.

Tuch, Steven A. 1987. "Urbanism, Region, and Tolerance Revisited: The Case of Racial Prejudice." *American Sociological Review* 52: 504–510.

Tumin, Melvin. 1985. *Social Stratification: The Forms and Functions of Social Inequality.* Englewood Cliffs, NJ: Prentice Hall.

Tumin, Melvin M. (ed.) 1970. *Readings on Social Statification.* Englewood Cliffs, NJ: Prentice Hall.

Tumin, Melvin M. 1953. "Some Principles of Stratification: A Critical Analysis." *American Sociological Review* 18: 378–394.

Turk, Amos, Janet T. Wittes, Jonathon Turk, and Robert E. Wittes. 1978. *Environmental Science,* 2nd ed. Philadelphia: Saunders.

Turkel, Studs. 1967. *Division Street: America.* New York: Pantheon.

Turner, Ralph, and Lewis M. Killian. 1987. *Collective Behavior,* 3rd ed. Englewood Cliffs, NJ: Prentice Hall.

Turner, Ralph H., and Lewis M. Killian. 1987. *Collective Behavior,* 3rd ed. Englewood Cliffs, NJ: Prentice Hall.

Turner, Ralph H., and Lewis M. Killian. 1972. *Collective Behavior,* 2nd ed. Englewood Cliffs, NJ: Prentice Hall.

Twaddle, Andrew C. 1979. *Sickness Behavior and the Sick Role.* Cambridge, MA: Schenkman.

Twaddle, Andrew C., and Richard Hessler. 1977. *A Sociology of Health.* St. Louis: C. V. Mosby.

Twentieth Century Fund. 1983. *Report of the Twentieth Century Fund Task Force on Federal Elementary and Secondary Education Policy.* New York: Twentieth Century Fund.

Tyree, Andrea, Moshe Semyonov, and Robert W. Hodge. 1979. "Gaps and Glissandos: Inequality, Economic Development, and Social Mobility in 24 Countries." *American Sociological Review* 44: 410–424.

Udry, J. Richard. 1988. "Biological Predispositions and Social Control in Adolescent Sexual Behavior." *American Sociological Review* 53: 709–722.

Udry, J. Richard, and John O. G. Billy. 1987. "Initiation of Coitus in Early Adolescence." *American Sociological Review* 52: 841–855.

Udy, Stanley H., Jr. 1959. "Bureaucracy and 'Rationality' in Weber's Organizational Theory: An Empirical Study." *American Sociological Review* 24: 791–795.

Unger, Irwin. 1989. *These United States: The Questions of Our Past,* 4th ed. Englewood Cliffs, NJ: Prentice Hall.

United Nations. 1988. *1986 Energy Statistics Yearbook.* New York: United Nations.

United Nations. 1985. *Demographic Yearbook 1983.* New York: United Nations.

United Nations. 1985b. *World Population Prospects: Estimates and Projections as Assessed in 1982.* New York: U.N. Department of International Economic an Social Affairs.

United Nations. 1954. "The Cause of the Aging of Populations: Declining Mortality or Declining Fertility?" *Population Bulletin of the United Nations* 4: 30.

U.S. Bureau of the Census. 1988a. *Current Population Reports: Population Estimates and Projections.* Series P-25, No. 1022. "United States Population Estimates by Age, Sex, and Race, 1980 to 1987." Washington, DC: U.S. Government Printing Office.

U.S. Bureau of the Census. 1988b. *Current Population Reports: Population Characteristics.* Series P-20, No. 431. "The Hispanic Population in the United States: March, 1988 (Advance Report)." Washington, DC: U.S. Government Printing Office.

U.S. Bureau of the Census. 1988c. *Current Population Reports: Consumer Income.* Series P-60, No. 180. "Poverty in the United States, 1986." Washington, DC: U.S. Government Printing Office.

U.S. Bureau of the Census. 1988d. *Current Population Reports,* Series P-20, No. 423. "Marital Status and Living Arrangements: March 1987." Washington, DC: Government Printing Office.

U.S. Bureau of the Census. 1988d. *Statistical Abstract of the United States, 1989.* Washington, DC: U.S. Government Printing Office.

U.S. Bureau of the Census. 1988e. *Current Population Reports,* Series P-20, No. 424. "Households and Family Characteristics: March 1987." Washington, DC: Government Printing Office.

U.S. Bureau of the Census. 1988e. *Current Population Reports: Consumer Income.* Money Income and Poverty Status of Families and Persons in the United States, 1987. (Advance Data from the March, 1988 Current Population Survey.) Washington, DC: U.S. Government Printing Office.

U.S. Bureau of the Census. 1988f. *Current Population Reports: Population Characteristics.* Series P-20, No. 431. The Hispanic Population in the United States: March, 1988 (Advance Report). Washington, DC: U.S. Government Printing Office.

U.S. Bureau of the Census. 1988g. *Current Population Reports: Consumer Income.* Money Income of Households, Families, and Persons in the United States, 1986. Washington, DC: U.S. Government Printing Office.

U.S. Bureau of the Census. 1988h. *Current Population Reports: Population Characteristics.* Series P-20, No. 423. Marital Status and Living Arrangements: March, 1987. Washington, DC: U.S. Government Printing Office.

U.S. Bureau of the Census. 1987a. *Current Population Reports: Consumer Income.* Series P-60, No. 157. "Money Income and Poverty Status of Families and Persons in the United States: 1986." (Advance Data from the March, 1987 Current Population Survey). Washington, DC: U.S. Government Printing Office.

U.S. Bureau of the Census. 1987b. *Current Population Reports: Population Characteristics.* Series P-20, No. 416. "The Hispanic Population in the United States: March, 1987 and 1986" (Advance Report). Washington, DC: U.S. Government Printing Office.

U.S. Bureau of the Census. 1987c. *Current Population Reports: Population Characteristics.* "Educational Attainment in the United States: March, 1982–1985." Washington, DC: U.S. Government Printing Office.

U.S. Bureau of the Census. 1987d. *Statistical Abstract of the United States, 1988.* Washington, DC: U.S. Government Printing Office.

U.S. Bureau of the Census. 1986a. *Current Population Reports: Population Characteristics.* Series P-20, No. 411. "Household and Family Characteristics: March, 1985." Washington, DC: U.S. Government Printing Office.

U.S. Bureau of the Census. 1986b. "Household Wealth and Asset Ownership." Washington, DC: U.S. Government Printing Office.

U.S. Bureau of the Census. 1986c. *1982 Census of Manufactures.* "Concentration Ratios in Manufacturing." Report No. MC82-S-7. Washington, DC: U.S. Government Printing Office.

U.S. Bureau of the Census. 1986d. *Current Population Reports: Population Estimates and Projections.* Series p-25, No. 995. Washington, DC: U.S. Government Printing Office.

U.S. Bureau of the Census. 1986e. *State and Metropolitan Area Data Book, 1986.* Washington, DC: U.S. Government Printing Office.

U.S. Bureau of the Census. 1983. *1980 Census of Population.* Characteristics of th Population, United States Summary. Report No. PC80-1-B1. Washington, DC: U.S. Government Printing Office.

U.S. Bureau of the Census. 1985. *Current Population Reports: Consumer Income.* "Money Income and Poverty Status of Persons and Families in the United States: 1984." Advance Data from the March, 1985 Current Population Survey. Series P-60, No. 149. Washington, DC: U.S. Government Printing Office.

U.S. Bureau of the Census. 1984. "Estimates of Poverty Including the Value of Non-Cash Benefits." Technical Paper No. 51. Washington, DC: U.S. Government Printing Office.

U.S. Bureau of the Census. 1984b. *Current Population Reports: Population Estimates and Projections:* Series P-25, No. 952. Washington, DC: U.S. Government Printing Office.

U.S. Bureau of the Census. 1984c. *Current Population Reports.* Series P-20, No. 395. "Fertility of American Women, June, 1983." Washington, DC: U.S. Government Printing Office.

U.S. Bureau of the Census. 1983. *1980 Census of the Population.* "Ancestry of the Population by State: 1980." Supplementary Report No. PC80-S1-10. Washington, DC: U.S. Government Printing Office.

U.S. Bureau of the Census. 1983b. *Current Population Reports: Population Characteristics.* "School Enrollment; Social and Economic Characteristics of Students" (Advance Report). Washington, DC: U.S. Government Printing Office.

U.S. Bureau of the Census. 1983c. *1980 Census of Poulation.* "Characteristics of the Population, General Population Characteristics, United States Summary." Report No. PC80-1-B1. Washington, DC: U.S. Government Printing Office.

U.S. Bureau of the Census. 1981. *1980 Census of the Population.* "Age, Sex, Race, and Spanish Origin of the Population by Regions, Divisions, and States: 1980." Report No. PC80-S1-1. Washington, DC: U.S. Government Printing Office.

U.S. Bureau of the Census. 1976. *Statistical Abstract of the United States, 1976.* Washington, DC: U.S. Government Printing Office.

U.S. Bureau of the Census. 1975. *Historical Statistics of the United States, Colonial Times to 1970.* Washington, DC: U.S. Government Printing Office.

U.S. Bureau of the Census. 1913. *Thirteenth Census of the United States: 1910.* Volume 1, Population: General Report and Analysis. Washington, DC: U.S. Bureau of the Census.

U.S. Bureau of Labor Statistics. 1988. U.S. Dept. of Labor, USDL 88-369, "Usual Weekly Earnings of Wage and Salary Workers: Second Quarter 1988."

U.S. Commission on Civil Rights. 1976. *Fulfilling the Letter and Sprit of the Law: Desegregation of the Nation's Schools.* Washington, DC: U.S. Government Printing Office.

U.S. Commission on Civil Rights. 1974. *Toward Quality Education for Mexican Americans.* Mexican American Study Report No. 4. Washington, DC: U.S. Government Printing Office.

U.S. Department of Education. 1987a. *Schools that Work: Educating Disadvantaged Children.* Washington, DC: U.S. Government Printing Office.

U.S. Department of Education. 1987b. *Elementary and Secondary Education Indicators in Brief.* Washington, DC: U.S. Government Printing Office.

U.S. Department of Education. 1987c. *The Condition of Education: A Statistical Report,* 1987 Edition. Washington, DC: U.S. Government Printing Office.

U.S. Department of Health, Education, and Welfare, National Cancer Institute, National Institute of Environmental Health Sciences, and National Institute of Occupational Safety and Health. 1978. *Estimates of the Fraction of Cancer in the United States Related to Occupational Factors.* Washington, DC: U.S. Government Printing Office.

U.S. Department of Housing and Urban Development. 1979. *Experimental Housing Allowance Program: A 1979 Report of Findings.* Washington, DC: U.S. Department of Housing and Ubban Development.

U.S. Department of Labor. 1988. "Current Labor Statistics," Table 47. *Monthly Labor Review* 111, 5: 105.

U.S. Department of Labor. 1965. *The Negro Family: The Case for National Action.* (The "Moynihan Report.") Washington, DC: U.S. Government Printing Office.

U.S. Environmental Protection Agency. 1984. *Draft National Environmental Report.* Washington, DC: U.S. Government Printing Office.

U.S. National Advisory Commission on Civil Disorders. 1968. *Report of the National Advisory Commission on Civil Disorders.* New York: New York Times Company, Bantam Books.

U.S. National Commission on the Causes and Prevention of Violence. 1968. *Report to the National Commission on the Causes and Prevention of Violence.* New York: Bantam Books.

U.S. Strategic Bombing Survey. 1947. *The Effects of Strategic Bombing on German Morale.* Washington, DC: U.S. Government Printing Office.

Useem, Michael. 1984. *The Inner Circle: Large Corporations and the Rise of Business Political Activity in the U.S. and U.K.* New York: Oxford University Press.

Useem, Michael. 1983. *The Inner Circle: Large Corporations and Business Politics in the U.S. and U.K.* New York: Oxford University Press.

Usher, Dan. 1981. *The Economic Prerequisites of Democracy.* New York: Columbia University Press.

Vago, Steven. 1989. *Social Change,* 2nd ed. Englewood Cliffs, NJ: Prentice Hall.

Vago, Steven. 1988. *Law and Society,* 2nd ed. Englewood Cliffs, NJ: Prentice Hall.

Van Arsdol, Maurice, Santo F. Camilleri, and Calvin F. Schmid. 1958. "The Generality of Urban Social Area Indices." *American Sociological Review* 23: 277–284.

Van de Kaa, Dirk J. 1987. "Europe's Second Demographic Transition." *Population Bulletin* 42, 1.

Van den Burghe, Pierre L. 1978. *Race and Racism: A Comparative Perspective*, 2nd ed. New York: John Wiley and Sons.

Vance, James E. 1976. "Cities in the Shaping of the American Nation." *Journal of Geography* (January): 41–52.

Vanek, Joann. 1973. "Keeping Busy: Time Spent in Housework, U.S., 1920–1970." Ph. D. dissertation, University of Michigan.

Vanfossen, Beth E., James D. Jones, and Joan Z. Spade. 1987. "Curriculum Tracking and Status Maintenance." *Sociology of Education* 60: 104–122.

Veblen, Thorstein. 1953. *The Theory of the Leisure Class*. New York: New American Library. [Originally published in 1899.]

Veblen, Thorstein. 1921. *Engineers and the Price System*. New York: Viking.

Veltfort, Helene Rank, and George E. Lee. 1943. "The Cocoanut Grove Fire: A Study in Scapegoating." *Journal of Abnormal and Social Psychology* 38: 138–154.

Vernon, Glenn. 1962. *Sociology and Religion*. New York: McGraw-Hill.

Veysey, Laurence. 1965. *The Emergence of the American University*. Chicago: University of Chicago Press.

Vold, George B., and Thomas J. Bernard. 1986. *Theoretical Criminology*, 3rd ed. New York: Oxford University Press.

Vrooman, John, and Stuart Greenfield. 1980. "Are Blacks Making It in the Suburbs?" *Journal of Urban Economics* 7: 155–167.

Waber, D. P. 1979. "Cognitive Abilities and Sex-Related Variations in the Maturation of Cerebral Cortical Functions." In M. A. Wittig and A. C. Peterson (eds.), *Sex-Related Differences in Congitive Functioning*. New York: Academic Press.

Waber, D. P. 1977. "Sex Differences in Mental Abilities, Hemispheric Lateralization, and Rate of Physical Growth at Adolescence." *Developmental Psychology* 12: 278–282; 13: 29–38.

Waite, Linda J. 1981. "U.S. Women at Work." *Population Bulletin* 36, 2.

Wallach, Michael A., Nathan Kogan, and Daryl J. Bem. 1962. "Group Influence on Individual Risk Taking." *Journal of Abnormal and Social Psychology* 65: 75–86.

Wallerstein, Immanuel. 1989. *The Modern World-System III: The Second Era of Great Expansion of the Capitalist World-Economy, 1730–1840*. New York: Academic Press.

Wallerstein, Immanuel. 1983. "An Agenda for World-Systems Analysis," Pp. 299–308 in William R. Thompson (ed.), *Contending Approaches to World System Analysis*. Beverly Hills: Sage.

Wallerstein, Immanuel. 1980. *The Modern World-System II: Mercantilism and the Consolidation of the European World Economy, 1600–1750*. New York: Academic Press.

Wallerstein, Immanuel. 1979. *The Capitalist World-Economy*. Cambridge: Cambridge University Press.

Wallerstein, Immanuel. 1976. "Modernization: Requiescat in Pace." Pp. 131–135 in Lewis Coser and Otto Larsen (eds.). *The Uses of Controversy in Sociology*. New York: The Free Press (reprinted as chapter 7 in Wallerstein 1979).

Wallerstein, Immanuel. 1974. *The Modern World-System: Capitalist Agriculture and the Origins of the European World Economy in the 16th Century*. New York: Academic Press.

Wallerstein, Immanuel. 1974a. "The Rise and Future Demise of the World Capitalist System: Concepts for Comparative Analysis." *Comparative Studies in Society and History* 16, 4: 387–415.

Wallerstein, Immanuel. 1974b. *The Modern World-System: Capitalist Agriculture and the Origins of European World-Economy in the Sixteenth Century*. New York: Academic Press.

Wallerstein, James S., and Clement J. Wyle. 1947. "Our Law-Abiding Law Breakers." Probation (April): 107–118.

Wallerstein, Judith S., and Joan B. Kelly. 1980. "California's Children of Divorce." *Psychology Today* 13. 8: 67–76.

Wallis, Roy. 1977. *The Road to Total Freedom: A Sociological Analysis of Scientology*. New York: Columbia University Press.

Wallis, Roy. 1975. *Sectarianism* New York: John Wiley.

Walster, E., and G. W. Walster. 1969. "The Matching Hypothesis." *Journal of Personality and Social Psychology* 6: 248–253.

Walton, John. 1977. "The Bearing of Social Science Research on Public Issues: Floyd Hunter and the Study of Power." Pp. 263–272 in John Walton and Donald E. Carns (eds.), *Cities in Change: Studies on the Urban Condition,* 2nd ed. Boston: Allyn and Bacon.

Walton, John. 1966. "Substance and Artifact: The Current State of Research on Community Power Structure." *American Journal of Sociology* 71: 430–438.

Waquant, Loic J. D., and William Julius Wilson. 1989. "The Cost of Racial and Class Exclusion in the Inner City." *The Annals of the American Academy of Political and Social Science* 501: 8–25.

Ward, Kathryn B. 1984. *Women in the World System*. New York: Praeger.

Ward, Kathryn B. 1988. "Women in the Global Economy." Pp. 17–48 in B. Gutek, Ann Strassberg, and Laurie Harwood (eds.). *Women and Work*. Beverly Hills: Sage.

Ward, Lester Frank. 1911. *Dynamic Sociology*, 2nd ed. New York: Appleton.

Warheit, G. J., C. E. Holzer, III, and J. J. Schwab. 1973. "An Analysis of the Social Class and Racial Differences in Depressive Symptomatology: A Community Study." *Journal of Health and Social Behavior* 14: 291–299.

Warner, Sam Bass. 1962. *Streetcar Suburbs*. Cambridge, MA: Harvard University and MIT Press.

Warner, W. Lloyd, Paul S. Hunt, Marchia Meekr, and Kenneth Eels. 1949. *Social Class in America*. New York: Harper.

Wasserman, Ira. 1984. "Imitation and Suicide: A Reexamination of the Werther Effect." *American Sociological Review* 49: 427–436.

Wasserman, Miriam. 1970. *The School Fix: NYC, USA*. New York: Outerbridge and Dienstfrey.

Watkins, Alfred J., and David W. Perry. 1977. "Regional Change and the Impact of Uneven Urban Development." Pp. 19–54 in David C. Perry and Alfred J. Watkins (eds.), *The Rise of the Sunbelt Cities,* Urban Affairs Annual Reviews, vol. 14. Beverly Hills, CA: Sage.

Watson, Andrew. 1988. "The Reform of Agricultural Marketing in China since 1978." *China Quarterly* 113: 1–28.

Wayne, Leslie. 1984. "The Irony and the Impact of Auto Quotas." *New York Times*, April 8, Section 3, p. 1.

Webb, Eugene J., Donald T. Campbell, Richard D. Schwartz, Lee Sechrest, and Janet Below Grove. 1981. *Nonreactive Measures in the Social Sciences,* 2nd ed. Boston: Houghton Mifflin.

Weber, C. U., P. W. Foster, and D. P. Weichert. 1978. "An Economic

Analsis of the Ypsilanti Perry Preschool Project." *Monographs of the High/Scope Educational Research Foundation 5.*

Weber, Max. 1968. *Economy and Society.* (Ephriam Fischoff et al., trs.) New York: Bedminster Press. Originally published in German in 1922.

Weber, Max. 1963. *The Sociology of Religion.* Ephraim Fischoff (tr.). Boston: Beacon. [Originally published in German, 1920.]

Weber, Max. 1962. *Basic Concepts in Sociology.* London: Peter Owen.

Weber, Max. 1958. *The Protestant Ethic and the Spirit of Capitalism.* New York: Scribner's. Originally published in German, 1904–1905.

Weber, Max. 1958. *The Protestant Ethic and the Spirit of Capitalism.* Talcott Parsons (tr.), with a forward by R. H. Tawney. New York: Scribner's.

Weber, Max. 1958. *The Protestant Ethic and the Spirit of Capitalism.* Talcott Parsons (tr.), New York: Scribner's Sons. [Originally published in German 1904–1905.]

Weber, Max. 1958. *The Religion of India.* Hans Gerth and Don Martindale (trs.). New York: Free Press. [Originally published in German, 1920.]

Weber, Max. 1952. *Ancient Judaism.* Hans Gerth (tr. & ed.). and Don Martindale. New York: Free Press. [Originally published in German in 1920.]

Weber, Max. 1951. *The Religion of China.* Hans Gerth (tr.). New York: Free Press. [Originally published in German, 1920.]

Weber, Max. 1946. *From Max Weber: Essays in Sociology.* Hans H. Gerth and C. Wright Mills (eds. and trs.). New York: Oxford University Press.

Webster, David S., Clifton F. Conrad, and Eric L. Jensen. 1988. "Objective and Reputational Rankings of Ph. D.-Granting Departments of Sociology, 1965–1982." *Sociological Focus* 21: 113–126.

Webster, David S. 1986. *Academic Quality Rankings of American Colleges and Universities.* Springfield, IL: C. C. Thomas.

Weeks, John R. 1986. *Population: An Introduction to Concepts and Issues,* 3rd ed. Belmont, CA: Wadsworth.

Weg, Ruth B. 1985. "Beyond Babies and Orgasm." Pp. 206–222 in Beth B. Hess and Elizabeth W. Markson (eds.), *Growing Old in America,* 3rd ed. New Brunswick, NJ: Transaction Books.

Weinberg, M. 1977. *Minority Students: A Research Appraisal.* Report to the Department of Health, Education, and Welfare, Office of Education. Washington, DC: System Development Corporation.

Weinstein, Bernard L., Harold T. Gross, and John Rees. 1985. *Regional Growth and Decline in the United States,* 2nd ed. New York: Praeger.

Weiss, Carol H. 1983. (reaction to women managers when 50% + female empl.)

Weiss, R. S. 1984. "The Impact of Marital Dissolution on Income and Consumption in Single-Parent Households." *Journal of Marriage and Family* 46: 115–127.

Weiss, Robert J. 1985. "Affirmative Action: A Brief History." *Journal of Intergroup Relations* 15, 2: 40–53.

Weitz, Rose, and Deborah A. Sullivan. 1986. "The Politics of Childbirth: The Re-Emergence of Midwifery in Arizona." *Social Problems* 33: 163–175.

Weitzman, Lenore. 1985. *Divorce Revolution: The Unexpected Social and Economic Consequences for Women and Children in America.* New York: Free Press.

Weitzman, Lenore J. 1985. *The Divorce Revolution: The Unexpected Social and Economic Consequences for Women and Children in America.* New York: Free Press.

Wekerle, Gerda. 1980. "Women in the Urban Environment." *Signs: Journal of Women in Culture and Society* 5, 3: S188–S214.

Wellisz, Slaneslaw H. 1971. "Economic Redevelopment and Urbanization." Pp. 39–58 in Leo Jakobson and Ved Prakash (eds.), *Urbanization and National Development.* Beverly Hills, CA: Sage.

Wellman, Barry. 1979. "The Community Question: The Intimate Networks of East Yorkers." *American Journal of Sociology* 84: 1201–1231.

Wennberg, John E. 1983. *A Study of the Nature, Costs, and Cost Implications of Hospital Market Variations in the Use of Inpatient Services,* Final Report. (Research Project Supported by Health Care Finance Administration.

Wennberg, John E., Klim McPherson, and Philip Caper. 1984. "Will Payment Based on Diagnostic-Related Groups Reduce Hospital Costs?" *New England Journal of Medicine* 311: 295–300.

Wesley, Charles H. 1927. *Negro Labor in the United States, 1850–1925.* New York: Vanguard.

Wheeler, Ladd. 1966. "Toward a Theory of Behavioral Contagion." *Psychological Review* 73: 179–192.

Whitaker, Mark. 1985. "Ten Ways to Fight Terrorism." *Newsweek* (July 1): 26–29.

White, L. K., and Alan Booth. 1985. "The Quality and Stability of Remarriages: "The Role of Stepchildren." *American Sociological Review* 50: 689–698.

White, Ralph K., and Ronald Lippitt. 1960. *Autocracy and Democracy.* New York: Harper and Row.

White, Sheldon. 1970. "The National Impact of Head Start." *Disadvantaged Child* 3: 163–184.

Whiting, Beatrice B., and Carolyn P. Edwards. 1976. "A Cross-Cultural Analysis of Sex Differences in the Behavior of Children Aged Three Through Eleven." In S. Cox (ed.), *The Emerging Self.* Chicago: Science Research Associates.

Whitley, Bernard E. 1983. "Sex-Role Orientation and Self-Esteem: A Critical Meta-Analytical Review." *Journal of Personality and Social Psychology* 44: 765–778.

Whorf, Benjamin Lee. 1956. *Thought and Reality: Selected Writings of Benjamin Lee Whorf.* John B. Carroll (ed.). Cambridge, MA: Technology Press of the Massachusetts Institute of Technology.

Whyte, Martin King and S. Z. Gu. 1987. "Popular Response to China's Fertility Transition." *Population and Development Review* 13, 3: 471–494.

Whyte, William Foote. 1981. *Street Corner Society,* 3rd ed. Chicago: University of Chicago Press. [Originally published in 1943.]

Wilensky, Harold L. 1967. *Organizational Intelligence: Knowledge and Policy in Government and Industry.* New York: Basic Books.

Wilensky, Harold L. 1964. *Complex Organizations: A Critical Essay,* 2nd ed. Glenview, IL: Scott, Foresman.

Wilkinson, David. 1987. "Central Civilization." *Comparative Civilization Review* 17: 31–59.

Will, J., P. Self, and N. Datan. 1974. Paper presented at the American Psychological Association.

Willard, W. 1972. *Curanderismo and Health Care.* Division of Social Perspectives in Medicine, University of Arizona, College of Medicine. (Mimeograph).

Williams, David R. 1986. "Socioeconomic Differentials in Health: The Role of Psychosocial Factors." Ph.D. Dissertation, The University of Michigan. *Dissertation Abstracts International* Abstract No. 3878A.

Williams, John E., and John R. Stabler. 1973. "If White Means Good, Then Black . . . " *Psychology Today* (July): 51–54.

Williams, Robin. 1977. "Competing Models of Multiethnic and Multiracial Societies: An Appraisal of Possibilities and Performances." Paper presented at plenary session of the American Sociological Association annual meeting, Chicago, IL.

Williams, Robin. 1970. *American Society: A Sociological Interpretation,* 3rd ed. New York: Alfred A. Knopf.

Williamson, John B., Anne Munley, and Linda Evans, with Barbara H. Vinick and Sharlene Hesse. 1980. *Aging and Society.* New York: Holt, Rinehart, and Winston.

Willie, Charles Vert. 1979. *The Caste and Class Controversey.* Bayside, NY: General Hall.

Willms, J. Douglas. 1987. "Patterns of Academic Achievement in Public and Private Schools: Implications for Public Policy and Future Research." Pp. 113–134 in Edward H. Haertel, Thomas James, and Henry M. Levin (eds.), *Comparing Public and Private Schools.* Volume 2, Student Achievement. New York: Falmer.

Wilson, Bryan. 1970. *Religious Sects.* New York: McGraw Hill.

Wilson, Bryan. 1961. *Sects and Society.* Berkeley: University of California Press.

Wilson, Bryan. 1959. "An Analysis of Sect Development." *American Sociological Review* 24: 2–15.

Wilson, Bryan R. 1985. "Secularization: The Inherited Model." In P. Hammond (ed.), *The Sacred in a Secular Age.* Berkeley: University of California Press.

Wilson, Edward O. 1978. *On Human Nature.* Cambridge, MA: Harvard University Press.

Wilson, Franklin D. 1988. "Aspects of Migration in Advanced Industrial Society." *American Sociological Review* 53: 113–126.

Wilson, Franklin D. 1985. "The Impact of School Desegregation Programs on White Public Enrollment, 1968–1976." *Sociology of Education* 58: 137–153.

Wilson, James Q., and Richard J. Herrnstein. 1985. *Crime and Human Nature.* New York: Simon and Schuster.

Wilson, James Q. 1980. *American Government: Institutions and Policies.* Lexington, MA: D. C. Heath.

Wilson, John. 1978. *Religion in American Society: The Effective Presence.* Englewood Cliffs, NJ: Prentice Hall.

Wilson, Kenneth L., and Anthony M. Orum. 1976. "Mobilizing People for Collective Action." *Journal of Political and Military Sociology* 4: 187–202.

Wilson, Susan. 1982. "A New Decade: The Gifted and Career Choice." *Vocational Guidance Quarterly* 31, 1: 53–59.

Wilson, William Julius. 1987. *The Truly Disadvantaged: The Inner City, the Underclass, and Public Policy.* Chicago: University of Chicago Press.

Wilson, William Julius. 1978. *The Declining Significance of Race: Blacks and Changing American Institutions.* Chicago: University of Chicago Press.

Wilson, William Julius. 1973. *Power, Racism, and Privilege.* New York: Free Press.

Wilson, William Julius, and Katherine O' Sullivan See. 1988. "Race and Ethnicity." Pp. 223–242 in Neil Smelser (ed.), *Handbook of Sociology.* Newbury Park, CA: Sage.

Winch, Robert F. 1958. *Mate Selection.* New York: Harper and Row.

Wirth, Louis. 1964. *On Cities and Social Life.* Chicago: University of Chicago Press.

Wirth, Louis. 1938. "Urbanism As a Way of Life." *American Journal of Sociology* 44: 1–24.

Wolf, Eric R. 1982. *Europe and the People Without History.* Berkeley: University of California Press.

Wolf, Richard. 1966. "The Measurement of Environments." In Anne Anastasi (ed.), *Testing Problems in Perspective.* Washington, DC: American Council on Education.

Wolfgang, Marvin E., and Frances Ferracuti. 1981. *The Subculture of Violence.* Beverly Hills, CA: Sage.

Wolkoff, Michael J. 1983. "The Nature of Property Tax Abatement Awards." *Journal of the American Planning Association* 49: 77–84.

Wolkoff, Michael J. 1982. "Chasing a Dream: The Use of Tax Abatements to Spur Urban Ecoomic Development." Discussion Paper No. 8206, Public Policy Analysis Program, University of Rochester.

Women on Words and Images. 1974. "Look Jane Look. See Sex Stereotypes." Pp. 159–177 in Judith Stacey, Susan Bereaud, and Joan Daniels (eds.), *And Jill Came Tumbling After: Sexism in American Education.* New York: Dell.

Woodward, K. L., E. Salholz, and J. Buckley. 1981. "The Church Versus the State." *Newsweek,* February 23, pp. 78–79.

Woodward, Kenneth L. 1989. "Religion: Searching for New Meaning about Heaven." *Newsweek,* March 27.

World Almanac. 1988. *World Almanac and Book of Facts,* 1988 ed.

World Bank. 1988. *World Development Report, 1988.* New York: Oxford University Press.

World Bank. 1986. *World Development Report, 1986.* New York: Oxford University Press.

World Bank. 1984. *World Development Report, 1984.* New York: Oxford University Press.

World Health Organization. 1973. *International Pilot Project in Schizophrenia.* Geneva, Switzerland: World Health Organization.

Worsley, Peter. 1984. *The Three Worlds: Culture & World Development.* Chicago: University of Chicago Press.

Wright, James D. 1976. *The Dissent of the Governed: Alienation and Democracy in America.* New York: Academic Press.

Wright, Richard. 1937. "The Ethics of Living Jim Crow." In Richard Wright, *Uncle Tom's Children.* New York: Harper and Row.

Wright, Sam. 1978. *Crowds and Riots: A Study in Social Organization.* Beverly Hills, CA: Sage.

Wrigley, E. A. 1969. *Population and History.* New York: McGraw Hill.

Yamagishi, Toshio, Mary R. Gilmore, and Karen S. Cook. 1988. "Network Connections and the Distribution of Power in Exchange Networks." *American Journal of Sociology* 93: 833–851.

Yamaguchi, Kazuo. 1986. "Models for Comparing Mobility Tables: Toward Parsimony and Substance." *American Sociological Review* 52: 482–494.

Yankelovich, Daniel. 1981. *New Rules: Searching for Self-Fulfillment in a World Turned Upside Down.* New York: Random House.

Yankelovich, Daniel. 1974. *The New Morality: A Profile of American Youth in the '70s.* New York: McGraw Hill.

Yinger, J. Milton. 1986. "Afterword. The Research Agenda: New Directions for Desegregation Studies." Pp. 229–254 in Jeffrey Prager, Douglas Longshore, and Melvin Seeman (eds.), *School Desegregation Research: New Directions in Situational Analysis*. New York: Plenum.

Yinger, J. Milton. 1982. *Countercultures: The Promise and Peril of a World Turned Upside Down*. New York: Free Press.

Yinger, J. Milton. 1970. *The Scientific Study of Religion*. New York: Macmillan.

Yinger, J. Milton. 1969. "A Structural Examination of Religion." *Journal for the Scientific Study of Religion* 8: 88–100.

Yinger, J. Milton. 1946. *Religion and the Struggle for Power*. Durham, NC: Duke University Press.

Yllo, K. 1983. "Sexual Equality and Violence against Wives in American States." *Journal of Comparative Family Studies* 14: 67–86.

Youniss, James. 1980. *Parents and Peers in Social Development*. Chicago: University of Chicago Press.

Yukl, G. 1981. *Leadership in Organizations*. Englewood Cliffs, NJ: Prentice Hall.

Zajonc, R. B. 1960. "The Concepts of Balance, Congruity, and Dissonance." *Public Opinion Quarterly* 24: 280–296.

Zald, Mayer N., and Robert Ash. 1966. "Social Movement Organizations: Growth, Decay, and Change." *Social Forces* 44: 327–340.

Zald, Mayer N., and John D. McCarthy (eds.). 1979. *The Dynamics of Social Movements: Resource Mobilization, Social Control, and Tactics*. Cambridge, MA: Winthrop.

Zald, Mayer N., and John D. McCarthy (eds.). 1975. "Organizational Intellectuals and the Criticism of Society." *Social Service Research* 49: 344–362.

Zald, Mayer N., and Burt Useem. 1987. "Movement and Countermovement Interaction: Mobliization, Tactics, and State Involvement." Pp. 247–272 in Mayer [376]. Zald and John D. McCarthy (eds.), *Social Movements in an Organizational Society*. New Brunswick, NJ: Transaction Books.

Zbrowski, Mark. 1969. *People in Pain*. San Francisco: Jossey-Bass.

Zeitlin, Irving M. 1987. *Ideology and the Development of Sociological Theory*, 3rd ed. Englewood Cliffs, NJ: Prentice-Hall.

Zeitlin, Maurice. 1984. *The Civil Wars in Chile (or the bourgeois revolutions that never were)*. Princeton: Princeton University Press.

Zeitlin, Maurice. 1974. "Corporate Ownership and Control: The Large Corporation and the Capitalist Class." *American Journal of Sociology* 79; 1073–1119.

Zetterberg, H. 1966. "The Secret Ranking." *Journal of Marriage and Family* 28: 136–142.

Zigler, Edward, E. F. Abelson, and V. Seitz. 1973. "Motivational Factors in the Performance of Economically Disadvantaged Children on the Peabody Picture Vocabulary Test." *Child Development* 44: 294–303.

Zill, Nicholas. 1984. National Survey conducted by Child Trends, Inc. Washington, DC: 1984, reported by Marilyn Adams, "Kids Aren't Broken by the Break Up." *USA Today*, p. 5D.

Zimbarbo, Philip G. 1971. "The Psychological Power and Pathology of Imprisomment." A statement prepared for the U.S. House of Representatives Committee on the Judiciary Subcommittee No. 3; Hearings on Prison Reform, San Francisco, California, October 25, cited and quoted in D. G. Myers, 1983, *Social Psychology*. New York: McGraw-Hill.

Zimmerman, Don H., and Candace West. 1975. "Sex Roles, Interruptions, and Silences in Conversation." In Barrie Thorne and Nancy Henley, *Language and Sex*. New York: Newbury House.

Zola, Irving. 1972. "Medicine as an Institution of Social Control." *Sociological Review* 20: 487–504.

Zola, Irving. 1966. "Culture and Symptoms: An Analysis of Patients' Presenting Complaints." *American Sociological Review* 31: 615–630.

Zopf, Paul E. 1984. *Population: An Introduction to Social Demography*. Palo Alto, CA: Mayfield.

Zwerdling, Daniel. 1978. *Workplace Democracy*. New York: Harper and Row.

Index

NAME INDEX

Abelson, E.F., 410
Aberle, D.F., 94
Abrahamson, M., 165
Abu-Lughod, J., 606
Ackland, H., 409
Aday, L., 476
Adler, T.F., 156
Adorno, T.W., 29, 48, 306-7, 574
Agree, E.M., 508, 509
Aguirre, B.E., 555, 566, 570
Ahmad, S., 498
Aiken, H., 38
Aiken, L.H., 474, 475
Aiken, M., 296
Akrne, G., 360
Aldrich, M., 173
Alexander, J.C., 68, 78
Alexander, K.L., 407, 409
Alexander, Y., 583
Alexis, M., 306
Alford, R.R., 296
Allen, W., 308, 316
Allison, P.P., 384
Allport, F.H., 559
Allport, G.W., 38, 307
Almond, G.A., 359
Altman, D., 571
Alwin, D.F., 405, 409
Ames, V.M., 120
Amin, S., 496
Anderson, O.W., 476
Anderson, P., 596
Anderson, R., 417, 476
Anderson, T.R., 541
Apple, M., 399
Arciniega, T., 409
Arendt, H., 574
Aries, P., 513, 519
Arluke, A., 513
Armor, D.J., 403
Arvidson, P., 568
Asch, S.E., 181
Ash, R., 572, 576
Astin, A.E., 417
Aviada, J.O., 437

Bachman, J.G., 99, 220
Backman, C.W., 74
Bain, D., 351
Bain, T., 158, 165
Bainbridge, W.S., 428
Bairoch, P., 606
Baj, J., 386
Baker, M.A., 155
Balakrishnan, T.R., 379
Baldassare, M., 535
Bales, R.F., 166, 185, 374
Baltzell, E.D., 294-95
Bancroft, J., 226
Bandura, A., 133
Bandura, M.M., 157
Bane, M.J., 248, 249, 392, 409
Banfield, E.C., 286
Banta, D., 471

Baratz, J.C., 402
Baratz, S.S., 402
Barkan, S.E., 579
Barlow, R., 6, 213, 223, 253, 264, 348
Barnes, R.D., 167
Baron, J.N., 163
Barrett, N., 158, 165
Bart, P., 515
Barth, G., 311
Bass, B., 187
Bastian, A., 399
Bastide, R., 315
Batts, V., 308
Bauer, R.A., 141
Beach, C.S., 108
Beach, F.A., 380
Bean, L.L., 541
Beck, P.A., 276
Beck, R.E., 416
Becker, G., 381
Becker, G.S., 398
Becker, H.S., 207
Bedau, H.A., 215
Beer, F.A., 339
Beez, W.V., 406
Behrens, W.W., 497
Bell, D., 113, 339, 340
Bell, W., 535, 541
Bellah, R., 426, 447-48, 452
Bem, D.J., 182
Benaske, N., 376
Benbow, C., 157
Bendix, R., 256, 599
Benford, R.D., 575
Bennett, N.G., 379
Bensman, J., 108
Bereaud, S., 407
Berger, B., 546
Berger, P., 71, 356, 358, 360, 465
Bergesen, A., 606
Berk, R.A., 559
Bernard, J., 157
Bernard, J.L., 375
Bernard, M.L., 375
Bernard, S.L., 375
Bernard, T.J., 215, 230
Berndt, H., 548
Bernstein, P., 189
Berrueta-Clement, J.R., 402
Berry, B.J.L., 542
Berscheid, E., 77
Best, R., 155, 157
Bettelheim, B., 117
Beuf, A., 156
Bianchi, S.M., 317, 389, 542, 543
Bidwell, C.E., 405, 409, 410
Bielby, D.D., 163
Bielby, W.T., 163
Biggar, J.C., 507
Billy, J.O.G., 124
Binstock, J., 411
Bishop, G.D., 183
Blalock, H.M., 313
Blanc, A.K., 379
Blascovish, J., 183
Blasi, A., 129
Blau, F.D., 153, 164, 173

Blau, P.M., 77, 193, 195, 196, 255, 256, 272
Blauner, R., 310, 315, 519
Blendon, R.J., 475
Block, H.A., 212
Block, J., 129
Bloom, D.E., 379
Blot, W., 462
Blumberg, P., 189
Blume, J., 136
Blume, M.E., 243
Blumer, H.G., 18, 57, 70, 72, 79, 194, 312, 558, 560, 569, 571, 573, 576
Blumstein, A., 215
Blumstein, P., 380
Boal, F.W., 542
Bobbio, N., 339, 359
Boberts, R.E., 311
Boffey, P.M., 291
Bogdanor, V., 277
Bogue, D.J., 497
Bolce, L.H.III., 105
Bolton, C.D., 575
Bonacich, E., 310, 311
Bond, K., 510, 516
Boocock, S.S., 406, 409
Booth, A., 386, 535
Bornschier, V., 606
Boskin, J., 316
Bosse, R., 516
Boucher, R.J., 218
Bourdieu, P., 399, 404
Bourne, L.S., 532
Bouvier, L.F., 492, 504, 505, 508, 509
Bowen, E., 282
Bowen, H.R., 417
Bowers, W.J., 215
Bowles, S., 135, 201, 351, 402, 404, 410, 411, 414
Boyer, E.L., 415-18
Braddock, J., 404
Braithwaite, J., 222, 385
Breault, K.D., 29
Breedlove, W.L., 606
Brenner, R., 606
Brinton, L.A., 462
Brischetto, R., 409
Brodsky, A., 471
Brody, D., 311
Brophy, J.E., 73, 305, 306, 406, 407
Broverman, D.M., 149
Broverman, I.K., 149
Brown, A.T., 530
Brown, B., 156, 402, 403
Brown, L.L., 405
Broyler, S.G., 113
Bruce-Briggs, B., 261
Brunton, M., 217
Brunvand, J.H., 567, 568
Bryan, J.H., 133
Bryan, M.M., 409
Buchele, R., 173
Bucher, R., 195
Buckley, W., 93
Bumpass, L., 35, 379, 381, 386, 389
Burch, P. Jr., 288

Burger, C., 196
Burgess, E.W., 16, 539, 573
Burnham, W.D., 277
Burrowes, R., 181
Burstein, P., 276
Burt, R., 346
Burtless, G., 291

Cahnman, W.J., 528
Caldwell, J., 496
Caldwell, S.B., 6
Calhoun, J.C., 534
Callahan, R.E., 398
Camilleri, S.F., 541
Campbell, A., 571
Campbell, E.Q., 401, 402, 406
Campbell, J., 438
Cancellier, P., 317, 505, 507, 508
Cantril, H., 568
Caper, P., 474
Cardell, M., 380
Carden, M.L., 574
Carlsmith, J.M., 6, 133, 308
Carmen, B., 167
Carnevale, J.D., 167
Carroll, J.W., 449
Carter, J., 186
Carter, T.P., 409
Castells, M., 539
Castro, F., 182
Cave, W.M., 398, 399
Chalfant, H.P., 437
Chambliss, W.J., 208, 214, 215, 225, 230
Charon, J., 71, 121
Chase-Dunn, C., 606
Chaucer, G., 136
Cherlin, A., 382
Chesler, M.A., 398, 399
Chesney-Lind, M., 228-29
Chiet, E.F., 415
Chilcote, R.H., 603
Childe, V.G., 526, 527
Chiricos, T.G., 215, 216
Chirot, D., 602, 603, 606
Choldin, H.M., 526, 530, 535, 536, 541, 545, 546
Christensen, H.T., 171, 391
Cicerelli, V.G., 402, 515
Cicourel, A., 407
Cipolla, C.M., 493
Clark, A.R., 542
Clark, C., 77, 465, 470
Clark, D., 340
Clark, K., 514
Clark, M., 469
Clarke, A.C., 227
Clarkin, C., 459
Clarkson, F.E., 149
Clausen, J.A., 470
Clawson, D., 292
Clay, P., 548
Cleckley, H., 217
Clelland, D.A., 100
Clements, J., 159
Clinard, M.B., 6, 212, 213
Clines, F.X., 592

SUBJECT INDEX